CALENDAR
of
PAPAL REGISTERS

GENERAL EDITOR
CHARLES BURNS OBE

Forma for Wolsey's investiture with the pallium as archbishop of York: NA, SC7 26/13 (Crown copyright photograph: reproduced by permission). Enclosed in entry no. 385 [B] below dated 25 Sept. 1514. The *Forma* was engrossed as letters-close and measures approx. 43x35 cms (reduced and cropped in the photograph); no plica; opened by cutting parchment, not seal cord. On the left: note by the *rescribendarius* (*Jo. Cheninart*) and *computator* (*Aloisius*); on the far left (not shown): contemporaneous note by the *rescribendarius* of the tax (VI [sc. *grossi* or *carlini*]) together with the signatures of the *rescribendarius* (*Jo. Cheninart*) and *computator* (*Aloisius*); on the far left (not shown): contemporaneous note by the *rescribendarius* of the month (*Sep*) in which the letter was taxed; on the right: signature of the *scriptor apostolicus* (*Jo. de Madrigal*) who engrossed the *Forma*. Unlike the registers, engrossments were always clearly written in the same basic script called *littera da bolle* or *bollatica*. On the dorse: the 'label' *Forma tradendi Pallium* (written by the grossator) and (at an edge) *viij* (of uncertain reference). With leaden *bulla* attached by hemp cord. On the method of folding and enclosure *see below* entry no. 385, note 10.

COIMISIÚN LÁMHSCRÍBHINNÍ NA hÉIREANN

CALENDAR
of
ENTRIES
in the
PAPAL REGISTERS
relating to
GREAT BRITAIN
&
IRELAND

PAPAL LETTERS, VOLUME XX
1513–1521
LEO X
LATERAN REGISTERS, PART ONE

edited by
ANNE P. FULLER

DUBLIN
IRISH MANUSCRIPTS COMMISSION
2005

Irish Manuscripts Commission
45 Merrion Square
Dublin 2
www.irishmanuscripts.ie

Typeset by December Publications
Printed by ColourBooks Ltd, Dublin

ISBN 1 874 280 789

CONTENTS

FOREWORD

The new series of *Calendar of Entries in the Papal Registers relating to Great Britain and Ireland, Papal Letters* has established itself as a remarkably full and reliable guide to the contents of one of the most valuable resources for British and Irish religious history in the later Middle Ages. It makes material from one of the world's greatest archives available to scholars in a way far beyond what is possible in the archive itself, and it has an established reputation for excellence and user-friendliness. It is, indeed, the largest-scale and most useful European project of its kind, with a scholarly relevance that extends far beyond these offshore islands.

The volumes in the series aim to provide full, and exhaustively indexed, calendars of all entries in the papal registers relating to Great Britain and Ireland, pontificate by pontificate. No other countries in Europe have a project of equivalent scope or thoroughness. These *Calendars* offer a resource that historians without direct access to the Vatican archive can use with confidence. They supply virtually all the information contained in the registers themselves, while glossing, identifying and annotating the material in ways that enormously enhance its historical value and usability. In addition to making available a unique and rich source for the late medieval ecclesiastical and social history of these islands, their editorial apparatus and introductory material provide an invaluable guide to changing procedure in the papal chancery in the late middle ages and renaissance.

Between the inauguration in 1970 of the new series of the *Calendar*, and the publication of the second volume of the *Calendar* for the pontificate of Alexander VI in 1998, the executive editors, Dr Michael Haren and Mrs Anne Fuller, completed between them seven volumes, comprising the Lateran registers of Popes Innocent VIII, Alexander VI, Pius III, and Julius II, covering the years 1484–1513. The present volume takes us on into the momentous pontificate of Leo X, and the age of the Reformation. The volume calendars rather more than half the surviving letters of British and Irish interest in the Lateran Registers of Leo X: in the process it brings before the reader many of the great and good (and not so good) of the period – Henry VIII, Catherine of Aragon, James V of Scotland, Cardinals Bainbridge and Wolsey, Archbishops Warham and Lee, and the humanists Colet and Linacre. The letters also illuminate the lives and careers of countless more obscure figures, and the editorial material disentangles many of the obscurities that surround them. Only those who have floundered with the bizarre and baffling transformations which Irish, English, Scottish and Welsh place and personal names frequently underwent at the hands of Italian renaissance clerks, can appreciate, and give due thanks for, the Herculean labours involved in identifying and indexing the people and places within this *Calendar*. Hence, for most purposes, this volume will be found far more useful to the historian than the original registers themselves.

It is appropriate therefore to acknowledge here in the warmest terms the superlative skills of the editor, Mrs Anne Fuller, who has laboured heroically to produce this volume within the very tight time-constraints which nowadays accompany all public funding. She has been able to call on the support, wise advice and long archival experience of Monsignor Charles Burns, formerly of the Vatican Archive. A friend and promoter of the new series of the *Calendar* since its inception in 1970, Monsignor Burns has now ably taken on the General Editorship of the series, following the death of the much-lamented Leonard Boyle OP.

Finally, this volume could not have been produced without the generous support of the Resource Enhancement Scheme of the Arts and Humanities Research Board, which funds Mrs Fuller's research and editorial work, and of the Irish Manuscripts Commission, which funds the production and distribution of the volumes. Our warmest gratitude goes to both these organisations, and to all those supporters of the CPR project who have helped to ensure the continuation of this superb scholarly resource.

Eamon Duffy
Chairman, CPR New Series Project

Magdalene College
Cambridge
Easter 2005

Other titles in the Calendar of Papal Registers *series*

PAPAL LETTERS

NEW SERIES PUBLISHED BY THE IRISH MANUSCRIPTS COMMISSION

SERIES PUBLISHED BY HMSO, LONDON

PETITIONS TO THE POPE

The sole volume of Petitions to the Pope *is an essential companion to volumes III and IV of
the* Papal Letters *series, which refer repeatedly to it. For the earlier volumes, the date in
parenthesis is that on the title page. Though proximate, it is not always that of publication.*

EDITOR'S PREFACE

Volume XIX of the *Calendar of Papal Letters*, edited by Michael Haren, covered the outstanding portion of the Lateran Registers of Julius II (d. 1513). The present volume of the Calendar takes the first eighty-one Lateran Registers of Leo X (1513-1521), namely *Reg. Lat.* 1276-1356. The remainder (*Reg. Lat.* 1357-1405; 1406, 2462 and 2464) will be covered in Vol. XXI. In addition to calendaring the Lateran Registers the present volume also collects the *rubricellae* of lost letters from all the relevant *Indici*, namely *Ind.* 350-355. In terms of the dates under which they are drawn the enregistered letters calendared below belong to 1-7 Leo; the letters represented by the *rubricellae* are drawn from the entire pontificate. The place-dates reflect Leo's itinerary. Most of the letters are dated at St Peter's, Rome (with a couple at the Lateran); a small proportion were given at places in the Patrimony and in Florence and Florentine territory. Several are dated at Magliana where there was a papal villa which served Leo as a hunting lodge; a few at Careggi and Poggio a Caiano where the Medici had villas. One was given at Bologna.

The registers covered by the present volume yielded 750 entries of British and Irish interest. Some 206 were known in outline from Hergenroether's *Regesta*; the rest are new. The *Indici* yielded a further 780 entries relating to letters in registers now lost, bringing the total haul to 1,530 letters.[1] All of them were expedited by the papal chancery and belong to the class of letter known as bulls – that is, they were issued *sub plumbo*. The bulk are letters of grace and justice issued in response to petitions; the rest are *consistoriales* – provisions to bishoprics and the greater abbeys, grants of the pallium, and other dispositions made by the pope in consistory. The selection illustrates, necessarily, the interface between the *Ecclesia Anglicana* and the other local churches on the one hand and the papacy and the Roman church on the other. As the letters imply there was a continuous stream of traffic between the two and a state, seemingly, of mutual and inextricable dependence. All parts of the British Isles are involved. Some 74% of the entries from the Lateran Registers are of English and Welsh interest; 17% are Irish; and 9% Scottish.[2] But the types of letter differ significantly and the percentages can mislead. The English and Welsh entries are typified by relatively short dispensations and indults; the Scottish and especially Irish by long and involved *beneficiales*. In terms of quantity of material as opposed to number of entries the Irish and Scottish entries contain, *pro rata*, vastly more information than the English and Welsh.

Though expedited by the papal chancery the letters were effectively initiated in Great Britain and Ireland and originated in the circumstances of those who impetrated them.

---

1   Strictly speaking, the total given here is somewhat understated: though one register entry normally equals one letter, a small proportion of entries (notably those concerning reservations of pensions and consistorial provisions) contain two or more letters.
2   The mix of *rubricellae* entries or lost bulls is virtually the same: 73% English and Welsh; 16% Irish; and 11% Scottish.

In consequence, they illuminate conditions in the British Isles and the Calendar brings to light a great mass of information about people and places which fills holes in our domestic records. Unlike the camera and the secretariate, the business handled by the chancery was essentially routine. Its letters were drawn in common form in accordance with a certain stilus and we cannot expect to find political letters and state secrets in the Lateran Registers. In general, the main strength of the selection lies in the abundance of biographical and topographical information. History book personalities are present. There is a letter in favour of Catherine of Aragon (no. 217); and we learn the name of the governess of Henry VIII (no. 1245 *note*). The ecclesiatical hierarchy, both current and prospective, is, of course, well represented. Of Englishmen, Bainbridge, Lee, Tunstal, Warham, and Wolsey all feature; so do Colet and Linacre. The Scots who appear include Betoun, Forman, the Hepburns, and Gavin Douglas. The careers of minor figures, like Richard Eden, clerk of the Henrician Privy Council, are also given further detail. More importantly, perhaps, the volume also rescues countless lives from oblivion, particularly parochial clergy *inter Hibernicos*. We are also told the names of Irishmen who are captains of their respective nations (no. 317). The topographical information is extremely varied, ranging from abbeys, cathedral churches, and other great establishments to rarely recorded parish churches and chapels. There is an impressive series of letters in favour, variously, of the abbot and convent of Oseney (nos. 11, 130, 133, 293, 360 and 567). And there are comprehensive grants in favour of the Augustinian monasteries of Bruton (nos. 154-5) and Bradenstoke (no. 494) whose abbots, perhaps significantly, had both been members of Cardinal Bainbridge's household in Rome.[3] We also note that the recently founded Savoy Hospital in London makes its first appearance (no. 661). Litigation can bring a small community into focus. We hear of a chapel of ease at Farrington in the parish of Chewton Mendip (Somerset) where the church wardens and parishioners were trying to compel the local vicar to provide them with a priest-chaplain (no. 223). Occasionally, the detailing can be very fine. We are told the names of farms in the Dorset parishes of Blandford Forum or Pimperne (no. 288) and of a bell at the parish church of Childrey, Berkshire (no. 580). There are also some items of exceptional technical or specialist interest. They include a fishing grant in favour of Felmeus OMulryan, noble on both sides, in which no less than ten benefices were targeted (no. 628); a supposed privilege of Lucius III (1181-1185) recited in the grant for Bradenstoke (no. 494); a rescript of justice in the protracted struggle between Prémontré and the English abbots (no. 521); and the provision of Andrew Forman, bishop of Moray, to the archbishopric of Bourges, to the effect that he remain bishop of Moray and be *utriusque earundem Bituricen. et Moravien. ecclesiarum verus presul et pastor* (nos. 171-2). Liturgical scholars will note that the relatively novel feast of the Name of Jesus is now established at Eastbourne (no. 426); and economic historians may delight in the "crane" and "kipe" at Colchester (no. 572). Because Wolsey tried to

---

3   Namely Gilbert and Walsh (*cf.* D.S. Chambers, *Cardinal Bainbridge in the Court of Rome 1509 to 1514* [Oxford, 1965], pp. 113-4). Both letters provided for prayers for Bainbridge.

upset it, the provision of Louis Guillart to the bishopric of Tournai has also been admitted to the selection (nos. 78-83).

Leo's pontificate saw the continuation and close of the V Lateran Council (1512-1517). Researchers expecting to find the council's decrees widely reflected in the letters below will be disappointed. The derogatoria, which was a routine part of letters expedited by the chancery and other departments, was, as we would expect, a graveyard of reform decrees issued by popes and approved by general councils. Constitutions of the III and IV Lateran Councils, for instance, are commonly incorporated (by reference) in the notwithstanding clauses of our letters. Ordinarily, they are overlooked by the Calendar and comprehended in 'Notwithstanding, etc.'. Although the V Lateran Council served as a forum for calls for reform and the condemnation of abuses the council is not noted for a large number of reform decrees. Conspicuously, sensitive topics like residence and the accumulation of benefices, which would have found their way into the chancery's formulary, were left untouched. The only reflection we have of the council is in no. 649, dated 14 May 1516, where the decree limiting exemptions approved by the council on 4 May 1515 was promptly set aside.

Leo's pontificate also saw Luther post his *Disputatio pro declaratione virtutis Indulgentiarum* (i.e. the celebrated ninety-five theses) at Wittenberg in 1517. The basic indulgences in favour of the rebuilding of St Peter's had been granted by Julius II (notably *Liquet omnibus* in 1510) and they could be given a clear field over the competition by revoking and suspending all other indulgences. Though the St Peter's indulgences were aggressively promoted under Leo we would not expect the relevant commissions to be expedited by the chancery and find their way into the Lateran Registers. Any further commissions to publish the indulgences in the British Isles,[4] as also the curia's response to Luther, must wait until the CPR Project takes on Leo's Vatican Registers and registers of briefs. In the meantime what we do have are a few indulgences (nos 155, 292, 426, 580 and 587) – all English – in which any revocations and suspensions designed to protect the St Peter's indulgences are effectively set aside. The exact significance of the derogation cannot be established until the registers of the camera and the secretariate have been surveyed; but it would appear that the pope was sometimes persuaded to spare a local rebuilding project or other worthy cause and allow it to compete with St Peter's, though not, of course, on an equal footing. If so, the knowledge is a useful corrective.[5]

Great historical enterprises need sponsors and set up. The UK funding environment is now intensely competitive and the chairmanship of the CPR has become a very testing

---

4   *Cf. CPL* XVIII, nos 39 and 94.

5   Though we note that the notwithstanding clauses in the generous and highly taxed indulgence in favour of the hospital of St Mary Rouncivall, London, granted by Julius and expedited by Leo, contain no such derogation (no. 168). Either Julius drew the line at it or the proctor slipped up. Whatever the reason, the indulgence was, on the face of it, particularly vulnerable to suspension and revocation.

office. The editor is greatly indebted to Professor Jane E. Sayers for successfully
launching the volume; and to Professor Eamon Duffy for keeping it afloat. The work
was made possible by a series of grants from the UK's Arts and Humanities Research
Board. The editor is grateful to the Board; to the School of Library, Archive and
Information Studies at University College London for adopting the project for the
duration of award; and to the Faculty of Divinity, University of Cambridge where the
project subsequently found shelter. Kerstin Michaels at UCL and Rosalind Paul at
Cambridge have, with their respective teams, provided administrative support and
relieved the editor of much tedious paperwork.

Preparing the Calendar is research-intensive and the editor relies heavily on archives
and libraries. The volume could not have been produced without the cooperation and
goodwill of the Archivio Segreto Vaticano where the original registers are kept. The
editor is also grateful to the staff of the Biblioteca Apostolica Vaticana; The British
Library; Cambridge University Library; The National Archives, Kew (particularly
Hugh Alexander of the Image Library); Archivio di Stato, Rome; Biblioteca Nazionale
Centrale, Rome; Biblioteca Vallicelliana, Rome; Institute of Historical Research,
London; Warburg Institute, London; Dr Williams's Library, London; and the library of
the Carmelite Friary, Aylesford. The lovely gold coin of Leo X reproduced on the dust
jacket is in the Department of Coins and Medals, The British Museum. Kirstin Munro
showed it to me; she and the relevant curator, Barrie Cook, identified it. Thanks are due
to them both.

The support and confidence of close colleagues has been crucial. In addition to his
numerous other commitments Professor Duffy has also served as Principal
Investigator. He has taken bombshells in his stride, made all the right decisions, and
kept the volume on course. The project and its editor could not have been better led.
The editor has also been extremely fortunate in her General Editors. The volume was
started under the direction of the late Professor Leonard Boyle, OP who gave so much
to the project. Monsignor Charles Burns, OBE, formerly Senior Archivist at the
Archivio Segreto Vaticano, has been the ideal successor. At her very first visit to the
Vatican he introduced the editor to the Lateran Registers and has encouraged the work
ever since. The editor is grateful to him for much kindness and expert guidance. His
careful reading of the proofs has greatly improved the volume. The editor alone is
responsible for the blunders.

The Irish Manuscripts Commission continues to be an effective partner and faithful
publisher. Mr James Maguire, the Commission's Chairman, and Dr Cathy Hayes, its
Administrator, have co-ordinated production of the volume in the final stages and
contributed to the preliminary matter. Paul Campbell and the staff of December
Publications have borne patiently with a very tiresome author. The firm has demonstrated
once again why it is Ireland's typesetter of choice for exacting publications.

A.P.F.

POSTSCRIPT

Note 13 to Calendar entry no. 385 considers the meaning of *sub eadem bulla* and *sub alia bulla*. In the course of collecting material for Vol.XXI the editor has noted that two different lead seals were used during the pontificate. One, illustrated in T. Frenz, *I Documenti Pontifici nel Medioevo e nell'Età Moderna*, ed. S. Pagano, Città del Vaticano, 1989, pp. 188-9 (TAV. 24 [13]); the other, illustrated in C. Serafini, *Le Monete e le Bolle Plumbee Pontificie del Medagliere Vaticano*, vol. I [= Collezioni Archeologiche, Artistiche e Numismatiche dei Palazzi Apostolici, vol. III], Milan, 1910, TAV. M (10), which notes the existence of different dies but gives no details (ibid., p. 195 [nos. 217-220]). Though basically similar, the two types differ in several minor points. Conspicuously, the latter has, on the obverse, five palle (not six); PA · PA (not PAPA); circular O (instead of oval O, tilted); and (?)47 beads around the circumference (not 60); on the reverse, semi-aureoles of 21 beadlets (not 18); and (?)48 circumference beads (instead of 49). Additionally, although they visibly belong to the same iconographic tradition, the heads are different. As we would expect, the two seals appear to have been used consecutively, not concurrently. Available evidence suggests that both dies (i.e. obverse and reverse) were changed c. 1515. Owing to delays in expedition, it is difficult to be precise; but what are probably the latest specimens known to the editor of the type illustrated in Frenz are appended to letters drawn under 25 Sept 1514 (NA, SC7 26/1 and NA, SC7 26/14: coincidentally the engrossments behind entry no. 385); likewise, the earliest example of the type illustrated in Serafini is appended to a letter drawn under 12 Feb 1516 (NA, SC7 26/16). As the two seals were not used concurrently, the thrust of note 13 is unaffected by the 'discovery'. However, in point of theory the existence of two seals could have had a bearing on the interpretation of *sub eadem bulla* and *sub alia bulla*. The new information should be read into the note but dismissed as irrelevant.

A.P.F

ABBREVIATIONS AND SYMBOLS

AH	*Archivium Hibernicum*
Annates, Ardfert	'Obligationes pro Annatis Diocesis Ardfertensis', ed. J. O'Connell, *AH*, XXI (1958), pp. 1-51
Annates, Cashel	'Obligationes pro Annatis Diocesis Cassellensis', ed. L. Ryan and W. Skehan, *AH*, XXVIII (1966), pp. 1-32
Annates, Cloyne	'Obligationes pro Annatis Diocesis Cloynensis', ed. D. Buckley, *AH*, XXIV (1961), pp. 1-30
Annates, Cork	'Obligationes pro Annatis Diocesis Corcagiensis', ed. Sister M. Angela Bolster, *AH*, XXIX (1970), pp. 1-32
Annates, Elphin	'Obligationes pro Annatis Diocesis Elphinensis', ed. G. Mac Niocaill, *AH*, XXII (1959), pp. 1-27
Annates, Killaloe	'Obligationes pro Annatis Diocesis Laoniensis, 1421-1535' ed. D.F. Gleeson, *AH*, X (1943), pp. 1-103
Annates, Ross	'Obligationes pro Annatis Diocesis Rossensis', ed. J. Coombes, *AH*, XXIX (1970), pp. 33-48
Annates, Tuam Province	'Obligationes pro Annatis Provinciae Tuamensis', transcribed by J.F. O'Doherty, *AH*, XXVI (1963), pp. 56-117
ASR	Archivio di Stato, Rome
ASV	Archivio Segreto Vaticano
BA	Bachelor of Arts
Banck	L. Banck, ed., *Taxa S. Cancellariae Apostolicae*, Franeker, 1651
BAV	Biblioteca Apostolica Vaticana
BC	*Bullarium Carmelitanum*, vol. I, ed. E. Monsignano, Rome, 1715
BDec	Bachelor of Canon Law
Bell	H. Idris Bell, 'A List of Original Papal Bulls and Briefs in the Department of Manuscripts, British Museum', Part II, *English Historical Review*, XXXVI (1921), pp. 556-583. References are to item-numbers.
BL	The British Library (London)
BOP	*Bullarium Ordinis FF. Praedicatorum*, edd. A. Brémond and T. Ripoll, tom. IV, Rome, 1732
Brady	W. Maziere Brady, *The Episcopal Succession in England, Scotland and Ireland, A.D.1400 to 1875*, I, II (Rome, 1876), III (Rome, 1877)
BTheol	Bachelor of Theology
C	century (e.g. C18 = the 18th century)

CPL	*Calendar of Entries in the Papal Registers relating to Great Britain and Ireland : Papal Letters*, ed. W.H. Bliss, C. Johnson, J.A. Twemlow, M.J. Haren and A.P. Fuller, 19 vols. to date, London and Dublin, 1893-1998. References to new series vols. (i.e. vol. XV onwards) are to calendar-entry numbers.
CUL	Cambridge University Library
d.	in *or* of the diocese of
DDec	Doctor of Canon Law
Dowden	J. Dowden, *The Bishops of Scotland*, ed. J. Maitland Thomson, Glasgow, 1912
ds.	in *or* of the dioceses of
DTheol	Doctor of Theology
EDR	Ely Diocesan Records
Emden, *Oxford*	A. B. Emden, *A Biographical Register of the University of Oxford to A.D. 1500*, 3 vols (continuously paginated), Oxford, 1957
Eubel	G. van Gulik and C. Eubel, *Hierarchia Catholica Medii et Recentioris Aevi*, vol. III : saeculum XVI ab anno 1503 complectens, 2nd. ed., ed. L. Schmitz-Kallenberg, Münster, 1923
Friedberg	*Corpus Iuris Canonici,* ed. Aemilius Friedberg, vol II, Leipzig, 1879 (repr. Graz, 1959). References are to column numbers.
Herg(enroether).	*Leonis X. Pontificis Maximi Regesta* , ed. Joseph Hergenroether, 2 vols. (the second incomplete), Freiburg im Breisgau, 1884 - 1891. References are to entry numbers.
HWRO	Hereford and Worcester Record Office (Worcester)
Ind.	ASV, *Indici*
L & I	Public Record Office. Lists and Indexes. No. XLIX. *List of Diplomatic Documents, Scottish Documents and Papal Bulls preserved in the Public Record Office* [*now* NA]. London, HMSO, 1923
L&P, F&D	*Letters and Papers, Foreign and Domestic, of the Reign of Henry VIII.,* vol. I : 1st ed., arranged and catalogued by J.S.Brewer, London, 1862; 2nd ed. (in three parts), revised and enlarged by R.H.Brodie, London, HMSO, 1920; vol. II (in two parts), arranged and catalogued by J.S.Brewer, London, 1864. Unless otherwise indicated references are to entry numbers.
LA	Lincolnshire Archives (Lincoln)
Liber cancellariae	BAV, Barb. Lat. 2825 (formerly Codex Barberinianus XXXV. 69; original MS for the late medieval and early modern period). Extracts from this and other MSS of the *Liber* printed by Tangl

	and by G.Erler (ed.), *Der Liber Cancellariae Apostolicae vom Jahre 1380 und der Stilus Palatii Abbreviatus Dietrichs von Nieheim*, Leipzig, 1888
Liber pontificalis	*Liber pontificalis* ed. by Augustinus Patritius de Piccolominibus, with corrections by Jacobus de Lutiis and Johannes Burchardus, Rome, Stephanus Plannck, 1497
LLB	Bachelor of Laws
LLD	Doctor of Laws
LPL	Lambeth Palace Library (London)
M.	Master
MA	Master of Arts
MTheol	Master of Theology
NA	The National Archives [*formerly* PRO] (Kew, Surrey)
NRO	Norfolk Record Office (Norwich)
OCarm	Carmelite Order
OCist	Cistercian Order
OClun	Cluniac Order
OESA	Augustinian Eremite Order
OFM	Franciscan Order
OP	Dominican Order
OPrem	Premonstratensian Order
OSA	Augustinian Order (canons regular)
OSB	Benedictine Order
OVict	Victorine Order
PRO	Public Record Office [*now* NA]
Reg. Audley	Register of Edmund Audley, bishop of Salisbury, 1502-1524
Reg. Campeggio	Register of Lorenzo Campeggio, bishop of Salisbury, 1524-1534
Reg. Lat.	ASV, *Registra Lateranensia*
Reg. Nykke	Register of Richard Nykke, bishop of Norwich, 1501-1535
Reg. Silvestro de' Gigli	Register of Silvestro de' Gigli, bishop of Worcester, 1499-1521
Reg. Suppl.	ASV, *Registra Supplicationum*
Reg. Swayne	*A Calendar of the Register of John Swayne, Archbishop of Armagh and Primate of Ireland, 1418-1439*, ed. D. A. Chart, Belfast, 1935
Reg. West	Register of Nicholas West, bishop of Ely, 1515-1533

Reg. Wolsey and Atwater	Register of Thomas Wolsey, bishop of Lincoln, 1514 and William Atwater, bishop of Lincoln, 1514-1521
Tangl	*Die Päpstlichen Kanzleiordnungen von 1200-1500*, collected and edited by M. Tangl, Innsbruck, 1894
UIB	Bachelor of both Laws
UID	Doctor of both Laws
Valor Ecclesiasticus	*Valor Ecclesiasticus Temp. Henr. VIII. Auctoritate Regia Institutus.*, 6 vols., Record Commission, 1810-1835
WRO	Wiltshire County Record Office (Trowbridge)

[ ]	encloses matter supplied by editor (except where used parenthetically)
< >	(1) *in* Calendar Text: encloses insertions by registry staff; (2) *in* Conspectus of the Registers: as stated (p. lxviii, note 32)
***	indicates omission in MS
|	indicates transition from one line to next
| |	indicates transition from one page to next
/	*in* Calendar Text: (1) indicates position of administrative notes in register entry, as follows: *to right at start of entry*: note of abbreviator's signature / *left margin at start of entry*: initial of *magister registri* and (very occasionally) note of secretary's signature / *end of entry*: subscription of *magister registri* (usually note of tax mark or gratis formula and, sometimes, date of expedition in the *bullaria* enclosed between initial and surname or title); (2) indicates a deleted letter (*cf.* p. 344). Otherwise the usage is normal.

CHRONOLOGICAL TABLE OF LETTERS

The letters, which are calendared below in register order, are here arranged in order of the dates under which they are drawn. Other particulars are included in the table so that the passage of a letter through the bureaucracy and the manner of its impetration can (in outline at least) be read at a glance. (*See CPL* XVI, p. lxiv). 'E&W' means that the letter is of English and Welsh interest; 'S' of Scottish interest; 'I' of Irish. The diocese and (if any) order is that of the petitioner. *Consistoriales* and related letters are asterisked and the diocese etc. then is that of the benefices concerned. Other information is self explanatory. Calendar entries nos 270, 285, 295, 361, 571, 621 and 639 are undated; and the dating of entries nos 277, 298, 336, 366-368, 443 and 645 is uncertain.

DATE Rome, St Peter's unless otherwise noted	DATE OF EXPEDITION IN THE *BULLARIA*	*REG. LAT.*	COUNTRY, DIOCESE, ORDER, ETC.	CAL. ENTRY NO.
1513, 19 Mar.	————	1279, fos 327^r-328^r	E&W (York; Lincoln)	52
"	————	1279, fos 331^v-333^v	E&W (Lincoln)	55
"	————	1279, fos 335^r-336^v	E&W (Salona)	57
"	————	1279, fos 372^v-374^r	E&W (Salisbury)	64
"	————	1281, fos 41^r-42^v	E&W (Rome; York)	73
"	————	1282, fos 145^r-146^r	E&W (Winchester)	128
"	————	1282, fos 247^v-249^r	E&W (Lincoln)	129
"	————	1283, fos 271^r-272^r	S (Glasgow)	135
"	————	1283, fos 272^r-273^v	S (St Andrews)	136
"	————	1283, fos 273^v-275^r	S (Aberdeen)	137
"	————	1283, fo 332^{r-v}	E&W (London)	138
"	————	1285, fos 263^r-265^v	E&W (*foreign*)	149
"	————	1287, fos 341^r-342^v	E&W (Bath & Wells; OSA)	155
"	————	1290A, fos 364^v-366^v	E&W (London)	168
"	————	1295, fo 164^{r-v}	E&W (Exeter)	179
"	————	1296, fos 284^v-285^v	E&W (Rochester)	203
"	————	1297, fos 16^r-17^r	E&W (Exeter)	214
"	————	1297, fos 387^v-388^r	E&W (Lincoln; OCist)	225
"	————	1307, fos 230^r-234^r	S (Brechin)	247
1513, 25 Mar.	————	1279, fos 333^r-334^v	E&W (London)	56
"	————	1279, fos 363^r-364^r	E&W (Exeter)	62
"	————	1279, fos 364^r-365^r	E&W (Chichester; OSB)	63
"	————	1283, fos 279^r-280^v & 253^{r-v}	E&W (Coventry & Lichfield; OSA)	134
"	————	1320, fos 329^r-330^v	E&W (Worcester)	321
1513, 30 Mar.	————	1279, fos 345^v-348^v	I (Leighlin)	60

DATE Rome, St Peter's unless otherwise noted	DATE OF EXPEDITION IN THE *BULLARIA*	*REG. LAT.*	COUNTRY, DIOCESE, ORDER, ETC.	CAL. ENTRY NO.
1513, 1 Apr.	———————	1279, fo 281^{r-v}	E&W (Lincoln; Order of St Lazarus)	43
"	1513, 14 Apr.	1284, fos 217^r-219^v	I (Limerick; OSA)	142
"	1513, 14 Apr.	1284, fos 219^v-223^r	I (Cloyne)	143
15[1]3, 1 Apr.	1513, 14 Apr.	1284, fos 223^r-226^r	I (Killaloe)	144
1513, 4 Apr.	———————	1279, fos 276^v-277^r	E&W (Bath & Wells; OSB)	40
"	———————	1279, fos 328^v-329^v	E&W (Coventry & Lichfield)	53
"	———————	1279, fos 330^r-331^r	E&W (Exeter)	54
"	———————	1279, fos 341^v-342^v	E&W (Lincoln)	58
"	———————	1279, fos 342^v-345^r	E&W (Coventry & Lichfield)	59
"	———————	1279, fos 352^r-354^v	I (Leighlin)	61
"	1513, 16 Apr.	1286, fos 302^v-305^v	I (Limerick)	152
1513, 6 Apr.	———————	1281, fos 139^v-142^r	S (St Andrews)*	97
"	———————	1281, fo 142^{r-v}	S (St Andrews)*	98
"	———————	1281, fos 142^v-143^r	S (St Andrews)*	99
"	———————	1281, fos 143^r-144^r	S (St Andrews)*	100
"	———————	1281, fos 144^r-145^r	S (St Andrews)*	101
"	———————	1281, fos 145^r-146^v	S (St Andrews)*	102
1513, 8 Apr.	———————	1296, fo 21^{r-v}	E&W (Coventry & Lichfield)	190
"	———————	1297, fos 120^v-121^v	I (Killala)	219
1513, 11 Apr.	———————	1284, fos 105^v-108^v	S (Glasgow)	140
1513, 15 Apr.	———————	1281, fos 47^r-49^r	E&W; S (Sodor)*	74
"	———————	1281, fo 49^{r-v}	E&W; S (Sodor)*	75
"	———————	1281, fo 50^v	E&W; S (Sodor)*	77
"	———————	1281, fos 89^r-90^r	E&W (?Prizren.)*	84
"	———————	1281, fos 90^v-91^r	E&W (?Prizren.)*	86
"	———————	1281, fos 91^r-92^r	E&W (?Prizren.; Lincoln)*	87
"	———————	1281, fo 92^{r-v}	E&W (?Prizren.; Lincoln)*	88
"	———————	1281, fos 103^r-105^v	E&W (St Asaph)*	89
"	———————	1281, fos 105^v-106^r	E&W (St Asaph)*	90
"	———————	1281, fos 135^r-136^r	E&W (Gallipoli)*	92
"	———————	1281, fos 136^r-137^r	E&W (Gallipoli; London)*	93

DATE Rome, St Peter's unless otherwise noted	DATE OF EXPEDITION IN THE *BULLARIA*	*REG. LAT.*	COUNTRY, DIOCESE, ORDER, ETC.	CAL. ENTRY NO.
1513, 15 Apr.	—————	1281, fo 138^{r-v}	E&W (Gallipoli; London)*	95
"	—————	1281, fos 138^v-139^r	E&W (Gallipoli)*	96
"	—————	1281, fos 313^r-314^r	E&W (Natura)*	122
"	—————	1281, fos 314^r-315^r	E&W (Natura)*	123
"	—————	1281, fos 315^r-316^r	E&W (Natura)*	124
"	—————	1281, fos 316^r-317^r	E&W (Natura)*	125
1513, 16 Apr.	—————	1281, fo 90^{r-v}	E&W (?Prizren.)*	85
"	—————	1281, fo 137^{r-v}	E&W (Gallipoli)*	94
"	—————	1281, fos 317^v-318^r	E&W (Natura)*	126
1513, 17 Apr.	—————	1281, fos 49^v-50^r	E&W; S (Sodor)*	76
"	—————	1281, fos 106^v-107^r	E&W (St Asaph)*	91
1513, 25 Apr.	—————	1297, fos 225^r-226^v	E&W (Forlì)	220
1513, 27 Apr.	1513, 10 June	1284, fos 309^r-312^v	I (Leighlin)	145
1513, 30 Apr.	—————	1297, fos 366^v-367^v	E&W (Norwich)	224
1513, 3 May	—————	1279, fos 288^v-289^v	E&W (Lincoln)	44
"	—————	1279, fos 289^v-290^v	E&W (Exeter)	45
"	—————	1279, fos 291^r-292^r	E&W (Salisbury)	46
"	—————	1279, fos 292^r-293^r	E&W (Chichester)	47
"	—————	1279, fos 293^v-294^r	E&W (Lincoln)	48
"	—————	1279, fos 298^v-299^v	E&W (Lichfield)	49
"	—————	1297, fos 23^v-24^r	E&W (Queen of England)	217
1513, 5 May	—————	1279, fo 301^{r-v}	E&W (Canterbury)	50
"	—————	1279, fo 302^{r-v}	E&W (Lincoln)	51
"	—————	1284, fos 96^v-97^v	E&W (Lincoln; OCist)	139
"	—————	1290A, fos 227^r-228^r	E&W (Salisbury)	164
1513, 6 May	—————	1287, fos 338^r-341^r	E&W (Bath & Wells; OSA)	154
1513, 7 May	—————	1297, fos 313^v-315^v	E&W (Exeter)	222
"	—————	1297, fos 315^v-316^v	E&W (Bath & Wells)	223
1513, 19 May	1513, 1 July	1285, fos 43^r-44^v	E&W (*foreign*)	146
1513, 20 May	—————	1281, fos 11^r-12^v	E&W; I (Leighlin)*	71
"	—————	1281, fo 13^r	E&W; I (Leighlin)*	72
1513, 26 May	—————	1285, fos 157^r-158^v	I (Kildare)	148
1513, 31 May	—————	1283, fos 93^v-95^v	E&W (Lincoln; OSA)	130
1513, 2 June	—————	1296, fos 161^r-162^r	E&W (Natura; Durham)	202
"	—————	1296, fos 370^r-371^r	E&W (Gallipoli)	208
"	—————	1297, fos 299^v-300^v	E&W (London)	221

DATE Rome, St Peter's unless otherwise noted	DATE OF EXPEDITION IN THE *BULLARIA*	*REG. LAT.*	COUNTRY, DIOCESE, ORDER, ETC.	CAL. ENTRY NO.
1513, 5 June	1513, 18 June	1284, fos 129ᵛ-134ʳ	I (Leighlin; OCist)	141
1513, 8 June	————————	1281, fos 51ʳ-53ʳ	E&W (Tournai)*	78
"	————————	1281, fo 53ᵛ	E&W (Tournai)*	79
"	————————	1281, fos 53ᵛ-54ʳ	E&W (Tournai)*	80
"	————————	1281, fo 54ᵛ	E&W (Tournai)*	81
"	————————	1281, fo 55ʳ	E&W (Tournai)*	82
"	1513, 5 July	1286, fos 166ʳ-168ᵛ	I ([Derry])	150
1513, 10 June	————————	1281, fos 55ʳ-56ʳ	E&W (Tournai)*	83
1513, 15 June	————————	1279, fos 269ᵛ-271ʳ	E&W (Salisbury)	35
"	————————	1279, fos 271ʳ-272ᵛ	E&W (Bath & Wells)	36
"	————————	1279, fos 272ᵛ-273ᵛ	E&W (York)	37
"	————————	1279, fos 274ʳ-275ʳ	E&W (Salisbury)	38
"	————————	1279, fos 275ʳ-276ʳ	E&W (Lincoln)	39
1513, 16 June[1]	————————	1279, fo 235ʳ⁻ᵛ	E&W (Canterbury)	30
1513, 17 June	————————	1339, fo 226ʳ⁻ᵛ	I (Leighlin)	573
1513, 18 June	————————	1276, fos 379ᵛ-381ʳ	E&W (Exeter)	22
"	————————	1279, fos 236ʳ-237ʳ	E&W (Lincoln)	31
"	————————	1279, fos 237ʳ-238ʳ	E&W (Lincoln)	32
"	1513, 28 June	1286, fos 204ᵛ-207ʳ	I (Kildare)	151
1513, 28 June	————————	1276, fos 121ʳ-122ᵛ	E&W (Thérouanne)	6
"	————————	1279, fos 139ᵛ-141ʳ	E&W (London)	26
"	————————	1279, fos 231ʳ-232ʳ	E&W (Lincoln)	27
"	————————	1279, fos 232ʳ-233ᵛ	E&W (Lincoln)	28
"	————————	1279, fos 233ᵛ-234ᵛ	E&W (Exeter)	29
"	————————	1279, fo 244ʳ⁻ᵛ	E&W (Norwich; OSB)	34
"	————————	1279, fos 277ᵛ-278ᵛ	E&W (Canterbury)	41
"	————————	1279, fos 279ʳ-280ᵛ	E&W (Winchester)	42
1513, 1 July	————————	1297, fos 17ʳ-18ᵛ	E&W (Lincoln)	215
"	————————	1297, fos 18ᵛ-19ᵛ	E&W (Lincoln)	216
"	————————	1297, fos 58ᵛ-60ᵛ	E&W (York)	218
1513, 2 July	1513, 18 July	1285, fos 80ᵛ-82ᵛ	E&W (*foreign*)	147
1513, 3 July	————————	1279, fos 238ᵛ-239ᵛ	E&W (Salisbury)	33
1513, 8 July	————————	1279, fos 136ʳ-137ᵛ	E&W (Lincoln)	25
1513, 13 July	————————	1296, fos 21ᵛ-22ᵛ	E&W (Chichester)	191
1513, 15 July	————————	1293, fos 1ʳ-4ᵛ	S (Bourges; Moray)*	171
"	————————	1293, fos 4ᵛ-6ʳ	S (Bourges; Moray)*	172
"	————————	1293, fos 6ᵛ-7ʳ	S (Bourges; Moray)*	173

---

1   The Lateran

DATE Rome, St Peter's unless otherwise noted	DATE OF EXPEDITION IN THE *BULLARIA*	*REG. LAT.*	COUNTRY, DIOCESE, ORDER, ETC.	CAL. ENTRY NO.
1513, 15 July	——————	1293, fo 7ʳ⁻ᵛ	S (Bourges; Moray)*	174
1513, 20 July	——————	1296, fo 3ʳ⁻ᵛ	E&W (Bath & Wells)	185
1513, 23 July	——————	1283, fos 113ʳ-114ᵛ	E&W (Lincoln; OSA)	133
1513, 27 July	——————	1281, fo 219ʳ⁻ᵛ	E&W (Panados)*	118
"	——————	1281, fo 220ʳ	E&W (Panados)*	119
"	——————	1281, fo 220ʳ⁻ᵛ	E&W (Panados)*	120
"	——————	1281, fo 221ʳ⁻ᵛ	E&W (Panados)*	121
1513, 3 Aug.	——————	1293, fos 7ᵛ-8ʳ	S (Bourges; Moray)*	175
"	——————	1293, fos 8ᵛ-9ʳ	S (Bourges; Moray)*	176
1513, 5 Aug.	——————	1296, fos 10ᵛ-11ᵛ	E&W (Lincoln)	186
1513, 6 Aug.	——————	1296, fos 23ᵛ-24ʳ	E&W (York; London)	193
1513, 14 Aug.	——————	1296, fo 16ʳ⁻ᵛ	E&W (Canterbury)	187
"	——————	1296, fos 16ᵛ-17ᵛ	E&W (York; OSA)	188
"	——————	1296, fos 18ᵛ-20ʳ	E&W (Canterbury)	189
"	——————	1296, fos 32ᵛ-34ʳ	E&W (Coventry & Lichfield)	195
"	——————	1296, fos 375ᵛ-376ʳ	E&W (Coventry & Lichfield)	209
1513, 17 Aug.	——————	1296, fos 22ᵛ-23ᵛ	E&W (London)	192
1513, 20 Aug.	——————	1290A, fo 297ʳ⁻ᵛ	E&W (London; OSA)	166
"	——————	1296, fos 27ʳ-28ʳ	E&W (Bath & Wells)	194
"	——————	1296, fo 122ʳ⁻ᵛ	E&W (Norwich)	200
"	——————	1296, fos 122ᵛ-123ᵛ	E&W (Exeter)	201
1513, 24 Aug.	1514, 14 Jan	1276, fos 82ʳ-83ʳ	S (Bourges)	5
1513, 31 Aug.	——————	1296, fos 299ᵛ-300ᵛ	E&W (?Prizren.; Lincoln)	205
1513, 5 Sep.	——————	1287, fos 395ᵛ-396ᵛ	E&W (Carlisle)	156
"	——————	1296, fos 294ᵛ-295ʳ	E&W (Canterbury)	204
1513, 6 Sep.	——————	1276, fos 264ʳ-265ᵛ	E&W (Lincoln)	15
1513, 17 Sep.	——————	1290A, fos 93ᵛ-94ᵛ	E&W (Carlisle)	160
1513, 18 Sep.	——————	1296, fos 102ʳ-103ᵛ	E&W (London)	199
"	——————	1296, fos 359ʳ-360ʳ	E&W (Hereford)	206
1513, 19 Sep.	——————	1296, fos 98ᵛ-99ʳ	E&W (Winchester; OSB)	196
"	——————	1296, fo 99ʳ⁻ᵛ	E&W (Norwich; OSB)	197
"	——————	1296, fos 99ᵛ-100ᵛ	E&W (Lincoln)	198
1513, 30 Sep.	——————	1276, fos 6ʳ-8ᵛ	E&W (Carlisle)	1
1513, 1 Oct.	——————	1296, fos 360ᵛ-361ʳ	E&W (Bath & Wells)	207
1513, 5 Oct.	——————	1296, fos 409ᵛ-410ᵛ	E&W (Exeter)	213

DATE Rome, St Peter's unless otherwise noted	DATE OF EXPEDITION IN THE *BULLARIA*	*REG. LAT.*	COUNTRY, DIOCESE, ORDER, ETC.	CAL. ENTRY NO.
1[5]13, 7 Oct.	———————	1290A, fos 69^r-70^r	E&W (Norwich)	159
1513, 7 Oct.	———————	1296, fos 376^v-377^r	E&W (Worcester)	210
"	———————	1296, fos 377^v-378^r	E&W (Norwich; OPrem)	211
"	———————	1296, fo 381^{r-v}	E&W (Salisbury)	212
1513, 14 Oct.[1]	———————	1276, fos 253^r-254^r	E&W (Lincoln)	11
1513, 24 Oct.	———————	1281, fos 211^r-213^r	I (Armagh)*	114
"	———————	1281, fo 213^v	I (Armagh)*	115
"	———————	1281, fos 214^v-215^v	I (Armagh)*	117
1513, 25 Oct.	———————	1281, fo 214^{r-v}	I (Armagh)*	116
1513, 26 Oct.	———————	1287, fos 319^v-320^v	E&W (Canterbury)	153
1513, 2 Nov.	———————	1276, fos 395^v-396^v	E&W (Coventry & Lichfield; OSB)	23
1513, 3 Nov.	———————	1276, fo 369^{r-v}	E&W (Salisbury)	19
"	———————	1276, fos 377^r-378^r	E&W (Salisbury)	20
"	———————	1276, fos 378^v-379^v	E&W (Bath & Wells)	21
1513, 7 Nov.[2]	———————	1276, fos 122^v-124^v	E&W (Lincoln)	7
1513, 11 Nov.[3]	———————	1276, fos 368^r-369^r	E&W (Worcester)	18
1513, 12 Nov.	———————	1299, fos 140^r-141^r	I (Ferns)	230
1513, 18 Nov.	———————	1280, fos 193^v-195^v	E&W (London)	69
1513, 1 Dec.	1513, 22 Dec.	1301, fos 264^r-265^v	S (Brechin)	232
"	———————	1301, fos 265^v-268^r	S (Brechin)	233
"	———————	1301, fos 268^r-270^v	S (Brechin)	234
1513, 2 Dec.	———————	1276, fo 296^{r-v}	I (Armagh)*	17
1513, 9 Dec.	———————	1276, fos 257^r-258^v	E&W (Exeter)	12
"	———————	1276, fos 258^v-259^v	E&W (Lincoln)	13
"	———————	1276, fos 260^r-261^r	E&W (London)	14
1513, 15 Dec.	———————	1276, fos 294^v-296^r	E&W (Panados; Ely)	16
1513, 17 Dec.	———————	1276, fos 192^v-193^v	E&W (Coventry & Lichfield)	10
"	———————	1287, fos 400^r-401^r	E&W (Carlisle)	157
1513, 18 Dec.[4]	———————	1276, fos 171^r-172^v	E&W (Lincoln)	9
1513, 21 Dec.	———————	1290A, fos 46^v-47^v	E&W (Exeter)	158
1514, 3 Jan.	———————	1290A, fos 141^r-142^r	E&W (London)	162
1514, 9 Jan.	———————	1281, fos 157^r-160^r	S (Glasgow)*	103
"	———————	1281, fo 160^{r-v}	S (Glasgow)*	104

1   Ostia
2   Palo
3   Civitavecchia
4   The Lateran

DATE Rome, St Peter's unless otherwise noted	DATE OF EXPEDITION IN THE *BULLARIA*	*REG. LAT.*	COUNTRY, DIOCESE, ORDER, ETC.	CAL. ENTRY NO.
1514, 9 Jan.	——	1281, fo 161ʳ	S (Glasgow)*	105
1514, 10 Jan.	——	1276, fos 163ᵛ-165ʳ	E&W (Norwich)	8
"	——	1283, fo 111ʳ⁻ᵛ	E&W (York)	131
"	——	1283, fo 112ʳ⁻ᵛ	E&W (Canterbury)	132
1514, 18 Jan.[1]	——	1298, fos 222ᵛ-224ᵛ	I (Elphin; OSB)	228
1514, 22 Jan.[2]	——	1290A, fos 312ᵛ-313ᵛ	E&W (York; OSA)	167
1514, 30 Jan.	——	1276, fo 11ʳ⁻ᵛ	E&W (Bath & Wells)	2
"	——	1276, fos 12ʳ-13ᵛ	E&W (Salisbury)	3
"	——	1290A, fos 225ᵛ-227ʳ	E&W (Lincoln)	163
1514, 1 Feb.	——	1280, fos 266ᵛ-268ʳ	E&W (York; OSA)	70
1514, 2 Feb.	——	1278, fos 43ʳ-46ᵛ	E&W (London)	24
1514, 3 Feb.	——	1276, fos 25ʳ-26ᵛ	E&W (Winchester)	4
1514, 6 Feb.	——	1281, fos 199ʳ-202ᵛ	E&W (Lincoln)*	106
"	——	1281, fos 202ᵛ-203ʳ	E&W (Lincoln)*	107
"	——	1281, fo 203ʳ⁻ᵛ	E&W (Lincoln)*	108
"	——	1281, fo 204ʳ⁻ᵛ	E&W (Lincoln)*	109
"	——	1281, fos 205ʳ-207ᵛ	I (Raphoe)*	110
"	——	1281, fos 207ᵛ-208ʳ	I (Raphoe)*	111
"	——	1281, fo 208ʳ⁻ᵛ	I (Raphoe)*	112
1514, 7 Feb.	——	1281, fos 208ᵛ-209ᵛ	I (Raphoe)*	113
1514, 8 Feb.	1514, 25 Feb.	1302, fos 6ʳ-10ʳ	I (Limerick)	237
1514, 9 Feb.	1514, 25 Feb.	1280, fos 138ʳ-140ʳ	S (Aberdeen)	65
"	——	1280, fos 140ᵛ-142ᵛ	S (St Andrews)	66
"	——	1280, fos 143ʳ-144ᵛ	S (St Andrews)	67
"	1514, 25 Feb.	1280, fos 144ᵛ-146ʳ	S (St Andrews)	68
1514, 13 Feb.	1514, 6 Mar.	1298, fos 355ʳ-357ᵛ	I (Limerick)	229
"	——	1302, fos 4ᵛ-6ʳ	I (Emly)	236
1514, 15 Feb.	——	1334, fos 134ᵛ-136ᵛ	S (St Andrews)	497
1514, 17 Feb.	——	1290A, fos 140ʳ-141ʳ	E&W (Bath &Wells)	161
"	——	1321, fo 269ʳ⁻ᵛ	E&W (Bath & Wells)	327
"	——	1321, fos 282ʳ-283ᵛ	E&W (Bath & Wells)	328
1514, 21 Feb.	——	1290A, fos 233ʳ-234ʳ	E&W (London; OCist)	165
1514, 13 Mar.	1514, 30 Mar.	1298, fos 105ᵛ-107ʳ	E&W (*foreign*)	226
"	1514, 30 Mar.	1298, fos 107ʳ-108ᵛ	E&W (*foreign*)	227
1514, 15 Mar.	——	1300, fos 232ʳ-233ᵛ	E&W (York)	231
1514, 17 Mar.	1514, 8 Apr.	1301, fos 278ʳ-280ʳ	E&W (*foreign*)	235
1514, 18 Mar.	1514, 1 Apr.	1310, fos 137ᵛ-139ʳ	I (Derry)	258

1   Canino
2   Corneto

DATE	DATE OF EXPEDITION IN THE *BULLARIA*	*REG. LAT.*	COUNTRY, DIOCESE, ORDER, ETC.	CAL. ENTRY NO.
Rome, St Peter's unless otherwise noted				
1514, 21 Mar.	————————	1331, fos 135^v-136^r	E&W (Norwich)	450
"	————————	1331, fos 136^v-137^v	E&W (Norwich; OFM)	451
"	————————	1331, fos 137^v-138^v	E&W (Lincoln)	452
"	————————	1331, fos 138^v-139^v	E&W (Ely)	453
(?)1514, 23 Mar.	————————	1321, fos 159^r-160^v	E&W (*foreign*)	322
1514, 23 Mar.	————————	1331, fos 356^v-357^v	E&W (Chichester)	469
1514, 26 Mar.	————————	1323, fos 241^v-243^v	E&W (*foreign*)	345
1514, 27 Mar.	————————	1331, fos 134^r-135^r	E&W (Salisbury; OSA)	449
1514, 31 Mar.	————————	1304, fos 30^r-31^v	S (Brechin)	238
1514, 4 Apr.	————————	1308, fos 327^r-328^r	E&W (Norwich)	251
"	————————	1308, fos 328^r-329^v	E&W (Norwich)	252
1514, 7 Apr.	————————	1331, fos 167^v-168^v	E&W (Worcester)	454
1514, 9 Apr.	————————	1331, fos 34^r-35^r	E&W (Hereford)	437
1514, 10 Apr.	————————	1312, fo 195^{r-v}	E&W (Salisbury; OCist)	280
"	————————	1331, fo 88^{r-v}	E&W (Norwich; OSA)	439
"	————————	1331, fos 94^r-95^r	E&W (Norwich)	440
"	————————	1331, fos 214^v-216^r	E&W (Lincoln)	457
1514, 11 Apr.	————————	1331, fo 5^{r-v}	E&W (*none*; OFM)	431
1514, 22 Apr.	————————	1331, fo 102^{r-v}	E&W (*none*; OFM)	444
"	————————	1331, fos 130^v-132^r	E&W (Bath & Wells)	448
1514, 25 Apr.	————————	1310, fos 88^r-90^r	I (Killaloe; OSA)	257
1514, 26 Apr.	————————	1331, fo 95^{r-v}	E&W (Rochester; OSB)	441
"	————————	1331, fo 96^{r-v}	E&W (Lincoln)	442
1514, 27 Apr.	1514, 13 May	1308, fos 207^r-209^r	I (Elphin)	248
"	————————	1308, fos 209^v-211^r	I (Elphin)	249
"	1514, 23 May	1311, fos 240^r-242^v	I (Ossory)	262
1514, 2 May	————————	1312, fos 223^v-224^r	E&W (Coventry & Lichfield)	282
"	————————	1331, fos 235^r-236^v	E&W (Thérouanne)	458
1514, 3 May	————————	1331, fos 25^v-26^r	E&W (York; OSA)	432
"	————————	1331, fo 26^{r-v}	E&W (Salisbury)	433
"	————————	1331, fos 168^v-170^r	E&W (Norwich; OFM)	455
"	————————	1331, fo 316^{r-v}	E&W (York)	459
1514, 11 May	————————	1331, fo 106^{r-v}	E&W (London; OSB)	445

DATE Rome, St Peter's unless otherwise noted	DATE OF EXPEDITION IN THE *BULLARIA*	*REG. LAT.*	COUNTRY, DIOCESE, ORDER, ETC.	CAL. ENTRY NO.
1514, 13 May	————	1331, fo 187^r-188^v	E&W (Exeter)	456
1514, 16 May	————	1331, fos 27^r-28^v	E&W (York; OCist)	434
1514, 17 May[1]	————	1331, fos 30^r-31^r	E&W (Lincoln)	435
"[1]	————	1331, fos 31^r-32^r	E&W (Exeter)	436
1514, 18 May[1]	————	1311, fos 209^v-210^v	S (Glasgow)	261
"	————	1312 , fo 3^{r-v}	E&W (Winchester; OSA)	267
1514, 19 May[1]	————	1331, fos 127^v-128^v	E&W (London)	446
"[1]	————	1331, fo 129^{r-v}	E&W (Lincoln)	447
1514, 22 May[1]	————	1331, fos 42^v -44^r	I (Meath)	438
"	————	1331, fos 337^v-339^v	E&W (*foreign*)	463
1514, 27 May	————	1331, fo 317^{r-v}	E&W (London)	460
1514, 2 June	————	1312, fos 135^v-136^r	E&W (Coventry & Lichfield; OSA)	278
1514, 3 June	1514, 3 June	1304, fos 31^v-34^r	S (Dunkeld)	239
"	1514, 23 June	1308, fos 276^v-279^r	I (Emly)	250
"	1514, 23 June	1311, fos 299^r-301^v	I (Killaloe)	263
"	1514, 23 June	1311, fos 302^r-304^v	I (Killaloe)	264
1514, 7 June	1514, 4 Aug.	1310, fos 219^r-221^r	E&W (*foreign*)	259
1514, (?)7 June	————	1331, fos 326^r-328^r	E&W (Exeter)	462
1514, 10 June	————	1331, fos 324^v-326^r	E&W (*foreign*)	461
1514, 13 June	————	1331, fos 358^r-359^r	E&W (London)	470
1514, 14 June	1514, 12 July	1311, fos 81^r-82^v	I (Killaloe)	260
1514, 16 June	————	1312, fos 20^v-22^v	E&W (York)	268
1514, 17 June	————	1312, fos 1^r-2^r	E&W (Exeter)	266
"	————	1331, fos 339^v-340^v	E&W (York)	464
"	————	1331, fos 352^r-353^r	E&W (Ely)	465
"	————	1331, fos 353^r-354^r	E&W (Canterbury)	466
"	————	1331, fos 354^r-355^r	E&W (Coventry & Lichfield)	467
"	————	1331, fos 355^r-356^v	E&W (Exeter)	468
"	————	1331, fos 359^r-360^r	E&W (Lincoln; OPrem)	471
1514, 19 June	————	1325, fos 31^v-33^v	I (Tuam)*	369
"	————	1325, fo 34^r	I (Tuam)*	370
1514, 20 June	————	1325, fo 34^v	I (Tuam)*	371
1514, 23 June	————	1312, fos 220^v-221^v	E&W (Selimbria; Exeter)	281
1514, 5 July	————	1312, fos 86^r-87^r	E&W (Salisbury)	269

---

1   Magliana

DATE Rome, St Peter's unless otherwise noted	DATE OF EXPEDITION IN THE *BULLARIA*	*REG. LAT.*	COUNTRY, DIOCESE, ORDER, ETC.	CAL. ENTRY NO.
1514, 6 July	————	1311, fos 326^r-329^v	I (Killaloe)	265
1514, 8 July	————	1312, fos 100^v-102^r	E&W (York)	271
1514, 14 July	————	1293, fos 246^v-248^v	E&W (Bologna; OSB)*	177
"	————	1293, fos 248^v-249^r	E&W (Bologna; OSB)*	178
"	————	1323, fos 256^r-258^r	E&W (*foreign*)	346
1514, 17 July	1514, 4 Aug.	1310, fos 33^v-36^v	I (Raphoe)	256
1514, 23 July	————	1309, fos 31^r-32^v	S (St Andrews; OSA)	253
1514, 24 July	————	1309, fos 230^v-231^v	E&W (Salisbury)	255
1514, 28 July	————	1314, fos 62^v-63^v	E&W (Winchester)	291
1514, 7 Aug.	1514, 13 Sep.	1312, fos 302^v-304^r	S (St Andrews)	284
(?)1514, 14 Aug.	1514, 31 Oct.	1322, fos 212^r-215^r	I (Limerick)	336
1514, 18 Aug.	————	1312, fos 108^v-109^r	E&W (Bangor)	272
"	————	1312, fos 115^r-116^r	E&W (Canterbury)	275
"	————	1312, fos 116^r-117^r	E&W (London)	276
1514, 21 Aug.	————	1312, fos 109^v-110^r	E&W (Bath & Wells; OSB)	273
"	————	1312, fo 112^{r-v}	E&W (*none*; OCarm)	274
1514, 25 Aug,	1514, 11 Sep.	1312, fos 268^r-269^v	S (St Andrews)	283
1514, 29 Aug.	————	1309, fos 202^v-204^r	E&W (York)	254
1514, 3 Sep.	————	1323, fos 91^r-92^r	E&W (Salisbury)	343
1514, 12 Sep.	————	1313, fos 134^v-136^r	E&W (Winchester; OSA; & Salisbury)	288
1514, 13 Sep.	————	1312, fos 153^r-154^r	E&W (Worcester or other)	279
1514, 15 Sep.	————	1325, fos 214^r-216^v	E&W (Lincoln)*	379
"	————	1325, fos 216^v-217^r	E&W (Lincoln)*	380
"	————	1325, fo 217^{r-v}	E&W (Lincoln)*	381
"	————	1325, fos 218^r-220^r	E&W (York)*	382
"	————	1325, fo 220^v	E&W (York)*	383
"	————	1325, fo 222^r	E&W (York)*	384
1514, 17 Sep.	————	1313, fos 9^r-10^v	I or S (Ross)	286
1514, 21 Sep.	————	1313, fos 12^r-14^v	E&W (Bath & Wells)	287
1514, 25 Sep.	————	1325, fos 221^v-222^v	E&W (York)*	385
1514, 29 Sep.	————	1314, fos 74^r-76^r	E&W (Lincoln; OSA)	293
1514, 1 Oct.[1]	————	1282, fo 135^{r-v}	E&W (Norwich)	127
" [1]	————	1314, fo 125^{r-v}	E&W (Salisbury)	294

---

1   Nepi

DATE Rome, St Peter's unless otherwise noted	DATE OF EXPEDITION IN THE *BULLARIA*	*REG. LAT.*	COUNTRY, DIOCESE, ORDER, ETC.	CAL. ENTRY NO.
1514, 3 Oct.[1]	————	1314, fos 73ʳ-74ᵛ	E&W (London; OCist)	292
1514, 4 Oct.[2]	————	1322, fos 221ᵛ-222ʳ	E&W (Bath & Wells; OSA)	337
1514, 12 Oct.[3]	————	1306, fo 53ʳ⁻ᵛ	E&W (Canterbury)	242
"[3]	————	1314, fos 61ʳ-62ʳ	E&W (Lincoln)	290
"[3]	1514, 2 Dec.	1322, fos 224ʳ-226ʳ	I (Lismore)	339
"[3]	1514, 14 Nov.	1322, fos 287ʳ-289ᵛ	I (Lismore)	342
1514, 13 Oct.[4]	1514, 30 Aug.	1322, fos 226ʳ-228ᵛ	I (Lismore)	340
"[4]	1514, 14 Nov.	1322, fos 284ᵛ-287ʳ	I (Cork)	341
1514, 15 Oct.[5]	————	1322, fos 153ᵛ-156ʳ	I (Lismore)	335
1514, 6 Nov.	————	1325, fos 231ᵛ-234ʳ	I (Kilfenora)*	386
"	————	1325, fo 234ᵛ	I (Kilfenora)*	387
1514, 7 Nov.	————	1325, fo 235ʳ⁻ᵛ	I (Kilfenora)*	388
1514, 9 Nov.	1515, 24 Mar.	1307, fos 25ʳ-26ʳ	E&W (*foreign*)	244
"	————	1315, fos 12ʳ-13ʳ	E&W (Salisbury)	296
1514, 10 Nov.	————	1315, fos 13ᵛ-14ʳ	E&W (York; OPrem)	297
1514, 11 Nov.	1514, 2 Dec.	1322, fos 222ᵛ-224ʳ	I (Clogher)	338
1514, 13 Nov.	————	1316, fos 104ʳ-108ᵛ	S (Dunblane; OSA)*	303
"	————	1316, fos 108ᵛ-109ᵛ	S (Dunblane; OSA)*	304
"	————	1316, fos 109ᵛ-110ʳ	S (Dunblane; OSA)*	305
1514, 22 Nov.	1514, 9 Dec.	1318, fos 78ʳ-81ʳ	I (Clogher)	310
1514, 28 Nov.	————	1314, fo 24ʳ⁻ᵛ	E&W (Coventry & Lichfield)	289
"	————	1318, fo 253ʳ⁻ᵛ	E&W (Worcester)	314
1514, 1 Dec.	————	1322, fos 133ʳ-136ʳ	I (Limerick)	333
1515, 9 Jan.	————	1306, fos 160ʳ-161ʳ	E&W (London)	243
1515, 11 Jan.	————	1317, fos 39ʳ-42ʳ	I (Meath; OCist)	307
1515, 12 Jan.	————	1318, fos 250ᵛ-251ᵛ	E&W (London)	312
1515, 25 Jan.[6]	————	1316, fos 102ʳ-104ʳ	E&W (Chichester)	302
1515, 28 Jan.	1515, 10 Feb.	1317, fos 258ʳ-260ʳ	I (Ross)	309
"	1515, 6 Feb.	1322, fos 118ʳ-120ʳ	I (Elphin?; OHosp)	331
1515, 31 Jan.	————	1318, fos 266ᵛ-267ᵛ	E&W (St David's)	315

1   Civita Castellana
2   Ronciglione
3   Viterbo
4   Montefiascone
5   Capodimonte
6   Magliana

DATE Rome, St Peter's unless otherwise noted	DATE OF EXPEDITION IN THE *BULLARIA*	*REG. LAT.*	COUNTRY, DIOCESE, ORDER, ETC.	CAL. ENTRY NO.
1515, 4 Feb.[1]	1515, 17 Feb.	1317, fos 242^r-245^r	I (Elphin)	308
" [1]	——————	1322, fos 122^r-123^r	E&W (Lincoln)	332
1515, 9 Feb.[2]	——————	1322, fos 152^v-153^r	I (Meath)	334
1515, 10 Feb.	1515, 18 July	1323, fos 95^v-97^r	S (Aberdeen)	344
1515, 22 Feb.	——————	1316, fos 1^r-3^v	E&W (Norwich)	299
"	——————	1316, fos 3^v-6^r	E&W (Lincoln)	300
"	——————	1316, fos 41^r-42^r	E&W (Chichester; OClun)	301
"	——————	1316, fos 281^r-283^r	S (*foreign*)	306
"	——————	1324, fos 267^v-270^v	E&W (Lincoln; OSA)	360
1515, 26 Feb.	——————	1291, fos 290^r-293^r	E&W (Exeter)	169
1515, 12 Mar.	——————	1307, fos 108^v-110^v	I (Elphin)	245
"	——————	1322, fos 10^v-13^v	I (Elphin)	330
1515, 13 Mar.	——————	1318, fos 249^v-250^v	E&W (Exeter)	311
"	——————	1318, fo 252^{r-v}	E&W (St David's)	313
"	——————	1321, fos 317^r-318^r	E&W (Norwich; OSA)	329
1515, 24 Mar.	——————	1328, fos 99^r-100^r	E&W (Exeter)	413
"	——————	1328, fo 116^{r-v}	E&W (Salisbury)	421
1515, 28 Mar.	——————	1328, fos 100^r-101^v	E&W (Winchester)	414
1515, 30 Mar.	1515, 14 Apr.	1307, fos 179^r-180^v	I (Tuam)	246
1515, 2 Apr.	——————	1334, fos 79^v-80^v	E&W (Salisbury)	496
1515, 5 Apr.	1515, 19 Apr.	1321, fos 220^r-222^r	I (Elphin)	323
"	——————	1328, fos 217^r-219^r	E&W (London; OPrem)	425
1515, 10 Apr.	——————	1326, fos 252^r-253^r	E&W (Lincoln)	398
1515, 11 Apr.	——————	1326, fos 253^r-254^r	E&W (Coventry & Lichfield)	399
1515, 19 Apr.	——————	1321, fos 222^v-223^v	B&W (Bangor)	324
1515, 20 Apr.	——————	1326, fos 260^r-261^r	E&W (Lincoln)	401
"	——————	1326, fos 261^v-262^v	E&W (Lincoln)	402
"	——————	1335, fos 27^r-28^r	I (Meath)	502
1515, 24 Apr.	——————	1332, fos 262^r-263^r	E&W (Exeter)	490
1515, 28 Apr.	——————	1321, fos 232^v-233^v	E&W (Canterbury)	325
1515, 3 May	1515, 26 May	1321, fos 237^v-240^r	I (Raphoe)	326
" [3]	——————	1324, fos 5^r-7^v	I (Raphoe)	347

1 Palo
2 Magliana
3 The Lateran

DATE Rome, St Peter's unless otherwise noted	DATE OF EXPEDITION IN THE *BULLARIA*	*REG. LAT.*	COUNTRY, DIOCESE, ORDER, ETC.	CAL. ENTRY NO.
1515, 7 May[1]	1515, 2 June	1324, fos 129^v-131^r	I (Raphoe)	354
1515, 12 May[1]	—————	1328, fos 121^v-122^r	E&W (Coventry & Lichfield)	422
"[1]	—————	1332, fos 37^v-39^v	E&W (London)	473
1515, 16 May	—————	1326, fos 256^r-257^r	E&W (Salisbury)	400
1515, 17 May	—————	1324, fos 97^r-99^r	I (Raphoe)	351
"	1515, (?) 14 June	1332, fos 91^v-94^r	I (Leighlin)	476
1515, 19 May	—————	1328, fos 124^v-125^r	E&W (Lincoln; OSB)	423
1515, 23 May	—————	1334, fos 26^r-33^v	E&W (Salisbury; OSA)	494
1515, 25 May	—————	1325, fos 134^r-136^r	S (Dunkeld)*	375
"	—————	1325, fo 136^v	S (Dunkeld)*	376
"	—————	1325, fos 137^v-138^v	S (Dunkeld)*	378
"	1515, 6 June	1332, fo 94^v-96^v	I (Ferns)	477
1515, 26 May	—————	1325, fo 137^{r-v}	S (Dunkeld)*	377
1515, (?)31 May	1515, 28 June	1324, fos 11^r-14^r	I (Leighlin)	349
1515, (?)2 June	—————	1324, fos 167^r-170^v	I (Ferns)	355
1515, 2 June	—————	1326, fos 231^r-232^r	E&W (London; OSA)	391
1515, 3 June	1515, 28 June	1324, fos 7^v-10^v	I (Leighlin)	348
1515, 4 June	—————	1324, fos 202^v-203^v	E&W (Chichester)	356
"	—————	1324, fos 203^v-205^r	E&W (Norwich)	357
"	—————	1326, fo 251^{r-v}	E&W (Worcester)	397
"	—————	1326, fos 267^r-268^r	E&W (Norwich)	403
"	—————	1326, fos 268^r-269^r	E&W (Ely)	404
"	—————	1326, fos 269^v-270^v	E&W (St David's)	405
"	—————	1326, fos 270^v-271^v	E&W (London)	406
"	—————	1326, fos 271^v-272^v	E&W (Coventry & Lichfield)	407
"	—————	1326, fo 273^{r-v}	E&W (York; OSA)	408
"	—————	1328, fos 103^r-104^r	E&W (Norwich)	415
"	—————	1328, fos 105^r-106^v	E&W (Exeter)	417
"	—————	1328, fos 107^r-108^v	E&W (London)	418
"	—————	1328, fo 125^{r-v}	E&W (York)	424
1515, 6 June	—————	1334, fos 231^v-232^v	E&W (Coventry & Lichfield)	498
1515, 7 June	1515, 7 July	1324, fos 99^r-102^r	I (Ossory)	352

1   Magliana

DATE Rome, St Peter's unless otherwise noted	DATE OF EXPEDITION IN THE *BULLARIA*	*REG. LAT.*	COUNTRY, DIOCESE, ORDER, ETC.	CAL. ENTRY NO.
1515, 7 June	1515, 23 June	1324, fos 212ᵛ-214ʳ	I (Tuam)	358
"	———————	1334, fo 56ʳ⁻ᵛ	E&W (Exeter)	495
1515, 8 June	———————	1328, fos 104ᵛ-105ʳ	E&W (Salisbury; OSA)	416
"	———————	1328, fos 108ᵛ-109ᵛ	E&W (Norwich; OSA)	419
"	———————	1328, fos 110ʳ-111ʳ	E&W (Bath & Wells)	420
1515, 9 June	———————	1335, fos 209ʳ-210ʳ	E&W (Lincoln)	509
1515, 18 June	———————	1330, fo 49ʳ⁻ᵛ	E&W (Chichester)	426
1515, 22 June	———————	1336, fos 244ʳ-245ʳ	E&W (Lincoln)	518
1515, 23 June	———————	1326, fos 232ᵛ-233ᵛ	E&W (London)	392
"	———————	1326, fos 233ᵛ-234ᵛ	E&W (Salisbury)	393
"	———————	1326, fos 235ʳ-236ʳ	E&W (Norwich)	394
"	———————	1326, fos 236ʳ-237ʳ	E&W (Coventry & Lichfield)	395
"	———————	1326, fos 237ʳ⁻ᵛ	E&W (Coventry & Lichfield; OSA)	396
"	———————	1332, fos 170ᵛ-172ʳ	E&W (Salisbury)	486
1515, 28 June	1515, 5 July	1324, fos 17ʳ-19ʳ	I (Connor)	350
1515, 2 July	1515, 7 July	1324, fos 102ʳ-105ʳ	I (Raphoe)	353
1515, 3 July	———————	1332, fos 9ᵛ-10ᵛ	E&W (Exeter)	472
"	———————	1332, fos 197ʳ-198ʳ	E&W (Worcester)	488
"	———————	1332, fos 207ʳ-208ʳ	E&W (York)	489
1515, 10 July	———————	1324, fos 309ʳ-310ᵛ	E&W (Lincoln)	365
1515, 21 July	———————	1332, fos 138ʳ-139ʳ	E&W (Norwich)	481
1515, 23 July	———————	1333, fos 151ʳ-152ᵛ	E&W (York)	493
1515, 26 July	———————	1324, fos 292ᵛ-293ᵛ	E&W (York)	363
"	———————	1324, fos 293ᵛ-294ᵛ	E&W (Exeter)	364
"	———————	1332, fos 39ᵛ-40ᵛ	E&W (Salisbury)	474
"	———————	1332, fos 101ʳ-102ᵛ	E&W (Coventry & Lichfield)	478
"	———————	1332, fos 139ᵛ-140ᵛ	E&W (London)	482
"	———————	1332, fos 140ᵛ-142ʳ	E&W (St David's)	483
1515, 27 July	———————	1325, fos 52ʳ-54ʳ	E&W (Ely)*	372
"	———————	1325, fo 55ʳ⁻ᵛ	E&W (Ely)*	374
1515, 28 July	———————	1325, fos 54ᵛ-55ʳ	E&W (Ely)*	373
1515, 29 July	———————	1332, fos 110ʳ-111ᵛ	E&W (Bath & Wells; OSA)	479
1515, 16 Aug.	———————	1326, fos 157ʳ-158ʳ	E&W (Chichester; OCarm)	390

DATE Rome, St Peter's unless otherwise noted	DATE OF EXPEDITION IN THE *BULLARIA*	*REG. LAT.*	COUNTRY, DIOCESE, ORDER, ETC.	CAL. ENTRY NO.
1515, 16 Aug.[1]	———————	1339, fos 39^r-40^r	E&W (Canterbury)	536
1515, 17 Aug.	———————	1324, fos 246^v-247^v	E&W (St David's)	359
"	———————	1332, fos 156^v-157^v	E&W (Exeter)	485
1515, 20 Aug.	———————	1337, fos 57^r-58^v	E&W (Durham)	519
"	———————	1341, fos 246^r-247^r	S (St Andrews; OSA)	584
"	1516, 7 Apr.	1341, fos 247^v-249^r	S (St Andrews; OSA)	585
1515, 21 Aug.	———————	1332, fos 125^v-126^r	E&W (Winchester; OSB)	480
1515, 23 Aug.	———————	1332, fos 67^v-69^r	E&W (Norwich)	475
1515, 25 Aug.	———————	1326, fos 23^r-24^r	E&W (Chichester)	389
1515, 26 Aug.	———————	1332, fos 155^r-156^r	E&W (Hereford)	484
1515, 1 Sep.	———————	1332, fo 176^{r-v}	E&W (Norwich)	487
1515, 12 Sep.	———————	1335, fos 30^v-32^r	E&W (Durham)	503
1515, 13 Sep.	———————	1333, fos 120^v-122^v	I (Dublin; OSA)	491
1515, 15 Sep.	1515, 16 Nov.	1327, fos 282^r-283^v	S (Moray)	411
1515, 17 Sep.	———————	1324, fos 276^r-277^r	E&W (Chichester)	362
"	———————	1335, fos 32^v-33^v	E&W (Coventry & Lichfield)	504
"	———————	1335, fos 34^r-35^r	E&W (St Asaph)	505
"	———————	1335, fos 43^v-44^v	E&W (Hereford)	506
1515, 19 Sep.	———————	1335, fo 46^{r-v}	E&W (Coventry & Lichfield)	507
1515, 23 Sep.	———————	1333, fos 123^r-124^v	I (Dublin; OSA)	492
1515, 30 Sep.	———————	1339, fo 12^{r-v}	E&W (Coventry & Lichfield)	533
1515, 10 Oct.[2]	———————	1335, fos 125^v-127^r	E&W (Ascalon; Worcester)	508
1515, 19 Oct.[3]	———————	1339, fos 159^r-160^v	E&W (Lincoln; OSA)	567
1515, 20 Oct.[3]	1515, 16 Nov.	1337, fos 162^v-164^r	S (St Andrews; OSA)	520
1515, 21 Oct.[4]	———————	1327, fo 285^{r-v}	S (St Andrews)	412
1515, 25 Oct.[5]	———————	1335, fos 12^r-13^v	E&W (Worcester)	501
1515, 2 Nov.[2]	———————	1335, fos 6^r-7^r	E&W (Lincoln)	499
"[2]	———————	1335, fos 7^r-8^v	E&W (Lincoln)	500
"[2]	———————	1339, fos 157^v-159^r	E&W (Salisbury)	566

1   Florence
2   Viterbo
3   Toscanella
4   Corneto
5   Civitavecchia

DATE Rome, St Peter's unless otherwise noted	DATE OF EXPEDITION IN THE *BULLARIA*	*REG. LAT.*	COUNTRY, DIOCESE, ORDER, ETC.	CAL. ENTRY NO.
1515, 10 Nov.[1]	———————	1327, fos 29ʳ-30ʳ	E&W (Bath & Wells; OSA)	409
"[1]	———————	1327, fos 30ʳ-31ʳ	E&W (Lincoln)	410
"[1]	———————	1335, fos 211ᵛ-212ʳ	E&W (St Asaph; OCist)	510
"[1]	———————	1335, fos 215ᵛ-217ʳ	E&W (Worcester)	511
"[1]	———————	1335, fos 233ʳ-234ʳ	E&W (London)	512
"[1]	———————	1335, fos 236ʳ-237ʳ	E&W (Lincoln)	513
"[1]	———————	1335, fos 237ᵛ-238ᵛ	E&W (Canterbury)	514
"[1]	———————	1335, fos 238ᵛ-239ᵛ	E&W (Chichester)	515
"[1]	———————	1335, fos 240ʳ-241ʳ	E&W (Exeter)	516
"[1]	———————	1335, fos 241ʳ-242ᵛ	E&W (St David's)	517
1515, 12 Dec.[2]	———————	1338, fos 120ʳ-121ʳ	E&W (OPrem)	521
1515, 22 Dec.[3]	———————	1339, fo 140ʳ⁻ᵛ	E&W (London)	556
"[3]	———————	1339, fo 149ʳ⁻ᵛ	E&W (Salisbury)	557
"[3]	———————	1339, fo 150ʳ⁻ᵛ	E&W (Worcester)	558
"[3]	———————	1339, fo 151ʳ⁻ᵛ	E&W (Lincoln)	559
"[3]	———————	1339, fo 155ᵛ	E&W (*none*; OFM)	563
"[3]	———————	1339, fo 156ʳ⁻ᵛ	E&W (Norwich; OSB)	564
1515, 23 Dec.[3]	1516, 15 Jan.	1340, fos 118ʳ-120ʳ	I (Achonry)	575
1515, 29 Dec.[3]	———————	1330, fo 97ʳ-98ʳ	E&W (Hereford)	427
"[3]	———————	1338, fos 301ʳ-302ʳ	S (St Andrews)	530
"[3]	———————	1339, fos 80ʳ-81ʳ	E&W (London; OSA)	542
"[3]	———————	1339, fos 152ʳ-153ʳ	E&W (Exeter)	560
"[3]	———————	1339, fos 153ʳ-154ʳ	E&W (Lincoln)	561
"[3]	———————	1339, fos 154ʳ-155ʳ	E&W (Coventry & Lichfield)	562
"[3]	———————	1339, fos 156ᵛ-157ᵛ	E&W (Worcester)	565
"[3]	1516, 30 Apr.	1341, fos 103ᵛ-105ʳ	I (Lismore)	581
1516, 5 Jan.[3]	———————	1339, fos 75ᵛ-77ʳ	E&W (Norwich)	541
1516, 7 Jan.[3]	———————	1338, fos 155ʳ-156ʳ	E&W (Winchester)	524
"[3]	———————	1338, fos 156ᵛ-157ᵛ	E&W (Hereford)	525
1516, 8 Jan.[3]	———————	1339, fo 275ʳ	E&W (Norwich; OSA)	574
1516, 9 Jan.[3]	———————	1339, fos 85ᵛ-86ʳ	E&W (Lincoln; OPrem)	543
"[3]	———————	1339, fos 109ʳ-110ʳ	E&W (Exeter)	546

1   Montefiascone
2   Bologna
3   Florence

DATE Rome, St Peter's unless otherwise noted	DATE OF EXPEDITION IN THE *BULLARIA*	*REG. LAT.*	COUNTRY, DIOCESE, ORDER, ETC.	CAL. ENTRY NO.
1516, 9 Jan.[1]	—————	1339, fos 111^r-112^r	E&W (London)	547
"[1]	—————	1339, fos 112^r-113^r	E&W (London)	548
"[1]	—————	1339, fos 113^r-114^r	E&W (London)	549
"[1]	—————	1339, fos 118^r-119^r	E&W (Coventry & Lichfield)	550
"[1]	—————	1339, fos 119^r-120^r	E&W (Exeter)	551
"[1]	—————	1339, fos 120^v-121^r	E&W (Lincoln)	552
"[1]	—————	1339, fos 123^v-124^v	E&W (York; OCist)	555
"[1]	—————	1339, fo 169^{r-v}	E&W (Exeter)	568
"[1]	—————	1339, fos 171^v-172^r	E&W (Worcester; OSVictor)	569
"[1]	—————	1339, fos 175^r-176^v	E&W (York)	570
1516, 10 Jan.[1]	—————	1338, fos 143^r-144^v	S (Aberdeen)	522
1516, 11 Jan.[2]	—————	1338, fos 149^v-150^r	E&W (Salisbury; OSB)	523
"[2]	—————	1338, fos 322^r-323^r	E&W (Salisbury)	532
1516, 14 Jan.[1]	—————	1338, fos 320^v-321^v	E&W (Exeter)	531
1516, 15 Jan.[1]	—————	1339, fos 30^v-32^r	E&W (London)	535
1516, 17 Jan.[1]	—————	1330, fos 104^v-106^r	E&W (Coventry & Lichfield)	429
"[1]	—————	1339, fos 47^v-48^v	E&W (Lincoln)	537
"[1]	—————	1339, fos 121^v-122^r	E&W (Canterbury)	553
"[1]	—————	1339, fos 122^v-123^v	E&W (Coventry & Lichfield)	554
1516, 20 Jan.[3]	1516, 1 Feb.	1339, fos 15^v-18^r	I (Ross)	534
1516, 30 Jan.[1]	—————	1330, fos 98^r-99^r	E&W (Worcester)	428
1516, 7 Feb.[1]	—————	1341, fos 117^v-118^v	E&W (Lincoln)	582
1516, 10 Feb.[1]	—————	1338, fo 202^{r-v}	E&W (London)	527
"[1]	—————	1338, fos 203^r-204^r	E&W (Coventry & Lichfield)	528
"[1]	—————	1338, fos 204^r-205^r	E&W (Lincoln; OSB)	529
1516, 15 Feb.[1]	—————	1338, fos 201^r-202^r	E&W (Lincoln)	526
1516, 16 Feb.[2]	—————	1339, fos 48^v-50^r	E&W (Lincoln)	538
"[2]	—————	1339, fos 97^v-98^v	E&W (Lincoln)	545
1516, 4 Mar.	1516, 19 Mar.	1341, fos 25^r-26^v	I (Armagh)	577
"	—————	1341, fos 27^r-29^r	I (Clogher)	578

1   Florence
2   Careggi
3   Poggio a Caiano

DATE Rome, St Peter's unless otherwise noted	DATE OF EXPEDITION IN THE *BULLARIA*	*REG. LAT.*	COUNTRY, DIOCESE, ORDER, ETC.	CAL. ENTRY NO.
1516, 8 Mar.	1516, 13 Nov.	1330, fos 177^v-179^v	E&W (*foreign*)	430
1516, 9 Mar.	——————	1339, fos 195v-196v	E&W (London)	572
1516, 12 Mar.	——————	1341, fo 94^{r-v}	E&W (Salisbury)	580
1516, 14 Mar.	——————	1339, fos 60^v-61^v	E&W (St David's)	539
"	——————	1339, fo 62^{r-v}	E&W (Ely)	540
1516, 16 Mar.	——————	1339, fo 87^{r-v}	E&W (York; OSA)	544
1516, 25 Mar.[1]	——————	1341, fos 188^v-190^r	E&W (St David's)	583
1516, 26 Mar.	——————	1345, fos 52^r-55^v	I (Killaloe)	618
1516, 27 Mar.	1516, 11 Apr.	1345, fos 57^v-60^r	I (Clogher)	619
"	1516, 7 Apr.	1345, fos 223^v-226^r	I (Armagh)	629
1516, 28 Mar.	——————	1345, fos 170^r-174^r	I (Lismore)	627
1516, 31 Mar.	——————	1345, fos 148^v-152^v	I (Cloyne)	625
1516, 7 Apr.	——————	1345, fos 97^v-98^v	E&W (York)	622
"	——————	1352, fos 155^r-156^r	E&W (Hereford)	697
"	——————	1353, fos 95^r-96^r	E&W (Lincoln)	717
"	——————	1345, fos 182^r-187^r	I (Emly)	628
1516, 9 Apr.	——————	1341, fos 274^v-275^v	S (Moray)	586
"	——————	1341, fos 365^r-366^v	E&W (*none*; Order of Knights of Holy Sepulchre)	587
1516, 10 Apr.	——————	1341, fos 92^v-93^v	E&W (Panados; St David's; Coventry & Lichfield)	579
1516, 13 Apr.[1]	——————	1345, fos 22^r-23^r	E&W (Norwich; OSA)	617
1516, 14 Apr.	——————	1345, fos 152^v-155^v	I (Lismore)	626
1516, 16 Apr.	——————	1341, fos 19^v-21^r	I (Armagh)	576
1516, 18 Apr.[1]	——————	1345, fos 335^v-336^v	E&W (Canterbury)	630
1516, 22 Apr.[2]	——————	1345, fos 21^r-22^r	E&W (Norwich)	616
"[2]	——————	1345, fos 128^r-132^r	I (Kildare)	624
1516, 23 Apr.[2]	——————	1345, fos 125^r-127^v	I (Leighlin)	623
1516, 24 Apr.[2]	——————	1344, fos 141^r-144^r	I (*none*; OSA)	611
1516, 25 Apr.[2]	——————	1352, fos 158^r-159^r	E&W (Salisbury)	698
1516, 29 Apr.	——————	1345, fos 84^v-85^v	I (Meath)	620
1516, 30 Apr.	——————	1355, fos 349^r-351^r	E&W (Lincoln)	745
1516, 9 May	——————	1346, fos 97^v-98^r	E&W (Worcester; OSA)	637
1516, 14 May	——————	1342, fos 175^r-177^v	S (St Andrews; OPrem)*	588

1   Magliana
2   Palo

DATE Rome, St Peter's unless otherwise noted	DATE OF EXPEDITION IN THE *BULLARIA*	*REG. LAT.*	COUNTRY, DIOCESE, ORDER, ETC.	CAL. ENTRY NO.
1516, 14 May	——————	1342, fo 178^r	S (St Andrews; OPrem)*	589
"	——————	1342, fos 178^r-179^v	S (St Andrews; OPrem)*	590
"		1346, fos 210^r-212^v	S (Moray)	649
1516, 16 May	1516, 12 June	1344, fos 93^v-96^r	I (Connor)	603
"		1344, fos 103^v-105^v	I (Connor)	606
1516, 19 May	1516, 21 June	1346, fos 273^r-274^v	I (*foreign*)	650
1516, 20 May		1346, fos 133^r-134^r	E&W (Lincoln)	638
"		1346, fo 135^{r-v}	E&W (Bath & Wells)	640
"		1346, fos 135^v-136^v	E&W (Exeter)	641
"		1346, fos 136^v-137^v	E&W (Lincoln; OSA)	642
"		1346, fos 147^v-148^r	E&W (London; OCist)	643
"		1352, fo 68^{r-v}	E&W (London; OSA)	681
1516, 21 May		1344, fos 118^v-122^v	I (Emly)	609
1516, 26 May[1]		1344, fos 131^r-133^v	I (Tuam)	610
"		1353, fos 410^r-415^v	E&W (*foreign*)	735
1516, 30 May	1516, 14 June	1344, fos 107^r-109^r	I (Killaloe)	607
1516, 1 June	1516, 14 June	1344, fos 98^v-100^v	I (Tuam)	604
1516, 2 June		1346, fos 163^v-164^r	E&W (York)	644
1516, 3 June	1516, 14 June	1344, fos 100^v-103^r	I (Tuam)	605
"	1516, 23 June	1344, fos 116^r-118^v	I (Killaloe)	608
1516, 9 June		1346, fos 184^v-185^r	E&W (Bath & Wells)	646
"		1346, fos 185^r-186^r	E&W (Exeter)	647
"		1353, fos 332^v-333^v	E&W (Salisbury; OSB)	733
1516, 10 June		1319, fos 331^r-334^v	I (Emly; OCist)	317
1516, 12 June	1516, 21 June	1344, fos 12^r-13^v	I (Clogher)	597
"	1516, 21 June	1344, fos 14^r-16^r	I (Kilmore)	598
"		1344, fos 77^r-78^v	E&W (Llandaff; OSB)	602
"		1346, fos 47^v-48^v	E&W (Salisbury)	631
"		1346, fos 49^r-50^r	E&W (Winchester)	632
"		1346, fos 50^v-51^v	E&W (Coventry & Lichfield)	633
"		1346, fo 53^{r-v}	E&W (York; OSA)	635

1 Rome

DATE Rome, St Peter's unless otherwise noted	DATE OF EXPEDITION IN THE *BULLARIA*	*REG. LAT.*	COUNTRY, DIOCESE, ORDER, ETC.	CAL. ENTRY NO.
1516, 13 June	——————	1346, fo 52^{r-v}	E&W (Winchester; OSB)	634
1516, 14 June	1516, 26 June	1319, fos 334^v-336^v	I (Killaloe)	318
"	——————	1319, fos 337^r-339^r	I (Killaloe)	319
1516, 17 June	——————	1346, fos 205^v-206^v	E&W (York)	648
1516, 18 June	——————	1344, fos 188^r-189^v	E&W (Exeter)	613
1516, 19 June	——————	1344, fos 261^r-262^v	E&W (Norwich)	614
1516, 22 June	——————	1344, fos 186^v-187^v	E&W (Rochester)	612
"	——————	1344, fos 311^r-312^r	E&W (Lincoln)	615
"	——————	1346, fos 61^r-62^r	E&W (Bath & Wells)	636
1516, 26 June	——————	1352, fos 134^v-135^r	E&W (Lincoln; OSA)	688
"	——————	1352, fo 135^{r-v}	E&W (Canterbury; OSA)	689
"	——————	1352, fos 135^v-136^v	E&W (Worcester)	690
1516, 30 June	——————	1292, fo 72^r	E&W (Worcester; OSA)	170
1516, 1 July	——————	1319, fos 339^v-341^v	S (Glasgow)	320
"	1516, 15 July	1344, fos 37^v-40^r	I (Waterford)	599
"	1516, 16 Aug.	1348, fos 12^r-14^r	I (Cashel)	652
"	1516, 27 Aug.	1348, fos 20^r-23^r	I (Cashel)	655
"	——————	1348, fos 303^v-307^v	I (Leighlin)	658
"	1516, 21 July	1351, fos 321^v-325^v	I (Derry)	668
1516, 7 July	——————	1344, fos 40^r-43^v	I (Ossory)	600
"	——————	1344, fos 44^r-47^r	I (Killaloe)	601
1516, 8 July	1516, 29 July	1351, fos 318^r-321^v	I (Lismore)	667
1516, 14 July	——————	1353, fos 106^v-107^r	E&W (Bath & Wells; OSA)	719
1516, 16 July	1516, 16 Aug.	1348, fos 17^r-20^r	I (Cashel)	654
1516, 21 July	1516, 12 Aug.	1348, fos 300^r-303^r	I (Lismore)	657
1516, 23 July	1516, 26 Aug.	1348, fos 14^v-16^v	I (Kildare; OCist)	653
1516, 25 July	——————	1352, fos 144^v-145^v	E&W (Coventry & Lichfield; OCist)	696
1516, 31 July	——————	1295, fos 275^v-277^r	E&W (Lincoln)	180
"	——————	1295, fos 277^r-279^r	E&W (St David's)	181
"	——————	1295, fo 279^{r-v}	E&W (Chichester; OPrem)	182
"	——————	1295, fos 279^v-280^r	E&W (*none*; OP)	183
"	——————	1349, fos 333^v-334^v	E&W (Norwich?; OSB)	662
"	——————	1352, fos 140^v-141^r	E&W (Exeter)	691

DATE Rome, St Peter's unless otherwise noted	DATE OF EXPEDITION IN THE *BULLARIA*	*REG. LAT.*	COUNTRY, DIOCESE, ORDER, ETC.	CAL. ENTRY NO.
1516, 31 July	——————	1352, fos 141^v-142^r	E&W (Chichester)	692
"	——————	1352, fo 142^{r-v}	E&W (Salisbury)	693
"	——————	1352, fo 143^{r-v}	E&W (Lincoln)	694
"	——————	1352, fos 143^v-144^v	E&W (York)	695
"	——————	1352, fo 167^{r-v}	E&W (Lincoln; OSB)	699
"	——————	1352, fos 167^v-168^v	E&W (Lincoln; OCist)	700
"	——————	1352, fo 211^{r-v}	E&W (London; OCist)	709
"	——————	1353, fos 110^r-111^r	E&W (Durham)	720
1516, 2 Aug.	——————	1295, fo 280^{r-v}	E&W (Canterbury)	184
1516, 28 Aug.	1516, 20 Sep.	1348, fos 86^v-88^v	I (Cashel; OCist)	656
1516, 9 Sep.	——————	1352, fo 48^{r-v}	E&W (London)	675
"	——————	1352, fo 170^{r-v}	E&W (Coventry & Lichfield)	701
"	——————	1355, fos 119^v-120^v	E&W (London)	736
1516, 15 Sep.	——————	1353, fo 84^{r-v}	E&W (York)	713
"	——————	1353, fo 85^{r-v}	E&W (York)	714
1516, 20 Sep.[1]	1516, 25 Sep.	1348, fos 413^v-417^r	I (Tuam)	659
1516, 25 Sep.[2]	——————	1352, fo 194^{r-v}	E&W (Bath & Wells)	702
"[2]	——————	1352, fo 195^{r-v}	E&W (Lincoln)	703
1516, 27 Sep.[2]	——————	1353, fo 83^{r-v}	E&W (York)	712
"[2]	——————	1353, fos 86^r-87^r	E&W (London)	715
"[2]	——————	1353, fo 87^{r-v}	E&W (Chichester)	716
"[2]	——————	1353, fo 99^{r-v}	E&W (*none*; OCarm)	718
"[2]	——————	1356, fos 218^r-219^r	E&W (Worcester)	750
1516, 10 Oct.[3]	——————	1349, fos 142^v-143^r	E&W (Norwich; OSB)	660
"[3]	——————	1352, fo 72^{r-v}	E&W (Salisbury)	682
1516, 17 Oct.[4]	——————	1352, fos 67^v-68^r	E&W (Winchester; OSB)	680
1516, 28 Oct.	——————	1352, fos 51^v-52^r	E&W (Exeter)	676
"	——————	1352, fo 107^{r-v}	E&W (Chichester)	684
"	——————	1352, fo 108^{r-v}	E&W (Winchester)	685
"	——————	1352, fos 115^v-116^r	E&W (York)	686
"	——————	1352, fos 116^r-117^r	E&W (Hereford)	687

1 Monterosi
2 Viterbo
3 Corneto
4 Magliana

DATE	DATE OF EXPEDITION IN THE *BULLARIA*	*REG. LAT.*	COUNTRY, DIOCESE, ORDER, ETC.	CAL. ENTRY NO.
Rome, St Peter's unless otherwise noted				
1516, 31 Oct.	——————	1352, fo 104^{r-v}	E&W (Bangor)	683
1516, 3 Nov.	——————	1353, fos 334^r-335^r	E&W (Lincoln)	734
1516, 15 Nov.[1]	——————	1355, fos 208^r-209^v	E&W (Durham)	738
1516, 16 Nov.[1]	——————	1352, fo 33^{r-v}	E&W (Norwich)	669
" [1]	——————	1352, fos 42^r-43^r	E&W (Exeter)	670
" [1]	——————	1352, fos 43^v-44^v	E&W (Exeter)	671
" [1]	——————	1352, fo 45^{r-v}	E&W (Ely; OSB)	672
" [1]	——————	1352, fo 64^{r-v}	E&W (Lincoln)	677
" [1]	——————	1352, fo 65^{r-v}	E&W (Coventry & Lichfield; OSA)	678
" [1]	——————	1352, fos 65^v-66^r	E&W (Coventry & Lichfield)	679
1516, 2 Dec.	——————	1352, fos 45^v-47^r	E&W (Coventry & Lichfield)	673
"	——————	1352, fo 47^{r-v}	E&W (London)	674
1516, 5 Dec.	——————	1353, fo 138^v	E&W (Bath & Wells)	723
1516, 10 Dec.	——————	1353, fo 128^{r-v}	E&W (Worcester)	722
"	——————	1355, fos 193^r-195^v	E&W (London)	737
1516, 12 Dec.	——————	1319, fos 172^r-173^v	E &W (Bath & Wells)	316
1516, 26 Dec.	——————	1352, fos 206^r-207^r	E&W (Worcester)	704
"	——————	1352, fos 207^r-208^r	E&W (Lincoln)	705
"	——————	1352, fos 208^r-209^r	E&W (London)	706
"	——————	1352, fo 209^{r-v}	E&W (Ely)	707
"	——————	1352, fos 210^{r-v}	E&W (Winchester)	708
"	——————	1352, fos 220^v-221^v	E&W (Chichester)	710
"	——————	1352, fos 222^r-223^r	E&W (Worcester)	711
1517, 7 Jan.	——————	1353, fo 162^{r-v}	E&W (York)	724
"	——————	1353, fos 163^v-164^r	E&W (Exeter)	726
1517, 8 Jan.	——————	1347, fos 5^v-7^r	E&W (Winchester; Ely)	651
1517, 16 Jan.	——————	1353, fos 164^v-165^r	E&W (Lincoln)	727
"	——————	1353, fos 165^r-166^r	E&W (Lincoln)	728
1517, 23 Jan.	——————	1353, fo 163^{r-v}	E&W (Norwich; OSB)	725
1517, 1 Feb.	——————	1353, fos 284^v-286^r	E&W (Lincoln)	732
1517, 5 Feb.	1517, 26 Feb.	1353, fos 227^r-229^v	E&W (Killala)	729
1517, 6 Feb.	——————	1353, fo 124^{r-v}	E&W (York)	721
1517, 13 Feb.	——————	1353, fos 306^r-307^r	I (Clogher; OSA)	739
	——————	1355, fos 339^v-341^v	E&W (London)	743

1   Magliana

DATE Rome, St Peter's unless otherwise noted	DATE OF EXPEDITION IN THE *BULLARIA*	*REG. LAT.*	COUNTRY, DIOCESE, ORDER, ETC.	CAL. ENTRY NO.
1517, 20 Feb.	———————	1353, fos 260ᵛ-263ᵛ	I (Elphin)	731
1517, 26 Feb.	———————	1353, fos 258ʳ-260ᵛ	I (Ardfert)	730
1517, 5 Mar.[1]	———————	1355, fos 335ʳ-336ᵛ	E&W (Norwich)	740
1517, 6 Mar.[1]	———————	1355, fos 338ʳ-339ᵛ	E&W (Lincoln)	742
"[1]	———————	1355, fos 341ᵛ-342ᵛ	E&W (Rochester)	744
1517, 7 Mar.[1]	———————	1355, fos 336ᵛ-338ʳ	E&W (London)	741
1517, 9 Mar.	———————	1349, fos 143ʳ-144ʳ	E&W (London)	661
1517, 28 Mar.	1520, 17 Mar.	1305, fos 102ʳ-104ʳ	S (St Andrews)	240
1517, 4 May	———————	1342, fos 205ʳ-206ʳ	E&W (Megara) *	591
"	———————	1342, fos 206ʳ-207ʳ	E&W (Megara)*	592
"	———————	1342, fos 207ʳ-208ʳ	E&W (Megara)*	593
"	———————	1342, fo 208ʳ⁻ᵛ	E&W (Megara)*	594
"	———————	1342, fos 208ᵛ-210ᵛ	E&W (Megara)*	595
1517, 8 May	———————	1350, fos 21ʳ-23ʳ	I (Killaloe)	663
"	1517, 28 May	1350, fos 23ᵛ-24ᵛ	I (Cashel)	664
1517, 27 July	———————	1356, fos 167ᵛ-169ʳ	E&W (Norwich; OSB)	749
1517, 12 Aug.	1517, 7 Sep.	1350, fos 375ʳ-376ᵛ	S (St Andrews)	666
1517, 17 Sep.	———————	1350, fos 174ʳ-177ʳ	E&W (Lincoln)	665
1517, 14 Dec.	———————	1356, fos 28ʳ-30ʳ	S (St Andrews; OSB)	746
1517, 29 Dec.	———————	1356, fo 122ʳ⁻ᵛ	E&W (Lincoln)	748
1518, 17 Sep.[2]	———————	1356, fos 92ᵛ-94ᵛ	S (Glasgow)	747
1519, 1 Jan.[1]	1519, 29 Jan.	1343, fos 69ᵛ-70ʳ	I (Armagh)	596
1519, 20 Oct.[3]	1520, 6 Nov.	1305, fos 153ʳ-155ʳ	S (St Andrews)	241

[1] Magliana
[2] Stimigliano
[3] Cerveteri

CONSPECTUS OF THE REGISTERS

Leo's pontificate generated some 227 chancery or Lateran registers as they came to be known.[1] Of the original complement, 130 have come down to us, viz. *Reg. Lat.* 1276-1290, 1290A, 1291-1328,[2] and 1330-1405.[3] The remaining 97 registers – approx. 43% of the original total – have been lost. One register had apparently been lost before the registers were renumbered in the 1640s;[4] a further two may have been lost before the re-rubrication of the registers in the C18.[5] The bulk were evidently lost when portions of the papal archives were sold as waste and wrapping paper at Paris in 1817 in preparation for the removal of the archives back to Rome.[6]

The destruction of a large proportion of Leo's registers necessarily hangs a question mark over the representativeness of the survivors; and it focuses attention on the ancient *Indici* as a means of helping to make good the loss. Our main concern here must obviously be to determine the incidence of loss and identify precisely which registers have perished; and also to facilitate use of the *rubricellae* of lost letters (below, pp. 525-579) by matching the C18 Index references with the parent registers. It would also, of course, be helpful to establish the concordance between the current numeration of the extant registers, the references in Hergenroether's *Regesta* (below, pp. lxxv, lxxvi), and the original designations. Ideally, we need a comprehensive conspectus.

Responsibility for assembling the gatherings or quinterns completed by the registry into bound registers or *libri*, arranging them in series, and indexing or rubricating them, rested with the keeper or *custos registri bullarum* (*cf. CPL* XVI (pp. xlix-liv). The important point to note here is that Leo's pontificate saw a fundamental change in the manner in which the registers were archivally ordered. The change, which was presumably archive led, was no doubt the outcome of the emergence, in the last quarter of the C15, of the *custodia* as a separate office with responsibility for duties previously performed by the registry. But for present purposes we must focus sharply on the early *signaturae*. Hitherto, registers had always been ordered by *materia* into separate series for each pontifical year. For example the registers of 2 Alexander VI were evidently arranged in at least three series: we have *Quintus de Vacantibus Anno Secundo*; *Quintus de Diversis Anno Secundo*; and *Quintus de Vacantibus et Diversis Anno Secundo*.[7] Under Leo the system of designation, which had already lost much of its elaboration by Alexander's pontificate,[8] was further simplified. Ordering by *materia* was abandoned altogether and registers were arranged in a single sequence for each year, or group of years, irrespective of content. Initially, the registers were still designated (but not ordered) by matter: thus *xxx diversarum bullarum Anno primo Leonis X (Reg. Lat.* 1290); *XXXIII· DE MIXTIS AN· PRIMI D· LEO · PP · X · (Reg. Lat.* 1277); and *XXXIIII VA · ET DI AN · I · D · LEO · X (Reg. Lat.* 1278) – all demonstrably part of the same annual series. But this relic of the past was soon dropped and from about the summer of 1516 onwards the registers were designated by number and year alone: *· I · AN · V · LEO · X (Reg. Lat.* 1358); *II · AN · V · D · LEo X (Reg. Lat.* 1360); and so on.[9] The change presupposes, of course, a corresponding change in the manner in which *libri* were assembled. Quinterns *de diversis* and quinterns *de vacantibus*, which previously had often been formed into separate registers, were now regularly formed into the same register.[10] And the component gatherings were now usually headed simply with the name of the pope and the pontifical year.[11] Description of the *materia* was now redundant and headings describing it became rare.[12] The only exception to the new system were the gatherings of consistorial provisions – never, of course, very numerous – which continued to be formed into dedicated registers which were still designated and ordered as a separate series.[13] Thus *primus de provisionibus prelatorum .d. Leonis . pape x^{mi} ANNI PRIMI* (*Reg. Lat.* 1281); *II · DE PROVI· D · LEO · · X ·* (*Reg. Lat.* 1342); and so on. By the end of the pontificate there were eighteen separate series: nine annual series; eight multi-year series; and one series *de provisionibus prelatorum.*

The change in the manner in which the registers were ordered and designated was accompanied by a change in the mode of expression and graphics. We might say that the title was 'modernised'. As the original bindings have not survived our remarks are limited to the inscription on the cuts. From the fourth year onwards Roman numerals were consistently used in place of words. Thus 'I' replaced 'primus' and 'primo', 'II' 'secundus', 'secundo'; and so on. And from the third year onwards cursive script was replaced by inscriptional Roman capitals: letters were shaded and serifed; words were abbreviated without marks of abbreviation;[14] and the interpunction was recognisably in the fashionable antique manner.[15] Somewhat incongruously, the 'L' (of 'LEO') was sometimes decorated in the 'Gothic' style.[16] The new graphics proclaimed the new system.

The new system of ordering the registers persisted until (at the least) the later C18.[17] In this respect, Leo's registers stand at the point of transition between the old system and the new, the 'medieval' and the 'modern'. The importance of this for the Calendar is that we are able, for the first time, to reconstruct the original holding with near certainty. With basically only one series of registers for each year, or group of years, the titles and numbers of the registers which have been lost can readily be conjectured from the titles of the survivors. They are implied by the numeration. Thus the existence of [9 AN. 5] to [12 AN. 5] is implied by *VIII · AN · V · D · LEO · X ·* (*Reg. Lat.* 1350) and *XIII · AN · V · D ·|· LEO · X ·* (*Reg. Lat.* 1362). Determining the end of each series is obviously more difficult: *XVII AN VII D LEO X* (*Reg. Lat.* 1383) – the highest of the extant registers of year 7 – does not imply [18 AN. 7] or [19 AN. 7] as conjectured. But we also know the total number of registers and can establish the relationship between the reference scheme of the C18 index and the original designations. The limits of each series can be determined from the overall framework.

The conspectus which follows is based, in the main, on the titles inscribed on the cuts of extant registers and on the implication of the numeration; on what is, I think, essentially a stocktaking list (at fos 44^r-48^v of *Ind.* 355) compiled probably in C17 which gives the titles of the registers as rubricated and the numeration applied to them in the 1640s (or thereabouts) during the keepership of Nicholas Thierry; and on the index which was produced in the mid C18 when the registers were re-rubricated (*Ind.* 350-354). As the main purpose of the conspectus is to enable readers to discipline the *rubricellae* of lost letters, entries have been ordered according to the scheme of the C18 index (i.e. I Anni I to II Anni IX). The editor's headings, however, reflect the original titles. Sometimes it has been possible to confirm the correspondence between successive designations from other sources (notably *BOP*). To enhance its utility the conspectus also gives the titles and other marks on the present bindings; and wherever possible it matches Hergenroether's references and the current designation.

Not unexpectedly, the incidence of loss is uneven. As can be seen from the following table, no series or year has escaped; but some have suffered more than others. The overall loss of 43% conceals some extremes: while only 4 of the 17 registers of year 6 have been lost (approx. 24%) 12 of the 23 registers (approx. 52%) of year 4 have perished. Owing to the change in the manner in which registers were assembled and designated the incidence of loss in terms of *materia* cannot be readily illustrated or determined. We can, however, be specific about the registers of consistorial provisions: 3 out of the original total of 9, or 33%, have been lost. As we would expect of the manner in which the registers were dispersed – sold as wrapping paper to grocers and the like and subsequently recovered in part from the buyers – the incidence of loss is random and there is no reason to assume that what survives is in any way unrepresentative of the original holding.

Leo X (1513, [11, 17, &] 19 March - 1521, 1 Dec): chancery registers

Annual series	Total number	Number extant	Number lost	% Loss	Date
I	34	21	13	38	**1513-14**
I & II	5	3	2	40	1513-15
I, II, & III	13	7	6	46	1513-16
I, II, III & IV	2	1	1	50	1513-17
II	25	16	9	36	**1514-15**
II & III	3	2	1	33	1514-16
III	17	11	6	35	**1515-16**
III & IV	2	1	1	50	1515-17
IV	23	11	12	52	**1516-17**
V	21	9	12	57	**1517-18**
IV, V & VI	1	1	—	—	1516-19
IV & V	1	1	—	—	1516-18
VI	17	13	4	24	**1518-19**
VII	19	10	9	47	**1519-20**
VIII	20	10	10	50	**1520-21**
IX	8	5	3	37	**1521**
Various	7	2	5	71	
Provisions	9	6	3	33	
	227*	130*	97		

* Excludes *Reg. Lat.* 1406 (shared with other popes).

In addition to identifying the registers which have been lost the conspectus also shows the correspondence between the original and subsequent designations. As can be seen, the C17 numeration follows the original numeration of the successive annual series and the natural order of the pontifical years. Multi-year volumes are incorporated at appropriate points in the sequence; and the registers of consistorial provisions, which, as we have seen, formed a separate series, are grouped together (actually at the end). The only exceptions occur among the registers of a multi-year series, namely years 1, 2, & 3. No. 48 was applied to *liber* [12 AN. 1, 2, & 3] where the original sequence calls for *liber* [9 AN. 1, 2, & 3]; and no. 49 was applied to a register of consistorial provisions – · *I* · *DE PROVI* · *PRELA* | *AN* · *I* · *II* & *III* · *LEO* · | · *X* · – which, though in the right multi-year series, we would have expected to find with the other registers of provisions (nos. 219-226). In all probability, the C17 numeration preserves the shelf order of the registers in the 1640s when it was applied.[18]

The re-rubricatiion project of the C18 was discussed (in outline) in *CPL* XVI (pp. l-li). When the *custodia* re-rubricated the medieval registers which lacked *rubricellae* they did not use the historic *signaturae* but – probably for ease of administration – they re-designated the registers after the manner of the scheme then in use for the designation and rubrication of newly formed registers. That is, the registers of each pope were simply designated by number and pontifical year. *II* · *AN* · *II* · *CL* · *XII* (*Reg. Lat.* 2071) – a *liber* of 1731 – and *L . 5 . A . XI . SS . D .N . B . PP . XIV* (*Reg. Lat.* 2091) – a *liber* of 1752 – illustrate the current system. Although, as we have seen, that simplified system originated in Leo's pontificate the C18 rubricators nevertheless invented an artificial scheme of designation for Leo's registers. Perhaps they were deceived by the descriptive element in the titles of the first three or four years and thought they were ordered in complicated fashion like the earlier registers. Perhaps they recognised the difference but were put off by the number of multi-year series. Whatever the reason, Leo's registers were divided artificially into nine annual series the first of 50 registers (*I Anni I* to *XXXXX Anni I*), the second to the eighth of 25 registers each (*I Anni II* to *XXV Anni II*, etc.), the ninth of 2 registers (*I Anni IX* and *II Anni IX*). However, although the C18 rubricators devised new *signaturae* the scheme they used visibly shadows the C17 numeration. Even the registers misplaced in C17 retain position: No. 48 in Thierry's numeration became *XXXXVIII Anni I*; and No. 49 became *XXXXIX Anni I*. But there are a few oddities due, presumably, to inadvertence. Nos 89 and 90 are reversed in the C18 index; so are 94 and 95; 148 and 149; and 223 and 224. Nos. 204, 205, and 206 are all misplaced; and if they equate with *XXV Anni VIII* and *I Anni IX*, so are nos. 186 and 210. Overall, however, there is a remarkable degree of coincidence. Wrinkles apart, via the C17 numeration the original arrangement is preserved, incognito, behind the C18 scheme.

In the early modern period the registers were kept in dedicated premises in the Vatican palace.[19] Simplicity of relationship between reference, collocation, and mark on the volume – that is, effectively, between finding aid, shelf mark, and register – ensured a well ordered archive. The original arrangement was straightforward enough. The titles, which were almost certainly inscribed on the original bindings (now lost) as well as on the cuts and sometimes on the recto of the first leaf, probably served as shelf marks;

and they were unquestionably used as references in the *rubricellae*. Thus the bottom cut of what is now *Reg. Lat.* 1293 is inscribed: *I · DE PROVI · PRELA | AN · I · ET · II · D · PP X | LEO ·*; and the same register was originally rubricated under *Primus de Provisionibus Prelatorum Annorum Primi et Secundi D. Leonis PP X (Ind.* 355, fo 10ʳ). The serial numbers (1-226 / I-CCXXVI) which were applied to the volumes during the keepership of Thierry in the 1640s and remained current until the earlier C18 were almost certainly inscribed on the original bindings (probably the spines) and intended primarily as shelf marks. Being shorter than the original titles, they naturally replaced them as a means of reference.[20]

The artificiality of the C18 index scheme, which perplexes *studiosi* and frustrates research, has previously been explained in terms of officialdom protecting the income from searches. There was, it is suggested, a closely guarded concordance between index reference and register.[21] Possibly. However, the pressure from litigants on current as opposed to medieval registers was likely to have been far higher and here the relationship between finding aid and register was totally transparent. The registers of Benedict XIV (1740-58), for example, were indexed under the *signaturae* inscribed on the volumes.[22] Thus *L · X · A · XVII · BENED · PP XIV (Reg. Lat.* 2094) was indexed under *X Anni XVII*. We have already noted that the artificiality of the scheme is explicable in terms of adherence to current practice. In the circumstances it makes sense to assume that the new *signaturae* were inscribed on the bindings of the medieval registers (Leo's included) when they were re-rubricated. Certainly, the registers were cited by the new C18 designations.[23] The apparent want of correspondence between C18 index reference and register must, I think, be dismissed as an illusion created by the subsequent loss of the bindings on which the *signatura* was inscribed. Put another way, although we cannot now move from C18 index to register without the help of a concordance we only need it because the registers have since been rebound.

The conspectus also shows the C19 designations. The upheavals of the Napoleonic era meant a definite break with the past. The removal of the papal archives to Paris in 1810-13 marked the end of continuous custody; and the loss there of a large part of the *Archivum Bullarum* created an unprecedented situation. The destruction of well over a third of the registers represented a massive loss of administratively valuable information. Finding aids were also lost. However, the immediate problem confronting the *custodia* was that the 2,100 or so registers which made the return journey to Rome in 1817 were, we surmise, disbound.[24] They needed rebinding; and the rebound volumes needed designations. The practice of the datary, who at that time nominated the *custos* and dictated his duties, was to have newly-formed registers properly bound in parchment.[25] But binding was costly and understandably the 2,100 registers recovered from grocers at Paris were rebound, technically cased, in economy bindings. Two different patterns were used, suggestive of different dates and contracts. The majority were bound in coarse, off-white, paper with two pairs of blue or buff fabric ties; the remainder in red paper (now faded pink) with a single pair of red fabric ties. Curiously, the red registers do not form a bloc but are scattered about the different pontificates. Leo, who has 108 white registers and 22 red, is not untypical. From the viewpoint of archive administration, the main chore was giving titles to the volumes.

The original title was, of course, still inscribed on the cuts; but the loss of the original bindings meant the loss of the subsequent *signaturae*: the C17 numeration and, arguably, the vital C18 index reference. In the event, new titles were invented. Formulation and language differed with the batch. The titles on the white registers – that is, the vast majority – incorporated a reading (not always accurate) of the *liber* number and pontifical year number of the original title and introduced a new element, namely the year date.[26] The titles on the red registers employed Latin, not Italian, and omitted the *liber* number. The lettering, which was done in manuscript on the spines, was presumably done by the binder in accordance with the keeper's instruction.[27] In the case of the modern registers, which had not been re-rubricated, the original title was a safe basis on which to proceed and the new titles corresponded, in the case of the ones cased in white, with the references in the *rubricellae*. Thus *BENEDETTO |* *XIV |* *<1752>*[28] *| Anno JJ · | Lib · 5 ·* written on the spine of what is now *Reg. Lat.* 2091 (a white register) followed *L[iber] . 5 . A . XI . SS . D . N . B . PP. XIV* on the bottom cut and accords with the reference *V Anni XI* in the contemporary C18 index. However, in the case of the medieval registers which, as we have seen, had been re-rubricated under new designations, following the original superseded titles made no sense whatever. But the office's corporate memory failed with the passage of time and the blow dealt by Napoleon. The subtleties of the C18 re-rubrication project had evidently been forgotten by the early C19 and the curia treated the medieval registers just like the modern ones, inventing new titles based on the original ones inscribed on the cuts. The result, of course, was chaos: a devastating mismatch between index reference and register reference. Leo's registers were among the casualties. Thus *XXV VA · ET DI ·* *AN | II D · LEO · X* (*Reg. Lat.* 1323), which had been re-rubricated under *V Anni III*, was nevertheless given the title *LEONO*[123] *| X | J5J4 | Anno. 2. | Lib. 25*. And *V VA · ET* *DI · AN | III D · LEO · X* (*Reg. Lat.* 1324), which had been indexed under *XIII Anni III*, was given the title *LEONE | X | <1514-15> | Anno. 3. | Lib. 5*. In short, the index reference now led to the wrong register. Except fortuitously, as in the case of the first thirty-four of Leo's registers, register and finding aid disagreed. Effectively, the letters in the medieval registers could not be accessed and they remained inaccessible until the concordance with the C18 index references was re-established by the ASV in the early C20.[29]

The registers which made the return journey from Paris to Rome in 1817 were eventually housed in the Lateran palace until transfer to their present home around 1890. The last two columns of the conspectus show the designations given to the registers by Cardinal Hergenroether in the 1880s; and by the ASV in 1900. As we have seen, the C17 and C18 schemes derived from the original: the *signaturae* changed but the order remained virtually the same. And as we have just seen, the titles invented in the early C19 when the registers were rebound also derived from the original titles. The shelf order at the Lateran was by pope and pontifical year.[30] However, the new designations of the late C19 were in no way informed by the previous arrangement and, as can be seen, the relationship between Hergenroether's *signaturae* (restricted, of course, to Leo's registers) and the previous ones is totally arbitrary; likewise the ASV's. Not surprisingly, they broke with the past. The order inherent in the ASV's numeration is chronological within achievable limits; but Hergenroether's is more complicated. All Leo's Lateran registers are chancery in origin and belong to the same series; but owing to accidents of rebinding, 22 are bound in red paper covers, 108 in white. The *signaturae* which Hergenroether invented for his *Regesta* split the registers into two series: the red ones were designated by letter (A to [V] or perhaps [W]); the white ones by number ([1] to 110[!]). Thus: Arch. Lat. vol. A (4753); Arch. Lat. tom. 31 (10207). Sometimes his references are written on the spines; otherwise the concordance has to be established by matching *Regesta* entries (limited, of course, to 1-3 Leo) with entries in the actual registers. Owing to the random relationship between the *Regesta*'s *signaturae* and the historic ones they cannot readily be conjectured and there are considerable gaps in our knowledge. The conspectus gives Hergenroether's *signaturae* for seven of the red registers and forty seven of the white. The ASV's long closure periods for modern records make a mystery of the recent past. We know more about the C16 than the C19.

Original Title[31]	C17 No.[35]	C18 Index Reference[36]	C19 Title[32]	Herg.[33]	Reg.[34] Lat.

YEAR 1 (1513, March 19-1514, March 18)

Original Title[31]	C17 No.[35]	C18 Index Reference[36]	C19 Title[32]	Herg.[33]	Reg.[34] Lat.
[1 div. bull. a. 1][37]	1	I Anni I	—	—	lost
Secu(n)d(us) divers(arum) bullar(um) | anno p(ri)mo Leonis · x ·mi[39]	2	II Anni I	LEONE | X | < 1512-13 >[38] | Anno. J. | Lib. 2.	[fig.]	1284
Terci(us) diversar(um) bullar(um) | anno p(ri)mo Leonis · X ·mi[40]	3	III Anni I	<1512-13> | An. I. | Leo. | X (red)	E	1279
[4 div. bull. a. 1][41]	4	IV Anni I	—	—	lost
Qui(n)t(us) Divers(arum) bulla(rum) | anno p(ri)mo leonis x·mi[42]	5	V Anni I	LEONE | X | J5J3 | Anno. J. | Lib. 5	14[43]	1296
[6 div. bull. a. 1][44]	6	VI Anni I	—	—	lost
[7 div .bull. a. 1][45]	7	VII Anni I	—	—	lost
viij·us divers(arum) bullar(um) | anno p(ri)mo leonis x·mi	8	VIII Anni I	LEONE | X | <1512-13> | Anno. J. | Lib. 8	15[46]	1285
[9 div. bull. a. 1][47]	9	IX Anni I	—	—	lost
[10 div. bull. a. 1][48]	10	X Anni I	—	—	lost
Vndecim(us) divers(arum) bullar(um) | Anno p(ri)mo leonis x·mi	11	XI Anni I	LEONE | X | J5J3 | Anno. J. | Lib. J2.[49]	7	1297
[12 div. bull. a. 1][50]	12	XII Anni I	—	—	lost
[13 div. bull. a. 1][51]	13	XIII Anni I	—	—	lost
xiiii·us diversar(um) bullar(um) | Anno p(ri)mo Leonis · X ·	14	XIV Anni I	<1512-13> | An. I. | Leo | X. (red)	A	1276
xv·us divers(arum) bullar(um) | A(n)no p(ri)mo Leonis · x ·	15[52]	XV Anni I	LEONE | X | <1512-13> | Anno. J. | Lib. J5.	[fig.]	1286
[16 div. bull. a. 1][53]	16	XVI Anni I	—	—	lost
xvii divers(arum) bullar(um) | Anno p(ri)mo leonis · x ·	17	XVII Anni I	<1513> | Anno I | Leonis | X (red)	G	1280
xviij·us divers(arum) bullarum | Anno p(ri)mo Leonis x·mi	18	XVIII Anni I	LEONE | X | <1512-13> | Anno. P. | Lib. J8	9	1287
[19 div. bull. a. 1][54]	19	XIX Anni I	—	—	lost
xx·us divers(arum) bullar(um) | anno primo Leonis x	20	XX Anni I	LEONE | X | J5J3 | Anno. J. | Lib. 20	17[55]	1298
xxi·us divers(arum) bullarum | Anno p(ri)mo Leonis · x ·	21	XXI Anni I	LEONE | X | J5J3 | Anno. J. | Lib. 2J.	[fig.]	1300
[22 div. bull. a. 1][56]	22	XXII Anni I	—	—	lost
[23 div. bull. a. 1][57]	23[58]	XXIII Anni I	—	—	lost
(?)xxiiij diversar(um) bullar(um) | (?)anno prim[o] Leonis · x ·	24	XXIV ANNI I	LEONE | X | <1512-13> | Anno. J. | Lib. J.	2[59]	1283
xxv·us divers(arum) bullar(um) | anno p(ri)mo Leonis · x ·[60]	25	XXV Anni I	LEONE | X | J5J3 | Anno J. | Lib. 20.	[fig.]	1299
xxvi·us diversar(um) Bullar(um) | anno p(ri)mo leonis· decimi[61]	26	XXVI Anni I	LEONE | X | <1513> | Anno. J. | Lib. 26	19	1302
xxvij·us divers(arum) bullar(um) | Anno primo Leonis · x ·	27	XXVII Anni I	LEONE | X | J5J3 | Anno. J. | Lib. 27.	[fig.]	1301

Original Title	C17 No.	C18 Index Reference	C19 Title	Herg.	Reg. Lat.
xxviij. diversar(um) bullar(um) a[n]no | primo Leonis· decimi·	28[62]	XXVIII Anni I	LEONE | X | <1512-13> | Anno. J. | Lib. 28.	21[63]	1288
xxix[us] divers(arum) bullar(um) | anno p(rim)o Leonis X[mi]	29	XXIX Anni I	LEONE | X | <1512-13> | Anno. J.[65] | Lib. 29	22[64]	1289
xxx diversar(um) bullar(um) | Anno p(rimo) Leonis X	30	XXX Anni I	LEONE | X | <1512-13> | Anno. J. | Lib. 30	[fig.]	1290
xxxi[us] bullar(um) anno | p(rim)o Leonis x[mi]	31	XXXI Anni I	LEONE | X | <1512-13> | Anno. J. | Lib. 3J	23.[66]	1290A
[32 bull. a. 1][67]	32	XXXII Anni I	—	—	lost
XXXIII · DE MIXT | IS AN •[68] PRIMI D• LEO · PP · X ·	33	XXXIII Anni I	<1512-13> | An. I. | Leo | X (red)	C.[69]	1277
XXXIIII VA • ET DI | AN • I · D • LEO • X[69bis]	34	XXXIV Anni I	<1512-13> | An. I. | Leonis | X (red)	[letter]	1278

YEARS 1 & 2 (1513, March 19-1515, March 18)

Original Title	C17 No.	C18 Index Reference	C19 Title	Herg.	Reg. Lat.
PRIMVS DE MIX | TIS AN • I ET II | D • LEO • PP • X •	35	XXXV Anni I	LEONE | X | <1512-14> | Anno. J.[70] | Lib..J[o].	[fig.]	1291
[2 DE MIXTIS AN. 1 & 2][71]	36[72]	XXXVI Anni I	—	—	lost
III • VA • & DI • AN • | • I & II • D • LEO • X[75]	37	XXXVII Anni I	<1512-13> | An. I.[73] | Leo | X. (red)	B.[74]	1282
IIII AN I & II | D LEO • X	38	XXXVIII Anni I	LEONE | X | <1512-14> | Anno. J.[76bis] | Lib. 4	5.[76]	1292
[5 VA. & DI. AN. 1 & 2][77]	39	XXXIX Anni I	—	—	lost

YEARS 1, 2 & 3 (1513, March 19-1516, March 18)

Original Title	C17 No.	C18 Index Reference	C19 Title	Herg.	Reg. Lat.
PRIMVS VACAN • ET | DIVERS • AN • PRIMI | II • ET III • D • LEO • X	40	XXXX Anni I	LEONE | X | <1513-15> | Anno. J | Lib. J.	27[78]	1321
[2 VAC. & DIV. AN. 1, 2, & 3][79]	41	XXXXI Anni I	—	—	lost
III · VA • ET DI • AN | I · II ET III LEO	42[80]	XXXXII Anni I	LEONE | X | <1514-15> | Anno. 3[81]	43	1326
IIII VA • ET DI • | AN• I · II · ET III · LEON • | X[82]	43	XXXXIII Anni I	LEONE | X <1514-15> | Anno. J.2.3 | Lib. 4 | Misto[83]	44	1327
[5 VAC. & DIV. AN. 1, 2, & 3][84]	44	XXXXIV Anni I	—	—	lost
[6 VAC. & DIV. AN. 1, 2, & 3][85]	45	XXXXV Anni I	—	—	lost
VII • AN • I • II & III | D • LEO • X •	46	XXXXVI Anni I	LEONE | X | <1512-15> | Anno. 3. | Lib. 7.	[fig.]	1320
VIII • AN • I • II & | III • D • LEO • X	47	XXXXVII Anni I	LEONE | X | <1512-16> | Anno J. | Lib. 8.	16.[86]	1295
[12 AN. 1, 2, & 3][87] *misplaced*	48	XXXXVIII Anni I	—	—	lost
• I • DE PROVI • PRELA | AN • I • II & III • LEO • | • X •[90]	49[88]	XXXXIX Anni I	LEONE | X | <1514-15>[89] | Anno. 2. 3. | Lib. J.	40	1325

Original Title	C17 No.	C18 Index Reference	C19 Title	Herg.	Reg. Lat.
[9 AN. 1,2, & 3][91] *misplaced*	50	XXXXX Anni I	—	—	*lost*
X • AN • I II III • D | LEO • X• *misplaced*	51	I Anni II	LEONE | X | <1512-15> | Anno. J. | Lib. J0	6.[92]	1294
[11 AN. 1, 2, & 3][93] *misplaced*	52	II Anni II	—	—	*lost*
XIII AN • I II III | D LEO X	53	III Anni II	LEONE | X | <1512-16> | Anno. 4. | Lib. J3.	47[94]	1354

YEARS 1, 2, 3 & 4 (1513, March 19 - 1517, March 18)

[1 AN. 1, 2, 3, & 4][95]	54	IV Anni II	—	—	*lost*
II AN I II III IIII | D LEO X[96]	55	V Anni II	[LEONE | X | 1516 | Anno 4 | Lib 1][97]	[fig.]	1343

YEAR 2 (1514, March 19 - 1515, March 18)

(?)prim(us) divers(arum) bulla | ru(m) anno 2º leonis x	56	VI Anni II	LEONE | X | J5J5 | Anno. 2. | Lib. J.	28	1331
[2 div. bull. a. 2][98]	57	VII Anni II	—	—	*lost*
Tertius diversar(um) | bullar(um) anno secu[n]do Leonis · x ·	58	VIII Anni II	LEONE | X | J5J4 | Anno. 2. | Lib. 3	26	1308
Quartus divers(arum) bullar(um) | a(n)no secu(n)do Leonis · x ·[101]	59	IX Anni II	LEONE | X | <1513-14> | Anno 2[99] | Lib. 4.[100]	[fig.]	1304
[5 div. bull. a. 2][102]	60	X Anni II	—	—	*lost*
Sextus diversar(um) Bullar(um) | anno secu(n)do Leonis x	61	XI Anni II	LEONE | X | J5J4 | Anno. 2. | Lib. 6.	30	1311
(?)vii[us] diversar(um) bullar(um) | Anno 2º Leonis · X ·	62[103]	XII Anni II	1514 | An.II | Leonis | X (*red*)	H	1310
[8 div. bull. a. 2][104]	63	XIII Anni II	—	—	*lost*
Nonus diversar(um) Bullar(um) | anno Secu(n)do Leonis · x ·	64	XIIII Anni II	LEONE | X | J5J4 | Anno. 2. | Lib. 9.	31	1312
decimus diversar(um) bullar(um) anno | 2º Leonis pp. X[mi]	65	XV Anni II	LEONE | X | J5J4 | Anno 2. | Lib. J0	33	1313
[11 div. bull. a. 2][105]	66	XVI Anni II	—	—	*lost*
(?)xii diversar(um) bullar(um) anno | 2º Leonis X.[mi]	67	XVII Anni II	LEONE | J5J4 | Anno 2. | Lib. J0[106]	32	1314
[13 div. bull. a. 2][107]	68[108]	XVIII Anni II	—	—	*lost*
[14 div. bull. a. 2][109]	69	XIX Anni II	—	—	*lost*
xv divers(arum) bullar(um) anno (?)2.º | Leoni(s) xmi	70	XX Anni II	1514 | An. II. | Leo | X. (*red*)	K	1306
· XVI · DIVER(SORUM) · AN· II · | D · LEO ·:· —	71[110]	XXI Anni II	LEONE | X | J5J4. | Anno. 2. | Lib. J6.	[34]	1315
xvij divers(arum) bullar(um) anno | 2º Leonis p(a)p(e) x[mi]	72	XXII Anni II	1514 | An. II. | Leonis | X[111] (*red*)	[letter]	1309

Original Title	C17 No.	C18 Index Reference	C19 Title	Herg.	Reg. Lat.
[18 div. bull. a. 2][112]	73	XXIII Anni II	—	—	lost
xix^us divers(arum) bullar(um) anno | 2º Leonis x^mi[113]	74	XXIV Anni II	LEONE | X | J5J4 | Anno. 2. | Lib. J9.	35	1316
xx divers(arum) bullar(um) anno | 2º Leonis x^mi[116]	75[114]	XXV Anni II	LEONE | X | J5J4 | Anno 2: | Lib. 20	[36][115]	1317
[21 div. bull. a. 2][117]	76[118]	I Anni III	—	—	lost
[22 MIXT. AN. 2][119]	77	II Anni III	—	—	lost
XXIII • MIXTVS | AN • II • D • LEO • PP • X •	78[120]	III Anni III	LEONE | X | J5J4 | Anno. 2. | Lib. 23. | Misto	37	1322
XXIIII MIXTVS AN | II D(OMI)NI[121] LEONIS PP | • X •	[79][122]	IV Anni III	LEONE | X | <1514> | Anno. 2. | Lib. 24.	18	1318
XXV VA • ET DI • AN | II D • LEO • X	80	V Anni III	LEONO[123] | X | J5J4 | Anno. 2. | Lib. 25.[124]	38	1323

YEARS 2 & 3 (1514, 19 March - 1516, 18 March)

Original Title	C17 No.	C18 Index Reference	C19 Title	Herg.	Reg. Lat.
PRIMVS MIXTVS | AN • II • ET • III • | D • LEONIS PP • X •[125]	81	VI Anni III	LEONE | X | J5J4 | Anno. 2. 3 | Lib. J.	[fig.]	1307
SECVNDVS · MIXT • | AN • SECVN • ET TER • | D· LEONIS · PP · X	82	VII Anni III	LEONE | X | <1514-15> | Anno. 2[126] | Lib: Misto	39	1328
[3 VAC. & DIV. AN. 2 & 3][127]	83	VIII Anni III	—	—	lost

YEAR 3 (1515, 19 March - 1516, 18 March)

Original Title	C17 No.	C18 Index Reference	C19 Title	Herg.	Reg. Lat.
[1 Vac. & Div. a. 3][128]	84	IX Anni III	—	—	lost
[2 Vac. & Div. a. 3][129]	85	X Anni III	—	—	lost
III VA • ET DI • A | III D • LEO • X	86	XI Anni III	LEONE | X | J5J5 | Anno. 3. | Lib. 3.[130]	49	1332
IIII VA • ET DI • A • | III D • LEO • X	87[131]	XII Anni III	LEONE | X | J5J5 | Anno. 3. | Lib. 4.	50	1333
V VA • ET DI • AN | III D • LEO • X	88	XIII Anni III	LEONE | X |<1514-15>| Anno. 3. | Lib. 5.	51	1324
VII VA • ET DI • AN | III D • LEO • X *misplaced*	90	XIV Anni III	LEONE | X | J5J5 | Anno. 3. | Lib. 7	[fig.]	1334
[6 VAC. & DIV. AN. 3][132] *misplaced*	89[133]	XV Anni III	—	—	lost
VIII VA • ET DI • AN | III D • LEO • X	91	XVI Anni III	LEONE | X | J5J5 | Anno 3 | Lib. 8.[134]	53	1335
IX VA • ET DI • AN | III D • LEO • X	92	XVII Anni III	LEONE | X | J5J5 | Anno. 3. | Lib. 9.	54	1336
X VA • ET DI • AN | III D • LEO • X[135]	93	XVIII Anni III	LEONE | X | J5J5 | Anno 3 | Lib. J0.	[fig.]	1337
XII • VA • & DI • AN • | III D • LEON • X[138] *misplaced*	95[136]	XIX Anni III	LEONN[137] | X | J5J5 | Anno. 3. | Lib. J2.[139]	[fig.]	1338

Original Title	C17 No.	C18 Index Reference	C19 Title	Herg.	Reg. Lat.
[11 VAC. & DIV. AN. 3][140] *misplaced*	94	XX Anni III	—	—	*lost*
XIII VA & DI AN | III D • LEO • X[141]	96	XXI Anni III	LEONE | X | J5J5. | Anno 3 | Lib. J3.	[fig.]	1339
XIIII VA • ET DI | AN • III • D • LEO • X	97	XXII Anni III	LEONE | X | J5J5 | Anno. 3. | Lib. J4.	[fig.]	1340
[15 VAC. & DIV. AN. 3][142]	98	XXIII Anni III	—	—	*lost*
[16 VAC. & DIV. AN. 3][143]	99	XXIV Anni III	—	—	*lost*
XVII • AN • III • D | LEO • X •	100	XXV Anni III	<1515> | An. III | Leonis | X. (*red*)	[letter]	1330

YEARS 3 & 4 (1515, March 19 - 1517, March 18)

Original Title	C17 No.	C18 Index Reference	C19 Title	Herg.	Reg. Lat.
I • VA • & DI • AN • | III & IIII • D • LEO[145]	101[144]	I Anni IV	LEONE | X | <1515-16> | Anno. ?3[146] | Lib. J.	[fig.]	1341
[2 VAC. & DIV. AN. 3 & 4][147]	102[148]	II Anni IV	—	—	*lost*

YEAR 4 (1516, March 19 - 1517, March 18)

Original Title	C17 No.	C18 Index Reference	C19 Title	Herg.	Reg. Lat.
• I • VA • ET DI • AN • | • IIII • D • LEO • X[150]	103	III Anni IV	LEONE | X | J5J6 | Anno. 4 | Lib. J.	61.[149]	1345
II • VA & DI • AN • | IIII • D • LEO • X	104	IV Anni IV	LEONE | X | J5J6 | Anno 4 | Lib. 2.	62[151]	1346
III • VA & DI • AN | • IIII • D • LEO • X	105[152]	V Anni IV	1516 | An. IV | Leo | X (*red*)	[letter]	1344
IIII AN IIII | D LEO • X	106	VI Anni IV	LEONE | X | J5J6 | Anno. 4. | Lib. 4.	63[153]	1347
V AN IIII | D LEO (?)PP · X	107	VII Anni IV	[LEONE | X | 1516 | Anno. 4. | Lib. J.[154]][155]	[fig.]	1319
[6 DIV. BULL. AN. 4][156]	108	VIII Anni IV	—	—	*lost*
VII AN IIII | D LEO • X	109	IX Anni IV	LEONE | X | J5J6 | Anno. 4. | Lib. 7.	65[157]	1348
[8 AN. 4][158]	110	X Anni IV	—	—	*lost*
IX AN IIII | D LEO X	111[159]	XI Anni IV	LEONE | X | <1516> | Anno. 4. | Lib. 9.	[fig.][160]	1351
X AN IIII | D • LEO • X	112	XII Anni IV	LEONNE[161] | X | <1516> | Anno 4 | Lib. J0.	[fig.]	1352
XI • AN IIII | D • LEO • X	113	XIII Anni IV	LEONE | X | <1516> | Anno 4 | Lib. JJ.[163]	67[162]	1353
[12 AN. 4][164]	114	XIV Anni IV	—	—	*lost*
[13 AN. 4][165]	115	XV Anni IV	—	—	*lost*
[14 AN. 4][166]	116	XVI Anni IV	—	—	*lost*
[15 AN. 4][167]	117	XVII Anni IV	—	—	*lost*
[16 AN. 4][168]	118	XVIII Anni IV	—	—	*lost*
[17 AN. 4][169]	119	XIX Anni IV	—	—	*lost*

Original Title	C17 No.	C18 Index Reference	C19 Title	Herg.	Reg. Lat.
XVIII AN • IIII | D • LEO • X[170]	120	XX Anni IV	LEONE | X |<1516> | Anno. 4. | Lib. J8.	[fig.]	1355
XIX • AN • IIII • D • | LEO • X •[171]	121	XXI Anni IV	LEONE | X | J5J6 | Anno. 4. | Lib. J9.[173]	69[172]	1349
[20 AN. 4][174]	122	XXII Anni IV	—	—	lost
[21 AN. 4][175]	123	XXIII Anni IV	—	—	lost
[22 AN. 4][176]	124	XXIV Anni IV	—	—	lost
[23 AN. 4][177]	125	XXV Anni IV	—	—	lost

VARIOUS YEARS

Original Title	C17 No.	C18 Index Reference	C19 Title	Herg.	Reg. Lat.
[1 DIVERS. AN.][178]	126[179]	I Anni V	—	—	lost
[2 DIVERS. AN.][180]	127	II Anni V	—	—	lost
[3 DIVERS. AN.][181]	128	III Anni V	—	—	lost
[4 DIVERS. AN.][182]	129	IV AN V	—	—	lost
V DIVER • AN • | D • LEO • X	130	V Anni V	LEONE | X | <1513-19> | Anno <1-8> | Lib. 5.	[fig.]	1305

YEAR 5 (1517, March 19 - 1518, March 18)

Original Title	C17 No.	C18 Index Reference	C19 Title	Herg.	Reg. Lat.
• I • AN • V • LEO • | X	131	VI Anni V	LEONE | X | J5J7 | Anno 5 | Lib. J.	[fig.]	1358
II • AN • V • D • LEo | X	132	VII Anni V	1517 | An. V. | Leonis | X. (*red*)	[letter]	1360
[3 AN. 5][183]	133	VIII Anni V	—	—	lost
IIII • AN • V • D • LEO | • X •	134	IX Anni V	LEONE | X | J5J7 | Anno. 5. | Lib. 4.	[fig.]	1359
V • AN • V D • LEO • | X	135	X Anni V	LEONE | X | J517. | Anno. 5. | Lib. 5.[184]	[fig.]	1361
[6 AN. 5][185]	136	XI Anni V	—	—	lost
[7 AN. 5][186]	137	XII Anni V	—	—	lost
VIII • AN • V • D • | LEO • X •	138	XIII Anni V	LEONE | X | J5J7 | Anno. 5. | Lib. 8.	[fig.]	1350
[9 AN. 5][187]	139	XIV Anni V	—	—	lost
[10 AN. 5][188]	140	XV Anni V	—	—	lost
[11 AN. 5][189]	141[190]	XVI Anni V	—	—	lost
[12 AN. 5][191]	142[192]	XVII Anni V	—	—	lost
XIII • AN • V • D • | • LEO • X •	143	XVIII Anni V	LEONE | X | J5J7 | Anno[193] | Lib. J3.	[fig.]	1362
[14 AN. 5][194]	144	XIX Anni V	—	—	lost
XV • AN • V • D • | LEO • X •	145	XX Anni V	LEONE | X | J5J7 | Anno . V. | Lib. J5.	[fig.]	1363
XVI • AN • V • D • | LEO • X •	146	XXI Anni V	LEONE | X | J5J7 | Anno. 5. | Lib. J6[195]	[fig.]	1364

Original Title	C17 No.	C18 Index Reference	C19 Title	Herg.	Reg. Lat.
[17 AN. 5][196]	147	XXII Anni V	—	—	lost
[19 AN. 5][197] *misplaced*	149[198]	XXIII Anni V	—	—	lost
[18 AN. 5][199] *misplaced*	148[200]	XXIV Anni V	—	—	lost
XX AN V	LEO • X	150	XXV Anni V	*newly rebound in parchment*[201]	[?]	1357
[21 AN. 5][202]	151	I Anni VI	—	—	lost

YEARS 4, 5, & 6 (1516, March 19 - 1519, March 18)

Original Title	C17 No.	C18 Index Reference	C19 Title	Herg.	Reg. Lat.
I AN IIII V VI	D LEO X	152	II Anni VI	<1517-18>	An. VI	Leonis	X. (*red*)	[letter]	1365

YEARS 4 & 5 (1516, March 19 - 1518, March 18)

Original Title	C17 No.	C18 Index Reference	C19 Title	Herg.	Reg. Lat.
I AN • IIII · V	D • LEO X	153[203]	III Anni VI	LEONE	X	<1516-18>[204]	Anno. (?)4[206]	Lib. J.	60.[205]	1356

YEAR 6 (1518, March 19 - 1519, March 18)

Original Title	C17 No.	C18 Index Reference	C19 Title	Herg.	Reg. Lat.
I AN • VI	LEO • X	154	IV Anni VI	1518	An. VI.	Leonis	X. (*red*)	[letter]	1369
II AN VI	LEO • X	155	V Anni VI	1518	An. VI	Leonis	X. (*red*)	[letter]	1366
[3 AN. 6][207]	156[208]	VI Anni VI	—	—	lost
IIII AN • VI	LEO • X	157	VII Anni VI	LEONE	X	J5J8.	Anno 6	Lib. 4.	[fig.]	1370
V AN VI	LEO • X •	158[209]	VIII Anni VI	LEONE	X	J5J8	Anno. 6.	Lib. 5.	[fig.]	1371
VI AN • VI	LEO • X	159	IX Anni VI	1518	An. VI	Leo	X (*red*)	[letter]	1367
VII AN VI	LEO • X •	160	X Anni VI	LEONE	X	J5J8	Anno. 6.	Lib. 7.	[fig.]	1372
VIII AN • VI •	• D • LEO • X	161[210]	XI Anni VI	LEONE	X	J5J8	Anno. 6.	Lib. 8	[fig.]	1373
IX AN VI	LEO • X	162	XII Anni VI	1518	An. VI	Leo	X. (*red*)	[letter]	1368
X AN VI	LEO • X	163	XIII Anni VI	LEONE	X	J5J0[211]	Anno 6.	Lib. J0.[212]	[fig.]	1374
XI AN VI	LEO • X	164	XIV Anni VI	LEONE	X	J5J8	Anno. 7[213]	Lib. JJ.[214]	[fig.]	1375
[12 AN. 6][215]	165[216]	XV Anni VI	—	—	lost
XIII AN VI	D LEO X	166	XVI Anni VI	LEONE	X	(?)J5J4[217]	Anno. 6.	Lib. J3.	[fig.]	1376
[14 AN. 6][218]	167	XVII Anni VI	—	—	lost
XV AN VI	D LEO X	168	XVIII Anni VI	LEONE	X	J5J8	Anno. VI.	Lib. J5.	[fig.]	1377

Original Title	C17 No.	C18 Index Reference	C19 Title	Herg.	Reg. Lat.
[16 AN. 6][219]	—	—	—	—	lost
XVII AN VI | D LEO X	169	XIX Anni VI	LEONE | X | J5J8 | Anno. 6. | Lib. J7.	[fig.]	1378

VARIOUS YEARS

Original Title	C17 No.	C18 Index Reference	C19 Title	Herg.	Reg. Lat.
VI DIVER • AN • | D • LEO • X	170[220]	XX Anni VI	<1513-14> | An. 11[221] | Leonis | X (*red*)	[letter]	1303
[7 DIVERS. AN.][222]	171	XXI Anni VI	—	—	lost

YEAR 7 (1519, March 19 - 1520, March 18)

Original Title	C17 No.	C18 Index Reference	C19 Title	Herg.	Reg. Lat.
I AN VII | D LEO X[223]	172	XXII Anni VI	LEONE | X | J5J9 | Anno. 7. | Lib. J	[fig.]	1379
[2 AN. 7][224]	173	XXIII Anni VI	—	—	lost
[3 AN. 7][225]	174	XXIV Anni VI	—	—	lost
IIII AN •[226] VII | D LEO • X[227]	175	XXV Anni VI	LEONE | X | J520 | Anno. 7. | Lib. 4.	[fig.]	1388
[5 AN. 7][228]	176	I Anni VII	—	—	lost
[6 AN. 7][229]	177[230]	II Anni VII	—	—	lost
VII AN • VII | D LE • X[231]	178	III Anni VII	LEONE | X | J5J9 | Anno. 7. | Lib. 7. [232]	[fig.]	1380
[8 AN. 7][233]	179	IV Anni VII	—	—	lost
IX AN VII | D LEO X	180	V Anni VII	LEONE | X | J5J9 | Anno. 7. | Jib.[234] 9.	[fig.]	1381
X AN • VII | D LEO • X[235]	181	VI Anni VII	LEONE | X | J5J9 | Anno. 7 | Lib. X	[fig.]	1382
[11 AN. 7][236]	182	VII Anni VII	—	—	lost
XII AN • VII | D LEO • X[237]	183	VIII Anni VII	LEONE | X | J5J9 | Anno. 7. | Lib. J2.	[fig.]	1384
XIII AN • VII | D LEO •[238] X[239]	184	IX Anni VII	LEONE | X | J5J9 | Anno. 7. | Lib. J3.	[fig.]	1385
XIIII AN • VII | D LEO •[240] X[241]	185	X Anni VII	LEONE | X | J5J9 | Anno 7. | Lib. J4.	[fig.]	1386
[15 AN. 7][242]	186	—[243]	—	—	lost
XVI AN VII | D LEO •[244] X[245]	187	XI Anni VII	LEONE | X | 15J9 | Anno. 7. | Lib. J6	[fig.]	1387
XVII AN VII | D LEO X	188[246]	XII Anni VII	1519 | An. VII | Leonis | X. (*red*)	[letter]	1383
[18 AN. 7][247]	189	XIII Anni VII	—	—	lost
[19 AN. 7][248]	190	XIV Anni VII	—	—	lost

Original Title	C17 No.	C18 Index Reference	C19 Title	Herg.	Reg. Lat.

YEAR 8 (1520, 19 March - 1521, 18 March)

Original Title	C17 No.	C18 Index Reference	C19 Title	Herg.	Reg. Lat.
[1 AN. 8][249]	191	XV Anni VII	—	—	*lost*
II AN • VIII | D LEO •[250] X[251]	192	XVI Anni VII	LEONE | X | J520 | Anno. 8. | Lib. 2.	[fig.]	1391
III AN • VIII | D • LEO • X[252]	193	XVII Anni VII	LEONE | X | <1520> | Anno. 8. | Lib. 3.	[fig.]	1392
IIII AN • VIII | D • LEO • X	194[253]	XVIII Anni VII	LEONE | X | J520 | Anno 8. | Lib. 4.	[fig.]	1393
V AN • VIII | D • LEO • X[254]	195	XIX Anni VII	<1520> | An. VIII | Leonis | X. (*red*)	[letter]	1397
[6 AN. 8][255]	196	XX Anni VII	—	—	*lost*
VII AN • VIII | D • LEO • X[256]	197	XXI Anni VII	LEONE | X | J520 | Anno. 8. | Lib. 7.	[fig.]	1394
VIII AN • VIII | D • LEO • X[257]	198	XXII Anni VII	LEONE | X | J520 | Anno 8 | Lib. 8.	[fig.]	1395
[9 AN. 8][258]	199	XXIII Anni VII	—	—	*lost*
X AN • VIII | D • LEO • X[259]	200	XXIV Anni VII	1520 | An. VIII | Leo | X (*red*)	[letter]	1389
[11 AN. 8][260]	201	XXV Anni VII	—	—	*lost*
[12 AN. 8][261]	202	I Anni VIII	—	—	*lost*
XIII AN • VIII | D • LEO • X	203	II Anni VIII	LEONE | X | J520 | Anno. 8. | Lib. J3.	[fig.]	1396
XV AN • VIII | D • LEO • X[262] *misplaced*	205	III Anni VIII	LEONE | X | <1520> | Anno. 8. | Lib. J5.[263]	[fig.]	1398
[16 AN. 8][264] *misplaced*	206[265]	IV Anni VIII	—	—	*lost*
[14 AN. 8][266] *misplaced*	204	V Anni VIII	—	—	*lost*
XVII AN VIII | D LEO X	207	VI Anni VIII	1520 | An. VIII | Leo | X (*red*)	[letter]	1390
[18 AN. 8][267]	208	VII Anni VIII	—	—	*lost*
[19 AN. 8][268]	209	VIII Anni VIII	—	—	*lost*
[20 AN. 8][269]	210	—[270]	—	—	*lost*

YEAR 9 (1521, 19 March - 1521, December 1)

Original Title	C17 No.	C18 Index Reference	C19 Title	Herg.	Reg. Lat.
[1 AN. 9][271]	211	IX Anni VIII	—	—	*lost*
[2 AN. 9][272]	212	X Anni VIII	—	—	*lost*
III • AN • IX | D • LEO • X[273]	213	XI Anni VIII	LEONE | X | J52J | Anno. 9 | Lib. 3.	[fig.]	1401
IIII AN • IX | D • LEO • X	214[274]	XII Anni VIII	LEONE | X | J52J | Anno. 9. | Lib. 4.	[fig.]	1402
V AN • IX | D • LEO • X	215	XIII Anni VIII	LEONE | X | J52J | Anno. 9. | Lib. 5	[fig.]	1403
[6 AN. 9][275]	216	XIV Anni VIII	—	—	*lost*
VII AN • IX | D • LEO • X[276]	217	XV Anni VIII	LEONE | X | J52J | Anno 9 | Lib. 7.	[fig.]	1404

Original Title	C17 No.	C18 Index Reference	C19 Title	Herg.	Reg. Lat.
VIII AN • IX | D • LEO • X[277]	218	XVI Anni VIII	LEONE | X | J52J | Anno. 2. | Lib. 8.	[fig.]	1405

[YEARS 1-9]: DE PROVISIONIBUS PRELATORUM

Original Title	C17 No.	C18 Index Reference	C19 Title	Herg.	Reg. Lat.
prim(u)s de pro(visioni)bus prelator(um) | .d. Leonis . p(a)pe x[mi] | ANN[I] PRIMI[280]	219[278]	XVIII Anni VIII	LEONE[279] | X | <1512-13> | Anno. J. | Lib. J.	12	1281
I • DE PROVI • PRELA | AN • I • ET • II • D • PP X | LEO •[285]	220[281]	XVIII Anni VIII	LEONE | X | <1512-15>| Anno. J.[283] | Lib. I.[284]	3[282]	1293
II • DE PROVI • D · | LEO • • X .[286]	221	XIX Anni VIII	LEONE | X | <1515-17> | Anno. 4[287] | Lib. 2.	[fig.]	1342
[3 DE PROV.][288]	222[289]	XX Anni VIII	—	—	*lost*
[5 DE PROV.][290] *misplaced*	224[291]	XXI Anni VIII	—	—	*lost*
[4 DE PROV.][292] *misplaced*	223	XXII Anni VIII	—	—	*lost*
VI DE PROVI • | D: LEO: X[293]	225[294]	XXIII Anni VIII	LEONE | X | <1518-21> | Anno 9[296] | Lib. 6.	110[295]	1400
VII DE (?)PROVI • | D • LEO • X[297]	226[298]	XXIV Anni VIII	[?LEONE] | [X][299] | <1517-21> | Anno 8[301] | Lib.[302]	90.[300]	1399

REMNANT

Original Title	C17 No.	C18 Index Reference	C19 Title	Herg.	Reg. Lat.
[diverse matter; not provisions of prelates][304]	—	XXV Anni VIII[303] —		—	*lost*

MISCELLANEOUS

Original Title	C17 No.	C18 Index Reference	C19 Title	Herg.	Reg. Lat.
[diverse matter][305]	—	I Anni IX[306]	—	—	*lost*
L (IBE)R VNICVS DIVERSOR(VM) PONT.·ET | AN • VIZ ALEX . VI . IVLII | II . ET LEONIS X	—	II Anni IX	ALES. VI | GIULIO.II. | LEONE X | Lib. un.[307]	[fig.]	1406

1 Thus our reconstruction of the original archive. The figure is corroborated by other records. The *Lista Librorum existentium in Registro Litterarum Apostolicarum publico* dated 13 Oct 1617 puts Leo's *libri* at 227 (BAV, Fondo Borghese, Serie IV, tom. 44, fos 268ʳ-269ʳ). The C17 list headed *Incipiuntur Rubricelle litterarum Apostolicarum .D. Leonis pape X Ab Anno primo et Die XIX Mensis Martii MDXIII Usque ad Annum Nonum & Ultimum sui pontificatus ac Diem 2. Mensis Decembris Anni MDXXI* (hereafter 'stocktaking list') at fos 44ʳ-48ᵛ of *Ind.* 355 refers (effectively) to 226 numbered *libri* plus one lost *liber* which is explicitly unnumbered (*below*, note 219). And the C18 Index (*Ind.* 350-354) refers to 227 *libri* (*I Anni I* to *II Anni IX*) – that is, the 226 numbered *libri* known to the stocktaking list plus *Reg. Lat.* 1406 (a *liber* shared with other popes and not previously reckoned among Leo's registers).

2 *Reg. Lat.* 1329 is probably a ghost. The official note *manca* against *Reg. Lat.* 1329 (M. Giusti, *Studi sui Registri di Bolle Papali* [Collectanea Archivi Vaticani, 1], Città del Vaticano, 1979, p. 154 presumably following the ASV's modern inventory of the Lateran registers [*Ind.* 1040, p. 36]) could be taken to mean that a volume known to the ASV is missing. However, the concordance which the Archive compiled when the registers were accessioned and numbered has (under *vetus Signatura*): 1515 and (under *recens Signatura*): Reg. 1329. *Deest propter defectum signaturae.* (*Ind.* 705 [dated 1900], fo 141ʳ). The note is somewhat cryptic and open to different interpretation. As 1515 was merely the date element in the old title and insufficient to identify a particular register there was arguably a mishap in the accessioning. The note probably means that 1329 is vacant.

3 In addition, there are some Leo gatherings in *Reg. Lat.* 1406 (shared with Alexander and Julius); and letters (or fragments of letters) at fos 190ʳ-191ʳ and 222ᵛ-223ᵛ of *Reg. Lat.* 2462 and fos 117ʳ-238ʳ of *Reg. Lat.* 2464 – both modern made-up volumes. The material in the modern-made up volumes appended to the RL series (as Appendice voll. I - V) in 1926 was formerly item 209 in the Fondo Santini (acquired by the ASV in 1909). *Cf. Ind.* 1066. In all probability all the leaves come from known volumes. (For an example *see CPL* XVI, p. xlix, note 2).

4 Namely *Decimus sextus An(ni) sexti* (*below*, note 219). No Leo chancery registers appear to have been lost in the Sack of 1527.

5 Namely *Quintus Decimus An(ni) Septimi* and *Vigesimus An(ni) Octavi*. But if, as seems not improbable, they equate with *XXV Anni VIII* and *I Anni IX* of the C18 index, they belong to the bulk lost at Paris.

6 The sale of certain administratively useless records was sanctioned by the curia in a cost cutting exercise; but the sale of the chancery registers, which were regarded as indispensable, was the outcome, seemingly, of communication failure between the curia and the papal agent at Paris. *See* R. Ritzler, 'Die Verschleppung der Päpstlichen Archive nach Paris unter Napoleon I. und deren Rückführung nach Rom in den Jahren 1815 bis 1817', *Römische Historische Mitteilungen*, 6 und 7 Heft, 1962/63 & 1963/64, Graz-Köln, 1964, pp. 144-190 (esp. pp. 156-157). A few of the chancery registers dispersed at Paris found their way to Trinity College, Dublin (*cf.* L.E.Boyle, *A Survey of the Vatican Archives and of its Medieval Holdings* [Toronto, 1972], pp. 145-148). None of Leo's registers is among them.

7 *Cf. CPL* XVI, pp. cxiii-cxvi; *CPL* XVII Part I, pp. lxiii-lxvii.

8 The classifications employed by the registry for the component gatherings and reflected in the titles of the *libri*, from Boniface IX to Hadrian VI, are tabulated in H. Diener, *Die grossen Registerserien im Vatikanischen Archiv (1378-1523)* [= Quellen und Forschungen aus Italienischen Archiven und Bibliotheken, Band 51], 1972, pp. 22-23 [= 322-323].

9 The change can be observed in the first seven registers of the fourth year (nos. 103 to 109 in the C17 numeration).

10 Although it might be supposed that letters of diverse *materia* could now be enregistered promiscuously in the same gathering, scribes continued, perhaps from habit, perhaps for other reasons, to enregister mandates *de providendo* and the like in separate quinterns.

11 Thus (typically): *Anni Tertii D. Leonis decimi* (*Reg. Lat.* 1333, fo 199ʳ); *Anni Tertii D. Leonis* (ibid., fo 303ʳ). Sometimes the pope's name was omitted and only the year stated: thus *Anno Tertio* (*Reg. Lat.* 1332, fo 127ʳ). Unless (as often) the leaf has been removed in binding the heading is found on the recto of the first leaf of the quintern or gathering. The rest of the page, which usually bears the name of the relevant *scriptor registri*, is usually occupied by a list, which served as an index, of the names of the grantees of letters enregistered in the quintern. The verso is ordinarily blank. Other examples of headings which specify only the pontifical year (or group of years) and also, usually, the pope's name are at *Reg. Lat.* 1282, fo 237ʳ; 1284, fo 337ʳ; 1287, fo 163ʳ; 1301, fo 106ʳ; 1305, fo 283ʳ (*de Annis diversorum .d. Le(onis) p(a)p(e) X*); 1311, fo 211ʳ; 1313, fo 232ʳ; 1332, fo 217ʳ; 1336, fo 205ʳ; 1343, fo 269ʳ; 1346, fos 141ʳ, 155ʳ; 1351, fo 25ʳ; 1352, fo 354ʳ; 1355, fos 215ʳ, 241ʳ; 1361, fos 71ʳ, 217ʳ; 1366, fo 267ʳ; 1368, fo 1ʳ; 1369, fo 405ʳ; 1382, fo 327ʳ; 1383, fos 171ʳ, 245ʳ; 1384, fos 281ʳ, 331ʳ; 1391, fos 195ʳ, 221ʳ; 1392, fos 79ʳ, 315ʳ, 341ʳ; – all first pages of quinterns in Leo registers.

12   Aside from gatherings of consistorial provisions, the only ones spotted by the editor are at *Reg. Lat.* 1306,
      fo 271ʳ (headed *Vacan. II*) and *Reg. Lat.* 1316, fo 313ʳ (headed *Vavacantium[!] secundo Leonis*) – both
      registers of 2 Leo X created before description of the *materia* was finally dropped from the titles in 1516.
      Thus the position under Leo; but we must not overstate the case. Under Clement VII, for instance, some
      quintern headings do specify the *materia* (e.g. *Diversis* at fos 52ʳ, 100ʳ, 226ʳ, and 304ʳ of *Reg. Lat.* 1585).
13   *See* conspectus, nos 49 and 219-226 in the C17 numeration. Gatherings which contained consistorial
      provisions were still regularly headed with a note of the *materia* as well as, usually, of the pope's name and
      sometimes of the pontifical year. Thus: *provisionibus* (*Reg. Lat.* 1325, fo 253ʳ); *de provisionibus prelatorum*
      (*Reg. Lat.* 1293, fo 25ʳ); *De Provisionibus prelatorum D. Leo(nis). X* (*Reg. Lat.* 1400, fo 340ʳ). Most of the
      'wrapper' leaves – that is, the leaf which carried (on the recto) the heading and (usually) contents and its
      conjoint leaf – were evidently removed, before binding, from the gatherings which went to form *Reg. Lat.*
      1293, *Reg. Lat.* 1325, and *Liber Tertius de Provisionibus* (lost) and are now bound in *Ind.* 355, as fos 84-
      108, 52-83, and 109-138 respectively. *Ind.* 355, fo 52 (the recto of which is headed: *Provisiones Prelatorum
      An. 1. 2 et 3ⁱʲ D. Leonis .X.*) and its conjoint leaf (fo 83) once formed the first and last leaves of the first
      gathering (fos 1-23) in *Reg. Lat.* 1325.
14   Except once (*see* note 121).
15   *See* notes 39, 68, and 226. The placing of the interpuncts – commonly mid-height – is reproduced in the
      Conspectus.
16   *Cf.* inscriptions on cuts of *Reg. Lat.* 1363, 1366, 1367, 1368, 1369, 1370, 1371, 1374, 1375, 1380; and
      possibly 1303, 1356, 1357, 1372, 1379, 1384, 1385, 1386, 1387. At *Reg. Lat.* 1382 the E of LEO is also
      decorated.
17   *Cf. I AN I | D CLE VII* (*Reg. Lat.* 1424: bottom cut); *IIII . An. P.ᵐⁱ PII . V . (Reg. Lat.* 1866A: bottom cut);
      III · A · I · BEN · XIII (*Reg. Lat.* 2067: bottom cut); *II · AN · II · CL · XII* (*Reg. Lat.* 2071: bottom cut); *L[iber]
      . 5 . A . XI . SS . D . N. B . PP . XIV* (*Reg. Lat.* 2091: top cut); *L · X · A · XVII · BENED · PP XIV* (*Reg. Lat.*
      2094: top cut). Eventually, the potentially tiresome Leonine practice of ordering registers in multi-year series
      seems to have died out; otherwise, minor variations of detail apart, the later designations all conform to the
      system established under Leo.
18   In Thierry's numeration the registers are ordered as follows: year 1; years 1 & 2; years 1, 2 & 3; years 1, 2,
      3 & 4; year 2; year 2 & 3; year 3; year 3 & 4; year 4; *primus* to *quintus diversorum annorum*; year 5; years
      4, 5 & 6; years 4 & 5; year 6; VI & [7] *diversorum annorum*; year 7; year 8; year 9; and *de provisionibus
      prelatorum*. This could well have been an historic shelf order. The order inherent in the stocktaking list (at
      Ind. 355, fos 44ʳ-48ᵛ) of what were almost certainly the original *rubricellae* is close to the order preserved
      in the C17 numeration. As the letters in each register were evidently rubricated under pontifical year the list
      repeats the titles of multi-year registers. Assuming that the first occurrence of such titles reflects the true
      order we find that the order in which the registers are taken by the *rubricellae* is largely the same as the order
      preserved in Thierry's numeration. The only difference – and it could easily be a mistake of the compiler of
      the list – is that where Thierry's numeration has: *primus* to *quintus diversorum annorum*; year 5; years 4, 5
      & 6; years 4 & 5 the list has: years 4, 5 & 6; years 4 & 5; *primus* to *quintus diversorum annorum*; and year
      5. In other words the first two series and the last two are reversed. Otherwise the order preserved in Thierry's
      numeration and the order of the *rubricellae* coincide, even down to the splitting of the seven *diversorum*
      registers into two separated groups (of 5 vols. and 2). Given the number of possible variables the coincidence
      is remarkable. It argues that the shelf order of the 1640s dates from the time, presumably in the earlier C16,
      when the registers were first rubricated.
19   In 1636 the registers were described as being in *Palatio Vaticano et duabus cameris designatis* (*Ind.* 1, fo
      692ʳ). The description perhaps fits the CVSTODIA REGISTRI BVLLARVM (thus the inscription over the
      door) in the cortile of Sixtus V (A. Mercati, 'Complementi al "Bullarium Franciscanum" ', *Archivum
      Franciscanum Historicum*, XLIII, 1950, pp. 161-180, 335-359). In 1820 – by which time, presumably, the
      surviving registers had been transported back from Paris – the registers were still being archived in the
      Vatican. *Cf.* attestation dated 17 July 1820: "... Similmente attestiamo, che i Quinterni e i Tomi dei Registri
      correnti delle Bolle Pontificie, le quali di mano in mano si spediscono nella Cancellaria si conservano, e si
      custodiscono IN UNA STANZA della Dataria A BELLA POSTA assegnata per simile oggetto a cui esercita
      l'officio di Custode del Registro delle Bolle, e che da ppoi[!] simili Registri vengono trasportati
      sull'Archivio della STESSA DATARIA ESISTENTE NEL PALAZZO VATICANO." (ASR, Camerale II, 34
      Dataria e Vacabili, busta 9: folder 16 . Dataria. Collegio dei Maestri del Registro delle bolle e dei Registratori
      delle medesime, 1737-1823: Papers [mostly printed] concerning Franciscus Livius, *custos regestri*
      [nominated 1805] and litigant); *and* " 1. Presta l'opera sua all'Officio della Custodia delli due Archivj. L'uno
      più vasto presso il Vaticano, e l'altro presso la Dataria Apostolica, delli quali ha le Chiavi sotto la più stretta
      responsabilità." (NOTA Delle Ingerenze, che il Custode pro tempore del Registro delle Bolle disbriga in

servizio della Dataria, ibid.). The smaller archive, where the current registers were kept, was presumably at the Palazzo della Dataria near the Quirinal.

20   Both *BOP* and *BC* cite the registers by Thierry's numeration. *See below*, notes 52, 58, 62, 80, 88, 103, 108, 110, 114, 118, 120, 133, 148, 152, 159, 190, 198, 200, 203, 209, 210, 216, 220, 230, 246, 253, 265, 274, 278, 294; and especially notes 72, 192, 281, and 291 where *BOP*'s reference is quoted. The reference is also quoted in notes 109 and 133 to the *Rubricellae* of Lost Letters, below, pp. 578 and 579. Wadding cites some earlier medieval registers by the same numeration (*cf. CPL* XVI, p. lii).

21   *CPL* XI, p. viii. The explanation remains perfectly plausible; but it is based on the assumption that the medieval registers received their present bindings (which do *not* bear the *signaturae* of the C18 indexes) *before* they were re-rubricated in the C18. For the arguments for a rebinding date of post 1817 *see below*, note 24.

22   *Ind.* 406-415. According to their title pages, *Ind.* 406 and 411 were edited by the then *custos regesti bullarum*, Bartolomeo Terzi (active mid C18 [*cf. CPL* XVI, p. l, note 13]).

23   For example, *XX Anni VIII* (lost) was cited as *Reg. Bullar.* [Leonis X.] *in Arch. Dat. A. VIII. T. XX.* by G. Marini, *Degli Archiatri Pontifici*, I (Rome, 1784), p. 231. *Cf. XIX Anni II* (*lost*) of Alexander VI cited as *Reg. in Arch. Dat. A. II. Tom. XIX* (ibid., p. 230). The same register is cited by Garampi as *AB* [= Archivum Bullarum]. *Al. VI. 2. T. 19.* (*Ind.* 553 [*Schedario Garampi*], fo. 187^r). The concordance between Garampi's references and the Lateran Registers as currently numbered is given in *Sussidi*, pp. 145-190. The reversal in Marini's and Garampi's reference of the *liber* and year numbers as given in the relevant C18 index (*Ind.* 339 [*cf. CPL* XVI, p. l]) – 'Anni II Tom. XIX' instead of 'XIX Anni II' – is interesting and has the effect of bringing the pontifical year into prominence. As the year must have been the main unit of collocation giving it priority would have facilitated shelving. It is possible that the references reflect the form of the *signatura* on the spine (A. II . T. XIX if not II | XIX) and that it served as a shelf mark. However, we should note that the old manuscript label (paper) on the spine of *Reg. Lat.* 1866A (*see* next note) is in the form *4* | *AN I* | *PII* | *PP V* (*cf. IIII . AN. P(RI)MI PII. V.* on bottom cut). The spine of 1866A is divided by the raised bands into four compartments. The fact that the *4* is the only occupant of the top or first compartment and that the rest of the *signatura* occupies the second gives decided prominence to the *liber* number.

24   At one time the Lateran Registers were almost certainly all properly bound. *Reg. Lat.* 1866A – a register of 1 Pius V (1566-1572) which has been out of custody and escaped rebinding – perhaps typifies the original bindings of the late medieval and early modern registers: green parchment (over boards); five raised bands on the spines forming four compartments; gatherings fastened to the bands. However, except for 1866A and *Reg. Lat.* 1198A (a register of Julius II, bound in cream (?)kid, which had strayed into another series), the only registers which are now bound in parchment are the registers of 7 Pius VII (1800-1823) onwards, viz. *Reg. Lat.* 2107 - 2460. Exceptions apart, the bulk of the series, viz. *Reg. Lat.* 1 (a register of Boniface IX [1389-1404]) to *Reg. Lat.* 2106 (5 Pius VII), is now bound, or rather cased, in paper (over card). As a previous editor, whose judgement deserves considerable respect, has stated that the Lateran Registers were re-bound "apparently in the 17th century." (*CPL* XI, p. v) we must note the arguments for a rebinding date of post 1817. In the absence of specific records (and the editor knows of none) determining the date when the medieval and early modern registers, Leo's included, received their present bindings is a matter of weighing up a number of more or less competing indicia. Certainty is beyond reach and the best we can expect is an on balance determination. The evidence is all more or less circumstantial; but it is quite compelling in its cumulativeness. In the first place, the date when the paper covered registers stop and the parchment ones begin – 1804-5 x 1806-7 – surely points to the approximate date when the registers were rebound. The registers (but probably not those of 7-10 Pius VII which may not then have been permanently archived [*cf.* above, note 19]) were removed to Paris in 1810-1813. When they were sold to grocers and the like as wrapping paper in 1817 they were probably asset-stripped and the registers which were recovered and eventually returned to Rome could well have been disbound. Contemporary exchanges between the curia and its agents in Paris refer repeatedly to the dispersal of the *Bollario legato in verde* (Marini to Mauri, 11 June 1817 [with the further reference to *i registri delle Bolle legati in verde*], in Ritzler, op. cit. [*above*, note 6] pp. 187-8; *cf.* Consalvi to Marini, 24 July 1817 [*bolle legate in verde*] in M. Marini, *Memorie Storiche dell' occupazione, e restituzione degli Archivii della S. Sede ...* in *Regestum Clementis Papae V*, Rome, 1885, pp. cclxxii-cclxxiii; the registers were clearly colour coded, green evidently meaning indispensable: *Io veggo che non mi era ingannato nel crederli necessarii, arguendolo dalla sola circostanza della legatura in cui si tenevano custoditi* [Consalvi to Marini, 19 July 1817, ibid., pp. cclxxv-cclxxvi]) – and the expression unquestionably refers to the Lateran Registers; and to the series as a whole and not just to a small date-limited section (*cf. l'alienazione seguita di tali Regesti contenenti bolle di molti secoli* [ibid.]). We know that the surviving representative of the registers as originally bound (*Reg. Lat.* 1866A) is bound in green parchment; *Reg. Lat.* 2107-2109 are bound in blue or blue-green parchment; and *Reg. Lat.* 2110-2121 are

bound in green parchment; and there is evidence that some if not all of the other registers were similarly bound (*cf.* small fragments of green parchment beneath the spine of *Reg. Lat.* 1078 [a register of Alexander VI now cased in white paper]; green stains and smudges, which may be related, are common in the registers of Alexander; another small scrap of green parchment is bound in at the bottom before the first quintern of *Reg. Lat.* 1314 – a register of Leo X; and the top cut of *Reg. Lat.* 1405 – another Leo register —— is stained blue or blue green). If the registers had already received their present bindings of red and white paper (*infra*) the exchanges about the *Bollario legato in verde* become utterly unintelligible. And, since the generality of C18 registers would not yet have needed rebinding by the time they were removed to Paris, the use of economy bindings for newly formed registers would need explaining. The fiasco at Paris provides the only possible occasion we know of for a massive rebinding operation. Alternative theories raise too many questions. <u>Secondly</u>, all the registers seem to have been rebound at much the same time. Aside from *Reg. Lat.* 189, which is bound in blue paper (the underlining, perhaps, of a register once covered in white paper), there are only two patterns of binding. The majority of the registers are bound in white paper, lettered on the spine in Italian between double rules; the remainder are bound in red paper, lettered differently on the spine in Latin. The lettering on both is MS. Obviously, the registers suffered wear and tear from searches and arranging for their repair (if not rebinding) must have been one of the *custodia*'s periodic housekeeping exercises. For example, the list of 1617 (above, note 1) notes that of Leo's 227 *libri* or registers 122 were due for repair (*resarcien(dos)*). However, the overall similarity of the present bindings – just two types over 2, 106 registers – argues that the rebinding was occasioned by a circumstance common to all the registers rather than to random wear and tear. In short, we seem to be looking at an exceptional blanket operation rather than routine maintenance by the *custos* of individual registers. <u>Thirdly</u>, the paper bindings are cheap. The off-white paper in which most of the registers are cased is of coarse quality, with inclusions and unbleached fibres, and was in common use in Italy for economy binding in the C18 (if not earlier) and early C19. The use of economy bindings is again suggestive of one or two large scale contracts rather than occasional piecemeal maintenance. We might add that it is not uncharacteristic of a government department suddenly faced with a need for significant outlay. <u>Fourthly</u>, the old bindings are not bound in. In an archive, where the reference means everything, that is a curious circumstance. <u>Fifthly</u>, a rebinding date of post 1817 provides, in my view, a more convincing explanation of why the *signaturae* of the C18 index are not inscribed on the present bindings of the medieval registers (Leo's included) and of the consequent want of accord between finding aid and register. The *signaturae* were inscribed on the bindings; but the bindings they were inscribed on were subsequently lost. <u>Finally</u>, a rebinding date of post 1817 would also explain the rather odd titles which are inscribed on the bindings of the medieval registers. The titles on the white paper bindings – that is the majority – evidently embody a reading of the *liber* number and year in the original title on the cut: thus the spine of *Reg. Lat.* 1323 is lettered *LEONO* | *X* | *J5J4* | *Anno. 2.* | *Lib. 25* reading the numbers in *XXV VA • ET DI • AN* | *II D • LEO • X* on the cut. But why invent a novel title incorporating an obsolete reference? From the 1640s to the early C18 the current reference was Thierry's: 'Liber 80'. More importantly, from the mid C18 when the register was re-rubricated the crucial reference elements in the original title – XXV and AN II – had been superseded by the reference V Anni III of the C18 index. The answer has to be that the spines were lettered at a late date, when the original bindings were not available and relevant knowledge had been lost.

We must hedge the argument with an important qualifier. It is that the sheer extent of the Lateran Registers sets practical limits to our knowledge. Though she has had sight of all the registers the editor has handled only a fraction of them. There could well be some surprises. Others may be justified in reaching different conclusions.

25 Evident from *Reg. Lat.* 2107-2121 (early C19) which are in their original bindings (*see* previous note). *Reg. Lat.* 2122 onwards are in plain, not green, parchment. The keeper's duties included: " 6. Di poi riuscire detti quinterni cosi (?)registrati, ed ogni trenta di questi ne forma tanti Tomi, e li consegna al Libraro della Dataria per legarli secondo il consueto stile tutto a spese della medesima numera tutte le pagini ..." (NOTA Delle Ingerenze, che il Custode pro tempore del Registro delle Bolle disbriga in servizio della Dataria in ASR, Camerale II, 34 Dateria e Vacabili, busta 9, etc.[*as specified in* note 9 above]). The datary had purchased the *custodia* (an *officium vacabile*) from the then proprietors in 1753 (ibid.); the chancery registers were kept in the archivio della dataria.

26 The dates were later subjected to correction by the ASV: *see below*, notes 28, 32, and 38.

27 The oblong slips (below, note 100) may relate to an earlier exercise of which we are wholly ignorant. The history of the *custodia* is not at all well documented and there are huge holes in our knowledge. The bindings of both the registers and the *rubricellae* are a prime source of information.

28 Corrected by the ASV: original date obscured by white label stamped *1752*.

29 *See* note 36.

30   The conditions there in November 1885 are vividly described by T. von Sickel, *Römische Erinnerungen*, ed.
     L. Santifaller, Vienna, 1947, pp. 79-82 (Erinnerungen I), 210-211 (official report of 4 Dec. 1885). He noted
     that volumes were misplaced; and that the titles on the spines were variously incorrect. The archivist insisted
     there was no catalogue. Leo's registers, which Hergenroether had been able to borrow in small lots for home
     reading, were all together (ibid., pp. 208, 210).

31   Unless otherwise stated, written in ink on bottom cut. Note that owing to mis-alignment of the leaves the title
     is not always readily legible and variant readings are possible. Capitalisation and punctuation (in
     approximated form) have been retained (*cf.* note 15 above, notes 39, 68, and 226 below). Where the title
     occupies more than one line the division from one line to the next is marked with a downstroke (|) .
     Conjectured titles are supplied in short-title form.

32   That is, the title as originally written, in ink, on spine of extant early C19 (post 1817) covers (directly onto
     the cover in the case of the white ones, often onto a white paper label in the case of the red). In its use of 'J'
     for '1/ I' and (as often) punctuation with triangular pellets, the lettering on the white covers is reminiscent
     of that on the title pages of the mid C18 indexes (notably *Ind.* 332, 333.335, 337, 338, and 357, dated
     [variously] 1758-62); but those conditioned by C18 fashions lived on into the C19. The lettering on the red
     covers exhibits no such features. Not infrequently, part of the title has been altered, occasionally by
     overwriting, usually by means of a superimposed stamped label. Where part of the C19 title is concealed by
     a label angled brackets [< >] enclose the revised matter. Other alterations are noted in the footnotes. Visibly,
     the most sensitive elements were the dates and these were presumably revised after transfer to the ASV,
     probably when the series was surveyed by G.- M. Laurent for his inventory (*Ind.* 1039-1040 which bears the
     explicit 21.iii. 1939). The identification of the titles (& covers) as early nineteenth century is qualified: *see*
     note 24 above.

33   The reference to the registers as given in Hergenroether's *Regesta* (below, pp. lxxv, lxxvi). Unless otherwise
     stated, the concordance between Hergenroether's designation and the current *Reg. Lat.* number is based on
     the match between entries covered by the present volume and entries in the *Regesta* (*see* Concordance,
     below, pp. lxxvii, lxxviii). Sometimes the reference is written on the spine. References in brackets are
     conjectural. Where the concordance has not been established 'letter' or 'figure' has been supplied as
     appropriate.

34   Current designation. Applied by the ASV when the registers were transferred from the Lateran. Established
     by early C20. (*cf. Ind.* 705: Inventarium Regestorum Lateranensium seu de Dataria in Tabularium Vaticanum
     iussu Leonis XIII P.M. translatorum [dated Anno Iubilaei MDCCCC]). The inventory gives, under Signatura,
     the concordance between vetus and recens, e.g. 1515 | an. 3 | lib 3 = 1332.

35   Numbers (from *Ind.* 355, fos 44ʳ-48ᵛ) applied to registers in mid seventeenth century during the keepership
     of Nicholas Thierry (*cf. CPL* XVI, p. lii, note 25). The numeration was evidently still current in the early
     C18 when it was used by both *BOP* and *BC.*

36   That is, the reference to the *liber* as given in the mid eighteenth century index (*Ind.* 350-354); not found on
     present bindings but probably inscribed on original bindings (now lost). The concordance between the index
     references and the registers (and thus, of course, the original designations on the cuts) was established by
     ASV staff soon after the arrival of the registers from the Lateran. A concordance was produced, namely
     Concordantia Numeri Rubricellarum Regestorum Lateranensium seu veteris cum novo numero (*Ind.* 319A;
     cf. CPL XI, p. viii); and the index ref. was written on the front endpaper of each register, and the number of
     the register (or Deest) was, where appropriate, written in the index. A similar concordance is printed in
     Sussidi per la Consultazione dell'Archivio Vaticano, I, Rome, 1926, pp. 169-172 (the Indicaz. Garampi
     equates with the index ref.; but note that 1234 is a misprint: I.2 = 1284).

37   Rubricated as *Primus Anni primi* (*Ind.* 355, fo 44ʳ).

38   Here, and in similar cases below, the concealed part of the C19 title is probably '1513'.

39   On the top cut. Unless otherwise stated, the punctuation represented by the small full stop is a round point.

40   On the top cut.

41   Rubricated as *Quartus Anni primi* (*Ind.* 355, fo 44ʳ).

42   On the top cut.

43   Written in pencil near base of spine.

44   Rubricated as *Sextus Anni primi* (*Ind.* 355, fo 44ʳ).

45   Rubricated as *Septimus Anni primi* (*Ind.* 355, fo 44ʳ).

46   as note 43 above

47   Rubricated as *Nonus Anni primi* (*Ind.* 355, fo 44ʳ).

48   Rubricated as *Decimus Anni primi* (*Ind.* 355, fo 44ʳ).

49   *sic*

50   Rubricated as *Duodecimus Anni primi* (*Ind.* 355, fo 44ʳ).

51   Rubricated as *Tertius Decimus Anni primi* (*Ind.* 355, fo 44^r).
52   *BC*, pp. 449-450 (Const. I) = *XV Anni I* (*Ind.* 350, fo 246^r).
53   Rubricated as *Sextus Decimus Anni primi* (*Ind.* 355, fo 44^r).
54   Rubricated as *Decimus Nonus Anni primi* (*Ind.* 355, fo 44^r).
55   as note 43 above
56   Rubricated as *Vigesimus secundus Anni primi* (*Ind.* 355, fo 44^r).
57   Rubricated as *Vigesimus Tertius Anni primi* (*Ind.* 355, fo 44^r).
58   *BOP*, p. 304 (entry xiii) = *XXIII Anni I* (*Ind.* 350, fo 353^r).
59   as note 43 above
60   A leaf at front has *xxv divers(arum) Bullar(um) Anno primo Leonis p(a)p(e) x^{mi}* in a contemporary hand.
61   The front endpaper has *Vicesimussext(us) diversarum Bullarum Anno Primo d(omi)ni Leonis x^{mi}* in a contemporary hand.
62   *BOP*, pp. 302-3 (entry x.) = Herg. 7237.
63   Herg. 3616-7 = *Reg. Lat.* 1288, fos 184^r-185^v.
64   Herg. 5831 = *Reg. Lat.* 1289, fos 275^r-277^r.
65   Contemporaneously corrected (by erasure) from *29*.
66   as note 43 above
67   Rubricated as *Trigesimus secundus Anni primi* (*Ind.* 355, fo 44^v). (The next register [i.e. no. 33 in the C17 numeration] is rubricated as *Trigesimus tertius de mixtis Anni primi* [ibid.]).
68   Unless otherwise stated, the interpunction represented by the larger full stop is in the form of a reversed and elongated 's' either centred on a triangle or pellet, or with a short horizontal stroke through it. Triangle and pellet are solid.
69   Written in ink near base of spine.
69bis   *sic*; but rubricated as *Trigesimus quartus de vacantibus et diversis An. primi et 2^{di}* (*Ind.* 355, fo 44^v).
70   *2* added here (modern stamping).
71   Rubricated as *secundus de Mixtis an. p. et 2.* (*Ind.* 355, fo 48^r); *and see* next note.
72   *BOP*, pp. 315-316 (entry xxviii [*ex Archivo Apostolico Libro II de mixtis An. I, & II Leonis X*]) = *XXXVI Anni I* (*Ind.* 350, fo 253^r). *BOP*'s manner of reference here is exceptional: as a rule it refers to registers by their C17 numeration, not by their original titles.
73   as note 70 above
74   as note 69 above
75   On the top cut.
76   as note 43 above
76bis   as note 70 above
77   Rubricated as *Quintus de Vacantibus et diversis An. primi et secundi* (*Ind.* 355, fo 44^v).
78   Herg. 15340-15341 = *Reg. Lat.* 1321, fos 135^v-138^r.
79   Rubricated as *Secundus Vacantium et diversorum An. 1. 2^{di} et 3^{ii}* (*Ind.* 355, fos 44^v, 45r, 45^v).
80   *BOP*, pp. 304-5 (entry xiv.) = Herg. 11183.
81   *2* and *3* superimposed (by modern stamping) on original *3*.
82   Or possibly *LEO PP· | X*.
83   Contemporary; but perhaps added later.
84   Rubricated as *Quintus Vacantium et diversorum An. I. 2^{di} et 3^{ii}* (*Ind.* 355, fos 44^v, 45^r, 45^v, 48^r).
85   Rubricated as *Sextus Vacantium et diversorum An. I. 2^{di} et 3^{ii}* (*Ind.* 355, fos 44^v, 45^r, 45^v, 48^r).
86   as note 43 above
87   The register rubricated as *Duodecimus An. pr(imi) 2^{di} et 3^{ii}* was numbered *48* (*Ind.* 355, fos 44^v, 45^r; *and see* 45^v). As the compilers of the C18 Index evidently followed the C17 numeration, it probably corresponds to *XXXXVIII Anni I*.
88   *BOP*, pp. 399-400 (F. Jo. de Witte) = Herg. 8737-8739.
89   The label is pealing away and *5* is visible.
90   Described in the fragments of early *rubricellae* as *Liber Primus de Provisionibus Prelatorum Annorum 1, 2 & 3 Leonis PP X^{mi}* (*Ind.* 355, fos 37^r-40^r). *Reg. Lat.* 1325 contains sixteen gatherings or quinterns. The sixteen bifolia which originally 'wrapped' the gatherings (as the first and last leaves) were evidently detached before the register was bound and are now fos 52-83 of *Ind.* 355. The content of each gathering is listed (by provisee) on the recto of the first leaf of the relevant bifolium. The recto of fo 52 – once the first leaf of the register – is headed: *Primus de Provisionibus prelatorum Ann(orum) Primi Secundi et Tertii D. Leonis PP X* (*cf.* ibid., 65^r).
91   The register rubricated as *Nonus An. primi 2^{di} et 3^{ii}* was numbered *50* (*Ind.* 355, fos 44^v, 45^r; *and see* 45^v). It probably corresponds to *XXXXX Anni I* (*cf.* note 87 above).

92   as note 43 above

93   The register rubricated as *Undecimus An. primi 2di et 3ii* was numbered *52* (*Ind.* 355, fos 44ᵛ, 45ʳ; *and see* 45ᵛ). It probably corresponds to *II Anni II* (*cf.* note 87 above).

94   as note 43 above

95   Rubricated as *Primus An. primi 2di 3ii et 4i* (*Ind.* 355, fos 44ᵛ, 45ʳ, 46ʳ).

96   Not punctuated; of uncertain date.

97   Rebacked; modern inscription probably reproduces original; below: *1513 al 1518* | *varii anni.*

98   Rubricated as *Secundus diversarum bullarum An. Secundi* (*Ind.* 355, fo 44ᵛ).

99   *1* and *2* superimposed (by modern stamping) on original *2.*

100 What may well be the instruction to the binder for the lettering is preserved on an oblong slip of coarse paper stuck on the front endpaper: *Leone 10* = | *1512* = | *Anno 2º Lib. 4º*; ink. The script is ?C18; the hand could, of course, be later. There are similar slips in *Reg. Lat.* 1323, 1335, 1361, 1364, 1380, and 1398 – all bound in white paper. (There are no slips in any of the red registers.)

101 Or possibly *Leonis p.*

102 Rubricated as *Quintus diver(sarum) bullar(um) An. Secundi* (*Ind.* 355, fo. 44ᵛ).

103 *BOP*, pp. 303-304 (entry xi.) = Herg. 7705.

104 Rubricated as *Octavus diversar(um) bullar(um) An. Secundi* (*Ind.* 355, fo 44ᵛ).

105 Rubricated as *Undecimus diversar(um) bullar(um) An. Secundi* (*Ind.* 355, fo 44ᵛ).

106 *sic*; beneath: *Lib (?)... * in red crayon.

107 Rubricated as *Decimus tertius diversar(um) bul. An. Secundi* (*Ind.* 355, fo 44ᵛ).

108 *BOP*, pp. 308-310 (entry xxi) = *XVIII Anni II* (*Ind.* 351, fo 7ᵛ).

109 Rubricated as *Decimus [Tertius:* del.] *Quartus diversar(um) bullar(um) An. Secundi* (*Ind.* 355, fo. 45ʳ).

110 *Cf. BOP*, p. 400 (F. Didacus Fernandez) = Herg. 12832-12836.

111 Beneath: *Lib. 17* in red crayon.

112 Existence corroborated: *cf.* near contemporary reference to a *liber xviij diversis anni 2i Leonis pp x.* (*Ind.* 355, fo 62ʳ); rubricated as *Decimus octavus diversar(um) bullar(um) An. Secundi* (*Ind.* 355, fo 45ʳ).

113 *Cf. Quere libro 19 divers(arum) bullar(um) Anni 2 D. Leo X* (*Ind.* 355, fo 11ᵛ).

114 *BOP*, pp. 305-306 (entry xvi) = *XXV Anni II* (*Ind.* 351, fo 161ʳ).

115 *Cf.* Herg. 14383; *BOP*, pp. 305-6 (Pro Coenobio Lugdunensi).

116 Thus the bottom cut; the top has: *XX Anº 2º*; of uncertain date.

117 Rubricated as *Vigesimus primus diversar(um) bul. An. Secundi* (*Ind.* 355, fo 45ʳ).

118 *BOP*, p. 305 (entry xv) = *I Anni III* (*Ind.* 351, fo 98ᵛ).

119 Rubricated as *Vigesimus secundus Mixtus An. Secundi* (*Ind.* 355, fo 45ʳ).

120 *BOP*, p. 315 (entry xxvii.) = Herg. 13932.

121 The form of the abbreviation mark is epigraphic: not unlike a sombrero in profile.

122 Evident error in MS: the register rubricated as *Vigesimus quartus Mixtus An. Secundi* is numbered *78* (*Ind.* 355, fo 45ʳ). It should be numbered '79': the previous item (*Vigesimus Tertius Mixtus An. Secundi*) is correctly numbered 78 (ibid.); the next (*Vigesimus quintus vacan(tium) et diver(sorum) An. Secundi* 80 (ibid.).

123 *sic*

124 On an oblong slip of white paper stuck on the front endpaper: *Leone X* | *1514:* | *Anno II. Lib: 25=*; *cf.* above, note 100.

125 Named in a contemporary reference: *Quere Lº primo Mixt. An(norum) S(e)c(un)di et tertii D. Leonis X. fol. 239* (*Ind.* 355, fo. 53ʳ).

126 *3* added (by modern stamping).

127 Rubricated as *Tertius Vacan(tium) et diversor(um) An. Secundi et tertii* (*Ind.* 355, fo 45ʳ; *and see* 45ᵛ).

128 Rubricated as *Primus Vacan(tium) et diversor(um) an. tertii* (*Ind.* 355, fo 45ʳ).

129 Rubricated as *Secundus Vacan(tium) et diversor(um) An. tertii* (*Ind.* 355, fo 45ʳ).

130 *Cf.* note 34 above.

131 In an exercise of this kind a few unresolved contradictions must be expected. *BOP*'s entry xxxiii (p.319) *ex Archivo Apostolico Libro LXXXVII* fol. 199 = Herg. 15736 from Arch. Lat. tom. 51, f. 199 and *BOP*, p. 319. But *liber* 87 equates with *Reg. Lat.* 1333; tom. 51 with *Reg. Lat.* 1324.

132 Rubricated as *Sextus Vacan(tium) et dive(rsorum) An. tertii* and numbered 89 (*Ind.* 355, fo 45ᵛ).

133 *BOP*, pp. 320-321 (entry xxxiv) = *XV Anni III* (*Ind.* 351, fo 276ʳ).

134 On an oblong slip of white paper stuck onto front endpaper: *Leone X.* | *1515* | *Anno III. Lib. VIII.*; *cf.* above, note 100.

135 *Cf. Decimus de Va(cantibus) et di(versis) Anni Tertij D. Leonis p(a)p(e) X* on recto of unnumbered leaf at front of register.

136 The register rubricated as *Duodecimus Vacan(tium) et diver(sorum) An. tertii* was numbered 95 (*Ind.* 355, fo 45ᵛ).

137 *sic*

138 On the top cut.

139 The first and third lines perhaps changed by erasure.

140 Rubricated as *Undecimus Vacan(tium) et diver(sorum) An. tertii* and numbered *94* (*Ind.* 355, fo 45ᵛ).

141 On the top cut.

142 Rubricated as *Decimus quintus vacan(tium) et diver(sorum) An. tertii* (*Ind.* 355, fo 45ᵛ).

143 Rubricated as *Decimus sextus vacan(tium) et diver(sorum) An. tertii* (*Ind.* 355, fo 45ᵛ).

144 *Primus vacan(tium) et dive(rsorum) An. 3 et quarti* occurs (with trivial differences of expression) three times in the list of *rubricellae* of Leo's letters. At one occurrence *101* replaces *126* deleted (*Ind.* 355, fo 46ʳ).

145 On the top cut.

146 *3* and *4* superimposed (by modern stamping); *An. 3* in pencil at base of spine.

147 Rubricated as *Secundus Vacan(tium) et dive(rsorum) An. 3 et 4* (*Ind.* 355, fos 45ᵛ, 46ʳ, 48ʳ). At one occurrence *102* replaces *127* deleted (ibid., fo 46ʳ).

148 *BOP*, pp. 328-329 (entry xlii) = *II Anni IV* (*Ind.* 352, fo 139ʳ).

149 as note 43 above

150 On the top cut.

151 as note 43 above

152 *BOP*, p. 344 (entry lvi) = *V Anni IV* (*Ind.* 352, fo 3ʳ).

153 as note 43 above

154 *sic*

155 Rebacked; modern inscription probably reproduces the original (or attempts to).

156 Rubricated as *Sextus dive(rsarum) bullar(um) An. quarti* (*Ind.* 355, fo 46ʳ).

157 as note 43 above

158 Rubricated as *Octavus An. quarti* (*Ind.* 355, fo 46ʳ).

159 *BOP*, pp. 331-332 (entry xlv) = *XI Anni IV* (*Ind.* 352, fo 6ʳ).

160 A number which is not 67 but capable of being so read is written in pencil near the base of the spine; the '6' is certain; by elimination 64, 66, or 68.

161 *sic*

162 as note 43 above

163 Below: *IV* (in pencil).

164 Rubricated as *Duodecimus An. quarti* (*Ind.* 355, fo 46ʳ). *Cf.* contemporary references: *quere Lᵒ xij Va et Di D. Leonis X An. quarto* and *lib. xij an. 4 D. Leonis X.* (*Ind.* 355, fo. 112ʳ). The references are to Jacobus Electus Moravien. at folio 72. *Cf.* C18 index reference to same letter at no. 1027 below.

165 Rubricated as *Tredecimus An. quarti* (*Ind.* 355, fo 46ʳ).

166 Rubricated as *Quatuordecimus An. quarti* (*Ind.* 355, fo 46ʳ).

167 Rubricated as *Decimus quintus An. quarti* (*Ind.* 355, fo 46ʳ).

168 Rubricated as *Decimus sextus An. quarti* (*Ind.* 355, fo 46ʳ).

169 Rubricated as *Decimus Septimus An quarti* (*Ind.* 355, fo 46ʳ).

170 On the top cut.

171 On the top cut.

172 as note 43 above

173 Below: *IV* (in pencil).

174 Rubricated as *Vigesimus An. quarti* (*Ind.* 355, fo 46ʳ).

175 Rubricated as *Vigesimus primus An quarti* (*Ind.* 355, fo 46ʳ).

176 Rubricated as *Vigesimus Secundus An. quarti* (*Ind.* 355, fo 46ʳ).

177 Rubricated as *Vigesimus Tertius An. quarti* (*Ind.* 355, fo 46ʳ).

178 Rubricated as *primus diversorum Annorum* (*Ind.* 355, fo 46ʳ).

179 Written over *154* (*Ind.* 355, fo 46ʳ). The context argues that *154* was just a slip.

180 Rubricated as *Secundus diversorum Annor(um)* (*Ind.* 355, fo 46ʳ).

181 Rubricated as *Tertius diversor(um) Annor(um)* (*Ind.* 355, fo 46ʳ).

182 Rubricated as *Quartus diversor(um) Annor(um)* (*Ind.* 355, fo 46ʳ).

183 Rubricated as *Tertius An. quinti* (*Ind.* 355, fo 46ᵛ).

184 On an oblong slip stuck on to front endpaper: *Leone 10 | 1517: | Anno 5ᵒ Lib: 5ᵒ*—; *cf. above*, note 100.

185 Rubricated as *Sextus An. quinti* (*Ind.* 355, fo 46ᵛ).

186 Rubricated as *Septimus An. quinti* (*Ind.* 355, fo 46ᵛ).

187 Rubricated as *No [nus] An. quinti* (*Ind.* 355, fo 46ᵛ).

188 Rubricated as *Decimus An. quinti* (*Ind.* 355, fo 46ᵛ).

189 Rubricated as *Undecimus An. quinti* (*Ind.* 355, fo 46ᵛ).

190 *BOP*, pp. 356-357 (entry lxxiii) = *XVI Anni V* (*Ind.* 352, fo 340^r).

191 Rubricated as *Duodecimus An. quinti* (*Ind.* 355, fo 46^v).

192 *BOP*, pp. 350-351 (entry lxiv): *ex Archivo Apostolico Libro CXLII fol. 347* = *XVII Anni V*, fo 357. Both items concern the Dominican house at Seville. Despite the difference of folio number they probably refer to the same letter.

193 *V* entered in pencil.

194 Rubricated as *Quartus decimus An. quinti* (*Ind.* 355, fo 46^v).

195 On an oblong slip stuck on to front endpaper: *Leone X.* | *1517:* | *Anno V. Lib: 16* —; *cf. above*, note 100.

196 Rubricated as *Decimus septimus An. quinti* (*Ind.* 355, fo 46^v).

197 Rubricated as *Decimus Nonus An[n]i quinti* and numbered *149* (*Ind.* 355, fo 46^v).

198 *BOP*, pp. 353-354 (entries lxviii & lxix) = *XXIII Anni V* (*Ind.* 352, fo 220^r).

199 Rubricated as *Decimus octavus An quinti* and numbered *148* (*Ind.* 355, fo 46^v).

200 *BOP*, pp. 346 (entry lix) and 348-349 (entry lxi) = *XXIV Anni V* (*Ind.* 352, fos 24^v and 181^r).

201 Spine blank save for " REG. LAT. | 1357" ; old paper cover not preserved.

202 Rubricated as *Vigesimus primus An. quinti* (*Ind.* 355, fo 46^v).

203 *BOP*, pp. 351-352 (entry lxv) and 355-356 (entry lxxi) = *III Anni VI* (*Ind.* 353, fos 138^r and 258^r).

204 *(1512-15)* written in ink immediately beneath.

205 as note 43 above

206 *6* added (by modern stamping).

207 Rubricated as *Tertius An. Sexti* (*Ind.* 355, fo 46^v).

208 *See* no. 1245 below.

209 *BOP*, p. 362 (entry lxxx) = *VIII Anni VI* (*Ind.* 353, fo 285^r); *BC*, pp. 474-476 (const. xx) = *VIII Anni VI* (*Ind.* 353, fo 260^v).

210 *BOP*, pp. 364-365 (entry lxxxiv) = *XI Anni VI* (*Ind.* 353, fo 286^v).

211 *sic*

212 The *0* possibly changed (by erasure).

213 *6* written (in near black crayon) over the '7'.

214 *An 6* written in pencil towards base of spine.

215 Rubricated as *Duodecimus An. sexti* (*Ind.* 355, fo 47^r).

216 *BOP*, pp. 376-377 (entry xcvii) = *XV Anni VI* (*Ind.* 353, fo 265^r).

217 The '4' now largely erased and highly uncertain; overstamped (?) *8* (itself now largely erased); *1518* written in pencil near base of spine.

218 Rubricated as *Decimus quartus An. sexti* (*Ind.* 355, fo 47^r).

219 Against *Decimus sextus An. sexti* in the list of *rubricellae* of Leo's letters is the note: + *Non adest ideo non fuit numeratus* (*Ind.* 355, fo 47^r). The note arguably refers not to the *rubricellae* but to the register which was evidently lost or mislaid by the 1640's when the registers were re-numbered (*cf. CPL* XVI, p. lii note 25); but after 1617 (*see above*, note 1).

220 *BOP*, p. 379 (entries c & ci) = *XX Anni VI* (*Ind.* 353, fo 291^v) = *Reg. Lat.* 1303, fo 240^v (245^v mech.).

221 *sic*

222 Rubricated as *Septimus Diversorum An. D[omini Leonis]* (*Ind.* 355, fo 47^r).

223 *Cf. Primus An. Septimi D. Leonis . X.* in contemporary hand on recto of leaf at front of register. The hand appears to be the same as that of the titles written at the fronts of *Reg. Lat.* 1385-1389, 1391, 1392, 1394, 1395, 1397, 1398, 1401, and also, perhaps, 1404 and 1405. The leaves on which the titles are written are usually some 5-7 cms. narrower than the other leaves in the register. Typically, the page bearing the title is otherwise blank.

224 Rubricated as *Secundus An. Septimi* (*Ind.* 355, fo 47^r).

225 Rubricated as *Tertius An. Septimi* (*Ind.* 355, fo 47^r).

226 Here, and in the inscriptions on the cuts of *Reg. Lat.* 1380, 1382, 1384-1387, and 1391, the interpunction may be a cornucopia (vessel only); but owing to wear and mis-alignment of the leaves it is rather mis-shapen and difficult to make out. The interpunction found on the monument to CHERVBINO BONANNO PISANO (died 1546) in the Minerva (facade wall) is not unlike it.

227 *Cf. Quartus An Septimi D. Leo. X* at front of register; *see* note 223 above.

228 Rubricated as *Quintus An. Septimi* (*Ind.* 355, fo 47^r).

229 Rubricated as *Sextus An. Septimi* (*Ind.* 355, fo 47^r).

230 *BOP*, pp. 384-385 (entry cviii) = *II Anni VII* (*Ind.* 353, fos 150^v, 294).

231 as note 226 above

232 On an oblong slip (approx. 6 x 3.75 cm) stuck on to front endpaper: *Leone. 10.* | *1519* | *an. 7 lib. 7*; *cf. above*, note 100.

233   Rubricated as *Octavus An. Septimi* (*Ind.* 355, fo 47^r).

234   *sic*

235   as note 226 above

236   Rubricated as *Undecimus An. Septimi* (*Ind.* 355, fo 47^r).

237   as note 226 above

238   as note 226 above

239   *Cf. Tertiusdecimus An vij D Leo. x.* at front of register; *see* note 223 above.

240   as note 226 above

241   *Cf. Quartus decimus (?)D. An. Septimi D. Leo .x.* at front of register; *see* note 223 above.

242   Rubricated *Quintus Decimus An. Septimi* and numbered *186* (*Ind.* 355, fo 47^v).

243   Unless it equates with *XXV Anni VIII* or *I Anni IX*, the register was lost or mislaid after the registers were renumbered in the 1640s (*cf. CPL* XVI, p. lii, note 25) and before they were re-rubricated in the C18 (ibid., pp. l-li).

244   as note 226 above

245   *Cf. Sextus decimus An. Septimi D. Leo. x.* at front of register; *see* note 223 above.

246   *BOP*, p. 380 (entry cii) = *XII Anni VII* (*Ind.* 353, fo 297^r).

247   Rubricated as *Decimus Octavus An. Septimi* (*Ind.* 355, fo 47^v).

248   Rubricated as *Decimus Nonus An. Septimi* (*Ind.* 355, fo 47^v).

249   Rubricated as *Primus An. Octavi* (*Ind.* 355, fo 47^v).

250   as note 226 above

251   *Cf. S(e)c(un)dus An. 8. D. Leo* and (below it) *Secundus a(n)ni .8. d Leonis decimi* at front of register; *see* note 223 above.

252   *Cf. Tertius An. Octavi D. Leo. x.* at front of register; *see* note 223 above.

253   *BOP*, pp. 390-391 (entry cxiii) = *XVIII Anni VII* (*Ind.* 353, fo 276^r).

254   *Cf. Quintus An. 8. D. Leo. x.* at front of register; *see* note 223 above.

255   Rubricated as *Sextus An. Octavi* (*Ind.* 355, fo 47^v).

256   *Cf. Sextus* [del.] *Septimus An Octavi D. Leo. p(a)p(e) x.* at front of register; *see* note 223 above.

257   *Cf. Octavus An. Octavi D. Leo. x* at front of register; *see* note 223 above.

258   Rubricated as *Nonus An. Octavi* (*Ind.* 355, fo 47^v).

259   *Cf. Decimus. An. Octavi D. Leo. x* at front of register; *see* note 223 above.

260   Rubricated as *Undecimus An. Octavi* (*Ind.* 355, fo 47^v).

261   Rubricated as *Duodecimus An. Octavi* (*Ind.* 355, fo 47^v).

262   *Cf. Quintusdecimus An. Octavi D. Leo. x.* at front of register; *see* note 223 above.

263   On an oblong slip stuck on to front endpaper: *Leone X.* | *1521:* | *Anno VIII Tom: XV*; *cf.* note 100 above.

264   Rubricated *Decimus sextus An. Octavi* and numbered *206* (*Ind.* 355, fo 47^v).

265   *BOP*, p. 391 (entry cxiv) = *IV Anni VIII* (*Ind.* 354, fo 106^r).

266   Rubricated as *Decimus quartus An. Octavi* and numbered *204* (*Ind.* 355, fo 47^v).

267   Rubricated as *Decimus Octavus Anni Octavi* (*Ind.* 355, fo 47^v).

268   Rubricated as *Decimus Nonus An. Octavi* (*Ind.* 355, fo 47^v).

269   Rubricated as *Vigesimus An. Octavi* and numbered *210* (*Ind.* 355, fo 47^v).

270   as note 243 above

271   Rubricated as *Primus An. Noni* (*Ind.* 355, fo 47^v).

272   Rubricated as *Secundus An. Noni* (*Ind.* 355, fo 47^v).

273   *Cf. Tertius An. ix. D. Leo. x* at front of register; *see* note 223 above.

274   *BC*, pp. 506-508 (const. xxxviii) = *XII Anni VIII* (*Ind.* 354, fo 119^r).

275   Rubricated as *Sextus An. Noni* (*Ind.* 355, fo 47^v).

276   *Cf. Septimus An. noni D. Leo. x.* at front of register; *see* note 223 above.

277   *Cf. Octavus An. noni D. Leo. x.* at front of register; *see* note 223 above.

278   *Cf. BOP*, p. 398 (F. Michael de Natera ; F. Dominicus de Cornaria) ; Herg. 2557-2560 and 5604 respectively.

279   Or *LEON P.*

280   *Cf.* heading of near contemporary *rubricellae*: *Liber Primus de Provision(ibus) Prelator(um) D. Leonis PP x. Anni Primi* (*Ind.* 355, fo 6^r).

281   *BOP*, p. 403 cites the provision, dated 26 Oct 1519, of Jo. Parisoti to Hierapolis *Ex Archivo Apostolico Lib. CCXX fol. 92*. But the provision in question, rubricated under *XXIV Anni VIII* (*Ind.* 354, fo 85^v), is at fo 92^{r-v} (modern mech. 99^{r-v}) of *Reg. Lat.* 1399 – that is, no. 226 in the C17 numeration, not 220. A misreading?

282   as note 43 above

283   *3* added here (by modern stamping).

284 At the base of the spine (below the pencilled *3*): *Liber I de provisionibus prelatorum Anno I et II Leo X*.; ink; of uncertain date.

285 *Cf.* heading of near contemporary *rubricellae*: *Primus de Provision(ibus) Prelator(um) Annorum Primi et Secundi D. Leonis PP X* (*Ind.* 355, fo 10ʳ); and inscription of uncertain date on a leaf at front of register: *Secundus* [deleted] *Primus de provisionibus p(re)lator(um) Annor(um) primi et secundi D. Leonis p(a)p(e) x.* 'Wrapper' bifolia (*cf.* note 90 above) from the gatherings in *Reg. Lat.* 1293 are at *Ind.* 355, fos 84-108. The recto of fo 84 – once the first leaf of the register – is marked: *Secundus* [del.] *Primus de provision(ibus) prelatorum Annorum primi et Secundi domini Leonis pape x.*

286 *Cf.* heading of near contemporary *rubricellae*: *Secundus de Provisionibus Prelatorum D. Leonis PP. X* (*Ind.* 355, fo 13ʳ).

287 Overstamped: *3.4.*

288 Existence corroborated: *cf.* heading of near contemporary *rubricellae*: *Liber Tertius de Provisionibus Prelatorum D. Leonis PP. X^{mi}* (*Ind.* 355, fo. 39ʳ; *cf.* 17ʳ). 'Wrapper' bifolia (*cf.* note 90 above) from this register (which evidently contained fifteen quinterns) are at *Ind.* 355, fos 109-138. The recto of fo 109 – once the first leaf of the register – is marked: *Hic liber intitulatur Tercius de provisionibus D. Leo X.*

289 The register rubricated as *Tertius de Provisionibus Prelatorum D. Leonis X* was numbered *222* (*Ind.* 355, fo 48ʳ); *and see below*, no. 1457 and note.

290 Existence corroborated: *cf.* heading of near contemporary *rubricellae*: *Quintus de Provisionibus Prelatorum D. Leonis X* (*Ind.* 355, fo. 22ʳ). The register rubricated as *Quintus de Provisionibus Prelatorum D. Leonis X* was numbered *224* (*Ind.* 355, fo 48ʳ).

291 *BOP*, p. 403 (provision of Jo. Kiperia to Gallipoli): *Ex Archivo Apostolico Lib. CCXXIV fol. 252 = XXI Anni VIII* (*Ind.* 354, fo 44ᵛ) = *Quintus de Provisionibus Prelatorum D. Leonis X* (*Ind.* 355, fos 22ʳ, 25ʳ).

292 Existence corroborated: *cf.* heading of near contemporary *rubricellae*: *Quartus De Provisionibus Prelatorum D(omi)ni Leonis x.* (*Ind.* 355, fo 43ᵛ; *cf.* 21ᵛ, 85ʳ). The register rubricated as *Quartus de Provisionibus Prelatorum D. Leonis X* was numbered *223* (*Ind.* 355, fo 48ʳ). For the correspondence between the original title and the C18 index reference *cf. Ind.* 355, fo 42ᵛ (original *rubricellae* of provision of John Veysey to Exeter and related letters at fo 22 of *Quartus de Provisionibus Prelatorum D. Leonis X*) and nos. 1501-1503 below.

293 *Cf.* heading of near contemporary *rubricellae*: *Sextus de Provision(ibus) Prelatorum D. Leonis X^{mi}* (*Ind.* 355, fo 27ʳ). The register rubricated as *Sextus de Provisionibus Prelatorum D. Leonis X* was numbererd *225* (*Ind.* 355, fo 48ʳ).

294 *BOP*, p. 404 (provision of William Hogeson to Darien.) = *Reg. Lat.* 1400, fo 185 (old foliation).

295 as note 43 above

296 *5* and *9* added (by modern stamping).

297 *Cf.* heading of near contemporary *rubricellae*: *LIBER VII de Provision(ibus) Prelatorum D. Leonis X^{mi}* (*Ind.* 355, fo. 32ᵛ). The register rubricated as *Liber Septimus de Provisionibus Prelatorum D. Leonis X* was numbered *226* (*Ind.* 355, fo 48ʳ). For the correspondence between the original title and the C18 index reference. *cf. Ind.* 355, fo 35ʳ (original *rubricellae* of provision of William [Sutton] to Panados and related letters at fo 237 of *Liber VII de Provisionibus Prelatorum D. Leonis X^{mi}*) and *Ind.* 354, fo 136ᵛ (re-rubrication of same under *XXIV Anni VIII*).

298 *See* previous note.

299 the C19 spine preserved; but upper part lost. Lettering on spine of recent paper cover reads: *LEO | X | 1517 | Anno V-IX | LIB. V* [*sic*].

300 as note 43 above

301 *5* and *9* added (by modern stamping).

302 No number.

303 May well equate with no. 186 or 210 in the C17 numeration: *see* note 243 above.

304 *Cf.* nos. 1511-1529 below.

305 *Cf. rubricellae* of *liber I Anni IX* (*Ind.* 354, passim).

306 as note 303 above

307 Below: *Divers. ann.* (ink) | *1492-1521* (modern stamping).

CONCORDANCE

Abstracts of entries in Leo's Lateran Registers are included in the *Leonis X. Pontificis Maximi Regesta* (Herder, Freiburg im Breisgau, 1884, 1885, etc) edited by a team under Joseph Hergenroether, ecclesiastical historian, cardinal, and archivist of the Holy See. The arrangement is chronological and the coverage comprehensive. Besides the Lateran Registers Hergenroether covers several other register series now in the ASV (notably the Vatican Registers) as well as published collections (e.g. *BOP*) and miscellaneous other sources, both printed and manuscript. The project was highly ambitious and not surprisingly it did not survive Hergenroether's death in 1890. The last instalment to be published was Fasciculus VII-VIII (= pp. 1-216 of volume II) which appeared in 1891 and stops abruptly at entry no. 18,070. As it stands the work covers no more than the first third of the pontificate, ending with entries dated 16 October 1515, Anno Tertio.

Incomplete though it is the *Regesta* is an immensely rich quarry which has supported research for over a century and will continue to do so. A typical *Regesta* entry gives an abstract of the letter, the time and place date under which it is drawn, its incipit, the names (usually) of the officials (but not, except rarely, the tax marks or the *bullaria* expedition dates), and the archival reference. Thus under '1513., 15. Junii. (XVII. Kal. Jul.) Romae apud S. Petrum' : ' (3198) Johanni Bulle perpet. vicario chorali nuncupato in eccl. collegiata de Suthwell Eboracen. dioec. indultum quoad beneficia et residentiam concedit. "Vitae ac morum" (O. de Cesis | Campania) Arch. Lat. vol. E f. 270, b.' (vol. I, p. 186). However, there are severe inconveniences. In the first place, as we would expect of an abandoned work, there is no index and the *Regesta* must be searched by chronology. Unless the user has the relevant date or is prepared to trawl 18,070 entries the material remains virtually inaccessible. Secondly, though it evidently aimed to be comprehensive there are numerous omissions. In the late nineteenth century the Archives were not as well ordered and user friendly as they are today and some registers which came within the scope of the work are not covered. Others are only partially covered. The *Regesta* includes 206 letters of British and Irish interest drawn from the Lateran Registers. For the relevant period – that is, from the beginning of the pontificate to the date when the *Regesta* was cut off (16 October 1515) – the Calendar has already found 483 letters. In addition to the major weaknesses there are minor drawbacks. Since Hergenroether's day the registers have been re-foliated (mechanically) and given new press marks. In consequence, the *Regesta*'s archival references can appear obscure (*cf.* above, p. liii). Also, standards have changed over the intervening decades. The *Regesta* was ahead of its time in giving the names of officials; but its summaries are sometimes too condensed for modern purposes. And inevitably with record publications on this scale, there are a few imperfections which are no doubt the outcome of difficult working conditions. As the arrangement is chronological correctness of dates is imperative and of particular interest to us here. As can be seen, now and again a date is misread and the abstract misplaced in the chronology. And very occasionally the same letter can be summarised twice, even under different dates. It happens. Given the monumental scale of the enterprise the overall level of accuracy is surprisingly high.

The bi-directional concordance which follows should enable readers to use the Calendar in conjunction with the *Regesta* and other works which refer to it. With the aid of the concordance researchers using the 2nd edition of vol. I of *L&P, F&D*, which incorporates the British and Irish entries in Hergenroether, can readily find the Calendar entry in question. And those using the Calendar can quickly turn up the relevant entry in Hergenroether. This can be unexpectedly rewarding . The remarkable provision of Andrew Forman, bishop of Moray, to the archbishopric of Bourges on 15 July 1513 (no. 171 below) is, with its conclusions, dealt with by the *Regesta* at nos. 3654-3659. At no. 3653 under the same date we are referred to a related letter of great interest in a Vatican Register (cited by Hergenroether as L. 993). Even when the *Regesta* omits an entry a search under the relevant date can be productive. Thus Hergenroether does not have the executory dated 2 February 1514 in favour of the hospital of St Thomas the Martyr of Acon, London (no. 24 below). But under the same date at no. 6532 he tells us, effectively, where the statute and ordinance recited in the executory is to be found, namely in a Vatican Register cited as L. 1014. For all its shortcomings the *Regesta* is invaluable and will never be entirely superseded.

CALENDAR TEXT – HERGENROETHER

1	4753	106	6596-6602	258	7356	387	12571
4	6567	107	6595	259	9429-9430	388	12596
8	6244	108	6641	262	8207	392	16087
9	5837	109	6603	263	9335	393	16088
10	5822	110	6606-6612	264	9336	394	16089
11	4989	111	6604	268	9697	395	16090
12	5664	112	6655	269	10207	396	16091
13	5518 & 5665[1]	113	6605	271	10310	398	14926
14	5666	114	5070-5076	273	11125	399	14945
16	5772	115	5069	276	11092	403	15769
17	5599-5600	116	5078	281	9925	404	15770
18	5360	117	5077	289	12975	405	15771
19	5195	118	3819	290	12236	406	15773
20	5196	119	3818	292	12095	407	15772
21	5197	120	3845[4]	293	12037	408	15774
25	3554	121	3820	294	12078	411	17616
26	3405	146	2722	303	12722-12726	414	14777
27	3426	154	2460	304	12721	418	15775
28	3427	158	5913	305	12727	421	14720
29	3403 & 3428[2]	159	4884	306	14191	434	8771
30	3220	160	4530	311	14533	445	8661
31	3241	162	6064	312	13662	446	8891
32	3242	165	6934	314	12974	455	8445
33	3487	167	6367	327	6873	456	8693
34	3404 & 3425[3]	171	3654-3659	338	12654-12655	457	7901
35	3201	172	3660	339	12232	459	8441
36	3202	174	3652	343	11380-11381	460	9085
37	3198	175	3943	344	14059	469	7519
38	3199	176	3944	345	7544	472	16266
39	3200	177	10408-10410	346	10416	474	16688
41	3423	178	10407	359	17049	478	16687
42	3424	185	3725	360	14195	479	16736
44	2408	186	3957	362	17606[9]	480	17123
45	2407	187	4217[5]	363	16692	481	16576
46	2406	189	4218[6]	364	16693	482	16690
47	2405	192	4143	365	16408	483	16691
48	2404	193	3988	369	9776-9782	484	17197
49	2409	196	4567	370	9775	485	17058
50	2431	197	4566	371	9841	486	16084
51	2432	198	4568	372	16706-16712	487	17313
65	6702-6703	202	2965	373	16725	488	16267
66	6704-6705	217	2410	374	16705	493	16611
67	6706-6707	226	7232	375	15607-15613	504	17603[11]
70	6804	227	7233	376	15606	505	17604[12]
71	2757-2763	228	6334	379	11695-11701	506	17605[13]
72	2756	235	7300	380	11694	507	17678
78	3059-3065	236	6674[7]	381	11750	508	17965
79	3057	237	6675	382	11684-11690	509	15851
80	3058	242	12213[8]	383	11683	518	16075
81	3066	244	12618	384	11691	533	17857
82	3067	256	10473	385	11692-11693[10]		
83	3133	257	8180	386	12572-12578		

HERGENROETHER – CALENDAR TEXT

2404	48	4218	189[6]	8180	257	14533	311
2405	47	4530	160	8207	262	14720	421
2406	46	4566	197	8441	459	14777	414
2407	45	4567	196	8445	455	14926	398
2408	44	4568	198	8661	445	14945	399
2409	49	4753	1	8693	456	15606	376
2410	217	4884	159	8771	434	15607-15613	375
2431	50	4989	11	8891	446	15769	403
2432	51	5069	115	9085	460	15770	404
2460	154	5070-5076	114	9335	263	15771	405
2722	146	5077	117	9336	264	15772	407
2756	72	5078	116	9429-9430	259	15773	406
2757-2763	71	5195	19	9697	268	15774	408
2965	202	5196	20	9775	370	15775	418
3057	79	5197	21	9776-9782	369	15851	509
3058	80	5360	18	9841	371	16075	518
3059-3065	78	5518	13[1]	9925	281	16084	486
3066	81	5599-5600	17	10207	269	16087	392
3067	82	5664	12	10310	271	16088	393
3133	83	5665	13[1]	10407	178	16089	394
3198	37	5666	14	10408-10410	177	16090	395
3199	38	5772	16	10416	346	16091	396
3200	39	5822	10	10473	256	16266	472
3201	35	5837	9	11092	276	16267	488
3202	36	5913	158	11125	273	16408	365
3220	30	6064	162	11380-11381	343	16576	481
3241	31	6244	8	11683	383	16611	493
3242	32	6334	228	11684-11690	382	16687	478
3403	29[2]	6367	167	11691	384	16688	474
3404	34[3]	6567	4	11692-11693	385[10]	16690	482
3405	26	6595	107	11694	380	16691	483
3423	41	6596-6602	106	11695-11701	379	16692	363
3424	42	6603	109	11750	381	16693	364
3425	34[3]	6604	111	12037	293	16705	374
3426	27	6605	113	12078	294	16706-16712	372
3427	28	6606-6612	110	12095	292	16725	373
3428	29[2]	6641	108	12213	242[8]	16736	479
3487	33	6655	112	12232	339	17049	359
3554	25	6674	236[7]	12236	290	17058	485
3652	174	6675	237	12571	387	17123	480
3654-3659	171	6702-6703	65	12572-12578	386	17197	484
3660	172	6704-6705	66	12596	388	17313	487
3725	185	6706-6707	67	12618	244	17603	504[11]
3818	119	6804	70	12654-12655	338	17604	505[12]
3819	118	6873	327	12721	304	17605	506[13]
3820	121	6934	165	12722-12726	303	17606	362[9]
3845	120[4]	7232	226	12727	305	17616	411
3943	175	7233	227	12974	314	17678	507
3944	176	7300	235	12975	289	17857	533
3957	186	7356	258	13662	312	17965	508
3988	193	7519	469	14059	344		
4143	192	7544	345	14191	306		
4217	187[5]	7901	457	14195	360		

NOTES

1   Due to variant readings of the dating clause the same letter appears twice in the *Regesta*: at no. 5518 where the date is read as "V. Kal. Dec." (27 Nov); and at no. 5665 where it is read as "V. Id. Dec." (9 Dec). The MS is somewhat equivocal; but the latter is almost certainly the correct reading.

2   The *Regesta* has two entries for the same letter: one at no. 3403; the other at no. 3428. The outcome, presumably, of duplicated effort. Both abstracts are under the same date.

3   The *Regesta* has two different abstracts for the same letter: a concise one at no. 3404; a fuller one at no. 3425. The outcome, presumably, of uneven teamwork. Both abstracts are under the same date.

4   MS has *sexto Kalendas Augusti* (27 July) (*cf.* below, no. 120 *note*): explicitly corrected by Hergenroether to 'V. Kal. Aug.' (28 July) and entered in the *Regesta* under the latter date. While the date might well be argued to be erroneous the stated grounds for correcting it to 28 July are not altogether convincing: the incipit is *Cum nos pridem* (as correctly read by Hergenroether) not 'Cum nos pridie'. The 28 July is certainly a possibility; but if correction is needed the correct date could be two or more days after the date of provision (27 July).

5   MS has *decimo nono Kalendas Septembris* (14 Aug); misread by Hergenroether as 'IX. Kal. Sept.' (24 Aug) – a slip which is easily made – and the abstract placed by him under that date.

6   as previous note

7   MS has (clearly) *Idibus Februarii* (13 Feb); misplaced in the *Regesta* under 'VI. Id. Febr.' (8 Feb). An error, perhaps, of printer rather than editor; but the effect is the same.

8   With certain scribes and scripts 'quarto' and 'quinto' are difficult to tell apart. MS has *quarto* or *quinto Idus Octobris*. Hergenroether reads 'V. Id. Oct.' (11 Oct). On different occasions the editor has read both *quarto Idus* (12 Oct) and *quinto*. In view of the peculiarities of the hand (particularly the characteristic formation of the letter 'a') the editor is inclined, on balance, to prefer *quarto* to *quinto*; but her reading is certainly disputable. As Leo was evidently at Viterbo on both 11th and 12th October the place date is not helpful.

9   MS has *quintodecimo Kalendas Octobris* (17 Sept); misread by Hergenroether as 'XVII. Kal. Oct.' (15 Sept.).

10   MS has *septimo Kalendas Octobris* (25 Sept); misplaced in the *Regesta* under 'XVII. Kal. Oct.' (15 Sept. 1514) – the date of Wolsey's translation.

11   as note 9 above

12   as note 9 above

13   as note 9 above

CALENDAR TEXT

1   **30 September 1513**   *Reg. Lat.* 1276, fos 6ʳ-8ᵛ

Approval and confirmation, as below. A recent petition to the pope on the part of the noblemen Henry, temporal lord of the places of Clifford and Westinorlande, Thomas Worthon, and Edward Mosgraue, and the magnates (*procerum*), nobles, residents, and inhabitants of the vill of Burghe, d. Carlisle, stated that John Burmschales, layman of the said vill, mindful of his own salvation and wishing to change earthly things into heavenly and transitory into eternal, had, with the special licence of the then bishop of Carlisle, caused a certain oratory to be constructed and built in the said vill in honour of the Most Glorious Virgin Mary and by it a hospital for the reception, recreation, and use of poor pilgrims and of those coming to the oratory and otherwise visiting the vill; had equipped the hospital with beds and other necessaries; had ordained that one chaplain, who would for ever celebrate mass and other divine offices in the said oratory, one person learned in Latin (*grammatica*), who would teach those wanting to learn Latin, and two menials or servants (*famuli sive servitores*), who would serve the pilgrims, were to be placed and appointed in the hospital after a suitable portion had been assigned by John from his own goods for the maintenance of the chaplain, Latin master, and servants; and had willed that Richard, bishop of Ely, who, by apostolic concession and dispensation, held the monastery of Shappe[1], OPrem, said d., *in commendam* and, after his death, the abbots or perpetual commendators of the said monastery for the time being, were to place and appoint the said chaplain and master under a certain manner and form then expressed; that afterwards, at another time, when a lawsuit had arisen over the oblation and other matters then expressed between Thomas Rigge, perpetual vicar of the parish church of the said vill, who alleged that by right of the said church the oblations belonged to him, and the then chaplain of the said oratory – divine service having so increased in the oratory and (on account of the frequent daily concourse to the oratory of the faithful of both sexes) the number of the vill's inhabitants having so increased that buildings and houses were newly built and more oblations were made in the oratory than usual[2] – the said Thomas – carefully taking into consideration that the increase in tithes, funeral dues (*funeralia*), and other things which had so far come about because of the oratory had brought the greatest utility to the said church, that the oblations were being directed towards the ornament and increase of divine service, and that if anything else was done the devotion and veneration of the faithful could cool, the oratory could be demolished totally (*in suis structuris et edificiis*), and the tithes and funeral dues could be diminished – for himself and his successors, vicars of the said church, provided the bishop of Carlisle's decree and consent for it were forthcoming, ceded the oblations and the right of collecting them in favour of the oratory and granted and gave them to it, in the best legal manner and form, on this agreement and condition: that each year in which the said oblations rise to the sum of 8 legal marks of the money of those parts a pension of 20 legal shillings of the said money was to be paid to the vicar of the said church for the time being, one half at the feast of St Martin, the other half at the feast of Pentecost, and in the event of non-payment in full the vicar was to be allowed, after ten days reckoned from the date when payment was due and not made (*a cessatione solutionis huiusmodi faciende*), to collect and gather the oblations on his own authority and keep them until the pension was paid to him in full; that thereafter the then official of Carlisle – to whom Roger bishop of Carlisle had committed the business of the approval and confirmation at the instance of the said Henry, Thomas, Edward, magnates, etc, who were requesting that the said cession, grant, and gift be approved and confirmed by the bishop on ordinary authority – by proclamation (*per preconem*) [(?)warned and ordered][3] the then master and members (*collegiales*) of the Queen's college in the university (*universitate studii generalis*) of Oxford,[4] to which the said church is perpetually united, and the said Thomas (all of whom bishop Roger had first caused to be summoned before him for this by public edict affixed to the doors of the said church) and all others disputing the interest in the foregoing, to appear before the said official within a certain suitable term then expressed, to say why the requested approval and confirmation ought not to be done; and that finally, upon the said Thomas consenting to it and the master and members of the college, and the others who had been summoned, not appearing within the said term, the official – proceeding in the business of the confirmation and approval [which had been committed][5] to him – approved and confirmed the said cession, grant, and gift by ordinary authority, as is said to be more fully stated in public instruments or letters-patent drawn up in that regard, the tenors of which the pope wills and decrees to be deemed inserted and expressed in the presents. At the supplication on the part of the said Henry, Thomas, Edward, and magnates, etc, to add the strength of apostolic confirmation to the said cession, grant, gift, confirmation and approval, to establish them more firmly, the pope, by apostolic authority, hereby approves and confirms the said cession, etc, and, insofar as they concern them, everything contained in the said instruments and letters and whatever is lawful and honest which has followed therefrom, supplying all defects (if any) in them. Notwithstanding, etc.

Ad perpetuam rei memoriam. Ex iniuncto nobis desuper apostolice servitutis officio … *.J. Benzon. / JoA: / : JoA: xxxx: Nardinus*

1   or *Schappe*
2   *cum in dicto oratorio divinus cultus et ob frequentem utriusque sexus Christifideles ad illud in dies concursum habitatorum dicte ville numerus adeo crevisset ut in eadem villa plura edificia et domos de novo construerentur pluresque solito oblationes in eodem oratorio fierent*
3   MS wants 'moneri fecit et mandavit eisdem' (or suchlike).
4   diocese not stated
5   MS wants 'commisso' (or suchlike).

2   30 January 1514   *Reg. Lat.* 1276, fo 11[r-v]

To William Walcher, rector of the parish church of St George, Bekyngton', d. Bath and Wells. Dispensation and indult – at his supplication – to receive and retain for life, together with the above parish church,[1] one, and without them, any two other benefices, with cure or otherwise mutually incompatible, even if parish churches or their perpetual vicarages, or chantries, free chapels, hospitals or annual services, usually assigned to secular clerics in title of a perpetual ecclesiastical benefice, or dignities, *personatus*, administrations or offices in cathedral, even metropolitan, or collegiate churches, even if the dignities in question should be major *post pontificalem* in cathedral, even metropolitan, churches, or principal in collegiate churches, or a combination, and even if the dignities etc. should be customarily elective and have cure of souls, if he obtains them otherwise canonically, to resign them, at once or successively, simply or for exchange, as often as he pleases, and in their place receive up to two other, similar or dissimilar, incompatible benefices and retain them together for life, as above; and, for life, while attending a *studium generale* or residing in the Roman curia or any one of his benefices, not to be bound to reside in his other benefices nor to be liable to be compelled to do so by anyone against his will. Notwithstanding etc. With the proviso that the above church[2] and other incompatible benefices shall not, on this account, be defrauded of due services and the cure of souls in the church and (if any) the other incompatible benefices shall not be neglected; but that customary burdens of those benefices in which he shall not reside shall be supported.

Vite ac morum honestas …
.O. de Cesis. / JoA: / JoA: LX: Nardinus

1 Other entries of this type (i.e. dispensation *ad duo* with indult for non-residence) relating to England and Wales are summarised in the present volume in an abridged form and refer to this entry as to the fully extended prototype.
   When necessary, a term appropriate to the previous content of the entry should be substituted here; e.g. for entries (such as no. 12) where the addressee is a perpetual vicar read 'perpetual vicarage of the above parish church' for 'above parish church'.
2 As indicated in note 1, when necessary (as in no. 12) read here 'vicarage' for 'church'.

3   30 January 1514   *Reg. Lat.* 1276, fos 12ʳ-13ᵛ

Union etc.; with indult for non-residence. At a recent petition on the part of John Estmond', MA, rector of the parish church of Lokyng, d. Salisbury, the pope hereby unites etc. the perpetual vicarage of the parish church of Haney, d. Salisbury (whose annual value does not exceed 16 pounds sterling), with all its rights and appurtenances, to the above church of Lokyng, which John holds together with the vicarage of Haney, for as long as he holds the church of Lokyng, to the effect that he may, on his own authority, in person or by proxy, take, or continue in, and retain corporal possession of the vicarage and the rights and appurtenances aforesaid, for as long as he holds the church of Lokyng, and convert its fruits etc. to his own uses and those of the vicarage of Haney and the church of Lokyng, without licence of the local diocesan or of anyone else. And the pope indulges John, for life, while attending a *studium generale*, or residing in the Roman curia or any one of his benefices, not to be bound to reside in his other benefices, nor to be liable to be compelled to do so by anyone against his will. Notwithstanding etc. The pope's will is, however, that the vicarage and other benefices in question shall not, on account of this union etc.,[1] be defrauded of due services and the cure of souls in the vicarage and (if any) the other benefices shall not be neglected; but that customary burdens of the vicarage and other benefices in which he shall not reside shall be supported; and that on John's death or his resignation etc. of the church of Lokyng the union etc. shall be dissolved and so deemed and the vicarage shall revert to its original condition and be deemed vacant automatically.

Ad futuram rei memoriam. Romanum decet pontificem votis illis et cetera …
P. lambertus / JoA: / JoA: xxxv:- Nardinus

---

1   usually: 'unionem annexionem et incorporationem'; but in this instance 'et incorporationem' does not occur.

---

4   3 February 1514   *Reg. Lat.* 1276, fos 25ʳ-26ᵛ

Union etc. At a recent petition on the part of John Harden, rector of the parish church of Worthymortemer [also spelt *Vorthymortemer*], d. Winchester, the pope hereby unites etc. the parish church of Louellevpton' [also spelt *Louellevpton*], d. Salisbury, (whose annual value does not exceed 10 English pounds), with all its rights and appurtenances, to the above church of Worthymortemer, which John holds together with that of Louellevpton' by apostolic dispensation, for as long as he holds Worthymortemer, to the effect that he may, on his own authority, in person or by proxy, take anew, or continue in, and retain corporal possession of the church of Louellevpton' and of the rights and appurtenances aforesaid, for as long as he holds the church of Worthymortemer, and convert its fruits etc. to his own uses and those of the said churches without licence of the local diocesan or of anyone else. Notwithstanding etc. The pope's will is, however, that the church of Louellevpton' shall not, on account of this union etc., be defrauded of due services and the cure of souls therein shall not be neglected; but that its customary burdens shall be supported, and that on John's death or his resignation etc. of the church of Worthymortemer the union etc. shall be dissolved and the church of Louellevpton' shall revert to its original condition and be deemed vacant automatically.

Ad futuram rei memoriam. Romanum decet et cetera.
.P. Lambertus / JoA: / JoA: xxxv: Nardinus

---

5   24 August 1513   *Reg. Lat.* 1276, fos 82ʳ-83ʳ

To Robert Blachadier, canon of Bourges. Collation and provision of a canonry of the church of Bourges – since, as the pope has learned, it is said to be expressly stipulated in the church's statutes and customs that no-one can hold a dignity, *personatus*, administration or office in it unless he is a canon – for the sole purpose of holding a dignity etc. in the church. Notwithstanding constitutions etc. and those concerning a fixed number of canons etc.

    Executory to the abbot of the monastery of St. Ambrose within and the prior of the secular and collegiate church of Castro without the walls of Bourges and the official of Bourges, or two or one of them, acting in person or by proxy.

Vite ac morum honestas ... The executory begins: *Hodie dilecto filio Roberto Blachadier* ...
.P. Lambertus..; .G. de Prato. / JoA. / JoA: xij: x: Nardinus[1] *Decimo nono k(a)l(endas) februarij: Anno primo* [14 January 1514[2]], *Had(riani)*[3]

1   written here; ordinarily placed after the pontifical year
2   1514 if Leo; but, if Hadrian, *probably* 1523 (reckoning the year from the coronation) *possibly* 1522 (reckoned from election)
3   apparently; not readily legible as 'Nard(inus)'

6   28 June 1513   *Reg. Lat.* 1276, fos 121[r]-122[v]

To Robert[1] Gundys, BDec, rector of the parish church of Boccarde [also spelt *Boccarre*], d. Thérouanne, dispensation. Some time ago, Julius II by his letters dispensed Robert to receive and retain for life, together with one incompatible benefice perhaps held by him at the time, another, and without them, any two benefices, with cure or otherwise mutually incompatible, even if parish churches or their perpetual vicarages, or chantries, free chapels, hospitals or annual services, usually assigned to secular clerics in title of a perpetual ecclesiastical benefice, or dignities, *personatus*, administrations or offices in cathedral, even metropolitan, or collegiate churches, even if the dignities in question should be major *post pontificalem* in cathedral, even metropolitan, churches, or principal in collegiate churches, or a combination, and even if the dignities etc. should be customarily elective and have cure of souls, if he obtained them otherwise canonically, to resign them, at once or successively, simply or for exchange, as often as he pleased, and in their place receive up to two other, similar or dissimilar, incompatible benefices, and retain them together for life, as is more fully contained in those letters.[2] The pope – at his supplication – hereby dispenses Robert, who, as he asserts, holds by virtue of the said dispensation the parish church of Boccarde aforesaid and Clare portion (one of the four portions of the parish church of Tyuerton', d. Exeter, usually ruled by four rectors) which were canonically collated to him, to receive and retain for life, together with the church of Boccarde and the portion aforesaid, or two other incompatible benefices held by him at the time by the said dispensation, any third benefice, with cure or otherwise incompatible, even if a parish church or its perpetual vicarage, or a chantry, free chapel, hospital or annual service, usually assigned to secular clerics in title of a perpetual ecclesiastical benefice, or a dignity, *personatus*, administration or office in a cathedral, even metropolitan, church, or a collegiate church, even if the dignity in question should be major *post pontificalem* in a cathedral, even metropolitan, church, or principal in a collegiate church, and even if the dignity etc. should be customarily elective and have cure of souls, if he obtains it otherwise canonically, to resign it, simply or for exchange, as often as he pleases, and in its place receive another, similar or dissimilar, benefice – provided that of three such benefices not more than two be parish churches or their perpetual vicarages – and retain it for life, as above. Notwithstanding etc. With the proviso that this third incompatible benefice shall not, on this account, be defrauded of due services and the cure of souls in it (if any) shall not be neglected.

Litterarum scientia, vite ac morum honestas …
.J. Benzon.' / JoA / JoA: Lxx: Nardinus

1   Directly after *Roberto, Rect* is deleted initialled *JoA*
2   unknown to the *CPL*

7   7 November 1513   *Reg. Lat.* 1276, fos 122ᵛ-124ᵛ

Union etc., with indult for non-residence, as below. At a recent petition on the part of
John Whyt,[1] MTheol, rector of the parish church of Assheton Flamwyle[2] *alias*
Burbege, d. Lincoln, the pope hereby unites etc. the parish church of B. Mary the
Virgin, Thrandeston', d. Norwich – which is of lay patronage and for which at one time
when it was vacant *certo modo* John was presented by its then patron (who was in
peaceful quasi-possession of the right of presenting a suitable person for B. Mary's at
a time of vacancy to the local ordinary within the lawful time) – assuming John were
to be canonically instituted at this presentation in the rectorship of the church of B.
Mary, whose annual value does not exceed 4 pounds sterling, with all its rights and
appurtenances, to the above church of Assheton', which John holds, for as long as he
does so, to the effect that he may, on his own authority, in person or by proxy, take and
retain corporal possession of B. Mary's and of the rights and appurtenances aforesaid,
for as long as he holds Assheton', and convert its fruits etc. to his own uses and those
of the said churches without licence of the local diocesan or of anyone else. With indult
to John, for life, while attending a *studium generale* or residing in the Roman curia or
any one of his benefices, not to be bound to reside in his other benefices, nor to be
liable to be compelled by anyone to do so against his will. Notwithstanding etc. The
pope's will is, however, that the church of B. Mary and the other benefices in question
shall not, on this account, be defrauded of due services and the cure of souls in B.
Mary's and (if any) the other benefices shall not, on this account, be neglected; but that
customary burdens of B. Mary's and of those benefices in which he shall not reside
shall be supported, and that on the death of John or his resignation of Assheton' the
union etc. shall be dissolved and so deemed and B. Mary's shall revert to its original
condition and be deemed vacant automatically. Given at Palo, d. Porto.[3]

Ad futuram rei memoriam. Romanum et cetera provideri.
.J. Benzon' / JoA: / JoA: xxxxv: Nardinus

1   both prongs of the 'y' dotted
2   thus in the first instance only; thereafter simply referred to as *Assheton'*
3   *Rome apud Sanctum Petrum* deleted in line; with *Pali Portuen. diocesis* inserted in margin; initialled *JoA*

8   10 January 1514   *Reg. Lat.* 1276, fos 163ᵛ-165ʳ

Union etc. At a recent petition on the part of Rowland Baxter, MA, rector of the parish church of Usforth, d. Norwich, the pope hereby unites etc. the parish church of BB. Peter and Paul, Redlay, d. Rochester, (whose annual value does not exceed 5 pounds sterling), with all its rights and appurtenances, to the above church of Usforth, which Rowland holds together with that of Redlay, for as long as he holds Usforth, to the effect that he may, on his own authority, in person or by proxy, take, or continue in, and retain corporal possession of the church of Redlay and of the rights and appurtenances aforesaid, for as long as he holds Usforth, and convert its fruits etc. to his own uses and those of the said churches without licence of the local diocesan or of anyone else. Notwithstanding etc. The pope's will is, however, that the church of Redlay shall not, on account of this union etc., be defrauded of due services and the cure of souls therein shall not be neglected; but that its customary burdens shall be supported, and that on Rowland's death or his resignation etc. of the church of Usforth the union etc. shall be dissolved and the church of Redlay shall revert to its original condition and be deemed vacant automatically.

Ad futuram rei memoriam. Romanum decet pontificem et cetera.
.P. Lambertus / JoA. / JoA: xxxv: Nardinus

9   18 December 1513   *Reg. Lat.* 1276, fos 171ʳ-172ᵛ

To William Clerke, MA, perpetual chaplain, called the inferior (*secundario*) of the two chaplains in the parish church of Tawcetur [also spelt *Taucetur*], d. Lincoln, relaxation, dispensation and indult etc., as below. As the pope has learned, in the foundation of the perpetual chaplaincy, called the inferior (*secundarie*) of the two chaplaincies in the above parish church, it is said to be expressly stipulated that anyone who holds the chaplaincy cannot hold another benefice with it, and that if he peacefully acquires another benefice, with or without cure, he shall be bound – within a month calculated from the day of its acquisition – to resign it or the chaplaincy, or to cede all right belonging to him in or to one of them, otherwise, after the month has elapsed, the chaplaincy shall fall vacant by the acquisition of the other benefice; and William, as he asserts, holds the chaplaincy and on acquiring it swore to inviolably observe the above foundation. Relaxing the oath for this once only, the pope hereby dispenses William – at his supplication – to receive and retain for life, together with the above chaplaincy, one, and without it, any two other benefices etc. [as above, no. 2 to '… retain them together for life, as above']; and indulges him, also for life, while residing in the Roman curia or any one of his benefices or attending a *studium generale*, to have his chaplaincy served by any suitable priest; and, meanwhile, not to be bound to reside in the said church nor to be liable to be compelled to do so by anyone against his will. Notwithstanding etc. and [notwithstanding] the said foundation which (otherwise remaining in force) the pope hereby specially and expressly derogates (even if, for its sufficient derogation, special, specific, express and individual mention – verbatim and not by means of general clauses importing the same – or any other expression of the foundation and its whole tenor ought to be had or other uncommon form ought to be observed), deeming the tenors as expressed by the presents, as if they were inserted verbatim; and [notwithstanding] anything else to the contrary. With the proviso that the above chaplaincy and the other incompatible benefices in question shall not, on this account, be defrauded of due services and the cure of souls in them ([if] any) shall not be neglected; but that the customary burdens of the chaplaincy shall be supported. Given at the Lateran.

Litterarum scientia, vite ac morum honestas …
.P. Lambertus / Jo. A: / Jo. A: Lxxx: Nardinus

10   17 December 1513   *Reg. Lat.* 1276, fos 192^v-193^v

To Richard Weston', cleric, d. Coventry and Lichfield. Dispensation and indult – at his supplication – to him, who, as he asserts, is less than eighteen years of age, to receive and retain for life, as soon as he reaches his eighteenth year, one, and with it on reaching his twentieth, another, and without them, any two other benefices, with cure or otherwise mutually incompatible, even if parish churches or their perpetual vicarages, or chantries, free chapels, hospitals or annual services, usually assigned to secular clerics in title of a perpetual ecclesiastical benefice, or dignities, *personatus*, administrations or offices in cathedral, even metropolitan, or collegiate churches, even if the dignities should be major *post pontificalem* in cathedral, even metropolitan, churches or principal in collegiate churches, or a combination, even if the dignities etc. should be customarily elective and have cure of souls, if he obtains them otherwise canonically, to resign them, at once or successively, simply or for exchange, as often as he pleases, and in their place receive up to two other, similar or dissimilar, incompatible benefices, viz.: one when he reaches his said eighteenth year and another when he reaches his twentieth, and retain them for life, as above; and, for life, while residing in the Roman curia or any one of his benefices or attending a *studium generale*, not to be bound to reside in his other benefices nor to be liable to be compelled to do so by anyone against his will. Notwithstanding the said defect of age which he will suffer in his eighteenth year and his twentieth, etc. With the proviso that the incompatible and other benefices in question shall not, on this account, be defrauded of due services and the cure of souls therein (if any) shall not be neglected; but that the customary burdens of those benefices in which he shall not reside shall be supported.

Vite ac morum honestas …
.Z. Benzon / JoA: / JoA: Lxxxx: Nardi(nus)

11[1]   **14 October 1513**   *Reg. Lat.* 1276, fos 253[r]-254[r]

Validation, etc as below. Some time ago – when it was explained to the pope on the part of the present abbot and convent of the monastery of B Mary the Virgin, Oseney, at Oxford (*de Osneya iuxta Oxoniam*), OSA, d. Lincoln, that the rectories of the parish churches of Cudgtinglon' [and][2] Hokenoiton', said d., had already (*antea*) been united etc to the said monastery in perpetuity and that if the perpetual vicarages of the said churches were also united etc in perpetuity to the monastery the abbot and convent would thereby obtain some relief to ease their maintenance and could more conveniently discharge the burdens incumbent on them and apply themselves to the divine will with more tranquillity – the pope, at their supplication, united etc the said vicarages, with all their rights and appurtenances, to the said monastery in perpetuity; to the effect that when the [then] present possessors of the vicarages ceded, even to bring about the union, died, or otherwise resigned, at once or successively, the abbot and convent could, in person or by proxy, on their own authority, freely take corporal possession of the vicarages and their rights and appurtenances, retain them in perpetuity, and, without the licence of the local diocesan or anyone else, cause the vicarages to be served[3] in things divine and the cure of souls of the parishioners of the said parish churches to be exercised by one of the canons of the monastery, appointable and removable at their pleasure, as is more fully stated in the pope's letters drawn up in this regard in which it was expressed that the fruits etc of the vicarages did not exceed an annual value of 12 marks sterling.[4] However, as a recent petition to the pope on the part of the abbot and convent stated, the fruits etc of the vicarages do not (and did not then) exceed an annual value of 12 pounds sterling (and not 12 marks sterling), and the abbot and convent accordingly fear that the said letters are of no use to them and that they could be molested in this connection in the future. At the abbot and convent's supplication, the pope wills and grants that the said letters and the union etc brought about by them of the vicarages to the monastery and whatsoever followed therefrom are valid from the date of the presents and enjoy full force and the abbot and convent can rely on them without limitation, just as if it had been expressed in the letters that the fruits etc of the vicarages did not exceed an annual value of 12 pounds (and not 12 marks) sterling; and that the said abbot and convent may cause the vicarages to be served in things divine and the cure of souls of the said parishioners to be exercised not only by one of the canons of the monastery but also by a suitable secular priest, similarly appointable and removable at their pleasure, without the licence of the said diocesan or anyone else, as above. Notwithstanding, etc. Given at Ostia.[5]

Ad perpetuam rei memoriam. Ad ea ex paterne caritatis officio libenter intendimus …
.P. Lambertus. / JoA / JoA: xvj: Nardinus

1   A copy of this letter in NA, E 164/26 (formerly Exchequer K. R., Misc. Books, Series I, no. 26), fos 91[v]-93[v]
    mech., is printed by H. E. Salter, *Cartulary of Oseney Abbey*, III (Oxford, 1931) [= Oxford Historical
    Society, vol. XCI], pp. 356-358. The source of the copy, which is near contemporary, is unclear; it ends:
    'Datum Ostie pridie Idus Octobris. '
2   MS wants 'et'.
3   MS: *deservire*; *recte*: 'deserviri'?

4   *See below*, no. 130.
5   *Ro* [the start of Rome (?) *apud Sanctum Petrum*] has been deleted, initialled *JoA*

12   9 December 1513   *Reg. Lat.* 1276, fos 257ʳ-258ᵛ

To John Holwell, MA, perpetual vicar of the parish church of St Petroc, Bedmynye, d.
Exeter. Dispensation and indult etc. [as above, no. 2].

Litterarum scientia, vite ac morum honestas …
.P. Lambertus / JoA: / JoA: Lx: Nardinus

13   9 December 1513[1]   *Reg. Lat.* 1276, fos 258ᵛ-259ᵛ

To John Wyon, perpetual vicar of the parish church of Ocley, d. Lincoln. Dispensation
and indult etc. [as above, no. 2].

Vite ac morum honestas …
O. d(e) Cesis / JoA / JoA: L:.[2] *Nardinus*

1   The dating clause (*Rome … primo*) is written in the same hand as the preceding text, but with a finer nib and
     could have been added later. *Cf.* next entry.
2   Letters were taxed according to the nature of their content. Thus the English dispensations *ad duo* commonly
     met with in the Calendar (e.g. no. 161 below) were made up of three or four elements: a basic dispensation
     ad incompatibilia, for life (taxed at 35 *grossi*) + extension of eligible benefices to include parish churches
     and major or principal dignities (5 *grossi*) + clause of exchange (10 *grossi*): total 50 *grossi* or *carlini* (*cf.*
     Banck, pp. 32-33). Normally, dispensations *ad duo* combined with indults for non-residence (e.g. no. 2
     above) were taxed at 60. However, the present volume includes nineteen such letters — approx. 12% of the
     relevant total — that were taxed at 50 (L), not 60 (LX), viz. nos. 13, 14, 39, 45, 47, 48, 54, 131, 159, 160,
     198, 209, 254, 400, 421, 435, 452, 458, and 466. No doubt occasionally an 'X' was inadvertently omitted by
     the *magister registri* when he noted the tax (*cf. CPL* XVI, pp. xxiii-xxiv); but the extensiveness of the
     phenomenon argues a definite change or oddity in taxation rather than laxity in the registry. At the other
     extreme, we also note that one dispensation *ad duo* with indult for non-residence (no. 525) was taxed at 70
     (LXX), not 60. The matter has not been investigated; and it is dangerous to argue from the evidence of a
     selection. However, there is no reason to suppose that in respect of taxation our selection is unrepresentative.
     As the bulk of such letters were, seemingly, still taxed at 60 the unexpected tax is unlikely to reflect a formal
     change of policy and revision of the tariff. In all probability it is attributable to inadvertence or eccentricity
     of the *rescribendarius* who taxed the letters (*cf. CPL* XVI, p. xix, note 30). Certainly, English dispensations
     combined with indults for non residence were now more common than uncombined dispensations and this
     may well be part of the explanation. In the present selection there are 154 of the former as against just 14 of
     the latter. Since the indult was tacked onto the end of the dispensation they could easily be mistaken for a
     straight *ad duo* by a careless or hard-pressed official. There may even have been a measure of discretion.

14   9 December 1513[1]   *Reg. Lat.* 1276, fos 260ʳ-261ʳ

To William Fell', rector of the parish church of Thaydon' at Mount,[2] d. London. Dispensation and indult etc. [as above, no. 2].

Vite ac morum honestas …
.O. de Cesis. / JoA: / Jo A: L:.[3] *Nardinus*

1   Part of the dating clause – [*me … primo*] (i.e. the last two letters of the place-date Rome up to and including the number of the pontifical year) – is written in the same hand as the preceding text, but with a finer nib and could have been added later. *Cf.* previous entry.
2   Unusually, MS has the vernacular 'at Mount' (instead of a Latin equivalent).
3   *See above*, no. 13, note 2.

15   6 September 1513   *Reg. Lat.* 1276, fos 264ʳ-265ᵛ

To James Malet, MA, rector of the parish church of Ezby [also spelt *Heby*], d. Lincoln. Some time ago, Julius II by his letters dispensed James to receive and retain for life any two benefices, with cure or otherwise mutually incompatible etc. [as above, no. 6, to '… as is more fully contained in those letters']¹. The pope – at his supplication – hereby dispenses James, who, as he asserts, holds by the said dispensation the parish church of Ezby and the perpetual vicarage of the parish church of Burrhuan, d. Lincoln, which were canonically collated to him at another time while vacant *certo modo*, to receive and retain for life, together with the said church and vicarage, or with any two other incompatible benefices held by him at the time by the said dispensation, any third benefice, with cure or otherwise incompatible etc. [as above, no. 6].

Litterarum scientia, vite ac morum honestas…
.P. Lambertus - / JoA: / JoA: Lxx: Nardinus

1   *See CPL*, XVIII, no. 313.

16   15 December 1513   *Reg. Lat.* 1276, fos 294ᵛ-296ʳ

To William, bishop of Panados (*Panaden.*). Dispensation – at his supplication – to him who, as he asserts, holds the hospital of St John, Ely,¹ d. Ely, by apostolic dispensation, and receives nothing from his episcopal *mensa*, to receive and retain *in commendam* for life, together with the church of Panados (which is located *in partibus infidelium* and over which he is understood to preside) and the above hospital, any other benefice, with or without cure, secular or regular of any order, even if the secular benefice should be a parish church or its perpetual vicarage, or a chantry, free chapel, hospital or annual service, usually assigned to secular clerics in title of a perpetual ecclesiastical benefice, or a canonry and prebend, dignity, *personatus*, administration or office in a cathedral, even metropolitan, or collegiate church, even if the dignity in question should be major *post pontificalem* in a cathedral, even metropolitan, church, or principal in a collegiate church, and even if the regular benefice should be a priory, *prepositura*, *prepositatus*, dignity (even conventual), *personatus*, administration or office, and even if the priory, *prepositura*, *prepositatus*, dignity, *personatus*, administration or office should be customarily elective and have cure of souls, if he obtains it otherwise canonically, to resign the benefice as often as he pleases and cede the commend and in its place receive another, similar or dissimilar, benefice, with or without cure, secular or regular of any order (provided that such regular benefice be not a claustral office), and retain it for life *in commendam*, as above; he may – due and customary burdens of this benefice having been supported – make disposition of the rest of its fruits etc. just as those holding it *in titulum* could and ought to do, alienation of immovable goods and precious movables being however forbidden. Notwithstanding etc. With the proviso that the benefice shall not, on this account, be defrauded of due services and the cure of souls therein (if any) shall not be neglected; but that its aforesaid burdens shall be supported.

Personam tuam nobis et apostolice sedi devotam et cetera oportuna.
.J. Benzon. / JoA: / JoA: Lx: Nardinus

1   MS: … *sancti Johannis Dely*; for 'sancti Johannis de Ely'

17   2 December 1513   *Reg. Lat.* 1276, fo 296[r-v]

Note. This entry combines, unusually, two mandates which are commonly enregistered separately (*cf.* nos. 175 and 176 below), namely that to the archbishop-elect informing him of the despatch of the pallium, etc (=[A]) and that to the two bishops charging them to assign the pallium, etc (=[B]). The second mandate is *Dat. ut supra*

[A] To John archbishop-elect[1] of Armagh. Since the pallium, namely the symbol of the plenitude of pontifical office, had, with becoming urgency, been requested from the pope on John's part by M. Aloisius Gibraleon, the pope's scriptor and familiar and John's envoy (*nuncium*), the pope – at John's supplication – has caused the said pallium, which has been taken from the tomb (*corpore*) of B. Peter and is to be assigned by the bishops of London and Winchester, to be delivered (*destinandum*) by Aloisius, so that the said bishops (or one of them) assign it to John in accordance with the form which the pope is sending to them enclosed (*introclusam*)[2] under his *bulla* and receive from John, in the name of the pope and the Roman church, the usual oath of fealty, in accordance with the form which the pope is sending under the same (*eadem*) *bulla*.[3] John is to use the pallium inside his church (*intra ecclesiam*)[4] of Armagh only on those days which are expressly stated in the privileges of the said church; and so that the symbol does not differ from the person who bears it, [but rather][5] John heeds inwardly what he wears externally, the pope hereby reminds and exhorts John attentively and commands that he shall aim to observe humility and justice and take care to augment the church of Armagh spiritually and temporally.

[B][6] To the bishops of London and Winchester, mandate. Since the pallium, [namely][7] the symbol [of the plenitude of pontifical office], [has, with becoming urgency, been requested from the pope] on the part of John, archbishop[8] of Armagh, by [M. Aloisius Gibraleon, the pope's scriptor and familiar and John's envoy], the pope, at Aloisius's entreaties (*ipsius precibus*), has caused the said pallium – [which has been taken from the tomb of B. Peter and is to be assigned to John by the above two (or one of them), in accordance with the form which the pope sends enclosed under his *bulla*] – to be delivered (*destinandum*) [by the said Aloisius]. The pope [hereby] commands that the above two (or one of them) shall take care to assign the pallium to John in accordance with the above form,[9] and receive from him, in the name of the pope and the Roman church, the usual oath of fealty, under the form which the pope is sending under the same (*eadem*) [*bulla*][10]. They shall, moreover, cause the form of oath which archbishop[8] John takes to be sent, verbatim, to the pope, at once, by their own [messenger][11] by his letters patent, marked with his seal.

[A] *Cum pallium insigne* … [B] *Cum palium insigne* …
.P. de Castello / JoA / JoA: xij: x: Nardinus

1   *sic*
2   *Cf.* below, nos. 384, note 4; 385, note 5.
3   *Cf.* below, no. 385, note 13.
4   For the meaning, *see* below, no. 176, note 6.
5   MS: *vel*; *recte*: 'sed'
6   This letter is introduced by the formula *Simili modo*.
7   As enregistered, this letter is abbreviated (by *et cetera*) in several places; particulars supplied from surrounds; rest from common form.
8   *sic*
9   The 'Forma dandi (or tradendi) pallium', is not enregistered.
10   MS: *forma*; *recte*: 'bulla'. The 'Forma iuramenti pro archiepiscopo in traditione pallii' is not enregistered. *Cf.* below, no. 385, notes 10, 12 & 13.
11   MS wants 'nuntium'.

18   11 November 1513   *Reg. Lat.* 1276, fos 368[r]-369[r]

To Richard Harrys, rector of the parish church of the Holy Trinity, Doynton, d. Worcester. Dispensation and indult etc. [as above, no. 2]. Given at Civitavecchia, d. Viterbo.[1]

Vite ac morum honestas …
.P. de. Castello. / JoA: / JoA: Lx: Nardinus

1   *Rome apud sanctum Petrum* deleted, initialled *Jo*; *Civitatis vetule Viterbien. diocesis* inserted in margin, initialled *JoA*

19   3 November 1513   *Reg. Lat.* 1276, fo 369^{r-v}

To John Ymberley, monk of the monastery of St Sampson the Bishop, Midelton [also spelt *Middelton*], OSB, d. Salisbury. Dispensation and indult – at his supplication – to receive and retain any benefice, with or without cure, usually held by secular clerics, even if a parish church or its perpetual vicarage, or a chantry, free chapel, hospital or annual service, usually assigned to secular clerics in title of a perpetual ecclesiastical benefice, of lay patronage and of whatsoever tax or annual value, if he obtains it otherwise canonically; to resign it, simply or for exchange, as often as he pleases, and in its place receive and retain another, similar or dissimilar, benefice, with or without cure, defined as above; and – even after he has acquired the said benefice – to receive the usual monachal portion received by monks of the above monastery, OSB, of which he is a monk and is, as he asserts, expressly professed of the order, and to have, for life, a stall in the choir and also a place and an active and a passive voice in the chapter of the said monastery and otherwise as before, without limitation, just as if he had not acquired the benefice. Notwithstanding etc.

Religionis zelus, vite ac morum honestas ...
.Phi. de. Agnellis / JoA / JoA. L: Nardinus

20[1]   **3 November 1513**   *Reg. Lat.* 1276, fos 377^r-378^r

To John Waytt, MA, rector of the parish church of St Nicholas, Nembery, d. Salisbury. Dispensation and indult etc. [as above, no. 2].

Litterarum scientia, vite ac morum honestas ...
.O. de Cesis. / JoA: / JoA: Lx: Nardinus

1   The engrossment is LPL, no. 117.

21   3 November 1513   *Reg. Lat.* 1276, fos 378^v-379^v

To John Wallgraue, BTheol, rector of the parish church of St Mary, Charteton Macrelle [also spelt *Cartheton Macrelle*], d. Bath and Wells. Dispensation and indult etc. [as above, no. 2].

Litterarum scientia, vite ac morum honestas ...
.O. de. Cesis / JoA: / JoA: Lx:- Nardinus

22   18 June 1513   *Reg. Lat.* 1276, fos 379ᵛ-381ʳ

Union etc. At a recent petition on the part of Robert Weston, rector of the parish church of St Dominica the Virgin, d. Exeter, the pope hereby unites etc. the perpetual vicarage of the parish church of Budley, d. Exeter, (whose annual value does not exceed 10 pounds sterling), with all its rights and appurtenances, to the above church of St Dominica the Virgin, which Robert holds together with the vicarage of Budley by apostolic dispensation, for as long as he holds the above church of St Dominica the Virgin, to the effect that he may, on his own authority, take anew, or continue in, and retain corporal possession of the vicarage and of the rights and appurtenances aforesaid, for as long as he holds the above church, and convert its fruits etc. to his own uses and those of the said vicarage and church without licence of the local diocesan or of anyone else. Notwithstanding etc. The pope's will is, however, that the said vicarage shall not, on account of this union etc., be defrauded of due services and the cure of souls therein shall not be neglected; but that its customary burdens shall be supported, and that on the death of Robert or his resignation etc. of the said church the union etc. shall be dissolved and the vicarage shall revert to its original condition and be deemed vacant automatically.

Ad futuram rei memoriam. Romanum decet pontificem votis illis gratum prestare assensum ...
.P. Lambertus / JoA: / JoA: xxxv: Nardinus

23   2 November 1513   *Reg. Lat.* 1276, fos 395ᵛ-396ᵛ

To Thomas Eccleston', monk of the monastery of St Thomas the Martyr, Holland', OSB, d. Coventry and Lichfield, indult. Some time ago, Thomas was, as he asserts, dispensed by apostolic authority[1] to receive and retain any benefice, with or without cure, usually held by secular clerics etc. [as above, no. 19, to '... annual value'], if he obtained it otherwise canonically. The pope – at his supplication – hereby indulges Thomas, for life, to wear the usual habit worn by monks of the above monastery, OSB, of whose number he is and is, as he asserts, expressly professed of the order, under an honest garment or robe,[2] of black or other honest colour; and not to be bound to wear the habit otherwise nor to be liable to be molested over this by anyone even a superior of the said order. Notwithstanding etc.

Religionis zelus, vite ac morum honestas ...
.P. Lanbertus.[3] */ JoA: / JoA: xx: Nardinus*

---

1   by Julius II. *See CPL*, XVIII, no. 893.
2   MS: *Thoma*; *recte*: 'toga'
3   or possibly 'Lambertus' with the final stroke of the 'm' fused with the 'b'

24[1]   **2 February 1514**   *Reg. Lat.* 1278, fos 43[r]-46[v]

To the archbishop of Canterbury, the bishop of Norwich, and the abbot of the monastery of Westminster (*Westmonasterii*), d. London, executory mandate. Letters of the following tenor have this day been issued by the pope:

> *Leo et cetera. Ad perpetuam rei memoriam. Commissum nobis desuper apostolice servitutis officium ...*

Statute and ordinance as below. A recent petition to the pope on the part of John Yong, master, and the brethren of the house or hospital of St Thomas the Martyr of Acon, d. London, in which, as the pope has learned, one master and several religious, called brothers, live under the rule of St Augustine, and of the *confratres* of the confraternity of the mercers in the church of the said house, stated that although, from its original foundation and erection, the said house was sufficiently and richly endowed so that its master and the brethren living therein for the tiime could properly maintain themselves and properly discharge the burdens falling on the house, nevertheless the revenues and proceeds of the house have been so reduced by the negligence, carelessness, or bad government of several masters who in the past have had the care of the house, or otherwise, that the house, its possessions, and goods, both movable and immovable are found to be crushed by <debts>[2] of 800 marks sterling and more; that but for the subvention to the house of the alms of the faithful – especially of the said *confratres* who have in the church of the house their own altar, called a chapel, which they cause to be served by two secular priests who celebrate there daily for the welfare of the souls of the said *confratres*, and above the chapel a great hall, built some time ago at the expense of the then *confratres* of the confraternity, in which the muniments, writings, and other privileges (*iura*) and chirographs (*cerografa*) belonging and appertaining to the mercers are found and where the *confratres* frequently meet for the sound management of the confraternity – the house, as could easily be comprehended, would have got into a worse state long ago (*longe*) and unless other thought be taken for it the house would in a short time be threatened with total ruin. At the supplication to the pope on the part of John, the brethren, and the *confratres*, the pope, whenever the express assent [of] John, the present brethren of the house, and the *confratres* of the confraternity, is forthcoming in accordance with the promise (*fides*) lawfully made to the pope by public documents,[3] hereby establishes and ordains[4] that henceforth, for all time, as often as a vacancy in the mastership of the house occurs, by death[5], resignation (*seu quamvis aliam dimissionem*), or by deprivation carried out by ordinary authority, the nomination (*nominatio*)[6] of two or three upright men suited by learning and morals, seculars or[7] brothers of the said house, shall belong to the wardens and assistants (*assisten(tes)*) of the confraternity for the time being; and that the said nominees thus[8] nominated from time to time by the wardens and assistants shall be bound to communicate the said nomination to the said brethren[9] within two months, reckoned from the date of the vacancy of the said mastership[10]; and the said brethren[11] shall be bound to present one of the nominees to the bishop of London for the time being within the eight days immediately following the intimation to them of the said nomination[12]; and the said bishop shall be bound to institute as master of the said house the person thus nominated and presented to him from time to time; and that if he does not come from the midst of the said house, the person thus nominated, presented, and instituted from time to time must at his admission, take a corporal oath on the gospels to profess[13] the said order within eight days reckoned from the date of his admission, to render a faithful account each year of his deeds and administration to the brethren and *confratres* of the confraternity for the time being, and not to squander the goods of the said house; that if the wardens and assistants neglect to make the nomination within two months or the said brothers neglect to present one of the nominees within the said eight days the right of nominating[14] or of presenting one of the nominees shall, for that turn, devolve, respectively, to those of the said *confratres* or brothers who have nominated or presented from time to time[15]; and that the said *confratres* shall be[16] the defenders and protectors or patrons and advocates of the said house for ever and in all cases (*in omnibus*) be deemed as such; and that the master and brethren of the house, now and for the time being, together with the *confratres*, may make reasonable and honest statutes, ordinances or constitutions, not contrary to the sacred canons, concerning the prosperous and happy rule of the house and its advantage and growth, and amend and reform for the better statutes etc already made and ordained whenever they are opposed to the religious state (*relligioni*), honesty, or the utility of the house.[17] Notwithstanding, etc.

Given at St Peter's, Rome, 1513, fourth day before the nones of February, first year [2 February 1514]

The pope [hereby] commands that the above three (or two, or one of them), acting in person or by proxy – assisting the said John, brethren, and *confratres* with the protection of an effective defence in the above, and solemnly publishing the said letters wherever and whenever they are requested to on the part of John, the brethren, and *confratres*, or some of them – shall, on the pope's authority, cause John, the brethren, and *confratres* to peacefully have the use and enjoyment of the pope's statute and ordinance and cause the same to be inviolably observed for all time, not permitting John, the brethren, and *confratres* to be unlawfully molested in connection with them by anyone. [Curbing] gainsayers, etc. Notwithstanding, etc.

Hodie emanarunt …
.J. Benzon. / JoA: / JoA: XX: Nardinus

1   The letter recited in the present executory appears to have been expedited by the Camera and enregistered in what is now a Vatican Register. *Cf.* Hergenroether, no. 6532.
2   marginal insertion initialled *JoA*
3   MS: *cum ad hoc Johannes* [!] *et modernorum fratrum domus ac confratrum confraternitatis huiusmodi prout nobis per publica documenta* (?)*ut legitime facta fides expressus accedit assensus*
4   The mention of the 'statutes and ordinances' in the operative part follows that in the narrative part almost verbatim. Oddities and minor differences between the two are only noted in the Calendar where they affect the sense.
5   The narrative has *cessum*, the operative part has *decessum*

6   thus operative part; the narrative has *dominatio*
7   thus narrative (*vel*); the operative part has *et*
8   *sic* occurs in the operative part but not in the narrative.
9   thus operative part (*dictis fratribus*); the narrative has *dilectis fillis fratribus eiusdem domus in ea pro*
     tempore degentibus
10   thus narrative (*a die vacationis ipsius magistratus computan(dos)*); with evident reference to this the
     operative part has *ut prefertur computan(dos)*.
11   The narrative has at this point: *ad quos electio seu presentatio persone idoney ad magistratum predictum*
     dum pro tempore vacat de antiqua et cetera confirmatione pertinet
12   The narrative has: *infra octo dies dicta nominationem eis intimatam immediate sequentes*; the operative part:
     infra octo dies a dicta nominatione eis intimata immediate sequentes
13   narrative: *profitebit*; operative part: *profitebitur*
14   *ius nominandi* occurs at this point in the narrative but is wanting in the operative part.
15   *et si guardiani et assistentes in nominando infra duos menses vel fratres prefati in unum ex nominatis*
     huiusmodi presentando infra octo dies predictos negligentes fuerint ius nominandi vel unum ex nominatis
     presentandi ea vice ad illos ex ipsis confratribus vel fratribus qui pro tempore nominaverint vel
     presentaverint respective de[vol]lvatur: thus narrative; but for minor differences of wording, the
     corresponding passage in the operative part is the same.
16   thus operative part (*existant*); the narrative has *insistant*
17   The narrative concludes: *ex hoc profecto statui dicte domus et fratrum in ea pro tempore degentium salubriter*
     consuletur ipsaque domus utilium personarum fulcta presidio votiva in spiritualibus et temporalibus
     susciperet incrementa; the conclusion inappropriate to the operative part and not reproduced in it.

25   8 July 1513[1]   *Reg. Lat.* 1279, fos 136^r-137^v

Union etc. At a recent petition on the part of Griffin (*Gryffini*) Dauyd Duy, rector of
the parish church of St Giles the Abbot, Wendylbury, d. Lincoln, the pope hereby unites
etc. the perpetual vicarage of the parish church of St ?Miliceus (*Sancti Mylycey*),
Lauarth, d. St David's, (whose annual value does not exceed 6 pounds, 6 shillings and
8 pence sterling), with all its rights and appurtenances, to the above church of St Giles,
which Griffin holds together with the said vicarage, for as long as he holds St Giles's,
to the effect that he may, on his own authority, in person or by proxy, take, or continue
in, and retain corporal possession of the vicarage and of the rights and appurtenances
aforesaid, for as long as he holds the church of St Giles,[2] and convert its fruits etc. to
his own uses and those of St Giles's without licence of the local diocesan or of anyone
else. Notwithstanding etc. The pope's will is, however, that the said vicarage shall not,
on account of this union etc., be defrauded of due services and the cure of souls therein
shall not be neglected; but that its customary burdens shall be supported, and that on
Griffin's death or his resignation etc. of the church of St Giles the union etc. shall be
dissolved and the vicarage shall revert to its original condition and be deemed vacant
automatically.

Ad futuram rei memoriam. Romanum decet pontificem votis illis gratum prestare
assensum ...
O. de Cesis.[3] */ JoA: / JoA: xxxv. de Nardinis*

1   part of date (*octavo idus Julii*) written in another hand? (if not also *anno primo*)
2   *Blas* deleted before *Egidii*
3   *Phi de Agnelis* is deleted and initialled *JoA*; *O. de Cesis*, written in a different hand and ink, is squeezed in
     below.

26   28 June 1513   *Reg. Lat.* 1279, fos 139ᵛ-141ʳ

Union etc. At a recent petition on the part of Thomas Sewell',¹ DDec, canon of London, the pope hereby unites etc. the parish church of Leynborne [also spelt *Leynbourc, Leynbouc*], d. Rochester, (whose annual value, as Thomas asserts, does not exceed 10 pounds sterling and with which, as he asserts, he holds by apostolic dispensation the perpetual vicarage of the parish church of B. Mary the Virgin, Reyc, d. Chichester), with all its rights and appurtenances, to the canonry and prebend of Hoxton of the church of London, d. London, which Thomas holds together with the church of Leynborne, for as long as he holds the canonry and prebend, to the effect that he may, on his own authority, in person or by proxy, take anew, or continue in, and retain corporal possession of Leynborne and of the rights and appurtenances aforesaid, for as long as he holds the canonry and prebend, and convert its fruits etc. to his own uses and those of the church of Leynborne and the canonry and prebend aforesaid without licence of the local diocesan or of anyone else. Notwithstanding etc. The pope's will is, however, that the church of Leynborne shall not, on account of this union etc., be defrauded of due services and the cure of souls therein shall not be neglected; but that its customary burdens shall be supported, and that on Thomas's death or his resignation etc. of the canonry and prebend the union etc. shall be dissolved and the church of Leynborne shall revert to its original condition and be deemed vacant automatically.

Ad futuram rei memoriam. Romanum decet pontificem votis illis prestare assensum …
O. de Cesis / JoA / JoA. xxxv de Nardinis

1   the 'w' read sympathetically

27   28 June 1513   *Reg. Lat.* 1279, fos 231ʳ-232ʳ

To Robert Marton', rector of the parish church of Pylhm', d. Lincoln. Dispensation and indult etc. [as above, no. 2].

Vite¹ ac morum honestas …
O. de Cesis / JoA: / JoA lx de nardinis.²

1   The 'e' is caudata. The feature is a marked characteristic of the *scriptor registri* who transcribed this letter and almost certainly does not reflect the writing of the draft or engrossment behind the entry. If there is a reflection it is coincidental. Save in this instance the phenomenon is not noted in the Calendar and for convenience here, as elsewhere, the implied dipthong is suppressed and e caudata is transcribed as *e* not *ae*.
2   The various forms of Nardini's signature, or what purports to be his signature, are collected in the Index of Persons and Places. As can be seen, the form *JoA de nardinis* is uncommon, as is *JoA de Nardinis*; and *JoAnd de nardinis* is unique in our selection. Additionally, the hand of the signature is unlike that normally associated with the common forms (e.g. *JoA Nardinus*); likewise elements of the script: the construction of the capital A, for instance, differs. In short, there are grounds for supposing that the 'signature' is not autograph. On occasion, registry scribes acted as substitutes for the masters and signed explicitly *pro magistris* (*cf. CPL* XVI, p. xxiii, note 54). It would not be surprising if sometimes scribes signed in the master's name, more or less successfully simulating his signature. No more than administrative irregularity need be involved: observance of formalities is not always convenient.

28   **28 June 1513**   *Reg. Lat.* 1279, fos 232^r-233^v

To John Hall', rector of the parish church of St Vincent, Catherp, d. Lincoln.
Dispensation and indult etc. [as above, no. 2].

Vite ac morum honestas ...
.O. de Cesis / JoA / JoA. Lx. de nardinis:

29   **28 June 1513**   *Reg. Lat.* 1279, fos 233^v-234^v

To Roger Scherman, perpetual vicar of the parish church of Plenynte, d. Exeter.
Dispensation and indult etc. [as above, no. 2].

Vite ac morum honestas ...
O. de Cesis. / JoA: / JoA. Lx: de Nardinis.

30   **16 June 1513**   *Reg. Lat.* 1279, fo 235^r-v

To John Rothelay, penitentiary of the church of Sowthe Mallyng, d. Canterbury, indult.
The pope has learned that in the statutes and customs of the church of Sowthe Mallyng,
d. Canterbury, it is expressly stipulated that the penitentiary of the said church for the
time being is bound: to reside personally and continually in the church; to be present
at matins, vespers, and the other canonical hours, like the other canons of the church;
to celebrate one mass daily for the parishioners of the church, which is also parochial,
between matins and high mass, particularly on Sundays and other feastdays;[1] and to
visit the parish church of Stanmer, said d., which is perpetually annexed to the
penitentiaryship of the church of Sowthe Mallyng, for three or four days (or more or
less, as necessary) at each one of the *quatuor tempora*.[2] At the supplication of John
(who, as he asserts, holds *inter alia* the said penitentiaryship and has been warned and
required by the archbishop of Canterbury, the local ordinary, or by his commissary to
reside therein personally within a certain term then expressed and to visit, as above,
and to do the other things which are required in accordance with the said statutes, and
who wants to study) the pope hereby grants indult to him not to be bound, for a seven-
year term reckoned from the date of the presents, while residing in the Roman curia or
in one of the benefices, with cure or without, held by him for the time, or while
attending a *studium generale*, personally to reside and make the visitations in the said
churches, as above, and not to be coerced by anyone to do so against his will, but to
cause the said penitentiaryship to be served by a sufficient vicar and, if he thinks
proper, by any one of the three prebended vicars of the church of Sowthe Mallyng, and
to cause the cure of souls of the said parishioners to be exercised. Notwithstanding the
above statutes and customs (whose tenors the pope deems to be sufficiently expressed
by the presents, as if they were inserted verbatim, and which, otherwise remaining in

force, the pope, for this once only, specially and expressly derogates) and the other statutes and customs of the church of Sowthe Mallyng, etc. Given at the Lateran.

Vite ac morum honestas
P. Lambertus / JoA / JoA: xx de Nardinis

1   MS: *et quottidie presertim dominicis et aliis festivis diebus inter matutinas et maiorem missam parochianis dicte ecclesie que etiam parochialis existit unam missam celebrare*
2   MS: *ac parochialem ecclesiam de Stanmer ... singulis quattuor anni temporibus per tres aut quattuor dies aut plus vel minus prout necessitas postulabit visitare*

31   18 June 1513   *Reg. Lat.* 1279, fos 236ʳ-237ʳ

To John Furner, rector of the parish church of St Martin, Withcall' [also spelt *Withcall*], d. Lincoln. Dispensation and indult etc. [as above, no. 2].

Vite ac morum honestas ...
L. Puccius / . Phi. / . Phi. Lx. de Senis

32   18 June 1513   *Reg. Lat.* 1279, fos 237ʳ-238ʳ

To William Totild, rector of the parish church of Kyng Ripton, d. Lincoln. Dispensation and indult etc. [as above, no. 2].

Vite ac morum honestas ...
L. Puccius / . Phi. / Phi. Lx. de Senis

33   3 July 1513[1]   *Reg. Lat.* 1279, fos 238ᵛ-239ᵛ

To Robert Gaskin, rector of the parish church of the Holy Trinity, Dorchestre, d. Salisbury, dispensation, as below. This day representation was made to the pope on Robert's part that at another time when he was holding the above parish church (which had been canonically collated to him while vacant *certo modo*), he acquired the perpetual vicarage of the parish church of St Nicholas, Milton' Abbot, said diocese, (which had been collated to him by ordinary authority while vacant *certo modo*) and detained the vicarage and the above church of the Holy Trinity together, without having obtained a dispensation in this regard, for three and a half years or thereabouts, receiving fruits (but not exceeding 12 pounds sterling) from them, albeit *de facto*, contracting disability; and then, when he had resigned the vicarage, he detained the said church of the Holy Trinity (as he did then), celebrating mass and other divine offices, but not in contempt of the keys. Rehabilitating Robert on account of all

disability and infamy contracted by reason of the foregoing, the pope, by other letters
of his, granted that Robert could retain the church of the Holy Trinity without
limitation, just as if, when he acquired the vicarage, he had been sufficiently dispensed
to hold two incompatible benefices together, as is more fully contained in the pope's
letters. At Robert's supplication, the pope hereby dispenses him to receive and retain
for life, together with the church of the Holy Trinity, one, and without them, any two
other benefices etc. [as below, no. 161 to '… Notwithstanding etc. ']. With the proviso
that the church of the Holy Trinity and the other incompatible benefices in question
shall not, on this account, be defrauded of due services and the cure of souls in the
church of the Holy Trinity and (if any) the other incompatible benefices shall not be
neglected.

Vite ac morum honestas …
P. Lambertus / JoA: / JoA: L de Nardinis

1   Part of the dating clause, namely the part *quinto nonas Julii anno primo*, which starts a new line, is written
     in a hand unlike both that of the enregistering scribe and that of the magistral subscription.

34   28 June 1513   *Reg. Lat.* 1279, fo 244[r-v]

To John Colchestre *alias* Neblond, monk of the monastery of St Edmund, Bury,[1] OSB,
d. Norwich. Dispensation and indult – at his supplication – to receive and retain for life
any benefice, with or without cure, usually held by secular clerics, etc. [as above, no.
19, to '… if he obtains it otherwise canonically']; and to wear the usual habit worn by
the monks of the above monastery, OSB, of whose number he is and is, as he asserts,
expressly professed of the order, under a robe or garment of any honest and decent
colour; and also to preach the word of God wherever he pleases, but under licence of
the local ordinaries or other relevant persons; and not to be bound to wear the habit
otherwise.[2] Notwithstanding etc.

Religionis zelus, vite ac morum honestas …
.P. Lamb(er)tus / JoA: / JoA: L de Nardinis

1   In the first instance, both prongs of the 'y' are dotted; in the second neither.
2   reading *al(ia)s*; uncertain: last letter changed by overwriting

35   15 June 1513   *Reg. Lat.* 1279, fos 269[v]-271[r]

To Thomas Scanceby, MA, perpetual vicar of the parish church of Brode Thalke, d.
Salisbury. Some time ago, Julius II dispensed Thomas to receive and retain for life,
together with the perpetual vicarage of the above parish church, which, as he asserted,
he was then holding, one, and without them, any two other benefices, with cure or
otherwise mutually incompatible etc. [as above, no. 6, to '… retain them together for

life, as above'], as is more fully contained – since Julius II died before his letters were drawn up – in the pope's letters drawn up in this regard.[1] The pope – at his supplication – hereby dispenses Thomas, who is a priest and, as he asserts, holds by the said dispensation the above vicarage still and the perpetual chantry of St Thomas in the church of York, d. York (which is incompatible with another incompatible benefice), to receive and retain for life, together with the said vicarage and chantry, which he holds, or with any two other incompatible benefices held by him at the time by the said dispensation, any third benefice, etc. [as above, no. 6].

Litterarum scientia, vite ac morum honestas ...
P. Lambertus / M / M Lx de Campania

1   *below*, no. 64

36   15 June 1513   *Reg. Lat.* 1279, fos 271ʳ-272ᵛ

Union etc. At a recent petition on the part of John Baker, BTheol, rector of the parish church of Lymyngton', d. Bath and Wells, the pope hereby unites etc. the perpetual vicarage of the parish church of Yvingho, d. Lincoln, (whose annual value does not exceed 10 pounds sterling), with all its rights and appurtenances, to the above church of Lymyngton', which John holds together with the above vicarage of Yvingho, for as long as he holds the church of Lymyngton', to the effect that he may, on his own authority, in person or by proxy, take, or continue in, and retain corporal possession of the vicarage and the rights and appurtenances aforesaid, and convert its fruits etc. to his own uses and those of the church of Lymyngton' without licence of the local diocesan or of anyone else. Notwithstanding etc. The pope's will is, however, that the said vicarage shall not, on account of this union etc., be defrauded of due services and the cure of souls therein shall not be neglected; but that its customary burdens shall be supported, and that on John's death or his resignation etc. of the church of Lymyngton' the union etc. shall be dissolved and the said vicarage shall revert to its original condition and be deemed vacant automatically.

Ad futuram rei memoriam. Romanum decet pontificem votis illis gratum prestare assensum ...
P. Lambertus / M / M xxxv de Campania

37   15 June 1513   *Reg. Lat.* 1279, fos 272ᵛ-273ᵛ

To John Bulle, perpetual vicar, called a vicar choral, in the collegiate church of Suthwell', d. York (who, as he asserts, holds a perpetual vicarage, called a vicarage choral, in the above collegiate church, which is incompatible with another incompatible benefice). Dispensation and indult etc. [as above, no. 2].

Vite ac morum honestas ...
O. de Cesis / M / M Lx de Campania

38   15 June 1513   *Reg. Lat.* 1279, fos 274^r-275^r

To William Geffrey, perpetual vicar of the parish church of Ergaston' *alias* Estgarston', d. Salisbury. Dispensation and indult etc. [as above, no. 2].

Vite ac morum honestas ...
O. de Cesis / M / M Lx de Campania

39   15 June 1513   *Reg. Lat.* 1279, fos 275^r-276^r

To John Cumberegge, rector of the parish church of Colsteruuorth', d. Lincoln. Dispensation and indult etc. [as above, no. 2].

Vite ac morum honestas ...
P. Lambertus / M / M L^1 de Campania

1   *See above*, no. 13, note 2.

40   4 April 1513   *Reg. Lat.* 1279, fos 276^v-277^r

To Alexander Colyn, monk of the monastery of B. Mary the Virgin, Glanstynbury [also spelt *Glanstybury*], OSB, d. Bath and Wells, indult as below. Some time ago, as he asserts, he was dispensed by apostolic authority[1] to receive and retain any benefice, with or without cure, usually held by secular clerics, etc. [as above, no. 19, to '...and in its place receive and retain another, similar or dissimilar, benefice, with or without cure, usually held by secular clerics']; and to have a stall in the choir and a place and voice in the chapter together with a room in the above monastery, OSB, of which he is a monk and is, as he also asserts, expressly professed of the order) in accordance with his seniority, and with a monachal portion of the said monastery. The pope – at his supplication – hereby indulges Alexander, for life, while residing in the Roman curia or in any benefice (defined as above) canonically held by him at the time or in the said monastery or while attending a *studium generale*, not to be bound to reside in other benefices held by apostolic dispensation by him at the time, nor to be liable to be compelled to do so by anyone against his will. Notwithstanding etc. With the proviso that the said benefices shall not, on this account, be defrauded of due services and the cure of souls therein (if any) shall not be neglected, but that their customary burdens shall be supported.

Religionis zelus, vite ac morum honestas ...
P. Lambertus / M / M xx de Campania

1   by Julius II. *See CPL*, XIX, no. 866.

41   28 June 1513   *Reg. Lat.* 1279, fos 277ᵛ-278ᵛ

To John Collys, MA, perpetual vicar of the parish church of Stone, d. Canterbury. Dispensation and indult etc. [as above, no. 2].

Litterarum scientia, vite ac morum honestas ...
P. Lambertus / JoA: / JoAnd¹ lx de nardinis

1   *sic*

42   28 June 1513   *Reg. Lat.* 1279, fos 279ʳ-280ᵛ

To Henry Asshaton', rector of the parish church of Qwarlay [also spelt *Quuarlay*], d. Winchester. Dispensation and indult etc. [as above, no. 2].

Vite ac morum honestas ...
.O. de Cesis / JoA: / JoA: Lx de nardinis

43   1 April 1513   *Reg. Lat.* 1279, fo 281ʳ⁻ᵛ

To William Frankysche, brother of the house of Burton', Order of St Lazarus, d. Lincoln. Dispensation – at his supplication – to him, who is a priest, and is, as he asserts, expressly professed of the above order which is not an order of mendicants,¹ to receive and retain any benefice, with or without cure, usually held by secular clerics, even if a parish church or its perpetual vicarage, or a chantry, free chapel, hospital or annual service, usually assigned to secular clerics in title of a perpetual ecclesiastical benefice, and of lay patronage and of whatsoever tax or annual value, if he obtains it otherwise canonically, to resign it, simply or for exchange, as often as he pleases, and in its place receive and retain another, similar or dissimilar, benefice, with or without cure, defined as above. Notwithstanding etc.

Religionis zelus, vite ac morum honestas ...
P. Lambertus / M / M xxx de Campania

1   This information comes from a notwithstanding clause.

44   **3 May 1513**   *Reg. Lat.* 1279, fos 288ᵛ-289ᵛ

To William Tayllour, rector of the parish church of Queryngton, d. Lincoln.
Dispensation and indult etc. [as above, no. 2].

Vite ac morum honestas ...
A. de S(anc)to Severino / A / A. Lx. Colotius:-

45   **3 May 1513**   *Reg. Lat.* 1279, fos 289ᵛ-290ᵛ

To Nicholas Henshaw, rector of the parish church of St George, Clist, d. Exeter.
Dispensation and indult etc. [as above, no. 2].

Vite ac morum honestas ...
A. de s(anc)to Severino / . A. / A. L.¹ Colotius:-

1   *See above*, no. 13, note 2.

46¹   **3 May 1513**   *Reg. Lat.* 1279, fos 291ʳ-292ʳ

To John Bellynghm', cantor of the chantry of St Catherine in the church of B. Mary the
Virgin, Gyllyngm', d. Salisbury. Dispensation etc. [as below, no. 161].

Vite ac morum honestas ...
A. de s(anc)to Severino / A. / A. L. Colotius: –

1   copy (enregistered from engrossment?) in WRO, Reg. Campeggio, fo. 79ʳ

47   **3 May 1513**   *Reg. Lat.* 1279, fos 292ʳ-293ʳ

To Thomas Pyere, LLB, perpetual vicar of the parish church of Barsted', d.
Chichester.¹ Dispensation and indult etc. [as above, no. 2].

Litterarum scientia, vite ac morum honestas ...
A. de s(anc)to Severino / A / ² L.³ Colotius: –

1   locally; a Canterbury peculiar
2   Magistral subscription lacks initial (here 'A') before tax mark (here 'L').
3   *See above*, no. 13, note 2.

48   3 May 1513   *Reg. Lat.* 1279, fos 293ᵛ-294ʳ

To Richard Woode, perpetual vicar of the parish church of Brakley,[1] d. Lincoln. Dispensation and indult etc. [as above, no. 2].

Vite ac morum honestas …
A. de s(anc)to Severino / A / A. L.[2] Colotius: –

1   thus, clearly, the second occurrence of the name; the first occurrence is unclear because the letters between 'B' and 'k' have been reworked, now possibly best read as '-rea-'.
2   *See above,* no. 13, note 2.

49   3 May 1513   *Reg. Lat.* 1279, fos 298ᵛ-299ᵛ

To William Webbe, sacrist of the church of Lichfield (who, as he asserts, holds the sacristship of the above church which is an administration or simple office and is incompatible with another incompatible benefice). Dispensation and indult etc. [as above, no. 2].

Vite ac morum honestas …
A. de s(anc)to Severino / A / A. Lx. Colotius: –

50   5 May 1513   *Reg. Lat.* 1279, fo 301ʳ⁻ᵛ

To Michael Wauugh, rector of the parish church of St Michael the Archangel, Harbaldoune, d. Canterbury. Dispensation and indult etc. [as above, no. 2].

Vite ac morum honestas …
P. lambertus / Phi. / Phi. Lx. de Senis

51   5 May 1513   *Reg. Lat.* 1279,fo 302ʳ⁻ᵛ

To Robert Leyff,[1] rector of the parish church of Isenhm'sted Theyne[2] [also spelt *Isenhiiisted[3] Theyne*], d. Lincoln. Dispensation and indult etc. [as above,no.2].

Vite ac morum honestas …
P. Lambertus / Phi. / Phi. Lx. d(e) Senis

1   both prongs of the 'y' dotted
2   both prongs of the 'y' dotted
3   the three minims after 'h' all dotted

52[1]   **19 March 1513**   *Reg. Lat.* 1279, fos 327[r]-328[r]

To the abbot of the monastery of B Mary outside the walls, York,[2] commission and mandate in favour of Edward Sanage, layman, d. York, and Alice Knyght, woman (*mulieris*), d. Lincoln. The text of a petition recently presented to the pope on Edward and Alice's part stated that, at another time, after the death of his first wife[3] Edward– not unaware that Alice [was related][4] to him in the second and third degrees[5] of affinity (the relationship arising from the fact that, at another time, when Edward's first wife was alive, Edward had often had sexual intercourse with, and got offspring by, Elisabeth Slylay[6], Edward's mistress (*mulierem*), d. York, who was related to Alice in the second and third degrees of consanguinity, being descended from the same stock) – lawfully[7] contracted marriage with Alice (who was then perhaps in ignorance), *de facto* and publicly, *per verba de presenti* and consummated it with connexion, the said Elisabeth marrying another man; that Edward and Alice cannot remain in the said marriage any longer as no apostolic dispensation has been obtained for it; and that, as the said petition added, if there were to be a divorce between them and the necessary business (which is a secret in those parts) was published the said women (*mulieres*) would be defamed forever and other great scandals could in all likelihood arise. At Edward's supplication (who asserts that Elisabeth had first married someone else), the pope, for the above and certain other reasons which have been explained to him, commissions and commands that the above abbot, if what is stated is true, shall, [for this once][8] only, in the customary form of the church, absolve the said Edward and Alice, if they so request, from the said excess, sentence of excommunication, and guilt of incest, having, however, enjoined on them, under the strength of an oath[9] to be taken by them, that in future they will not commit such things nor give help, counsel, or favour to those committing them, and also a salutary penance proportional to the fault, and other things which by law ought to be enjoined; further, if the said Alice has not been abducted[10] on this account, the above abbot shall dispense Edward and Alice[11] to secretly contract marriage, notwithstanding the said impediment, decreeing any existing and future offspring of the marriage to be legitimate, having, however, first separated them for a period of time at the abbot's discretion. Notwithstanding, etc.

Oblate nobis nuper pro parte ... petitionis series ...
p. lambertus / A. / A. xxv. Colotius: –

---

1   The entry is ill-written and marred by several deletions and (arguably) one sizeable omission. Only those
     shortcomings which directly affect the summary are noted. Unhappily, the same incompetent and illiterate
     scribe was responsible for other entries (e.g. no. 59 below).
2   *dioc(esis)* deleted occurs after *Eboracen.*
3   reading *et dicta prima uxore vita functa*
4   MS perhaps wants 'fore coniunctam' (or suchlike).
5   MS: *grandibus* for 'gradibus'
6   initial 'S' written over 'E'
7   MS: (*per verba*) *legitima* (*de presenti*); *recte*: 'legitime'
8   MS: *ac vere duntaxat*; *recte*: 'hac vice duntaxat'
9   reading *sub virtute iuramenti*; *virtute* is very doubtful.
10   MS: *racta*; *recte*: 'rapta'
11   MS: *eiusdem Eduuardi et Alitie*; *recte*: 'cum eisdem Eduuardo et Alitia'?

53   **4 April 1513**   *Reg. Lat.* 1279, fos 328ᵛ-329ᵛ

To John Thomas, BA, rector of the parish church of B. Mary, Muckulston', d. Coventry and Lichfield. Dispensation and indult[1] to receive etc. [as above, no. 2].

Litterarum scientia,[2] *vite ac morum honestas ...*
O. Cesis / . A. / . A. Lx. Colotius: –

1   'tuis in hac parte supplicationibus' does not occur.
2   Unusual: the proem in this form was ordinarily reserved for graduates and the BA was not regarded by the chancery as a degree.

54   **4 April 1513**   *Reg. Lat.* 1279, fos 330ʳ-331ʳ

To Thomas Ricardus *alias* Ricardis, MA, rector of the parish church of B. Mary the Virgin, Kelly, d. Exeter. Dispensation and indult etc. [as above, no. 2].

Litterarum scientia, vite ac morum honestas ...
O. Cesis / . A. / A. L.[1] *Colotius: –*

1   *See above*, no. 13, note 2.

55   **19 March 1513**   *Reg. Lat.* 1279, fos 331ᵛ-333ᵛ

To Edward Darby, MA, archdeacon of Stowe in the church of Lincoln, effectuation of Julius II's dispensation in his favour. Some time ago – after Alexander VI, by his letters, had dispensed Edward to receive and retain together for life any two benefices, etc. [as above, no. 6, to '...retain them together for life'], as is more fully contained in those letters[1] – Julius II, under the date 14 November, eighth year [1511] – at the supplication of Edward (who, as he asserted, was holding the archdeaconry of Stowe in the church of Lincoln and the perpetual vicarage of the parish church of Charelbery, d. Lincoln, by Alexander's above dispensation) – further dispensed him to receive and retain for life, together with the above archdeaconry and vicarage, or any two other incompatible benefices held by him at the time by the said dispensation, any third benefice, etc. [as above, no. 6, to '... retain it for life, as above']. Notwithstanding etc. With the proviso that this third incompatible benefice should not, on this account, be defrauded of due services and the cure of souls therein (if any) should not be <neglected>.[2] Since however Julius II died before his letters to this effect were drawn up, the pope hereby wills and decrees that the present letters shall everywhere be sufficient proof of the said dispensation etc.

Rationi congruit et cetera.
p Lambertus / . A. / A Lxx Colotius:

1   *See CPL*, XVII Part I, no. 806.
2   *negligatur* with *re* above -*at*- deleted in line; *negligeretur* inserted in margin, initialled *A*. Many such oddities occur in the entry – some neither deleted nor corrected.

56   25 March 1513   *Reg. Lat.* 1279, fos 333ᵛ-334ᵛ

To Edward Orenge, cleric, d. London. Dispensation and indult – at his supplication – to him, who, as he asserts, is in his nineteenth year[1] of age, to receive and retain any benefice, with cure or otherwise incompatible, even if a parish church or its perpetual vicarage, or a chantry, free chapel, hospital or annual service, usually assigned to secular clerics in title of a perpetual ecclesiastical benefice, or a dignity, *personatus*, administration or office in a cathedral, even metropolitan, or collegiate church, even if the dignity in question should be major *post pontificalem* in a cathedral, even metropolitan, church, or principal in a collegiate church, even if the dignity etc. should be customarily elective and have cure of souls, if he obtains it otherwise canonically, to resign it, simply or for exchange, as often as he pleases, and in its place receive and retain another, similar or dissimilar, incompatible benefice; and, for life, not to be bound, while residing in the Roman curia or any one of his benefices or attending a *studium generale*, to reside in his other benefices; and also not to be bound, by reason of any benefices with cure or otherwise requiring sacred, even priest's, orders held by him at the time – until he is in his <twenty-fifth>[2] year – to be promoted to any of the sacred orders, even of the subdiaconate; nor to be liable to be compelled to do so by anyone against his will. Notwithstanding the said defect of age etc. With the proviso that the benefice with cure or otherwise incompatible and the other benefices in question shall not, on this account, be defrauded of due services and the cure of souls therein (if any) shall not be neglected; but that customary burdens of those benefices in which he shall not reside shall be supported.

Vite ac morum honestas …
p. lambertus / M / M xxxxvj de Campania

1   'vel circa' (which might be expected here) is deleted (but without initial).
2   (?)*vigintiquinque* is deleted in line, initialled *M*; *vigesimumquintum* inserted in margin, initialled *M*

57   19 March 1513   *Reg. Lat.* 1279, fos 335ʳ-336ᵛ

To William, bishop of Salona (*Salonen.*), who, as he asserts, holds the canonry and prebend of Bemester Prima, church of Salisbury, and the parish church of Monkyston' [also spelt *Monkyston*] alias Anebek, and also the perpetual vicarage of the parish church of Bridford,[1] ds. Winchester and Salisbury [respectively], by apostolic dispensation. Dispensation – at his supplication – to receive together with the church of Salona (which is in *partibus infidelium* and over which he is understood to preside), and the canonry and prebend, church of Monkyston' and vicarage aforesaid, any other benefice, with or without cure, secular or regular of any order, even if the secular benefice should be a parish church or its perpetual vicarage, or a chantry, free chapel, hospital or annual service, usually assigned to secular clerics in title of a perpetual ecclesiastical benefice, or a canonry and prebend, dignity, *personatus*, administration or office in a cathedral, even metropolitan, or collegiate church, even if the dignity in question should be major *post pontificalem* in a cathedral, even metropolitan, church, or principal in a collegiate church, and the regular benefice should be a priory, *prepositura*, *prepositatus*, dignity (even conventual), *personatus*, administration or office, and of lay patronage and of whatsoever tax or annual value, and even if the priory etc. should be customarily elective and have cure of souls, if he obtains it otherwise canonically, and retain it *in commendam* for life; to resign it, simply or for exchange, as often as he pleases, and cede the commend and in its place receive another, similar or dissimilar, benefice, with or without cure, secular or regular of any order (provided that the regular benefice be not a claustral office), and retain it *in commendam* for life, as above; he may – due and customary burdens of this benefice having been supported – make disposition of the rest of its fruits etc. just as those holding it *in titulum* could and ought to do, alienation of immovable goods and precious movables being however forbidden. Notwithstanding etc. With the proviso that the benefice shall not, on this account, be defrauded of due services and the cure of souls therein (if any) shall not be neglected; but that its aforesaid burdens shall be supported.

Personam tuam nobis et apostolice sedi devotam tuis exigentibus meritis paterna benivolentia prosequentes illa tibi libenter concedimus ...
p Lambertus / A / A. C. Colotius

1   or *Budford*; or *Burford*

58   4 April 1513   *Reg. Lat.* 1279, fos 341ᵛ-342ᵛ

To John Wittwod', rector of the parish church of Alscott, d. Lincoln. Dispensation etc. [as below, no. 161].[1]

Vite ac morum honestas ...
p. lambertus[2] */ M / M L de Campania*

1   textual oddities in the present entry (which do not affect the tenor) apart
2   occurs, appropriately, to the right at the start of the entry – i.e. in the position kept for the name of the expediting abbreviator.
     The name of another abbreviator, *phi de Agnellis*, occurs at the top right hand corner of fo. 342ᵛ. The name, which is deleted, presumably 'belongs' to the next entry (no. 59 below) which begins near the bottom of the page. Both entries are the work of the same registry scribe.

59[1]   **4 April 1513**   *Reg. Lat.* 1279, fos 342[v]-345[r]

Indult as below. A recent petition to the pope on the part of John Lenglon, cleric, d. Coventry and Lichfield, stated that some time ago the late Thomas Bownd, citizen and merchant of the town of Coventry (*Conventrie*), said d., making testamentary disposition of his goods in his last will,[2] willed and ordained *inter alia* that from certain annual fruits, etc then assigned by him for the purpose, a doctor or at least bachelor in theology, who [was (bound) to][3] reside continuously in the said town and preach the word of God to the faithful and teach them the true way of living well and chastely[4], was to receive annually the sum of 20 marks sterling, as <is said>[5] to be more fully stated in a certain public instrument drawn up in that regard; and that, as the said petition added, if it were granted that John[6], who has been appointed to the office of preacher under the will of the said testator and who has exercised the office and exercises it at present, and his successors appointed to the office under the will from time to time and exercising it in the said town, as above, could receive, for life, all the fruits etc of their ecclesiastical benefices, they would be better able to execute the office. At [John's][7] supplication the pope hereby grants indult to John and his successors in the said office from time to time that henceforth, for all time, John and the successors exercising the office in accordance with the will of the said testator, as above, may receive, for life, all the fruits etc of any ecclesiastical benefices, with and without cure, held from time to time in [any] churches or places – even if they are canonries and prebends, dignities, *personatus*, administrations, or offices, in cathedral, even metropolitan, or collegiate churches, and the said dignities are major *post pontificales* in cathedral even metropolitan churches or principal ones in collegiate churches and the dignities etc should be customarily elective and have cure of souls, or they are parish churches or their perpetual vicarages, chantries, free chapels, hospitals, or annual services customarily assigned to secular clerics in title of a perpetual ecclesiastical benefice, or a combination of such – with the same completeness, daily distributions alone excepted, with which they would have received them had they been personally resident in the [said][8] churches or places; and that they are not bound to reside meanwhile in the same and may not be coerced into doing so by anyone against their will. Notwithstanding that John and the successors may not have made the first customary personal residence in the said churches or places, Boniface VIII's constitution that such grants are not allowed to be made without limit of time,[9] etc and the statutes and customs of the churches, etc, even if John should perhaps happen to have hitherto taken, and the successors in the future take, in person or by proxy, an oath to observe the statutes etc and not to impetrate apostolic letters against them and not to use such letters even impetrated by another or others or otherwise granted in any way; or if there has been a grant by the apostolic see to the local ordinaries, or if there is one in the future, that they may, by withdrawal of the proceeds of their ecclesiastical benefices or otherwise, compel canons, rectors, and persons of churches and places of their cities and dioceses, even ones appointed to dignities, *personatus*, administrations, or offices, to reside personally in them; or if there is an indult from the apostolic see to the local ordinaries and the chapters of their churches, in common or separately, or if there is one in the future, that they are not bound, in the absence of canons, rectors, and persons of their churches or places, even ones appointed to dignities, *personatus*, administrations, or offices, and not residing in them, or who have not made the customary first personal residence in them, to administer the fruits etc of their ecclesiastical benefices for them, and that they cannot be compelled to do so by apostolic letters which do not make full and express mention, verbatim, of the said indult; and any other privileges, etc. With the proviso that the said benefices shall not be defrauded of due services; and the cure of souls in them (if any) shall not be neglected, but diligently exercised and laudably served therein in things divine, by good and sufficient vicars maintained from the proceeds of the said [benefices][10].

Ad perpetuam rei memoriam. Cum inter cetera ...
phi de Agnellis[11] */ M / M Cxx de Campania*

1   The entry includes several deletions and other textual oddities; only those with a direct bearing on the Calendar text are noted; same illiterate scribe as no. 52 above.
2   MS: *condens de bonis suis in eius ultima voluntate testamentum*
3   MS: (?)*te veru(m)*; *recte*: 'teneretur'?
4   MS: *cesteque*; for 'casteque'
5   *dicitur* inserted in margin, initialled *M*
6   MS: *si dictus Johannes ... ac successoribus suis ad officium ... deputatis et ... officium ... exercentibus ... fructus ... percipere possent concederet*; *recte*: 'dicto Johanni'?
7   lacuna in MS supplied conjecturally: *... exequi valerent* [pro parte dicti Johannis nobis] *fuit humiliter supplicatum ...* The omission could be more extensive.
8   MS: *eiusdem*; *recte*: 'eisdem'
9   *Cf. Sext*, I. 3. 15 (Friedberg, 943).
10   MS: (*de*) *bene et(iam)* (*eorundem proventibus*); *recte*: ' beneficiorum'
11   *See* previous entry, note 2.

60   **30 March 1513**   *Reg. Lat.* 1279,fos 345[v]-348[v]

To Edmund Mocody and John Cantwell',canons of the church of Ossory, mandate in favour of Cornelius Offechna,canon of the church of Leighlin. The pope has learned that the archdeaconry of the church of Leighlin and the prebend,called the rectory of Poyneston [also spelt *Pyoneston*, *P<o>yneston*[1]], in the same church,and also the perpetual vicarage of the parish church of Thunoch,[2] d. Leighlin,are vacant *certo modo* at present and have been vacant for so long that by the Lateran statutes their collation has lawfully devolved on the apostolic see,although the chapter of the church of Leighlin has detained the prebend, and Patrick Ollatre,[3] has detained the archdeaconry,and Malachy Omone,[4] the vicarage – bearing themselves as clerics[5] – with no title, at least no canonical title,for a certain time,but short of a three-year period, as they still do. At a recent petition on the part of Cornelius (who holds a canonry and prebend of the church of Leighlin; and who asserts that the annual value of the archdeaconry does not exceed 6, of the prebend of Poyneston, 5, and of the vicarage, 7, marks sterling) to the pope to unite etc. the archdeaconry,the prebend of Poyneston and the vicarage to the canonry and prebend which he holds, for as long as he holds the latter,the pope hereby commands that the above three (or two or one of them),[6] if,having summoned the chapter, Patrick,Malachy and others concerned, they find the archdeaconry (which is a dignity not however major *post pontificalem*), the vicarage and the prebend of Poyneston (which has cure of souls) to be vacant (howsoever etc.) shall unite etc. them (even if specially reserved etc.),with all their rights and appurtenances, to the said canonry and prebend, for as long as Cornelius holds the latter; to the effect that Cornelius may, on his own authority, in person or by proxy, take corporal possession of the archdeaconry, the prebend of Poyneston and the vicarage and the said rights and appurtenances, and retain them for as long as he holds the said canonry and prebend,and convert their fruits etc. to his own uses and those of the archdeaconry, canonry and prebends,[7] and vicarage, without licence of the local diocesan or of anyone else. Notwithstanding etc. The pope's will is, however, that the archdeaconry, said united [prebend] and vicarage shall not, on account of this union etc., be defrauded of due services and the cure of souls in the vicarage and (if any) the archdeaconry shall not be neglected; but that the customary burdens of the archdeaconry, vicarage and united prebend shall be supported; and that on Cornelius's death or his resignation etc. of the said canonry and prebend this union etc. shall be dissolved and be so [deemed] and the prebend of Poyneston, the archdeaconry and the vicarage shall revert to their original condition and be deemed vacant automatically.

Ex iniuncto nobis desuper apostolice servitutis officio ad ea libenter intendimus ...
phi de Agnellis / M / M xxv de Campania

1   the 'o' written above the 'y'
2   the four minims here read as -*un*- variously readable
3   last three letters uncertain
4   the 'ne' read sympathetically
5   MS: *qui se gerunt pro clerico*; *recte*: '... clericis'
6   MS: *vos vel duo aut unus vestrum* – i.e. the phrase appropriate for three mandataries – though only two are addressed above. The same discrepancy occurs below in the next entry.
7   MS: *preben'* arguably for *preben(darum)* i.e. referring to both the prebend (of the canonry and prebend) Cornelius already holds and to the prebend (of Poyneston) he wants.

61   4 April 1513   *Reg. Lat.* 1279, fos 352ʳ-354ᵛ

To the prior of the monastery, usually governed by a prior, of St. Columba,[1] Inistehoc, d. Ossory,[2] and Edmund Macody, canon of the church of Ossory, mandate in favour of Patrick Yfegna, treasurer of the church of Leighlin (who, as he asserts, holds the treasurership of the church of Leighlin, which is a dignity, not however major *post pontificalem*, and has cure of souls, and to which, for as long as he holds it, the rectory of the parish church of Sleti and the perpetual vicarage of the parish church of Kelalban, d. Leighlin, are united by apostolic authority).[3] The pope has learned that the perpetual vicarage of the parish church of Glendessel [also spelt *Glandessell*], d. Leighlin, which is of lay patronage, is vacant *certo modo* at present and has been vacant for so long that by the Lateran statutes its collation has lawfully devolved on the apostolic see, although Donat Offeachna,[4] who bears himself as a priest, has detained the vicarage of Glendesssel with no title or support of law, of his own temerity and *de facto*, for a certain time, as he does. He hereby commands that the above three (or two or one of them),[5] if, having summoned Donat and others concerned, they find the vicarage of Glendessel, whose annual value does not exceed 7 marks sterling, to be vacant (howsoever etc.) shall collate and assign it (even if specially reserved etc.), with all its rights and appurtenances, to Patrick, inducting him etc., having removed Donat and any other unlawful detainer, and causing Patrick (or his proctor) to be admitted and its fruits etc., rights and obventions to be delivered to him. [Curbing] gainsayers etc. Notwithstanding etc. Also the pope dispenses Patrick to retain the said treasurership for life, together with the vicarage of Glendessel, if conferred on him by virtue of the presents and he acquires it, notwithstanding etc. With the proviso that the treasurership and the vicarage of Glendessel shall not, on this account, be defrauded of due services and the cure of souls therein shall not be neglected.

Vite ac morum honestas …
p. lambertus / M / M xxx sexto decimo k(a)l(endas) maij an(n)o primo [16 April 1513], *de Campania*

1 *Sancte* [*recte*: 'Sancti'] *Columbe*
2 *Sal* [deleted, initialled *M*] – probably the premature start of 'Salutem' – occurs directly after *Ossorien. diocesis*
3 *Cf. CPL* XVIII, no. 745.
4 the *-na* uncertain; perhaps *-nec*
5 MS: *vos vel duo aut unus vestrum* – i.e. the phrase appropriate for three mandataries – though only two mandataries are addressed above. (The deletion in the address clause [above, note 2] may be indicative of some confusion as to the mandataries.) A like discrepancy occurs above (no. 60).

62   25 March 1513   *Reg. Lat.* 1279, fos 363[r]-364[r]

To Richard Com, rector of the parish church of Parecomb', d. Exeter. Dispensation and indult etc. [as above, no. 2].[1]

Vite ac morum honestas …
p. lambertus / M / M Lx de Campania

1 scribal errors (e.g. the indult for non-residence has *retinere* instead of 'residere') apart

63   25 March 1513   *Reg. Lat.* 1279, fos 364ʳ-365ʳ

To Thomas Mylys,[1] monk of the monastery, called priory or house, of Boxg've [also spelt *Boxg'ne*], OSB, d. Chichester. Dispensation and indult – at his supplication – to receive and retain any benefice, with or without cure, usually held by secular clerics, etc. [as above, no. 19].

Religionis zelus, vite ac morum honestas ...
p. lambertus / M / M L de Campania

1   written *Mijlijs*

64   19 March 1513   *Reg. Lat.* 1279, fos 372ᵛ-374ʳ

To Thomas Scawceby, MA,[1] perpetual vicar of the parish church of Brode Chalke,[2] d. Salisbury, decree as below. Some time ago, Julius II, under the date 5 March, ninth year [1512], dispensed and indulged Thomas (who was then a priest[3] and, as he asserted, holding the perpetual vicarage of the above parish church) – at his supplication – to receive and retain for life, together with the above vicarage, one, and without them, any two other benefices etc. [as above, no. 2, with appropriate changes of tense, to '... retain them together for life, as above']; and, for life, while attending a *studium generale* or residing in the Roman curia or any one of his benefices, not to be bound to reside in his other benefices nor to be liable to be compelled to do so by anyone against his will. Notwithstanding etc. Since however Julius II died before his letters to this effect were drawn up, the pope hereby wills and decrees that the present letters shall everywhere be sufficient proof of the said dispensation etc.

Rationi congruit et cetera.
p. lambertus / M / M Lx de Campania

1   'Litterarum scientia' – the formula used for degree-holders – occurs in the narrative of Julius II's intended
     dispensation and indult which suggests that Thomas had received his degree by the date there stated (5
     March 1512).
2   In the second occurrence of *Chalke* the k's ascender is stunted; perhaps *-ltie*
3   MS: *presbyteratus*; in error for 'presbyter eras'?

65   9 February 1514   *Reg. Lat.* 1280, fos 138ʳ-140ᵛ

To John Pennycuyk,[1] MA, canon of Aberdeen, collation and provision. Following the pope's reservation some time ago of all canonries and prebends and other benefices vacated then and in the future at the apostolic see to his own collation and disposition, the canonry and prebend of Bancquhory de Vy[nik],[2] church of Aberdeen, became vacant by the free resignation of Thomas Halkerston, lately a canon of the church, which he held at the time, made through Adam Symson, cleric, d. Dunkeld, his specially appointed proctor, spontaneously into the pope's hands, and admitted by the pope at the said see, and is vacant at present, being reserved as above. The pope hereby collates and makes provision of the canonry and prebend, whose annual value does not exceed 30 pounds sterling (whether vacant as above, or howsoever etc.; even if they have been vacant for so long that by the Lateran statutes their collation has lawfully devolved on the apostolic see, etc.), with plenitude of canon law and all their rights and appurtenances, to John. Notwithstanding etc.

Executory to the bishop of Cavaillon, the archdeacon of the church of Dunblane, and the official of St Andrews, acting in person or by proxy.

Litterarum scientia, vite ac morum honestas ... The executory begins: *Hodie dilecto filio Johanni Pannycuyk* ...
P. Lambert(us); G. de prato / JoA: / JoA: xij: x: Quinto kalendas Martii Anno primo: [25 February 1514], *Nardinus*

1   spelt *Pannycuyk* in the executory
2   the 'y' doubtful; followed by a short blank – enough for three or four letters. This blank supplied from the executory where the name is spelt: *Vynik* – the three minims here read as '- ni-' being capable of other readings. *Cf. also* the spellings which occur in the next entry.

66   9 February 1514   *Reg. Lat.* 1280, fos 140ᵛ-142ᵛ

To Thomas Halkerston,[1] cleric, d. St Andrews, reservation of fruits of resigned canonry and prebend, with indult for re-entry, as below. This day Thomas has spontaneously and freely resigned into the pope's hands the canonry and prebend called Bancquhory de Vinyk,[2] church of Aberdeen, which he was then holding, through a certain proctor of his, and the pope admitting the resignation, by other letters of his, made provision of the said canonry and prebend, then vacant by the said resignation and previously reserved to apostolic disposition, to John Pannycuyk,[3] a canon of the church, as is more fully contained in those letters.[4] Lest Thomas should suffer excessive loss by this resignation, the pope hereby reserves [grants and assigns][5] – with John's express consent – to Thomas all the canonry and prebend's fruits etc. which are to be received, exacted and levied by him for life, on his own authority, in person or by proxy, and to be converted to his own uses in place of an annual pension; and indulges Thomas that he may – on John's death or his resignation etc. of the said canonry and prebend, and in whatever way they are vacant, even at the apostolic see – have free re-entry to the canonry and prebend and take corporal possession of them, on his own authority, in person or by proxy, and retain them as before, as much by virtue of the presents as by his earlier title, without other new provision of them having to be made to him, without limitation, just as if he had not resigned them at all. Notwithstanding etc. The pope's will is, however, that Thomas is, meanwhile, bound to discharge all burdens incumbent on the canonry and prebend out of the said fruits etc.

Executory to the bishop of Cavaillon, the archdeacon[6] of Dunblane, and the official of St Andrews, or two or one of them, acting in person or by proxy.

Vite ac morum honestas ... The executory begins: *Hodie cum dilectus filius Thomas Harcuhaston ...*

P. Lambert(us); G.[7] *de Ces(is) / JoA / JoA: xxx: x Nardinus*

1 spelt *Harcuhaston* in the executory
2 likewise executory; sympathetic reading – in both occurrences the three minims are capable of various readings
3 spelt *-cuyk* or *-cyk* in the executory
4 above, no. 65
5 MS does not have 'concedimus et assignamus' after *reservamus*; however, all three verbs occur together in the corresponding passage in the executory; and the *Nulli* clause in the main letter refers to *reservationis concessionis assignationis*
6 'ecclesie' does not occur.
7 *sic*; *recte*: 'O'?

67   9 February 1514   *Reg. Lat.* 1280, fos 143ʳ-144ᵛ

To Thomas Halkerscon,[1] cleric, d. St Andrews, reservation of fruits of resigned parish church, with indult for re-entry, as below. This day Thomas has spontaneously and freely resigned into the pope's hands the parish church of (?)Ben[ham],[2] d. St Andrews, which he was then holding, through a certain specially appointed proctor of his, and the pope, admitting the resignation, by other letters of his, made provision of the said church, then vacant by the said resignation and previously reserved to apostolic disposition, to Adam Hoppau, its rector, as is more fully contained in those letters.[3] Lest Thomas should suffer excessive loss by this resignation, the pope hereby reserves, grants and assigns to Thomas – with Adam's express consent – all the church's fruits etc., even tithe,[4] to be received, exacted and levied by him for life, on his own authority, in person or by proxy, and to be converted to his own uses in place of an annual pension; and indulges Thomas that he may – on the death of Adam or his resignation etc. of the said church and in whatever way it is vacant, even at the apostolic see – have free re-entry to the church and take corporal possession of it, on his own authority, in person or by proxy, and retain it as before, by virtue of his earlier title, without other provision of it having to be made to him, without limitation, just as if he had not resigned it at all. Notwithstanding etc. The pope's will is, however, that meanwhile Thomas is bound to discharge all burdens incumbent on the church out of the said fruits etc.

Executory to the bishop of Cavaillon, the archdeacon of the church of Dunblane, and the official of St Andrews, or two or one of them, acting in person or by proxy.

Vite ac morum honestas ... The executory begins: *Hodie cum dilectus filius Thomas Halkerston ...*

P. Lambert(us); O de Ces(is) / JoA. / JoA: xxx: x: Nardinus

1 spelt *Halkerston* in the executory
2 After the 'B' (which is certain) there are, apparently, two more letters, possibly 'en' or 'cu'. However, the name is spelt *Benham* in the executory.
3 *See below*, no. 68.
4 *(fructus) decimales*

68   **9 February 1514**   *Reg. Lat.* 1280, fos 144ᵛ-146ʳ

To the archdeacon of the church of Dunblane, mandate in favour of Adam Hopper, cleric, d. St Andrews. Following the pope's reservation some time ago of all benefices, with and without cure, vacated then and in the future at the apostolic see, the parish church of Benhan, d. St Andrews, fell vacant by the free resignation of Thomas Halkeston, lately its rector, which he held at the time, made through John Lokert, cleric, d. Glasgow, his specially appointed proctor, spontaneously into the pope's hands, and admitted by the pope at the said see, and is vacant at present, being reserved as above. The pope hereby commands the above archdeacon, if by diligent examination he finds Adam to be suitable – concerning which the pope burdens the archdeacon's conscience – to collate and assign the church, whose annual value does not exceed 30 pounds sterling (vacant as above or in any other way etc.; even if it has been vacant for so long that by the Lateran statutes its collation has lawfully devolved on the apostolic see etc.), with all its rights and appurtenances, to Adam, inducting him etc. having removed any unlawful detainer and causing the church's fruits etc., rights and obventions to be delivered to him. Curbing gainsayers etc. Notwithstanding etc.

Dignum arbitramur et cetera.
p. *Lambert(us) / JoA / JoA: xx: Quinto K(a)l(endas) martii Anno primo* [25 February 1514], *Nardinus*

69   **18 November 1513**   *Reg. Lat.* 1280, fos 193ᵛ-195ᵛ

To Christopher Joye, cleric, d. London, dispensation and indult. The pope (who, some time ago, decreed and declared that provisions or grants or mandates of provision to canonries and prebends of cathedral churches to persons who have not completed their fourteenth year of age shall be of no force except by consent of the apostolic see) hereby dispenses Christopher (who, as he asserts, is a nephew, by sister german, of Christopher, cardinal priest of the title of S. Prassede; and is in his twelfth[1] year or thereabouts) – at his supplication – to receive, henceforth: any canonries and prebends of any cathedral, even metropolitan, churches and a dignity of a cathedral, metropolitan or collegiate church; and, without the dignity in question, in his fifteenth[2] year: one [benefice with cure]; and in his nineteenth[3] year: another with it; and, in his twenty-third[4] year: a further one, and without them, any three other benefices, with cure or otherwise mutually incompatible, even if parish churches or their perpetual vicarages, chantries, free chapels, hospitals or annual services usually assigned to secular clerics in title of a perpetual simple ecclesiastical benefice, or dignities, *personatus*, administrations or offices in cathedral, even metropolitan, or collegiate churches, and of the patronage of laymen or clerics, or a combination of clerics and laymen, and of whatsoever tax or annual value, and even if the individual dignities, *personatus*, administrations or offices are customarily elective and have cure of souls, if he obtains them otherwise canonically, and retain them together, and if the third benefice should be a parish church or its perpetual vicarage [retain it] for a year[5] calculated from the day of acquiring peaceful possession of it, but if the third should be another incompatible secular[6] benefice [retain it] for life; to resign them, at once or successively, simply or for exchange, as often as he pleases, and in their place receive other, similar or dissimilar, benefices viz.: henceforth: any canonries and prebends of any cathedral, even metropolitan, churches and a dignity, *personatus*, administration or office of a cathedral, metropolitan or collegiate church; and, without the dignity in question, in his fourteenth[7] year: one; and in his nineteenth[8] year: another with it; and in his twenty-third[9] year: a further one, and without them, any three other benefices, with cure or otherwise mutually incompatible, defined as above, and retain them together, and if the third incompatible should be a parish church or its perpetual vicarage, [retain it] for a year calculated from the day of acquiring peaceful possession of it, but if the third benefice should be another incompatible benefice [retain it] for life, as above. And the pope indulges Christopher, also for life, not to be bound, while residing in the Roman curia or any one of his benefices or attending a *studium generale*, to reside in his other benefices, nor to be liable to be compelled to do so by anyone against his will. Notwithstanding the above defect of age and also the pope's above decree and declaration, etc. With the proviso that the canonries and prebends and the incompatible and other benefices shall not, on this account, be defrauded of due services and the cure of souls in them shall not be neglected; but that customary burdens of those benefices in which he shall not reside shall be supported. And the pope's will is that – within the said year – Christopher shall exchange the third parish church or its perpetual vicarage for another benefice, compatible or incompatible, which may not be a parish church or its perpetual vicarage; otherwise the pope decrees that – after the said year has passed – Christopher is bound to resign the parish church or perpetual vicarage in question as soon as he acquires it and that it is thenceforth vacant.

Laudabilia tue puerilis etatis indicia …
[…][10] / *JoA:* / *:JoA: Gratis p(ro) nepot(e) Nardinus*

1   MS: *xij °* i.e. 'duodecimo'; (words – not Roman numerals – are most often used to state age; and generally
      give rise to fewer errors)
2   MS: *xv °*; *cf.* below, note 7.
3   MS: *xix* (wants superscript 'o'); *cf.* below, note 8).
4   MS: *xxiij °*
5   MS: *unum; recte*: 'annum'?
6   reading *se(cu)la(r)e* (appropriate here; but not essential and not repeated in the corresponding passage below)
7   MS: *xiiij °*; *cf.* above, note 2.
8   MS: *xix °*
9   MS: *xxiij °*
10   no abbreviator's name

70   13 February 1514   *Reg. Lat.* 1280, fos 266ᵛ-268ʳ

To John Bolton,[1] canon of the monastery of Bolton' in Craven',[2] OSA, d. York. Dispensation to him, who, as he asserts, suffers a defect of birth as the son of an unmarried man and an unmarried woman, and is, as he also asserts, expressly professed of the above order[3] – at his supplication – to receive any benefice, with or without cure, regular, of the order of St Augustine or of any other order, or secular or usually held by secular clerics, [even][4] if the regular benefice should be a monastery, priory, *prepositura, prepositatus*, dignity ([even][5] conventual or major *post pontificalem*), or *personatus*, administration or office (even claustral and in a cathedral or metropolitan church), and the secular benefice should be a parish church or its perpetual vicarage, or a chantry, free chapel, hospital or annual service, usually assigned to secular clerics in title of a perpetual ecclesiastical benefice, [even][6] if of lay patronage and of whatsoever tax or annual value, and in the kingdom of England only,[7] and even if the priory, *prepositura, prepositatus*, dignity, *personatus*, administration or office should be customarily elective and have cure of souls, if he obtains it otherwise canonically, and to retain the regular benefice *in titulum* and the secular *in commendam*, for life, to resign it, simply or for exchange, as often as he pleases, and cede the commend, and in its place receive likewise another, similar or dissimilar, benefice, with or without cure, regular, of the above order of St Augustine or of any other order, or secular, and retain the regular (even if defined as above) *in titulum*, and the secular *in commendam*, for life, as above; he may – due and customary burdens of the secular benefice having been supported – make disposition of the rest of its fruits etc., just as those holding it *in titulum* could and ought to do, alienation of immovable goods and precious movables being however forbidden. Notwithstanding the above defect, etc. With the proviso that the above secular benefice shall not, on this account, be defrauded of due services and the cure of souls therein (if any) shall not be neglected; but that its customary burdens shall be supported.

Religionis zelus, vite ac morum honestas ...
p. Lambert(us) / JoA: / JoA: L: Nardinus

1   *sic*
2   thus, clearly, the second occurrence; the first is obscured by a descender from the line above.
3   This information comes from a notwithstanding clause.
4   MS: *et*; 'etiam'?
5   as note 4
6   as note 4
7   MS: *et in regno Anglie dumtaxat*; uncommon in a letter of this type

71   20 May 1513   *Reg. Lat.* 1281, fos 11ʳ-12ᵛ

To Thomas, elect of Leighlin. Consistorial provision of him – cleric of Lincoln; UID; papal notary; in the priesthood; and of lawful age – to the church of Leighlin, vacant by the death, outside the Roman curia, of the late bishop Nicholas, during whose rule the pope specially reserved the said church to his own disposition; and appointment of Thomas as bishop, committing to him the care and administration of the church in spiritualities and temporalities.
Conclusions to (i) the chapter of the church of Leighlin; (ii) the clergy of the city and

diocese of Leighlin; (iii) the people of the said city and diocese; (iv) the vassals of the said church; (v) the archbishop of Dublin; (vi) Henry, king of England.

Divina disponente clementia ... The conclusions begin: (i) *Hodie ecclesie vestre Leglinen.*; (ii), (iii), (iv) *Hodie ecclesie Leglinen. et cetera*; (v) *Ad cumulum et cetera*; (vi) *Gratie divine premium et cetera.*
L Puccius / JoA: / JoA xx. xxxxxx. de Nardinis

72   20 May 1513   *Reg. Lat.* 1281, fo 13ʳ

To Thomas Alsey, UID, cleric of Lincoln, papal notary and familiar. Since the pope, on the advice of the cardinals, intends this day to make provision of Thomas to the church of Leighlin, vacant *certo modo*, and to appoint him bishop, he hereby absolves him from any sentences of excommunication, suspension and interdict and other ecclesiastical sentences, censures and pains under which he may perhaps lie, so far only as regards the taking effect of the said provision and appointment and each of the relevant letters. Notwithstanding etc.

Apostolice sedis circumspecta benignitas de statu personarum ecclesiasticarum quarumlibet ...
L Puccius / JoA. / JoA xx de Nardinis

73   19 March 1513   *Reg. Lat.* 1281, fos 41ʳ-42ᵛ

To Christopher, cardinal priest of the title of S Prassede. Commendation of the monastery of St Stephen, Bologna, OSB – which, at the time of his elevation to the papacy, the pope was holding *in commendam* by apostolic concession and dispensation, and which, on the ceasing of this commend through his elevation, is vacant still in the way it was vacant when it was commended to him. Wishing to provide a capable and suitable governor to the monastery to rule and direct it as well as to assist cardinal Christopher to conveniently keep up his position in accordance with the lofty rank of the cardinalate and to better support the expenses which, of necessity, he has continually to incur, the pope[1] – *motu proprio* – [hereby commends][2] the monastery (whose annual value does not, as the pope has learned, exceed 70 gold ducats of the camera) to cardinal Christoper for life, to be held, ruled and governed by him, even together with S Prassede (which is the title of his cardinalate) and with [the church] of York (over which he is understood to preside by apostolic concession and dispensation) and also with each and every one of the other churches, monasteries, priories, *prepositure*, canonries and prebends, dignities, *personatus*, administrations and offices and other benefices, with and without cure, secular and regular of any order, which he holds and shall hold *in titulum* or *commendam* by any apostolic concessions and dispensations, and with annual pensions assigned and to be assigned to him on any ecclesiastical fruits etc. which he receives and shall receive in the future, committing to him the care, rule and administration of the monastery in spiritualities and temporalities. The pope's will is, however, that divine worship in the said monastery shall not, on account of this commend, be neglected and the usual number of monks and ministers [be diminished][3] and that cardinal Christopher may – due and customary burdens of the said monastery and its convent having been supported – make disposition of the rest of its fruits etc. just as abbots of the monastery could and ought to do, alienation of the monastery's immovable goods and precious movables being however forbidden.

Conclusions to: (i) the convent of the monastery of St Stephen, Bologna, OSB; (ii) the vassals of the said monastery; (iii) the bishop of Bologna.

Romani pontificis providentia circumspecta ... The conclusions begin: (i), (ii) *Hodie motu proprio monasterium* ... (iii) *Hodie motu proprio et cetera.*
[–][4] / M / M Grat(is) p(ro) Car(dina)li de Campania

1   The principal letter mentions only the pope; but the conclusion to the convent includes the cardinals, deploying the standard formula: *de fratrum nostrorum consilio* (repeated – by means of *et cetera* – in the other two conclusions).
2   *commendavimus*; *recte*: 'commendamus'. [The conclusion to the convent has *commendavimus* (repeated – by means of *et cetera* – in the other two conclusions) – correctly, of course, in referring to what has been done by the principal letter.]
3   MS: *divinus cultus ac solitus monachorum et ministrorum numerus nullatenus negligatur*; 'minuatur' – in respect of the number of monks and ministers – wanting?
4   abbreviator's name or abbreviators' names wanting

74   15 April 1513   *Reg. Lat.* 1281, fos 47ʳ-49ʳ

To Hugh, elect of Sodor. Consistorial provision of him – cantor called chaplain of the chantry or chapel of B. Mary, Lufford, d. Coventry and Lichfield; MA – to the church of Sodor, vacant by the death, outside the Roman curia, of the late bishop Huanus, during whose rule the pope specially reserved the said church to his own disposition; and appointment of Hugh as bishop, committing to him the care and administration of the church in spiritualities and temporalities
    Conclusions to: (i) the chapter of the church of Sodor; (ii) the clergy of the city and diocese of Sodor; (iii) the people of the said city and diocese; (iv) the vassals of the said church; (v) the archbishop of Nidaros;[1] (vi) Henry, king of England.

Apostolatus officium meritis licet imparibus nobis ex alto commissum ...
The conclusions begin: (i) *Hodie ecclesie vestre Sodoren.* ... (ii), (iii), (iv) *Hodie ecclesie Sodoren. et cetera.* (v) *Ad cumulum et cetera.* (vi) *Gratie divine premium et cetera.*
P d(e) Castello / . A. / A. xx. x. x. x. x. x. x. Colotius

1   MS: *Indresien*; *recte*: 'Nidrosien.'

75 15 April 1513 *Reg. Lat.* 1281, fo 49^{r-v}

To Hugh, elect of Sodor, whom the pope has this day provided to the church of Sodor (then without a pastor *certo modo*), appointing him bishop, as is more fully contained in his letters drawn up in that regard.[1] Since, as the pope has learned, at the time of the said provision and appointment Hugh was holding, as he does, the chantry or free chapel, of B. Mary, Rufford, d. Coventry and Lichfield, the pope – wishing to assist him to keep up his position in accordance with pontifical dignity – hereby dispenses Hugh – *motu proprio* – after he has acquired, on the strength of the said provision and appointment, peaceful quasi-possession of the rule and administration and of the goods of the church of Sodor or the greater part of them and has received consecration – to retain as before the said chantry or chapel,[2] (whose annual value does not exceed 7 English pounds), even if it has cure of souls, together with the said church of Sodor, for as long as he presides over the latter; notwithstanding etc.; decreeing that the chantry or free chapel, is not made vacant on this account. With the proviso that the chantry or free chapel, shall not, on this account, be defrauded of due services and the cure of souls therein (if any) shall not be neglected; but that its customary burdens shall be supported.

Personam tuam nobis et apostolice sedi devotam tuis exigentibus meritis paterna benivolentia prosequen(tes) illa tibi favorabiliter concedimus ...
P de Castello / A. / . A. L. Colotius: –

1 above, no. 74
2 In this instance the scribe has not written 'liberam' before *capellam*.

76 17 April 1513 *Reg. Lat.* 1281, fos 49^{v}-50^{r}

To Hugh, elect of Sodor. Since the pope has recently made provision of Hugh to the church of Sodor, appointing him bishop, as is more fully contained in his letters drawn up in that regard,[1] he hereby grants faculty to Hugh – at his supplication – to receive consecration from any catholic bishop of his choice in communion with the apostolic see, assisted by two or three catholic bishops similarly in communion; and to the bishop concerned to consecrate him, having first received from him in the name of the pope and the Roman church the usual oath of fealty in accordance with the form noted in the presents. The pope decrees, however, that if the bishop consecrates Hugh without receiving the said oath and Hugh receives consecration they shall both be suspended automatically. Moreover it is the pope's will that Hugh shall send him, at once, by his own messenger, the form of oath taken by him, verbatim, by his letters patent, marked with his seal; and that the above shall not be to the prejudice of the archbishop of Nidaros[2] to whom the aforesaid church is understood to be subject by metropolitan law. With the form of oath.[3]

Cum nos pridem ...
P de Castello / A / A. xxviij Colotius:-

77   15 April 1513   *Reg. Lat.* 1281, fo 50ᵛ

To Hugh Hesketh, MA, cantor, called chaplain, of the chantry, or free chapel, of B.
Mary, Rufford, d. Coventry and Lichfield. Since the pope, on the advice of the
cardinals, intends this day to make provision of Hugh to the church of Sodor, at present
without a pastor *certo modo*, and to appoint him bishop, he hereby absolves him from
any sentences of excommunication, suspension and interdict and other ecclesiastical
sentences, censures and pains under which he may perhaps lie, so far only as regards
the taking effect of the said provision and appointment and each of the relevant letters.
Notwithstanding etc.

Apostolice sedis consueta clementia ne dispositiones ...
P de Castello / A. / A. xx. Colotius:-

78[1]   8 June 1513   *Reg. Lat.* 1281, fos 51ʳ-53ʳ

To Louis Guillart, elect of Tournai. Consistorial appointment of Louis – cleric of Paris,
in his twenty-second year of age or thereabouts and in minor orders only – as
administrator in spiritualities and temporalities of the church of Tournai – vacant at the
apostolic see because Charles, recently bishop of Tournai, had ceded the rule and
administration of the said church over which he was then presiding, into the hands of
the pope who admitted the cession; and reserved to the pope's disposition under his
reservation of provisions to all churches vacated then and in the future at the said see
– until Louis reaches his twenty-seventh year; and then, when he reaches his said
twenty-seventh year, from now onwards as from then onwards and from then onwards
as from now onwards, provision of Louis to the said church and appointment of him
as bishop, committing to him the care and administration of the church – even during
the said administration – in spiritualities and temporalities, and granting that Louis
may – even during this interim administration – make disposition of the fruits etc. of
the *mensa* (even communal) of Tournai, and convert them to his own uses and those of
the said church, just as bishops of Tournai for the time being could and ought to do,
alienation of immovable goods and precious movables being however forbidden. The
pope's will is, however, that before Louis involves himself in any way in the rule and
administration by reason of the said appointment [as administrator] he shall give the
usual oath of fealty into the hands of the bishops of Paris and Amiens (in accordance
with the form noted in the letters of consecration) both and each one of whom the pope
has by other letters of his[2] commanded to receive the oath from Louis in his name and
that of the Roman church.
    Conclusions to (i) the chapter of the church of Tournai; (ii) the clergy of the city

and diocese of Tournai; (iii) the people of the said city and diocese; (iv) the vassals of the said church; (v) the archbishop of Reims (vi) Louis, king of the Franks.

Apostolatus officium meritis licet inparibus ex alto nobis commissum …
The conclusions begin: (i), (ii), (iii), (iv) *Hodie dilectum filium …* (v) *Ad cumulum et cetera.* (vi) *Gratie divine et cetera.*
Jo copis / JoA: / JoA Lx. xxxxx³ de nardinis⁴

1   Contemporary copies of the principal letter and of two of the conclusions, viz. those to the chapter and to the clergy, are in England among the State Papers: NA, SP 1/230, fos. 26ʳ-35ᵛ (*cf. L&P, F&D*, I², no. 2197, i, v, and vi). The same paper also contains copies of nos. 79-81 below (ibid., no. 2197, ii-iv). The copies may have been prompted by Wolsey. It would be illuminating to know their source. Wolsey's designs on the bishopric are discussed in detail by C.G. Cruickshank, *The English Occupation of Tournai 1513-1519* (Oxford, 1971), esp, chapter VI. 'The Battle of the Bishops' (pp. 143-187).
2   below, no. 83
3   The point after *Lx* separates the taxation of the principal letter from that of the conclusions. However, unusually, the taxation figures for the conclusions are not themselves separated by points; and there is one 'x' short.
4   unusual form and script: *cf.* above, no. 27, note 2.

79¹   8 June 1513   *Reg. Lat.* 1281, fo 53ᵛ

To Louis Guillart, cleric of Paris. Since the pope, on the advice of the cardinals, intends this day to constitute and appoint Louis administrator in spiritualities and temporalities of the church of Tournai, vacant *certo modo* at present, *sub certis modo et forma*, and then make provision of him to the said church and appoint him bishop, he hereby absolves him from any sentences of excommunication, suspension and interdict and other ecclesiastical sentences, censures and pains under which he may perhaps lie, so far only as regards the taking effect of the said appointment as administrator and the said provision and appointment as bishop and each of the relevant letters. Notwithstanding etc.

Apostolice sedis consueta clementia ne dispositiones …
Jo copis / JoA: / JoA xx de Nardinis²

1   Contemporary copy exists: *see above*, no. 78, note 1.
2   unusual form and script: *cf.* above, no. 27, note 2.

80¹   8 June 1513   *Reg. Lat.* 1281, fos 53ᵛ-54ʳ

To Louis Guillart, cleric of Paris. Since the pope, on the advice of the cardinals, intends this day to constitute and appoint Louis (who, as the pope has learned, is in his twenty-second year of age or thereabouts) administrator in spiritualities and temporalities of the church of Tournai (vacant *certo modo* at present), until he reaches his twenty-seventh year, and, thereafter, make provision of him to the said church and appoint him bishop, he – *motu proprio* – hereby dispenses Louis when[2] he reaches his twenty-seventh year, to be appointed to and preside over the said church as bishop, to rule and govern it in the said spiritualities and temporalities, and to receive consecration and make use of it. Notwithstanding the defect of age, which he will suffer even in his twenty-seventh year, etc.

Divina supereminens largitas …
Jo copis / JoA: / JoA xxx de Nardinis[3]

1   Contemporary copy exists: *see above*, no. 78, note 1.
2   *unacum*; *recte*: 'cum'
3   unusual form and script; *cf.* above, no. 27, note 2.

81[1]   **8 June 1513**   *Reg. Lat.* 1281, fo 54[v]

To Louis, elect of Tournai, indult as below. This day the pope, on the advice of the cardinals, has constituted and appointed Louis administrator in spiritualities and temporalities of the church of Tournai (which was then vacant at the apostolic see because Charles, recently bishop of Tournai, spontaneously and freely ceded the rule and administration of the said church, over which he was then presiding, into the hands of the pope, who admitted the cession) up to a certain point in time stated by law; and, from [now][2] onwards as from that day [when he reaches his twenty-seventh year] onwards, has thereafter made provision of Louis to the said church and appointed him bishop, committing to him the care and administration of the church in spiritualites and temporalities, as is more fully contained in his letters drawn up in that regard.[3] The pope – who some time ago willed that if anyone suffering infirmity should resign any benefice and afterwards die from the infirmity within twenty days and the benefice be collated through resignation made in this way, the collation in question shall be null and the benefice shall in no wise be deemed vacant by death[4] – hereby indulges Louis – *motu proprio* – that if bishop Charles were to die from an infirmity (should he perhaps be suffering one at present) within twenty days after this cession, nevertheless the above appointment as administrator and provision and appointment as bishop shall be valid and efficacious; and the said church shall be deemed to have been vacated by the cession, and not by the death. Notwithstanding the pope's above will, etc.

Exigentibus meritis tue devotionis inducimur …
Jo copis / JoA / JoA: xx de Nardinis[5]

1   Contemporary copy exists: *see above*, no. 78, note 1.
2   *tunc*; *recte*: 'nunc'
3   above, no. 78
4   The reference here is to an established rule of chancery, namely the *Regula de viginti diebus*
5   unusual form and script; *cf. above*, no. 27, note 2.

82   8 June 1513   *Reg. Lat.* 1281, fo 55ʳ

To the bishops of Paris and Amiens, commission and mandate. Since the pope has this day [constituted and appointed]¹ Louis, elect of Tournai, in his twenty-second year of age or thereabouts, administrator in spiritualities and temporalities of the church of Tournai (vacant *certo modo* at the time), until he reaches his twenty-seventh year, and made provision of him to the said church and appointed him bishop, committing to him the care and administration of the church in the said spiritualities and temporalities, as is more fully contained in his letters drawn up in that regard,² he – wishing to spare Louis elect, who lives in those parts, the labour and expense of being compelled on that account to come in person to the apostolic see – hereby commissions and commands that the above two (or one of them) shall – by reason of the above appointment³ [as administrator] – receive the usual oath of fealty from Louis, elect and adminstrator, in the name of the pope and the Roman church in accordance with the form which the pope sends noted in other letters of his⁴ granted to Louis elect in respect of a faculty to receive consecration, and shall cause the form of oath which Louis elect takes to be sent, verbatim, to the pope, at once, by his own messenger, by his letters patent, marked with his seal.

Cum nos hodie …
[–]⁵ / *JoA.* / *JoA xvj de Nardinis*⁶

1   'constituerimus' and 'deputaverimus' do not occur; *see* note 3.
2   above, no. 78
3   MS: *constitutionis et deputationis predictorum*; *sic*; *see* note 1.
4   below, no. 83
5   no abbreviator's name
6   unusual form and script; *cf.* above, no. 27, note 2.

83   10 June 1513   *Reg. Lat.* 1281, fos 55ʳ-56ʳ

To Louis, elect of Tournai. Since the pope, on the advice of the cardinals, has recently constituted and appointed Louis, then in his twenty-second year of age or thereabouts, administrator in spiritualities and temporalities of the vacant church of Tournai, until he reaches his twenty-seventh year; and, from now¹ onwards as from the day that he reaches his said twenty-seventh year onwards, has thereafter made provision of him to the said church, appointing him bishop and committing to him the care and administration of the church in spiritualities and temporalities, as is more fully contained in his letters drawn up in that regard,² he hereby grants faculty to Louis (who, as he asserts, is in minor orders only) – at his supplication – to be promoted by any catholic bishop of his choice in communion with the apostolic see on three Sundays or double feasts, even outside the times established by law, successively to the orders of the subdiaconate, diaconate and priesthood otherwise duly; and also to receive consecration from the same or another catholic bishop similarly in communion assisted by two or three catholic bishops similarly in communion, in his said twenty-seventh year; and the pope also grants faculty to the said bishop to bestow consecration on Louis having first received from him in the name of the pope and the Roman church the usual oath of fealty in accordance with the form noted in the presents. The pope decrees, however, that if the bishop consecrates Louis without receiving the said oath and Louis receives consecration they shall both be suspended automatically. Moreover, it is the pope's will that Louis shall send him, at once, by his own messenger, the form of oath taken by him, verbatim, by his letters patent, marked with his seal; and that the above shall not be to the prejudice of the archbishop of Reims, to whom the aforesaid church is understood to be subject by metropolitan law. With the form of oath.[3]

Cum nos pridem ...
Jo copis / JoA. / JoA: xxviij de nardinis[4]

1   *tunc*; *recte*: 'nunc'
2   above, no. 78
3   not recited in full; *cf.* below, no. 377.
4   unusual form and script; *cf.* above, no. 27, note 2.

84[1]   15 April 1513   *Reg. Lat.* 1281, fos 89r-90r

To Thomas, elect of ?Prizren (*Purien.*) Consistorial provision of him – prior of the priory of St Augustine, Daventre, OSB, d. Lincoln, in the priesthood and of lawful age – to the church of ?Prizren, vacant *certo modo*, and appointment of him as bishop, committing to him the care and administration of the church in spiritualities and temporalities. The pope's will is, however, that Thomas shall – after he has had the present letters expedited – travel to the said church and reside in person at it; and that he shall not be able to exercise the pontifical office outside his city and diocese.

Apostolatus officium quanquam insufficientibus meritis nobis ex alto commissum ...
I BenZon[2] */ JoA / JoA: L: Nardinus*

1   Principal letter only enregistered (i.e. no conclusions).
2   *Cf. below*, no. 88, note 2.

85   16 April 1513   *Reg. Lat.* 1281, fo 90r-v

To Thomas, elect of ?Prizren (*Purien.*) Since the pope has recently made provision of Thomas to the church of ?Prizren, appointing him bishop, as is more fully contained in his letters drawn up in that regard,[1] he hereby grants faculty to Thomas – at his supplication – to receive consecration from any catholic bishop of his choice in communion with the apostolic see, assisted by two or three catholic bishops similarly in communion; and to the bishop concerned to consecrate him, having first received from him in the name of the pope and the Roman church the usual oath of fealty in accordance with the form noted in the presents. The pope decrees, however, that if the bishop consecrates Thomas without receiving the said oath and Thomas receives consecration they shall both be suspended automatically. Moreover it is the pope's will that Thomas shall send him, [at once],[2] by his own messenger, the form of oath taken by him, verbatim, by his letters patent, marked with his seal; and that the above shall not be to the prejudice of the archbishop of ?Prjeslav (*Procamen.*), to whom the aforesaid church is understood to be subject by metropolitan law. With the form of oath.[3]

Cum nos pridem ...
I BenZon[4] */ JoA / . JoA: xxviij: Nardinus*

1   *See above*, no. 84.
2   MS: *quam totiens; recte:* 'quamtotius'
3   not recited in full; *cf. below*, no. 377.
4   *Cf. below*, no. 88, note 2.

86   15 April 1513   *Reg. Lat.* 1281, fos 90ᵛ-91ʳ

To Thomas, prior of the priory of St Augustine, Daventre, OSB, d. Lincoln. Since the pope, on the advice of the cardinals, intends this day to make provision of Thomas to the church of ?Prizren (*Purien.*), at present vacant *certo modo*, and to appoint him bishop, he hereby absolves him from any sentences of excommunication, suspension and interdict and other ecclesiastical sentences, censures and pains under which he may perhaps lie, so far only as regards the taking effect of the said provision and appointment and each of the relevant letters. Notwithstanding etc.

Apostolice sedis circumspecta benignitas ad ea libenter intendit ...
I BenZon[1] */ JoA / :JoA: xx: Nardinus*

1   *Cf.* below, no. 88, note 2.

87   15 April 1513   *Reg. Lat.* 1281, fos 91ʳ-92ʳ

To Thomas, elect of ?Prizren (*Purien.*) This day the pope made provision of Thomas to the church of ?Prizren, which was then vacant, appointing him bishop, willing *inter cetera* that Thomas – as soon as he has had the apostolic letters in respect of this provision and appointment expedited – shall go to the said church and reside in person at it; and that he shall not be able to exercise the pontifical office outside his city and diocese, as is more fully contained in the pope's letters drawn up in that regard.[1] Since however, as the pope has learned, Thomas is unable to travel conveniently to the said church, which is *in partibus infidelium*, and reside in person at it, the pope – at his supplication – hereby indulges him not to be bound to go to the said church or to reside at it; and to be able – after he has received consecration – to exercise the pontifical office in the city and diocese of Lincoln only, while required to do so by the present and any future bishop of Lincoln and with the bishop's special licence. Notwithstanding the pope's will aforesaid etc.

Sincere devotionis affectus …
I BenZon[2] */ JoA / JoA: xxx: Nardinus*

1   above, no. 84
2   *Cf.* below, no. 88, note 2.

88   15 April 1513   *Reg. Lat.* 1281, fo 92[r-v]

To Thomas, elect of ?Prizren (*Purien.*) Since the pope has this day made provision of Thomas to the church of ?Prizren, appointing him bishop, as is more fully contained in his letters drawn up in that regard;[1] and, as the pope has learned, at the time of the said provision and appointment, Thomas was holding, as he does, the priory of St Augustine, Daventre, OSB, d. Lincoln, the pope – wishing to assist Thomas (who receives nothing from the fruits and proceeds of the said church which is *in partibus infidelium*) to keep up his position in accordance with pontifical dignity – hereby dispenses Thomas – *motu proprio* – to retain as before – even after he has received consecration and acquired, on the strength of the said provision and appointment, peaceful quasi-possession of the rule and administration and of the goods of the said church or the greater part of them – the said priory, which is conventual and whose annual value does not exceed 40 English pounds sterling, even if it is customarily elective and has cure of souls, for life, even together with the above church, for as long as he presides over the latter; notwithstanding etc.; decreeing that the priory is not made vacant on this account. With the proviso that the priory shall not, on this account, be defrauded of due services and the cure of souls therein (if any) shall not be neglected; but that its customary burdens shall be supported.

Personam tuam nobis et apostolice sedi devotam tuis exigentibus meritis paterna benivolentia prosequen(tes) illa tibi libenter concedimus …
I Benzon[2] */ JoA / JoA: L: Nardinus*

1   *See above*, no. 84.
2   unexpectedly, not in hand of enregistering scribe (*cf. CPL* XVI, p. xix); perhaps enregistered prematurely from a draft (*cf.* ibid., pp. xxiv-xxxi); likewise the others in the group (nos. 84-87 above)?

89   15 April 1513   *Reg. Lat.* 1281, fos 103[r]-105[v]

To Edmund Brychehede, elect of St Asaph. Consistorial provision of him – professor OFM and of theology and in the priesthood – to the church of St Asaph, vacant by the death, outside the Roman curia, of the late bishop David, during whose rule the pope specially reserved the said church to his own ordinance and disposition; and appointment of Edmund as bishop, committing to him the care and administration of the church in spiritualities and temporalities.

Conclusions to (i) the chapter of St Asaph; (ii) the clergy of the city and diocese of St Asaph; (iii) the people of the said city and diocese; (iv) the vassals of the said church; (v) the archbishop of Canterbury; (vi) Henry, king of England.

Apostolatus officium meritis licet imparibus nobis ex alto commissum ...
The conclusions begin: (i) *Hodie ecclesie vestre Assanen.* ... (ii), (iii), (iv) *Hodie ecclesie Assanen.* ... (v) *Ad cumulum ...* (vi) *Gratie divine premium ...*
f. Bregeon / M / M xx x x x x x x[1] *de Campania*

1   *sic*; i.e. no points between the tax marks

---

90   15 April 1513   *Reg. Lat.* 1281, fos 105ᵛ-106ʳ

To Edmund Brikehede, professor OFM and of theology. Since the pope, on the advice of the cardinals, intends this day to make provision of Edmund to the church of St Asaph, at present bereft of a pastor *certo modo*, and to appoint him bishop, he hereby absolves him from any sentences of excommunication, suspension and interdict and other ecclesiastical sentences, censures and pains under which he may perhaps lie, so far only as regards the taking effect of the said provision and appointment and each of the relevant letters. Notwithstanding etc.

Apostolice sedis providentia circumspecta ...
f. Bregeon / M / M xx de Campania

---

91   17 April 1513   *Reg. Lat.* 1281, fos 106ᵛ-107ʳ

To Edmund, elect of St Asaph. Since[1] the pope has recently made provision of Edmund to the church of St Asaph (then bereft of a pastor by the death, outside the Roman curia, of the late bishop David), appointing him bishop, as is more fully contained in his letters drawn up in that regard,[2] he hereby grants faculty to Edmund – at his supplication – to receive consecration from any catholic bishop of his choice in communion with the apostolic see, assisted by two or three catholic bishops similarly in communion; and to the bishop concerned to consecrate him, having first received from him in the name of the pope and the Roman church the usual oath of fealty in accordance with the form noted in the presents. The pope decrees, however, that if the bishop consecrates Edmund without receiving the said oath and Edmund receives consecration they shall both be suspended automatically; that Edmund shall send him, at once, by his own messenger, the form of oath taken by him, verbatim, by his letters patent, marked with his seal; and that the above shall not be to the prejudice of the archbishop of Canterbury, to whom the aforesaid church is understood to be subject by metropolitan law. With the form of oath.[3]

Dum[4] *nos pridem ...*
f. Bregeon / M / M xxviij de Campania

1   MS: *Dum*; *recte* 'Cum'
2   above, no. 89
3   not recited in full; *cf.* below, no. 377.
4   *See above*, note 1.

92[1]   **15 April 1513**   *Reg. Lat.* 1281, fos 135[r]-136[r]

To John, elect of Gallipoli (*Calipolen.*) Consistorial provision of him – rector, called master, of the hospital, called house or mastership, of St Thomas the Martyr of Acon, London, OSA; and in the priesthood – to the church of Gallipoli, vacant *certo modo*, and appointment of him as bishop, committing to him the care and administration of the church in spiritualities and temporalities. The pope's will is, however, that John shall – after he has had the present letters expedited – travel to the said church and reside in person at it; and that he shall not be able to exercise the pontifical office outside his city and diocese.

Apostolatus officium quamquam insufficientibus meritis nobis ex alto commissum ...
L. Puccius / C / C L. Barotius

1   Principal letter only (i.e. no conclusions).

93   **15 April 1513**   *Reg. Lat.* 1281, fos 136[r]-137[r]

To John, elect of Gallipoli (*Calipolen.*) Since the pope has this day made provision of John to the church of Gallipoli, vacant *certo modo*, appointing him bishop, as is more fully contained in his letters drawn up in that regard;[1] and, as the pope has learned, at the time of the said provision and appointment, John was holding, as he does, the hospital, called house or mastership, of St Thomas the Martyr of Acon, London, OSA, the pope – wishing to assist John (who receives nothing from the fruits and proceeds of the said church which is *in partibus infidelium*) to keep up his position in accordance with pontifical dignity – hereby dispenses John – *motu proprio* – to retain as before – even after he has received consecration and peacefully acquired, on the strength of the said provision and appointment, quasi-possession of the rule and administration and of the goods of the said church or the greater part of them – the said hospital, whose annual value does not exceed 35 English pounds sterling, even if it is customarily elective and has cure of souls, together with the said church, for as long as he presides over the latter, notwithstanding etc.; decreeing that the hospital is not made vacant on account of the said provision, appointment, consecration and acquisition. With the proviso that the hospital shall not, on this account, be defrauded of due services and the cure of souls therein (if any) shall not be neglected.

Personam tuam nobis et apostolice sedi devotam tuis exigentibus meritis
paterna benevolentia prosequentes illa tibi libenter concedimus ...
L. Puccius / C / C L. Barotius

1   above, no. 92

94   16 April 1513   *Reg. Lat.* 1281, fo 137[r-v]

To John, elect of Gallipoli (*Calipolen.*) Since the pope has recently made provision of John to the church of Gallipoli, appointing him bishop, as is more fully contained in his letters drawn up in that regard,[1] he hereby grants faculty to John – at his supplication – to receive consecration from any catholic bishop of his choice in communion with the apostolic see, assisted by two or three catholic bishops similarly in communion; and to the bishop concerned to consecrate him, having first received from him in the name of the pope and the Roman church the usual oath of fealty in accordance with the form noted in the presents. The pope decrees, however, that if the bishop consecrates John without receiving the said oath and John receives consecration they shall both be suspended automatically. Moreover it is the pope's will that John shall send him, at once, by his own messenger, the form of oath taken by him, verbatim, by his letters patent, marked with his seal; and that the above shall not be to the prejudice of the archbishop of Heraclea (*Irachien.*),[2] to whom the aforesaid church is understood to be subject by metropolitan law. With the form of oath.[3]

Cum nos pridem ...
L. Puccius / C / C. xxviij Barotius

1   above, no. 92
2   the -*ch*- doubtful
3   not recited in full; *cf.* below, no. 377.

95   15 April 1513   *Reg. Lat.* 1281, fo 138[r-v]

To John, elect of Gallipoli (*Calipolen.*) This day the pope by other letters of his made provision of John to the church of Gallipoli, then vacant *certo modo*, appointing him bishop, as is more fully contained in the said letters[1] in which the pope willed that John – as soon as he has had those letters expedited – shall go to the said church and reside in person at it; and that he shall not be able to exercise the pontifical office outside his city and diocese of Gallipoli. Since however, as the pope has learned, John is unable to travel conveniently to the said church, which is *in partibus infidelium*, and reside in person at it, the pope – at his supplication – hereby indulges him not to be bound to go to the said church and reside in person at it; and to be able – after he has received consecration – to exercise the pontifical office in the city and diocese of London only, if he should be required to do so by the present and any future bishop of London and with the bishop's special licence. Notwithstanding the pope's will aforesaid etc.

Sincere devocionis affectus ...
L. Puccius / C / C xxx Barotius

1   above, no. 92

96   15 April 1513   *Reg. Lat.* 1281, fos 138[v]-139[r]

To John Yong, rector, called master, of the hospital, called house or mastership, of St Thomas the Martyr of Acon, London, OSA. Since the pope, on the advice[1] of the cardinals, intends this day to make provision of John to the church of Gallipoli (*Calipolen.*), vacant *certo modo*, and to appoint him bishop, he hereby absolves him from any [sentences] of excommunication etc. under which he may perhaps lie, so far only as regards the taking effect of the said appointment and provision[2] and each of the relevant letters. Notwithstanding etc.

Apostolice sedis circumspecta benignitas de statu personarum[3] quarumlibet ...
L. Puccius / C / C. xx Barotius

1   *concilio*; *recte*: 'consilio'
2   MS: *prefectio et provisio predicte*; i.e. the usual word-order is reversed.
3   'ecclesiasticarum' does not occur.

97   6 April 1513   *Reg. Lat.* 1281, fos 139[v]-142[r]

To Patrick Paniter, abbot of the monastery of Cambuskynet [also spelt *Cambuskynet*'], OSA, d. St Andrews. Consistorial provision as below to him – cleric, d. Brechin; secretary of James, king of Scots; in minor orders and of lawful age – whom, also this day, the pope, *motu proprio*, by other letters of his,[1] has dispensed to be appointed abbot of the above monastery – even without having taken the habit usually worn by the canons of the monastery and without having made the profession usually made by them – and to preside over the monastery – even without having taken the habit and made his profession – for a year calculated from the date of having peaceful possession of the monastery's rule, administration and goods, or the greater part of them. The pope, on the advice of the cardinals, hereby makes provision of Patrick to the monastery, vacant by the death, outside the Roman curia, of the late abbot Andrew, during whose rule the pope specially reserved the monastery to his own ordinance and disposition, and appoints Patrick abbot, committing the care, rule and administration of the monastery to him in spiritualities and temporalities. The pope's will is, however, that Patrick shall be bound – within the said year – to take the habit and make his profession; otherwise – after the year has elapsed – the pope decrees the monastery vacant automatically.

Conclusions to: (i) the convent of the above monastery; (ii) the vassals of the monastery; (iii) James, king of Scots; (iv) the archbishop of St Andrews.

Summi disposicione rectoris ad regimen universalis ... The conclusions begin: (i) *Hodie monasterio vestro* ... (ii) *Hodie et cetera.* (iii), (iv) *Hodie et cetera plenius continetur.*
f. Bregeon / . A. / A. xvj. viij. viij. viij. viij. Colotius: –

1   *See below*, no. 98.

98   6 April 1513   *Reg. Lat.* 1281, fo 142^{r-v}

To Patrick Paniter, cleric, d. Brechin. Since the pope, on the advice of the cardinals, intends this day to make provision of Patrick to the monastery of Cambuskynet, OSA, d. St Andrews, at present vacant *certo modo*, and appoint him abbot, he – *motu proprio* – hereby dispenses Patrick to be appointed abbot – even without having taken the habit usually worn by the canons and without having made the profession usually made by them – and to preside over the monastery – even without having taken the habit and made his profession – for a year calculated from the date of having peaceful possession of its rule and administration and goods or the greater part of them, and to rule and govern it in spiritualities and temporalities. Notwithstanding etc. The pope's will is, however, that Patrick shall be bound – within the said year – to take the habit and make his profession; otherwise – after the year has elapsed – the monastery shall be deemed vacant automatically.

Exigit tue devotionis sinceritas ...
f. Bregeon / [...]¹ / A. xx. Colotius

1   no magistral initial

99   6 April 1513   *Reg. Lat.* 1281, fos 142^v-143^r

To Patrick Paniter, cleric, d. Brechin. Since the pope, on the advice of the cardinals, intends this day to make provision of Patrick to the monastery of Cambuskynet, OSA, d. St Andrews, at present vacant *certo modo*, and to appoint him abbot, he hereby absolves him from any [sentences] of excommunication etc. under which he may perhaps lie, so far as regards the taking effect of the said provision and appointment and each of the relevant letters. Notwithstanding etc.

Apostolice sedis consueta clemencia ne dispositiones …
f. Bregeon / . A. / A. xvj. Colotius

100   6 April 1513   *Reg. Lat.* 1281, fos 143ʳ-144ʳ

To Patrick, abbot of the monastery of Cambuskynet, OSA, d. St Andrews. Since this day the pope has made provision of Patrick to the above monastery, then vacant *certo modo*, appointing him abbot, as is more fully contained in his letters drawn up in that regard,[1] he hereby grants faculty to Patrick, who is in minor orders only – at his supplication – to receive from any catholic bishop (or bishops) of his choice in communion with the apostolic see on any three Sundays or feast days, even outside the times established by law, the orders, successively, of the subdiaconate, diaconate and priesthood, and from one of these bishops (or another likewise in communion with the apostolic see) blessing; and to the bishop (or bishops) concerned to bestow the said orders and blessing. The pope's will is, however, that the bishop who bestows benediction on Patrick shall, after he has bestowed it, receive from Patrick in the name of the pope and the Roman church the usual oath of fealty in accordance with the form[2] the pope sends enclosed under his *bulla*;[3] and Patrick shall send him, at once, by his own messenger, the form of oath taken by him, verbatim, by his letters patent, marked with his seal; and that the above shall not be to the prejudice of the archbishop of St Andrews, to whom the monastery is understood to be subject by ordinary law.

Cum nos hodie …
f. Bregeon / A / A. Xvj. Colotius

1   above, no. 97
2   unusually, form of oath not recited
3   *Cf.* below, no. 384, note 4.

101   6 April 1513   *Reg. Lat.* 1281, fos 144ʳ-145ʳ

To the deans of the churches of Glasgow and Brechin and the archdeacon of the church of Moray, mandate in favour of Patrick Paniter, cleric, d. Brechin. The pope has learned that Patrick wishes to enter the monastery of Cambuskynet, OSA, d. St Andrews, under the regular habit. Wishing to encourage Patrick (who, as he has learned, is secretary of James, king of Scots), the pope hereby commands that the above three, or two or one of them, in person or by proxy, shall receive Patrick – if he is suitable and there is no canonical obstacle – as a canon in the monastery and shall bestow the regular habit on him in accordance with the custom of the monastery, and cause him to be given charitable treatment therein; and, if Patrick spontaneously wishes to make the usual profession made by the canons, receive and admit it. [Curbing] gainsayers etc. Notwithstanding etc.

Cupientibus vitam ducere regularem apostolicum decet esse presidium ...
f. Bregeon / A. / . A. xvj. Colotius

102 6 April 1513   *Reg. Lat.* 1281, fos 145ʳ-146ᵛ

To Patrick, abbot of the monastery of Cambuskynet, OSA, d. St Andrews. This day the pope, on the advice of the cardinals, has made provision of Patrick to the above monastery, vacant *certo modo* at the time, and appointed him abbot, and dispensed him to be so appointed and to preside over the monastery as abbot for up to a year without taking the habit and making the regular profession, as is more fully contained in the pope's various letters drawn up in that regard.[1] And the pope has learned that at the time of the said provision and appointment Patrick had a right in the preceptory of Torsihen, of the Hospital of St John of Jerusalem, said d. St Andrews (which at another time, when it was vacant *certo modo*, had been commended [to him] to be held, ruled and governed by him for up to six months calculated from the day of taking peaceful possession of it, and thereafter, provision of it had been made to him on condition he took the habit and made his profession timeously) and was litigating (as he is now) over the preceptory in the Roman curia before a certain auditor of causes of the apostolic palace, in the third instance, against a certain adversary of his who had intruded into the said preceptory, and Patrick is still within the term of the commend; and all the fruits etc. of the archdeaconry of Moray, of the canonry and prebend of Chynel, [of the church][2] of St Salvator within the city of St Andrews, and also of the parish church of Convecht, of the same diocese, and 40 pounds Scots on the fruits etc. of the parish church, called a prebend, of Federesso within the church of St Mary called of the Rock (*de Rupe*), of the city of St Andrews, were reserved to Patrick for life to be received, exacted and levied by him on his own authority; and re-entry and entry etc (*regressus et accessus seu ingressus*) to the archdeaconry, to the canonry and prebend and to the said churches of Convecht and Federesso in certain eventualities was granted to him. Wishing to assist Patrick to keep up his position in accordance with abbatial dignity the pope — *motu proprio* — hereby dispenses him — even after he has taken the habit and made his profession and acquired, on the strength of the said provision and appointment, peaceful quasi-possession of the rule [and] administration of the said monastery and of its goods or the major part of them — to prosecute the right belonging to him in or to the said preceptory (whose annual value does not exceed 300 pounds sterling), to raise in court what has not yet been raised (*non deductum deducere*), and, if he wins and acquires the preceptory, to retain it *in commendam*, for life; and also to receive and levy the fruits etc. assigned to him as above, and to use the rights of re-entry and entry (*regrediendi et accedendi*) to the archdeaconry, to the canonry and prebend and also to the churches of Convecht and Federesso (whose annual value, as the pope has also learned, does not exceed 70 pounds sterling), granted to him, and, in the event of re-entry and entry etc (*in illorum eventu*) to retain the archdeaconry (which is a dignity not however major *post pontificalem*), even if it should be customarily elective and have cure of souls, and the canonry and prebend and parish churches in question for a year calculated from the day of taking peaceful possession of them, together with the said monastery. Notwithstanding etc. the statutes etc of the said Hospital and of the said [churches] of Moray, St Salvator and St Mary of the Rock; and also the establishments, uses and natures, privileges and indults granted by the apostolic see to the said Hospital and to its Master and convent and also to the monastery and order aforesaid and confirmed and renewed, under whatsoever tenors and forms of words so granted, confirmed and renewed, and anything else to the contrary. With decree that the right in the preceptory belonging to Patrick shall not, on this account, become vacant; and also that the reservation and assignment of fruits etc. shall not cease and the right of re-entry and entry shall not expire. With the proviso that the preceptory and, in the event of re-entry and entry etc, the canonry and prebend and the parish church[3] shall not, on this account, be defrauded of due services and the cure of souls in the said parish churches and (if any) in the archdeaconry shall not be neglected; but that their customary burdens and those of the canonry and prebend shall be supported. The pope's will is, however, that Patrick shall be bound to resign utterly the archdeaconry, canonry and prebend and parish churches within one year of peaceful acquisition, and the pope has decreed them to be vacant thenceforth.

Personam tuam nobis et apostolice sedi devotam ...
f. Bregeon / A / A . C . x . Colotius:—

1   The principal letter is no. 97 above; the dispensation is no. 98.
2   'ecclesie' does not occur.
3   MS: *parrochialis ecclesia*; *recte*: 'parrochiales ecclesie'?

103   9 January 1514   *Reg. Lat.* 1281, fos 157[r]-160[r]

To James, archbishop of Glasgow, consistorial surrogation and commend as below. Some time ago a dispute arose between William Bwuch,[1] monk of the monastery of B. Mary, Kylwynyn, OSB, d. Glasgow, and John Forman, who bears himself as a cleric or as a monk of the said order, over the rule and administration of the said monastery to which William asserted he had at one time been provided by apostolic authority, when it was vacant *certo modo*, and been appointed its abbot; and had, by virtue of this provision and appointment, acquired quasi-possession of the monastery's rule and administration, and had been despoiled of them afterwards by John; and William and John each asserted that the rule and administration rightfully belonged to himself. The pope committed the case of disputed title and spoliation (*causam petitorii et spolii*) to Achille, cardinal priest of the title of S. Sisto; and next, because of Achille's absence from the Roman curia, to Antonio, cardinal priest of the title of S. Vitale, to be heard and duly determined; and Cardinals Achille and Antonio are said to have proceeded successively in this case to several acts, perhaps even – at William's instance – to a conclusion of it by Cardinal Antonio. Moreover since this day, while the said suit was thus pending undecided before the said Cardinal A.,[2] William, spontaneously and freely, ceded the suit and case and all right belonging to him in or to the said rule and administration into the pope's hands and the pope admitted the cession, the pope – lest, with the case undefended, the monastery be detained by someone unlawfully; and wishing to provide a capable and suitable governor for it, as well as to assist archbishop James to keep up his position in accordance with pontifical dignity – on the advice of the cardinals, surrogates archbishop James in and to all right which William had (or could have had) in any way to the rule and administration of the monastery at the time of his cession, grants James such right and admits him to it and to the prosecution and defence of the said right, suit, and case, even the case of spoliation, in the state in which William was at the time of his cession and could and ought to be admitted as if he had not ceded, and the pope wills and commands that he be so admitted. And the pope, likewise on the advice of the cardinals, commends the monastery, vacant howsoever, to archbishop James to be held, ruled and governed by him for life, even together with [the church of] Glasgow, over which he is understood to preside, and any other cathedral, even metropolitan, [church] to which he might be translated; and also with all other churches, monasteries, priories, *prepositure*, canonries and prebends, dignities, *personatus*, administrations and offices and other ecclesiastical benefices, with and without cure, secular and regular of any orders, which he holds and shall hold in the future *in titulum* and *commendam* and otherwise by any apostolic grants and dispensations; and with annual pensions assigned and to be assigned to him on any ecclesiastical fruits etc. which he receives and shall receive in the future, committing the care, rule and administration of the monastery to him in spiritualities and temporalities. The pope's will is, however, that divine worship and the usual number of monks and ministers in the said monastery shall not, on account of this commend, be diminished; but that the customary burdens of the monastery and its convent shall be supported and that archbishop James may – the burdens in question having been supported – make disposition of the rest of the monastery's fruits etc. just as abbots of the monastery could and ought to do, alienation of its immovable goods and precious movables being however forbidden; and that archbishop James shall – before involving himself in the monastery's rule and administration in any way – take the usual oath of fealty before the bishops of Whithorn, chapel royal, Stirling[3], and of Dunblane (or one of them) in accordance with the form the pope sends enclosed (*introclusam*) under his *bulla*[4]; and the pope, by other letters of his, commands the said bishops that they (or one of them) shall receive the oath from archbishop James in his name and that of the Roman church.

Conclusions to: (i) the convent of the monastery of Kylwynyn, OSB, d. Glasgow; (ii) the vassals of the said monastery; (iii) James, king of Scots.

Romani pontificis providencia circumspecta ... The conclusions begin: (i) *Hodie cum d. f. Wilhelmus Dwuch* ... (ii), (iii) *Hodie cum d. f. Wilhelmus et cetera.*
. F. Brigon' / JoA: / . JoA: C: viij: viij: viij: Nardinus

1   spelt *Dwuch* in conclusion (i)
2   thus in MS
3   *in manibus ... Candide Case cappelle regie Sterlingen. et Dunblanen. episcoporum*
4   *Cf.* below, no. 384, note 4.

104   9 January 1514   *Reg. Lat.* 1281, fo 160[r-v]

To James, archbishop of Glasgow. Since this day William Bwuch, monk of the
monastery of B. Mary, Kylwynyn, OSB, d. Glasgow, [has ceded the above
monastery];[1] and the pope, on the advice of the cardinals, intends, also this day, to
surrogate archbishop James in and to all right in or to the [monastery's][2] rule and
administration which belonged or could have belonged in any way to William, and to
commend the monastery to archbishop James to be held, ruled and governed by him
for life – the pope hereby absolves archbishop James from any [sentences][3] of
excommunication etc. under which he may perhaps lie, so far only as regards the
taking effect of the said surrogation and commend and each of the relevant letters.
Notwithstanding etc.

Apostolice sedis circumspecta clementia ne dispositiones ...
.F. Brigon' / JoA: / JoA: xvj: Nardinus

1   MS has *et cetera* referring to the content of the principal letter (above no. 103).
2   MS: *predictis* – referring to the passage covered by *et cetera, see above*, note 1.
3   Again MS has *et cetera* – but here simply to abridge common form.

105   9 January 1514   *Reg. Lat.* 1281, fo 161[r]

To the bishops of Whithorn, chapel royal, Stirling,[1] and of Dunblane. This day the pope
– [following a dispute] between William Bwuch, monk of the monastery of B. Mary,
Kylwynyn, OSB, d. Glasgow and John Forman – [surrogated James archbishop of
Glasgow in the monastery's rule and administration and commended the monastery to
him] – [as] is [more fully] contained [in the pope's letters drawn up in that regard].[2]
Wishing to spare archbishop James, who lives in those parts, the labour and expense
of going in person to the apostolic see, the pope hereby commands the above bishops
that both or one of them, shall receive the usual oath of fealty from archbishop James
in the name of the pope and the Roman church in accordance with the form which the
pope sends enclosed (*introclusam*) under his *bulla*; and that they shall send the pope,
at once, by their own messenger, the form of oath which archbishop John takes before
them verbatim, by his letters patent, marked with his seal.

Cum nos hodie ...
F. Brigon' / JoA: / . JoA: xij: Nardinus

1   MS: *Candide Case capelle regie Sterlingen.*
2   MS: *et cetera* referring to the content of the principal letter (above, no. 103)

106[1]   **6 February 1514**   *Reg. Lat.* 1281, fos 199^v-202^v

To Thomas, elect of Lincoln. Consistorial provision of him – dean of the chapel of St
Stephen within the royal palace of Westminster (*Westmonasterii*), d. London; almoner
and counsellor of Henry, king of England; and in the priesthood – to the church of
Lincoln, vacant by the death, outside the Roman curia, of the late bishop William,
during whose rule the pope specially reserved the said church to his own disposition;
and appointment of Thomas as bishop, committing to him the care and administration
of the church in spiritualities and temporalities.

    Conclusions to (i) the chapter of the church of Lincoln; (ii) the vassals of the said
church; (iii) the clergy of the city and diocese of Lincoln; (iv) the people of the said
city and diocese; (v) the archbishop of Canterbury; (vi) Henry, king of England.

Divina disponente clementia ... The conclusions begin: (i) *Hodie ecclesie vestre* ... (ii)
Hodie ecclesie Lincolinen. tunc per obitum et cetera. (iii), (iv) *Hodie ecclesie
Lincolinen. et cetera.* (v) *Ad cumulum* ... (vi) *Gratie divine premium* ...
.J. Benzon' / JoA: / JoA: xx: x: x: x: x: x: x: Nardinus

1   The engrossments are NA, SC7 26/6 (principal letter); SC7 26/11 (conclusion to chapter); SC7 26/10 (concl.
     to vassals); SC7 26/12 (concl. to clergy); SC7 26/9 (concl. to people); and SC7 26/7 (concl. to king). *Cf.*
     L&P, F&D, I^2, no. 2629 (items 2-7); L&I p. 318.

107[1]   **6 February 1514**   *Reg. Lat.* 1281, fos 202^v-203^r

To Thomas Vlcey, dean of the chapel of St Stephen within the royal palace of
Westminster (*Westmonasterii*), d. London. Since the pope [...]^2 intends this day to
make provision of Thomas to the church of Lincoln, which is without a pastor *certo
modo*, and to appoint him bishop, he hereby absolves him from any [...]^2 sentences and
censures under which he may perhaps [lie]^2, so far only as regards the taking effect of
the said provision and appointment and each of the relevant letters. Notwithstanding
etc.

*Apostolice sedis circumspecta benignitas de statu personarum ecclesiasticarum
quarumlibet* ...
.J. Benzon / JoA: / JoA: xx: Nardi(nus)

1   The engrossment is NA, SC7 26/5; *cf. L&P, F&D,* I^2, no. 2629 (item 1); L&I p. 318.
2   This letter (at least in its enregistered form) does not wholly conform to type and is occasionally muddled.
     In particular, the passages: 'on the advice of the cardinals' and 'sentences of excommunication, suspension
     and interdict and other' – *cf.*, for instance, above, no. 90 – are wanting. Moreover, the entry has: *vel irretus*
     where 'ecclesiasticis irretitus' might be expected.

108[1]   **7 February 1514**   *Reg. Lat.* 1281, fo 203[r-v]

To Thomas, elect of Lincoln. Since the pope, on the advice of the cardinals, has
recently made provision of Thomas to the church of Lincoln, appointing him bishop,
as is more fully contained in his letters drawn up in that regard,[2] he hereby grants
faculty to Thomas – at his supplication – to receive consecration from any catholic
bishop of his choice in communion with the apostolic see, assisted by two or three
catholic bishops similarly in communion; and to the bishop concerned to consecrate
him, having first received from him in the name of the pope and the Roman church the
usual oath of fealty in accordance with the form noted in the presents. The pope
decrees, however, that if the bishop consecrates Thomas without receiving the said
oath and Thomas receives consecration they shall both be suspended automatically.
Moreover, it is the pope's will that Thomas shall send him, at once, by his own
messenger, the form of oath taken by him, verbatim, by his letters patent, marked with
his seal; and that the above shall not be to the prejudice of the archbishop of
Canterbury, to whom the aforesaid church is understood to be subject by metropolitan
law. With the form of oath.[3]

Cum nos pridem ...
.J. Benzon / JoA. / JoA: xxviij: Nardinus

1   The engrossment is NA, SC7 26/4 (marked *Concordat*); *cf. L&P, F&D*, I², no. 2635 (but 'enclosing' is
      misleading); L&I p. 318.
2   above, no. 106
3   not recited in full; *cf.* below, no. 377, notes 3 and 4.

109   **6 February 1514**   *Reg. Lat.* 1281, fo 204[r-v]

To Thomas, elect of Lincoln. Since the pope [has] this day [made provision of Thomas]
to the church of Lincoln [appointing him bishop] as is [more fully] contained [in the
pope's letters drawn up in that regard];[1] and has learned that at the time of the said
provision and appointment Thomas was holding, as he does, the deanery of the chapel
of St Stephen within the royal palace of Westminster (*Vestmonasterij*), d. London, the
pope – wishing to assist him to keep up his position in accordance with pontifical
dignity – hereby dispenses Thomas – *motu proprio* – to retain as before – even after he
has received consecration and peacefully acquired, on the strength of the said provision
and appointment, quasi-possession of the rule and administration and of the goods of
the church of Lincoln or the greater part of them – the said deanery, which is a principal
dignity in the said chapel, even if it is customarily elective and has cure of souls, (the
annual value of which and of annexes thereto does not exceed 69 pounds sterling),
together with the said church, for as long he presides over the latter; notwithstanding
etc.; decreeing that the deanery is not made vacant through the provision, appointment,
consecration and acquisition aforesaid. With the proviso that the deanery shall not, on
this account, be defrauded of due services and the cure of souls therein (if any) shall
not be neglected.

Personam tuam nobis et apostolice devotam sedi tuis exigentibus meritis paterna benivolentia prosequen(tes) illa tibi favorabiliter concedimus ...
.J. Benzon / JoA: / JoA. Lx: Nardinus

1   MS: *Cum itaque nos hodie ecclesie Lincolinen. et cetera continetur.* Supplied in much abridged form from principal letter (no. 106 above).

110   6 February 1514   *Reg. Lat.* 1281, fos 205^r-207^v

To Cornelius Okahan', elect of Raphoe. Consistorial provision as below to him – cleric of Derry (*Deren.*), BDec, and of lawful age, on whose behalf Henry, king of England, has petitioned the pope. Following the pope's reservation some time ago of provisions of all churches vacated then and in the future at the apostolic see to his own ordinance and disposition, the church of Raphoe fell vacant at the said see because Menelanus, its recent bishop, spontaneously and freely ceded the rule and administration of the said church over which he was then presiding into the pope's hands and the pope admitted the cession. On the advice of the cardinals, the pope hereby makes provision of Cornelius to the said church, reserved as above, and appoints him bishop, committing to him the care and administration of the church in spiritualities and temporalities.

Conclusions to: (i) the chapter of the church of Raphoe; (ii) the vassals of the said church; (iii) the clergy of the city and diocese of Raphoe; (iv) the people of the said city and diocese; (v) the archbishop of Armagh; (vi) Henry, king of England.

Apostolatus officium nobis meritis licet insuffien(tibus)[1] *ex alto commissum ...* The conclusions begin: (i) *Hodie ecclesie vestre Rapoten* ... (ii), (iii), (iv) *Hodie ecclesie Rapoten. et cetera.* (v) *Ad cumulum* ... (vi) *Gratie divine premium* ...
.A. De Sancto severino / JoA: / JoA: xx: x: x: x: x: x: x: Nardinus

1   *sic*

111   6 February 1514   *Reg. Lat.* 1281, fos 207^v-208^r

To Cornelius Okahan, cleric, d. [Derry].[1] Since the pope, on the advice of the cardinals, intends this day to make provision of Cornelius to the church of Raphoe, at present vacant *certo modo*, and to appoint him bishop, he hereby absolves him from any [sentences] of excommunication etc. under which he may perhaps lie, so far only as regards the taking effect of the said provision and appointment and each of the relevant letters. Notwithstanding etc.

Apostolice sedis consueta clementia ne dispositiones ...
.A. de. Sancto severino / JoA. / :JoA: xx: Nardinus

1   MS: *Daren.* (Kildare); *recte*: 'Deren.'

112   6 February 1514   *Reg. Lat.* 1281, fo 208^{r-v}

To Cornelius Okahan, cleric, d. [Derry].[1] *Motu proprio* dispensation to Cornelius –
since the pope intends this day [to provide him] to the church of Raphoe [and appoint
him bishop][2] – (who, as the pope has learned, notwithstanding a defect of birth as the
son of a professed layman and an unmarried woman, herself the offspring of an
incestuous union, has been duly marked with clerical character), to be provided to and
preside over the said church; receive its care and administration; perform and exercise
that care and administration in spiritualities and temporalities; and receive and make
use of consecration. Notwithstanding the said defect etc.

Divina supereminens[3] *largitas …*
A. de. Sancto severino / JoA. / JoA: xxx: Nardinus

1   MS: *Daren.* (Kildare); *recte*: 'Deren.'
2   MS: *et cetera. Cf.* principal letter (above, no. 110).
3   *sic*; *cf.* 'superveniens'.

113   7 February 1514   *Reg. Lat.* 1281, fos 208^v-209^v

To Cornelius, elect of Raphoe. Since the pope has recently made provision of
Cornelius to the church of Raphoe, as is [more fully] contained in his [letters drawn up
in that regard],[1] he hereby grants faculty to Cornelius[2] to receive consecration from any
catholic bishop of his choice in communion with the apostolic see, assisted by two or
three catholic bishops similarly in communion; and to the bishop concerned to
consecrate him, having first received from him in the name of the pope and the Roman
church the usual oath of fealty in accordance with the form noted in the presents. The
pope decrees, however, that if the bishop consecrates Cornelius without receiving the
said oath and Cornelius receives consecration they shall both be suspended
automatically. Moreover it is the pope's will that Cornelius shall send him, at once, by
his own messenger, the form of oath taken by him, verbatim, by his letters patent,
marked with his seal; and that the above shall not be to the prejudice of the archbishop
of Armagh, to whom the aforesaid church is understood to be subject by metropolitan
law. With the form of oath.[3]

Cum nos pridem …
.A de. Sancto severino / JoA: / JoA: xxviij: Nardinus

1   MS: *et cetera. Cf.* principal letter (above, no. 110).
2   MS wants 'tuis in hac parte supplicationibus inclinati'.
3   not recited in full; *cf.* below. no. 377.

114   24 October 1513   *Reg. Lat.* 1281, fos 211ʳ-213ʳ

To John, elect of Armagh. Consistorial provision of him – canon of the churches of
Salisbury and of Credyngton', d. Exeter; rector of the parish church of St Stephen in
Walbruk, d. London; in the priesthood and of lawful age – to the church of Armagh,
vacant by the death, outside the Roman curia, of the late archbishop Octavian, during
whose rule the said church was specially reserved by the pope to his own ordinance
and disposition, and appointment of John as archbishop, committing to him the care
and administration of the said church in spiritualities and temporalities.

   Conclusions to: (i) the chapter of the church of Armagh; (ii) the vassals of the said
church; (iii) the people of the city and diocese of Armagh; (iv) the clergy of the said
city and diocese; (v) the suffragans of the said church; (vi) Henry, king of England.

Apostolatus officium quamquam insufficient(ibus) meritis nobis ex alto commissum ...
The conclusions begin: (i) *Hodie ecclesie vestre ...* (ii), (iii), (iv), (v) *Hodie ecclesie
Armachan ...;* (vi) *Gratie divine premium ...*
.P. de. Castello. / JoA / JoA xxijij::xij xij: xij: xij: xij: xij:[1] *Nardinus*

1   The tax marks were variously altered. The first – (?)*xxiiij* – is deleted; the second – now *xxijij* – has the 'x'
     at the beginning and the 'ij' at the end written in a darker ink, probably indicating they were added later (i.e.
     to an existing 'xij'); the third, written somewhat in the margin at the start of a new line and in a darker ink,
     was also probably added later and perhaps after the 'xij' immediately before *Nardinus* was blotched.
     The alterations resulted, correctly, in one tax mark for the principal letter and a further six (each of half the
     amount for the principal letter) for the six conclusions.

115   24 October 1513   *Reg. Lat.* 1281, fo 213ᵛ

To John Ryte,[1] canon of Salisbury. Since the pope, on the advice of the cardinals,
intends this day to make provision of John[2] to the church of Armagh, vacant by the
death, outside the Roman curia, of the late archbishop Octavian, and to appoint him
archbishop, he hereby absolves John from any [sentences] of excommunication etc.
under which he may perhaps lie, so far only as regards the taking effect of the said
provision and appointment and each of the relevant letters. Notwithstanding etc.

*Apostolice sedis providentia circumspecta de statu personarum ecclesiasticarum
quarumlibet ...*
.P. de. Castello. / JoA: / JoA: xxiiij[3] *Nardinus*

1   *sic*
2   MS: *de persona*; wanting 'tua'
3   *L* deleted at start of tax mark.

116   25 October 1513   *Reg. Lat.* 1281, fo 214[r-v]

To John, elect of Armagh. Since the pope has recently made provision of John to the church of Armagh, appointing him archbishop, as is more fully contained in his letters drawn up in that regard,[1] he hereby grants faculty to John – at his supplication – to receive consecration from any catholic bishop of his choice in communion with the apostolic see, assisted by two or three catholic bishops similarly in communion; and to the bishop concerned to consecrate him, having first received from him in the name of the pope and the Roman church the usual oath of fealty in accordance with the form noted in the presents. The pope decrees, however, that if the bishop consecrates John without receiving the said oath and John receives consecration they shall both be suspended automatically. Moreover it is the pope's will that John shall send him, at once, by his own messenger, the form of oath taken by him, verbatim, by his letters patent, marked with his seal. With the form of oath.[2]

Cum nos pridem …
.P. de. Castello. / JoA: / JoA: xviij: Nardinus

1   above, no. 114
2   not recited in full; *cf.* below, no. 377.

117   24 October 1513   *Reg. Lat.* 1281, fos 214[v]-215[v]

To John, elect of Armagh. This day the pope, on the advice of the cardinals, made provision of John to the church of Armagh, appointing him archbishop, as is more fully contained in his letters drawn up in that regard.[1] Since, however, as the pope has learned, at the time of the said provision and appointment, John was holding, as he does at present, canonries of the churches of Salisbury and of Credyngton' [also spelt *Credyngto'*], d. Exeter, and the prebends of Stratton in the church of Salisbury and of Allare in the church of Credyngton', and also the parish church of St Stephen in Walbruk, d. London, whose annual values altogether do not exceed 97$\frac{1}{2}$ marks sterling, the pope – wishing to assist him to keep up his position in accordance with archiepiscopal dignity – hereby dispenses John – *motu proprio* – to retain as before – even after he has received consecration and acquired, on the strength of the said provision and appointment, peaceful quasi-possession of the rule and administration and of the goods of the said church of Armagh or the greater part of them – the canonries and prebends and the parish church aforesaid, together with the said church of Armagh, for as long as he presides over the latter; notwithstanding etc.; decreeing that the canonries and prebends and parish church are not made vacant on this account. With the proviso that the canonries and prebends and parish church shall not, on this account, be defrauded of due services and the cure of souls in the parish church shall not be neglected; but that the customary burdens of the canonries and prebends shall be supported.

Personam tuam nobis et apostolice sedi devotam tuis exigentibus meritis paterna
benivolen(tia) prosequen(tes) illa tibi favorabiliter concedimus ...
.P. de. Castello. / JoA / JoA: Lxx: Nardinus

1   above, no. 114

118[1]   **27 July 1513**   *Reg. Lat.* 1281, fo 219[r-v]

To William Graunt,[2] elect of Panados (*Panaden.*). Consistorial provision of him –
professor OESA and of theology; and in the priesthood – to the church of Panados,
vacant *certo modo*, and appointment of him as bishop, committing to him the care and
administration of the church in spiritualities and temporalities. The pope's will is,
however, that William shall – after he has had the present letters expedited – travel to
the said church and reside in person at it; and that he shall not be able to exercise the
pontifical office outside his city and diocese.

Apostolatus officium quanquam insufficien(tibus) meritis nobis ex alto commissum ...
.L. Pucius / M[3] */ JoA: L: Nardinus*[4]

1   principal letter only (i.e. no conclusions)
2   *Graut'*; the bar over the 'ut'
3   *sic*: magistral initial at start of entry that of M. de Campania; magistral subscription at end that of JoA.
     Nardinus
4   Scrawled beneath the signature is *Simili Modo* (written in another hand) deleted, initialled *JoA*

119   27 July 1513   *Reg. Lat.* 1281, fo 220[r]

To William Graunt,[1] professor OESA and of theology. Since the pope, on the advice of
the cardinals, intends this day to make provision of William to the church of Panados
(*Panaden.*), vacant *certo modo*, and to appoint him bishop, he hereby absolves William
from any [sentences] of excommunication etc. under which he may perhaps lie so far
only as regards the taking effect of the said provision and appointment and each of the
relevant letters. Notwithstanding etc.

Apostolice sedis circumspecta benignitas de statu personarum et cetera.
.L. Pucius / JoA / JoA: XX: Nardinus

1   *Graut'*

120   27 July 1513   *Reg. Lat.* 1281, fo 220[r-v]

To William, elect of Panados (*Panaden.*) Since the pope has recently made provision
of William to the church of Panados appointing him bishop, as is more fully contained
in his letters drawn up in that regard,[1] he hereby grants faculty to William – at his
supplication – to receive consecration from any catholic bishop of his choice in
communion with the apostolic see, assisted by two or three catholic bishops similarly
in communion; and to the bishop concerned to consecrate him, having first received
from him in the name of the pope and the Roman church the usual oath of fealty in
accordance with the form noted in the presents. The pope decrees, however, that if the
bishop consecrates William without receiving the said oath and William receives
consecration they shall both be suspended automatically. Moreover it is the pope's will
that William shall send him, at once, by his own messenger, the form of oath taken by
him, verbatim, by his letters patent, marked with his seal; and that the above shall not
be to the prejudice of the archbishop of Constantinople (*Constantinopolitan.*), to whom
the aforesaid church is understood to be subject by metropolitan law. With the form of
oath.[2]

Cum nos pridem[3] ...
.L. Pucius. / JoA / JoA: xxviij: Nardinus

1   above, no. 118
2   not recited in full; *cf.* below. no. 377.
3   Unquestionably drawn under the same date as the letter of provision (no. 118 above). However, as the incipit
     (the usual one for this form of letter) suggests, faculties for consecration *a quocunque* were normally granted
     under a later date (*cf.* nos. 76, 85, 91 above). At some stage, presumably, an error was made and the date
     might be argued to stand in need of correction; but without knowledge of the correct date we cannot emend
     it (*see above*, p. lxxix, note 4). The incipit is *Cum nos pridem* not *Cum nos pridie*, let alone *Cum nos hodie.*

121   27 July 1513   *Reg. Lat.* 1281, fo 221[r-v]

To William, elect of Panados (*Panaden.*). This day the pope made provision of William
to the church of Panados, which was vacant at the time, appointing him bishop, willing
inter cetera that William – as soon as he has had the apostolic letters in respect of this
provision and appointment expedited – shall go to the said church and reside in person
in it; and that he shall not be able to exercise the pontifical office outside his city and
diocese, as is more fully contained in the pope's letters drawn up in that regard.[1] Since
however, as the pope has learned, William is unable without personal inconvenience to
travel conveniently[2] to the said church, which is *in partibus infidelium*, and reside in
person in it, the pope – at his supplication – hereby indulges him not to be bound to go
to the said church or reside at it; and to be able – after he has received consecration –
to exercise the pontifical office in the city and diocese of Ely <only>[3], while required
to do so by the present and any future bishop of Ely and with the bishop's special
licence. Notwithstanding the pope's will aforesaid etc.

Sincere devotionis affectus ...
.L. Pucius / JoA / JoA: xxx: Nardinus

1   above, no. 118
2   MS: ... *absque personali incommodo commode nequeas* ...
3   *dumtaxat* inserted in margin, initialled *JoA*

122[1]   **15 April 1513**   *Reg. Lat.* 1281, fos 313[r]-314[r]

To Richard Sclater, elect of Natura (*Naturen.*). Consistorial provision of him – canon
of the monastery of Gyseburn', OSA,[2] d. York; and in the priesthood – to the church
of Natura, vacant *certo modo*, and appointment of him as bishop, committing to him
the care and administration of the said church in spiritualities and temporalities. The
pope's will is, however, that Richard shall – after he has had the present letters
expedited – go to the said church and reside in person at it; and that he shall not be able
to exercise the pontifical office outside his city and diocese.

Apostolatus officium quamquam insufficientibus meritis nobis ex alto commissum ...
L. putius / M / M L de Campania

1   Principal letter only (i.e. no conclusions).
2   Order corrected (by order of the regent of the chancery) to OSA, viz: *Benedicti*, in line, deleted and initialled
     JoA; *Augustini* inserted in margin and initialled *JoA*; with the note (in hand of Nardini): *Cass(atum) et*
     correctu(m) de man(da)to D: Regentis Nardi(nu)s

123   **15 April 1513**   *Reg. Lat.* 1281, fos 314[r]-315[r]

To Richard Sclater, canon of the monastery of Gyseburn', OSB,[1] d. York. Since the
pope, on the advice of the cardinals, intends this day to make provision of Richard to
the church of Natura (*Naturen.*), vacant *certo modo*, and to appoint him bishop, he
hereby absolves Richard from any [sentences] of excommunication etc. under which
he may perhaps lie so far only as regards the taking effect of the said provision and
appointment and each of the relevant letters. Notwithstanding etc.

Apostolice sedis circumspecta benignitas de statu personarum quarumlibet ...
L. putius / M / M xx de Campania

1   *sic* (i.e. not corrected); *cf.* previous entry, note 2.

124   15 April 1513   *Reg. Lat.* 1281, fos 315ʳ-316ʳ

To Richard, elect of Natura (*Naturen.*) This day the pope by other letters of his made provision of Richard to the church of Natura, then vacant *certo modo*, appointing him bishop, as is more fully contained in the said letters[1] in which the pope willed that Richard – as soon as he has had those letters expedited – shall go to the said church and reside in person at it; and that he shall not be able to exercise the pontifical office outside his city and diocese of Natura. Since, however, as the pope has learned, Richard is unable – without personal danger – to go to the said church (which is *in partibus infidelium*) conveniently and reside in person at it, the pope hereby indulges Richard – at his supplication – not to be bound to go to the said church and reside in person at it; and to be able – after he has received consecration – to exercise the pontifical office in the city and diocese of Durham only, if he should be required to do so by the present and any future bishop of Durham and with the bishop's special licence. Notwithstanding the pope's will aforesaid etc.

Sincere devotionis affectus …
L. putius / M / M xxx de Campania

1   above, no. 122

125   15 April 1513   *Reg. Lat.* 1281, fos 316ʳ-317ʳ

To Richard, elect of Natura (*Naturen.*), dispensation as below. The pope has this day made provision of Richard to the church of Natura appointing him bishop, vacant *certo modo*, appointing him bishop, as is more fully contained in his letters drawn up in that regard;[1] and, as the pope has learned, at the time of the said provision and appointment, Richard was holding, as he does, the perpetual vicarage of the parish church of Strancton', d. Durham. Wishing to assist Richard, (who, as the pope has also learned, receives nothing from the fruits and proceeds of the said church of Natura which is *in partibus infidelium*), to keep up his position more fittingly in accordance with pontifical dignity, the pope, *motu proprio*, hereby dispenses Richard for life to retain as before – even after he has received consecration and, on the strength of the said provision and appointment, acquired peaceful quasi-possession of the rule and administration and of the goods of the said church of Natura or the greater part of them – the said vicarage, (whose annual value does not exceed 50 marks sterling, equivalent to 150 gold ducats of the camera or thereabouts), even together with the said church of Natura, for as long as he presides over the latter. Notwithstanding etc. Decreeing that the vicarage is not made vacant by the said provision, appointment, consecration and acquisition. With the proviso that the vicarage shall not, on this account, be defrauded of due services and the cure of souls therein shall not be neglected; but that its customary burdens shall be supported.

Personam tuam nobis et apostolice sedi devotam tuis exigentibus meritis paterna

benivolentia prosequentes illa tibi favorabiliter concedimus …
L putius / M / M L de Campania

1   above, no. 122

---

126   16 April 1513   *Reg. Lat.* 1281, fos 317ᵛ-318ʳ

To Richard, elect of Natura (*Naturen.*). Since the pope has recently made provision of
Richard to the church of Natura, appointing him bishop, as is more fully contained in
his letters drawn up in that regard,[1] he hereby grants faculty to Richard – at his
supplication – to receive consecration from any catholic bishop of his choice in
communion with the apostolic see, assisted by two or three catholic bishops similarly
in communion; and to the bishop concerned to consecrate him, having first received
from him in the name of the pope and the Roman church the usual oath of fealty in
accordance with the form noted in the presents. The pope decrees, however, that if the
bishop consecrates Richard without receiving the said oath and Richard receives
consecration they shall both be suspended automatically. Moreover it is the pope's will
that Richard shall send him, at once, by his own messenger, the form of oath taken by
him, verbatim, by his letters patent, marked with his seal; and that the above shall not
be to the prejudice of the archbishop of Constantinople (*Constantinopolitan.*), to whom
the aforesaid church is understood to be subject by metropolitan law. With the form of
oath.[2]

Cum nos pridem …
L putius / M / xxviij³ de Campania

1   above, no. 122
2   not recited in full; *cf.* below, no. 377.
3   before it: *xxxv* deleted and initialled *M*

---

127   1 October 1514   *Reg. Lat.* 1282, fo 135ʳ⁻ᵛ

To Richard Edyn', rector of the parish church in Waldyngfyldemagna, d. Norwich. A
recent petition to the pope on Richard's part stated that at another time – after he had
been dispensed on apostolic authority by letters of the pope's penitentiary not to be
bound, while attending a *studium generale* and studying in the legally permitted
faculties,[1] to be promoted to any of the sacred orders, for a five-year period, calculated
from that time,[2] by reason of the above parish church, which he was then holding, or
by reason of any benefices held by him during the said five-year period, nor to be liable
to be compelled by anyone to do so against his will, provided that within the first two
years of this five-year period he has himself promoted to the subdiaconate – Julius II,
by letters of his *in forma brevis*, extended and prolonged the said two-year period,
(which Richard was then still within), for another two-year period calculated from the

end of the first two-year period, to the effect that Richard was not, in the interim,[3] bound by reason of the said church and other benefices, to be promoted to the subdiaconate and other sacred orders, even the order of the priesthood, even while [applying himself][4] to the service of Henry, king of England, or of someone else, as is said to be more fully contained in each of the letters aforesaid; and that the end of the said prolonged two-year period (within which Richard still is) is understood to be up in the near future, and he still holds the said church and does not expect to be able to be conveniently promoted to the said orders within that period. At Richard's supplication, the pope hereby further extends and prolongs the five-year period and the prolonged two-year period for another five-year period calculated from the end of the earlier five-year period, during which, while applying himself to the aforesaid service, he is not bound to be promoted to any of the said orders, nor to be liable[5] to be compelled by anyone to do so against his will, provided that he is a subdeacon within the two-year period calculated from the end of the prolonged two-year period. Notwithstanding etc.[6] Given at Nepi.

Vite ac morum honestas …
.P. Lambertus / JoA: / JoA: xx: Nardinus

1   *in facultatibus a iure permissis* – effectively, branches of learning other than civil law or medicine for the study of which indult /dispensation needed. *Cf. Decretals*, III. 50.10 (Friedberg, 660).
2   i.e. the date of the dispensation
3   i.e. in the period between the date of the brief and the end of the penitentiary's biennium
4   MS: *existen(tis)*; *recte*: 'insistendo'?
5   MS wants 'valeas' or 'possis'.
6   The notwithstanding clauses of the recited letters are incorporated by reference.

128   19 March 1513   *Reg. Lat.* 1282, fos 145[r]-146[r]

To James Denton, UID, rector of the parish church of St Olave the Martyr in Gnthwark,[1] d. Winchester, effectuation of Julius II's dispensation and indult in his favour. Some time ago, Julius II dispensed and indulged James – at his supplication – under date 10 March, fifth year [1508] to receive and retain for life, together with St Olave's, two, and without them, any three other benefices, with cure or otherwise mutually incompatible, even if dignities, *personatus*, administrations, or offices in cathedral, even metropolitan, or collegiate, churches, even if the dignities in question should be major *post pontificalem* in cathedral, even metropolitan, churches, or principal in collegiate churches, or chantries, free chapels, hospitals or annual services, usually assigned to secular clerics in title of a perpetual ecclesiastical benefice, or two of them be parish churches or their perpetual vicarages, or a combination, even if the dignities etc. should be customarily elective and have cure of souls, if he obtained them otherwise canonically; to resign them, at once or successively, simply or for exchange, as often as he pleased, and in their place retain for life up to three mutually incompatible benefices – provided that of three such benefices not more than two be parish churches or their perpetual vicarages – and retain them together for life as above; and while residing in the Roman curia or one of his benefices, with or without cure, which he has been holding or shall hold in future, or attending a *studium generale*, not to be bound to reside in the other benefices held by him at the time, nor to be liable to be compelled to do so by anyone against his will. Notwithstanding etc. With the proviso that the above church and other, even incompatible, benefices shall not, on this account, be defrauded of due services and the cure of souls in the church and (if any) the other, even incompatible, benefices aforesaid shall not be neglected; but that customary burdens of those benefices in which he does not reside shall be supported. Since, however, Julius died before his letters to this effect were drawn up, the pope hereby decrees that the present letters shall everywhere be sufficient proof of the said dispensation and indult.

Rationi congruit et cetera.
.P. Lambertus / JoA: / JoA: Cx: Nardi(nus): –

1   in the first occurrence capital *S* changed to *G* or vice versa; in the second definitely *G~*

129   19 March 1513   *Reg. Lat.* 1282, fos 247^v-249^r

To Walter Jeffrey, rector of the parish church of All Saints, Reddewell' [also spelt *Raddewell'*], d. Lincoln, effectuation of Julius II's dispensation in his favour. Some time ago, Julius II under date 9 August, second year [1505] dispensed Walter – at his supplication – to receive and retain for life, together with the above church, one, and without them, any two other benefices, etc. [as above, no. 6, to '… usually assigned to secular clerics in title of a perpetual ecclesiastical benefice'], and of lay patronage,[1] or dignities, etc. [as above, no. 6, to '… and retain them together for life as above']. Notwithstanding etc. With the proviso that the above church and other incompatible benefices should not, on this account, be defrauded of due services and the cure of souls in the above church and (if any) the other incompatible benefices should not be neglected. Since, however, Julius died before his letters to this effect were drawn up, the pope hereby decrees that the present letters shall everywhere be sufficient proof of the said dispensation.

Rationi congruit et cetera.
G de prato / JoA: / JoA: L: Nardinus

1   *sic*; unexpected in a dispensation *ad duo* for a secular cleric; common in a dispensation for a religious to hold a secular benefice

130   31 May 1513   *Reg. Lat.* 1283, fos 93^v-95^v

Perpetual union, as below. A recent petition to the pope on the part of the present abbot and the convent of the monastery of B Mary the Virgin, Oseney, at Oxford (*de Osneya iuxta Oxoniam*), OSA, d. Lincoln, stated that at another time the rectories of the parish churches of Cudgtington' and Hokenorton', said d., were united etc. to the said monastery in perpetuity and that if the perpetual vicarages of the said churches were also[1] united etc. in perpetuity to the monastery the abbot and convent would thereby obtain some relief to ease their maintenance and could more conveniently discharge the burdens incumbent on them from time to time and apply themselves to the divine will with more tranquillity. At the supplication on the part of the abbot and convent, who assert that the annual value of the vicarages together does not exceed 12 marks sterling,[2] the pope hereby[3] unites etc. the said vicarages, with all their rights and appurtenances, to the said monastery in perpetuity; to the effect that when [the present possessors][4] of the vicarages cede, even to bring about the union, die, or otherwise resign, at once or successively, the abbot and convent may, in person or by proxy, on their own authority[5], take corporal possession of the vicarages and their rights and appurtenances, and retain them in perpetuity; and they are allowed to reserve, establish and assign to the possessors of the vicarages for life – if they want to cede to bring about the union – a suitable portion from the fruits etc. of the vicarages and also, at their discretion, to reserve, establish and assign a part of the said fruits (but not more than a one third part of them) to the present bishop of Lincoln and the present[6] archdeacon of the church of Exeter (*Oxomen.*) or to any other person concerned; and they are allowed otherwise to convert the fruits etc. to their own uses and and those of the monastery and said vicarages; and they are allowed to cause the said vicarages to be served in things divine and the cure of souls of the parishioners of the said parish churches to be exercised by one of the canons of the monastery, appointable and [removable][7] at their pleasure, without licence of the local diocesan or of anyone else. Notwithstanding etc. With the proviso that the said vicarages shall not, on account of the said union etc., be defrauded of due services and the cure of souls in them shall not be neglected; but that their customary burdens shall be supported.

Ad perpetuam rei memoriam. Ad apostolice dignitatis apicem divina disponente vocati
...
.A: de Sancto seve(ri)no / M / M C de Campania

1   MS: (?)*et(iam)*; perhaps deleted
2   corrected to '12 pounds sterling' in a validation: *see* no. 11 above.
3   The chancery rule *de unionibus* made expression of the true annual values of the benefice(s) to be united and of the benefice to which it was to be united a requirement for valid union. In practice, only expression of the value of the benefice(s) to be united was required (as here), and, as usual in unions, the rule is recited (in part) at the opening of the operative part preliminary to its nullification by a 'pro expressis' clause. The recital is ordinarily ignored by the Calendar.
4   MS: *itaquod cedentibus etiam ad effectum unionis huiusmodi vel decedentibus* [illarum modernis possessoribus] *seu illas alias quomodolibet dimittentibus*; omission supplied from validation (no. 11 above)
5   MS: *nomine propria auctoritate*; *nomine*, which does not occur in the summary of this letter in the validation, looks redundant, but is not deleted.
6   MS: *dilecto filio moderno pro tempore existenti archidiacono* ...; *tempore* appears to be deleted; but not *pro* and *existenti*
7   MS: *admictendum*; *recte*: ' amovendum' (thus no. 11 above)

131   10 January 1514   *Reg. Lat.* 1283, fo 111ʳ⁻ᵛ

To Robert Boswell, perpetual vicar of the parish church of Scherborn, d. York.
Dispensation and indult etc. [as above, no. 2].

Vite ac morum honestas ...
.O. de Cesis / JoA. / JoA: L¹ Nardinus

1   *See above*, no. 13, note 2.

132   10 January 1514   *Reg. Lat.* 1283, fo 112ʳ⁻ᵛ

To John Respis, MA, rector of the parish church of BB. Peter and Paul, Eythorne, d.
Canterbury. Dispensation and indult etc. [as above, no. 2].

Litterarum scientia, vite ac morum honestas ...
.O. de Cesis. / JoA: / JoA: Lx: Nardinus

133   23 July 1513   *Reg. Lat.* 1283, fos 113ʳ-114ᵛ

To <William>¹ abbot of the monastery of B Mary, Oseney, at Oxford (*de Osneya yuxta²
Oxoniam*), OSA, d. Lincoln. Licence and faculty to him (who, as he asserts, was
dispensed by apostolic authority *inter alia* to receive, together with the above
monastery, over which he was then presiding, or together with another monastery
which he should happen to preside over in the future, one, or without them, any two
other [ecclesiastical benefices]³, with or without cure, regular of the said or any other
order, or secular, even if the regular benefices be priorships (*prioratus*), *prepositatus*,
dignities, *personatus*, administrations, or offices, or the secular benefices be parish
churches or their perpetual vicarages, chantries, free chapels, hospitals, or annual
services customarily assigned to secular clerics⁴, and even if they were in William's
patronage or another's, whatever their value, and they appertained to William's
collation or another's, and even if the said priorships, *prepositatus*, dignities,
personatus, administrations, or offices, were elective and had cure of souls, provided
they were otherwise canonically collated to him, and to retain them *in commendam* for
life, and who, under the said dispensation, holds *in commendam* the perpetual vicarage
of the parish church of St Mary Magdalen, vill of Oxford [*Oxomen.*] said d.) – at his
supplication – of resigning, outside the Roman curia and without the licence of the
apostolic see and of anyone else, the said vicarage and every other ecclesiastical
benefice, with or without cure, secular and regular of the said or any other order, which
he happens to hold at the time, *in titulum* or *in commendam*, under the said or any other
apostolic dispensation, at once or successively, simply or in exchange for another or
other, similar or dissimilar, ecclesiastical benefices with those wishing to exchange

with him, in which, however, there shall be no unlawful agreement or simony, into the hands of any local ordinaries or canons of metropolitan or other cathedral [churches] or of other ecclesiastical dignitaries, chosen by William for the purpose; and of ceding the commends of the vicarage and other benefices held by him from time to time *in commendam*; and licence and faculty to the ordinaries, canons, and ecclesiastical dignitaries: of receiving and admitting, on apostolic authority, outside the Roman curia, the said resignations, [made] simply or for exchange, and the said cessions of commends; of collating, on the same authority, to suitable persons to be nominated by William or his proctor, even to persons who hold and expect any ecclesiastical benefices, the benefices which William has resigned simply or whose commends he has ceded, and of making provision of them; of collating, on the same authority, the benefices resigned by William for exchange to the persons exchanging with him and the benefices resigned (but only for exchange) by the persons exchanging with him – even if they are qualified as above (provided they are not major dignities *post pontificales* in <cathedral>[5] even metropolitan churches or principal ones in collegiate churches, and the benefices of the persons exchanging with William who do not have a similar faculty are not generally reserved to apostolic disposition or affected) – to William, to be retained by him *in titulum* or *in commendam* for life, in accordance with the tenor of the dispensations[6] granted to him, just as he used to hold the benefices then resigned by him or whose commends he ceded, and of making provision of them; of reserving, establishing, and assigning, by the said authority – so that William does not suffer excessive loss through ceding the commend of the said vicarage – an annual pension on the fruits etc of the vicarage (provided it does not exceed a third part of them) payable in full [to William], each year, by him to whom provision of the vicarage happens to be made when it is vacant by William's cession and the commend stops and by his successors holding the vicarage from time to time, at the terms and places then to be established and under the ecclesiastical censures, sentences and pains customarily included in such things; and of doing and executing all other things which are necessary or in any way opportune in the above matters and in connection with them. Notwithstanding, etc. It is the pope's will, however, that if the fruits etc of the vicarage and of other benefices whose commends William cedes and also of individual benefices destined to be resigned [by him] simply, exceed an annual value of 24 gold florins of the camera, the persons collating them and those to whom they are collated, or – if the resignations are made by reason of exchange and their fruits etc and the fruits etc of the benefices collated to William in exchange are unequal and there is an excess, even if the difference does not exceed 24 like florins – the said collators and those to whom the benefices of greater value have been collated, are to certify the names and surnames of the persons, the names of the benefices, and the dates the collations were made, to the personnel of the apostolic camera or the collectors or sub-collectors of the fruits and proceeds due to the camera appointed from time to time in those parts, and they must do so within one month if the collations have been made on this side of the Alps, within three months if made beyond the Alps, in accordance with certain letters of Sixtus IV and Innocent VIII published in this connection;[7] otherwise the benefices thus collated shall be deemed to be vacant automatically.

Personam tuam nobis et apostolice sedi devotam ...

.P. Lambertus / JoA / JoA: Lxv: Nardinus

1   *Willelmo* inserted in margin, initialled *JoA*
2   *sic*
3   MS wants 'beneficia ecclesiastica'.
4   'in titulum perpetui beneficii ecclesiastici' does not occur.
5   *in cathedralibus* inserted in margin, initialled *JoA*; insertion in same hand as initial
6   MS: *dispensationem*; *recte*: 'dispensationum'
7   i.e. *Ad perpetuam rei memoriam. Sicut bonus pastor* of Sixtus, dated 27 Sept 1480 (published in the chancery
     on 27 Sept 1480 and in the *audientia litterarum contradictarum* on 10 Oct 1480 [BAV, Barb. Lat. 2825, pp.
     466-470]); and *Ad perpetuam rei memoriam. Sicut bonus pastor* of Innocent, dated 27 Sept 1491 (published
     in the chancery on 6 Oct 1491[ibid., pp. 515-517]).

134   25 March 1513   *Reg. Lat.* 1283, fos 279r-280v;253[r-v1]

To the prior of the priory of Bernewell', d. Ely, Henry Mataell', canon of the church of
York, and Edward Wnderuuode, canon of the church of London, mandate in favour of
John Barton', prior of the monastery customarily governed by a prior of St Nicholas,
Burstogh', OSA, d. Coventry and Lichfield. A recent petition to the pope on John's part
stated that although, some time ago, he had acquired the priorship of the monastery,
which had been canonically collated to him when it was vacant *certo modo*, and was
holding and possessing it peacefully and quietly, as he had for some time, and had
never committed anything on account of which he ought to be deprived, Geoffrey,
bishop of Coventry and Lichfield, unaccountably obstructed him contrary to justice so
that he was unable to peacefully possess the priory and in this connection bishop
Geoffrey variously molested and disturbed him and *de facto* often threatened that he
would deprive John of the priory; that prior John – feeling *inter alia* unduly aggrieved
as a result of these and certain other sufficient gravamina then expressed inflicted *de
facto* and threatened by bishop Geoffrey – appealed to William, archbishop of
Canterbury, primate of all England and legate born of the apostolic see in those parts;
that bishop Geoffrey – proceeding wrongly to further matters in the case regardless of
the appeal of which he was not ignorant and while prior John was still well within the
time for prosecuting it – promulgated (albeit *de facto* and temerariously attempting) an
unjust, definitive (as he said) sentence by which he *inter alia* deprived John of the
priory; that in the cause of the said appeal and over bishop Geoffrey's attempts
(*attemptatis*) after it had been lodged and their revocation prior John caused bishop
Geoffrey to be summoned to judgement before Cuthbert Tu'nstall', auditor of causes
of the archiepiscopal court of Canterbury, as the local metropolitan court[2]; that
although the said auditor had by his letters correctly inhibited bishop Geoffrey from
proceeding further against prior John in the above connection while the suit was thus
pending, the bishop – scornful of the inhibition and other things above and
notwithstanding them – nevertheless *de facto* collated and made provision of the said
priory, as if it was vacant by deprivation (as he said), to Robert Harwy[3], who bears
himself as a canon of the said order; and that although lawful requests had been made
on prior John's part at a suitable time and place the aforesaid auditor unlawfully
refused to proceed to further matters in the cause, to administer justice to John in

connection with the above, or to cause delivery of the priory's fruits to be made to prior John (as he was bound to do), for John's sustentation and for the prosecution of the suit, while it lasted; that prior John, feeling *inter alia* unduly aggrieved thereby, appealed to the apostolic see and impetrated apostolic letters concerning this appeal and the principal matter to the bishop of Norwich, the archdeacon of the church of Worcester, and the dean of the church of Leicester (*Leicestrie*), d. Lincoln, their proper names not expressed, with the clause 'that they or two or one of them should proceed in the causes of the later appeal and of the principal matter'; that after the bishop of Lincoln had, at the instance of bishop Geoffrey, been joined to the cause for decision, so that the trial should proceed without suspicion, and after prior John had, on the strength of the said letters, caused bishop Geoffrey and Robert Harwy to be summoned to judgement in the cause of the later appeal before Thomas Alcok, UID, archdeacon of the church of Worcester, and after archdeacon Thomas had, in the cause of the later appeal, proceeded to several acts (short, however, of a conclusion) the bishop of Lincoln – who was supporting the cause almost as if it was his own – committed his powers, jointly and severally, to John Veysey[4], dean, and Richard Thollet, canon, of the church of Exeter, Henry Wilcok, canon of the church of Lincoln, John Wardrop' [also spelt *Wardrop, Vardrop*], canon of the church of Exeter or other cathedral church, and Thomas Haniball', vicar general in spirituals of the bishop of Worcester or official of Worcester, to the end that they (or he) should proceed in the cause of the later appeal together with archdeacon Thomas; that although archdeacon Thomas and, by pretext of this commission, Thomas, the vicar or official, and John Wardrop', the canon, had assigned to the said parties a certain term then expressed for proceeding further in the cause of the later appeal, Thomas, the vicar or official, and John Wardrop', the canon, nevertheless, when the term which had been thus assigned came about, maliciously absented themselves from the place appointed by them for the decision of the cause and the administration of justice to the parties, thereby purposely protracting the cause, no other suitable place having been assigned for this to the parties, to the considerable prejudice of prior John; and that, as the said petition added, canon John Wardrop' has removed himself by thirty miles (or thereabouts) from the place thus appointed, as above, and has been away from it for some time and it is feared that he is still, it is said, absent. At prior John's supplication to the pope to call in the cause of the later appeal and the other causes from the archdeacon, canon John Wardrop', Thomas the vicar or official, and other judges aforesaid; to commit them to some upright men in those parts, to be resumed in due state and, with all their incident, dependent, emergent, and connected matters, heard further, examined, and duly determined, even summarily, simply, and informally, without the formality and formulas of legal proceedings, factual accuracy alone being considered (*sola facti veritate inspecta*) and to order that the archdeacon, Thomas the vicar or official, canon John Wardrop', and any other judges and persons, be inhibited, as often as necessary, even under ecclesiastical censures, the pope – hereby calling in the said causes from the archdeacon, Thomas the vicar or official, canon John Wardrop', and the other judges aforesaid, and deeming their states to be sufficiently expressed by the presents – hereby commands that the above three, (or two, or one of them), having summoned bishop Geoffrey and Robert Harwy and others concerned and having inhibited the archdeacon, Thomas the vicar or official, canon John Wardrop', and any other judges and persons, as often as necessary and inasmuch as it is just, even under ecclesiastical censures, resuming the causes in due state, shall, on the pope's authority, hear the causes, with all their incident, dependent, emergent, and connected matters, even summarily, etc, and, having heard both sides, taking cognizance even of the principal matter, duly determine and decide them, causing by ecclesiastical censure what they have decreed to be strictly observed, and moreover compel witnesses, etc. Notwithstanding etc.

Humilibus supplicum votis libenter annuimus ...
Jo: Copis / A / A. xx Colotius: –

1   The entry has been misbound.
2   MS: ... *auditore causarum curie archiepiscopalis qua*(m) *Canthurien. loci metropolitice ...*
3   written *HarWij*
4   written *Veijseij*

135   19 March 1513   *Reg. Lat.* 1283, fos 271ʳ-272ʳ

To the provost of the church of Dunbertan', d. Glasgow, and Patrick Elphynstoum', canon of the church of Glasgow, mandate in favour of Margaret Dowglas, noblewoman, damsel of the place of Carlile, d. Glasgow. A recent petition to the pope on Margaret's part stated that, at another time, when a law-suit had arisen, not by apostolic delegation, concerning certain rights of jurisdiction or sums of money, goods, and other things then expressed, between herself and certain others, her co-litigants, on the one side, and the nobleman William, temporal lord of the said place, on the other, before the official of Glasgow, a competent judge for this, the official, proceeding correctly in the case, promulgated an absolutory sentence in favour of the co-litigants and against William, from which on William's part – falsely alleging that the sentence was unjust – appeal was made to the apostolic see and in connection with the appeal William impetrated[1] apostolic letters under a certain form to the archdeacon of Lothian (*Laudomie*) of the church of St Andrews, his proper name not expressed, and certain other colleagues of his in that regard, and by pretext of them he caused Margaret to be summoned to judgement in the cause of the appeal before William Wawane, canon of Aberdeen, to whom, by pretext of the letters and commission, the archdeacon had committed his powers in the matter; and canon William, proceeding wrongly in the case, promulgated a certain unjust sentence by which he revoked the aforesaid sentence,[2] from which on Margaret's part appeal was made to the apostolic see. At the supplication to the pope to order that Margaret be absolved *ad cautelam* from the sentence of excommunication and other censures and pains by which she is perhaps deemed bound by reason of the foregoing and also to commit to some upright men in those parts the causes: of the aforesaid latest appeal and of anything attempted and innovated after and against it; of the nullity of the said sentence and of the whole process had by canon William concerning this matter; of each and every other thing done in any way by canon William and any other judges and persons to Margaret's [prejudice][3] in the above connection; and of the principal matter, the pope <hereby> commands that <the above two>[4] (or one of them), having summoned the nobleman

William and others concerned, shall, on the pope's authority, for this once only, bestow
on Margaret, if she so requests, the benefit of absolution *ad cautelam* from the said
sentence of excommunication and the other sentences, censures, and pains, if and as it
is just, having, however, first received from her suitable security in connection with
that for which she is deemed excommunicate and caught by the other sentences,
censures and pains, that if they find the said sentence of excommunication, etc to have
been justly inflicted on her she will obey their mandates and those of the church; and
as to the other things, having heard both sides, lawfully taking cognizance even of the
principal matter, [shall decree what is just, without appeal, causing by ecclesiastical
censure what they have decreed to be strictly] observed;⁵ [and moreover compel]
witnesses, etc. Notwithstanding etc.

Humilibus et cetera.
f. Bregion / M / M xij de Campania

1   MS: (?) *impetrarunt*; *recte*: 'impetravit'
2   required by the context; but MS muddled: *quamdam per (?)quadam sententiam predictas revocavit*
    sententiam promulgarunt iniquas
3   MS: *precedent'*; *recte*: 'preiudicium'
4   *discretioni vestre per apostolica scripta* inserted in margin; the insertion initialled *M*
5   MS: *quod iustum fuerit et cetera observari*. Supplied from common form.

136   19 March 1513   *Reg. Lat.* 1283, fos 272ʳ-273ᵛ

To Adam Coguaone and George de Montgu'ri, canons of the church of Glasgow, and
William Vaven'¹, canon of the church of Aberdeen, mandate in favour of the nobleman
Adam Creichtoini of Ravent², knight, and the noblewoman Jonet³ Lile, damsel, relict
of the late James Ogilvi [also spelt *Ogilbi*] of Arlit, knight, d. St Andrews, executors of
the testament or last will of the said James, co-litigants in this regard. A recent petition
to the pope on the part of the co-litigants stated that some time ago, when a law-suit
had arisen, not by apostolic delegation, between the said executors on the one side and
the noblemen Thomas Ogilvi, knight, and Malcolm (*Marchu' Coluu'*) Ogilvi, laymen,
said d., joint parties in that regard, on the other, over the validity or invalidity of the
said testament, sums of money, goods, and other matters then expressed, before the
then official of St Andrews, who was, it was said, a competent judge for this, the said
official – proceeding wrongly in the case – promulgated a definitive sentence, as he
said, in favour of the joint parties and against the co-litigants, from which appeal was
made on the co-litigants' part to the apostolic see; but since the co- litigants were
prevented by lawful impediment from prosecuting their appeal within the due time and
had not prosecuted it, the joint parties – falsely alleging that on account of its non-
prosecution the aforesaid appeal had been abandoned and that the said sentence ought
to be put into execution – sued the co- litigants before the aforesaid official over the
desertion of the appeal; and the official – having recklessly rejected certain objections
(which in law ought to have been admitted) put before him on the part of the co-
litigants at a suitable time [and place]⁴ and proceeding wrongly in the case of the

appeal desertion, promulgated[5] an unjust interlocutory sentence by which he declared that the said appeal had been and was abandoned, from which on the part of the co-litigants (who felt *inter alia* unduly aggrieved thereby) appeal was made to the apostolic see; but the said official – regardless of the said appeal of which he was not ignorant and while the co-litigants were still well within the time for prosecuting it – recklessly [proceeded][6] to further matters and perhaps to the execution of the sentences inflicted by him, attempting temerariously and *de facto*; wherefore on the part of the co- litigants (who felt *inter alia* unduly aggrieved thereby) appeal was made to the apostolic see. At the supplication to the pope to order that the said co-litigants be absolved *ad cautelam* from sentence of excommunication and other sentences, censures, and pains by which they are perhaps deemed bound by the said official on the above occasion and also to commit to some upright men in those parts the causes: of the individual appeals and of anything attempted and innovated after and against them and each one of them; of the nullity of the said sentences and of the whole process conducted in this connection by the said official, and of each and every other thing done in any way by the official and any other judges and persons to the prejudice of the co-litigants in connection with the above; and of the whole principal matter, the pope [hereby] commands that the above three (or two or one of them), having summoned the said joint parties and others concerned, shall, on the pope's authority, for this once only, bestow on the said co-litigants, if they so request, the benefit of absolution *ad cautelam* from the said sentence of excommunication and other sentences, censures, and pains, if and as it is just, having, however, first received from them suitable security in respect of that for which they are deemed caught by the said sentence of excommunication, etc, that if the above find that the sentence of excommunication and other censures and pains were justly inflicted on them, they will obey the mandates of the above and those of the church; as to the other things, if what is stated about the said impediment is true, having heard[7] both sides, taking cognizance even of the principal matter, [shall decree] what is just, [without appeal, causing what they have decreed to be strictly] observed;[8] [and moreover compel] witnesses, etc. Notwithstanding the said lapse of time, etc.

Humilibus et cetera.
f. bregion / M / M xvj de Campania

1   or *Raven'*: initial letter changed by overwriting
2   or *Vavent*: initial letter changed by overwriting
3   sympathetic reading; MS: *Jontte* (for 'Jonete')
4   MS: *congr(uo) liceret tempore*; *recte*: 'congruis loco et tempore'?
5   MS: *promulgarunt*; *recte*: 'promulgavit'
6   wanting in MS
7   MS: *auditoribus*; *recte*: 'auditis'
8   MS: *quod iustum fuerit et cetera observari*. Supplied from common form.

137   19 March 1513   *Reg. Lat.* 1283, fos 273ᵛ-275ʳ

To the abbot of the monastery of Balmormotht[1], d. St Andrews, David Spens, canon of
the church of Moray, and William Yslande[2], canon of the church of Dunkeld, mandate
in favour of James Stevont, canon of Aberdeen. A recent petition to the pope on James'
part stated that some time ago – after he had canonically acquired the canonry and the
prebend, called the rectory, of Kynkel, of the church of Aberdeen, which were [then][3]
vacant by the death, outside the Roman curia, of the late Adam Georddunn, canon, of
the said church – he sued <Patrick>[4] *etiam*[5] Gordown', layman of Aberdeen, who had
accepted the executorship of the testament or last will of the said Adam, before the late
John Ӡonug', canon of Dunkeld –subconservator appointed [by a certain][6] conservator
(himself appointed by letters of the apostolic see) of the privileges and rights granted
to all the scholars [and][7] rectors of the *studium* of the city of St Andrews (among whom
James was then numbered) against those molesting <and>[8] damaging[9] them in respect
of [their][10] interests and goods (*in rebus et bonis*) and having, by the said letters, special
power of taking cognizance even of those matters which [require][11] judicial
investigation – suing him on the strength of the said letters and appointment, praying
inter alia that Patrick – who was refusing to hand over and assign to him Adam's
movable goods, called utensils or household goods, or to cause provision to be made
of the other goods left by Adam at the time of his death, or to cause the churches of the
prebend and annexes and their houses and buildings in need of repair to be thoroughly
(*in eorum structuris et edificiis*) repaired and restored, or to cause provision to be made
of the usual ornaments for the said churches, even though[12] by ancient, approved, and
hitherto peacefully observed custom Patrick was bound to hand over and assign the
movable goods, repair and restore the churches, houses, and buildings, and provide the
said ornaments[13] – be excommunicated and coerced and compelled to hand over and
assign to him the moveable goods, repair and restore the said churches and houses, and
provide the said ornaments for the churches; and that when John the subconservator
had duly proceeded in the cause to several acts then expressed and appeal had been
made to the apostolic see on the part of Patrick (who falsely alleged that he was unduly
aggrieved by [certain][14] gravamina inflicted on him, [as][15] he said, by canon John),
Patrick impetrated apostolic letters under a certain form <in connection with>[16] his
appeal to Robert Elpainstone', Alexander Galtoluar [also spelt *Gallowai*[17]], and
William Elpainstone', canons of the church of Aberdeen, and he caused James to be
summoned to trial before Alexander Caluanen' [also spelt *Cullanen', Cullonen'*],
canon of the church of Aberdeen, and Alexander Hai, canon of the church of Moray (to
whom, [as][18] he said, the aforesaid Robert, Alexander Galtoluar, and William, had fully
committed their powers in this matter, causing him to be summoned to trial by pretext
of the said letters and commission; and that Alexander Caluanen' and Alexander Hai,
proceeding wrongly in the cause, promulgated an <unjust>[19], definitive (as was said)
sentence in favour of Patrick and against James, from which, on James' part, appeal
was made to the apostolic see. At James' supplication to the pope to commit to some
upright men in those parts the causes: of the latest appeal and of anything attempted
and innovated after and against it; of the nullity of the sentence inflicted by Alexander
Caluanen' and Alexander Hai, and of the whole process conducted by them concerning
this matter, and of each and every other thing done in any way by them and by any

other judges and persons to James' prejudice in connection with the above; and of the principal matter, the pope [hereby] commands that the above three (or two, or one of them), having summoned Patrick and others concerned and having heard both sides, taking cognizance even of the principal matter, shall decree what is just, without appeal, causing [by ecclesiastical censure what they have decreed to be strictly] observed,[20] [and moreover compel] witnesses, etc. Notwithstanding etc.

Humilibus et cetera.
f. bregion / M / M xij de Campania

1   final letter(s) altered and uncertain: reading 't' written over 'ar' or possibly 'er'
2   in the line after it: *Islande* (or possibly *Irlande*) deleted
3   MS: *nunc*; *recte*: 'tunc'
4   in the line *Franciscum* deleted; *Patricium* inserted in the margin (the insertion initialled *M*)
5   despite the difference of spelling, implies that Patrick has the same surname as Adam
6   in the line a word (or words) deleted and now illegible; in the margin *asserto*; *recte*: 'a certo'; the marginal insertion initialled *M*. *Cf.* note 14 below.
7   MS: *scolaribus rectoribus*; or 'scholar-rectors'
8   *et* inserted in margin; not initialled
9   MS: *inferentes ... molestias <et> recturas* (*recte*: 'iacturas')
10   MS wants 'suis'; but implied.
11   MS: *regunt recte*: ' requirunt'
12   MS: *liceat*; *recte*: 'licet'
13   order of MS text (which is somewhat tortuous) not followed here; the complaint against Patrick is stated before mention of the subconservator to whom it was made.
14   MS: *assertis*; *recte*: 'a certis'. *Cf.* note 6 above.
15   MS wants 'ut'
16   *super* inserted in margin, initialled *M*
17   ending altered and uncertain
18   MS: *et*; *recte*: 'ut'
19   *iniquam* inserted in margin, initialled *M*
20   MS: *facientes et cetera observari*. Supplied from common form.

138   19 March 1513   *Reg. Lat.* 1283, fo 332[r-v]

To Richard Spynnell',[1] brother of the hospital of St Catherine[2] by the tower, London, OSA, d. London. Dispensation – at his supplication – to him, who, as he asserts, is expressly professed of the above order,[3] to receive and retain any benefice, with or without cure, usually held by secular clerics, etc. [as above, no. 43, to '… receive and retain another, similar or dissimilar, benefice, with or without cure'], usually held by secular clerics.[4] Notwithstanding etc.

Religionis zelus, vite ac morum honestas ...
A. de Alvaroctis / . A. / A xL. Colotius: –

1   written *Spijnnell'*
2   MS: *Sancte Catherine iuxta Turrim*
3   This information comes from a notwithstanding clause.
4   Of course, this latter phrase reflects a variation from no. 43 merely in the formulation – not the tenor – of the Latin.

139   5 May 1513   *Reg. Lat.* 1284, fos 96ᵛ-97ᵛ

To John, abbot of the monastery of B. Mary the Virgin, *de Regali Loco* [Rewley] at
Oxford (*iuxta Oxonia(m)*), OCist, d. Lincoln. Dispensation – at his supplication – to
receive and retain *in commendam* for life together with the above monastery over
which he presides, or with any other monastery over which he may preside in the
future, any two regular or secular benefices, with or without cure, of the above or any
other order, even the Cluniac, even if the regular benefices should be priories,
prepositur[e],[1] *prepositatus*, dignities, *personatus*, administrations or offices[2] and the
secular benefices should be parish churches or their perpetual vicarages, or chantries,
free chapels, hospitals or annual services usually assigned to secular clerics in title of
a perpetual ecclesiastical benefice, and the secular as well as the regular benefices
should be of lay patronage and of whatsoever tax or annual value, and even if the
priories etc. should be customarily elective and have cure of souls, if he obtains them
otherwise canonically, to resign them, at once or successively, simply or for exchange,
as often as he pleases, and cede the commend, and in their place receive up to two
other, similar or dissimilar, regular or secular, benefices, with or without cure, of the
above Cistercian or any other order – provided that the regular benefices be not
conventual dignities or claustral offices – and retain them *in commendam* for life, even
together with the said monastery, as above; he may – due and customary burdens of
these benefices having been supported – make disposition of the rest of their fruits etc.
just as those holding them *in titulum* could and ought to do, alienation of the
immovable goods and precious movables of the said benefices being however
forbidden. Notwithstanding etc. With the proviso that these benefices shall not, on this
account, be defrauded of due services and the cure of souls in them (if any) shall not
be neglected; but that their aforesaid burdens shall be supported.

*Personam tuam nobis et apostolice sedi devotam tuis exigentibus meritis paterna
benevolentia prosequentes illa tibi libenter concedimus ...*
P. lambert(us) / M / M C de Campania

1   MS: *prepositura*; *recte*: '-e'
2   changed to *officia* from *officiu(m)*; *cf.* note 1.

140   11 April 1513   *Reg. Lat.* 1284, fos 105ᵛ-108ᵛ

To James Carnythell, cleric, d. Glasgow, reservation, constitution and assignment of a
pension, as below. A recent petition to the pope on James's part stated that at another
time he had spontaneously and freely resigned, outside the Roman curia, the perpetual
vicarage, called *pensionaria*, in the church of Carnvo,[1] d. Glasgow, which he was then
holding, into the hands of its ordinary collator, who, after admitting this resignation
outside the said curia by ordinary authority, collated and provided the vicarage, then
vacant through this resignation, by the same authority, to John Weyr, perpetual vicar in
the said church, and John acquired the vicarage by virtue of this collation and

provision. Lest James should suffer excessive loss by this resignation, the pope hereby reserves, constitutes and assigns an annual pension of 10 marks Scots on the fruits etc. (of which this pension does not, as James asserts, exceed one half) of the perpetual ecclesiastical benefice, called prebend, of Carnvo, in the church of Glasgow, which Alexander Inglis, treasurer of the church of Glasgow, holds canonically, payable in full to James for life, or to his specially mandated proctor, by Alexander (whose express assent to this is given – in view of the fact that, as James also asserts, another annual pension of 10 pounds Scots reserved on the same fruits at another time for the said John by apostolic authority has been nullified and extinguished by the same apostolic authority with John's consent – through Leonard Bertini, scriptor and papal familiar, Alexander's specially appointed proctor) and by his successors as holders of the said benefice at the time, each year, one half on the Nativity of B. John the Baptist and the other on that of Jesus Christ. With decree that if Alexander (or any one of his successors) fails to make payment on the said feasts or at least within the thirty days immediately following, he shall, after this time has elapsed, incur sentence of excommunication, from which he cannot be absolved, except on the point of death, until he shall have made satisfaction in full or reached agreement in respect of it with James (or his proctor) and, if he remains obdurate under that sentence for a further six months, he shall thereupon be deprived in perpetuity of the said benefice, which shall be deemed vacant automatically. Notwithstanding etc.

Executory to the bishops of Cavaillon and Agrigento and the official of Glasgow, or two or one of them, acting in person or by proxy.

Vite ac morum honestas ... The executory begins: *Hodie dilecto filio Jacobo Carnythell* ...
P. lambertus; G. prato[2] */ C / C. xij x Barotius*

1   The first occurrence readable either as *Carnwo* or *Carnvo*; but the second (and only other occurrence in the
     principal letter) is clearly *Carnvo*; spelt *Carnwo* in the executory.
2   The two names occur together at the top of the entry to the right.

141   5 June 1513   *Reg. Lat.* 1284, fos 129ᵛ-134ʳ

To the abbot of the monastery of B. Mary, Monasteranenagh (*de Magio*), d. Limerick, mandate in favour of Donat Olecluir [also spelt *Olecluyr, Olecluer*[1]], monk of the monastery of St. Mary, *de Legedei* [Abbeyleix], OCist., d. Leighlin. The pope has learned that the above monastery of St Mary, *de Legedei*, and the <perpetual vicarages>[2] of the parish churches of the places of Tymolk[3] [also spelt *Tymoik*] *alias de Villafontis*, and of Scrabo[4] *alias* Syan and of Kilcolmonan[5] [also spelt *Kilcolmavan*] and Disseacthenis d. Leighlin, are vacant *certo modo* at present and have been vacant for so long that by the canonical sanctions the provision of the monastery and by the Lateran statutes the collation of the perpetual vicarages have lawfully devolved on the apostolic see, although Donat Omorro has detained the monastery, Malachy Omorro the vicarage of Tymolk, John Olecluir that of Scrabo, David Olecluir that of Kilcolmonan and Patrick Olecluir that of Disseacthenis – bearing themselves as priests

– with no title or support of law, of their own temerity and *de facto*, for a certain time, as they do. A petition on the part of Donat Olecluir was made recently to the pope to unite etc.[6] the said vicarages to the above monastery, for as long as he presides over the monastery (in the event of his provision thereto by virtue of the presents and his appointment as abbot) – asserting that recently (after he had, at another time, contracted marriage *per verba de presenti* with a virgin, prohibited to him by law (*a iure*), and had, perhaps, consummated the marriage by connexion, and afterwards, having been separated from her by a judge of the church, when the country (*patria*) was invaded by enemies, for the necessary defence of himself and the country he had been present at a conflict in which – to avoid danger of death and for the country's necessary defence – he had killed and, perhaps, mutilated some men, and then had been present at other wars and conflicts in which several men had been mutilated and others indeed killed, although he had not killed or mutilated anyone with his own hands and had not lent counsel, help or favour for this) he had been absolved by apostolic authority from any [sentences] of excommunication and other censures and pains, even ecclesiastical, if he incurred any on account of the foregoing, and from the crimes and excesses of the homicides and mutilations; and that, by the said authority, he had been dispensed for irregularity contracted by him on account of the foregoing and to be promoted – the foregoing notwithstanding – to all, even sacred, orders and the order of the priesthood, and – after promotion – to minister in them, even as a minister before the altar, and to receive and retain any compatible benefices conferred on him canonically; and that he had been rehabilitated on account of all disability and infamy arising from the foregoing; and that the annual value of the above monastery does not exceed 24, and of the vicarages together, 32, marks sterling. Wishing to provide the monastery – lest it be exposed to the inconvenience of a long vacation – with a capable and suitable person to rule and direct it, and not having certain knowledge[7] of the merits and suitability of Donat Olecluir (who, as he asserts, is expressly professed of the order), the pope hereby commands [the above abbot],[8] if, having summoned Donat Omorro, Malachy, John, and also David and Patrick[9] and others concerned, he finds the said monastery and vicarages to be vacant (howsoever etc.), and Donat Olecluir fit to rule the monastery, having diligently informed himself in this regard – concerning which the pope burdens the abbot's conscience – make provision of him to the monastery (which is not consistorial) and appoint him abbot, committing the care, rule and administration of the monastery to him in spiritualities and temporalities, and causing him to be given due obedience and reverence by the convent and customary services and rights by the vassals and other subjects of the monastery; and to unite etc. the vicarages (even if specially reserved etc.), with all their rights and appurtenances, to the monastery, for as long as Donat Olecluir presides over the monastery (in the event of his provision and appointment to it); having removed Donat Omorro, Malachy, John, David, Patrick and any other unlawful detainers from them; to the effect that Donat Olecluir may, on his own authority, in person or by proxy, take corporal possession of the vicarages and rights and appurtenances aforesaid and retain possession for as long as he presides over the monastery as above; and convert their fruits etc. to his own uses and those of the monastery and vicarages aforesaid, without licence of the local diocesan or of anyone else. [Curbing] gainsayers etc. Notwithstanding etc. Also the pope hereby grants that Donat Olecluir may – in the event of his provision and appointment as above – receive blessing from any catholic bishop of his choice in communion with the apostolic see; and that the bishop concerned may bestow it. The pope's will is, however, that the said vicarages shall not, on account of this union etc., be defrauded of due services and the cure of souls in them shall not be neglected, but that their customary burdens shall be supported; and that on the death of Donat Olecluir or his resignation etc. of the said monastery this union etc. shall be dissolved and be so deemed and the vicarages shall revert to their original condition automatically.

Sollicite considerationis indagine …
P. lambertus / M / M L quarto decimo k(a)l(endas) Julij an(n)o [18 June 1513], *de Campania*

1   or possibly -*uir*
2   *perpetue vicarie* inserted in margin; *JoA* before it; *aditum de ma(n)dato d(omi)ni Regentis de nardinis* after
     it. The insertion is in the hand of Nardini.
3   The 'l' is written over a 'y'.
4   second occurrence possibly spelt *Scrubo*
5   the first 'o' changed from a (?)'b'; the second doubtful: perhaps an 'a'
6   MS: *uniretur annecteretur*; wanting 'et incorporaretur'. Such small-scale deviations from common form and
     other textual oddities (and also many small-scale deletions) occur throughout the entry.
7   assuming standard formulary: 'cert[a]m [notitiam] non habentes' by reading *certam* (rather than 'certum')
     and supplying 'notitiam'.
8   MS: *discretioni et cetera mandamus*

142   1 April 1513   *Reg. Lat.* 1284, fos 217ʳ-219ᵛ

To the treasurer and William Nagill, canon, of the church of Limerick, and the official of Limerick, mandate in favour of Thomas Offlayff, canon of the monastery, usually governed by a prior, of B. Mary, Ragell,¹ OSA, d. Limerick, (who, as he asserts, is expressly professed of the said order and, notwithstanding a defect of birth as the son of a priest and an unmarried woman, has been duly promoted to all, even sacred, orders). The pope has learned that the priory of the said monastery is vacant *certo modo* at present and has been vacant for so long that by the Lateran statutes its collation has lawfully devolved on the apostolic see, although Thomas Okeyth, who bears himself as a canon of the monastery, has detained it, with no title or support of law, of his own temerity and *de facto*, for a certain time, as he does. He hereby commands that the above three (or two or one of them), if, having summoned Thomas Okeyth and others concerned, they find the priory, which is conventual and whose annual value does not exceed 12 marks sterling, to be vacant (howsoever etc.), shall collate and assign it (even if specially reserved, or generally reserved (because it is conventual) etc.), with all its rights and appurtenances, to Thomas Offlayff, inducting him etc. having removed Thomas Okeyth and any other unlawful detainer and causing Thomas Offlayff (or his proctor) to be admitted to the priory and its fruits etc., rights and obventions to be delivered to him. [Curbing] gainsayers [etc.] Notwithstanding etc. Also the pope dispenses Thomas Offlayff to receive and retain the priory, if conferred on him by virtue of the presents, notwithstanding the above defect etc.

Religionis zelus, vite ac morum honestas ...
P. lambertus / . A. / A. xxv Decimo octavo K(a)l(endas) maij anno primo [14 April 1513], *Colotius: –*

---

1   sympathetic reading: readable as *Re-*

---

143   1 April 1513   *Reg. Lat.* 1284, fos 219[v]-223[r]

To <Peter Valetio>[1] and Donat Machaulli[2] and Cormac Machari, canons of the [church][3] of (?)Cloyne (*Cluenen.*), mandate in favour of William Osichan, cleric, d. Cloyne (*Cluenen.*)[4]. The pope has learned that the mutually united perpetual vicarages of the parish churches of the places of Castellon Magner and Moiranoach[5], which are of lay patronage, and of Roschin [also spelt *Roschino*], d. Cloyne (*Eluenen.*)[6] are vacant *certo modo* at present and have been vacant for so long that by the Lateran statutes their collation has lawfully devolved on the apostolic see, although David Mainer, who bears himself as a cleric, has detained the said vicarages with no title or support of law, of his own temerity and *de facto*, for a certain time, as he does. At a recent petition on William's part to the pope to unite etc. the vicarage of Roschin to the said mutually united vicarages, for as long as William holds the latter, if conferred on him as above – asserting that he, notwithstanding a defect of birth as the son of a priest and an unmarried woman, has been duly marked with clerical character; and that the annual value of the said vicarages together does not exceed 12 marks sterling – the pope hereby commands that the above three (or two or one of them), if, having summoned David and others concerned, they find the said vicarages to be vacant (howsoever etc.) shall collate and assign the mutually united vicarages to William and unite etc. Roschin to the mutually united vicarages (even if they are specially reserved etc.), for as long as William holds the latter, if conferred on him as above, with all their rights and appurtenances, inducting him etc. having removed David and any other unlawful detainers and causing William (or his proctor) to be admitted to the mutually united vicarages, and the fruits etc., rights and obventions of each of the said vicarages to be delivered to him. [Curbing] gainsayers [etc.] Notwithstanding etc. Also the pope dispenses William to receive and retain the said mutually united vicarages, if conferred on him on the strength of the presents, notwithstanding the above defect etc. The pope's will is, however, that the vicarage of Roschin shall not, on account of this union etc., be defrauded of due services and the cure of souls in it shall not be neglected; but that its customary burdens shall be supported; and that on William's death or his resignation etc. of the mutually united vicarages the said union etc. shall be dissolved and the vicarage of Roschin shall revert to its original condition automatically.

Vite ac morum honestas ...
P. lambertus / A / A. xxij Decimo octavo K(a)l(endis) maij anno primo. [14 April 1513], *Colotius: –*

1   *Willelmo (?)Omurchu Artificen.* [*recte*: 'Artferten.' (Ardfert)] deleted and initialled *A*; with *Petro Valetio* [the
   'ti' uncertain; readable also as 'ri'] inserted in margin (in the master's hand) initialled *A*
2   thereafter *canonico* deleted; not initialled
3   MS: *ecclesiarum*; *recte* (on deletion of *Artificen.* [*see above*, note 1]): 'ecclesie'
4   the corresponding Annates entry has *Clunenensis*: *Annates, Cloyne*, pp. 29-30 (no. 102).
5   the *-oa-* uncertain
6   *recte*: 'Clonen.' the three benefices are in d. Cloyne; *Annates* op.cit.

144   **1 April 15[1]3[1]**   *Reg. Lat.* 1284, fos 223[r]-226[r]

To[2] William Ochonimochan', canon <of the church>[3] of Killaloe,[4] <and the official of
Killaloe>,[5] mandate in favour of Conay Macnamari, canon of Killaloe, (who, some
time ago, as he asserts, was dispensed by apostolic authority notwithstanding a defect
of birth as the son of an unmarried man and an unmarried woman to be promoted to
all, even sacred, orders and to hold a benefice, even if it should have cure of souls, and
afterwards was duly marked with clerical character and holds a canonry and prebend
of the said church, which was canonically collated to him when vacant *certo modo*).
The pope has learned that the treasurership of the church of Killaloe is vacant *certo
modo* at present and has been vacant for so long that by the Lateran statutes [its][6]
collation has lawfully devolved on the apostolic see, although Roderick Macnamari,
who bears himself as a cleric, has detained it, with no title and no support of law, of his
own temerity and *de facto*, for a certain time, as he does. He hereby commands that the
above three, or two or <one >[7] of them, if, having summoned Roderick and others
concerned, they find the treasurership (which is a dignity, not however major *post
pontificalem*, whose annual value does not exceed 10 marks sterling) to be vacant
(howsoever etc.) shall collate and assign it (even if specially reserved etc.), with all its
rights and appurtenances, to Conay, inducting him etc. having removed Roderick and
any other unlawful detainer and causing Conay (or his proctor) to be admitted to the
treasurership and its fruits etc., rights and obventions to be delivered to him. [Curbing]
gainsayers [etc.] Notwithstanding etc. Also the pope dispenses Conay to receive and
retain the treasurership, if conferred on him by virtue of the presents, notwithstanding
the above defect etc.

Vite ac morum honestas ...
P. lambertus / A / A. xxij. Decimo octavo K(a)l(endas) maij anno primo [14 April
1513], *Colotius:* –

1   MS: *millesimo quingentesimo tertio kalendis Aprilis ...*; arguably wanting 'decimo' after *tertio*
2   The names of both mandataries (and their churches) have been changed, involving several deletions and
   marginal insertions. After *dilectis filiis*, MS has *Thesaurario et Villelmo Nagell canonico Limerycen. ac*
   deleted (initialled *A* in two places). And *see below* notes 3, 4 and 5; *cf.* also note 7.
   As usual, the background to the alterations is not explained; and cannot be readily established.
3   *ecclesie* inserted in margin initialled *A*
4   *ecclesiarum* deleted (*cf. above*, note 2)
5   *ac offitiali Laonen.* inserted in margin initialled *A*
6   'eius' (or suchlike) wanting
7   At this point confusion arises because alterations have not been carried through consistently. Above, the
   address clause – itself altered, *see above*, note 2 – as it now stands has two mandataries. Here *vos vel duo*

aut unus vestrum – i.e. the phrase appropriate for three mandataries – was written originally; and then *unus vestrum* was deleted (initialled *A*); with *alter* inserted in the margin (also initialled *A*). The result: *vos vel duo aut alter* – an unhappy mix of the formulary for two mandataries and for three.

145   27 April 1513   *Reg. Lat.* 1284, fos 309[r]-312[v]

To the abbots of the monasteries of Hylcule,[1] d. Ossory,[2] and *de Lege dei* [Abbeyleix], d. Leighlin, and Maurice Obechayn, canon of the church of (?)Kildare,[3] mandate in favour of Richard Oleclayr,[4] (?)coarb (?*converbus*) of Clueneynec, cleric, d. Leighlin. The pope has learned that the perpetual vicarages of the parish churches of the places of Clueneynec [also spelt *Cluenenec, Cluenenynec*] and of Muyena and Kilsayalid [also spelt *Kilsalyalid*], d. Leighlin, have been vacant *certo modo* and are vacant at present, although Niellanus Oleclayr has detained the vicarage of Clueneynec and William Ocluna *alias* Okella that of Muyena and Kilsayalid – bearing themselves as clerics – with no title or support of law, of their own temerity and *de facto*, for a certain time, as they do. At a recent petition on Richard's part to the pope to unite etc. the vicarage of Muyena and Kilsayalid to that of Clueneynec, for as long as Richard holds the latter (if it is conferred on him by virtue of the presents and he acquires it) – asserting that notwithstanding a defect of birth as the son of an unmarried man and an unmarried woman he has been duly marked with clerical character; and that the annual value of the said vicarages together does not exceed 24 marks sterling – the pope hereby commands that the above three (or two or one of them), if, having summoned Niellanus and William and others concerned, they find the vicarages of Clueneynec [and of Muyena and Kilsayalid] to be vacant (howsoever etc.) shall collate and assign the vicarage of Clueneynec to Richard; and unite etc. the vicarage of Muyena and Kilsayalid, with all its rights and appurtenances, to that of Clueneynec, for as long as Richard holds the latter, if conferred on him as above (even if they [i.e. both vicarages] have been vacant for so long that by the Lateran statutes their collation has lawfully devolved on the apostolic see etc.); inducting him etc. having removed Niellanus from Clueneynec and William from Muyena and Kilsayalid and any other unlawful detainers and causing Richard (or his proctor) to be admitted to the vicarage of Clueneynec and its fruits etc., rights and obventions and those of the united vicarage [of Muyena and Kilsayalid] to be delivered to him. [Curbing] gainsayers etc. Notwithstanding etc. Also the pope dispenses Richard to be promoted to all, even sacred, orders – outside the Roman curia however[5] – and to receive and retain the vicarage of Clueneynec, if conferred on him by virtue of the presents; notwithstanding the above defect etc. The pope's will is, however, that the above vicarage of Muyena and Kilsayalid shall not, on account of this union etc. (if created by virtue of the presents) be defrauded of due services and the cure of souls in it shall not be neglected; but that its customary burdens shall be supported; and that on the death of Richard or his resignation etc. of the vicarage of Clueneynec this union etc. shall be dissolved and so deemed and the vicarage of Muyena and Kilsayalid shall revert to its original condition automatically.

Vite ac morum honestas ...
P. Lambertus / M / M xxv quarto id(us) Iunii an(n)o primo [10 June 1513], *de Campania*

1   the '-cu-' uncertain; possibly 'ni'
2   Kilcooly appears to have been on the Cashel side of the border with Ossory.
3   reading *Daren.*; but '*Deren.* ' also possible
4   the 'la' badly formed and uncertain; perhaps Olechyr
5   MS: *extra t(ame)n Romanam curiam*; a curious qualification in this context.

146   19 May 1513   *Reg. Lat.* 1285, fos 43ʳ-44ᵛ

Mandate to collate and assign to Paulus Nicolai Guidottis de <Guinzano>¹ – cleric of Lucca and (as he asserts) a continual commensal familiar of Sixtus, cardinal priest of the title of St Peter ad Vincula, vicechancellor of the holy Roman church – the priorship (which is a non-principal dignity) of the secular and collegiate church of St Donatus just outside the walls of Lucca (whose annual value does not exceed 160² gold ducats of the camera). Silvester, bishop of Worcester, who was recently holding the priorship *in commendam* by apostolic concession and dispensation, has this day freely and spontaneously ceded the commend into the pope's hands, the pope has admitted the cession, and the priory is known to be vacant at present still in the way it was vacant before it was commended. The letter, which is addressed to three mandataries, is of no other interest to the Calendar.

Vite ac morum honestas ...
.A. d(e) alvarottis / A / A xx. K(a)l(endis) Julij a(n)no primo [1 July 1513], *Colotius:* –

1   marginal insertion replacing (?)*Vinzano* altered to (?)*Ginzano* and then deleted; initialled *A*
2   originally written *centum quinquaginta*; *quinquaginta* then deleted and *sexaginta* inserted in the margin; initialled *A*

147   2 July 1513   *Reg. Lat.* 1285, fos 80ᵛ-82ᵛ

Some time ago the pope ordered the mandataries to collate and assign the parish church, called priory, of St Stephen, Tasignano, d. Lucca (of lay patronage), which was then vacant but unlawfully occupied by a detainer, to Hercules de Ciampantibus, cleric of Lucca, continual commensal familiar of the pope and in the service of Sixtus, cardinal priest of the title of St Peter ad Vincula and vicechancellor of the holy Roman church. A suit then arose over the church between Hercules and the detainer, namely Paulus Nicolai de Guidottis, and the pope committed it to an auditor of causes (named) of the apostolic palace who proceeded to several acts but short of a conclusion. The detainer has this day ceded the suit, cause, and his right in and to the church into the hands of the pope and the pope has admitted the cession. The pope – calling-in the suit and extinguishing it and, for this once only, derogating the right of patronage – orders the mandataries to decree that the former mandate (which has not been presented to the executors and executed) is valid from the date of the presents and to execute it as if the pope had ordered that provision be made of the church to Hercules as simply vacant *certo modo*, without the clause *vocatis dicto Paulo et cetera* and without the disposition of the devolution of the collation to the apostolic see.

The 'bishop of Worcester' was one of the three mandataries in the former mandate and is one of the three mandataries of the present mandate. Entry otherwise of no interest to the Calendar.

Grata familiaritatis obsequia …
P. pla(n)ca / JoA. / JoA xxx Quinto decimo K(a)l(endas) Agusti[1] *Anno primo* [18 July 1513], *de Nardinis*

1   *sic*

148   26 May 1513   *Reg. Lat.* 1285, fos 157ʳ-158ᵛ

To the prior of the monastery, usually governed by a prior, of Villehe, d. Kildare, and James Odun, canon of the church of Kildare, mandate in favour of Donald Ybecan', perpetual vicar of the parish church of Kilclonsert, d. Kildare. The pope has learned that the rectory of the above parish church, which is of lay patronage, is vacant *certo modo* at present and has been vacant for so long that by the Lateran statutes its collation has lawfully devolved on the apostolic see, although John Ouiana,[1] who bears himself as a priest, has detained it, without any title or support of law, of his own temerity and *de facto*, for a certain time, as he does. At a recent petition on Donald's part (which stated that the fruits etc. of the perpetual vicarage of the said church, which Donald (?)detains,[2] are so meagre that there is not sufficient to keep up hospitality therein and support the other burdens incumbent on him by reason of the vicarage) to the pope to unite etc. the rectory to the vicarage, for as long as Donald holds the latter, to enable him the more easily to maintain hospitality and discharge the burdens in question – asserting that the annual value of the rectory does not exceed 12 marks sterling – the pope hereby commands that the above two (or one[3] of them), if, having summoned John and others concerned, they find the rectory to be vacant (howsoever etc.), shall unite etc. it (even if specially reserved etc.), with all its rights and appurtenances, to the vicarage, for as long as Donald holds the latter; to the effect that he may, on his own authority, in person or by proxy, take corporal possession of the rectory and its rights and appurtenances aforesaid, and retain it as above for as long as he holds the vicarage, and convert its fruits etc. to his own uses and those of the vicarage and rectory, without licence of the local diocesan or of anyone else. Notwithstanding etc. The pope's will is, however, that the above rectory shall not, on account of this union etc., be defrauded of due services and the cure of souls in it shall not be neglected; but that its customary burdens shall be supported; and that on the death of Donald or his resignation etc. of the rectory this union etc. shall be dissolved and be so deemed and the rectory shall revert to its original condition automatically.

Romanum decet pontificem votis illis gratum prestare assensum ...
.P. lambert(us). / . A / A. xv. Colotius:-

1   the '-ui-' doubtful
2   Surprisingly, MS has (?)*detinet* here – the verb normally used for unlawful occupation of benefices, and the one used to describe John's detention of the rectory. Elsewhere in the letter, however, *obtinuerit* is consistently used of Donald's holding of the vicarage, in accordance with normal usage for benefices held lawfully. Perhaps (?)*obtinet* is the better reading.
3   MS: *vos vel alter vestrum*, with *duo* deleted (without initial) after *vel* – i.e. the scribe began the very common formula for three mandataries ('vos vel duo aut unus vestrum'); but replaced it with that – needed here – for two.

149   19 March 1513   *Reg. Lat.* 1285, fos 263ʳ-265ᵛ

Effectuation of Julius II's appointment of Blanchus de Blanchis, cleric of Lucca, as vicar in the rule and administration of the parish church, called *plebs*, of St Mary, Villa Basilica, d. Lucca (over which he had been litigating in the Roman curia before an auditor of causes of the apostolic palace and in and to which he had ceded all right into Julius' hands) and reservation for him of pension on the fruits of the said church, under date 9 November, ninth year [1512]; both for life. With concurrent executory mandate.

  The 'bishop of Worcester' is one of the three mandataries. Entry otherwise of no interest to the Calendar.

Rationi congrui[t] et cetera. The executory begins: *Dudum felicis recordationis Julius papa II predecessor noster ...*
.A. d(e) S(an)c(t)o Severi(n)o; . P. Blanca¹ / Phi. / Phi. xxx. x. de Senis

1   *sic*

150   8 June 1513   *Reg. Lat.* 1286, fos 166ʳ-168ᵛ

To the abbot of the monastery of St Peter, [Derry]¹, and the priors of the monasteries, usually governed by priors, of Dungefyn and Agefye, d. [Derry], mandate in favour of Terence Macnarthan', cleric, d. [Derry] (who, some time ago, as he asserts, was dispensed by apostolic authority, notwithstanding a defect of birth as the son of a priest and an unmarried woman, to be promoted to all, even sacred, orders and to the order of the priesthood, and to hold a benefice, even if it should have cure of souls; and who afterwards was duly marked with clerical character). The pope has learned that the parish church, called rectory, of Capachac, d. [Derry], is vacant *certo modo* at present and has been vacant for so long that by the Lateran statutes its collation has lawfully devolved on the apostolic see, although Emundus Magnacman, who bears himself as a cleric, has detained the rectory, with no title or support of law, but of his own temerity and *de facto*, for certain time, as he does. At a recent petition on Terence's part to the pope to erect and institute a canonry in the church of [Derry] and the said parish church into a simple prebend of that church, for his lifetime (during which the number of ministers in the church would be increased) – asserting that the annual value of the parish church does not exceed 5 marks sterling – the pope hereby commands that the above three (or two or one of them), if, having summoned Emundus and others concerned, they find the parish church to be vacant (howsoever etc.), shall erect and institute a canonry in the said church of [Derry] and the said parish church into a simple prebend of that church (even if the parish church be specially reserved etc.), for Terence's lifetime only and without prejudice to anyone; and in that event collate and assign the newly erected canonry and prebend, being vacant, to Terence, with plenitude of canon law and all their rights and appurtenances; inducting him etc. having removed Emundus and any other unlawful detainer and causing Terence (or his proctor) [to be admitted] to the prebend and received as a canon, and a stall in the choir and a place in the chapter of the church of [Derry] [to be assigned] to him, with plenitude of canon law, and the fruits etc., rights and obventions of the canonry and prebend to be delivered to him. [Curbing] gainsayers etc. Notwithstanding etc. Also the pope dispenses Terence to receive and retain the said canonry and prebend, if conferred on him by virtue of the presents, notwithstanding the above defect of birth etc. The pope's will is, however, that on Terence's death or his resignation etc. of the said parish church this erection and union shall be extinguished and be so deemed and the parish church shall revert to its original condition automatically.

Apostolice sedis providentia circumspecta ad ea que in singulis ecclesiis presertim cathedralibus ...
P lambertus / A / . A. xxj. Tertio non(as) Julij anno primo [5 July 1513], *Colotius:-*

1   Here, and throughout, MS has *Daren.*; *recte*: 'Deren.'.

151   18 June 1513   *Reg. Lat.* 1286, fos 204ᵛ-207ʳ

To the abbot of the monastery *de Legedei* [Abbeyleix] and the prior [of the monastery][1] *de Insula Viventium* [Monaincha], <ds. >[2] Leighlin and [Killaloe][3] [respectively], and Peter Obechan, canon of the church of Kildare, mandate in favour of Patrick Macostela *alias* Negala, cleric, d. Kildare (who, some time ago, as he asserts, was dispensed by apostolic authority, notwithstanding a defect of birth as the son of a priest and an unmarried woman, to be promoted to all, even sacred, orders and the order of the priesthood, and to hold a benefice, even if it should have cure of souls, and to resign it, simply or for exchange, as often as he pleased, and in its place hold likewise another, similar or dissimilar, benefice, even with cure; and who [afterwards][4] was duly marked with clerical character). The pope has learned that the perpetual vicarage of the parish church of Lega,[5] said diocese [of Kildare], which is of lay patronage, is vacant *certo modo* at present and has been vacant for so long that by the Lateran statutes its collation has lawfully devolved on the apostolic see, although Thady Macostella *alias* Negala, who bears himself as a priest, has detained it, with no title or support of law, of his own temerity and *de facto*, for a certain time, as he still does. He hereby commands that the above three (or two or one of them), if, having summoned Thady and others concerned, they find the vicarage, whose annual value (as Patrick also asserts) does not exceed 10 marks sterling, to be vacant (howsoever etc.), shall collate and assign it (even if specially reserved etc.), with all its rights and appurtenances, to Patrick, inducting him etc. having removed Thady and any other unlawful detainer and causing Patrick (or his proctor) to be admitted to the vicarage and its fruits etc., rights and obventions to be delivered to him. [Curbing] gainsayers etc. Notwithstanding etc.

Vite ac morum honestas ...
phi d(e) agnellis / A / A xv quarto k(a)l(endas) Julij anno primo [28 June 1513], Colotius

1   'monasterii (per priorem soliti gubernari)' does not occur.
2   *dioc(esium)* inserted in margin (Colocci's hand?) initialled *A*
3   *Leglinen. et et* [both ampersands] *Legalen.* [*recte*: 'Laonen.'?]
4   'postmodum' might be expected; but possibly was overlooked by scribe turning overleaf.
5   or *Lege*

152   4 April 1513   *Reg. Lat.* 1286, fos 302ᵛ-305ᵛ

To the prior of the monastery, usually governed by a prior, of St Mary, Ragell', d. Limerick, and the official of Limerick, mandate in favour of Gerald Omolcoarkiry, canon of Limerick (who, as he asserts, is in his twenty-second year of age, or thereabouts; and, some time ago, was dispensed by apostolic authority, notwithstanding a defect of birth as the son of a cleric and an unmarried woman, to be promoted to all, even sacred, orders, and to hold a benefice, even if it should have cure of souls; and who afterwards was duly marked with clerical character and holds a canonry and prebend of the said church which were canonically collated to him when vacant *certo modo*). The pope has learned that the chancellorship of the church of Limerick is vacant *certo modo* at present and has been vacant for so long that by the Lateran statutes its collation has lawfully devolved on the apostolic see, although Philip Omolcoarkyri, who bears himself as a priest, has detained it, as he does, without any canonical title or support of law, for more than a year, but short of a three-year period. He hereby commands that the above two (or one of them), if, having summoned Philip and others concerned, they find the chancellorship, which is a dignity, not however major *post pontificalem*, and whose annual value does not exceed 60 marks sterling,[1] to be vacant (howsoever etc.) shall collate and assign it (even if specially reserved etc.), with all its rights and appurtenances, to Gerald, inducting him etc. having removed Philip and any other unlawful detainer and causing Gerald (or his proctor) to be admitted to the chancellorship and its fruits etc., rights and obventions to be delivered to him. [Curbing] gainsayers etc. Notwithstanding etc. Also the pope dispenses Gerald – who in regard to holding the chancellorship suffers the said defects of birth and (in his twenty-second year) of age – to receive and retain the chancellorship, if conferred on him by virtue of the presents; and not to be bound – by reason of the chancellorship, if he acquires it – to be promoted to any of the sacred orders for a seven-year period, calculated from the end of the year granted to him by law, provided that he is a subdeacon within the first two years; nor to be liable to be compelled to do so by anyone against his will. Notwithstanding the above defects etc. With the proviso that the chancellorship and other benefices in question shall not, on this account, be defrauded of due services and the cure of souls in it (if any) shall not be neglected.

Vite ac morum honestas …
P. lambertus / M / M xxx sexto decimo k(a)l(endas) maij an(n)o primo [16 April 1513], *de Campania*

1   *librarum sterlingorum* has been deleted, initialled *M*

153   26 October 1513   *Reg. Lat.* 1287, fos 319ᵛ-320ᵛ

To Thomas Colman', cleric, d. Canterbury, validation as below. Some time ago, Julius II by letters of his dispensed Thomas, then, as he asserted, in his twenty-second year of age, to receive and retain together for life any two benefices, with cure or otherwise mutually incompatible, even if parish churches or their perpetual vicarages, chantries, free chapels, hospitals or annual services, usually assigned to secular clerics in title of a perpetual[1] benefice, or dignities, *personatus*, administrations or offices in cathedral, even metropolitan, or collegiate churches, even if the dignities should be major *post pontificalem* in cathedral, even metropolitan, churches, or principal in collegiate churches, or a combination, and even if the dignities etc. should be customarily elective and have cure of souls, if he obtained them otherwise canonically, to resign them, at once [or][2] successively, simply or for exchange, as often as he pleased, and in their place receive up to two other, similar or dissimilar, mutually incompatible benefices, and retain them together for life as above, as is more fully contained in the said letters.[3] However, as a recent petition to the pope on Thomas's part stated – after he, then attending a *studium generale* and believing that he had been sufficiently dispensed in this regard, had, by pretext of the said dispensation, acquired the perpetual vicarage of the parish church of St Michael, Harenhyll, d. Canterbury, which was collated to him by ordinary authority, but otherwise canonically, when vacant *certo modo*, and detained it for a certain time, receiving fruits from it, but in good faith – since it had come to Thomas's notice that at the time of the said letters he was only in his twentieth year, Thomas resigned the vicarage and fears that, on account of the foregoing, the said letters are surreptitious and everywhere less useful with the passage of time. Lest the effect of the said letters be frustrated, the pope grants to Thomas (who, as he asserts, is in his twenty-fourth year and is a student at the university of the *studium generale* of Bologna) – at his supplication – that the letters and dispensation aforesaid with clauses of exchange and all the other clauses in them are valid from the date of the presents and have full force and support him without limitation, just as if it had been expressed in the said letters that Thomas had been in his said twentieth year and had been dispensed for the defect of age in question. Notwithstanding etc.

Vite ac morum honestas ...
Phi de Agnellis[4] / *JoA:* / *JoA: xxiiij: Nardinus*

1   'ecclesiastici' does not occur.
2   'vel' (or suchlike) does not occur.
3   *Cf. CPL*, XIX, no. 1955, from *rubricellae* of a lost register of Julius (which, predictably, affords even fewer details than the present Leo register).
4   shaved along top

154   6 May 1513   *Reg. Lat.* 1287, fos 338[r]-341[r]

Reception, licence, faculty, decree, declaration, and indult, as below. Some time ago – after Sixtus IV had, by his letters,[1] granted to the then prior of the monastery customarily governed by a prior of B. Mary of the place of Brenton [also spelt *Bre'ton*], OSA, d. Bath and Wells, and to his successors, that they could use the pastoral staff, grey almuce, ring, and other pontifical inignia, and after it had been explained to Julius II on the part of William Gilberd, MTheol, prior of the said monastery, *inter alia* that in Sixtus's letters the priorship of B. Mary, Brenton was [designated] the priorship of a monastery customarily governed by a prior and that in certain other extremely old letters, even apostolic ones, the priory was [designated] conventual and the prior was [designated] prior of a priory – not prior of a monastery or prior of the church of the said B. Mary (the expression not being prior of a monastery or of a priory but prior of a church)[2] — and that it was unclear from the foregoing whether it was a priorship of a monastery or a church or a conventual priory, and whether it ought to be called priorship of a monastery or prior of a priory – Julius, at William's supplication, by other letters,[3] decreed, established, and ordained that thenceforth, for all time, the priory of B. Mary, Brenton was (and was to be called) a "monastery" and the said William and his successors were (and were to be called) "abbots" of the said monastery, and that on the strength of his letters, without other provision being made of his person to the monastery, William was true abbot of the monastery and at the head of it; and he granted to William and his successors licence and faculty, *inter alia*, of blessing clothing, or sandals, and other vestments, or any sacred priestly furniture, and also necessary and appropriate altars for the use of mass and divine office in the said monastery and its annexes (*annexis menbris*) and in churches and chapels subject to it, even ones not subject to it by full authority; and he granted relaxation of twenty-five years and as many quarantines of enjoined penance to all the faithful of both sexes who, annually, being truly penitent, devoutly visited the church of the monastery and the chapel of B. Mary on the feasts of the Ascension and Corpus Christi, and on the second, third, and fourth weekdays in the octave of Easter, and on the first Sunday of each month and there devoutly recited or said the Lord's Prayer and the Angelic Salutation for the salvation of William's soul and the souls of the late Otto and Isabel his parents (*parentum*), and of his predecessors and successors in the monastery; and he also granted both to the abbot and canons as also to the brethren and sisters of the monastery, then present and future, and granted indult, that they could and ought to use, have, and enjoy all the privileges, indults, indulgences, and even apostolic letters, which the members of the Lateran congregation, OSA, and its monasteries and places, and their abbots, priors and provosts (*prepositi*), and the rectors, diffinitors, and persons of the congregation, used, had, and enjoyed by law or custom; as is more fully stated in the individual letters aforesaid. However, as a recent petition to the pope on abbot William's part stated, [several persons][4] interpret Julius' letters as empty (*vano modo*) and it is doubted by some whether William and his successor abbots can, by the grant of the faculty of blessing, also bless virgins, canonesses of the said order, and chapels, bells, crosses, and images of the monastery and of churches subject to it, and some are of opinion that the faithful cannot obtain the indulgence unless they have visited the church and chapel one day after another, without missing one (*continue nullo dierum predictorum omisso*); that there are several brothers and sisters in the monastery, pure laity (*meri laici*), who, even while living in their houses, by ancient immemorial custom, without having taken the profession, are made partakers of the prayers and suffrages which are performed in the monastery, and they are called brothers and sisters of the monastery by everyone, and it could be doubted whether Julius's grant and indult extends to these brothers and sisters; and that for a certain number of years in the monastery the manner of reciting the canonical hours in accordance with its ancient custom has in some part been altered. At abbot William's supplication, the pope hereby receives William and his successor abbots as his sons and sons of the apostolic see and grants licence and faculty to William and his successors: of ruling, governing and administering the said monastery, in all its rights and goods, spiritual and temporal, just as if an abbot had been instituted in it and set over it from the beginning of its foundation; of blessing virgins, canonesses of the said order, and chapels, bells, crosses, images, and any other things necessary for the use of the mass, both in the monastery and in the churches and chapels subject to it, even ones not subject to it by full authority; of reconciling cemeteries, churches, and chapels polluted by blood or semen, the water having, however, first been blessed by any catholic bishop in communion with the apostolic see; of absolving each and every parishioner of the parish church (which is annexed or appropriated to the monastery) of the place of Bauwel, said d. (in which place abbot William and his predecessors in the monastery, its priors for the time being, have been accustomed to have jurisdiction, just as abbot William has and exercises jurisdiction), by themselves or by their vicar or vicars appointed for the purpose by abbot William and his successors, just as they can, under the privileges granted to them by the apostolic see, in person or by proxy, absolve the parishioners of the church of the said monastery, which is also a parish church; of granting licence to any persons, both clerics and religious, who are honest and imbued with sufficient learning, of preaching the word of God to the people in the said monastery and in the churches and chapels subject to it, even ones not subject by full authority; and the pope grants licence and faculty to William: of correcting [and] improving the canonical hours and the divine office in conformity with the older custom (*antiquiori consuetudine*) of the said monastery; of causing and ordering[5] feasts of saints which are not celebrated in the monastery to be celebrated, to the glory of the divine name, according to the ancient custom (*antiquam ... consuetudinem*) of the monastery and order, as seems expedient for the divine service; of drawing up and making, [in accordance with][6] the regular institutes of St Augustine, any statutes and ordinances which are otherwise lawful, honest, and not opposed to the sacred canons; and, with the consent of a majority of the convent of the monastery, of correcting, making anew, and reviving (*erigendi*) its ancient offices (*antiqua ... officia*). Moreover, the pope hereby decrees, declares and grants indult: that everything which is reformed, established, ordained, interpreted and done by abbot William with regard to those things must be inviolably observed by everyone there for ever and binds and constrains them as if the reforms etc. had been confirmed by the apostolic see; that no one, of whatever dignity, standing, degree, or dignity[7] is allowed to keep or hide canons or other religious and lay brothers (*conversos*) of the monastery who leave the enclosure (*septa*) of the monastery without the licence of its abbot for the time being, and both those leaving thus and those thus keeping or hiding them or [giving][8] them help, counsel or favour to leave the monastery shall automatically incur sentence of excommunication from which they cannot be absolved unless they have obeyed the mandates of the abbot of the monastery for the time being or they are on the point of death; that the abbot for the time being can, by ecclesiastical censure, compel objectors [and] detainers or defenders of fugitives to hand them over; that the abbot and convent of the monastery may not be compelled, by any far-fetched pretext, even on apostolic authority, to receive someone as a canon or religious of the said monastery, except with the consent of the abbot and a majority of the convent, and those received and admitted otherwise, if the abbot or a majority of the convent object, are not to be considered canons or religious of the monastery, and if they have been warned by the abbot to depart from the monastery on that account and they stubbornly neglect to obey, they automatically incur sentence of excommunication after three days have passed, from which they can only be absolved by authority of the apostolic see; that all the faithful of both sexes who visit the said church and chapel, even just once, or repeatedly at intervals (*interpellatis vicibus*), or after a break (*ex intervallo*), obtain the said indulgence for each one of the said days (*pro qualibet dierum predictarum*) on which they have visited, as above; that the brothers, sisters, familiars, and officials of the said monastery, whoever they are, present and future, have and enjoy all the privileges, indulgences, and indults granted by Julius' letters just as if it had been expressed in Julius' letters (*eisdem prioribus litteris*) that the brothers and sisters dwell outside the monastery and live as seculars (*seculari more*) in their own houses; and that the abbot for the time being and convent shall use, have and enjoy, and can and ought to use, have and enjoy, the same apostolic privileges, indults, indulgences, and graces which, by law or custom, the abbot for the time being and convent of the monastery of Cirencester (*de Cirencestria*), OSA, d. Worcester, use, have and enjoy.

Ad perpetuam rei memoriam. Superna dispositione cuius inscrutabili providentia ordinationem suscipiunt universa ...
P lambertus / JoA: / JoA: CC: Nardinus

---

1   *Cf. CPL* XIII, p. 892 (a lost bull).
2   As it stands the meaning here is particularly elusive. The full MS context is: ... *expossito* [!] *quod in predictis*
      [sc. Sixtus's letters] *quod prioratus eiusdem Beate Marie de Bre'ton prioratus monasterii per priorem*

gubernari soliti et quibusdam aliis antiquissimis litteris etiam apostolicis quod prioratus conventualis et
prior prioratus non autem monasterii vel prior ecclesie eiusdem Beate Marie (?)non exprimendo prior
monasterii vel prioratus sed prior ecclesie *existeret et ex premissis non appareret clare si esset prioratus*
monasterii vel ecclesie aut prioratus conventualis et dici deberet prioratus monasterii vel prior prioratus ...
There are no reversal marks in the passage I have underlined; but the terms seem to be reversed; 'prior
ecclesie sed (prior) prioratus' would fit the context.

3   *CPL* XIX, no. 610
4   MS: *nulli*; *recte*: 'nonnulli'?
5   reading, tentatively, *man-* | *dandi*
6   MS: *iusta*; *recte*: 'iuxta'
7   MS: *dignitatis ... dignitatis*; the second occurrence presumably an error (perhaps pure repetition; perhaps for
     another word, e.g. 'conditionis', 'ordinis', or 'nobilitatis', etc which sometimes occur in elaborated versions
     of this clause).
8   MS: *impedientes*; *recte*: 'impendentes'?

155   19 March 1513   *Reg. Lat.* 1287, fos 341^r-342^v

Effectuation of remission, faculty, and decree, as below. Some time ago, Julius II –
wishing that the monastery of B Mary, Brenton, OSA, [d.][1] Bath and Wells (to which
William, then abbot of the monastery, was singularly devoted) was suitably honoured
and held in due veneration and that its buildings (*in suis structuris et edificiis*) were
duly repaired, conserved and maintained, and also that Christ's faithful flock willingly
to the monastery church out of devotion and therein contribute readily to the above
because they see themselves thereby abundantly refreshed there with the gift of
celestial grace – assured of the mercy of Almighty God and of the authority of His
Apostles BB. Peter and Paul, under date 28 June tenth year [1513] granted plenary
remission of all their sins, delicts, crimes, and excesses, which had been orally
confessed and for which they were sincerely contrite, to all the faithful of either sex,
being truly penitent and confessed, who devoutly visited the said church in person, and
also to those, including monks and nuns, from the city and diocese of Bath and Wells
only, who, prevented by old age, sickness, or otherwise, could [not][2] conveniently
reach the church in person, devoutly visited the church by proxy, on the third Sunday
of Lent, from first vespers to sunset of the following day. Further, in order that the
faithful, even those visiting by proxy, partook the more easily of the said indulgence
and remission, Julius granted: to William and his successors, the abbots of the said
monastery for the time being, full and unfettered faculty of appointing suitable
confessors in the said church, seculars or regulars of any order, even of mendicants, at
his discretion, to hear the confessions of those coming to obtain the indulgence; and to
the said persons appointed, full and unfettered faculty: of hearing the confessions of
those coming at the time of the indulgence and on the three previous days, and, when
their confessions had been diligently heard, of absolving them from each and every one
of their sins, delicts, and excesses, even ones reserved to the apostolic see (except for
those contained in the bull customarily read aloud *in Coena Domini*), of enjoining on
them a salutary penance in proportion to their sins etc., and also of commuting into
other works of piety any vows taken by them from time to time (with the exception
only of the vows of visiting the Holy Land, the tombs of the Apostles Peter and Paul
and of St James at Compostella, and also the vows of religion and chastity); and to the

faithful prevented from visiting the church full and unfettered faculty of choosing similar confessors who were to similarly absolve them and also able to commute vows, as above; and Julius decreed that the said indulgence was in no wise to be comprehended under any rules of the apostolic chancery and any revocations of similar indulgences, made and destined to be made from time to time, in any way and under any forms and tenors of words and clauses, even clauses derogatory of derogatory clauses, and not even under rules and revocations made for the duration of the indulgence granted by Julius and the apostolic see for the fabric of the basilica of the prince of the apostles, Rome, and for the crusade, but was always to be accounted exempt from them, and that unless the name and surname of abbot William had been expressed it was never to be accounted derogated and was not to be accounted suspended; and had Julius' letters been drawn up in this regard they were to last for all time. Since however Julius died before his letters to this effect were drawn up, the pope hereby wills and decrees that the said grant etc. are valid and take effect from the said 28 June; and that the present letters shall everywhere be sufficient proof of the said grant etc.

Universis Christifidelibus presentes litteras inspecturis ... Romanorum gesta pontificum salutem animarum presertim concernentia super quibus illorum superveniente obitu littere confecte non fuerint recenseri iustum reputamus et rationi consonum ut illa universis Christifidelibus innotescant.
F Bregeon / A.gratiadei[3]; JoA / JoA: CCCC: Nardinus.

1   MS wants 'diocesis' or 'diocesium'.
2   MS wants 'non'.
3   By special arrangement, indulgences, though expedited by the chancery, were signed by papal secretaries (*cf.* *CPL* XVI, p. xvii, note 8). But effectuations of such grants tested the arrangement. Hence, perhaps, the register notes of two signatures (noted presumably from the engrossment), viz.: that of Antonius Gratiadei (as *secretarius apostolicus*) and that of Franciscus Bregeon (as *abbreviator de parco maiori*). The names are noted in the register in their conventional positions – secretaries in the left margin at the start of the entry, abbreviators in the right margin.

156[1]   5 September 1513   *Reg. Lat.* 1287, fos 395ᵛ-396ᵛ

To Miles Spensar, cleric, d. Carlisle (who, as he asserts, is in his nineteenth year of age and is a nephew of Christopher, cardinal priest of the title of S. Prassede, the issue of his sister german), dispensation and indult. The pope – at his supplication – hereby dispenses Miles to receive and retain together – henceforth – any two benefices, and – when he reaches his twenty-third year – with them any other, with cure or otherwise mutually incompatible, even if chantries, free chapels, hospitals or annual services, usually assigned to secular clerics in title of a perpetual ecclesiastical benefice, or dignities, *personatus*, administrations or offices in cathedral, even metropolitan, or collegiate churches, even if the dignities in question should be major *post pontificalem* in cathedral, even metropolitan, churches, or principal in collegiate churches, or three parish churches or their perpetual vicarages, and of lay or clerical patronage, or a combination, and even if the dignities etc. should be customarily elective and have cure of souls, if he obtains them otherwise canonically, [retaining the two benefices together for life and] the third – if it should be a parish church (or its perpetual vicarage) – for a year calculated from the day of taking peaceful possession of it, or – if it be another incompatible secular benefice – for life, to resign them, at once or successively, simply or for exchange, as often as he pleases, and in their place [receive and] retain up to three other, similar or dissimilar, mutually incompatible, benefices, viz.: two – henceforth – and – when he reaches his twenty-third year – with them any other, [retaining] the third incompatible benefice – if it should be a parish church (or its perpetual vicarage) – for a year etc., or – if it be other than a parish church – for life, as above. And the pope indulges him not to be bound, by reason of any benefices, with cure or otherwise requiring sacred and priest's orders by statute or foundation, held by him at the time, to have himself promoted to any of the said sacred orders for a seven-year period calculated from the end of the year fixed by law, provided that he is a subdeacon within the first two years, nor to be liable to be compelled to do so by anyone against his will; and also, for life, while residing in the Roman curia or either[2] of his benefices, or attending a *studium generale*, not to be bound to reside in the said benefices, nor to be liable to be compelled to do so by anyone against his will. Notwithstanding the defect of age which he suffers in his nineteenth year and shall suffer in his twenty-third, etc. With the proviso that the incompatible and other benefices in question shall not, on this account, be defrauded of due services and the cure of souls in them ([if] any) shall not be neglected; but that the customary burdens of benefices in which he shall not reside shall be supported. The pope's will is, however, that – within the said year – he shall be bound to exchange any such [third] parish church (or its perpetual vicarage) for another benefice, compatible or incompatible, which may not be a parish church (or its perpetual vicarage); otherwise he shall – after the said year has elapsed – be bound to resign the parish church (or its perpetual vicarage) which he has acquired first and which the pope decrees thenceforth vacant.

Vite ac morum honestas …
P lambertus / JoA: / Jo. A. Gratis p(ro) nepot(e) Car(dina)lis Nardin(us)

1   Engrossment is BL Stowe Charter 585; *cf. L&P, F&D*, I², no. 2236; Bell, no. 252.
2   reading *altero* (ill-written); (unexpected in the context of *three* – rather than two – benefices) *Cf.* no. 157.

157   17 December 1513   *Reg. Lat.* 1287, fos 400ʳ-401ʳ

To Christopher Colynson, cleric, d. Carlisle (who, as he asserts, is in his twenty-third year of age and is a nephew of Christopher, cardinal priest of the title of S. Prassede, the issue of his sister german), dispensation and indult. The pope – at his supplication – hereby dispenses Christopher to receive and retain together any three benefices, with cure or otherwise mutually incompatible, even if parish churches or their perpetual vicarages, or chantries, free chapels, hospitals or annual services, usually assigned to secular clerics in title of a perpetual ecclesiastical benefice, or dignities, *personatus*, administrations or offices in cathedral, even metropolitan, or collegiate churches, even if the dignities in question should be major *post pontificalem* in cathedral, even metropolitan, churches, or principal in collegiate churches, and of lay or clerical patronage, or a combination, and even if the dignities etc. should be customarily elective and have cure of souls, if he obtains them otherwise canonically, [retaining two of the benefices together for life and] the third – if it should be a parish church (or its perpetual vicarage) – for a year calculated from the day of taking peaceful possession of it, or – if it be another incompatible secular benefice – for life, to resign them, at once or successively, simply or for exchange, as often as he pleases, and in their place receive and retain together up to three other, similar or dissimilar, mutually incompatible benefices, [retaining] the third incompatible benefice – if it should be a parish church (or its perpetual vicarage) – for a year etc., or – if it be other than a parish church – for life, as above. And the pope indulges him not to be bound, by reason of any benefices, with cure or requiring sacred orders by statute or foundation or otherwise, held by him at the time, to have himself promoted to any of the said sacred orders for a seven-year period calculated from the end of the year granted to him by law, provided that he is a subdeacon within the first two years, nor to be liable to be compelled to do so by anyone against his will; and also, for life while residing in the Roman curia or either[1] of his benefices, or attending a *studium generale*, not to be bound to reside in the said benefices, nor to be liable to be compelled to do so by anyone against his will. Notwithstanding the defect of age which he suffers in his twenty-third year, etc. With the proviso that the incompatible and other benefices in question shall not, on this account, be defrauded of due services and the cure of souls in them ([if] any) shall not be neglected, but that the customary burdens of benefices in which he shall not reside shall be supported. The pope's will is, however, that – within the said year – he shall be bound to exchange any such third parish church (or its perpetual vicarage) for another benefice, compatible or incompatible, which may not be a parish church (or its perpetual vicarage); otherwise he shall – after the said year has elapsed – be bound to resign the parish church (or its perpetual vicarage) which he has acquired first and which the pope decrees thenceforth vacant.

Vite ac morum honestas ...
P[2] *de Cesis / M / M Grat(is) p(ro) nepot(e) Car(dina)lis de Campania*

1   MS: *altero* (unexpected in the context of *three* – rather than two – benefices)
2   uncertain

158   21 December 1513   *Reg. Lat.* 1290A, fos 46ᵛ-47ᵛ

To Nicholas Morton, rector of the church, called chapel, of the college of Slapton' [also spelt *Slapton*], d. Exeter, indult, derogation and relaxation, as below. The pope has learned that in the foundation of the above church it is expressly stipulated that anyone who holds it ought and is bound to: reside in it personally; assist in the celebration of mass and other divine offices at fitting times; and preside over the priests and clerics living in the said college and received in it for the time and preside over their rule. At his supplication, the pope hereby indulges Nicholas, who, as he asserts, holds the above church and the perpetual vicarage of the parish church of Lodeswell', d. Exeter, not to be bound, for life, while residing in the Roman curia or one of his benefices or attending a *studium generale*, to reside in the vicarage or in the above church of Slapton' or the other benefices aforesaid, nor to be liable to be compelled to do so by anyone against his will. Notwithstanding etc. and notwithstanding the oath perhaps[1] taken by him perhaps[1] on acquisition of the said vicarage and the above church of Slapton' or the other benefices aforesaid to reside at them; and [notwithstanding] anything else to the contrary. And even if, for the derogation of the said foundation, special, specific, express, and individual mention or any other expression ought to be made of it and of its whole tenor, verbatim and not by means of general clauses importing the same, or some other uncommon form ought to be observed, the pope – deeming the tenors of the foundation as sufficiently expressed and inserted – hereby, for this once only, specially and expressly derogates the said foundation which shall otherwise remain in force; and relaxes the said oath in this regard. With the proviso that customary burdens of the vicarage, the above church of Slapton' and the other benefices aforesaid in which Nicholas shall not reside shall be supported.

Vite ac morum honestas …
.P Lambertus. / M / M xxv de Campania

1   *sic*

159   7 October 1<5>13[1]   *Reg. Lat.* 1290A, fos 69[r]-70[r]

To Robert Hoon, rector of the parish church of B. Mary, Thodenham by Eklyngham, d. Norwich. Dispensation and indult etc. [as above, no. 2].

Vite ac morum honestas …
.P. Lambertus. / M / M L[2] *de Campania*

1   MS: *millesimo tertio decimo* … in line, with *quingentesimo* inserted in margin initialled *M*; the insertion is in the master's hand.
2   (?) *non(is)*, which is written after the tax mark (L), deleted and initialled *M*. For the tax mark *see above*, no. 13, note 2.

160   17 September 1513   *Reg. Lat.* 1290A, fos 93[v]-94[v]

To George Crakanthort, rector of the parish church of Newbiggynge, d. Carlisle. Dispensation and indult etc. [as above, no. 2].

Vite ac morum honestas …
.P. Lambertus. / JoA: / Jo. A: L:[1] *Nard(inus):*

1   *See above*, no. 13, note 2.

161   17 February 1514   *Reg. Lat.* 1290A, fos 140ᵛ-141ʳ

To John Clerk, DDec, rector of the parish church of Porteshet,[1] d. Bath and Wells. Dispensation – at his supplication – to receive and retain for life, together with the above parish church, one, and without them, any two other benefices, with cure or otherwise mutually incompatible, even if parish churches or their perpetual vicarages, or chantries, free chapels, hospitals or annual services, usually assigned to secular clerics in title of a perpetual ecclesiastical benefice, or dignities, *personatus*, administrations or offices in cathedral, even metropolitan, or collegiate churches, even if the dignities in question should be major *post pontificalem* in cathedral, even metropolitan, churches, or principal in collegiate churches, or a combination, and even if the dignities etc. should be customarily elective and have cure of souls, if he obtains them otherwise canonically, to resign them, at once or successively, simply or for exchange, as often as he pleases, and in their place receive up to two other, similar or dissimilar, incompatible benefices and retain them together for life, as above. Notwithstanding etc. With the proviso that the above parish church[2] and other incompatible benefices shall not, on this account, be defrauded of due services and the cure of souls in the parish church and (if any) the other incompatible benefices shall not be neglected.

Litterarum scientia, vite ac morum honestas …
.P. Lambertus. / C / C. L. Barotius

1   or -*er*
2   Other entries of this type (i.e. dispensations *ad duo*) relating to England and Wales are summarised in the present volume in an abridged form and refer to this entry as to the fully extended prototype.
     When necessary, a term appropriate to the content of the entry should be substituted here; e.g. for no. 442 where the addressee is a cantor read 'chantry'.

162   3 January 1514   *Reg. Lat.* 1290A, fos 141ʳ-142ᵛ

Union etc. At a recent petition on the part of Thomas[1] Wodyngton', DDec, rector of the parish church of Bockyng [also spelt *B<o>*[2]*ching, Doching, Boching*], d. London,[3] (who asserts that he holds a canonry and prebend of the church of London), the pope hereby unites etc. the parish church of Sowthchirche [also spelt *Sowtchirche, Sowchirche*], said diocese,[4] (whose annual value does not exceed 18 pounds sterling), with all its rights and appurtenances, to the above church of Bockyng, which Thomas holds together with the church of Sowthchirche by apostolic dispensation, for as long as he holds Bockyng, to the effect that he may, on his own authority, in person or by proxy, take anew or continue in and retain corporal possession of the church of Sowthchirche, and of the rights and appurtenances aforesaid, for as long as he holds the church of Bockyng, and convert its fruits etc. to his own uses and those of the said churches without licence of the local diocesan or of anyone else. Notwithstanding etc. The pope's will is, however, that the church of Sowthchirche shall not, on account of this union etc., be defrauded of due services and the cure of souls in it shall not be neglected; but that its customary burdens shall be supported; and that on Thomas's death or his resignation etc. of the church of Bockyng this union etc. shall be dissolved and be so deemed and the church of Sowthchirche shall revert to its original condition automatically.

Ad futuram rei memoriam. Romanum decet pontificem et cetera.
.P. Lambertus / C. / C. xxxv. Barotius

1   MS: *Tho<me>*; the 'me' is a supralinear insertion by the enregistering scribe.
2   supralinear insertion by the enregistering scribe
3   *sic*; actually a Canterbury peculiar
4   *sic*; another Canterbury peculiar in d. London

163   30 January 1514   *Reg. Lat.* 1290A, fos 225^v-227^r

To Richard Mabot, MA, perpetual chaplain [of the perpetual chaplaincy] of two chaplains called "Spones' Chauntrey"[1] in the parish church of Tawcestre, d. Lincoln, dispensation, indult and relaxation, as below. As the pope has learned, in the foundation of the perpetual chaplaincy called "Spones' Chauntrey" it is said to be expressly stipulated that anyone who holds the chaplaincy cannot hold another benefice with it or even burden himself with the service of another benefice either continuously for more than a week or discontinuously for more than a month in any one year, and that if he peacefully acquires any other benefice, with or without cure, he shall be bound – within a month calculated from the day of its acquistion – to resign it or the chaplaincy, or cede all right belonging to him in or to one of them, otherwise, after the said month has elapsed, the chaplaincy shall fall vacant by the acquisition of the other benefice; and Richard, as he asserts, holds the chaplaincy and on his acquisition of it swore (before his local ordinary) to inviolably observe the above foundation. Relaxing the oath in this regard, the pope hereby dispenses Richard – at his supplication – to receive and retain for life, together with the chaplaincy, one, and without them, any two other benefices, etc. [as above, no. 2, to '… retain them together for life, as above']; and for life, while residing at the chaplaincy, or in the Roman curia or any one of his benefices, or attending a *studium generale*, not to be bound to reside in his other benefices, nor to be liable to be compelled to do so by anyone against his will. Notwithstanding etc. and [notwithstanding] the said foundation which (otherwise remaining in force) the pope, for this once only, hereby specially and expressly derogates (even if, for its sufficient derogation, full, special, specific, express and individual mention – verbatim and not by means of general clauses importing the same

– or any other expression of the foundation and its whole tenor ought to be had or other uncommon form ought to be observed), deeming the tenors as expressed by the presents, as if they were inserted verbatim; and [notwithstanding] anything else to the contrary. With the proviso that the benefices held and the incompatible and other benefices in question shall not, on this account, be defrauded of due services and the cure of souls in them ([if] any) shall not be neglected; but that customary burdens of the chaplaincy and of other benefices in which he shall not reside shall be supported.

Litterarum scientia, vite ac morum honestas …
.J. Benzon / JoA. / JoA: Lx: Nard(inus)

1　　somewhat sympathetic reading: readily readable as *Chanutrey*

164　　5 May 1513　　　　　　　　　　　　　　　*Reg. Lat.* 1290A, fos 227^r-228^r

Union etc. At a recent petition on the part of John Wylcokk',[1] MTheol, rector of the parish church of Corsfrastell' [also spelt *Corsfrestell'*], d. Salisbury, the pope hereby unites etc. the perpetual vicarage of the parish church of the Holy Cross, vill of Sudha<m>[2]ten', d. Winchester, (whose annual value does not exceed 10 English pounds sterling), with all its rights and appurtenances, to the above church of Corsfrastell', which John holds together with the said vicarage by apostolic dispensation, for as long as he holds Corsfrastell', to the effect that he may, on his own authority, in person or by proxy, take or continue in and retain corporal possession of the vicarage and of the rights and appurtenances aforesaid, for as long as he holds Corsfrastell', and convert its fruits etc. to his own uses and those of Corsfrastell' and the said vicarage without licence of the local diocesan or of anyone else. Notwithstanding etc. The pope's will is, however, that the said vicarage shall not, on account of this union etc., be defrauded of due services and the cure of souls in it shall not be neglected; but that its customary burdens shall be supported; and that on John's death or his resignation etc. of the church of Corsfrastell' this union etc. shall be dissolved and be so deemed and the vicarage shall revert to its original condition automatically.

Ad futuram rei memoriam. Romanum decet pontificem et cetera.
.P. Lambertus / JoA. / . JoA. xxxv. Nardinus

1　　written *Wijl-* with the lower fork of the second 'k' developed into a loop
2　　supralinear insertion above (?)*nn* deleted

165　　21 February 1514　　　　　　　　　　　*Reg. Lat.* 1290A, fos 233^r-234^r

To Richard Prehest, abbot of the monastery of Graces (*de Gratiis*)[1] by the tower of London, OCist, d. London, approval and confirmation. A recent petition to the pope on

Richard's part stated that at another time, when the monastery of B Mary Graces by the tower of London, OCist, d. London, (which is immediately subject to the apostolic see), was vacant by the death, outside the Roman curia, of the late John Langton, formerly abbot of the said monastery, the convent of the said monastery, with the consent of Thomas, abbot of the monastery of B Mary, Beaulieu Regis (*de bello loco regis*), OCist, d. Winchester, father-abbot and visitor of the monastery of Graces, meeting, as is the custom, in one body for the election of the future abbot, on the day which had been fixed beforehand for the election, harmoniously elected Richard – then prior of the monastery of Graces, expressly professed of the said order, and a priest – as abbot of the monastery of Graces, and the said Thomas the father-abbot, by ordinary authority, approved [and] confirmed the election of Richard when the election- decree had been presented to him, and he appointed Richard abbot of the said monastery of Graces, fully committing the care, rule, and administration of the said monastery of Graces to him in spiritualities and temporalities; and thereafter, by virtue of the election and appointment aforesaid, Richard has acquired quasi -possession of the rule, administration, and goods of the said monastery of Graces. The pope – at the supplication to him to add the strength of apostolic confirmation to the aforesaid election and confirmation, for their greater sufficiency – hereby approves and confirms the said election and subsequent confirmation of the father-abbot and whatsoever ensued therefrom [provided that][2] the said election belongs by law to the said convent, supplying all defects (if any) in the same. Notwithstanding etc.

Ad ea ex apostolice servitutis officio libenter intendimus ...
O. de Cesis. / JoA: / JoA: L: Nardinus

1   'Beate Marie' does not occur in the address clause. In the body of the letter the monastery is once referred
    to as *Beate Marie de Gratiis iuxta Turrim Londen.*, six times as simply *de Gratiis*
2   MS: *... ac inde secuta quecunque quarum electio huiusmodi de iure ad eosdem conventum pertineat ...* Where
    MS has *quarum* we would expect 'dummodo' (or suchlike). Either *quarum* is a mistake or there is an
    omission at this point.

166   20 August 1513   *Reg. Lat.* 1290A, fo 297[r-v]

To Henry[1] Trotter, canon of the monastery, called priory or house, of St John the Evangelist, Lega, OSA, d. London. Dispensation – at his supplication – to him, who, as he asserts, is expressly professed of the above order,[2] to receive and retain any benefice, with or without cure, usually held by secular clerics, etc. [as above, no. 43].

Relligionis[3] zelus, vite ac morum honestas ...
.P. Lambertus / M / M xxx de Campania

1   written *hEnrico*: the 'h' an afterthought
2   This information comes from a notwithstanding clause.
3   *sic*

167[1]   **22 January 1514**   *Reg. Lat.* 1290A, fos 312ᵛ-313ᵛ

To Thomas Barcher, prior of the monastery, usually governed by a prior, of Newburgh (*de Novo Burgo*), OSA, d. York (who, as he asserts, by apostolic concession and dispensation,[2] holds the priorship of the said monastery, which is conventual, *in titulum* and the parish church of Epweth', d. Lincoln – which belongs at a time of vacancy to the presentation of the prior for the time being and convent of the said priory by ancient and approved custom hitherto observed – *in commendam*). Dispensation – at Thomas's supplication – to the said prior for the time being to be able, in perpetuity, to be presented for the said church, within the lawful time, whenever it falls vacant, by the sub-prior of the said monastery for the time being and convent or by anyone else who, by concession of the prior and convent or sub-prior and convent aforesaid, has the right of presenting for it; and, at such presentation, he must be instituted as rector of the said church by the local ordinary or his vicar general or by the administrator (*custodem*) of the church of Lincoln when the see is vacant; and to retain the church *in commendam* together with the priory for as long as he is its prior; he may – due and customary burdens of the said parish [church][3] having been supported – make disposition of the rest of its fruits etc. just as those holding it *in titulum* could and ought to do, alienation of the parish church's [immovable goods and precious movables][4] being however forbidden. Notwithstanding etc. With the proviso that while the said parish church is held *in commendam* it shall not, on this account, be defrauded of due services and the cure of souls in it shall not be neglected; but that its aforesaid burdens shall be supported. Given at Corneto.

Ad perpetuam rei memoriam. Sincere devotionis affectus ...
.A. de. Sancto severino / JoA: / JoA: LXXXX: Nardinus

1   Copy in LA, Reg. Wolsey and Atwater, fo. 55ᵛ/65ᵛ; the dating clause is incomplete: only the place-date (Corneto) and year date (1513) are recorded. Impetration licensed by king: *cf. L&P, F&D*, I², no. 2484 (2).
2   Julius II's dispensation to Thomas to hold two benefices with cure *in commendam* with the priorship is summarised in *CPL*, XVIII at no. 715.
3   MS wants 'ecclesie'.
4   MS: *alienatione tamen et cetera* Supplied from common form.

168   19 March 1513   *Reg. Lat.* 1290A, fos 364ᵛ-366ᵛ

Effectuation of Julius II's confirmation etc. and statute etc. in favour of the master, guardians and all the members (*confratres*) of the confraternity in the chapel of the hospital of B. Mary the Virgin, Rowncydewall', close outside the walls of London. Some time ago, representation was made to Julius II on the part of the above master, guardians and members that at another time several citizens and others of Christ's faithful of the city and district of London, led by piety, had instituted and established a certain notable confraternity of persons of both sexes in the chapel of the above hospital and had produced certain praiseworthy and honest constitutions and ordinances, in conformity with the sacred canons, for the maintenance and direction of

the confraternity; and supplication was made on the part of the said master etc. to Julius
to add the strength of apostolic confirmation to the said institution and constitutions
and ordinances for their greater support. Julius – who intended that works of piety and
pious ordinances enacted by the devotion of the faithful should endure for all time and
who fostered the pious prayers (*suffragia*) of the faithful with heavenly gifts so that
they be made more worthy of divine grace and much more devoted to charity – at this
supplication under date 17 December, tenth year [1512] approved and confirmed the
said institution and constitutions etc. and also all privileges, liberties, immunities,
concessions, donations, bounties (*largitiones*) and indults whatsoever granted and
made in any way to the hospital and chapel and to the confraternity and its members
by any of Leo's (at that time Julius's) predecessors and by the apostolic see as well as
by any kings and princes and others of the faithful and decreed this confirmation to
hold good in perpetuity, supplying any defects in the same. And Julius established and
ordained that all members (of both sexes) of the confraternity at that time and for the
time being who, from the goods conferred on them by God, every year[1] paid 4 English
pence annually[1] towards the maintenance of the confraternity and the support and
sustenance of the ministers of the poor and infirm in the said hospital for the time
being, may choose any suitable priest, secular or regular of any order, even mendicant,
who may – after he has, within the said chapel or hospital, heard their confessions on
each of the feasts of the Conception, Nativity, Annunciation, Visitation, Purification
and Assumption of B. Mary the Virgin, and of the Resurrection of Our Lord and of
Pentecost, Corpus Christi, and of St James the Apostle, and the feast of the dedication
of the said chapel and of the celebration of All Saints – absolve the members and each
one of them, being truly confessed and contrite, from all their sins however grievous,
except those reserved to the apostolic see; and enjoin a salutary penance on them for
the sins etc. committed; and may grant plenary remission of all their sins on the said
feasts of the Annunciation and Assumption of B. Mary; and that it is permissible for
the said members (of both sexes) at that time and for the time being to have a portable
altar on which, in fitting places, without prejudice to anyone in law, when pressure of
affairs dictates, they may cause mass and other divine offices to be celebrated, in their
presence and in that of their household, by any secular or regular priest, even before
day-break (though about that time), but faultlessly, and if in places laid under interdict
on ordinary authority, then behind closed doors with the interdicted and
excommunicated kept out, without bell-ringing and in a low voice; and that the priest,
as well as any others, duly confessed and contrite, may, as many times as they wish,
receive the sacrament of the Eucharist in the said chapel (saving always the right of the
parish church and of anyone else in all things); and that, at a time of interdict, it is
permissible for the members to hear, behind closed doors with the excommunicated,
suspended and interdicted kept out, as above, without bell-ringing and in a low voice,
mass and other divine offices, and, as above, receive other things even ecclesiastical
sacraments; and for the priests of the said hospital and confraternity for the time being
to administer the said sacraments to them; and also that the bodies of those dying in
the said hospital or within its precinct may be assigned for ecclesiastical burial in the
said chapel or its cemetery and the bodies of those members (of both sexes) dying at a
time of interdict may, without funeral pomp, be assigned for ecclesiastical burial in the
said chapel and the cemetery of the same or in any other church or cemetery not

specially under interdict where they choose to be buried; and that all members (of both sexes) present at that time and all future members and also others of the faithful who, on the Fridays of Lent, visited the said chapel and, kneeling, devoutly said and recited five times the Lord's Prayer with the Angelic Salutation and the Apostles' Creed (*simbolo apostolorum*) would obtain all the indulgences and remissions of sins which they would obtain if they were to personally visit the stational churches in Rome (*Urbis*) and outside its walls, at Lent and at the other station times and days in the year; and also that those who on any of the said feasts firstly gave to the said hospital 4 English pence on behalf of their father, mother, wife, sons, daughters, blood-relations or friends in purgatory, and [then] gave the same amount on behalf of any one of them to any priest-member of the said confraternity to recite once the entire Psalter of B. Mary the Virgin on behalf of any one of the same, would obtain the same indulgences and remissions of sins by way of intercession (*per modum suffragii*) which they would obtain if they were to personally visit the chapel of B. Mary, *Schala Celi*, close by the monastery of St. Anastasia[2] at Tre Fontane (*ad Tres Fontes*), OCist, outside the walls of Rome. Notwithstanding etc. Since, however, Julius died before his letters to this effect were drawn up, the pope wills and decrees that Julius's confirmation etc. and statute etc. shall take effect from the said 17 December and that the present letters shall everywhere be sufficient proof thereof.

Ad perpetuam rei memoriam. Rationi congruit et cetera.
.P. Lambertus / M / M CCCC De Campania

1   MS: *qui singulis annis ... annuatim solverent*
2   MS: *Sancte Anastasie*; *recte* 'Sancti Anastasii'

169   26 February 1515   *Reg. Lat.* 1291, fos 290[r]-293[r]

To the bishop of Exeter and Richard Gilbert and Richard Tollet, canons of the church of Exeter, mandate in favour of John Elys and John Trobulfild, laymen, d. Exeter, joint parties in this regard. A recent petition to the pope on the part of the joint parties stated that some time ago Henry Fayrman, who bears himself as rector of the parish church of Honyton, said d. – falsely alleging that the joint parties had, against the wishes (*preter et contra voluntatem*) of Henry the rector, audaciously presumed, to the great prejudice of Henry the rector and of the said church, *de facto* to cut down, split up, and take away several trees and branches growing within the bounds or precinct of the cemetery of the said church, automatically and culpably incurring the sentence of greater excommunication and the other ecclesiastical sentences, censures, and pains promulgated generally, as he said, against such persons under the provincial constitutions of Canterbury[1] – sued the joint parties over this, not by apostolic delegation, before Thomas Wodyngton', the then official, called president, of Canterbury, who was, he said, a competent judge for this, requesting *inter alia* a declaration that the right of taking up and cutting down trees and branches appertains solely to the said Henry and the rector of the said church for the time being and that Henry the rector has, as above, been recklessly and *de facto* robbed of them and that the joint parties have therefore automatically incurred the sentence of greater excommunication and the other sentences, censures, and pains contained in the said constitution; that the said official, proceeding wrongly in the case, promulgated an unjust, definitive (as he said) sentence by which he declared that the right of taking up and having[2] all the trees and branches growing within the precinct or bounds of the cemetery of the said church belongs to Henry (and the rector of the said church for the time being) and that by rashly and *de facto* pulling out and cutting down the said trees and branches against Henry the rector's wishes the joint parties and each one of them had, as he said, automatically incurred the sentence of excommunication and the other sentences, censures, and pains contained in the said constitution and that they (and each one of them) had been and were excommunicate, and he publicly denounced them as such and ordered that they were to be strictly avoided by everyone, condemning them as well in the expenses run up in the case the taxation of which was reserved to the official in the future; and that on the joint parties' part appeal was made from the sentence to the apostolic see, but because the official unlawfully refused to recognize the appeal (which in law should have been recognized) appeal was again made to the said see on the joint parties' part. At the supplication to the pope to order that the joint parties and each one of them be absolved *ad cautelam* from the [sentence][3] of excommunication and from the other ecclesiastical [sentences], censures, and pains promulgated[4] against them on the above occasion, and also to commit to some upright men in those parts the causes: of the aforesaid appeals and of everything perhaps attempted and innovated [after][5] and against them and each one of them; of the nullity of the process and sentence of the said official and of each and every other thing done in any way to the prejudice of the joint parties and each one of them in connection with the above; and of the whole principal matter, the pope hereby commands that the above three (or two or one of them), having summoned Henry and the others concerned, shall, on the pope's authority, for this once only, bestow on the joint parties and each one of them, if they so request, the benefit of absolution *ad cautelam* from the said sentence of excommunication and other sentences, censures, and pains, inasmuch as it is just, having, however, first received from them suitable security in respect of that for which they are perhaps deemed excommunicate and caught by the other sentences, censures, and pains, that if the above find that the said sentence of excommunication and the other sentences censures and pains were justly inflicted on them they will obey the mandates of the above and those of the church; as to the other things, having heard both sides, taking cognizance even of the principal matter, shall decree what is just, without appeal, causing [by ecclesiastical censure] what they have decreed to be [strictly] observed[6]; [and moreover compel] witnesses, etc. Notwithstanding etc.

Humilibus et cetera.
J Benzon / M / M xvj De Campania

1   *Cf.* W. Lyndwood, *Provinciale*, Lib. III, Tit. 28, cap. 6. *Quia Divinis* (ed. Oxford, 1679, pp. 267-8).
2   MS: *habendi*; *recte*: 'amputandi'?
3   MS wants 'sententiis'
4   *sic*
5   MS wants 'post'
6   MS: *facientes quod decreveritis et cetera observari*. Supplied from common form.

170   30 June 1516[1]   *Reg. Lat.* 1292, fo 72[r]

To William Burford *alias* Lambard, canon of the monastery of St Mary, Cirencestrie[2] [also spelt *Cire(n)cestrie*[3]] *alias* Ccessetur, OSA, d. Worcester. Dispensation – at his supplication – to him, who, as he asserts, is expressly professed of the above order,[4] to receive and retain any benefice, with or without cure, usually held by secular clerics etc. [as above, no. 138].[5]

Relligionis[6] *zelus, vite ac morum honestas...*
P. Lambertus / JoA: / JoA: xxx: Nardinus

1   Relating to the pontifical year, MS has: *anno* [*p* – the start of 'primo'? – deleted] *quarto*
2   MS: *de Cirencestrie*. Possibly *Cirencestrie* is Latin, the *de* being erroneous; but the alias (= the local pronunciation), especially as it is not introduced by 'de', perhaps argues that *Cirencestrie* is (or is treated as) a vernacular form.
3   MS: *Cire'cestrie*
4   This information comes from a notwithstanding clause.
5   Save for a slight difference of formulation, viz.: no. 138 repeats the phrase 'usually held by secular clerics'; whereas the present entry deploys 'defined as above'.
6   *sic*

171   15 July 1513   *Reg. Lat.* 1293, fos 1[r]-4[v]

To Andrew, bishop of Moray, archbishop-elect of Bourges. Consistorial provision of him – bishop of Moray – to the church of Bourges, vacant by the death, outside the Roman curia of the late archbishop Michael, during whose rule Julius II specially reserved the said church to his own disposition (after which Julius did not otherwise dispose of the said church before his own death; and the pope has declared that provisions of all cathedral and metropolitan churches reserved by Julius, but vacant at the time of his death, have remained and do remain covered by Julius's said reservation); and appointment of bishop Andrew as archbishop of Bourges, committing to him the care and administration of the church of Bourges in spiritualities and temporalities; on condition, however, that he shall not, because of this, cease to be bishop of Moray, but shall be true head (*presul*) and pastor of the churches of both Bourges and Moray. The pope's will is, however, that before bishop Andrew involves himself in the rule and administration of the church of Bourges in any way he shall take the usual oath of fealty before the bishops of Paris and Angoulême, or one of them, in accordance with the form which the pope is sending enclosed (*introclusam*) under his *bulla*[1]; and by other letters of his the pope has commanded that the above bishops of Paris and Angoulême (or one of them) shall receive the oath from bishop Andrew in the name of the pope and the Roman church.[2]
    Conclusions to (i) the chapter of the church of Bourges; (ii) the clergy of the city and diocese of Bourges; (iii) the people of the said city and diocese; (iv) the vassals of the said church; (v) Louis, king of the Franks; (vi) the suffragans of the said church.

Divina disponente clemencia ... The conclusions begin: (i) *Hodie*[3] *ecclesie vestre*

Bitturicen. ...; (ii), (iii), (iv), (vi) *Hodie ecclesie Bitturicen.*[4]... (v) *Gratie divine premium* ...

L. Puccius / JoA. / JoA: Cxx: xij: xij: xij: xij: xij: Nardinus

1   Cf. below, no. 384, notes 3 and 4.
2   below, no. 173
3   following *Hodie, dilecto filio* is deleted (without initial).
4   or (in one instance) *Bituricen.*

172   15 July 1513   *Reg. Lat.* 1293, fos 4ᵛ-6ʳ

To Andrew, bishop of Moray, archbishop-elect of Bourges, whom the pope has this day, on the advice of the cardinals, provided to the church of Bourges (then bereft of a pastor *certo modo*) and appointed archbishop, committing the care and administration of the church of Bourges to him in spiritualities and temporalities – on condition, however, that he should not, because of this, cease to preside over the church of Moray, over which he was then presiding; but should be the true head (*presul*) and pastor of the churches of both Bourges and Moray – as is more fully stated in the pope's letters drawn up in that regard.[1] Since, as the pope has learned, at the time of the said provision and appointment Andrew was holding *in commendam*, as he does, the monastery of Driburght [also spelt *Driburghat*], and the priory of Pettinweynn, Augustinian and Premonstratensian Orders,[2] both d. St Andrews, and also the parish church of Cottingahan, d. York, by apostolic concession and dispensation, the pope – wishing to assist him to keep up his position in accordance with pontifical dignity – hereby dispenses Andrew – *motu proprio* – after he has acquired, on the strength of the said provision and appointment, peaceful quasi-possession of the rule and administration of the said church of Bourges and of [its][3] goods or the greater part of them – to retain for life as before the parish church and the priory (which is conventual), whose annual value together does not exceed 100 pounds sterling, and also the monastery, even if the priory is customarily elective and has cure of souls, together with the churches of Bourges and Moray, for as long as he presides over them; and – having been granted entry (*accessu*) to the monastery of Bellzo[4] *alias* Kelso (*de Calco*), OSB, d. St Andrews, some time ago by the said apostolic authority – in event of this entry to retain for life the monastery of Bellzo *alias* Kelso (the fruits etc. of which and of the aforesaid monastery of Driburght the pope wills to be had as expressed) likewise *in commendam*. Notwithstanding etc. With decree that the commends of the monastery of Driburght, the priory and the parish church aforesaid shall not cease and the entry in question shall not expire. With the proviso that divine worship in the monasteries and the usual number of monks and ministers shall not be diminished and the priory and parish church shall not be defrauded of due services and the cure of souls in the parish church and (if any) in the priory shall not be neglected; but that customary burdens of the said monasteries and priory and their convents and of the parish church aforesaid shall be supported.

Personam tuam nobis et apostolice sedi devotam tuis exigentibus meritis paterna

benevolentia prosequentes illa tibi favorabiliter concedimus ...
L. Puccius / JoA / JoA: C: XX: Nardinus

1   above, no. 171
2   thus the word-order of the register
3   *illorum*; *recte*: 'illius'
4   the letter here transcribed as 'z' perhaps yogh

173   15 July 1513   *Reg. Lat.* 1293, fos 6ᵛ-7ʳ

To the bishops of Paris and Angoulême mandate. This day the pope provided Andrew, bishop of Moray, archbishop-elect of Bourges, to the church of Bourges, appointing him archbishop and committing the care and administration of Bourges to him in spiritualities and temporalities, as is more fully contained in his letters drawn up in that regard.[1] Wishing to spare bishop Andrew, archbishop-elect, who lives[2] in those parts, the labour and expense of going in person to the apostolic see, the pope hereby commands the above bishops that both or one of them shall receive the usual oath of fealty from bishop Andrew, archbishop-elect, in the name of the pope and the Roman church in accordance with the form which the pope is sending enclosed (*introclusam*) under his *bulla*,[3] and that they shall send the pope, at once, by their own messenger, the form of oath which bishop Andrew takes as archbishop-elect before them, verbatim, by his letters patent, marked with his seal.[4]

Cum nos hodie ...
L. Puccius / JoA: / JoA: xvj: Nardi(nus)

1   above, no. 171
2   *commorantibus*; *recte*: 'commorantis'?
3   *Cf.* below, no. 384, notes 3 and 4.
4   *sigillo* – changed (by overwriting) from *signo*

174   15 July 1513   *Reg. Lat.* 1293, fo 7ʳ⁻ᵛ

To Andrew, bishop of Moray. Since the pope, on the advice of the cardinals, intends this day to make provision of Andrew to the church of Bourges, at present vacant *certo modo*, and to appoint him archbishop, he hereby absolves him from any [sentences] of excommunication [etc.][1] under which he may perhaps lie, so far only as regards the taking effect of the said provision and appointment and each of the relevant letters. Notwithstanding etc.

Apostolice sedis consueta clementia ne disposiciones ...
L. Puccius / JoA: / JoA xxiiij Nardinus

1   omission of passage of common form (perhaps triggered by the scribe turning overleaf)

175   3 August 1513   *Reg. Lat.* 1293, fos 7ᵛ-8ʳ

To the bishops of Paris and Angoulême, mandate. Since the pallium, namely the symbol of the plenitude of pastoral office[1], has, with becoming urgency, been requested from the pope on the part of Andrew, bishop of Moray, archbishop-elect of Bourges (whom the pope, on the advice of the cardinals, has provided to the church of Bourges and appointed archbishop, as is more fully contained in the pope's letters drawn up in this regard)[2] by M. Thomas Nudre, archdeacon of the church of Moray, the pope's notary and Andrew's envoy (*nuncium*), the pope, at Thomas's entreaties (*ipsius precibus*), has caused the said pallium – which has been taken from the tomb (*de corpore*) of B Peter and is to be assigned to Andrew by the above two (or one of them), in accordance with the form which the pope is sending enclosed (*introclusam*) under his *bulla*[3] – to be delivered (*destinandum*) by the said Thomas. The pope hereby commands that the above two (or one of them) shall take care to assign the pallium to Andrew in accordance with the above form, and receive from him, in the name of the pope and the Roman church, the usual oath of fealty, under the form which the pope is sending (*dirigimus*) under another (*alia*) *bulla*.[4] They shall, moreover, take care to immediately forward to the pope, by their own courier (*nuncium*), the form of oath which archbishop Andrew takes, verbatim, by his letters patent, fortified with his seal.

Cum pallium insigne videlicet ...
L. puccius / JoA / JoA xij: Nardinus

1   MS: *pastoralis officii*; *recte*: 'pontificalis officii'?
2   above, no. 171
3   The 'forma dandi (*or* tradendi) pallium' not enregistered; *cf.* below, no. 385, note 10.
4   The 'forma iuramenti pro archiepiscopo in traditione pallii' is not enregistered; *Cf.* below, no. 385, note 13.

176   3 August 1513   *Reg. Lat.* 1293, fos 8ᵛ-9ʳ

To Andrew, bishop of Moray, archbishop-elect of Bourges, mandate. Since, recently, the pope, on the advice[1] of the cardinals, made provision of Andrew to the church of Bourges, then vacant, appointing him archbishop, as is more fully stated in the pope's letters drawn up in this regard;[2] and since, afterwards, the pallium, namely the symbol of the plenitude of pontifical office,[3] had, with becoming urgency, been requested from the pope on Andrew's part by M. Thomas Nudre, archdeacon of the church of Moray, the pope's notary and Andrew's envoy (*nuncium*), the pope – at Andrew's supplication – has caused the said pallium, which has been taken from the tomb (*corpore*) of B Peter and is to be assigned by the bishops of Paris and Angoulême, to be delivered (*destinandum*) by Thomas, so that the said bishops (or one of them) assign[4] it to Andrew in accordance with the form which the pope is sending (*dirigimus*) enclosed (*introclusam*) under his *bulla* and receive from Andrew, in the name of the pope and the Roman church, the usual oath of fealty, under the form which the pope is sending under the said (*eadem*) *bulla*.[5] Andrew is to use the pallium inside his church (*intra ecclesiam*)[6] of Bourges only on those days which are expressly stated in the privileges of the said church; and so that the symbol does not differ from the person who bears it, but rather Andrew heeds inwardly what he wears externally, the pope hereby reminds and exhorts Andrew attentively and commands that he shall aim to observe humility and justice and take care to augment the church of Bourges spiritually and temporally.

Cum pridem ecclesie Bituricen. ...
L. Puccius / JoA. / JoA: x: Nardinus

1   MS: *consisio*; *recte*: 'consilio'
2   above, no. 171
3   *pontificalis officii*; *see* previous entry.
4   MS: *assignare*; *recte*: 'assignent'
5   Neither form is enregistered in this entry; *cf.* below, no. 385, note 13; *and see* nos. 384 notes 3 and 4; 385 notes 5 and 10.
6   On the meaning of this expression, *see Decretals*, I. 8. especially caps. 1, 5, and 6 (Friedberg, 100-102).

177   14 July 1514   *Reg. Lat.* 1293, fos 246ᵛ-248ᵛ

To M. Richard Pace (*Paceo*), cleric of York, papal notary, consistorial commend as below. Wishing to provide the monastery of St Stephen, Bologna, OSB – which the late Christopher, cardinal priest of the title of S. Prassede, held *in commendam* by apostolic concession and dispensation while he lived; and which (the commend having ended when cardinal Christopher died at the apostolic see) is vacant still in the way in which it was vacant when it was commended to cardinal Christopher – with a capable and suitable governor; as well as to assist Richard, the pope, on the advice of the cardinals, hereby commends the monastery, thus vacant, to Richard, to be held, ruled and governed by him for life, even together with all the benefices, with and without cure, secular and regular of any order, which he holds by any apostolic concessions and dispensations *in titulum* and *in commendam*, and shall hold in the future, and with annual pensions assigned to him on any ecclesiastical fruits etc. which he receives and shall receive in the future, committing the care, rule and administration of this monastery to him in spiritualities and temporalities. The pope's will is, however, that divine worship and the usual number of monks and ministers in the said monastery shall not, on account of this commend, be diminished; but that customary burdens of the monastery and its convent shall be supported; and that Richard may – after the burdens in question have been duly supported – make disposition of the rest of the fruits etc. (upon which divers annual pensions up to a total of 400 gold ducats of the camera are assigned by apostolic authority to certain ecclesiastical persons who receive them annually[1])– just as abbots of the said monastery could and ought to do, alienation of the monastery's immovable goods and precious movables being however forbidden; and that Richard is specially[2] bound to pay the said pensions.

Conclusions to: (i) to the bishop of Bologna (to whom the monastery of St Stephen, Bologna, is understood to be subject by ordinary law); (ii) the convent of the said monastery.

Romani pontificis providentia circumspecta ... The conclusions begin: (i), (ii) *Hodie monasterium Sancti Stephani Bononien.* ...
f Bregeon / C / C xvj viij viij Barotius

1 MS affected by bleed through; tentatively reading: *annuatim percipiunt dicta auctoritate assignate existant*
2 reading: (?)*specialiter*

178[1] **14 July 1514**   *Reg. Lat.* 1293, fos 248ᵛ-249ʳ

To M. Richard Pace (*Paceo*), cleric of York,[2] papal notary. Since the pope, on the advice of the cardinals, intends this day to commend the monastery of St Stephen, Bologna, OSB, vacant *certo modo* at present, to Richard to be held, ruled and governed by him for life, he hereby absolves him from any [sentences] of excommunication *et cetera* under which he may perhaps lie, so far only as regards the taking effect of the said commend and each of the relevant letters. Notwithstanding etc.

Apostolice sedis consueta clementia ad ea libenter intendit ...
f Bregeon / C / C xvj Barotius

1 Entire entry very badly affected by bleed through.
2 *clerico Eboracen.* (i.e. 'diocesis' does not occur)

179   19 March 1513   *Reg. Lat.* 1295, fo 164ʳ⁻ᵛ

To John Moor', perpetual vicar of the parish church of Burlescombe, d. Exeter, effectuation. Some time ago, Julius II under date 26 December, ninth year [1511] [granted] John (who, as he asserted, was holding the perpetual vicarage of the above parish church) dispensation and indult etc. [as above, no. 2, with appropriate changes of tense]. Since Julius died before his letters to this effect were drawn up, the pope hereby wills and decrees that the present letters shall everywhere be sufficient proof of the said dispensation etc.

Rationi congruit et cetera.
.P. lambertus / A[1] */ JoA: L: Nardinus*

1 *sic*; in view of the subscription 'JoA:' expected here. The 'A' formed like the 'A' in *JoA* in the subscription.

180   31 July 1516   *Reg. Lat.* 1295, fos 275^v-277^r

To William Geyll',[1] rector of the parish church of Ardeley, d. Lincoln. Dispensation and indult etc. [as above, no. 2].

Vite ac morum honestas ...
.P. lambertus / JoA: / :JoA: Lx: Nardinus

1   *Willemo Geyll'* appears to have been entered later in a gap left for the purpose.

181   31 July 1516   *Reg. Lat.* 1295, fos 277^r-279^r

To William Stradling, chancellor of the church of St David's, dispensation. Some time ago, Julius II by his letters dispensed William to receive and retain together for life any two benefices, etc. [as above, no. 6, to '... as is more fully contained in those letters'].[1] The pope – at his supplication – hereby dispenses William, who, as he asserts, holds by the said dispensation the chancellorship of the church of St David's (which is a dignity, perhaps major *post pontificalem*) and the parish church of St Catherine the Virgin and Martyr,[2] d. Llandaff, to receive and retain for life, together with the chancellorship and parish church aforesaid, or with any two other incompatible benefices <held>[3] by him at the time by virtue of the said dispensation, any third benefice, etc. [as above, no. 6].

Vite ac morum honestas ...
.P. Lambertus. / JoA: / :JoA: Lxx: Nar(dinus)

1   *CPL* XIX, no. 394
2   If our identification is correct the dedication was misread, seemingly, by the Valor as *Sancte Tatha*^{e}. (*Valor Ecclesiasticus*, IV, p. 353); dedication then subsequently further corrupted as St Athanasius with invented name 'St Aithan alias Tathan' dedicated to St Athanasius (Willis, *Parochiale* [1733], p. 200); 'Tatha *alias* St Tathan's' ded. St Athanasius (Ekton, *Thesaurus* [1742], p. 652); 'Tatha, alias St Tathan, alias St Athan's' ded. St Athanasius (Bacon, *Liber Regis* [1786], p. 1083); and St Athan (Crockford's *Clerical Directory*, 1971-72 [1973], p. 1267).
3   *obtemptis* in line deleted and initialled *JoA.* (with a cross [signalling error?] above the deletion); *obtentis* inserted in margin (in hand of enregistering scribe) initialled *JoA*

182   31 July 1516   *Reg. Lat.* 1295, fo 279^{r-v}

To Henry Skenner, canon of the monastery, called house, of B. Mary and St John the Baptist, Darforth [also spelt *Darfort*], OPrem, d. Chichester, (who, as he asserts, is expressly professed of the said order)[1]. Dispensation – at his supplication – to receive and retain for life any benefice, with or without cure, usually held by secular clerics, even[2] if a parish church or its perpetual vicarage, etc. [as above, no. 43].

Religionis zelus et cetera.
P lambertus. / JoA: / JoA: xxx: Nardinus

1   This information comes from a notwithstanding clause.
2   MS: *et*; *recte*: 'etiam'

183   31 July 1516   *Reg. Lat.* 1295, fos 279ᵛ-280ʳ

To Edmund de Nuy, professor OP. Dispensation – at his supplication – to receive and retain for life any benefice, with or without cure, usually held by secular clerics, etc. [as above, no. 43, to '... Notwithstanding etc. '] and [notwithstanding] the constitutions of Otto and Ottobuono, formerly legates of the apostolic see in the kingdom of England etc.[1]

Religionis zelus et cetera.
P lambertus. / JoA: / :JoA: xxxx: Nardinus

1   The inclusion of these constitutions gives de Nuy the option of holding his secular benefice in England.

184   2 August 1516   *Reg. Lat.* 1295, fo 280ʳ⁻ᵛ

To Cuthbert Punscal, rector of the parish church of Harou [also spelt *Haron*], d. Canterbury, extension and amplification of indult, etc. At another time Cuthbert was, as he asserts, indulged by apostolic authority, for life, while residing at a *studium generale* or [applying himself][1] to the service of a second bishop in whose diocese he was beneficed,[2] or while residing in the Roman curia or any one of his benefices, not to be bound to reside in his other benefices, nor to be liable to be compelled to do so by anyone against his will, as is more fully contained in the apostolic letters drawn up in that regard.[3] By virtue of this indult, Cuthbert was, for a certain time, auditor of causes of William, archbishop of Canterbury, in whose diocese he is beneficed; and, afterwards, he transferred to the service of the present king of England and has been received as master and keeper of the king's archive and rolls (*in cuius scriniorum et voluminum magistrum et custodem*). At the supplication of Cuthbert (who, as he asserts, holds the above parish church and the perpetual vicarage of the parish church of Kyrkbi, <in Kendal, d. York>,[4] by apostolic dispensation), the pope hereby extends and amplifies the indult and the letters drawn up in that regard with every one of the clauses contained in them concerning this, so that Cuthbert, for life, is not bound – while in the said king's service – to reside in any of his benefices, nor is he liable to be compelled to do so by anyone against his will. Notwithstanding etc. With relaxation of the oath to reside at the said vicarage which Cuthbert took when he acquired it.

Vite ac morum et cetera.
.P. lambertus. / JoA: / : JoA: xx: Nardinus

1   MS wants an appropriate verb (i.e. in addition to 'residendo'); 'insistendo' can be found in a not greatly
    dissimilar context.
2   *serviciis alterius episcopi in cuius dioc(esi) beneficiatus esses* – alluding, possibly, to York (even though no
    bishop [or archbishop] has yet been particularised in the present entry; and despite the use of 'episcopi').
3   unknown to the *CPL*.
    On 6 May 1501 Tunstal had been dispensed to hold a second (unidentified) benefice with the rectory of
    Claughton, d. York (*CPL*, XVII, Part I, no. 521); but the letters for that do not comprehend an indult for non-
    residence.
    Maybe the "unknown" indult for non-residence cited in the entry above was issued *in forma brevis* (*cf. CPL*,
    XVII, Part II, p. cxxxv).
    It might be helpful to compare both indults for non-residence described in the present entry against the usual
    form of indult which, by Leo's pontificate, was commonly issued together with a dispensation *ad duo*
    (above, no. 2). Plainly, the additional passages here reflect Tunstal's own special circumstances and
    requirements.
4   *in Kendal Eboracen. diocesis* inserted in margin (hand of enregistering scribe) initialled *JoA*.

185   20 July 1513   *Reg. Lat.* 1296, fo 3[r-v]

Union etc. At a recent petition on the part of Peter Trott, perpetual vicar of[1] the parish
church of Cuttrombe[2] [also spelt *Contrombe, Contrombre,*[3] *C<u>trombe,*[4]
Cuttro(m)be,[5]] d. Bath and Wells, the pope hereby unites etc. the perpetual vicarage of
the parish church of Wynnysford [also spelt *Wynnisford*], said diocese, (whose annual
value does not exceed 4 English pounds), with all its rights and appurtenances, to the
vicarage of the above parish church of Cuttrombe, which Peter holds together with the
vicarage of Wynnysford by apostolic dispensation, for as long as he holds that of
Cuttrombe, to the effect that he may, on his own authority, in person or by proxy,
continue in, or take anew, and retain corporal possession of the vicarage of Wynnysford
and the rights and appurtenances aforesaid, for as long as he holds that of Cuttrombe,
and convert its fruits etc. to his own uses and those of the said vicarages, without
licence of the local diocesan or of anyone else. Notwithstanding etc. The pope's will
is, however, that the vicarage of Wynnysford shall not, on account of this union etc.,
be defrauded of due services and the cure of souls in it shall not be neglected; but that
its customary burdens shall be supported; and that on Peter's death or his resignation
etc. of the vicarage of Cuttrombe the union etc. shall be dissolved and be so deemed
and the vicarage of Wynnysford shall revert to its original condition and be deemed
vacant automatically.

*Ad futuram rei memoriam. Romanum decet pontificem votis illis gratum prestare
assensum ...*
.P. Lambertus / JoA: / JoA xxxv: Nardinus

1   MS: ... *perpetui vicarii in* [!] *parrochialis ecclesie ...*
2   Later, in two instances of this spelling, a second 'r' (written after the 'b') has been deleted.
3   *sic*; i.e. the second 'r' has not been deleted; *cf.* above, note 2.
4   after 'C', *ou* deleted, with 'u' inserted above the line
5   written *Cuttrobe'*

186[1]   **5 August 1513**   *Reg. Lat.* 1296, fos 10ᵛ-11ᵛ

To M.[2] Richard Robert, LLB, rector of the parish church of Bigrave, d. Lincoln. Dispensation and indult etc. [as above, no. 2].

Litterarum scientia, vite ac morum honestas …
.P. Lambert(us) / JoA: / JoA LX: Nardinus

1   Various textual oddities which this entry has in common with no. 187 below indicate that both entries were enregistered from one and the same draft. Both entries have *…. in quibusvis* (where 'quibus' is needed) *et ad que* …; and, later on, *admittere* where 'dimittere' is needed; furthermore, 'aut' or (suchlike) and 'in loco' are wanting at the same points in the text of both. Enregistration of batches of like letters from a single draft is the subject of Appendix II in *CPL*, XVI, at pp. xli-xlviii.
2   *sic*; unclear from the letter why he should be addressed as 'magister'. He is not described as a papal notary or other curial official accorded the title of master.

187[1]   **14 August 1513**   *Reg. Lat.* 1296, fo 16ʳ⁻ᵛ

To Thomas Grey, rector of the parish church of St Augustine, Snawe, d. Canterbury. Dispensation and indult etc. [as above, no. 2].[2]

Vite ac morum honestas …
.P. Lambert(us) / JoA: / JoA L[3]*: Nardinus*

1   *See above*, no. 186, note 1.
2   Marginal insertion of text is frequently found in entries enregistered from drafts as the practice tended to result in oversights. Through the present entry some five passages of various lengths are inserted (variously: not initialled; or initialled *JoA*; or sandwiched between: *JoA* and *Nard(inus)*; or *JoA* and *JoA*).
3   *See above*, no. 13, note 2.

188   **14 August 1513**   *Reg. Lat.* 1296, fos 16ᵛ-17ᵛ

To Gilbert Whittehede, canon of the monastery, called house, of B. Mary the Virgin, Beydlynton' [also spelt *Beydlyngton'*], OSA, d. York. Dispensation – at his supplication – to receive and retain any benefice, with or without cure, usually held by secular clerics, even if a parish church or its perpetual vicarage, or a chantry, free chapel, hospital or annual service, usually assigned to secular clerics in title of a perpetual ecclesiastical benefice, and of lay patronage and of whatsoever tax or annual value, if he obtains it otherwise canonically; to resign it, simply or for exchange, as often as he pleases, and in its place receive another, similar or dissimilar, benefice, with or without cure, defined as above; and – even after he has acquired the said benefice – to receive the usual canonical portion received by canons of the above monastery, OSA, of which he is a canon and is, as he asserts, expressly professed of the order, and to have, for life, a stall in the choir and also a place and an active and a passive voice in the chapter of the said monastery, and otherwise as before, without limitation, just as if he had not acquired the benefice. Notwithstanding etc.

Religionis zelus, vite ac morum honestas …
.P. lambert(us) / JoA: / JoA: LXX: Nardinus

189   14 August 1513   *Reg. Lat.* 1296, fos 18ᵛ-20ʳ

Union etc. At a recent petition on the part of Thomas Bascharche, rector of the parish church of Newyngton [also spelt *Newyngton'*], d. Canterbury, the pope hereby unites etc. the perpetual vicarage of the parish church of B. Mary the Virgin, Almondesbury, d. Worcester, (for which recently, when it was vacant *certo modo*, Thomas was presented by the abbot and convent of the monastery of St Augustine[1] near Bristol (*prope Bristolliam*), said diocese – since the presentation of a suitable person for the said vicarage at a time of vacancy pertains to the abbot for the time being and the convent by ancient, approved and hitherto <peacefully>[2] observed custom – to the then bishop of Worcester or his vicar general within the lawful time), if at this presentation Thomas is canonically instituted into the perpetual vicarage of B. Mary's, (the annual value of which and of any annexes does not exceed 12[3] pounds sterling), with the annexes in question and all its rights and appurtenances, to the church of Newyngton, (which Thomas holds), for as long as he holds it, to the effect that he may, on his own authority, in person or by proxy, take corporal possession of the vicarage, annexes and rights and appurtenances aforesaid, retain it for as long as he holds Newyngton, and convert its fruits etc. to his own uses and those of the church of Newyngton and the vicarage aforesaid, without licence of the local diocesan or of anyone else. Notwithstanding etc. The pope's will is, however, that the said vicarage shall not, on account of this union etc., be defrauded of due services and the cure of souls in it shall not be neglected; but that its customary burdens shall be supported; and that on Thomas's death or his resignation etc. of the church of Newyngton this union etc. shall be dissolved and so deemed and the vicarage shall revert to its original condition automatically.

Ad futuram rei memoriam. Romanum decet pontificem votis[4] gratum prestare assensum…
.P. Lambert(us) / JoA / JoA XXXX: Nardinus

1   MS: *Sancte Augusti*; *recte*: 'Sancti Augustini'
2   *pacifice* inserted in margin, initialled *JoA*
3   *x* deleted; *duodecim* substituted
4   following *votis*, *subvenire* is deleted, initialled *JoA*

190   8 April 1513   *Reg. Lat.* 1296, fo 21[r-v]

To the bishop of Coventry and Lichfield, commission and mandate. A petition presented to the pope on the part of Andrew Barton'[1] and Agnes Stauley,[2] woman, d. Coventry and Lichfield, stated that, on certain reasonable grounds, they desire to be joined together in marriage, but that – because they are mutually related in the third and fourth degrees of consanguinity, springing from the same stock – they cannot fulfil their desire in this matter without an apostolic dispensation. At their supplication, the pope – on each of the aforesaid reasonable grounds demonstrated to him – hereby commissions and commands the above bishop, if it is so and Agnes has not been abducted[3] on this account, to dispense Andrew and Agnes, the impediment of consanguinity notwithstanding, to contract marriage together and solemnize it *in facie ecclesie*, and, after it has been contracted, remain therein, declaring the offspring [of the marriage] legitimate. Notwithstanding etc.

Oblate nobis pro parte ... petitionis series continebat ...
.P. Lambert(us) / JoA / JoA XXV: Nardinus

1   'laici' does not occur.
2   or possibly *Stanley*
3   MS: *capta*; *recte*: 'rapta'?

191[1]   13 July 1513   *Reg. Lat.* 1296, fos 21[v]-22[v]

To John Gcynyssh, rector of the parish church of Estangmaryng, d. Chichester.[2] Dispensation etc. [as above, no. 161].[3]

Vite ac morum honestas ...
L. Pucius / JoA / JoA: L: Nardinus

1   The chancery registers were kept by twelve *scriptores registri* (*cf. CPL* XVI, p. xix). Hands varied, naturally, as did the precise specification of the script (*cf.* ibid., pp. cvi-cvii). As a rule each scribe habitually used only one script (e.g. a humanist cursive). However, one *scriptor* – actually the one given to e caudata (above, no. 27, note 1) – sometimes deployed two scripts when copying the same letter. In the present entry parts of the address clause (... *dilecto filio Johanni Gc ... rectori parrochialis* ...) and of the dating clause (*Dat. Rome apud Sanctum Petrum anno incarnationis dominice millesimo quingentesimo tertio decimo* ...) and also the words *duo du(n) taxat* in the body of the letter are in a script which looks virtually 'printed' – i.e. upright and scarcely ligatured and also quite thick – reminiscent of the script used for engrossments, that is (in contemporary terminology) *lettera da bolle* or *bollatica* (*cf.* frontispiece). The remainder of the letter is in a slanting cursive. In effect, crucial parts of the letter were highlighted.
2   *Estangmaryng Cicestren. dioc(esis)* occurs twice in the course of the entry, apparently added later.
3   Save that the prototype (rightly) has: 'clericis secularibus' whereas the present entry (like no. 192 below, which immediately follows it in the register) has: *ecclesiis secularibus*

192¹   17 August 1513   *Reg. Lat.* 1296, fos 22ᵛ-23ᵛ

To Ralph Woolfe, perpetual cantor at the altar of St Catherine in the church of St Paul, London, d. London. Dispensation – at his supplication – to receive and retain for life, together with the perpetual chantry at the above altar (which is incompatible with another incompatible benefice), one, and without them, any two other benefices etc. [as above, no. 2, to '… retain them together for life, as above']²; and indult, for life, while attending a *studium generale* etc. [as above, no. 2].

Vite ac morum honestas …
.P. Lambertus / JoA / JoA: LX: Nardinus

1   Bollatica deployed at start of address clause and in most of dating clause. The remainder of the letter is in a slanting cursive. *Cf.* previous entry, note 1.
2   Save that the prototype (rightly) has: 'clericis secularibus' whereas the present entry (like no. 191 above, which immediately precedes it in the register) has: *ecclesiis secularibus*

193   6 August 1513   *Reg. Lat.* 1296, fos 23ᵛ-24ʳ

To the bishop of London, commission and mandate. A petition presented to the pope on the part of Robert Swyllyngton', layman, d. York, and Margaret Bewyk, widow, d. London, stated that, on certain reasonable grounds, they desire [to be joined]¹ together in marriage, but that – because Robert was godfather of a son of Margaret – they cannot fulfil their desire in this matter without an apostolic dispensation. At their supplication, the pope – on each of the aforesaid and certain other reasonable grounds demonstrated to him – hereby commissions and commands the above bishop, if it is so and Margaret has not been abducted² on this account, to dispense them – the impediment of the spiritual relationship arising from the foregoing notwithstanding – to contract marriage together and solemnize it *in facie ecclesie* and, after it has been contracted, remain therein, declaring the offspring of the marriage legitimate. Notwithstanding etc.

Oblate nobis pro parte … pet[it]ionis series continebat …
.P. Lambert(us) / JoA: / JoA LX. Nardinus

1   'copulari' (or suchlike) wanting
2   MS: *capta*; *recte*: 'rapta'?

194   20 August 1513   *Reg. Lat.* 1296, fos 27ʳ-28ʳ

To Christopher Gomuldo', perpetual vicar of the parish church of Kewstolre, d. Bath and Wells, dispensation and indult. Some time ago, Julius II by his letters dispensed Christopher to receive and retain together for life any two benefices etc. [as above, no.

6, to '… as is more fully contained in those letters'].[1] The pope – at his supplication – hereby further dispenses Christopher, who, as he asserts, holds the perpetual vicarage of the above parish church and the chantry of St Catherine at the altar of B. Mary the Virgin in the church of Wells by the said dispensation, to receive and retain for life together with the said chantry and vicarage, or any two other incompatible benefices held by him by the above dispensation, any third benefice etc. [as above, no. 6, to '… retain it for life, as above']; and, for life, while attending a *studium generale* or residing in the Roman curia or any one of his benefices, not to be bound to reside in his other benefices nor to be liable to be compelled to do so by anyone against his will. Notwithstanding etc. With the proviso that the third incompatible benefice and the other benefices in question shall not, on this account, be defrauded of due services and the cure of souls in them (if any) shall not be neglected; but that customary burdens of those benefices in which he shall not reside shall be supported.

Vite ac morum honestas …
.P. Lambertus / JoA / JoA: Lxxx: Nardinus

1   CPL, XVIII, no. 231.

195[1]   **14 August**[2] **1513**   *Reg. Lat.* 1296, fos 32ᵛ-34ʳ

Union etc. At a recent petition on the part of Thomas Leson, BDec, canon of the church of St Chad[3] in Shrewsbury (*Salopia*), d. Coventry and Lichfield, the pope hereby unites etc. the parish church of Helbelina [also spelt *Ewelinc, Elbelinc, Eweline*], (whose annual value does not exceed 12[4] pounds sterling), and the parish church of Benlhij' [also spelt *Benthon'*], within the archdeaconry of Rityemundie [later spelt *Ritzunode,*[5] *Retzennude*[6]],[7] respectively d. Coventry and Lichfield[8] and d. York, (whose annual value does not exceed 20[9] pounds sterling) (which is of lay patronage and for which, when it was vacant *certo modo*, he was presented by its true and only patron who was in peaceful quasi-possession of the right[10] of presenting a suitable person for it at a time of vacancy, to the then archbishop of York or his vicar general, [within the lawful time][11]), if at the time of this presentation he is canonically instituted into the rectory of Benlhij', with all their rights and appurtenances, to the canonry and prebend of Lemute of the above church of St Chad, which Thomas holds, for as long as he holds the canonry and prebend; to the effect that he may, on his own authority, in person or by proxy, take and retain corporal possession of the parish churches and the rights and appurtenances aforesaid, for as long as he holds the canonry and prebend, and convert their fruits etc. to his own uses and those of the canonry and prebend and of the parish churches aforesaid, without licence of the local diocesan or of anyone else. Notwithstanding etc. The pope's will is, however, that the said parish churches shall not, on account of this union etc., be defrauded of due services and the cure of souls in them shall not be neglected; but that on Thomas's death or his resignation etc of the canonry and prebend the union etc. shall be dissolved and so deemed and the parish churches shall revert to their original condition automatically.

Romanum decet pontificem votis illis gratum [prestare][12] ...
.P. Lambert(us) / JoA / JoA xxxv: Nardinus

1   Bollatica deployed for first line and for start of dating clause; remainder in a slanting cursive. *Cf.* above no. 191, note 1.
2   The day-date has been altered: from ... *decimo septimo kalendas Septembris* ... (by the deletion of *septimo*) to ... *decimo nono* ... (by the marginal insertion of *nono*, initialled *JoA*).
3   or, possibly, St Ched; MS: *Sancti Thedde or Tedde*
4   MS: *xij.*
5   the 'z' probably yogh
6   the 'z' probably yogh; the minims '-nnu-' capable of various readings; but unless two letters are compounded not readable as '-mun-'.
7   Inexplicably, the name of the archdeaconry is later twice substituted in the narrative for that of the parish church.
8   *sic*; *recte*: 'Lincoln'?
9   MS: *xx.*
10 (?)*intus* for 'iuris'?
11 *de sui t(em)p(or)is legi.* ...: *legi.* followed by an illegible scrawl – perhaps just a space-filler – of approx. a word's length. A corruption of 'infra tempus legitimum'?
12 MS: *pres | tastare*

196   19 September 1513   *Reg. Lat.* 1296, fos 98ᵛ-99ʳ

To William Sloo, monk of the monastery of St Saviour, Barmondesey, <in Southwrk>[1] [also spelt *Sonthwerk*], OSB,[2] d. Winchester (who, as he asserts, is expressly professed of the above order).[3] Dispensation – at his supplication – to receive and retain any benefice, with or without cure, usually held by secular clerics, etc. [as above, no. 43].

Religionis zelus, vite ac morum honestas ...
O. de. Cesis. / JoA: / JoA: xxx: Nardinus

1   marginal insertion initialled *JoA:*
2   *sic*; *recte*: OClun
3   This information comes from a notwithstanding clause.

197   19 September 1513   *Reg. Lat.* 1296, fo 99ʳ⁻ᵛ

To Robert Colchester *alias* Cuper, monk of the monastery of St Benedict, Hulme (*de Hulmo* [also spelt *Ulmo*]), OSB, d. Norwich. Dispensation – at his supplication – to him, who, as he asserts, is expressly professed of the above order,[1] to receive and retain any benefice, with or without cure, usually held by secular clerics, etc. [as above, no. 43].

Religionis zelus, vite ac morum honestas ...
.O. de. Cesis. / JoA / JoA: xxx: Nardinus

1   This information comes from a notwithstanding clause.

198[1]   **19 September 1513**   *Reg. Lat.* 1296, fos 99ᵛ-100ᵛ

To Giles <Bachon>,[2] perpetual vicar of the parish church of B. Mary the Virgin, Narthaston, d. Lincoln. Dispensation and indult etc. [as above, no. 2].[3]

Vite ac morum honestas ...
.O. de[4] *Cesis. / JoA / JoA: L:*[5] *Nardinus:*

1   The script of the first line (*LEO et cetera dilecto filio Egidio perpetuo vicario parrochialis*) is inclined to be upright and looks 'printed'; and the 'E' of *Egidio* is recognisably in bollatica. The remainder of the letter (including the dating clause) is in a slanting cursive. *Cf.* above, no 191, note 1.
2   marginal insertion by enregistering scribe; not initialled. In the body of the letter the enregistering scribe has made a couple of small marginal insertions, which are initialled (*JoA*).
3   Save that the present entry has *onera antedicta*, though 'onera' had not been mentioned and 'onera consueta' is appropriate (*cf.* no. 209 below).
4   Unusually, there is a stroke after *de*
5   *See above*, no 13, note 2.

199   18 September 1513   *Reg. Lat.* 1296, fos 102ʳ-103ᵛ

Union etc. At a recent petition on the part of William Ricardson, rector of the parish church of Onger Alta,[1] d. London, the pope hereby unites etc. the perpetual vicarage of the parish church of Heghington'[2] [also spelt *Heghinton'*, *Heghnigton'*], d. Durham,[3] (for which recently, when it was vacant *certo modo*, William was presented by the prior and convent [of the monastery][4] of St Cuthbert, Dumelum,[5] [d.][6] Durham,[7] OSB – to whom the presentation of a suitable person for the said vicarage at a time of vacancy belongs by ancient, approved and hitherto peacefully observed custom – to the local ordinary within the proper time), if at this presentation William is instituted into the perpetual vicarage of Heghington' (whose annual value does not exceed <13>[8] pounds, 6 shillings and 8 pence sterling) by the said ordinary or it is otherwise canonically conferred on him, with all its rights and appurtenances, to the church of Onger Alta, (which William holds [?canonically][9]), for as long as he holds the latter, to the effect that he may, on his own authority, in person or by proxy, take corporal possession of the vicarage and of the rights and appurtenances aforesaid, retain the vicarage for as long as he holds the church of Onger Alta, and convert its fruits etc. to his own uses and those of the said church and vicarage, without licence of the local diocesan or of anyone else. Notwithstanding etc. The pope's will is, however, that the said vicarage shall not, on this account, be defrauded of due services and the cure of souls in it shall not be neglected; but that its customary burdens shall be supported; and that on the death of William or his resignation etc. of the church of Onger Alta this union etc. shall be dissolved and be so deemed and the vicarage shall revert to its original condition automatically.

Ad futuram rei memoriam. Romanum decet pontificem[10] *votis illis gratum prestare assensum ...*
.P. lambertus / C. / C. xxxv Barotius

1   MS: *alta* or *Alta*; and (once): *alia*
2   sympathetic reading; the 'in' variously readable; none of the minims dotted
3   *Demolenen.* (the 'D' read sympathetically)
4   'monasterii' (or 'domus', or suchlike) wanting
5   the final 'um' variously readable; none of the minims dotted
6   wanting (probably through the scribe's oversight as he turned overleaf)
7   *Dunulinen.*; the 'unu' variously readable; none of the minims dotted
8   *xiij* deleted in line; *terdecim* [*sic*] inserted in margin;. *C* before it, *Ba* after
9   *ea vice*; for 'canonice'?
10   *et cetera providere* deleted and initialled *C*

200   20 August 1513   *Reg. Lat.* 1296, fo 122^r-v

To Gregory Mawer, DDec, rector of the parish church of Ecclys Ep(iscop)i,[1] d.
Norwich. Dispensation and indult etc. [as above, no. 2].[2]

Litterarum scientia, vite ac morum honestas …
.L. Pucius. / JoA / JoA: Lx: Nardi(nus)

1   written *Ecclijs Epi'* in the first instance; and *Ecclijs' Epi'* in the second
2   However, the present entry contains a few textual oddities, including two (*ute te* changed by deletion of 'e'
     to *ut te*; and *absque aliis* for 'absque illis') that are echoed in the next entry in the register (no. 201 below)
     and again later (no. 204). This is suggestive of linkage between the three entries – all were certainly
     enregistered by the same scribe, perhaps from one and the same draft.
     Enregistration of batches of like letters from a single draft is the subject of Appendix II in *CPL*, XVI, at pp.
     xli-xlviii.

201   20 August 1513   *Reg. Lat.* 1296, fos 122^v-123^v

To Gerendus Roms, BTheol, rector of the parish church [of] Absinten' [also spelt
Absynten'], d. Exeter. Dispensation and indult etc. [as above, no. 2].[1]

Litterarum scientia, vite ac morum honestas …
.L. Pucius. / JoA / JoA: Lx: Nardinus

1   However, the present entry contains a couple of small textual oddities (*ute* for 'ut te'; *absque aliis* for 'absque
     illis') found too in no. 204. *Cf.* also the previous entry in the register, above no. 200.

202   2 June 1513   *Reg. Lat.* 1296, fos 161^r-162^r

To Richard, elect of Natura (*Naturen.*), dispensation. Recently the pope made provision
of Richard to the church of Natura, then vacant *certo modo*, appointing him bishop, and
dispensed him to retain for life as before – even after he has received consecration and,
on the strength of the said provision and appointment, acquired peaceful quasi-

possession of the rule and administration and of the goods of the said church, or the greater part of them – the perpetual vicarage of the parish church of Stremton',[1] d. Durham, which he was then holding, even together with the said church of Natura, for as long as he presides over the latter, as is more fully contained in the pope's various letters drawn up in this regard.[2] Wishing to assist Richard to keep up his position more fittingly in accordance with pontifical dignity, the pope – at his supplication – hereby dispenses him to receive and retain in commendam for life together with the above church and vicarage, any two other benefices, with or without cure, secular or regular of any order, even the Cluniac or Cistercian, even if the secular benefices should be parish churches or their perpetual vicarages, chantries, free chapels, hospitals or [annual][3] services usually assigned to secular clerics in title of a perpetual ecclesiastical benefice, or canonries and prebends, dignities, personatus, administrations or offices in cathedral, even metropolitan, or collegiate churches, even if the dignities should be major post pontificalem in cathedral, even metropolitan, churches, or principal in collegiate churches, and even if the regular benefices should be priories, prepositure, prepositatus, dignities (even conventual), personatus, administrations or offices in cathedral, even metropolitan, [churches],[4] or a combination, and even if the priories etc. should be customarily elective and have cure of souls, if he obtains them otherwise canonically, to resign them, at once or successively, when he pleases and cede their commends and in their place receive up to two other, similar or dissimilar, benefices, with or without cure, secular or regular of any order, even the Cluniac or Cistercian – provided that the regular benefices be not claustral offices – and retain them in commendam for life as above; he may – due and customary burdens of these secular or regular benefices held in commendam having been supported, make disposition of the rest of their fruits etc. [just as][5] those holding them in titulum at the time could and ought to do, alienation of immovable goods and precious movables of the benefices retained in commendam being however forbidden. Notwithstanding etc. With the proviso that the secular and regular benefices in question shall not, on this account, be defrauded of due services and the cure of souls in them shall not be neglected; but that their aforesaid burdens shall be supported.

Personam tuam nobis et apostolice sedi devotam tuis exigen(tibus) meritis …
.P. Lambertus. / JoA. / JoA: C: Nardinus

1   readable as *Stranton'* – but only sympathetically
2   above, nos. 122-126
3   *alia*; *recte*: 'annualia'
4   *regularibus*; *recte*: 'ecclesiis'?
5   MS wants 'sicuti' or 'prout' – probably latter: omission triggered by *pro(ventibus)*?

203   19 March 1513   *Reg. Lat.* 1296, fos 284ᵛ-285ᵛ

To Nicholas Methast, archdeacon of the church of Rochester, effectuation. Some time ago, Julius II by his letters dispensed Nicholas to receive and retain for life any two benefices etc. [as above, no. 6, to '… more fully contained in those letters' with appropriate changes of tense]. And – at his supplication – Julius under date 10 January, tenth year [1513] further dispensed Nicholas (who, as he asserted, was holding the archdeaconry of the above church, which is a dignity, perhaps major *post pontificalem*, and the parish church of Henlen [also spelt *Henlen'*] super Tauusiazo,[1] d. Lincoln, by the above dispensation) to receive and retain for life, together with the above archdeaconry and the church of Henlen, or without them, with any two other incompatible benefices held by him at the time by virtue of the above dispensation, any third benefice etc. [as above, no. 6, with appropriate changes of tense].[2] Since Julius died before his letters to this effect were drawn up, the pope hereby wills and decrees that the present letters shall everywhere be sufficient proof of the said [latter] dispensation etc.

Rationi congruit et cetera.
.Vanzon'. / JoA / JoA: Lxx: Nardi(nus):

1   or possibly *Tamisiazo* (though the first 'i' is not dotted): an interesting case of corruption. What must have
    originated as 'super Tamisiam [*cf. CPL* XIII, pp. 775, 861]' (perhaps written 'Tamisiaz' where the 'z' was a
    mark of abbreviation for 'm') has somehow acquired a final o, turning the abbreviation for m into a z or
    yogh, and super + acc. into super + abl. The script of *Henlen super T~* somewhat larger than that of adjacent
    text: entered later in blank space?
2   Save that here and elsewhere the present entry contains various small slips (e.g. *postea*; *recte*: 'perpetua').

204   5 September 1513   *Reg. Lat.* 1296, fos 294ᵛ-295ʳ

To Richard Bull', perpetual vicar of the parish church of Broklondon [also spelt *Broklongon*], d. Canterbury. Dispensation and indult etc. [as above, no. 2].[1]

Vite ac morum honestas …
O. de. Cesis / JoA / JoA: Lx: Nardinus

1   However, the present entry contains a few small textual oddities, including two (*ute* for 'ut te'; *absque aliis*
    for 'absque illis') found too in no. 201. *Cf.* also no. 200.

205   31 August[1] 1513   *Reg. Lat.* 1296, fos 299ᵛ-300ᵛ

To Thomas, elect of ?Prizren (*Purien.*), dispensation. Recently the pope on the advice of the cardinals by certain letters[2] made provision of Thomas to the church of ?Prizren, then bereft of a pastor *certo modo*, appointing him bishop, and by other letters[3] of his dispensed Thomas – *motu proprio* – to retain for life as before – even after he has received consecration and, on the strength of the said provision and appointment, acquired peaceful quasi-possession of the rule and administration and of the goods of the said church, or the greater part of them – the priory of St Augustine, Daventre, OSB, d. Lincoln (which, as the pope has learned, he was then holding) even together with the said church, for as long as he presides over the latter, as is more fully contained in the said letters. Wishing to assist Thomas (who, as he asserts, receives no fruits from the said church which is *in partibus infidelium*) – to keep up his position more fittingly in accordance with pontifical dignity – the pope hereby dispenses him – at his supplication – to receive and retain *in commendam* for life – even after the aforesaid consecration and acquisition – together with the above church [and][4] priory, any two, and without them, with the said church, any three other benefices,[5] secular, with or without cure, or regular, of the above or any other order, even the Cluniac or Cistercian, even if the secular benefices should be dignities, *personatus*, administrations or offices in cathedral, even metropolitan, or collegiate [churches], and even if the dignities should be major *post pontificalem* in cathedral, even metropolitan, churches, or principal in collegiate churches, or chantries, free chapels, hospitals or annual services usually assigned to secular clerics in title of a perpetual ecclesiastical benefice, or two of them be parish churches or their perpetual vicarages, and the regular benefices should be priories, *prepositure*, *prepositatus*, dignities, even conventual, *personatus*, administrations or offices, or a combination, and of whatsoever tax or annual value, even if the priories etc. should be customarily elective and have cure of souls, if he obtains them otherwise canonically, to resign them, at once or successively, simply or for exchange, as often as he pleases, and cede the commend, and in their place receive up to three other, similar or dissimilar, benefices, secular, with or without cure, or regular of the above order of St Benedict or any other order, even the Cluniac or Cistercian – provided that of three such secular benefices not more than two be parish churches or their perpetual vicarages and that any regular benefices be not claustral offices – and retain them *in commendam* for life as above; he may – due and customary burdens of the benefices having been supported – make disposition of the rest of their fruits etc., just as those holding them *in titulum* could and ought to do, alienation of immovable goods and movable valuables being however forbidden. Notwithstanding etc. With the proviso that the benefices in question shall not, on this account, be defrauded of due services and the cure of souls in them shall not be neglected; but that their aforesaid burdens shall be supported.

Personam tuam nobis et apostolice sedi devotam tuis exigen(tibus) meritis paterna benivolentia prosequentes illa tibi favorabiliter concedimus …
.P. Lambert(us) / JoA / JoA: C: Nardinus

1   date as corrected in MS; viz.: '… *pridie kalendas* followed by *Augusti* deleted, with *Septembris* inserted in the margin (in hand of enregistering scribe), initialled *JoA*
2   above, no. 84
3   above, no. 88
4   wants 'et' or suchlike
5   i.e. in either case a maximum of four benefices

206   **18 September 1513**   *Reg. Lat.* 1296, fos 359^r-360^r

Union etc. At a recent petition on the part of Thomas Milling, UIB, canon (*canonici*)[1] of the church of Bromiard', d. Hereford, the pope hereby unites etc. the parish church of B. Mary the Virgin, Pacchyng', d. Chichester, (whose annual value does not exceed 11 pounds sterling), with all its rights and appurtenances, to the canonry and prebend[2] of the church of Bromiard' which (and, by apostolic dispensation, the perpetual vicarage of the parish church of St Michael the [Arch]angel, Conmor,[3] d. Salisbury) Thomas holds together with the above parish church of B. Mary, for as long as he holds the canonry and prebend, to the effect that he may, on his own authority, in person or by proxy, continue in, or take anew, and retain corporal possession of B. Mary's and the rights and appurtenances aforesaid, for as long as he holds the canonry and prebend, and convert its fruits etc. to his own uses and those of the canonry and prebend and of B. Mary's, without licence of the local diocesan or of anyone else. Notwithstanding etc. The pope's will is, however, that the said church of B. Mary shall not, on account of this union etc., be defrauded of due services and the cure of souls in it shall not be neglected; but that its customary burdens shall be supported; and that on Thomas's death or his resignation etc. of the canonry and prebend this union etc. shall be dissolved and be so deemed and B. Mary's shall revert to its original condition automatically.

Ad futuram rei memoriam. Romanum decet pontificem votis illis gratum prestare assensum …
.P. lambertus / JoA / JoA: xxxv: Nardinus

1   sic; recte: 'portionarii'? See below, note 2.
2   sic: canonicatui et prebende (& thus, variously inflected, throughout). A near contemporary domestic record shows that the rectory of Bromyard was divided into three portions; and that Thomas Myllyng, *clericus prebendarius*, held the first portion (*Valor Ecclesiasticus*, III, p. 42). Though the portioners were sometimes called prebendaries the church does not appear to have been collegiate (*cf. VCH*, Hereford, II, Part I, pp. 79-81).
3   or perhaps *Comnor*; none of the minims is dotted.

207[1]   1 October 1513   *Reg. Lat.* 1296, fos 360ᵛ-361ʳ

To the archbishop of Canterbury and the bishop of Durham,[2] executory as below. Some time ago, Julius II[3] by his letters indulged William Cusin, DDec, dean of the church of Wells, to receive, exact and levy in full – while resident in the said church for six months only, continuously or intermittently – each and every one of the fruits etc. distributed at the end of the year between resident canons of the church and holders of dignities in it by reason of the deanery of the said church (which he holds by apostolic dispensation together with the archdeaconry of Bedford (*Belforden.*) of the church of Lincoln), just as if he had resided for eight months in the said church of Wells, in accordance with its statutes and customs, and not to be liable to be compelled to reside in the same – other than for six months as above – by anyone against his will; and if – while on visitation of the said archdeaconry, or residing personally in any one of his benefices, or absenting himself for the sake of his health, or while in the service of Henry, king of England, or absenting himself on any other honest or useful ground – he happens to fall short in some way of six months of residence, he should not, nevertheless, lose all the fruits distributed to an individual canon at the end of the year by reason of residence, but a portion of them should be deducted in accordance with the short-fall in the six months residence, as is more fully contained in the said letters.[4] Executory to the above two (or one of them), if and after the said letters be presented to them, acting in person or by proxy, to cause the above fruits etc. to be given in full to William, in accordance with the tenor of the above indult, not permitting him to be compelled by the bishop and chapter of Wells or any others to reside in the said church of Wells longer than the six months in question, or otherwise be molested in any way contrary to the tenor of the above indult. [Curbing] gainsayers etc. Notwithstanding all that Julius II willed in the said letters to be notwithstanding.

Dudum felicis recordationis Julius papa .iy. ...
.P. lambertus. / JoA: / JoA XX: Nardinus

1   The present entry – recording Leo's mandate to the archbishop of Canterbury and the bishop of Durham to execute an indult granted to William 'Cusin' by Julius II – evidently has a bearing on the indult granted by Julius to William 'Consyn' summarised in *CPL*, XIX at no. 265. For, as will be readily perceived, both indults – though differing considerably in detail – reflect concern to receive the fruits of the deanery without full compliance with the established local requirement of personal residence.
     However, the particular Julius indult to which the present Leo executory relates is unknown to the Calendar; as are the circumstances in which this executory was issued.
     Consequently, the content of the present entry is here given in a less summary form than usual for an executory.
2   *Durmonen.* (for 'Dunelmen' or suchlike); the third letter of *Durmonen.* (a blotched 'r'?) is deleted; *r* above it.
3   MS: *iy.*; for 'II'
4   unknown; *see above*, note 1.

208   2 June 1513   *Reg. Lat.* 1296, fos 370ʳ-371ʳ

To John, elect of Gallipoli (*Calipolen.*), dispensation. Recently the pope made provision of John to the church of Gallipoli, then vacant *certo modo*, appointing him bishop, and dispensed him to retain for life as before – even after he has received consecration and acquired, on the strength of the above provision and appointment, peaceful quasi-possession of the rule and administration and of the goods of the said church, or the greater part of them – the hospital, called house or mastership, of St Thomas the Martyr of Acon, London, OSA, which he was then holding, even together with the said church, for as long as he presides over the latter, as is more fully contained in the pope's various letters drawn up in this regard.[1] Wishing to assist John to keep up his position more fittingly in accordance with pontifical dignity, the pope – at his supplication – hereby dispenses John to receive and retain *in commendam* for life, together with the above church and hospital, any two other benefices, secular, with or without cure, or regular, of any order, even the Cluniac and Cistercian, even if the secular benefices should be parish churches or their perpetual vicarages, or chantries, free chapels, hospitals or annual services usually assigned to secular clerics in title of a perpetual ecclesiastical benefice, or canonries and prebends, dignities, *personatus*, administrations or offices, in cathedral, even metropolitan, or collegiate churches, even if the dignities should be major *post pontificalem* in cathedral, even metropolitan, churches or principal in collegiate churches, even if the regular benefices should be priories, *prepositure*, *prepositatus*, dignities, even conventual, *personatus*, administrations or offices even in cathedral, even metropolitan, churches, or a combination, and even if the priories etc. should be customarily elective and have cure of souls, if he obtains them otherwise canonically, to resign them, at once or successively, when he pleases, and cede their commends and in their place receive up to two other, similar or dissimilar, benefices, secular, with or without cure, or regular, of any order, even the Cluniac or Cistercian – provided that the regular benefices in question be not claustral offices – and retain them *in commendam* for life as above; he may – due and customary burdens of the secular or regular benefices retained *in commendam* having been supported – make disposition of the rest of their fruits etc. just as those holding them *in titulum* at the time could and ought to do, alienation of the immovable goods and movable valuables of the benefices to be retained *in commendam* being however forbidden. Notwithstanding etc. With the proviso that the secular and regular benefices in question shall not, on this account, be defrauded of due services and the cure of souls in them shall not be neglected, but that their aforesaid burdens shall be supported.

Personam tuam nobis et apostolice sedi devotam tuis exigentibus meritis paterna benevolentia prosequentes illa tibi libenter concedimus ...
.P Lambertus / JoA: / JoA: C: Nardinus

1   above, nos. 92-95

---

209   14 August 1513   *Reg. Lat.* 1296, fos 375[v]-376[r]

To Richard[1] Bulle, cantor of the chantry, called chapel, of B. Mary the Virgin, Wolnerhampton' Pyxwell, d. Coventry and Lichfield. Dispensation – at his supplication – to receive and retain for life, together with the above chantry (which is incompatible with another[2] benefice), one, and without them, any two other benefices etc. [as above, no. 2, to '... retain them together for life, as above']; and indult, for life, while attending a *studium generale* etc. [as above, no. 2].

Vite[3] ac morum honestas ...
.P. Lambertus. / JoA / JoA: L[4]: Nardinus

1   *Ric<ardo>* (the 'ardo' inserted above the line in hand of enregistering scribe, initialled *JoA*)
2   'incompatibile' (inserted in next entry) does not occur in this instance.
3   the 'V' bollatica; the remainder of the word – and entry – in humanist cursive; *cf.* above, no. 191, note 1.
4   *See above*, no. 13, note 2.

210   7 October[1] 1513   *Reg. Lat.* 1296, fos 376[v]-377[r]

To William Brown,[2] BDec, cantor of the chantry of Wyntbora', d. Worcester. Dispensation – at his supplication – to receive and retain for life, together with the above chantry (which is incompatible with another <incompatible> benefice),[3] one, and without them, any two other benefices etc. [as above, no. 2 to '… retain them together for life, as above']; and indult, for life, while attending a *studium generale* etc. [as above, no. 2].

Litterarum scientia, vite ac morum honestas …
.O. de. Cesis / JoA / JoA: Lx: Nardinus

1   The day-date has been altered by the deletion (not initialled) of the *decimo* in *tertiodecimo nonis Octobris*
2   very sympathetic reading; readily readable as *Beowu*
3   *que cum alio <incompatibilis[!]> beneficio ecclesiastico incompatib[i]le[!] existit*. Inflections or word order unhappy. *incompatibilis* is inserted in margin in hand of enregistering scribe, initialled *JoA*

211   7 October[1] 1513   *Reg. Lat.* 1296, fos 377[v]-378[r]

To Robert Freman' *alias* Fuller, canon of the monastery, called house, of B. Mary the Virgin, Wendlyng, OPrem, d. Norwich. Dispensation – at his supplication – to receive and retain any benefice, with or without cure, usually held by secular clerics, even if a parish church or its perpetual vicarage, or a chantry, free chapel, hospital or annual service, usually assigned to secular clerics in title of a perpetual ecclesiastical benefice, of lay patronage and of whatsoever tax or annual value, if he obtains it otherwise canonically, to resign it, simply or for exchange, as often as he pleases and in its place receive and retain another, similar or dissimilar, benefice, with or without cure, defined as above; and – even after he has acquired the said benefice – to receive the usual canonical portion received by the canons of the above monastery, OPrem, of which he is a canon and, as he asserts, expressly professed of the order; and to have, for life, a stall in the choir and a place and an active and a passive voice in the chapter of the said monastery and otherwise as before, without limitation, just as if he had not acquired the benefice. Notwithstanding etc.

Relligionis[2] zelus, vite ac morum honestas …
.P. La(m)bertus / JoA / JoA Lxx: Nardinus

1   *nonis Octobris* is written in a different hand from and on a larger scale than the rest of the date; apparently entered later in a space deliberately left blank.
2   *sic*

212   7 October 1513   *Reg. Lat.* 1296, fo 381[r-v]

To Thomas Lathum', rector of the parish church of Englefeld',[1] d. Salisbury.
Dispensation and indult etc. [as above, no. 2].[2]

Vite ac morum honestas ...
O. de. Cesis. / JoA: / JoA: Lx: Nardinus

1   sympathetic reading: in both instances written *Eu* -
2   Save that the present entry has *perpetue cap(p)ele* where the prototype (rightly) has *libere cappelle*

213   5 October 1513   *Reg. Lat.* 1296, fos 409[v]-410[v]

To Henry Tredenek, rector of the parish church of Bokonck [also spelt *Bokonock*], d.
Exeter. Dispensation and indult etc. [as above, no. 2].[1]

Vite ac morum honestas ...
.P. Lamtus[2] / JoA: / JoA: Lx: Nardinus

1   save for a few textual oddities in the present entry (e.g. 'dimittere et loco' – summarised in the prototype as
     'to resign and in their place' – wanting)
2   *sic*; 'Lambertus'?

214   19 March 1513   *Reg. Lat.* 1297, fos 16[r]-17[r]

To Thomas Bryant,[1] rector of the parish church of South'pole, d. Exeter, effectuation
of Julius II's dispensation and indult in his favour. Some time ago Julius II dispensed
and indulged Thomas (who was holding, as he asserted, the above parish church) – at
his supplication – under date 19 June, ninth year [1512], to receive etc. [as above, no.
2,[2] to '... but that customary burdens of those benefices in which he does not reside
shall be supported.' with appropriate changes of tense]. Since, however, Julius died
before his letters to this effect were drawn up, the pope hereby decrees that the present
letters shall everywhere be sufficient proof of the said dispensation and indult etc.

Racioni congruit et cetera.
f. Bregeon / C / C. Lx Barotius

1   written *Brijant*
2   as to content; however the order of clauses in the indult is not identical.

215   1 July 1513   *Reg. Lat.* 1297, fos 17ʳ-18ᵛ

To the bishop of St Asaph, the dean of the church of Salisbury, and Richard Rosten',
canon of the church of Lincoln, mandate in favour of Thomas Belschaw, rector of the
parish church of Nayleson *alias* Nayleston', d. Lincoln. A recent petition to the pope
on Thomas' part stated that some time ago a law-suit had arisen, not by apostolic
delegation, between Thomas on the one side and Robert Browne, who bore himself as
rector of the said church, on the other, over the said church (provision of which, when
it was vacant *certo modo*, had been canonically made to Thomas some time ago) and
other matters then expressed, before Henry Wilkok', vicar general in spirituals of
William, bishop of Lincoln; that Thomas appealed from sufficient grievances then
expressed inflicted on him *de facto* in the case by Henry the vicar, to William,
archbishop of Canterbury, primate of all England and legate born of the apostolic see
in those parts, and in the cause of this appeal he caused Robert to be summoned to
judgement before Cuthbert Tunstall', auditor of causes of the court of the said
archbishop; that Cuthbert the auditor, proceeding correctly in the case, promulgated a
definitive sentence in favour of Thomas and against Robert, from which Robert –
falsely alleging that it was unjust – appealed to the apostolic see, and in connection
with the later appeal he impetrated apostolic letters under a certain form to the abbots
of the monasteries of Garaden' and of Ffevershm', said or other d., [and]¹ John Coole,
an ecclesiastical dignitary, and by pretext of the letters caused Thomas to be summoned
to judgement, in the cause of the later appeal, before John Coole; that John –
proceeding suddenly and *de facto* in the case of the later appeal, regardless of the order
of law – unjustly decreed that Cuthbert the auditor and Thomas ought to be inhibited
under a certain manner and form then expressed, and inhibited them, and he caused
Thomas to be cited to appear before him even on a certain holiday then expressed and
he was not ashamed to harass him, putting him to effort and expense, and inflict *de
facto* several other sufficient grievances on him then expressed; and that on the part of
Thomas, who felt *inter alia* unduly aggrieved thereby, appeal was made to the
apostolic see. At the supplication to the pope to commit to some upright men in those
parts the causes: of the latest appeal and of anything perhaps attempted and innovated
after and against it; of the nullity of the said decree, inhibition, and citation; of the
gravamina inflicted on Thomas by the vicar and by John, as above; of their processes
and of each and every other thing done in any way by them and any other judges and
persons to Thomas' prejudice in connection with the foregoing; and of the whole
principal matter, the pope [hereby] commands that the above three (or two, or one of
them), having summoned Robert and the others concerned and having heard both
sides, taking cognizance even of the principal matter, [shall decree] what is just,
[without appeal, causing by ecclesiastical censure what they have decreed to be
strictly] observed;² [and moreover compel] witnesses, etc. Notwithstanding etc.

Humilibus et cetera.
Jo. Copis / . Phi. / . phi. xij. de Senis

1   MS: *ad*; *recte*: 'ac'
2   MS: *quod iustum fuerit et cetera observari*. Supplied from common form.

216   I July 1513   *Reg. Lat.* 1297, fos 18ᵛ-19ᵛ

To the bishop of Ely, the abbot of the monastery of St Peter, Westmon', d. London, and the abbot of the monastery of B Mary, Redyng, d. Salisbury, mandate in favour of Robert Massam, rector of the parish church of Retherhed, d. Lincoln. A recent petition to the pope on Robert's part stated that some time ago Nicholas Metcalse[1], bearing himself as rector of the parish church of Henaley[2], said d. – falsely alleging that the tithes and ecclesiastical dues (*iura*) then expressed and lawfully appertaining [to][3] Robert by reason of the said church belonged by law to him and that Robert had wrongly kept the tithes and dues to himself – sued Robert over this before Cuthbert Tunstall', UID, auditor of causes of the court of William, archbishop of Canterbury, primate of all England, and legate born of the apostolic see in those parts (who, as he said, [was] a competent judge for this), praying *inter alia* that the tithes and dues be adjudged his and that Robert be coerced and compelled to give to him the tithes and dues which had been taken away and to desist from taking them away further; and that Cuthbert the auditor, proceeding wrongly in the case, promulgated an unjust, definitive (as he said) sentence, in favour of Nicholas and against Robert, from which, on Robert's part, appeal was made to the apostolic see. At Robert's supplication to the pope to commit to some upright men in those parts the causes: of the aforesaid appeal and of anything perhaps attempted and innovated after and against it; of the nullity of the process and sentence of Cuthbert the auditor; and of the principal matter, the pope [hereby] commands that the above three (or two, or one of them), having summoned Nicholas and others concerned and having heard both sides, taking cognizance even of the principal matter, [shall decree] what is just, without appeal, [causing by ecclesiastical censure what they have decreed to be strictly] observed,[4] [and moreover compel] witnesses, etc. Notwithstanding etc.

Humilibus et cetera.
P. Lambertus / . Phi. / . Phi. xij. de Senis

1   The 's' is long; but cannot be read as an 'f'.
2   the 'y' double dotted
3   MS: *et; recte*: 'ad'
4   MS: *quod iustum fuerit appellatione remota et cetera observari.* Supplied from common form.

217[1]   3 May 1513   *Reg. Lat.* 1297, fos 23ᵛ-24ʳ

To Catherine, queen of England. Indult – at her supplication[1] – to her, for life, to choose and depute six suitable priests as her chaplains who may say and recite the canonical hours, mass and other divine offices, day and night, according to the use, rite and custom of the Roman church, for as long as they are in her service; and to the said chosen and deputed chaplains, for as long as they are in her service, as above, to receive all fruits etc. of any benefices which they hold at the time in any churches or places, the daily distributions alone excepted, as if they were resident personally in the said churches or places, and not to be bound meanwhile to reside in them, and not to be liable to be compelled to do so by local ordinaries or anyone else. Notwithstanding the constitution of Boniface VIII prohibiting grants of this type without a limit set on their duration,[2] etc.

Exigit tue devocionis...
P. lambert(us) / . A. / A. Lx. Colotius: –

1   Silvester de' Gigli, bishop of Worcester, the king's agent at the curia, sent Catherine a supplication and draft letter when he reported to her on 13 May 1513 (NA, SP1/4, fo 7[r-v]; summarised by *L&P, F&D*, I[2], no 1872).
2   *Cf. Sext*, I.3.15 (Friedberg, 943).

218   1 July 1513   *Reg. Lat.* 1297, fos 58[v]-60[v]

To the abbot of the monastery of Swhynesched' and the prior of the monastery customarily governed by a prior of Spaldyng, d. Lincoln, and Thomas Haniball', canon of the church of York, mandate in favour of William Magelyn [also spelt *Magelyn'*, *Magelym*], layman, d. Lincoln. A recent petition to the pope on William's part stated that some time ago he sued, not by apostolic delegation, Cicely Choney, woman, said d., who had lawfully contracted marriage with him *per verba de presenti*, before William Sthmydt, archdeacon of the church of Lincoln (to whom cognizance [*punitio*] of similar causes which arise from time to time between similar persons living within the jurisdiction of the archdeacon of the said church for the time being and within the bounds of the archdeaconry of the said church belongs by ancient, approved, and hitherto peacefully observed custom), praying in this connection *inter alia* that she be adjudged his lawful wife, coerced and compelled to solemnize the said marriage in the face of the church, cohabit with him, and show marital affection; that after there had been proceedings before the said archdeacon to several acts in the case (but short of the conclusion), when the suit was pending thus, undecided, before the said archdeacon, William Dawson [also spelt *Dawson'*], layman, said d. – falsely alleging that he had previously contracted marriage *per verba de presenti*[1] with the said Cicely – similarly sued Cicely before the said archdeacon, praying in this connection *inter alia* that she be adjudged his lawful wife,[2] that the marriage contracted with William Magelyn be declared null and invalid, and that the marriage duly contracted with him (as he said) be declared valid; that because the said archdeacon, who was unduly favouring William Dawson and suspending the case for too long, expressly and unlawfully refused to decide and determine the case within the lawful time (as he was bound) and to administer justice to William Magelyn (although he had often been lawfully asked to do so on William Magelyn's part at a suitable time and place), William Magelyn, feeling *inter alia* unduly aggrieved thereby, appealed to the local metropolitan court of Canterbury and caused the aforesaid William Dawson and Cicely (who had been united [*copulata*] to William Dawson while the suit was pending) to be summoned to trial in the cause of the said appeal before the then president of the said [court][3]; that the president duly inhibited the said archdeacon under a certain manner and form then expressed and, at William's instance, caused William Dawson and Cicely, who were due to appear in the cause of the appeal, to be cited to appear;[4] that a certain libel had been presented in the cause of the appeal on William Magelyn's part and there had been proceedings to several acts in the cause (but short of the conclusion); that although William Magelyn had then put forward before the president, at a suitable time and place, several lawful objections (which in law should have been approved and admitted) against the persons of certain witnesses produced before him and examined in the cause of the appeal on the part of William Dawson and Cicely and against their testimony and statements afterwards published, the president – having rejected the objections (at least tacitly) and without observing the order of law, proceeding wrongly to further matters in the cause of the appeal – nevertheless promulgated an unjust, definitive (as he said) sentence by which he declared *inter alia* that the marriage contracted (as he said) between William Dawson and Cicely was valid and he adjudged her to be the lawful wife of William Dawson, and he also freed William Dawson and Cicely from William Magelyn's claim, and, further he condemned William Magelyn in the expenses run up before him, from which sentence appeal was made on William Magelyn's part to the apostolic see. At the supplication to the pope to commit to some upright men in those parts, even to men below the rank of bishops, the causes, with all their incident, dependent, and connected matters: of the aforesaid last appeal and of anything perhaps attempted and innovated after and against it; of the nullity of the refusal and rejection of the said objections, of the process and sentence of the said president, and of each and every other thing done in any way by him and by the said archdeacon to the prejudice of William Magelyn in connection with the above; and of the whole principal matter, the pope, deeming the state of the cause sufficiently expressed in the presents, hereby commands that the above three (or two or one of them), having summoned William Dawson and Cicely and others concerned, shall hear the individual causes aforesaid, with all their incident, dependent, and connected matters, and, having heard both sides, taking cognizance even of the principal matter, decree what is canonical, without appeal, causing by ecclesiastical censure what they have decreed to be strictly observed. Notwithstanding that the above are not of the class of persons to whom similar causes have been customarily committed, etc.

Humilibus et cetera.
Jo. Copis / C / C xvj Barotius

1   MS: *per similia verba*
2   MS muddled: ... *eam sibi in uxorem legitimam uxorem iudicare* ...
3   MS wants 'curie'.
4   MS very ill-written at this point and the section 'and, at William's instance, caused ... to be cited to appear' is accordingly tentative. The underlying reading: *ad dicti Willermi instantiam citari fecerat* may be particularly unsafe where I have underlined it.

219   8 April 1513   *Reg. Lat.* 1297, fos 120ᵛ-121ᵛ

To the bishop of Clonfert, the abbot of the monastery of Bullis, d. Elphin (*Olfenen.*), and the prior of the monastery, customarily governed by a prior, of Acris, d. Killala, mandate in favour of Richard (*Risard–*, *Riscard–*, *Ristard–*), bishop of Killala. A recent petition to the pope on Richard's part stated that although, some time ago, Julius II had, by certain letters of his, provided him to the church of Killala (then destitute *certo modo* of a pastor) and appointed him bishop, fully committing the care, rule, and administration of the said church to him in spiritualities and temporalities, as is more fully stated in the said letters,[1] Malachy (*Malchias*) Cluhan, who bears himself as bishop – claiming, albeit falsely, that the right in or to the rule and administration of the said church belonged to him – has nevertheless hitherto presumed and is presuming to obstruct bishop Richard contrary to justice (although Richard is able to peacefully acquire quasi-possession of the rule, administration and goods of the said church and preside over it) and he has often agitated *de facto* over this, and agitates, to the peril of his soul and to the considerable prejudice and injury of bishop Richard and of the said church. At bishop Richard's supplication to the pope to commit to some upright men in those parts, to be heard, examined, duly determined and decided, even summarily, simply, and informally, without the formality and formulas of legal proceedings, factual accuracy [alone] being considered ([sola][2] *facti veritate inspecta*), each and every cause, with all their incident, emergent, dependent, and connected matters, which bishop Richard intends to move, jointly and severally, against Malachy and any others, clerics and laymen, in common or separately, disputing his interest in the above matters, over the rule and administration of the said church, over the unlawful obstruction and agitation, over the damage which bishop Richard has suffered, over the expenses which he has run up, and over other matters; and to order the inhibition of any judges and persons as often as necessary and insofar as it is just, the pope [hereby] commands that the above three (or two, or one of them), having summoned Malachy and others concerned and having inhibited any judges and persons as often as necessary, etc shall, on the pope's authority, hear the said causes[3], with all their incident, dependent, and connected matters, even summarily, etc, and having heard both sides, duly determine and decide them, without appeal, causing, by the pope's authority in bishop Richard's case, by ecclesiastical censure in the case of others, what they have decreed to be strictly observed, [and moreover compel] witnesses, etc. Notwithstanding etc.

Humilibus et cetera.
P. Lambertus / M / M x de Campania

1   *CPL*, XIX, no. 606
2   wanting in MS
3   MS: *causa*; *recte*: 'causas'

220   25 April 1513   *Reg. Lat.* 1297, fos 225[r]-226[v]

To Peter, bishop of Forlì (who is a scriptor of the archive of the Roman curia). The pope (who, some time ago, willed that provisions or mandates of provision or grants of an expective grace concerning a parish church made to any person shall be of no force unless that person understands the language of the place where the church in question is located and speaks it intelligibly) wishing to assist the above bishop to keep up his position more fittingly in accordance with pontifical dignity – at his supplication – hereby dispenses and indulges him to receive and retain *in commendam* for life, together with the church of Forlì, (over which he is understood to preside), and with all the benefices, with and without cure, secular or regular which he holds,[1] and also with the annual pensions which he receives,[2] any two other benefices, with or without cure, secular or regular of any order, even if located in the kingdom of England, and even if the secular benefices should be parish churches or their perpetual vicarages, or chantries, free chapels, hospitals or annual services usually assigned to secular clerics in title of a perpetual ecclesiastical benefice, or canonries and prebends,[3] dignities, *personatus*, administrations or offices in cathedral, even metropolitan, or collegiate churches, even if the dignities should be major *post pontificalem* in cathedral, even metropolitan, churches, or principal in collegiate churches, and even if the regular benefices should be priories, *prepositure*,[4] dignities (even conventual), *personatus*, administrations or offices, or a combination, and of lay patronage and of whatsoever[5] annual value, and even if the priories, *prepositure*,[6] *personatus*, administrations or offices should be customarily elective and have cure of souls, if he obtains them otherwise canonically, to resign them, at once or successively, when he pleases, and cede their commends and in their place receive up to two other, similar or dissimilar, benefices, with or without cure, secular or regular of any order, provided that the regular benefices be not claustral offices, and as above retain them *in commendam* for life; he may – due and customary burdens of the secular or regular benefices retained *in commendam* having been supported – make disposition of their fruits etc. just as those holding them *in titulum* at the time could and ought to do, alienation of immovable goods and precious movables being however forbidden. Notwithstanding the pope's earlier volition aforesaid and any other apostolic constitutions etc. and [notwithstanding] that the above bishop neither understands the English language nor knows how to speak it intelligibly, and [notwithstanding] anything else to the contrary. With the proviso that the secular and regular benefices in question shall not, on account of this commend, be defrauded of due services and the cure of souls in them shall not be neglected; but that the aforesaid burdens shall be supported.

Personam tuam nobis et apostolice sedi devotam tuis exigentibus meritis paterna benevolentia prosequentes ...
P. lambertus / M / M Grat(is) p(ro) scriptor(e) archivij de Campania

1   The 'pro expressis habentes' clause rightly includes secular and regular benefices, both held and expected, *in titulum* or *commendam*; and also annual pensions.
2   *See* note 1.
3   *canonicatus et prebende* unusual here
4   'prepositatus' does not occur here or below.
5   MS: *cuiuscunque annui valoris*; i.e. not (as usual) 'cuiuscunque taxe seu annui valoris'
6   'dignitates' does not occur here.

221   2 June 1513   *Reg. Lat.* 1297, fos 299ᵛ-300ᵛ

To Christopher Swale, MA, perpetual vicar of the parish church of Messyng, d. London. Dispensation and indult etc. [as above, no. 2].

Litterarum scientia, vite ac morum honestas …
L. Puccius / . Phi. / . Phi. L.¹ de Senis

1   *See above*, no. 13, note 2.

222   7 May 1513   *Reg. Lat.* 1297, fos 313ᵛ-315ᵛ

To William Wylton', canon of the church of Salisbury, and Robert Dykar, canon of the church of Wells, mandate in favour of John Pannffordt, Henry Heoke, John Attrock, Thomas Pannfford, and John Thorn', clerics or laymen, d. Exeter, co-litigants in this regard. A recent petition to the pope on the co-litigants' part stated that, at another time, Richard Tolleth, LLD, bearing himself as a commissary of the present bishop of Exeter, had, *ex officio* and *de facto*, caused the co-litigants to be cited to appear before him, on a certain day and in a certain place then expressed, to reply to several articles or interrogatories concerning, as he said, the welfare of their souls and the correction or improvement of their lives; that the co-litigants, appearing on this account before Richard the commissary, but before the prolongation of his jurisdiction, had, with due instance and at a suitable time and place, requested a copy of the articles or interrogatories to be handed over to them by Richard at their cost and expense; that Richard the commissary, unlawfully refusing to hand over, or cause to be handed over, a copy to the co- litigants, as above, and to hear them in their defence, excommunicated them without reasonable ground, recklessly and *de facto*; that the co- litigants, feeling *inter alia* unduly aggrieved thereby, appealed to the local metropolitan court of Canterbury or expounded their complaint over these things before Thomas Wodyngton', DDec, the then president of the said court, and in the cause of this appeal or complaint they caused Richard the commissary to be summoned to judgement before Thomas the president; and that Thomas the president – proceeding wrongly in the cause of this appeal or complaint – promulgated an unjust or null, definitive (as he said) sentence by which *inter alia* he freed Richard the commissary from the co-litigants' claim, from which, on the co-litigants' part, appeal was made to the apostolic see. At the supplication to the pope to order that the co- litigants and each one of them be absolved *ad cautelam* from the said sentence of excommunication and any other ecclesiastical sentences, censures and pains perhaps promulgated against them by Richard the commissary and any other judges and persons on the above occasion and to commit to some upright men in those parts the causes: of the said later appeal and of anything perhaps attempted and innovated after and against it; of the nullity of the excommunication and refusal and of the whole process and sentence of Richard the commissary and Thomas the president; of each and every other thing done in any way by them and any other judges and persons to the prejudice of the co-litigants and of each one of them in connection with the foregoing; and of the whole principal matter, the pope [hereby] commands that the above two (or one of them), having summoned Richard the commissary and others concerned, shall, on the pope's authority, bestow on the co-litigants and each one of them, for this once only, if they so request, the benefit of absolution *ad cautelam* from the said sentence of excommunication and other ecclesiastical sentences, censures, and pains, if and as it is just, having, however, first received from them suitable security in regard to that for which they are held excommunicate and perhaps caught by the said censures, that if it appears to the above that the sentence of excommunication and other ecclesiastical sentences etc were justly inflicted on them they will obey the above's mandates and those of the church; and as to the other matters, having heard both sides, taking cognizance even of the principal matter, decree what is just, without appeal, causing what they have decreed to be strictly observed; [and moreover compel] witnesses, etc. Notwithstanding etc.

Humilibus et cetera.
P. lambert(us) / C / C. xx. Barotius

223   7 May 1513   *Reg. Lat.* 1297, fos 315ᵛ-316ᵛ

To the bishop of Exeter, the abbot of the monastery of Westmon', d. London, and Roger Church, canon of the church of Bath, mandate in favour of Thomas Springar and Walter Abraham, guardians or churchwardens (*gardianorum sive iconomorum*), and John Jamys, Roger Johannis, Robert Henton', John Lane, Edmund Martyn, Thomas Colyat, Richard Smyth', William and John Hele, John Henton' the younger, and William Nasche, laymen, parishioners of the chapel called the chapel of Ffaryngtun'[1] (which is also parochial) situated within the boundary of the parish church of Chewton', d. Bath and Wells co-litigants in this regard. A recent petition to the pope on the co-litigants' part stated that although by ancient, approved, and hitherto peacefully observed custom the rector[2] of the said church for the time being is bound and has been accustomed, from time immemorial, to provide for them and appoint a priest-chaplain to celebrate mass and other divine offices in the said chapel on at least each feast day and to administer the ecclesiastical sacraments to them; that because Thomas Lane, perpetual vicar[3] of the said church – falsely alleging that he was not bound to this – was unlawfully refusing to provide for them and appoint a priest-chaplain who would celebrate mass and other divine offices in the said chapel and administer the ecclesiastical sacraments to the co-litigants, as above, they sued Thomas the vicar over this before Cuthbert Tusculanus[4], auditor of causes of the court of William, archbishop of Canterbury, primate of all England and legate born of the apostolic see in those parts, praying *inter alia* that he be coerced and compelled to provide for them and appoint a priest-chaplain, as above; and that Cuthbert the auditor – proceeding wrongly in the case – promulgated an unjust, definitive (as he said), sentence by which *inter alia* he freed Thomas the vicar from the co-litigants claim, from which, on the part of the co-litigants, appeal was made to the apostolic see. At the supplication to the pope to commit to some upright men in those parts the causes: of the aforesaid appeal and of anything perhaps attempted and innovated after and against it; of the nullity of Cuthbert's process and sentence; and of the whole principal matter, the pope [hereby] commands that the above three (or two or one of them), having summoned Thomas the vicar and others concerned and having heard both sides, taking cognizance even of the principal matter, shall decree what is just without appeal, causing by ecclesiastical censure what they have decreed to be strictly observed; [and moreover compel] witnesses, etc. Notwithstanding etc.

Humilibus et cetera.
P. lambertus / C / . C. xij Barotius

1   the '-un' uncertain
2   *sic*
3   *sic*
4   MS: *coram dilecto filio Coberto Tusculano*

224   30 April 1513   *Reg. Lat.* 1297, fos 366ᵛ-367ᵛ

To the abbot of the monastery of Bury and the priors of the priories of Westakyr and Yxworth, d. Norwich, mandate in favour of Cuthbert Sebby, layman of the parish of the parish church of Tuddenhm', d. Norwich. A recent petition to the pope on Cuthbert's part stated that some time ago Robert Hone, who bears himself as rector of the said church – falsely alleging that Cuthbert had wrongly taken away certain tithes due to him (as he said) by reason of the said church – sued Cuthbert over this, not by apostolic delegation, firstly before Thomas Woddingten', DDec, [dean][1] of the church of B Mary le Bow (*de Arcubus*), London, and then before the said Thomas as official of Canterbury, who was, he [Robert] said, a competent judge for this; and that Thomas the official, proceeding wrongly in the case, promulgated an unjust, definitive (as he said) sentence in Robert's favour and against Cuthbert, also condemning Cuthbert in the costs run up in the case, from which, on Cuthbert's part, appeal was made to the apostolic see. At the supplication to the pope to commit to some upright men in those parts the causes: of the aforesaid appeal and of anything perhaps attempted and innovated after and against it; of the nullity of the process and sentence of Thomas the official; and of the whole principal matter, the pope [hereby] commands that the above three (or two or one of them), having summoned Robert and others concerned and having heard both sides, taking cognizance even of the principal matter, shall decree what is just, without appeal, causing by ecclesiastical censure what they have decreed to be strictly observed; [and moreover compel] witnesses, etc. Notwithstanding etc.

Humilibus et cetera.
P. lambert(us) / C / C. xij. Barotius

1   MS: *decime*; *recte*: 'decano'

225   19 March 1513   *Reg. Lat.* 1297, fos 387ᵛ-388ʳ

To Edward Gyllete, monk of the monastery of Kyrkestede [also spelt *Kerkestete*],
OCist, d. Lincoln, effectuation of Julius II's dispensation in his favour. Some time ago,
Julius II, under the date 23 October, ninth year [1512], dispensed Edward (who, as he
asserted, was a monk of the above monastery and professed of the above order)¹ – at
his supplication – to receive and retain any benefice, with or without cure, usually held
by secular clerics, even if a parish church or its perpetual vicarage, or a chantry, free
chapel, hospital or annual service, usually assigned to secular clerics in title of a
perpetual ecclesiastical benefice, of lay or clerical or mixed patronage and of
whatsoever tax or annual value, if he obtained it otherwise canonically; to resign it,
simply or for exchange, as often as he pleased and in its place receive and retain
another, similar or dissimilar, benefice, with or without cure, usually held by secular
clerics. Notwithstanding etc. Since however Julius II died before his letters to this
effect were drawn up, the pope hereby wills and decrees that the present letters shall
everywhere be sufficient proof of the said dispensation etc.

Racioni congruit et cetera.
p. lambert(us) / [–]² / C xxx Barotius

1   This information comes from a notwithstanding clause.
2   no magistral initial

226   13 March 1514   *Reg. Lat.* 1298, fos 105ᵛ-107ʳ

Mandate to collate and assign to Panthaleon Salvago – cleric of Genoa, scriptor of the
archive of the Roman curia, continual commensal familiar of the pope, and in the
service of Christopher, cardinal priest of the title of S Prassede – the parish church of
St Laurence, Caualˡ, d. Barcelona, at present vacant by the death outside the Roman
curia of its rector (named), whose annual value does not exceed 24 gold ducats of the
camera. The letter, which is addressed to three mandataries, is of no other interest to
the Calendar.

Grata devotionis et familiaritatis obsequia …
.P. la(m)bert(us) / JoA. / .JoA. Gratis p(ro) Scriptor(e) Archivij tertio k(a)l(endas)
aprilis Anno Secundo [30 March 1514]: *Nard(inus)*

1   or *Canal* or *Caral*

227   13 March 1514   *Reg. Lat.* 1298, fos 107ʳ-108ᵛ

Mandate to collate and assign to Panthaleon Salvago – cleric of Genoa, scriptor of the
archive of the Roman curia, continual commensal familiar of the pope, and in the

service of Christopher, cardinal priest of the title of S Prassede – the parish church of St Michael, Marmellario, d. Barcelona, at present vacant by the death outside the Roman curia of its rector (named), whose annual value does not exceed 24 gold ducats of the camera. The letter, which is addressed to three mandataries, is of no other interest to the Calendar.

Grata devotionis et familiaritatis obsequia ...
.P. la(m)bert(us) / JoA / JoA: Gratis p(ro) Scriptor(e) Archivii tertio K(a)l(endas) Aprilis Anno Secundo [30 March 1514]: *Nardinus*

228   18 January 1514   *Reg. Lat.* 1298, fos 222ᵛ-224ᵛ

To the priors of the monasteries, usually governed by priors, of Cluntoskeyt nasyna[1] and Runduyn, d. Elphin, and Tyhius Offalleryn, canon of the church of Elphin, mandate in favour of John Okellay *alias* Okernain junior, monk of the monastery, usually governed by a prior, of Sts Peter and Paul, Athlone (*de Anocentia*)[2] at Alnym,[3] OSB,[4] d. Elphin. It has been referred to the pope's audience by the said John Okellay junior that John Okellay senior[5], cleric, who holds the priorship of the said monastery *in commendam* by apostolic concession and dispensation, has dared to commit homicide and to alienate and dilapidate *de facto* the goods of the said monastery. The pope – considering that if the foregoing is true John senior has rendered himself unworthy of the priorship; and wishing to give a special grace to John junior (who is a priest and, as he asserts, expressly professed of the above order; and who, some time ago was dispensed by apostolic authority notwithstanding a defect of birth as the son of a priest, a monk expressly professed of the above order, and an unmarried woman, to hold a benefice, even if it should have cure of souls) – hereby commands that the above three (or two or one of them), if John junior will accuse John senior before them over the above related matters and proceed in form of law, thereafter, having summoned John senior and others concerned, shall make inquiry into the above related matters and, if they find the truth of them to be substantiated, deprive John senior of the priorship and remove him from it; and, in that event, collate and assign the priorship, (which is conventual and whose annual value does not exceed 16 marks sterling), then vacant howsoever etc.; even if specially reserved or generally reserved because it is conventual, and even if it is customarily elective and has cure of souls etc., with all its rights and appurtenances, to John junior, inducting him etc. having removed any unlawful detainer and causing John junior (or his proctor) to be admitted to the priorship and its fruits etc., rights and obventions to be delivered to him. [Curbing] gainsayers etc. Notwithstanding etc. Also the pope dispenses John junior to receive and retain the priorship, if conferred on him by virtue of the presents, notwithstanding the above defect etc. Given at Canino, d. Castro.

Religionis zelus, vite ac morum honestas ...
.Je. venzon. / JoA: / JoA xx:- Nardinus

1   perhaps one word: the name is written over two lines, with *nasyna* at the start of the second.
2   *sic*; *recte*: 'Innocentia'
3   follows a deleted spelling
4   *sic*
5   *Johannes etiam Okellay* ['alias Okernain'?] senior

229   13 February 1514   *Reg. Lat.* 1298, fos 355ʳ-357ᵛ

To the treasurer and William Rogill' and James Bauod,[1] canons of the church of
Limerick, mandate in favour of Maurice Felany, priest, d. Limerick. A recent petition
to the pope on Maurice's part stated that at another time – after he had been dispensed
by apostolic authority notwithstanding a defect of birth as the son of a cleric and an
unmarried or (*alias*) married woman to be promoted to all, even sacred, orders and to
receive and retain together for life three benefices, with or without cure, even if they
should be canonries and prebends in cathedral churches or two of them be parish
churches or their perpetual vicarages, if conferred on him otherwise canonically; and
he had been duly marked with clerical character the then bishop of Limerick, by
ordinary authority, collated to Maurice the perpetual vicarage of the parish church of
the place of Tancartistam and the perpetual vicarage of the parish church of BB. Peter
and Paul the Apostles of the place of Killochia,[2] d. Limerick (which were vacant *certo
modo*) and made provision of them. However, as the said petition added, Maurice fears
that for certain reasons the said collation and provision do not hold good; and, as the
pope has learned, the said perpetual vicarages are understood to be vacant still as
above; and also the perpetual vicarages of the parish churches, which are of lay
patronage, of Alekary,[3] a place, d. Limerick and of B. Mary the Virgin and St John the
Evangelist, Stagno, a place, d. Emly, are understood to be vacant at present (that of
Alekary, by the death, outside the Roman curia, of its perpetual vicar Theodoric
Ocanuirej, who held it while he lived, and that of Stagno from the outset of its
erection). The said petition added that if a canonry was to be erected and instituted in
the church of Emly and all the said vicarages were to be erected and instituted into a
simple prebend of it, for Maurice's lifetime, it would be of advantage to the church of
Emly (with increase of divine worship) and to Maurice. The pope – not having certain
knowledge of the foregoing and wishing to give Maurice a special grace – hereby
commands that the above three (or two or one of them), if the matter is as stated and
the express assent for it is forthcoming from those concerned and, with respect to the
two vicarages mentioned second, from the said patrons, shall erect and institute in the
said church of Emly a canonry and all the said vicarages (vacant howsoever etc.; even
if they have been vacant for so long that by the Lateran statutes their collation has
lawfully devolved on the apostolic see etc.) into a simple prebend of the church of
Emly, for Maurice's lifetime, as above, without prejudice to anyone; and, in the event
of this erection and institution by virtue of the presents, shall collate and assign the
newly erected canonry and prebend, whose annual value does not exceed 24[4] marks
sterling, being then vacant, with plenitude of canon law and all their rights and
appurtenances, to Maurice, inducting him etc. having removed any unlawful detainer
and causing Maurice (or his proctor) to be received as a canon in the church of Emly;

and shall assign him, with plenitude of the said law, a stall in the choir and a place in the chapter of the said church of Emly and [causing] all the fruits etc., rights and obventions of the vicarages to be delivered to him. [Curbing] gainsayers etc. Notwithstanding etc. The pope's will is, however, that the said vicarages shall not, on this account, be defrauded of due services, and the cure of souls in them shall not be neglected; but that their customary burdens shall be supported; and that on Maurice's death or his resignation etc. of the canonry and prebend this erection and institution shall be dissolved and so deemed and the vicarages shall revert to their original condition automatically.

Apostolice sedis circumspecta benignitas ad ea libenter intendit ...
.phi. d(e) agnellis / *JoA:* / *JoA: xxv: pridie non(as) martii Anno primo* [6 March 1514], *Nard(inus)*

1   Though there is a dot above the second 'minim' of the 'u'.
2   reading 'K' sympathetically (formed very like an 'R')
3   written *Alekarij*; the 'r' somewhat uncertain
4   *viginti quatuor* written in larger characters, seemingly in another hand: entered later in a space left blank?

230   12 November 1513   *Reg. Lat.* 1299, fos 140[r]-141[r]

To Richard Newyll', cleric, d. Ferns. Some time ago, Alexander VI by other letters[1] of his dispensed Richard – who formerly, as he asserted, had been dispensed by apostolic authority, notwithstanding a defect of birth as the son of a bishop and an unmarried woman, to be promoted to all, even sacred, orders and to hold a benefice, even if it had cure of souls – to receive and retain for life, together with the said benefice, one, and without them, any two other benefices, with cure or otherwise mutually incompatible, and also [any number][2] of benefices, with and without cure, compatible[3] mutually and with the said incompatible benefices, even if the incompatible benefices should be parish churches or their perpetual vicarages and they as well as the compatible benefices should be canonries and prebends, dignities, *personatus*, administrations or offices in cathedral, even metropolitan, or collegiate churches, even if the dignities should be major *post pontificalem* in cathedral, even metropolitan, churches, or principal in collegiate churches, or a combination, even if they should be [in churches] over which his father was presiding at that time or should preside in the future, and even if the dignities etc. should be customarily elective and have cure of souls, if he obtained them otherwise canonically, to resign them, at once or successively, simply or for exchange, as often as he pleased and in their place receive up to two other, similar or dissimilar, incompatible benefices and any number of compatible benefices, with and without cure, as above, and retain them together for life as above, as is more fully contained in those letters in which it was expressed that he was a cleric. However, a recent petition to the pope on Richard's part stated that at the date of the said letters he was a scholar and not a cleric (although he is now duly marked with clerical character) and had not been dispensed for the said orders and to hold a benefice [even][4] if it had cure of souls, but there had only been a mandate *de dispensando* on apostolic authority, and on this account Richard fears that the said letters and dispensation are vitiated by surreption and of no use to him and that he could be molested over them in time to come. Lest the effect of the said letters be frustrated, the pope – at Richard's supplication – hereby wills and grants that Alexander's letters and dispensation, with the clause of exchange and all the other clauses contained in them, shall be valid from the date of the presents and have full force and that Richard can rely on them without limitation, just as if it had been stated in the said letters that Richard was only a [scholar][5] and, not that he had been dispensed, but that there had been a mandate for dispensing him [for] the said orders and to hold one [benefice][6], even if it had cure of souls. Notwithstanding the above defect etc.

Vite ac morum honestas …
phi de agnel[lis][7] / JoA: / JoA: xx: Nardinus

1   *Cf.* Index entry for Richard Kawall, d. Ferns, dispensation for illegitimacy. *CPL*, XVII, Part I, no. 1299. On the unreliability of the surnames given in the mid-eighteenth century index from which this reference comes, *see CPL*, XVI, p. li, note 19.
2   'quotcunque' wanting here (though it occurs below)
3   here and below: *compascientia*; for 'compatientia'?
4   MS wants 'etiam'.
5   MS: *clericus*; *recte*: 'scolaris'?
6   MS wants 'beneficium ecclesiasticum'.
7   shaved

231   15 March 1514   *Reg. Lat.* 1300, fos 232[r]-233[v]

To Thomas Fforune, perpetual chaplain, called cantor, at the altar of St Christopher in the church of York. Dispensation – at his supplication – to receive and retain for life, together with the perpetual chaplaincy, called a chantry, at the above altar, (which is incompatible with another incompatible benefice), one, and without them, any two other benefices etc. [as above, no. 2, to '… retain them together for life, as above']; and indult for life, while attending a *studium generale* etc. [as above, no. 2].

Vite ac morum honestas …
P. lambertus / JoA: / :JoA: Lx: Nardinus

232   1 December 1513   *Reg. Lat.* 1301, fos 264[r]-265[v]

To the official of Brechin. Following the pope's reservation of all benefices, with and without cure, vacated then or in the future at the apostolic[1] see to his own collation and disposition, the perpetual vicarage of the parish church of the town of Dunde, d. Brechin, became vacant by the free resignation of John Barre senior (recently perpetual vicar, who was holding the vicarage at the time) made by John Fagnoy, cleric, d. Cambrai, his specially appointed proctor, spontaneously into the pope's hands and admitted by the pope at the said see, and is vacant at present, being reserved as above. Wishing to give John Barre junior, cleric, said d. <Brechin>[2] (who is, as he asserts, in sacred orders) a special grace, the pope hereby commands the above official, if by diligent examination he finds John junior to be suitable – concerning which the pope burdens the official's conscience – to collate and assign the vicarage, whose annual value does not exceed 30 pounds sterling, (vacant as above or in any other way etc.; even if it has been vacant for so long that by the Lateran statutes its collation has lawfully devolved on the apostolic see, even if reserved specially or otherwise, even generally because, as is asserted, John senior was holding it as collector of the fruits and proceeds due to the apostolic camera in those parts, etc.), with all its rights and appurtenances, to John junior, inducting him etc. having removed any detainer[3] and causing John junior (or his proctor) to be admitted to the vicarage and its fruits etc., rights and obventions to be delivered to him. [Curbing] gainsayers etc. Notwithstanding etc.

Dignum et cetera.
.P. lambert(us) / JoA: / JoA. XX: undecimo k(a)l(endas) Januarij Anno Primo [22 December 1513], *Nardinus*

1   *sedem predictam*; *sedes apostolica* (indicated, in this instance, by *et cetera*) had occurred in the proem.
2   marginal insertion in hand of enregistering scribe initialled *JoA*
3   'illicito' does not occur.

233   1 December 1513   *Reg. Lat.* 1301, fos 265ᵛ-268ʳ

To John Barre, priest, d. Brechin, reservation, constitution and assignment of a pension, as below. This day John resigned, spontaneously and freely, the parish church of Culase, d. St Andrews, which he was then holding, through a certain specially appointed proctor of his, into the pope's hands and the pope admitted the resignation and commanded by other letters of his that provision of the church, (then vacant by the said resignation and previously reserved to apostolic disposition), be made to Henry Barre, cleric, d. Brechin, as is more fully contained in those letters.[1] Lest John (who, as he asserts, has passed his sixty-first year of age or thereabouts) should suffer excessive loss on this account, the pope hereby reserves, constitutes and assigns an annual pension of 30 marks of the money current in the kingdom of Scotland, not exceeding 6 pounds sterling of the said money, on the church's fruits etc., of which this pension does not exceed, as John asserts, one half, payable in full in the town of Dunde, d. Brechin, to John, for life, or to his specially mandated proctor, by Henry, who has expressly assented to this, and by his successors as rectors of the said church for the time being, each year, viz.: one half of the said pension on the feast of Pentecost and the other on that of St Martin in November. With decree that Henry and his successors are obliged to make full payment of the pension to John in accordance with the said reservation etc. and establishing that if Henry or any one of his successors fails to make payment on either of the said feasts or at least within the thirty days immediately following he shall, after this time has elapsed, incur sentence of excommunication from which he cannot be absolved, except on the point of death, until he has made satisfaction in full or reached agreement in respect of it with John (or his proctor); and if Henry remains obdurate for a further six months immediately after the said thirty days he shall thereupon be deprived of the church in perpetuity and it shall be deemed vacant automatically. Notwithstanding etc.

Executory to the bishop of Cavaillon and the archdeacon of La Hesbaye in the church of Liège and the official of St Andrews, or two or one of them, acting in person or by proxy.

Vite ac morum honestas ... The executory begins: *Hodie dilecto filio Johanni Barre* ... *.P. lambert(us); Ge d(e) prato. / JoA: / JoA: xij: x: Nardinus*

1   *Cf.* below, no. 807.

234   1 December 1513   *Reg. Lat.* 1301, fos 268ʳ-270ᵛ

To John Barre senior, priest, d. Brechin, reservation, constitution and assignment of a pension, as below. This day John senior resigned, spontaneously and freely, the perpetual vicarage of the <parish church>[1] of the town of Dunde, d. Brechin, which he was then holding, through a certain specially appointed proctor of his, into the pope's hands; and the pope, by other letters of his, admitted the resignation and made provision of the vicarage, (then vacant by the said resignation and previously reserved to apostolic disposition), to John Barre junior, cleric, <said>[2] diocese, as is more fully contained in those letters.[3] Lest John senior (who, as he asserts, has passed his sixty-first year of age or thereabouts), should suffer excessive loss on this account, the pope hereby reserves, constitutes and assigns an annual pension of <90>[4] marks of the money current in the kingdom of Scotland, not exceeding <15>[5] pounds sterling of the said money, on the vicarage's fruits etc., (of which this pension does not exceed, as John asserts, one half), payable in full, in the town,[6] to John senior, for life, or to his specially mandated proctor, by John junior, who has expressly assented to this, and by his successors <holding>[7] the vicarage at the time, each year, viz.: one half of the said pension on the <feast>[6] of Pentecost and the other on the <feast>[6] of St Martin in November. With decree that John junior and his successors are obliged to make full payment of the pension in accordance with the said reservation etc. and establishing that if John junior or any one of his successors fails to make payment on either of the said feasts or within the thirty days immediately following he shall, after this time has elapsed, incur sentence of excommunication from which he shall not be absolved, except on the point of death, until he has made satisfaction in full or reached agreement in respect of it with John senior (or his proctor), and if he remains obdurate for a further six months he shall thereupon be deprived of the vicarage in perpetuity and it shall be deemed vacant automatically. Notwithstanding etc.

Executory to the bishop of Cavaillon and the archdeacon of La Hesbaye in the church of Liège and the official of St Andrews, Brechin,[8] or two or one of them, acting in person or by proxy.

Vite ac morum honestas ... The executory begins: *Hodie dilecto filio Jo(hanni) Barre* ...
.P. lambert(us); Ge. de prato / JoA / JoA: xij: x: Nardinus

1   *parrochialis ecclesie* is inserted in margin initialled *JoA*
2   *Berchinen.* [*sic*; spelt as in address clause] deleted in line; *dicte* inserted in margin, initialled *JoA*
3   above no. 232
4   *triginta* deleted in line; *nonaginta* inserted in margin; both deletion and insertion initialled *JoA*. Similarly the
    executory.
5   *sex* deleted in line; *quindecim* inserted in margin, initialled *JoA*
6   originally written: ... *mensis Novembris* | *dicto oppido de . . . . dicte Berchinen. diocesis* | *integre*
    persolvendam ...; the text here underlined then deleted (initialled *JoA*) and *festivitatibus in* (initialled *JoA*)
    inserted in left margin opposite *dicto*. The blank space occupied by the four dots never filled. 'Dunde' would
    fit nicely.
7   originally written: *et successores suos dicte vicarie rectores pro tempore existentes annis singulis*; changed,
    by deletion and marginal insertion, to: *et successores suos dictam vicariam pro tempore <obtinentes> annis*
    singulis; the insertion initialled *JoA*
8   MS: *ac officiali Sancti Andree Brechinen.*

235   17 March 1514   *Reg. Lat.* 1301, fos 278ʳ-280ʳ

Mandate to collate and assign to John Rolla, cleric, d. Valencia, the canonry and
prebend of the church of B Mary, Xatina and the parish church of the place of Castillo,
d. Valencia, whose annual values together do not exceed 90 gold ducats of the camera,
(all formerly held by his father Ansias Bolla), vacant at the apostolic see by their
resignation into the pope's hands of Hadrian, cardinal priest of the title of S Crisogono,
and previously reserved to the pope's disposition. When, at another time, they were
vacant *certo modo* provision of the canonry and prebend and parish church had (with
suitable dispensation to hold them) been made by apostolic authority to cardinal
Hadrian but he had not had possession. The letter, which is addressed to a single
mandatary, is of no other interest to the Calendar.

Dignum et cetera.
.Je. Venzon / JoA. / JoA: xxxv: Sexto Id(us) aprilis Anno Secundo [8 April 1514],:
Nardinus

1   *sic*; *recte*: 'Rolla'?

236   13 February 1514   *Reg. Lat.* 1302, fos 4ᵛ-6ʳ

To the noble John, son of Thomas de Gueraldinis, the earl of Desmond (*de Simonie*)[1],
de Gueraldinis, temporal lord of the place of Ane, d. Emly, reservation etc. of the right
of patronage and presentation, as below. A recent petition to the pope on John's part
stated that the parish churches of the places of his temporal lordship of Ane,
Kareketaeyll', and Glinogroe and also of Frademur and Torlarbreghe [also spelt

Tolarbreh, Tolarbregh], ds. Emly and Limerick, are in great need of repair; and also
that the fruits etc. of the rectory of the said parish church of Torlarbreghe and of the
perpetual vicarages of Torlarbreghe and the other parish churches aforesaid are so
slight that they scarcely amount in total to an annual value of 30 pounds sterling, that
the said parish churches cannot be repaired from them, and also that the said rectory
and vicarages cannot conveniently support those holding them at the time; and that
John, on account of the singular devotion which he bears towards these parish
churches, is prepared – from the goods conferred on him by God – to cause the said
parish churches to be fittingly repaired and restored and to increase by one half the
endowments of the rectory and vicarages respectively, if the right of patronage of the
rectory and vicarages and of presenting suitable persons to the rectory and each of the
vicarages, as often as they fall vacant, be reserved and granted – after the restoration
and increase – in perpetuity to him and, after his death, to the males of his house and
family existing at the time. At this supplication, the pope – if and after John causes the
said parish churches to be re-built and increases by one half the endowments of the
rectory and of each of the vicarages aforesaid, as above – hereby reserves and grants
in perpetuity to John, and to the aforesaid males of his house and family, the right of
patronage and of presenting to the bishops of Emly and Limerick for the time being
suitable persons to be instituted by them at the presentation in question as rector of
Torlarbreghe and as perpetual vicars of Torlarbreghe and each of the other aforesaid
parish churches, as often as they fall vacant, thenceforth for all time. Notwithstanding
etc.

Sincere devotionis affectus …
phi d(e) agnellis / JoA. / JoA: xxxx: Nard(inus)

1   MS: *Johanni Thome comitis de Simonie de Gueraldinis domino temporali …*

237   8 February 1514   *Reg. Lat.* 1302, fos 6ʳ-10ʳ

To the treasurer and William Negeyll' and Maurice Felavyn, canons, of the church of
Limerick, mandate in favour of James son of John son of Thomas de Gueraldinis, earl
of Desmond (*de Simonie*),[1] cleric, d. Limerick. The pope has learned that the
archdeaconry of the church of Lismore and the canonry and prebend of Differt Laorais
of the church of Emly, and also the perpetual vicarages of the parish churches of the
places of Kayrillei [also spelt *Kayrelley*,[2] *Rayrelley*], Lugden', Rosestuim[3] [also spelt
Rosystuim] and Raychsuredan' [also spelt *Raychsuredan*], d. Emly, are vacant *certo
modo* at present and have been vacant for so long that by the Lateran statutes their
collation has lawfully devolved on the apostolic see, although Maurice, archbishop of
Cashel, has detained the archdeaconry, William Olledy, the canonry and prebend and
the vicarage of Kayrillei, Philip Sanch, the vicarage of Lugden', Richard de Burgo, that
of Rosestuim, and Donald Obegnuim[4] that of Raychsuredan' – bearing themselves as
clerics and priests respectively – with no title or support of law, of their own temerity
and *de facto*, for a certain time, as they still do. At the supplication of James (who

asserts that he is in his eighteenth year of age and that the annual value of the archdeaconry, canonry and prebend and vicarages aforesaid together does not exceed 30 marks sterling) to the pope to unite etc. the vicarages to the canonry and prebend, for as long as he holds the latter, the pope hereby commands that the above three (or two or one of them), if, having summoned archbishop Maurice, and William, Philip, Richard and Donald and others concerned and those interested in the union, they find the archdeaconry (which in the church of Lismore is a dignity not however major *post pontificalem*) and the canonry and prebend and the vicarages to be vacant (howsoever etc.), shall unite etc. the vicarages to the canonry and prebend, for as long as James holds the latter, as above, and collate and assign the canonry and prebend and the archdeaconry (even if they and the said vicarages be specially reserved etc.), with plenitude of canon law and with the annexes in question and all their rights and appurtenances, to James, inducting him etc. having removed archbishop Maurice from the archdeaconry, William from the canonry and prebend and the vicarage of Kayrillei, Philip from the vicarage of Lugden', Richard from that of Rosestuim and Donald from that of Raychsuredan' and any other unlawful detainers, and causing James (or his proctor) to be received as a canon in the said church of Emly, and shall assign him a stall in the choir and a place in the chapter of the church of Emly, with plenitude of canon law, and [causing James] to be admitted to the archdeaconry, and the fruits etc., rights and obventions of the archdeaconry, the canonry and prebend and the said vicarages to be delivered to him. [Curbing] gainsayers by [the pope's] authority etc. Notwithstanding etc. Also the pope dispenses James to receive and retain the archdeaconry, if conferred on him by virtue of the presents, notwithstanding the above defect of age, etc. With the proviso that the archdeaconry and vicarages shall not, on this account, be defrauded of due services and the cure of souls in the archdeaconry (if any) and the vicarages shall not be neglected, but that their customary burdens shall be supported; and that on James's death or his resignation etc. of the canonry and prebend this union etc. shall be dissolved and so deemed and the vicarages shall revert to their original condition and be deemed vacant automatically.

Vite ac morum ac morum[5] *honestas* ...
phi de agnellis / *JoA:* / *JoA. xxxx. Quinto K(a)l(endas) Martij Anno Primo:* [25 February 1514], *Nardinus*

1   *Jacobus Johannis Thome comitis de Simonie de Gueraldinis*
2   bar through the '-ll-' deleted
3   uncertain
4   final letter uncertain: 'm' or possibly 'n'?
5   *sic*

238   31 March 1514   *Reg. Lat.* 1304, fos 30[r]-31[v]

To William Meldrum, perpetual vicar of the parish church of Dunithtyn [also spelt *Dunthin*] d. Brechin, dispensation as below. Some time ago, Alexander VI by his letters dispensed William to receive and retain for life together with the chantership (*cantoria*) of the church of Brechin, (which was a dignity not however major *post pontificalem*, which had cure of souls and which, as he asserted, he was then holding), one, and without them, any two other benefices, with cure or otherwise mutually incompatible, even if parish churches or their perpetual vicarages, or dignities, etc. [as above, no. 6, to '… retain them together for life …'], as is more fully contained in those letters.[1] The pope hereby dispenses William (who, as he asserts, having resigned the above chantership, holds the perpetual vicarages of the parish churches of Dunithtyn and Montrois,[2] d. Brechin, by the said dispensation) – at his supplication – to receive and retain for life together with the above chantership or with any other dignity held by him at the time in the said church of Brechin (or in another cathedral, even metropolitan, church or in a collegiate church), the canonry and prebend called the vicarage of Brechin, or any other canonry and prebend under the roof of Brechin (or of another cathedral, even metropolitan, church, or of a collegiate church), and also together with the said benefices held [i.e. the vicarages of Dunithtyn and Montrois] (or with any two other incompatible benefices held by him at the time by virtue of the said dispensation), any third benefice, with cure or otherwise incompatible, even if a parish church or its perpetual vicarage, or a dignity, etc. [as above, no. 6, to '… if he obtains it otherwise canonically'], to resign them, at once or successively, simply or for exchange, as often as he pleases, and in their place receive and retain together for life, as above, another, similar or dissimilar, third incompatible benefice, and also another canonry and prebend and another dignity located under one and the same roof of one and the same church, provided that among all of them not more than three[3] be incompatibles and among these three incompatibles not more than two be parish churches or their perpetual vicarages. Notwithstanding etc. With the proviso that the third incompatible benefice and the dignity and also the canonry and prebend located under the [same] roof shall not, on this account, be defrauded of due services and the cure of souls in the third incompatible benefice shall not be neglected; but that the customary burdens of the dignity and of the canonry and prebend located under the same roof shall be supported.[4]

Vite ac morum honestas …
p. lambert(us) / JoA: / JoA. Lxxx: Nard(inus)

1   unknown to the *CPL*
2   uncertain reading; the 'r' especially doubtful
3   MS: *dummodo inter omnia illa ultra tria incompatibilia et inter ipsa tria incompatibilia plures quam due parrochiales ecclesie vel earum perpetue vicarie insimul non existant*
4   The terms of this dispensation are much defined and, perhaps, a little confusing. To recapitulate: while holding the chantership [or precentorship] of Brechin cathedral, Meldrum was dispensed *ad duo* by Alexander VI; he later resigned the chantership, and currently holds two vicarages under Alexander's dispensation; he is now dispensed to hold (i) the chantership he had resigned (or another dignity) in Brechin cathedral (or another cathedral or collegiate church); (ii) a named (or another) canonry and prebend of Brechin (or of another cathedral or collegiate church) – provided these two benefices are under the same roof; and (iii) together with the two vicarages he holds or other two incompatibles under Alexander's dispensation, a third incompatible, on condition that not more than three of all the benefices are incompatibles, and not more than two of the incompatibles are parish churches or their perpetual vicarages. That is, altogether he is dispensed, maximally, for up to five benefices; but with strictly limiting provisos.

239   3 June 1514   *Reg. Lat.* 1304, fos 31ᵛ-34ʳ

To M. William Cassador, papal chaplain and auditor of causes of the apostolic palace, mandate in favour of Adam Symson, cleric, d. Dunkeld. A recent petition to the pope on Adam's part stated that some time ago – when a law-suit had arisen between Adam and James Wilson, cleric,[1] over the perpetual vicarage of the parish church of Dron, d. Dunblane, which, when it was vacant *certo modo* at another time, Adam asserted he had accepted within the lawful time and had had provision of it made to him on the strength of certain letters of expectative grace granted to him by Julius II, whose form had enabled him to (*prout ex illarum forma poterat*), and asserted that, contrary to justice, James had opposed the said acceptance and provision, and was opposing [Adam's] right, had obstructed and was obstructing it, and had taken action and was taking action,[2] so that the acceptance and provision had not obtained, and were not obtaining, their due effect and Adam had not been able to acquire the vicarage and asserted that James had detained, and was then detaining, it unlawfully occupied; James, however, asserted that by law the vicarage belonged to him – Julius II, at Adam's instance,[3] committed the case which Adam was intending to move over the vicarage against James and all others disputing his interest – notwithstanding that it had not lawfully devolved to the Roman curia and was not, by necessity of law, to be treated and brought to a finish there – to John, bishop, then elect, of Sibenik (*Sibinicen.*), who by the pope's mandate, then by Julius II's, was holding the place of one of the auditors of causes of the apostolic palace, to be heard and duly determined; that after bishop John, *locumtenens* auditor, had proceeded in the case to the decree of citation and the citation had been put into execution against James and, on the strength of the clause *omnesque alios* incorporated in the commission, against Patrick Mediton'[4] who, bearing himself as a cleric, had *de facto* despoiled James of possession of the vicarage[5] and intruded himself in it, just as he is intruded, and after bishop John, *locumtenens* auditor, proceeding wrongly to further matters between Adam and Patrick, had promulgated an unjust definitive sentence by which he absolved Patrick from Adam's claim, and, when appeal from the sentence had been made on Adam's part to the apostolic see, after Julius II had committed the case of the appeal to the above M. William, to be heard and duly determined, bishop John, *locumtenens* auditor, having suspended the petitory action in the possessory case between Patrick and James, proceeding duly, promulgated a definitive sentence, for restitution of possession of the vicarage, in favour of James and against Patrick, and by virtue of certain letters of Innocent VIII he sequestrated the fruits of the vicarage; and that when appeal from the later sentence had been made on Patrick's part to the apostolic see, the pope (who had been elevated on the death, in the interim, of Julius II) committed the case of the later appeal to the above M. William to be heard and duly determined, and M. William has said that he has proceeded in the cases between, respectively, the said individuals to several acts but short of the conclusion. However, since James has, by Gilbert Stracthanthyn, canon of Brixen,[6] his proctor, specially appointed by him for the purpose, this day – with the suit still pending thus undecided before bishop John, *locumtenens* auditor, with respect to the petitory action[7] between Patrick and James, and before the above M. William, between Adam and Patrick – spontaneously and freely ceded into the pope's hands the said suit and cause and all right in any way belonging to him in or to the vicarage, and the pope has admitted the cession, the pope – wishing to provide for Adam (who, as he asserts, notwithstanding the defect of birth which he suffers as the son of a priest and an unmarried woman, was dispensed some time ago by apostolic authority *inter alia* to be promoted to all even sacred orders and the priesthood and to receive and retain any benefices with or without cure or mutually incompatible if they were[8] otherwise canonically collated to him) lest a new adversary is surrogated against him in the case and wishing to grant him a special grace – calling in the case pending before bishop John, [hereby] commands that the above M. William, having summoned Patrick and others concerned, shall resume the called-in case in due state, hear it further and duly determine and decide it, causing by ecclesiastical censure what he has decreed to be strictly observed; and moreover compel witnesses, etc. and, provided Adam has not intruded into the vicarage, surrogate him in and to all the right which in any way belonged or could have belonged to James in or to the vicarage, collate the right to him and make provision of it, and admit Adam, and cause him to be admitted, as is the custom, to the right and also to the prosecution and defence of the right, suit, case, and spoliation, in the state in which James was at the time of the cession and ought and could have been in if he had not ceded; further, collate and assign the vicarage (whose annual value does not exceed 9 pounds sterling), with all its rights and appurtenances, to Adam, howsoever vacant, even if it is still vacant by the death outside the Roman curia of the said[9] John 3oumge, formerly perpetual vicar of the said church, or by the like cession of James, etc, inducting, personally or by proxy, Adam or his proctor in his name, into corporal possession of the vicarage and its appurtenances, defending him when he has been inducted, having removed any unlawful detainer, and causing Adam or his proctor on his behalf to be admitted to the vicarage, as is the custom, and a full account to be made to him of its fruits, etc. Curbing gainsayers, etc. Notwithstanding etc.

Vite ac morum honestas …
p. lambert(us) / JoA: / :JoA: xx: tertio non(as) Junij Anno Secundo [3 June 1514]:
Nardinus

1   awkwardness and possible omission in MS: *inter eum et dilectum filium Jacobum Wilson clericum qui super perpetua vicaria …* As the entry stands, *qui* is redundant. It may have introduced a clause which was lost in the act of enregistration, perhaps one containing further particulars of JW (possibly in the form 'qui se gerit pro …'); it could equally be a scribal aberration or a relict of a superseded draft which somehow found its way into the register. For a possible indicator of omission, *see below*, note 9.

2   MS: *dictumque Jacobum acceptation(i) et provision(i) predictis contra justiciam se opposuisse et iur(i) oponere inpedivisseque et inpedire ac fecisse et facere*

3   MS: *ad id ipsius Ade instantiam*; treating *id* as redundant

4   first two, perhaps three, letters uncertain

5   MS: *qui … contra prefatum Jacobum possessione ipsius vicarie de facto spoliaverat*; *contra* seems redundant

6   MS: *Brixinen.* (or perhaps *Brexinen.*); *recte*: 'Brechinen.'

7   MS: *petorium*; *recte*: ' petitorium'

8   MS: *conferantur*; 'conferrentur' ?

9   *sic* (*eiusdem*). As the entry stands, this is the first mention of John 3oumge; but if a passage has been lost (*cf.* above, note 1) there may have been an earlier mention.

240   28 March 1517   *Reg. Lat.* 1305, fos 102[r]-104[r]

To the official of St Andrews, mandate in favour of Alexander Fothringham, cleric, d. St Andrews. Some time ago, by a certain constitution of his published in the apostolic chancery on 28 November in the second year of his pontificate [1514],[1] the pope generally reserved to his collation and disposition all ecclesiastical benefices, with and without cure, qualified in a certain way and comprised under a certain annual value then expressed, falling vacant, in January and certain other months then expressed, from that time onwards up to a certain time then expressed which has not yet run out; and thereafter, by a certain other constitution of his published in the apostolic chancery on 19 April in the third year of his pontificate [1515],[2] the pope extended the aforesaid constitution to all other ecclesiastical benefices, whatever the annual value of their fruits; and successively, by a subsequent constitution of his published in the apostolic chancery on 29 April in the fourth year of his pontificate [1516],[3] the pope renewed the said reservation of benefices and its extension, and in renewing it he made a wholly similar reservation.[4] Afterwards, the parish church of Cullace, d. St Andrews, which the late Henry Barre, rector of the church, held while he lived, fell vacant and is vacant at present by his death last January[5] outside the Roman curia, being reserved as above. The pope – wishing to bestow a gracious favour on Alexander (who asserts that Robert Monorgond, who bears himself as a cleric, has detained the said church for a certain time, but short of a year, and is detaining it) – [hereby] commands that the above official shall, on the pope's authority – if by diligent examination he finds that Alexander is suitable (concerning which the pope burdens the official's conscience) and having summoned Robert and others concerned – collate and assign the church (whose annual value does not exceed 10 pounds sterling) with all its rights and appurtenances, to Alexander, whether it is vacant as above or by the said Henry's resignation, etc, personally or by proxy inducting Alexander etc. having removed Robert and any other unlawful detainer, and causing its fruits etc rights and obventions to be delivered to Alexander; [curbing] gainsayers, etc. Notwithstanding etc.

Dignum et cetera.
Jo Ingenwinckel / JoA / JoA xx: sextodecimo k(a)l(endas) aprilis Anno septimo [17 March 1520]*: Nardinus*

---

1   *Cf.* pamphlet entitled *Regula Cancellarie noviter publicata de Reservatione beneficiorum vacaturorum in mensibus Apostolicis* (contemporary imprint; but undated and without place or printer's name; attributed to M. Silber, Rome [F. Ascarellli, *Le Cinquecentine Romane* (Milan, 1972), p. 44]); prefaced with the rubric: *Reservatio beneficiorum in antea vacaturorum in mensibus apostolicis cum inhibitione & decreto quod Ordinarii nec alii etiam auctoritate Apostolica de illis sic in dictis mensibus vacantibus se intromittere non debeant*; and with the authenticating notes at the end: *Placet publicetur & describatur in Cancellaria. I.* ['I' = Johannes (Medices) = Leo X] and *Lecta & publicata fuit suprascripta Regula Rome in Cancellaria Apostolica Die Vicesimaoctava mensis Novembris. Anno Incarnationis Dominice M. D. XIIII. Pontificatus prefati Sanctissimi domini nostri Pape Anno Secundo.* There is a copy in the Biblioteca Nazionale Centrale, Rome (collocazione: 14. 25. M. 18, item 4). The 'apostolic months' were November, January, March, May, July, and September. The rule provided that collations and provisions of the reserved benefices made by the pope or on his authority were null and void *nisi in litteris desuper conficiendis presens reservatio dispositive enarrata fuerit* – hence, presumably, the very unusual inclusion in a papal letter of such specific references to rules of chancery.

2   *Cf.* pamphlet entitled *Regula revocationis Facultatum Legatis Nunciis et aliis quibuscunque Collatoribus etc*

de conferendis beneficiis concessarum in Mensibus Apostolicis (as previous note [Ascarelli, p. 45]); prefaced with the rubric: *Regula revocationis facultatum Legatis etc de conferendis beneficiis concessarum*; and with the authenticating notes at the end: *Placet publicetur & describatur. I.* and *Lecta & publicata fuit suprascripta Regula Romae in Cancellaria Apostolica Anno Incarnationis dominice Millesimoquingentesimoquintodecimo. Die Decinona* [!] *mensis Aprilis. Pontificatus prefati Sanctissimi domini nostri Pape Anno tertio.* (BNCR, 14. 25. M. 18, item 6).

3   *Cf.* pamphlet entitled *Regula Cancellarie Apostolice extensionis et ampliationis omnium Revocationum quarumcunque Reservationum et Facultatum etc.* (as note 1 above [Ascarelli, p. 45]); no prefacing rubric; with the authenticating notes at the end: *Placet publicetur & describatur. I.* and *Lecta & publicata fuit suprascripta Regula Rome in Cancellaria apostolica, Die. xxix. mensis Aprilis, Anno Incarnationis dominice Millesimoquingentesimo sextodecimo, Pontificatus prefati Sanctissimi domini nostri Pape Anno Quarto.* (BNCR, 14. 25. M. 18, item 13).

4   MS: ... *innovamus et innovando similem penitus reservacionem fecimus*; as printed the rule (identified in previous note) actually says: ... *innovavit & innovando similes penitus illis Constitutionibus continentur, beneficiorum reservationem, & illius extensionem, ac Gratiarum expectativarum etc revocationem fecit.*

5   i.e. an 'apostolic month'. Papal letters disposing of benefices vacant *per obitum* rarely disclose the relevant date of death.

241   20 October 1519   *Reg. Lat.* 1305, fos 153^r-155^r

To the bishop of Brechin and the treasurer of the church of Brechin, mandate in favour of Thomas Hau, MA, cleric, d. St Andrews. Following the pope's reservation some time ago of all major dignities *post pontificalem* in cathedral churches vacated then and in the future to his own collation and disposition, the deanery of the church of Brechin, which is a major dignity *post pontificalem* and which Patrick Paniter, its late dean, held while he lived, fell vacant by his death outside the Roman curia and is vacant at present, being reserved as above. Wishing to give a special grace to Thomas, who asserts that he is the secretary of the nobleman, John, duke of Albany (*Albanie*), who is the tutor of James, king of Scots (a minor), and the governor of the kingdom of Scotland; and that Alexander Stewart, who bears himself as a cleric, has detained the deanery after the said vacation, with no title or support of law, of his own temerity and *de facto*, for a certain time, but short of a year, and detains it still,[1] the pope hereby commands that the above two (or one of them), having summoned Alexander and others concerned, shall collate and assign the deanery, the annual value of which and of any annexes thereto, does not exceed 40 pounds sterling, (whether vacant as above, or howsoever etc.; even if it has been vacant for so long that by the Lateran statutes its collation has lawfully devolved on the apostolic see, etc.), with the said annexes and all their rights and appurtenances, to Thomas, inducting him etc. <having previously received the usual oath from him>[2] into corporal possession of the deanery, annexes and rights and appurtenances aforesaid, having removed Alexander and any other unlawful detainer and causing Thomas (or his proctor) to be admitted to the deanery and causing the fruits etc., rights and obventions of the deanery and of the annexes in question to be delivered to him. [Curbing] gainsayers etc. Notwithstanding etc. Given at Cerveteri, d. Porto.

Litterarum scientia, vite ac morum honestas ...
Jo. danielo / M / M xxx octavo id(us) novemb(ris) an(n)o octavo [6 November 1520], *de Campania*

1   *ad uc*; for 'adhuc'
2   *recepto prius ab eo solito iuramento* inserted in margin initialled *M*

242   12¹ October 1514   *Reg. Lat.* 1306, fo 53ʳ⁻ᵛ

To the prior of the church of Canterbury and the official of Canterbury, mandate in favour of Edward Ponyng, nobleman, captain of Henry, king of England, undoubted (*certi*) temporal lord of the lordship of Folston.² A recent petition to the pope on Edward's part stated that although, by reason of the lordship, he is patron of the monastery of St Radegund, OPrem, d. Canterbury, recently, when the monastery was destitute of the rule of its abbot, the convent nevertheless– without informing Edward of the vacancy (which it ought to have done in accordance with the monastery's foundation and ancient, approved, and hitherto peacefully observed custom) – perhaps elected William (who bears himself as the monastery's present abbot) as their and the monastery's abbot; and that the then abbot of the monastery of Newerque,³ OPrem, said or other d. – bearing himself as visitor of the monastery of St Radegund – presumed, without obtaining Edward's consent in this connection, to confirm the said election or otherwise to appoint William as abbot of the monastery of St Radegund, to Edward's considerable prejudice and injury. At Edward's supplication to the pope to commit to some upright men in those parts the causes which Edward intends to move over the above matters both against the abbot and the convent and William as also against others, in common or separately, disputing his interest, the pope [hereby] commands that the above two (or one of them), having summoned the abbot and the convent and William and others concerned and having heard both sides, [shall decree] what is just [without appeal, causing by ecclesiastical censure what they have decreed to be strictly] observed,⁴ [and moreover compel] witnesses, etc. Notwithstanding etc. Given at Viterbo.⁵

Humilibus supplicum et cetera.
phi de agnell(is) / C / C. x. Barotius

1   For the day-date *see above*, p. lxxix, note 8.
2   no diocese mentioned
3   or just possibly *Welberque*
4   MS: … *quod iustum fuerit et cetera observari*. Supplied from common form.
5   The place date has been altered: *Rome apud Sanctum Petrum* deleted (though surprisingly the deletion has not been initialled by the registrar (i.e. Cristoforus Barotius); *Viterbii* inserted in the margin (hand of enregistering scribe).

243   9 January 1515   *Reg. Lat.* 1306, fos 160ʳ-161ʳ

To the bishop of Winchester, the abbot of the monastery of B Peter, Westminster (*West monasterii*), London, and the prior of the priory of Merton, d. Winchester, mandate in favour of Dominic Cini, rector of the parish church of Suth Wokyngton, d. London. A recent petition to the pope on Dominic's part stated that although, some time ago, when he had held and possessed the said church for some time (having acquired it with canonical title when it was vacant *certo modo*), and was holding and possessing it, peacefully and quietly, William Tyrrell, cleric or layman,[1] London or other city or diocese – claiming, albeit falsely, that the church was vacant and that Dominic was an intruder and detaining it unlawfully occupied – nevertheless sued Dominic over this before the then official of London, praying *inter alia* that the church be declared vacant and perhaps be collated to him; that after he had proceeded to several acts short, however, of a conclusion the said official committed the case (as is said) to Robert Bryght', cleric, to be resumed in due state and duly determined; and that Robert the commissary, proceeding in the case without warning or citing Dominic, promulgated a null or unjust, definitive (as is also said) sentence in William's favour and against Dominic, from which, on Dominic's part, as soon as he had knowledge of it, appeal was made to the apostolic see. At the supplication to the pope to commit to some upright men in those parts the causes: of the said appeal and of anything attempted and innovated after and against it; of the said nullity and of each and every other thing done in any way by the official and Robert the commissary and any other judges and persons to Dominic's prejudice in connection with the above; and of the whole principal matter, the pope [hereby] commands that the above three (or two or one of them), having summoned William and others concerned and having heard both sides, taking cognizance even of the principal matter, [shall decree] what is just, [without appeal, causing by ecclesiastical censure what they have decreed to be strictly observed],[2] [and moreover compel] witnesses, etc. Notwithstanding etc.

Humilibus et cetera.
phi de Agnell(is) / JoA. / : JoA: xij: Nardinus

1   MS: (?)*layeus clericus seu laycus*
2   MS: *quod iustum fuerit et cetera.* Supplied from common form.

244   9 November 1514   *Reg. Lat.* 1307, fos 25ʳ-26ʳ

Mandate to collate and assign to Claudius Perrot de Lavantio – cleric, d. Besançon, a continual commensal familiar (as he asserts) of Hadrian, cardinal priest of the title of S Crisogono – the perpetual chaplaincy at the altar of B Mary the Virgin in the parish church of B Mary, Mont-sous-Vaudrey (*de Monte subtus Valdrenum*), d. Besançon, which is without cure and whose annual value does not exceed 24 gold ducats of the camera, vacant by the death in the Roman curia of Ludovicus Esteueno, himself a continual commensal familiar of cardinal Hadrian. The letter, which is addressed to three mandataries, is of no other interest to the Calendar.

Vite ac morum honestas …
Ge. de Prato / JoA: / :JoA. xx: Quarto k(a)l(endas) aprilis Anno tertio [29 March 1515]: *Nard(inus):*

245   12 March 1515   *Reg. Lat.* 1307, fos 108ᵛ-110ᵛ

To the prior of the monastery, usually governed by a prior, of B. Mary, Darean, OSA,[1] d. Elphin, and Roger Omoitani,[2] canon of the church of Achonry (*Arcaden.*), and Walter Macgereden,[3] canon of the church of Tuam, mandate in favour of William Maclaroy', canon of the church of Elphin. The pope has learned that the rectory and perpetual vicarage of the parish church of Fieria,[4] d. Elphin, are vacant *certo modo* at present and have been vacant for so long that by the Lateran statutes their collation has lawfully devolved on the apostolic see, although Andrew Machyldrony has detained the rectory and John Machyldrony the vicarage – bearing themselves as clerics – with no title and no support of law, of their own temerity and *de facto*, for a certain time, as they still do. At a recent petition on the part of William – who asserts that some time ago he was dispensed by ordinary authority, notwithstanding a defect of birth as the son of a priest and a married woman, to be marked with clerical character and to receive and retain a benefice without cure, even a canonry and prebend in a cathedral church, if conferred on him otherwise canonically; that afterwards, by virtue of this dispensation, he was marked with clerical character and holds a canonry of the said [church][5] of Elphin; and that the annual value of the rectory and vicarage together does not exceed 12 marks sterling – to the pope to erect and institute the said rectory and vicarage and the feudal fruits of the town of Trosde,[6] d. Elphin, (which belong to the prior of the monastery, usually governed by a prior, of Rostomat', OSA, d. Elphin), into a simple prebend of the church of Elphin, for William's lifetime, the pope – not having certain knowledge of the foregoing – hereby commands that the above three (or two or one of them), if it is so, having summoned the bishop and chapter of Elphin and Andrew and John and others concerned, shall erect and institute the rectory, (which is without cure), and the vicarage, (howsoever they are vacant etc.; even if specially reserved etc.), and also the feudal fruits – with the consent of the said prior, after the usual annual pension has been paid to him – into a simple prebend of the church of Elphin, for William's lifetime, without prejudice to anyone; and, in the event of this erection and institution, collate and assign the newly erected prebend, being then vacant, to William, with all rights and appurtenances, inducting him etc. having removed Andrew from the rectory and John from the vicarage and any other unlawful detainers and causing William (or his proctor) to be admitted to the prebend and its fruits etc., rights and obventions to be delivered to him. [Curbing] gainsayers etc. Notwithstanding etc. The pope's will is, however, that the above rectory and vicarage shall not, on this account, be defrauded of due services and the cure of souls in the vicarage shall not be neglected; but that its customary burdens and those of the rectory shall be supported; and that on William's death or his resignation etc. of the canonry and prebend this erection and institution shall be extinguished and be so deemed and the rectory and vicarage shall revert to their original condition automatically.

Apostolice sedis circumspecta benignitas ad ea libenter intendit ...
Phi de agnell(is) / JoA. / JoA: xxv: Nardinus

---

1   outside *stilus*: it is most unusual for religious houses to be identified by their order in the address clause of mandates.

2   very uncertain: especially the 't' and whatever precedes it
3   doubtful (the 'c', 'r' and 'n' especially)
4   only the 'F' and 'a' certain
5   'ecclesie' does not occur.
6   doubtful (the 'd' especially)

246[1]   **30 March 1515**   *Reg. Lat.* 1307, fos 179[r]-180[v]

To Walter Macrden, canon of the church of Tuam, and William Ostyn[g]in'[2] and John On.cadam[3], canons of the church of Ossory, mandate in favour of James Ohelly [also spelt *Yhelly*], cleric, d. Tuam. The pope has learned that the perpetual vicarage of the parish church of Cillurquur *alias* Racurnay, d.Tuam, is vacant *certo modo* at present and has been vacant for so long that by the Lateran statutes its collation has lawfully devolved on the apostolic see, although William Omurcu, canon of the monastery of St Michael, Mayo, OSA, d. Tuam, has detained it with no title or support of law, of his own temerity and *de facto*, for a certain time, as he still does. Recently, supplication was made on the part of James (who asserts that some time ago he was dispensed by apostolic authority, notwithstanding a defect of birth as the son of a priest and an unmarried woman, to be promoted to all, even sacred and priest's, orders and to hold a benefice, even if it should have cure of souls; that, by virtue of this dispensation, he was marked with clerical character; and that the annual value of the said vicarage does not exceed 10 marks sterling) to the pope to cause the fruits etc. of the episcopal fourth of the place of Tirnectin[4] and also of the chapel of Cullicolman, d.Tuam (which is united etc. in perpetuity to the above monastery), which are, respectively, accustomed to be given and granted for a certain annual pension, after the said pensions have been paid by him, to be applied and assigned to the said vicarage, for James's lifetime. Whereat the pope hereby commands that the above three (or two or one of them), if, having summoned William and others concerned, they find the vicarage to be vacant (howsoever etc.) shall collate and assign it (even if specially reserved etc.), with all rights and appurtenances, to James; and also, with the consent of the archbishop of Tuam and of the abbot and convent of the said monastery and after the customary annual pensions have been paid to them (and to the archbishop of Tuam for the time being) apply and assign the fruits etc. of the fourth and of the chapel to the vicarage, for as long as James holds the latter, if conferred on him by virtue of the presents, inducting him etc. into corporal possession of the vicarage and rights and appurtenances aforesaid, having removed William and any other unlawful detainer and causing James (or his proctor)[5] to be admitted to the vicarage and its fruits etc., rights and obventions to be delivered to him. [Curbing] gainsayers etc. Notwithstanding etc.

Vite ac morum honestas ...
phi de Agnell(is) / JoA. / :JoA: xx: Decimo octauo K(a)l(endas) maj Anno tertio [14 April 1515], *Nardinus*

1   The entry is badly affected by ink bleed and the obvious caveats apply.
2   the letter read as 'g' obscured by the descender of the 'p' of *phi de Agnell(is)*
3   third letter illegible – so much so that it is unclear whether it has ascender or descender.

4   uncertain reading
5   In MS: (?)*procuratorem suum eius nomine in corporalem possessionem vicarie iuriumque et pertinentiarum predictorum* is written twice, the second instance being deleted and initialled *JoA* at the beginning and end of the deleted passage. The second instance is separated from the first by sixteen words.

247[1]   **19 March 1513**   *Reg. Lat.* 1307, fos 230[r]-234[r]

To William Paniter *alias* Lam, cleric,[2] d. Brechin, effectuation of Julius II's reservation etc. in his favour. Some time ago, representations on William's part were made to Julius II that at another time William had, spontaneously and freely, resigned the canonry and prebend of Duchel[3] of the church of Moray, which he was then holding, into the hands of the local ordinary (or his vicar general), outside the Roman curia, with a view to Thomas Atkison [also spelt *At Cason,* (?)*Dekson*],[4] canon of Aberdeen, acquiring the canonry and prebend of Torrays [also spelt *Toray, Torrayf, Torres*][5] of the church of Aberdeen; and the said ordinary (or vicar – having, as he asserted, special faculty for this from the ordinary by his letters – by virtue of that faculty) having admitted this resignation, outside the said curia, by ordinary authority, had provided the said canonry and prebend of Duchel, then vacant by the said resignation, to a certain ecclesiastic nominated at the time by Thomas; and Thomas himself had afterwards acquired the above canonry and prebend of Torrays (which had been canonically collated to him while vacant *certo modo*). Lest William suffer excessive loss from this resignation, Julius II, under date 7 February, ninth year [1512], reserved, established and assigned an annual pension of 50 pounds Scots on the fruits etc. of the said canonry and prebend of Torrays, (of which this pension did not exceed one third or, at all events, one half), payable to William (or to William's specially mandated proctor), for life – or until, through Thomas's efforts,[6] provision of the canonry and prebend of Duchel (or provision of another, more fruitful, benefice) was canonically made to William and he peacefully acquired them (or it), in which case this pension would be cancelled and extinguished and be so deemed – by the said Thomas (whose assent thereto had been expressly given through his specially appointed proctor, Thomas Midre, cleric, d. Brechin) and by his successors holding the canonry and prebend of Torrays at the time, in full, each year, viz.: one half of the said pension on the feast of the Nativity of B. John the Baptist and the other on that of Jesus Christ. With decree that if Thomas Atkison (or any one of his successors) fails to make payment on the said feasts or at least within the thirty days immediately following, he shall, after this time has elapsed, incur sentence of excommunication from which he cannot be absolved, except on the point of death, until he shall have made satisfaction in full or reached agreement in respect of it with William (or his proctor) and, if he remains obdurate under that sentence for a further six months, he shall thereupon be deprived in perpetuity of the canonry and prebend of Torrays which shall be deemed vacant automatically. Notwithstanding etc. Since, however, Julius died before his letters to this effect were drawn up, the pope hereby wills and decrees that the said reservation etc. shall take effect from the said 7 February, just as if Julius's letters under the same date had been drawn up, as narrated above; and that the present letters shall everywhere be sufficient proof of the said reservation etc.

Executory to the bishop of Cavaillon and the archdeacon of Moray and the dean of the church of Lestarik, d. St Andrews, or two or one of them, acting in person or by proxy.

Rationi congrui[7] *et cetera.*
.P. La(m)berti;. Jo Danielo / JoA: / JoA: xij: x: Nard(inus): –

1   Note in the narrative the unusual complexity of the dealings among the various Scots; which, in turn, affected the detail of Julius's reservation.
2   Here: *Willielmo Paniter* [or *Painter* or even *Pamter* (since none of the three minims is dotted)] *alias Lam clerico* ... Cf. the executory: *Wilhelmo Paniter clerico alias Lam clerico* ... ('clerico' is repeated, oddly).
3   or possibly *Ducliel* (here) and *Duclief* (below)
4   so written (here and once below); spelt *Atchason* in the executory
5   the last occurrence in the main letter altered from *Torrays* to *Torray* by deletion of the final letter – a long 's'? – after the 'y'; in the executory the name is definitely spelt *Torray*
6   reading *procurante* after *dicto Thoma*
7   *sic*; *recte*: 'congruit'

248   27 April 1514   *Reg. Lat.* 1308, fos 207ʳ-209ʳ

To John Macgillarnay[1] and John Flanus (?)Osqihyn[2] and Malachy Obern, canons of the church of Elphin, mandate in favour of William Okelay, canon without a prebend (*canonicus non prebendatus*) of the church of Elphin. The pope has learned that the prebend, called canonical, of Vrauinathe, in the said church, and the priory of Roschoman, OSA, d. Elphin, are vacant *certo modo* at present and have been vacant for so long that by the Lateran statutes their collation has lawfully devolved on the apostolic see, although Peter Osqhyn[3] has detained the prebend, and he and Eugene Mecsuyne – bearing themselves as clerics – the priory, with no title or support of law, of their own temerity and *de facto*, for a certain time, dividing the fruits between themselves, as they do. He hereby commands that the above three (or two or one of them), if, having summoned Peter and Eugene and others concerned, they find the prebend (whose annual value does not exceed 4 marks sterling) and the priory (which is conventual and usually held *in commendam* and whose annual value does not exceed 30 marks sterling), to be vacant (howsoever etc.), shall collate and assign the prebend and commend the priory, (even if they are specially or generally reserved, even if the priory is generally reserved because it is conventual, as above, and is customarily elective and has cure of souls, etc.) to be held, ruled and governed by William for life, with all their rights and appurtenances; he may – due and customary burdens of the priory having been supported make disposition of the rest of its fruits etc., just as those holding it *in titulum* at the time could and ought to do, alienation of immovable goods and precious movables being however forbidden; inducting William etc. into corporal possession of the prebend and priory and the said rights and appurtenances, having removed Peter and Eugene and any other unlawful detainers and causing William (or his proctor) to be admitted to the prebend and priory and their fruits etc., rights and obventions to be delivered to him. [Curbing] gainsayers by the pope's authority etc. Notwithstanding etc. With the proviso that the priory shall not, on account of this commend, be defrauded of due services and the cure of souls in it (if any) shall not be neglected; but that its aforesaid burdens shall be supported.

Vite ac morum honestas …
.phi. de agnell(is) / JoA: / JoA: xxx: tertio Id(us) Maij Anno Secundo: [13 May 1514], *Nard(inus)*

1   written *Magillarnaij* with *c* above the 'g'; *cf.* next entry.
2   also readable as *Osquhyn*: apparently originally written Osquyn; an (?)'h' was then inserted, leaving the first minim of the 'u' visible, but covering the second.
3   unaltered and clearly written

249   27 April 1514   *Reg. Lat.* 1308, fos 209ᵛ-211ʳ

To John Macgillarnay,[1] William Odonullan and Cormac Odumur, canons of the church of Elphin, mandate in favour of Andrew Macgillarnay,[2] rector of the parish church, called prebend, of Ferta and Cilcumata[3] *alias* Maentemayn,[4] d. Elphin. The pope has learned that the perpetual vicarage of the parish church of Tiatsarara, d. Elphin, is vacant *certo modo* at present and has been vacant for so long that by the Lateran statutes its collation has lawfully devolved on the apostolic see, although Malachy Okelay, who bears himself as a priest,[5] has detained it, with no title or support of law, temerariously and *de facto*, for a certain time, as he still does. At a recent petition on Andrew's part – asserting that the annual value of the vicarage does not exceed 4, and of the church held by him, also 4, marks sterling – to the pope to unite etc. the vicarage to the church, he hereby commands that the above three (or two or one of them), if, having summoned Malachy and others concerned and those interested in the union, they find the vicarage to be vacant (howsoever etc.), shall unite etc. it (even if specially reserved etc.), with all its rights and appurtenances, to the church held by him, for as long as he holds the latter, inducting Andrew etc. having removed Malachy and any other unlawful detainer and causing the fruits etc., rights and obventions of the vicarage to be delivered to him. [Curbing] gainsayers by ecclesiastical censure etc. Notwithstanding etc. The pope's will is, however, that the vicarage shall not, on account of this union etc., be defrauded of due services and the cure of souls in it shall not be neglected; but that its customary burdens shall be supported; and that on Andrew's death or his resignation etc. of the above church this union etc. shall be dissolved and the vicarage shall revert to its original condition and be deemed vacant automatically.

[6]*Votis fidelium omnium ex quibus precipue eorum commoditatibus consulitur libenter annuimus …*
.phi. d(e) agnell(is): / JoA: / JoA: xv: Nardinus

1   written *Macgillarnaij*
2   changed (by overwriting) from *Mar-*; the ending written *-ij* (as above)
3   (?)*Cir* deleted but not initialled
4   the 'm' doubtful

5   *clerico* deleted (but not initialled) before *presbytero*
6   *Vite ac morum* deleted (initialled *JoA:*) before *Votis* ...

250   3 June 1514   *Reg. Lat.* 1308, fos 276ᵛ-279ʳ

To the dean of Cashel and Robert Offlahauaym and William Oduygyn, canons of the
churches of Lismore and Killaloe, mandate in favour of Richard Macbryen, cleric, d.
Emly. The pope has learned that the deanery of Emly and the perpetual vicarages of
the parish churches of the places of Vlay and Theoclugyn, d. Emly, are vacant *certo
modo* at present and have been vacant for so long that by the Lateran statutes their
collation has lawfully devolved on the apostolic see, although William Macbryen
junior, who bears himself as a priest, has detained the deanery and vicarages with no
title or support of law, of his own temerity and *de facto*, for a certain time, as he does
still. At a supplication made to the pope on Richard's part – asserting that the annual
value of the deanery and vicarages together does not exceed 15 marks sterling; and that
Richard has, notwithstanding a defect of birth as the son of a priest and an unmarried
woman, been marked by ordinary authority with clerical character otherwise however
duly – to unite etc. the vicarages to the deanery, for as long as Richard should hold the
latter, if conferred on him by virtue of the presents, the pope hereby commands that the
above three (or two or one of them), if, having summoned William and others
concerned, they find the deanery (which is a dignity major *post pontificalem* in the
church of Emly and has cure of souls) and the vicarages to be vacant (howsoever etc.),
shall collate and assign the deanery to Richard and unite etc., with all their rights and
appurtenances, the vicarages to the deanery, (even if specially reserved etc.), for as
long as Richard should hold the latter, inducting him etc. having removed William and
any other unlawful detainers and causing Richard (or his proctor) to be admitted to the
deanery and its fruits etc., rights and obventions and those of the annexed vicarages to
be delivered to him. [Curbing] gainsayers by the pope's authority etc. Notwithstanding
etc. Also the pope dispenses Richard, notwithstanding his above defect of birth, to
receive the deanery, if conferred on him by virtue of the presents, and to retain it with
the annexes in question; and to be promoted to all, even sacred and priest's, orders and
thereafter to minister in them even as a minister before the altar, notwithstanding the
above defect etc. The pope's will is, [however], that the said vicarages shall not, on
account of this union etc., be defrauded of due services and the cure of souls in them
shall not be neglected; but that their customary burdens shall be supported; and that on
Richard's death or his resignation etc. of the deanery this union etc. shall be dissolved
and the vicarages shall revert to their original condition and [be deemed]¹ vacant
automatically.

Vite ac morum honestas ...
.Phi. d(e) agnell(is) / C / C xxxx Nono k(a)l(endas) Julij Anno Secundo [23 June 1514],
Barotius

1   'censeantur' wanting

251   4 April 1514   *Reg. Lat.* 1308, fos 327^r-328^r

To John Betesson, rector of the parish church of Ryngsfyld, d. Norwich. Dispensation and indult – at his supplication – to receive and retain for life, together with the above parish church, one, and without them, any two other benefices, etc. [as above, no. 2, to '... or a combination'], even of lay patronage and of whatsoever tax or annual value,[1] and even if the dignities etc. should be customarily elective etc. [as above, no. 2, to '... retain them together for life, as above']; and, for life, while residing in the Roman curia or either of his parish churches,[2] or attending a *studium generale*, not to be bound to reside personally[3] in his other benefices etc. [as above, no. 2].[4]

Vite ac morum honestas ...
P. lambert(us) / . Phi. / . Phi. Lx. de Senis

1   *etiam de iurepatronatus laicorum et cuiuscunque taxe seu annui valoris illorum fructus red(ditus) et pro(ventus)*: unexpected in a dispensation *ad incompatibilia* for a secular cleric; the formulary belongs to dispensations for religious to hold secular benefices. *Cf.* next entry (also Norwich).
2   *altero ex parrochialibus ecclesiis ... obtentis*; usually 'aliquo beneficiorum ... obtentorum' (or variants of it). The present formulation is not only very restrictive – vicarages, for example, are not included – but also unusual and raises the suspicion that it derives ultimately from the petitioner rather than the chancery.
3   *personaliter*; unusual here; *cf.* next entry and no. 325.
4   Otherwise the tenor of the indult for non-residence is as no. 2 (thought the word order departs slightly).

252   4 April 1514   *Reg. Lat.* 1308, fos 328^r-329^v

To John London,[1] rector of the parish church of Goysbek, d. Norwich. Dispensation and indult – at his supplication – to receive and retain for life, together with the above parish church, one, and without them, any two other benefices, etc. [as above, no. 2, to '... or a combination'], even of lay patronage and of whatsoever tax or annual value,[2] and even if the dignities etc. should be customarily elective etc. [as above, no. 2].[3]

Vite ac morum honestas ...
P. lambert(us) / . Phi.[4] / . Phi. Lx. de Senis

1   or perhaps *Loudon*
2   as in no. 251; *see* note 1 particularly.
3   i.e. hereafter the present entry conforms to the usual formulation for a dispensation *ad duo* (summarised more fully in no. 2). The tenor of the indult for non-residence is the same as no. 2; but like no. 251 the present entry is unusual in having *personaliter*, though unlike no. 251 it has *altero beneficiorum ... obtentorum* and not the abnormal 'altero ex parrochialibus ecclesiis ... obtentis'.
4   Though the first 'point' is more of a short slanting line.

253   23 July 1514   *Reg. Lat.* 1309, fos 31ʳ-32ᵛ

To David Farlis, canon regular of the church of St Andrews, OSA. Dispensation – at his supplication – to him (who, as he asserts, holds the perpetual vicarage of the parish church of Dow, d. Dunkeld, usually held by Augustinian canons; and who is, as he also asserts, expressly professed of the said Augustinian order[1]) to receive, together with the above vicarage, one, and without them, any two other benefices, with or without cure, usually held by canons of the above order or by monks of any other, even the Cluniac, order, or with one of the two, or without them, one secular benefice with cure, even if the benefices usually held by the above canons or monks should be parish churches or their perpetual vicarages, or priories, *prepositure, prepositatus*, dignities, *personatus*, administrations or offices, or the secular benefice should be a parish church or its perpetual vicarage, and even if the priories, *prepositure, prepositatus*, dignities etc. should be customarily elective and have cure of souls, if he obtains them otherwise canonically, and to retain for life whichever one of the said regular benefices he chooses (even if it should be a priory, *prepositura*[2] or other conventual dignity or a claustral office) *in titulum*, and the other regular benefice or a secular benefice *in commendam*; to resign them, at once or successively, simply or for exchange, as often as he pleases, and cede the commend and in their place receive up to two other, similar or dissimilar, benefices, with or without cure, usually held by Augustinian canons or by monks of any other, even the Cluniac, order, or with one of them, or without them, one secular benefice with cure, and to retain for life whichever one of the regular benefices he chooses *in titulum* and the other regular benefice (which may not, however, be a priory or other conventual dignity or a claustral office) or a secular benefice *in commendam*, as above; he may – due and customary burdens of the benefice retained *in commendam* having been supported – make disposition of the rest of its fruits etc. just as those holding it *in titulum* could and ought to do, alienation of immovable goods and precious movables being however forbidden. Notwithstanding etc. With the proviso that the benefice retained *in commendam* shall not, on this account, be defrauded of due services and the cure of souls in it (if any) shall not be neglected; but that its aforesaid burdens shall be supported.

Religionis zelus, vite ac morum honestas …
p. lambert(us) / JoA. / JoA. xxxx: Nardinus

1   This latter information comes from a notwithstanding clause.
2   'prepositatus' does not occur here.

254   29 August 1514   *Reg. Lat.* 1309, fos 202ᵛ-204ʳ

To John Somerby, perpetual vicar of the parish church of Muston',[1] d. York. Dispensation and indult etc. [as above, no. 2].[2]

Vite ac morum honestas …
P. lambertus / C / C. L.[3] *Barotius*

1   here (and below) possibly *Muscoy*
2   Save that the present indult wants 'curia' after *Romana*
3   *See above*, no. 13, note 2.

255   24 July 1514   *Reg. Lat.* 1309, fos 230ᵛ-231ᵛ

To John Clyffi, rector of the parish church of Whaddon', d. Salisbury. Dispensation and
indult etc. [as above, no. 2].¹

Vite ac morum honestas …
P. de Castello / JoA. / JoA: Lx: Nardinus

1   save for a few textual oddities (e.g. *simpliciter*; *recte*: 'similiter')

256   17 July 1514   *Reg. Lat.* 1310, fos 33ᵛ-36ᵛ

To the archdeacon of Clogher and Peter Oduygny, canon of the church of Ossory, and
Cormac Omurysci, canon of the church of Derry, mandate in favour of Rory Odonaill,
cleric, d. Raphoe. The pope has learned that the deanery of Raphoe and the rectories of
the parish churches of Enuyrnaal¹ [also spelt *Ennyrnaal*] and Termancrona and also the
vicarage of the parish church of Raynrayhaenay² – which [i.e. the rectories and
vicarage] are, as is asserted by some, of lay patronage – d. Raphoe, are vacant *certo
modo* at present and have been vacant for so long that by the Lateran statutes their
collation has lawfully devolved on the apostolic see, although Laurence Ogallcuyr has
detained the deanery, Laurence Macgillage *alias* Ogallcuyr, the rectory of Enuyrnaal,
and Gelasius Oducan that of Termancrona, and Roger Omoran³ has detained the
vicarage – bearing themselves as priests – with no title and no support of law, of their
own temerity and *de facto*, for a certain time, as they still do. At a recent petition on
the part of Rory (who asserts that he is in his twenty-third year of age and,
notwithstanding a defect of birth as the son of an unmarried man and an unmarried
woman, has been duly marked with clerical character; and that the annual value of the
deanery does not exceed 30, and of the rectories and vicarage together, 20 marks
sterling) to the pope to unite etc. the rectories and vicarage to the deanery, for as long
as Rory holds the latter, the pope hereby commands that the above three (or two or one
of them), if, having summoned Laurence Ogallcuyr, Laurence Macgillage, Gelasius,
Roger and others concerned, they find the deanery (which is a dignity major *post
pontificalem*) and the rectories and vicarage to be vacant (howsoever etc.) shall collate
and assign them (even if specially reserved and the deanery (as a major dignity)
generally reserved, etc.) to Rory and unite etc. the rectories and vicarage, with all their
rights and appurtenances, to the deanery, for as long as Rory holds the latter, inducting
him etc. having removed Laurence Ogallcuyr, Laurence Macgillage, Gelasius and
Roger respectively and any other unlawful detainers and causing Rory (or his proctor)
to be admitted to the deanery and the fruits etc., rights and obventions of the deanery

and annexes aforesaid to be delivered to him. [Curbing] gainsayers by the pope's authority etc. Notwithstanding etc. Also the pope dispenses and indulges Rory – who suffers the above defect of birth and (in his above twenty-third year) a defect of age for holding the deanery – to receive and retain the deanery, if conferred on him by virtue of the presents, and to be promoted to all, even sacred and priest's, orders; and, while attending a *studium particulare* (at the least) in Ireland[4] or a *studium generale* elsewhere, not to be bound, by reason of the above deanery or of any other benefices with cure or otherwise requiring sacred orders by law, statute, custom, foundation or otherwise, to have himself promoted for a period of up to five years, calculated from the end of the year prefixed by law – provided that within the first two years he is a subdeacon – to any other sacred order; and not to be liable to be compelled to do so by anyone against his will, notwithstanding the said defects of age and birth. It is the pope's will, however, that the deanery, rectories and vicarage shall not, on this account, be defrauded of due services and the cure of souls in the rectories and vicarage and (if any) the deanery shall not be neglected; but that their customary burdens shall be supported; and that on Rory's death or his resignation etc. of the deanery, this union etc. shall be dissolved and the rectories and vicarage shall revert to their original condition and be deemed vacant automatically.

Vite ac morum honestas ...
.Phi. d(e) agnell(is):. / JoA. / JoA: L: pridie non(as) Agusti[5] *Anno Secundo.* [4 August 1514], *Nardinus*

1 the third letter uncertain: somewhat enlarged
2 the '-nr-' uncertain: the 'n' perhaps 'm'; the 'r' indistinct
3 the medial 'o'and the 'a' read sympathetically
4 MS: *in partibus Ibernie*; not 'province' (*cf.* nos. 262, 265)
5 *sic*

257   25 April 1514   *Reg. Lat.* 1310, fos 88ʳ-90ʳ

To the prior of the monastery, usually governed by a prior, of St John at Lenaenach, d. Killaloe, and William Oduygyn' and Rory Oduygyn', canons of the churches of Killaloe and (?)Clonmacnois[1], mandate in favour of Donald Omeachyr, prior of the monastery, usually governed by a prior, of the Holy Cross, *de Insula Viventium* [Monaincha], OSA, d. Killaloe. The pope has learned that the perpetual vicarages of the parish churches of the places of Liamocaemoc,[2] and of St James, Burgeslia, and of B. Mary, Amaryn, and also of St Nicholas, Boyston, d. Cashel, are vacant *certo modo* at present and have been vacant for so long that by the Lateran statutes their collation has lawfully devolved on the apostolic see, although Cornelius Olach.. an,[3] who bears himself as a cleric, has detained them with no title and no support of law, of his own temerity and *de facto*, for a certain time, as he does still. At a recent petition on Donald's part to the pope to unite etc. the vicarages to the priory of the above monastery of the Holy Cross, for as long as he holds the priory (which Donald – who has a defect of birth as the son of a prior of the said order and an unmarried woman –

holds by apostolic dispensation; and which is conventual) – asserting that the annual value of the vicarages together does not exceed 12 marks sterling – the pope hereby commands that the above three (or two or one of them), if, having summoned Cornelius and others concerned, they find the vicarages to be vacant (howsoever etc.), shall unite etc. them (even if specially reserved etc.), with all their rights and appurtenances, to the priory, for as long as Donald holds the latter; to the effect that Donald may, on his own authority, in person or by proxy, take corporal possession of the vicarages and the rights and appurtenances aforesaid, and retain them for as long as he holds the priory, and convert their fruits etc. to his own uses and those of the vicarages and priory, without licence of the local diocesan or of anyone else. Notwithstanding etc. The pope's will is, however, that the vicarages shall not, on this account, be defrauded of due services and the cure of souls in them shall not be neglected; but that their customary burdens shall be supported; and that on Donald's death or his resignation etc. of the priory this union etc. shall be dissolved and so deemed and the said vicarages shall revert to their original condition and be deemed vacant automatically.

Votis illis ex quibus ecclesiasticarum quarumlibet religionis presertim iugo astrictarum personarum commoditatibus consulitur libenter annuimus …
.phi. d(e) agnell(is) / JoA: / JoA: xxv: Nardi(nus)

1   MS: *Cluonen.*; *recte*: 'Cluanen.'?
2   the second 'm' unhappy: perhaps -*aeinoc*
3   blotched; the unreadable letters (possibly 'ra') without ascenders or descenders

258   18 March 1514   *Reg. Lat.* 1310, fos 137ᵛ-139ʳ

To Bernard Obugill and John Macrathagairt,[1] canons of the church of Derry, mandate in favour of Magonius Ygarme Leigaydh, perpetual vicar of the parish church of Funnaydh,[2] d. Derry. The pope has learned that the rectory of the parish church of Cyllcairill, d. Derry, is vacant *certo modo* at present and has been vacant for so long that by the Lateran statutes its collation has lawfully devolved on the apostolic see, although Thoroletus Magrath, who bears himself as prior of the priory of St Patrick's Purgatory (*de Lacu rubio Sancti Patritii*), OSA, d. Clogher, has detained the rectory with no title or support of law, of his own temerity and [de][3] *facto*, for a certain time, as he does. At a recent petition on the part of Magonius to the pope to unite etc. the rectory to the perpetual vicarage of the above parish church of Funnaydh, which he holds – asserting that the rectory's annual value does not exceed 3 marks sterling – the pope hereby commands that the above two [or one of them],[4] if, having summoned Thoroletus and others concerned, they find the rectory to be vacant (howsoever etc.) shall unite etc. it (even if specially reserved etc.), with all its rights and appurtenances, to the vicarage, for as long as Magonius holds the latter, having removed Thoroletus and any other unlawful detainer; to the effect that Magonius may, on his own authority, in person or by proxy, take corporal possession of the rectory and the said rights and appurtenances, and retain them for as long as he holds the vicarage, and convert its fruits etc. to his own uses and those of the vicarage and rectory, without licence of the local diocesan or of anyone else. [Curbing] gainsayers etc. Notwithstanding etc. The pope's will is, however, that the rectory shall not, on account of this union etc., be defrauded of due services and the cure of souls in it shall not be neglected; but that its customary burdens shall be supported; and that on the death of Magonius or his resignation etc. of the vicarage this union etc. shall be dissolved and so deemed and the rectory shall revert to its original condition automatically.

Romanum decet pontificem votis illis gratum prestare assensum ...
.p. lambert(us) / JoA. / JoA. x: K(a)l(endis) aprilis Anno Secundo: [1 April 1514], *Nardinus*

1   the 'c' uncertain
2   the minims capable of various readings
3   wanting
4   MS: *discretioni vestre et cetera mandamus.* Supplied from common form.

259   7 June 1514   *Reg. Lat.* 1310, fos 219ʳ-221ʳ

To Raynaldus[1] de Prato, rector of the parish church of St Michael, Viraga,[2] d. Vicenza (who, as he asserts, is a continual commensal familiar of Christopher, cardinal priest of the title of S Prassede), collation and provision as below. Following the pope's reservation of all benefices, with and without cure, vacated then and in the future at the apostolic see to his own collation and disposition, the above parish church fell vacant by the free resignation of its recent rector, Silvester de Podio Catini, who was holding it at the time, made spontaneously into the hands of the pope who admitted it at the said see, and is vacant at present, being reserved as above. Cardinal Christopher – asserting that at another time it had been commanded by apostolic authority that the above church (vacant by the death of its former rector James Bertini, outside the Roman curia) [be commended to cardinal Christopher to] be held, ruled and governed by him for life – has this day, spontaneously and freely, ceded all right belonging to him in or to the said church into the hands of the pope who has admitted the cession. The pope hereby collates and makes provision of the above church – whose annual value (of which one annual pension of 12, and another of 18, gold ducats of the camera are reserved by apostolic authority to certain ecclesiastical persons who respectively receive the said pensions) does not exceed 60 like gold ducats – whether vacant as above, or howsoever etc. or by a like resignation of Silvester, etc.; even if it has been vacant for so long that by the Lateran statutes its collation has lawfully devolved on the apostolic see, etc. – with all rights and appurtenances, to Raynaldus. Notwithstanding etc.
Executory to the bishops of Cavaillon and Alessandria and to the vicar general of the bishop of Vicenza, or two or one of them, acting in person or by proxy.

Vite ac morum honestas ...
G d(e) prato; O d(e) Cesis / JoA: / JoA: Gratis de man(da)to: pridie non(as) Agusti[3]

Anno secundo: [4 August 1514], *Nardinus*

1   thus in the executory; however, he is addressed as (?)*Rainandus* in the principal letter.
2   *Viraga* occurs thrice; *Vigar* is written directly before the second occurrence of *Viraga* but is evidently just a
      misfire (even though not deleted).
3   *sic*

260   14 June 1514   *Reg. Lat.* 1311, fos 81ʳ-82ᵛ

To the dean and John Fangni, canon, of the church of Limerick and the official of
Killaloe, mandate in favour of Dermot Okely, priest, d. Killaloe. A recent petition to
the pope on Dermot's part stated that at another time when the vicarage of the parish
church of Kilhynfyyij, d. Killaloe, was vacant by the death, outside the Roman curia,
of Dermot Mackynrachdy, its sometime vicar, the then bishop of Killaloe collated the
vicarage, vacant as above, to the above Dermot Okely, by ordinary authority, and made
provision of the same; and Dermot Okely acquired possession of the vicarage by virtue
of this collation and provision. However, as the said petition added, Dermot Okely
fears that for certain reasons this collation and provision do not hold good, and, as the
pope has learned, the said vicarage is understood to be vacant still as above. The pope
hereby commands that the above three (or two or one of them), in person or by proxy,
shall collate and assign the vicarage, whose annual value does not exceed 8 marks
sterling, (whether vacant as above, or in any other way etc. or by the free resignation
of the said Dermot <Mackynrachdy>¹ or anyone else etc.; even if vacant for so long
that by the Lateran statutes its collation has lawfully devolved on the apostolic see
etc.), with all rights and appurtenances, to Dermot Okely, inducting him etc. having
removed any unlawful detainer and causing Dermot Okely (or his proctor) to be
admitted to the vicarage and its fruits etc., rights and obventions to be delivered to him.
[Curbing] gainsayers by [the pope's] authority etc. Notwithstanding etc.

Vite ac morum honestas …
Phi d(e) agnellis / M / M x quarto id(us) Julii an(n)o secundo [12 July 1514], *de
Campania*

1   marginal insertion initialled *M*

261   18 May 1514   *Reg. Lat.* 1311, fos 209ᵛ-210ᵛ

To Matthew Stewart, perpetual vicar of the parish church of Maybol, d. Glasgow.
Dispensation – at his supplication – to receive and retain for life, together with the
perpetual vicarage of the above parish church, one, and without them, any two other
benefices, with cure or otherwise mutually incompatible, even if parish churches or
their perpetual vicarages, or dignities, *personatus*, administrations or offices in
cathedral, even metropolitan, or collegiate churches, even if the dignities in question

should be major *post pontificalem* in cathedral, even metropolitan, churches, or principal in collegiate churches, or a combination, and even if the dignities etc. should be customarily elective and have cure of souls, if he obtains them otherwise canonically, to resign them, at once or successively, simply or for exchange, as often as he pleases, and in their place receive up to two other, similar or dissimilar, incompatible benefices and retain them together for life, as above. Notwithstanding etc. With the proviso that the above perpetual vicarage and the other incompatible benefices shall not, on this account, be defrauded of due services and the cure of souls in the vicarage and (if any) the other incompatible benefices shall not be neglected. Given at Magliana, d. Porto.

Vite ac morum honestas ...
P lambert(us) / M / M xxxx de Campania

262   27 April 1514   *Reg. Lat.* 1311, fos 240ʳ-242ᵛ

To the prior of the monastery, usually governed by a prior, of the Holy Cross, *de Insula Viventium* [Monaincha], d. Killaloe, William Oduygyn', canon of the church of Killaloe, and Rory Oduygyn, canon of the church of (?)Clonmacnois[1], mandate in favour of Edmund Rutiler, cleric, d. Ossory (who, as he asserts, suffers a defect of birth as the son of a married man and a married woman,[2] and in ignorance of this was marked with clerical character, otherwise however duly; and is in his twenty-first year of age or thereabouts). The pope has learned that the archdeaconries of the churches of Ossory and Cashel, are vacant *certo modo* at present and have been vacant for so long that by the Lateran statutes their collation has lawfully devolved on the apostolic see, although Robert Oheyden has detained <the archdeaconry>[3] of Ossory and Gerald de Geraldinis <the archdeaconry>[3] of Cashel – bearing themselves as clerics – with no title or support of law, of their own temerity and *de facto*, for a certain time as they do still. He hereby commands that the above three (or two or one of them), if, having summoned Robert and Gerald and others concerned, they find the archdeaconries, which are dignities in the said churches, not however major *post pontificalem*, and whose annual value together does not exceed 80 marks sterling, to be vacant (howsoever etc.) shall collate and assign them (even if specially reserved etc.), with all their rights and appurtenances, to Edmund, inducting him etc. having removed Robert from the archdeaconry of Ossory and Gerald from that of Cashel and any other unlawful detainers and causing Edmund (or his proctor) to be admitted to the archdeaconries and their fruits etc., rights and obventions to be delivered to him. [Curbing] gainsayers by [the pope's] authority etc. Notwithstanding etc. Also the pope dispenses Edmund, in respect of his above defects of birth and age, to receive and retain the said archdeaconries together for life, if conferred on him by virtue of the presents, and while attending a *studium generale* outside the province of Ireland or a *studium particulare* (at the least) in the said province,[4] not to be bound – [by reason][5] of the said archdeaconries or of any other benefices with cure or otherwise requiring sacred, even priest's, orders by law, custom or statute,[6] foundation or otherwise – for a five-year period calculated from the end of the year prefixed by law, to have himself promoted to any other of the said orders, provided that he is a subdeacon within the first two years; and not to be liable to be compelled to do so by anyone against his will. Notwithstanding the above defects etc. With the proviso that the archdeaconries and other benefices shall not, on this account, be defrauded of due services and the cure of souls in them (if any) shall not be neglected; but that their customary burdens shall be supported.

Vite ac morum honestas …
phi d(e) agnellis / M / M xxxx decimo k(a)l(endas) Junij an(n)o secundo [23 May 1514], *de Campania*

1   MS: *Cluonen.*; *recte*: 'Cluanen.'?
2   MS: *de coniugato genitus et coniugata*; evidently, by implication, not married to each other, or, at least, not so as to spare Edmund the defect.
3   Corrected by order of the regent of the chancery. *archidiaconatus* is inserted in margin; *phi.* before it; *Additu(m) et correctu(m) de m(anda)to d(omi)ni regen(tis). d(e) Senis* after it; in hand of master concerned.
4   MS: *… quodque litterarum studio extra Ibernie provinciam* [(?) *in* deleted] *in loco ubi generale aut intra dictam provinciam ubi illud saltem particulare vigeat …*
5   'ratione' wanting?
6   *ordinatione* has been deleted after *statuto*, initialled *M*

263   3 June 1514   *Reg. Lat.* 1311, fos 299ʳ-301ᵛ

To the dean and John Fangyn and William Rangil,[1] canons, of the church of Limerick, mandate in favour of Donat Macnamara, cleric, d. Killaloe. The pope has learned that the canonry and prebend of Tanigrenecronan[2] of the church of Killaloe and also the perpetual vicarages of the parish churches of Riltenayn, of Clomarean [also spelt *Clomarcan*] *alias* Stradnali and of Rilei [also spelt *Riley*], ds. Limerick and Killaloe, are vacant *certo modo* at present and have been vacant for so long that by the Lateran statutes their collation has lawfully devolved on the apostolic see, although Thomas Ogradi has detained the canonry and prebend, John Macunamara has detained the vicarage of Riltenayn, William Omolrean that of Clomarean and Cornelius *alias* Cuinea nacuamara[3] that of Rilei – bearing themselves as clerics – with no title and no support of law, of their own temerity and *de facto*, for a certain time, as they do. At the supplication of Donat – who asserts that the annual value of the canonry and prebend does not exceed 20, and of the vicarages together, 32, marks sterling – to the pope to unite etc. the said vicarages to the canonry and prebend, for as long as he holds the latter, if conferred on him and acquired by him by virtue of the presents, the pope hereby commands that the above three (or two or one of them), if, having summoned Thomas, John, William and Cornelius and others concerned, they find the canonry and prebend and the vicarages to be vacant (howsoever etc.), shall collate and assign them ([even] if specially reserved etc.) to Donat, with plenitude of canon law; and unite etc. the vicarages to the canonry and prebend, with all their rights and appurtenances, for as long as Donat should hold the latter, inducting him etc. having removed Thomas, John, William and Cornelius and any other unlawful detainers and causing Donat (or his proctor) to be received as a canon in the church of Killaloe; and shall assign him a stall in the choir and a place in the chapter of the said church of Killaloe, with plenitude of canon law, [causing] the fruits etc., rights and obventions of the canonry and prebend and the said vicarages to be delivered to him. [Curbing] gainsayers by the pope's authority etc. Notwithstanding etc. The pope's will is, however, that the said vicarages shall not, on account of this union etc., be defrauded of due services and the cure of souls in them shall not be neglected; but that their customary burdens shall be supported; and that on Donat's death or his resignation etc. of the canonry and prebend this union etc. shall be dissolved and the vicarages shall revert to their original condition and be deemed vacant automatically.

Vite ac morum honestas ...
.Phi. de agnell(is):. / M / M xxx nono k(a)l(endas) Julij anno secundo [23 June 1514], *de Campania*

1   initial letter somewhat doubtful
2   The element *-cronan*, which is here grafted onto the end of the name, comes from the name of the associated
     property: the termon lands of St Cronan (*cf. Annates, Killaloe*, pp. 15 and 20 and *CPL* VIII, p. 81).
3   written *Cuineanacuamara*

264   3 June 1514   *Reg. Lat.* 1311, fos 302^r^-304^v^

To Andrew Creagh, John Fangyn and William Rangil, canons of the church of Limerick, mandate in favour of Laurence Macnamara, cleric, d. Killaloe. The pope has learned that the canonry and prebend of Tulacuasbuc of the church of Killaloe and the perpetual vicarage of the parish church of Tulac, d. Killaloe, are vacant *certo modo* at present and have been vacant for so long that by the Lateran statutes their collation has lawfully devolved on the apostolic see, although Matthew Obryeyn has detained the canonry and prebend and John Thatei Macnamara[1] the vicarage – bearing themselves as clerics – with no title or support of law, of their own temerity and *de facto*, for a certain time, as they do. At the supplication of Laurence – who asserts that the annual value of the canonry and prebend does not exceed 20 and of the vicarage, likewise 20, marks sterling – to the pope to unite etc. the vicarage to the canonry and prebend, for as long as he holds the latter, if conferred on him by virtue of the presents, the pope hereby commands that the above three (or two or one of them), if, having summoned Matthew and John and others concerned, they find the canonry and prebend and vicarage to be vacant (howsoever etc.; even if specially reserved etc.) shall collate and assign the canonry and prebend to Laurence and unite etc. the vicarage to the said canonry and prebend, for as long as Laurence holds the latter, with plenitude of canon law and all their rights and appurtenances, inducting him etc. having removed Matthew and John and any other unlawful detainers and causing Laurence (or his proctor) to be received as a canon in the church of Killaloe; and shall assign to him a stall in the choir and a place in the chapter of the said church, with plenitude of canon law, [causing] the fruits etc., rights and obventions of the canonry and prebend and annexed vicarage to be delivered to him. [Curbing] gainsayers by the pope's authority etc. Notwithstanding etc. The pope's will is, however, that the vicarage shall not, on account of this union etc., be defrauded of due services and the cure of souls in it shall not be neglected; but that its customary burdens shall be supported; and that on the death of Laurence or his resignation etc. of the canonry and prebend this union etc. shall be dissolved and the vicarage shall revert to its original condition and be deemed vacant automatically.

Vite ac morum honestas ...
.phi. d(e) agnellis / JoA / JoA. xxv: non(o) k(a)l(endas) Julij Anno Secundo [23 June 1514]*, Nardi(nus)*

1   written *Chateymacnamara*

265   6 July 1514   *Reg. Lat.* 1311, fos 326ʳ-329ᵛ

To the abbot of the monastery of the Holy Cross¹ *de Aurecampo* [Kilcooly], d. Cashel, and the prior of the monastery, usually governed by a prior, of the Holy Cross¹ *de Insulla*² *Viventium* [Monaincha], d. Killaloe, and (?)Rory³ Oduygyn,⁴ canon of the church of (?)Clonmacnois (*Clunen.*), mandate in favour of Peter Iduygyn, cleric, d. Killaloe. The pope has learned that the rectory of the parish church of the place of Delge and also the rectory of the parish church of St Patrick, of the place of Donachinor, and the perpetual vicarage of the parish church of St Michael, of the place of Erich, which are both of lay patronage, d. Ossory, are vacant *certo modo* and have been vacant for so long that by the Lateran statutes their collation has lawfully devolved on the apostolic see, although Donald Odnygyn has detained the rectory of Delge, Theodoric Maegilpadric has detained that of St Patrick, and sometimes John Ohely and sometimes William Astackin *alias* Maccoda have detained the vicarage – bearing themselves as clerics and priests – with no title and no support of law, of their own temerity and *de facto*, for a certain time, as they still do. Recently a petition on the part of Peter (who asserts that he is in his twenty-third year of age; and that at another time – notwithstanding the defect of birth he suffers as the son of a cleric and an unmarried woman, related, as is asserted, by consanguinity or affinity – he was marked with clerical character, not by his own ordinary and without having obtained a relevant licence or mentioning the defect, but otherwise duly; and that at another time – being unable to obtain certain letters, called letters of safe conduct (*conductitias*) without which no one is allowed to come to the Roman curia from those parts – he swore an oath under a certain manner and form then expressed that he would not impetrate the said rectory of Delge and would not molest Donald over it, but not, however, with the intention of actually observing the oath but only of obtaining the said letters [sc. of safe conduct]⁵; and that the annual value of the said rectories and vicarage together does not exceed 32 marks sterling) was made to the pope to erect and institute a canonry in the said church of Ossory and the said vicarage into a simple prebend, for Peter's lifetime. The pope – not having certain knowledge of the foregoing; wishing to give a special grace to Peter; and relaxing the above oath for the purpose of the present letters taking effect and only to that extent – hereby commands that the above three (or two or one of them), if it is thus and, having summoned Donald, Theodoric, John and William and, as regards the erection,[6] the bishop and chapter of Ossory, and others concerned, they find the rectories and vicarage to be vacant (howsoever etc.) shall (even if the rectories and vicarage are specially reserved etc.) erect and institute a canonry in the church of Ossory and the said vicarage into a simple prebend, for Peter's lifetime, without prejudice to anyone; and shall collate and assign the newly erected canonry and prebend, then being vacant, and the said rectories to Peter, with plenitude of canon law and all their rights and appurtenances, inducting him etc. into corporal possession of the canonry and prebend, the rectories and the rights and appurtenances aforesaid, having removed Donald, Theodoric, John and William and any other unlawful detainers, and causing Peter (or his proctor) to be received as a canon of the church of Ossory; and shall assign him a stall in the choir and a place in the chapter of the church of Ossory, with plenitude of the said law, and [causing] him to be admitted to the rectories, and their fruits etc., rights and obventions and those of the canonry and prebend to be delivered to him. [Curbing] gainsayers by the pope's authority etc. Notwithstanding etc. Also the pope dispenses Peter – who suffers a defect of age for holding the rectories and a defect of birth for holding them and the canonry and prebend – to use the said clerical character and to be promoted to all, even sacred and priest's, orders, and to receive and retain together for life the erected canonry and prebend and also the rectories, if conferred on him by virtue of the presents, and without the said rectories, any two other benefices, with cure or otherwise mutually incompatible, even if parish churches or their perpetual vicarages, or dignities, *personatus*, administrations or offices in cathedral, even metropolitan, or collegiate churches, even if the dignities etc. should be customarily elective and have cure of souls, if he obtains them otherwise canonically, to resign them, at once or successively, simply or for exchange, as often as he pleases, and in their place receive and retain up to two other, similar or dissimilar, incompatible benefices, and retain them together for life, as above;[7] and, while attending a *studium particulare* in the province of Ireland (*Iberni<e>*[8]) or a *studium generale* elsewhere,[9] not to be bound by reason of the said rectories and of any other benefices – with cure or requiring sacred orders by law, statute or custom or otherwise – held by him at the time, to be promoted to the orders in question for a five-year period calculated from the end of the year prefixed by law, provided that he is a sub-deacon within the first two years, nor to be liable to be compelled to be so promoted by anyone against his will. Notwithstanding the above defects of age and birth, etc. The pope's will is, however, that the rectories and vicarage and other incompatible benefices in question shall not, on this account, be defrauded of due services and the cure of souls in the rectories and vicarage and (if any) the other incompatible benefices shall not be neglected; and that on Peter's death or his resignation etc. of the said canonry and prebend this erection and institution shall be dissolved and be so deemed and the said vicarage shall revert to its original condition automatically.

Apostolice sedis circumspecta benignitas ad ea libenter intendit ...
.Phi. d(e) agnell(is):. / JoA: / JoA: L: Nardinus

1   *sic*; MS: *Sancte Crucis* in both cases

2   the *first* 'l' possibly deleted
3   MS: *Zuorico*; a misread 'R'?
4   the 'gy' heavily inked in, apparently over other letter(s)
5   MS: *non tamen animo id opere adimplendi sed dictas litteras consequendi dumtaxat iurasse*
6   'et institutionem' does not occur.
7   Note that this dispensation *ad duo* (at least as enregistered) does not contain all the content in the prototype (no. 2 above).
8   The *e* is supralinear, above the deletion of one (or possibly two) letters in the line.
9   MS: ... *alibi vero ubi vigeat generale* ...; the tenor of the passage is certainly indicative of a lack of a *studium generale* in Ireland.

266   17 June 1514   *Reg. Lat.* 1312, fos 1ʳ-2ʳ

To Thomas Colcot *alias* Colocot, rector of the parish church of Pelleton', d. Exeter (who, as he asserts, holds the above parish church <and is a BA>[1]). Dispensation and indult etc. [as above, no. 2].

Vite ac morum honestas ...
.P. Lambertus. / JoA. / JoA. Lx: Nardinus

1   marginal insertion initialled *JoA*

267   18 May 1514   *Reg. Lat.* 1312, fo 3ʳ⁻ᵛ

To Richard Moyne *alias* Hampton', canon of the priory, called Christchurch, Twynhm', OSA, d. Winchester. Dispensation – at his supplication – to him, who, as he asserts, is expressly professed of the above order,[1] to receive and retain any benefice, with or without cure, usually held by secular clerics, etc. [as above, no. 43].[2] Given at Rome, St Peter's.[3]

Relligionis[4] zelus, vite ac morum honestas ...
.P. Lambertus. / JoA: / JoA: xxx: Nardinus

1   This information comes from a notwithstanding clause.
2   Save that where no. 43 has: *de iure patronatus laicorum* in MS (rendered as 'of lay patronage' in the Calendar) the present entry wants 'laicorum'.
3   *sic*; possible but improbable in view of the chronology: *see above*, p. xxxi
4   *sic*

268[1] **16 June 1514**   *Reg. Lat.* 1312, fos 20^v-22^v

To the bishops of Winchester, Durham (*Dunclinen.*), and Lincoln, mandate in favour
of Thomas Dalby, LLB, archdeacon of Richmond (*Richmundie*) in the church of York.
A recent petition to the pope on Thomas's part stated that although, as far as human
frailty allows, he has abstained from illicit acts and never perpetrated anything on
account of which he could lawfully be deprived of the archdeaconry of Richmond in
the said church, the provostship of the church of St John, Beverley (*Beverlacen.*), d.
York, and the parish church of Bucotbrogkton', d. Lincoln, all canonically collated to
him, or on account of which he could be investigated or proceeded against like a rebel
or someone disobedient to his superior, nevertheless, some time ago, at the false
relation of several persons who envied Thomas his untroubled position (*quieto statui*)
and aspired to his benefices, Brian Hicgdon, LLD, who bears himself as official or
vicar of the court of York, had, by certain letters of his of a certain tenor, warned and
ordered Thomas (who had previously been dispensed some time ago by apostolic
authority to retain together, for life, the provostship of the church of St John, which is
a simple office therein, the parish church of Bucotbrogkton', and the said
archdeaconry, which is a dignity but not major *post pontificalem*) to appear before him,
within a certain term then expressed which was clearly much too short, and show him
the titles to the archdeaconry, provostship, and parish church, and the faculties for
holding them together; that although several lawful declinatory objections against the
jurisdiction of the said official or vicar, and reasons for mistrusting and objecting to his
person, had been put before him at a suitable time and place, which by right should
have been admitted, the official or vicar – unlawfully refusing to hear Thomas over this
and having rejected the said objections, at least tacitly – warned and ordered Thomas
again, under sentence of excommunication and perhaps other ecclesiastical sentences,
censures, and pains then expressed, to appear before him [(?)or][2] his deputy, within a
certain peremptory term then expressed, to prove that he was lawfully dispensed to
retain the archdeaconry, provostship, and parish church together, and he threatened that
he was minded to deprive Thomas forever of the archdeaconry, provostship, and parish
church, and he perhaps deprived him forever of them, *de facto* and contrary to justice;
and that on the part of Thomas, who felt *inter alia* unduly aggrieved thereby, appeal
was made to the apostolic see, but the said official or vicar, proceeding to further
matters, regardless of the appeal of which he was not ignorant and while Thomas was
still well within the time for prosecuting it, sequestered, as is said, the fruits, revenues,
proceeds, dues, and emoluments of the provostship, albeit *de facto* and temerariously
attempting, and Thomas, who felt *inter alia* similarly unduly aggrieved thereby,
therefore appealed, extra-judicially, to the apostolic see. At the supplication[3] to the
pope to order that Thomas be absolved *ad cautelam* from the sentence of
excommunication and other ecclesiastical sentences, censures, and pains perhaps
promulgated against him by the said official, vicar, or deputy, and by any other judges
and persons, on the above occasion, and that the official, vicar, or deputy, and any other
judges and persons be inhibited [as appropriate][4] and as often as necessary, even under
ecclesiastical censures; and to commit to some upright men in those parts the causes:
of each appeal and of anything attempted and innovated after and against them and
each one of them; of the nullity of the process, monition, citation, decree, declaration,

sequestration, deprivation,[5] and each and every other thing done in any way by the said official, vicar, or deputy, to Thomas's prejudice [in connection with][6] the above; and of the whole principal matter, the pope [hereby] commands that the above three (or two or one of them), having summoned the said official, vicar, or deputy, and others concerned, shall, on the pope's authority, for this once only, bestow on Thomas, if he so requests, the benefit of absolution *ad cautelam* from the sentence of excommunication and other sentences, censures, and pains, inasmuch as it is just, having, however, first received from him suitable security in respect of that for which he is perhaps deemed caught by the said sentence of excommunication and other sentences, censures, and pains, that if they find that the sentence of excommunication etc were justly inflicted on him, he will obey their mandates and those of the church; as to the other things, having inhibited the official, vicar, or deputy, even under ecclesiastical censures, in accordance with the law, and having heard both sides, taking cognizance even of the principal matter, [decree] what is just [without appeal, causing by ecclesiastical censure what they have decreed] to be strictly observed,[7] [and moreover compel] witnesses, etc. Notwithstanding etc.

Humilibus et cetera.
.Jo. Copis. / JoA. / : JoA: xx: Nardinus

1   a prior draft of this letter entered (incompletely) at fo 92[r-v] of same register (below, no. 270)
2   MS: *ad*; *recte*: 'vel'?
3   The enregistered copy of a corresponding supplication is at *Reg. Suppl.* 1455, fos 66[r]-67[r].
4   MS wants 'inhibendum'.
5   MS: *monitionis citationis decreti declarationis sequestri privationis*. But there is no explicit mention of any citation, decree, or declaration in the preceding narrative.
6   MS: *contra*; *recte*: 'circa'
7   MS: *quod iustum fuerit et cetera firmiter observari*. Supplied from common form.

269   5 July 1514   *Reg. Lat.* 1312, fos 86[r]-87[r]

To the bishop of Exeter, the dean, and Richard Tollett[1], canon, of the church of Exeter, mandate in favour of Walter Gill', layman, vill of Shaftesbury (*ville Shatonie*), d. Salisbury, executor of the testament or last will of the late Ralph Byry, perpetual vicar of the parish church of St James, said vill. A recent petition to the pope on Walter's part stated that some time ago Thomas Pottere, priest, who bears himself as the present perpetual vicar of the said church – falsely alleging that the principal house of the vicar of the said church, called the manse, the kitchen, stable, barn, and its other buildings, which had been built and assigned for the habitation and use of the vicar of the said church for the time being, became ruinous and abandoned while the said Ralph was holding the vicarage, through his carelessness, fault, delay, and neglect, and, after his death, similarly by the carelessness, fault, delay, and neglect of Walter the executor – sued the said Walter over this, not by apostolic delegation, before Cuthbert Twstall', UID, auditor of William, archbishop of Canterbury, who was, he said, a competent judge for this, praying *inter alia* that Walter be condemned and compelled to restore, repair, and rebuild the said house, kitchen, stable, barn, and other buildings; and that the said Cuthbert, proceeding wrongly in the case, promulgated an unjust, definitive (as he said) sentence, by which he condemned Walter the executor in the sum of 12 pounds sterling of English money, and also condemned him in the costs run up in the case, from which sentence appeal was made on Walter's part to the apostolic see. At the supplication to the pope to order that Walter be absolved *ad cautelam* from the sentence of excommunication [and other ecclesiastical] sentences, [censures] and pains[2] perhaps inflicted on him by Cuthbert the auditor and any other judges and persons on the above occasion and to commit to some upright men in those parts the causes: of the said appeal and of anything perhaps attempted and innovated after and against it; of the nullity of the process of the said auditor and of each and every other thing done in any way by the auditor and any other judges and persons to Walter's prejudice in connection with the above; and of the whole principal matter, the pope [hereby] commands that the above three (or two or one of them), having summoned the said Thomas and others concerned, shall, on the pope's authority, bestow on Thomas, for this once only, if he so requests, the benefit of absolution *ad cautelam* from the said sentence of excommunication and other ecclesiastical sentences, censures, and pains,[3] inasmuch as it is just, having, however, first received from him suitable security in respect of that for which he is perhaps deemed excommunicate and caught by the other sentences, censures, and pains, that if they find the said sentence of excommunication etc was justly inflicted on him, he will obey their mandates and those of the church; as to the other things, having heard both sides, taking cognizance even of the principal matter, decree what is just, without appeal, causing [by ecclesiastical censure] what [they have decreed to be strictly] observed,[4] [and moreover compel] witnesses, etc. Notwithstanding etc.

Humilibus et cetera.
Jo. Copis. / . JoA. / JoA: xiiij: Nardinus

1   or *Tollet*
2   MS: ab *excommunicationis* [aliisque ecclesiasticis] *sententiis* [censuris] *et penis*; conjectured omissions supplied tentatively from below (*cf* next note)
3   MS: *ab excommunicationis aliisque ecclesiasticis sententiis censuris et penis* (i.e. the usual formulation here)
4   MS: *facientes quod et cetera observari.* Supplied from common form.

270   [–]¹   *Reg. Lat.* 1312, fo 92ʳ⁻ᵛ

Abortive entry: start only of rescript of justice in favour of Thomas Dalby, LLB, concerning his loss, by deprivation by Brian Higdon, LLD, official or vicar of the court of York, of his archdeaconry in the church of York, provostship of Beverley, d. York, and the parish church of Brant Broughton, d. Lincoln.

Thirty-one lines, occupying the lower part of fo 92ʳ and all of 92ᵛ. Though well launched the narrative is incomplete, stopping at the end of the last line on fo 92ᵛ. The entry may well have continued on another leaf, now lost. An unrelated entry begins at the top of fo 93ʳ.

No magistral initial or subscription; but with the note of the abbreviator's name: .*Jo. Copis*.

Deleted (by slanting strokes) with the explanatory note *Alibi* [sc. 'scripta' or 'registrata'] in another hand (a master's?). No attempt at correction.

From the viewpoint of a student of the 'background papers' and the process of impetration and enregistration this is a quite interesting fragment. It is obviously of related interest to the rescript in Dalby's favour enregistered (by the same scribe) at fos 20ᵛ-22ᵛ of the same register (no. 268 above), and there attributed to the same abbreviator, Johannes Copis. So far as it goes the text of present entry is in large part the same as the other one. However, there are some significant differences and the document immediately behind the present entry visibly differed from the document immediately behind the other entry. The two texts are arranged in parallel columns below. As can be seen there are telling differences of word order, stilus, and statement. For instance, where the abortive entry has *que canonice obtinet* the successful one has *canonice sibi collatis*. Additionally, blanks – each long enough (approx. 18-27 mm) for the insertion of a word – have been left in the present entry in four places. The first two were obviously left blank for the name of the archdeaconry (*Richmundie*). We are given a glimpse of the paperwork behind the official register. Clearly, the letter was first enregistered, prematurely, from an unrevised draft; then again from a corrected draft or the engrossment.

Moreover, as a corresponding petition (at *Reg. Suppl.* 1455, fos 66ʳ-67ʳ) contains the name of the archdeaconry (*Richmundie*) it would appear – assuming the same proctor was behind both drafts – that the draft from which the letter was originally enregistered pre-dated the composition of the petition. The letter may even have been enregistered at the incipient stage, before the petition was granted. In all probability, it was enregistered afresh because of the number of corrections needed; but it may have been done for another reason. The scribes were human and explanations in terms of bureaucratic efficiency are not always convincing.

---

1   Entry does not reach dating clause.

ENREGISTERED FROM DRAFT

Reg. Lat. 1312, fo 92ʳ⁻ᵛ (present entry)
.Jo. Copis.

[–]¹
.Alibi.
LEO et cetera venerabilibus fratribus
Vintonien. et Lincolinen.² ac
Lincolinen.² episcopis salutem et cetera.

Humilibus et cetera.

Exhibita siquidem nobis nuper pro parte
d(ilecti) f(ilii) Thome D a l b y
archidiaconi <u>BLANK</u>³ in ecclesia
Eboracen. bachalarii in legibus petitio
continebat quod licet ipse ab illis⁴
quantum [fo 92ᵛ] humana sinit fragilitas
semper se abstinuerit nec unquam
aliquid propter quod archidiaconatu
<u>BLANK</u> in dicta ecclesia in dicta
ecclesie⁵ et prepositura ecclesie Sancti
Johannis B e v e r l a c e n . Eboracen.
diocesis ac parrochiali ecclesia de
B u r n t h b r o g k t o n ' Lincolinen.
diocesis que canonice obtinet de iure
privari aut contra eum tanquam rebellem
et innobedientem superiori suo inquiri
seu procedi possit perpetraverit tamen
cum olim Brianus H i g d o n legum
doctor qui pro officiali seu vicario curie
Eboracen. se gerit ad <u>BLANK</u> qui dicti
Thome quieto statui invidebant et ad
ipsius beneficia aspirabant falsam
relationem eundem Thomam cum quo
dudum antea ut cum

1   not signed: no magistral initial at start of entry
2   *sic*; the initial *L* over *D* in the first occurrence
3   this and the others a word's length
4   *sic*; *recte* 'illicitis'
5   *in dicta ecclesia in dicta ecclesia*] *sic*

**ENREGISTERED FROM REVISED
DRAFT OR ENGROSSMENT**

Reg. Lat. 1312, fos 20ᵛ-22ᵛ (no. 268 above)
.Jo. Copis.

JoA.

LEO et cetera venerabilibus fratribus
Wintonien. et Dunclinen. ac
Lincholinen. episcopis salutem et cetera.

Humilibus et cetera.

Exhibita siquidem nobis ⁶ pro parte
d(ilecti) filii Thome D a l b y
archidiaconi R i c h m u n d i e in
ecclesia Eboracen. bachalarii in legibus
[fo 21ʳ] petitio continebat quod licet ipse
ab illicitis quantum humana sinit
fragilitas se abstinuerit neque umquam
aliquid propter quod archidiaconatu
R i c h m u n d i e in dicta ecclesia et
prepositura ecclesie Sancti Johannis
B e u e r l a c e n . Eboracen. diocesis ac
parrochiali ecclesia de
B u c o t b r o g k t o n ' Lincolinen.
diocesis canonice sibi collatis de iure
privari aut propter quod contra eum
tanquam superiori suo rebellem et
inhobedientem inquiri seu procedi posset
perpetraverit tamen cum olim d(ilectus)
f(ilius) Brianus H i c g d o n legum
doctoris⁷ qui pro officiali seu vicario
curie Eboracen. se gerit ad nonnullorum
qui dicti Thome quieto statui invidebant
et ad ipsius beneficia aspirabant falsam
relationem eundem Thomam cum quo
dudum antea ut cum

6   'nuper' does not occur.
7   *sic*; *recte* 'doctor'

archidiaconatu predicto que[8] dignitas ibi
non tamen post pontificalem maior
existebat preposituram dicte ecclesie
Sancti Johannis que simplex in eo[9]
officium existit ad[10] parrochialem
ecclesiam de B u r n t h b r o k t o n
huiusmodi quoadviveret retinere libere
et licite valeret apostolica fuerat
auctoritate dispensatum quamvis infra
certum tunc expressum terminum
notorie minus[11] brevem coram eo
compareret tibique[12] archidiaconatus et
prepositure ac parrochialis ecclesie
huiusmodi titulos illaque simul retinendi
facultates et <u>BLANK</u> litteras exhiberet
per quasdam suas certi tenoris litteras
monuisset et mandasset et quamvis non
nonnulle legitime exceptiones
declinatorie contrahi[13] iurisdictionem
suam et suspitionem ac recusationem
causa[14] in eius[15] personam pro parte dicti
Thome coram eo congruis loco et
tempore exhibere fuissent que de iure
admittende erant idem officialis vel
vicarius dictum Thomam super hoc
audire [*ends*]

archidiaconatu predicto qui dignitas inibi
non tamen post pontificalem maior
existebat preposituram dicte ecclesie
Sancti Johannis que simplex officium in
ea existit ac parrochialem ecclesiam de
de[16] B u c o t b r o g k t o n ' huiusmodi
quoadviveret retinere libere et licite
valeret apostolica fuerat auctoritate
dispensatum q(ua)t(en)us infra certum
tunc expressum //////[17] notorie nimis
brevem terminum coram eo compareret
sibique archidiaconatus et prepositure ac
parrochialis ecclesie huiusmodi titulos
illaque insimul retinendi facultates[18]
exhiberet per quasdam suas certi tenoris
litteras monuisset et mandasset eidem et
quamvis pro parte dicti Thome nonnulle
legitime exceptiones declinatorie contra
iurisdictionem dicti officialis seu vicarii
et suspitionum ac recusationum cause in
ipsius personam que de iure admittende
erant coram eo congruis loco et tempore
exhibite [fo 21ᵛ] fuissent idem officialis
seu vicarius dictum Thomam super hoc
audire indebite recusans huiusmodi
exceptionibus saltem tacite reiectis ...

8   *sic*; 'qui'?
9   *sic*; ea'?
10   *sic*; *recte* 'ac'
11   *sic*; *recte* 'nimis'
12   *sic*; *recte* 'sibique'
13   *sic*: written *co(n)-* | *trahi*; *recte* 'contra'
14   *suspitionem ... causa*] *sic*
15   *sic*

16   *de de*] *sic*
17   *tempus* deleted
18   or possibly *-em*

271   8 July 1514   *Reg. Lat.* 1312, fos 100ᵛ-102ʳ

To the bishops of Winchester and Lincoln and the dean of the church of Salisbury, mandate in favour of John Perott, BDec, precentor of the church of York, and Christopher Gill', chaplain, vicar choral, succentor, and warden of the college of vicars choral, said church, joint parties in this regard. A recent petition to the pope on the part of the joint parties stated that although by apostolic privilege, which has in no point been derogated, and by ancient and approved custom, which has been lawfully prescribed from time immemorial, the said joint parties have been and are utterly exempt from every kind of jurisdiction of the archbishop of York and his officials, vicars, commissaries, and deputies for the time being and totally subject to the dean for the time being and, when there is no dean, to the chapter, of the said church; and although the dean and chapter of the said church have, from time immemorial, been in peaceful quasi-possession of the correction and punishment of excesses and of the exercise of every kind of jurisdiction over the individual persons and the subjects of the said chapter among whom the joint parties were and are numbered, Edward Keller, DDec, who bears himself as commissary or deputy of the official of the court or consistory of York, nevertheless, by certain letters of his of a certain tenor, warned and ordered the joint parties, in contempt of the said privileges and immunities and although the said exemption, which was common knowledge, was well known to him, to appear personally, within an excessively short term then expressed, to reply to certain articles and positions produced before him, as he said, on the part of John Ffisher[1]; that then, having rejected (at least tacitly) several lawful declinatory objections to his jurisdiction produced at a suitable time and place by the said Christopher both in his own name and in the names of John Perott and of the joint parties, which in law should have been admitted, he again caused the joint parties to be similarly warned and also ordered them afresh to appear personally before him, within another short term, to reply to the said articles, and he decreed and declared that the said joint parties and each one of them ought to be suspended *a divinis*[2], and he actually suspended them; and that an appeal on the part of the joint parties, who felt *inter alia* unduly aggrieved thereby, was therefore made, extra-judicially, to the apostolic see. At the [supplication][3] to the pope to order that the joint parties, and each one of them, be absolved *ad cautelam* from the sentences of excommunication, suspension, and interdict[4], and from the other ecclesiastical sentences, censures, and pains, perhaps promulgated against them and each one of them by the said commissary or deputy and any other judges and persons on the above occasion and that the commissary or deputy and any other judges and persons be inhibited, as often as necessary, even under ecclesiastical censures; and to commit to some upright men in those parts, with each and every one of their incident, dependent, emergent, annexed, and connected matters, the causes: of the said appeal and of anything attempted and innovated after and against [it][5]; of the nullity of the process of the said commissary or deputy, of the said warning, order, decree, declaration, and suspension, and of each and every other thing done in any way by the commissary and any other judges and persons to the prejudice of the joint parties and each one of them in connection with the above; and of the principal matter, the pope [hereby] commands that the above three (or two or one of them), having summoned Edward and John Ffisher and any others concerned, shall, on the pope's authority, for this once only, inasmuch as it is just, bestow on the said joint parties and each one of them,[6] the benefit of absolution *ad cautelam* from the said sentence of excommunication [and][7] other ecclesiastical sentences, censures, and pains, having, however, first received from them suitable caution in respect of that by which they are perhaps held excommunicate and caught by the other ecclesiastical sentences, censures, and pains aforesaid, that if the above find that the said sentence of excommunication and the other sentences, censures and pains were justly inflicted on them they will obey the above's mandates and those of the church; as to the other things, when the above have inhibited the commissary or deputy and any other judges and persons, as often as necessary, even under ecclesiastical censures, insofar as it is just, and after they have heard both sides, taking cognizance even of the principal matter, decree what is just, without appeal, causing by ecclesiastical censure, what they have decreed to be strictly observed, [and moreover compel] witnesses, etc. Notwithstanding etc.

Humilibus et cetera.
.Jo. Copis. / JoA. / :JoA: xviij: Nardinus

1   makes an abrupt appearance, without explanation or identification
2   uncertain reading: ill-written
3   *appellatum*; *recte*: 'supplicatum'
4   *sic*; the various mentions of ecclesiastical sentences at different points in the letter are not entirely consistent.
5   MS: *illas*; *recte*: 'illam'
6   'si hoc humiliter petierint' does not occur; the omission is probably inadvertent.
7   MS wants 'et' (or suchlike).

272   18 August 1514   *Reg. Lat.* 1312, fos 108ᵛ-109ʳ

To Maurice Glyn', UIB, archdeacon of the church of Bangor. Dispensation and indult – at his supplication – to him (who, as he asserts, holds the archdeaconry of the above church, which is a dignity perhaps major *post pontificalem*) to receive and retain for life together with the above archdeaconry, two, and without them, any three other benefices, with cure or otherwise mutually incompatible, even if they should be dignities, *personatus*, administrations or offices in cathedral, even metropolitan, or collegiate churches, even if the dignities should be major *post pontificalem* in cathedral, even metropolitan, churches or principal in collegiate churches, or chantries, free chapels, hospitals or annual services usually assigned to secular clerics in title of a perpetual ecclesiastical benefice, or two of them be parish churches or their perpetual vicarages, or a combination, even if the dignities etc. should be customarily elective and have cure of souls, if he obtains them otherwise canonically, to resign them, at once or successively, simply or for exchange, as often as he pleases, and in their place receive up to three other, similar or dissimilar, incompatible benefices, provided that not more than two be parish churches or their perpetual vicarages, and retain them together for life, as above; and, while attending a *studium generale* or residing in the Roman curia or any one of his benefices, not to be bound to reside in his other

benefices, and not to be liable to be compelled to do so by anyone against his will.
Notwithstanding etc. With the proviso that the archdeaconry and other incompatible
benefices in question shall not, on this account, be defrauded of due services and the
cure of souls in them (if any) shall not be neglected; but that customary burdens of
those benefices in which he shall not reside shall be supported.

Litterarum scientia, vite ac morum honestas …
.P. Lambertus / JoA. / JoA: CX: Nard(inus):

273   21 August 1514   *Reg. Lat.* 1312, fos 109ᵛ-110ʳ

To John Selwoode *alias* Tanner, monk of the monastery of B. Mary the Virgin,
<Glaston'>,[1] OSB, d. Bath and Wells. Dispensation [and indult][2] – at his supplication
– to receive and retain any benefice, with or without cure, usually held by secular
clerics, etc. [as above, no. 19, to '… and in its place receive and retain another, similar
or dissimilar, benefice, with or without cure, defined as above']; and to wear the usual
habit worn by monks of the above monastery, OSB, of which he is a monk and, as he
asserts, expressly professed of the order, beneath the honest garment or robe of a priest
or secular cleric, of any honest colour, without any apostasy or incurring ecclesiastical
censure; and not to be bound to wear the habit in another way, nor to be liable to be
compelled by anyone to do so against his will. Notwithstanding etc.

Relligionis³ zelus, vite ac morum honestas …
.P. lambertus / JoA. / JoA: xxxxL: Nard(inus):

1   *de Glaston'* inserted in margin; *C* before it; *Additu(m) de m(anda)to .R. P. D. Regen(tis) Barotius* after it;
     insertion and note in the hand of the master concerned
2   'tibique pariter indulgemus' does not occur; *cf.* correlative (*indulti*) in 'Nulli ergo' clause.
3   *sic*

274   21 August 1514   *Reg. Lat.* 1312, fo 112ʳ⁻ᵛ

To Thomas Lyell', <BTheol>,[1] professor OCarm. Dispensation and indult – at his
supplication – to receive and retain any benefice, with or without cure, usually held by
secular clerics, even if a parish church or its perpetual vicarage, or a chantry, free
chapel, hospital or annual service, usually assigned to secular clerics in title of a
perpetual ecclesiastical benefice, and of lay patronage and of whatsoever tax or annual
value, if he obtains it otherwise canonically, to resign it, simply or for exchange, as
often as he pleases, and in its place receive and retain another, similar or dissimilar,
benefice, with or without cure, defined as above; and to receive for life – even after he
has acquired the said benefice – the usual conventual portion received by brothers of a
house of the above order, of which he is a professor and in which he has made the usual
profession made by the brothers; and to have – as before – an active and a passive voice

in the said order; and also to use, possess and enjoy each and every one of the apostolic privileges, indults, graces and letters granted in any way to the said order and which the other brothers of the order use, possess and enjoy and may use, possess and enjoy in any way in the future, without limitation, just as if he had not acquired the benefice. Notwithstanding etc. and [notwithstanding] the constitutions of Otto and Ottobuono, formerly legates of the apostolic see in the kingdom of England etc.[2]

Relligionis[3] zelus, vite ac morum honestas …
.P. Lambertus. / JoA. / JoA. Lx: Nardinus

1   corrected by order of the regent of the chancery. In line: *et theologia* (written before *professori*) is deleted and initialled *JoA*. In margin: *bacalario in theologia* is inserted; *JoA*. before it; *cassat(um) et aditu(m) de man(da)to D. Regentis Nardinis* after it.
2   The inclusion of these constitutions gives Lyell' the option of holding his secular benefice in England.
3   *sic*

275   18 August 1514   *Reg. Lat.* 1312, fos 115ʳ-116ʳ

To Thomas Pierson,[1] B<Dec>,[2] perpetual vicar of the parish church of Boxley, d. Canterbury. Dispensation and indult etc. [as above, no. 2, to '… by anyone against his will. '] Notwithstanding etc. and [notwithstanding] constitutions etc. in which it is said to be expressly stipulated that those (?)instituted[3] in or holding perpetual vicarages of parish churches shall be bound to maintain continual residence in them, otherwise the vicarages shall be deemed vacant and may be conferred on others, the which constitutions etc. the pope specially and expressly derogates for this once only; and notwithstanding the constitutions etc. of Otto and Ottobuono etc., and the oath perhaps taken by Thomas on acquiring the vicarage of Boxley to reside there in the flesh, the which oath the pope hereby relaxes in this regard; and notwithstanding anything else to the contrary. With the proviso that the above vicarage and the other, even incompatible, benefices in question shall not, on this account, be defrauded of due services and the cure of souls in the vicarage and (if any) the other, even incompatible, benefices shall not be neglected; but that customary burdens of these benefices in which he shall not reside shall be supported.

Litterarum scientia, vite ac morum honestas …
.P. Lambertus. / JoA: / JoA. Lxx: Nardinus

1   the *n* above a deleted letter
2   *legibus* deleted and initialled *JoA* twice; *decretis* inserted in margin above it: *JoA*; beneath: *cassat(um) et correctu(m) de man(da)to D(omi)ni Regentis Nard(inus)*
3   slightly uncertain; reading *instituti*

276   18 August 1514   *Reg. Lat.* 1312, fos 116ʳ-117ʳ

Union etc. At a recent petition on the part of Thomas Welkynson, rector of the parish church of St Nicholas within the vill of Colchester (*Colcestrie*), d. London, the pope hereby unites etc. the parish church of B. Mary the Virgin at the Walls within the said vill, said diocese, (whose annual value does not exceed 6 pounds sterling after deduction of all expenses), with all its rights and appurtenances, to the above church of St Nicholas, which Thomas holds by apostolic dispensation together with that of B. Mary the Virgin, for as long as he holds St Nicholas's, to the effect that he may, on his own authority, in person or by proxy, take anew,[1] or continue in, and retain corporal possession of B. Mary's and the rights and appurtenances aforesaid, for as long as he holds St Nicholas's, and convert its fruits etc. to his own uses and those of the said churches, without licence of the local diocesan or of anyone else. Notwithstanding etc. The pope's will is, however, that B. Mary's shall not, on account of this union etc., be defrauded of due services and the cure of souls in it shall not be neglected, but that its customary burdens shall be supported; and that on Thomas's death or his resignation etc. of St Nicholas's this union etc. shall be dissolved and so deemed and B. Mary's shall revert to its original condition automatically.

Ad futuram rei memoriam. Romanum decet pontificem votis illis et cetera provideri.
.P. Lambertus. / JoA. / JoA. xxxv: Nardinus

1   *deno*; for 'denuo' ('de novo')?

277¹   1514 [or potentially 1515]²   *Reg. Lat.* 1312, fos 132ʳ-133ᵛ

To Robert Dykar, UIB, chancellor of the church of Wells, d. Bath and Wells, indult. The pope has learned that in a certain statute or ordinance of the above church of Wells, published, as is asserted, by the late Ralph, bishop of Bath and Wells, with the consent of the chapter, the chancellor of the said church for the time being is bound, in perpetuity, each year on lecture-days to lecture in theology or the decretals, in person or by proxy at his expense, if there is no lawful impediment;³ and whoever is to be received and admitted to the chancellorship of this church (which is a dignity or office, and which Robert holds), must, at his reception and admission, take a corporal oath on the gospels to give the lecture. And a recent petition to the pope on Robert's part stated that for forty years and more, or even from time immemorial, there have, successively, been many chancellors of the said church, Robert's predecessors in the said chancellorship, who have not lectured in the said church, in person or by proxy at their expense, and consequently the said statute has probably never been received or observed in the said church, or at least, as custom is opposed to it – there being no lecture for such a long time, as above – the statute has probably been utterly abrogated; and that the said predecessors have not, at their reception and admission to the chancellorship, taken a corporal oath specifically and expressly to observe the said statute or ordinance of bishop Ralph, but only a general oath about fulfilling and observing the statutes, ordinances and laudable customs of the church, just as Robert, at his reception and admission, took only a general oath about observing the statutes and customs, and not a specific one; and that hitherto Robert has held and possessed the chancellorship free and immune from all burden of the lecture, just as his predecessors in their time have successively held and possessed it, and as he holds and possesses it at present; and that the fruits of the chancellorship are more than usually diminished and nothing was granted and assigned to the chancellorship for the burden of the lecture by bishop Ralph or other bishops of Bath and Wells. The pope hereby indulges Robert – at his supplication – not to be in any way bound to cause the lecture to be given in the said church, by himself or by proxy at his expense, nor to be liable to be compelled to do so by anyone against his will or be deprived of the chancellorship on this account. Notwithstanding etc. and [notwithstanding] the aforesaid statute and the other statutes and customs of the said church which the pope, specially and expressly, derogates for this once only, even if [for their derogation] special, specific, express, and individual mention or any other expression was to be made of them and their whole tenors, verbatim and not by general clauses, or even if some other uncommon form for this purpose was to be observed. And [notwithstanding] that Robert, having been summoned about this before the present bishop of Winchester[4] who had been appointed by apostolic authority, has acknowledged judicially that he was bound to lecture in accordance with the aforesaid statute except insofar as he was dispensed by the apostolic see; and [notwithstanding] any process conducted or undertaken against Robert in this connection by the said bishop or any other judges, delegate or ordinary; and anything else to the contrary.

Litterarum scientia, vite ac morum honestas ...
[–]⁵ / [–]⁶ / [–]⁷

1   The enregistration of this entry is incomplete (*see below*, note 2) and wants the authenticating marks of officials (*see below*, notes 5, 6 and 7). And at one point there is an odd hiatus in the text (*see below*, note 4).
2   Dating clause left incomplete; viz: ... *millesimo quingentesimo quartodecimo*: ends thus, leaving the month-date and day-date wanting.
3   The *ordinatio lecture in ecclesia Wellensi* dated 4 Dec. 1335 is printed in *The Register of Ralph of Shrewsbury, Bishop of Bath and Wells, 1329-1363*, ed. T.S. Holmes, 1896 [=Somerset Record Society, vols. 9 and 10], pp. 340-341.
4   MS: *moderno episcopo* [*Bathonien.* deleted, but not initialled] *Wintonien.* [then a blank space of about the length of a word] *apostolica auctoritate deputato*
5   name of abbreviator wanting
6   master's initial wanting
7   magistral subscription wanting

278   2 June 1514   *Reg. Lat.* 1312, fos 135ᵛ-136ʳ

To William Mallerey, canon of the monastery, called house, of B. Mary the Virgin, Erdebure [also spelt *Erdebur'*], OSA, d. Coventry and Lichfield. Dispensation and indult – at his supplication – to receive and retain any benefice, with or without cure, usually held by secular clerics, etc. [as above, no. 19, to '... and in its place receive and retain another, similar or dissimilar, benefice, with or without cure, defined as above'];

and to wear the usual habit worn by the canons of the above monastery, OSA, of which
he is a canon, and, as he asserts, expressly professed of the order, beneath the honest
garment or robe of a priest or secular cleric, of any honest colour, without any apostasy
or incurring ecclesiastical censure. Notwithstanding etc.

Relligionis[1] *zelus, vite ac morum honestas* ...
.*P. Lambertus.* / *JoA:* / *JoA: xxxx: Nardinus*

1   *sic*

---

279   **13 September 1514**   *Reg. Lat.* 1312, fos 153[r]-154[r]

To Cuthbert Tunstall', canon of the church of <Lincoln>,[1] and William Wylton' and
John Bakdee, canons of the church of Salisbury, mandate in favour of Richard Hill' and
John Bewe, laymen, Worcester or other d., executors of the testament or last will of the
late Alice Buryman', woman, parishioner of Stowe St Edward the King,[2] said d. A
recent petition to the pope on the part of Richard and John stated that, some time ago,
in connection with the validity, probate (*verificatione*), formalities (*solemnitate*), and
other legal requirements of the said testament, which was not erased, damaged,
cancelled, or suspect in any part but on the face of it utterly without defect and in no
way suspicious, and which the said Richard and John, its executors lawfully appointed
therein by the said <testatrix>[3], had previously exhibited before him for the purpose of
public enregistration and of putting the testator's[4] will into actual execution without
delay, John Mogerii, BDec, general commissary of Silvester, bishop of Worcester,
refused or unduly delayed – contrary to justice, when he had been lawfully asked at a
suitable time and place and when no lawful objector had appeared – to admit certain
witnesses who were beyond objection and fit to be heard, at least for summary
information of the above, produced before him on the part of the said executors, and
to swear and examine them or order them to be examined, and to assign some
competent term for other witnesses to be similarly produced before him concerning the
above; that Thomas Wodington', DDec, official of the primatial court of Canterbury,
had, at the instance of the said executors, by certain letters of his of a certain tenor,
warned the commissary, or ordered and caused him to be warned, to receive the said
witnesses within a certain term then expressed, swear and examine them or cause them
to be examined, and also to assign some other competent term for the other witnesses
to be produced; that the said commissary, opposing the said warning and order, then
appeared before the said official within the prefixed term or the term extended for him
for the purpose, with a view to proving his right; that by a certain interlocutory
sentence of his the said official[5], to the great prejudice of the said executors and
obstruction and delay of the execution, admitted several irrelevant and inapplicable –
actually diverse and mutually repugnant – reasons or objections then expressed
exhibited before him on the part of John the commissary, which in law ought,
deservedly, to have been rejected; and that on the part of the said executors, who felt
inter alia unduly aggrieved thereby, appeal was made to the apostolic see. At the

supplication to the pope to order that the said commissary and official and any others be inhibited as often as it is a necessity, even under ecclesiastical censures, and to commit to some upright men in those parts, with each and every one [of their][6] incident, dependent, emergent, annexed, and connected matters, the causes: of the said appeal and of anything perhaps attempted and innovated after and against it; of the nullity of the said commissary's process and the official's interlocution and sentence, and of each and every other thing done in any way to the prejudice of the said executor's in connection with the above; and of the whole principal matter, the pope [hereby] commands that the above three (or two or one of them), having summoned the said commissary and others concerned, inhibited the said commissary and official and any others who ought to be inhibited, even under ecclesiastical censures, in accordance with the law, and having heard both sides, taking cognizance even of the principal matter, [shall decree] what is just, [without appeal, causing by ecclesiastical censure what they have decreed to be strictly] observed,[7] [and moreover compel] witnesses, etc. Notwithstanding etc.

Humilibus et cetera.
.P. de Castello. / M / M xij de Campania

1   marginal insertion, initialled *M*
2   MS: *de Stowe Sancti Edwardi Regis*
3   *testatricem* inserted in margin; in the line: *testatore*[m] deleted
4   MS: *dicti testatoris*
5   MS: *officiales predictos*; *recte*: 'officialis predictus'
6   MS: *illatis*; *recte*: 'illarum' ?
7   MS: *quod iustum et cetera observari*. Supplied from common form.

280   10 April 1514   *Reg. Lat.* 1312, fo 195[r-v]

To the abbot[1] of the monastery of Bindon (*de Benedona*), O. Cist., d. Salisbury. Dispensation – at his supplication – to receive and retain *in commendam* for life, together with the above monastery, over which he presides, any benefice, with or without cure, usually held by secular clerics, even if a parish church or its perpetual vicarage, or a chantry, free chapel, hospital or annual service, usually assigned to secular clerics in title of a perpetual benefice,[2] and of lay patronage and of whatsoever tax or annual value, if he obtains it otherwise canonically, to resign it as often as he pleases and cede the commend and in its place receive another, similar or dissimilar, benefice, with or without cure, usually held by secular clerics and retain it *in commendam* for life as above; he may – due and customary burdens of the benefice having been supported – make disposition of the rest of its fruits etc. just as those holding it *in titulum* at the time could and ought to do, alienation of the benefice's immovable goods and precious movables being however forbidden. Notwithstanding etc. With the proviso that the benefice in question shall not, on this account, be defrauded of due services and the cure of souls in it (if any) shall not be neglected; but that its aforesaid burdens shall be supported.[3]

Personam tuam nobis et apostolice sedi devotam tuis exigentibus meritis paterna benevolentia prosequentes illa tibi favorabiliter concedimus …
.P. Lambertus. / C / C. L. Barotius

1   not named. As the grant is personal the absence of a name is distinctly odd.
2   MS: *perpetui beneficii*; 'ecclesiastici' which we would expect here, does not occur.
3   The *Nulli* clause includes: *indulti ac voluntatis*; though the preceding text contains no corresponding passages.

281   23 June 1514   *Reg. Lat.* 1312, fos 220ᵛ-221ᵛ

Union etc. At a recent petition on the part of Thomas, bishop of Selimbria (*Solubrien.*), the pope hereby unites etc. the parish church of Parva Torynton', d. Exeter (whose annual value does not exceed 5 pounds sterling), with all its rights and appurtenances, to the priory, called cell, of Carswell', OClun, d. Exeter, which, together with the above parish church, bishop Thomas holds *in commendam* by apostolic dispensation, for as long as he holds the priory *in commendam*, to the effect that he may, on his own authority, in person or by proxy, freely continue in, or take anew, and retain corporal possession of the church and rights and appurtenances aforesaid, for as long as he holds the priory as above, and convert the church's fruits etc. to his own uses and those of the priory and the church, without licence of the local diocesan or of anyone else. Notwithstanding etc. The pope's will is, however, that the church shall not, on account of this union etc., be defrauded of due services and the cure of souls in it shall not be neglected, but that its customary burdens shall be supported; and that on bishop Thomas's death or his resignation etc. of the priory this union etc. shall be dissolved and so deemed and the church shall revert to its original condition automatically.

Ad futuram rei memoriam et cetera.¹ Romanum decet pontificem votis illis gratum prestare assensum …
.P. Lambertus. / JoA. / JoA. xxxv:- Nardinus

1   *sic*; the formula 'Ad futuram rei memoriam' is complete and 'et cetera' is redundant here; presumably a scribal slip.

282   2 May 1514   *Reg. Lat.* 1312, fos 223ᵛ-224ʳ

To Thomas Stanley, cleric, Coventry and Lichfield,¹ extension etc. as below. Some time ago,² Julius II by letters of his dispensed Thomas, (who, as he asserted, was then in his thirteenth year of age and, notwithstanding a defect of birth as the son of a cleric of noble birth and an unmarried woman, had been marked with clerical character otherwise however duly), [to receive and retain] thereafter the parish church of Cotnam³ [also spelt *Cotnan*], d. Ely, *in commendam* until his eighteenth year, and thenceforth *in titulum*; and when he should reach his twentieth year to receive and retain for life with the above parish church, one other, or without them, any two other benefices, etc. [as above, no. 6, to '…to resign them, at once or successively, simply or for exchange, as often as he pleased'], and cede the commend and in their place receive up to two other, similar or dissimilar, incompatible benefices and retain them together for life, as above, as is more fully contained in those letters.[4] Wishing to give Thomas (who, as he asserts, is now in his sixteenth year or thereabouts and as yet has no hope of acquiring, or even of being able to acquire, the said church of Cotnam) a more ample grace, the pope – at Thomas's supplication – hereby extends and enlarges the dispensation and letters aforesaid (with clauses of exchange and of ceding the commend and with everything else contained in them in this regard) to enable Thomas even as from now to receive and retain [*in commendam*][5] – in place of the church of Cotnam – any other benefice, with cure or otherwise incompatible, otherwise defined as above, if he obtains it otherwise canonically, until his eighteenth year; and thereafter to retain it *in titulum* otherwise in accordance with the tenor of the said letters, notwithstanding his above defect of birth and the defect of age which he shall suffer when he is in his eighteenth year, etc.

Vite ac morum honestas …
.P. Lambertus. / JoA. / JoA. xij: Nardinus

1   'dioc'' does not occur.
2   Directly prior to *Dudum*, a short passage – *Hinc est quod nos* (?)*te* – has been deleted and initialled *JoA*
3   or *Cotuam*
4   *CPL*, XIX, no. 806 – from which it is clear that in addition to dispensing Thomas Stanley for tenure of benefice(s) Julius had dispensed him for non-promotion to orders and indulged him for non-residence. However, neither issue is raised in the present letter – presumably because the petitioner's recourse to Leo had been prompted simply by failure to get Cotnam.
5   *in commendam* does not occur.

283[1]   **25 August 1514**   *Reg. Lat.* 1312, fos 268ʳ-269ᵛ

To the archdeacon of the church of Dunblane, mandate in favour of Adam Hepburne, cleric, d. St Andrews (who, as he asserts, is in his sixteenth year of age or thereabouts and, notwithstanding a defect of birth as the son of a canon [regular],[2] OSA, of noble birth, and an unmarried woman, has been duly marked with clerical character). Following the pope's reservation of all benefices, with and without cure, vacated then and in the future at the apostolic see to his own collation and disposition, the perpetual vicarage of the parish church of Hathington, d. St Andrews, fell vacant by the free resignation of George Hepbuene,[3] its recent perpetual vicar, who was holding it at the time, made spontaneously through his specially appointed proctor Gilbert Strathanchm', canon of Brechin, into the hands of the pope who admitted the resignation at the said see, and is vacant at present, being reserved as above. The pope hereby commands the above archdeacon, if through diligent examination he finds Adam to be otherwise suitable for this – concerning which the pope burdens the archdeacon's conscience – to collate and assign the vicarage (whose annual value does not exceed 12 pounds sterling) (whether vacant as above or in any other way etc.; even if it has been vacant for so long that by the Lateran statutes its collation has lawfully devolved on the apostolic see etc.), with all its rights and appurtenances, to Adam, inducting him etc. having removed any unlawful detainer and causing Adam (or his proctor) to be admitted to the vicarage and its fruits etc., rights and obventions to be delivered to him. Curbing gainsayers etc. Notwithstanding etc. Also the pope dispenses Adam to receive and retain the vicarage, if conferred on him by virtue of the presents, notwithstanding the above defects of birth and age etc. With the proviso that the vicarage shall not, on this account, be defrauded of due services and the cure of souls in it shall not be neglected.

Dignum arbitramur et cetera.
G. de prato / C / C xxxx Tertio Id(us) Sept(embris) Anno secundo [11 September 1514], *Barotius*

1   What appears to be an abortive entry of this letter is at no. 285 below.
2   'regulari' (which occurs at this point in next entry) wanting
3   the antepenultimate *e* not easily read as an 'r'

284   7 August 1514   *Reg. Lat.* 1312, fos 302ᵛ-304ʳ

To the archdeacon of the church of Dunblane, mandate in favour of Alexander Hepburne, cleric, d. St Andrews (who, as he asserts, is in his seventeenth year of age or thereabouts and, notwithstanding a defect of birth as the son of a canon regular,[1] OSA, of noble birth, and an unmarried woman, has been marked with clerical character otherwise duly). Following the pope's reservation of all benefices, with and without cure, vacated then and in the future at the apostolic see to his own collation and disposition, the perpetual vicarage of the parish church of Ga(m)mery,[2] d. Aberdeen, fell vacant by the free resignation of Henry Preston, its recent perpetual vicar, who was holding it at the time, made spontaneously through his specially appointed proctor Gilbert Strathanthm, canon of Brechin, into the hands of the pope who admitted the resignation at the said see, and is vacant at present, being reserved as above. The pope hereby commands the above archdeacon, if through diligent examination he finds Alexander to be suitable for this – concerning which the pope burdens the archdeacon's conscience – to collate and assign[3] the vicarage (whose annual value does not exceed 12 pounds sterling) (whether vacant as above or in any other way etc.; even if it has been vacant for so long that by the Lateran statutes its collation has lawfully devolved on the apostolic see etc.), with all its rights and appurtenances, to Alexander, inducting him etc. having removed any unlawful detainer and causing Alexander (or his proctor) to be admitted to the vicarage and its fruits etc., rights and obventions to be delivered to him. Curbing gainsayers etc. Notwithstanding etc. Also the pope dispenses Alexander to receive and retain the vicarage, if conferred on him by virtue of the presents, notwithstanding the above defects of birth and age etc. With the proviso that the above vicarage shall not, on this account, be defrauded of due services and the cure of souls in it shall not be neglected.

Dignum arbitramur et cetera ...
A. de S(an)cto Seve(ri)no[4] */ C / C. xxxx. Id(ibus) Sept(embris) Anno Secundo* [13
September 1514], *Barotius*

1   *... canonico regulari ...* (*cf.* previous entry)
2   written *Ga'mery*
3   *conferri et assignari*; *recte*: -'re'? Other small-scale textual oddities (e.g. superfluous repetition of words or
     phrases) are to be found through the entry.
4   *G. de prato* deleted and initialled *C*

285   [–][1]   *Reg. Lat.* 1312, fo 304[r]

Abortive entry: start only of mandate of provision in the form *Dignum* – a form
appropriate for a provisee who is not present at the curia – addressed to the archdeacon
of the church of Dunblane. The benefice in question appears to be the perpetual
vicarage of the parish church of Haddington which, judging from the opening of the
recital, is vacant at the apostolic see and, in consequence, reserved to the collation and
disposition of the pope. As it stands the entry does not reach that part of the letter where
the provisee would be named.

Occupies nine lines at the foot of the page and scarcely gets beyond the start of the
detailed narrative: *Cum itaque postmodum perpetua vicaria parrochialis ecclesie de
Hathington* [ends]

Hathington is at the end of the last line; but, curiously, text not continued on verso
which is blank. The previous entry (same scribe) is no. 284 above. The following entry
(again same scribe) is an unrelated letter drawn under 15 August 1514 (fos 305[r]-306[v]).

No administrative notes: no abbreviator's name; and no initial or subscription of a
registry master. The proem is: *Dignum arbitramur et cetera.*

Cancelled by two intersecting diagonal lines forming a large 'St Andrews' cross; but
without explanatory note. However, at fos 268[r]-269[v] of the same register (above, no.
283) there is a provisory mandate ordering the collation of the vicarage of Haddington
to Adam Hepburn. The text of the present entry, so far as it goes, matches that of the
other entry.[2] If the other entry (which was made by the same scribe) was made earlier
it could explain why the present entry was abandoned.

1   Text does not extend to dating clause.
2   Apart, that is, from the repetition of *et dispositioni* in the opening narrative of no. 283.

286   **17 September 1514**   *Reg. Lat.* 1313, fos 9[r]-10[v]

To James Condour,[1] scholar, d. Ross, dispensation and indult as below. The pope (who,
some time ago, willed that provisions or grants or mandates of provision to canonries
and prebends of cathedral churches to persons who have not completed their fourteenth
year of age shall have no force except by consent of the apostolic see) – at the
supplication of James (who, as he asserts, is coming up to his fourteenth year; suffers

a defect of birth as the son of a priest and an unmarried woman; and desires to become a cleric) – hereby dispenses and indulges him to be marked with clerical character; and, at the lawful age, to be promoted to all, even sacred and priest's, orders; and, likewise after he has been duly marked with the said character, to receive and retain any number of mutually compatible benefices without cure; and, at the said lawful age, even with cure; and, when[2] he reaches his eighteenth year, one benefice with cure or otherwise incompatible, even if the compatible benefices should be canonries and prebends, dignities, *personatus*, administrations or offices in cathedral, even metropolitan, <or collegiate>[3] churches, and [even if] the benefice with cure or otherwise incompatible should be a parish church or its perpetual vicarage, or a combination of such benefices, and even if the dignities etc. should be customarily elective and have cure of souls, if he obtains them otherwise canonically; to resign them, at once or successively, simply or for exchange, as often as he pleases, and in their place receive and retain, hereafter, any number of other, similar or dissimilar, compatible benefices without cure, even canonries and prebends in cathedral, even metropolitan, churches; and, at the lawful age, even with cure, as above; and, in his said eighteenth year, one benefice with cure or otherwise incompatible – provided that the dignities in question be not major *post pontificalem* in cathedral, even metropolitan, churches, or principal in collegiate churches. Notwithstanding the above defects of birth and age etc. With the proviso that the canonries and prebends which he may hold before he has completed his said fourteenth year in cathedral, even metropolitan, churches, and the incompatible benefice in question shall not, on this account, be defrauded of due services and the cure of souls in the incompatible benefice (if any) shall not be neglected; but that customary burdens of the said canonries and prebends shall (?)meanwhile[4] be supported.

Laudabilia tue puerilis etatis inditia ...
Je Benzon / C / C. Lxx. Barotius

1   first letter uncertain
2   reading *et cum*
3   *vel collegiatis* inserted in margin initialled *C* and *Ba*
4   MS: (?) *interim*

287   21 September 1514   *Reg. Lat.* 1313, fos 12ʳ-14ᵛ

To the bishop of Winchester, the abbot of the monastery of St Peter, Westmon', London, and the dean of the church of Windsor (*de Windesora*), d. Salisbury, mandate in favour of Reginald West, sub-dean, and Peter Cuselegh', John Bekehem, John Edimundi, William Mors, and Thomas Lovell', canons, of the church of Wells, co-litigants in this regard. A recent petition to the pope on the co-litigants' part stated that although under the statutes of the said church certain fruits, revenues and proceeds have been accustomed to be distributed at the end of the year among those holding dignities in it and keeping due residence in the said church for eight months continuously or intermittently and among the canons, called residentiaries, of the church and keeping due residence in it for six months continuously or intermittently, in such a way that if residence is short by one day no portion is proper but accrues to those keeping the said residence, to be divided among them; and although the dean of the church for the time being has been accustomed to keep residence continuously or [?intermittently][1] for eight months, as above, and, when the bishop is away from time to time, on principal feasts in place of the bishop, on Sundays, and on each Saturday, to attend the chapter of the said church and to hear and duly determine causes appertaining to the said chapter, and, bound by his own oath, to defend the rights of the said church, to observe the statutes and customs, and to cause other things to be done and executed which are useful and necessary; nevertheless, at another time, William Wilton, chancellor of the church of Salisbury – on the strength (as it was said) of certain letters surreptitiously and obreptitiously impetrated from Julius II by William Cosyn, dean of the said church of Wells, [and] of other letters directed to the then archbishop of Canterbury and the bishop of Durham, their proper names not expressed, concerning the execution of the first mentioned letters,[2] and at the instance, as it is believed, of dean William – by the affixing of certain other letters of William the sub-executor,[3] warned and ordered Hadrian, cardinal priest of the title of S Crisogono (but without mentioning that he was a cardinal), who is known to preside over the church of Wells by apostolic concession and dispensation, and the said chapter, that they, or any of them, were not to obstruct dean William in any way over the receipt of the said fruits, etc due by reason of the said residence if dean William were to serve in the church of Wells for six months, as above, and they were not to compel dean William to serve in the church of Wells more than six months; and, in the event of their not obeying the said warning and order he interdicted them [ab] *ingressu ecclesie*, as of then, and he perhaps bound them by sentence of excommunication and other ecclesiastical sentences, censures, and pains, going beyond the tenor of Julius's letters; and that appeal was made to the apostolic see on the part of the said co-litigants (who felt *inter alia* unduly aggrieved thereby), both for themselves and for those wishing to join them[4]. At the supplication to the pope [to order][5] that they and each one of them be absolved from the said sentence of excommunication and the other sentences, censures, and pains perhaps inflicted on them by William the sub-executor and any others on the above occasion; that the said interdict be relaxed; and that William the chancellor and William the dean and any other judges and persons be inhibited as appropriate; and to commit to some upright men in those parts, to be heard, examined, decided, and duly determined, with their annexed, connected, and dependent matters, the causes: of the aforesaid appeal and of anything attempted and innovated after and against it; of the nullity of the said warning, mandate, and censures, and also of the subreption and obreption of the first-mentioned letters, and of each and every other thing done in any way by William the chancellor and William the dean and any other judges and persons to the prejudice of the co-litigants and of those wishing to join them, in connection with the above; and of the whole principal matter, the pope hereby commands that the above three (or two or one of them), having summoned William the dean and others concerned, shall, on the pope's authority, bestow on the co-litigants and those wishing to join them, for this once only, if they so request, the benefit of absolution *ad cautelam* from the said sentence of excommunication and other sentences, censures, and pains, if and as it is just – having, however, first received from them suitable security in respect of that for which they are perhaps deemed excommunicate and caught by the other sentences, censures, and pains, that if the above find that the said sentence of excommunication and the other sentences, etc. were justly inflicted on them they will obey the above's mandates and those of the church – and relax the said interdict; as to the other things, when they have inhibited William the chancellor and William the dean and any other judges and persons, as appropriate, under the pains and censures aforesaid, in accordance with the law, as often as necessary, and after they have heard both sides, taking cognizance even of the principal matter, shall decree what is just, without appeal, causing by ecclesiastical censure what they have decreed to be strictly observed; and moreover compel witnesses, etc. Notwithstanding etc.

Humilibus supplicum votis libenter annuimus ...
phi de agnell(is) / C / C. xvj. Barotius

1   MS: *continue seu per octo menses*; wants 'interpellatim'?
2   MS: *quarumdam litterarum a felicis recordationis Julio papa II predecessore nostro per dilectum filium*
      Willermum Cosyn decanum dicte ecclesie Wellen. surrepticie et obrepticie impetratarum ut dicebatur vigore
      aliarum litterarum ad tunc archiepiscopum Cantuarien. et episcopum Dunelmen. eorum propriis nominibus
      non expressis super primo dictarum litterarum executione directarum
3   As well as William Cosyn, dean of Wells, and William Mors, canon of Wells, the letter refers, variously to
      Willermus cancellarius (i.e. William Wilton, chancellor of Salisbury) and to a 'William the sub-executor'.
      The first mention of the latter is *ipsius Willermi subexecutoris* which, by virtue of the *ipsius*, seems to refer
      to 'William the chancellor' who has already been mentioned. But further on a distinction would appear to be
      drawn between them: *Et deinde nobis humiliter supplicatum ut ipsos* [sc. the petitioners] *et eorum quemlibet*
      ab excommunicationis et aliis sententiis ... in eos per ipsum Will(el)mum subexecutorem et quoscunque alios
      forsan premissorum occasione promulgatis absolvi ... et dictis Will(er)mo cancellario et Will(er)mo decano
      ac quibusvis aliis iudicibus et personis quibus inhibendum fuerit inhiberi [mandare] ... It is not absolutely
      clear whether 'William the chancellor' and 'William the sub-executor' are different persons; or whether a
      distinction is being drawn between different capacities of the same person. If they are not the same person
      the surname of 'William the sub-executor' is not given.
4   reading, very tentatively [p]*ro se et eis adherere volentibus*
5   MS wants 'mandare'.

288   12 September 1514   *Reg. Lat.* 1313, fos 134ᵛ-136ʳ

To the archdeacon of Suffolk (*Suffolchie*) of the church of Norwich, William Wylton', canon of the church of Salisbury, and Richard Tollet, canon of the church of Exeter, mandate in favour of the prior and convent of the monastery of Twynlya, OSA, d. Winchester, and William Cressall', perpetual vicar of the parish church of Blanford Fori, d. Salisbury, co-litigants in this regard. A recent petition to the pope on the co-litigants' part stated that although the tithes of all the lambs (and their wool) born and feeding in Ffonnage[1], in Noosend[2], in Hurles Plaic[3], in the holding of John Gilyngton', and in the holding of Thomas Wyghman', places, called farms, situated within the boundaries of the parish of the said church, which is united, annexed, and incorporated to the said monastery, wholly appertain, by reason of the said church, to the said prior and convent, by ancient, approved, and hitherto peacefully observed custom, and although both they and previous priors and convents of the monastery, have, from time immemorial, been in peaceful quasi-possession of the right of gathering in the tithes in their entirety, Peter Rodericus, who bears himself as rector of the parish church of Pymporu' [also spelt *Pymporum*], d. Salisbury – claiming, albeit falsely, that the said places are within the boundaries of the parish church of Pymporu', that half the said tithes belong to him by reason of the parish church of Pymporu', and that William (to whom the prior and convent had granted the tithes in farm and who, on the strength of this grant, had at some time collected and gathered them in) had robbed Peter of the tithes and unlawfully gathered them in and collected them – nevertheless sued William over these matters, not by apostolic delegation, before Cuthbert Tunstall' who was, he said, auditor of causes and matters of the court of the archbishop of Canterbury, primate of all England, and legate born of the apostolic see; and that Cuthbert, proceeding wrongly in the case, without observing the order of law, promulgated a null or unjust, definitive ([as][4] he said), sentence, by which *inter alia* he restored Peter to the gathering in of half the tithes and condemned William to restore to Peter the half part then gathered in by him and in the expenses run up on Peter's part in the case before him; from which, on the co-litigants' part, appeal was made to the apostolic see. At the supplication to the pope to commit and entrust[5] to some upright men in those parts, to be heard, examined, decided, and duly determined, with their annexed, connected, and dependent matters, the causes: of the said appeal and of anything attempted and innovated after and against it; of the nullity of the said process and sentence and of each and every other thing done in any way by Cuthbert and Peter and any other judges and persons to the co-litigants' prejudice in connection with the above; and of the whole principal matter, the pope hereby commands that the above three (or two or one of them), having summoned Peter and others concerned and having heard both sides, taking cognizance even of the principal matter, shall decree what is just, without appeal, causing, by ecclesiastical censure, what they have decreed to be strictly observed; and moreover compel witnesses, etc. Notwithstanding etc.

Humilibus supplicum votis libenter annuimus ...
phi de agnell(is) / M / M xij de Campania

1   or perhaps *Fformage*
2   or *Norsendi*
3   or *Plare*
4   MS: *et*; *recte*: 'ut'
5   MS: *committere et mandare*; unusual formulation here.

289[1]   **28 November 1514**   *Reg. Lat.* 1314, fo 24[r-v]

To the bishop of Coventry and Lichfield, commission and mandate. A recent petition to the pope on the part of Robert Dodde, layman, and Cicely Coton', woman, d. Coventry and Lichfield, stated that for certain sensible reasons they want to marry, but because at another time Robert stood godfather to a certain male child of Cicely's by a former husband now deceased, Robert and Cicely are unable to fulfil their desire in the matter without an apostolic dispensation. In view of the above and certain other reasons expressed to him, the pope – at Robert and Cicely's supplication – hereby commissions and commands the above bishop – if it is so and Cicely has not been abducted on this account – to dispense Robert and Cicely, the impediment of the spiritual relationship arising from the foregoing notwithstanding, to contract marriage and remain therein, declaring any offspring of the marriage legitimate.

Oblate nobis nuper pro parte ... petitionis series continebat ...
.P. Lambertus. / M / M L de Campania

1   *Cf.* below, no. 295 (abortive).

290   12 October 1514   *Reg. Lat.* 1314, fos 61ʳ-62ʳ

Union etc. At a recent petition on the part of John Denham, BTheol, rector of the parish church of Northkyllvorth [also spelt *Northkylvorth, Northkylwort, Northkylworth, Northkilvorth*] *alias* Kyllvorthrabbas, d. Lincoln, the pope hereby unites etc. the parish church of Tynwell, d. Lincoln, (whose annual value does not exceed 6 English pounds), provision of which was made canonically to John at another time when it was vacant *certo modo*, if he acquires it, with all its rights and appurtenances, to the above church of Northkyllvorth, which he holds, for as long as he does so, to the effect that John may, on his own authority, in person or by proxy, freely take and retain corporal possession of the church of Tynwell and the rights and appurtenances aforesaid, for as long as he holds Northkyllvorth, and convert its fruits etc. to his own uses and those of the said churches without licence of the local diocesan or of anyone else. Notwithstanding etc. The pope's will is, however, that the said church of Tynwell shall not, on account of this union etc., be defrauded of due services and the cure of souls in it shall not be neglected, but that its customary burdens shall be supported; and that on John's death or his resignation etc. of Northkyllvorth this union etc. shall be dissolved and so deemed and Tynwell shall revert to its original condition automatically. Given at Viterbo.[1]

Ad futuram rei memoriam. Romanum decet pontificem votis illis gratum prestare assensum ...
.P. Lambertus. / M / M xxxv de Campania

1   the 'V' converted from an 'R' (which had been the start, probably, of 'Rome apud Sanctum Petrum')

291   28 July 1514   *Reg. Lat.* 1314, fos 62ᵛ-63ᵛ

To William Stynt,[1] rector of the parish church of Halbant[2], d. Winchester, dispensation. Some time ago, Julius II by letters of his dispensed William to receive and retain together for life any two benefices, etc. [as above, no. 6, to '...retain them together for life, as above'], as is more fully contained in those letters.[3] The pope – at his supplication – hereby further dispenses William (who, as he asserts, holds the parish churches of Halbant and Meonstoke [also spelt *Me'stoke*], d. Winchester, by the said dispensation) to receive and retain for life together with the said churches,[4] or with any two other incompatible benefices held by him by virtue of the said dispensation, any third benefice, etc. [as above, no. 6].

Vite ac morum honestas …
.P. Lambertus. / M / M Lxx de Campania

1   *See* note 3 below.
2   second occurence written *Albant* with a small 'h' above the 'A'
3   Summarised in *CPL*, XVIII, at no. 820, where William Stynt, rector of *Hawant*, is designated LLB in the address clause, and where the incipit of his letter (an *ad duo* dispensation with indult for non-residence) is (as appropriate for a degree-holder): *Litterarum scientia, vite…* However, the present entry contains no indication whatever of Stynt having a degree of any sort. The discrepancy may well be simply an outcome of the supplications for the two letters being handled by different – more or less well-informed – proctors. Technically, possession of a degree put the petitioner into a preferred category and so it would always be sound business practice to mention it. The grantee was in fact LLB by April 1501 (Emden, *Oxford*, p. 1812).
4   *de Halbant et Me'stoke* is inserted in margin at end of line, initialled *M*

292   3 October 1514   *Reg. Lat.* 1314, fos 73ʳ-74ᵛ

Indulgences as below. Wishing that the church of the monastery of B. Mary the Virgin of Graces (*de Gratiis*) by the citadel or tower of London, OCist, d. London, (in which, as the pope has learned, the head of B. Anne, the mother of the said B. Mary the Virgin, is, as is piously believed, honourably conserved and continually venerated by Christ's faithful on the feast of St Anne as well as on other days of the year, and to which [sc. the church] abbot Richard and <the convent>[1] of the said monastery are singularly devoted), be held in greater veneration, that it be duly repaired, conserved, and maintained in its structural parts and buildings, that its ecclesiastical furnishings and ornaments necessary for divine service be decently supported; and that the faithful flock willingly to the said church out of devotion and contribute there for the above because they see themselves thereby abundantly refreshed there with the gift of heavenly grace, the pope – assured of the mercy of Almighty God and of the authority of His Apostles BB. Peter and Paul – hereby grants to all the faithful, of both sexes, who, being truly penitent and contrite,[2] have devoutly visited the said church from noon on the Vigil of the feast of St Anne until sunset on the day immediately following the said feast of St Anne, viz.: <for two>[3] days and a half, and likewise from noon on the Vigil of the feast of the Annunciation of B. Mary until sunset on the feast of the Annunciation itself, and also on the Wednesday, Thursday, Friday and Saturday after the first Sunday of Lent; and who have contributed to the repair, conservation, maintenance and support aforesaid; and also who have devoutly said the Lord's Prayer with the Angelic Salutation or the Psalm *de Profundis* for the salvation of the souls of the late John Langton', formerly abbot of the said monastery, of the others whose bodies rest in the said church and its cemetery, and of all the other faithful departed:

for each time they have done it, all the indulgences and remissions of sins which have been granted to those visiting the Lateran, St Peter's, St Paul's and the other basilicas and churches of the stations of Rome and outside its walls, at Lent and the other times of the year in which the said stations are celebrated, and which they would and could obtain if they were to personally visit the basilicas and churches of Rome and outside its walls on the station days. Further, the pope hereby grants to abbot Richard and to the abbot of the said monastery for the time being and, when it is vacant, to the prior of the said monastery for the time being or his deputy, faculty of appointing <as many>[4] suitable confessors as seems to be expedient, seculars or regulars, or a combination of seculars and regulars, who, on the said days, when they have diligently heard the confessions of the faithful flocking to the said church to obtain the said indulgences may absolve them and each one of them from all their sins, crimes, excesses and delicts, in any cases even in ones reserved to the apostolic see (except for those contained in the bull customarily read on Holy Thursday [in *die Cene Domini*] and enjoin a salutary penance on them for the sins etc. committed; and who may also commute any vows into other works of piety – with the exception only of the Holy Land vow, the vow of the visit of the tombs of the Apostles Peter and Paul and of St James in Compostella and the vows of chastity and religion – and relax any oaths, without prejudice to anyone. And the pope decrees that the said indulgences must be deemed to be in no way comprehended under any revocations or suspensions of any indulgences made for the time by the pope and the apostolic see, even ones made while the indulgence for the fabric of St Peter's and for the crusade lasts, under whatsoever tenors and with any clauses, even ones derogatory of derogatory clauses, but are always to be excepted from any revocations etc. The present letters are to be valid for all time. Given at Civita Castellana.

Universis Christifidelibus presentes litteras inspecturis[5] ... *Pastoris eterni qui non vult mortem sed conversionem peccatoris vices meritis licet imparibus gerentes ...*
.P. Lambertus / JoA: / JoA: C: Nardinus

1   *canonicus* deleted in line, initialled *JoA.*; *conventus* inserted in margin, initialled *JoA.*
2   MS: *contritis*; 'confessis', which is often found at this point, would not be required here as letter makes special provision for confession.
3   *predictos* deleted in line, initialled *JoA*; *per duos* inserted in margin, initialled *JoA.*
4   *tot* inserted in margin; initialled *JoA*
5   *Universis ... inspecturis* is written in bollatica; and – with *LEO et cetera* – forms the first line of the entry. Bollatica is also used for the capital 'C' of *Cupientes* and (once) for the 'M' of *Marie. Cf.* above, no. 191, note 1.

293[1]   **29 September 1514**   *Reg. Lat.* 1314, fos 74ᵛ-76ʳ

To William, abbot of the monastery of B. Mary, Oseney at Oxford (*iuxta Oxoniam*),[2] OSA, d. Lincoln, dispensation as below. Some time ago, Julius II by letters of his dispensed abbot William to receive and retain *in commendam* for life together with the above monastery, over which he was then presiding, or with any other monastery over which he might preside in the future, one, and without them, any two other benefices, with or without cure, regular of the aforesaid or any other order, or secular, even if the [regular]³ benefices should be priories, *prepositure, prepositatus, personatus*, dignities, administrations or offices, and the secular benefices should be parish churches or their perpetual vicarages, or chantries, free chapels, hospitals or annual services usually assigned to secular clerics in title of a perpetual ecclesiastical benefice, and of abbot William's patronage, as much by reason of himself personally as of his monastery, or of the patronage of any other ecclesiastic or lay persons, and of whatsoever tax or annual value, even if the priories, *prepositure, prepositatus*, dignities, *personatus*, administrations or offices were customarily elective and had cure of souls and pertained to abbot William's collation, presentation or provision, if he obtained them otherwise canonically, to resign them, at once or successively, as often as he pleased, and cede the commends and in their place receive up to two other, similar or dissimilar, benefices, with or without cure, regular of the aforesaid or any other order, or secular – provided that the regular benefices be not conventual dignities or claustral offices – and retain them *in commendam* for life, as above, as is more fully contained in those letters.⁴ At his supplication, the pope hereby further dispenses abbot William to receive and retain *in commendam* for life together with the above monastery, over which he is understood to preside still, with another [benefice] now, perhaps, or with any two other benefices held by him at the time by virtue of the said dispensation, any third secular benefice, with or without cure, even if a parish church or its perpetual vicarage, or a chantry, free chapel, hospital or annual service, usually assigned to secular clerics in title of a perpetual ecclesiastical benefice, and of lay patronage and of whatsoever tax or annual value, if he obtains it otherwise canonically, to resign it as often as he pleases and cede the commend and in its place receive another, similar or dissimilar, secular benefice, with or without cure – provided that of three such benefices not more than two be parish churches or their perpetual vicarages – and retain it *in commendam* for life as above. Notwithstanding etc. With the proviso that this third benefice shall not, on this account, be defrauded of due services and the cure of souls in it (if any) shall not be neglected; but that its customary burdens shall be supported.

Personam tuam nobis et apostolice sedi devotam tuis exigentibus meritis paterna benivolentia prosequen(tes) illa tibi favorabiliter concedimus ...
.P. Lambertus. / JoA: / JoA: Lxx: Nardinus

1   The first line of the entry (*LEO et cetera ... Beate*) is written in a script reminiscent of bollatica; likewise the dating clause (*Dat. ... anno secundo*). Cf. above, no. 191, note 1.
2   sympathetic reading; written *Oxoma'*
3   *secularia*; *recte*: 'regularia'?
4   unknown to the *CPL*

294¹ 1 October 1514   *Reg. Lat.* 1314, fo 125ʳ⁻ᵛ

To Thomas Dayly *alias* Doyly, perpetual vicar of the parish church of All Saints, Marcham [also spelt *Mercham*], d. Salisbury. Indult – at his supplication – to Thomas – who, as he asserts, is in his sixtieth year of age or thereabouts and has no strength left in his body and, on this account, cannot conveniently serve the perpetual vicarage of the above parish church (which he holds) in things divine – while residing in any one of the benefices held by him now and at the time or in the Roman curia or attending a *studium generale*, not to be bound to reside in other benefices held by him, with or without cure, even if they should be parish churches or their perpetual vicarages, nor to be liable to be compelled to do so by anyone against his will. Notwithstanding etc. With the proviso that the above vicarage and other benefices in question shall not, on this account, be defrauded of due services; and that the cure of souls in the vicarage and (if any) the other incompatible benefices shall not be neglected, but that it [sc. the cure] shall be diligently exercised and the vicarage served in things divine by good and capable vicars to whom suitable sustenance shall be given from the proceeds of the vicarage and other benefices; and that customary burdens of the other benefices shall be supported. Given at Nepi.

Vite ac morum honestas ...
.P. Lambertus / JoA: / JoA: xx: Nard(inus):

1   A corresponding petition is at *Reg. Suppl.* 1468, fo. 79ᵛ.

295   [–]¹   *Reg. Lat.* 1314, fo 126ᵛ

Abortive entry: start only of marriage dispensation in *forma commissoria* addressed to the bishop of Coventry and Lichfield in favour of Robert Dodde, layman, and Cicely Coton', woman, both of d. Coventry and Lichfield.

Occupies lower half of page and extends, for thirteen lines, to opening of operative part of letter: *Nos igitur ex premissis et certis aliis nobis expositis causis huiusmodi supplicationibus inclinati fraternitati tue de qua in hiis et aliis specialem in domino fiduciam obtinemus* [ends]

obtinemus is at the end of the last line of the page (the last of the quintern). A new entry begins at top of fo 127ʳ (the first page of a new quintern). The original foliation is continuous. However, the surrounds argue that the entry probably continued on another page, now lost (perhaps discarded when the liber was assembled and bound). The upper half of fo 126ᵛ is occupied by the end of an unrelated letter drawn under 30 October 1514.

No administrative notes: no abbreviator's name; and no initial or subscription of a registry master. The proem is the usual one for letters of this class: *Oblate nobis ...*

The entry is cancelled by two diagonal strokes; but there is no explanatory note. Trifling differences of spelling apart, the entry matches, so far as it goes, the dispensation in favour of Cotton and Dodd enregistered by the same scribe at fo 24ʳ⁻ᵛ of the same register (no. 289 above). Presumably the same document was behind both entries and all we are looking at is a clerical hiccup.

1   Entry does not extend to dating clause.

296   9 November 1514   *Reg. Lat.* 1315, fos 12ʳ-13ʳ

To John Crone, perpetual vicar of the parish church of Brappole [first spelt *Brap'ole*], d. Salisbury. Dispensation and indult etc. [as above, no. 2].[1]

Vite ac morum honestas ...
.P. Lambertus / JoA. / JoA: L²: Nardinus

1   Save for small textual oddities (e.g. (?)*unam* where 'una cum' occurs, rightly, in no. 2).
2   *See above*, no. 13, note 2.

297   10 November 1514   *Reg. Lat.* 1315, fos 13ᵛ-14ʳ

To Thomas Boltou,[1] canon of the monastery, called house, of B. Mary, Cou'han, OPrem, d. York (who, as he asserts, is expressly <professed>[2] of the order).[3] Dispensation – at his supplication – to receive and retain any benefice, with or without cure, usually held by secular clerics, etc. [as above, no. 43].

Religionis zelus, vite ac morum honestas ...
.P. Lambertus / JoA: / JoA: xxx: Nardinus

1   final letter formed as 'u' (rather than 'n')
2   *p(ro)fexus ex* deleted and initialled *JoA*; *professus* inserted in margin initialled *JoA*
3   This information comes from a notwithstanding clause.

298   19 March 1514 x 18 March 1515   *Reg. Lat.* 1315, fos 47ʳ-50ᵛ

The entry, which is abortive, comprises seven items, viz.

[1] To Alexander Steuuart, cleric, d. St Andrews. Absolution preliminary to the commend to him of the Augustinian monastery of Inchaffray (*Insule Missarum*), d. Dunblane. The dating clause is incomplete: *Dat. Rome apud Sanctum Petrum anno et cetera millesimo quingentesimo quartodecimo* ...... [about half a line left blank in MS] *pontificatus nostri anno secundo*. (*Cf.* no. 304 below)

[2] To same. Consistorial commend of Inchaffray. *Dat. ut supra.* (*Cf.* no. 303 below)

[3] Conclusion to the convent of Inchaffray. *Dat. ut supra.* (*Cf.* no. 303 (i) below)

[4] To the bishops of Dunkeld and Brechin. Mandate to receive from Alexander the usual oath of fealty. *Dat. ut supra.* (*Cf.* no. 305 below)

[5] Conclusion to James, king of Scots. *Dat. ut supra.* (*Cf.* no. 303 (iii) below)

[6] Conclusion to the vassals of the monastery of Inchaffray. *Dat. ut supra.* (*Cf.* no. 303 (ii) below)

[7] Conclusion to the bishop of Dunblane. *Dat. ut supra.* (*Cf.* no. 303 (iv) below)

In the right margin at the start of the entry – the position reserved for abbreviators – the enregistering scribe has noted five names: *A de alverottis; .L. Dalago; .G. de gibraleon'; .H. Berna(r)di;* and *Hie Millinus.* In the left margin at the start: *JoA;* beneath it (in the master's hand?): *No(n) fuit ap(ro)bat(um) quia fuit error;* and again (in the left margin of fo 50ᵛ, near the end of the entry): *No(n) fuit ap(ro)bat(um) quia fuit Error. Est scriptu(m) i(n) aliu(m) Qui(n)ternu(m).* In conformity with the note there is no magistral subscription. Though clearly empty the entry has not, however, been struck through.

The entry has abnormal features and it might be argued that they explain why the entry was not approved. Normally, the principal letter and conclusions ([2], [3], and [5]-[7]), the absolution ([1]), and the 'commissio receptionis iuramenti' ([4]) were enregistered separately (as indeed these were elsewhere) and the combination made an unusual enregistration entity. It was also unusual (though not unknown) for the registry scribe to note the names of the minor abbreviators who expedited the conclusions. Ordinarily, the name of the senior abbreviator (here Alvarottis) who expedited the principal letter (as also the absolution and the commissio) sufficed. Additionally, the space left blank in the dating clause suggests that the principal letter and, since they are *Dat. ut supra,* the other letters, may have been enregistered prematurely from drafts (a common enough practice) raising the possibility that the text was erroneous. However, dating clause and trifling verbal differences apart, the letters as enregistered here do not differ from the successful enregistrations at nos 303-305 below. Despite the points of interest the explanation for the non-approval would appear to be the prosaic one: that the items had been enregistered elsewhere (i.e. in the quintern which now forms part of *Reg. Lat.* 1316) and that the present entry was simply a mistake. Indeed, although it is somewhat ambiguous, that is the obvious interpretation of the explanatory note.

299   22 February 1515   *Reg. Lat.* 1316, fos 1ʳ-3ᵛ

Union etc. At a recent petition on the part of Henry Glover, rector of the parish church of B. Mary the Virgin, Whatfelde[1] [also spelt *Whatfeld*], d. Norwich, the pope hereby unites etc. the parish church of St Margaret, Downehm',[2] d. London (whose annual value does not exceed 5 English pounds), with all its rights and appurtenances, to the above church of Whatfelde, which Henry holds by apostolic dispensation together with that of Downehm', for as long as he holds Whatfelde, to the effect that he may, on his own authority, in person or by proxy, take [anew][3] or continue in, and retain corporal possession of Downehm' and the rights and appurtenances aforesaid, for as long as he holds Whatfelde, and convert its fruits etc. to his own uses and those of the said churches, without licence of the local diocesan or of anyone else. Notwithstanding etc. The pope's will is, however, that the said church of Downehm' shall not, on account of this union etc., be defrauded of due services and the cure of souls in it shall not be neglected, but that its customary burdens shall be supported; and that on Henry's death or his resignation etc. of the church of Whatfelde this union etc. shall be dissolved and be so deemed and that of Downehm' shall revert to its original condition automatically.

Ad futuram rei memoriam. Romanum decet pontificem votis illis gratum prestare assensum ...
.P. La(m)bertu[s] / JoA: / : JoA. xxxv: Nardinus

1   in one instance written *dWhatfelde*; evidently for 'd[e] Whatfelde'
2   The name is spelt thus throughout; but in two instances 'de' is wanting before *Downehm'*
3   *dono*; for 'denuo' ('de novo')?

300   22 February 1515   *Reg. Lat.* 1316, fos 3ᵛ-6ʳ

To John Hichecok, rector of the parish church of Brongh'ton' [also spelt *Brough'ton'*], d. Lincoln. Dispensation and indult etc. [as above, no. 2].

Vite ac morum honestas ...
.P. Lambertus / JoA: / : JoA: L:¹ Nardinus

1   *See above*, no. 13, note 2.

301   22 February 1515   *Reg. Lat.* 1316, fos 41ʳ-42ʳ

To John Bristowe, monk of the monastery, called house, of Leuuen',¹ OClun, d. Chichester (who, as he asserts, is expressly professed of the above order).² Dispensation – at his supplication – to receive and retain any benefice, with or without cure, usually held by secular clerics, etc. [as above, no. 43].

Religionis zelus, vite ac morum honestas ...
.P. La(m)bertus / JoA: / : JoA: xxx: Nard(inus):

1   Thus the second occurrence, where MS has: *d(e) Leuuen'* – an improvement on the evident confusion in the address clause, viz.: (?)*dlew* (deleted) *Deleuuen'* (the first 'e' being squeezed in, as an afterthought, between the 'D' and the 'l').
2   This information comes from a notwithstanding clause.

302   25 January 1515   *Reg. Lat.* 1316, fos 102ʳ-104ʳ

To William Robynson', perpetual vicar of the parish church of Sydelesham, d. Chichester. Dispensation and indult etc. [as above, no. 2]. Given at Magliana, d. Porto.

Vite ac morum honestas ...
.P. Lambert(us) / JoA: / JoA: Lx: Nardinus

303[1]   13[2] November 1514   *Reg. Lat.* 1316, fos 104[r]-108[v]

To Alexander Steuuar',[3] cleric, d. St Andrews, consistorial commend. Some time ago, during the rule of the late abbot Laurence, the pope specially reserved provision to the monastery of Inchaffray (*Insule Missarum*), OSA, d. Dunblane, to his own disposition; and afterwards the monastery was left vacant by abbot Laurence's death outside the Roman curia; and the pope – *motu proprio* – under date 3 October, first year [1513], granted it, thus vacant, to be commended to Peter, cardinal priest of the title of S Eusebio, to be held, ruled and governed by him for life. However, cardinal Peter has this day, spontaneously and freely, ceded the grant of this commend – in respect of which apostolic letters had not been drawn up – into the hands of the pope who has admitted the cession; and, on this account, the said monastery is understood to be vacant still as above, provision thereto being reserved as above. Wishing to make provision of a capable and suitable governor to the monastery to rule and direct it [as well as to assist Alexander to be supported more conveniently],[4] the pope, on the advice of the cardinals, hereby commends the monastery, thus vacant, with all its rights and appurtenances, to Alexander to be held, ruled and governed by him for life – even together with all benefices, with and without cure, secular or regular (of any military and other order) which, even by any apostolic grants and dispensations, he holds now and in the future, *in titulum* and *commendam*, or otherwise; and with annual pensions which he receives now and in the future – committing to him the care, rule and administration of the monastery in spiritualities and temporalities. The pope's will is, however, that divine worship and the usual number of monks and ministers in the said monastery shall not, on account of this commend, be diminished; but that the customary burdens of the monastery and its convent shall be supported and that – when all other charges have been deducted and, if Alexander's *mensa* is separate and apart from the conventual one, after a fourth part of all the monastery's fruits has been bestowed annually on the restoration of the fabric, or on the purchase of ornaments, vestments, and sacred furniture, or on the sustenance and maintenance of the poor, according to the greater need, or, if the *mensa* is common, after a third part of all the monastery's fruits has been bestowed annually on the restoration of the fabric etc. and on the maintenance of the monks – Alexander may – the said due burdens having been supported – make disposition of the rest of the monastery's fruits etc. just as abbots could and ought to do, alienation of the monastery's immovable goods and precious movables being however forbidden; and that, before he involves himself in the rule and administration of the monastery in any way, Alexander shall take the usual oath of fealty before the bishops of Dunkeld and Brechin (or one of them) in accordance with the form which the pope is sending enclosed (*introclusam*) under his *bulla*;[5] and the pope, by other letters of his,[6] commands that the said bishops (or one of them) shall receive the oath from Alexander in the name of the pope and the Roman church.

    Conclusions to: (i) The convent of the monastery of Inchaffray; (ii) the vassals of the monastery; (iii) James, king of Scots; (iv) the bishop of Dunblane.

Romani pontificis providentia circumspecta ... The conclusions begin:
(i) *Hodie monasterium vestrum* ... (ii), (iii), (iv) *Hodie monasterium et cetera* ...
A De Alverottis;. G. De Gibralion / JoA: / JoA: xvj: viij: viij: viij: viij:
Nardinus

1   There is an aborted enregistration of this commend (together with the absolution to which it gave rise) in
     another register (*see above*, no. 298). The tenor of the two entries (which may have been made by different
     scribes) is the same. However, the aborted entry supplies additional names of authenticating officials. And
     there are a few small-scale textual discrepancies (e.g. as in note 4, below); and the orthography is not
     identical.
2   MS: *Idus*; reading *Id(ib)us*; but there may be an omission before *Idus*. In the absence of corroborative
     evidence the day-date cannot be regarded as totally safe. The dating clause of the abortive entry (note 1
     above) has a blank in it.
3   spelt *Steuuart* in the conclusion to the convent (the only other occurrence of the name)
4   'quam tibi ut commodius substentari valeas' (which occurs, as usual, in the abortive entry, above, no. 298)
     is wanting in the present entry.
5   *Cf.* below, no. 384, note 4.
6   below, no. 305

304[1] **13**[2] **November 1514**   *Reg. Lat.* 1316, fos 108ᵛ-109ᵛ

To Alexander Steuart, cleric, d. St Andrews. Since the pope, on the advice of the
cardinals, intends this day to commend the monastery of Inchaffray (*Insule Missarum*),
OSA, d. Dunblane, at present without an abbot *certo modo*, to Alexander to be held,
ruled and governed by him for life, he hereby absolves him from any [sentences] of
excommunication, suspension and interdict etc. under which he may perhaps lie, so far
only as regards the taking effect of the said commend and each of the relevant [letters].[3]
Notwithstanding etc.

Apostolice sedis consueta clementia ad ea libenter intendit ...
A d(e) Averottis[4] / *JoA:* / :*JoA: xvj: Nardinus*

1   There is an aborted enregistration of this absolution (together with the commend which gave rise to it) in
     another register (*see above*, no. 298).
2   as note 2 of previous entry
3   *littere* wanting
4   *sic*; beneath it *G de Gibralio(n)* deleted

305   13[1] **November 1514**   *Reg. Lat.* 1316, fos 109ᵛ-110ʳ

To the bishops of Dunkeld and Brechin, mandate. Since the pope [has] this day
[commended] the monastery of Inchaffray (*Insule Missarum*) [to Alexander Steuuar']
etc., [as] is more fully contained [in his letters drawn up in that regard],[2] he – wishing
to spare Alexander the commendator, who lives in those parts, the labour and expense
of being compelled on that account to come in person to the apostolic see – hereby
commands that the above two (or one of them) shall receive from him in the name of
the pope and the Roman church the usual oath of fealty in accordance with [the form][3]
the pope is sending enclosed (*introclusam*) under his *bulla*[4] and shall cause the form of
oath which Alexander takes to be sent, verbatim, to the pope, at once, by their own
messenger, by his letters patent, marked with his seal.

Cum nos hodie ...
.A. De alverottis / JoA. / : JoA: xij: Nardinus

1   as note 2 of no. 303 above
2   MS: *monasterium Insule Missarum et cetera plenius continetur*, referring to the principal letter (no. 303 above)
3   *formam* wanting (just one of many small oddities)
4   *Cf.* below, no. 384, note 4.

306   22 February 1515   *Reg. Lat.* 1316, fos 281ʳ-283ʳ

Mandate to commend to Claude de Mirabel, cleric, d. Limoges, the priory of Blankafort, OSA, d. Bourges, (whose annual value does not exceed 24 gold ducats of the camera), which Walter (*Galterus*) Stuart, was recently holding *in commendam* by apostolic concession and dispensation and which Walter has this day spontaneously and freely ceded through his specially appointed proctor Andrew Cave, cleric, d. Paris, into the hands of the pope who admitted this cession.

   "Walter Stuart" is not identified beyond the details given above.[1] Entry otherwise of no interest to the Calendar.

Nobilitas generis, vite ac morum honestas ...
G. d(e) prato. / JoA: / Jo: xxx: Nard(inus): –

1   i.e. not even his diocese is supplied

307   11 January 1515   *Reg. Lat.* 1317, fos 39ʳ-42ʳ

To the abbot of the monastery *de Flumine Dei* [Abbeyshrule], d. Ardagh[1] *alias* Meath, and Fergal Osyridean, canon of the church of Kilmore, and Maurice Macochluyn, canon of the church of Clonmacnois[2], mandate in favour of Ross, abbot of the monastery of B. Mary, *de Benedictione Dei* [Kilbeggan], OCist, d. Meath.[3] The pope has learned that the rectory of the parish church of St James and the perpetual vicarage of the parish church of St David, of the places of Newtown [*de Villanova*] and Armirchayr, d. Meath, have been vacant *certo modo* and are vacant at present, although Walter Macvalront' has detained the rectory and Tuahlanus Okyngay the vicarage – bearing themselves as priests – with no title or support of law, of their own temerity and *de facto*, for a certain time, as they do. At a recent petition on the part of abbot Ross (who asserts that the annual value of the rectory does not exceed 12, and of the vicarage, 30, marks sterling), the pope [– not having certain knowledge of the foregoing – hereby commands that the above three (or two or one of them), if, having summoned Walter and Tuahlanus and others concerned,][4] they find the rectory and vicarage to be vacant (howsoever etc.) shall unite etc. them (even if they have been vacant for so long that by the Lateran statutes their collation has lawfully devolved on the apostolic see etc.), with all their rights and appurtenances, to the said monastery, for as long as abbot Ross presides over it; to the effect that abbot Ross may, on his own authority, in person or by proxy, take and retain corporal possession of the rectory and vicarage and the said rights and appurtenances, for as long as he presides over the monastery; and convert their fruits etc. to his own uses and those of the monastery and of the rectory and vicarage, without licence of the local diocesan or of anyone else, having removed Walter and Tualhanus and any other unlawful detainers. [Curbing] gainsayers etc. Notwithstanding etc. The pope's will is, however, that the rectory and vicarage shall not, on account of the said union etc., be defrauded of due services and the cure of souls in them shall not be neglected; but that their customary burdens shall be supported; and that on abbot Ross's death or his resignation etc. of the monastery this union etc. shall be dissolved and be so deemed and the rectory and vicarage shall revert to their original condition automatically.

Apostolice sedis providentia circumspecta ...
p la(m)bert(us) / JoA: / :JoA: xxv: Nardinus

1   *Arch* deleted (not initialled) before *Ardachaden'*
2   MS: *Cluonen.*; *recte*: 'Cluanen'
3   MS: *dicte diocesis* – evidently referring to Meath
4   evident omission in MS suppliable conjecturally: *dicti Valterus et Tuahlanus rectoriam et vicariam predictas detinuerint presentibus pro expressis habentes (ac certam notitiam non habentes) huiusmodi supplicationibus inclinati discretioni vestre per apostolica scripta mandamus quatenus vos vel duo aut unus vestrum si vocatis dictis Valtero et Tuahlano et aliis qui fuerint evocandi*

308   4 February 1515   *Reg. Lat.* 1317, fos 242ʳ-245ʳ

To the preceptor of the house of St John the Baptist, Ruidum,¹ d. Elphin, and Fergal Osyrideair, canon of the church of Kilmore, and the official of Elphin, mandate in favour of Hobert Okellay, canon of the church of Elphin. The pope has learned that Malachy Okellay, perpetual vicar of the parish church of Ahassagrachaman [also spelt *Ahaffagrachaman, Ahassgrachaman*], d. Elphin, spontaneously and freely, resigned the perpetual vicarage of the said parish church, which he was then holding, before a certain notary and witnesses, outside the Roman curia; and that the perpetual vicarage of the parish church of Theachbuy [also spelt *Teachbuy*], d. Elphin, is vacant *certo modo* at present and has been vacant for so long that by the Lateran statutes its collation has lawfully devolved on the apostolic see, although Thyus Offlalluyn, who bears himself as a priest, has detained it, with no title and no support of law, of his own temerity and *de facto*, for a certain time, as he still does. At a recent petition on the part of Hobert (who asserts that he holds a canonry of the above church of Elphin; that this canonry is worthless;² and that the annual value of the fruits etc. of the vicarage of Ahassagrachaman does not exceed 8, and of Theachbuy, 5, marks sterling), to the pope to erect and institute the vicarage of Ahassagrachaman into a simple prebend of the said church of Elphin and unite etc. the vicarage of Theachbuy to the said canonry and erected prebend, for Hobert's lifetime, the pope – not having certain knowledge of the foregoing – hereby commands that the above three (or two or one of them) – if it is thus and when the matter of the resignation has been lawfully established before them – shall admit the resignation, for this once only, insofar as it was not duly admitted; and, after it has been admitted by them, having summoned the bishop and chapter of Elphin and Thyus and others concerned and those interested in the union, shall erect and institute the vicarage of Ahassagrachaman into a simple prebend of the church of Elphin, without prejudice to anyone; and unite etc. the vicarage of Theachbuy (howsoever the vicarages are vacant etc., even if Ahassagrachaman has been vacant for so long that by the Lateran statutes its collation has lawfully devolved on the apostolic see, and even if it and Theachbuy are specially reserved etc.) to the said canonry and prebend, for Hobert's lifetime; and, in the event of this erection, institution and union etc., collate and assign the newly erected prebend, being vacant, with the annex in question and all rights and appurtenances, to Hobert; inducting him etc. having removed Thyus and any other unlawful detainers from them and causing Hobert (or his proctor) to be admitted to the prebend and causing its fruits etc., rights and obventions and those of the annex to be delivered to him. [Curbing] gainsayers etc. Notwithstanding etc. The pope's will is, however, that the said vicarages shall not, on this account, be defrauded of due services and the cure of souls in them shall not be neglected; but that their customary burdens shall be supported; and that on Hobert's death or his resignation etc. of the canonry and prebend the said erection, institution and union etc. shall be extinguished and be so deemed and the vicarages shall revert to their original condition automaticaly. Given at Palo, d. Porto.

Apostolice sedis circumspecta benignitas ad ea libenter intendit ...
phi de Agnell(is) / *JoA:* / *:JoA: xxx: tertio decimo k(a)l(endas) Martij Anno secundo:*
[17 February 1515]*, Nardinus*

1   the minims variously readable
2   literally 'that there are no fruits etc. of this canonry'

309   28 January 1515   *Reg. Lat.* 1317, fos 258ʳ-260ʳ

To the archdeacon of Achadeo, Thady[1] Osullywan, canon of the church of Ardfert, and Donat Okcallachan, canon of the church of Cork, mandate in favour of Cornelius Ohullachan, priest, d. Ross. The pope has learned that the perpetual vicarage of the parish church of Cillcrochan, d. Cork, has been vacant *certo modo* and is vacant at present, although Richard Omathunna, who bears himself as a priest, has detained it, with no title and no support of law, of his own temerity and *de facto*, for a certain time, as he still does. He hereby commands that the above three (or two or one of them), if, having summoned Richard and others concerned, they find the vicarage (whose annual value does not exceed 16 marks sterling) to be vacant (howsoever etc.), shall collate and assign it (even if it has been vacant for so long that by the Lateran statutes its collation has lawfully devolved on the apostolic see etc.), with all its rights and appurtenances, to Cornelius, inducting him etc. having removed Richard and any other unlawful detainer and causing Cornelius (or his proctor) to be admitted to the vicarage and its fruits etc., rights and obventions to be delivered to him. [Curbing] gainsayers etc. Notwithstanding etc.

Vite ac morum honestas …
phi de agnell(is) / JoA: / JoA: xv: Quarto Id(us) februarij Anno Se(cun)do: [10 February 1515], *Nardinus*

1   MS: *Thaeo*; for 'Thateo'?

310   22 November 1514   *Reg. Lat.* 1318, fos 78^r-81^r

To the prior of the monastery, <usually>[1] governed by a prior, of St Mary, ?Drumlane (*de Torsolato*), d. Kilmore, and the archdeacon of the church of Kilmore, and the official of Kilmore, mandate in favour of Maurice Macdonnallynd, cleric. d. [Clogher].[2] The pope has learned that the rectory of the parish church, called *plebs*, of St Congall (*Sancti Cogally*), of the places of Gaulum[3] [and] Darteny, and the perpetual vicarage of the parish church, called *plebs*, of St Tiernach of the places of Cluenos and Clanchellovyd, d. Clogher, are vacant *certo modo* at present and have been vacant for so long that by the Lateran statutes their collation has lawfully devolved on the apostolic see, although Patrick Magnihauna, who bears himself as a priest, has detained the rectory and vicarage, with no title and no support of law, of his own temerity and *de facto*, for a certain time, as he still does. At a recent petition on Maurice's part to the pope to erect and institute a canonry in the church of Clogher and the said rectory and vicarage and also the episcopal fourth of the parish of Drommyche', said diocese (which is customarily given in farm at the pleasure of the bishop of Clogher for the time, to some ecclesiastical person, for a certain annual payment or pension) into a simple prebend of the said church of Clogher, for Maurice's lifetime, the pope – not having certain knowledge of the foregoing; and wishing to give a special grace to Maurice (who asserts that at another time he was dispensed by apostolic authority, notwithstanding a certain accidental homicide perpetrated by him out of fear, to receive and retain any number of mutually compatible benefices, with or without cure, even if they should be canonries and prebends in cathedral churches, if conferred on him otherwise canonically), hereby commands that the above three (or two or one of them), if it is thus, having summoned the above bishop and the chapter of Clogher and Patrick and others concerned, shall erect and institute a canonry in the church of Clogher and the said rectory and vicarage (vacant howsoever etc.; even if specially reserved etc.) and also – with the consent of the present bishop of Clogher and after the usual pension has been paid to him and to the bishops of Clogher his successors – the said episcopal fourth into a simple prebend of the church of Clogher, for Maurice's lifetime, as above, without prejudice to anyone; and, in the event of this erection and institution, shall collate and assign the newly erected canonry and prebend (whose annual value does not exceed 35 marks sterling), being then vacant, with plenitude of canon law and all rights and appurtenances, to Maurice, inducting him etc. having removed Patrick and any other unlawful detainer and causing Maurice (or his proctor) to be received as a canon in the church of Clogher; and shall assign him a stall in the choir and a place in the chapter of the church of Clogher, with plenitude of canon law, and [causing] the fruits etc., rights and obventions of the canonry and prebend to be delivered to him. [Curbing] gainsayers by [the pope's] authority etc. Notwithstanding etc. The pope's will is, however, that the rectory and vicarage shall not, on this account, be defrauded of due services and the cure of souls in them shall not be neglected; but that their customary burdens shall be supported; and that on Maurice's death or his resignation etc of the canonry and prebend this erection and institution shall be extinguished and be so deemed and the rectory and vicarage shall revert to their original condition automatically.

Apostolice sedis circumspecta benignitas ad ea libenter intendit ...
Phi d(e) agnellis / M / M xx quinto id(us) decembris an(n)o secundo [9 December 1514], *de Campania*

1   (?)*sliti* in line deleted and initialled *M*; *soliti* inserted in margin initialled *M*
2   MS: *dicte diocesis* – evidently referring to Clogher.
3   the 'um' uncertain: the five minims (none dotted) capable of various readings

311 13 March[1] 1515						*Reg. Lat.* 1318, fos 249[v]-250[v]

Union etc. At a recent petition on the part of Richard Carlion', canon of the church of Glaysney, d. Exeter, the pope hereby unites etc. the perpetual vicarage of the parish church of Glumaco,[2] said diocese, (whose annual value does not exceed 16 pounds sterling), with all its rights and appurtenances, to the canonry and prebend of the above church, (to which canonry and prebend the parish church of Lansalose,[3] said diocese, is united by apostolic authority, for as long as Richard holds the canonry and prebend) which Richard holds together with the said vicarage, for as long as he holds the canonry and prebend, to the effect that he may, on his own authority, in person or by proxy, take and retain corporal possession of the vicarage and the rights and appurtenances aforesaid, for as long as he holds the canonry and prebend, and convert its fruits etc. to his own uses and those of the canonry and prebend and the vicarage, without licence of the local diocesan or of anyone else. Notwithstanding etc. The pope's will is, however, that the vicarage shall not, on account of this union etc., be defrauded of due services and the cure of souls in it shall not be neglected, but that its customary burdens shall be supported; and that on Richard's death or his resignation etc. of the canonry and prebend this union etc. shall be dissolved and be so deemed and the vicarage shall revert to its original condition automatically.

Ad futuram rei memoriam. Romanum decet pontificem votis illis gratum prestare assensum ...
.P. Lambertus. / JoA. / JoA. xxxv: Nardinus

1   (?) *Martii* altered to *Mai* in line deleted, initialled *JoA*; *Martii* inserted in margin initialled *JoA*
2   *recte*: '(de) Gluviaco'
3   third letter readable as 'n' or 'u'

312   12 January 1515   *Reg. Lat.* 1318, fos 250ᵛ-251ᵛ

Union etc. At a recent petition on the part of Richard Rawlyns, canon of the church of London, professor of theology (who asserts that he is almoner and counsellor of Henry, king of England), the pope hereby unites etc. the parish church of B. Mary the Virgin, Wolnoth' within the city of London, d. London (whose annual value does not exceed 24 pounds sterling; and to which [the parish church] of B. Mary the Virgin, Woforde, d. Worcester, is united by apostolic authority, for as long as Richard holds Wolnoth'), with all its rights and appurtenances, to the canonry and prebend of Bonnys[1] at Willesdon'[2] in the church of London, which Richard holds together with the above church of Wolnoth', for as long as he holds the canonry and prebend, to the effect that he may, on his own authority, in person or by proxy, take anew, or continue in, and retain corporal possession of the church of Wolnoth' and the rights and appurtenances aforesaid, for as long as he holds the canonry and prebend, and convert its fruits etc. to his own uses and those of the canonry and prebend and the church of Wolnoth', without licence of the local diocesan or of anyone else. Notwithstanding etc. The pope's will is, however, that the church of Wolnoth' shall not, on account of this union etc., be defrauded of due services and the cure of souls in it shall not be neglected, but that its customary burdens shall be supported; and that on Richard's death or his resignation etc. of the canonry and prebend this union etc. shall be dissolved and be so deemed and the church of Wolnoth' shall revert to its original condition automatically.

Ad futuram rei memoriam. Romanum decet pontificem votis illis gratum prestare assensum ...
.P. Lambertus. / JoA: / JoA: xxxv: Nardinus

1   or possibly *G-*; if Bonnys, possibly a corruption of 'bonis'
2   the first 'l' changed from a long 's'

313   13 March 1515   *Reg. Lat.* 1318, fo 252 ʳ⁻ᵛ

To Henry ApWillmsohn',[1] scholar, d. St David's. Dispensation – at his supplication – to him (who, as he asserts, is less than eighteen but more than fourteen years old; suffers a defect of birth as the son of a married man and an unmarried woman; and desires to become a cleric) to be promoted at the lawful age to all, even sacred and priest's, orders, and (after he has been duly marked with clerical character) as soon as he reaches his eighteenth year, to receive and retain any benefice, with cure or otherwise incompatible, and, hereafter, any benefice without cure, and, at the said lawful age, also any number of benefices, even with cure, otherwise compatible mutually and with the said cured or incompatible benefice, even if the benefice with cure or incompatible should be a parish church or its perpetual vicarage, and it as well as the compatible[2] benefices in question should be canonries and prebends, dignities, *personatus*, administrations or offices in cathedral, even metropolitan, or collegiate churches, or chantries, free chapels, hospitals or annual services usually assigned to

secular clerics in title of a perpetual ecclesiastical benefice, even if the dignities etc.
should be customarily elective and have cure of souls, if he obtains them otherwise
canonically, to resign them, at once or successively, simply or for exchange, as often
as he pleases, and in their place receive other, similar or dissimilar, benefices, viz.: one
with cure or otherwise incompatible in his said eighteenth year, and, hereafter, [one]
without cure, and, at the said lawful age, any number of compatible benefices, even
with cure, provided that the dignities in question be not major *post pontificalem* in
metropolitan or other cathedral churches or principal in collegiate churches – and
retain them as above. Notwithstanding the above defects of birth and age etc. With the
proviso that the incompatible benefice in question shall not, on this account, be
defrauded of due services and the cure of souls in it shall not be neglected.

Vite ac morum honestas …
.P. Lambertus. / JoA: / JoA: L: Nardinus

1   with additional *n* above the *m*
2   originally written *incompatibilia*; then, seemingly, the *in* deleted

314   28 November 1514   *Reg. Lat.* 1318, fo 253ʳ⁻ᵛ

To William Tony, rector of the parish church of St Helen, <Worcester>,[1] d. Worcester.
Dispensation and indult etc. [as above, no. 2].

Vite ac morum honestas …
.P. Lambertus / JoA: / JoA: Lx: Nard(inus):-

1   *Wigornien.* inserted (in enregistering scribe's hand) in left margin beneath the magistral initial (*JoA:*); below
     the insertion: *Nard(inus)*. The omission was apparently spotted quickly – just four lines below (in the
     narrative) *Wigornien. Wigornien. dioc(esis)* is written in line.

315   31 January 1515   *Reg. Lat.* 1318, fos 266ᵛ-267ᵛ

To Henry Ap Rice, BDec, rector of the parish church of Llaij[1] Goydmore [also spelt
Llaijgoydmore,[2] *Llaij*[3]], d. St David's, dispensation and indult. Some time ago, Henry,
as he asserts, was dispensed by apostolic authority, notwithstanding a defect of birth as
the son of a priest and an unmarried woman, to be promoted to all, even sacred and
priest's, orders, and to receive and retain any two mutually compatible benefices, with
or without cure, if conferred on him otherwise canonically, to resign them, at once or
successively, simply or for exchange, as often as he pleased, and in their place receive
and retain up to two other, similar or dissimilar, compatible benefices; and afterwards
he was duly promoted to the said orders by virtue of this dispensation and holds the
above parish church and also the free chapel, called royal, within the castle of
Carin'dine, d. St David's (which is compatible with another, even incompatible,

benefice) which were canonically collated to him when vacant *certo modo*. Dispensation and indult etc. [as above, no. 2].[4]

Litterarum scientia, vite ac morum honestas ...
.P. Lambertus. / JoA: / JoA: Lx: Nardinus

1   written *LL-*
2   written *LL-*
3   written *LL-*
4   Save that the order of clauses in the indult is not identical; and also that the issue of the grantee having a
     defect of birth (catered for, rightly, among the notwithstanding clauses) arises in the present instance, but not
     in no. 2.

316[1]   12 December 1516   *Reg. Lat.* 1319, fos 172ʳ-173ᵛ

To the archdeacon of Cornwall (*Corunbien.*), church of Exeter, and Francesco Chiericati (*?Ch[ier]agato*),[2] canon of the church of (?Castonen.)[3] living in the city or diocese of London, mandate in favour of John (?)Mone and Joan his wife, married couple of the parish of the parish church of Dychet, d. Bath and Wells. A recent petition to the pope on the married couple's part stated that although, at another time, they had been dispensed by apostolic letters or letters of the pope's sacred penitentiary in such way that if there was any impediment [(?)between them] so that they could not contract marriage with one another or remain in the marriage perhaps then contracted by them, they could, the impediment notwithstanding, freely and lawfully contract marriage or remain in the marriage already perhaps contracted; that the said married couple have lawfully contracted marriage with one another *per verba de presenti*, solemnized it in the face of the church, and begotten offspring from it; that Thomas Loell, who bears himself as vicar general in spirituals of the bishop of Bath and Wells, proceeding *ex officio*, as he said, nevertheless, by certain letters of his of a certain tenor, warned and ordered the married couple to appear before him, at a certain time and place which were not suitable, to reply personally to certain articles or interrogatories concerning the said marriage; that when, afterwards, the married couple had appeared before Thomas the vicar [(?) at the said time] and place, even at their inconvenience, and had exhibited the said apostolic letters or letters of the penitentiary before him and they had requested, at a suitable time and place and with due instance: that the letters be registered in the acts and [(?)then inserted in them]; that a copy of the articles be granted to them; that a suitable term be assigned them for replying to the articles; and that their marriage be pronounced and declared to be true and lawful, Thomas the vicar – refusing (at least tacitly) [(?)to hear them] – falsely declared that they [(?)ought to be] excommunicated and imprisoned and threatened to inflict great damage on them; and that appeal was therefore made to the apostolic see on the part of the married couple who felt *inter alia* thereby unduly aggrieved. At the supplication to the pope to order that they and each one of them be absolved from the sentence of excommunication and other ecclesiastical sentences, censures, and pains perhaps promulgated against them on the above occasion and to order that Thomas the vicar be compelled to desist from the false declarations and molestations, even under ecclesiastical sentences, censures, and pains; and to commit to some upright men in those parts, even to men below episcopal rank, the causes, with all their annexed, connected, and dependent matters: of the aforesaid appeal and of anything attempted and innovated after and against it; of the nullity and nullities of the whole of the foregoing and also of each and every other thing done in any way by Thomas the vicar and any other judges and persons to the married couple's prejudice in connection with the above; and of the whole principal matter, the pope [hereby] commands that the above two or one of them, having summoned Thomas and others concerned, shall[4] bestow on the married couple[5], for this once only, if they so request, the benefit of absolution *ad cautelam* from the sentence of excommunication and other sentences, censures, and pains, if and as it is just, having, however, first received from them suitable security in respect of that for which they are perhaps deemed excommunicates and caught by the other ecclesiastical sentences, censures, and pains, that if the above find that the sentence of excommunication etc. were justly inflicted on them, they will obey the above's mandates and those of the church; as to the other things, when Thomas the vicar has been inhibited by the above, even under ecclesiastical sentences, censures, and pains, [and] when they have heard both sides, taking cognizance even of the principal matter, decree what is canonical, without appeal, causing [by ecclesiastical censure what they have decreed to be strictly] observed[6]. Notwithstanding etc.; and that the above are not of the class of persons to whom matrimonial causes are customarily committed, etc.

Humilibus et cetera.
.Jo. Copis / M / M xx de Campania

1   The leaves are badly waterstained and in places affected by mould and the entry is not readily legible; hence the occasional tentativeness.
2   or *Ch[ier]egato*
3   *canonico* (?)*Castonen. ecclesiarum* ... Church unidentifiable; canonry unknown to Chiericati's biography in the *Dizionario Biografico degli Italiani*. Unless the MS is seriously corrupt, the problematic designation is difficult to resolve. However, some two months before Chiericati was sent to England in December 1515 (*L&P, F&D*, II, no. 1228) Henry and Wolsey had been told to expect Francis [of Sassello, OFM], bishop of Castoria (*Castorien.*) (ibid., nos. 926 and 928). Castoria was a titular see (*cf. CPL* XIX, nos. 530-534), without, of course, a cathedral chapter. Fanciful resolutions are unhelpful; but the possibility of bureaucratic confusion cannot be ruled out.
4   'on the pope's authority' does not occur.
5   'and each one of them' does not occur.
6   MS: ...*facientes et cetera observari*. Supplied from common form.

317   10 June 1516   *Reg. Lat.* 1319, fos 331[r]-334[v]

To the abbot of the monastery of B Mary, *de Arvicampo* [Kilcooly], d. Cashel, Robert Offlahyuayn, canon of the church of Lismore, and Malachy Ohogayn, canon of the church of Killaloe, mandate in favour of the present abbot and convent of the monastery of B Mary, *de Wothnia* [Abington], OCist, d. Emly. A recent petition to the pope on the abbot and convent's part stated that, at another time, William Omolryayn[1], who bears himself as a cleric, led, seemingly, by the devil, by pretext of a certain apostolic rescript forged by him or by another at his instance,[2] has not been afraid – to the peril of his soul and as a pernicious example and scandal to the many and also to the prejudice and detriment of the said monastery – to waste the monastery, or the greater part of it, even to the extent of burning it (*etiam cum illius incendio*), and to (?)physically undermine it[3] and to pillage and carry off numerous things and, recklessly and *de facto*, violently and by force, to occupy and detain occupied, several other goods of the monastery and its dependencies (*membrorum*) and also of the ecclesiastical benefices belonging to the monastery, and the benefices themselves, and to inflict divers other injuries on the monastery, or to cause the same to be wasted, pillaged, carried off, occupied, detained, and inflicted, on account of which divine service and the customary number of monks in the monastery, and the alms-giving and other pious works customarily performed by the said abbot and convent, have been greatly reduced. At the abbot and convent's supplication, the pope – wishing, by means of justice, to curb the enterprises of the rash so that others do not presume to commit similar things – [hereby] commands that the above three (or two or one of them), if and when the foregoing, which has been represented to the pope, has been established before them, summarily, simply, and informally, even extrajudicially, shall, on the pope's authority, remove and search for, and cause to be removed and searched for, the said William and his accomplices and also those giving him help, counsel, and favour in the foregoing matters, publicly or secretly, directly or indirectly, by any far-fetched pretext, of whatever dignity, standing, degree, order, or condition, even if they are distinguished by archiepiscopal or any other ecclesiastical or secular (*mundana*) dignity, under sentence of excommunication and other ecclesiastical sentences [and] censures and under penalty of deprivation of ecclesiastical benefices held by them and of disqualification (*inhabilitationis*) for holding them and others in the future, and, if they are not ecclesiastical persons (*seculares*), under penalty of deprivation of the fiefs and all rights held by them as feudatories from churches[4]; and, within a suitable term to be previously fixed for them by the above three (or one of them), William and his accomplices shall restore all the movable goods and (?)livestock (*bona mobilia ac se moventia*) carried off by them and shall give up [and] yield vacant, free, and ready possession of the immovable goods and benefices which have been occupied; also William and accomplices shall make suitable amends[5] and give full and due satisfaction in respect of the fruits etc collected by them from those places, the injuries inflicted by them as above, and the expenses and interest incurred by the abbot and convent by reason of the foregoing; and those giving counsel, help and favour shall utterly and altogether desist from giving it; and, by the same authority, the above three shall inhibit and order Peter Butyller, Marianus Okuarwayll, Odo Okynnedy, Philip *etiam* Okynnedi, Donat Obryen, and William Omarryayn, captains,[6] and any other lords of those parts, both spiritual and temporal, by whatever name they are called and by whatever dignity they are distinguished, not to assist William and accomplices with help, counsel, or favour, directly or indirectly, by any far-fetched pretext, while the said law-suit is pending. Further, the above three shall declare that those who appear to them to have contravened the said warning and inhibition and not obeyed them have incurred the said censures; and in the event of such declaration, when the relevant lawful processes have been observed, the above three shall take care to aggravate the said sentences, repeatedly and as often as necessary, and they are to place under ecclesiastical interdict any places in which those contravening the warning etc (*eos*) happen to stay or go to and in which they have been knowingly allowed to remain[7], and to cause it to be strictly observed for a period of three days after their departure [from that place][8], having, if necessary, even called in the aid of the secular arm for the purpose; and having summoned Willliam and the accomplices and others concerned, having heard both sides on each and every one of the foregoing matters,[9] jointly and severally, the above three shall decree [what][10] is just, without appeal, causing by ecclesiastical censure what they have decreed to be strictly observed. The pope hereby grants to the above three full and free faculty: of citing, as often as necessary, William and the accomplices and all those mentioned above and any others, jointly or severally, disputing the abbot and convent's interest (*interesse putantes*); of inhibiting everyone it is necessary to inhibit; of compelling, by ecclesiastical censure, named witnesses to testify to the truth and notaries to produce documents concerning the foregoing which are in their possession; and of doing, ordering, and executing all other things which are necessary and in any way opportune in the above matters and in connection with them; and if, by relevant summary information to be had by the above three, it appears to them that the warnings, formal demands (*requisitionibus*), and citations of William, the accomplices, and the others disputing the abbot and convent's interest, cannot be safely undertaken by the above three (or one of them) the pope also grants full and free faculty to them of performing the said warnings and formal demands and any citations and inhibitions by public edicts to be affixed in public places where it is probable they will come to the notice of those cited; and the pope wills and by apostolic authority decrees that the warnings, formal demands, and citations bind those warned, those subjected to formal demands, and those cited, just as if they had been made and communicated to them personally. Notwithstanding etc.

Ad compescendos perversorum nefarios conatus et sacrilegorum ...
G [? de Prato][11] / M / M xiiij de Campania

1   though readable as *Omokyayn*
2   MS: ... *pretextu ac* [!] *certi rescripti apostolica* [!] *per eum vel alium ad eius instantiam falso confecti ...*
3   MS: *minisque deformare*: the context perhaps argues mining or rather sapping operations rather than disfigurement by battlements; but the interpretation is uncertain: either seems possible. Though the fourth and seventh minims are clearly dotted, it is, of course, always possible that *minisque* is a corruption; 'nimisque' *deformare* – 'and to greatly disfigure it' [i.e. by fire] would make sense in the context.
4   MS: ... *et si seculares fuerint feudorum et iurium omniumque ab ecclesiis recognoscunt penis ...*
5   MS: *condigna emenda*; there is an equivocal mark over the 'a' of *condigna*; *recte*: 'condignam emendam'
6   i.e. of their respective nations: *cf. State Papers*. Volume II. *Henry VIII*. Part III. *Correspondence between the Governments of England and Ireland, 1515-1538* [State Papers Commission], 1834, pp. 3, 7, and 25.
7   reading: ... *et in quibus scienter stare permissi fuerint*
8   reading: ... *post eorum* [exinde *or* abinde] *discessum*: MS affected by waterstaining and ink-bleed and in places illegible
9   *ac vocatis Willelmo et complicibus prefat(is) ac aliis qui fuerint evocandi super premissis omnibus et singulis tam coniunctim quam divisim auditis hinc inde propositis*
10   MS: *quo* for 'quod'
11   conjectural: rest of abbreviator's name obscured by waterstaining and ASV oval stamp

318   14 June 1516   *Reg. Lat.* 1319, fos 334ᵛ-336ᵛ

To the abbot of the monastery of B. Mary, *de Wothuna*[1] [Abington], d. Emly, and
Malachy Ohogayn, canon of the church of Killaloe, and Dermot Omulrrian, canon of
the church of Emly, mandate in favour of John Macosti, priest, d. Killaloe. The pope
has learned that the perpetual vicarage of the parish church of Brugesrayhtriyll',[2] d.
Killaloe,[3] is vacant *certo modo* at present and has been vacant for so long that by the
Lateran statutes its collation has lawfully devolved on the apostolic see, although Rory
Macosti, who bears himself as a priest, has detained it, with no title and no support of
law, of his own temerity and *de facto*, for a certain time, as he still does. He hereby
commands that the above three (or two or one of them), if, having summoned Rory and
others concerned, they find the vicarage (whose annual value does not exceed 3 marks
sterling) to be vacant (howsoever etc.) shall collate and assign it (even if specially
reserved etc.), with all rights and appurtenances, to John, inducting him etc. having
removed Rory and any other unlawful detainer and causing John (or his proctor) to be
admitted to the vicarage and its fruits etc., rights and obventions to be delivered to him.
[Curbing] gainsayers etc. Notwithstanding etc.

Vite ac morum honestas ...
Phi de Agnellis / M / M x Sexto k(a)l(endas) Julij anno quarto [26 June 1516], *de
Campania*

1   the minims here read as 'un' capable of various readings; but none dotted [next entry has *-nia*]
2   the 'ru' and 'ri' uncertain
3   MS: *dicte diocesis* – evidently referring to Killaloe

319   14 June 1516   *Reg. Lat.* 1319, fos 337ʳ-339ʳ

To the abbot of the monastery of B. Mary, *de Wothnia* [Abington], d. Emly, and
Malachy Ohogayn, canon of the church of Killaloe, and Dermot Omoltyayn, canon of
the church of Emly, mandate in favour of John Okearwayll, cleric, d. [Killaloe][1] (who
asserts that, some time ago, he was dispensed by ordinary authority notwithstanding a
defect of birth as the son of a married man, of noble birth, and a married woman, to be
marked with clerical character, and by virtue of this dispensation he was duly marked
with the said character). The pope has learned that the perpetual vicarage and the
rectory (which, as is asserted, is of lay patronage) of the parish church of
Domacdrchyny[2] [also spelt *Demacdrchyny*,[3] *Mac[dr]⁴chyny*],[5] and the rectory of the
parish church of Leacharachaurayn,[6] d. Killaloe, are vacant *certo modo* at present and
have been vacant for so long that by the Lateran statutes their collation has lawfully
devolved on the apostolic see, although Cornelius Okearwayll[7] has detained the
vicarage and rectory of Domacdrchyny and Rory Okymedy,[8] the rectory of
Leacharachaurayn – bearing themselves as clerics – with no title or support of law, of
their own temerity and *de facto*, for a certain time, as they still do. At a recent petition
on John's part to the pope to erect and institute a canonry in the church of Killaloe and
the vicarage into a simple prebend of it and unite etc. the said rectories to the said

erected canonry and prebend, for the lifetime of John – who asserts that the annual value of the vicarage and rectories together does not exceed 40 marks sterling – the pope – not having certain knowledge of the foregoing – hereby commands that the above three (or two of one of them), if, having summoned Cornelius and Rory and as regards the erection the bishop and chapter of Killaloe and others concerned and those interested in the union, they find the vicarage and rectories to be vacant (howsoever etc.), shall erect and institute a canonry in the church of Killaloe and the vicarage into a simple prebend of it, without prejudice to anyone, and <unite>,[9] annex etc. the said rectories (even if specially reserved etc.) to the said canonry and prebend, for John's lifetime; and, in the event of this erection and institution and union etc., shall collate and assign the newly erected canonry and prebend, being vacant, to John, with plenitude of canon law and the annexes in question and all their rights and appurtenances, inducting him etc., having removed Cornelius and Rory and any other unlawful detainers and causing John (or his proctor) to be received as a canon in the church of Killaloe, and shall assign him a stall in the choir and a place in the chapter of the said church and [causing] the fruits etc., rights and obventions of the said canonry and prebend and annexes to be delivered to him. [Curbing] gainsayers etc. Notwithstanding etc. Also the pope dispenses John, on account of his defect of birth, to receive and retain the said canonry and prebend, if conferred on him by virtue of the presents, notwithstanding etc. The pope's will is, however, that the vicarage and rectories shall not, on this account, be defrauded of due services and the cure of souls in them shall not be neglected; but that their customary burdens shall be supported; and that on John's death or his resignation etc. of the canonry and prebend, the said erection and institution shall be extinguished and the said union and incorporation shall be dissolved and be so deemed and the vicarage and rectories shall revert to their original condition automatically.

Apostolice sedis circumspecta benignitas ad ea libenter intendit...
Phi de agnellis / JoA / JoA: xxx: Nardinus

1   MS: *dicte diocesis* evidently referring to Killaloe
2   possibly 'De-' and '-ynn'; there may also be a letter between the 'r' and 'c' in '-drc-'.
3   the '-ma-' uncertain
4   largely lost in cleavage; supplied from other occurrences
5   occurs in marginal insertion: <*et rectorie de Mac[dr]chyny collatio devoluta sit*> initialled *JoA*
6   the 'n' read sympathetically
7   in the first occurrence the '-ar-' uncertain
8   the 'm' uncertain; perhaps 'n'
9   marginal insertion initialled *JoA*

320   1 July 1516   *Reg. Lat.* 1319, fos 339ᵛ-341ᵛ

To the archdeacon of the church of St Andrews, the provost of Crethon, d. St Andrews, and Archibald Steuuart, canon of the church of Glasgow, mandate in favour of William, nobleman, temporal lord of the place [of][1] Carlile, farmer (*arrendatarii*) of the tithe-fruits (*fructuum decimalium*) of the parish church of Torthowald, d. Glasgow. A recent petition to the pope on William's part stated that, at another time, he sued Margaret Dowglas, damsel, and certain other co-litigants in this regard then expressed, clerics or laymen, said d. (who were legally bound to give and pay to him by way of rent (*fictu*) several tithe-fruits, called sheaves (*garbales*), [due] to him by reason of the farm of the said fruits, and who were unlawfully refusing to give and pay them to him) before John Sprente, to whom the archbishop of Glasgow had, as was said, committed the case, praying *inter alia* that they be condemned and coerced and compelled to give and pay the tithe-fruits to him; that John, proceeding wrongly in the case, promulgated a certain unjust or null sentence, by which he absolved Margaret and the co- litigants from, as he said, William's claim, and from which William, feeling *inter alia* unduly aggrieved thereby, appealed to the apostolic see, and in connection with his appeal he impetrated apostolic letters to William Wawane [also spelt *Wawame*], canon of Aberdeen, and on the strength of the letters caused Margaret and the co-litigants to be summoned to trial in the cause of the appeal before William Wawane; that William Wawane, proceeding correctly in the case of the appeal, promulgated a definitive sentence by which *inter alia* he revoked the said sentence, from which, on the part of Margaret and the co-litigants, falsely alleging that the sentence was unjust, appeal [was made] to the apostolic see [and] in connection with their appeal Margaret and the co-litigants impetrated apostolic letters under a certain form to the provost of the church of Dun'brata' [also spelt *Dunnbertan*], d. Glasgow, his proper name perhaps not expressed, and Patrick Elphinen', canon of the church of Glasgow, and by pretext of the letters caused William the farmer to be summoned to trial before Walter Abermeti, provost of the church of Dun'brata' [and] the said canon Patrick; and that provost Walter and canon Patrick, proceeding wrongly in the case of the latest appeal, promulgated a certain unjust or null sentence in favour of Margaret and the co-litigants and against William the farmer by which *inter alia* they overturned (*infirmarunt*) the sentence of William Wawane, from which on the part of William the farmer, feeling *inter alia* unduly aggrieved thereby, appeal was made to the apostolic see, but detained, as he asserts, by lawful impediment, William the farmer did not, perhaps, prosecute his later appeal within the lawful time. At William the farmer's supplication to the pope [to order][2] that he be absolved from the sentence of excommunication and other ecclesiastical sentences, censures, and pains perhaps promulgated against him on the above occasion and, notwithstanding the lapse of time, to commit to some upright men in those parts the causes: of the aforesaid later appeal and of anything attempted and innovated after and against it; of the nullity and nullities of the process and sentence of John Sprente [and] of the provost and canon Patrick, and of each and every other thing done in any way by them and any other judges and persons to William the farmer's prejudice in connection with the above; and of the whole principal matter, the pope [hereby] commands that the above three (or two or one of them), having summoned Margaret and the co-litigants and others concerned, shall bestow on William the farmer, for this once only, if he so requests, the benefit of absolution *ad cautelam* from the sentence of excommunication and other sentences, censures, and pains, if and as it is just, having, however, first received from him suitable security in respect of that for which he is perhaps deemed excommunicate and caught by other sentences, censures, and pains that if they find the sentence of excommunication etc were justly inflicted on him he will obey their mandates and those of the church; as to the other things, if what is said about the impediment is true, having heard both sides, taking cognizance even of the principal matter, decree what is just, without appeal, causing [by ecclesiastical censure what they have decreed to be strictly] observed,[3] [and moreover compel] witnesses, etc. Notwithstanding etc.

Humilibus et cetera.
P. Lanb(er)tus / JoA: / :JoA: xiiij: Nardinus

1   MS wants 'de'.
2   MS wants 'mandare'.
3   MS: *facientes et cetera observari.* Supplied from common form.

321   25 March 1513   *Reg. Lat.* 1320, fos 329ʳ-330ᵛ

Union etc. At a recent petition on the part of Richard Skypwith, canon of the church of B. Mary the Virgin, Warwick (*Warwici*), d. Worcester, the pope hereby unites etc. the parish church of St Alban in Wodstret, city of London, d. London,[1] (whose annual value does not exceed 11 pounds sterling), with all its rights and appurtenances, to the canonry and prebend of St Michael of the above church of B. Mary, which Richard holds together with St Alban's, for as long as he holds the canonry and prebend, to the effect that he may, on his own authority, in person or by proxy, continue in, or take anew, and retain [corporal possession of]² St Alban's and of the rights and appurtenances aforesaid, for as long as he holds the canonry and prebend, and convert its fruits etc. to his own uses and those of the canonry and prebend and of St Alban's, without licence of the local diocesan or of anyone else. Notwithstanding etc. The pope's will is, however, that the church of St Alban shall not, on account of this union etc., be defrauded of due services and the cure of souls in it shall not be neglected; but that its customary burdens shall be supported; and that on Richard's death or his resignation etc. of the canonry and prebend this union etc. shall be dissolved and be so deemed and St Alban's shall revert to its original condition automatically.

Ad futuram rei memoriam. Romanum decet pontificem votis illis gratum prestare assensum ...
P. lanbertus / M / M xxxv. de Campania

1   MS: ... *Wodstret civitatis Londonien. diocesis canonicatui* ...
2   'corporalem possessionem' wanting

322   23 March (?)1514[1]   *Reg. Lat.* 1321, fos 159ʳ-160ᵛ

Reservation, grant, and assignment, for life, to Peter Rolla, priest, d. Valencia, and (as he asserts) continual commensal familiar of Hadrian, cardinal priest of the title of S Crisogono, of the fruits etc, in lieu of annual pension, of the parish church of Villaiosa and of the simple perpetual ecclesiastical benefice, called *servitorium*, under the invocation of the Virgin Mary in the church of Ayora, d. Valencia and Orihuela, which Peter has this day resigned into the pope's hands and which – thus vacant and previously reserved to apostolic disposition – the pope has made provision of and collated to Ieronimus Rolla (who has consented to the reservation, etc); and indult to have re-entry on the resignation or death etc of Ieronimus. With separate concurrent executory. Entry of no other interest to the Calendar.

Vite ac morum honestas ... The executory begins: *Hodie cum dilectus filius Petrus Rolla* ...
.F. Bregon.; Phi. de Agnellis / JoA: / JoA: xij: x: Nardinus

1   There is a contradiction between the year of the incarnation and the year of the pontificate: *millesimo quingentesimo tertio decimo decimo kalendas Aprilis anno primo* [*recte*: 'secundo'?]. The pontifical year began on 19 March, that of the incarnation on 25 March.

323   5 April 1515   *Reg. Lat.* 1321, fos 220^r-222^r

To Edmund Oflanagay' and John Ohargadaynis,[1] canons of the church of Elphin,[2] mandate in favour of Theodoric Odenenir,[3] dean of the church of Elphin. The pope has learned that the perpetual vicarage of the parish church of Cillmenecayr,[4] d. Elphin, is vacant *certo modo* at present and has been vacant for so long that by the Lateran statutes its collation has lawfully devolved on the apostolic see, although Maurice Ohardgoda',[5] who bears himself as a cleric, has detained it with no title and no support of law, of his own temerity and *de facto*, for a certain time, as he still does. At a recent petition on the part of Theodoric (who holds the deanery of the above church of Elphin, which is a dignity major *post pontificalem*; and who asserts that the annual value of the vicarage does not exceed 3 marks sterling and that the fruits etc. of the deanery are so meagre that they do not even suffice for his sustenance) to the pope to unite etc. the vicarage to the deanery, for as long as Theodoric holds the latter, the pope hereby commands that the above two (or one of them), if, having summoned Maurice and others concerned, [they find that] the vicarage is vacant (howsoever etc.), shall unite etc. it (even if specially reserved etc.), with all rights and appurtenances, to the deanery, for as long as Theodoric holds the latter, inducting him etc. having removed Maurice and any other unlawful detainer and causing the vicarage's fruits etc., rights and obventions to be delivered to him. Curbing gainsayers by apostolic authority etc. Notwithstanding etc. The pope's will is, however, that the vicarage shall not, on this account, be defrauded of due services and the cure of souls in it shall not be neglected; but that its customary burdens shall be supported; and that on Theodoric's death or his resignation etc. of the said [deanery][6] this union etc. shall be dissolved and be so deemed and the vicarage shall revert to its original condition and be deemed vacant automatically.

Apostolice sedis providentia circumspecta ad ea libenter intendit ...

/ M; P. Lambert(us)⁷ / M x terciodecimo k(a)l(endas) maij anno tercio [19 April 1515],
de Campania

1   the three minims (none dotted) here read as *-ni-* capable of various readings
2   here *Olfinen.*; elsewhere *Elfinen.*
3   *Cf. Annates, Elphin,* no. 100.
4   the second 'e' doubtful; possibly converted to a 'd'
5   the 'o' uncertain: blotched
6   'decanatum' wanting
7   not, as usual, in the right hand margin but in the left (beneath the magistral initial [*M*])

324   19 April 1515   *Reg. Lat.* 1321, fos 222ᵛ-223ᵛ

To William Glen, BDec, priest, d. Bangor, dispensation. Some time ago, Julius II by
other letters of his dispensed him to receive and retain together for life any two
benefices, with cure or otherwise incompatible,[1] even if parish churches or their
perpetual vicarages,[2] or dignities etc. [as above, no. 2[3], with appropriate changes of
tense, to '... retain them together for life, as above'], as is more fully contained in those
letters.[4] The pope – at his supplication – hereby dispenses William (who is a priest) to
receive and retain for life, together with any two incompatible benefices perhaps held
by him now and at the time by virtue of the said dispensation, any third benefice, with
cure or otherwise incompatible, even if a parish church or its perpetual vicarage, or a
dignity etc. [as above, no. 6].

Litterarum sientia,[5] vite ac morum honestas et cetera.
P.[6] de Cesiis / JoA: / JoA: Lx: Nard(inus): –

1   'invicem' does not occur.
2   *sic*; i.e. the passage 'or chantries ... a perpetual ecclesiastical benefice' (*cf.* above, no. 2) does not occur here.
3   Though, most unusually, the constitutions of Otto and Ottobuono (ignored by the Calendar save in
     exceptional cases) are not mentioned in the notwithstanding clauses. The omission is, presumably, due to
     inadvertence by the draftsman.
4   *Cf.* index entry transcribed in *CPL* XIX, at no. 1932.
5   *sic*
6   *sic; recte:* 'O'

325[1]   28 April 1515   *Reg. Lat.* 1321, fos 232ᵛ-233ᵛ

To Henry Tankard, rector of the parish church of Berfreyston, d. Canterbury.
Dispensation and indult – at his supplication – to receive and retain for life, together
with the above parish church, one, and without them, any two other benefices, with
cure or otherwise mutually incompatible, even if dignities, *personatus*, administrations
or offices in cathedral, even metropolitan, or collegiate churches, even if the dignities
in question should be major *post pontificalem* in cathedral, even metropolitan,
churches, or principal in collegiate churches, or parish churches or their perpetual

vicarages, or chantries, free chapels, hospitals or annual services, usually assigned to secular clerics in title of a perpetual ecclesiastical benefice, and of lay patronage and of whatsoever tax or annual value, and even if the dignities etc. should be customarily elective and have cure of souls, if he obtains them otherwise canonically, to resign them, at once or successively, simply or for exchange, as often as he pleases, and in their place [likewise][2] receive up to two other, similar or dissimilar, incompatible benefices and retain them together for life, as above; and, for life, while residing in the Roman curia or any one of his benefices or attending a *studium generale*, not to be bound to reside personally[3] in his other benefices, nor to be liable to be compelled to do so by anyone against his will. Notwithstanding etc. With the proviso that the above church and other incompatible benefices shall not, on this account, be defrauded of due services and the cure of souls in the church and (if any) the other incompatible benefices shall not be neglected; but that customary burdens of those benefices in which he shall not reside shall be supported.

Vite ac morum honestas ...
P Lambert(us) / JoA: / JoA: Lx: Nard(inus): –

1   This entry – essentially a dispensation *ad duo* with indult for non-residence – is calendared at length because of its odd formulation. Comparison with no. 2 above (the prototype – in this volume – for a letter of this type) shows that the order of the two main passages listing types of benefices (*dignities ... collegiate churches* and *parish churches ... ecclesiastical benefices*) is reversed. Furthermore, the *absence* here of the standard phrase calendared as 'or a combination' is unexpected. And the *presence* of 'and of lay patronage and of whatsoever tax or annual value' is decidedly strange – being normally found in dispensations (typically *ad unum*) for religious to hold secular benefices.
2   *simpliciter*; *recte*: 'similiter'
3   *personaliter* (often [as no. 2] not present); *cf.* above, nos. 251 and 252.

326   3 May 1515   *Reg. Lat.* 1321, fos 237ᵛ-240ʳ

To William Omurissa and Nillanus Oceruelan, canons of the church of Derry, and Dermot Oflag'am, canon of the church of Elphin, mandate in favour of John Marcoli,[1] cleric, d. Raphoe. A recent petition to the pope on John's part stated that, although at another time when the parish church of Ynysgyill, d. Raphoe, was vacant *certo modo* outside the Roman curia, the then bishop of Raphoe, by ordinary authority, collated and made provision of it, thus vacant, to John; by virtue of which he acquired possession of it; and, detained by lawful impediment, he was unable to have himself promoted to sacred orders within a year of this acquisition – nevertheless Odo Marcaluan [also spelt *Macaluam*], who bears himself as a priest, asserting that the said church was vacant, [...][2] "X" declared [...][2] promulgated an unjust sentence and collated and made provision of the church, thus vacant, to Odo; and appeal to the apostolic see was made on John's part from this sentence and also this collation and provision. Moreover, as the same petition added, it was asserted by some that the right in or to the said church belongs to neither John nor Odo. At the supplication on the part of John (who asserts that the annual value of the parish church does not exceed 5 marks sterling) to the pope to erect and institute a canonry in the church of Raphoe and the said parish church into

a simple prebend of it, the pope – not having certain knowledge of the foregoing –
hereby commands that the above three (or two or one of them), having summoned Odo
Marcaluan and, as regards the erection, the said bishop and the chapter of Raphoe and
others concerned, shall hear, decide and duly determine the causes of the appeal and of
the principal matter, causing what they decree to be strictly observed by ecclesiastical
censure without appeal; and, moreover, compel witnesses etc. And if through the
outcome of the suit it is established by them that neither John nor Odo has the right in
or to the said parish church, the above three (etc.) shall erect and institute a canonry in
the church of Raphoe and the parish church (vacant howsoever etc.; even if it has been
vacant for so long that by the Lateran statutes its collation has lawfully devolved on
the apostolic see etc.) into a simple prebend, for John's lifetime, without prejudice to
anyone; and, in the event of this erection and institution, shall collate and assign the
newly erected canonry and prebend, being vacant, with plenitude of canon law and all
their rights and appurtenances, to John; inducting him etc. having removed any
unlawful detainer and causing John (or his proctor) to be received as a canon of the
church of Raphoe, and shall assign him a stall in the choir and a place in the chapter
of the church of Raphoe, with plenitude of canon law, and [causing] the fruits etc.,
rights and obventions of the canonry and prebend to be delivered to him. [Curbing]
gainsayers etc. Notwithstanding etc. The pope's will is, however, that the above parish
church shall not, on this account, be defrauded of due services and the cure of souls
[in] it shall not be neglected; but that its customary burdens shall be supported; and that
on the death of John or his resignation etc. of the canonry and prebend this erection and
institution shall be extinguished and be so deemed and the parish church shall revert to
its original condition automatically.

Apostolice sedis circumspecta benignitas ad ea libenter intendit …
P. de Agnellis / JoA: / : JoA: xv: Sept(imo) k(a)l(endas) Junij Anno tertio: [26 May
1515], *Nardinus*

1   The final minim (read as an 'i') is topped with a flourish (which could be read as a bar, signalling
     abbreviation).
2   MS: … *asserens ecclesiam predictam vacare declaravit sententiam promulgavit iniquam* … Omission(s) in
     the vicinity of *vacare?*

327   17 February 1514   *Reg. Lat.* 1321, fo 269ʳ⁻ᵛ

To John Clerk, DDec, rector of the parish church of Porteshed', d. Bath and Wells.
Dispensation and indult – at his supplication – not to be bound by reason of the said
church or of any other benefices with cure or requiring sacred orders by statute or
foundation or otherwise held by him at the time to be promoted to any of the sacred
orders in question for a two-year period calculated from the end of the year allowed by
law, and not to be liable to be compelled to be so promoted by anyone against his will.
Notwithstanding etc. With the proviso that the church and other benefices in question
shall not, on this account, be defrauded of due services and the cure of souls in the
church and (if any) the other benefices shall not be neglected.

Litterarum scientia, vite ac morum honestas ...
.P. Lambertus / JoA: / JoA: xij: Nard(inus): –

328   17 February 1514   *Reg. Lat.* 1321, fos 282ʳ-283ᵛ

To John <Clerk>,[1] DDec, rector of the parish church of Porteshed, d. Bath and Wells, dispensation and indult as below. This day the pope by other letters of his dispensed John to receive and retain for life, together with the above parish church (which, as he asserted, he was holding at the time), one, and without them, any two other benefices, etc. [as above, no. 6, to '... retain them together for life'], as is more fully contained in those letters.[2] He hereby dispenses and indulges John – at his supplication – to receive, together with the above parish church (which he still holds) and one other, or with any two other incompatible benefices held by him at the time by virtue of the said dispensation, any third benefice etc. [as above, no. 6, to '... if he obtains it otherwise canonically']; and, if the third benefice should be a parish church or its perpetual vicarage, retain it for one year only (calculated from the day of acquiring peaceful possession), but if it should be another incompatible benefice, retain it for life; to resign it, simply or for exchange, as often as he pleases, and in its place receive another, similar or dissimilar, third incompatible benefice, and if the third should be a parish church or its perpetual vicarage retain it for a year calculated as above, but if it should be another incompatible benefice retain it for life, provided that of three such incompatible benefices – after the said year – not more than two be parish churches or their perpetual vicarages; and, while residing in the Roman curia or any one of his benefices or attending a *studium generale*, not to be bound to reside in his other benefices, nor to be liable to be compelled to do so by anyone against his will. Notwithstanding etc. The pope's will is, however, that the third incompatible benefice and the benefices in which John shall not reside shall not, on this account, be defrauded of due services and the cure of souls in them ([if] any) shall not be neglected; but that customary burdens of those benefices in which he shall not reside shall be supported; and that John shall be bound – within the said year – to exchange the said parish church or perpetual vicarage for another (even incompatible) benefice, which, however, may not be a parish church or its perpetual vicarage; otherwise John shall be bound to resign it altogether and the pope decrees it thenceforth vacant.

Litterarum scientia, vite ac morum honestas ...
.P. Lambertus. / JoA. / JoA: Lxxx: Nardinus

1   *Clerck* deleted in line, initialled *JoA*; with *Clerk* inserted above
2   above, no. 161

329   13 March 1515   *Reg. Lat.* 1321, fos 317ʳ-318ʳ

To William Loweth, canon of the monastery, usually governed by a prior, of B. Mary, Walsyngham, OSA, d. Norwich, (who, as he asserts, is expressly professed of the order),[1] dispensation and indult as below. At another time William had, as he asserts, spontaneously and freely resigned, outside the Roman curia, the priorship of the above monastery, which he was then holding, into the hands of the then bishop of Norwich (or his vicar general in spirituals); and the said bishop (or his vicar – by virtue of a special faculty for it which he had, as he asserted, from the bishop by letters), when the said resignation [had been admitted][2] by the person in question (*eum*) by ordinary [authority][2] outside the said curia and so that William should not suffer excessive loss on account of it, with the express consent of the then prior and convent, reserved, established and assigned by the said ordinary authority a certain annual pension (of English money) then expressed to be received and levied by William for life, on the fruits etc. of the said monastery and also a certain house situated within the precinct of the monastery to be inhabited by William for life. Hereby the pope dispenses and indulges William – at his supplication – to receive and retain any benefice, with or without cure, secular or regular of the aforesaid or any other order, even the Cluniac, even if the secular benefice should be a parish church or its perpetual vicarage, or a chantry, free chapel, hospital or annual service, usually assigned to secular clerics in title of a perpetual ecclesiastical benefice, or the regular benefice should be a priory, *prepositura, prepositatus,* dignity (even conventual), *personatus,* administration or office (even claustral), and even if the priory etc. should be customarily elective and have cure of souls, if he obtains it otherwise canonically, to resign it, simply or for exchange, as often as he pleases, and in its place receive and retain another, similar or dissimilar, benefice, with or without cure, secular or regular of the aforesaid order of St Augustine or any other order, even the Cluniac; and, for life, to receive the said pension along with the benefice, for life, and also receive the canonical portion usually received by canons of the said monastery even after he has acquired the benefice; and to have a stall in the choir and an active and passive voice and place in the chapter of the monastery, for life, otherwise as before, without limitation, just as if he had not acquired the benefice. Notwithstanding etc.

Relligionis[3] *zelus, vite ac morum honestas ...*
.P. Lambertus. / Phi. / . Phi. Lxxx. de Senis

1   This information comes from a notwithstanding clause.
2   evident lacuna in MS: ... *extra dictam curiam ordinaria* ∗∗∗ *ne propterea* ...; 'auctoritate admissa' supplied
     conjecturally
3   *sic*

330   12 March 1515   *Reg. Lat.* 1322, fos 10ᵛ-13ᵛ

To the prior of the monastery, usually governed by a prior, of B. Mary, Doran, d.
Elphin, and Philip Macruran and Walter Macredere, canons of the church of Tuam,
mandate in favour of David de Bergo, canon of [the church of][1] Elphin (who asserts
that some time ago he was dispensed by ordinary authority, notwithstanding a defect
of birth as the son of an unmarried man and an unmarried woman, to be marked with
clerical character and to hold any benefice without cure, by virtue of which he was duly
marked with the said character; and that he was received in the church of Elphin as a
supernumerary canon by the bishop and chapter). The pope has learned that the rectory
of the parish church of Raharam and the [perpetual][2] vicarage of the parish church of
Kylldery, [d.][3] Tuam, are vacant *certo modo* at present and have been vacant for so long
that by the Lateran statutes their collation has lawfully devolved on the apostolic [see],[4]
although Charles Ocuncenayn[5] has detained the rectory and William Ocunoenayn the
vicarage – bearing themselves as clerics – with no title and no support of law, of their
own temerity and *de facto*, for a certain time, as they still do. At a recent petition on
the part of David – who asserts that the annual value of the rectory and vicarage
together does not exceed 12 marks sterling – to the pope to erect and institute the
rectory and vicarage and the episcopal fourth of the rectory into a simple prebend of
the church of Elphin, for his lifetime, the pope – not having certain knowledge of the
foregoing – hereby commands that the above three (or two or one of them), if it is thus
and, having summoned the bishop and chapter and also Charles and William and others
concerned, they find the rectory and vicarage to be vacant (howsoever etc.), shall erect
and institute them (even if specially reserved etc.) and also – with the consent of the
archbishop of Tuam and after the usual annual pension has been paid to him and to his
successors the archbishops of Tuam for the time being – the said episcopal fourth into
a simple prebend of the church of Elphin, for David's lifetime, without prejudice to
anyone; and, in the event of this erection and institution, collate and assign the newly
erected prebend, being vacant, to David, with all rights and appurtenances, inducting
him etc. having removed Charles and William and any other unlawful detainers and
causing David (or his proctor) to be admitted to the prebend and its fruits etc., rights
and obventions to be delivered to him. [Curbing] gainsayers by [the pope's] authority
etc. Notwithstanding etc. The pope's will is, however, that the rectory and vicarage
shall not, on this account, be defrauded of due services and the cure of souls in them
shall not be neglected; but that their customary burdens shall be supported; and that on
David's death or his resignation etc. of the prebend this erection and institution shall
be extinguished and so deemed and the rectory and vicarage shall revert to their
original condition automatically.

Apostolice sedis circumspecta benignitas ad ea libenter intendit …
phi d(e) agnellis / JoA / JoA. xx: Nardinus

1   'ecclesie' does not occur.
2   'perpetua' does not occur.
3   'diocesis' wanting
4   'sedem' wanting
5   the second 'c' doubtful; possibly an 'o'

331   28 January 1515   *Reg. Lat.* 1322, fos 118ʳ-120ʳ

To the abbot of the monastery of B. Mary, *de Benedictione Dei* [Kilbeggan], d. Meath, and Malachy Okellay and Odo Obernd, canons of the church of Elphin, mandate in favour of Donald Okellay, brother of the hospital of St John of Jerusalem. The pope has learned that the priorship of the house of St John the Baptist, Rayndduin, called *cruciferorum*, of the said hospital, d. Elphin, is vacant *certo modo* at present and has been vacant for so long that by the Lateran statutes its collation has lawfully devolved on the apostolic see, although William Okellay,[1] who bears himself as prior, has detained the priorship with no title and no support of law, of his own temerity and *de facto*, for a certain time, as he still does. He hereby commands that the above three (or two or one of them), if, having summoned William and others concerned, they find the priorship (whose annual value does not exceed 24 pounds sterling) to be vacant (howsoever etc.), shall collate and assign it (even if specially reserved etc.), with all its rights and appurtenances, to Donald, inducting him etc. having removed any other unlawful detainer and causing Donald (or his proctor) to be admitted to the priorship and its fruits etc., rights and obventions to be delivered to him. [Curbing] gainsayers by [the pope's] authority etc. Notwithstanding etc.

Religionis zelus, vite ac morum honestas ...
Phi. de agnellis / M / M xv octavo id(us) februarij an(n)o secundo [6 February 1515], *de Campania*

1   sympathetic reading; readable as *Okellan*

332   4 February 1515   *Reg. Lat.* 1322, fos 122ʳ-123ʳ

To Thomas Cade, rector of the parish church of All Saints, Bukvorte[1] [also spelt *Bukvorthe*],[2] d. Lincoln. Dispensation and indult etc. [as above, no. 2, to '... shall be supported. '].[3] Given at Palo, d. Porto.

Vite ac morum honestas ...
G. d(e) prato / JoA: / JoA: Lx: Nard(inus): –

1   fourth letter altered; 'b' written over 'v' or vice versa
2   third letter altered; 'k' written over 'B' or perhaps vice versa
3   But note that, though the tenor is the same as no. 2, the formulation (of a short passage in the dispensation and of much of the indult for non- residence) is different.

333   1 December 1514   *Reg. Lat.* 1322, fos 133ʳ-136ʳ

To the bishop of Cloyne and the precentor and the dean of the church of Lismore, mandate in favour of John de Ylongayn, priest, d. [Limerick].[1] The pope has learned that the perpetual vicarages of the parish churches of Clonenicrevo[2] [also spelt *Clonenicrello*,[3] *Clenenicrew*,[4] *Clonenicrew*[5]], Chorkymoyr[6] [also spelt *Corchimoyr*] and Ardpadrig [also spelt *Ardpradig*] and also – which are of lay patronage – the perpetual vicarage of the parish church of Dermachno[7] and the rectory of the parish church of Kyllflyn and the chapels, called particles of land, of the places of Dwnyrys and Dulgadmac and also of Martyll[8] and Snychayly,[9] d. Limerick, are vacant *certo modo* at present and have been vacant for so long that by the Lateran statutes their collation has lawfully devolved on the apostolic see, although James Redmundi de Geraldinis has detained the vicarage of Chorkymoyr, Cormac Offilayn[10] that of Dermachno and Gerald de Leow that of Ardpadrig, and Thomas Mertell[11] has detained the rectory and Gerald Roche has detained the said chapels – bearing themselves as clerics and priests respectively – with no title or support of law, of their own temerity and *de facto*, for a certain time, as they still do. At a recent petition on John's part to the pope to erect and institute a canonry in the church of Limerick and the said vicarages, rectory and chapels into a simple prebend of it, for John's lifetime, the pope – not having certain knowledge of the foregoing – hereby commands that the above three (or two or one of them), if it is thus, having summoned the bishop and chapter of Limerick and James, Cormac, Gerald de Leow, Thomas [Mertell] and Gerald Roche and others concerned, shall erect and institute a canonry in the church of Limerick and the said vicarages, rectory and chapels (whose annual value does not exceed 32 marks[12] sterling) – howsoever vacant, [even if] the vicarage of Clonenicrevo is vacant by the death at the apostolic see of James Oreanayn,[13] formerly vicar of this church, and [even if] it and the other vicarages and the rectory and chapels are vacant by resignation etc. – into a simple prebend of the church of Limerick, for John's lifetime, without prejudice to anyone; and, in the event of this erection and institution by virtue of the presents, collate and assign the newly erected canonry and prebend, being then vacant, with plenitude of canon law and all rights and appurtenances, to John, inducting him etc. into corporal possession of the canonry and prebend and rights and appurtenances aforesaid, having removed any unlawful detainer, and causing John (or his proctor) to be received as a canon of the church of Limerick, and shall assign him a stall in the choir and a place in the chapter of this [church] of Limerick, with plenitude of canon law, and [causing] the fruits etc., rights and obventions of the canonry and prebend to be delivered to him. [Curbing] gainsayers by [the pope's] authority etc. Notwithstanding etc. The pope's will is, however, that the above vicarages, rectory and chapels shall not, on this account, be defrauded of due services and the cure of souls in the vicarages and rectory shall not be neglected; but that their customary burdens and those of the said chapels shall be supported; and that on John's death or his resignation etc. of the canonry and prebend the said erection and institution shall be extinguished and so deemed and the vicarages, rectory and chapels shall revert to their original condition automatically.

Apostolice sedis circumspecta benignitas ad ea libenter intendit …
Phi d(e) agnellis / JoA / JoA: xxx: Nardinus

1   MS: *dicte diocesis*, evidently referring to Limerick
2   the '-cr' uncertain

3   or -creW
4   or possibly -crello
5   or possibly -crello
6   or possibly -oyt
7   the penultimate letter perhaps a 'u'
8   the '-ar-' uncertain
9   the 'n' uncertain
10   the 'i' doubtful and perhaps non-existent
11   the 'r' uncertain
12   librarum has been deleted and initialled JoA just before marcharum
13   very uncertain reading

334   9 February 1515   *Reg. Lat.* 1322, fos 152[v]-153[r]

To the abbot of the monastery *de beneditione dei* [Kilbeggan], d. Meath, and Fergal
Osiriden, canon of the church of Kilmore, and Maurice Machochlayn,[1] canon of the
church of Clonmacnois[2], mandate in favour of Conchofanus Ocerbre, priest, d. Meath.
A recent petition to the pope on Conchofanus's part stated that if to him, for life, all the
fruits etc., rights and obventions of the parish church of Vastina, d. Meath, (united etc.
in perpetuity to the monastery of B. Mary, Molyndkearr, OSA, d. Meath), which are
customarily leased – at the pleasure of the prior for the time being and the convent of
the said monastery (which is usually governed by a prior) – to a single priest who
exercises the cure [of souls][3] of the parishioners of the said church under a certain
annual payment, were to be leased and assigned under the same annual payment; and
[faculty and licence][4] were to be granted to administer the ecclesiastical sacraments to
the said parishioners and otherwise exercise the cure of souls, it would be of advantage
to Conchofanus (who does not have a benefice from which to support himself
conveniently), and the said cure of souls would be exercised more diligently. At this
supplication, the pope hereby commands that the above three (or two or one of them)
– if the present prior and convent give their express assent to this – shall lease and
assign to Conchofanus, for life, all the fruits etc., rights and obventions of the said
church under the same usual annual payment; and shall, meanwhile, grant licence[5] to
him to administer the ecclesiastical sacraments of the said parishioners and otherwise
exercise the cure of their souls. Notwithstanding etc. Given at Magliana.[6]

*Ex debito pastoralis offitii vota personarum humilium ad exauditionis gratiam libenter
admictimus …*
I. Benzon / JoA: / : JoA. x: Nardinus

1   or possibly -bayn
2   MS: *Cluonen.*; *recte*: 'Cluanen.'
3   'animarum' does not occur at this point.
4   'facultatem et licentiam' (or suchlike) wanting here; *cf.* note 5.
5   MS: *licentiam*
6   'Portuen. dioc.' wanting

335   15 October 1514   *Reg. Lat.* 1322, fos 153ᵛ-156ʳ

To Thady Orronan, canon of the church of Lismore, and Thomas Okyellyry, canon of the church of Cloyne, and the official of Cork, mandate in favour of James Redimundi de Geraldinis, canon of the church of Lismore. The pope has learned that the perpetual vicarages of the parish churches of Sts Peter and Paul, Kyllochia, and of Brury, of Tankarryschnyn¹ [also spelt *Tankariwscuym*]² *alias* Baletancana³ and of Effyngyn [also spelt *Effyngin*, *Effygyn*], (which is of lay patronage), d. Limerick, and also of Sandronin,⁴ d. Cloyne, are vacant *certo modo* at present and have been vacant for so long that by the Lateran statutes their collation has lawfully devolved on the apostolic see, although Maurice Offellan has detained the vicarages of Kyllochia and Tankarryschnyn, and William Odonayll has detained Effyngyn – bearing themselves as priests – and Hugh de Loyz *alias* Ulich⁵ has detained the vicarages of Brury and Sandronin – bearing himself as a cleric – with no title or support of law, of their own temerity and *de facto*, for a certain time, as they do. At a recent petition on James's part to the pope to unite etc., for his lifetime, the said vicarages to the canonry and prebend of the church of Lismore which James holds – asserting that the annual value of the vicarages together does not exceed 50, and of his canonry and prebend, 10, marks sterling – the pope hereby commands that above three (or two or one of them), if, having summoned Hugh, Maurice and William and others concerned and those interested in the union, they find the vicarages to be vacant (howsoever etc.) shall unite etc. the vicarages (even if specially reserved etc.), with all their rights and appurtenances, to the canonry and prebend, for as long as James holds the latter; to the effect that James may, on his own authority, in person or by proxy, take and retain corporal possession of the vicarages, for as long as he holds the canonry and prebend, and convert their fruits etc. to his own uses and those of the canonry and prebend and vicarages aforesaid, without licence of the local diocesan or of anyone else. Notwithstanding etc. The pope's will is, however, that the vicarages shall not, on account of this union etc., be defrauded of due services and the cure of souls in them shall not be neglected, but that their customary burdens shall be supported; and that on James's death or his resignation etc. of the canonry and prebend this union etc. shall be dissolved and so deemed and the vicarages shall revert to their original condition automatically. Given at Capodimonte, d. Montefiascone.

Vite ac morum honestas …
Phi d(e) agnellis / JoA: / JoA: xxv: Nardinus

1   the second 'r' doubtful, the first 'y' reworked, and the 'c' doubtful
2   the 'ri' uncertain; a cross (signalling error) above the name and another opposite in the right margin
3   the final 'a' uncertain
4   the 'nin' uncertain; readable as 'rem'
5   *sic*; *not* 'Hugh *alias* Ulick de Loyz' (*cf. CPL* XVIII, no. 482)

336 (?)1514, 19 Kal. Aug. a. 2[1]   *Reg. Lat.* 1322, fos 212ʳ-215ʳ

To the dean and Thady Oronan, canon, of the church of Lismore, and John Olyche',
canon of the church of Cloyne, mandate in favour of Maurice Omulchorrcha, cleric, d.
[Limerick].[2] The pope has learned that the priory of the monastery, usually governed
by a prior, of B. Mary, Rahgelny, OSA, and the perpetual vicarages of the parish
churches of Killseanall [also spelt *Killscanall, Kyllscanall*] and Croch (which is of lay
patronage), d. Limerick, are vacant *certo modo* at present and have been vacant for so
long that by the Lateran statutes their collation has lawfully devolved on the apostolic
see, although Thomas Offlayn [also spelt *Offilayn*], who bears himself as prior of the
said monastery, has detained the priory, and Thomas Rorre [also spelt *Norre*], who
bears himself as a priest, has detained the vicarage of Croch, with no title and no
support of law, of their own temerity and *de facto*, for a certain time, as they still do.
At a recent petition on Maurice's part to the pope to erect and institute a canonry in the
church of Limerick and the said vicarages into a simple prebend of it, for his lifetime,
the pope hereby commands that the above three (or two or one of them), if it is thus,
having summoned the bishop and chapter of Limerick, shall erect and institute a
canonry in the church of Limerick; and [having summoned] Thomas Offlayn and
Thomas Rorre and others concerned, if they find the priory (which is conventual and
has cure of souls, and whose annual value does not exceed 12 marks sterling), and the
vicarages of Killseanall and Croch (whose annual values do not exceed 5 and 8 marks
sterling), to be vacant (howsoever etc.) shall (even if they are specially reserved or the
priory, because it is conventual, is generally reserved, etc.) erect and institute the
vicarages into a simple prebend of the church of Limerick, for Maurice's lifetime,
without prejudice to anyone; and also shall, with plenitude of canon law and all rights
and appurtenances, collate and assign the newly erected canonry and prebend, being
vacant, to Maurice, and commend the priory to him to be held, ruled and governed by
him for life; (Maurice may – due and customary burdens of the priorship having been
supported – <make disposition>[3] of the rest of its fruits etc. just as those holding it *in
titulum* at the time could and ought to do, alienation of immovable goods and precious
movables being however forbidden); inducting Maurice etc. into corporal possession
of the canonry and prebend and priory and rights and appurtenances aforesaid having
removed any unlawful detainers, and causing Maurice (or his proctor) to be received
as a canon in the church of Limerick; and shall assign Maurice a stall in the choir and
a place in the chapter of the church of Limerick, with plenitude of canon law, [causing]
him to be admitted to the priory and its fruits etc., rights and obventions and those of
the canonry and prebend to be delivered to him. [Curbing] gainsayers by [the pope's]
authority etc. Notwithstanding etc. The pope's will is, however, that the vicarages and
priory shall not, on this account, be defrauded of due services and the cure of souls in
them shall not be neglected; but that customary burdens of the priory and vicarages
shall be supported; and that on Maurice's death or his resignation etc. of the canonry
and prebend, the said erection and institution shall be extinguished and be so deemed
and the vicarages shall revert to their original condition automatically.

Apostolice sedis clementia circumspecta ad ea libenter intendit …
Phi d(e) agnellis / JoA: / : JoA: xxxx[4] *pridie k(a)l(endas) novebris*[5] *Anno Secundo.* [31

October 1514], *Nardinus*

1 MS: *millesimo quingentesimo quartodecimo decimonono kalendas Augusti anno secundo.* Impossible date: XIX Kal. cannot be of *Augusti*; *Januarii*, *Februarii*, or *Septembris* are the only candidates. Of the three, XIX Kal. Septembris [= 14 August 1514] suggests itself [unless the year of the Incarnation is wrong]. The others are ruled out by the bullaria expedition date which necessarily post-dates the date under which the letter is drawn.
2 MS: *dicte diocesis* – evidently referring to Limerick
3 *disponere et ordinare sucuti* [*sic*] inserted in margin, initialled *JoA.* and perhaps in his hand – just one of several marginal insertions. There are also deletions in line and various other small-scale alterations.
4 (?)*v* deleted here
5 *sic*

337   4 October 1514   *Reg. Lat.* 1322, fos 221ᵛ-222ʳ

To Robert Kakilworthi,[1] canon of the priory of Sts Peter and Paul, Taunton',[2] OSA, d. Bath and Wells. Dispensation and indult – at his supplication – to receive and retain any benefice, with or without cure, usually held by secular clerics, even if a parish church or its perpetual vicarage, or a chantry, free chapel, hospital or annual service, usually assigned to secular clerics in title of a perpetual ecclesiastical benefice, and of lay patronage and of whatsoever tax or annual value, if he obtains it otherwise canonically, to resign it, simply or for exchange, as often as he pleases and in its place receive and retain another, similar or dissimilar, secular benefice, with or without cure; and – even after he has acquired the said benefice – to receive the canonical portion usually received by the canons of the above priory of which he is a canon and, as he asserts, expressly professed of the order and to have, for life, a stall in the choir and also a place and an active and a passive voice in the chapter of the said priory and otherwise as before, without limitation, just as if he had not acquired the benefice. Notwithstanding etc. Given at Ronciglione, d. Sutri.

Religionis zelus, vite ac morum honestas …
P. lambert(us) / JoA: / JoA: Lx: Nardinus

1 the first 'i' doubtful; possibly 'a'
2 the '-un-' a sympathetic reading

338   11 November 1514   *Reg. Lat.* 1322, fos 222ᵛ-224ʳ

To John Ochonant, perpetual vicar of the perpetual vicarage of the parish church[1] of St Cormac, Drumonilche, d. Clogher, (who is a priest). Following the pope's reservation some time ago of all benefices, with and without cure, vacated then and in the future at the apostolic see to his own collation and disposition, the perpetual vicarage of the above parish church, which Maurice <Macdonnallynd>,[2] lately[3] perpetual vicar of this perpetual vicarage,[4] was then holding, became vacant by his free resignation made spontaneously into the hands of the pope and admitted by him at the said see, and is vacant at present, being reserved as above. The pope hereby collates and makes provision of the vicarage (whose annual value does not exceed 8 marks sterling) (vacant as above or howsoever etc.; even if it has been vacant for so long that by the Lateran statutes its collation has lawfully devolved on the apostolic see etc.), with all rights and appurtenances, to John. Notwithstanding etc.

Executory to the bishops of Cavaillon and Ascoli and the dean of the church of Clogher, or two or one of them, acting in person or by proxy.[5]

Vite ac morum honestas … The executory begins: *Hodie dilecto filio Johanni Ochonant* …
P. d(e) Castello; P. planca / M / M vij: v: quarto non(as) decembris an(n)o secundo [2 December 1514], *de Campania*

1   *perpetuo vicario perpetue vicarie parrochialis ecclesie.* Odd formulation; usually simply 'perpetuo vicario parrochialis ecclesie'; *cf.* below, note 4.
2   *Donaldi* in line deleted and initialled *M*; *Macdonnallynd* inserted in margin initialled *M*. The same deletion in line and insertion in margin are repeated in the executory, the marginal insertion likewise being initialled *M*
3   A curious deletion (initialled *M*) occurs after *nuper ipsius* namely: *ecclesie rectoris de.* There is no suggestion of a rector or rectory elsewhere in the entry.
4   *perpetue vicarie perpetui vicarii.* Cf. above, note 1.
5   A curious deletion occurs in the executory between *facientes eundem* and *Johannem ad vicariam huiusmodi ut est moris admicti* namely: *Franciscum* [*sic*] *vel procuratorem suum eius nomine.* The deletion is not initialled; but there is a cross (signalling error?) above the deleted passage and another in the margin opposite. There is no suggestion of a "Francis" elsewhere in the entry.

339   12 October 1514   *Reg. Lat.* 1322, fos 224[r]-226[r]

To the dean and the chancellor of the church of Cashel and the official of Cashel, mandate in favour of Gerald Johannis de Geraldinis, precentor of the church of Lismore. A recent petition to the pope on Gerald's part stated that at another time, when the archdeaconry of the church of Cashel was vacant *certo modo*, the then archbishop of Cashel, by ordinary authority, collated and made provision of it, thus vacant, to Gerald; and, furthermore, that Gerald fears that, for certain reasons, this collation and provision do not hold good; and, as the pope has learned, the archdeaconry is understood to be vacant still as above. At the supplication on the part of Gerald – who asserts that the annual value of the above archdeaconry does not exceed 20, and of the precentorship of the said church of Lismore (to which the rectory of the parish church of Ardinore, d. Lismore, is united etc. in perpetuity), 40, marks sterling – to the pope to unite etc. the archdeaconry to the precentorship, which Gerald holds, for as long as he does so, the pope hereby commands that the above three (or two or one of them), having summoned those interested, shall unite etc. the archdeaconry, which is a dignity, not however major *post pontificalem*, (vacant howsoever etc.; even if it has been vacant for so long that by the Lateran statutes its collation has lawfully devolved on the apostolic see, etc.), with all its rights and appurtenances, to the precentorship, for as long as Gerald holds the latter; to the effect that he may, on his own authority, in person or by proxy, freely take and retain corporal possession of the archdeaconry and the rights and appurtenances aforesaid, for as long as he holds the precentorship, and convert its fruits etc. to his own uses and those of the archdeaconry and precentorship without licence of the local diocesan or of anyone else. Notwithstanding etc. The pope's will is, however, that the archdeaconry shall not, on this account, be defrauded of due services and the cure of souls in it (if any) shall not be neglected; but that its customary burdens shall be supported; and that on Gerald's death or his resignation etc. of the precentorship this union etc. shall be dissolved and be so deemed and the archdeaconry shall revert to its original condition and be deemed vacant automatically. Given at Viterbo.

Romanum decet pontificem votis illis gratum prestare assensum …
Phi d(e) agnellis / M / M xij quarto non(as) decembris an(n)o secundo [2 December 1514], *de Campania*

340 13 October 1514[1]   *Reg. Lat.* 1322, fos 226ʳ-228ᵛ

To the precentor of the church of Cashel and Thady Oronan, canon of the church of Lismore, and Philip Omulkochory,[2] canon of the church of Limerick, mandate in favour of William Ylahaffayn,[3] canon of the church of Lismore. A recent petition to the pope on William's part stated that at another time when the perpetual vicarages of the parish churches of Kyllimyloch,[4] Kyllscyech[5] *alias* Colman and Kyllbracha, d. Cashel, were vacant *certo modo*, the then archbishop of Cashel, by ordinary authority, united etc. them altogether,[6] thus vacant, for William's lifetime, and collated and made provision of them, thus united, to William, by the said authority. At the supplication on the part of William – who asserts that he holds a canonry and prebend of the church of Lismore – to the pope to erect and institute a canonry in the church of Cashel and the said vicarages into a simple prebend, for his lifetime, the pope – not having certain knowledge of the foregoing – hereby commands that the above three (or two or one of them), if it is thus, having summoned the archbishop and chapter of Cashel and others concerned, shall erect and institute a canonry in the church of Cashel and the vicarages, whose annual value together does not exceed 8 marks sterling, (vacant howsoever etc.; even if they have been vacant for so long that by the Lateran statutes their collation has lawfully devolved on the apostolic see etc.), into a simple prebend of the said church of Cashel, for William's lifetime, without prejudice to anyone; and in the event of this erection and institution, shall collate and assign the newly erected canonry and prebend, being vacant, with plenitude of canon law and all rights and appurtances, to William, inducting him etc. having removed any unlawful detainer and causing William (or his proctor) to be received as a canon of the church of Cashel; and shall assign him a stall in the choir and a place in the chapter of the said church of Cashel, with plenitude of canon law, [causing] the fruits etc., rights and obventions of the erected canonry and prebend to be delivered to him. [Curbing] gainsayers by [the pope's] authority etc. Notwithstanding etc. The pope's will is, however, that the vicarages shall not, on this account, be defrauded of due services and the cure of souls in them shall not be neglected; but that their customary burdens shall be supported; and that on William's death or his resignation etc. of the erected canonry and prebend this erection and institution shall be extinguished and be so deemed and the vicarages shall revert to their original condition automatically. Given at Montefiascone.

Apostolice sedis circumspecta benignitas ad ea libenter intendit …
Phi d(e) agnellis / M / M xxx tercio k(a)l(endas) septembris an(n)o secundo [30 August 1514],[7] *de Campania*

1   *sic*; corroborated by place-date; but conflicts with bullaria expedition date
2   uncertain: there may be a letter between the 'o' and 'c' in *och*; or perhaps the 'o' in question is an 'a'.
3   the 'l' formed not unlike a capital 'P'
4   the 'm' uncertain
5   the first 'c' and the 'e' uncertain
6   *invicem* (the context here being a union of three – not, as commonly, two – benefices)
7   *sic*; probably incorrect. The bullaria expedition date should, of necessity, post-date the date under which the letter is drawn.

341   13 October 1514   *Reg. Lat.* 1322, fos 284ᵛ-287ʳ

To the dean and Thady Oronan, canon, of the church of Lismore, and the official of Cork, mandate in favour of Eugene Odalig, cleric, d. Cork. The pope has learned that the canonry and prebend of Kyllynella [of the church] of Cork and the perpetual vicarage of the parish church of Lysanclery and also the rectory (which is of lay patronage) of the parish church of Kyllnyde, d. Cork, are vacant *certo modo* at present and have been vacant for so long that by the Lateran statutes their collation has lawfully devolved on the apostolic see, although Rory Offlayn has detained the canonry and prebend and David Oconyll', the rectory – bearing themselves as clerics – and John Hogan has detained the vicarage – bearing himself as a canon, OSA – with no title and no support of law, of their own temerity and *de facto*, for a certain time, as they still do. At the supplication on the part of Eugene – who asserts that the annual value of the canonry and prebend and the rectory and vicarage altogether does not exceed 16 marks sterling – to the pope to unite etc. the rectory and vicarage to the canonry and prebend, for as long as Eugene holds the latter, if conferred on him by virtue of the presents, the pope hereby commands that the above three (or two or one of them), if, having summoned Rory, David and John and others concerned and those interested in the union, they find the canonry and prebend and the rectory and vicarage to be vacant (howsoever etc.; even if specially reserved etc.) shall collate and assign the canonry and prebend, with plenitude of canon law, to Eugene, and unite etc. the rectory and vicarage, with all rights and appurtenances, to the canonry and prebend, for as long as Eugene holds the latter, if conferred on him as above; inducting him etc. having removed Rory, David and John and any other unlawful detainers and causing Eugene (or his proctor) to be received as a canon of the church of Cork; and shall assign him a stall in the choir and a place in the chapter of the church of Cork, with plenitude of canon law; [causing] him to be admitted to the rectory and vicarage and [causing] the fruits etc., rights and obventions of the rectory and vicarage and the canonry and prebend to be delivered to him. [Curbing] gainsayers by [the pope's] authority etc. Notwithstanding etc. The pope's will is, however, that the rectory and vicarage shall not, on account of this union etc., be defrauded of due services and the cure of souls in them shall not be neglected; but that their customary burdens shall be supported; and that on Eugene's death or his resignation etc. of the canonry and prebend this union etc. shall be dissolved and be so deemed and the rectory and vicarage shall revert to their original condition and be deemed vacant automatically. Given at Montefiascone.

Vite ac morum honestas ...
Phi d(e) agnellis / JoA: / Jo:A.[1] *xxx: Decimo octavo k(a)l(endas) decenbris Anno Secundo:* [14 November 1514], *Nardinus*

1   *sic*; oddly punctuated; usually: 'JoA:' (occasionally ':JoA:', 'JoA.' etc.)

342   12 October 1514   *Reg. Lat.* 1322, fos 287ʳ-289ᵛ

To Thady Oronan and Rubertus[1] Offlahamayn, canons of the church of Lismore, mandate in favour of Edmund de Geraldinis, cleric, d. Lismore. The pope has learned that the perpetual vicarages of the parish churches of Acydymoyr and Lisgeynayn, d. Lismore, are vacant *certo modo* at present and have been vacant for so long that by the Lateran statutes their collation has lawfully devolved on the apostolic see, although James Macgyllymury has detained one of the vicarages and Edmund Breayn the other – bearing themselves as priests – with no title or support of law, of their own temerity and *de facto*, for a certain time, as they still do. At a recent petition on the part of Edmund de Geraldinis to the pope to erect and institute a canonry in the church of Lismore and the said vicarages into a simple prebend, for his lifetime, the pope – not having certain knowledge of the foregoing – hereby commands that the above three (or two or one of them), if it is thus [and], having summoned James and also Edmund Breayn and others concerned,[2] they find the vicarages (whose annual values together do not exceed 20 marks sterling) to be vacant howsoever etc., shall erect and institute a canonry in the church of Lismore and the said vicarages (even if specially reserved etc.) into a simple prebend of the said church, for the lifetime of Edmund de Geraldinis, without prejudice to anyone, and collate and assign the newly erected canonry and prebend, with plenitude of canon law and with all their rights and appurtenances, to Edmund de Geraldinis, inducting him etc. having removed James and also Edmund Breayn and any other unlawful detainers and causing Edmund de Geraldinis (or his proctor) to be received as a canon of the church of Lismore; and shall assign him a stall in the choir and a place in the chapter of the said church, with plenitude of canon law, and [causing] the fruits etc., rights and obventions of the canonry and prebend to be delivered to him. [Curbing] gainsayers by [the pope's] authority etc. Notwithstanding etc. The pope's will is, however, that the said vicarages shall not, on this account, be defrauded of due services and the cure of souls in them shall not be neglected; but that their customary burdens shall be supported; and that on the death of Edmund de Geraldinis or his resignation etc. of the canonry and prebend this erection and institution shall be dissolved[3] and be so deemed and the vicarages shall revert to their original condition automatically. Given at Viterbo.

Apostolice sedis circu[m]specta benignitas ad ea libenter intendit ...
Phi d(e) agnellis / JoA. / JoA: xxx: Decimo octavo k(a)l(endas) decenbris Anno
Secundo: [14 November 1514], *Nardinus*

1   *sic*; for Robert?
2   no express mention of summoning the bishop of Lismore and the chapter
3   *dissolute sint* – unexpected choice of verb ('dissolvere' usual in respect of a union; 'extinguere' usual in respect of an erection)

343   3 September 1514   *Reg. Lat.* 1323, fos 91^r-92^r

To M. Richard Pace (*Paceo*), archdeacon of Dorset (*Dorsetie*) in the church of Salisbury, papal notary. Indult[1] for life – at his supplication – to visit by suitable deputy the churches, monasteries and other ecclesiastical places within the limits of the archdeaconry of Dorset and their personnel, in which the office of visitation falls, by law or custom, to him as archdeacon, as often as the time of visitation shall occur, even two, three or more of the said places in the same day, and to receive the limited (*moderatas*) procurations due to him on visitation in ready money.[2] Notwithstanding the constitutions of Innocent IV and Gregory X,[3] and of Otto and Ottobuono,[4] etc. It is, however, the pope's intention that no-one shall be compelled, by pretext of this indult, to pay a procuration beyond his means.

Executory to the archbishop of York and the bishops of Cavaillon and Ascoli, or two or one of them, acting in person or by proxy.

Meruit tue devotionis sinceritas ... The executory begins: *Hodie d(ilecto) f(ilio)*
magistro Richardo Paceo ...
phi. de Agnellis; O. de Cesis. / JoA: / JoA: xxx: xx: Nardinus

1   Omission in the narrative: *Hinc est quod nos* [...] *tuis in hac parte supplicationibus inclinati* ...: there is no *absolutio ad effectum* (and, corroboratively, no reference to it in the final clauses: *Nulli et cetera nostri indulti infringere et cetera*). The omission is probably explicable in terms of defective drafting rather than scribal error. Further particulars of the grantee may also have been inadvertently omitted from the narrative.
2   No maximum limit stated for the daily total (usually – as in *CPL*, XVII Part 1, no. 371 – explicitly set at '30 silver tournois, of which 12 are worth one gold florin of Florence' [*cf. Extra. Comm.*, III. 10 (Friedberg, 1280–1284)]). Instead the entry has *procurationes ... moderatas*.
3   *Cf. Sext*, III. 20.1 and 2 respectively (Friedberg, 1056–1058).
4   *Constitutiones Legatinae ... Othonis* and *Othoboni, Cardinalium, & Sedis Romanae in Anglia Legatorum*, Oxford, 1679, pp. 114–115 (*Naturalis dispositionis* of Ottobuono).

344   10 February 1515   *Reg. Lat.* 1323, fos 95ᵛ-97ʳ

To the dean <of the church>[1] of Glasgow, mandate in favour of Thomas Thawmer,[2] cleric, d. Aberdeen.[3] Following the pope's reservation some time ago of all dignities and offices and other benefices, with and without cure, vacated then [and in the future] at the apostolic see [to his own collation and disposition],[4] the succentorship of the church of Moray became vacant by the free resignation of the recent succentor Andrew Forman (who was holding the succentorship at the time) made spontaneously through John Thomson,[5] cleric, d. St Andrews (his specially appointed proctor), into the hands of the pope, who admitted the resignation at the said see, and is vacant at present, being reserved as above. The pope hereby commands the above dean, if by diligent examination he finds Thomas to be suitable – concerning which the pope burdens the dean's conscience – to collate and assign the succentorship, (which is a dignity, not however major *post pontificalem*, or an office; and whose annual value does not exceed 26 pounds sterling) – whether vacant as above or still by the death outside the Roman curia of former succentor John Syms,[6] or in any other way etc., or by similar resignation of Andrew or John aforesaid, etc.; even if [it has been vacant] for so long etc.), with all its rights and appurtenances, to Thomas; inducting him etc. having removed any detainer[7] and causing Thomas (or his proctor) to be admitted to the succentorship and its fruits etc., rights and obventions to be delivered to him. [Curbing] gainsayers etc. Notwithstanding etc.

Dignum et cetera.
.P. Lambertus[8] / *JoA:* / *JoA: xxv: Quintodecimo K(a)l(endas) Agusti*[9] [18 July 1515], *Nardinus*

1   *ecclesie* inserted in margin initialled *JoA.* (and perhaps in his hand)
2   the initial 'T' definite: not readable as a 'C'
3   *Aberinnen.*
4   common form indicated in MS by *et cetera*
5   read sympathetically; strictly: *Thonison* as the third minim is dotted.
6   read sympathetically; strictly: *Syins* as the first minim is dotted.
7   *illicito* does not occur.
8   written in 'semi' bollatica; *cf.* above, no 191, note 1.
9   or *A'gusti* (reading a possible bar over the 'g')

345[1]   26 March 1514   *Reg. Lat.* 1323, fos 241ᵛ-243ᵛ

Mandate to collate and assign to Francesco Chiericati (*Cheregatus*), cleric of Vicenza, the perpetual chaplaincy at the altar of St Mary in the parish church of St Mary, Cologna Veneta (*loci Colonie*), d. Vicenza, which, by apostolic concession and dispensation, the late John, bishop of Cattaro (*Catharen.*), held *in commendam*, is, with the ending of the commend by his death outside the Roman curia, still vacant at present in the way in which it was vacant before it was commended. All right in and to the said chaplaincy (which is with cure and whose annual value does not exceed 40 gold ducats of the camera), has this day been freely and spontaneously ceded into the hands of the pope (and the pope has admitted the cession) by Christopher, cardinal priest of the title of S Prassede, the cardinal of York, who did not have possession of it and who asserts that at another time he had, within the lawful time, accepted the said chaplaincy, then vacant as above, on the strength of certain letters of general reservation granted to him by the pope (as he was able under their form) and had had it commended to him. The letter, which is addressed to three mandataries, is of no other interest to the Calendar.

Vite ac morum honestas ...
[–]² / [–] / [–]³

1   The status of this entry is uncertain. Though it lacks the usual administrative notes (*cf.* below, notes 2 and 3) it has not been struck out. Unhappily, there is no explanatory note.
2   no name of abbreviator
3   The letter is unsigned: registry master's intial (at start of entry) and subscription are both wanting.

346¹   14 July 1514   *Reg. Lat.* 1323, fos 256ʳ-258ʳ

Mandate, *motu proprio*, to commend to M. Giuliano de' Tornabuoni (*de Tornabonis*), cleric of Florence, the pope's notary and continual commensal familiar, the monastery of S. Nicandro, order of St Basil, d. Messina (whose annual value does not exceed 24 gold ducats of the camera) which, by apostolic concession and dispensation, the late Christopher, cardinal priest of the title of S Prassede, held *in commendam* and which, with the ending of the commend by his death at the apostolic see, is known to be vacant at present [still] in the way it was vacant before it was commended. The letter, which is addressed to three mandataries, is of no other interest to the Calendar.

Romani pontificis providentia circumspecta ...
[–]² / [–] / [–]³

1   The status of this entry is unclear. Though without the usual administrative notes (*cf.* below, notes 2 and 3) the entry is not deleted. Unfortunately, there is no explanatory note. Bainbridge died during the night of 14 July 1514 – the date under which this letter is drawn. On the date and circumstances of his death *see* D.S. Chambers, *Cardinal Bainbridge in the Court of Rome 1509 to 1514* (Oxford, 1965), p. 131 foll.
2   no abbreviator's name
3   The entry is unsigned: wants registry master's initial (at start of entry) and subscription.

347¹   3 May 1515   *Reg. Lat.* 1324, fos 5ʳ-7ᵛ

To Dermot Oflanagam,¹ canon of the church of Elphin, and Bernard Maccarinne² and Felmeus Odonaill', canons of the church of Raphoe, mandate in favour of Nillanus Omullfayl,³ canon [of the church] of Raphoe. It has been referred to the pope's audience by Nillanus that Conatius Oseegil,⁴ abbot of the monastery of *Celemegre*,⁵ [Derry], OCist,⁶ d. Derry, has dared to dilapidate several of the monastery's immovable goods, to commit perjury, and also to receive a certain sum of money to collate a certain benefice or office (then vacant and pertaining to the collation and provision of the abbot for the time being), as he subsequently did, incurring simony and the sentence of excommunication, and other censures and pains promulgated against such persons. Considering that, if the above related matters are true, abbot Conatius has rendered himself unworthy of the rule and administration of the said monastery over which he presides; and wishing to provide a capable and suitable governor to rule and direct the monastery as well as to assist Nillanus – who asserts that he holds a canonry of the church of Raphoe and the prebend of Tualaeligle (to which the rectory of the parish church of Raygfem, d. Raphoe, is united by apostolic authority, for as long as he holds the prebend) – to be supported more conveniently, the pope hereby commands that the above three (or two or one of them), if Nillanus will accuse abbot Conatius before them over the above related matters and proceed in form of law, thereafter, having summoned abbot Conatius and others concerned, shall make inquiry into these matters and, if they find the truth of them to be substantiated, deprive abbot Conatius of the said rule and administration and remove him from them; and, in that event, commend the monastery (whose annual value does not exceed 16 marks sterling) (vacant at that time by this deprivation and removal, or at another time howsoever, etc.; even if its provision pertains specially or generally to the apostolic see, etc.), with all rights and appurtenances, to Nillanus to be held, ruled and governed by him for life, even together with the above canonry and prebend and all the other benefices, with and without cure, secular and regular, which Nillanus holds as above and shall hold in the future, and with the annual pensions which he receives and shall receive in the future; he may – after due and customary burdens of the monastery and its convent have been supported; and, if the abbatial *mensa* is separated from the conventual *mensa*, after a fourth part of all the monastery's fruits has been bestowed annually on the restoration of the fabric, or on the purchase or repair of the ornaments, vestments and sacred furniture, or on the sustenance and maintenance of the poor, according to the greater need, or, if the *mensa* is common, after a third part of all its fruits, has been bestowed annually on the support and sustenance of the monks, called canons, of the monastery – make disposition of the rest of its fruits etc. just as abbots of the monastery could and ought to do, alienation of immovable goods and precious movables being however forbidden; committing the care, rule and administration of the monastery to Nillanus in spiritualities and temporalities, and causing due obedience and reverence to be given him by the convent and customary services and rights by the vassals and other subjects of the monastery. [Curbing] gainsayers etc. Notwithstanding etc. With the proviso that divine worship and the usual number of monks, called canons, and ministers in the said monastery shall not, on account of this commend, be diminished; but that the aforesaid burdens shall be supported. Given at the Lateran.

Romani pontificis providentia circumspecta …
Ge de prato / JoA: / JoA: xxxv: Nardinus

1   The 'f' does not have a bar through it and resembles a long 's'; but the initial 'f' of *filiis* (previous word but one) is similarly formed.
2   uncertain (esp. *-inn-*)
3   uncertain (esp. *mu-*)
4   uncertain: the first 'e' perhaps converted from a 'y'

5   or possibly *Celemigre*; for 'Celle nigre'
6   *sic*; *recte*: OSA

348   3 June 1515   *Reg. Lat.* 1324, fos 7ᵛ-10ᵛ

To the abbot of the monastery of Dubusge, d. Ossory, and Cornelius Olachnaym, canon
of the church of Cashel, and Gerald Macdubgayll, canon of the church of Leighlin,
mandate in favour of Donald Omakassa, perpetual vicar of the parish church of
Kykynail, d. Leighlin.[1] The pope has learned that the perpetual vicarages of the parish
churches of Eleysdum [also spelt *Elesdum*] and Hachacha, d. Leighlin, are vacant *certo
modo* at present and have been vacant for so long that by the Lateran statutes their
collation has lawfully devolved on the apostolic see, although Edmund Oneda[2] and
John Debrena[3] have detained the vicarages of Eleysdum and Hachacha respectively –
bearing themselves as priests – with no title and no support of law, of their own
temerity and *de facto*, for a certain time, and do so. At a recent petition on the part of
Donald (who asserts that the annual value of the said vicarages together does not
exceed 12 marks sterling) to the pope to erect and institute a canonry in the church of
Leighlin and the perpetual vicarage of the said church of Kykynail (which Donald
holds) into a simple prebend of it, for his lifetime, and to unite etc., likewise for his
lifetime, the vicarages of Eleysdum and Hachacha to the canonry and prebend thus
erected, after provision of the canonry and prebend has been made to Donald and he
has acquired them, the pope hereby commands that the above three (or two or one of
them), if, having summoned Edmund and John and the bishop and chapter of Leighlin
(as regards the erection) and others concerned, they find the vicarages of Eleysdum and
Hachacha to be vacant (howsoever etc.), shall erect and institute a canonry in the
church of Leighlin and the vicarage of Kykynail into a simple prebend of it, for
Donald's lifetime, without prejudice to anyone; and unite etc. the vicarages of
Eleysdum and Hachacha (even if specially reserved etc.) to the canonry and prebend
thus erected, likewise for his lifetime, without prejudice to anyone; and, in the event of
this erection and institution and union etc., shall collate and assign the newly erected
canonry and prebend, being then vacant, to Donald, with plenitude of canon law and
the annexes in question and all rights and appurtenances, inducting him into corporal
possession of the canonry and prebend and annexes and rights and appurtenances
aforesaid, having removed Edmund and John and any other unlawful detainers, and
causing Donald (or his proctor) to be received as a canon in the church of Leighlin, and
shall assign him a stall in the choir and a place in the chapter of the church of Leighlin,
with plenitude of <canon>[4] law, and [causing] the fruits etc., rights and obventions of
the canonry and prebend and those of the said annexes to be delivered to him.
[Curbing] gainsayers etc. Notwithstanding etc. and notwithstanding that there may be
an indult from the apostolic see to the abbot and convent of the monastery of Dubusge,
OCist, d. Ossory, and also to the prioress and convent of the monastery, usually
governed by a prioress, of Grane, OSA, d. Dublin *alias* Glendalough, to whom, it is
asserted, the presentation of suitable persons for the said vacant vicarages at a time of
vacancy respectively belongs by ancient and approved custom hitherto peacefully

observed, that they are not bound to the reception or provision of anyone and cannot be compelled to it, etc.[5] The pope's will is, however, that the said vicarages shall not, on account of this erection, institution and union etc., be defrauded of due services and the cure of souls in them shall not be neglected, but that their customary burdens shall be supported; and that on Donald's death or his resignation etc. of the canonry and prebend this erection and institution shall be extinguished and union etc. dissolved and be so deemed and the vicarages shall revert to their original condition automatically.

Apostolice sedis providentia circumspecta personarum ecclesiasticarum votis …
p lambertus / JoA: / : JoA: xxxv: Quarto k(a)l(endas) Julij Anno tertio: [28 June 1515], *Nard(inus)*

1　MS: *dicte diocesis* evidently referring to Leighlin
2　highly doubtful reading; only the 'd' safe
3　another highly doubtful reading; only the 'D' safe
4　*canonici* inserted in margin, initialled *JoA*.
5　Ordinarily this notwithstanding clause is disregarded by the Calendar. It is summarised here because (unusually) it contains definite particulars.

349　(?)31 May 1515[1]　　　　　　　　　　　　*Reg. Lat.* 1324, fos 11ʳ-14ʳ

To the precentor[2] of the church of Ossory and Gerald Macdubllgayll, canon of the church of Leighlin, and Donald Lassy, canon of the church of Ferns, mandate in favour of Maurus Kamanach, canon of [the church of][3] <Leighlin>.[4] The pope has learned that the archdeaconry of the church of Leighlin and the rectory of the parish church of Clendesyll,[5] d. Leighlin, are vacant *certo modo* at present and have been vacant for so long that by the Lateran statutes their collation has lawfully devolved on the apostolic see, although Patrick Olechluyr,[6] Cornelius Ofeona[7] [also spelt *Offecna, Offeolna,*[8] (?)*Offeona*[9]] and Gerard Obroyn[10] have detained the archdeaconry, dividing its fruits between themselves, and Cornelius Offeckna[11] [also spelt *Offeckana*] has detained the rectory – bearing themselves as priests – with no title and no support of law, of their own temerity and *de facto*, for a certain time, as they still do. At a recent petition on the part of Maurus (who asserts that he is more than seventeen years of age; and that, notwithstanding a defect of birth as the son of a cleric of noble birth and an unmarried woman, he has been dispensed by apostolic authority to be marked with clerical character; to be promoted to all, even sacred, orders; to minister in them, even before the altar; and to hold a benefice, even if it should be a canonry and prebend in a cathedral church; and that, by virtue of this dispensation, he has been duly marked with clerical character and holds a canonry and prebend of the said church of Leighlin; and that the annual value of the archdeaconry and rectory together does not exceed 16 marks sterling) to the pope to unite etc. the above rectory to the said archdeaconry, for as long as Maurus holds the latter, if conferred on him as above, the pope hereby commands that the above three (or two or one of them) if, having summoned Patrick and Cornelius Ofeona and Gerald and also Cornelius Offeckna and others concerned, they find the archdeaconry (which is a dignity, not however major *post pontificalem,* and perhaps is cured and elective) and the rectory to be vacant (howsoever etc.), shall unite etc. the rectory to the archdeaconry, for as long as Maurus holds the latter, if conferred on him as above; and shall collate and assign the archdeaconry (even if specially reserved etc.) to Maurus, with all rights and appurtenances, inducting him etc. into corporal possession of the archdeaconry and the annex and rights and appurtenances aforesaid, having removed the aforesaid and any other unlawful detainers and causing Maurus (or his proctor) to be admitted to the archdeaconry and its fruits etc., rights and obventions and those of the annex to be delivered to him. [Curbing] gainsayers etc. Notwithstanding etc. Also the pope dispenses Maurus to receive and retain the archdeaconry, if conferred on him by virtue of the presents, notwithstanding the above defects of birth and age, etc. The pope's will is, however, that the archdeaconry and rectory shall not, on this account, be defrauded of due services and the cure of souls in the rectory and (if any) the archdeaconry shall not be neglected; but that customary burdens shall be supported; and that on Maurus's death or his resignation etc. of the archdeaconry this union etc. shall be dissolved and the rectory shall revert to its original condition and be deemed vacant automatically.

Vite ac morum honestas …
phi de Agnell(is) / JoA: / JoA: xxxx Quarto k(a)l(endas) Julij Anno tertio [28 June 1515], *Nardinus*

1   reading *kalendas* (*idus* just possible)
2   *Dilectis fillis precenptori* upright script, much less cursive than the rest of the entry: same scribe?
3   'ecclesie' does not occur.
4   (?)*Leglen.* in line deleted and initialled *JoA*; *Leglien.* inserted in margin initialled *JoA*.
5   uncertain (especially the second 'e')
6   uncertain
7   the second 'o' (if it is an 'o') perhaps deleted; just possibly readable as *Ofechna*
8   uncertain; the *-ol-* particularly doubtful
9   uncertain (especially the 'o')
10   uncertain
11   uncertain

350   28 June 1515[1]   *Reg. Lat.* 1324, fos 17[r]-19[r]

To dean Maablosgid and archdeacon Macblosgid[2] of the church of Derry, and Nillanus Omul'fail, canon of the church of Raphoe, mandate in favour of Donat Omuri, cleric, d. Connor[3] (who, some time ago, as he asserts – after he had been duly marked with clerical character, notwithstanding a defect of birth as the son of a priest and an unmarried woman – was dispensed by apostolic authority – this defect notwithstanding – to be promoted to all, even sacred, orders and to hold a benefice, even if it should have cure of souls). The pope has learned that the rectory of the parish church of Cukam[4] *alias* Tempul padrig, said diocese, is vacant *certo modo* at present and has been vacant for so long that by the Lateran statutes its collation has lawfully devolved on the apostolic see, although Philip Omuri, who bears himself as a cleric, has detained it, with no title and no support of law, of his own temerity and *de facto*, for a certain time, and does so. He hereby commands that the above three (or two or one of them) if, having summoned Philip and others concerned, they find the rectory (whose annual value and that of the perpetual vicarage of the said church, which is annexed to the rectory, do not exceed 4 marks sterling) to be vacant (howsoever etc.) shall collate and assign the rectory (even if specially reserved, etc.), with the annexed vicarage and all rights and appurtenances, to Donat, inducting him etc. into corporal possession of the rectory and annexed vicarage and rights and appurtenances aforesaid, having removed Philip and any other unlawful detainer and causing Donat (or his proctor) to be admitted and the rectory's fruits etc., rights and obventions and those of the annexed vicarage to be delivered to him. [Curbing] gainsayers etc. Notwithstanding etc.

Vite ac morum honestas …
Ge de prato | JoA: | JoA: xv: tertio non(as) Julij Anno tertio:- [5 July 1515], *Nardinus*

1   reading *kalendas* (*idus* just possible)
2   *Sic*. It is most unusual in an address clause to further designate cathedral dignitaries by surname.
3   *Condoren.* (*cf. episcopo Conderen.*, which occurs just once below)
4   possibly *Cukarm* or *Crikarm*

351   17 May 1515[1]   *Reg. Lat.* 1324, fos 97[r]-99[r]

To Nillanus[2] Omulfail[3] and Felmeus Odonilmarch.elle,[4] canons of the church of Raphoe, mandate in favour of Odo Macgillabride, rector of the parish church of Tullacbigle, d. Raphoe. At a recent petition on the part of Odo (who asserts that at another time he was dispensed by apostolic authority, notwithstanding a defect of birth as the son of a priest and an unmarried woman, to be promoted to all, even sacred, orders and to hold a benefice, even if it should have cure of souls; and that, by virtue of this dispensation, he was duly promoted to the said orders and acquired the rectory of the above parish church, which was vacant *certo modo* at that time and was canonically collated to him; and also that the annual value of the said rectory and of the perpetual vicarage of the parish church of Regefenom,[5] d. Raphoe, which is perpetually annexed to the rectory, does not exceed 6 marks sterling) to the pope to erect and institute a canonry in the church of Raphoe and the rectory into a simple prebend, for Odo's lifetime, the pope hereby commands that the above three (or two or one of them) if it is thus, having summoned the bishop and chapter of Raphoe and others concerned, shall erect and institute a canonry in the church of Raphoe and the said rectory into a simple prebend, for Odo's lifetime, without prejudice to anyone; and, in the event of this erection and institution, shall collate and assign the newly erected canonry and prebend, then being vacant, with plenitude of canon law and with the annexes and all rights and appurtenances, to Odo, inducting him etc. into corporal possession of the canonry and prebend and annexes[6] and rights and appurtenances aforesaid having removed any unlawful detainer and causing Odo (or his proctor) to be received as a canon of the church of Raphoe, and shall assign him a stall in the choir and a place in the chapter of the church of Raphoe, with plenitude of canon law, and [causing] the fruits etc., rights and obventions of the said canonry and prebend and annexes[7] to be delivered to him. [Curbing] gainsayers etc. Notwithstanding etc. Also the pope dispenses Odo to receive and retain the canonry and prebend, if erected and conferred on him by virtue of the presents, as above, and with them, another benefice, even if it should have cure of souls, if conferred on him otherwise canonically; to resign them, simply or for exchange, and in their place receive and retain up to two other benefices likewise; notwithstanding the said defect (of birth) etc. The pope's will is, however, that the said rectory shall not, on this account, be defrauded of due services and the cure of souls in it shall not be neglected; but that its customary burdens shall be supported; and that on Odo's death or his resignation etc. of the canonry and prebend this erection and institution shall be extinguished and be so deemed and the rectory shall revert to its original condition automatically.

Apostolice sedis circumspecta benignitas ad ea libenter intendit …
phi de Agnell(is) / JoA: / JoA: xxv: Nardinus

1 There is a sizeable well-inked cross – resembling an ill-formed cross crosslet (or possibly cross potent) – in the left margin opposite the space between the last line of the dating clause and the magistral subscription. Crosses (usually signalling error) are not uncommon; but the form and size of this one is unusual.
2 or perhaps *Nillanius*
3 the 'il' read sympathetically
4 The 'onil' uncertain as is the letter after the 'h'.
5 uncertain reading
6 MS: *annexis*; *recte*: 'annexa'? (since only a perpetual vicarage is stated to be annexed)
7 MS: *annexorum*; *recte*: 'annexe'? (*Cf.* above, note 6)

352   7 June 1515   *Reg. Lat.* 1324, fos 99^r-102^r

To the prior of the priory of St Columba,[1] Instyghog, d. Ossory, and James Canchowll and William Maggylpadyk, canons of the church of Ossory, mandate in favour of William Arstekin, priest, d. Ossory. A recent petition to the pope on William's part stated that although, at another time, when the perpetual vicarage of the parish church of the place of Erke, said diocese, was vacant *certo modo*, the prior and brethren of the house of Kylmaynan of the Hospital of St John of Jerusalem, d. Dublin, had – since by ancient, approved, and hitherto peacefully observed custom the presentation of a suitable person for the vicarage at a time of vacancy belongs to the prior of the said house for the time being and the said brethren – presented William for the said vicarage, vacant as above, to the then bishop of Ossory within the lawful time and the said bishop, at this presentation, had instituted William as perpetual vicar, and he, by virtue of the said presentation and institution, had acquired possession of the vicarage, nevertheless John Ohelli, who bears himself as a cleric – claiming (albeit falsely) that the vicarage was vacant and that William was detaining it unlawfully – impetrated apostolic letters under a certain form over this to Henry Ollac, canon of the church of Cashel, and perhaps certain other colleagues of his in this regard, and by pretext of them[2] caused William to be summoned to trial before canon Henry, praying that the vicarage be adjudged his and that perpetual silence be imposed on William concerning it; and canon Henry, proceeding wrongly in the said cause, pronounced an unjust definitive sentence in favour of John and against William, from which William appealed to the apostolic see and impetrated apostolic letters concerning the said appeal to certain judges mentioned in the letters and, by virtue of the letters, caused John to be summoned to trial before the said judges in the cause of the said appeal; and the judges, proceeding lawfully in the cause of the said appeal, promulgated a definitive sentence by which they revoked[3] the sentence brought in by canon Henry; from which on John's part – asserting that the sentence was unjust – appeal was made to the apostolic see; and, when the cause of the later appeal had not yet been committed, the said bishop, taking the cause to himself *ex officio* (as he said), having summoned William and John, pronounced a null or unjust definitive sentence by which he declared that the right in or to the said vicarage belonged to neither William nor John; from which William, as regards the part of the sentence brought in against him, appealed again to the apostolic see and thereafter he had himself (albeit *de facto*) again presented for the vicarage by the said prior and brethren and again instituted by the said bishop. However since, as the said petition added, it is alleged by several persons that the right in or to the vicarage belongs to neither William nor John, the pope hereby commands that the above three (or two or one of them), having summoned John and others concerned, shall hear, duly decide and determine the causes of the last two appeals, causing by ecclesiastical censure, without appeal, what they have decreed to be strictly observed; [and moreover compel] witnesses, etc.; and, further, if it is established before them that the right in or to the said vicarage belongs to neither William nor John, they shall collate and assign the vicarage (whose annual value does not exceed 9 marks sterling), howsoever vacant etc, even if it has been vacant for so long that by the Lateran statutes its collation has lawfully devolved on the apostolic see, etc, with all its rights and appurtenances, to William, inducting him etc. having removed any unlawful detainer and causing William (or his proctor) to be admitted to the vicarage and its fruits etc., rights and obventions to be delivered to him. [Curbing] gainsayers etc. Notwithstanding etc.

Vite ac morum honestas …
phi de Agnell(is) / JoA: / :JoA: x: non(is) Julij Anno tertio: [7 July 1515], *Nardinus*

1   MS: *Sancte[!] Columbe*
2   MS: redundant: *… ac illarum pretextu … litterarum earundem pretextu …*
3   MS: *revocavit … promulgavit*

353   2 July 1515   *Reg. Lat.* 1324, fos 102[r]-105[r]

To Philip Omoran, Nilanus Omulfail and Bernard Macarama,[1] canons of the church of Raphoe, mandate in favour of Trollerus Macsrinne,[2] cleric, d. Raphoe. It has been referred to the pope's audience by Trollerus that Aeneas Odonil,[3] canon of the church of Raphoe – after the erection and institution of a canonry in the said church and of the parish church of the place of Clamdacbocdoc, d. Raphoe, (vacant *certo modo* at the time), into a simple prebend of that church, for as long as Aeneas should hold the said canonry and prebend; and after provision of the canonry and prebend, thus erected, had been made to Aeneas by apostolic authority[4] – Aeneas committed perjury and was judicially convicted of it, and incurred sentence of excommunication. The pope – considering that, if the foregoing is true, Aeneas has rendered himself unworthy of the said canonry and prebend which he holds; and wishing to give a special grace to Trollerus (who asserts that he is in his eighteenth year of age or thereabouts; and that, notwithstanding a defect of birth as the son of an unmarried man and an unmarried woman, he has been marked with clerical character, otherwise however duly); and extending and prolonging the erection and institution in question for the lifetime of Trollerus – hereby commands that the above three (or two or one of them), if Trollerus will accuse Aeneas over the above related matters and proceed in form of law, thereafter shall, having summoned Aeneas and others concerned, make inquiry into the above related matters, and if they find the truth of them to be substantiated, deprive Aeneas of the canonry and prebend and remove him from them; and, in that event, shall collate and assign the canonry and prebend (whose annual value does not exceed 12 marks sterling) (whether vacant by the above deprivation and removal or howsoever etc.; even if they have been vacant for so long that by the Lateran statutes their collation has lawfully devolved on the apostolic see, etc.), with plenitude of canon law and all rights and appurtenances, to Trollerus, inducting him etc. having removed any unlawful detainer and causing Trollerus (or his proctor) to be received as a canon in the church of Raphoe, and shall assign him a stall in the choir and a place in the chapter of the church of Raphoe, with plenitude of canon law, and [causing] the fruits etc., rights and obventions of the said canonry and prebend to be delivered to him. [Curbing] gainsayers etc. Notwithstanding etc. Also the pope dispenses Trollerus to receive and retain the said canonry and prebend, if conferred on him on the strength of the presents, notwithstanding the said defect etc. The pope's will is, however, that the above parish church shall not, on this account, be defrauded of due services and the cure of souls in it shall not be neglected; and that on the death of Trollerus or his resignation etc. of the canonry and prebend this erection, institution, prolongation and extension shall be extinguished and be so deemed and the parish church shall revert to its original condition automatically.

Vite ac morum honestas …
phi de Agnell(is) / JoA: / JoA: xx: non(is) Julij Anno tertio: [7 July 1515], *Nardinus*

1   or *-rmua* or *-ruma*
2   or *Macsunne*: the six minims between the 's' and 'e' capable of various readings
3   uncertain
4   *CPL* XIX, no. 166

354   7 May 1515   *Reg. Lat.* 1324, fos 129[v]-131[r]

To Felmeus Odonel, Bernard Manarmacha and Odo Maguile,[1] canons of the church of Raphoe, mandate in favour of Trollerus Machellbride, cleric of Raphoe,[2] (who, some time ago, as he asserts, notwithstanding a defect of birth as the son of an unmarried man and an unmarried woman, was dispensed by apostolic authority to be promoted to all, even sacred, orders, and to hold a benefice, even if it should have cure of souls, and afterwards was duly marked with clerical character). The pope has learned that the rectory of the parish church of Culmacuenam,[3] d. Raphoe, is vacant *certo modo* at present and has been vacant for so long that by the Lateran statutes its collation has lawfully devolved on the apostolic see, although Thady[4] Ofribel,[5] who bears himself as a priest, has detained it without any title or support of law, of his own temerity and *de facto*, for a certain time, as he does. He hereby commands that the above three (or two or one of them), if, having summoned Thady and others concerned, they find the rectory (whose annual value does not exceed 9 marks sterling) to be vacant (howsoever etc.), shall collate and assign it (even if specially reserved etc.) to Trollerus, inducting him etc. having removed Thady and any other unlawful detainer, and causing Trollerus (or his proctor) to be admitted to the rectory and its fruits etc., rights and obventions to be delivered to him. [Curbing] gainsayers etc. Notwithstanding etc. Also the pope dispenses Trollerus to resign the rectory, if [conferred] on him by virtue of the presents, simply or for exchange, as often as he pleases, and in its place receive and retain another similar benefice, if he obtains it otherwise canonically. Notwithstanding etc. Given at Magliana, d. Porto.

Vite ac morum honestas …
G. *de prato* / *JoA:* / *:JoA: xx: Quarto non(as) Junij Anno: tertio:* [2 June 1515], *Nardinus*

1   the 'ui' doubtful; the three minims (none dotted) capable of various readings
2   'diocesis' does not occur.
3   uncertain reading
4   In this instance, *Tatheus* follows the deletion of *Tha*
5   uncertain reading, especially the 'ri'

355 (?)2[1] June 1515

Reg. Lat. 1324, fos 167[r]-170[v]

To the abbot of the monastery of Dusque *alias* St Saviour [*de Sancto Salvatore*], d. Ossory, the prior of the priory of St John the Evangelist at Inisforthy, d. Ferns, and Cornelius Olochanyn,[2] canon of the church of Cashel, mandate in favour of Patrick Ygyhyn, cleric, d. Ferns. The pope has learned that the perpetual vicarage of the parish church of Karmilla[3] *alias* Karnodia and the rectories of the parish churches of Issertkainain[4] [also spelt *Issertkaman*] and Preben and also a certain perpetual ecclesiastical benefice, called a prebend, which is customarily conferred on one of the numerary canons of the church of Ferns, in the parish church of Tuoym, d. Ferns, are vacant *certo modo* at present and have been vacant for so long that by the Lateran statutes their collation has lawfully devolved on the apostolic see, although Nicholas Ogemnan[5] has detained the vicarage, Maurice Ostosgat has detained the rectory of Issertkainain and William Lacy that of Preben, and the said William Lacy and Thomas Quenurthwn[6] have detained the benefice – bearing themselves as priests – with no title and no support of law, of their own temerity and *de facto*, for a certain time, and do so. At a recent petition on the part of Patrick (who asserts that some time ago – after he, notwithstanding a defect of birth as the son of an unmarried man and an unmarried woman, had had himself marked with clerical character without having obtained a canonical dispensation for it – he was dispensed by apostolic authority to use the said character, to be promoted to all, even sacred and priest's, orders, and to hold a benefice, even if it should have cure of souls, notwithstanding the said defect; and that the annual value of the said vicarage and rectories and the benefice of Tuoym and annexes to it together does not exceed 29 marks sterling) the pope hereby commands that the above three (or two or one of them), if, having summoned Nicholas, Maurice, William and Thomas and, as regards the erection, the bishop and chapter of Ferns, and others concerned, they find the vicarage and rectories and the benefice of Tuoym (which is without cure and sacerdotal) to be vacant (howsoever etc.) shall erect and institute a canonry in the church of Ferns and the said vicarage and rectories and the benefice of Tuoym into a simple prebend of the church of Ferns (even if they are specially reserved etc.), for Patrick's lifetime, without prejudice to anyone; and, in the event of the said erection and institution, collate and assign the newly erected canonry and prebend, being then vacant, to Patrick, with plenitude of canon law and the annexes in question and all their rights and appurtenances, inducting him etc. into corporal possession of the canonry and prebend and of the annexes and rights and appurtenances aforesaid, having removed Nicholas, Maurice, William and Thomas and any other unlawful detainers and causing Patrick (or his proctor) to be received as a canon of the church of Ferns; and shall assign him a stall in the choir and a place in the chapter of the church of Ferns, with plenitude of canon law, and [causing] the fruits etc., rights and obventions of the canonry and prebend and annexes aforesaid to be delivered to him. [Curbing] gainsayers etc. Notwithstanding etc. and notwithstanding that there may be an indult from the apostolic see to the abbess and convent of the monastery of nuns of Grane, OSA, d. Dublin *alias* Glendalough, to whom, it is asserted, the presentation of a suitable person to the said vicarage at a time of vacancy belongs by ancient and approved custom hitherto peacefully observed, that they are not bound to the reception or provision of anyone and cannot be compelled to it, etc.[7] Also the pope dispenses Patrick to receive and retain the said canonry and prebend, if conferred on him by virtue of the presents, and to resign them, at once or successively, simply or for exchange, as often as he pleases and in their place likewise receive and retain another, similar or dissimilar, benefice, even if it should have cure of souls, notwithstanding the above defect etc. The pope's will is, however, that the vicarage and rectories and the benefice of Tuoym shall not, on account of the above erection and institution, be defrauded of due services and the cure of souls in the vicarage and rectories shall not be neglected, but that their customary burdens and those of the benefice of Tuoym shall be supported; and that on Patrick's death or his resignation etc. of the canonry and prebend this erection and institution shall be utterly extinguished and be so deemed and the vicarage and rectories and the benefice of Tuoym shall revert to their original condition automatically.

Apostolice sedis providentia circumspecta personarum ecclesiasticarum votis ...
p lambertus / JoA: / JoA: xxxx: Nard(inus): –

1　　MS: ... *quarto non(as) Julii* ...; but the word here read as *non(as)* (in preference to 'idus') is blotched and uncertain.

2   the 'O' doubtful; possibly 'C'
3   the '-mi-' variously readable
4   the '-in-'s variously readable
5   the minims read as '-mn-' capable of various readings
6   very uncertain
7   *See above*, no. 348, note 5.

356   4 June 1515   *Reg. Lat.* 1324, fos 202ᵛ-203ᵛ

To John Fransbysh,[1] <perpetual vicar>[2] of the parish church of Rugewyk[3] <d. Chichester>.[4] Dispensation and indult etc. [as above, no. 2].[5]

Vite ac morum honestas …
phi de agnellis / JoA: / JoA: Lx: Nard(inus): –

1   the 'b' slightly uncertain
2   *perpetuo vicario* inserted at end of line; initialled *JoA.*
3   occurs thus twice; in both occurrences the 'k' is doubtful
4   *Cistrenen.' diocesis salutem et cetera* inserted in margin, initialled *JoA.*
5   Save for a few small textual oddities unique to this entry (e.g. once where the context requires 'et dignitates' *et digni* has been deleted and initialled *JoA.* leaving only *tates* [!]). And – referring to the kingdom of England – this entry has (?)*Scitilie* (or suchlike) instead of 'Anglie'. Note also that the order of phrases in the present indult does not correspond exactly with that of no. 2.

357   4 June 1515   *Reg. Lat.* 1324, fos 203ᵛ-205ʳ

Union etc. At a recent petition on the part of Thomas Gresham, rector of the parish church of Southe[1] [also spelt *Sote'*,[2] *Soute*, *Sonte*] Reppes,[3] d. Norwich, the pope hereby unites etc. the parish church of Wyffton',[4] d. Norwich (whose annual value does not exceed 9 pounds sterling), with all rights and appurtenances, to the above church of Southe Reppes, which he holds together with Wyffton' by apostolic dispensation, for as long as he holds Southe Reppes, to the effect that he may, on his own authority, in person or by proxy, continue in, or take anew, and retain corporal possession of Wyffton' and the rights and appurtenances aforesaid, for as long as he holds Southe Reppes, and convert its fruits etc. to his own uses and those of the said churches, without licence of the local diocesan or of anyone else. Notwithstanding etc. The pope's will is, however, that the church of Wyffton' shall not, on account of this union etc., be defrauded of due services and the cure of souls in it shall not be neglected; but that its customary burdens shall be supported; and that on Thomas's death or his resignation etc. of the church of Southe Reppes this union etc. shall be dissolved and be so deemed and Wyffton' shall revert to its original condition automatically.

Ad futuram rei memoriam. Romanum decet pontificem votis illis gratum prestare assensum …

p la(m)bert(us) / JoA: / : JoA: xxxv: Nardinus

1   the second occurrence of the name; *see* note 2.
2   This spelling in fact occurs first; but, in this instance, the 'So-' is blotched and doubtful.
3   The first 'p' is uncertain in two (out of eight) occurrences.
4   here and below the '-ff-' uncertain: perhaps '-ss-'

358   7 June 1515   *Reg. Lat.* 1324, fos 212ᵛ-214ʳ

To David Oculeayn and William Ohuluyn, canons of the church of Tuam, and William[1]
Omochayn, canon of the church of Killala, mandate in favour of Robert Omale *alias*
Baret, cleric, d. Tuam (who, as he asserts, notwithstanding a defect of birth as the son
of a cleric and an unmarried woman, has been duly marked with clerical character).
The pope has learned that the perpetual vicarage of the parish church of Villgaiphair,[2]
d. Tuam,[3] is vacant *certo modo* at present and has been vacant for so long that by the
Lateran statutes its collation has lawfully devolved on the apostolic see, although
Monan Oduchard, who bears himself as a priest, has detained the vicarage, with no (at
least no canonical) title or support of law, for a certain time, but short of a year, as he
does. He hereby commands that the above three (or two or one of them), if, having
summoned Monan and others concerned, they find the vicarage, whose annual value
does not exceed 3 marks sterling, to be vacant (howsoever etc.), shall collate and assign
it (even if [(?)specially][4] reserved etc.), with all rights and appurtenances, to Robert,
inducting him etc., having removed Monan and any other unlawful detainer, and
causing Robert (or his proctor) to be admitted to the vicarage and its fruits etc., rights
and obventions to be delivered to him. [Curbing] gainsayers etc. Notwithstanding etc.
Also the pope dispenses Robert[5] to receive and retain the vicarage, if conferred on him
by virtue of the presents, notwithstanding the above defect etc.

Vite ac morum honestas …
p lambertus / JoA: / JoA: xv: non(o) k(a)l(endas) Julij Anno tertio: [23 June 1515],
Nardinus

1   MS: (?)*Illialmo*; the first letter very uncertain; perhaps a 'V'
2   the 'h' doubtful
3   MS: *dicte diocesis* – evidently referring to Tuam.
4   'specialiter' does not occur; but the omission is not necessarily deliberate as it coincides with the point of
     transition between one line and the next.
5   Directly after *Robertus*, MS has: *presens non fuerit ad prestandum de observandis statutis et consuetudinibus
     dicte ecclesie solitum iuramentum* deleted and initialled *JoA* in five places and *Nard(inus)* in one. The
     deleted passage was certainly inappropriate here: it belongs to the formulary of provisions to cathedral (and
     the like) benefices (e.g. canonry and prebend) – not to parochial benefices.

359   17 August 1515   *Reg. Lat.* 1324, fos 246ᵛ-247ᵛ

To Philip Joh'ns, BDec, rector of the parish church of Cantres',[1] d. St David's.
Dispensation and indult etc. [as above, no. 2].

Litterarum scientia, vite ac morum honestas …
.P. Lambertus. / JoA: / JoA: Lx: Nardinus

1 In both occurrences the final letter is a long 's' with a diagonal stroke through it (which resembles the abbreviated form for 'ser').

360[1]   22 February 1515   *Reg. Lat.* 1324, fos 267ᵛ-270ᵛ

To all archbishops, bishops, abbots, and other ecclesiastical dignitaries, and also canons of cathedral churches, and the vicars general in spirituals of the said archbishops and bishops, letters conservatory. At the supplication of abbot William and the convent of the monastery of B Mary the Virgin, Osney at Oxford (*de Oseneya iuxta Oxoniam*), OSA, d. Lincoln, who have complained that several archbishops etc[2] have occupied and unlawfully detain towns (*castra*), vills, etc[2] of the said monastery and that several persons molest the abbot and convent and their familiars and servants (*servitoribus*) over the towns, vills, etc, the pope hereby commands that the above addressees (or two or one of them), acting in person or by proxy, even if the abbot and convent are outside the places in which they are appointed conservators and judges, shall defend the abbot and convent etc and not allow them to be unlawfully molested over these things etc and they are to be prepared to administer justice when required by the abbot and convent or their proctors in respect of the aforesaid and any other persons with regard to the restitution of the towns, vills, etc and in respect of any molestations etc, summarily, simply, and informally, without the formality and formulas of legal proceedings, in those cases which require judicial investigation, in others as their quality demands, on the pope's authority compelling occupiers etc of whatever dignity etc, whenever and as often as expedient, by ecclesiastical censure, without appeal, having, if necessary, even called in the aid of the secular arm; and, when the relevant lawful processes to be conducted by the above addressees have been observed, they shall take care to aggravate, repeatedly and as often as necessary, the censures and pains inflicted by them against those who, it appears, have incurred them; furthermore, if by summary information, it also appears to the addressees that the places in which the occupiers etc are to be summoned are, apparently, unsafe of access for the due warning and citing of the occupiers etc, the pope hereby grants faculty to the addressees of performing any warnings and citations by public edict affixed in public places in those parts, in places nearby where there is a probability that they will come to the notice of those cited and warned; and the pope wills and decrees that warnings and citations thus made bind those cited and warned just as if they had been notified and communicated to them in person. Notwithstanding etc. and [notwithstanding] that only archbishops, bishops, and ecclesiastical dignitaries can be appointed conservators, and that the above canons and vicars are not of the class of persons who can be appointed conservators, etc.[3] With the usual decree as to the jurisdiction and procedure of the addressees and each one of them.[4] The present letters shall be valid only so long as the said abbot William lives.

Militanti ecclesie licet immeriti disponente domino presidentes ...
.P. Lambertus / JoA: / JoA: L: Nardinus

1   As they usually followed a standard form letters conservatory were normally enregistered in a much abridged
     form. Unusually, the text is here enregistered in full.
2   Though variously elaborated, the formulation of letters conservatory was, as noted, fairly standard and
     designed to cover a wide range of circumstances. Particular words did not necessarily have special
     application to the complainant's case.
3   *Cf. Sext*, I. 14. 15 (Friedberg, cols. 982-983).
4   *Cf.* M. Tangl, *Die Päpstlichen Kanzleiordnungen* (Innsbruck, 1894), pp. 323-324 (*Ceterum volumus et
     auctoritate apostolica decernimus ... in contrarium edita non obstante*); but with minor verbal differences.

361   [–][1]   *Reg. Lat.* 1324, fo 271[r]

Abortive entry: start only of indult, for life, to visit, by proxy, churches etc in his
archdeaconry addressed to (and in favour of) 'Richard Pace (*Paceo*) archdeacon of
Dorset (*Dorsetie*) in the church of Salisbury, notary of the pope'. The main body of the
letter is truncated:

> *Hinc est quod nos tuis in hac parte supplicationibus inclinati ut quoadvixeris
> ecclesias monasteria et alia loca ecclesiastica infra limites archidiaconatus
> Dorsetie in ecclesia Saresbirien. quem obtines consistentia eorumque personas in
> quibus tibi ratione dicti archidiaconatus visitationis officium de iure* [stops]

Entry occupies upper half of page; stops at start of tenth line; start of unconnected
letter (drawn under 9 March 1515 and expedited in the bullaria on 28 June 1515)
beneath. The previous letter is drawn under 22 February 1515 (= no. 360 above).

No administrative notes: no abbreviator's name; no magistral initial or subscription.
The proem is the usual one for letters of this class: *Meruit tue devotionis sinceritas ...*

Struck through repeatedly by diagonal strokes in both directions, forming diamond
pattern; but no explanatory note. Matchable to the indult in favour of Pace enregistered
by the same scribe at no. 343 above (in a different register). In the present entry Pace
is not designated *magistro*; otherwise, so far as it goes, the text agrees with that of no.
343 and is similarly defective. Perhaps abandoned because the item had already been
enregistered and the scribe realised it.

1   Entry does not reach dating clause.

362   17 September 1515   *Reg. Lat.* 1324, fos 276[r]-277[r]

To John Pachyng, cantor of the chantry of B. Mary, Stanyng, d. Chichester.
Dispensation and indult – at his supplication – to receive and retain for life, together
with the above chantry (which is incompatible with another incompatible benefice),
one, and without them, any two other benefices etc. [as above, no. 2].[1]

Vite ac morum honestas ...

.P. Lambertus. / JoA: / JoA: Lx: Nard(inus): –

1   to end; i.e. including indult for non-residence

363   26 July 1515   *Reg. Lat.* 1324, fos 292ᵛ-293ᵛ

To Robert Syngleton', subdeacon, d. York. Dispensation and indult – at his supplication – to him (who, as he asserts, is a subdeacon; and is in a year [of age] which is less than his nineteenth, but greater than his fourteenth) to receive and retain, as soon as he reaches his nineteenth year, any benefice, with cure or otherwise incompatible, even if a parish church or its perpetual vicarage, or a chantry, free chapel, hospital or annual service, usually assigned to secular clerics in title of a perpetual ecclesiastical benefice, or a dignity, *personatus*, administration or office in a cathedral, even metropolitan, or collegiate church, even if the dignity should be major *post pontificalem* in a cathedral, even metropolitan, church, or principal in a collegiate church, even if the dignity etc. should be customarily elective and have cure of souls, if he obtains it otherwise canonically, to resign it, simply or for exchange, when he pleases, and in its place receive and retain another, similar or dissimilar, benefice, with cure or otherwise incompatible; and not to be bound, by reason of any benefices with cure or requiring sacred, even priest's, orders by statute, custom or otherwise, held by him at the time, to be promoted – until he reaches the lawful age – to any orders of the diaconate and priesthood; and not to be liable to be compelled by anyone to do so against his will, notwithstanding the above defect of age which he will – [even] in his said nineteenth year – suffer for holding the incompatible benefice, etc. With the proviso that the incompatible benefice and the other benefices in question shall not, on this account, be defrauded of due services and the cure of souls in them ([if] any) shall not be neglected.

Vite ac morum honestas …
.P. Lambertus. / JoA: / JoA: xxx: Nard(inus): –

364   26 July 1515   *Reg. Lat.* 1324, fos 293ᵛ-294ᵛ

To Richard Ceack,[1] cleric, d. Exeter. Dispensation and indult – at his supplication – to him (who, as he asserts, is in a year [of age] which is less than his twenty-first, but greater than his fourteenth) to receive and retain, as soon as he reaches his twenty-first year, any benefice, etc. [as above, no. 363, to '… in its place receive and retain another, similar or dissimilar, benefice, with cure or otherwise incompatible']; and not to be bound, by reason of any benefices with cure or requiring sacred, even priest's, orders, by statute, custom, foundation, endowment, privilege or otherwise, even of lay patronage, held by him at the time, to be promoted – provided that he is a deacon[2] within a two-year period[3] – to any of the other sacred orders in question until he reaches his twenty-eighth year;[4] and not to be liable to be compelled by anyone to do so against his will, notwithstanding the above defect of age which he will – even in his said twenty-first year – suffer for holding the incompatible benefice, etc. With the proviso that the incompatible benefice and the other benefices in question shall not, on this account, be defrauded of due services, and the cure of souls in them ([if] any) shall not be neglected.

Vite ac morum honestas ...
.P. Lambertus. / JoA: / JoA: xxx:-[5] Nardinus

1   the penultimate letter (here read as *c*) very doubtful; above it (and perhaps joined to it) an ascender, deleted
2   *sic*; *recte*: subdeacon?
3   reckoned, of course, from the date Richard acquires peaceful possession of a benefice
4   Set by reference to his age in the absence of other framework: Richard is, as yet, unbeneficed.
     The twenty-eighth year would appear generous for non-promotion to orders above the ?[sub]diaconate.
5   *xxx.* occurs (in another hand) towards bottom right hand corner of page; *cf. CPL* XVI, pp. xxiii-xxiv.

365   10 July 1515   *Reg. Lat.* 1324, fos 309[r]-310[v]

To Richard Edon', LLB, rector of the parish church of Cranofelde,[1] d. Lincoln, (who, as he asserts, is clerk of Henry, king of England, and of his privy council [*Henrici ... regis ... et sui concilii secreti clericus*]), dispensation as below. Some time ago, Julius II by letters of his dispensed Richard to receive and retain for life, together with the above parish church, (which he was then holding), one, and without them, any two other benefices, etc. [as above, no. 6, to '... to retain them together for life'], as is more fully contained in those letters.[2] The pope hereby further dispenses Richard – at his supplication – to receive and retain for life, together with the above parish church (which he [still] holds) and with another incompatible benefice perhaps held by him now, or with any two other incompatible benefices held by him at the time by the said dispensation, or without them, any two other benefices, with cure or otherwise mutually incompatible, even if parish churches or their perpetual vicarages, or chantries, free chapels, hospitals or annual services usually assigned to secular clerics in title of a perpetual ecclesiastical benefice, or dignities, *personatus*, administrations or offices in cathedral, even metropolitan, or collegiate churches, even if the dignities should be major *post pontificalem* in cathedral, even metropolitan, churches, or principal in collegiate churches, or a combination, and even if the dignities etc. should be customarily elective and have cure of souls, if he obtains them otherwise canonically, to resign them, at once or successively, simply or for exchange, as often as he pleases and in their place receive up to two other, similar or dissimilar, incompatible benefices, provided that of four such incompatible benefices not more than three together be parish churches or their perpetual vicarages. Notwithstanding etc. With the proviso that the last [two] said incompatible benefices shall not, on this account, be defrauded of due services and the cure of souls in them (if any) shall not be neglected.

Litterarum scientia, vite ac morum honestas …
.P. Lambertus / JoA: / Jo A: C: Nardinus

1   the 'n' a sympathetic reading; here and below readable as a 'u'
2   not known to the *CPL* volumes covering the pontificate of Julius II. However, many Julius registers are now
     lost; and the compilers of the eighteenth century *Indici* volumes (on which we necessarily rely for lost
     material) sometimes overlooked the indexing of dispensations *ad duo*.

366[1]   **[1514 / potentially 1515]**[2]   *Reg. Lat.* 1325, fos 24r-26r

To David, bishop of Lismore, 'consistorial' commend as below. At another time –
when the monastery of Blenluce,[3] OCist, d. Whithorn, which the late Cuthbert Balzhe,[4]
cleric,[5] was holding *in commendam* by apostolic concession and dispensation while he
lived, was vacant (on the ending of the commend by Cuthbert's death outside the
Roman curia) still in the way it was vacant when it was commended to him – the pope
– *motu proprio* – granted under date 3 October, first year [1513] that the monastery,
vacant as above, be commended to be held, ruled and governed by Peter, cardinal priest
of the title of S. Eusebio, for life. This day, cardinal Peter has, spontaneously and
freely, ceded the grant of this commend (in respect of which apostolic letters had not
been drawn up) into the hands of the pope who has admitted the cession. Wishing to
provide the monastery with a capable and suitable governor to rule and direct it as well
as to assist bishop David to keep up his position in accordance with pontifical dignity,
the pope, on the advice of the cardinals, hereby commends the monastery (all of whose
fruits etc. are reserved by apostolic authority to Dominic, bishop of Porto, to be
received, exacted and levied by him for life[6]), howsoever vacant, with all rights and
appurtenances, to bishop David to be held, ruled and governed by him for life – even
together with the church of Lismore, over which he is understood to preside –
committing the care, rule and administration of the monastery to him in spiritualities
and temporalities. The pope's will is, however, that divine worship and the usual
number of monks and ministers in the monastery shall not, on account of this
commend, be diminished; but that the customary burdens of the monastery and its
convent shall be supported; and that – when all other charges have been deducted and,
if bishop David's *mensa* [sc. abbatial *mensa*] is separate and apart from the conventual
mensa, after a fourth part of all the fruits of the monastery has been bestowed annually
on the restoration of the fabric, or on the purchase or repair of ornaments, vestments
and sacred furniture, or on the sustenance and maintenance of the poor, according to
the greater need, or, if the *mensa* is common, after a third part of all the fruits of the
monastery has been bestowed annually on the restoration of the fabric etc. and on the
maintenance of the monks – bishop David may – the monastery's said burdens having
been supported – make disposition of the rest of its fruits etc.[7] just as abbots of the
monastery could and ought to do, alienation of its immovable goods and precious
movables being however forbidden; and that before he involves himself in the rule and
administration of the monastery in any way, bishop David shall take the usual oath of
fealty before the bishops of Dunkeld and Brechin (or one of them) in accordance with
the form which the pope is sending enclosed (*introclusam*) under his *bulla*[8]; and the

pope by other letters[9] commands that the said bishops (or one of them) shall receive the oath in his name and that of the Roman church.

Conclusions to: (i) the convent of the above monastery of Blenluce; (ii) the vassals of the monastery; (iii) the bishop of Whithorn; (iv) James, king of Scots.

Romani pontificis providentia circumspecta ... The conclusions begin: (i) *Hodie monasterium vestrum* ... (ii), (iii), (iv) *Hodie monasterium* ...
[–][10] / [–][11] / [–][12]

1   The entry – probably based on a draft – is arguably empty: though not deleted it is unsigned and the dating clause is incomplete (below, note 2). There is no explanatory note. The letter – if there was one – may not have been expedited (at least by the chancery[cf. *Ind.* 355, fos 53 and 82 (conjoint leaves once wrapped around the relevant quintern, sc. fos 24ʳ-47ᵛ mech. of *Reg. Lat.* 1325) where David, bp Lismore is effectively removed from the list of items in the quintern]). Moreover, the reference to the commend of Glenluce by the pope on the advice of the cardinals may well be the draftsman anticipating the outcome of consistory. In short, the evidential value of the entry is not that of an approved entry. The background is exciting: *see* D.E.R. Watt and N.F.Shead (edds.), *The Heads of Religious Houses in Scotland from Twelfth to Sixteenth Centuries* (Edinburgh, 2001), pp. 88-89.

2   Dating clause left incomplete to be completed later: *Dat. Rome apud Sanctum Petrum anno et cetera millesimo quingentesimo quartodecimo* [ends] i.e. the year of the Incarnation is given, but no month- or day-date, and no pontifical year. A half line has been left blank between *quartodecimo* and *Simili modo* which introduces the first of the conclusions (all of which are *Dat. ut supra*). As it stands, datable to 25 March 1514 x 24 March 1515. We cannot, of course, date what may be an imaginary letter. The draft behind the entry was presumably framed after 5 August 1514 when Hamilton was recommended for Glenluce by James V (*L&P, F&D*, I², no. 3119). And it is obviously datable from Accolti's cession mentioned in the entry. The date when he ceded his right to both Dunfermline and Inchaffray – 13 November 1514 (Hergenroether, nos. 12699-12702; above, no. 303) — may be an indicator.

3   spelt in the conclusions: *Glenluce* (in the first instance the 'G' written over a 'B') and (four times) *Glanluce*

4   the letter here transcribed as *z* probably yogh; the 'h' possibly readable as a 'b'

5   diocese or other designation not stated

6   MS: ... *monasterium predictum cuius fructus redditus et proventus venerabili fratri nostro Dominico episcopo Portuen. per eum quoadviveret percipiendi et exigendi et levandi apostolica auctoritate reservati existunt.* This is the only mention of Grimani and of the reservation of the fruits. There is no reference whatever to any consent of his in this or any other connection.

7   MS: ... *de residuis ipsius monasterii fructibus redditibus et proventibus illius oneribus predictis debite supportatis disponere et ordinare libere et licite valeas* – i.e. the usual formulation. The prior reservation of all fruits to Grimani is not mentioned here.

8   *Cf.* below, no. 384, note 4.

9   *Cf.* below, no. 368 (but addressed to bishops of Dunkeld and Aberdeen).

10   no abbreviator's name

11   no magistral initial

12   no magistral subscription

367[1]   **[1514 / potentially 1515]**[2]   *Reg. Lat.* 1325, fo 26ʳ⁻ᵛ

To David, bishop of Lismore. Since the pope, on the advice of the cardinals, intends this day to commend the monastery of Glanluce, OCist, d. Whithorn, at present bereft of the rule of an abbot *certo modo*, to bishop David to be held, ruled and governed by him for life, he hereby absolves him from any [sentences] of excommunication etc. under which he may perhaps lie, so far only as regards the taking effect of the said commend and each of the relevant letters. Notwithstanding etc.

Apostolice sedis consueta clementia ad ea libenter intendit ...
[–]³ / [–]⁴ / [–]⁵

1   This entry, like the adjacent ones (above, no. 366, below, no. 368), is arguably empty: though not deleted, it
    is unsigned and the dating clause is incomplete. No explanatory note. *See above*, no. 366, note 1.
2   Dating clause left incomplete: *Dat. Rome apud Sanctum Petrum anno et cetera millesimo quingentesimo
    quartodecimo* [ends]. Letter clearly framed to be drawn under the same date as the principal one (no. 366
    above). On the datability of the entry, *see above*, no. 366, note 2.
3   no abbreviator's name (as in nos. 366 and 368)
4   no magistral initial (as in nos. 366 and 368)
5   no magistral subscription (as in nos. 366 and 368)

368¹   [1514 / potentially 1515]²   *Reg. Lat.* 1325, fos 26ᵛ-27ʳ

To the bishops of Dunkeld and Aberdeen,³ mandate. Since the pope has this day
commended the monastery of Glanluce, OCist, d. Whithorn, vacant *certo modo* at the
time, to David, bishop of Lismore, to be held, ruled and governed by him for life, as is
more fully contained in his letters drawn up in that regard,⁴ he – wishing to spare
bishop David, who lives in those parts, the labour and expense of being compelled on
that account to come in person to the apostolic see – hereby commands that the above
two (or one of them) shall receive from him in the name of the pope and the Roman
church the usual oath of fealty in accordance with the form the pope sends enclosed
(*introclusam*) under his *bulla*⁵ and shall cause the form of oath which bishop David
takes to be sent, verbatim, to the pope, at once, by their own messenger, by his letters
patent, marked with his seal.

Cum nos hodie ...
[–]⁶ / [–]⁷ / [–]⁸

1   This entry, like the draft grant of commend itself (*above*, no. 366) and the draft absolution (no. 367 above),
    is arguably empty: though not deleted, it is unsigned and the dating clause is incomplete. There is no
    explanatory note. *See above*, no. 366, note 1.
2   Dating clause left incomplete: *Dat. Rome apud Sanctum Petrum anno et cetera millesimo quingentesimo
    quartodecimo* [ends]. Clearly framed to be drawn under the same date as the principal letter (no. 366 above).
    On the datability of the entry, *see above*, no. 366, note 2.
3   *sic*; the draft principal letter (no. 366 above) refers to the commission for the receipt of the oath (= present
    letter) as being addressed to the bishops of Dunkeld and Brechin.
4   *above*, no. 366
5   *Cf.* below, no. 384, note 4.
6   no abbreviator's name (as in nos. 366 and 367)
7   no magistral initial (as in nos. 366 and 367)
8   no magistral signature (as in nos 366 and 367)

369   19 June 1514   *Reg. Lat.* 1325, fos 31ᵛ-33ᵛ

To Thomas, lately bishop of [Clonmacnois],[1] archbishop-elect of Tuam. Consistorial translation, though absent,[2] from the church of [Clonmacnois] to that of Tuam, vacant by the death, outside the Roman curia, of the late archbishop Maurice, during whose rule the said church of Tuam was specially reserved by the pope to his own disposition. The pope hereby appoints Thomas archbishop, committing to him the care and administration of the church of Tuam in spiritualities and temporalities and granting him licence to transfer thereto. His will is, however, that – before Thomas receives quasi-possession of the rule and administration and of the goods of the said church – he shall take the usual oath of fealty before the bishops of Clonfert and Killala (or one of them), in accordance with the form the pope is sending enclosed (*introclusam*) under his *bulla*[3]; and the pope, by other letters,[4] commands the said bishops that they (or one of them) shall receive the oath from Thomas in his name and that of the Roman church.

Conclusions to: (i) the chapter of the church of Tuam; (ii) the people of the city and diocese of Tuam; (iii) the clergy of the city and diocese; (iv) the vassals of the said church; (v) the suffragans of the said church; (vi) Henry, king of England.

Romani pontificis quem pastor ille celestis ... The conclusions begin: (i) *Hodie venerabilem fratrem nostrum Thomam* ... (ii), (iii), (iv) *Hodie et cetera.* (v) *Hodie venerabilem et cetera.* (vi)[5] *Gratie divine premium et cetera.*
.F. Bregon' / JoA: / JoA: xxiiij: xij: xij: xij: xij: xij: Nard(inus):

1   MS: *Clonen.* (Cloyne) throughout; *recte*: 'Cluanen.'
2   i.e. from the Roman curia; *cf.* below, no. 371.
3   *Cf.* below, no. 384, note 4.
4   below, no. 371
5   *Hodie et cetera* deleted (initialled *JoA.*) precedes *Gratie* ...

370   19 June 1514   *Reg. Lat.* 1325, fo 34ʳ

To Thomas, bishop of [Clonmacnois][1]. Since the pope, on the advice of the cardinals, intends this day to translate Thomas from the church of [Clonmacnois], over which he is understood to preside, to that of Tuam, vacant *certo modo* at present, and to appoint him archbishop, he hereby absolves him from any [sentences] of excommunication etc. under which he may perhaps lie, so far only as regards the taking effect of the said translation and appointment and each of the relevant letters. Notwithstanding etc.

Apostolice sedis consueta clementia ne dispositiones ...
.F. Bregon.[2] / *JoA: / JoA: xxiiij Nardinus*

1   MS: *Clonen.* (Cloyne) throughout; *recte*: 'Cluanen.'
2   *sic*

371   20 June 1514   *Reg. Lat.* 1325, fo 34^v

To the bishops of Clonfert and Killala, mandate. Since the pope has recently translated Thomas, lately bishop of [Clonmacnois][1], from the church of [Clonmacnois] to that of Tuam, appointing him archbishop, as is more fully contained in his letters drawn up in that regard,[2] he – wishing to spare Thomas elect, who lives in those parts, the labour and expense of being compelled on that account to come in person to the apostolic see – hereby commissions and commands that the above two (or one of them) shall receive from him in the name of the pope and the Roman church the usual oath of fealty in accordance with the form the pope is sending enclosed (*introclusam*) under his *bulla*;[3] and shall cause the form of oath which Thomas elect takes to be sent, verbatim, to the pope, at once, by their own messenger, by his letters patent, marked with his seal.

Cum nos nuper..
.*F.*[4] *Bregon.* / *JoA.* / JoA. xvj: Nard(inus): –

1   MS: *Clonen.* (Cloyne) throughout; *recte*: 'Cluanen.'
2   above, no. 369
3   *Cf.* below, no. 384, note 4.
4   perhaps converted from *P*

372   27 July 1515   *Reg. Lat.* 1325, fos 52^r-54^r

To Nicholas, elect of Ely. Consistorial provision of him – dean of the church, called chapel royal, of Windsor (*de Windesora*), d. Salisbury; UID; and in the priesthood – to the church of Ely, vacant by the death, outside the Roman curia, of the late bishop James, during whose rule the said church was specially reserved by the pope to his own disposition; and appointment of Nicholas as bishop, committing to him the care and administration of the church of Ely in spiritualities and temporalities.

   Conclusions to: (i) the chapter of the church of Ely; (ii) the clergy of the city and diocese of Ely; (iii) the people of the said city and diocese; (iv) the vassals of the said church; (v) the <arch>[1]bishop of Canterbury; (vi) Henry, king of England.

Apostolatus officium quamquam insufficientibus meritis nobis ex alto commissum ...
The conclusions begin: (i) *Hodie ecclesie vestre ...* (ii), (iv) *Hodie ecclesie Elien. et cetera ...* (iii) *Hodie ecclesie Elien. per obitum et cetera ...* (v) *Ad cumulum et cetera.*
(*vi*) *Gratie divine premium et cetera.*
.*P. de Castello.* / *JoA:* / *JoA. xx: x: x: x: x: x: x: Nardinus*

1   *archi* inserted in margin initialled *JoA*

373   28 July 1515   *Reg. Lat.* 1325, fos 54ᵛ-55ʳ

To Nicholas, elect of Ely. Since the pope has recently made provision of Nicholas to the church of Ely, appointing him bishop, as is more fully contained in his [letters drawn up in that regard[1]],[2] he hereby grants faculty to Nicholas – at his supplication – to receive consecration from any catholic bishop of his choice in communion with the apostolic see, assisted by two or three catholic bishops similarly in communion; and to the bishop concerned to consecrate him, having first received from him in the name of the pope and the Roman church the usual oath of fealty in accordance with the form noted in the presents. The pope decrees, however, that if the bishop consecrates Nicholas without receiving the said oath and Nicholas receives consecration they shall both be suspended automatically. Moreover it is the pope's will that Nicholas shall send him, at once, by his own messenger, the form of oath taken by him, verbatim, by his letters patent, marked with his seal; and that the above shall not be to the prejudice of the archbishop of Canterbury, to whom the aforesaid church is understood to be subject by metropolitan law. With the form of oath.[3]

Cum nos pridem ...
.P. de Castello / JoA: / JoA: xxviij[4]: Nardinus

1   MS: *in nostris et cetera continetur*
2   above, no. 372
3   not recited in full; *cf.* below, no. 377, notes 3 and 5.
4   changed from (?)*xxviiij*

374[1]   27 July 1515   *Reg. Lat.* 1325, fo 55ʳ⁻ᵛ

To Nicholas West, UID, dean of the church, called chapel royal, of Windsor (*de Windesora*), d. Salisbury. Since the pope, on the advice of the cardinals, intends this day to make provision of Nicholas to the church of Ely, vacant by the death, outside the Roman curia, of the late bishop James, and to appoint Nicholas bishop, he hereby absolves him from any [sentences] of excommunication etc. under which he may perhaps lie, so far only as regards the taking effect of the said provision and appointment and each of the relevant letters. Notwithstanding etc.

Apostolice sedis consueta benignitas ad ea libenter intendit ...
.P. de Castello. / JoA: / JoA: xx: Nardinus

1   The engrossment is BL, Vit. B.ii. fo. 191; summarised by *L&P, F&D*, II, no. 755; *cf.* Bell, no. 262.

375   25 May 1515   *Reg. Lat.* 1325, fos 134ʳ-136ʳ

To Gavin, elect of Dunkeld. Consistorial provision of him – provost of the church of
St Giles, Edinburgh, d. St Andrews; of noble (even illustrious) birth; and in the
priesthood[1] – to the church of Dunkeld, vacant by the death, outside the Roman curia,
of the late bishop George, during whose rule the pope specially reserved the said
church to his own disposition; and appointment of Gavin as bishop, committing to him
the care and administration of the church in spiritualities and temporalities.

Conclusions to[2]: (i) James king of Scots; (ii) the archbishop of St Andrews; (iii) the
chapter of the church of Dunkeld; (iv) the clergy of the city and diocese of Dunkeld;
(v) the people of the city and diocesis of Dunkeld; (vi) the vassals of the church of
Dunkeld.

Apostolatus officium meritis licet imparibus nobis ex alto commissum ... The
conclusions begin: (i) *Gratie divine premium ...* (ii) *Ad cumulum tue ...* (iii) *Hodie
ecclesie vestre ...* (iv), (v), (vi) *Hodie ecclesie ...*
A. de Alvarott(is) / JoA: / JoA: xxviij: x: x:- |[3] *JoA: x: x:*[4] *x: x: x:*[5] *Nardinus*

1   The phrase 'litterarum scientia' (which is appropriate for degree- holders) occurs below, although there is no
    mention of his having a degree.
2   The order in which the conclusions are enregistered (followed in the present summary) deviates from the
    standard (*cf.* above, no. 372, for instance).
3   editorial end of line marker: not part of signature
4   *JoA: x: x:* in left margin: added later? Normally, the tax marks are sandwiched between initial and surname.
    The intrusion of the extra initial is corroborative of subsequent addition.
5   i. e. a total of eight tax marks (representing, presumably, principal letter plus seven conclusions) are
    enregistered; but there are only the six conclusions we would expect. A seventh is improbable: so it follows
    that one 'x' too many was written in error (perhaps when *JoA: x: x:* was added later; *see above*, note 4).

376   25 May 1515   *Reg. Lat.* 1325, fo 136ᵛ

To Gavin Douglas, provost of the church of B. Giles, Edinburgh, d. St Andrews. Since
the pope, on the advice of the cardinals, intends this day to make provision of Gavin
to the church of Dunkeld, vacant *certo modo* at present, and to appoint him bishop, he
hereby absolves him from any [sentences] of excommunication etc. under which he
may perhaps lie, so far only as regards the taking effect of the said provision and
appointment and each of the relevant letters. Notwithstanding etc.

Apostolice sedis consueta clementia ne dispositiones ...
A de Alvarott(is) / JoA: / :JoA. xx: Nardinus

377   26 May 1515   *Reg. Lat.* 1325, fo 137[r-v]

To Gavin, elect of Dunkeld. Since the pope has recently made provision of Gavin to the church of Dunkeld, appointing him bishop, as is more fully contained in his letters drawn up in that regard,[1] he hereby grants faculty to Gavin (who is in the priesthood) – at his supplication – to receive consecration from any catholic bishop of his choice in communion with the apostolic see, assisted by two or three catholic bishops similarly in communion; and to the bishop concerned to consecrate him, having first received from him in the name of the pope and the Roman church the usual oath of fealty[2] in accordance with the form noted in the presents.[3] The pope decrees, however, that if the bishop consecrates Gavin without receiving the said oath and Gavin receives consecration they shall both be suspended automatically. Moreover it is the pope's will that Gavin shall send him, at once, by his own messenger, the form of oath taken by him, verbatim, by his letters patent, marked with his seal;[4] and that the above shall not be to the prejudice of the archbishop of St Andrews, to whom the aforesaid church is understood to be subject by metropolitan law. With the form of oath.[5]

Cum pridem ecclesie[6]...
A. de Alvarott(is) / JoA: / :JoA: xxviij: Nardinus

1   above, no. 375
2   MS: *recepto prius per eum nostro et Romane ecclesie nomine a te fidelitatis debite solito iuramento.* Whether by accident or design the papal requirement was satisfied: Douglas is recorded as taking the oath immediately *before* his consecration. The formalities were recorded in letters of the consecrator, namely Andrew Forman, archbishop of St Andrews (G. Donaldson and C. Macrae, edd., *St. Andrews Formulare, 1514-1546* [Stair Society], Vol. I [Edinburgh, 1942], pp. 183-184: [no. 173]). Forman's letters appear to have recited the present letters, i.e. Leo's faculty; but in the form in which they are preserved – an entry in a precedent book – the form of oath is not given. The entry in the *Formulare* is caveated by Dowden, pp. 84, 430-431.
3   MS: *iuxta formam presentibus annotatam.* The practice of reciting or noting down the form of oath in the faculty *a quocunque* itself only became the norm towards the end of the fifteenth century. Previously, it was usually noted on a separate document *sub plumbo* enclosed in the faculty. The development can, in outline, be traced in the Calendar. For example, of the eight relevant faculties in *CPL* XI (1455-64) the form was recited in only one (at p. 473); in the rest it was enclosed (pp. 31, 309, 310, 323, 324, 359, and 360). Similarly, of the eighteen faculties in *CPL* XIII (1471-84) just two forms (both at p. 657) are recited, the rest enclosed (pp. 148, 154, 471, 522, 523, 591, 743, 744, 798, 813, 824, 825, 826, 827, 846, and 847). Under Innocent VIII, however, the position changes dramatically. *CPL* XV (1484-92) has ten faculties and in all of them the form is recited in the faculty itself. Likewise all the faculties in *CPL* XVI, XVII Part I; all the relevant faculties in *CPL* XVIII and XIX; and all the faculties in the present volume (nos. 76, 83, 85, 91, 94, 108, 113, 116, 120, 126, and 373 above; and 381, 388, and 593 below). So far as faculties for consecration *a quocunque* are concerned the recited form of oath has ousted the enclosed form. However, the enclosed form *sub plumbo* remained the norm when reception of the oath was committed to specified mandataries, commonly bishops of named sees. (*Cf.* nos. 173, 305, 368, and 371 above; and no. 384 below. No. 82 is an exception; but the circumstances were unusual.)
4   MS: *Preterea volumus quod formam huiusmodi a te tunc prestiti iuramenti nobis de verbo ad verbum per tuas patentes litteras sigillo tuo signatas per proprium nuntium quantotius destinare procures.* Satisfaction of the requirement may have involved sending the actual document on which the oath was taken and not just the text. The letters-patent of Hugh Pavy by which he certified the oath of fealty and obedience he had taken, as bishop-elect of St David's, at his consecration in 1485 were copied into his register: *The Episcopal Registers of the Diocese of St David's 1397 to 1518*, [edited] and translated by R.F.Isaacson, vol II [Cymmrodorion Record Series No. 6], London 1917, pp. 458-461 (incomplete). (As we should expect at this date [above, note 3], the form of oath was noted in the faculty for consecration *a quocunque* [*CPL* XV, no. 97]) Pavy's letters-patent refer to the oath having been taken *secundum omnem vim formam et effectum in*

bulla vestre sanctitatis [i.e. the faculty] *inclusam*. The letters-patent which were forwarded to the pope may well have been the actual document used by the bishop-elect when he took the oath. In comparable circumstances, namely the oath taken by a bishop to his metropolitan, the Roman Pontifical envisages the document being sealed during the ceremony of consecration. The rubric runs: *Quo facto* [sc. the oath] *sigillum suum littere iuramenti huiusmodi pro maiori illius robore appendebat seu appendi faciebat*. (*Liber pontificalis*, fo xl) On arrival in Rome the letters-patent were presumably kept – at least until the bishop's death (when they ceased to have practical value), if not permanently. When Henry broke with Rome the oath formed an obvious point of reference for both the episcopate and the papacy. At Cranmer's trial under Mary the court focused on it (*cf.* below, no. 384, note 3).

5   The form invariably occupies the final position in the letter, immediately before the dating clause. It was presumably tacked on to an existing form of letter when the practice of recital developed (above, note 3). The form of oath followed a prescribed form and as usual the enregistration is much abridged: *Ego Gawinus electus Dunkelden. ab hac hora et cetera sic me deus adiuvet et hec sancta dei evangelia*. The exemplars were kept in the chancery's 'statute-book', the *Liber cancellariae*. An unabridged specimen of a prescribed form [Roman obedience] from the period of the Great Schism is printed (from the *Liber*) in Tangl, *Kanzleiordnungen*, pp. 51-52).

6   *sic*; *recte*: 'Cum nos pridem ecclesie…'

378   25 May 1515   *Reg. Lat.* 1325, fos 137ᵛ-138ᵛ

To Gavin, elect of Dunkeld. This day, the pope [has made provision] of Gavin to the church of Dunkeld, then vacant *certo modo*, [and appointed him bishop], as is more fully contained [in his letters drawn up in that regard].[1] And, as the pope has learned, at the time of the said provision and appointment, Gavin was holding, as he does, the provostship (*prepositura*) of the church of B. Giles, Edinburgh [also spelt *Du'bergh*], d. St Andrews, (which is a dignity and of the patronage of the king of Scots for the time being by apostolic privilege which has not been set aside), and the canonry and prebend of the church of Dunbar[2] *alias* Hanch, d. St Andrews, (which are of the patronage of other laymen). Wishing to assist Gavin to keep up his position more fittingly in accordance with pontifical dignity, the pope – *motu proprio* – hereby dispenses him to retain as before – even after he has, on the strength of the said provision and appointment, acquired quasi-possession of the rule and administration of the church of Dunkeld and of its goods, or the greater part of them, and received consecration – the provostship and the canonry and prebend aforesaid (whose annual value together, as the pope has also learned, does not exceed 125 pounds sterling), even if the provostship should have cure of souls, even together with the said church of Dunkeld, for as long as he presides over the latter. Notwithstanding etc. Decreeing that the provostship and the canonry and prebend shall not, on this account, be vacated. With the proviso that the provostship and the canonry and prebend shall not, on this account, be defrauded of due services and the cure of souls in the provostship (if any) shall not be neglected; but that its customary burdens and those of the canonry and prebend shall be supported.

Personam tuam nobis et apostolice sedi devotam …
A. de Alvarott(is) / JoA: / JoA: Lx: Nardinus

1   MS: *tuorum et cetera plenius continetur. Cf.* principal letter (*above*, no. 375).
2   'de' does not occur unless we read *de Ubar*

379   15 September 1514   *Reg. Lat.* 1325, fos 214ʳ-216ᵛ

To William, elect of Lincoln. Consistorial provision of him – dean of the chapel royal
of Henry, king of England; dean of the church of Salisbury; MTheol; in the priesthood;
and counsellor and confessor of the said king and most pleasing and acceptable to him[1]
– to the church of Lincoln[2] – vacant by the translation this day of Thomas, bishop of
Lincoln, to the church of York (vacant *certo modo* at the time), and his appointment as
archbishop – and appointment of William as bishop, committing to him the care and
administration of the church of Lincoln in spiritualities and temporalities.

    Conclusions to: (i) the chapter of the church of Lincoln; (ii) the clergy of the city
and diocese of Lincoln; (iii) the people of the said city and diocese; (iv) the vassals of
the said church; (v) the archbishop of Canterbury; (vi) Henry, king of England.

Apostolatus officium quamquam meritis insufficientibus nobis ex alto commissum ...
The conclusions begin: (i), (iii), (iv) *Hodie ecclesie vestre ... (ii) Hodie ecclesie ...*
(v) Ad cumulum tue ... (vi) Gratie divine premium ...
.P. de Castello. / C / C. xx. x. x. x. x. x. x. Barotius

1   MS: *eidemque regi plurimum gratum et acceptum.* The inclusion of these words – extraordinary in the
     context – would appear to suggest that the king had taken a particularly close interest in securing this
     provision.
2   Remarkably, there is no mention of the provision to Lincoln having been reserved in any way.

380   15 September 1514   *Reg. Lat.* 1325, fos 216ᵛ-217ʳ

To William Atwater, dean of the church of Salisbury. Since the pope, on the advice of
the cardinals, intends this day to make provision of William to the church of Lincoln,
vacant *certo modo*, and to appoint him bishop, he hereby absolves him from any
[sentences] of excommunication etc. under which he may perhaps lie, so far only as
regards the taking effect of the said provision and appointment and each of the relevant
letters. Notwithstanding etc.

Apostolice sedis circumspecta benignitas de statu personarum ecclesiasticarum
quarumlibet ...
.P. de Castello. / C / C. xx. Barotius

381   16 September 1514   *Reg. Lat.* 1325, fo 217ʳ⁻ᵛ

To William, elect of Lincoln. Since the pope has recently made provision of William
to the church of Lincoln, appointing him bishop, as is more fully contained in his
letters drawn up in that regard,[1] he hereby grants faculty to William – at his
supplication – to receive consecration from any catholic bishop of his choice in
communion with the apostolic see, assisted by two or three catholic bishops similarly

in communion; and to the bishop concerned to consecrate him, having first received from him in the name of the pope and the Roman church the usual oath of fealty in accordance with the form noted in the presents. The pope decrees, however, that if the bishop consecrates William without receiving the said oath and William receives consecration they shall both be suspended automatically. Moreover it is the pope's will that William shall send him, at once, by his own messenger, the form of oath taken by him, verbatim, by his letters patent, marked with his seal; and that the above shall not be to the prejudice of the archbishop of Canterbury, to whom the aforesaid church is understood to be subject by metropolitan law. With the form of oath.[2]

Cum nos pridem ...
.P. de Castello / C / C. xxviij. Barotius

1   above, no. 379
2   not recited in full; *cf.* above, no. 377.

382[1]   **15 September 1514**   *Reg. Lat.* 1325, fos 218[r]-220[r]

To Thomas, lately bishop of Lincoln, archbishop elect of York. Consistorial translation, though absent,[2] from the church of Lincoln to that of York (which – following the pope's reservation of all metropolitan churches vacated then and in the future at the apostolic see to his own disposition – became vacant by the death, at the apostolic see, of the late Christopher, cardinal priest of S. Prassede, who by apostolic concession and dispensation presided over it while he lived, and is reserved as above). The pope hereby appoints Thomas archbishop, committing to him the care and administration of the church of York in spiritualities and temporalities and granting him licence to transfer thereto. His will is, however, that – before Thomas involves himself in the rule and administration of the church of York in any way – he shall take the usual oath of fealty before the bishops of Winchester and Norwich (or one of them) in accordance with the form the pope is sending enclosed under his *bulla*[3]; and the pope, by other letters,[4] commissions the said bishops that they (or one of them) shall receive the oath from Thomas in his name and that of the Roman church.

Conclusions to: (i) the chapter of the church of York; (ii) the clergy of the city and diocese of York; (iii) the people of the said city and diocese; (iv) the vassals of the said church; (v) the suffragans of the said church; (vi) Henry, king of England.

Romani pontificis quem pastor ille celestis ... The conclusions begin: (i), (ii) *Hodie venerabilem fratrem nostrum Thomam ...* (iii), (iv), (v) *Hodie venerabilem fratrem nostrum et cetera.* (vi) *Gratie divine premium ...*
.P. de Castello. / C / :C. xxiiij. xij. xij[.] xij. xij. xij. xij. Barotius

1   The engrossment of the principal letter is NA, SC7 26/2; variously summarised in *L&P, F&D*, I[2], no. 3276 and L & I, p. 318. The top right hand corner of the face of the engrossment – the position reserved by the chancery for notes by the *auscultator* – is blank: 'Concordat' is not written anywhere on the document.
2   i.e. from the Roman curia; *cf.* below, no. 384.

3   MS: *iuxta formam quam sub bulla nostra mittimus introclusam*. The formulary is misleading: no form was
      enclosed in the present letter. The clause refers to enclosure in the *commissio receptionis juramenti* (no. 384
      below, *q.v.*) which was drawn under the same date. The *Forma juramenti* was a standard document and had
      to be collated with the prescribed form kept by the chancery. Had a copy been enclosed in the present letter
      the *auscultator* would have written 'Concordat' on the engrossment to show that the *Forma* had been duly
      processed (*Cf.* above, note 1; below, no. 384, notes 1, 3 and 4).
4   below, no. 384

383[1]   **15 September 1514**   *Reg. Lat.* 1325, fo 220ᵛ

To Thomas, bishop of Lincoln. Since the pope, on the advice of the cardinals, intends
this day to translate Thomas from the church of Lincoln, over which he is understood
to preside, to that of York, vacant *certo modo* at present, and to appoint him archbishop,
he hereby absolves him from any [sentences] of excommunication etc. under which he
may perhaps lie, so far only as regards the taking effect of the said translation and
appointment and each of the relevant letters. Notwithstanding etc.

Apostolice sedis consueta clementia ne dispositiones ...
.P. de Castello. / C / C. xvj.[2] *Barotius*

1   The engrossment is NA, SC7 26/3; grotesquely misinterpreted by *L&P, F&D*, I, no. 5411; misinterpretation
      repeated in *L&P, F&D*, I², no. 3275; summarised, briefly but correctly, in L & I, p. 318.
2   The tax mark on the engrossment is *xxiiij*; the tax mark in the register should be a copy of it. The discrepancy
      may be explicable in terms of premature enregistration from a draft: *cf. CPL* XVI, pp. xxiii-xxiv.

384[1]   **15 September 1514**   *Reg. Lat.* 1325, fo 221ʳ

To the bishops of Winchester and Norwich, commission and mandate. Since the pope
has this day translated Thomas, bishop of Lincoln at the time, from the church of
Lincoln to that of York, vacant *certo modo*, appointing him archbishop, as is [more
fully] contained in his [letters drawn up in that regard],[2] he – wishing to spare Thomas
elect, who lives in those parts, the labour and expense of coming in person on that
account to the Roman curia – hereby commissions and commands that the above two
(or one of them) shall receive from him in the name of the pope and the Roman church
the usual oath of fealty in accordance with the form[3] the pope sends enclosed under his
bulla;[4] and shall cause the form of oath which Thomas elect takes to be sent, verbatim,
to the pope, at once, by their own messenger, by his letters patent, marked with his seal.

Cum nos hodie ...
.P. de Castello. / C / C. xxiiij Barotius

1   The engrossment is NA, SC7 26/ 8; summarised in *L&P, F&D*, I², no. 3277 and L&I, p. 319. On what, when
      it was folded, was one of the two outer sides of the document is the contemporary description (in a curial
      hand): *Co(m)missio receptionis Juramenti*. Opened out, the parchment measures approx. 43 x 25.5 cms
      (exclusive of plica); the plica is approx. 7 cms. In the top right hand corner of the face – that is, in the position

reserved for notes by the *auscultator* – is the note: *Concordat.*

2   MS: *in nostris et cetera continetur. Cf.* principal letter (above, no. 382).

3   not enregistered. Ordinarily, archbishops in the making were required to take two oaths of fealty and
     obedience to the Roman church and the papacy: one on appointment (i.e. the *Forma juramenti pro episcopo
     vel archiepiscopo, et patriarcha*, taxed at 12 *grossi* [*cf.* L. Banck, *Taxa S. Cancellariae Apostolicae,*
     Franecker, 1651, p. 10]); the other on bestowal of the pallium (i.e. the *Forma juramenti pro archiepiscopo
     in traditione pallii*, taxed at 8 grossi [ibid., p. 11]). The former oath, which was to be taken *before* he involved
     himself in the rule and administration of the church (*cf.* no. 382 above) – or, if the archbishop-elect was not
     a bishop, *before* consecration – was drawn in the name of the archbishop-elect; the latter oath, which was
     shorter, was taken when the pallium was bestowed (*see below*, no. 385, note 11). (The forms are expansions
     of that in *Decretals*, II. 24.4 [Friedberg, 360]; *cf.* Tangl, pp. 50-52. Not surprisingly, it was a hot text during
     the Schism and much elaborated. Near contemporary examples of the two oaths are among the records of
     Cranmer's trial in *The Works of Thomas Cranmer, Archbishop of Canterbury*, ed. by J.E.Cox, vol. 2:
     Miscellaneous Writings and Letters [The Parker Society], Cambridge, 1846, pp. 559-562). The Wolsey
     engrossments in the NA include one *Forma juramenti*, namely SC7 26/15 (briefly summarised in *L&P,
     F&D*, I², no. 3277 (2); L&I, p. 319). The document begins: *Ego Thomas episcopus nuper Lincolinen. in
     archiepiscopum Eboracen. electus ab hac hora inantea fidelis et obediens ero...* Both from the tax mark
     (XII), as also from the form, it is identifiable as the one to be taken on appointment and referred to in the
     present letter and in no. 382 above. Tantalisingly, both letters, using identical wording, describe the *forma
     juramenti* as 'enclosed' – *iuxta formam quam sub bulla nostra mittimus introclusam* – raising the possibility
     that there were two copies of the form, one enclosed in each letter. Fortunately, we can settle the point from
     the engrossments. It was chancery procedure for the *auscultator* to write *Concordat* on the engrossment in
     which the *forma* (a standard document) was inserted or enclosed (*Cf.* T. Frenz, *Die Kanzlei der Päpste der
     Hochrenaissance (1471-1527)*, Tübingen, 1986, p. 160 and below, no. 385, note 5). In its engrossed form
     (i.e. NA, SC7 26/8) the present letter is marked *Concordat*; the principal letter (i.e. NA, SC7 26/2 [= no. 382
     above]) is not. In short, there was only one copy of the form and it was enclosed in the present letter.
          As we should expect of a *forma juramenti* enclosed in a *commissio receptionis juramenti* it is engrossed
     as letters-close *sub plumbo*. (A specimen of 1472 is conveniently described and illustrated in A. Brackmann,
     Papsturkunden [= Urkunden und Siegel, 2 Heft], Leipzig and Berlin, 1914, p. 29 and Taf. XIII a-b). Various
     methods of folding *litterae clausae* are known (*cf.* diagrams and references in Russian work by N.
     Lichatschev, *Una lettera di Pio V allo zar Ivan il Terribile in connessione colla questione dei Brevi papali*
     [= translation of Russian title] , St Petersburg, 1906, esp. pp. 14-18). The *Forma juramenti* (i.e. SC7 26/15),
     which was enclosed in the present letter, measures approx. 48 x 34 cms. Owing to flattening and re-folding
     by the PRO the original creases cannot be determined with certainty; but it appears to have been folded three,
     perhaps four, times. Firstly, with the document face up, in 'landscape' position, it was folded vertically down
     the centre, the left half being folded down over the right half; secondly, the document was again folded
     vertically down the centre, this time the right half over the left half; the parchment was now a tall four-ply
     strip measuring approx. 12 x 34 cms, with the first fold overlaid by two free edges down the left-hand side;
     thirdly, the document was folded horizontally across the centre, the upper half over the lower. The parchment
     was now eight-ply and, thus folded, measured approx. 12 x 17 cms. The description *Forma juramenti*, which
     occurs on the dorse, will now be found to be written across the upper part of the document thus folded. The
     eight thicknesses of parchment were then punctured by two holes for the cord. The holes, which were approx.
     7.5 cms apart, were roughly centred in both directions – that is, they were both half way between the top and
     bottom edges; and each one was equidistant from its own side. The two ends of the hemp seal cord, which
     was approx. 143 cms long, were both passed through the two holes from the side inscribed *Forma juramenti*
     and secured on the other side by the leaden seal. The document may also have been folded a fourth time,
     again horizontally across the centre, in the line of the two cord holes. It would then have measured approx.
     12 x 8.5 cms and been 16-ply. Thus sealed, the document could not be opened and read without either cutting
     the parchment, cutting the seal cord, or tampering with the seal itself. As the genuineness of a bull was in
     part attested by the seal, recipients no doubt preferred, understandably, to open the document by cutting the
     parchment rather than the seal cord. Methods of cutting naturally varied. The *Forma tradendi Pallium*
     (below, no. 385, note 10) was probably folded in the same way as the *Forma juramenti*. Though cut in
     different places, the cuts were in both cases designed to enable the document to be unfolded while leaving
     the cord intact and the seal attached.

4   *Bulla* here refers to the lead seal appended to the *Forma juramenti* (*cf.* previous note). But what exactly does
     'enclosed' mean? Unhappily, no contemporary description of the method of enclosure is known to the editor;
     but the possibilities are obviously largely determined by the physical realities. Judging from the creases and
     other indicia the *Commissio* measured, in its folded state, approx. 14 x 10 cms; the *Forma juramenti* 12 x 17

cms (8-ply); perhaps 12 x 8.5 cms (16-ply) (*cf.* previous note); lead seal and approx. 143 cms of cord added to the form's bulk. Though not absolutely decisive the measurements argue forcibly that the *forma* was not enclosed in the *Commissio* as a letter is in an envelope. Rather we should envisage the *forma* being wrapped up or bundled with the *commissio*. The free ends of the cord below the seal – 45 cms in the case of the *forma*, 52 cms in the case of the *Commissio* – were perhaps wound round the bundle to secure it. We recall the contemporary practice of issuing commissions in the form of briefs *supplicatione introclusa* (*cf.* C.Cenci, ed., *Bullarium Franciscanum*, Nova Series, Tomus IV-1 (1484-1489) [Grottaferrata, 1989], nos. 62, 111, 144, *et passim*; G. Gualdo, 'Il "Liber brevium de Curia anni septimi" di Paolo II', in *Mélanges E. Tisserant*, I V (Vatican City, 1964) [Studi e Testi 234], p. 329); and we note that the supplications in question could be appreciably larger in one dimension than the briefs which 'enclosed' them: plate 38 of *Exempla Scripturarum* fasc. III: *Acta Pontificum*, collected by I. Battelli, 2nd ed. (Vatican Library, 1965), shows a supplication of 1552 measuring 25.3 x 21.5 cms granted *Et per breve... hac supplicatione introclusa*; plate 39a shows the resultant brief which measures 12 x 45 cms and refers to the supplication as *presentibus introclusam*. The accompanying text (pp. 40-42) is superb; but unfortunately we are not told how, if at all, the supplication was enclosed.

385   25 September 1514   *Reg. Lat.* 1325, fos 221^v-222^v

Note. This entry combines, unusually, two mandates which are commonly enregistered separately (*cf.* nos. 175 and 176 above), namely that to the archbishop-elect informing him of the despatch of the pallium, etc (=[A]) and that to the two bishops charging them to assign the pallium, etc (=[B]). The second mandate is *Dat. ut supra*

[A][1] To Thomas, recently bishop of Lincoln, archbishop-elect of York, mandate. Since, recently, the pope, on the advice of the cardinals, has translated Thomas, bishop of Lincoln at the time, from the church of Lincoln to that of York, then vacant, appointing him archbishop, as is more fully contained in the pope's letters drawn up in that regard;[2] and since, afterwards, the pallium, namely the symbol of the plenitude of pontifical office, had, with becoming urgency, been requested from the pope on Thomas's part by Andrea Gentile, citizen of Genoa,[3] Thomas's envoy (*nuncium*) the pope, at Thomas's supplication, has caused the said pallium, which has been taken from the tomb (*corpore*) of B Peter and is to be assigned by the bishops of Winchester and Norwich, [to be delivered][4] by Andrea so that the said bishops (or one of them) assign it to Thomas under the form which the pope is sending to them enclosed under his *bulla*[5] and receive from Thomas, in the name of the pope and the Roman church, the usual oath of fealty, under the form which the pope is sending under the same (*eadem*) *bulla*.[6] Thomas is to use the pallium inside his church (*intra ecclesiam*)[7] only on those days which are expressly stated in the privileges of the said church;[8] and so that the symbol does not differ from the person who bears it, but rather Thomas heeds inwardly what he wears externally, the pope hereby reminds and exhorts Thomas attentively and commands that he shall aim to observe humility and justice and take care to augment the church of York spiritually and temporally.

[B][9] To the bishops of Winchester and Norwich, mandate. Since the pallium, namely the symbol of the plenitude of pontifical office, has, with becoming urgency, been requested from the pope on the part of Thomas, then bishop of Lincoln, archbishop-elect of York, by Andrea Gentile, citizen of Genoa, Thomas's envoy (*nuncium*), the pope, at Andrea's entreaties (*ipsius precibus*), has caused the said pallium – which has been taken from the tomb (*de corpore*) of B Peter and is to be assigned to Thomas by the above two (or one of them) in accordance with the form which the pope sends enclosed (*introclusam*) under his *bulla*[10] – to be delivered (*destinandum*) by Andrea. The pope hereby commands that the above two (or one of them) shall assign the pallium to Thomas in accordance with the above form, and receive from him, in the name of the pope and the Roman church, the usual oath of fealty,[11] under the form[12] which the pope is sending under the same (*eadem*) *bulla*.[13] They shall, moreover, send the pope, at once, by their own courier (*nuncium*) , the form of oath which Thomas the [archbishop-] elect takes, verbatim, by his letters patent, marked with his seal.

[**A**] *Cum nuper te...* [**B**] *Cum pallium insigne videlicet...*
.P. de Castello / *C* / *.C: xij. x. Barotius*

1   The original engrossment is NA, SC7 26/1; date misread by *L&P, F&D*, I[1], no. 5414 where the letter is briefly (and somewhat misleadingly) described under 15 [!] Sept 1514; error perpetuated by *L&P, F&D*, I[2], no. 3278; date and description corrected by L&I, p. 319. The face of the engrossment is marked *Concordat* in the top right hand corner – that is, in the position reserved for notes by the *auscultator* (*cf.* note 5 below). On the dorse of the engrossment, on what, when it was originally folded, was one of the two outer sides, is the contemporary description: *Destinatio pallii*. The dorse also bears the number given to the document by the *L&P, F&D* team in the mid C19: *5414* (pencil).

2   above, no. 382

3   elsewhere described as a Genoese merchant following the Roman court (*L&P, F&D*, I[2], pp. 1525-1527). For the background to his involvement with the pallium, *see* ibid., no. 3166.

4   MS: *detestan(dum)*; engrossment has (correctly) *destinandum*

5   MS: *sub forma quam eis sub bulla nostra mittimus introclusam*. The *L&P* team surely erred when it implied that the *Forma tradendi Pallium* was transmitted with this letter (*L&P, F&D*, I[1], no. 5414 (2); ibid. I[2], no. 3278 (2); *cf*. *5414/ 2* pencilled on the dorse of the *Forma* [NA, SC7 26/13] in mid C19 when the first ed. was being prepared). As correctly stated by L&I, p. 319, the form was transmitted with the mandate (i.e. 385 [**B**]) and the text here is to be understood in that sense. No forms were enclosed in this letter. Before they were expedited standard letters had to be collated by the *auscultator* with the prescribed forms kept by the chancery. As both the *Forma juramenti pro archiepiscopo in traditione pallii* and the *Forma tradendi Pallium* were standard forms it might be supposed that the *Concordat* which appears on the engrossment (above, note 1) evidences the enclosure of the forms (*cf*. above, no. 384, note 3). However, the *Destinatio pallii* or letter notifying the archbishop of the despatch of the pallium was itself a standard letter – an exemplar was entered in the *Liber cancellariae* (*cf*. Tangl, p. 320) – and *Concordat* here merely indicates that the letter itself had been collated. (*Cf*. Frenz, op. cit. [above, no. 384, note 3] , p. 160, (e) where, however, the focus is on the collation of letters concerning the pallium rather than on the standard nature of the letters in question.)

6   MS: *sub forma quam sub eadem bulla derigimus fidelitatis debite solitum recipiant iuramentum*. Like the reference to the *Forma tradendi Pallium* (*cf*. previous note) the text here refers to the *Forma iuramenti pro Archiepiscopo in traditione pallii* enclosed in the accompanying mandate (i.e. [**B**]). *Cf*. notes 12 and 13 below.

7   For the meaning *see above*, no. 176, note 6.

8   The *Forma tradendi Pallium* (below, note 10) specifies 'apostolic privileges'. For privileged days on which the pallium was worn *cf*. *Liber Pontificalis Chr. Bainbridge Archiepiscopi Eboracensis*, ed. Dr. Henderson [Surtees Society, vol. LXI], 1875, pp. 384-385. A similar (but not identical) list of the days is given in the Roman pontifical (*Liber pontificalis*, fo xliii[v]).

9   The original engrossment is NA, SC7 26/14; briefly described by *L&P, F&D*, I, no. 5415 (which, however, mis-corrects the date to 15 [!] Sept 1514); mis-correction perpetuated in *L&P, F&D*, I[2], no. 3279; briefly summarised by L&I, p. 319 under the correct date (i.e. 25 Sept 1514). The engrossment is marked *Concordat* in the top right hand corner of the face; on the dorse: *Pallium* and *5415* (in pencil). *Cf*. note 1 above. The forms of the letter and of the two enclosures were prescribed (*cf*. exemplars in Tangl, pp. 50, 51, 321 printed from the *Liber cancellariae*); hence the *Concordat* (*cf*. notes 1 and 5 above).

10 The form, which was engrossed as letters-close *sub plumbo* like the *Forma juramenti* (above, no. 384, note 3), is NA, SC7 26/13. *See* note 5 above. The text, which is headed *Forma tradendi Pallium*, runs: *Ad honorem dei omnipotentis et beate Marie Virginis ac beatorum Apostolorum Petri et Pauli et domini pape*

Leonis x. et sancte Romane ecclesie necnon Eboracen. ecclesie tibi commisse tradimus tibi Pallium de corpore beati Petri sumptum plenitudinem videlicet Pontificalis officii ut utaris eo infra ecclesiam tuam certis diebus qui exprimuntur in privilegiis ei ab apostolica sede concessis. Minor differences apart, the text matches specimens from the *Liber cancellariae* (Erler, p. 154; Tangl, p. 321); but in one or two places it differs appreciably from that in the Roman Pontifical (*Liber pontificalis*, fo xliii^r). Like the *Formae juramenti* (above, no. 384, note 3; below, note 12), the *Forma tradendi Pallium* is not enregistered. Essentially, perhaps, for the basic reason that in the routeing of letters the registry was the stop *after* the bullaria and when letters-close arrived there they had already been sealed and were effectively unopenable. The *Forma* was, of course, opened after its arrival in England, presumably for the *traditio*, and in its opened state is reproduced as the frontispiece (*q.v.*) to the present volume. Though it was cut in different places to open it, the *Forma tradendi Pallium* was probably folded and (enclosed) in much the same way as the *Forma juramenti* enclosed in the *Commissio receptionis juramenti* (*cf.* no. 384 above, notes 3 and 4).

11   Unlike faculties *a quocunque*, which clearly and consistently stipulated that the oath of fealty must be received from the bishop-elect *before* he was consecrated (*cf.* above, no. 377, note 2), mandates to bestow the pallium (of which the present is a specimen) do not appear to lay down the order of events. The internal indications we have are slight and contradictory. Because the command to bestow the pallium precedes the command to receive the oath it might be supposed that the events were thereby ordered; but the statements are joined by a simple conjunction and arguably there is no order beyond the order of the words. The letter does, however, refer to the oath *quod dictus Thomas electus prestabit* which argues that the oath was to be taken before the bestowal of the pallium (below, note 12). If we had the form of oath that was enclosed it might strengthen this argument; but unfortunately we do not have it (ibid.). Although the letter seems on the whole to leave the order of events up to the mandataries, the contemporary Roman pontifical clearly envisages the oath being taken *before* the pallium is bestowed. The rubric (under *De pallio*) is unambiguous: *Deinde... episcopi... capiunt iuramentum fidelitatis nomine sedis apostolice ab ipso electo Patriarcha vel Archiepiscopo... iuxta formam per litteras apostolicas eis traditam. Quo prestito episcopi surgunt... et ambo simul pallium hinc inde de altari recipientes senior eorum solus illud super humeros electi patriarche vel Archiepiscopi... imponit* (*Liber pontificalis*, fo xliiii^r). However, observance of the Roman pontifical did not become obligatory until 1596 and local practice varied. When David Betoun received the pallium as archbishop of St Andrews in 1539 he took the oath beforehand. The mandatary's record runs: *Idcirco Apostolica auctoritate nobis commissa... recepto primitus* [my emphasis] *per nos a... David Archiepiscopo... Sanctissimi Domini nostri Pape et Sancte Romane Ecclesie nomine, solito... iuramento* (*Processus traditionis Pallii Archiepiscopo consecrato vigore commissionis Apostolice desuper facte* printed from the St Andrews Formulare by Joseph Robertson, ed., *Concilia Scotiae, Ecclesiae Scoticanae Statuta tam provincialia quam synodalia que supersunt MCCXXV-MDLIX*, Edinburgh 1866 [Bannatyne Club, no. 113], tom. I, pp. cxvii-cxviii [note 1]; *cf. St Andrews Formulare 1514-1546* [The Stair Society], edd. G. Donaldson and C. Macrae, vol. II (Edinburgh, 1944), pp. 165 [no. 429] and 389). But when Cranmer was made archbishop of Canterbury in 1533 he seems to have taken the oath *after* investiture with the pallium. (Thus the interpretation in D. MacCulloch, *Thomas Cranmer* [New Haven and London, 1996], p. 89; but the trial record [cited in note 3 to no. 384 above] is not absolutely clear. Certainly the oath he took, as recorded, was drawn in the name of the archbishop, not archbishop-elect. The form is: *Ego Thomas Archiepiscopus Cantuarien. ab hac hora...*). Much earlier, in 1414, Chichele is clearly recorded as taking the oath *after* he received the pallium: the form, noted in his register under the heading *Juramentum domini post recepcionem pallei*, runs: *Ego Henricus Archiepiscopus Cantuarien. ab hac hora...* (E.F. Jacob, ed., *The Register of Henry Chichele, Archbishop of Canterbury, 1414-1443*, vol. I [Oxford, 1943], p. 17).

12   As we would expect of an enclosure, especially one in the form of letters-close, the *forma* is not enregistered (*cf.* note 10 above); and the engrossment is not known to be extant (*cf.* above, no. 384, note 3). We do not, therefore, know whether the form was drawn in the name of the archbishop or the archbishop-elect. The bestowal of the pallium was regarded by canonists and the papacy as conferring the title of archbishop (*cf.* R.L. Benson, *The Bishop-Elect: A Study in Medieval Ecclesiastical Office* [Princeton, 1968], pp. 171, 175-177). Since practice varied and the oath was, seemingly, sometimes taken before investiture with the pallium, sometimes after (*cf.* previous note), we infer that chancery practice was variable and that sometimes the required form was drawn in the name of the archbishop-elect, sometimes of the archbishop. There is a possible reflection of this in our letters. As noted (above, note 11) the present letter expects the oath to be taken by 'Thomas, [archbishop-] elect'; but no. 17 above has *quam* [sc. forma] *dictus Johannes archiepiscopus prestabit*; and no. 175 has *quod* [sc. iuramentum] *dictus Andreas archiepiscopus prestabit*. In this connection we should note that the form printed from the *Liber cancellariae* is drawn in the name of the archbishop, *not* archbishop-elect (Tangl, pp. 50-51); but the form is an old one – it had already entered the *Liber* by 1380 (*cf.* G. Erler, *Der Liber Cancellariae Apostolicae vom Jahre 1380 und der Stilus Palatii*

Abbreviatus Dietrichs von Nieheim [Leipzig, 1888], p. 155) – and was perhaps no longer invariably applicable. Though it directs that the oath is to be taken before the bestowal of the pallium the *Liber pontificalis* does not give the form of oath. The rubric simply says that the mandataries are to take it *iuxta formam per litteras apostolicas eis traditam* (above, note 11). Eventually, when observance of the Roman pontifical became obligatory, the form of oath was incorporated in the text. In conformity with the rubrics which required the oath to be taken before the pallium was bestowed and with the doctrine that the title of archbishop was conferred with the pallium the incorporated oath was in the form: *Ego N. Electus Ecclesiae N. ab hac hora... (Cf. Pontificale Romanum Clementis VIII. ac Urbani VIII. jussu editum, inde vero a Benedicto XIV. recognitum et castigatum,* Pars Prima [Mechliniae, 1845], p. 124).

13   The expression *sub eadem bulla* is somewhat perplexing. The formulary runs: *mandamus quatenus ... pallium ipsum iuxta premissam formam* [sc. quam sub bulla nostra mittimus introclusam] *sibi assignare curetis et ab ipso nostro et Romane ecclesie nomine sub forma quam <u>sub eadem bulla</u>* [my emphasis] *derigimus fidelitatis debite solitum recipiatis ... iuramentum* (thus also the engrossment [*cf.* note 9 above]). Comparable formulary is deployed in the companion letter addressed to Wolsey (no. 385 [A] above): *ut hiidem episcopi* [sc. bps Winchester and Norwich] *... illud* [sc. pallium] *tibi assignent sub forma quam eis sub bulla nostra mittimus introclusam et a te nostro et Romane ecclesie nomine sub forma quam <u>sub eadem bulla</u> derigimus fidelitatis debite solitum recipiant iuramentum* (thus also,again,the engrossment [*cf.* note 1 above]). The two mandates were standard letters – exemplars had been entered in the *Liber cancellariae* by 1380 (*cf.* Tangl, pp. 320-1) – and the formulary is found commonly (*cf.* nos. 17 [A] and [B] above; *Reg. Lat.* 1129, fos 204r-v, 204v-205r; E.F .Jacob, ed., *The Register of Henry Chichele, Archbishop of Canterbury, 1414-1443,* vol. I [Oxford,1943], p. 16). *Eadem bulla* refers, clearly, to the *bulla* already mentioned, namely the pope's *bulla (bulla nostra)* or leaden seal. Since 'idem' often means 'said' the obvious interpretation is that the expression is generic and has no more precise meaning than 'under the said [sc. the pope's] *bulla*'. However, the formulary deployed in a similar context elsewhere, namely in no. 175 above, induces us to consider an alternative interpretation. While the notification (no. 176) has the expected *sub eadem bulla* the accompanying mandate (no. 175),which we would expect to echo it has,instead, *sub alia bulla* [my emphasis; the reading is certain]. The *bullae* used to seal Leo letters issued *sub plumbo* were all of the same type. In practice, therefore, *alia bulla* could only mean another specimen of the same type rather than another *bulla* of a different type. The corollary of this is that *sub eadem bulla* might signify 'under the very same *bulla*'. In other words, it might mean that the *Forma tradendi Pallium* and the *forma iuramenti in traditione pallii* were physically under one and the same seal. Of course, formulary has an independent currency of its own; but to the extent that it assumes meaning from the factual context we can test this interpretation. It does not fit: although we do not have the *Forma iuramenti* it is evident from the *Forma tradendi Pallium* (above, note 10) that both forms were engrossed separately and that each had its own seal. We must, accordingly, dismiss the alternative explanation as fanciful: *sub eadem bulla* means 'under the said (or same) seal' in a generic and not specific sense.

Nevertheless,we are still left with *sub alia bulla.* We do not know what form the *formae* enclosed in no. 175 took; but probably the practice exemplified here was followed there and they were engrossed separately, each with its own *bulla.* It would therefore seem possible that in no. 175 the language deployed was specific and accurately described the facts of the case. However, significant deviation from the standard would be unusual and we have already noted that the accompanying notification (no.176) has *sub eadem* (not 'alia') *bulla* – that is, it accords with the standard. On the available evidence we can reach no definite conclusion; but *alia* might well be a mistake of draftsman or copyist.

386   6 November 1514   *Reg. Lat.* 1325, fos 231ᵛ-234ʳ

To Maurice Okillyd, elect of Kilfenora. Consistorial provision of him – professor OFM and of theology; in the priesthood – to the church of Kilfenora, vacant by the death, outside the Roman curia, of the late bishop Theodoric, during whose rule the pope specially reserved the said church to his own disposition; and appointment of Maurice as bishop, committing to him the care and administration of the church in spiritualities and temporalities.

Conclusions to (i) the chapter of the church of Kilfenora; (ii) the clergy of the city and diocese of Kilfenora; (iii) the people of the said city and diocese; (iv) the vassals of the said church; (v) the archbishop of Cashel; (vi) Henry, king of England.

Divina disponente clementia ... The conclusions begin: (i) *Hodie ecclesie vestre Finaboren.* ...; (ii), (iii), (iv) *Hodie ecclesie Finaboren.* ...; (v) *Ad cumulum tue* ...; (vi) *Gratie divine premium* ...
.J. Benzon. / M / M xx [xx]:[1] */ xx / xx / xx / xx / xx / xx²* *de Campania*

1   The *xx* here enclosed in brackets is deleted and initialled *M*
2   i. e. the tax marks are separated by oblique strokes instead of (as usually) by punctuation. Note that the taxation of the conclusions is somewhat unexpected: normally they are taxed at less than the principal letter (often at 'xii').

387   6 November 1514   *Reg. Lat.* 1325, fo 234ᵛ

To Maurice Okaillyd', professor OFM and of theology. Since the pope[1] intends this day to make provision of Maurice to the church of Kilfenora, vacant *certo modo*, and to appoint him bishop, he hereby absolves him from any [sentences] of excommunication etc. under which he may perhaps lie, so far only as regards the taking effect of the said provision and appointment and each of the relevant letters. Notwithstanding etc.

Apostolice sedis circumspecta benignitas de statu personarum ecclesiasticarum quarumlibet ...
.J. Benzon. / M / . M xx de Campania

1   MS contains no reference to the pope acting 'on the advice of the cardinals'. (The standard formulation includes: '... et fratribus nostris ... de fratrum predictorum consilio'.) *Cf.*, for example, no. 380.

388   7 November 1514   *Reg. Lat.* 1325, fo 235ʳ⁻ᵛ

To Maurice Okaillyd', elect of Kilfenora. Since the pope has recently made provision of Maurice to the church of Kilfenora, appointing him bishop, as is more fully contained in his letters drawn up in that regard],[1] he hereby grants faculty to Maurice – at his supplication – to receive consecration from any catholic bishop of his choice in communion with the apostolic see, assisted by two or three catholic bishops similarly in communion; and to the bishop concerned to consecrate him, having first received from him in the name of the pope and the Roman church the usual oath of fealty [in accordance with][2] the form noted in the presents. The pope decrees, however, that if the bishop consecrates Maurice without receiving the said oath and Maurice receives consecration they shall both be suspended automatically. Moreover, it is the pope's will that Maurice shall send him, at once, by his own messenger, the form of oath taken by him, verbatim, by his letters patent, marked with his seal; and that the above shall not be to the prejudice of the archbishop of Cashel, to whom the aforesaid church is understood to be subject by metropolitan law. With the form of oath.[3]

Cum nos pridem …
.J. Benzon. / M / M xxviij de Campania

1   above, no. 386
2   'iuxta' wanting
3   not recited in full; *cf.* above, no. 377, notes 3 and 5.

389   25 August 1515   *Reg. Lat.* 1326, fos 23^r-24^r

To the bishop of [?Rochester][1], the abbot of the monastery of Boxley, and the prior of the priory [of][2] Eomu bryge, d. Canterbury, mandate in favour of William Henauge[3], cleric or layman, d. Chichester. A recent petition to the pope on William's part stated that some time ago Simon Fowler, perpetual vicar of the parish church of Arlyngton', said d. – falsely alleging that William had taken away or detained, and was then detaining, certain tithes then expressed – sued William over this and perhaps other matters then expressed, not by apostolic delegation, before the official of Canterbury who was, Simon said, a competent judge for these matters; and that the official, proceeding wrongly in the case, adhering to the deposition of witnesses produced in the case who furnished false testimony, promulgated a null or unjust definitive sentence by which *inter alia* he condemned William in certain tithes then expressed and in the expenses run up in the case on Simon's part, from which William appealed to the apostolic see. At William's supplication to the pope [to order][4] that he be absolved *ad cautelam* from the sentence of excommunication and other ecclesiastical sentences, censures, and pains perhaps promulgated against him on the above occasion and to commit to some upright men in those parts, to be heard, examined, and duly determined, together with the annexed, connected, and dependent matters, the causes: of the aforesaid appeal and of anything attempted and innovated after and against [it][5]; of the nullity and nullities of the said process and sentence and of each and every other thing done in any way in connection with the above;[6] and of the whole principal matter, the pope [hereby] commands that the above three (or two or one of them), having summoned Simon and others concerned, shall, on the pope's authority, bestow on William, for this once only, if he so requests, the benefit of absolution *ad cautelam* from the sentence of excommunication and other sentences, censures, and pains, if and as it is just, having, however, first received from him suitable security in respect of that for which he is perhaps deemed excommunicate and caught by other sentences, censures, and pains that if it is lawfully established before them that the sentence of excommunication and other sentences etc were justly inflicted on him he will obey their mandates and those of the church; as to the other things, having heard both sides, taking cognizance even of the principal matter, decree what is just, without appeal, causing [by ecclesiastical censure what they have decreed to be strictly] observed[7], [and moreover compel] witnesses, etc. Notwithstanding etc.

Humilibus et cetera.
Jo Copis / JoA: / : JoA: xiiij: Nardinus

1   MS: *Rossen.* (Ross); *recte*: 'Roffen. ' (Rochester) ?
2   'de' does not occur.
3   or *Henange*
4   MS wants 'mandare'.
5   MS wants 'eam' (or suchlike).
6   MS: *ac omnium et singulorum aliorum* [per officialem prefatum et quoscunque alios iudices et personas in ipsius Willermi preiudicium] *circa premissa quomodolibet gestorum*; the passage supplied conjecturally here, which we would expect at this point, does not occur.
7   MS: *facientes et cetera observari.* Supplied from common form.

390   16 August 1515   *Reg. Lat.* 1326, fos 157[r]-158[r]

To Richard Coke *alias* Reve, professor OCarm.[1] Dispensation – at his supplication – to him (who, as he asserts, is expressly professed in the house, called priory, of Scale, OCarm, d. Chichester)[2] to receive and retain any benefice, with or without cure, etc. [as above, no. 43, to '… receive and retain another, similar or dissimilar, benefice, with or without cure'], usually held by secular clerics.[3] Notwithstanding etc.[4]

Religionis zelus, vite ac morum honestas …
.P. Lamberti / JoA: / JoA: xxxx: Nardinus

1   MS: *Richardo Coke alias Reve* [(?)*fratri* (?)*domus* (?)*prioratus* (?)*nuncupate de Scale* heavily deleted and initialled *JoA* in two places] *ordinis fratrum Beate Marie* [*virginis* heavily deleted and initialled *JoA*] *de Monte Carmelo professori.* Compare this address clause (including its deletions) with the corresponding passage in the body of the letter, below, note 2.
2   MS: *te qui ut asseris in domo prioratu nuncupata de Scale ordinis fratrum Beate Marie Virginis Carmelitarum de Monte Cormello* [*sic*] *Cisterien.* [originally (?)*Cicest*- the 'ce' being heavily deleted] *diocesis ordinem ipsum expresse professus existis. Cf.* above, note 1.
3   Of course, this latter phrase reflects a variation from no. 43 merely in the formulation – not the tenor – of the Latin.
4   Heavily inked deletions (initialled *JoA*) apparently corresponding (in part or whole) to passages deleted above (*see* notes 1 and 2) occur among the notwithstanding clauses.

391   2 June 1515   *Reg. Lat.* 1326, fos 231[r]-232[r]

To William Bolton', prior of the monastery, usually governed by a prior, of St Bartholomew, in Westsmythfeld, OSA, d. London. Dispensation and indult – at his supplication – to receive together with the priory of the above monastery, two, and without them, any three other benefices, with or without cure, regular, of the above order or the order of St Benedict or of any other order, even the Cluniac or Cistercian, or secular, even if the regular benefices should be priories, *prepositure, prepositatus,* dignities, *personatus,* administrations or offices, and even if the secular benefices should be chantries, free chapels, hospitals or annual services, usually assigned to secular clerics in title of a perpetual ecclesiastical benefice, or canonries and prebends, dignities, *personatus,* administrations or offices in cathedral, even metropolitan, or collegiate churches, and even if two of the secular benefices should be parish churches or their perpetual vicarages, or a combination, and even if the priories etc. should be customarily elective and have cure of souls, if he obtains them otherwise canonically, and to retain the regular benefices *in titulum* and the secular benefices *in commendam*, for life, to resign them, at once or successively, simply or for exchange, as often as he pleases, and cede the commend and in their place receive up to three other, similar or dissimilar, benefices, with or without cure, regular of the above order or the order of St Benedict or of any other order, even the Cluniac or Cistercian, or secular – provided that of three such secular benefices not more than two be parish churches or their perpetual vicarages – and to retain the regular benefices together *in titulum* and the secular benefices *in commendam*, for life, as above; (he may – due and customary burdens of the benefices retained *in commendam* having been supported – make disposition of the rest of their fruits etc. just as those holding them *in titulum* at the time could and ought to do, alienation [of immovable goods and precious movables being] however [forbidden]); and to wear – outside the said monastery only – the habit usually worn by the canons of the said order of St Augustine or its sign under an honest garment or robe of a priest or secular cleric, of any honest colour, without any apostasy or incurring ecclesiastical censure. Notwithstanding etc. With the proviso that the benefices retained *in commendam* shall not, on this account, be defrauded of due services and the cure of souls in them (if any) shall not be neglected; but that the aforesaid burdens shall be supported.

Relligionis[1] *zelus, vite ac morum honestas ...*
.P. Lambertus. / JoA. / JoA: Cx: Nardinus

1   *sic*

392   23 June 1515   *Reg. Lat.* 1326, fos 232ᵛ-233ᵛ

To Thomas Laynde, rector of the parish church of Hornemede P(ar)va, d. London. Dispensation and indult etc. [as above, no. 2].

Vite ac morum honestas ...
.P. Lambertus. / JoA. / JoA. Lx: Nard(inus):-

393   23 June 1515   *Reg. Lat.* 1326, fos 233ᵛ-234ᵛ

To John Burdewx, rector of the parish church of Stratford' Tony [also spelt *Stratford Toni*], d. Salisbury. Dispensation and indult etc. [as above, no. 2].

Vite ac morum honestas ...
.P. Lambertus / JoA: / JoA: Lx: Nard(inus):-

394   23 June 1515   *Reg. Lat.* 1326, fos 235ʳ-236ʳ

To William Jenkynson', rector of the parish [church][1] of Alby, d. Norwich. Dispensation and indult etc. [as above, no. 2].

Vite ac morum honestas …
.P. Lambertus. / JoA: / JoA: Lx: Nardinus

1   'ecclesie' wanting here in the address clause (but present in the text below)

395   23 June 1515   *Reg. Lat.* 1326, fos 236ʳ-237ʳ

To George Billyngton', rector of the parish church of Redcliffe,[1] d. Coventry and Lichfield. Dispensation etc. [as above, no. 161].

Vite ac morum honestas …
.P. Lambertus. / JoA: / JoA: L: Nardinus

1   the final 'e' read sympathetically

396   23 June 1515   *Reg. Lat.* 1326, fo 237ʳ⁻ᵛ

To William Marston' *alias* Clerk, canon of the monastery, called house, of the Holy Trinity, Reppyngdon', OSA, d. Coventry and Lichfield. Dispensation – at his supplication – to him, who, as he asserts, is expressly professed of the above order,[1] to receive and retain any benefice, with or without cure, usually held by secular clerics, etc. [as above, no. 43].

Relligionis² zelus, vite ac morum honestas …
.P. Lambertus. / JoA: / JoA: xxx: Nard(inus):

1   This information comes from a notwithstanding clause.
2   *sic*

397   4 June 1515   *Reg. Lat.* 1326, fo 251ʳ⁻ᵛ

To Humphrey Poyntz,[1] cleric, d. Worcester. Dispensation – at his supplication – to him, who, as he asserts, is in his twenty-second or twenty-third year of age, to receive and retain any benefice, with cure or otherwise incompatible, even if a parish church or its perpetual vicarage, or a chantry, free chapel, hospital or annual service, usually assigned to secular clerics in title of a perpetual ecclesiastical benefice, or a dignity, *personatus*, administration or office in a cathedral, even metropolitan, or collegiate church, even if the dignity in question should be major *post pontificalem* in a cathedral, even metropolitan, church, or principal in a collegiate church, even if the dignity etc. should be customarily elective and have cure of souls, if he obtains it otherwise canonically, to resign it, simply or for exchange, when he pleases, and in its place receive and retain another, similar or dissimilar, benefice, with cure or otherwise incompatible, notwithstanding the above defect of age which he suffers in his twenty-second or twenty-third year, etc. With the proviso that the benefice in question shall not, on this account, be defrauded of due services and the cure of souls in it (if any) shall not be neglected.

Vite ac morum honestas …
.P. Lambertus. / JoA: / JoA: xv: Nardinus

1   or *Poynez*

398   10 April 1515   *Reg. Lat.* 1326, fos 252^r-253^r

Union etc., with indult for non-residence. At a recent petition on the part of John Carter, rector of the parish church of Rerysby[1] [also spelt *Rerysbi*], d. Lincoln, the pope hereby unites etc. the parish church of Petirtany[2] [also spelt *Petratani*,[3] *Periatani*,[4] *Petirtani*, *Petretani*], d. Exeter (whose annual value does not exceed 9 pounds and 10 shillings sterling), with all rights and appurtenances, to the above parish church of Rerysby, which he holds together with Petirtany by apostolic dispensation, for as long as he holds Rerysby, to the effect that he may, on his own authority, in person or by proxy, take anew, or continue in, and retain corporal possession of Petirtany and the rights and appurtenances aforesaid, for as long as he holds Rerysby, and convert its fruits etc. to his own uses and those of the said churches, without licence of the local diocesan or of anyone else. With indult for life to John, while attending a *studium generale* or residing in the Roman curia or any one of his benefices, not to be bound to reside in his other benefices nor to be liable to be compelled to do so by anyone against his will. Notwithstanding etc. The pope's will is, however, that the church of Petirtany and other benefices shall not, on account of this union etc., be defrauded of due services and the cure of souls in it and (if any) in the other benefices aforesaid shall not be neglected; but that customary burdens of the church of Petirtany and of other benefices in which he shall not reside shall be supported; and that on John's death or his resignation etc. of the church of Rerysby this union etc. shall be dissolved and be so deemed and Petirtany shall revert to its original condition automatically.

Ad futuram rei memoriam. Romanum decet pontificem votis illis gratum prestare assensum …
.P Lambertus. / M / M xxxxv de Campania

1   consistently read as *R-* (though the first letter occasionally resembles 'K')

2   The name has been altered: the letter read as 'i' was probably originally an 'r'; the letter read as 'r' is written
     directly above a deleted 'a'; and the letter read as 'n' could be read as 'u'.
3   the letter read as 'n' could be read as 'u'
4   the first 'a' indistinct and uncertain

399   11 April 1515   *Reg. Lat.* 1326, fos 253ʳ-254ʳ

To Edward Molyneux, rector of the parish church of Seston', d. Coventry and
Lichfield. Dispensation and indult etc. [as above, no. 2].

Vite ac morum honestas ...
.P. Lambertus. / JoA: / JoA: Lx: Nardinus

400   16 May 1515   *Reg. Lat.* 1326, fos 256ʳ-257ʳ

To Edmund Edylston, rector of the parish church of Yatenden [also spelt *Yanteden*], d.
Salisbury. Dispensation and indult etc. [as above, no. 2].

Vite ac morum honestas ...
.P. Lambertus / JoA: / JoA: L.¹ Nardinus

1   *See above*, no. 13, note 2.

401   20 April 1515   *Reg. Lat.* 1326, fos 260ʳ-261ʳ

Union etc. At a recent petition on the part of Arthur Wernon', rector of the parish
church of St Peter, Shele, d. Lincoln, the pope hereby unites etc. the parish church of
St Andrew, Bonsherston', d. St David's (whose annual value does not exceed 8 pounds
sterling), with all rights and appurtenances, to the above church of St Peter, which he
holds together with St Andrew's by apostolic dispensation, for as long as he holds St
Peter's, to the effect that he may, on his own authority, in person or by proxy, take
anew, or continue in, and retain possession¹ of St Andrew's and the rights and
appurtenances aforesaid, for as long as he holds St Peter's, and convert its fruits etc. to
his own uses and those of the said churches, without licence of the local diocesan or of
anyone else. Notwithstanding etc. The pope's will is, however, that St Andrew's shall
not, on account of this union etc., be defrauded of due services and the cure of souls in
it shall not be neglected, but that its customary burdens shall be supported; and that on
Arthur's death or his resignation etc. of St Peter's this union etc. shall be dissolved and
be so deemed and St Andrew's shall revert to its original condition automatically.

Ad futuram rei memoriam. Romanum decet pontificem votis illis gratum prestare

assensum ...
.P. Lambertus. / JoA: / JoA: xxxv: Nard(inus):

1 'corporalem' does not occur.

402 20 April 1515   *Reg. Lat.* 1326, fos 261ᵛ-262ᵛ

To Henry Lussell', perpetual vicar of the parish church of Wystow, d. Lincoln. Dispensation and indult etc. [as above, no. 2].

Vite ac morum honestas ...
.P. Lambertus. / JoA: / JoA: Lx: Nardinus

403 4 June 1515   *Reg. Lat.* 1326, fos 267ʳ-268ʳ

To Geoffrey Bnyght',[1] MTheol, rector of the parish church of Styfkey St Johns,[2] d. Norwich. Dispensation and indult etc. [as above, no. 2].

Litterarum scientia, vite ac morum honestas ...
.P. Lambertus / JoA; / JoA: Lx: Nardinus

1 or *Buyght'*
2 MS: *Styfkey Sancti Johannis* (with, in the first instance, *Styfchey* deleted and initialled *JoA.* before *Styfkey*)

404 4 June 1515   *Reg. Lat.* 1326, fos 268ʳ-269ʳ

To Geoffrey W<h>arton,[1] BDec, perpetual vicar of the parish church of Todelow, d. Ely. Dispensation and indult etc. [as above, no. 2].

Litterarum scientia, vite ac morum honestas ...
.P. Lambertus. / JoA: / JoA: Lx: Nard(inus):-

1 the 'h' written above the 'a'

405 4 June 1515   *Reg. Lat.* 1326, fos 269ᵛ-270ᵛ

To Owen Ap' Meredith', rector of the parish church of St Michael the Archangel, Castop, [d.][1] St David's. Dispensation and indult etc. [as above, no. 2].

Vite ac morum honestas …
.P. Lambertus. / JoA: / JoA: Lx: Nard(inus):

1   'diocesis' wanting here in the address clause (but present in the text below)

406   4 June 1515   *Reg. Lat.* 1326, fos 270^v-271^v

To John Huys, MA, rector of the parish church of Langham, d. London. Dispensation and indult etc. [as above, no. 2].

Litterarum scientia, vite ac morum honestas …
P. Lambertus / JoA: / JoA: Lx: Nardinus

407   4 June 1515   *Reg. Lat.* 1326, fos 271^v-272^v

To Gilbert Hecton', perpetual vicar of the parish church of Legh', d. Coventry and Lichfield. Dispensation and indult etc. [as above, no. 2].

Vite ac morum honestas …
.P. Lambertus. / JoA: / JoA: Lx: Nardinus

408   4 June 1515   *Reg. Lat.* 1326, fo 273^r-v

To Robert Norcliffe, canon of the monastery of St Nicholas, Drax, OSA, d. York. Dispensation – at his supplication – to him, who, as he asserts, is expressly professed of the above order,[1] to receive and retain for life any benefice, with or without cure, usually held by secular clerics, etc. [as above, no. 43].

Relligionis[2] zelus, vite ac morum honestas …
.P. Lambertus / JoA: / JoA: xxx: Nardinus

1   This information comes from a notwithstanding clause.
2   *sic*

409   10 November 1515   *Reg. Lat.* 1327, fos 29^r-30^r

To Nicholas Peper, prior of the priory of Peter and Paul the Apostles, Taunton', OSA, d. Bath and Wells. Dispensation – at his supplication – to receive and retain *in commendam* for life, together with the above priory, any benefice, with or without cure, usually held by secular clerics, even if a parish church or its perpetual vicarage, or a chantry, free chapel, hospital or annual service, usually assigned to secular clerics in title of a perpetual ecclesiastical benefice, and of lay patronage and of whatsoever tax or annual value, if he obtains it otherwise canonically, to resign it, simply or for exchange, as often as he pleases and cede the commend and in its place receive and retain *in commendam* for life another, similar or dissimilar, benefice, with or without cure, defined as above; he may – due and customary burdens of this benefice having been supported – make disposition of the rest of its fruits etc. just as those holding it *in titulum* could and ought to do, alienation of immovable goods and precious movables being however forbidden. Notwithstanding etc. With the proviso that the above benefice shall not, on this account, be defrauded of due services and the cure of souls in it (if any) shall not be neglected; but that the aforesaid burdens shall be supported. Given at Montefiascone.

Religionis zelus, vite ac morum honestas …
I. Benzon / JoA: / :JoA: L: Nardinus

410   10 November 1515   *Reg. Lat.* 1327, fos 30ʳ-31ʳ

To Thomas Angyll',[1] rector of the parish church of <Barwell>[2] [also spelt *Barwell'*][3] d. Lincoln. Dispensation etc. [as above, no. 161]. Given at Montefiascone.

Vite ac morum honestas …
I. Benzon / JoA: / JoA: L: Nardinus

1 the 'y' written *-ij-*
2 *Sorwell'* in line deleted and initialled *JoA*; with *Barwell* inserted in margin: *JoA* above it; *cassat(um) et correctu(m) de man(da)to D(omi)ni Regentis Nardinus* beneath. The same deletion and insertion occurs in the narrative below, with *JoA* above it; *cassat(um) et correctu(m) de man(da)to R(everendissimi) D(omini) Regentis Nardinus* beneath.

411   15 September 1515   *Reg. Lat.* 1327, fos 282ʳ-283ᵛ

To the official of Aberdeen, mandate in favour of Nicholas Paterson, cleric, d. Moray. Following the pope's reservation some time ago of all benefices, with and without cure, vacated then and in the future at the apostolic see to his own collation and disposition, the perpetual vicarage of the parish church of Kyrinerny, d. Aberdeen, fell vacant by the free resignation of John Toncht,[1] lately vicar, who was then holding the vicarage, made spontaneously through Adam Simson,[2] cleric, d. Dunkeld, his specially appointed proctor, into the hands of the pope who admitted the resignation at the said see, and is vacant at present, being reserved as above. The pope hereby commands the above official, if by diligent examination he finds Nicholas to be suitable – concerning which the pope burdens the official's conscience – to collate and assign the vicarage, whose annual value does not exceed 9 pounds sterling, (vacant as above or in any other way etc.; even if it has been vacant for so long that by the Lateran statutes its collation has lawfully devolved on the apostolic see etc.), with all rights and appurtenances, to Nicholas, inducting him etc. having removed any unlawful detainer and causing Nicholas (or his proctor) to be admitted to the vicarage and its fruits etc., rights and obventions to be delivered to him. [Curbing] gainsayers etc. Notwithstanding etc.

Dignum arbitramur et congruum et cetera.
Jo. Copis / JoA: / :JoA: xx: Sexto decimo k(a)l(endas) decenbris Anno tertio: [16 November 1515], *Nardinus*

1   highly uncertain
2   Though the last minim of the 'm' appears dotted.

412   21 October 1515   *Reg. Lat.* 1327, fo 285[r-v]

To George Hepburn, cleric, d. St Andrews. Dispensation – at his supplication – to him, who, as he asserts, is in his eighteenth year of age or thereabouts, to receive and retain any benefice, with cure or otherwise incompatible, even if a parish church or its perpetual vicarage, or a dignity, *personatus*, administration,[1] or office[2] in a cathedral, even metropolitan, or collegiate church, even if major *post pontificalem* in a cathedral, even metropolitan, church or principal in a collegiate church, even if the dignity, *personatus*, administration or office should be customarily elective and have cure of souls, if he obtains it otherwise canonically, to resign it, simply or for exchange, as often as he pleases and in its place receive and retain another, similar or dissimilar, benefice, with cure or otherwise incompatible, notwithstanding the above defect of age, etc. With the proviso that the benefice in question shall not, on this account, be defrauded of due services and the cure of souls in it shall not be neglected. Given at Corneto.

Vite ac morum honestas …
p. lambert(us) / JoA: / :JoA: xxiiij: Nardinus

1   *dignitates … administrationes*; *recte*: 'dignitas … administratio'
2   *officia* is deleted and initialled *JoA* before *officium* (ending this confusion of the singular and plural cases).

413   24 March 1515   *Reg. Lat.* 1328, fos 99[r]-100[r]

Union etc. At a recent petition on the part of Thomas Wyse, LLB, canon of the church of St Carantocus (*Sancti Carantoci*),[1] d. Exeter, the pope hereby unites etc. the parish church of St Euninus (*Sancti Eunini*),[2] d. Exeter, (whose annual value does not exceed 10 pounds sterling), with all rights and appurtenances, to the canonry and prebend of the above church of St Carantocus, which he holds together with the said church of St Euninus, for as long as he holds the canonry and prebend, to the effect that he may, on his own authority, in person or by proxy, <continue in or> take <anew>[3] and retain corporal possession of the church of St Euninus and the rights and appurtenances aforesaid, for as long as he holds the canonry and prebend, and convert its fruits etc. to his own uses[4] and those of the canonry and prebend and the church of St Euninus, without licence of the local diocesan or of anyone else. Notwithstanding etc. The pope's will is, however, that the church of St Euninus shall not, on account of this union etc., be defrauded of due services and the cure of souls in it shall not be neglected; but that its customary burdens shall be supported; and that on Thomas's death or his resignation etc. of the canonry and prebend this union etc. shall be dissolved and so deemed and the church of St Euninus shall revert to its original condition automatically.

Ad futuram rei memoriam. Romanum decet pontificem votis illis gratum prestare assensum ...
.P. Lambertus. / JoA. / JoA. xxxv: Nard(inus):

1   In the first occurrence the 'r' is written directly above 'x' deleted.
2   Here (and in occurrences below) the minims are capable of various readings; the fifth and the last (elongated) are dotted.
3   *continuare seu de novo* inserted in margin initialled *JoA*
4   'usus et utilitatem' expected here; MS just has: *utilitatem*

414   28 March 1515   *Reg. Lat.* 1328, fos 100[r]-101[v]

Union etc. A recent petition to the pope on the part of Henry Tuker, BDec, rector of the parish church of Cludysden'[1] [also spelt *Cludysdeum*], d. Winchester, stated that if the parish [church][2] of Chilton' Caudener[3] [also spelt *Chilton' Kaudener, Chilton' Chaudener, Chilton Caudener*], d. Winchester, and the perpetual chantry of St Catherine in the parish church of St Peter, Marbow, d. Salisbury (which is of lay patronage, and [for] which recently, when it was vacant *certo modo*, Henry was presented by its lay patron within the lawful time) assuming he were to be canonically instituted in the chantry at this presentation, were to be united etc. to the above church of Cludysden', which Henry holds together with the said church of Chilton' Caudener by apostolic dispensation, for as long as he holds Cludysden', it would be of advantage to him. At the supplication on the part of Henry (who asserts that the annual value of the above church of Chilton' Caudener does not exceed 3, and of the above chantry, also 3, pounds sterling) the pope hereby unites etc. the church of Chilton' Caudener and the chantry (if Henry is canonically instituted in it at this presentation, as above), with all rights and appurtenances, to the said church of Cludysden', for as long as Henry holds the latter, to the effect that he may, on his own authority, in person or by proxy, take corporal possession of the church of Chilton' Caudener and the chantry and the rights and appurtenances aforesaid, or continue in and retain [corporal possession] of this united church, for as long as he holds the church of Cludysden', and convert the fruits etc. to his own uses and those of the churches of Cludysden' and Chilton' Caudener and the chantry aforesaid, without licence of the local diocesan or of anyone

else. Notwithstanding etc. The pope's will is, however, that the church of Chilton'
Caudener and the chantry shall not, on account of this union etc., be defrauded of due
services and the cure of souls in the church of Chilton' Caudener shall not be neglected;
but that its customary burdens and those of the above chantry shall be supported; and
that on Henry's death or his resignation etc. of the church of Cludysden' this union etc.
shall be dissolved and be so deemed and the church of Chilton' Caudener and the
chantry shall revert to their original condition automatically.

Ad futuram rei[4] *memoriam. Romanum decet pontificem votis illis gratum prestare
assensum ...*
.P. Lambertus / JoA: / JoA: xxxx: Nardinus

1   The 'en' is clear in some instances; but doubtful in others.
2   'ecclesia' does not occur here.
3   the 'u' and 'n' are also readable as 'n' and 'u' respectively.
4   *Ad futuram rei* written in 'semi' bollatica; *cf.* above, no. 191, note 1.

415   4 June 1515   *Reg. Lat.* 1328, fos 103[r]-104[r]

Union etc. At a recent petition on the part of Geoffrey Knygth, MTheol, rector of the
parish church of Styfkey St Johns [also spelt simply <*Styskey*>,[1] *Styfkei, Stifkei*], d.
Norwich, the pope hereby unites etc. the parish church of Pensthorpe [also spelt
Penstorpe], d. Norwich, (which is of lay patronage; is of annual value not exceeding 5
pounds sterling; and for which at another time, when it was vacant *certo modo*,
Geoffrey was presented by its true patron – who was in peaceful quasi-possession of
the right of presenting a suitable person for the said church, at a time of vacancy –
within the lawful time, perhaps to the local ordinary), assuming Geoffrey were to be
canonically instituted as rector at this presentation, with all rights and appurtenances,
to the above church of Styfkey, which Geoffrey holds, for as long as he does so, to the
effect that he may, on his own authority, in person or by proxy, take and retain corporal
possession of Pensthorpe and the rights and appurtenances aforesaid, for as long as he
holds Styfkey, and convert its fruits etc. to his own uses and those of the said churches,
without licence of the local diocesan or of anyone else. Notwithstanding etc. The
pope's will is, however, that the church of Pensthorpe shall not, on account of this
union etc., be defrauded of due services and the cure of souls in it shall not be
neglected; but that its customary burdens shall be supported; and that on Geoffrey's
death or his resignation etc. of the church of Styfkey this union etc. shall be dissolved
and be so deemed and Pensthorpe shall revert to its original condition automatically.

*Ad futuram rei memoriam. Romanum decet pontificem votis illis gratum prestare
assensum ...*
.P. Lambertus. / JoA: / JoA: xxxv: Nardinus

1   This spelling occurs in a marginal insertion; the second 's' is written long, i.e. like an 'f' without a bar.

416 8 June 1515[1]   *Reg. Lat.* 1328, fos 104^v-105^r

To Richard Jeuyn',[2] prior of the priory <called house>,[3] of B. Mary the Virgin, Madynbredlegh, OSA, d. Salisbury. Indult – at his supplication – to wear the usual rochet or habit worn by canons of the said order under an honest garment or other vestment of a priest or secular cleric, of any honest colour, without any apostasy or incurring ecclesiastical censure; and not to be bound to wear the above habit otherwise, and not to be liable to be compelled by anyone to do so against his will. Notwithstanding etc.

Exigunt tue devotionis merita …
.P. Lambertus. / JoA: / JoA: xx:- Nardinus[4]

1   *See below*, note 4.
2   the 'u' readable as 'n'
3   *domus nuncupati* inserted in margin, initialled *JoA.*
4   As a rule, the magistral subscription simply followed the dating clause. In this case date (in the enregistering scribe's hand) and subscription (in the master's) are, puzzlingly, intermingled: *Dat. Rome* ‖ [fo 105r] *apud Sanctum Petrum anno et cetera millesimo quingentesimo quinto | decimo* JoA: *sexto idus Junii anno tertio.* xx:- | Nardinus. Additionally, xx *deleted* occurs in the right hand margin opposite the penultimate line. The freak subscription was no doubt the outcome of procedural irregularity in the registry (*cf. CPL* XVI, pp. xxi-xxiv); but in the absence of further data the exact circumstances which produced it must remain a matter of guesswork. Whatever the explanation, a close collaboration between master and scribe would appear to be indicated.

417[1]   **4 June 1515**   *Reg. Lat.* 1328, fos 105^r-106^v

Union etc. A recent petition to the pope on the part of Nicholas Henshaw,[2] canon of the church of St Mary, Otery, d. Exeter, stated that if the perpetual vicarage of the parish church of Thornerton' [also spelt *Thornerton*], said diocese, were to be united etc. to the canonry and prebend of the said church of St Mary, which Nicholas holds *inter alia* together with the said vicarage [of Thornerton'], for as long as he holds the canonry and prebend, it would be of advantage to him. Wherefore supplication was made on Nicholas's part – asserting that he also holds *inter alia* the perpetual vicarage of the parish church of Holboton', said diocese, by apostolic dispensation; and that the annual value of the said vicarage of Thornerton' [*sic*] does not exceed 13 pounds 6 shillings and 8 pence sterling – to the pope to unite etc. the vicarage of Thornerton' to the canonry and prebend, for as long as Nicholas holds the latter. The pope (having the annual value of the vicarage of Holboton' [*sic*] as expressed in the presents) – at this supplication – hereby unites etc. the above vicarage of Holboton', with all rights and appurtenances, to the canonry and prebend, for as long as Nicholas holds the latter, to the effect that he may, on his own authority, in person or by proxy, take anew, or continue in, and retain corporal possession of the vicarage of Holboton' and the rights and appurtenances aforesaid, for as long as he holds the said canonry and prebend, and convert its fruits etc. to his own uses and those of the canonry and prebend and also of the vicarage of Holboton', without licence of the local diocesan or of anyone else.

Notwithstanding etc. The pope's will is, however, that the vicarage of Holboton' shall
not, on account of this union etc., be defrauded of due services and the cure of souls in
it shall not be neglected; but that its customary burdens shall be supported; and that on
Nicholas's death or his resignation etc. of the canonry and prebend this union etc. shall
be dissolved and so deemed and the vicarage of Holboton' shall revert to its original
condition automatically.

*Ad futuram rei memoriam. Romanum decet pontificem votis illis gratum prestare
assensum ...*
P. Lambertus. / JoA: / JoA: xxxv: Nardinus

1   This entry contradicts itself: the operative part unites Holboton' vicarage to the petitioner's canonry and
    prebend; but the narrative envisages union of Thornerton' vicarage. To enable the reader to follow the
    contradiction as it evolves, the somewhat repetitious formulation of the Latin has been adhered to more
    closely than is our practice in the calendaring of English unions. A corresponding petition is for the union of
    Thorverton (*Tarvertan*) to Henshaw's canonry and prebend. As we would expect, Holbeton is not mentioned
    (*Reg. Suppl.* 1491, fo. 134ᵛ).
2   written: *hEnshaW*

418   4 June 1515   *Reg. Lat.* 1328, fos 107ʳ-108ᵛ

To John Collet, MTheol, dean of the church of London, dispensation and indult. Some
time ago, Innocent VIII by his letters dispensed him to receive and retain together for
life any two benefices, with cure or otherwise mutually incompatible, even if parish
churches or their perpetual vicarages or chantries, free chapels, hospitals or annual
services usually assigned to secular clerics in title of a perpetual ecclesiastical
benefice, or dignities, *personatus*, administrations or offices in cathedral, even
metropolitan, [or collegiate]² churches, etc. [as above, no. 6, to '... retain them together
for life'], as is more fully contained in those letters.³ The pope therefore – at his
supplication – hereby dispenses John, who, as he asserts, holds the deanery of the
above church of London (which is perhaps a dignity major *post pontificalem*) and the
parish church of St Mary, Donynglon', d. Norwich, by the said dispensation, to receive
and retain for life, together with the above deanery and the church of B.⁴ Mary, or any
two other incompatible benefices held by him at the time by virtue of the said
dispensation, any third benefice, etc. [as above, no. 6, to '... in its place receive
another'], similar or dissimilar, third incompatible benefice – provided that of three
such benefices not more than two be parish churches or their perpetual vicarages – and
retain it for life, as above. With indult for life to John, while atttending a *studium
generale* or residing in the Roman curia or any one of his benefices, not to be bound
to reside in his other benefices nor to be liable to be compelled to do so by anyone
against his will. Notwithstanding etc. With the proviso that the third incompatible
benefice and those benefices in which he shall not reside shall not, on this account, be
defrauded of due services and the cure of souls in them ([if] any) shall not be neglected;
but that customary burdens of those benefices in which he shall not reside shall be
supported.

Litterarum scientia, vite ac morum honestas …
.P. Lambertus / JoA: / JoA: Lxxx:- Nardinus

1   A corresponding petition is at *Reg. Suppl.* 1491, fo. 136ʳ.
2   MS: *… in cathedralibus etiam metropolitanis * et dignitates ipse in cathedralibus etiam metropolitanis post pontificales maiores …* The asterisk is mine and marks the spot where *post* is deleted and 'vel collegiatis' ought to have been written but, presumably through inadvertence, was not.
3   *CPL*, XV, no. 335.
4   here: *Beate*; the two other occurences: *Sancte*

419   8 June 1515   *Reg. Lat.* 1328, fos 108ᵛ-109ᵛ

To Thomas Clerke, prior of the priory, called house, of B. Mary the Virgin and All Saints, Westacre [also spelt *Vestacre*], OSA, d. Norwich. Dispensation and indult – at his supplication – to receive and retain *in commendam* together with the above priory, or any other priory, monastery, dignity or office of the said order held by him at the time, one, and without them, any two other benefices, secular, with or without cure, even if parish churches or their perpetual vicarages, or chantries, free chapels, hospitals or annual services usually assigned to secular clerics in title of a perpetual ecclesiastical benefice, and of lay patronage and of whatsoever tax or annual value, and [even if] pertaining in any way to his collation, provision, presentation or any other disposition [even]¹ and by reason of the said priory if conferred on him otherwise canonically, to resign them, at once or successively, as often as he pleases, and cede the commend, and in their place receive up to two other, similar or dissimilar, secular benefices, with or without cure, and retain them *in commendam* for life, as above; he may – due and customary burdens of the said benefices having been supported – make disposition of the rest of their fruits etc. just as those holding them *in titulum* at the time could and ought to do, alienation [of immovable goods and precious movables being] however [forbidden]²; and, for life, while attending a *studium generale*, or residing in the Roman curia or any one of his benefices, not to be bound to reside in his other benefices, nor to be liable to be compelled to do so by anyone against his will. Notwithstanding etc. With the proviso that the benefices to be held *in commendam* and others in which he shall not reside shall not, on this account, be defrauded of due services and the cure of souls in them ([if] any) shall not be neglected; but that customary burdens in benefices retained *in commendam* and others in which he shall not reside shall be supported.

Relligionis³ zelus, vite ac morum honestas …
.P. Lambertus / JoA: / JoA: Lx: Nardinus

1   MS: *et*; *recte*: 'etiam'
2   MS: *alienatione tamen et cetera.* Supplied from common form.
3   *sic*

420   8 June 1515   *Reg. Lat.* 1328, fos 110ʳ-111ʳ

To William Niwton, rector of the parish church of Hygham, d.[1] Bath and Wells.
Dispensation and indult etc. [as above, no. 2].

Vite ac morum honestas ...
.P. Lambertus. / JoA: / JoA: Lx: Nardinus

1   *dioc'* present in the address clause but not below

421   24 March 1515   *Reg. Lat.* 1328, fo 116ʳ⁻ᵛ

To John Fflooke, MA, rector of the parish church of Sulham, d. Salisbury. Dispensation
and indult etc. [as above, no. 2].

Litterarum scientia, vite ac morum honestas ...
.P. Lambertus / C / C. L.[1] Barotius

1   *See above*, no. 13, note 2.

422   12 May 1515   *Reg. Lat.* 1328, fos 121ᵛ-122ʳ

To Giles Dewhurst, perpetual vicar of the parish church of Merston' [also spelt
Merston], d. Coventry and Lichfield. Indult for life – at his supplication – to him, who,
as he asserts, holds the perpetual vicarage of the above parish church, not to be bound,
while attending a [*studium*][1] *generale* etc. [as below, no. 433]. Given at Magliana, d.
Porto.

Vite ac morum honestas ...
.P. Lambertus. / JoA. / JoA: xx: Nardinus

1   'studio' wanting in MS

423   19 May 1515   *Reg. Lat.* 1328, fos 124ᵛ-125ʳ

To John Asseby,[1] monk of the monastery of B. Mary, St Benedict and All Holy Virgins,
Ramesen, OSB, <county of Huntyngdon[2]>,[3] d. Lincoln. Dispensation – at his
supplication – to him, who, as he asserts, is expressly professed of the above order,[4] to
receive and retain any benefice, with or without cure, usually held by secular clerics,
etc. [as above, no. 43].

Relligionis[5] zelus, vite ac morum honestas …
.P. Lambertus / JoA: / :JoA: xxx: Nardinus

1   the 'b' converted from a long 's'?
2   written *Hungtyngdon* with the first 'g' struck through
3   *comitatus Hun(g)tyngdon* (*see* note 2) is inserted in the margin, initialled *JoA*.; the county name is repeated
     below (in a notwithstanding clause) – but within the line of text and the name is spelt *Huntyngdon* (i.e. not
     requiring alteration).
4   This information comes from a notwithstanding clause.
5   *sic*

424   4 June 1515   *Reg. Lat.* 1328, fo 125[r-v]

To M. John Newman, canon of York,[1] papal notary. Indult for life – at his supplication
– to him who, as he asserts, holds canonries and prebends of the churches of York [and]
Osmanderlay [also spelt *Osmo(n)derlay*],[2] and also the perpetual vicarage of the parish
church[3] of St Andrew, Ocborne, ds. <York>[4] and Salisbury, not to be bound, while
attending a *studium generale* etc. [as below, no.433, to '… served by good and
sufficient vicars maintained from the proceeds of the vicarage and other benefices'];
and customary burdens of the canonries and prebends and other benefices shall be
supported.

Grata devotionis obsequia …
.P. Lambertus. / JoA: / JoA: xx: Nard(inus):–

1   *sic*; i.e. 'ecclesie' (which might be expected) does not occur.
2   written *Osmo'derlay*
3   *ecclesie* (deleted) occurs after *parrochialis*, the deletion initialled *C* (at the start) and *Ba* (at the finish).
     ecclesie was redundant as *ecclesiarum* occurs at the end of the enumeration of benefices.
4   *Eboracen.* inserted in the margin; above it: *C*; beneath: *cassatum et additu(m) de man(da)to R. p. D.*
     Regent(is) et concordat. Barotius. The insertion replaces *Dunelmen.* deleted in the line; the deletion initialled
     C (at the start) and *Ba* (at the finish). Osmotherley was a Durham peculiar in the d. York. In view of the
     variable treatment of peculiars (*cf.* nos. 30, 47, 162, 184, 189, 206, and 473) the formal alteration is
     interesting. In a corresponding petition *Dunelmen. diocesis* has not been altered and, significantly, *immediate*
     is deployed before *Saresbirien. diocesis* (*Reg. Suppl.* 1491, fos 260[v]-261[r]). The petition, which is captioned
     de non residendo, is dated 4 June 1515.

425   5 April 1515   *Reg. Lat.* 1328, fos 217[r]-219[r]

To the bishop of Norwich, the prior of the monastery customarily governed by a prior
of St Bartholomew in Wostsmythfelid in the suburbs of London, and Cuthbert
Tunstall', canon of the church of Lincoln, commission [and mandate][1] in favour of
John Coposhosso, canon of the monastery of B Mary and St Nicholas, Bildgh [also
spelt *Bildgh*.[2]], OPrem, d. London. A recent petition to the pope on John's part stated
that some time ago – after Henry Purforte, canon of the said monastery (who, by
apostolic dispensation, was holding the perpetual vicarage of the parish church of

Wltyng and the rectory with cure of the church of St Laurence, Dansoy, said d., which are in the patronage of the abbot and convent of the said monastery) had been canonically elected abbot of the monastery of Langlei, OPrem, d. Norwich (then destitute of the rule of an abbot) by its convent, and, consenting to the election when the election-decree was presented to him, had had it confirmed (not, however, by apostolic authority) by him to whom the confirmation of such elections appertained and had peacefully acquired the rule and administration of the said monastery and its annexes;[3] and after the said rectory had, by the said acquisition, become vacant, and the abbot and convent of the monastery of Bildgh had, within the lawful time, presented John to the bishop of London [for][4] the church of St Laurence – the said bishop or his vicar or commissary ordered and caused Henry to be cited to adduce before him the reasons why, at the presentation which had been made to him, John ought not to be instituted; that the said bishop or his vicar or commissary ordered Henry or his proctor to reply to certain pertinent or relevant positions (to which in law reply was due) produced before him on John's part at a suitable time and place, and Henry – falsely alleging that he was thereby unduly aggrieved – then appealed to the local metropolitan court of Canterbury, and in the cause of the said appeal, caused John to be summoned to trial before the official, called president, of the said court; that the said official or president found that Henry had appealed frivolously and by a certain interlocutory of his, sent back the cause to the judge from whom Henry had appealed, to be resumed by him in its original state, further heard, and duly determined; that when the cause had been resumed in due state by William Horslei[5], DDec, the commissary-judge of the bishop from whom appeal had been made on Henry's part, and both the (?)witnesses[6] as also the instruments aforesaid had been received, and the witnesses on John's part had been sworn and examined by the said vicar or commissary, and their testimony published, for the purpose of establishing John's claim, the vicar or commissary lawfully refused to grant Henry a certain competent term of his choosing (*ad ipsius Henrici voluntatem*) to prove several frivolous and irrelevant objections unlawfully put forward on Henry's part against the witnesses and instruments; that Henry, falsely alleging that he was *inter alia* thereby unduly aggrieved, appealed to the apostolic see; and that, as the said petition added, Henry is neglecting and delaying to prosecute the later appeal. At John's supplication to the pope to commit to some upright men in those parts the causes, with each and every one of their incident, dependent, emergent, annexed, and connected matters, of the later appeal lodged on Henry's part and of the whole principal matter, the pope [hereby] enjoins [and commands][7] that the above three (or two or one of them), having summoned Henry and others concerned and having heard both sides, taking cognizance even of the principal matter, [shall decree] what is just, [without appeal, causing by ecclesiastical censure what they have decreed to be strictly] observed,[8] [and moreover compel] witnesses, etc. Notwithstanding the constitution of Innocent IV beginning "Oblite" concerning *inter alia* one day's journey, the constitution of Boniface VIII,[9] and the constitution on two day's journey published in the general council, provided that by authority of the presents no one is summoned more than four day's journey.

Humilibus et cetera.

Jo Copis / JoA: / :JoA: xv: Nard(inus):–

1   MS: *comittimus et cetera*. Supplied from common form.
2   final letter or mark illegible
3   MS: *ac regiminis et administrationis ipsius monasterii ac annexorum eiusdem pacifice assequatus fuerat*
4   MS wants 'ad'
5   the '-le-' uncertain
6   reading (?)*testibus*; but ill-formed and uncertain
7   MS: *comittimus et cetera*. Supplied from common form.
8   MS: *quod iustum fuerit et cetera observari*. Supplied from common form.
9   MS muddled: *Non obstantibus felicis recordationis Innocentii pape IIII que incipit "Oblite" qua inter alia cavetur ne quis extra suam civitatem vel diocesim nisi in certis exceptis casibus et in illis ultra unam dietam a fine sue diocesis ad iudicium evocetur seu ne iudices ... vices suas committere presumant ac pie memorie Bonifatii pape VIII predecessorum nostrorum et de duabus dietis in concilio generali edita ... et aliis constitutionibus apostolicis ... .* The constitution touching one day's journey is Boniface VIII's (*cf.* Friedberg 941-2; 982-3), not Innocent IV's; the constitution "Oblite" (= Oblatae), which concerns delayed appeals (not dietae), is Innocent III's (Friedberg 435-7), not Innocent IV's. The reference to the constitution on two day's journey (not muddled) is to that published in the general council (*cf. Decretals*, I, 3.28 [Friedberg, 31]; *Clem.* II.2. [Friedberg, 1144-5]).

426   18 June 1515   *Reg. Lat.* 1330, fo 49[r-v]

Relaxation and grant of faculty and licence as below. The pope – wishing that the confraternity of Christ's faithful of both sexes, dedicated to the Name of Jesus [and] St [S]citha (*Sancte Cithe*) the Virgin,[1] instituted in the parish church of Estburne, d. Chichester, [to][2] which, as the pope has learned, John Cosyng, priest, the present chaplain, and all the members of the said confraternity are singularly devoted, is increased, conserved, and maintained; and that the said church is suitably honoured and held in due veneration; and that, out of devotion, the said faithful willingly enter the said confraternity and contribute readily to its maintenance, increase and conservation because they see themselves abundantly refreshed thereby with the gift of celestial grace – assured of the mercy of Almighty God and of the authority of BB. Peter and Paul His Apostles, mercifully grants, to all the said faithful who, being truly penitent and confessed, shall have devoutly visited the said church annually on the several feasts of the Name of Jesus, of St [S]citha, of the Assumption and Nativity of B Mary the Virgin, and of the dedication of the said church, and also on the Sundays immediately following the feast of the said dedication, from first vespers to second vespers of the several feasts and days, inclusively, and shall have contributed to the said maintenance, increase, and conservation, ten years and as many quarantines of enjoined penance for the several feasts and days aforesaid, [as often as][3] they shall have done it; and to those who shall have been present at solemn mass and at the antiphon in honour of the Name of Jesus to be sung in the said church on Fridays and the other customary days or who shall have proposed to be present but, detained by lawful impediment, shall have been unable to be present; and also to those who shall have contributed from their own goods, to the chaplain for the time being of the said confraternity who celebrates mass and the other divine offices therein each day, something for his keep, one hundred days and as many quarantines of enjoined penance as often as they shall have done it; and the pope grants licence and faculty that the guardians and keepers (*guardiani et custodes*) of the said confraternity appointed from time to time, having summoned five or six members of the confraternity, may, after the death of the said John and successively at their discretion, elect and appoint another as their and the confraternity's chaplain to celebrate mass and other divine offices at the altar under the said dedication [sc. the Name of Jesus and St [S]citha the Virgin], without the licence of the rector or vicar of the said church for the time being or of anyone else; and the pope strictly inhibits, under sentence of excommunication, the said rector and vicar and any others, from accepting anything from the oblations made from time to time to the said confraternity or involving themselves in anything without the licence of the said guardians or keepers or from molesting, upsetting, or disturbing the said chaplain and confraternity members in connection with the above; and he declares that the said indulgence cannot be comprehended under any revocations or suspensions which have emanated from the apostolic see from time to time of similar or dissimilar indulgences, even revocations or suspensions in favour of the basilica of the Prince of the Apostles, Rome (*de Urbe*) or the crusade and with any clauses derogatory of derogatory clauses and other highly efficacious clauses, but is always to be excepted from them. The present letters shall last for all time.

Universis Christifidelibus presentes litteras inspecturis ... Fildelium animarum ... / Gratiadei; JoA. / JoA: Lxxx: Nard(inus)

1   *Cf.* F. Procter and C. Wordsworth (edd.), *Breviarium ad usum insignis ecclesiae Sarum*. Fasciculus III. *Sanctorale cum Accentuario* (Cambridge, 1886), Indices, &c, p. xxxix.
2   MS: *ac*; *recte*: 'ad'
3   MS: *quibus*; *recte*: 'quoties'

427   29 December 1515   *Reg. Lat.* 1330, fos 97ʳ-98ʳ

To Ranulph Pole, canon of[1] Hereford, validation. Some time ago, following representations on Ranulph's part to Julius II to unite etc. the parish church of St Nicholas, Sontham', d. Coventry and Lichfield, to the canonry and prebend of Wythyngton' of the church of Hereford, which he was then holding together with the said parish [church],[2] for as long as he should hold the canonry and prebend, Julius united etc. the parish [church],[3] with all rights and appurtenances, to the canonry and prebend, for as long as Ranulph should hold the latter, as is more fully contained in his letters drawn up in that regard,[4] in which it was expressed that the annual value of the said parish church did not exceed 6 pounds 13 shillings and 4 pence sterling of the money of those parts, equivalent to 30 gold ducats of the camera or thereabouts. Since however, as a recent petition to the pope on Ranulph's part stated, the prebend was not then (and is not) called <Wythyngton'>[5] but <Ewithyngton'>[6] [also spelt *Ewythyngton'*]; and it is asserted by some that the fruits etc. of the parish church even then were (and are at present) worth more, although they did not (and do not) exceed 16 pounds sterling; and, on this account, Ranulph fears that the said letters could be surreptitious and be rendered less useful to him and that he could be molested over them in time to come. Wishing to provide lest the effect of the said letters be frustrated, the pope – at Ranulph's supplication – hereby wills and grants that the letters, with all the clauses contained in them, and the said union etc. of the parish church to the canonry and prebend made by them, and whatsoever ensued therefrom shall be valid from the date of the presents and have full force and support Ranulph without limitation, just as if it had been expressed in those letters that the said prebend was called Ewithyngton' and that the fruits of the said parish church did not exceed 16 pounds sterling. Notwithstanding etc. Given at Florence.

Vite ac morum honestas …
.P. Lambertus / . JoA: / JoA: xvj: Nardinus

1   *ecclesie* does not occur.
2   MS: *et(iam)*; *recte*: 'ecclesiam'?
3   *ecclesiam* does not occur.
4   unknown to the *CPL*
5   marginal insertion; before it: *JoA*; after it: *cassat(um) et correctu(m) de man(da)to D(omi)ni Regentis Nar.* In line *Wynthyngton'* has been deleted by a horizontal stroke; initialled *JoA*; and the first 'n' has been deleted by a vertical stroke … (as note 6 below).
6   marginal insertion; before it: *JoA*; after it: *cassat(um) et correctu(m) de mandato Domini Regentis Nar.* In line *Ewynthyngton'* has been deleted by a horizontal stroke; initialled *JoA*; and the first 'n' has been deleted by a vertical stroke; perhaps the deletion of the 'n' was made when the letter was first enregistered and predates the deletion of the entire word ordered by the regent of the chancery.

428   30 January 1516   *Reg. Lat.* 1330, fos 98ʳ-99ʳ

Union etc. At a recent petition on the part of Thomas Hall', rector of the parish church of Suckeley, d. Worcester, the pope hereby unites etc. the parish church of St Michael the Archangel on the Hill, Bristol (*Bristollie*), d. Worcester (whose annual value does not exceed 4 pounds sterling), with all rights and appurtenances, to the above parish church of Suckeley, which he holds together with St Michael's by apostolic dispensation, for as long as he holds Suckeley, to the effect that he may, on his own authority, in person or by proxy, continue in, or take anew, and retain corporal possession of St Michael's and the rights and appurtenances aforesaid, for as long as he holds Suckeley, and convert its fruits etc. to his own uses and those of the said churches, without licence of the local diocesan or of anyone else. Notwithstanding etc. The pope's will is, however, that St Michael's shall not, on account of this union etc., be defrauded of due services and the cure of souls in it shall not be neglected; but that its customary burdens shall be supported; and that on Thomas's death or his resignation etc. of Suckeley this union etc. shall be dissolved and be so deemed and St Michael's shall revert to its original condition automatically. Given at Florence.

Ad futuram rei memoriam. Romanum decet pontificem et cetera.
.P. Lambertus. / JoA: / JoA: xxxv: Nardinus

429   **17 January 1516**   *Reg. Lat.* 1330, fos 104ᵛ-106ʳ

Union etc., as below, in favour of M.¹ Robert Haldesworth', MTheol, canon of the
church, called chapel royal, of B. Mary, Stafford, d. Coventry and Lichfield. A recent
petition to the pope on Robert's part stated that if the perpetual vicarage of the parish
church of Barkeley [also spelt *Barheley*], d. Worcester, were to be united etc. to the
canonry and prebend of Sandwall', of the said church of B. Mary, which he holds *inter
alia* together with the said vicarage, for as long as he holds the canonry and prebend,
it would be of advantage to him. And Robert asserts that he holds *inter alia* – by the
dispensation below – the parish church of Hampton Episcopi, d. Worcester (to which
the perpetual vicarage of the parish church of Blocley, d. Worcester, is united by
apostolic authority, for as long as he holds Hampton Episcopi)²; and that the annual
value of the vicarage of Barkeley does not exceed 20 pounds sterling. Robert is also a
DDec; and some time ago Julius II, by certain letters, dispensed him to receive any four
benefices, with cure or otherwise mutually incompatible, even if dignities, *personatus*,
administrations or offices in cathedral, even metropolitan, or collegiate churches, even
if the dignities in question should be major *post pontificalem* in cathedral, even
metropolitan, churches, or principal in collegiate churches, or even if three of them
should be parish churches or their perpetual vicarages, or chantries, free chapels,
hospitals or annual services, usually assigned to secular clerics in title of a perpetual
ecclesiastical benefice, or a combination, and even if the dignities etc. should be
customarily elective and have cure of souls, if he obtained them otherwise canonically,
and to retain three of them for life, even if two should be parish churches or their
perpetual vicarages, but if the third be a parish church [to retain it] for six months only,
and [to retain] the fourth incompatible benefice for a two-year period only, calculated
[in each case] from the day of his having peaceful possession; to resign them, at once
or successively, simply or for exchange, as often as he pleased, and in their place
receive up to four [other, similar or dissimilar]³, incompatible benefices, of which two
parish churches or their perpetual vicarages should be for life and three for six months,
and the fourth incompatible benefice be for a two-year period, calculated as above, and
retain three incompatibles for life, as above.⁴ And, thereafter, Julius II, by other letters
of his, extended and prolonged the dispensation and earlier letters aforesaid, with
clauses of exchange and all other clauses contained in them respecting this, to enable
Robert to retain the fourth incompatible benefice for life and the third benefice, if it be
a parish church, for another six-month period after the expiry of the first, as is more
fully contained in each of the aforesaid letters.⁵ At Robert's supplication, the pope
hereby unites etc. the above vicarage of Barkeley, with all rights and appurtenances, to
the said canonry and prebend, for as long as Robert holds the latter, to the effect that
Robert may, on his own authority, in person or by proxy, continue in, or take anew, and
retain corporal possession of the vicarage of Barkeley and the rights and appurtenances
aforesaid, for as long as he holds the canonry and prebend, and convert its fruits etc. to
his own uses and those of the canonry and prebend and the vicarage of Barkeley,
without licence of the local diocesan or of anyone else. Notwithstanding etc. The
pope's will is, however, that the vicarage of Barkeley shall not, on account of this union
etc., be defrauded of due services and the cure of souls in it shall not be neglected, but
that customary burdens shall be supported; and that on Robert's death or his

resignation etc. of the canonry and prebend this union etc. shall be dissolved and so deemed and the vicarage of Barkeley shall revert to its original condition automatically. Given at Florence.

Ad futuram rei memoriam. Romanum decet pontificem et cetera provideri.
.P. Lambertus. / JoA: / :JoA. xxxv: Nardinus

1   Though, curiously, there is no mention of it in the letter, Holdysworth was a papal notary (*cf. CPL*, XIX, no. 471) – hence the title *magistri*.
2   *Cf. CPL*, XIX, no. 471 where the formulation is: 'for his life'.
3   MS: *dimissi et cetera ecclesiastica quatuor.* Supplied from common form.
4   formulated thus (with rather less clarity) here
5   Julius II's prolongation and extension of his (unusually generous) dispensation to hold four incompatibles is summarised in *CPL*, XIX, at no. 471. Although the entry in Julius's register and the account of it in Leo's register have much in common; there are a few obvious differences of detail or formulation (for example, *see above*, notes 1 and 2).

430   8 March 1516   *Reg. Lat.* 1330, fos 177ᵛ-179ᵛ

Collation and provision of French secular benefice (named) to [Nicholas] Frital, who, as he asserts, holds the perpetual chaplaincy at the altar of St Thomas of Canterbury in the parish church of Argentueil (*de Agentolio*), d. Paris. Entry otherwise of no interest to the Calendar. With separate concurrent mandate to induct, etc.

Vite ac morum honestas ... The concurrent executory begins: *Hodie dilecto filio Nicolao Frital* ...
G de prato; O. de Cesis / M / M xx: xv Id(ibus) novembris a(n)no quarto [13 November 1516], *de Campania*

1   first name wanting in letter of provision; supplied from executory
2   or *Fatal* or even *Futal*

431   11 April 1514   *Reg. Lat.* 1331, fo 5ʳ⁻ᵛ

To John Mowtter, professor OFM. Dispensation – at his supplication – to receive and retain any benefice, with or without cure, usually held by secular clerics, etc. [as above, no. 43, to 'notwithstanding etc.'] and [notwithstanding] the constitutions of Otto and Ottobuono, formerly legates of the apostolic see in the kingdom of England etc.[1]

Relligionis² zelus, vite ac morum honestas ...
.P. Lambertus. / JoA: / JoA: xxxx: Nardinus

1   The inclusion of these constitutions gives Mowtter the option of holding his secular benefice in England.
2   *sic*

432   3 May 1514   *Reg. Lat.* 1331, fos 25ᵛ-26ʳ

To John Butler, canon of the monastery, called house, of Nawbrugh' [also spelt *Newbrugh'*], OSA, d. York. Dispensation and indult – at his supplication – to receive and retain any benefice, with or without cure, usually held by secular clerics, etc. [as above, no. 188].

Relligionis¹ zelus, vite ac morum honestas ...
.P. Lambertus / JoA: / JoA: L: Nardinus

1   *sic*

433   3 May 1514   *Reg. Lat.* 1331, fo 26ʳ⁻ᵛ

To Richard Marshall',¹ LLB, rector of the parish church of St Romuald (*Romwaldi*), Shaftesbury (*Shastome*),² d. Salisbury. Indult for life – at his supplication – to him, who, as he asserts, holds the above parish church and the perpetual vicarage of the parish church of Baschcurche,³ d. Coventry and Lichfield, by apostolic dispensation, not to be bound – while attending a *studium generale* or residing in the Roman curia or any one of his benefices, to reside in his other benefices, nor to be liable to be compelled to do so by anyone against his will. Notwithstanding etc. With the proviso that the above church and vicarage⁴ and other benefices in question shall not, on this account, be defrauded of due services and the cure of souls in the church and vicarage and (if any) other benefices shall not be neglected; but that [the cure] shall be exercised and things divine served by good and sufficient vicars maintained from the proceeds of the church and vicarage and other benefices; and that customary burdens of the other benefices shall be supported.

Litterarum scientia, vite ac morum honestas ...
.P. Lambertus / JoA: / : Jo A. xx:⁵ Nardinus

1   or possibly *Marshatt'*
2   evidently a corruption of 'Shaftonie'
3   the middle 'c' uncertain; possibly 'e'
4   Other entries of this type (i.e. indult for non-residence) relating to England and Wales are summarised in the present volume in an abridged form and refer to this entry as to the fully extended prototype.
     When necessary, the term(s) appropriate to the previous content of the entry should be substituted here; e.g. for nos. 422 and 424 read only 'vicarage'.
5   apparently originally *xL*; then changed (by writing the second 'x' over *L*) to *xx*; the alteration initialled *JoA*

434   16 May 1514   *Reg. Lat.* 1331, fos 27ʳ-28ᵛ

To the abbots of the monasteries of Fountains (*de Fontibus*), Meaux (*de Melsa*), and
Byland (*Bella landa*), d. York, mandate in favour of Alexander Banke, abbot of the
monastery of B Mary, Furness (*de Furnesio*), OCist, archdeaconry of Richmond
(*Richmu'die*), d. York. A recent petition to the pope on Alexander's part stated that
although he was of good life, honest conversation, and untarnished reputation and was
not bound by any sentence of suspension, excommunication, or interdict, or accused of
any crime, and was always ready to obey the lawful and honest commands and
precepts of his ordinaries and their delegates, subdelegates, and commissaries; and
although he had done nothing on account of which he ought to be cited to appear
personally or to be deprived of the aforesaid monastery to which, at another time, when
it was vacant *certo modo*, he was canonically provided, and appointed abbot, and on
the strength of the said provision and appointment he acquired possession or quasi-
possession of the rule, administration, and goods of the said monastery and has
presided over it, peacefully and laudably, for ten years and more, as he does at present;
nevertheless William – bearing himself as abbot of the monastery of B Mary, Stratford,
OCist, d. London and as visitor and reformer, appointed by apostolic authority, of the
said monastery of Furness – at the instigation or sollicitation, perhaps, of the present
earl of La Darbi, nobleman and (?)governor (*regente*) of the town of Lancaster
(*Lancastrie*), said or another d., abbot Alexander's capital enemy, firstly ordered abbot
Alexander to appear personally before him in the chapter-house (*loco capitulari*) of the
Dominican house of the said town (a place which was well known to be unsafe for
Alexander to appear in personally and in which he was not bound by law to appear),
assigning him a certain term for this which was too short; and he caused abbot
Alexander to be cited (as is said) by public edict (even though it was clear that he could
be safely approached) and Alexander was not otherwise summoned or cited, at least
lawfully; and thereafter – proceeding against abbot Alexander while he was absent
(and not through contumacy) – by his sentence William deprived Alexander (as is said)
of the aforesaid monastery and appointed John Dalton' (who bore himself as a monk
of the monastery of Furness or as a cleric) as abbot of the said monastery and intruded
him in it, albeit *de facto*. Wherefore on the part of abbot Alexander (who, as soon as
he had knowledge of these things, felt himself to be unduly aggrieved as a result of
these gravamina and several others, then expressed, with which he was threatened)
appeal was made to the apostolic see. At Alexander's supplication to the pope to order
that he be absolved from the sentence of excommunication and other sentences
censures and pains perhaps promulgated against him on the above occasion, and to
commit to some upright men in those parts the causes, with their incident, dependent,
and connected matters: of the aforesaid appeal and of anything attempted and
innovated after and against it; of the iniquity and injustice of all the foregoing; of the
nullity of the aforesaid citation, process, sentence, and appointment made by abbot
William and of everything else done in any way by him and by any other judges and
persons to abbot Alexander's prejudice in connection with the above; and of the whole
principal matter, the pope [hereby] commands that the above three (or two or one of
them), having summoned abbot William, the earl, and John Dalton' aforesaid and any
others who are concerned, shall, on the pope's authority, bestow on Alexander, for this

once only, if he so requests, the benefit of absolution *ad cautelam* from the said sentence of excommunication and the other sentences, censures, and pains, if and as it is just, having, however, first received from him suitable security in respect of that for which he is perhaps deemed to be caught by the said sentence of excommunication, etc, that if they find that the said sentence of excommunication and other ecclesiastical sentences, censures, and pains perhaps promulgated against him on the above occasion were justly inflicted on him, he will obey their mandates and those of the church; as to the other things, when abbot William, the earl, and John, and any other judges and persons who ought to be inhibited, even under the censures aforesaid and under a fine, have been inhibited by them, as is just, and after they have heard both sides, taking cognizance even of the principal matter, [shall decree][1] what is just [without appeal, causing by ecclesiastical censure what they have decreed] to be [strictly] observed, invoking the aid of the secular arm for this if necessary, [and moreover compel] witnesses, etc. Further, if, from summary information, it is clear to the above that for the purpose of citing them there is no safe access to abbot William, the earl, and John aforesaid, the pope hereby grants full and free facultry to the above of making the citations by public edicts affixed in public places where it is probable that they can come to the notice of those cited; and the pope wills and decrees that the citations made thus shall bind those cited just as if the citations had been communicated to them personally. Notwithstanding etc.

Humilibus et cetera.
.Jo. Copis. / C / C. xvj. Barotius

1   MS: *quod iustum fuerit et cetera observari.* Supplied from common form.

435   17 May[1] 1514   *Reg. Lat.* 1331, fos 30ʳ-31ʳ

To Richard Bedoo, MA, perpetual vicar of the parish church of Lewkener,[2] d. Lincoln. Dispensation and indult etc. [as above, no. 2]. Given at Magliana, d. Porto.

Litterarum scientia, vite ac morum honestas ...
.P. Lambertus / -JoA: / JoA: L:[3] Nardi(nus)

1   The date has been altered. MS: ... *sexto decimo kalendas* [*Julii* deleted, but not initialled] *Junii* ...
2   first occurrence: *Ludquenel* deleted (initialled *JoA:*) with *Lewkener* written immediately after it
3   *See above*, no. 13, note 2.

436   17 May 1514   *Reg. Lat.* 1331, fos 31ʳ-32ʳ

To Adam Travesse, perpetual vicar of the parish church of Wynkelley, d. Exeter. Dispensation etc. [as above, no. 161]. Given at Magliana, d. Porto.

Vite ac morum honestas …
.P. Lambertus / JoA: / JoA: L: Nardinus

437   9 April 1514   *Reg. Lat.* 1331, fos 34ʳ-35ʳ

To Thomas Myllyng, UIB, portionary of the church [of] <Bromiard>,[1] d. Hereford,
validation. Some time ago, in response to representations on Thomas's part, the pope
united etc. the parish church of B. Mary the Virgin, Pacchyng, d. Chichester, (whose
annual value did not exceed 11 pounds sterling), with all rights and appurtenances, to
the canonry and prebend of the church of Bromiard, which Thomas holds with the
above parish church, as is [more fully contained] in his [letters].[2] However, as a recent
petition to the pope on Thomas's part stated, at the time of the said letters Thomas was
holding (as he does) not a canonry and prebend but a portion of the above church of
Bromiard; and on this account he fears that the said letters are surreptitious and of little
use to him, and that he could be molested over them in time to come. The pope,
wishing to provide lest the effect of the said letters be frustrated, hereby wills and
grants that the letters with the union etc. and other clauses contained in them and
whatsoever ensued therefrom shall be valid and have full force from the date of the
presents and shall support Thomas without limitation, just as if it had been expressed
in those letters that he was holding not a canonry and prebend but the portion in
question; and that the said parish church had been united etc. by the pope to the said
portion and not to a canonry and prebend. Notwithstanding etc.

Litterarum scientia, vite ac morum honestas …
.P. de. Castello / JoA. / JoA: xvj: Nardinus

1   The first occurrence of Bromiard was ill-written and was deleted (initialled *JoA*) and rewritten in the margin.
2   MS: *in nostris et cetera continetur.* Supplied from common form. The letters in question are calendared at
     no. 206 above.

438   22 May 1514   *Reg. Lat.* 1331, fos 42ᵛ-44ʳ

To the bishop of Meath and the priors of the priories of St Peter by Trym and B Mary,
Morligbyter[1], d. Meath, mandate in favour of Patrick Mawyrte, layman, d. Meath. A
recent petition to the pope on Patrick's part stated that some time ago – when a law-
suit had arisen, not by apostolic delegation, between Patrick on the one side and
Matilda Walshe, woman, d. Armagh, on the other, over a marriage contract and other
matters concerning the ecclesiastical forum, before Octavian, archbishop of Armagh,
primate of all Ireland – the said archbishop, proceeding wrongly in the case,
promulgated an unjust, definitive (as was said) sentence in favour of Matilda and
against Patrick, from which Patrick appealed to the apostolic see; that in connection
with the said appeal Patrick impetrated apostolic letters under a certain form to the
prior of the monastery customarily governed by a prior of Ffowyt, d. Meath, his proper

name not expressed, and it may be (*forsan*) other colleagues of his in that regard, with
the clause 'that they or two or one of them' were to execute the letters,[2] and on the
strength of them Patrick caused Matilda to be summoned to trial, in the cause of the
appeal, before the said prior; that the prior, proceeding correctly in the case,
promulgated a definitive sentence by which he revoked the archbishop's sentence and
declared that Patrick was the lawful husband of Margaret Symon, woman, d. Armagh,
from which Matilda – falsely alleging that the sentence was unjust and that she had
appealed to the apostolic see – impetrated apostolic letters under a certain form in
connection with her appeal, as she said, to the prior of the priory of the monastery
customarily governed by a prior[3] of the Most Blessed Virgin Mary, Lowcht, d. Armagh,
his proper name not expressed, and perhaps (*forsan*) other colleagues of his in that
regard, and by pretext of them she caused Patrick to be summoned to trial in the cause
of her appeal, as she said, before the said prior of Lowcht; and that the prior of Lowcht,
proceeding similarly wrongly in the cause of the said appeal, promulgated a similarly
unjust, definitive (as he said) sentence, by which he confirmed the archbishop's
sentence, revoked the sentence of the prior of Ffowyt, and declared that no lawful
marriage subsisted between Patrick and Margaret; from which later sentence appeal
was made on Patrick's part to the apostolic see. At the supplication to the pope to
commit to some upright men in those parts, even to men below the rank of bishop, the
causes, with each and every one of their incident, dependent, emergent, annexed, and
connected matters: of the later appeal and of everything perhaps attempted and
innovated after and against it; of the nullity of the process and sentence of the prior of
Lowcht and of each and every other thing done in any way both by the archbishop and
by the prior of Lowcht to Patrick's prejudice in connection with the above; and of the
whole principal matter, the pope [hereby] commands that the above three (or two or
one of them), having summoned Matilda and the others [concerned, and having heard
both sides],[4] taking cognizance even of the principal matter, [shall decree] what is
canonical, [without appeal, causing by ecclesiastical censure what they have decreed
to be strictly] observed.[5] Notwithstanding etc.; and that the above priors are not of the
class of persons to whom similar cases are customarily committed by the apostolic see,
etc. Given at Magliana, d. Porto.

Humilibus et cetera.
.P. de Castello. / JoA: / JoA: xij: Nardinus

1   the 't' perhaps an 'r'; penultimate letter (? *n*) deleted; final letter probably an 'r'
2   MS: *cum clausula quatenus ipsi vel duo aut unus eorum ad exhecutionem procederent*
3   MS: *ad dilectum filium priorem prioratus monasterii per priorem soliti gubernari*
4   MS: *vocatis dicta Matilda et aliis et cetera.* Supplied from common form.
5   MS: *quod canonicum fuerit et cetera observari.* Supplied from common form.

439   10 April 1514[1]   *Reg. Lat.* 1331, fo 88[r-v]

To Geoffrey Barnes, canon of the monastery of St Peter, Gyppwyey, OSA, d. Norwich.
Dispensation – at his supplication – to him, who, as he asserts, is expressly professed

of the above order,[2] to receive and retain any benefice, with or without cure, usually held by secular clerics, etc. [as above, no. 43].

Relligionis[3] zelus, vite ac morum honestas …
.P. Lambertus / - JoA: / JoA: xxx: Nardinus

1   In conformity with this date, the pontifical year (at the end of the dating clause as usual) has been altered: from *primo* (deleted and initialled *JoA.*) to *secundo.*
2   This information comes from a notwithstanding clause.
3   *sic*

440   10 April 1514   *Reg. Lat.* 1331, fo 94[r]-95[r]

To William Stilington, rector of the parish church of Blowfold [also spelt *Blowfeld*], d. Norwich. Dispensation and indult – at his supplication – to receive and retain for life, together with the above parish church, two, and without them, any three other benefices etc. [as above, no. 272].

Vite ac morum honestas …
.P. Lambertus / JoA: / JoA: C: Nardinus

441   26 April 1514[1]   *Reg. Lat.* 1331, fo 95[r-v]

To Robert Smyth, monk of the monastery of St Andrew, Rochester,[2] OSB, d. Rochester. Dispensation and indult – at his supplication – to receive and retain any benefice, with or without cure, usually held by secular clerics, etc. [as above, no. 19].

Relligionis[3] zelus, vite ac morum honestas …
.P. Lambertus. / JoA: / :JoA: L:- Nardinus

1   The end part of the date – *sexto kalendas Maii anno secundo* – is graphically all of a piece with the magistral subscription.
2   written *Rochestester* with the first '-ste' deleted; the deletion not initialled
3   *sic*

442   26 April 1514   *Reg. Lat.* 1331, fo 96[r-v]

To John Galyen, rector of the parish church of Broghton', d. Lincoln. Dispensation etc. [as above, no. 161].

Vite ac morum honestas …
.P. Lambertus. / JoA: / JoA: L: Nardinus

443[1]   **1514 / potentially 1515**[2]   *Reg. Lat.* 1331, fos 100ᵛ-101ᵛ

Union etc. A recent petition to the pope on the part of George Crowmer[3] *alias* Cromer, MA, master of the college or chantry of Cobham [also spelt *Cohoham*], d. Rochester, stated that if the parish church of Guldeford[4] [also spelt *Guldeforde*] *alias* Nova Guldeford, d. Chichester, which is of lay patronage and for which George was recently presented within the lawful time when it was vacant *certo modo* – assuming he were to be instituted as rector at this presentation – and also the perpetual vicarage of the parish church of Benynden', d. Canterbury, were to be united etc. to the mastership of the college or chantry of Cobham which George holds by apostolic dispensation together with the said vicarage, it would be of advantage to him. At the supplication of George (who asserts that he is of noble birth and is chaplain to Henry VIII,[5] king of England; and that the annual value of the church of Guldeford does not exceed 14, and of the vicarage, 18, pounds sterling, after deduction of all their charges), the pope hereby unites etc. the church of Guldeford – if George is instituted at this presentation, as above – and the vicarage, with all rights and appurtenances, to the said mastership or chantry, for as long as George holds the latter, to the effect that he may, on his own authority, in person or by proxy, take and retain corporal possession of the church of Guldeford and the vicarage and the rights and appurtenances aforesaid, for as long as he holds the mastership or chantry, and convert their fruits etc. to his own uses and those of the mastership or chantry and of the church of Guldeford and the vicarage, without licence of the local diocesan or of anyone else. Notwithstanding etc. The pope's will is, however, that the church of Guldeford and the vicarage shall not, on account of this union etc., be defrauded of due services and the cure of souls in them shall not be neglected, but that their customary burdens shall be supported; and that on George's death or his resignation etc. of the mastership or [chantry][6] this union etc. shall be dissolved and be so deemed and the church of Guldeford and the vicarage shall revert to their original condition automatically.

Ad futuram rei memoriam. Romanum decet pontificem votis illis gratum prestare assensum ...
[–]⁷ / [–]⁸ / [–]⁹

1   The entry has been left unsigned and not fully dated (*cf.* notes 2, 7, 8 and 9); and is marked *alibi registrata* (hand of enregistering scribe) in left margin at start of entry. The other registration is, however, unknown to the registers covered by the present volume.
2   dating clause not complete: ... *millesimo quingentesimo quartodecimo* [ends] i.e. no month or day-date
3   the editor's preferred reading; but just possibly readable as *Gowmer*
4   The 'e' is blotched and rewritten above the line.
5   MS: *Henrici VIII*; the inclusion of numerals after the king's name is unusual.
6   *vicariam*; *recte*: 'cantariam'
7   no abbreviator's name
8   no magistral initial
9   no magistral subscription

444   22 April 1514   *Reg. Lat.* 1331, fo 102[r-v]

To John Damyan', professor OFM. Dispensation – at his supplication – to receive and
retain any benefice, with or without cure, usually held by secular clerics, etc. [as above,
no. 43, to '... and in its place receive and retain another, similar or dissimilar, benefice,
with or without cure, defined as above']. Notwithstanding etc. and [notwithstanding]
the constitutions of Otto and Ottobuono, formerly legates of the apostolic see in the
kingdom of England etc.;[1] and also [notwithstanding] any apostolic privileges, indults
and letters for the said order and its general, or minister, for the time being, granted,
renewed and confirmed by any of the preceding Roman pontiffs, or even by the pope,
in any way and of whatever tenors; and anything else to the contrary. And even if, for
the derogation of the said privileges etc. special, specific, individual and express
mention or any other expression ought to be made of them and of their whole tenors,
verbatim and not by means of general clauses importing the same, or some other
uncommon form ought to be observed, the pope – deeming the tenors of the privileges
etc. as sufficiently expressed – hereby, for this once only, specially and expressly,
derogates the said privileges etc. which shall otherwise remain in force.

Relligionis[2] *zelus, vite ac morum honestas ...*
.P. Lambertus. / JoA: / :JoA: L: Nardi(nus)

1   The inclusion of these constitutions gives Damyon the option of holding his secular benefice in England.
2   *sic*

445   11 May 1514   *Reg. Lat.* 1331, fo 106[r-v]

To John Whytley, monk of the monastery of St John the Baptist, Colchester
(*Colchestrie*), OSB, d. London. Dispensation and indult – at his supplication – to
receive and retain together for life any two benefices, with or without cure, regular, of
the order of St Benedict or of any other order, or usually held by secular clerics, even
if the regular benefices should be priories, *prepositure,*[1] *personatus*, dignities,
administrations or offices, and the secular should be parish churches or their perpetual
vicarages, or chantries, free chapels, hospitals or annual services, usually assigned to
secular clerics in title of a perpetual ecclesiastical benefice, and of lay patronage and
of whatsoever tax or annual value, even if the priories etc. should be customarily
elective and have cure of souls, if he obtains them otherwise canonically, to resign
them, at once or successively, simply or for exchange, as often as he pleases, and in
their place receive up to two other, similar or dissimilar, benefices, with or without
cure, regular, of the above order of St Benedict or of any other order, or usually held
by secular clerics, provided that the regular benefices in queston be not priories or
other conventual dignities, <or claustral offices>,[2] and retain them together for life, as
above; and to wear the usual habit worn by the monks of the above monastery, OSB,
of which he is a monk and, as he asserts, expressly professed of the above order, under
an honest garment or robe of a priest or secular cleric, of any honest colour, without

any apostasy or incurring ecclesiastical censure; and, for life, while residing in the Roman curia or any one of his benefices, or attending a *studium generale*, not to be bound to reside in his other benefices, nor to be liable to be compelled to do so by anyone against his will. Notwithstanding etc. With the proviso that the benefices in question shall not, on this account, be defrauded of due services and the cure of souls in them (if any) shall not be neglected; but that customary burdens of those benefices in which he shall not reside shall be supported.

Relligionis[3] zelus, vite ac morum honestas ...
.P. Lambertus. / JoA: / JoA: Lx: Nardinus

1   'prepositatus' does not occur.
2   *aut officia claustralia* inserted in margin (in enregistering scribe's hand) initialled *JoA:*
3   *sic*

446   19 May 1514   *Reg. Lat.* 1331, fos 127ᵛ-128ᵛ

To William Danson,[1] MA, rector of the parish church of All Saints, Magna Fordham,[2] d. London. Dispensation and indult etc. [as above, no. 2]. Given at Magliana, d. Porto.

Litterarum scientia, vite ac morum honestas ...
.P. Lambertus / JoA. / JoA: Lx: Nardinus

1   or *Dauson*
2   The first occurrence has a bar through the upper part of the 'f' (= F~).

447   19 May 1514   *Reg. Lat.* 1331, fo 129ʳ⁻ᵛ

To William Digne, layman, d. Lincoln. Dispensation – at his supplication – to him (who, as he asserts, at another time was married to a certain widow, now deceased, and had offspring by her; and who desires to become a cleric and make his profession in any of the approved orders) – after he has entered the monastery of St Saviour and Sts Mary the Virgin and Bridget, Syon, OSA,[1] d. London, and has expressly made his profession in the said order – to be marked with clerical character and be promoted to all sacred, even priest's, orders; and, after promotion, to minister in them, even as a minister before the altar; and also to perform and exercise any offices of the said order. Notwithstanding etc. Given at Magliana, d. Porto.

Apostolice sedis circumspecta benignitas ...
.P. Lambertus / JoA: / JoA. xx: Nardinus

1   *sic*; *recte*: order of St Saviour *alias* St Bridget under the rule of St Augustine (*cf. CPL* XVII, Part II, no. 91)

448   22 April 1514   *Reg. Lat.* 1331, fos 130ᵛ-132ʳ¹

To John Caluelen, MA, perpetual vicar of the parish church of [St]² Cuthbert, Wellie,³ d. Bath and Wells, dispensation. Some time ago, Julius II by his letters dispensed him to receive and retain for life any two benefices, with cure etc. [as above, no. 6, to '… retain them together for life'], as is more fully contained in those letters.⁴ The pope therefore – at his supplication – hereby dispenses John, who, as he asserts, holds, by the said dispensation, the perpetual vicarage of the above parish church of St Cuthbert, and a certain perpetual simple ecclesiastical benefice, called keepership (*custodia*) or wardenship (*guardianatus*), (which is incompatible with another incompatible benefice), in the church of St Boniface, Bunbrery, d. Coventry and Lichfield, to receive and retain for life, together with the vicarage and benefice aforesaid or with any two other [in]compatible⁵ benefices held by him at the time by virtue of the said dispensation, any third benefice etc. [as below, no. 6].

Litterarum scientia, vite ac morum honestas …
.P. Lambertus / JoA / JoA. Lxx: Nardinus

1   Excluding the first line of fo. 131ʳ which is the start of an unconnected letter, viz.: *LEO et cetera Dilecto filio Juliano Cencio rectori par*; the fragment is deleted and initialled *JoA.*
2   *Sancti* does not precede *Cuthberti* at this point; but does in the text below.
3   MS: *de Wellie*
4   *Cf. CPL*, XIX, no. 827.
5   MS: *compatibilibus*; *recte*: 'incompatibilibus'?

449   27 March 1514   *Reg. Lat.* 1331, fos 134ʳ-135ʳ

To Richard Jenyn,¹ prior of the priory of B. Mary the Virgin, Maydenebradlegh', OSA, d. Salisbury. Dispensation – at his supplication – to receive together with the above priory, or with any monastery of the above order held by him at the time, two, and without them, any three other benefices, with or without cure, regular, of the above or any other order, even the Cluniac or Cistercian, or secular, even if the regular benefices should be priories, *prepositure*, *prepositatus*, dignities, *personatus*, administrations or offices, and the [secular]² should be chantr[ies],³ free chapels, hospitals or annual services, usually assigned to secular clerics in title of a perpetual ecclesiastical benefice, and two of the secular benefices should be parish churches or their perpetual vicarages, and [even if] the secular as well as the regular benefices should be of lay patronage and of whatsoever tax or annual value, and pertain in any way to his collation, provision, presentation or any other disposition, even by reason of the said priory, and even if the priories etc. should be customarily elective and have cure of souls, if he obtains them otherwise canonically, and to retain one of the said regular benefices – even if it should be conventual or claustral – *in titulum*, and the other two regular benefices, or the secular benefices, *in commendam*, for life; and to resign them, at once or successively,⁴ as often as he pleases, and cede the commend, and in their place receive up to three other, similar or dissimilar, benefices, with or without cure, regular, of the above or any other order, even the Cluniac or Cistercian, or secular, and retain whichever one of the said regular benefices he chooses *in titulum*, and the other two regular benefices – which may not be conventual or claustral – or the secular benefices – provided that of the secular benefices not more than two be parish churches or their perpetual vicarages – *in commendam*, for life, as above; he may – due and customary burdens of the benefices retained *in commendam* having been supported – make disposition of the rest of their fruits etc., just as those holding them *in titulum* could and ought to do, alienation of immovable goods and precious movables being however forbidden. Notwithstanding etc. With the proviso that the benefices retained *in commendam* shall not, on this account, be defrauded of due services and the cure of souls in them (if any) shall not be neglected; but that their aforesaid burdens shall be supported.

Relligionis[5] zelus, vite ac morum honestas ...
P. Lambertus. / JoA. / JoA. C: Nardinus

1   the first 'n' readable as a 'u' or 'v'
2   *regularia*; *recte*: 'secularia'
3   *cantaria*; *recte*: 'cantarie'
4   'simpliciter vel ex causa permutationis' does not occur.
5   *sic*

450   21 March 1514   *Reg. Lat.* 1331, fos 135^v-136^r

To Robert Chapman, rector of the parish church of St John the Baptist, Trymynghm', d. Norwich. Dispensation and indult etc. [as above, no. 2].

Vite ac morum honestas ...
O. de. Cesis. / JoA: / JoA: Lx: Nardinus

451   21 March 1514   *Reg. Lat.* 1331, fos 136^v-137^v

To John Smyth', rector of the parish church of Chellisworth', d. Norwich. Dispensation and indult etc. [as above, no. 2].

Vite ac morum honestas ...
O. de Cesis. / JoA: / JoA: Lx: Nard(inus)

452   21 March 1514   *Reg. Lat.* 1331, fos 137ᵛ-138ᵛ

To Alexander Cutler, perpetual vicar of the parish church of St Botolph, Saxhilby,[1] d. Lincoln. Dispensation and indult etc. [as above, no. 2].

Vite ac morum honestas ...
.O. de. Cesis / JoA: / JoA: L.[2] Nardinus

1   thus the second occurrence; the first may have a bar through the upper part of the 'h'.
2   *See above*, no. 13, note 2.

453[1]   21 March 1514   *Reg. Lat.* 1331, fos 138ᵛ-139ᵛ

To William Buckynham, MTheol, perpetual vicar of the parish church of the Holy Sepulchre within the vill of Cambridge (*Cantibriggie*), d. Ely. Dispensation and indult etc. [as above, no. 2].

Litterarum scientia, vite ac morum honestas ...
.O. de. Cesis. / JoA. / JoA: Lx: Nard(inus)

1   copy in NRO, Reg. Nykke, DN. Reg/9/15, fos. 118ᵛ-120ʳ

454   7 April 1514   *Reg. Lat.* 1331, fos 167ᵛ-168ᵛ

To Richard[1] Stafford', rector of the parish church of St Andrew, Cornehall', d. Worcester. Dispensation etc. [as above, no. 161].

Vite ac morum honestas ...
.P. Lambertus. / JoA: / JoA: L: Nardi(nus)

1   *Johani'* now deleted (initialled *JoA:*) was written before *Richardo*

455   3 May 1514   *Reg. Lat.* 1331, fos 168ᵛ-170ʳ

To Thomas Rodyng, professor OFM and of theology, absolution, dispensation, rehabilitation, grant and indult etc. as below. A recent petition to the pope on Thomas's part stated that at another time – after he (even then a professor OFM) had been dispensed by apostolic authority to hold any secular benefice with cure; and had been promoted in the Roman curia to the degree of master in theology, without his superior's licence, but otherwise duly; and, by virtue of the said dispensation, had acquired the perpetual vicarage of the parish church of Wykham, d. Norwich, then vacant *certo modo* and canonically collated to him – he – perhaps believing he was allowed to – wore a priestly robe (*togam presbyteralem*) (of a decent colour however), without having a faculty to do so, for seventeen years or thereabouts, as, perhaps, he does at present, incurring apostasy and the sentence of excommunication and the other sentences, censures and pains inflicted on such persons in accordance with the canonical sanctions and the regular ordinances (*institutiones*) of the said order. At the supplication of Thomas (who asserts that he still holds the said vicarage; and that he is unable, perhaps, to prove his promotion to the degree of master in theology seeing that the letters to him drawn up in that regard were carried off by the then minister of the order or by someone appointed by him), the pope hereby absolves Thomas from apostasy and also from the sentence of excommunication and the other ecclesiastical sentences, censures and pains which he incurred in any way by occasion of the foregoing; and dispenses him on account of the said irregularity[1] if he contracted it by celebrating mass and other divine offices or by taking part in them, while bound by the censures in question; and rehabilitates Thomas on account of all disability and infamy contracted by him by the said occasion. And the pope grants and indulges Thomas to serve the said vicarage in things divine by a suitable priest, removable by him at will, and to cause the cure of souls to be exercised; and also to wear the robe in question, or the habit usually worn by friars of the said order under the said robe or the honest garment of a priest or secular cleric (of a dark, or any other decent, colour), without any apostasy or incurring ecclesiastical censure, and without the licence of anyone else; and the pope also grants and indulges Thomas to use, possess and enjoy all the privileges, grants, graces, favours, prerogatives, immunities and indults which other professors of the order who have been promoted to the said degree of master in theology by licence of their superiors and otherwise duly use, possess and enjoy in any way now and in the future, without limitation, just as if Thomas had been promoted to the said degree of master by licence of his superior and is able to prove his promotion lawful; and not to be bound to reside in the said church and to wear the habit in another way, nor to be liable to be compelled to do so by anyone against his will. Notwithstanding etc. and [notwithstanding] the statutes and customs of the said order, and the apostolic privileges and indults granted to it under any tenor which the pope – deeming their tenors to be expressed by the presents – for this once only specially and expressly derogates, the privileges etc. otherwise remaining in force. The pope's will is, however, that Thomas shall be bound to perform the penance for the foregoing enjoined on him by the confessor whom he chooses for this purpose.

Apostolice sedis circumspecta benignitas …
.P. Lambertus / JoA: / JoA: xxx. Nardinus

---

1   MS: *super dicta irregularitate*. Despite the 'dicta' this is the first express mention of 'irregularity'.
      The letter is ambivalent: it does not envisage Rodyng actually contracting irregularity unless and until he has celebrated or involved himself in the divine offices; at the same time the 'dicta' seems to concede that the irregularity arose when he became an apostate. As the holder of a vicarage he may well have celebrated frequently (the priestly robe implies he was a priest); but it is not admitted in the narrative. The dispositive just takes care of the probability.

456   13 May 1514   *Reg. Lat.* 1331, fos 187ʳ-188ᵛ

Union etc. A recent petition to the pope on the part of Thomas Michell', professor of theology, perpetual vicar of the parish church of Stauerton' [also spelt *Stauerton*], d. Exeter, stated that if the perpetual vicarage of the parish church of Alternon [also spelt *Alternon'*, *Altermon*], d. Exeter, and the perpetual vicarage of the parish church of Ipellpen' [also spelt *Ipellpen*],[1] d. Exeter – which at a time of vacancy pertains to the presentation of the warden (*custos*) for the time being and the chapter of the church of B. Mary, Otray, d. Exeter, by ancient and approved custom hitherto peacefully observed, and is vacant *certo modo* at present and has been vacant for so long that its collation has lawfully devolved on the local ordinary – assuming the vicarage of Ipellpen' were to be canonically conferred on him by the said ordinary, were to be united etc. to the vicarage of the said church of Stauerton', which Thomas holds together with the said vicarage of Alternon by apostolic dispensation, for as long as Thomas holds that of Stauerton', it would be of advantage to him. At the supplication on the part of Thomas (who asserts that the annual value of the vicarage of Alternon' does not exceed 15, and of Ipellpen', 20, pounds sterling) the pope hereby unites etc. the perpetual vicarages of Alternon' and – if conferred on him as above – of Ipellpen', with all rights and appurtenances, to the vicarage of Stauerton', for as long as Thomas holds the latter, to the effect that he may, on his own authority, in person or by proxy, take, continue in, and retain corporal possession of the vicarages of Alternon and Ipellpen' and the rights and appurtenances aforesaid, and convert their fruits etc. to his own uses and those of the said vicarages, without licence of the local diocesan or of anyone else. Notwithstanding etc. The pope's will is, however, that the vicarages of Alternon and Ipellpen' shall not, on this account, be defrauded of due services and the cure of souls in them shall not be neglected; but that their customary burdens shall be supported; and that on Thomas's death or his resignation etc. of the vicarage of Stauerton' this union etc. shall be dissolved and be so deemed and the vicarages of Alternon' and Ipellpen' shall revert to their original condition automatically.

Ad futuram rei memoriam. Romanum decet pontificem et cetera provideri.
.P. Lambertus / JoA. / JoA: xxxx: Nardinus

1   In some instances, the formation of the second 'p' closely resembles a 'y'.

457   10 April 1514   *Reg. Lat.* 1331, fos 214ᵛ-216ʳ

To Thomas Ffalke, LLB, rector of the parish church of Ffarndon',[1] d. Lincoln. Dispensation and indult etc. [as above, no. 2].

Litterarum scientia, vite ac morum honestas …
J Benzon / JoA: / : JoA: Lx: Nardinus

1   or possibly *-den'* (in both occurrences)

458   2 May 1514   *Reg. Lat.* 1331, fos 235ʳ-236ᵛ

To Dominic de Corsis, rector of the parish church of St Peter, near Calais (*prope Callesium*), d. Thérouanne. Dispensation and indult – at his supplication – to him, who, as he asserts, is in his twenty-fourth year of age or thereabouts, and holds the above parish church by apostolic dispensation, to receive and retain for life, together with the above parish church, one, and without them, any two other benefices, etc. [as above, no. 2, to '… retain them together for life, as above']; and, for life, while residing in the Roman curia or any one of his benefices or attending a *studium generale*, not to be bound to reside in his other benefices nor to be liable to be compelled to do so by anyone against his will. Notwithstanding etc.[1] The pope's will is, however, that the above church of St Peter and the other, even incompatible, benefices shall not, on this account, be defrauded of due services and the cure of souls in St Peter's and (if any) the other, even incompatible, benefices shall not be neglected; but that their customary burdens shall be supported.

Vite ac morum honestas …
P. lambertus / JoA / JoA: L:[2] Nardinus

1   As usual in letters relating to England, the notwithstanding clauses include reference to the constitutions of
     Otto and Ottobuono, legates in the kingdom of England.
2   *See above*, no. 13, note 2.

459   3 May 1514   *Reg. Lat.* 1331, fo 316ʳ⁻ᵛ

To James Blyeth', cleric, d. York. Dispensation – at his supplication – to him, who, as he asserts, is in his twenty-first year of age or thereabouts, to receive and retain any benefice, with cure or otherwise incompatible, even if a parish church or its perpetual vicarage, or a chantry, free chapel, hospital or annual service, usually assigned to secular clerics in title of a perpetual ecclesiastical benefice, or a dignity, *personatus*, administration or office in a cathedral, even metropolitan, or collegiate church, even if the dignity in question should be major *post pontificalem* in a cathedral, even metropolitan, church, or principal in a collegiate church, even if the dignity etc. should be customarily elective and have cure of souls, if he obtains it otherwise canonically, to resign it, simply or for exchange, as often as he pleases, and in its place receive and retain another, similar or dissimilar, benefice, with cure or otherwise incompatible. Notwithstanding the above defect of age, etc. With the proviso that the benefice in question shall not, on this account, be defrauded of due services and the cure of souls in it (if any) shall not be neglected.

Vite ac morum honestas …
.P. Lambertus. / JoA: / JoA. xv: Nardi(nus)

460   27 May 1514   *Reg. Lat.* 1331,fo 317^(r-v)

Relaxation as below. The pope – wishing that the parish church of St Clement Danes without the bars of New Temple, London, and the chapel of St John the Baptist situate in it (in which, as the pope has learned, an admirable confraternity under the dedication of St Clement is established and to which the members of the confraternity (*confratres*) are singularly devoted) are held in due veneration and suitably honoured by Christ's faithful and are duly repaired in their structural parts and buildings and wishing that both the chapel (*illaque*) and confraternity are conserved and maintained and that the faithful flock willingly to the church and chapel out of devotion and contribute readily to the above because they see themselves thereby abundantly refreshed there with the gift of celestial grace – assured of the mercy of Almighty God and of the authority of BB. Peter and Paul His Apostles, grants relaxation of four years and four quarantines of enjoined penance to all the faithful of both sexes who, being truly penitent and confessed, shall have devoutly visited the above church and chapel on the feasts of the Resurrection of Our Lord Jesus Christ, of St James and of St Clement and also on the feast of the Decollation of St John the Baptist and the feast of St Anne, and throughout their octaves, and also on the Wednesday of the second week of Lent, from first vespers to sunset on the feasts, octaves, and Wednesday aforesaid, inclusively, and shall have contributed to the said repair, conservation, and maintenance. The present letters shall last for all time.

Universis Christifidelibus presentes litteras inspecturis ... De salute gregis dominici ... P¹ / .P. Blund(us); JoA. / JoA. xxv: Nardinus

1   though not deleted almost certainly written in error. As a rule chancery letters were expedited by abbreviators and by convention the name of the responsible abbreviator was noted to the right at the start of an entry. Thus conditioned the registry scribe started to note the name in the right hand position. One (and the major) exception to the rule were indulgences which, though processed by the chancery, were commonly expedited by apostolic secretaries whose names, by convention, were noted to the left at the start of an entry. In this case the scribe quickly realised his mistake, noted the name in the correct position, but failed to delete his false start.

461   10 June 1514   *Reg. Lat.* 1331, fos 324^v-326^r

Mandate to commend etc. the parish church of St Geminianus, Courrono, d. Lucca – vacant at present at the apostolic see by the free resignation of Galeatius de Nellinis, recently its rector, made into the pope's hands (and admitted by him) by Silvester, bishop of Worcester, his specially appointed proctor, and previously reserved to apostolic disposition – to Geminianus Damiani de Nellinis, scholar, d. Lucca, in his fifteenth year (or thereabouts), after he has been duly marked with clerical character, and then, if he is suitable, to collate and assign it to him in his eighteenth year; with dispensation to hold it at that age. The letter, which is addressed to a single mandatary, is of no other interest to the Calendar.

Dignum et cetera.
Phi. de Agnellis / JoA: / JoA: xxxv: Nardinus

462   (?)7 June 1514[1]   *Reg. Lat.* 1331, fos 326^r-328^r

To the present bishop of Selimbria (*Solubrien.*) resident in the city or diocese of London, the abbot of the monastery of Dunkiswell', d. Exeter, and John Simyth', canon of the church of London, mandate in favour of Richard Tollett [also spelt *Tollett'*], LLD, precentor of the church of Credithon, d. Exeter. A recent petition to the pope on Richard's part stated that when, some time ago, Hugh, bishop of Exeter, had ordered that Edward Gridson' (who also bears himself as precentor of the said church and has not been ashamed to wickedly transgress and violate its constitutions and statutes and to perpetrate several excesses and crimes then expressed) be cited to appear personally before him to reply to certain articles and positions and Richard, by special commission of the said bishop, *ex officio* or otherwise, had turned to the investigation against Edward over these things, Edward – falsely claiming that he was unduly aggrieved on account of certain insufficient gravamina drawn up and inflicted on him *de facto*, as he said, in the case by Richard – appealed firstly to the apostolic see and then, for easier relief, as he said, [to][2] the court of Canterbury as the local metropolitan court, and in the cause of the said appeal he caused Richard to be summoned to judgement before Thomas Wudyngton', the then official or president of the said court; that because Thomas the official or president of the court declared that the appeal was frivolous and had been lodged for insufficient gravamina and that in accordance with the stilus and custom of the court Edward was fit to be condemned and he perhaps condemned him, Edward – falsely alleging that he was *inter alia* similarly aggrieved thereby – appealed anew to the apostolic see and in connection with his later appeal he impetrated apostolic letters under a certain form to the bishop of Norwich, the abbot of the monastery of Evesaham, Worcester,[3] and the archdeacon of Derby (*Derbie*) of the church of Lichfield, their proper names not expressed, and by pretext of the letters he caused Richard to be summoned to judgement, in the cause of the later appeal, before William Wylton', canon of the church of Salisbury, to whom the bishop of Norwich had totally committed his powers after he had begun to take cognizance of the case, and Richard Newport' and John Baker', canons of the church of Salisbury; that the said canon William warned and ordered Richard Tollett that he was to reply to several irrelevant and notoriously criminous articles and claims exhibited before him on Edward's part – to which Richard Tollett replied once, sufficiently enough (although he was not bound to do so in law), in order to overcome the malice of his adversary and fearing to be caught[4] by the sentence of excommunication and the other ecclesiastical sentences, censures, and pains promulgated against him by William in the event of a reply being refused – and warned and ordered him, under similar sentence of excommunication and other ecclesiastical sentences, censures, and pains then expressed, to reply within a certain term also then expressed, and to cause the register or acts done in this matter before Richard Tollett, or a copy,[5] to be brought before him, and, to Richard Tollett's great prejudice, he taxed at no small sum the expenses to be laid out for the hire and labours of the notary, at least as regards Edward's part, for which the notary was due to be properly paid, and he assigned a term which was not long for paying them to Edward; and that on the part of Richard Tollett, who felt *inter alia* unduly aggrieved thereby, appeal was made to the apostolic see. At the supplication to the pope to commit to some upright men in those parts the causes: of the said appeal and of anything perhaps attempted and innovated after and against it; of the nullity of the process of canon William and of each and every other thing done in any way by William and any other judges and persons to the prejudice of Richard Tollett in connection with the above; and of the whole principal matter, the pope [hereby] commands that the above three (or two or one of them), having summoned Edward and others concerned, and having heard both sides, taking cognizance even of the principal matter, [shall decree] what [is] just [without appeal, causing what they have decreed to be strictly] observed,[6] [and moreover compel] witnesses, etc. Notwithstanding etc.

Humilibus et cetera.
.P. de Castello / JoA. / . JoA. xij: Nardinus

1   MS: *Dat. Rome apud Sanctum Petrum anno et cetera millesimo quingentesimo quartodecimo secundo* [sic] *id(us) Junii anno secundo.* As the chancery adhered to the descriptive method of the Roman calendar the likelihood is that *secundo id(us)* is a mistake for 'septimo idus' (7 June) rather than a novel alternative to 'pridie idus Junii' (12 June). The previous entry is dated 1514, IV Id. Julii, a. II, the next 1514, VII Id. Junii, a. II.
2   MS: *ac*; *recte*: 'ad'
3   'diocesis' does not occur.
4   MS: *illa q(ue) reari* for 'illaqueari'
5   MS: *et registrum seu acta … coram se trasportari seu reproduci …*
6   MS: *quod iustum et cetera observari.* Supplied from common form.

463   22 May 1514   *Reg. Lat.* 1331, fos 337ᵛ-339ᵛ

Collation and provision to Bartholomew de Soncinellis,[1] who, as he asserts, is a continual commensal familiar of Sixtus, cardinal priest of the title of St Peter ad Vincula, vicechancellor of the Holy Roman Church, of a perpetual chaplaincy in the church of St Andrew, Mantua, vacant at the apostolic see and previously reserved to the pope's disposition. With separate concurrent mandate to induct, etc. Given at Magliana, d. Porto.
The 'bishop of Worcester' is one of the three mandataries. Entry otherwise of no interest to the Calendar.

Vite ac morum honestas … The executory begins: *Hodie dilecto filio Bartholomeo de Goncinellis …*
Ge. de Prato.; O. de. Cesis. / JoA. / JoA: xij: x: Duodecimo K(a)l(endas) Julij Anno Secundo: [20 June 1514], *Nardinus*

1   spelt *Goncinellis* in the executory

464   17 June 1514   *Reg. Lat.* 1331, fos 339ᵛ-340ᵛ

To Thomas Schaw, MA, rector, called master, of the hospital of the Holy Trinity in
Ffosgate, York. Dispensation and indult – at his supplication – to receive and retain for
life, together with the above hospital, which is incompatible with another incompatible
benefice, one, and without them, any two other benefices etc. [as above, no. 2].

Litterarum scientia, vite ac morum honestas ...
.P. Lambertus. / JoA: / JoA: Lx: Nardinus

465   17 June 1514   *Reg. Lat.* 1331, fos 352ʳ-353ʳ

To Henry Cundall', BDec, perpetual vicar of the parish church of Berton', d. Ely.
Dispensation and indult etc. [as above, no. 2].

Litterarum scientia, vite ac morum honestas ...
.P. Lambertus / JoA. / JoA. Lx: Nardinus

466   17 June 1514   *Reg. Lat.* 1331, fos 353ʳ-354ʳ

To Edward Bowdon', MA, rector of the parish church of St Mildred, Canterbury
(*Cantuarien.*). Dispensation and indult etc. [as above, no. 2].

Litterarum scientia, vite ac morum honestas ...
.P. Lambertus / JoA: / JoA. L:¹ Nardinus

1   *See above*, no. 13, note 2.

467   17 June 1514   *Reg. Lat.* 1331, fos 354ʳ-355ʳ

To William Henne, rector of the parish church of Dreycot' Delemoers¹ [also spelt
Dreycot Delemoer], d. Coventry and Lichfield. Dispensation and indult etc. [as above,
no. 2].

Vite ac morum honestas ...
.P. Lambertus / JoA: / JoA Lx: Nardinus

1   final letter readable as an 's' or a 'b'

468   17 June 1514   *Reg. Lat.* 1331, fos 355^r-356^v

To Simon Chridlegh',[1] cleric, d. Exeter. Dispensation and indult – at his supplication – to him, who, as he asserts, is under eighteen, to receive and retain – as soon as he reaches his eighteenth year of age – one benefice, and – when he reaches his twentieth – another with it, or without them, any two other benefices, with cure or otherwise mutually incompatible, even if parish churches or their perpetual vicarages, or chantries, free chapels, hospitals or annual services, usually assigned to secular clerics in title of a perpetual ecclesiastical benefice, or dignities, *personatus*, administrations or offices in cathedral, even metropolitan, or collegiate churches, even if the dignities in question should be major *post pontificalem* in cathedral, even metropolitan, churches, or principal in collegiate churches, or a combination, even if the dignities etc. should be customarily elective and have cure of souls, if he obtains them otherwise canonically, to resign them, at once or successively, simply or for exchange, as often as he pleases, and in their place receive and retain for life other, similar or dissimilar, benefices, viz.: – as soon as he reaches his eighteenth year – one, and – when he reaches his twentieth – another with it, or without them, two mutually incompatible benefices; and not to be bound, by reason of any benefices with cure or requiring sacred orders by statute or foundation or otherwise held by him at the time, to be promoted to any of the said orders until the said age[2]; and, for life, while attending a *studium generale* or residing in the Roman curia or any of his benefices, to reside in his other benefices, and not to be liable to be compelled to do so by anyone against his will. Notwithstanding the above defect of age which he will suffer even in his eighteenth and twentieth year, etc. With the proviso that the incompatible and other benefices in question shall not, on this account, be defrauded of due services and the cure of souls in them ([if] any) shall not be neglected; but that customary burdens of those benefices in which he shall not reside shall be supported.

Vite ac morum honestas ...
.P. Lambertus. / JoA / JoA Lxxx: Nard(inus)

1   or possibly *Chrudlegh'* (but with a dot above the 'u')
2   MS: *usque ad etatem huiusmodi* – as it stands obscure; with reference, presumably, to 'ad etatem legitimam' (or 'etate tibi suffragante legitima') which does not occur but ordinarily finds place in dispensations for minors to hold benefices requiring sacred orders.

469   23 March 1514[1]   *Reg. Lat.* 1331, fos 356^v-357^v

Union etc. At a recent petition on the part of Edward Stephynson, canon of the church, called college, of Bashani,[2] d. Chichester, the pope hereby unites etc. the parish church of Musgrabe,[3] d. Carlisle (whose annual value does not exceed 13 [?pounds][4] 6 shillings and 8 pence sterling), with all rights and appurtenances, to the canonry and prebend of Apul Idram[5] of the said church of Bashani, which Edward holds together with the above parish church, for as long as he holds the canonry and prebend, to the effect that he may, on his own authority, in person or by proxy, continue in, or take

anew, and retain corporal possession of the parish church and the rights and
appurtenances aforesaid, for as long as he holds the canonry and prebend, and convert
its fruits etc. to his own uses and those of the canonry and prebend and parish church
aforesaid, without licence of the local diocesan or of anyone else. Notwithstanding etc.
The pope's will is, however, that the above parish church shall not, on account of this
union etc., be defrauded of due services and the cure of souls in it shall not be
neglected; and that on Edward's death or his resignation etc. of the canonry and
prebend this union etc. shall be dissolved and be so deemed and the parish church shall
revert to its original condition automatically.

Ad futuram rei memoriam. Romanum decet pontificem et cetera.
.P. Lambertus / JoA: / JoA: xxxv: Nard(inus):

1   The year-date has been altered: by deletion in line before *decimo* of *quarto* (initialled *JoA*); and insertion in
     margin of *tertio* (initialled *JoA:*).
2   The name occurs twice in MS and in both cases the third minim is dotted; presumably *-ham*
3   the 'b' only readable as a 'v' very sympathetically
4   MS: *tredecim sex solidorum* ...; i.e. 'librarum' (or 'marcharum') does not occur.
5   or *Apulidram*: spread over two lines; but no hyphen at end of *Apul*

470   13 June 1514[1]   *Reg. Lat.* 1331, fos 358[r]-359[r]

To Roger Sondeforth', DDec, rector of the parish church of [St][2] Clement without the
bars of New Temple, London, dispensation. Some time ago, Alexander VI by his letters
dispensed him to receive and retain for life any two benefices, etc. [as above, no. 6, to
'... retain them together for life'], as is more fully contained in those letters.[3] The pope
– at his supplication – hereby dispenses Roger, who, as he asserts, holds, by the said
dispensation, the above parish church of St Clement and the parish church of
Morcherde Episcopi [also spelt *Merchede Episcopi*], d. Exeter, to receive and retain for
life, together with the said parish churches, or any two other incompatible benefices,
held by him at the time by virtue of the said dispensation, any third benefice, etc. [as
above, no. 6].

Litterarum scientia, vite ac morum honestas ...
.P. Lambertus. / JoA: / JoA: Lxx: Nardinus

1   *idibus Junii anno secundo* is written in a different hand with a larger nib and on a larger scale than the
     preceding part of the dating clause (and the body of the letter). Entered later?
2   *Sancti* wanting here; but does occur below.
3   *See CPL*, XVII, Part 1, no. 565.

471   17 June 1514   *Reg. Lat.* 1331, fos 359ʳ-360ʳ

To George Ffa'coner, canon of the monastery of B. Mary the Virgin and St John the
<Baptist>,[1] Lavenden', OPrem, d. Lincoln. Dispensation and indult – at his
supplication – to receive and retain any benefice, with or without cure, usually held by
secular clerics, etc. [as above, no. 211, to '… and to have, for life, a stall in the choir
and a place and an active and passive voice in the chapter'] and a room in the convent
(*in conventu*)[2] of the monastery, and otherwise as before, without limitation, just as if
he had not acquired the benefice. Notwithstanding etc. and [notwithstanding] the
statutes, customs and privileges granted, renewed and confirmed by any indults and
apostolic letters to the said order and its general or to the abbot for the time being of
the monastery of Welbeke,[3] said order, d. York, of which Lavenden' is perhaps a
dependency, by any of the preceding Roman pontiffs, or even by the pope, in any way
and of whatever tenors; and [notwithstanding] anything else to the contrary. And even
if, for the derogation of the said privileges etc. special, specific, individual and express
mention or any other expression ought to be made of them and of their whole tenors,
verbatim and not by means of general clauses importing the same, or some other
uncommon form ought to be observed, the pope – deeming the tenors of the privileges
etc. as sufficiently expressed – hereby, for this once only, specially and expressly,
derogates the said privileges etc. which shall otherwise remain in force.

Relligionis[4] *zelus, vite ac morum honestas …*
.P. Lambertus. / JoA. / JoA. Lx: Nardinus

1   Dedication corrected by order of the regent of the chancery: *Evangeliste* in line deleted and initialled *JoA.*;
    with *Baptiste* inserted in margin; before the insertion: *JoA.*; after it: *cassat(um) et aditu(m) de man(da)to D.*
    Rege(n)tis Nardinus. The same deletion and insertion occurs in the narrative below, with *JoA.* before the
    insertion and *cassat(um) ut supra Nard(inus)* after it.
2   i.e. 'conventus' is used of conventual building: in a chancery letter this usage is unexpected. Ordinarily, 'in
    dormitorio' (or other part of building) is specified.
3   *Velbech* deleted but not initialled
4   *sic*

472   3 July 1515   *Reg. Lat.* 1332, fos 9ᵛ-10ᵛ

To John Powne, rector of the parish church of Chymleght, d. Exeter. Dispensation and
indult etc. [as above, no. 2].

Vite ac morum honestas …
.P. Lambertus. / JoA: / JoA: Lx: Nardinus

473   12 May 1515   *Reg. Lat.* 1332, fos 37[v]-39[v]

To Robert Wykes, rector of the parish church of B. Mary the Virgin, Chelmesford, d. London, dispensation and indult. Some time ago, Alexander VI by his letters dispensed him to receive and retain together for life any two benefices, etc. [as above, no. 6, to '... retain them together for life'], as is more fully contained in those letters.[1] The pope hereby dispenses Robert, who, as he asserts, holds the above parish church of B. Mary the Virgin, Chelmesford (to which the parish church of St Michael, Smerden', d. Canterbury, is united by apostolic authority,[2] for as long as he holds B. Mary's) and the parish church of St Martin,[3] Wybaldown,[4] d. Canterbury, by the said dispensation – at his supplication – to receive and retain for life, together with B. Mary's and St Martin's, or any two other incompatible benefices held by him at the time by virtue of the said dispensation, the deanery of the church of Southmallyng [also spelt *Southmallyng'*, *Sonthmallyng'*[5]], d. Canterbury,[6] which is perhaps a principal dignity, or any other third benefice, with cure or otherwise incompatible, even if a dignity, *personatus*, administration or office in a cathedral, even metropolitan, or collegiate church, even if the dignity in question should be major *post pontificalem* in a cathedral, even metropolitan, church, or principal in a collegiate church, or a parish church or its perpetual vicarage, or a chantry, free chapel, hospital or annual service, usually assigned to secular clerics in title of a perpetual ecclesiastical benefice, and of lay patronage and of whatsoever [tax][7] or annual value, even if the deanery or dignity etc. should be customarily elective and have cure of souls, if he obtains it otherwise canonically, to resign it, simply or for exchange, as often as he pleases, and in its place receive and retain together for life another, similar or dissimilar, incompatible benefice – provided that of three such incompatible benefices not more than two be parish churches or their perpetual vicarages; and, while residing in the Roman curia or any one of his benefices or attending a *studium generale*, not to be bound to reside in the said church of Southmallyng or in his other benefices; nor to be liable to be compelled by anyone to do so against his will. Notwithstanding etc. and [notwithstanding] the statutes and customs of the church of Southmallyng, even if it is expressly stipulated therein that its dean for the time being cannot – without lawful impediment – absent himself from the church for more than forty days at the most, the which statutes etc. the pope hereby specially and expressly derogates for this once only, and [notwithstanding] the statutes etc. of other churches in which perhaps another third incompatible and the said other benefices may be. And the pope relaxes the oath to reside at the third incompatible and other benefices taken at the time by Robert on their acquisition. With the proviso that the deanery (or other third incompatible benefice) and the other benefices in which he shall not reside shall not, on this account, be defrauded of due services and the cure of souls in them (if any) shall not be neglected; but that their customary burdens shall be supported. Given at Magliana, d. Porto.[8]

Vite ac morum honestas ...
.P Lambertus[9] / JoA. / JoA: C: Nard(inus): –

1   unknown to the *CPL*; presumably enregistered in one of Alexander's registers now lost; and not comprehended by the Index volumes
2   *CPL*, XIX, nos. 951 and 1457

3   MS: *Sancti Martini*: safe reading
4   follows *Wb* (deleted but not initialled)
5   This spelling occurs first; but only the once.
6   a Canterbury peculiar situated in d. Chichester
7   'taxe' wanting
8   follows *Rome* | *apud* (the start of: 'Rome apud Sanctum Petrum') deleted; initialled *JoA.* and *JoA*
9   in a large "printed" script

474   26 July 1515   *Reg. Lat.* 1332, fos 39ᵛ-40ᵛ

To James Etton, rector of the parish church of Longbredy,[1] d. Salisbury. Dispensation and indult etc. [as above, no. 2].

Vite ac morum honestas ...
.P. Lambertus / *JoA:* / *JoA: Lx: Nardinus*

1   The second occurrence altered; viz.: *Long* [(?)*m* deleted] *bredy*

475   23 August 1515   *Reg. Lat.* 1332, fos 67ᵛ-69ʳ

To the bishop of London, the prior of the priory of B Mary, Walfynghm', d. Norwich, and the prior of the church of Norwich, mandate in favour of Denise Bolte, woman, d. Norwich. A recent petition to the pope on Denise's part stated that after Henry More, cleric or layman, said or other d., had seized Denise and carried her off to a certain place then expressed and after Denise, driven by force and fear which could overcome a steadfast woman, had contracted marriage with the said Henry and had, perhaps, solemnized it in the face of the church, and after she had run away from him as soon as she conveniently could, Henry – falsely claiming that Denise was his lawful wife and that he was robbed by her of possession of his conjugal services (*obsequiorum conjugalium*) –sued Denise before Cuthbert Tu'stall', auditor of causes and matters appointed by William, archbishop of Canterbury, primate of all England and legate born of the apostolic see, a competent judge for this (as Henry said), praying *inter alia* that she be compelled to cohabit with Henry and bestow conjugal services on him and that he be restored to possession of them; and that Cuthbert the judge, proceeding wrongly in the case, promulgated a null or unjust, definitive (as he said) sentence by which *inter alia* he pronounced that Denise should be restored to Henry and coerced and compelled to cohabit with him and stick to him as her husband and spouse; from which appeal was made on Denise's part to the apostolic see but prevented, as she asserts, by lawful impediment she has not, perhaps, prosecuted her appeal within the due time. At Denise's supplication to the pope [to order][1], notwithstanding the lapse of time, that Denise be absolved *ad cautelam* from the sentence of excommunication and other ecclesiastical sentences, censures, and pains perhaps promulgated against her on the above occasion and that the said Cuthbert and any other judges and persons be inhibited as appropriate and to commit to some upright men in those parts, even to men

below the rank of bishop, to be heard, examined, decided and duly determined, with
their annexed, connected, and dependent matters, the causes: of the aforesaid appeal
and anything attempted and innovated after and against it; of the nullity and nullities
of the said process and sentence and of each and every other thing done in any way by
Cuthbert and any other judges and persons to Denise's prejudice in connection with the
above; and of the whole principal matter, the pope [hereby] commands that the above
three (or two or one of them), having summoned Henry and others concerned, shall, on
the pope's authority, for this once only, bestow on Denise, if she so requests, the benefit
of absolution *ad cautelam* from the said sentence of excommunication and any other
ecclesiastical sentences, censures, and pains, if and as it is just[2], having, however, first
received from her suitable security in respect of that for which she is perhaps deemed
excommunicate and caught by the said sentences, censures, and pains, that if it appears
to them that the sentence of excommunication etc were justly[3] inflicted on her she will
obey their mandates and those of the church; as to the other things, if what is put
forward about the said impediment is true, having inhibited Cuthbert and any other
judges and persons who ought to be inhibited, under ecclesiastical censures and pains,
as required by law, and having heard both sides, taking cognizance even of the
principal matter, decree what is canonical, without appeal, causing [by ecclesiastical
censure what they have decreed to be strictly] observed[4]. Notwithstanding the said
lapse of time etc., and that the above priors are not of the class of persons to whom
similar cases are customarily committed by the apostolic see, etc.

Humilibus et cetera.
.Jo. Copis. / JoA: / JoA: xvj: Nard(inus): –

1   MS wants 'mandare'.
2   MS *iuxtum* for 'iustum'
3   MS *iuxte* for 'iuste'
4   MS *facientes et cetera observari.* Supplied from common form.

476   17 May 1515   *Reg. Lat.* 1332, fos 91ᵛ-94ʳ

To the abbot of the monastery of[1] Dwsq(ue) *alias* St Saviour, d. Ossory, the prior of the
monastery, usually governed by a prior, of St John the Evangelist at Ynisscorthy, d.
Ferns, and Gerard Macduyll', canon of the church of Leighlin, mandate in favour of
Thady Omnuzyhy[2] [also spelt *Omnusyhy*], cleric, d. Leighlin. The pope has learned
that the rectory of the parish church of Carygwaspayn and the parish churches called
vicarages[3] of Ballyn' and of Rahemur, d. Leighlin, are vacant *certo modo* at present
[and have been vacant] for so long [that by the Lateran statutes their collation has
lawfully devolved on the apostolic see],[4] although Thady Ocuzryhyn and Thady
Ocuzryhyn[5] and Odo Oedian, who bear themselves as priests, have detained the rectory
and the churches called vicarages[6] respectively, with no title or support of law, of their
own temerity and *de facto*, for a certain time, and do so. On the part of Thady
Omnuzyhy – who asserts that some time ago, he was dispensed by apostolic authority,
notwithstanding a defect of birth as the son of a cleric and an unmarried woman related

in the fourth degree of consanguinity, to be promoted to all, even sacred and priest's, orders; and to hold, first, one benefice, even if it should have cure of souls, and then, if he cannot conveniently support himself from its fruits, another benefice, compatible with it; and that afterwards he was duly marked with clerical character; and that the annual value of the said rectory and the churches called vicarages[7] and of annexes to them together does not exceed 15 marks sterling – supplication was made to the pope to unite etc. the churches called vicarages of Ballyn' [and of Rahemur][8] to the said rectory, for as long as he, Thady Omnuzyhy, holds the rectory, if conferred on him as above. The pope, therefore, hereby commands that the above three (or two or one of them), if, having summoned Thady Ocuzryhyn and Thady Ocuzryhyn[9] and Odo Oedian and others concerned, they find the rectory and the churches called vicarages to be vacant (howsoever etc.), shall collate and assign the rectory to Thady Omnuzyhy; and unite etc. the churches called vicarages, even if generally reserved etc., to the rectory, for as long as Thady Omnuzyhy holds the latter, if conferred on him as above, with the annexes in question [and] with all rights and appurtenances, inducting him etc. having removed Thady Ocuzryhyn and Thady Ocuzryhyn and Odo Oedian and any other unlawful detainers and causing Thady Omnuzyhy to be admitted to the rectory and its fruits etc., rights and obventions and those of the united churches and annexes aforesaid to be delivered to him. [Curbing] gainsayers etc. Notwithstanding etc. and [notwithstanding] that there may be an indult from the apostolic see to the abbot and convent of the monastery of St Thomas the Martyr, OVict, d. Dublin [to whom][10], as it is asserted, the presentation of a suitable person for the church of Rahemur at a time of vacancy belongs by ancient, approved and hitherto peacefully observed custom, that they are not bound to the reception or provision of anyone and cannot be compelled to it, etc. The pope's will is, however, that the said churches called vicarages shall not, on account of this union etc., be defrauded of due services and the cure of souls in them shall not be neglected, but that customary burdens shall be supported; and that on the death of Thady Omnuzyhy or his resignation etc. of the rectory this union etc. shall be dissolved and be so deemed and the said churches called vicarages shall revert to their original condition automatically.

Vite ac morum honestas ...
.P. Lambertus. | JoA: | :JoA: xxxv: Decimo non(o) k(a)l(endas) Julij Anno tertio: [? 14 June 1515],[11] *Nardinus*

1   MS: *abbati DWsq(ue) ... monasteriorum*; i.e. 'de' does not occur – unless merged with place name. The size of 'W' in MS need not signify that it starts the name.
2   Just before this spelling, *Omw* is deleted and initialled *JoA:* Note also that the letter transcribed in this and other names here and below as a 'z' resembles yogh.
3   MS: *parrochiales ecclesie vicarie nuncupate. Cf.* below, notes 6 and 7.
4   MS: *et tanto et cetera devoluta*
5   *sic*; unless it is a mistake, the first and second detainers have the same name (*cf.* below, note 9).
6   MS: *ecclesias vicarias nuncupatas predictas. Cf.* above, note 3 and below, note 7.
7   MS: *vicariarum nuncupatarum ecclesiarum predictarum. Cf.* above, notes 3 and 6.
8   *... ecclesias vicarias de Ballyn' nuncupatas predictas eidem rectorie ...* i.e. Ballyn' is the only name at this point. Judging by the previous text, the name wanting here is Rahemur.
9   *sic; cf.* above, note 5.
10   There is a contemporary cross above the 'p' of *presentatio* and another in the margin opposite. The crosses probably signal error; but no corrective action has been taken. 'ad quos' supplied by the editor.
11   'xix Kal. Jul. ' is unknown to the Roman calendar; perhaps an error for 'xviii Kal. Jul. '

477   25 May 1515   *Reg. Lat.* 1332, fos 94ᵛ-96ᵛ

To the prior of the monastery, usually governed by a prior, of St John the Evangelist at Ynisscorthy, d. Ferns, and Cornelius Olachuayn, canon of the church of Cashel, and William Sutton, canon of the church of Ferns, mandate in favour of John Laules *alias* Lelas, cleric, d. Ferns. The pope has learned that the rectory of the parish church of B. Mary, Vyterriros, and the perpetual vicarage of the parish church of Clomor, d. Ferns, are vacant *certo modo* at present and have been vacant for so long [that by the Lateran statutes their collation has lawfully] devolved [on the apostolic see][1] although Maurice Macinurchu, who bears himself as a priest, has detained the vicarage, with no title and no support of law, of his own temerity and *de facto*, for a certain time, as he still does; and that if the vicarage and rectory were collated to John and united for as long as he held them it would be of advantage to him. At John's supplication the pope hereby commands that the above three (or two or one of them), having summoned Maurice and others concerned and those interested in the union, shall unite etc. the vicarage and rectory (whose annual value together does not exceed 15 marks sterling), (vacant howsoever etc.; even if specially reserved etc.), and collate and assign them thus united, with all rights and appurtenances, to John, inducting him etc. having removed Maurice and any other unlawful detainers from them, and causing John (or his proctor) to be admitted to the vicarage and its fruits etc., rights and obventions and those of the rectory to be delivered to him. [Curbing] gainsayers etc. Notwithstanding etc. The pope's will is, however, that the vicarage and rectory shall not, on account of this union etc., be defrauded of due services and the cure of souls in them shall not be neglected; but that their customary burdens shall be supported; and that on John's death or his resignation etc. of the vicarage and rectory this union etc. shall be dissolved and so deemed and the vicarage and rectory shall revert to their original condition automatically.

Vite ac morum honestas ...
phi. de Agnellis. / *JoA:* / *JoA: xxx: octavo id(us) Junij: Anno tertio:* [6 June 1515], *Nardinus*

1   MS: *tanto tempore vacaverint et cetera devoluta.* Supplied from common form.

478   26 July 1515   *Reg. Lat.* 1332, fos 101ʳ-102ᵛ

Union etc. A recent petition to the pope on the part of Philip Agard, DDec, canon of the church of Lichfield, d. Coventry and Lichfield, stated that if the parish church of Sandhirst [also spelt *Sandirst*], d. Canterbury, of which provision was recently made to Philip by ordinary authority when it was vacant *certo modo*, but which he has not had possession of, were to be united etc. to the canonry and prebend of Pipa Parua, church of Lichfield, which Philip holds, for as long as he does so, it would be of advantage to him. At the supplication on the part of Philip (who asserts that he holds the parish churches of Asheton' super Trent [also spelt *Asheton*] and Rolston [also spelt *Rolston'*],

d. Lichfield and Coventry, by apostolic dispensation; and that the annual value of Sandhirst does not exceed 8 pounds sterling) the pope hereby unites etc. Sandhirst, with all rights and appurtenances, to the said canonry and prebend, for as long as Philip holds the latter, to the effect that Philip may, on his own authority, in person or by proxy, take and retain corporal possession of Sandhirst and the rights and appurtenances aforesaid, for as long as he holds the canonry and prebend, and convert its fruits etc. to his own uses and those of the canonry and prebend and also the church of Sandhirst, without licence of the local diocesan or of anyone else. Notwithstanding etc. The pope's will is, however, that the church of Sandhirst shall not, on account of this union etc., be defrauded of due services and the cure of souls in it shall not be neglected; but that its customary burdens shall be supported; and that on Philip's death or his resignation etc. of the canonry and prebend this union etc. shall be dissolved and be so deemed and the church of Sandhirst shall revert to its original condition automatically.

Ad futuram rei memoriam. Romanum decet pontificem votis illis gratum prestare assensum ...
.P. Lambertus. / JoA: / JoA: xxxv: Nardinus

479   29 July 1515   *Reg. Lat.* 1332, fos 110ʳ-111ᵛ

To Thomas Byrde, prior of the monastery, usually governed by a prior, of St Nicholas, Barlyche [also spelt *Barliche*], OSA, d. Bath and Wells. Dispensation – at his supplication – to receive together with the priory of the above monastery, one, and without them, any two other regular benefices, with or without cure, of the above order or of the order of St Benedict or of any other order, or with one of the regular benefices, or without them, one secular benefice, with or without cure, even if the regular benefices should be priories, *prepositure*, *prepositatus*, dignities, *personatus*, administrations or offices, and the secular benefice should be a parish church or its perpetual vicarage, or a chantry, free chapel, hospital or annual service, usually assigned to secular clerics in title of a perpetual ecclesiastical benefice, and even if the priories etc. should be customarily elective and have cure of souls, if he obtains them otherwise canonically, and to retain whichever one of the regular benefices he chooses (even if it should be a priory or other conventual dignity or a claustral office) *in titulum*, and the other regular benefice or the secular benefice *in commendam*, for life; [to resign]¹ them, at once or successively, simply or for exchange, as often as he pleases, and cede the commend, and in their place receive up to two other, similar or dissimilar, regular benefices, of the above order of St Augustine or of St Benedict or of any other order, or with one of them, or without them, one secular benefice, with or without cure; and to retain whichever one of the regular benefices he chooses *in titulum* and the other regular benefice (which may not be a conventual dignity or a claustral office) or the secular benefice *in commendam*, for life, as above; he may – due and customary burdens of the benefice retained *in commendam* having been supported – make disposition of the rest of its fruits etc. just as those holding it *in titulum* could and ought to do, alienation [of immovable goods and precious movables being] however [forbidden].[2] Notwithstanding etc. With the proviso that the benefice retained *in commendam* shall not, on this account, be defrauded of due services and the cure of souls in it (if any) shall not be neglected; but that its aforesaid burdens shall be supported.

Relligionis[3] zelus, vite ac morum honestas ...
.P. Lambertus. / JoA: / JoA: L: Nardinus

1   'dimittere' wanting
2   MS: *alienatione tamen et cetera.* Supplied from common form.
3   *sic*

480   21 August 1515   *Reg. Lat.* 1332, fos 125[v]-126[r]

To William Sloo, monk of the monastery, called house, of St Saviour, Bermondesey in So'thwerk [also spelt *Southwerk*], OSB,[1] d. Winchester. Indult – at his supplication – to wear the usual habit worn by the monks of the above monastery, OSB,[1] (of which he is a monk and is, as he asserts, expressly professed of the order), under an honest robe or other garment of a priest or secular cleric, of any honest colour, without any apostasy or incurring ecclesiastical censure; and not to be bound to wear the habit openly[2] nor to be liable to be compelled to do so by anyone against his will. Notwithstanding etc.

Relligionis[3] zelus, vite ac morum honestas ...
.P. Lambertus. / JoA: / JoA: xx: Nardinus

1   *sic*; *recte*: OClun
2   reading, very tentatively, *m(an)i(fest)e*; in other contexts we would unhesitatingly read *minime.*
3   *sic*

481   21 July 1515   *Reg. Lat.* 1332, fos 138[r]-139[r]

To Nicholas Carre, UIB, rector of the parish church of Sterston' [also spelt *Sterston*], d. Norwich. Dispensation and indult etc. [as above, no. 2].

Litterarum scientia, vite ac morum honestas ...
.P. Lambertus / JoA: / JoA: Lx: Nardinus

482   26 July 1515   *Reg. Lat.* 1332, fos 139ᵛ-140ᵛ

To Alexander Archer, BDec, rector of the parish church of Wenden' Lowtis, d. London. Dispensation and indult etc. [as above, no. 2].

Litterarum scientia, vite ac morum honestas …
.P. Lambertus¹ / JoA: / JoA: Lx: Nardinus

1   the 'er' read sympathetically

483   26 July 1515   *Reg. Lat.* 1332, fos 140ᵛ-142ʳ

To John Lewys, LLB, rector of the parish church of Llandeylo, d. St David's. Dispensation and indult etc. [as above, no. 2].

Litterarum scientia, vite ac morum honestas …
.P. Lambertus / JoA: / JoA: Lx: Nardinus

484   26 August 1515   *Reg. Lat.* 1332, fos 155ʳ-156ʳ

To Thomas Slade, rector of the parish church of Oniburi,¹ d. Hereford. Dispensation and indult etc. [as above, no. 2].

Vite ac morum honestas …
.P. Lambertus / JoA: / JoA: Lx: Nardinus

1   sympathetic reading: the third minim is not dotted in MS.

485   17 August 1515   *Reg. Lat.* 1332, fos 156ᵛ-157ᵛ

Union etc. At a recent petition on the part of Edward Higgyns, DDec, rector of the parish church of Lanteglos, d. Exeter, the pope hereby unites etc. the parish church of Chesilchurst [also spelt *Chesilhurst, Chesilierst, Chesilchierst, Chesilchist,*¹ *Chesihierst, Cheislichierst*], d. Rochester,² (whose annual value does not exceed 13 pounds sterling), with all rights and appurtenances, to the above church of Lanteglos, (to which the perpetual vicarage of the parish church of Stepulashton, d. Salisbury, is united by apostolic authority, for as long as Edward holds Lanteglos), which he holds together with Chesilchurst by apostolic dispensation, for as long as he holds Lanteglos, to the effect that Edward may, on his own authority, in person or by proxy, take, or continue in, and retain corporal possession of the church of Chesilchurst and the rights and appurtenances aforesaid, for as long as he holds Lanteglos, and convert its fruits etc. to his own uses and those of the said churches of Lanteglos and Chesilchurst, without licence of the local diocesan or of anyone else. Notwithstanding etc. The pope's will is, however, that the church of Chesilchurst shall not, on account of this union etc., be defrauded of due services and the cure of souls in it shall not be neglected, but that its customary burdens shall be supported; and that on Edward's death or his resignation etc. of the church of Lanteglos this union etc. shall be dissolved and be so deemed and Chesilchurst shall revert to its original condition automatically.

Ad futuram rei memoriam. Romanum decet pontificem votis illis gratum prestare assensum ...
.P. Lambertus / JoA: / JoA: xxxv: Nardinus

1   the ending *-ist* very uncertain: compacted: written at the end of a line
2   reading *Roffen.* sympathetically (in preference to 'Kuffen. ')

486   23 June 1515   *Reg. Lat.* 1332, fos 170^v-172^r

Union etc. At a recent petition on the part of Thomas Martyn', rector of the parish church of Ffonleston [also spelt *Ffo'leston'*,[1] *Ffonleston'*, *Ffonston'*[2]], d. Salisbury, the pope hereby unites etc. the parish church of Wylly [also spelt *Willi*, *Wylli*], d. Salisbury, (whose annual value does not exceed 12 pounds sterling), with all rights and appurtenances, to the above church of Ffonleston, (to which the parish church of St John the Baptist, Berewyk, d. Salisbury, is united by apostolic authority, for as long as Thomas holds Ffonleston), which he holds together with Wylly by apostolic dispensation, for as long as he holds Ffonleston, to the effect that Thomas may, on his own authority, in person or by proxy, take and retain corporal possession of the church of Wylly and the rights and appurtenances aforesaid, for as long as he holds Ffonleston, and convert its fruits etc. to his own uses and those of the said churches without licence of the local diocesan or of anyone else. Notwithstanding etc. The pope's will is, however, that the church of Wylly shall not, on account of this union etc., be defrauded of due services and the cure of souls in it shall not be neglected, but that its customary burdens shall be supported; and that on Thomas's death or his resignation etc. of the church of Ffonleston this union etc. shall be dissolved and be so deemed and Wylly shall revert to its original condition automatically.

Ad futuram rei memoriam. Romanum decet pontificem votis illis gratum prestare assensum ...
.P. Lambertus. / JoA: / JoA: xxxv: Nardinus

1   This spelling occurs first in MS.
2   *sic*; written at the end of a line

487   1 September 1515   *Reg. Lat.* 1332, fo 176^{r-v}

To Richard Fferyby, rector of the parish church of Stradford, d. Norwich. Dispensation etc. [as above, no. 161].

Vite ac morum honestas ...
.P. Lambertus. / JoA: / JoA: L: Nard(inus):-

488   3 July 1515   *Reg. Lat.* 1332, fos 197^r-198^r

To Thomas Parker, BA, perpetual vicar of the parish church of Hertbury [also spelt *Hartbury*], d. Worcester. Dispensation and indult etc. [as above, no. 2].

Vite ac morum honestas ...
.P. Lambertus. / JoA: / J. oA:[1] Lx: Nard(inus):-

1   *sic*; (usually *JoA:*)

489   3 July 1515   *Reg. Lat.* 1332, fos 207^r-208^r

To Charles Fsarrer',[1] cantor of the chantry of St Nicholas in the church of York, d. York. Dispensation and indult – at his supplication – to receive and retain for life, together with the above chantry, which is incompatible with another incompatible benefice, one, and without them, any two other benefices, etc. [as above, no. 2[2]].

Vite ac morum honestas ...
.P. Lambertus / JoA: / JoA: Lx: Nardinus

1   the 's' long – its formation closely resembling an 'f' wanting its horizontal bar; but the initial is unambiguously a capital F. The capital F of English script usually occurs as 'ff' (i.e. two minuscule 'f's) in the registers.
2   i.e. dispensation *ad duo* with indult for non-residence

490   24 April 1515   *Reg. Lat.* 1332, fos 262^r-263^r

To John Calwodley, scholar, d. Exeter. Dispensation to him, who, as he asserts, is in his sixteenth year of age,[1] suffers a defect of birth as the son of a married man and an unmarried woman, and desires to become a cleric – at his supplication – to be marked with clerical character; and to receive and retain henceforth – after he is duly marked with the said character – any benefice without cure, or[2] – as soon as he reaches his seventeenth year – any benefice with cure or otherwise incompatible, even if the benefice with cure or incompatible should be a parish church or its perpetual vicarage, or a chantry, free chapel, hospital or annual service, usually assigned to secular clerics in title of a perpetual ecclesiastical benefice, or a dignity, *personatus*, administration or office in a cathedral, even metropolitan, or collegiate church, even if the dignity etc. should be customarily elective and have cure of souls, if he obtains it otherwise canonically, to resign it, simply or for exchange, as often as he pleases, and in its place receive and retain another, similar or dissimilar, benefice, viz.: henceforth – after he is marked with the said character as above – one without cure, or[2] – when he reaches his seventeenth year – one with cure or otherwise incompatible – provided that it be not a major dignity *post pontificalem* in a cathedral, even metropolitan, church, or a principal dignity in a collegiate church. Notwithstanding the above defects of birth and (for holding an incompatible benefice in his seventeenth year) of age, etc. With the proviso that the benefice with cure or otherwise incompatible shall not, on this account, be defrauded of due services and the cure of souls in it (if any) shall not be neglected.

Vite ac morum honestas …
.P. Lambertus. / JoA: / JoA: xx: Nardinus

1   'vel circa' ('or thereabouts') does not occur.
2   MS: *aut*; though 'et' or 'ac' (or suchlike) might be expected.

491   13 September 1515   *Reg. Lat.* 1333, fos 120ᵛ-122ᵛ

To the abbot of the monastery of St Thomas the Martyr and the prior of the priory of All Saints by the city of Dublin, and the chancellor of the church of Dublin, mandate in favour of William Fowille', prior of the house, called hospital, of St John *cruciferorum*, OSA, outside the new gate of the city of Dublin. A recent petition to the pope on William's part stated that although, at another time, when the priorship of the said house was vacant *certo modo*, the members of the convent, meeting, as is the custom, as one body to elect the house's future prior – on the day which had been previously fixed for the election and after everyone who had wanted or rather ought properly to be present at the election had been summoned – had harmoniously elected William as their and the house's prior and William, [prior-]elect – agreeing to the election-decree when it was presented to him – had had it confirmed by him[1] to whom, by law or ancient, approved, and so far peacefully observed custom, confirmation of the election belonged, and, having acquired the priorship on the strength of the said election and confirmation, had held and possessed it for some time, as he was then holding and possessing it, John Theodorici, who bears himself as a cleric – falsely alleging that by law the priorship belonged to him and that William was detaining it unlawfully occupied – nevertheless caused William to be summoned to trial over this before Walter Wellysley who was, John asserted, the judge appointed for this by certain apostolic letters [addressed], as John said, to Walter and some other colleagues of his in this regard impetrated over this under a certain form by John; that after he had assigned William a too short term for setting forth all the peremptory or dilatory (*dilatorias*) objections which were to be set forth before him in the cause by William and after William had set forth before Walter the grounds of his suspicion and refusal and other lawful objections, declinatory (*declinatorias*) or against his jurisdiction and against the said letters which were surreptitious and obreptitious, and after William had prayed with due instance that (?)they[2] be remitted to Walter's colleagues or to another competent judge who would take cognizance of them, Walter unlawfully refused to do it and proceeded *de facto* to further matters in the cause; and that appeal was therefore made to the apostolic see on the part of William, who felt *inter alia* unduly aggrieved thereby, but prevented, as he asserts, by lawful impediment he has not perhaps prosecuted the appeal within the due time. At William's supplication to the pope, to commit to some upright men in those parts, notwithstanding the said lapse of time, the causes: of the aforesaid appeal and of anything perhaps attempted and innovated after and against it; of the nullity of the refusal and whole process of the said Walter; of the surreption and obreption of the said letters; of each and every other thing done in any way by Walter and any other judges and persons to William's prejudice in connection with the above; and of the whole principal matter, the pope [hereby] commands that the above three (or two or one of them), if what is set forth about the said impediment is true, having summoned John and others concerned and having heard both sides, taking cognizance even of the principal matter, shall decree what is just, without appeal, causing by ecclesiastical censure what they have decreed to be strictly observed [and moreover compel] witnesses, etc. Notwithstanding etc.

Humilibus et cetera.
Phi. de Agnell(is) / JoA: / :JoA: xij: Nard(inus): –

1   tentatively reading *per eum*; MS is affected by ink bleed.
2   reading (?)*eas*; that is the letters if not also William's objections

492[1]   **23 September 1515**   *Reg. Lat.* 1333, fos 123ʳ-124ᵛ

To the abbot of the monastery of St Thomas the Martyr and the prior of the priory of All Saints by the city of Dublin, and the chancellor of the church of Dublin, mandate in favour of William Fowille', prior of the house, called hospital, of St John *cruciferorum*, OSA, outside the new gate of the city of Dublin. A recent petition to the pope on William's part stated that, at another time, John Theodorici, bearing himself as collector of the fruits and revenues due to the apostolic camera in the parts of Ireland, caused William to be cited *de facto* to appear before him to do or adduce (*allegandum*) something then expressed or see to the same (to which William was not in law bound),[2] and – recklessly regardless of a certain appeal from John then lodged by William of which John was not ignorant and while William was still well within the time for prosecuting it – erroneously and *de facto* excommunicated William, suspended and interdicted him *a divinis* and sequestrated the fruits, revenues, and proceeds of the said priory; that appeal was therefore made to the apostolic see on the part of William (who, in the cause of the priory,[2] felt *inter alia* unduly aggrieved thereby); but prevented, as he alleges, by lawful impediment, he has not, perhaps, prosecuted the said appeal within the due time. At William's supplication to the pope to order that he be absolved *ad cautelam* from the sentence of excommunication, suspension, and interdict and other ecclesiastical sentences, censures, and pains perhaps promulgated (?)against him in any way by John or any other judges and persons on the above occasion; and also, notwithstanding the lapse of time, to commit to some upright men in those parts the causes: of the aforesaid appeals and of anything perhaps attempted and innovated after and against them[3]; of the nullity of the said citation, excommunication, suspension, and interdict, and of John's whole process and of each and every other thing done in any way by him and any other judges and persons to the prejudice of William and the priory[4] in connection with the above; and of the whole principal matter, the pope [hereby] commands that the above three (or two or one of them), if what is set forth about the said impediment is true, having summoned John and others concerned, shall, on the pope's authority, bestow on William, for this once only, if he so requests, the benefit of absolution *ad cautelam* from the said sentence of excommunication, suspension, and interdict and other ecclesiastical sentences, censures, and pains, if and as it is just, having, however, first received from him suitable security in respect of that for which he is held excommunicate, suspended, and interdicted, and perhaps caught by the other censures, that if it appears to them that the said sentence of excommunication, etc were justly inflicted on him, he will obey their mandates and those of the church; as to the other things, having heard both sides, taking cognizance even of the principal matter, decree what is just, without appeal, causing by ecclesiastical censure what they have decreed to be strictly observed, [and moreover compel] witnesses, etc. Notwithstanding etc.

Humilibus et cetera.
Phi. de Agnell(is) / JoA: / : JoA: xiiij: Nardinus

1   The leaves are badly affected by ink bleed, the entry not readily legible, and the calendar accordingly
     tentative.
2   MS: *sentientis … indebite se ad dictum prioratum gravari*; an unusual qualification in this clause; its
     presence perhaps explicable in terms of the parallel action (*see* previous entry); *cf.* below, note 4.
3   reading *appellationum predictarum ac post et contra illas*
4   *sic*: in *Willelmi et prioratus huiusmodi preiudicium*; the inclusion of the benefice or institution here is an
     unusual qualification; *cf.* above, note 2.

493   23 July 1515   *Reg. Lat.* 1333, fos 151ʳ-152ᵛ

To John Musshe, perpetual vicar of the parish church of Burn',[1] d. York. Dispensation and indult etc. [as above, no. 2].

Vite ac morum honestas …
A. de S. severino / JoA: / JoA: Lx: Nardinus

1   uncertain; possibly *Buni'*

494   23 May 1515   *Reg. Lat.* 1334, fos 26^r-33^v

Some time ago letters of the following tenor were issued by Lucius III[1]:

[*Great or solemn privilege. At the request of prior Matthew and the
brethren, Lucius III takes the church of Bradenstoke under his protection
and that of B Peter; confirms its liberation from the church of Cirencester,
its possessions (enumerated) and its exemption from tithe; ratifies its
immunities; and regulates various other matters including reception of
brethren, celebration at time of interdict, burial in the church, arrangements
for serving its parish churches, etc. Granted at Veroli, 13 May 1184*]

Lutius episcopus servus servorum dei dilectis filiis Matheo priori de
B r a d e n e s t o t eiusque fratribus tam presentibus quam futuris
regularem vitam professis in perpetuum.

Religiosam vitam eligentibus apostolicam[2] debet presidium impartiri[3] ne
forte cuiuslibet temeritatis incursus aut eos a proposito revocet aut robur
quod absit sacre religionis infringat.

Ea propter dilecti in domino filii vestris iustis postulationibus clementer
annuamus[4] et prefatam ecclesiam de B r a d e n e s t o t in qua divino estis
obsequio mancipati sub beati Petri et nostra protectione suscipimus et
presentis scripti privilegio communimus.

In primis siquidem statuentes vobis libertatem et emancipationem a
iurisdictione Cirencestren. ecclesie de qua ordinem vestrum sumpsistis ut
ordo canonicus qui secundum deum et beati Augustini regulam in ecclesia
vestra institutus est[5] perpetuis ibidem temporibus inviolabiliter observetur.

Preterea quascunque possessiones quecumque bona eadem ecclesia in
presentiarum iuste et canonice possidet aut in futurum concessione
pontificum largitione regum vel principum oblatione fidelium seu aliis
iustis modis prestante domino poterit adipisci firma vobis vestrisque
successoribus et illibata permaneant.

In quibus hec propriis duximus exprimenda vocabulis: ex dono [fo 26^v]
Gualteri de S a r e s b u r i a totam villam de B r a d e ' n e s t o t et
quicquid ad illam pertinet cum ecclesia eiusdem ville et unam hidam terre
in E c h e l i n g e n t u n ' et quicquid ad eam pertinet capellam de
L a c h a cum omnibus pertinentiis suis; ex dono comitis Patricii totam
villam de V i l e c h o t a et quidquid[6] ad eam pertinet ecclesiam eiusdem
ville cum omnibus pertinentiis suis et salinam quandam in C h a n e s o t o
que est apud W u a l d e[7] F l e t a y n cum omnibus pertinentiis suis; ex
dono comitis Guillelmi de S a r e s b u r i a ecclesiam de C h a n e f o r o
cum omnibus pertinentiis suis capellam Sancti Andree de C e t r a ; ex dono
Winhelmi de L i t l e c o t a terram illam de D a n e que adiacet vicinius et
competentius terre de B r a d e n e s t o t; ex donatione Guillelmi
M a l c o v e n a t' unam virgatam terre; ex dono Richardi de C o t a l[8] unam
virgatam terre in villa de L a c h a apud H e s t o n a m ecclesiam eiusdem
ville cum omnibus pertinentiis suis; ex dono Guillelmi de H e s t o n a

quinquaginta achas[9] de inlanda sua cum cessione[10] Osberti filii sui cum tribus mansuris et unam virgatam terre in eadem villa quam canonici de B r a d e'n e s t o t   rationabiliter   concordaru(n)t[11]   a   Reginaldo   de S a n c t o   P a u l o; ex donatione Rogerii filii Gualfridi unam hidam terre apud C o t s t o a n' et quicquid ad eam pertinet; ex dono Stephani de L a n g e f o r e t dimidiam hidam //// ///[12] terre apud C e t r a m cum omnibus pertinentiis suis et unam virgatam terre in villa de L a n g e f o r o et quicquid ad eam pertinet et W i l t o n tres solidatus terre; ex dono Nigelli de M o r d o n a unam virgatam terre in eadem villa.

Sane novalium vestrorum que propriis manibus vel sumptibus colitis sive de nutrimentis animalium vestrorum nullus a vobis decimas exigere vel extorquere presumat.

Liceat quoque vobis clericos vel laicos ex secula[13] fugientes liberos et absolutos ad conversionem recipere et eos absque contraditione aliqua retinere.

Prohibemus insuper ut nulli fratrum vestrorum post factam in eodem [fo 27ʳ] loco professionem phas sit de eodem loco absque licentia sui prioris nisi arctioris religionis obtentu discedere; discedentem vero sine communium litterarum cautione nullus audeat retinere.

Cum autem generale interdictum terre fuerit liceat vobis clausis ianuis non pulsatis campanis exclusis excommunicatis et interdictis subpressa voce divina offitia celebrare.

Sepulturam preterea ipsius ecclesie liberam esse decernimus ut eorum devotioni et extreme voluntati qui se illic sepeliri deliberaverint nisi forte excommunicati vel interdicti sint nullus //(///)//[14] obsistat salva tamen iustitia illarum ecclesiarum a quibus mortuorum corpora assumuntur.

In parrochialibus autem ecclesiis quas habetis liceat vobis quatuor vel tres aut duos de canonicis vestris ponere et unum diocesano episcopo presentare cui sit[15] idoneus fuerit episcopus curam animarum committat ut ei ex[16] spiritualibus vobis de temporalibus debeat respondere.

Libertates etiam et immunitates ecclesie vestre pia devotione concessas et rationabiles consuetudines hattenus observatas ratas habemus et eas perpetuis temporibus illibatas permanere sancimus[17].

Preterea novas et indebitas exactiones ab archiepiscopis episcopis archidiaconis seu decanis aliisve personis ecclesiasticis vobis et ecclesiis vestris omnino fieri prohibemus.

Ad hec presenti decreto santimus ut nemini censerit[18] sine iuditio et manifesta ac rationabili causa ecclesias vestras interdicto supponere vel in personas vestras excommunicationis sententiam promulgare.

Presenti quoque pagina duximus statuend(um) ut possessiones et alia in morte sive in vita ecclesie vestre pia devotione iuxta collata a fidelibus Christi recipiendi vobis ac retinendi libera sit facultas.

Apostolica insuper auctoritate sancemus ut omnes ecclesie vestre canonici in loco [fo. 27ᵛ] ipso priori suo professionem fatiens[19] proprio non utantur et toto vite sue tempore sub regularis vite districtione permaneant nec alicui phas sit ponere in ecclesia vestra canonicos nisi prioris et conventus prebeatur assensus.

Obeunte vero te nunc eiusdem loci priore vel tuorum quolibet successorum nullus ibi qualibet surrection(is)[20] astutia seu violentia preponatur nisi quem fratres communi consensu vel fratrum pars consilii sanioris secundum dei timorem et beati Augustini regulam providerint eligend(um).

Ad hoc[21] quoniam ecclesia C i r e n c e s t r i e a qua ordinem suscepistis per interventum nobilis viri Guillelmi comitis S a r e s b r i g i e post institutionem ecclesiam vestram liberam reddidit et quietam nos absolutionem ipsam que a iam dicta ecclesia C i r e n c e s t r e n s i facta esse dignoscitur auctoritate apostolica confirmamus.

Decernimus ergo ut nulli omnino hominum liceat prefatam ecclesiam temere p(er)turbare aut eius possessiones conferre[22] vel ablatas retinere minuere seu quibuslibet vexationibus fatigare sed omnia integra conserventur eorum pro quorum gubernatione ac sustentatione concessa sunt usibus omnimodis profutura salva sedis apostolice auctoritate et diocesani episcopi canonica iustitia.

Si qua igitur in futurum ecclesiastica secularisve persona hanc nostre constitutionis paginam sciens contra eam temere venire tentaverit secundo tertiove commonita nisi reatum suum congrua satisfactione correxerit p[otes]tatis honorisque sui careat dignitate reamque se divino iuditio existere de perpetrata iniquitate cognoscat et a sacratissimo corpore ac sanguine dei et domini redentoris nostri Jesu Christi aliena fiat atque in extremo examinatione divine[23] ultioni subiaceat.

Cunctis autem eidem loco [fo 28ʳ] sua iura servantibus sit pax domini nostri Jesu Christi quatenus et hic fructum bone actionis percipiant et apud districtum iudicem premia eterne pacis inveniat[24]. Amen.[25]

Dat. V e r u l i s per manum Alberti Sancte Romane Ecclesie presbyteri Cardinalis et cancellarii tertio idus Maii indictione secunda incarnationis dominice anno millesimo centesimo octuagesimo quarto pontificatus vero d(omi)ni Lutii pape tertii anno tertio.

Thereafter, when it had been explained to Julius II on the part of M. Thomas Vallesche, prior of the monastery customarily governed by a prior of B Mary, Brade'nestot [also spelt *Bradenestot, Bra.*, and *Dra.* or *Gra.*],[26] said order, d. Salisbury, and a notary of the pope (then of Julius), that by virtue of a grant on apostolic authority the prior of the monastery for the time being could use the mitre, staff, and other pontifical insignia and that the monastery was distinguished and honoured with many privileges, Julius – at Thomas's supplication – granted to him and his successors, the priors of the monastery for the time being, faculty of absolving, in person or by his vicar or vicars appointed from time to time for the purpose, any parishioners of the monastery and of its annexes, chapels, and dependencies (*membrorum*), and of the other [places] united, appropriated, or subject to the monastery or its priorship, even ones not subject by full authority, from all their sins, excesses, and delicts, however serious (provided they were not reserved to the apostolic see), having enjoined on the parishioners and each one of them a salutary penance, etc; and on the said authority, by special grace, he granted indult to Thomas and the priors of the monastery for the time being, and to the canons or brothers, that he and they and each one of them could, except for the said exemption,[27] use, have and enjoy each and every privilege, indult, indulgence, and apostolic letter which by law or custom the members of the congregation of the Lateran, said order, and the monasteries of S Maria della Pace, Rome (*Sancte / Beate Marie de Pace de Urbe*) and S Maria in Porto, Ravenna (*Sancte / Beate Marie in Porticu Ravenaten.*) and the other monasteries and places of the said congregation and order and their abbots, priors, provosts and the rectors, diffinitors, and visitors of the said congregation, and other superiors and persons, were using, having, and enjoying, and would be able to use, have, and enjoy in any way in the future, as is more fully stated in Julius's letters drawn up in this regard.[28] However, as a recent petition to the pope on Thomas's part stated, although the use and carrying of the pastoral staff and other pontifical insignia have been granted to the said prior for the time being, as above, nevertheless the grant of the use of the mitre is not specially and expressly clear and on this account Thomas fears that Julius's letters could be surreptitious and of no use to him in time to come; that it is doubted by some persons whether those who visit the church of the monastery of Brade'nestot from time to time obtain the same indulgences as those who from time to time visit the churches of S Maria della Pace and S Maria in Porto and the churches of the other monasteries of the Lateran congregation; and that there are also several purely lay brothers and sisters (*fratres et sorores mere laici*) who, in accordance with immemorial custom observed in all the religious houses (even mendicant ones) throughout the kingdom of England, are made partakers of the prayers and suffrages which are performed in the monastery of Brade'nestot while living in their own dwelling-houses (*propriis domibus*) and [without] having made the profession[29], and they are reputed (*reportantur*) and called brothers and sisters of the convent or chapter of the monastery of Brade'nestot by everyone. At the supplication to the pope of Thomas (who asserts that the abbots and priors of the monasteries of the kingdom of England to whom use of the mitre and the other pontifical insignia has been granted by apostolic privilege use the said pontifical insignia not only in their monasteries and in places directly or indirectly subject to them but also in the general or provincial chapters of their orders and at the obsequies of noblemen and that they bestow benediction on the people) to add the strength of his approval to Julius's letters and extend and enlarge the privileges and indults granted by Julius to the priors and canons of the monastery of Brade'nestot for the time being, as above, to the lay-brothers (*conversos*), familiars, officials, and tenants, and also to the so-called brothers and sisters of the convent or chapter of the monastery who are purely lay, the pope wills and grants to Thomas and to the prior of the monastery of Brade'nestot for the time being that Julius's letters and each and every clause contained in them and his faculty, grant, and indult, and whatsoever has ensued therefrom are valid from the date of the presents and possess full force and shall, without limitation, support Thomas and the prior for the time being and the convent, canons, and brothers of the monastery, just as if there had been an express grant in Julius's letters to the prior of the monastery for the time being that he could use the mitre. Further, the pope hereby grants to Thomas and the prior of the monastery for the time being that they may: use the mitre, even one embellished and ornamented with gold foil (*laminis aureis*) and gems, and the other pontifical insignia, like the other abbots and priors of the monasteries of the said kingdom, in places directly or indirectly subject to them, in addition to (*preter*) the places granted to them by apostolic authority at another time, and in the general and provincial chapters of their order and at the obsequies of noblemen, as often as requisite, and, after mass and the solemnities of the other divine offices, freely bestow solemn benediction on the people then and there present, provided no legate of the apostolic see or his [sc. the prior's] metropolitan or diocesan is present, or, if present, after he has expressly assented to it; also, as often as the prior for the time being confers solemn benediction on the people by apostolic authority, to relax one hundred days and ten quarantines of penance enjoined on them and each one of them; to duly mark with clerical character and to promote to the four minor orders at the legally established times both canons of the monastery of Brade'nestot as also other persons (*alios*) from (*ex*) the parishes subject to the monastery of Brade'nestot (even ones not subject by full authority) and also any others who, with letters-dimissory of their own bishops, have approached the prior of the monastery of Brade'nestot for the time being with a view to (*gratia*) taking clerical character and minor orders, and to confer the said orders on them; and if, at any time, the priest-canons of the monastery of Brade'nestot are not adequate for celebrating mass in the monastery, or if for some other good reason it seems expedient to the prior for the time being, to cause to be promoted to the priesthood, without other obstacle (*oppositione*) or examination, by any catholic bishop of the prior's choice in communion with the apostolic see, those who among the canons of the monastery in subdeacon's and deacon's orders have reached their twenty-second year of age;to reconcile cemeteries, churches, and chapels subject to the prior (*sibi*), as above, which have been polluted by effusion of blood or semen, the water having, however, first been blessed by any bishop in communion with the apostolic see; to bless bells, chalices, images, vestments, and other ecclesiastical ornaments in churches and places subject to the prior (*sibi*); also prior Thomas may: correct and reform the canonical hours and other divine offices customarily celebrated there; appoint feasts for the praise of God which have not hitherto been celebrated there and cause them to be observed and celebrated; and, with the consent of a majority of the members of the convent of the monastery of Brade'nestot, change its ancient offices and ordain and appoint new ones; on condition, however, that, if they are made, the corrections or reforms of the divine offices and the changes of the ancient ones and ordaining of new ones and the appointment of feasts, shall not deviate from the sacred canons, otherwise they shall not be binding and ought not to be observed by anyone; and also make, publish, and draw up, in accordance with the regular institutes of the order, any other statutes and ordinances, which, however, are to be otherwise just and honest and not repugnant to the sacred canons; and everything which has been corrected, reformed, appointed, changed, ordained, made, published, and drawn up by Thomas, as above, must forever be inviolably observed by every one of his successors, the priors of the monastery of Brade'nestot for the time being, and shall tie and bind them as if everything corrected etc had been confirmed and approved by the apostolic see; and the pope grants indult: to the prior for the time being and convent that they may use, have, and enjoy, the privileges, graces, grants, favours, indulgences, and indults, which, by law, custom, or otherwise, the abbot for the time being and convent of Cirencester (*Ciri.*), said order, d. Worcester, (of which, though it [sc. Cirencester] was (?)secular from its foundation, the priory of

Brade'nestot, was formerly a dependency, having been separated and exempted from it by apostolic authority)[30] use, have, and enjoy in any way and will be able to use, have, and enjoy in any way in the future; and to the said bishop to confer the order of the priesthood on the said canons in subdeacon's and deacon's orders; and the pope decrees: that no one is allowed to build or cause to be built any oratory or church (*basilicam*) within the bounds and limits of the parishes of the parish churches which are subject to the monastery of Brade'nestot (even ones which are not subject by full authority) without the consent and licence of the prior and local diocesan for the time being; that no one is allowed to keep or hide canons or lay-brothers of the said monastery who run away from the precincts of the monastery without the licence of the prior for the time being; that both the runaways as also those keeping or hiding them or those giving or [bestowing][31] counsel, help, or favour on them to run away from the said monastery or not return, shall automatically incur sentence of excommunication from which they cannot be absolved unless they obey the orders of the prior for the time being or are on the point of death; that the prior for the time being can, by ecclesiastical censures and other suitable legal remedies (having, if necessary, called in the aid of the secular [arm][32] for this), compel the objectors and those hiding, detaining, and defending the fugitives and those giving them help, counsel, or favour, to give them up and release them and to desist from the above; that the prior for the time being and convent cannot under any pretext, even on apostolic authority, be coerced into receiving someone as a canon or religious in the monastery of Brade'nestot without the consent of the prior and a majority of the convent of the monastery, and that those received and admitted otherwise are not deemed to be canons and religious of the monastery , and if – after they have been accordingly warned by the prior for the time being to depart from the monastery – they stubbornly object, neglect or delay to obey, they shall, when a period of three days has elapsed[33], automatically incur sentence of excommunication from which they cannot be absolved except by authority of the apostolic see; and that when the three days period has elapsed, the prior for the time being may excommunicate them, even publicly, declare them excommunicated, and denounce them publicly as excommunicates, to be duly deemed and treated as such and strictly avoided by everyone. Also, the pope hereby enlarges and extends all the privileges, indults, indulgences, and letters granted and conceded (*indulta*) by Julius to the [then][34] priors, canons, and brethren aforesaid [and][34] to the priors, etc for the time being, as above, [to][35] the lay brothers (*conversos*), servants (*servitores*), officials, and tenants, of the monastery of Brade'nestot, and also to all the brothers [and] sisters, called brothers [and] sisters of the convent or chapter of the monastery of Brade'nestot, now and for the time being, although the brothers and sisters have been purely lay (*mere laici*) and have lived and dwelt (as they do) in their own houses, now and from time to time, without having taken the profession, but have simply (*duntaxat*), after a ceremony[36] in the said chapter, been made partakers of the prayers and suffrages which are [performed][37] in the monastery of Brade'nestot from time to time.[38] Further, the pope hereby decrees and declares that everyone visiting the church of the monastery of Brade'nestot from time to time may freely and lawfully use, have and enjoy all the indulgences (but not the plenary ones) which those visiting the monasteries of S Maria della Pace, Rome and S Maria in Porto, Ravenna and the other monasteries and places of the Lateran congregation and their churches use, have and enjoy and will be able to use, have and enjoy in any way in the future; and that the prior, canons, brothers and sisters of the chapter of the monastery of Brade'nestot for the time being – and only they – may also freely and lawfully use, have and enjoy all the plenary indulgences which those visiting the monasteries of S Maria della Pace etc use, have and enjoy etc. And the pope hereby establishes and ordains that henceforth, for all time, everyone of Christ's faithful of either sex who visits the church of the monastery of Brade'nestot on the feasts of the Nativity, Annunciation, Visitation, and Assumption of B Mary the Virgin and on the Tuesday after Easter or on some or any one of the said feasts or the Tuesday and there devoutly says and recites the Lord's Prayer five times and as many Angelic Salutations for the salvation of the souls of the late Christopher, cardinal priest of the title of S Prassede, the cardinal of York, of Thomas, bishop of Winchester, and Edmund, bishop of Salisbury, and also of prior Thomas and the founders and benefactors and brothers and sisters of the monastery of Brade'nestot, and also even of the parents of all the afore-named benefactors, [39] shall obtain thirty years and as many quarantines of enjoined penance, for each feast and Tuesday on which they have visited and prayed; and that all the faithful who also continually (*perpetuo*) visit the said chapel of The Holy Trinity and B Mary the Virgin built and maintained within the church of the monastery of Brade'nestot and pray there, as above, or who cause masses and prayers to be said and celebrated there by others, and also if masses and prayers are said there for any who have departed this life and died in a state of grace or in whom there were apparent signs of repentance, then both those visiting the chapel as also those for whom the prayers are performed, alive or dead, shall enjoy, have and benefit from, and can and ought to benefit from, have and enjoy, all the said graces, indulgences, pardons, and even remissions of sins which those who visit the church of S Prassede, Rome or, as they please (*quamvis*), also the chapel or church of S Anastasio or the chapel of B Mary the Virgin called *Scala Coeli* at Tre Fontane (*apud Tres Fontes*) from time to time and pray in them or any one of them, or those for whom there will be celebration or prayer in them or any one of them, use, have, benefit from, and enjoy, or will be able to use, have, benefit from, and enjoy in any way in the future; and the said deceased shall share in them all by way of intercession (*per viam suffragii*). Finally, the pope hereby approves and confirms the letters of Julius and all other privileges and grants concerning (*de*) any possessions and goods granted, made, decreed, and conceded to the monastery of Brade'nestot and its prior for the time being and convent and to the canons and brothers for the time being, by any other popes and by kings, dukes, and princes and other faithful. Notwithstanding, etc. And because it would be difficult to carry the present letters and the other letters granted to the monastery of Brade'nestot and its prior, convent, canons, and brothers to every place in which it would be expedient, it is the pope's will and he also decrees that in court and outside court, wherever, absolutely the same trustworthiness shall attach to transumpts of the presents as also of any other letters and apostolic privileges [and] indults granted to them, now and from time to time, which have been subscribed by the hand of a public notary and strengthened by the seal of an ecclesiastical dignitary, as would attach to the original letters if they were exhibited or shown; and it is also the pope's will that if, at another time, some other indulgence, which is to last for ever or for a certain time which has not yet run out, has been granted by the pope to those visiting the church of the monastery of Brade'nestot and praying, as above, the present letters are of no force or moment as regards the said indulgences.

With concurrent executory, reciting the above (including the letters of Lucius III), [40] addressed to the archbishop of Canterbury and the bishops of Salisbury and Norwich.

Ad perpetuam rei memoriam. Pastoralis offitii cura meritis licet inparibus nobis ex alto commissi ... The executory begins: *Hodie a nobis emanarunt littere tenoris subsequentis ...*
p. lambert(us);O. de Cesis / JoA: / JoA: CCCC: L: Nardinus

1   engrossment not extant. Two supposed copies are entered in a Bradenstoke cartulary: BL, Stowe 925, viz. a copy of the C14 at fos 32^v-34^r; and a C16 copy, which includes particulars of extra grants, at fos 191^v-192^v. Both versions are printed by W. Holtzmann, *Papsturkunden in England*, II. Texte [Abhandlungen Der Gesellschaft Der Wissenschaften Zu Göttingen. Philologisch-Historische Klasse, Neue Folge, Bd. XXV.2], Berlin, 1931, pp. 496-500 (no. 220); summarised by V.C.M. London, ed., *The Cartulary of Bradenstoke Priory*, Wiltshire Record Society, 1979, nos. 19 (p. 33) and 581 (p. 176) respectively. On chronological grounds, Holtzmann detects false interpolations in both versions, especially in the C16 one. Minor verbal differences apart, the text recited in Leo's letter agrees with the C14 version, at fos 32^v-34^r of the cartulary.
2   *sic*; *recte*: 'apostolicum'
3   *sic*; 'impertiri'?
4   *sic*; *recte*: 'annuimus'
5   *sic*
6   *sic*; 'quicquid' ?
7   or *Cuualde*
8   or possibly *Cotel*
9   *sic*; *recte*: 'acras'
10 *sic*; 'concessione'?
11 *sic*
12 (?)*cete hid* deleted and initialled *JoA*
13 *sic*; *recte*: 'seculo'
14 *ex(ist)at* deleted; not initialled
15 *sic*; *recte*: 'si' ?
16 *sic*; 'de' ?
17 changed: the 'c' over a long 's'
18 or just possibly *censeat*; 'liceat'?
19 *sic*: for 'faciens'; 'faciant' ?
20 *sic*; ' surreptionis' ?
21 *sic*; 'hec'?
22 *sic*; *recte*: 'auferre' ?
23 *sic*; 'examine districte' ?
24 *sic*; *recte*: 'inveniant'
25 Note that, as recited and enregistered, certain authenticating features usually found in engrossed privileges of this class are wanting: there is only one 'Amen' (not three); and there are no subscriptions (of pope and cardinals). The diplomatic of solemn privileges (particularly in the form *Religiosam vitam eligentibus*) is discussed in two books by Jane E. Sayers: *Papal Government and England during the Pontificate of Honorius III (1216-1227)*, Cambridge, 1984, pp. 121-2; and *Original Papal Documents in England and Wales from the Accession of Pope Innocent III to the Death of Pope Benedict XI (1198-1304)*, Oxford, 1999, pp. lxii-lxvi, 487-490. See also Anne J. Duggan, 'The confirmation of Becket's primacy: *In apostolice sedis*, Lateran, 8 April 1166', *Journal of the Society of Archivists*, vol. 9, no. 4, Oct. 1988, pp. 197-209. A solemn privilege of 1163 is reproduced as the frontispiece of Robert Somerville, *Scotia Pontificia*, Oxford, 1982.
26 Thus the rest of Leo's letter; the spellings in the Lucius letter recited in it are as given in the transcription.
27 MS: *exemptione huiusmodi excepta*; of uncertain reference; perhaps the restriction of absolution to non-reserved cases is meant.
28 *Cf. CPL* XIX, no. 612.
29 MS: *in illa professione emissa*; *recte*: 'nulla professione ...'
30 MS: *a quo dictus prioratus olim dependebat, licet (?)seculari* [sc. Cirencester] *ab eius fundatione, ab illo*

dicta auctoritate separatus et exemptus fuerit. The punctuation is mine.

31   MS: *impedientes*; *recte*: 'impendentes'; curiously, the same error occurs in the Bruton grant (no. 154 above).
32   MS wants 'brachii'
33   MS: *exacto* (here and below); usually 'elapso'
34   MS: *prioribus ... et fratribus predictis (?)tot pro tempore existentibus*; *recte*: '... predictis tunc et pro tempore ...'
35   MS: *et*; *recte*: 'ad'
36   MS: *adhibitis ... Serimoniis* (a pronunciation spelling?)
37   MS: *sint*; *recte*: 'fiunt'
38   The brothers (and sisters) mentioned here, and in no. 154 above, are identifiable, essentially, as *fratres conscripti*. On the *confratres* and *consorores* and the admission ceremony *see* Edmund Bishop, 'Some Ancient Benedictine Confraternity Books', reprinted (from the *Downside Review* of Jan. 1885) in *Liturgica Historica* (Oxford, 1918), pp. 349-361 (esp. pp. 357-8).
39   MS: *... necnon etiam parentum et benefactorum omnium prenominatorum predictorum ...*; discarding *et*
40   enregistration of the recital abbreviated: *Lutius episcopus servus servorum dei et cetera*

495   7 June 1515   *Reg. Lat.* 1334, fo 56^{r-v}

To John Wilsen,[1] perpetual vicar of the parish church of Northpederten,[2] d. Exeter. Indult for life – at his supplication – to him, who, as he asserts, holds the perpetual vicarage of the above parish church, not to be bound, while residing in the Roman curia or one or other[3] of his benefices or attending a *studium generale*, to reside personally in his other benefices, nor to be liable to be compelled to do so by anyone against his will. Notwithstanding etc. With the proviso that the above vicarage and other benefices[4] shall not, on this account, be defrauded of due services and the cure of souls in the vicarage and (if any) the other benefices aforesaid shall not be neglected; but that the [cure] shall be exercised and things divine served by good and sufficient vicars maintained from the proceeds of the vicarage and other benefices; and that the aforesaid burdens of the other benefices shall be supported.

Vite ac morum honestas ...
p. lambert(us) / JoA: / :JoA. xx: Nard(inus):

1   the *-en* somewhat doubtful
2   or perhaps *-pedriten*
3   MS: *altero beneficiorum ... pro tempore obtentorum*; only *Northpederten* is mentioned.
4   *sic*

496   2 April 1515   *Reg. Lat.* 1334, fos 79^{v}-80^{v}

To Hugh Ap Griffith Ap Giryn', rector of the parish church of Byngesten' Baptist,[1] d. Salisbury. Dispensation and indult etc. [as above, no. 2].

Vite ac morum honestas ...
P. lambert(us) / JoA: / :JoA: Lx: Nardinus

1   referred to again as *Byngesten' Baptist*, then (twice) simply as *Byngesten'*

497   15 February 1514   *Reg. Lat.* 1334, fos 134ᵛ-136ᵛ

To Andrew Steward,[1] cleric, d. St Andrews, reservation etc. as below. A recent petition
to the pope on Andrew's part stated [that][2] at another time he – to avoid the tortuosity
of suits which were brewing between himself and Walter Beton, canon of Glasgow,
over the canonry and prebend of Gowan, church of Glasgow, which, he asserted, had
formerly (when vacant *certo modo*) been provided to him by ordinary authority and
rightfully belonged to him; and to spare labour and expense; and for the sake of peace
– spontaneously and freely ceded all right in any way belonging to him in or to the said
canonry and prebend into the hands of the local ordinary, outside the Roman curia, and
left Walter (as he is) in peaceful possession of the canonry and prebend. Lest Andrew
suffer excessive loss on this account, the pope hereby reserves, constitutes and assigns
to him an annual pension of 80 marks Scots, equivalent to 15[3] pounds sterling or
thereabouts, on the tithes and fruits etc. of the said canonry and prebend, (of which, as
Andrew asserts, this pension does not exceed one half), payable in full to Andrew for
life (or to his specially mandated proctor) by Walter (who has given his express assent
to this through Adam Symson, cleric, d. Dunkeld, his specially appointed proctor) and
his successors as holders of the canonry and prebend for the time being, each year, in
the church of Glasgow, viz.: one half of the said pension on the feast of the
Resurrection of Our Lord Jesus Christ and the other on that of St Peter ad Vincula.
With decree that if Walter (or any one of his successors) fails to make payment on the
said feasts or at least within the thirty days immediately following, he shall, after this
time has elapsed, incur sentence of excommunication from which he cannot be
absolved, except on the point of death, until he shall have made satisfaction in full or
reached agreement in respect of it with Andrew (or his proctor) and, if he remains
obdurate under that sentence for a further six months, he shall thereupon be deprived
in perpetuity of the canonry and prebend which shall be deemed vacant automatically.
Notwithstanding etc.

    Executory to the bishop of Cavaillon, and the dean of the church of Dunblane and
the provost of the church of Crethon, d. St Andrews.

Vite ac morum honestas … The executory begins: *Hodie dilecto filio*[4] *Stewal*[5] …
p. lambert(us); G. de prato / C / C. xij. x. Barotius

1   spelt *Stewal* (or perhaps *Stewad*; no 'r') in the executory
2   'quod' does not occur.
3   reading *quindecim*
4   first name ('Andree') wanting
5   *See above*, note 1.

498   6 June 1515   *Reg. Lat.* 1334, fos 231ᵛ-232ᵛ

To the dean and Richard Collet, canon, of the church of Exeter, and Henry Mart',
canon of the church of Hereford, mandate in favour of George Darwent[1], perpetual
vicar of the church[2] of Dulu',[3] d. Coventry and Lichfield. A recent petition to the pope

on George's part stated that at another time, Joan Athurley, woman, said d. – falsely
asserting that George was sexually incontinent and had perpetrated other excesses and
crimes then expressed – sued George, not by apostolic delegation, before Thomas
Filzherbert, who bore himself as the official or vicar general in spirituals[4] of the bishop
of Coventry and Lichfield, accusing George in this connection or denouncing him to
be guilty (*criminosum*) of the said crimes and praying *inter alia* that he be condemned
according to the penalties established by law against perpetrators of the same; that
Thomas, proceeding wrongly in the case, allowed (*admiserat*) Joan, George's capital
enemy, to make the accusation or denunciation and refused unlawfully to assign
George the competent term he sought for responding to Joan's 'libel' and refused to
admit several legitimate and declinatory objections to the 'libel' and to Thomas' person
put forward on George's part before Thomas at a suitable time and place which in law
ought to have been admitted; that George, feeling *inter alia* unduly aggrieved thereby,
then appealed to the court of Canterbury, the local metropolitan court, and in the cause
of the appeal caused Joan to be summoned to judgement before the official of the said
court; and that the official, proceeding wrongly in the case of the appeal, promulgated
an unjust definitive sentence in Joan's favour and against George, from which, on
George's part, appeal was made to the apostolic see, but the official, regardless of the
appeal of which he was not ignorant and while George was still well within the time
for prosecuting it, proceeded, perhaps, to further matters, albeit *de facto* and
temerariously attempting. At George's supplication to the pope to commit[5] to some
upright men in those parts the causes: of the latter appeal and of anything perhaps
attempted and innovated after and against it; of the nullity of the process and sentence
of the official of the said court and of each and every other thing done in any way by
the officials of Coventry and Lichfield and of the said court and by any other judges
and persons to George's prejudice in connection with the above; and of the whole
principal matter, the pope [hereby] commands that the above three (or two or one of
them), having summoned Joan and others concerned and having heard both sides,
taking cognizance even of the principal matter, shall, in matters not involving the
penalty of death or mutilation (*penam sanguinis*), decree what is just, without appeal,
causing [what they have decreed to be strictly][6] observed. Notwithstanding etc.

Humilibus et cetera.
Jo. copis / . Phi. / . phi: xiij. de Senis

1   or *Dacw–*
2   'parrochialis' does not occur.
3   or *Duln'*
4   MS: *vicario generali ... in spiritualibus generali* [!]
5   MS: *committere et mandare*
6   MS: *facientes et cetera observari.* Supplied from common form.

499   2 November 1515[1]   *Reg. Lat.* 1335, fos 6ʳ-7ʳ

To Adam Becansaw, rector of the parish church of Brington[2] [also spelt *Brengton'*], d.
Lincoln. Dispensation and indult etc. [as above, no. 2]. Given at Viterbo.

Vite ac morum honestas ...
.P. Lambertus. / JoA: / JoA: Lx: Nardinus

1   reading ... *quarto nonas* ...; but note that *quarto* is somewhat uncertain.
2   possibly *Brington'*

500   2 November 1515   *Reg. Lat.* 1335, fos 7ʳ-8ᵛ

To Edward Pennant, BDec, rector of the parish church of Sanlake [also spelt *Saulake*],
d. Lincoln. Dispensation and indult [as above, no. 2]. Given at Viterbo.

Litterarum scientia, vite ac morum honestas ...
.P. Lambertus. / JoA: / JoA: Lx: Nardinus

501   25 October 1515   *Reg. Lat.* 1335, fos 12ʳ-13ᵛ

Union etc. At a recent petition on the part of Thomas Han(n)ybale,[1] LLD, rector of the
parish church of Alchurche [also spelt *Alcurche, Arcurche, Alcurchie*[2]], d. Worcester,
the pope hereby unites etc. the parish church of Estysley [also spelt *Estisley, Estislei*],
d. Salisbury (whose annual value does not exceed 12 pounds sterling), with all rights
and appurtenances, to the above church of Alchurche, which he holds together with
Estysley by apostolic dispensation, for as long as he holds Alchurche, to the effect that
Thomas may, on his own authority, in person or by proxy, take, or continue in, and
retain corporal possession of Estysley and the rights and appurtenances aforesaid, for
as long as he holds Alchurche, and convert its fruits etc. to his own uses and those of
the said churches, without licence of the local diocesan or of anyone else.
Notwithstanding etc. The pope's will is, however, that the church of Estysley shall not,
on account of this union etc., be defrauded of due services and the cure of souls in it
shall not be neglected; but that its customary burdens shall be supported; and that on
Thomas's death or his resignation etc. of the church of Alchurche this union etc. shall
be dissolved and be so deemed and Estysley shall revert to its original condition
automatically.[3] Given at Civitavecchia.

*Ad futuram rei memoriam. Romanum decet pontificem votis illis gratum prestare
assensum ...*
.P. Lambertus / JoA: / JoA: xxxv: Nardinus

1   written *Han'ybale*

2   The only instance of this spelling occurs in a marginal insertion initialled *JoA*.
3   Final imprecatory clauses ('Nulli ergo … Si quis …') are wanting.
     (It is our policy to note these standard clauses in the Calendar only for some exceptional reason, as here.)

502   20 April 1515   *Reg. Lat.* 1335, fos 27[r]-28[r]

To William[1] Manw,[2] rector of the parish church of St David the Bishop, Gervenston, d. Meath. Dispensation – at his supplication – to receive and retain for life, together with the above parish church, one, and without them, any two other benefices, etc. [as above, no. 161].[3]

Vite ac morum honestas …
.P. Lambertus. / JoA: / JoA: L: Nardinus

1   G (perhaps *Gui*) deleted (but not initialled) directly before *Willelmo*
2   uncertain: badly affected by bleed-through
3   The Notwithstanding clauses include the constitutions of Otto and Ottobuono, formerly legates of the apostolic see in the kingdom of England, thereby giving Manw the option of holding benefices in England.

503   12 September 1515   *Reg. Lat.* 1335, fos 30[v]-32[r]

To Thomas Patenson, BTheol, dean of the church of St Andrew, Awkland, d. Durham. Dispensation and indult – at his supplication – to him, who, as he asserts, holds the deanery of the above church, which in the said church – which is also a parish [church] and in which, besides its dean, it is understood that there are twelve canons with prebends, called residentiaries – is the principal dignity, to receive and retain for life together with the above deanery, one, and without them, any two other benefices etc. [as above, no. 2, to '… retain them together for life, as above']; and, for life, while residing in the Roman curia or the said church of St Andrew or the manor of Aukland Episcopi *alias* Awkland Borrale' (located in the said diocese and lawfully pertaining, as he also asserts, to the said church of St Andrew or its capitular *mensa*, and a mile or so distant from the said church), or any one of his benefices, or attending a *studium generale*, not to be bound to reside in his other benefices, nor to be liable to be compelled to do so by anyone against his will. Notwithstanding etc. and [notwithstanding] the constitutions published, it is said, by the late Laurence, bishop of Durham, even those in which it is said to be expressly stipulated that the said dean and canons must reside continuously (*perpetuo*) not at the said church of St Andrew, but at the said manor,[1] and [notwithstanding the constitutions] of other churches in which the other benefices in question may perhaps be, etc., and [notwithstanding] the statutes and customs and also the foundation of the said church of St Andrew requiring personal residence at it, the which foundation and the statutes and customs aforesaid the pope hereby specially and expressly derogates; and he relaxes the oath to reside at the said church[2] perhaps taken by Thomas; and [notwithstanding] anything else to the contrary.

With the proviso that the deanery and other, even incompatible, benefices shall not, on this account, be defrauded of due services and the cure of souls in them shall not be neglected; but that customary burdens of those benefices in which he shall not reside shall be supported.

Litterarum scientia, vite ac morum honestas ...
.P. Lambertus. / JoA: / : JoA: Lxxx: Nard(inus): –

1   *sic*
2   *sic*

504   17 September 1515   *Reg. Lat.* 1335, fos 32ᵛ-33ᵛ

To John Bexwyk, perpetual vicar called vicar choral[1] in the church of B. Mary, Manc<e>ster[2] [also spelt *Ma'cester*], d. Coventry and Lichfield. Dispensation and indult – at his supplication – to him, who, as he asserts, holds a perpetual chaplaincy, called vicarage choral,[3] in the above church, to receive and retain for life together with the above chaplaincy (which is incompatible with another incompatible benefice), one, and without them, any two other benefices, etc. [as above, no. 2, to '... retain them together for life as above']; and, for life, while attending a *studium generale* or residing in the Roman curia or any one of his benefices, not to be bound to reside in his other benefices nor to be liable to be compelled to do so by anyone against his will. Notwithstanding etc. and [notwithstanding] the said B. Mary's foundation in which it is said to be expressly stipulated that no-one holding any benefice in B. Mary's can hold another benefice binding him to reside outside B. Mary's, the which foundation the pope, specially and expressly, derogates for this once only. With the proviso that the chaplaincy and other incompatible benefices shall not, on this account, be defrauded of due services and the cure of souls in them ([if] any) shall not be neglected; but that customary burdens of those benefices in which he shall not reside shall be supported.

Vite ac morum honestas ...
.P. Lambertus / JoA: / JoA: Lxx: Nard(inus): –

1   MS: *perpetuo vicario corali nuncupato*
2   the *e* inserted over the line, above (?)*c* indistinctly written in line
3   MS: *perpetuam* [*vicaria* deleted] *cappellaniam vicariam coram* [*sic*] *nuncupatam*; and below: *ac dicte capp(ellani)e* (a marginal insertion initialled *JoA.*)

505   17 September 1515   *Reg. Lat.* 1335, fos 34ʳ-35ʳ

To John Gyttyns, rector of the parish church of Eston', d. St Asaph. Dispensation and indult etc. [as above, no. 2].

Vite ac morum honestas …
.P. Lambertus / JoA: / JoA: Lx: Nardinus

506   17 September 1515[1]   *Reg. Lat.* 1335, fos 43ᵛ-44ᵛ

To Henry Marten, UIB, rector of the parish church of Tradley,[2] d. Hereford,
dispensation and indult. Some time ago, Julius II by his letters dispensed him to receive
and retain together for life any two benefices, etc. [as above, no. 6, to '… retain them
together for life'],[3] as is more fully contained in those letters.[4] The pope – at his
supplication – hereby further dispenses Henry, who, as he asserts, by virtue of the said
dispensation holds the parish churches of Tradley and of Radno'[5] Nova, d. Hereford,
to receive and retain together with the above parish churches, or with any two other
incompatible benefices held by him at the time by virtue of the said dispensation, any
third benefice, [with cure][6] or otherwise incompatible, etc. [as above, no. 6, to '…
retain it for life, as above']; and indulges him for life, while attending a *studium
generale* or residing in the Roman curia or any one of his benefices, not to be bound
to reside in his other benefices, nor to be liable to be compelled to do so by anyone
against his will. Notwithstanding etc. With the proviso that the third incompatible and
other benefices in question shall not, on this account, be defrauded of due services and
the cure of souls in the third incompatible and other benefices aforesaid (if any) shall
not be neglected; but that customary burdens of those benefices in which he shall not
reside shall be supported.

Litterarum scientia, vite ac morum honestas …
.P. Lambertus / JoA. / JoA: Lxxx: Na [rdinus]

1   The month has been altered: from *Augusti* (deleted in line, initialled *JoA*) to *Octobris* (inserted in margin,
    initialled *JoA*); i.e. this part of the date now reads: … *quintodecimo kalendas Octobris* …
2   Clearly written *T~* in each of the four instances of the name in the present entry. Cf. *CPL*, XIX, no. 375 which
    gives the spelling in Julius's register (as in the modern place-name) as *C~*
3   Save that 'aut talia mixtim fuerint' (rendered as 'or a combination') is wanting.
4   *CPL*, XIX, no. 375
5   in the first occurrence: a (?)*d* is deleted between the 'd' and 'n'
6   'curatum' wanting

507   19 September 1515   *Reg. Lat.* 1335, fo 46ʳ⁻ᵛ

To the bishop of Coventry and Lichfield, commission and mandate. A petition on the
part of Thomas Halisall', layman, and Joan Stanley, woman, d. Coventry and Lichfield,
stated that for certain good reasons they desire to be joined together in marriage, but
because they are related in the third degree of consanguinity they cannot fulfil their
desire in this matter without an apostolic dispensation. The pope therefore – at their
supplication – hereby commissions and commands the above bishop – if it is so and
Joan has not been abducted on this account – to dispense Thomas and Joan – the
impediment of this consanguinity notwithstanding – to contract marriage together and

remain therein, declaring the offspring of the marriage legitimate. Notwithstanding etc.

Sedis apostolice providentia circumspecta …
Phi. de Agnellis. / JoA: / :JoA: xx: Nard(inus): –

508   10 October 1515   *Reg. Lat.* 1335, fos 125ᵛ-127ʳ

Union etc. At a recent petition on the part of Ralph,[1] bishop of Ascalon (*Ascalonen.*),
the pope hereby unites etc. the perpetual vicarage of the parish church of Cropton', d.
Worcester, (whose annual value does not exceed 6 pounds sterling), with all rights and
appurtenances, to the parish church of Wethedon' [also spelt *Vethedon, Wethedon*], d.
Worcester, which bishop Ralph holds by apostolic dispensation together with the above
vicarage, for as long as he holds the church of Wethedon', to the effect that bishop
Ralph may, on his own authority, in person or by proxy, continue in, or take anew, and
retain corporal possession of the vicarage and rights and appurtenances aforesaid, for
as long as he holds Wethedon', and convert its fruits etc. to his own uses and those of
the vicarage and of the church of Wethedon', without licence of the local diocesan or
of anyone else. Notwithstanding etc. The pope's will is, however, that the said vicarage
shall not, on account of this union etc., be defrauded of due services and the cure of
souls in it shall not be neglected; but that its customary burdens shall be supported; and
that on bishop Ralph's death or his resignation etc. of the church of Wethedon' this
union etc. shall be automatically dissolved and be so deemed. Given at Viterbo.

*Ad futuram rei memoriam. Romanum decet pontificem votis illis gratum prestare
assensum …*
J. Benzon. / JoA: / JoA: xxxv: Nardinus

1   MS: *Radulphus* in the first instance; thereafter simply *.R.* or *R.*

509   9 June 1515   *Reg. Lat.* 1335, fos 209ʳ-210ʳ

Union etc. At a recent petition on the part of John Malteby, rector of the parish church
of Wassyngbueth' [also spelt *Whassyngb'ueth*],[1] d. Lincoln, the pope hereby unites etc.
the parish church of <Hemeswell'>[2] [also spelt *Hemeswell, Hemeswel*], d. Lincoln,
(whose annual value does not exceed 13 pounds 6 shillings and 8 pence sterling), with
all rights and appurtenances, to the above church of Wassyngbueth', which John holds
together with Hemeswell' by apostolic dispensation, for as long as he holds
Wassyngbueth', to the effect that John may, on his own authority, in person or by
proxy, take, or continue in, and retain corporal possession of Hemeswell', for as long
as he holds Wassyngbueth', and convert its fruits etc. to his own uses and those of the
said churches of Wassyngbueth' and Hemeswell', without licence of the local diocesan
or of anyone else. Notwithstanding etc. The pope's will is, however, that the church of

Hemeswell' shall not, on account of this union etc., be defrauded of due services and the cure of souls in it shall not be neglected; but that its customary burdens shall be supported; and that on John's death or his resignation etc. of the church of Wassyngbueth' this union etc. shall be dissolved and be so deemed and the church of Hemeswell' shall revert to its original condition automatically.

Ad futuram rei memoriam. Romanum decet pontificem votis illis gratum prestare assensum …
.P. Lambertus / JoA: / JoA: xxxv: Nardinus

1   subsequently simply written: *Whas*.
2   The first occurrence of *Hemeswell'* is inserted in margin, initialled *JoA*; replacing *Wassyngbueth* which had been written in line (mistakenly) and was then deleted, initialled *JoA*

510   10 November 1515   *Reg. Lat.* 1335, fos 211ᵛ-212ʳ

To Benjamin Godson, monk of the monastery of B. Mary the Virgin at Strata Marcella (*apud Stratam Marcellam*), OCist, d. St Asaph. Dispensation – at his supplication – to him, who, as he asserts, is expressly professed of the above order,[1] to receive and retain for life any benefice, with or without cure, usually held by secular clerics, etc. [as above, no. 43]. Given at Montefiascone.

Relligionis[2] *zelus, vite ac morum honestas …*
.P. Lambertus / JoA: / JoA: xxx: Nardinus

1   This information comes from a notwithstanding clause.
2   *sic*

511   10 November 1515   *Reg. Lat.* 1335, fos 215ᵛ-217ʳ

To John Stokylei,[1] DTheol, rector of the parish church of St John the Evangelist, Slimbrige, d. Worcester (who, as he asserts, is an MA). Dispensation and indult etc. [as above, no. 2]. Given at Montefiascone.

Litterarum scientia, vite ac morum honestas …
JoA: / . P. Lambertus / JoA: Lx: Nardi(nus)

1   the final letter doubtful; readable as a long 'i' written over (?)'r', or as an oddly formed 'y'

512   10 November 1515   *Reg. Lat.* 1335, fos 233ʳ-234ʳ

To Robert Thomson, BTheol, rector of the parish church of Coryngaym, d. London. Dispensation and indult etc. [as above, no. 2]. Given at Montefiascone.

Litterarum scientia, vite ac morum honestas ...
.P. Lambertus / . JoA: / JoA: Lx: Nardi(nus)

513 10 November 1515   *Reg. Lat.* 1335, fos 236ʳ-237ʳ

To William Hullyar, MA, rector of the parish church of Werketon', d. Lincoln. Dispensation and indult etc. [as above, no. 2]. Given at Montefiascone.

Litterarum scientia, vite ac morum honestas ...
P. Lambertus / JoA: / JoA: Lx: Nardi(nus)

514   10 November 1515   *Reg. Lat.* 1335, fos 237ᵛ-238ᵛ

To Richard Neell', perpetual vicar of the parish church of Westwell', d. Canterbury. Dispensation and indult etc. [as above, no. 2]. Given at Montefiascone.

Vite ac morum honestas ...
.P. Lambertus. / JoA: / JoA: Lx: Nardinus

515   10 November 1515   *Reg. Lat.* 1335, fos 238ᵛ-239ᵛ

To John Inskippe, perpetual vicar of the parish church of B. Mary the Virgin, Ffelgam [also spelt *Ffalgam*], d. Chichester. Dispensation and indult etc. [as above, no. 2]. Given at Montefiascone.

Vite ac morum honestas ...
.P. Lambertus[1] / JoA: / JoA: Lx: Nardi(nus)

516   10 November 1515   *Reg. Lat.* 1335, fos 240ʳ-241ʳ

To Richard Huntyngdu,[1] MA, perpetual vicar of the parish church of St Andrew, Plymmonth', d. Exeter. Dispensation and indult etc. [as above, no. 2]. Given at Montefiascone.

Litterarum scientia, vite ac morum honestas …
.P. Lambertus² / *JoA:* / *JoA: Lx: Nardinus*

1   a final letter (?)'n' deleted
2   reading the 'e' sympathetically

517   10 November 1515   *Reg. Lat.* 1335, fos 241ʳ-242ᵛ

Union etc. and indult. At a recent petition on the part of Thomas Kemey,¹ MA, rector
of the parish church of Newport, d. St David's, the pope hereby unites etc. the
perpetual vicarage of the parish church of Strugulior *alias* Chepstowe, d. Llandaff,
(whose annual value does not exceed 6 pounds sterling), with all rights and
appurtenances, to the above church of Newport, which Thomas holds by apostolic
dispensation together with the above vicarage, to the effect that Thomas may, on his
own authority, in person or by proxy, continue in, or take anew, and retain corporal
possession of the vicarage and rights and appurtenances aforesaid, for as long as he
holds the church of Newport, and convert its fruits etc. to his own uses and those of the
church of Newport and of [(?)the vicarage],² without licence of the local diocesan or
of anyone else. With indult to Thomas, for life, while attending a *studium generale* or
residing in the Roman curia or any one of his benefices, not to be bound to reside in
his other benefices nor to be liable to be compelled to do so by anyone against his will.
Notwithstanding etc. The pope's will is, however, that the said vicarage (on account of
this union etc.) and the said other benefices (on account of non-residence) shall not be
defrauded of due services and the cure of souls in the vicarage and (if any) the other
benefices aforesaid shall not be neglected; but that customary burdens of the vicarage
and of other benefices in which he shall not reside shall be supported; and that on
Thomas's death or his resignation etc. of the church of Newport this union etc. shall be
dissolved and so deemed and the vicarage shall revert to its original condition
automatically. Given at Montefiascone.

Ad futuram rei memoriam. Romanum decet pontificem votis illis gratum prestare
assensum …
.P. Lambertus. / *JoA:* / *JoA: xxxv: Nardinus*

1   possibly R~
2   MS: *… ecclesie de Newport ac ecclesie predictarum …*; *recte*: *ac* 'vicarie' *predictarum*

518   22 June 1515   *Reg. Lat.* 1336, fos 244r-245ʳ

To James Wylson',¹ rector of the parish church of Wokyngton¹ de Greue, d. Lincoln.
Dispensation and indult etc. [as above, no. 2].²

Vite ac morum honestas …

P Lambert(us) / JoA: / JoA: Lx: Nardinus

1   in both cases the 'W' written *Vu*
2   Save that – though the tenor is the same – the order of clauses in the indult for non-residence is not identical;
     and that the present entry contains a few scribal slips (e.g. *alia* where 'talia' occurs, rightly, in no. 2).

519   20 August 1515   *Reg. Lat.* 1337, fos 57^r-58^v

Union etc. A recent <petition>[1] to the pope on the part of William Frankeleyn, BDec,
canon of the church of Langehestre [also spelt *Langchestre*], d. Durham, stated that if
<one of the two portions of the parish church>[2] of All Saints, Hoghton Conguest,
<usually ruled by two rectors, and the parish church>[3] of St (*divi*) John the Baptist,
Bedford (*de Bedfordia*), d. Lincoln – which are of the patronage of laymen or clerics,
or of a combination of laymen and clerics; and for which at another time, while vacant
certo modo, the said William, <archdeacon>[4] of the church of Durham, was presented
by the patrons of those parish churches within the lawful time, or hopes to be presented
shortly[5] – were, after he was presented and therein instituted, to be united etc. to the
canonry and prebend of Ystune[6] of the said church of Langehestre, which William
holds, for as long as he holds the latter, it would be of advantage to him. Supplication
was made on the part of William – who asserts that he holds by apostolic dispensation
the archdeaconry of the said church of Durham and the hospital of St Giles, Kepyer,[7]
d. Durham; and that the annual value of the said parish churches together does not
exceed 43 pounds sterling – to the pope to unite etc. <the above portion and the above
church of St John>[8] to the said canonry and prebend, for as long as William holds the
latter. At this supplication, the pope hereby unites etc. <the portion and the church of
St John the Baptist aforesaid>[9] after William has been presented for them and
instituted, as above, with all rights and appurtenances, to the said canonry and prebend,
for as long as William holds the latter; to the effect that he may, on his own authority,
in person or by proxy, take corporal possession <of the portion and of the church of St
John the Baptist>[10] and the rights and appurtenances aforesaid, and retain them for as
long as he holds the canonry and prebend, as above, and convert their fruits etc. to his
own uses and those of the canonry and prebend [and] <of the portion and of the church
of St John the Baptist aforesaid>[11], without licence of the local diocesan or of anyone
else. Notwithstanding etc. The pope's will is, however, that <the portion and the church
of St John the Baptist aforesaid>[12] shall not, on this account, be defrauded of due
services and the cure of souls in them shall not be neglected; but that their customary
burdens shall be supported; and that on William's death or his resignation etc. of the
canonry and prebend, this union etc. shall be dissolved and this <portion and church of
St John the Baptist>[13] shall revert to their original condition and be deemed vacant
automatically.

*Ad futuram rei memoriam. Romanum decet pontificem votis illis gratum prestare
assensum ...*
Phi. de Agnell(is) / C / C. xxxx Barotius

1   *petitio* inserted in margin, initialled *JoA*. The insertion, which is made after *exhibita*, replaces *peticio*, deleted
    and initialled *JoA*, written in line before *exhibita*. Here and below the inserted words are in a third hand, that
    is, they are not in Nardini's hand and not in that of the enregistering scribe.

2   *altera portio parrochialis ecclesie* inserted in margin; *JoA* above insertion; *correctu(m) ut supra Nar*
    beneath. In a corresponding petition *seu altera portio dicte ecclesie Omnium Sanctorum* has been inserted
    (in the margin) after *Omnium Sanctorum de Houghton' Conguest* in the line. Accompanying the insertion is
    the note: *additu(m) de man(da)to R(everendissimi) Io(hannis) Casertan. p(ro)ut in originali p(er) me
    Ant(onium) de Baschenis*. (*Reg. Suppl.* 1498, fo 89ʳ⁻ᵛ: captioned *unio*). Johannes Baptista Boncian(n)us,
    bishop of Caserta, is noted in the entry (*Jo. Casertanus*) as the referendary who signed the supplication.

3   *per duos rectores regi solite et parrochialis ecclesie* inserted in margin; *JoA* above insertion; *cassat(um) et
    correctu(m) de man(da)to D(omi)ni Regentis Nar* beneath it. This replaces *parrochiales ecclesie* (deleted and
    initialled *JoA*) written in line a few words later, after *Lincolinen. diocesis*

4   *archidiaconus* inserted in right margin after *Willelmus* which ends a line; *JoA* above it; *correctu(m) ut sup(ra)
    Nar* beneath. This replaces *Archidiaconus* written in line before *Willelmus* and deleted, initialled *JoA*

5   *brevi*

6   the four minims variously readable

7   written *Kepijer*

8   *portionem et ecclesiam divi Jo(hannis) predictas* inserted in margin; *JoA* above it; *correctu(m) ut sup(ra) Nar*
    beneath. This replaces *dictas parrochiales ecclesias* written in line and deleted, initialled *JoA*

9   *portionem et ecclesiam divi Johannis Baptiste predictas* inserted in margin, *JoA* above it; *correctu(m) ut
    sup(ra) Nar* beneath it. This replaces *parrochiales ecclesias predictas* written in line and deleted, initialled
    JoA

10 *portionis et ecclesie divi Jo(hannis) Bap(tis)te* inserted in margin; *JoA* above it; *correctu(m) ut sup(ra) Nar*
    beneath it. This replaces *parrochialium ecclesiarum* in the line, deleted and initialled *JoA*

11 *portionis et ecclesie divi Jo(hannis) Bap(tis)te predictorum* inserted in margin; *JoA* above it; *correctu(m) ut
    supra Nar* beneath it. This replaces *et parrochialium ecclesiarum* in the line, deleted and initialled *JoA*

12 *portio et ecclesia divi Jo(hannis) Bapt(is)te predicte* inserted in margin; *JoA* above it; *correctu(m) ut sup(ra)
    Nar* beneath. This replaces *dicte parrochiales ecclesie* written in line and deleted, initialled *JoA*

13 *portio et ecclesia divi Jo(hannis) Bapt(is)te* inserted in margin; *JoA* above it; *correctu(m) ut sup(ra) Nar*
    beneath. This replaces *parrochiales ecclesie* written in the line and deleted, initialled *JoA*

520   20 October 1515   *Reg. Lat.* 1337, fos 162ᵛ-164ʳ

To the provost of the church of Crethton',[1] d. St Andrews, mandate in favour of John
Crethton' [also spelt *Crethton, Creton, Cre.*[2]], canon of the monastery of the Holy
Cross, near Edinburgh, OSA, d. St Andrews. A recent petition to the pope on the said
John's part stated that at another time, when the priory of St Mary, Insula Traill, OSA,
d. Whithorn, was vacant by the death of the late John Crauford, formerly its prior,
outside the Roman curia, the then abbot and convent of the said monastery of the Holy
Cross (from which the priory depends) – [since] to the said abbot for the time being
and convent of which the collation, provision and every sort of disposition of the priory
at a time of vacancy pertains by ancient, approved and hitherto peacefully observed
custom – by ordinary authority collated and made provision of the priory, vacant as
above, to the said John Crethton' – who, previously, after entering the said monastery,
had made the usual regular profession made by its canons; and (notwithstanding a
defect of birth as the son of an abbot, OSB, and an unmarried woman) had had himself
duly promoted to all, even sacred and priest's, orders; and (also notwithstanding the
above defect) had been dispensed by apostolic authority to receive and retain a
benefice, with or without cure, usually held by Augustinian canons, even if it should
be a priory or *prepositura*, if conferred on him otherwise [canonically][3] – and by virtue
of the said collation and provision John Crethton' did, perhaps, acquire possession of

the priory. Moreover since, as the said petition added, John Crethton' fears that for certain reasons the said collation and provision do not hold good; and, as the pope has learned, the priory is understood to be vacant still as above, the pope hereby commands the above provost, if by diligent examination he finds John Crethton' to be suitable – concerning which the pope burdens the provost's conscience – to collate and assign the priory (which is not conventual, is customarily held by canons of the said monastery, and whose annual value does not exceed 45 pounds sterling), (vacant as above or in any other way, etc.; even if it has been vacant for so long that by the Lateran statutes its collation has lawfully devolved on the apostolic see, etc.), with all rights and appurtenances, to John Crethton', inducting him etc. having removed any unlawful detainer, and causing John Crethton' to be admitted to the priory and its fruits etc., rights and obventions to be delivered to him. [Curbing] gainsayers etc. Notwithstanding etc. And the pope has commanded that – if John Crethton' is found suitable – provision of the priory be made to him from the date of the presents. Given at Toscanella.

Dignum arbitramur et congruum et cetera.
p. lambert(us) / JoA: / :JoA: xx: Sextodecimo K(a)l(endas) decenbris Anno tertio: [16 November 1515], *Nardinus*

1   Throughout, the 't's of *Crethton'* (and its variants) are read sympathetically, as the scribe is apt to be lax about crossing them.
2   *sic*
3   'canonice' does not occur.

521   12 December 1515   *Reg. Lat.* 1338, fos 120ʳ-121ʳ

To the officials of Cambrai, Thérouanne, and Arras, mandate in favour of Amatus de Fonte, canon, OPrem, syndic or proctor of the present father-abbot and of the whole general chapter, OPrem. A recent petition to the pope on Amatus' part stated that although the said father-abbot and general chapter [have been able][1] to exercise jurisdiction of all sorts over the abbots and convents of the monasteries of the Premonstratensian order within the kingdom of England in their entirety (*universi*), in accordance with the regular institutes of the order which have been hitherto peacefully observed, and although the said abbots and convents in their entirety are bound to show reverence and obedience to the father-abbot and general chapter and cannot or ought not to withdraw from them, nevertheless, by pretext of certain apostolic letters impetrated by them from Julius II[2] by *suggestio falsi* and *suppressio veri* and otherwise surreptitiously and obreptitiously, the abbots and convents of the said monasteries in their entirety have often *de facto* falsely declared[3] that they are exempt from the jurisdiction of the father-abbot and general chapter and perhaps from showing obedience and reverence, and they have perhaps withdrawn themselves from showing obedience and reverence; and that on this account Amatus the sydic or proctor, feeling that the father-abbot and general chapter were thereby unduly aggrieved, appealed to the apostolic see before a certain notary and trustworthy witnesses. At the supplication which Amatus caused to be made to the pope to commit to some upright men in those parts the causes: of the aforesaid appeal and of anything perhaps attempted and innovated after and against it; of the nullity of the false declarations and withdrawal; of the surreption and obreption and nullity and invalidity of the said letters; of each and every other thing done in any way in connection with the above by any judges and persons to the prejudice of the father-abbot and general chapter and their jurisdiction; and of the whole principal matter, the pope [hereby] commands that the above three (or two or one of them), having summoned the said abbots and convents in their entirety and others concerned, and having heard both sides, taking cognizance even of the principal matter, shall decree what is just, without appeal, causing by ecclesiastical censure what they have decreed to be strictly observed. Notwithstanding the constitution of Boniface VIII concerning *inter alia* one day's journey and the constitution touching two day's journey published in the general council, provided that by authority of the presents no one is summoned more than three day's journey beyond (*extra*) the said kingdom,[4] etc. Given at Bologna.

Humilibus et cetera.
I. Benzon / JoA: / : JoA: xiiij: Nardinus

1   MS wants 'potuerint' (or suchlike).
2   *Cf. CPL* XIX, no. 768.
3   reading *iactarunt*
4   Boniface VIII's constitution on judicial procedure (*cf. Sext*, I.3.11; I.14.15; Friedberg, 941-2; 982-3) and the constitution published in the general council (*cf. Decretals*, I.3.28; *Clem.* II.2; Friedberg, 31; 1144-5) – which regularly find place in the notwithstanding clauses of rescripts of justice and mandates *de providendo* and the like – are not, as a rule, noticed by the current volume of the Calendar. Though readily explicable in the circumstances of the letter the reckoning of the dietae from the frontier of the kingdom instead of the relevant diocesan boundary is a feature of exceptional interest and justifies mention of the constitutions in the present summary.

522   10 January 1516   *Reg. Lat.* 1338, fos 143ʳ-144ᵛ

To the archdeacon, treasurer, and Alexander Gallouay[1], canon, of the church of Aberdeen, mandate in favour of Alexander Haye, canon of Aberdeen. A recent petition to the pope on Alexander's part stated that some time ago William Lame *alias* Panter, who bears himself as a cleric of the city or d. Brechin – claiming that at another time an annual pension of 50 pounds of the money current in those parts on the fruits etc of the canonry and prebend of Turrer[2] of the church of Aberdeen, which Alexander holds canonically, had been reserved, constituted, and assigned to him by certain apostolic letters and that Alexander was bound to pay him the pension and had unlawfully stopped payment – caused Alexander, by pretext of the said surreptitious and obreptitious letters and of the processes (perhaps intimated to Alexander) conducted over them, to be warned and ordered *de facto*, by a certain executor, [as][3] he said, of the said letters, under sentence of excommunication and certain other ecclesiastical sentences, censures and pains then expressed, to pay him the pension within a certain term then expressed; that the executor perhaps declared, or threatened to declare, that

Alexander had incurred the said sentence of excommunication and the other ecclesiastical sentences, etc because he had not obeyed the said warning and order (which he was not in law bound to obey); and that on the part of Alexander, who felt unduly aggrieved thereby, appeal was made to the apostolic see. At the supplication to the pope to order that Alexander be absolved, simply or *ad cautelam*, from the aforesaid and any other ecclesiastical sentences, censures, and pains perhaps promulgated against him in any way by the executor and any other judges and persons on the above occasion, and that the executor, William, and any other judges and persons, be inhibited, even under ecclesiastical censures and pains, as often as necessary, and also to commit to some upright men in those parts the causes: of the aforesaid appeal and of anything perhaps attempted and innovated after and against it; of the nullity of the said warning and mandate; of the intimation of the said letters and processes; of the excommunication and any other ecclesiastical sentences, censures, and pains perhaps promulgated against Alexander in any way on the above occasion; of the executor's whole process; of the surreption and obreption of the said letters; of each and every other thing done in any way by the executor and any other judges and persons to Alexander's prejudice in connection with the above; and of the whole principal matter, the pope [hereby] commands that the above three (or two or one of them), having summoned William and others concerned, shall, on the pope's authority, [for this once][4] only, bestow on Alexander, if he so requests, the benefit of absolution, simply or *ad cautelam*, from the said sentence of excommunication and any other ecclesiastical sentences, etc., if and as it is just, having, however, first received from him suitable security in respect of that for which he is deemed excommunicate and perhaps caught by the said censures, that if it appears to them that the sentence of excommunication and other ecclesiastical sentences etc were justly inflicted on him he will obey their mandates and those of the church; as to the other things, having inhibited the executor, William, and any other judges and persons, even under ecclesiastical censures, as often as necessary and inasmuch as it is just, on the pope's authority hear the several causes, even the cause of the principal matter, without delaying payment of the pension, and, having heard both sides, duly terminate or decide them, causing by ecclesiastical censure what they have decreed to be strictly observed, [and moreover compel] witnesses, etc. Notwithstanding etc. Given at Florence.

Humilibus et cetera.
P. lambertus / JoA: / :JoA: xij: Nardinus

1   or *Gallonan*, etc
2   or *Turret*
3   MS wants 'ut'.
4   MS wants 'hac vice'.

523   11 January 1516   *Reg. Lat.* 1338, fos 149ᵛ-150ʳ

To Henry Radyng¹ *alias* Ffrenche, monk of the monastery of B. Mary the Virgin and BB. John and James the Apostles, Radyng,¹ OSB, d. Salisbury. Dispensation and indult – at his supplication – to receive and retain any benefice, with or without cure, usually held by secular clerics, even if a parish church or its perpetual [vicarage, or]² a chantry, free chapel, hospital or annual service, usually assigned to secular clerics in title of a perpetual ecclesiastical benefice, and of lay patronage and of whatsoever tax or annual value, if he obtains it otherwise canonically, to resign it, simply or for exchange, as often as he pleases, and in its place receive and retain another, similar or dissimilar, benefice, with or without cure, usually held by secular clerics; and also – [even] after he has acquired the said benefice – to receive a monachal portion of the above monastery, OSB, of which he is a monk and, as he asserts, expressly professed of the order, and to have³ a stall in the choir and also an active and a passive voice in the chapter of this monastery.⁴ Notwithstanding etc. Given at Careggi, d. Florence.

Religionis zelus, vite ac morum honestas …
p. de Castello / JoA: / JoA: Lxx: Nardinus

1   *sic*
2   'vicaria aut' wanting
3   'quoadvixeris' does not occur.
4   The clause: 'ac alias ut prius … in omnibus et per omnia perinde ac si beneficium huiusmodi nullatenus assecutus fuisses' (rendered in no. 19 as 'and otherwise as before, without limitation, just as if he had not acquired the benefice') does not occur in this entry.

524   7 January 1516   *Reg. Lat.* 1338, fos 155ʳ-156ʳ

To Miles Garnet, perpetual vicar of the parish church of Wymmeryng, d. Winchester. Dispensation and indult etc. [as above, no. 2]. Given at Florence.

Vite ac morum honestas …
P. de Castello / JoA: / :JoA: Lx: Nardinus

525   7 January 1516   *Reg. Lat.* 1338, fos 156ᵛ-157ᵛ

To Richard Parkurst, MA, perpetual vicar of the parish church of Rosse, d. Hereford. Dispensation and indult etc. [as above, no. 2]. Given at Florence.

Litterarum scientia, vite ac morum honestas …
P. de Castello / JoA: / JoA: Lxx:¹ Nardinus

1   *sic*; *cf.* above, no. 13, note 2.

526   15 February 1516   *Reg. Lat.* 1338, fos 201ʳ-202ʳ

To William Blakden, rector of the parish church of Wotton, d. Lincoln. Dispensation etc. [as above, no. 161]. Given at Florence.

Vite ac morum honestas ...
P. de Castello / JoA: / JoA: L: Nar(dinus)

527   10 February 1516   *Reg. Lat.* 1338, fo 202ʳ⁻ᵛ

To Robert Tailloure, canon of the monastery, called house or priory, of Typtre,[1] OSA, d. London. Dispensation – at his supplication – to him, who, as he asserts, is expressly professed of the above order,[2] to receive and retain any benefice, with or without cure, usually held by secular clerics, etc. [as above, no. 43]. Given at Florence.

Religionis zelus, vite ac morum honestas ...
P. lambert(us) / JoA: / :JoA: xxx: Nardinus

1   The second occurrence spelt *Typte* or possibly *Typtre* (the 'tre' merged).
2   This information comes from a notwithstanding clause.

528   10 February 1516   *Reg. Lat.* 1338, fos 203ʳ-204ʳ

To Robert Mayneweryng, rector of the parish church of Alderlay, d. Coventry and Lichfield. Dispensation and indult etc. [as above, no. 2]. Given at Florence.

Vite ac morum honestas ...
P. lambert(us) / JoA: / :JoA: Lx: Nardi(nus)

529   10 February 1516   *Reg. Lat.* 1338, fos 204ʳ-205ʳ

To Robert Eston', monk of the monastery, called house, of Peterborough (*de Burgo Sancti Petri*), OSB, d. Lincoln. Dispensation – at his supplication – to him, who, as he asserts, is expressly professed of the above order,[1] to receive and retain any benefice, with or without cure, usually held by secular clerics, etc. [as above, no. 43]. Given at Florence.

Religionis zelus, vite ac morum honestas ...
P. lamberti² / JoA: / : JoA: xxx: Nardinus

1   This information comes from a notwithstanding clause.
2   *sic*

530   29 December 1515   *Reg. Lat.* 1338, fos 301ʳ-302ʳ

To David Wauchop[1], William Yrlande, and Thomas Greig, canons of the church of Dunkeld, mandate in favour of Christine Wardlaw, relict of the late Robert Skerling, layman, widow,[2] d. St Andrews. A recent petition to the pope on Christine's part stated that some time ago Andrew Aytone', rector of the parish church of Spot[3], said or other d. – falsely alleging that the said Christine was bound on certain, albeit unlawful, grounds then expressed to give and pay to him a certain sum of money then expressed –caused Christine to be summoned to trial over this before Hugh Spens, sub-conservator appointed, as Andrew said, by a certain conservator (himself appointed by letters of the apostolic see) [of the privileges and rights granted][4] to all the doctors, masters, scholars, and subjects of the university (*universitatis studii generalis*) of St Andrews (among whom Andrew falsely said that he was numbered) against those molesting and damaging them in respect of their goods and interests (*in bonis et rebus suis*), and having, as the said Andrew also asserted, special faculty by the said letters of taking cognizance of those matters which require judicial investigation, and it was by pretext of the said letters and faculty that Andrew brought her to trial; and that Hugh the sub-conservator, proceeding wrongly in the case, promulgated an unjust, definitive (as he said) sentence, in favour of Andrew and against Christine, from which on Christine's part appeal was made to the apostolic see, but prevented, as she asserts, by lawful impediment she has not, perhaps, prosecuted the appeal within due time. At Christine's supplication to the pope to commit to some upright men in those parts the causes: of the aforesaid appeal and of anything perhaps attempted and innovated after and against it; of the nullity of the sentence and whole process of Hugh the sub-conservator and of each and every other thing done in any way by him and any other judges and persons to Christine's prejudice in connection with the above; and of the whole principal matter; the lapse of time notwithstanding, the pope [hereby] commands that the above three (or two or one of them), if what is put forward about the said impediment is true, having summoned Andrew and others concerned and having heard both sides, taking cognizance even of the principal matter, shall decree what is just, without appeal, causing by ecclesiastical censure, what they have decreed to be strictly observed, [and moreover compel] witnesses, etc. Notwithstanding the said lapse of time etc. Given at Florence.

Humilibus et cetera.
P. lambertus / JoA: / :JoA: xij: Nardi(nus)

1   or *Wanchop*
2   MS: *relicte ... vidue*
3   the 'o' doubtful; possibly an 'a' or even 'e'
4   MS wants ' privilegiorum et iurium ... concessorum' (or suchlike).

531   14 January 1516   *Reg. Lat.* 1338, fos 320ᵛ-321ᵛ

Union etc. At a recent petition on the part of Benedict Trego as,[1] MA, perpetual vicar
of the perpetual vicarage of the parish church[2] of St Paternus (*Sancti Paterni*), d.
Exeter, the pope hereby unites etc. the perpetual vicarage of the parish church of St Just
(*Sancti Justi*), d. Exeter, (whose annual value does not exceed 6 English pounds, not in
excess of a total of 24 gold ducats of the camera), which he holds together with the said
vicarage of the church of St Paternus by apostolic dispensation, with all rights and
appurtenances, to the vicarage of the church of St Paternus, for as long as Benedict
holds the latter; to the effect that he may, on his own authority, in person or by proxy,
take anew, or continue in, and retain corporal possession of the vicarage of the church
of St Just, for as long as he holds the vicarage of the church of St Paternus, and convert
its fruits etc. to his own uses and those of the said vicarages, without licence of the
local diocesan or of anyone else. Notwithstanding etc. The pope's will is, however, that
the said vicarage of the church of St Just shall not, on account of this union etc., be
defrauded of due services and the cure of souls in it shall not be neglected; but that its
customary burdens shall be supported; and that on Benedict's death or his resignation
etc. of the vicarage of the church of St Paternus this union etc. shall be automatically
dissolved and be so deemed and the vicarage of the church of St Just shall revert to its
original condition automatically. Given at Florence.

*Ad futuram rei memoriam. Ex iniuncto nobis desuper apostolice servitutis officio ad ea
liberenter*[3] *...*
P. de Castello / JoA: / :JoA: xxxv: Nar[4]

1   The first five letters are ligatured; likewise the last two; a slight gap between the two groups.
2   *perpetui vicarii perpetue vicarie parrochialis ecclesie*; unusual formulation
3   *sic*; *recte*: 'libenter'. The proem continues: *intendi(mus) per que personarum ecclesiasticarum
     commoditatibus valeat utiliter et salubriter provideri*. This is an unusual proem for a union *ad vitam* in this
     form; and in view of the grantee's degree we would have expected 'presertim litterarum scientia preditarum'
     (or suchlike) built into it (e.g. after *ecclesiasticarum*).
4   *Nar* is written without mark of abbreviation.

532   11 January 1516   *Reg. Lat.* 1338, fos 322ʳ-323ʳ

To John Warum,[1] rector of the parish church of St Leonard, Berwyke, d. Salisbury.
Dispensation and indult etc. [as above, no. 2]. Given at Careggi, d. Florence.

Vite ac morum honestas ...
P. de Castello / JoA: / :JoA: Lx: Nardinus

1   reading of minims uncertain; none dotted

533   30 September 1515   *Reg. Lat.* 1339, fo 12[r-v]

To the bishop of Coventry and Lichfield, commission and mandate in favour of Thomas Pylkynton,[1] layman, and Margaret Hulton, woman, a married couple, d. Coventry and Lichfield. A petition to the pope on Thomas and Margaret's part stated that at one time they – aware that they were related in the third degree of consanguinity – contracted marriage *per verba de presenti* (perhaps clandestinely), consummated it by connection, and cohabited for many years. Moreover, Thomas and Margaret cannot remain in their marriage, thus contracted, without an apostolic dispensation; and, as the same petition added, a permanent divorce between them could truly give rise to grave scandals. At their supplication to the pope to absolve them from the sentence of excommunication (which they incurred on account of the foregoing; and also, perhaps, in accordance with provincial and synodal constitutions on account, perhaps, of the said marriage having been contracted clandestinely and of the incest) and to grant them dispensation, the pope – for the aforesaid and certain other reasons explained to him, hereby commissions and commands the above bishop, if it is thus, to absolve Thomas and Margaret, if they so request, from the sentence of excommunication and the incest, for this once only, in the customary form of the church, having enjoined – on the strength of an oath to be taken by them not to repeat the offences nor to give help, counsel or favour to those committing them – a salutary penance on them etc.; and – if it seems expedient to the bishop to grant this dispensation and Margaret has not been abducted on this account – to dispense Thomas and Margaret – after a period of separation at his discretion – to contract marriage anew (notwithstanding the aforesaid impediment etc.), even in any church or private chapel, without the banns, proclamations or solemnities wont to be performed by the law or custom of those parts; and after contracting the marriage to remain therein, decreeing the present (if any) and future offspring of the marriage legitimate.

Oblate nobis pro parte ... petitionis series continebat ...
.P. Lambertus. / JoA: / :JoA: xxx: Nardinus

1   *Pyg* deleted (but not initialled) immediately before *Pylkynton*

534   20 January 1516   *Reg. Lat.* 1339, fos 15[v]-18[r]

To the chancellor and Donald Oedriscol and Darius Oegna, canons, of the church of Ross, mandate in favour of Donat Ohydscoll', priest, d. Ross. A recent petition to the pope on Donat's part stated that at another time – after he had been dispensed by apostolic authority, notwithstanding a defect of birth as the son of a priest and an unmarried woman, to be promoted to all, even sacred and priest's, orders and to hold a benefice, even if it should have cure of souls; and, by virtue of this dispensation, had been duly promoted to the said orders – the then bishop of Ross by ordinary authority collated and made provision of the perpetual vicarage of the parish church of Glunborchan', d. Ross, which was vacant *certo modo* at the time, to Donat; and, by virtue of this collation and provision, he acquired possession of it. Moreover, the same petition added that Donat fears that the said collation and provision do not, for certain reasons, hold good; and, as the pope has learned, the said [vicarage][1] is understood to be vacant still, as above; and the rectory of the parish church of Miros in ecclesiastical fee, d. Ross, is understood to be vacant *certo modo*, and has been vacant for so long [that by the Lateran statutes its collation has lawfully] devolved [on the apostolic see],[2] although Donal[3] Ohydscoll', who bears himself as a cleric, has detained the rectory with no title or support of law, of his own temerity, and *de facto*, for a certain time, and so does. At this petition on the part of Donat (who asserts that the annual value of the rectory and vicarage together does not exceed 24 marks sterling) to the pope to erect and institute a canonry in the church of Ross and the rectory into a simple prebend, for his lifetime, and to unite etc. the said vicarage to the canonry and prebend thus erected, also for his lifetime, the pope hereby commands that the above three (or two or one of them), if they find the vicarage and the rectory[4] – having summoned Donal and the bishop and chapter of Ross regarding the rectory and others concerned – to be vacant (howsoever etc.), shall erect and institute a canonry in the church of Ross and the rectory into a simple prebend, for Donat's lifetime, without prejudice to anyone; and shall unite etc. the said vicarage[5] to the canonry and prebend thus erected (even if the vicarage has likewise been vacant for so long *et cetera*,[6] and the (?)rectory[7] and vicarage are generally reserved etc.), likewise for Donat's lifetime; and, in the event of this erection, institution and union etc., collate and assign the newly erected canonry and prebend to Donat, with plenitude of canon law and all rights and appurtenances, inducting Donat etc. having removed Donal and any other unlawful detainers from the same, and causing Donat (or his proctor) to be received as a canon of the church of Ross, and assign him a stall in the choir and a place in the chapter of the church of Ross, with plenitude of canon law, and [causing] the fruits etc., rights and obventions of the canonry and prebend to be delivered to him. [Curbing] gainsayers etc. Notwithstanding etc. Also the pope dispenses Donat to receive the said canonry and prebend, if [conferred][8] on him by virtue of the presents, and any two benefices, with cure or otherwise mutually incompatible, and any number of other benefices, with and without cure, compatible mutually and with the incompatible benefices and the canonry and prebend aforesaid, even if the compatible benefices should be canonries and prebends, and the compatible as well as the incompatible benefices, should be dignities, *personatus*, administrations or offices in cathedral, even metropolitan, or collegiate churches, or parish churches or their perpetual vicarages, or a combination, and even if the dignities etc. should be customarily elective and have cure of souls, if he obtains them otherwise canonically, and retain even the incompatible benefices together for life; to resign them, at once or successively, simply or for exchange, as often as he pleases, and in their place receive up to two other incompatible benefices etc. – provided that the dignities be not major *post pontificalem* in metropolitan or other cathedral churches or principal in collegiate churches – and retain even the incompatible benefices together for life, as above. Notwithstanding the above defect etc. The pope's will is, however, that the rectory and vicarage and incompatible benefices in question shall not, on this account, be defrauded of due services and the cure of souls in the rectory and vicarage and (if any) the incompatible benefices shall not be neglected, but that the customary burdens of the rectory and vicarage shall be supported; and that on Donat's death or his resignation etc. of the canonry and prebend the erection and institution shall be utterly extinguished and the union etc. be dissolved and so deemed and the rectory and vicarage shall revert to their original condition automatically. Given at Poggio a Caiano, d. Florence.

Apostolice sedis providentia circumspecta …
.P. Lambertus / JoA: / :JoA: Lx: k(a)l(endis) feb(rua)rij Anno tertio: [1 February 1516], *Nardinus*

1   MS wants 'vicaria' after *dicta*
2   MS: *tanto tempore vacaverit et cetera devoluta.* Supplied from common form.
3   repeatedly *Donallus*; once *Danallus*
4   *rectorias*; *recte*: 'rectoriam'
5   *vicarias predictas*; *recte*: 'vicariam predictam'
6   *Cf.* above, note 2.
7   *illa et vicaria*; of uncertain reference; 'rectoria'?
8   'conferantur' does not occur here.

535   15 January 1516   *Reg. Lat.* 1339, fos 30ᵛ-32ʳ

To Gamaliel Cliston, canon of the church of York, and John Dolman and William Haringron, canons of the church of London, mandate in favour of Robert Hypping, layman, and Elisabeth Smyth, married couple of St Stephen's parish, London. A recent petition to the pope on the married couple's part stated that, at another time, after they had lawfully contracted marriage with one another *per verba de presenti* and had solemnized it in the face of the church and consummated it by connexion, and after they had remained in the said marriage, thus contracted, showing one other conjugal [affection][1], Godleua[2] Willa'd, woman, d. [Rochester][3] – falsely alleging that Robert had contracted marriage with her *per verba de presenti*[4] – sued Robert over this before Cuthbert[5] Cunstall', the auditor appointed to hear causes which, as was said, are moved from time to time in the court of Canterbury, by the archbishop of Canterbury, legate born of the apostolic see in those parts, and, as it was also said, a competent judge for this, praying *inter alia* that he be adjudged her husband; that Godleua, knowing that Robert and Elisabeth remained[6] in the marriage contracted between them, produced and caused to be examined false, perjured, corrupt, and unsuitable witnesses in the said case, while Elisabeth, whose prejudice and interest was considerably affected (*agebat(ur)*), was not summoned for this purpose; that Cuthbert, proceeding wrongly and in a null manner in the case, similarly without Elisabeth having been summoned for the purpose or cited, lawfully at least, but while she was absent (and not through contumacy), promulgated a null or unjust, definitive (as he said) sentence, by which *inter alia* he adjudged Robert to be Godleua's husband, from which Robert appealed to the apostolic see; that Cuthbert – after he had recklessly caused Robert, regardless of the appeal of which he was not ignorant and while Robert was still well within the time for prosecuting it, to be cited to argue before him why the said sentence should not be put into execution, and after both Robert (who had previously taken Elisabeth as his wife and was keeping her as his lawful wife) and Elisabeth had put forward before Cuthbert several lawful objections against, *inter alia*, the said witnesses and their statements, preventive of the execution of the said sentence, and after they had offered to prove the objections – decreed that his aforesaid sentence should be put into execution and appeal was therefore made to the apostolic [see][7] on the part of Elisabeth and perhaps Robert who felt *inter alia* unduly aggrieved thereby; and that Walter Stone, auditor of the said causes appointed, as was said, by the said archbishop, during Cuthbert's absence resuming the said case, as he said, again regardless of the appeal, by certain letters of his of a certain tenor recklessly warned and ordered Robert and Elisabeth, under pain of excommunication, that they were to obey the said sentence and that Robert was to solemnize marriage with Godleua in the face of the church, whence Robert and Elisabeth, feeling *inter alia* unduly aggrieved thereby, appealed again to the apostolic see. At the married couple's supplication to the pope to order that they and each one of them be absolved from the sentence of excommunication and other ecclesiastical sentences, censures and pains perhaps promulgated against them on the above occasion, and to commit to some upright men in those parts, even to men of a rank below bishops (to whom such causes have customarily been committed), the causes, with all their connected, annexed, and dependent matters: of the aforesaid appeals and of each one of them and of anything attempted and innovated after and against them; of the nullity of the said process and sentence and of each and every thing done in any way by Cuthbert and Walter and any other judges and persons to the married couple's prejudice in connection with the above; and of the whole principal matter, the pope [hereby] commands that the above three (or two or one of them), having summoned Godleua and others concerned, shall, on the pope's authority, for this once only, bestow on Robert and Elisabeth and on each one of them, if they so request, the benefit of absolution *ad cautelam* from the said sentence of excommunication and other sentences, censures, and pains, if and as it is just, having, however, first received from them suitable security in respect of that for which they are perhaps deemed bound by the said [sentence] of excommunication and other [sentences], censures and pains,[8] that if the above find that the said sentence of excommunication and the other sentences, censures, and pains were justly inflicted on them, they will obey the above's mandates and those of the church; as to the other things, having heard both sides, taking cognizance even of the principal matter, decree what is canonical, without appeal, causing [by ecclesiastical censure] what they have decreed to be [strictly] observed.[9] Notwithstanding the foregoing, etc.; and that the above are not of the class of persons to whom such cases have been customarily committed, etc. Given at Florence.

Humilibus et cetera.
Jo. Copis. | JoA: | JoA: xx: Nardinus

1   MS: *effectus*; *recte*: 'affectus'
2   or *Godlena*
3   MS: *Rossen.* (the '-ss-' both long); *recte*: 'Roffen.'
4   MS: *per similia verba*
5   MS: *Cutberto*; thereafter consistently *Gutbertus* (variously inflected)
6   reading *permanere*
7   MS wants 'sedem'

8   MS: *excommunicationis et aliis* [sententiis] *censuris et penis huiusmodi*
9   MS: *quod decreveritis et cetera observari*. Supplied from common form.

536   16 August 1515   *Reg. Lat.* 1339, fos 39ʳ-40ʳ

To the dean[1] and archdeacon of the church of Winchester and Andrew Ammonius[2], canon of the church of Salisbury, mandate in favour of John Sheff, cleric or layman, d. Canterbury. A recent petition to the pope on John's part stated that some time ago Margaret Tailer, woman, said d. – falsely alleging that the said John had lawfully contracted marriage with her *per verba de presenti* or otherwise and that he was therefore bound to marry her – sued him over this before Cuthbert Constal, the auditor appointed by the archbishop of Canterbury, legate born of the apostolic see in those parts, for hearing causes which are moved from time to time in the court of Canterbury, a competent judge for this, as she said; and that when Cuthbert was absent Walter Stone, auditor of the said causes also appointed, as she said, by the said archbishop – having resumed the cause and proceeding wrongly in it – firstly refused to admit several lawful [objections][3], which in law were bound to be admitted, against certain corrupt and false witnesses then expressed produced in the case on Margaret's part and against their testimony (*dicta*), although the [objections] had been put forward before him at a suitable time and place; and then, proceeding in a null manner to further matters, he promulgated a null or unjust, definitive (as he also said) sentence by which *inter alia* he adjudged John to be Margaret's husband, from which appeal was made on John's part to the apostolic see. At the supplication to the pope to command that he be absolved from the sentence of excommunication and other ecclesiastical sentences, censures, and pains perhaps promulgated against him on the above occasion and to commit to some upright men in those parts, even to men of a rank below bishops to whom such cases have customarily been committed, the causes, with the annexed, connected, and dependent matters: of the aforesaid [appeal][4] and of anything attempted and innovated after and against it; of the nullity of the said process and sentence and of each and every other thing done in any way by the said Cuthbert and Walter and any other judges and persons to John's prejudice[5]; and of the whole principal matter, the pope [hereby] commands that the above three (or two, or one of them), having summoned Margaret and others concerned, shall, on the pope's authority, for this once only, bestow on the said John, if he so requests, the benefit of absolution *ad cautelam* from the said sentence of excommunication and other sentences, censures, and pains, if and as it is just, having, however, first received from him suitable security in respect of that for which he is perhaps deemed bound by the said sentence of excommunication etc, that if they find that the said sentence of excommunication etc were justly inflicted on him, he will obey their mandates and those of the church; as to the other things, having heard both sides, taking cognizance even of the principal matter, decree what is canonical, without appeal, causing [by ecclesiastical censure] what they have decreed [to be strictly] observed.[6] Notwithstanding etc.; and that the above three are not of the class of persons to whom such causes have been customarily committed, etc. Given at Florence.[7]

Humilibus et cetera.
Lambertus[8] / *JoA:* / *JoA: xx: Nardinus*

1   *sic*: *decano et archidiacono Wintonien.* ...; perhaps the dean of Salisbury was intended but the intention was
     muddled by the draftsman or copyist; or possibly *decano* was written in error for 'priori'.
2   MS: *Am'onio*
3   MS: *cessiones*; *recte*: 'exceptiones'?
4   MS: *absolutionis*; *recte*: 'appellationis'
5   'circa premissa' does not occur
6   MS: *quod decreveritis et cetera observari*. Supplied from common form.
7   *sic*
8   *sic*: no initial

537   17 January 1516   *Reg. Lat.* 1339, fos 47ᵛ-48ᵛ

Union etc. Recently the pope was petitioned on the part of Robert Shorton',[1] MTheol,
rector of the parish church of Keteryng, d. Lincoln, to unite etc. the parish church of
Melford Longa,[2] d. Norwich, – for which Robert was recently presented, when it was
vacant *certo modo*, by its then patron, who was in peaceful quasi-possession of the
right of presenting a suitable person for it at a time of vacancy to the local ordinary
within the proper time – assuming he were to be instituted in Melford at this
presentation, to the above church of Keteryng, which he holds for as long as he does
so. At the supplication of Robert – who asserts that he also holds *inter alia* the
<perpetual>[3] vicarage of the parish church of Hoo, d. Rochester, by apostolic
dispensation; and that the annual value of the church of Melford does not exceed 20
pounds sterling – the pope hereby unites etc. the church of Melford, if Robert is
instituted in it as above, with all rights and appurtenances, to the church of Keteryng,
for as long as he holds the latter; to the effect that Robert may, on his own authority,
take and retain corporal possession of the church of Melford and the rights and
appurtenances aforesaid, for as long as he holds the church of Keteryng, and convert
its fruits etc. to his own uses and those of the churches of Keteryng and Melford,
without licence of the local diocesan or of anyone else. Notwithstanding etc. The
pope's will is, however, that the church of Melford shall not, on account of this union
etc., be defrauded of due services and the cure of souls in it shall not be neglected; but
that its customary burdens shall be supported; and that on Robert's death or his
resignation etc. of the church of Keteryng this union etc. shall be dissolved and be so
deemed and the church of Melford shall revert to its original condition automatically.
Given at Florence.

Ad futuram rei memoriam. Romanum decet pontificem et cetera.
.P. Lambertus. / *JoA:* / *JoA: xxxv: Nardinus*

1   the 'h' curiously formed; possibly 'c' written first and altered to 'h'
2   subsequently referred to simply as: Melford [also spelt *Malford*]
3   *perpetuam* inserted in margin, initialled *JoA*. This replaces a word – possibly *perpetuam* – miswritten in line,
     deleted, initialled *JoA*

538   16 February 1516   *Reg. Lat.* 1339, fos 48ᵛ-50ʳ

Union etc. At a petition on the part of Robert Brygth', LLD, rector of the parish church of St Peter, Nortampton', d. Lincoln, the pope hereby unites etc. the perpetual vicarage <of the parish church>¹ of St John in the Isle of Thanet (*Insula de Taneto*), d. Canterbury – for which at another time, when it was vacant *certo modo*, Robert was presented by the then abbot and convent of the monastery of St Augustine outside the walls of Canterbury (since the presentation of a suitable person for the said <vicarage>² at a time of vacancy pertains to the abbot for the time being and convent of the said monastery by ancient [approved and hitherto peacefully observed]³ custom) to the ordinary collator of it, within the proper time – if at this presentation Robert is canonically instituted <as perpetual vicar>⁴ [of the perpetual vicarage], whose annual value does not exceed 5 pounds 13 shillings and 4 pence sterling, with all rights and appurtenances, to the above church of St Peter, for as long as Robert holds the latter; to the effect that Robert may, on his own authority, in person or by proxy, take and retain corporal possession of <the vicarage>⁵ and the rights and appurtenances aforesaid, for as long as he holds the church of St Peter, and convert its fruits etc. to his own uses and those of the said <church of St Peter and the vicarage>⁶ without licence of the local diocesan or of anyone else. Notwithstanding etc. The pope's will is, however, that the said vicarage shall not, on account of this union etc., be defrauded of due services and the cure of souls in it shall not be neglected; but that customary burdens shall be supported; and that on Robert's death or his resignation etc. of the church of St Peter this union etc. shall be dissolved and so deemed and the said <vicarage>⁷ shall revert to its original condition automatically. Given at Careggi, d. Florence.

Ad futuram rei memoriam. Romanum decet pontificem et cetera.
.F.⁸ Benzon. / JoA: / . JoA: xxxv: Nardinus

1   Benefices (and related matter) corrected throughout the entry by order of the regent of chancery. The correction entails a sequence of fourteen deletions in the line with insertions in the margin. The tenor of the corrections is the same throughout; and therefore our usual form of summary has not been abandoned to reproduce all instances of correction. Corrections are, however, noted where they crop up naturally in the course of summarising. In the first instance of correction (which occurs close to the start of the narrative), *parrochialis ecclesia seu eius* has been deleted in the line (initialled *JoA*) directly before *perpetua vicaria*; with *parrochialis ecclesie* inserted in the margin, to come directly after *perpetua vicaria*. The insertion has *JoA* above it; *cassat(um) et correctu(m) de mandato D(omi)ni Regentis Nard(inus)* beneath. The script of the insertion differs both from the main body of the enregistered letter and from the explanatory magistral note in which it is sandwiched.

2   *ecclesiam Sancti Johannis* deleted in line (initialled *JoA*) with *vicariam* inserted in margin; *JoA* above insertion; *cassat(um) et correct(um) ut supra Nar* beneath. Scripts as note 1 above.

3   MS: *de antiqua et cetera consuetudine.* Supplied from common form.

4   *rectorem* deleted in line (initialled *JoA*) with *perpetuum vicarium* inserted in margin; *JoA* above insertion; *cassatu(m) et correctu(m) de man(da)to D(omi)ni Rege(n)tis Nardinus* beneath. Scripts as note 1 above.

5   *ecclesie Sancti Johannis* deleted in line with *vicarie* inserted in margin. Other details as note 2 above (save that MS here has *Nardi(nus)*, not *Nar*).

6   *ecclesiarum* deleted in line with *ecclesie Sancti Petri et vicarie* inserted in margin. Other details as note 2 above.

7   *ecclesia Sancti Johannis* deleted in line (initialled *JoA*) with *vicaria* inserted in margin; *JoA* above insertion; *cassat(um) et correctu(m) ut sup(ra) Nar.* beneath. Scripts as note 1 above.

8   *sic*; 'I' or 'J'?

539   14 March 1516   *Reg. Lat.* 1339, fos 60ᵛ-61ᵛ

To John Griffith', BDec,[1] treasurer of the church of St David's, dispensation. Some
time ago, Julius II by his letters dispensed him to receive and retain for life any two
benefices, etc. [as above, no. 6, to '... retain them together for life'],[2] as is more fully
contained in those letters.[3] The pope hereby further dispenses John, who, as he asserts,
holds by the said dispensation the treasurership of the church of St David's (which is
a dignity major *post pontificalem*) and the parish church of Burth'ofery, d. St David's
– at his supplication – to receive together with the above treasurership and parish
church, or with any two other incompatible benefices held by him at the time by virtue
of the said dispensation, any third benefice, etc. [as above, no. 6].[4]

Litterarum scientia, vite ac morum honestas ...
.P. Lambertus. / JoA: / JoA: Lxx: Nardi(nus)

1   MS: *bachalario in* [*the* deleted, but not initialled] *decretis* It looks, therefore, as if the scribe started to write
     theologia; but promptly realised his mistake.
2   Save for a few textual oddities which do not affect the tenor.
3   *Cf. CPL*, XIX, no. 1816.
4   as note 2 above

540   14 March 1516   *Reg. Lat.* 1339, fo 62ʳ⁻ᵛ

To John Wyot, perpetual vicar of the parish church of Wisbych', d. Ely. Indult for life
– at his supplication – to him – who, as he asserts, holds by apostolic dispensation[1] the
perpetual vicarage of the above parish [church][2] of Wisbych' and the parish church of
St Margaret, Cley next the Sea (*iuxta mare*), d. Norwich, and also the chantry of St
Leonard, d. York (to which, for as long as he holds it, the parish church of St Nicholas,
Ffoltwe'll, [d. Norwich], is united by apostolic authority) and [the mastership] of the
college of St Martin, Thomeston', d. [Norwich][3] – while attending a *studium generale*
or residing in the Roman curia or in any one of the aforesaid or other benefices he may
hold now or in the future, not to be bound to reside in other benefices held by him at
the time, nor to be liable to be compelled to do so by anyone against his will.
Notwithstanding etc. With the proviso that the vicarage and the churches of St
Margaret and St Nicholas and also the chantry [and mastership][4] and other benefices
in question shall not, on this account, be defrauded of due services; and that the cure
of souls in the vicarage and in the churches of St Margaret and St Nicholas and (if any)
in the chantry [and mastership][5] and other benefices aforesaid shall not be neglected;
but that the cure shall be exercised and things divine served by good and sufficient
vicars maintained from the proceeds of the parish churches; and that customary
burdens of the other benefices in question shall be supported.

Vite ac morum honestas ...
.P. Lambertus. / Jo.A.[6] */ JoA: xx: Nardinus*

1   *Cf. CPL* XVIII, no. 788.
2   'ecclesie' wanting here
3   MS is variously defective: *...Norwicen. necnon Sancti Leonardi cui quamdiu illam obtinueris parrochialis ecclesia Sancti Nicolai de Ffoltwe'll apostolica auctoritate unita existit ac (?)Migrantu(m) nuncupate collegii Sancti Martini de Thomeston' Eboracen. dioc(esium) cantarias ex dispensatione apostolica inter alia obtines* ... A corresponding petition has: ... *Johannes Wiot magister collegii sive cantarie Sancti Martini de Thomeston aut cantarius cantarie sive libere capelle Sancti Leonardi Eboracen. necnon ... Norwicen. ac ... Elien. diocesium (Reg. Suppl.* 1514, fo 167ᵛ). That is, the college is mistakenly located in d. York; but the mastership is not corrupted into a place name. The petition, which is for an indult for non-residence, is dated 14 March 1516.
4   MS: *cantarie*. The emendations incorporated in the summary are purely editorial and do not imply the existence of a correct text. If the enregistered copy is true the engrossment was equally defective.
5   MS: *cantoriis* [!]; *see above*, note 4
6   *sic*; usually *JoA.*; sometimes *JoA.*

541   5 January 1516   *Reg. Lat.* 1339, fos 75ᵛ-77ʳ

To the abbot of the monastery of Bury St Edmunds (*de Burgo Sancti Edmundi*) and the priors of the priories[1] of Thetfordi and Kyklyno', d. Norwich, mandate in favour of Thomas Balkey, cleric or layman, city or d. Norwich, executor of the testament or last will of the late John Walters, inhabitant of the said city. A recent petition to the pope on Thomas' part stated that although in the said testament or last will Thomas was appointed its executor, John Butler[2], cleric or layman, and Elisabeth Welters, woman, said d., joint parties in this regard – falsely asserting that in another testament or last will of the said John they were appointed its executors and that the testament or last will in which the joint parties had been given as executors, not the testament or last will in which Thomas had been appointed its executor, was the valid one – nevertheless sued Thomas over this, not by apostolic delegation, before the then official of Norwich, who was, it was said, a competent judge for this; that the said official, proceeding in a null manner and wrongly in the case, promulgated a certain null or unjust sentence [by][3] which *inter alia* he declared that the testament or last will of the said John in which the joint parties had been appointed its executors was the valid one and he committed the administration of the late John's goods to the said joint parties; that Thomas appealed from this sentence to the archbishop of Canterbury, legate born of the apostolic see in those parts, within the bounds of which legation the said parties lay, and he caused the joint parties to be summoned to trial in the cause of the appeal before Cuthbert Tunscall', one of the auditors appointed by the said archbishop of matters and of causes devolved from time to time to the said archbishop legate; that after Cuthbert the auditor had proceeded to several acts in the case of the appeal, Walter Stone, another of the said auditors, reassuming (*reassumens*) the case of the appeal and proceeding wrongly in it, promulgated a null or unjust sentence by [which][4] he declared that he was a competent judge in the said case, and also condemned Thomas in the expenses run up in the said case, taxed them at a certain very excessive sum, then expressed, and warned and ordered Thomas, under sentence of excommunication and other ecclesiastical sentences, censures, and pains, to pay them to the joint parties within a certain time then expressed; and that appeal was therefore made to the apostolic see on the part of Thomas, who felt *inter alia* thereby unduly aggrieved. At the supplication to the pope to order that Thomas be absolved from the said sentence of excommunication and other sentences, censures, and pains perhaps promulgated against him on the above occasion, and to commit to some upright men in those parts the causes, with annexed and dependent matters: of the aforesaid last appeal and of anything attempted and innovated [after][5] and against it; of the nullity of the said processes and sentences and of each and every other thing done in any way by the official and judges aforesaid and by any other judges and person[s] to Thomas' prejudice in connection with the above; and of the whole principal matter, the pope [hereby] commands that the above three (or two or one of them), having summoned the joint parties and others concerned,[6] shall bestow on Thomas,[7] if he so requests, the benefit of absolution *ad cautelam* from the said sentence of excommunication and other sentences, censures, and pains, if and as it is just, having, however, first received from him suitable security in respect of that for which he is deemed excommunicate and bound by the said other sentences and censures that if they find that the sentence of excommunication and other sentences, censures, and pains were justly inflicted on him he will obey their mandates and those of the church; as to the other things, having summoned the joint parties and others concerned[8] and having heard both sides, taking cognizance even of the principal matter, decree what is just,[9] causing by ecclesiastical censure what they have decreed to be strictly observed.[10] Notwithstanding etc. Given at Florence.

Humilibus et cetera.
.Jo. Copis. / JoA: / JoA: xvj: Nardinus

1   *sic* (MS: *prioratuum prioribus*); the stilus required 'priors of the monasteries customarily governed by priors'
2   or *Boeler*
3   MS: *preter*; *recte*: 'per'
4   MS: *suam*; *recte*: ' quam'
5   MS: *per se*; *recte*: 'post'
6   MS: *vocatis dictis adherentibus et aliis qui fuerint evocandi*; *see below*, note 8.
7   Oddly, 'auctoritate nostra' and 'hac vice dumtaxat', which we would expect at this point, do not occur.
8   MS: *vocatis dictis adherentibus et aliis qui fuerint evocandi*; the repetition of the 'vocatis' clause at this point is unusual; *see* note 6 above.
9   'appellatione remota' does not occur.
10   MS: ... *observari. Testes* [deleted and initialled *JoA*]. *Non obstantibus* ... That is, the start of the clause 'and moreover compel witnesses ...' (usually abbreviated in the register as 'Testes (autem) et cetera'), which we would expect here, has been struck out.

542   29 December 1515   *Reg. Lat.* 1339, fos 80ʳ-81ʳ

To Robert Belay, rector, called master, of the hospital of St Bartholomew in Westsmy'thfelde in the suburbs of London,[1] OSA, d. London[2] (who, as he asserts, holds the above hospital, usually assigned in title of a perpetual ecclesiastical benefice, and is expressly professed of the above order).[3] Dispensation – at his supplication – to receive together with the above hospital, two, and without them, any three other benefices, [with][4] or without cure, regular, of the aforesaid or any other order [even] the Cluniac or Cistercian, or with one of them or without them, any two secular benefices, even if the regular benefices should be priories, *prepositure, prepositatus*, dignities, *personatus*, administrations or offices, and the secular should be parish churches or their perpetual vicarages, or chantries, free chapels, hospitals or annual services, usually assigned to secular clerics in title of a perpetual ecclesiastical benefice, and [even if] the secular as well as the regular benefices should be of his patronage by reason of his own person or of the said hospital, or be of the patronage of any other ecclesiastical or secular persons, and of whatsoever tax or annual value, and [should pertain][5] to his collation, provision, presentation or any other disposition in any way at the time, and [even if] the priories etc. should be customarily elective and have cure of souls, if he obtains them otherwise canonically, and retain whichever one of the regular benefices he chooses, even if it should be a priory, *prepositura* or other conventual dignity or claustral office, *in titulum* and the other two regular benefices or the secular benefices *in commendam*, for life, to resign them, at once or successively, simply or for exchange, as often as he pleases, and cede the commend and in their place receive up to three other, similar or dissimilar, benefices, with or without cure, regular, of the aforesaid order of St Augustine or any other order, even the Cluniac or Cistercian, or with one of them, or without them, two secular benefices, and to retain whichever one of the regular benefices he chooses *in titulum* and the other two, which may not however be conventual or claustral, or the secular benefices *in commendam*, for life, as above; he may – due and customary burdens of the benefices retained *in commendam* having been supported – make disposition of the rest of their fruits etc. just as those holding them *in titulum* could and ought to do, alienation [of immovable goods and precious movables][6] being however forbidden. Notwithstanding etc. With the proviso that the benefices retained *in commendam* shall not, on this account, be defrauded of due services and the cure of souls in them (if any) shall not be neglected; but that their aforesaid burdens shall be supported. Given at Florence.

Relligionis[7] zelus, vite ac morum honestas …
.P. Lambertus. / JoA: / JoA: C: Nardi(nus): –

1   *in suburbiis Rondonien.* (thus in the address clause; and also (occurring once) in the body of the letter); *cf.* note 2.
2   *Londonien. diocesis* (thus in the address clause; and also (occurring once) in the body of the letter; *cf.* note 1.
3   The latter information comes from a notwithstanding clause.
4   'cum' wanting
5   *pro tuo aut*; *recte*: 'pertineant' ?
6   MS: *alienatione t(am)en et cetera.* Supplied from common form.
7   *sic*

543   9 January 1516   *Reg. Lat.* 1339, fos 85ᵛ-86ʳ

To John Maxe, abbot of the monastery of St Martial, Newsom *alias* Newhowse, OPrem, d. Lincoln. Dispensation – at his supplication – to receive together with St Martial's, over which he presides, or with another monastery over which he may

perhaps preside in the future or a priory of the said order which he may hold, any
benefice, with or without cure, secular or regular of the aforesaid or any other order,
even if the secular benefice should be a parish church or its perpetual vicarage, or a
chantry, free chapel, hospital or annual service, usually assigned to secular clerics in
title of a perpetual ecclesiastical benefice, and the regular should be a priory,
prepositura, prepositatus, dignity (even conventual), *personatus*, administration or
office (even claustral) and even if the [regular or secular][1] benefice should be of lay
patronage and of whatsoever tax or annual value, even if the priory etc. should be
customarily elective and have cure of souls, if he obtains it otherwise canonically, and
retain it *in commendam* for life; and resign it[2] as often as he pleases and cede the
commend and in its place receive another, similar or dissimilar, benefice, with or
without cure, secular or regular of the Premonstratensian order aforesaid or any other
order, and retain it *in commendam* for life, even together with St Martial's or with
another monastery over which he may perhaps preside or a priory which he may hold,
as above; he may – due and customary burdens of the benefice in question having been
supported – make disposition of the rest of its fruits etc. just as those holding it *in
titulum* at the time could and ought to do, alienation [of immovable goods and precious
movables][3] being however forbidden. Notwithstanding etc. With the proviso that the
benefice shall not, on this account, be defrauded of due services and the cure of souls
in it shall not be neglected; but that its aforesaid burdens shall be supported. Given at
Florence.

*Personam tuam nobis et apostolice sedi devotam tuis exigentibus meritis paterna
benevolentia prosequentes …*
.P. Lambertus. / JoA: / JoA: L: Nardinus

1   MS: *regulare vero prioratus … illudque aut regulare beneficium*; 'illud' here has to refer to 'regulare' and
     the final 'regulare' has to be an error for 'seculare'.
2   *illa*; *recte*: 'illud'
3   MS: *alienatione tamen et cetera*. Supplied from common form.

544   16 March 1516   *Reg. Lat.* 1339, fo 87[r-v]

To John Wilkyrrson', canon of the monastery of St Nicholas, Drakys [also spelt *Dakys*]
alias Drax, OSA, d. York. Dispensation – at his supplication – to him, who, as he
asserts, is expressly professed of the above order,[1] to receive and retain any benefice,
with or without cure, usually held by secular clerics, etc [as above, no. 43].

Relligionis[2] zelus, vite ac morum honestas …
.P. Lambertus / JoA: / JoA: xxx: Nardinus

1   This information comes from a notwithstanding clause.
2   *sic*

545   16 February 1516   *Reg. Lat.* 1339, fos 97ᵛ-98ᵛ

Union etc. At a recent petition on the part of Robert Leyf, rector of the parish church of Isenhamsted Cheyny [subsequently referred to simply as *Isenhamsted* (also spelt *Ise(nhamste)d*,[1] *Isenamsted)*], d. Lincoln, the pope hereby unites etc. the parish church of Tyngreyth'[2] [also spelt *Tyngreyth, Teyngreyth', Tyngreyt, Tingreyth'*], d. Lincoln – which is of lay patronage; and for which at another time, when it was vacant *certo modo*, Robert was presented by its then patron, who was in peaceful quasi-possession of the right of presenting a suitable person for the said church at a time of vacancy to the ordinary collator of it, within the lawful time – assuming Robert is instituted as rector at this presentation, and also the parish church of Broughton'[3] [also spelt *Brougthon', Bro'gtohon', Bro'gton', Brongton', Brougton'*], d. Lincoln, (the annual value of the said church of Tyngreyth' not exceeding 3 pounds, and of Broughton', 5 pounds 6 shillings and 8 pence), with all rights and appurtenances, to the church of Isenhamsted, which Robert holds together with the said church of Broughton' by apostolic dispensation, for as long as he holds Isenhamsted, to the effect that Robert may, on his own authority, in person or by proxy, continue in corporal possession of the church of Broughton', or take corporal possession of that church and of the church of Tyngreyth' (after he has been instituted as rector of the latter), and retain possession for as long as he holds Isenhamsted, and convert its fruits etc. to his own uses and those of the said churches without licence of the local diocesan or of anyone else. Notwithstanding etc. The pope's will is, however, that the said churches of Tyngreyth' and Broughton' shall not, on account of this union etc., be defrauded of due services and the cure of souls in them shall not be neglected; but that their aforesaid burdens[4] shall be supported; and that on Robert's death or his resignation etc. of the church of Isenhamsted this union etc. shall be dissolved and be so deemed and the said churches of Tyngreyth' and Broughton' shall revert to their original condition and be deemed vacant automatically. Given at Careggi, d. Florence.

Ad futuram rei memoriam. Romanum decet pontificem et cetera.
.P. Lambertus. / JoA: / JoA. xxxx: Nardi(nus): –

1   written *Ise.* ᵈ.
2   The third occurrence of this spelling was originally written (?)*Toyn-*; the (?)*o* then deleted.
3   originally written (?)*Broou-*; the second (?)*o* then deleted. Here and elsewhere 'u' readable as 'n'.
4   *onera antedicta*; *recte*: 'onera consueta' (since no mention of 'burdens' had been made in the preceding text)

546   9 January 1516   *Reg. Lat.* 1339, fos 109ʳ-110ʳ

To Edward Carminowe, rector of the parish church of Thorneby, d. Exeter. Dispensation and indult etc. [as above, no. 2]. Given at Florence.

Vite ac morum honestas …
.P. Lambertus / JoA: / JoA: Lx: Nardinus

547   9 January 1516   *Reg. Lat.* 1339, fos 111ʳ-112ʳ

To William Capol, BTheol, perpetual vicar of the parish church of Barckwey,[1] d. London. Dispensation and indult etc. [as above, no. 2]. Given at Florence.

Litterarum scientia, vite ac morum honestas …
.P. Lambertus / JoA: / JoA: Lx: Nardinus

1   The second occurrence has the 'w' written over a (second) 'k'.

548   9 January 1516   *Reg. Lat.* 1339, fos 112ʳ-113ʳ

To Richard Robynson, rector of the parish church of St John the Evangelist in Ffrydaystrete, London, d. <London>.[1] Dispensation and indult etc. [as above, no. 2].[2] Given at Florence.

Vite ac morum honestas …
.P. Lambertus / JoA. / JoA: Lx: Nardinus

1   *Londonien.'* inserted by the scribe in the margin; *Londonien.' Londonien.' diocesis* occurs without alteration in the text a few lines below.
2   Save that 'for life' ('quamdiu vixeris' or suchlike) is not repeated in the context of the indult.

549   9 January 1516   *Reg. Lat.* 1339, fos 113ʳ-114ʳ

To Nicholas Townley, perpetual vicar of the parish church of Strotford, d. London. Dispensation and indult etc. [as above, no. 2]. Given at Florence.

Vite ac morum honestas …
.P. Lambertus / JoA: / :JoA: Lx: Nardinus

550   9 January 1516   *Reg. Lat.* 1339, fos 118ʳ-119ʳ

To William Marshall' *alias* Baker, scholar, d. Coventry and Lichfield. Dispensation and indult – at his supplication – to him, who, as he asserts, is less than nineteen but [more][1] than fourteen years and desires to become a cleric, to receive – after he has been duly marked with clerical character and has reached his [nineteenth][2] year of age – one benefice, and together with it – after he has reached his twentieth year – another, and without them, any two other benefices, etc. [as above, no. 2, to '… as often as he pleases'], and in their place receive up to two incompatible benefices, viz.: one in his nineteenth year and the other one in his twentieth, and retain them together for life, as above; and, for life, while attending a *studium generale*, or residing in the Roman curia or one of his benefices, not to be bound to reside in his other benefices, nor to be liable to be compelled to do so against his will. Notwithstanding the above defect of age which he will suffer even in his nineteenth and twentieth years, etc. With the proviso that the incompatible and other benefices in question shall not, on this account, be defrauded of due services and the cure of souls in them ([if] any) shall not be neglected; but that customary burdens of those benefices in which he shall not reside shall be supported. Given at Florence.

Vite ac morum honestas …
.P. lambertus. / JoA: / JoA: Lxxxx: Nardinus

1   'maior' wanting
2   MS: *decimum unum*; i.e. 'nonum' wanting after *decimum*. (Elsewhere written in Roman numerals: *xviiij*.)

551   9 January 1516   *Reg. Lat.* 1339, fos 119ʳ-120ʳ

Union etc. At a recent petition on the part of Richard Carlyord, canon of the church of Glaysney, d. Exeter, the pope hereby unites etc. the perpetual vicarage of the parish church of Stratton [also spelt *Stratton'*], of the said diocese,[1] (whose annual value does not exceed 11 pounds sterling), with all rights and appurtenances, to the canonry and prebend of the said church of Glaysney (to which the parish church of Lansalose and also the perpetual vicarage of the parish church of Glyvmaco, d. Exeter, are united etc. by apostolic authority, for as long as Richard holds the canonry and prebend), which he holds together with the said vicarage of Stratton, likewise for as long as he holds the canonry and prebend, to the effect that Richard may, on his own authority, in person or by proxy, continue in, or take anew, and retain corporal possession of the vicarage of Stratton and the rights and appurtenances aforesaid, for as long as he holds the canonry and prebend, and convert its fruits etc. to his own uses and those of the canonry and prebend and of the vicarage of Stratton without licence of the local diocesan or of anyone else. Notwithstanding etc. and [notwithstanding] the oath to reside in the vicarage of Stratton taken by Richard on acquisition of it, which the pope relaxes in this regard. The pope's will is, however, that the vicarage of Stratton shall not, on account of this union etc., be defrauded of due services and the cure of souls in it shall not be neglected; but that its customary burdens shall be supported; and that on Richard's death or his resignation etc. of the canonry and prebend this union etc. shall be dissolved and so deemed and the vicarage of Stratton shall revert to its original condition automatically. Given at Florence.

Ad futuram rei memoriam. Romanum decet pontificem et cetera provideri.
.P. Lambertus / JoA: / :JoA: xxxx: Nardinus

1   MS: *Stratton cuius dicte diocesis …*; *recte*: 'eiusdem diocesis'?

552   9 January 1516   *Reg. Lat.* 1339, fos 120ᵛ-121ʳ

To Alexander Howers, scholar, d. Lincoln. Dispensation – at his supplication – to him – who, as he asserts, is less than eighteen[1] but more than fourteen years,[2] and desires to become a cleric – to receive and retain – after he has been duly marked with clerical character and reached his eighteenth year of age – any benefice, with cure or otherwise incompatible, even if a parish church or its perpetual vicarage, or a chantry, free chapel, hospital or annual service, usually assigned to secular clerics in title of a perpetual ecclesiastical benefice, or a dignity, *personatus*, administration or office in a cathedral, even metropolitan, or collegiate church, even if the dignity in question should be major *post pontificalem* in a cathedral, even metropolitan, church, or principal in a collegiate church, and even if the dignity etc. should be customarily elective and have cure of souls, if he obtains it otherwise canonically, to resign it, simply or for exchange, when he pleases, and in its place receive and retain another benefice with cure or otherwise incompatible. With indult for life, while attending a *studium generale* or residing in the Roman curia or any one of his benefices, not to be bound to reside in his other benefices, nor to be liable to be compelled to do so by anyone against his will. Notwithstanding the above defect of age (which as regards holding the said incompatible benefice he will suffer even in his eighteenth year), etc. With the proviso that the incompatible benefice and other benefices in question shall not, on this account, be defrauded of due services and the cure of souls in them ([if] any) shall not be neglected; but that customary burdens of those benefices in which he shall not reside shall be supported. Given at Florence.

Vite ac morum honestas ...
.P. Lambertus. / JoA: / :JoA: xxx: Nardinus

1   MS: *xviij*
2   MS: *xv xv* deleted (but not initialled); followed by *xiiij*

553   17 January 1516[1]   *Reg. Lat.* 1339, fos 121ᵛ-122ʳ

To Richard Cheppard, perpetual vicar of the parish church of Charryng [also spelt *Charrynd*], d. Canterbury. Dispensation and indult etc. [as above, no. 2]. Given at Florence.

Vite ac morum honestas ...
.P. Lambertus / JoA: / JoA: Lx: Nar(dinus)

1   Date altered from 22 December 1515 to 17 January 1516. In MS: *Millesimo quingentesimo quinto decimo* is followed by *Undecimo Kalendas Januarii anno Tercio* deleted and then *sestodecimo Kalendas februarii anno Tercio;* the deletion is initialled *JoA*

554   17 January 1516   *Reg. Lat.* 1339, fos 122ᵛ-123ᵛ

Union etc. At a recent petition on the part of John Mogriche, BDec, canon of the church, called chapel royal, of B. Mary, Strafford, d. Coventry and Lichfield, the pope hereby unites etc. the parish church of Wigginton' [also spelt *Wingginton'*, *Wington*,[1] *Wigginton*, *Wiggi'ton*], d. Lincoln, (whose annual value does not exceed 8 pounds 13 shillings and 8 pence sterling), with all rights and appurtenances, to the canonry and prebend of Swenam *alias* Wichenhm'[2] of the above church of B. Mary, which John holds together with the parish church of Wigginton', for as long as he holds the canonry and prebend, to the effect that John may, on his own authority, in person or by proxy, take, or continue in, and retain corporal possession of the church of Wigginton' and the rights and appurtenances aforesaid, for as long as he holds the canonry and prebend, and convert its fruits etc. to his own uses and those of the canonry and prebend and the church of Wigginton' without licence of the local diocesan or of anyone else. Notwithstanding etc. The pope's will is, however, that the church of Wigginton' shall not, on account of this union etc., be defrauded of due services and the cure of souls in it shall not be neglected; but that its customary burdens shall be supported; and that on John's death or his resignation etc. of the canonry and prebend this union etc. shall be dissolved and be so deemed and the church of Wigginton' shall revert to its original condition automatically. Given at Florence.

Ad futuram rei memoriam. Romanum decet pontificem et cetera provideri.
.P. lambertus / JoA: / . JoA: xxxv Nardinus

1   this spelling spread over two lines: *Win | gton*
2   wavy bar over the 'm'

555   9 January 1516   *Reg. Lat.* 1339, fos 123ᵛ-124ᵛ

To Robert Thornton, abbot of the monastery, called house, of B. Mary, Jervaulx (*de Jerovalle*)[1], OCist, d. York. Dispensation – at his supplication – to receive and retain *in commendam* for life, together with the above monastery, over which he presides, or with another Cistercian monastery, over which he might preside in the future, any benefice, with or without cure, secular or regular of the above or any other order, even if the secular benefice should be a parish church or its perpetual vicarage, or a chantry, free chapel, hospital or annual service, usually assigned to secular clerics in title of a perpetual ecclesiastical benefice, and [even if] the regular benefice should be a priory, *prepositura*, *prepositatus*, dignity, *personatus*, administration or office, and [even if] the regular or secular benefice should be of abbot Robert's patronage by reason of his own person as well as of the said monastery, or of the patronage of any other persons, ecclesiastical or secular[2], and of whatsoever tax or annual value, and [even if] the priory etc. should be customarily elective and have cure of souls, if he obtains it otherwise canonically, to resign it, as often as he pleases and cede the commend and in its place receive another, similar or dissimilar, benefice, with or without cure, secular or regular of the above Cistercian order, or of any other, and – provided that the regular benefice in question be not conventual or claustral – retain it *in commendam* for life, even together with the above monastery of B. Mary, or another over which he might preside as above; he may – due and customary burdens of the benefice in question having been supported – make disposition of the rest of its fruits etc. just as those holding it *in titulum* could and ought to do, alienation [of immovable goods and precious movables being][3] however [forbidden].[3] Notwithstanding etc. With the proviso that the benefice in question shall not, on this account, be defrauded of due services and the cure of souls in it shall not be neglected; but that the aforesaid burdens shall be supported. Given at Florence.

Personam tuam et cetera prosequen(tes) illa tibi et cetera oportuna.
.P. Lambertus. / JoA: / JoA: L: Nardinus

1   In the first occurrence, the 'J' is written over *G*
2   MS: *secularium. Cf.* below, nos. 569, 700 and 719.
3   MS: *alienatione tamen et cetera.* Supplied from common form.

556   22 December 1515   *Reg. Lat.* 1339, fo 140[r-v]

To Henry Myime, MA, rector of the parish church of Hadstocke [also spelt *Hadstochke*], d. London. Dispensation and indult etc. [as above, no. 2]. Given at Florence.

Litterarum scientia, vite ac morum honestas ...
.P. Lambertus- / JoA: / JoA: Lx: Nardinus

557   22 December 1515   *Reg. Lat.* 1339, fo 149[r-v]

To John Pontre, BTheol, rector of the parish church of Sonth'morton' [also spelt (?)*South'morton'*][1] d. Salisbury. Dispensation and indult etc. [as above, no. 2]. Given at Florence.

Litterarum scientia, vite ac morum honestas ...
.P. Lambertus. / JoA: / JoA: Lx: Nardi(nus)

1   The second occurrence equally readable as *Sonth'morton'*. Both occurrences have a bar over the 'th' and over the final 'n'.

558   22 December 1515   *Reg. Lat.* 1339, fo 150^{r-v}

To John Blamyre, rector of the parish church of Wytley, d. Worcester. Dispensation etc. [as above, no. 161]. Given at Florence.

Vite ac morum honestas …
.P. Lambertus / JoA: / JoA: L: Nardi(nus)

559   22 December 1515   *Reg. Lat.* 1339, fo 151^{r-v}

To Thomas Grene, perpetual vicar of the parish church of Nevntonluyll', d. Lincoln (who, as he asserts, is a BA). Dispensation and indult etc. [as above, no. 2]. Given at Florence.

Vite ac morum honestas …
.P. Lambertus / JoA: / JoA: Lx: Nardi(nus)

560   29 December 1515[1]   *Reg. Lat.* 1339, fos 152^{r}-153^{r}

To Walter Sonthcott, BDec, rector of the parish church of Brydfford, d. Exeter. Dispensation and indult etc. [as above, no. 2]. Given at Florence.

Litterarum scientia, vite ac morum honestas …
.P. La(m)bertus / JoA: / JoA: Lx Nardinus

1   Dating clause exhibits same features as no. 562 below, *q.v.*

561   29 December 1515[1]   *Reg. Lat.* 1339, fos 153^{r}-154^{r}

To Richard Gone, rector of the parish church of St Michael the Archangel, near the southern gate of the vill of Oxford (*Oxon'*), d. Lincoln. Dispensation and indult etc. [as above, no. 2]. Given at Florence.

Vite ac morum honestas …
.P. Lambertus / JoA: / JoA: Lx: Nardinus

1   Dating clause exhibits same features as no. 562 below, *q.v.*

562   29 December 1515[1]   *Reg. Lat.* 1339, fos 154ʳ-155ʳ

To Edward Lye, rector of the parish church of Bollas, d. Coventry and Lichfield. Dispensation and indult etc. [as above, no. 2]. Given at Florence.

Vite ac morum honestas ...
.P. Lambertus / JoA: / JoA: Lx: Nardinus

1   Differences of ink suggest date was entered later: the ink of *Dat'* matches body of letter; that of *Florentie ... anno Tertio* is different.

563   22 December 1515   *Reg. Lat.* 1339, fo 155ᵛ

To Nicholas Rodoke, professor OFM. Dispensation – at his supplication – to receive and retain any benefice, with or without cure, usually held by secular clerics, etc. [as above, no. 43, to '... Notwithstanding etc.'] and [notwithstanding] the constitutions etc. of Otto and Ottobuono formerly legates of the apostolic see in the kingdom of England etc.[1] Given at Florence.

Relligionis[2] *zelus, vite ac morum honestas ...*
.P. Lambertus. / JoA: / JoA: xxxx: Nardinus

1   The inclusion of these constitutions gives Rodoke the option of holding his secular benefice in England.
2   *sic*

564   22 December 1515   *Reg. Lat.* 1339, fo 156ʳ⁻ᵛ

To Richard Bochyng, monk of the monastery, called house or priory, of B. Mary the Virgin, Thedford [also spelt *Tedford*], OSB, d. Norwich. Dispensation – at his supplication – to him, who, as he asserts, is expressly professed of the above order,[1] to receive and retain any benefice, with or without cure, usually held by secular clerics, etc. [as above, no. 43]. Given at Florence.

Relligionis[2] *zelus, vite ac morum honestas ...*
.P. Lambertus / JoA: / JoA: xxx: Nardinus

1   This information comes from a notwithstanding clause.
2   *sic*

565   29 December 1515   *Reg. Lat.* 1339, fos 156^v-157^v

Union etc. At a recent petition on the part of Thomas Halle, perpetual vicar of the
parish church of Halbarton', d. Worcester, the pope hereby unites etc. the parish church
of St Michael the Archangel, Bristol (*Bristollie*), d. Worcester, (whose annual value
does not exceed 4^1 pounds sterling), with all rights and appurtenances, to the perpetual
vicarage of the above church of Halbarton', which Thomas holds together with St
Michael's by apostolic dispensation, for as long as he holds the vicarage, to the effect
that Thomas may, on his own authority, in person or by proxy, continue in, or take
anew, and retain corporal possession of St Michael's and the rights and appurtenances
aforesaid, for as long as he holds the vicarage, and convert its fruits etc. to his own uses
and those of the vicarage and of St Michael's without licence of the local diocesan or
of anyone else. Notwithstanding etc. The pope's will is, however, that the above church
of St Michael shall not, on account of this union etc., be defrauded of due services and
the cure of souls in it shall not be neglected; but that its customary burdens shall be
supported, and that on Thomas's death or his resignation etc. of the vicarage this union
etc. shall be dissolved and be so deemed and St Michael's shall revert to its original
condition automatically. Given at Florence.

Ad futuram rei memoriam. Romanum decet pontificem votis illis gratum prestare
assensum ...
.P. de Castello.^{2} / *JoA:* / *JoA: xxxx: Nardinus*

1   *viginti* deleted (initialled *JoA*) immediately before *quatuor*
2   *P. Lambertus.* deleted (not initialled)

566   2 November 1515   *Reg. Lat.* 1339, fos 157^v-159^r

Union etc. At a recent petition on the part of William Poxwel, rector of the parish
church of Child Okeford (North),^{1} d. Salisbury, the pope hereby unites etc. the parish
church of Ffised Newell', d. Salisbury – annual value not exceeding 26 shillings and 8
pence sterling – and the parish church of Child Okford (South), d. Salisbury – annual
value not exceeding 4 pounds sterling – (which is of lay patronage; and for which,
when it was vacant *certo modo*, William was lawfully presented by its then patron, who
was in peaceful quasi-possession of the right of presenting a suitable person for it at a
time of vacancy to the local ordinary within the lawful time), assuming William is
instituted as its rector at this presentation, to the first said church of Child [i.e. Child
Okeford (North)], which he holds together with Ffised Newell' by apostolic
dispensation, for as long as he holds the first said church of Child, to the effect that
William may, on his own authority, in person or by proxy, continue in, or take anew,
and retain corporal possession of the second and third of the said churches [i.e. Ffised
Newell and Child Okford (South)] and the rights and appurtenances aforesaid, for as
long as he holds the first said church, and convert their fruits etc. to his own uses and
those of the said churches^2 without licence of the local diocesan or of anyone else.

Notwithstanding etc. The pope's will is, however, that the said churches [i.e. Ffised Newell' and Child Okford (South)] united to the aforesaid church [i.e. Child Okeford (North)] shall not, on account of this union etc., be defrauded of due services and the cure of souls in them shall not be neglected, but that their customary burdens shall be supported; and that on William's death or his resignation etc. of the said first church [i.e. Child Okeford (North)] this union etc. shall be dissolved and be so deemed and the united churches shall revert to their original condition automatically. Given at Viterbo.

Ad futuram rei memoriam. Romanum decet pontificem votis illis gratum prestare et cetera provideri.
.P. Lambert(us) / JoA: / JoA: xxxx: Nardinus

1   MS: *parrochialis ecclesie de Child Okeford partis borealis*; and below: ... *Ffised Newell' ac ... etiam de Child Okford partis australis ... parrochiales ecclesie*
2   *dictarum ecclesiarum* – i.e. of all three churches. The church of Childe Okeford was divided into two moieties (each a rectory). Though the letter talks of three churches the reality was two churches (i.e. Childe Okeford and Fifehead Neville) but three benefices.

567   19 October 1515   *Reg. Lat.* 1339, fos 159ʳ-160ᵛ

To William, abbot of the monastery of B. Mary, Oseney, at Oxford (*iuxta Oxoniam*), OSA, d. Lincoln, extension etc. Some time ago – after Julius II by certain letters of his[1] had dispensed abbot William to receive and retain *in commendam* for life, together with the above monastery over which he was then presiding (or with another over which he might preside in the future), one, and without them, any two other benefices, with or without cure, regular, of the aforesaid or any other order, or secular, even if the regular benefices should be priories, *prepositure*, *prepositatus*, dignities, *personatus*, administrations or offices, and the secular benefices be parish churches or their perpetual vicarages, or chantries, free chapels, hospitals or annual services, [usually][2] assigned to secular clerics in title of a perpetual ecclesiastical benefice, and [even if] of his patronage, by reason of his own person as well as of the monastery in question, or of the patronage of any other ecclesiastic or lay persons, and of whatsoever tax or annual value, and [even if] the priories etc. should be customarily elective and have cure of souls, and should pertain to his collation, provision or presentation, if he obtained them otherwise canonically,[3] to resign them, at once or successively, as often as he pleased, and cede the commend, and in their place receive up to two other, similar or dissimilar, benefices, with or without cure, regular, of the aforesaid or any other order, or secular, and (provided that the regular benefices in question be not conventual dignities or claustral offices) retain them *in commendam* for life, as above – the pope by other letters of his dispensed abbot William to receive and retain *in commendam* for life, together with the above monastery, over which he was understood to be still then presiding and with another over which he might then be presiding, or with any two other benefices held by him at the time by virtue of the said dispensation, any third benefice, secular, with or without cure, even if a parish church or its perpetual vicarage, or a chantry, free chapel, hospital or annual service, usually assigned to secular clerics in title of a perpetual ecclesiastical benefice, and of lay patronage and of whatsoever tax or annual value, if he obtained it otherwise canonically, to resign it, as often as he pleased, and cede the commend, and in its place receive another, similar or dissimilar, secular benefice with or without cure – provided that of three such benefices not more than two be parish churches or their perpetual vicarages – and retain it *in commendam* for life as above, as is more fully contained in the said letters.[4] At abbot William's supplication the pope hereby extends and amplifies his dispensation and letters with the cedable commend and every one of the clauses contained in them to the end that abbot William may retain the third benefice (for which he is dispensed as above) *in commendam* for life – even if it is of his patronage by reason of his own person as well as of the monastery in question, or of the patronage of any other ecclesiastic or lay persons; and pertains to his collation, provision, presentation or any other disposition; otherwise in accordance with the tenor of the pope's said letters. Notwithstanding etc. Given at Toscanella.

Personam tuam nobis et apostolice sedi devotam tuis exigen(tibus) meritis paterna benivolentia prosequen(tes) illa tibi favorabiliter concedimus ...
.P. Lambertus / JoA. / :JoA: xx: Nardi(nus)

1   unknown to the *CPL*; possibly entered in a Julius register now lost and overlooked by the compilers of the eighteenth century indices
2   'solita' wanting
3   *si tibi alias canonice conferentur* inserted in margin, initialled *JoA*.; *vel alias assumereris ad illa et instituereris in eis* being written in line
4   *See above*, no. 293.

568   9 January 1516   *Reg. Lat.* 1339, fo 169[r-v]

To John Adams, rector of the parish church of Blakborowgh', d. Exeter. Dispensation and indult etc. [as above, no. 2]. Given at Florence.

Vite ac morum honestas ...
.P. Lambertus. / JoA: / JoA: Lx: Nardinus

569   9 January 1516   *Reg. Lat.* 1339, fos 171[v]-172[r]

To Robert Elyot, abbot of the monastery, called house, of St Augustine, at Bristol (*iuxta Brestolliam*), OSVictor, d. Worcester. Dispensation – at his supplication – to receive and retain *in commendam* for life, together with the above Victorine monastery over which he presides, or any other monastery of the said or any other order, over which he might preside in the future, any two benefices, with or without cure, usually held by secular clerics, even if parish churches or their perpetual vicarages, or chantries, free chapels, hospitals or annual services, usually assigned to secular clerics in title of a perpetual ecclesiastical benefice, and [even if] of abbot Robert's patronage, by reason of his own person as well as of the said monastery, and of the patronage of any other persons, ecclesiastic or secular[1], and of whatsoever tax or annual value, and [even if] the benefices pertain at the time in any way to his collation, provision, presentation or any other disposition, if he obtains them otherwise canonically, to resign them, at once or successively, simply or for exchange, as often as he pleases, and cede the commend, and in their place receive up to two other, similar or dissimilar, benefices, with or without cure, usually held by secular clerics, and retain them *in commendam* for life, even together with the monastery of St Augustine over which he presides, or with another monastery of the said [Victorine] order or of any other order over which he might preside in the future; he may – due and customary burdens of these benefices having been supported – make disposition of the rest of their fruits etc., just as those holding them *in titulum* at the time could and ought to do, alienation [of immovable goods and precious movables being][2] however [forbidden].[2] Notwithstanding etc. With the proviso that these benefices shall not, on this account, be defrauded of due services and the cure of souls in them (if any) shall not be neglected; but that the aforesaid burdens shall be supported. Given at Florence.

Personam tuam et cetera illa tibi et cetera oportuna.
.P. Lambertus. / JoA: / JoA: C: Nardinus

1   MS: *secularium. Cf.* above, no. 555 and below nos. 700 and 719.
2   MS: *alienatione tamen et cetera.* Supplied from common form.

570   9 January 1516   *Reg. Lat.* 1339, fos 175ʳ-176ᵛ

To Brian Higdon, LLD, archdeacon of the church of York, dispensation as below. Some time ago, Julius II dispensed Brian first, by certain letters,[1] to receive and retain for life, any two benefices, etc. [as above, no. 6, to '... retain them together for life']; and then, by other letters of his,[2] to receive together with any two incompatible benefices held by him at the time by virtue of the said dispensation, any third benefice, etc. [as above, no. 6, to '... even if the dignity etc. should be customarily elective and have cure of souls'], if he obtained it otherwise canonically, and to retain the third benefice simultaneously [with the above two incompatible benefices] – if it should be a parish church or its perpetual vicarage – for up to a year calculated from the date of his having peaceful possession of it; but – if it should be another incompatible benefice – for life; and to resign it, simply or for exchange, as often as he pleased, and in its place receive another, similar or dissimilar, benefice, with cure or otherwise incompatible, and retain the third benefice simultaneously – if it should be a parish church or its perpetual vicarage – for up to a year calculated as above; but – if it should be another incompatible benefice – for life, as above, as is more fully contained in each of the aforesaid letters. The pope – at his supplication – hereby further dispenses Brian (who, as he asserts, holds by the said dispensations the archdeaconry of the church of York and the sub[(?)deanery][3] of the church of Lincoln (which are dignities, perhaps major *post pontificalem*) and also the parish church of Nettillon, d. Lincoln (to which the parish church of Bukenehull', d. Lincoln, is united and incorporated by apostolic authority, for as long as he holds Nettillon) to receive and retain for life, together with the above archdeaconry, sub[(?)deanery][4] and church of Nettillon, or with any three other incompatible benefices held by him at the time by virtue of the said dispensations, any fourth benefice, with cure or otherwise incompatible, even if a parish church or its perpetual vicarage, or a chantry, free chapel, hospital or annual service, usually assigned to secular clerics in title of a perpetual ecclesiastical benefice, or a dignity, *personatus*, administration or office in a cathedral, even metropolitan, or collegiate church, even if the dignity in question should be major *post pontificalem* in a cathedral, even metropolitan, church or principal in a collegiate church, and even if the dignity etc. should be customarily elective and have cure of souls, if he obtains it otherwise canonically, to resign it, simply or for exchange, as often as he pleases, and in its place receive and retain for life another, similar or dissimilar, fourth incompatible benefice; provided that of these four incompatible benefices – in the aforesaid year for which he is dispensed to hold a third parish church – not more than three – and after that year – not more than two be parish churches or their perpetual vicarages. Notwithstanding etc. With the proviso that the fourth incompatible benefice shall not, on this account, be defrauded of due services and the cure of sous in it (if any) shall not be neglected. Given at Florence.[5]

Litterarum scientia, vite ac morum honestas …
.P. Lambertus. / JoA: / JoA: Lxxxx[6]: Nardi(nus): –

1   summarised (including an indult for non-residence) in *CPL*, XVIII at no. 661
2   summarised (including an indult for non-residence) in *CPL*, XIX at no. 632
3   MS: *subdia(cona)tu(m)*; *recte*: 'subdecanatum'; the 'habentes pro expressis' clause has *sub(diacona)tus*
4   MS: *sub(diacona)tu*; *recte*: 'subdecanatu'
5   Unlike the two Julius entries (*see above* notes 1 and 2), the present entry does not raise the issue of non-residence.
6   *Lxxxx* (the four 'x's stacked one on top of another in the angle of the 'L') occurs in the bottom inner corner of the page (i.e. fo 176ᵛ). On the significance *see CPL* XVI, p. xxiii.

571[1]   [...]²   *Reg. Lat.* 1339, fos 193ʳ-194ʳ

To Otto[3] Ochmagan, David Maclena and Malachy Ocheman, canons [...],[4] mandate in favour of Thomas Ochemcam, canon of the church of Killala. The pope has learned that the deanery of the church of Killala and the perpetual vicarages of the parish churches of Rafrana' [also spelt *Refrana'*, *Refra'na*, *Rafra'no*] and Rayrac, d. Killala, are vacant *certo modo* at present and have been vacant for so long that by the Lateran statutes their collation has lawfully devolved on the apostolic see, although Richard Baret has detained the deanery, John Omumcam[5] the vicarage of Rafrana', and Thady Odidchn that of Rayrac – bearing themselves as clerics – with no title or support of law, of their own temerity and *de facto*, for a certain time, as they still do. At a recent petition on the part of Thomas (who asserts that the annual value of the deanery does not exceed 6, and of the vicarages of Rayrac, 2, and Rafrana', 1, marks sterling) to the

pope to erect and institute the vicarage of Rayrac into a simple prebend of the canonry
of the church of Killala, which Thomas holds, for as long as he does so, and unite etc.
the vicarage of Rafrana' to the said deanery, for as long as Thomas [should hold] the
deanery, if provision of it be made [to him] by virtue of the presents, the pope hereby
commands that the above three (or two or one of them), if, having summoned Richard,
John and Thady and [others]⁶ concerned, they find the deanery (which is a major
dignity *post pontificalem*) and the vicarages to be vacant (howsoever etc.; even if
specially reserved etc.), shall erect and institute the vicarage of Rayrac into a simple
prebend of the said canonry, for as long as Thomas holds the canonry, without
prejudice to anyone; and [(?)shall unite etc.] the vicarage of Rafrana' to the said
deanery, for as long as Thomas should hold the deanery, if provision of the deanery be
made to him by the above three, and collate and assign them, with all rights and
appurtenances, to Thomas, inducting him etc. into corporal possession of the deanery
and prebend and annex and rights and appurtenances aforesaid, having removed …

Apostolice sedis providentia circumspecta …
[–] / [–] / [–]⁷

1   This entry is unfinished: that is it extends to the foot of fo 194ʳ ending in mid-sentence with the words
     deffendentes inductum amotis; (fos 194ᵛ and 195ʳ are left blank; and an entirely new entry starts at the top of
     fo 195ᵛ). The entire entry is struck through; there is no explanatory note.
2   No date. Insofar as an unfinished and cancelled letter of unknown antecedents is dateable, probably March
     1516 or thereabouts: in a register of the third year [1515 March 19 – 1516 March 18] (*see above*, p. lviii);
     and the next letter entered in the register is drawn under 9 March 1516 (no. 572 below).
3   MS: *Ottoni*; *recte*: 'Odoni'?
4   'ecclesie N' or 'ecclesiarum N et N' wanting
5   This reading is highly doubtful; only initial 'O' is certain.
6   'aliis' wanting
7   no abbreviator's name or magistral initial at start of entry; and, of course, no magistral subscription below
     the abrupt stop in the text

572   9 March 1516   *Reg. Lat.* 1339, fos 195ᵛ-196ᵛ

To <the abbots of the monasteries> of Stratford (*de Stratfordia*) [and] Bylley, d.
London,¹ and John Alyn, canon of the church of Lincoln living in the city of London,
mandate in favour of Ambrose Lowth', cleric or layman, vill of Colchester (*Colcestrie*)
, d. London. A recent petition to the pope on Ambrose's part stated that, at another time,
Robert Lownd, rector of the parish church of St Leonard, said vill and diocese – falsely
asserting that Ambrose was bound to give and pay him a tithe (*decimam*) of 40 pounds
sterling (as he said) <acquired>² by Ambrose in two years then expressed, clear of
overheads (*deductis oneribus*), by reason of a <certain>³ building <or house and a
contrivance (*machine*) called, in English, "a [crane]" and "[kipe]⁴">⁵ situate <within
the bounds>⁵ of the said church <and >⁶ by reason of the wares and merchandise⁷
conveyed there by various merchants and other men, (?)especially⁸ the warehousing
(*custodie*) and removal (*extractionis*) carried on by Ambrose or by others in his name
– caused him to be summoned to trial over this before Cuthbert Tunnschall', auditor of

matters and causes whose cognizance and decision belongs to the archbishop of Canterbury for the time being by reason of his office of legate born, appointed by William, archbishop of Canterbury, legate born of the apostolic see in those parts; and that when Cuthbert was absent, Walter Ston, auditor of the said causes appointed by archbishop William, proceeding wrongly in the case, promulgated a null or unjust, definitive (as he said) sentence, in favour of Robert and against Ambrose, from which, on Ambrose's part, appeal was made to the apostolic see. At the supplication to the pope to order that Ambrose be absolved *ad cautelam* from the sentence of excommunication and other ecclesiastical sentences, censures, and pains perhaps promulgated against him on the above occasion and to commit to some upright men in those parts the causes: of the aforesaid appeal and of anything attempted and innovated after and against it; of the nullity and nullities of the process and sentence and of each and every other thing done in any way by Walter and any other judges and persons to Ambrose's prejudice in connection with the above; and of the whole principal matter, the pope [hereby] commands that the above three (or two or one of them), having summoned Robert and others concerned, shall, on the pope's authority, bestow on Ambrose, for this once only, if he so requests, the benefit of absolution *ad cautelam* from the said sentence of excommunication and other ecclesiastical sentences, censures, and pains, if and as it is just, having, however, first received from him suitable security in respect of that for which he is perhaps deemed excommunicate and caught by the other sentences, censures, and pains, that if it appears to them that the said sentence of excommunication etc were justly inflicted on him he will obey their mandates and those of the church; as to the other things, having heard both sides, taking cognizance even of the principal matter, [decree] what is just, [without appeal, causing by ecclesiastical censure, what they have decreed to be strictly] observed,[9] [and moreover compel] witnesses, etc. Notwithstanding, etc.

Humilibus et cetera.
Jo Copis / JoA: / JoA: xiiij: Nardinus

1   As originally enregistered, the address clause ran: ... *dilectis filiis abbati monasterii de Stratfordia et priori prioratus de Bylley Londonien. diocesis* ...; *abbati monasterii* and *et priori prioratus* were then deleted (both deletions initialled *JoA*) and *monasteriorum abbatibus* was inserted after *diocesis*. After the insertion (which is made in the margin) is the note: *cassat(um) et correctu(m) de man(da)to D(omi)ni Rege(n)tis Nardinus*.

2   in the line: *acquisitarum* (ending reworked) deleted, initialled *JoA*; *acq(ui)sitarum* inserted in margin; above the insertion: *JoA.*; beneath: *cassat(um) et correctu(m) ut sup(ra) Nardi(nus)*

3   *certi* inserted in margin, initialled *JoA*

4   A kipe is a basket (*The Shorter Oxford English Dictionary*); evidently for use with the crane.

5   in the line: *machine Anglice nuncupate | in certa ripa tunc expressa infra limites*, deleted and initialled *JoA* in two places; *seu domus et Machine Anglice Arrane* [!] *et Ripe* [!] *infra fines nuncupate* inserted in the margin; *JoA* above the insertion; *cassat(um) et correctu(m) de man(da)to D(omi)ni Regentis Nar* after it.

6   in the line: *seu* deleted (not initialled); *ac* inserted in margin, initialled *JoA*

7   MS: *mertiu(m) et mercimoniu(m) per diversos mercatores et alios homines ibidem delatoru(m)*; *recte*: 'mercimonii' ?

8   reading hesitantly (?)*imprimis*

9   MS: *quod iustum fuerit et cetera observari*. Supplied from common form

573   17 June 1513   *Reg. Lat.* 1339, fo 226[r-v]

To Thomas, elect of Leighlin, dispensation and indult. Recently, the pope, on the
advice of the cardinals, made provision of Thomas to the church of Leighlin, then
vacant *certo modo*, appointing him bishop, as is more fully contained in his letters
drawn up in that regard.[1] And, as a recent petition to the pope on Thomas's part stated,
at the time of the said provision and appointment, Thomas was holding, as he does, the
office or place of one of the minor penitentiaries of St Peter's, Rome (*de Urbe*), and
the parish church of Draiton Paslow,[2] d. Lincoln; and he also had (as he still does) a
claim to the parish church of St Paul, Piacenza, which had been canonically provided
to him when it was vacant *certo modo*, but which he had not had possession of.
Wishing to assist Thomas to keep up his position more fittingly in accordance with
pontifical dignity, the pope hereby dispenses and indulges Thomas – at his supplication
– to retain for life – even [after] he, on the strength of the above provision and
appointment, peacefully acquires peaceful[3] quasi-possession of the rule and
administration and the goods of the said church of Leighlin, or the greater part of them,
and receives consecration – the said office or place, with its customary honours,
burdens and emoluments, at the pope's pleasure, and also the above church of Draiton
(whose annual value does not exceed 6 pounds sterling), as before, even together with
the church of Leighlin, for as long as he presides over the latter; to prosecute his claim
to the said church of St Paul (whose annual value does not exceed 24 gold ducats of
the camera); to raise in court what has not yet been raised; and, similarly, if he wins
and acquires the church of St Paul, to retain it for life, as above. Notwithstanding etc.
With decree that the office or place and the church of Draiton and also Thomas's claim
to St Paul's are not, on this account, voided. With the proviso that the above parish
churches shall not, on this account, be defrauded of due services and the cure of souls
in them shall not be neglected; but that their customary burdens shall be supported.

Personam tuam nobis et apostolice sedi devotam tuis exigentibus ...
p. lambert(us) / JoA: / :JoA: Grat(is) de man(da)to: Nardinus

1   above, no. 71
2   the first occurrence not clearly written, possibly: *Dunton Paslow*; thereafter (twice) simply referred to as:
     Draiton (clearly written)
3   MS: *pacificam possessionem vel quasi ... pacifice assecutus fueris*

574   8 January 1516   *Reg. Lat.* 1339, fo 275[r]

To Thomas Duttley,[1] canon of the monastery of B. Mary, Buttley,[2] OSA, d. Norwich.
Dispensation – at his supplication – to him, who, as he asserts, is expressly professed
of the above order,[3] to receive and retain [any][4] benefice, with or without cure, [usually
held][5] by secular clerics, etc. [as above, no. 43].[6] Given at Florence.

<Religionis zelus >,[7] vite ac morum honestas ...
p. lambert(us) / JoA: / :JoA: xxx: Nardinus

1   *sic*
2   *sic*
3   This information comes from a notwithstanding clause.
4   *quotcunque*; for 'quod-'
5   'teneri solitum' wanting
6   a small and insignificant difference of formulation apart
7   marginal insertion (hand of enregistering scribe) initialled *JoA*

575   23 December 1515   *Reg. Lat.* 1340, fos 118ʳ-120ʳ

To Matthew Oquari,[1] canon of the church of Elphin, and Odo Obrucam and Thomas Ohemanchan, canons of the church of Killala, mandate in favour of Odo Ohynaga',[2] priest, d. Achonry. The pope has learned that the perpetual vicarages of the parish churches of Cillassar and Cilsersgnaien, d. Achonry, are vacant *certo modo* at present and have been vacant for so long that by the Lateran statutes their collation has lawfully devolved on the apostolic see, although Donat Ocrun,[3] who bears himself as a priest, has detained them with no title and no support of law, of his own temerity and *de facto*, for a certain time, and does so. At a recent petition on Odo's part to him to mutually unite etc. the said vicarages (whose annual value together does not exceed 4 marks sterling), if conferred on Odo by virtue of the presents, the pope hereby commands that the above three (or two or one of them), if, having summoned Donat and others concerned, they find the vicarages to be vacant (howsoever etc.) shall mutually unite etc. them (even if specially reserved etc.), for as long as Odo holds them, if conferred on him as above; and collate and assign them, thus united, to Odo, with all rights and appurtenances, inducting him etc., having removed Donat and any other unlawful detainers, and causing Odo (or his proctor) to be admitted to the vicarages and their fruits etc., rights and obventions to be delivered to him. [Curbing] gainsayers etc. Notwithstanding etc. The pope's will is, however, that the above vicarages shall not, on account of this union etc., be defrauded of due services and the cure of souls shall not be neglected; but that their customary burdens shall be supported; and that on Odo's death or his resignation etc. of the vicarages this union etc. shall be dissolved and be so deemed and the vicarages shall revert to their original condition automatically. Given at Florence.

Vite ac morum honestas …
.P. Lanb(er)tus. / JoA: / : JoA: xx: decimoctavo[4] k(a)l(endas) februarij Anno tertio: [15 January 1516], *Nardinus*

1   or *Oquini*
2   After the '-ga-' there is a blotch, conceivably obscuring a letter (without ascender or descender); and there is definitely a bar over the 'ga' and the blotch.
3   final letter particularly doubtful; only the 'O' absolutely certain
4   *sic*

576   16 April 1516   *Reg. Lat.* 1341, fos 19ᵛ-21ʳ

To Ranellinus[1] Machellymor[2] and Conocius[3] Ohaed, canons of the church of Armagh,
and the official of Armagh, mandate in favour of Patrick Odonull,[4] priest, d. Armagh.
The pope has learned that the monastery of Sts Peter and Paul, Armagh, OSA, is vacant
certo modo at present and has been vacant for so long that by the Lateran statutes or
by other canonical sanctions its provision has lawfully devolved on the apostolic see,
although James Odo'null, who bears himself as abbot, has detained it, with no title and
no support of law (at least not canonical), of his own temerity and *de facto*, for a certain
time, as he does. Wishing to provide a capable and suitable governor to rule and direct
the monastery as well as to assist Patrick to be better supported, the pope hereby
commands that the above three (or two or one of them), if, having summoned James
and others concerned, they find the monastery (which is not customarily disposed of
consistorially; and whose annual value does not exceed 24 marks sterling) to be vacant
(in any way and by whatsoever person), shall commend it (even if its provision
pertains, specially or generally, to the apostolic see, etc.), with all rights and
appurtenances, to Patrick, to be held, ruled and governed by him for life, even together
with all other benefices, with and without cure, secular and regular, which he holds as
above and shall hold in the future; he may – due and customary burdens of the
monastery and its convent having been supported – make disposition of the rest of its
fruits etc. just as abbots of it could and ought to do, alienation of immovable goods and
precious movables being however forbidden; committing the care, rule and
administration of the monastery to Patrick in spiritualities and temporalities; and, in
person or by proxy, causing Patrick to be given obedience and reverence by the
convent and customary services and rights by the vassals and other subjects of the
monastery. [Curbing] gainsayers etc. Notwithstanding etc. With the proviso that divine
worship in the said monastery and the usual number of canons and ministers shall not,
on account of this commend, be diminished; but that the aforesaid burdens of the
monastery and convent shall be supported.

Romani pontificis providencia circumspecta ...
Phi. de Agnell(is) / JoA: / JoA: xxxvj: Nardinus

1   MS: *Ranellino* or *Ravellino*
2   the '-mor' somewhat uncertain
3   MS: *Conocio*
4   the 'u' doubtful; the letter(s) smudged and seemingly changed (from ?*ai*)

577   4 March 1516   *Reg. Lat.* 1341, fos 25ʳ-26ᵛ

To Magonius Mackrenyr, Patrick Macmahuna and John Oculean, canons of the
churches of Clogher and Armagh, mandate in favour of Conacius[1] Ohaed, rector of the
parish church of Achadluna,[2] d. Armagh. The pope has learned that Conacius,
prompted by certain rational considerations, desires that the union etc. of the said
parish church and its perpetual vicarage (which is united etc. to the parish church, for

as long as he holds the parish church) be dissolved; and that Conacius proposes to give his express consent <in this regard>³. Assenting to Conacius's entreaties in this matter and wishing to give a special grace to Patrick Johacd, cleric, d. Armagh, the pope hereby commissions and commands that the above three (or two or one of them), if Conacius has given his express consent to this, shall dissolve this union etc., and thereafter, collate and assign the vicarage (whose annual value does not exceed 4 marks <sterling>⁴) (whether vacant by this dissolution or in any other way etc.; even if it has been vacant for so long that by the Lateran statutes its collation has lawfully devolved on the apostolic see, etc.), with all rights and appurtenances, to Patrick, inducting him etc. having removed any unlawful detainer, and causing Patrick (or his proctor) to be admitted to the vicarage and its fruits etc., rights and obventions to be delivered to him. [Curbing] gainsayers etc. Notwithstanding etc. Furthermore – since it is not likely that anyone would, without reason, spontaneously resign his benefices (perhaps acquired with great labour) from which his livelihood may be derived – the above three shall take care lest there be any simony, or even corruption, in any consent given on the part of Conacius.

Apostolice sedis providencia circumspecta ...
I. Benzon / JoA: / JoA: x: Quarto decimo K(a)l(endas) aprilis Anno Quarto: [19 March 1516], *Nardinus*

1   repeatedly *Conacius*; once *Canacius*
2   the *-luna* uncertain
3   *in hoc* inserted in the margin, initialled *JoA*
4   marginal insertion initialled *JoA*; in the line (?)*argenti* deleted and initialled *JoA*

578   4 March 1516   *Reg. Lat.* 1341, fos 27ʳ-29ʳ

To the abbot of the monastery of B. Mary, OSA,¹ d. Clogher, and Patrick Macmahuna, canon of the church of Clogher, and Matthew Machean, canon of the church of Armagh, mandate in favour of Philip Macurdayl,² rector of the parish church of Tethalen [also spelt *Thethalen*], d. Clogher.³ The pope has learned that the parish church of Tethdannada [also spelt *Thetdannada*, *Tethannada*], d. Clogher, is vacant *certo modo* at present and has been vacant for so long that by the Lateran statutes its collation has lawfully devolved on the apostolic see, although Donat Occallen,⁴ who bears himself as a cleric, has detained it, with no title and no support of law, of his own temerity and *de facto*, as he still does. At a recent petition on the part of Philip (who asserts that the annual value of the above church of Tethdannada does not exceed 5 marks sterling), the pope hereby commands that [the above three (or two of one of them)]⁵, if, having summoned Donat and others concerned, they find the church of Tethdannada to be vacant (howsoever etc.) shall unite etc. it (even if specially reserved etc.), with all rights and obventions, to that of Tethalen, for as long as Philip holds the latter; to the effect that Philip may, on his own authority, in person or by proxy, take and retain corporal possession of the church of Tethdannada and the rights and appurtenances aforesaid, for as long as he holds Tethalen, and convert its fruits etc. to his own uses and those of Tethalen, without licence of the local diocesan or of anyone else. Notwithstanding etc. The pope's will is, however, that the above church of Tethdannada shall not, on account of this union etc., be defrauded of due services and the cure of souls in it shall not be neglected, but that its customary burdens shall be supported; and that on the death of Philip or his resignation etc. of the said church of Tethalen this union etc. shall be dissolved and be so deemed and the church of Tethdannada shall revert to its original state and be deemed vacant automatically.

Apostolice sedis providencia circumspecta votis illis gratum prestare assensum ...
I. Benzon / JoA: / :JoA: xxij. Nardi(nus)

1   outside stilus of chancery: when mandate addressed to head of religious house the order is not usually stated
2   or *Macardayl*
3   MS: *dicte diocesis* – evidently referring to Clogher
4   or maybe *Occullen*
5   MS: *discretioni et cetera mandamus*. Supplied from common form.

579   10 April 1516   *Reg. Lat.* 1341, fos 92ᵛ-93ᵛ

Exemplification in full from the register of Julius II at a recent petition to the pope on the part of Thomas, bishop of Panados (*Panaden.*) of the letter *Personam tuam et cetera oportuna*. (dated 21 April 1506),¹ as follows:
  Some time ago, Innocent VIII by his letters² dispensed bishop Thomas to receive and retain for life, together with the church of Panados (which is *in partibus infidelium* and over which he was then presiding), any two benefices, with cure or otherwise mutually incompatible, in the kingdom of England, even if parish churches or their perpetual vicarages, [or] chantries, free chapels, hospitals or annual services, usually assigned to secular clerics in title of a perpetual ecclesiastical benefice, or dignities, *personatus*, administrations or offices in cathedral, even metropolitan, or collegiate churches, even if the dignities in question should be major *post pontificalem* in cathedral, even metropolitan, churches, or principal in collegiate churches, or a combination, and even if the dignities etc. should be customarily elective and have cure of souls, if he obtained³ them otherwise canonically, to resign them, at once or successively, simply or for exchange, as often as he pleased, and in their place receive up to two mutually incompatible benefices and retain them together for life, as above, as is more fully contained in those letters. Julius II, wishing to assist bishop Thomas – who, as he asserts, holds the canonry and prebend of Rayte⁴ and Clero of the church of Abrigroilly, [d.]⁵ St David's (to which the parish church of Bryngoyn, said diocese, is united etc. for bishop Thomas's lifetime) and the perpetual vicarage of the parish church of Noneton', d. Coventry and Lichfield – to keep up his position more fittingly in accordance with pontifical dignity, hereby dispenses bishop Thomas – at his supplication – to receive and retain for life, together with the above church of Panados and the above canonry and prebend and vicarage, or with any two other benefices held by him at the time by virtue of the said dispensation, any third

benefice etc. [as above, no. 6].
The pope hereby decrees that this exemplification shall everywhere have the same
force as the original. His will is, however, that no new right be acquired through this;
only that the old be conserved.

Ad futuram rei memoriam. Provisionis et cetera.
.P. Lambertus / JoA: / JoA: xxxxviiij: Nard(inus): –

1 unknown to the *CPL*
2 unknown to the *CPL*
3 The present tense is used hereabouts in MS; though the context plainly requires the past.
4 the 'a' over-inked and uncertain
5 'diocesis' is not written here; yet may be indicated by the occurrence of *dicte diocesis*, directly after
   Bryngoyn

580   12 March 1516   *Reg. Lat.* 1341, fo 94^{r-v}

Indulgences as below. Wishing that salutary provision be made for the salvation of the
souls of the nobleman William Ffeteplace, knight, d. Salisbury, and of his wife
Elisabeth, and of the other faithful; and that in the hope of better attaining the salvation
of their own souls the faithful pray fervently to God for the prosperous estate of the
said William and Elisabeth in this life and, after their deaths, for the salvation of their
souls and the souls of the other faithful departed, the pope – assured of the mercy of
Almighty God and of the authority of His Apostles BB. Peter and Paul – hereby
relaxes, for all the faithful of both sexes who, being truly penitent and confessed, [1]
at the ringing of the bell called "La Coursewe"[1] in the bell-tower of the parish church
of the Assumption of B. Mary the Virgin, Chelerey, said diocese, which is wont to be
rung each day at the hour of vespers or at about dusk, have devoutly visited [the said
church][2] and devoutly said and recited once the Lord's Prayer with the Angelic
Salutation for the prosperous estate of William and Elisabeth in this life, and, after their
deaths, for the salvation of their souls and the souls of all the other faithful departed:
one hundred days of enjoined penance for each time they have done it; and [2] on
Sundays and other feastdays, at the tomb or monument of William and Elisabeth, have
devoutly said and recited once the Lord's Prayer with the Angelic Salutation for the
salvation of the souls of William and Elisabeth and of the other faithful departed: also
one hundred days of enjoined penance for each time they have done it. And the pope
decrees that the present letters, which are to be valid for all time, are to be in no way
comprehended under any revocations and suspensions of any indulgences, similar or
dissimilar, made by the pope and the apostolic see, or even ones in favour of the fabric
of St Peter's or of the crusade, but are to be excepted from them always, and as often
as any revocations etc. are issued the present letters are as often to be deemed restored
to their original state.

Universis Christifidelibus presentes litteras inspecturis […] Disideran(tes)[3] fidelium
omnium lucrifieri deo fideles ipsos ad salutis opera exercenda p(er) spiritualia munera

frequenter invitamus ...
/ *C. de Cesis; JoA:* / *JoA: xx: Nardinus*

1   or *Courfewe* (=curfew?); the scribe's 'f' and long 's' are virtually indistinguishable in this entry.
2   The passage (at least as enregistered) is ill-framed: *semel orationem dominicam cum salutatione angelica pro*
      felici statu Willelmi et Elisabeth predictorum quamdiu vitam duxerint in humanis et illis vita functis pro
      suarum et omnium aliorum Christifidelium defunctorum animarum salute devote visitaverint quoties id
      fecerint centum necnon qui dominicis et aliis festivis diebus ad tumulum seu monumentum eorundem
      Willelmi et Elisabeth similiter orationem dominicam cum salutatione angelica pro Willelmi et Elisabeth ac
      aliorum Christifidelium defunctorum animarum salute huiusmodi devote dixerint et recitaverint. Our
      interpretation supplies 'ecclesiam' as the express object of *visitaverint*; takes *semel* with *dixerint et*
      recitaverint; and, as required by the context, takes *dixerint et recitaverint* as applying to both sections.
3   *sic*; for 'Desideran(tes)'

581   29 December 1515   *Reg. Lat.* 1341, fos 103^v-105^r

To the abbot of the monastery of Suir (*de Surio*), d. Lismore, and the dean of the church
of Waterford and John Hamikan', canon of the church of Lismore, mandate in favour
of Nicholas Mackanryc, perpetual vicar of the parish church of the vill of Cloment', d.
Lismore. The pope has learned that, for certain reasons, Nicholas spontaneously and
freely proposes to resign the perpetual vicarage of the above parish church which he
holds. Assenting to Nicholas's entreaties in this regard and wishing to give a special
grace to Peter Whyte, cleric, said d. Lismore, as well as to assist Nicholas lest he suffer
excessive loss by this resignation, the pope hereby commands that the above three (or
two or one of them) shall receive and admit Nicholas's resignation (from Nicholas
himself or from his specially mandated proctor) into their hands (or the hands of
anyone of them) if Nicholas spontaneously and freely wishes to make it; and shall,
having received and admitted it, collate and assign the vicarage, whose fruits etc. do
not exceed an annual value of (?)8[1] pounds sterling, (whether vacant then by this
resignation or at another time in any other way, etc.; even if [vacant][2] for so long it has
devolved etc.), with all its rights and appurtenances, to Peter; and also reserve,
establish and assign an annual pension of 4 like pounds on the above fruits etc., of
which this pension does not exceed one half, to Nicholas (or his specially mandated
proctor), for life, payable by Peter and his successors as holders of the vicarage for the
time being, each year, in a place and in terms and under sentences, censures and pains
established for the purpose by the above three with the consent of Nicholas and Peter,
inducting Peter (or his proctor) into corporal possession of the vicarage and the rights
and appurtenances aforesaid, having removed any unlawful detainer and causing Peter
(or his proctor) to be admitted to the vicarage and its fruits etc., rights and obventions
to be delivered to him; and also shall cause the said pension to be delivered to Nicholas
in accordance with the above reservation etc. [Curbing] gainsayers etc.
Notwithstanding etc. Further, the above three shall take care lest there be any simony,
or even corruption, in this resignation on the part of Nicholas and Peter. And the pope
dispenses Peter while studying[2] not to be bound, by reason of the said vicarage, (if
conferred on him by virtue of the presents and he acquires it), or of any other benefices
with cure or requiring sacred, even priest's, orders by statute, custom, foundation or

otherwise, held by him at the time, to have himself promoted for a seven-year period calculated from the end of the year granted by law – provided that within the first two years of the said seven he is a subdeacon – to any of the other sacred orders, nor to be liable to be compelled to do so by anyone against his will. Notwithstanding etc. With the proviso that the vicarage and the benefices requiring the other sacred orders shall not, on this account, be defrauded of due services and the cure of souls in the vicarage and (if any) the other aforesaid benefices shall not be neglected; but that their customary burdens shall be supported. Given at Florence.

Apostolice sedis circumspecta benignitas et cetera recommendant.
.P. Lambertus. / JoA: / JoA: xxx: pridie k(a)l(andas) maj Anno Quarto [30 April 1516], *Nardinus*

1   tentatively reading *octo*
2   MS: *tanto et cetera devoluta.* Supplied from common form.
3   MS: ... *litterarum studio insistendo*; 'in loco ubi illud vigeat generale/particulare' (or suchlike) does not
     occur.

582[1]   **7 February 1516**   *Reg. Lat.* 1341, fos 117[v]-118[v]

Union etc. At a recent petition on the part of John Alyn, UID, canon [of the church][2] of Lincoln, the pope hereby unites etc. the parish church of Sowgh Wokyngton [also spelt *Sowgh Wokyngton', Sowgh' Wokyngton', Wgh*[3] *Wokymgton', S<w>ogh*[4] *Wokyngton'*], d. London – whose annual value does not exceed 16 pounds sterling, which is vacant *certo modo* at present, and provision of which he expects to be made to him shortly – assuming provision of it is made to him otherwise canonically, to the canonry and prebend of the church[5] of Lincoln, which he holds (and to which, for as long as he holds them, the perpetual vicarage of the parish church of Cheslet, d. Canterbury, is united etc. by apostolic authority), likewise for as long as he holds the canonry and prebend, to the effect that he may, on his own authority, in person or by proxy, take and retain corporal possession of the church of Sowgh Wokyngton, after provision of it has been made to him as above, and of the said rights and appurtenances, for as long as he holds the canonry and prebend, and convert its fruits etc. to his own uses and those of the canonry and prebend and also of the church of Sowgh Wokyngton, without licence of the local diocesan or of anyone else. Notwithstanding etc. The pope's will is, however, that the above church of Sowgh Wokyngton shall not, on account of this union etc., be defrauded of due services and the cure of souls in it shall not be neglected; but that its customary burdens shall be supported; and that on John's death or his resignation etc. of the canonry and prebend this union etc. shall be dissolved and be so deemed and the church of Sowgh Wokyngton shall revert to its original condition automatically. Given at Florence.

Ad futuram rei memoriam. Romanum decet pontificem et cetera provideri.
O. de Cesis. / JoA: / JoA: xxxv: Nardinus

1   engrossment exhibited: CUL, EDR, G/1/7 (Reg. West), fo. 36^{r-v}; *cf.* Anthony à Wood, *Athenae Oxonienses*,
     3rd ed., vol. I (London, 1813), cols. 76-78.
2   'ecclesie' wanting here (but *cf.* below, note 5)
3   *sic*
4   the 'w' inserted directly above the 'o' (the caret mark is beneath and to the left (not right) of the 'o')
5   *ecclesie* occurs (appropriately) here

583   25 March 1516[1]   Reg. Lat. 1341, fos 188ᵛ-190ʳ

To Richard, bishop of Hereford, the abbot of the monastery of Talley, d. St David's,
and Henry Martynn, canon of the church of Hereford, mandate in favour of Edward,
bishop of St David's. A recent petition to the pope on Edward's part stated that at
another time John Edimundi, who bears himself as a canon currently endowed with a
prebend, namely the prebend of Brordsburry, of the church of [London][2] – falsely
alleging that, at another time, while bishop Edward, then in < minor orders>[3], was
holding the said canonry and prebend, he was bound to repair certain buildings of the
prebend which, it was said, had become ruinous in his time and to restore to the
canonry and prebend and reinstate certain goods lawfully[4] belonging, as John
Edimundi said, to the prebend which, as he said, had been wasted by bishop Edward,
and give them to the estate and ownership (*ad ius et proprietatem*) of the canonry and
prebend – sued bishop Edward over this, not by apostolic delegation, before the
archbishop of Canterbury, who was, John Edimundi said, a competent judge for this,
praying *inter alia* that he be condemned and compelled to repair the said buildings and
to renew the canonry and prebend in respect of the wasted goods; and that after
Cuthbert Tunscal[5], UID, to whom the archbishop had committed the cause to be heard
and duly determined, had proceeded to several acts, Walter Stone, LLD, who was
bearing himself as Cuthbert's deputy, proceeding erroneously and wrongly in the case,
then promulgated an unjust, definitive (as he said) sentence, in favour of John and
against bishop Edward, also condemning him in the expenses run up in the case,
[from][6] which, on bishop Edward's part, appeal was made to the apostolic see. [At the
supplication to the pope][7] to commit to some upright men in those parts the causes: of
the aforesaid appeal and of anything perhaps attempted and innovated after and against
it; of the nullity of the said process and sentence and of each and every other thing done
in any way to the bishop's prejudice in connection with the above; and of the principal
matter, the pope [hereby] commands that the above three (or two or one of them),
having summoned John and others concerned and having heard both sides, [shall
decree] what is just, [without appeal, causing what they have decreed to be][8] strictly
observed, by the bishop, on the pope's authority, by others, by ecclesiastical censure,
[and moreover compel] witnesses, etc. Notwithstanding , etc. Given at Magliana, d.
Porto.

Humilibus et cetera.
Jo Copis / JoA: / JoA: xij: Nardinus

1   Pontifical year (reckoned from Leo's coronation on 19 March 1513) changed: originally written ... *anno*

tertio; *tertio* then deleted and *quarto* written; the alteration initialled *JoA*. The year of the Incarnation, used in the dating clause with the pontifical year, began on 25 March (the feast of the Annunciation).

2 MS: *Landaven* (Llandaff) or possibly *Londaven.*; *recte* 'Londonien.'
3 originally written *tunc in humanis existens*; *humanis* then deleted and *minoribus* [sc. 'ordinibus'] inserted in the margin; the insertion initialled *JoA*
4 MS: *legitime legitime*
5 or *Tunscali*
6 MS: *... condemnando* [a] *qua quidem sententia* ...; unless it is obscured by a near vertical stroke 'a' is wanting.
7 MS: *Et deinde et cetera ut appellationis ... Nos igitur et cetera mandamus* ... Supplied from common form
8 MS: *... et auditis hinc inde propositis quod iustum fuerit et cetera*. Supplied from common form; 'etiam de negotio principali huiusmodi cognoscentes legitime', which in such rescripts ordinarily occurs between 'propositis' and 'quod iustum' , surprisingly does not occur.

584   20 August 1515   *Reg. Lat.* 1341, fos 246^r-247^r

To Alexander Crawffo[r]d',[1] canon <of the house of St Anthony, near Leicht[2]>,[3] OSA, d. St Andrews (who, as he asserts, is expressly professed of the above order),[4] reservation etc. and re-entry, as below. This day Alexander spontaneously and freely resigned the preceptory of the above house, which he was then holding, through a certain proctor specially appointed by him for this, into the hands of the pope, who, admitting this resignation, commanded, by other letters, that provision of the preceptory, vacant at the time by the said resignation and previously reserved to apostolic disposition, be made to Richard Donyson,[5] preceptor of this house, as is more fully contained in those letters.[6] Lest Alexander should suffer excessive loss by this resignation, the pope hereby reserves, grants and assigns to him for life – with Richard's express consent – all the preceptory's fruits etc. to be received, exacted and levied by him, on his own authority, in person or by proxy, and to be converted to his own uses, in place of an annual pension; and grants indult to Alexander that on Richard's death or resignation etc., when the preceptory is vacant in any way, even at the apostolic see, Alexander shall be allowed to return to the preceptory and, on his own authority, in person or by proxy, take corporal possession of it and – by virtue of the presents as also by virtue of his earlier title, without any new provision being made to him – retain it as before, without limitation, just as if he had not resigned the preceptory. Notwithstanding etc. The pope's will is, however, that meanwhile Alexander shall be bound to bear all burdens incumbent on the said preceptory from the said fruits etc.

Executory to the bishop of Cavaillon, the provost of Crethten', d. St Andrews, and the official of St Andrews, or two or one of them, acting in person or by proxy.

Religionis zelus, vite ac morum honestas ... The executory begins: *Hodie cum dilectus filius Alexander Crawffurd* ...

p. lambert(us); phi. de agnellis / JoA. / JoA: xxx: x: Nardinus

1 The penultimate letter of the spelling in the address clause is badly blotched and supplied from the spelling in the executory, viz.: *Crawffurd*
2 spelt *Leitht* in the body of the letter and in the executory
3 *domus Sancti Antonii prope Leicht* inserted in margin initialled *JoA*.
4 This information comes from a notwithstanding clause.

5   spelt (?)*Thomsen* in the executory; the '-en' uncertain; but definitely *Tho-* (not 'Don-'); *cf.* below, no. 585
      where Richard's surname is spelt *Thomson'*
6   below, no. 585

585   20 August 1515   *Reg. Lat.* 1341, fos 247ᵛ-249ʳ

To the provost[1] of the church of Crethen', d. St Andrews, mandate in favour of Richard
Thomson', canon of the house of St Anthony near Leitht, OSA, d. St Andrews.
Following the pope's reservation of all preceptories and other benefices, with and
without cure, secular and regular of any order, vacated then and in the future at the
apostolic see, to his own collation and disposition, the preceptory of the above house
became vacant through the free resignation of Alexander Crawssins,[2] its recent
preceptor, who was holding it at the time, made spontaneously through his specially
appointed proctor, Adam Symson, cleric, d. Dunkeld, into the hands of the pope who
admitted the resignation at the said see, and is vacant at present, being reserved as
above. The pope hereby commands the above provost, if through diligent examination
he finds Richard to be suitable – concerning which the pope burdens the provost's
conscience – to collate and assign the above preceptory, which is conventual and
whose annual value does not exceed 30 pounds sterling (whether vacant as above or in
any other way etc.; even if it has been vacant for so long that by the Lateran statutes
its collation has lawfully devolved on the apostolic see, etc.), with all its rights and
appurtenances, to Richard, inducting him etc. – having first received from him in the
name of the pope and the Roman church the usual oath of fealty in accordance with the
form which the pope sends enclosed (*introclusam*)[3] under his *bulla* – having removed
any unlawful detainer, and causing Richard (or his proctor) to be admitted to the
preceptory and its fruits etc., rights and obventions to be delivered to him. [Curbing]
gainsayers etc. Notwithstanding etc.

Dignum arbitramur et congruum et cetera.
p. lambert(us) / JoA: / : JoA: xxx: Nardinus: Septimo Id(us)[4] aprilis Anno Quarto [7
April 1516] *Nar*[5]

1   MS: ... *dilecto filio Johanni* [deleted] *preposito* ... The deletion is initialled *JoA*. Why *Johanni* was ever
      written is unclear; it was not the first name of the then provost of Crichton (i.e. Thomas Halkerston: *cf.*
      D.E.R. Watt and A.L. Murray, *Fasti Ecclesiae Scoticanae Medii Aevi Ad Annum 1638* [revised ed.
      Edinburgh, 2003], p. 455).
2   the '-ssins-' doubtful; *cf.* above, no. 584 where Alexander's surname is spelt *Crawffo[r]d*
3   *Cf.* above, no. 384, note 4.
4   possibly *K(a)l(endas)*
5   Unusual construction: normally the tax mark and (when it occurs) the expedition date are both enclosed
      between the master's initial and surname (or title). In this case it looks as if the expedition date was omitted
      inadvertently then added; *Septimo ... Nar* forms the last line of the entry.

586   9 April 1516   *Reg. Lat.* 1341, fos 274ᵛ-275ᵛ

To Nicholas Patricii *alias* Paterson, perpetual vicar of the parish church of Kynner, d.
Moray. Dispensation etc. [as above, no. 261].

Vite ac morum honestas ...
p. lambert(us) / JoA: / :JoA: xxxx: Nardinus

587¹   9 April 1516   *Reg. Lat.* 1341, fos 365ʳ-366ᵛ

Relaxation, as below. At the report of John Pillet, Englishman, knight of the military
order of the Holy Sepulchre, the pope has learned that at another time, when John was
returning from Jerusalem (*Iherosolimis*), he was captured by the Moors (*Mauris*), the
enemies of the Christian religion, and coerced by them, by torture (*tormentis*) and
(?)threats² of an unthinkable death, either to deny the Christian faith and observe the
evil faith of the Mamelukes (*Mamelucorum*) or to pay the Moors many thousands of
ducats (*multa ducatorum millia*); and that John – preferring to be without the goods of
this world than deny the Christian faith and renounce the joy of the kingdom of heaven
– bound himself, so that he might be freed from prison and the said torture, in the sum
of 2,000 ducats, payable in a certain short time thereafter, to certain Venetian
merchants who have (?)actually (?)paid³ the aforesaid sum (*summam predictam*)⁴ to the
Moors in exchange for John's release; that, in accordance with the laudable ordinances
and statutes of the said order, as often as he is summoned by the present grand master
or grand master for the time being of the said order to come and (?)fight, for the
triumph of the faith of Christ, against the infidels, the cruel enemies of the Christian
religion, John is bound under oath, notwithstanding the great cost to himself, either to
go in person to the grand master or to send a suitable proxy, and he is similarly bound
to observe, as is proper, the state and honour of the said military order; that John is not
allowed to contravene the oath, vow, faith, promise, and obligation taken and made by
him when he professed the said military order; that in honesty, the merchants must be
paid and this can in no way be done without the alienation of John's immovable goods;
that John would not have the means or benefit of observing the vows and oaths he has
taken, as above, if he sells his immovable goods since they are necessary for his daily
use; and indeed if John were to sell his immovable goods he might well – since they
would not, perhaps, suffice for the payment – be compelled to beg, contrary to the
dignity and honour of the said religion and of John and the knights. The pope – wishing
that John be aided in the above matter and that Christ's faithful contribute readily to
the above because they expect thereby to attain the salvation of their souls – assured of
the mercy of Almighty God and of the authority of His Apostles BB. Peter and Paul –
grants, to all the faithful of both sexes who, being truly penitent and confessed, in
person or by proxy, shall have contributed towards the payment of the said sum by
giving pious alms from their own goods to John the knight and to those specially
appointed by him, fifteen years and as many quarantines of enjoined penance for each
such donation (*quotiens id fecerint*). The pope has willed and decreed that the present

letters (which will not be valid after the term of three years) are not to be comprehended under any revocations or suspensions of any indulgences made by the pope and the apostolic see, even revocations etc in favour of the fabric of St Peter's or of the crusade, but shall be excepted from them always; and that full and undoubted faith shall attach to transumpts of the present letters subscribed by the hand of a public notary and fortified with the seal of an ecclesiastical prelate, wherever they are due to be exhibited.

Universis Christifidelibus presentes litteras inspecturis... Licet in desideriis cordis nostri ea continue sollicitudo versetur ut Christifidelibus quibuslibet eorum presertim quos adversa fortune conditione preveniente⁵ dira Sarracenorum rabies oppressit quantum nobis pro virium facultate conceditur succurramus...
Jo. *danyelo* / JoA: /:JoA: *Grat(is) p(ro) Deo: Nardinus*

1   Without the engrossment we cannot be sure; but there appears to be a somewhat loose and selective English
     rendering of this letter (or one like it) in a contemporary royal proclamation printed by [R. Pynson, London]:
     Be it knowen to all Criste(n) people that syr John' Pyllet... w[as taken by] Mauris, etc (*cf.* A.W. Pollard and
     G.R. Redgrave, edd., *A Short-Title Catalogue of Books printed in England, Scotland, & Ireland and of
     English Books Printed Abroad 1475-1640*, 2nd. ed. by W. A. Jackson, F.S. Ferguson, and K.F.Pantzer, 3 vols.
     [London 1976-1991], no. 14077c.131 [formerly 7769]; reprinted [with modernised spelling] by P.L. Hughes
     and J.F. Larkin, edd., *Tudor Royal Proclamations*, vol. I: *The Early Tudors (1485-1553)* [New Haven and
     London, 1964], pp. 132-133). The proclamation contains further particulars of the fund-raising exercise.
2   reading (?) *minis*; but hesitantly. MS is affected by ink bleed and where it is not readily legible our summary
     is accordingly tentative.
3   reading: (?)*realiter* (?)*soluerint*.
4   Though it is not expressed as a definite sum, refers, seemingly, to *multa ducatorum millia* which precedes it
     in MS, not to *in summa duorum millium ducatorum* which comes after it. (Our summary necessarily departs
     from the word order of the Latin). The transactions are not entirely transparent. In view of the commercial
     background, presentational aspects may have carried weight with the draftsman.
5   *sic*; *recte*: 'premente'?

588   14 May 1516   *Reg. Lat.* 1342, fos 175ʳ-177ᵛ

Note. Exceptionally, this entry combines several items. They all concern the commend of Driburgh abbey to James Ogilvie, viz., **[A]** Derogation of privileges, etc; **[B]** the four conclusions to the principal letter (i.e. no. 590); and **[C]** the mandate for the reception of the oath of fealty. The derogation is dated in full; the subsequent items in the entry are all *Dat. ut supra.*¹ Ordinarily, conclusions are enregistered with the principal letter and the other items separately. As a registration entity, the combination is most unusual.

[A] Derogation of privileges, etc. The pope intends this day, on the advice of the cardinals, to commend the monastery of Driburgrh,² OPrem, d. St Andrews, vacant *certo modo* at present, to James Ogilvy, MA, canon of Aberdeen, to be held, ruled, and governed by him for life; and since, as the pope has learned, it is expressly stipulated in the privileges, indults, and apostolic letters granted to the Premonstratensian Order by Sixtus IV and renewed and confirmed by the apostolic see, *inter alia*: that no one, of whatever dignity, estate, degree, order, nobility, or condition, can hold any monastery of the said order *in commendam* unless he has expressly professed the order; that the convents of the monasteries of the order are not bound to receive any commendators and cannot, on that account, be suspended or the monasteries be placed under interdict and their individual persons be excommunicated; that all commends of the monasteries made from time to time, the letters expedited concerning them, and the processes conducted from time to time under the letters (*per eas*), even ones including any sentences, censures, and pains, together with all the sentences of excommunication, suspension, and interdict, and any other sentences, censures, and pains promulgated from time to time against the convents and monasteries or their persons by reason of the foregoing, are null and invalid and of no force or moment; and that the said privileges, indults, and letters shall in no way be deemed derogated by any apostolic letters, even ones *motu proprio*, *ex certa scientia*, and *de apostolice potestatis plenitudine*, issued from time to time by the apostolic see, of whatever tenor they are and including any stronger and more efficacious clauses derogatory of derogatory clauses, even clauses specifically and expressly derogating the said privileges etc., and rehearsing them verbatim, except when the pope for the time being has – by a group of three letters (*trinas litteras*) granted at different times, in the later of which mention is made of the earlier ones, sealed with the authentic pendant lead seal, specifically containing the text (*seriem*) of the privileges etc. – signified his intention to the said convents three times, at intervals, and with three different months between the month of the presentation of the letters,[3] to derogate the above on the occasion in question. Wishing to make provision so that the said commend may not on this account be obstructed in any way, the pope – *motu proprio* – hereby, for this once only, specially and expressly derogates the said privileges etc. (which shall otherwise remain in force) – deeming (solely to give effect to the commend and related letters) the tenors of the privileges etc. sufficiently expressed by the presents, as if they were inserted verbatim – and wills them to be derogated, even if they have been granted and approved *motu proprio*, *ex certa scientia*, and *de potestatis plenitudine*, and by way of statute and ordinance, and with any stronger, more efficacious, and unusual clauses derogatory of derogatory clauses, and with a decree (which there may be) that it ought to be adjudicated,[4] and other decrees, even decrees *irritantes*, and even if, for their sufficient derogation, they must be mentioned specifically, expressly, individually, and verbatim, and not by general clauses importing the same, or even if any other expression is to be had of them and their whole tenors, or other uncommon form for this purpose is to be observed. Notwithstanding the statutes and customs of the monastery of Driburgrh and of the said order, etc.

[B] Conclusions to: (i) the convent of the monastery of Driburgch [also spelt *Triburgrh*]; (ii) the vassals of the monastery; (iii) the abbot of the monastery of Prémontré, d. Laon; (iv) James, king of Scots.

[C] To the bishops of Dunblane and Whithorn, mandate. Since the pope [has] this day [on the advice of the cardinals, commended] the monastery of Driburgch, OPrem, d. St Andrews, then vacant *certo modo*, [to James Ogilvy, MA, canon of Aberdeen, to be held, ruled, and governed by him for life], as is more fully contained [in his letters drawn up in that regard][5] he – wishing to spare James the commendator, who lives in those parts, the labour and expense of being compelled on that account to come in person to the apostolic see – hereby commands that the above two (or one of them) shall receive from James, in the name of the pope and the Roman church, the usual oath of fealty, in accordance with the form which the pope sends enclosed (*introclusam*)[6] under his *bulla* and shall cause the form of oath which James takes to be sent, verbatim, to the pope, at once, by their own messenger, by his letters patent marked with his seal.

[A] *Ad futuram rei memoriam. Decet Romanum pontificem ne provisiones et commende ...*
[B] The conclusions begin: (i), (ii), (iii), (iv) *Hodie monasterium ...*
[C] *Cum nos hodie ...*
f. Bregeon / JoA: / JoA: xxv: x: x: x: x x[7]: Nardinus

1   as is, strangely, the relevant absolution which follows but as a separate entry (no. 589)
2   antepenultimate letter uncertain
3   *diversis mensibus tribus inter (?)mensem earum presentationum*
4   *quod sit iudicari debeat*
5   MS: *Cum nos hodie monasterium de Driburgch Premonstraten. ordinis Sancti Andree diocesis tunc certo modo et cetera plenius continetur.* Particulars supplied from surrounds; rest from common form.
6   As usual with enclosed forms, the form is not enregistered. *Cf.* above, no. 384, note 4; *and see* no. 385, note 10.
7   There are no points between the penultimate and final 'x'.

589   **[14 May 1516]**[1]   *Reg. Lat.* 1342, fo 178[r]

To James Ogilvy, MA, canon of Aberdeen. Since the pope, on the advice of the cardinals, intends this day to commend the monastery of Driburgrh,[2] OPrem, d. St Andrews, at present vacant *certo modo*, to James to be held, ruled and governed by him for life, he hereby absolves him from any [sentences] of excommunication etc. under which he may perhaps lie, [so far only as regards the taking effect of the said commend and each of the relevant letters[3]]. Notwithstanding etc.

Apostolice sedis consueta clementia ad ea libenter intendit ...
[–][4] / JoA: / JoA: xvj: Nardinus

1   Even though this is a separate entry in the register, it is subscribed: *Dat. ut supra* (*See above*, no. 588.)
2   As in no. 588 above, the antepenultimate letter is uncertain: here possibly a 'c' or even an 'i'.
3   MS: *a quibusvis excommunicationis et cetera fore nunctiamus.* Supplied from common form.
4   no abbreviator's name

590[1]   **14 May 1516**   *Reg. Lat.* 1342, fos 178[r]-179[v]

To James Ogilvy, MA, canon of Aberdeen, consistorial commend as below. This day Andrew, archbishop of St Andrews, has, spontaneously and freely, ceded the monastery of Driburgch, OPrem, d. St Andrews, which he was lately holding *in commendam* by apostolic concession and dispensation, into the hands of the pope who has admitted the cession (the monastery being vacant on this cession still in the way in which it was vacant when commended to archbishop Andrew). Wishing to provide the monastery with a capable and suitable governor as well as to assist James (who is of noble birth by both parents; and is a counsellor of James, king of Scots, and Master of Requests of the kingdom of Scotland) to be supported more conveniently, the pope, on the advice of the cardinals, hereby commends the monastery (vacant howsoever), with all rights and appurtenances, to James, to be held, ruled and governed by him for life, even together with the canonry and prebend of Kinckel of the church of Aberdeen, and with all other benefices, with and without cure, secular and regular of any order, which James holds (also by any apostolic concessions and dispensations) *in titulum* and *commendam* and otherwise[2] and shall hold in the future, and with annual pensions assigned to him on any ecclesiastical fruits etc. which he receives and shall receive in the future; committing the care, rule and administration of the monastery to him in spiritualities and temporalities. The pope's will is, however, that divine worship and the usual number of canons and ministers in the monastery shall not, on account of this commend, be diminished, but that the monastery's customary burdens and those of its convent shall be supported; and that James may – the aforesaid burdens having been supported – make disposition of the rest of the monastery's fruits etc., just as abbots could and ought to do, alienation of immovable goods and precious movables being however forbidden. And the pope commands, by other letters of his, that before James involves himself in the rule and administration of the monastery in any way he shall take the usual oath of fealty in accordance with the form which the pope sends enclosed (*introclusam*)[3] under his *bulla* before the bishops of Dunblane and Whithorn (or one of them); and that the bishops concerned (or one of them) shall receive the oath from James in the name of the pope and the Roman church.

Romani pontificis circumspecta et cetera oportune.
f Bregeon / JoA: / :JoA: xvj: Nardi(nus): –

1   Principal letter only. The conclusions are enregistered with the derogation in a separate entry: above, no. 588.
2   *alias* (but reworked)
3   *Cf.* above, no. 384, note 4.

591[1]   4 May 1517   *Reg. Lat.* 1342, fos 205ʳ-206ʳ

To Thomas, elect of Megara (*Megaren.*). Consistorial provision of him – prior of the priory, called house, of B. Mary and St Petroc, Bodmyn', OSA, d. Exeter; and in the priesthood – to the church of Megara, vacant at present, and appointment of him as bishop, committing to him the care and administration of the said church in spiritualities and temporalities. The pope's will is, however, that Thomas shall – after he has had the present letters expedited – go to the above church and reside personally in it; and that he shall not be able to exercise the pontifical office outside the city and diocese of Megara.

Apostolatus officium quamquam insufficientibus meritis nobis ex alto commissum ...

.Je. Benzon / M / M L de Campania

1   principal letter only (i.e. no conclusions)

592   4 May 1517   *Reg. Lat.* 1342, fos 206ʳ-207ʳ

To Thomas, elect of Megara (*Megaren.*). This day the pope by other letters of his made
provision of Thomas to the church of Megara, then vacant *certo modo*, appointing him
bishop; his will being, *inter cetera*, that – as soon as Thomas has had the said letters
expedited – he shall go to the above church and reside in person at it; and that he shall
not be able to exercise the pontifical office outside the city and diocese of Megara, as
is more fully contained in the said letters.[1] Since however, as the pope has learned,
Thomas is unable – without danger to his person – to go to the above church (which is
in partibus infidelium) and reside in person at it, the pope – at his supplication – hereby
indulges Thomas not to be bound to go there and reside in person at it; and – after he
has received consecration – to be able to exercise the pontifical office in the city and
diocese of Exeter with the express consent and special licence of its diocesan.
Notwithstanding the pope's will aforesaid etc.

Sincere devotionis affectus …
Je Benzon / M / M xxx de Campania

1   above, no. 591 (in which, incidentally, 'certo modo' does not occur)

593   5 May 1517   *Reg. Lat.* 1342, fos 207ʳ-208ʳ

To Thomas, elect of Megara (*Megaren.*). Since the pope has recently made provision
of Thomas to the church of Megara, appointing him bishop, as is more fully contained
in his letters drawn up in that regard,[1] he hereby grants faculty to Thomas – at his
supplication – to receive consecration from any catholic bishop of his choice in
communion with the apostolic see, assisted by two or three catholic bishops similarly
in communion; and to the bishop concerned to consecrate him, having first received
from him in the name of the pope and the Roman church the usual oath of fealty in
accordance with the form noted in the presents. The pope decrees, however, that if the
bishop consecrates Thomas without receiving the said oath and Thomas receives
consecration they shall both be suspended automatically. Moreover it is the pope's will
that Thomas shall send him, at once, by his own messenger, the form of oath taken by
him, verbatim, by his letters patent marked with his seal; and that the above shall not
be to the prejudice of the archbishop of Athens (*Atthenen.*), to whom the aforesaid
church is understood to be subject by metropolitan law. With the form of oath.[2]

Cum nos pridem …

Je Benzon / M / M xxviij de Campania

1   above, no. 591
2   not recited in full; *cf.* above, no. 377, notes 3 and 5.

594   4 May 1517   *Reg. Lat.* 1342, fo 208[r-v]

To Thomas Viniam, prior of the priory, called house, of B. Mary and St Petroc, Bodmyn', OSA, d. Exeter. Since the pope, on the advice of the cardinals, intends this day to make provision of Thomas to the church of Megara (*Megaren.*), vacant *certo modo* at present, and to appoint him bishop, he hereby absolves him from any sentences of excommunication, suspension and interdict and other ecclesiastical sentences, censures and pains under which he may perhaps lie, so far only as regards the taking effect of the said provision and appointment and each of the relevant letters. Notwithstanding etc.

Apostolice sedis circumspecta benignitas ad ea libenter intendit …
.Je. Benzon / M / M xx de Campania

595   4 May 1517   *Reg. Lat.* 1342, fos 208[v]-210[v]

To Thomas, elect of Megara (*Megaren.*). This day the pope made provision of Thomas to the church of Megara, vacant *certo modo*, and appointed him bishop, as is more fully contained in his letters drawn up in that regard.[1] However, as the pope has learned, at the time of this provision and appointment, Thomas was holding (as he does), by apostolic concession and dispensation, the priory, called house, of B. Mary and St Petroc, Bodmyn', OSA, *in titulum*, and the perpetual vicarage of the parish church of Eglishede,[2] d. Exeter, *in commendam*, (whose annual value together, as the pope has also learned, does not exceed 30 pounds sterling of English money). Wishing to assist Thomas (who, as the pope has likewise learned, is expressly professed of the above order of St Augustine)[3] to keep up his position more fittingly in accordance with pontifical dignity, the pope – *motu proprio* – hereby dispenses Thomas to receive and retain – even after he has received consecration on the strength of this provision and appointment – together with the said church of Megara, the above priory (which is conventual)[4] and vicarage, as before; and [to receive] with the said priory and vicarage, one, and with one of them, two, and without them, any three benefices, with or without cure, viz.: two secular benefices and one regular benefice of the said order of St Augustine, or of the Cluniac or Cistercian order or another order, even if the secular benefices should be parish churches or their perpetual vicarages, or chantries, free [chapels],[5] hospitals or annual services, usually assigned to secular clerics in title of a perpetual ecclesiastical benefice, [or][6] dignities, *personatus*, administrations or offices in cathedral, even metropolitan, or collegiate churches, even if the dignities in question should be major *post pontificalem* in cathedral, even metropolitan, churches, or principal in collegiate churches, and even if the regular benefice should be a monastery (not however consistorial), priory, *prepositura*[7] or other dignity (even conventual), *personatus*, administration or office, and even if the priory, *prepositura*, *prepositatus*, and the dignities, *personatus*, administrations or offices in question should be customarily elective and have cure of souls, if he obtains them otherwise canonically, and to retain the regular benefice *in titulum* and the secular benefices *in commendam* together for life; to resign them, at once or successively, simply or for exchange, as often as he pleases, and cede the commend, and in their place receive up to three other, similar or dissimilar, benefices, with or without cure, viz.: two secular benefices and one regular benefice of the above order of St Augustine, or of the Cluniac or Cistercian order or another order, and retain the regular benefice (which may not be a claustral office) *in titulum* and the secular benefices *in commendam* together for life; he may – due and customary burdens of the benefices held *in commendam* having been supported – make disposition of the rest of their fruits etc. just as those holding them *in titulum* could and ought to do, alienation of immovable goods and precious movables being however forbidden). Notwithstanding etc. With decree that the above priory and vicarage which Thomas holds are not made vacant and the commend does not cease on this account. With the proviso that the priory and vicarage he holds (or other benefices he may hold as above) shall not be defrauded of due services and the cure of souls in the vicarage and (if any) the priory (or other benefices) shall not be neglected; but that customary burdens of the priory and vicarage (or aforesaid burdens of other benefices) shall be supported.

Personam tuam nobis et apostolice sedi devotam tuis exigentibus meritis paterna benivolentia prosequentes illa tibi libenter concedimus ...
Je Benzon / M / M Cxxx de Campania

1   above, no. 591
2   or perhaps *Eglisherle*
3   This information comes from a notwithstanding clause.
4   'not conventual' perhaps written originally. For there is a deletion – (?) *non* – between *conventualis* and *est*, with *JoA* initialled above the deletion; and in the margin opposite a cross (signalling error) with *cassatu(m) de man(da)to D(omi)ni Regentis Nar* beneath it. The deletion is heavily done and no letters can be made out; but there are no ascenders or descenders and the length of the deletion is consistent with *non* and the sense is agreeable to it.
5   *cerpelle*; for 'ca(p)pelle'
6   'aut' or suchlike does not occur.
7   Though it occurs later, 'prepositatus' does not occur here.

596   1 January 1519   *Reg. Lat.* 1343, fos 69ᵛ-70ʳ

To the dean, the archdeacon and the treasurer of the church of Armagh, mandate in favour of Patrick Omulgira, priest, d. Armagh. The pope has learned that the rectory of the parish church of Oylledres[1] and the vicarage of the parish church of Iscerdagrych, said diocese, are vacant *certo modo* at present and have been vacant for so long that by the Lateran statutes their collation has lawfully devolved on the apostolic see, although

Terence Oconalan and Patrick Omulgira junior have detained the rectory, dividing its fruits between themselves, and James Magunsoram has detained the vicarage – bearing themselves as priests – with no title and no support of law, of their own temerity and *de facto*, for a certain time, as they still do. At a recent petition on the part of the first Patrick aforesaid (who asserts that the annual value of the rectory and vicarage does not exceed 6 marks sterling) the pope hereby commands that the above three (or two or one of them), if, having summoned Terence, the second Patrick and James aforesaid and others concerned, and those interested in the union, they find the rectory and vicarage to be vacant (howsoever etc.), shall collate and assign the rectory to the first Patrick and (even if the rectory and vicarage are specially reserved etc.) unite etc. the vicarage to the rectory, for as long as the first Patrick holds the rectory, with all rights and appurtenances, inducting him etc. having removed Terence, the second Patrick and James and any other unlawful detainers and causing the fruits etc., rights and obventions of the rectory and vicarage to be delivered to the first Patrick. [Curbing] gainsayers by the pope's authority etc. Notwithstanding etc. The pope's will is, however, that the vicarage shall not, on account of this union etc., be defrauded of due services and the cure of souls in it shall not be neglected; but that its customary burdens shall be supported; and that on the death of the first Patrick or his resignation etc. of the rectory, this union etc. shall be dissolved and be so deemed and the vicarage shall revert to its original condition and be deemed vacant automatically. Given at Magliana, d. Porto.

Vite ac morum honestas ...
Phy. de Agnellis. ~ / *Je- / Je xx Quarto K(a)l(endas) Februarij anno sexto* [29 January 1519], *De laporta–*

1   seventh letter altered and now doubtful; readable as 'r' or 'o' or even deleted

597   12 June 1516   *Reg. Lat.* 1344, fos 12ʳ-13ᵛ

To the abbot of the monastery of Sts Peter and Paul, Clones, d. Clogher, and Magonius Maccrenyr, canon of the church of Clogher, and James Curreyn, canon of the church of Dublin, mandate in favour of Terence Osyche, priest, d. Clogher. The pope has learned that the perpetual vicarage of the parish church of St Firmin (*Sancti Firmini*), Macgareroche, d. Clogher, has been vacant *certo modo* and is vacant at present, although John Meyayn,[1] who bears himself as a priest, has detained it with no title and no support of law, of his own temerity and *de facto*, for a certain time, as he still does. He hereby commands that the above three (or two or one of them), if, having summoned John and others concerned, they find the vicarage (whose annual value does not exceed 5 marks sterling) to be vacant (howsoever etc.), shall collate and assign it (even if it has been vacant for so long that by the Lateran statutes its collation has lawfully devolved on the apostolic see, etc.), with all rights and appurtenances, to Terence, inducting him etc., having removed John and any other unlawful detainer and causing Terence (or his proctor) to be admitted to the vicarage and its fruits etc., rights and obventions to be delivered to him. [Curbing] gainsayers etc. Notwithstanding etc.

Vite ac morum honestas ...
Phi Agnellis / JoA: / JoA: x: vndecimo k(a)l(endas) Julij Anno Quarto: [21 June 1516],
Nardinus

1   or perhaps *Megayn*

598 12 June 1516					*Reg. Lat.* 1344, fos 14ʳ-16ʳ

To the abbot of the monastery of Sts Peter and Paul, Clones, d. Clogher, and James
Curryn, canon of the church of Dublin, and Patrick Omablpadrig, canon of the church
of Kilmore, mandate in favour of Gilbert Macunradet,[1] perpetual vicar of the parish
church of Kyllualayn [also spelt *Kylldalayn*], d. Kilmore. The pope has learned that the
perpetual vicarage of the parish church of St Bridget, Dysertynyn, d. Kilmore, has been
vacant *certo modo* and is vacant at present, although Thomas Macunrada,[2] who bears
himself as a priest, has detained [it], with no title and no support of law, of his own
temerity and *de facto*, for a certain time, as he still does. Wishing to give a special grace
to Gilbert (who, as he asserts, holds the perpetual vicarage of the said church of
Kyllualayn), [the pope hereby commands that the above three (or two or one of them),
if, having summoned Thomas and others concerned],[3] they find the said vicarage of
Dysertynyn (whose annual value does not exceed 8 marks sterling) to be vacant
(howsoever etc.) shall collate and assign it (even if it has been vacant for so long that
by the Lateran statutes its collation has lawfully devolved on the apostolic see etc.),
with all rights and appurtenances, to Gilbert, inducting him etc. having removed
Thomas and any other unlawful detainer and causing Gilbert (or his proctor) to be
admitted to the vicarage of Dysertynyn and its fruits etc., rights and obventions to be
delivered to him. [Curbing] gainsayers etc. Notwithstanding etc. Also the pope
dispenses Gilbert to receive the vicarage of Dysertynyn, if conferred on him by virtue
of the presents, and retain it for life together with the vicarage [of Kyllualayn] which
he holds. Notwithstanding etc. With the proviso that the vicarage of Dysertynyn shall
not, on this account, be defrauded of due services and the cure of souls in it shall not
be neglected.

Vite ac morum honestas ...
Phi Agnellis / JoA: / :JoA: x: vndecimo k(a)l(endas) Julij Anno Quarto: [21 June
1516], *Nar*

1   the four minims here read as -*un*- variously readable
2   the '-ra-' ink clogged and uncertain
3   The passage in brackets is wanting in the register and is supplied from common form.

599   1 July 1516   *Reg. Lat.* 1344, fos 37ᵛ-40ʳ

To the abbot of the monastery of B. Mary, *de Aruica'po* [Kilcooly], d. Cashel, and
Thady Omuirisa, canon of the church of Ossory, and the official of Waterford, mandate
in favour of William Ymorosa, perpetual vicar of the parish church of Reske, d.
Waterford. The pope has learned that the precentorship of the church of Ferns is vacant
certo modo at present and has been vacant for so long that by the Lateran statutes its
collation has lawfully devolved on the apostolic see, although John Euuart,[1] who bears
himself as a priest, has detained it, with no title and no support of law, of his own
temerity and *de facto*, for a certain time, as he still does. At a recent petition on the part
of William (who asserts that the annual value of the precentorship does not exceed 12
marks sterling) to the pope to unite etc. the precentorship to the perpetual vicarage of
the above parish church, which William holds, for as long as he does so, the pope
hereby commands that the above three (or two or one of them), if, having summoned
John and others concerned, they find the precentorship (which is a dignity, not however
major *post pontificalem*) to be vacant (howsoever etc.) shall unite etc. it (even if
specially reserved etc.), with all rights and appurtenances, to the vicarage, for as long
as William holds the latter, and shall remove[2] John and any other unlawful detainer; to
the effect that William may, on his own authority, in person or by proxy, take and retain
corporal possession of the precentorship and the rights and appurtenances aforesaid,
for as long as he holds the vicarage, and convert its fruits etc. to his own uses and those
of the vicarage, without licence of the local diocesan or of anyone else.
Notwithstanding etc. The pope's will is, however, that the said precentorship shall not,
on this account, be defrauded of due services and the cure of souls in it (if any) shall
not be neglected; but that [its][3] customary burdens shall be supported; and that on
William's death or his resignation etc. of the vicarage this union etc. shall be dissolved
and be so deemed and the precentorship shall revert to its original condition and be
deemed vacant automatically.

*Vot(is) fidelium omnium ex quibus precipue eorum commoditatibus consulitur libenter
anuimus ...*
Phy de Agnellis / M / M xx Id(ibus) Julij a(n)no quarto [15 July 1516]*, de Campania*

1   the 'uu' read sympathetically
2   MS: *amoveatisque ... detentorum*: unusual construction; usually 'amotis ... detentore' etc.
3   MS: *eorum*; *recte*: 'eius'

600   7 July 1516   *Reg. Lat.* 1344, fos 40ʳ-43ᵛ

To the abbot of the monastery of B. Mary, *de Arnicampo* [Kilcooly], d. Cashel, and the
dean and Cornelius Olocuayn, canon, of the church of Cashel, mandate in favour of
Thady Omorissa, perpetual vicar of the parish church of Ponkoean [also spelt
Ponkoeam], d. Ossory.[1] The pope has learned that the perpetual vicarage of the parish
church of Fedun[2] and that of the parish church of Caryek [also spelt *Carick, Caryk*][3]

(which is, as is asserted by some, of lay patronage) and the rectory of the parish church of Kylinogunock[4] [also spelt *Kylmogunok*], d. Ossory, are vacant *certo modo* at present and have been vacant for so long that by the Lateran statutes their collation has lawfully devolved on the apostolic see, although John Bottilier [also spelt *Bothylier*,[5] *Bottiglier*] has detained the vicarage of Fedun, and John Branoc [also spelt *Beanor*, *Brauor*] that of Caryek, and Patrick Olocamahayn has detained the rectory of Kylinogunock – bearing themselves as clerics and priests[6] – respectively with no title and no support of law, of their own temerity and *de facto*, for a certain time, as they still do. A recent petition to the pope on the part of Thady – who asserts that some time ago he was dispensed by apostolic authority notwithstanding a defect of birth as the son of a subdeacon and an unmarried woman to be promoted to all, even sacred and priest's, orders, and to receive and retain the vicarage of the parish church of Ponkoean, d. Ossory, and the rectory of the parish church of Balymarytyn [also spelt *Ballimarrtyn*][7], d. Ossory; and that by virtue of this dispensation he had been duly marked with clerical character and had acquired the said vicarage and rectory (vacant *certo modo* at the time and canonically collated to him) which he holds; and also that the annual value of the "vacant" vicarages [of Fedun and Caryek] and the "vacant" rectory [of Kylimogunock] does not exceed 24 marks sterling – stated that if a canonry were to be erected and instituted in the church of Ossory and the rectory and vicarage which Thady holds into a simple prebend of that church, for his lifetime, and the rectory and vicarages which are vacant were to be united etc. to the canonry and prebend thus erected it would be to the advantage of Thady and to the increase of divine worship in the church of Ossory. The pope – not having certain knowledge of the foregoing – hereby commands – at this supplication – that the above three (or two or one of them), if, having summoned John Bottilier, John Branoc and Patrick and the bishop and chapter of Ossory (as regards the erection) and others concerned, they find the "vacant" vicarages and rectory to be vacant (howsoever etc.) shall erect and institute a canonry in the church of Ossory and the rectory and vicarage he holds into a simple prebend of that church, without prejudice to anyone; and unite etc. the vacant vicarages and rectory (even if specially reserved etc.) to the said canonry and prebend, for Thady's lifetime; and, in the event of this erection and institution and union etc., collate the newly erected canonry and prebend, being vacant, to Thady, with plenitude of canon law and the annexes in question and all rights and appurtenances, inducting him etc. into corporal possession of the canonry and prebend and annexes and rights and appurtenances aforesaid, having removed John Buthylier and John Branoc and Patrick and any other unlawful detainers and causing [Thady][8] (or his proctor) to be received as a canon in the church of Ossory, with plenitude of canon law, and the fruits etc., rights and obventions to be delivered to him. [Curbing] gainsayers etc. Notwithstanding etc. Also the pope dispenses Thady to receive and retain the said canonry and prebend, if conferred on him by virtue of the presents, notwithstanding the above defect of birth etc. The pope's will is, however, that the "vacant" rectory and vicarages shall not, on this account, be defrauded of due services and the cure of souls in the vicarage of Ponkoean and also in the "vacant" vicarages and rectory[9] shall not be neglected; but that their customary burdens and those of the rectory of Balymarytyn shall be supported; and that on Thady's death or his resignation etc. of the canonry and prebend this erection and institution shall be extinguished and union etc. shall be dissolved and be so deemed and these vicarages and rectories shall revert to their original condition automatically.

Apostolice sedis circumspecta benignitas ad ea libenter intendit …
Phy Agnellis / M / M xxxv de Campania

1   MS: *dicte diocesis* – evidently referring to Ossory
2   perhaps *Fedum* in one instance
3   Carrick was in d. Lismore, but near border with Ossory.
4   the first 'o' blotched and uncertain
5   in this, the first occurrence, the 'hy' oddly formed and uncertain
6   MS: *pro clericis et presbyteris*; but only three detainers
7   the first 'r' written over an 'l'?
8   'Tatheum' wanting
9   *rectoriis*; *recte*: 'rectoria'

601   7 July 1516   *Reg. Lat.* 1344, fos 44^r-47^r

To the abbot of the monastery of B. Mary, *de Arnicampo*[1] [Kilcooly], d. Cashel, and the dean and Cornelius Olacuayn, canon, of the church of Cashel, mandate in favour of Thady Ydugyn, cleric, d. Killaloe. The pope has learned that the rectories of the parish churches of Delig[2] and of St. Patrick, Doma'omer (which is of lay patronage), and the vicarage of the parish church of B. Mary, Katholona, d. Ossory, are vacant *certo modo* at present and have been vacant for so long that by the Lateran statutes their collation has lawfully devolved on the apostolic see, although Donald Oduygyn has detained the rectory of Delig, and Theodoric Mugyllaphadryg that of St Patrick, and William Offellayn has detained the said vicarage – bearing themselves as clerics or priests[3] respectively – with no title or support of law, of their own temerity, and *de facto*, for a certain time, as they still do. At a recent petition on the part of Thady (who asserts that he – having kept silent[4] about his defect of birth as the son of a beneficed cleric and an unmarried woman – has been marked with clerical character, otherwise however duly; and also that the annual value of the rectories and vicarage does not exceed 30 marks sterling) to the pope to erect and institute the rectory of St Patrick into a simple prebend of the church of Ossory for his lifetime, and to unite etc. to it, thus erected, the other rectory and the vicarage, the pope – not having certain knowledge of the foregoing – hereby commands that the above three (or two or one of them), if, having summoned Donald, Theodoric and William and, as regards the erection, the bishop and chapter of Ossory and others concerned, they find the rectories and vicarage to be vacant (howsoever etc.), shall erect and institute the rectory of St Patrick into a simple prebend of the church of Ossory, without prejudice to anyone; and shall unite etc. the other rectory and the vicarage (even if specially reserved etc.) to the said prebend, for Thady's lifetime; and, in the event of this erection and institution and union etc., shall collate and assign the newly erected prebend, then being vacant, and also a canonry of the church of Ossory, to Thady, with plenitude of canon law and all rights and appurtenances, inducting him etc. having removed Donald, Theodoric and William and any other unlawful detainers and causing Thady (or his proctor) to be

admitted to the prebend and received as a canon of the church of Ossory, and assign
him a stall in the choir and a place in the chapter, with plenitude of canon law, and
[causing] the fruits etc., rights and obventions of the canonry and prebend to be
delivered to him. [Curbing] gainsayers etc. Notwithstanding etc. Also the pope
dispenses Thady – on account of the above defect of birth – to use the said clerical
character and to receive and retain the said canonry and prebend, if conferred on him
by virtue of the presents, notwithstanding etc. The pope's will is, however, that the said
rectories and vicarage shall not, on this account, be defrauded of due services and the
cure of souls in them shall not be neglected; but that their customary burdens shall be
supported; and that on Thady's death or his resignation etc. of the canonry and prebend
this erection and institution shall be extinguished and union etc. be dissolved and be so
deemed automatically and the rectories and vicarage shall revert to their original
condition.

Apostolice sedis circumspecta benignitas ad ea libenter intendit …
Phy Agnellis / M / M xxxv de Campania

1   *sic*; for 'Arvicampo'
2   the '*lig*' uncertain; maybe '*-hij*', '*-hy*' etc.
3   MS: *pro clericis et presbyteris*; but only three detainers; *cf.* previous entry.
4   (?)*tatito*; for 'tacite'

602   12 June 1516   *Reg. Lat.* 1344, fos 77ʳ-78ᵛ

To the abbots of the monasteries of St Augustine near the vill of Bristol (*Bristollie*) and
Llanternam,[1] mandate in favour of Catherine Kunnes,[2] prioress of the nunnery of B.
Mary the Virgin, OSB, Uste, d. Llandaff. A recent petition to the pope on Catherine's
part stated that at another time, after the convent of the said house, or some of them,
had, when the [prioress-ship][3] of the said house was vacant *certo modo*, elected
Catherine as their and the said house's prioress, and after she had been dispensed by
apostolic authority, notwithstanding the fact that for certain reasons then expressed the
said election was null or invalid, to retain the said prioress-ship (of which she was then,
perhaps, in possession) Catherine – fearing, for certain likely and credible reasons, that
she would be *de facto* obstructed and molested over the possession, rule, and
administration of the said house or prioress-ship by Joan Harymany, who bears herself
as nun or prioress of the said house, and by certain other clerics or laymen, said d. –
appealed to the local metropolitan court of Canterbury to which by ancient, approved,
and hitherto peacefully observed custom it has been customary to appeal directly; that
after the appeal had been lawfully made known to Joan,[4] and, indeed, after Hopkyn ap
Pukyn', Thomas ap Johi', and Philip apLln, laymen, said d. (who were (?)then lending
[Joan] support in the above[5]), had been inhibited by the official, called president, of the
above court from attempting or innovating anything after or against the said appeal, the
said official, for some reason (*q(ua)r(e)*), refused, at least tacitly, to cancel certain
things then expressed attempted on Joan's part after and against the said appeal,
although he had been lawfully asked to on Catherine's part, at a suitable time and

place; and that appeal was made to the apostolic see on the part of Catherine who felt *inter alia* unduly aggrieved. At the supplication to the pope to order that Catherine be absolved *ad cautelam* from the sentence of excommunication and other ecclesiastical sentences, censures, and pains perhaps inflicted on her on the above occasion and to commit to some upright men in those parts the causes: of the said appeal and of anything perhaps attempted and innovated after and against it; of the nullity of the process of the said official and of each and every other thing done in any way to Catherine's prejudice in connection with the above; and of the whole principal matter, the pope hereby commands that the above two (or one of them), having summoned Joan and others concerned, shall, on the pope's authority, bestow on Catherine, for this once only, if she so requests, the benefit of absolution *ad cautelam* from the said sentence of excommunication and other sentences, censures, and pains, inasmuch as it is just, having, however, first received from her suitable security in respect of that for which she is perhaps deemed excommunicate and caught by the other sentences, censures, and pains, that if they find that the sentences, etc were [justly][6] inflicted on her she will obey their mandates and those of the church; as to the other things, having heard both sides, taking cognizance even of the said principal matter, [decree] what [is] just, [without appeal], causing [by ecclesiastical censure what they have decreed to be strictly] observed,[7] [and moreover compel] witnesses, etc. Notwithstanding etc.

Humilibus et cetera.
phi de angnell(is)[8] / JoA: / :JoA: xiiij: Nardi(nus)

1   diocese(s) not mentioned; *and see below*, note 8.
2   the six minims variously readable
3   MS: *priorissam* (*... vacante*); *recte*: 'priorissatu'?
4   MS: *appellationis* (*huiusmodi dicte Johanne intimata*); *recte*: ' appellatione'
5   MS: *qui tunc in premissis favebant*; *recte*: 'qui eam (or suchlike) in ...'?
6   MS: *iniuste*; *recte*: 'iuste'
7   MS: *quod iustum fuerit et cetera facientes et cetera observari*. Supplied from common form.
8   The note of the abbreviator's name was usually entered by the registry scribe when he transcribed the letter. In this instance the note is in the same hand as the magistral initial and subscription. In all probability, then, the name was not entered until the master signed the register entry. Taken with the hole in the address clause (*cf.* note 1 above) the circumstance is faintly suggestive of premature enregistration from a draft.

603   16 May 1516   *Reg. Lat.* 1344, fos 93ᵛ-96ʳ

To the abbot of the monastery of B. Mary, *de Deserto* [Kells], d. Connor, and the archdeacon and Odo Ochilla, canon, of the church of Connor, mandate in favour of William Oduruyn, cleric, d. Connor. The pope has learned that the rectories of the parish churches of Balananyun [also spelt *Balenanyur, Balenayur, Belenanynr*], Balmalmad [also spelt *Balemalmad, Balenahnad*] and Rassia [also spelt *Rassya*] *alias* Rasyi and also the perpetual vicarage of the parish church of Myblysg,[1] d. Connor, are vacant *certo modo* at present and have been vacant for so long that by the Lateran statutes their collation has lawfully devolved on the apostolic see, although Andrew Obyge and Dermot, John and Magonius Maquelurmna,[2] who bear themselves as priests, have detained the rectories and vicarage respectively, with no title and no support of law, temerariously and *de facto*, for a certain time, and do so. At a recent petition on the part of William (who asserts that some time ago he was dispensed by apostolic authority, notwithstanding a defect of birth as the son of a canon, OSA, and an unmarried woman, to be promoted to all, even sacred, orders, and to hold a benefice, even if it should have cure of souls; and that afterwards he was duly marked with clerical character; and that the annual value of the vicarage and rectories together does not exceed 8 marks sterling), to the pope to unite etc. the above rectories of Balmalmad and Rassia and the above vicarage to the above rectory of Balananyun, for as long as William holds the latter, if conferred on him by virtue of the presents, he hereby [commands]³ that the above three (or two or one of them), if, having summoned Andrew, Dermot, John and Magonius and others concerned, they find the rectories of the said churches of Balananyun, Balmalmad and Rassia and also the above vicarage to be vacant (howsoever etc.), shall collate and assign the rectory of Balananyun to William, and unite etc. the rectories and vicarage aforesaid (even if specially reserved etc.) to the rectory of Balananyun, for as long as William holds the latter, if conferred on him by virtue of the presents, with all rights and appurtenances, inducting William etc. into corporal possession of the rectory of Balananyun and of the annexes and rights and appurtenances aforesaid, having removed Andrew, Dermot, John and Magonius and any other unlawful detainers and causing the fruits etc., rights and obventions of the rectory of Balananyun and of the annexes in question to be delivered to him. [Curbing] gainsayers etc. Notwithstanding etc. The pope's will is, however, that the united vicarage and rectories shall not, on account of this union etc., be defrauded of due services and the cure of souls in them shall not be neglected; but that their customary burdens shall be supported; and that on William's death or his resignation etc. of the rectory of Balananyun this union etc. shall be dissolved and be so deemed and the united vicarage and rectories shall revert to their original condition automatically.

Apostolice sedis providentia circumspecta ...
.G de prato / phi. / .phi. xx. pridie Id(us) Junij Anno Quarto [12 June 1516], *de Senis*

1   the 'g' doubtful; perhaps 'ij' or 'n' or possibly 'y'
2   the 'q' perhaps a 'g'; and the '-mna-' uncertain
3   'mandamus' wanting

604   1 June 1516   *Reg. Lat.* 1344, fos 98ᵛ-100ᵛ

To [Nemeas]¹ Magnell, John de Burgo and Malachy Ohicgyn,² canons of the church of Tuam, mandate in favour of Thomas Omanay, cleric of Tuam (who, as he asserts, some time ago was dispensed by ordinary authority, notwithstanding a defect of birth as the son of a priest and a married woman, to be marked with clerical character; and then by apostolic authority, to be promoted to all, even sacred and priest's, orders, and to hold a benefice, even if it should have cure of souls; and by virtue of the said dispensation was duly marked with the said character). The pope has learned that a certain perpetual simple benefice, called semi-vicarage or semi-office or semi-stipend,³ in the church of

Tuam, is vacant *certo modo* at present and has been vacant for so long that by the Lateran statutes its collation has lawfully devolved on the apostolic see, although Richard Ohart, who bears himself as a cleric, has detained it, with no title and no support of law, of his own temerity and *de facto*, for a certain time, as he still does. He hereby commands that the above three (or two or one of them), if, having summoned Richard and others concerned, they find the benefice (whose annual value does not exceed 2 marks sterling) to be vacant (howsoever etc.), shall collate and assign it (even if specially reserved etc.), with all rights and appurtenances, to Thomas, inducting him etc. having removed Richard and any other unlawful detainer and causing Thomas (or his proctor) to be admitted to the benefice and its fruits etc., rights and obventions to be delivered to him. Curbing gainsayers by the pope's authority etc. Notwithstanding etc.

Vite ac morum honestas …
Phy Agnellis / M / M x decimo octavo k(a)l(endas) Julij a(n)no quarto [14 June 1516], *de Campania*

1   *Nunee; recte:* 'Nimee' (for 'Nemee'?)
2   the 'O' (written *o*) ink-clogged and doubtful
3   MS: *quoddam perpetuum simplex beneficium ecclesiasticum semi-vicaria aut semi-officium seu semi-stipendium nuncupatum Cf.* below, no. 605, note 2.

605   3 June 1516   *Reg. Lat.* 1344, fos 100ᵛ-103ʳ

To Magonius Omanay and Nemeas and David Ohallinan, canons of the church of Annaghdown, mandate in favour of John de Burgo, canon of Tuam. The pope has learned that the perpetual vicarage of the parish church of St Malachy, Adrignull,[1] d. Tuam, and a perpetual simple benefice, called semi-vicarage or semi-stipend,[2] in the church of Tuam, are vacant *certo modo* at present and have been vacant for so long that by the Lateran statutes their collation has lawfully devolved on the apostolic see, although Donald Macarsurlui,[3] who bears himself as a priest, has detained the vicarage and Odo Okurllay,[4] who bears himself as a cleric, has detained the said benefice, with no title and no support of law, of their own temerity and *de facto*, for a certain time, as they still do. At a recent petition on the part of John (who asserts that he holds a canonry of the said church of Tuam; and that the annual value of the vicarage and benefice together does not exceed 6 marks sterling) to the pope to erect and institute the vicarage and benefice into a simple prebend of the church of Tuam for his lifetime, the pope – not having certain knowledge of the foregoing – hereby commands that the above three (or two or one of them), if, having summoned Donald and Odo and, as regards the erection, the archbishop and chapter of Tuam, and others concerned, they find the vicarage and benefice to be vacant (howsoever etc.) shall erect and institute them (even if specially reserved etc.) into a simple prebend of the church of Tuam for John's lifetime, as above, without prejudice to anyone; and, in that event, collate and assign the newly erected prebend, being then vacant, to John, with all rights and appurtenances; inducting him etc. having removed Donald and Odo and any other unlawful detainers and causing John (or his proctor) to be admitted to the prebend and its fruits etc., rights and obventions to be delivered to him. [Curbing] gainsayers etc. Notwithstanding etc. The pope's will is, however, that the above vicarage and benefice shall not, on this account, be defrauded of due services and the cure of souls in the vicarage shall not be neglected; but that its customary burdens and those of the benefice shall be supported; and that on John's death or his resignation etc. of the prebend this erection [and] institution shall be extinguished and be so deemed and the vicarage and benefice shall revert to their original [condition] automatically.

Apostolice sedis providentia circumspecta benignitas ad ea libenter intendit ...
Phy Agnellis / M / M xv decimo octavo k(a)l(endas) Julij a(n)no quarto [14 June 1516],
de Campania

1   the minims (here read as *-nu-*) variously readable
2   MS: *perpetuum simplex beneficium ecclesiasticum semi-vicaria seu semi-stipendium nuncupatum* Cf. above,
      no. 604, note 3.
3   the 'ui' doubtful
4   the letters here read as *-ur-* readable as *-ui-, -ni-*, etc.

606   16 May 1516   *Reg. Lat.* 1344, fos 103ᵛ-105ᵛ

To the abbots of the monasteries of Moybile, d. Down, and of Gudbuerum, d. Connor, and James Cuirni, canon of the church of Leighlin, mandate in favour of Patrick Macgelarinun,¹ cleric, d. Connor. It has been referred to the pope's audience by Patrick that Odo Machrecani, perpetual vicar of the vicarage of the parish church of St. Archanata, Duochayn *alias* Dumdean,² and Magonius Macgelarinan, rector of the parish church of St Bridget, Killbride, d. Connor, have dared to dilapidate the rectory's goods and to commit fornication, perjury and simony; and supplication has been made on the part of Patrick (who asserts that the annual value of the vicarage and rectory together does not exceed 5 marks sterling; and that he has been dispensed by apostolic authority, notwithstanding a defect of birth as the son of an unmarried man and an unmarried woman, to be promoted to all, even sacred and priest's, orders, and to hold a benefice, even if it should have cure of souls) to the pope to unite etc. the rectory to the vicarage, for as long as Patrick should hold the latter, if conferred on him by virtue of the presents. Considering that if the foregoing is true Odo and Magonius have rendered themselves unworthy of the vicarage and the rectory, and wishing to give Patrick a special grace, the pope hereby commands that the above three (or two or one of them), if Patrick will accuse Odo and Magonius before them over the above related matters and proceed in form of law, thereafter, having summoned Odo and Magonius and others concerned and those interested in the union, shall make inquiry into these matters and, if they find the truth of them to be substantiated, shall deprive Odo of the vicarage and Magonius of the rectory and remove them from them; and, in the event of this deprivation and removal by virtue of the presents, shall collate and assign the vicarage to Patrick, and unite etc. the rectory (whether it and the vicarage are vacant by this deprivation and removal or in any other way, etc.; even if they have been vacant for so long that by the Lateran statutes their collation has lawfully devolved on the apostolic see, etc.), with all rights and appurtenances, to the vicarage, for as long as Patrick holds the latter, inducting him etc. into corporal possession of the vicarage and annexed rectory and rights and appurtenances aforesaid, having removed Odo and Magonius and any other unlawful detainers and causing Patrick (or his proctor) to be admitted to the vicarage and its fruits etc., rights and obventions and those of the annexed rectory to be delivered to him. [Curbing] gainsayers etc. Notwithstanding etc. The pope's will is, however, that the rectory shall not, on account of this union etc., be defrauded of due services and the cure of souls in it shall not be neglected; but that its customary burdens shall be supported; and that on the death of Patrick or his resignation etc. of the vicarage this union etc. shall be dissolved and be so deemed and the rectory shall revert to its original condition and be deemed vacant automatically.

Vite ac morum honestas ...
Phy Agnellis / M / M x de Campania

1   the seven minims at the end variously readable
2   the five minims here read as 'um' variously readable

607   30 May 1516   *Reg. Lat.* 1344, fos 107ʳ-109ʳ

To John Ohogayn and John Macnymarra, canons of the church of Killaloe, and (?)Denis[1] Omalryayn, canon of the church of Emly, mandate in favour of James *alias* Sida Macnymarra, cleric, d. Killaloe. The pope has learned that the rectory of the parish church of Killmirayn, of Fyckyll, Hyconyly, Ardhy [and] Chlelyn,[2] d. Killaloe, (which, as is asserted, is of lay patronage) is vacant *certo modo* at present and has been vacant for so long that by the Lateran statutes its collation has lawfully devolved on the apostolic see, although John Ocormacam, who bears himself as dean of the church of Killaloe, has detained the rectory, with no title and no support of law, of his own temerity and *de facto*, for a certain time, and does so. He hereby commands that the above three (or two or one of them), if, having summoned John and others concerned, they find the rectory (which is without cure and whose annual value does not exceed 22 marks sterling) to be vacant (howsoever etc.) shall collate and assign it (even if specially reserved etc.), with all rights and appurtenances, to James, inducting him etc. having removed John and any other unlawful detainer, and causing James (or his proctor) to be admitted to the rectory and its fruits etc., rights and obventions to be delivered to him. [Curbing] gainsayers etc. Notwithstanding etc.

Vite ac morum honestas ...
G de Prato / M / M xv decimo octavo k(a)l(endas) julij a(n)no quarto [14 June 1516], *de Campania*

1   MS: *Dornisio* or *Dorvisio*; *recte*: 'Dionisio'?
2   ... *rectoria parrochialis ecclesie de Killmirayn de Fyckyll Hyconyly Ardhy Chlelyn dicte diocesis* ... On the enumeration: *cf. CPL* VIII, p. 4; XIII, p. 609.

608   3 June 1516   *Reg. Lat.* 1344, fos 116ʳ-118ᵛ

To the precentor and Dermot Omulreayn, canon, of the church of Emly, and James
Ocurryn, canon of the church of Leighlin, mandate in favour of Thomas Ogrida, canon
of the church of Killaloe. The pope has learned that the treasurership of the church of
Killaloe and the perpetual vicarage of the parish church of Congiren' [also spelt
Congirenen[1]], d. Killaloe, are vacant *certo modo* at present and have been vacant for
so long that by the Lateran statutes their collation has lawfully devolved on the
apostolic see, although Cornelius Macnamara, who bears himself as a cleric, has
detained the treasurership and John Ograda, who bears himself as a priest, has detained
the vicarage, with no title and no support of law, of their own temerity and *de facto*, for
a certain time, as they do. On the part of Thomas (who asserts that some time ago –
after he had been duly marked with clerical character, notwithstanding a defect of birth
as the son of a cleric and an unmarried woman related in the third and fourth degrees
of consanguinity and affinity – he was dispensed by apostolic authority to be promoted
to all, even sacred and priest's, orders and to receive and retain the canonry and
prebend of Congiren' of the said church of Killaloe, then vacant *certo modo*, which
were to be conferred on him by apostolic authority; and that afterwards he had acquired
the said canonry and prebend which were conferred on him by the said authority while
vacant as above; and that the annual value of the above [treasurership?][2] does not
exceed 12, and vicarage, 6, marks sterling) petition[3] was made to the pope to unite etc.
the said treasurership and vicarage to the said canonry and prebend, for as long as
Thomas holds the latter.The pope, therefore, hereby commands that the above three (or
two or one of them), if, having summoned Cornelius and John and others concerned,
they find the treasurership (which is a dignity, not however major *post pontificalem*)
and the vicarage to be vacant (howsoever etc.) shall unite etc. them (even if specially
reserved etc.), with all rights and appurtenances, to the said canonry and prebend, for
as long as Thomas holds the latter, having removed Cornelius and John and any other
unlawful detainers from the said treasurership and vicarage; to the effect that Thomas
may, on his own authority, in person or by proxy, take and retain corporal possession
of the treasurership and vicarage and the rights and appurtenances aforesaid, for as
long as he holds the canonry and prebend, and convert their fruits etc. to his own uses
and those of the canonry and prebend and of the treasurership and vicarage without
licence of the local diocesan or of anyone else. [Curbing] gainsayers etc.
Notwithstanding etc. The pope's will is, however, that the treasurership and vicarage
shall not, on account of this union etc., be defrauded of due services and the cure of
souls in the vicarage [and] (if any) the treasurership shall not be neglected, but that
customary burdens shall be supported; and that on Thomas's death or his resignation
etc. of the canonry and prebend this union etc. shall be dissolved and be so deemed and
the treasurership and vicarage shall revert to their original condition automatically.

Romanum decet pontificem votis illis gratum prestare assensum …
G de Prato. / M / M XX nono k(a)l(endas) Julij anno quarto [23 June 1516]*, de*[4]
Campania

1 the 'C' over 'T'?
2 'thesaurarie' does not occur here: wanting?
3 'nuper' does not occur.
4 the 'd' reworked; originally a 'D'?

609   21 May 1516   *Reg. Lat.* 1344, fos 118ᵛ-122ᵛ

To the abbot of the monastery of B. Mary, *de Vuothaya* [Abington], d. Emly, and
Cormac Ochey and Maurice Omadyn, canons of the church of Emly, mandate in favour
of William Macbryen, cleric, d. Emly. Following the pope's reservation some time ago
of all benefices, with and without cure, vacated then and in the future at the apostolic
see to his own collation and disposition, the rectory of the parish church of Valt [also
spelt *Nalt*] *alias* Killmali and the perpetual vicarage of that [parish church] [and]¹ the
perpetual vicarage of the parish church of Killsyly [also spelt *Kyllsyly*,² *Kylsyli*,
Kyllsyli, *Kylsyly*], d. Emly, [became vacant] by the free resignation of Rory
Omarcacayn, recently rector of Valt and perpetual vicar of Valt and Killsyly, (which he
was then holding and which had been mutually united by ordinary authority for as long
as he should hold them) made spontaneously through Bernard Ochoyn, cleric of the
same diocese, his specially appointed [proctor], into the hands of the pope who
admitted this resignation at the said see. And the pope has learned that the
chancellorship of the church of Emly and the perpetual vicarage of the parish church
of Tempul Hybrydeayin³ [also spelt Tempul Hybrydeayn, Tempul Hybrydeyn, Tempul
Hybrydayn, Tempul Hybrydeayr], d. Emly, are vacant *certo modo* at present and the
said vicarage of Tempul Hybrydeayin has been vacant for so long that by the Lateran
statutes its collation has lawfully devolved on the apostolic see, although Maurice
Ococulayn, who bears himself as a priest, has detained the vicarage of Tempul
Hybrydeayin without any title (at least any canonical title), for a certain time, but short
of a year, and does so. And the above rectory of Valt and vicarages of Valt and Killsyly
are reserved as above. At a recent petition on the part of William (who asserts that some
time ago, notwithstanding a defect of birth as the son of a canon of the said church of
Emly and an unmarried woman, he was marked with clerical character otherwise
however duly; and that the annual value of the above chancellorship, vicarages and
rectory together does not exceed 9 marks sterling) to the pope to unite etc. the rectory
and vicarages to the chancellorship, for as long as William should hold the latter, if
conferred on him by virtue of the presents, the pope hereby commands that the above
three (or two or one of them) shall collate and assign the chancellorship (which is a
dignity, not however major *post pontificalem*) to William; and if, having summoned
Maurice and others concerned, they find the vicarage of the church of Tempul
Hybrydeayin to be vacant, unite etc. that vicarage and those of Valt and Killsyly and
also the rectory (whether the rectory of Valt and the vicarage of Killsyly are vacant in
the aforesaid or any other way; and howsoever etc. the chancellorship and the vicarage
of Tempul Hybrydeayin are vacant; even if the chancellorship, the rectory and the
vicarages of Valt and Killsyly have been vacant for so long that by the Lateran statutes
their collation has lawfully devolved on the apostolic see, and even if they and the
vicarage of Tempul Hybrydeayin are specially reserved etc.), with all rights and

appurtenances, to the said chancellorship, for as long as William should hold [the latter], if conferred on him as above; inducting William etc. into corporal possession of the chancellorship and annexed rectory and vicarages and rights and appurtenances aforesaid, having removed Maurice from the vicarage of Tempul Hybrydeayin and any unlawful detainers from the chancellorship and the rectory and remaining vicarages; and causing William (or his proctor) to be admitted to the chancellorship and its fruits etc., rights and obventions and those of the annexed rectory and vicarages to be delivered to him. [Curbing] gainsayers etc. Notwithstanding etc. Also the pope dispenses William to receive and retain the chancellorship, if [conferred] on him by virtue of the presents, for life, and with it, one, or without them, any two other benefices, with cure or otherwise mutually incompatible, and also any number of benefices, with and without cure, compatible mutually and with the said incompatible benefices, even if the compatible benefices should be canonries and prebends and they as well as the incompatible benefices should be dignities, *personatus*, administrations or offices in cathedral, even metropolitan, or collegiate churches, or these incompatible benefices should be parish churches or their perpetual vicarages, or a combination,[4] and even if the dignities etc. should be customarily elective and have cure of souls, if he obtains them otherwise canonically; to resign them, at once or successively, simply or for exchange, as often as he pleases, and in their place receive up to two other, similar or dissimilar, incompatible benefices and any number of other benefices, with or without cure, compatible mutually as above – provided that the dignities in question be not major *post pontificalem* in metropolitan or other cathedral churches or principal in collegiate churches; and retain even the incompatible benefices together for life, as above, notwithstanding the above defect of birth etc. The pope's will is, however, that the chancellorship and rectory and also the vicarages and other incompatible benefices aforesaid shall not, on this account, be defrauded of due services and the cure of souls in the rectory and vicarages and (if any) the chancellorship and other incompatible benefices shall not be neglected; but that customary burdens of the rectory and vicarages shall be supported; and that on William's death or his resignation etc. of the chancellorship this union etc. shall be dissolved and be so deemed and the rectory and vicarage[s] shall revert to their original condition automatically.

Vite ac morum honestas ...
G de Prato / phi / .phi. L. de Senis

1   MS: ... *rectoria de Valt alias de Killmali ac illius* ['et' wanting?] *de Killsyly perpetue vicarie parrochialium ecclesiarum* ...
2   This spelling occurs most frequently; in one instance, however, *Kyllysyly* was written first, and the second 'y' was deleted (but not initialled).
3   changed (by overwriting) from (?) -*deanyin*
4   The tenor of the entry is clear, despite several superfluous repetitions in the text (such as the passage rendered here as 'dignities, *personatus* ... combination').

610   26 May 1516   *Reg. Lat.* 1344, fos 131ʳ-133ᵛ

To Thomas de Burgo and Magonius Omanay and David Ohillman, canons of the church of Tuam,[1] mandate in favour of Thomas de Burgo, canon of Tuam. The pope has learned that the monastery of St Mary, Cong (*de Conga*), OSA, and the perpetual vicarage of the parish church of the Twelve Holy Apostles, Kilmeanbec, d. Tuam, are vacant *certo modo* at present and have been vacant for so long that the collation of the vicarage (by the Lateran statutes) and the provision of the monastery (by canonical sanctions) have lawfully devolved on the apostolic see, although Eneas Macdonayl, who bears himself as abbot, has detained the monastery, with no title and no support of law, of his own temerity and *de facto*, for a certain time, as he still does. At a recent petition on the part of Thomas de Burgo, canon of Tuam[2] (who asserts that he holds a canonry of the said church of Tuam, whose annual value is nil; and that the annual value of the vicarage does not exceed 3, and of the monastery, 50, marks sterling; and that Miler de Burgo, layman, is taking the vicarage's fruits) to the pope to erect and institute the vicarage into a simple prebend of the church of Tuam, and unite etc. the monastery to the prebend thus erected, for Thomas's lifetime, the pope hereby commands that the above three (or two or one of them), having summoned Eneas and, as regards the erection, the archbishop and chapter of Tuam and others concerned, and those interested in the union, shall erect and institute the vicarage into a simple prebend of the church of Tuam, without prejudice to anyone; and, in that event, collate and assign the newly erected prebend, being then vacant, to Thomas; and unite etc. the monastery (howsoever etc. the monastery and vicarage are vacant; even if the vicarage is specially reserved to apostolic disposition and provision of the monastery pertains specially or generally to the apostolic see, etc.) to the said canonry and prebend, with all rights and appurtenances, for Thomas's lifetime; inducting Thomas (or his proctor) into corporal possession of the prebend and annex and rights and appurtenances aforesaid, having removed Miler and Eneas and any other unlawful detainers and causing Thomas (or his proctor) to be admitted to the prebend and its fruits etc., rights and obventions and those of the monastery to be delivered to him. Curbing gainsayers by the pope's authority etc. Notwithstanding etc. The pope's will is, however, that divine worship and the usual number of canons and ministers in the said monastery shall not, on this account, be diminished; and the vicarage shall not be defrauded of due services and the cure of souls in it shall not be neglected, but that customary burdens of the vicarage and monastery shall be supported; and that on Thomas's death or his resignation etc. of the prebend this erection, institution and union etc. shall be extinguished and be so deemed automatically and the vicarage and monastery shall revert to their original condition. Given at Rome.[3]

Apostolice sedis circumspecta benignitas ad ea libenter intendit …
Phi Agnellis / JoA. / JoA: xxxv: Nardinus

1   spelt *Tumacen.* throughout the entry
2   The petitioner Thomas de Burgo, canon of Tuam, is not, of course, to be confused with the Thomas de Burgo, canon of Tuam, named in the address clause as one of the three mandataries.
3   MS: *Rome anno…*; wants 'apud Sanctum Petrum' after *Rome*?

611   24 April 1516   *Reg. Lat.* 1344, fos 141ʳ-144ʳ

To Felmeus Omulrean, canon of the church of Emly, William Offlauuan, canon of the church of Cashel, and the official of Kilfenora, mandate in favour of John Ymallayn, canon, OSA (who asserts that he, at another time, for certain reasons then expressed, had, by apostolic authority, been translated from the order of St Francis – of which he was expressly professed at the time – to the above Augustinian order; and been dispensed to receive and retain any benefices of the Augustinian order, even abbatial dignities, [if] conferred [on him] otherwise canonically). The pope has learned that the monastery of B. Mary, Killesama, OSA, and the perpetual vicarages of the parish churches of Kiltocorach [also spelt *Killthorach*] and Gleaneneach and also the perpetual vicarage of the parish church of Aglaysni in Ballayn [also spelt *Aglis in Ballayn*] (*alias* "the chaplaincy of the monks")[1], and of Cromlyn [also spelt *Cromlynd*] and of Kathblamac [also spelt *Katblame*], and also the rectory of the parish church of Aglinmena *alias* Nova, ds. Kilfenora and Killaloe, are vacant *certo modo* at present and have been vacant for so long that the provision of the monastery (by canonical sanctions) and the collation of the vicarages and rectory (by the Lateran statutes) have lawfully devolved on the apostolic see, although Maurus Obrien has detained the monastery [and the vicarages][2] of Cromlyn and Kathblamac, Cornelius Oconoanbar has detained [the vicarage] of Kiltocorach, and (?)Thady[3] Obrien [the vicarages] of Gleaneneach and Aglaysni in Ballayn, and Honorius Olochlynd has detained the rectory – bearing themselves as clerics of the said dioceses – with no title, temerariously and *de facto*, for a certain time, as they still do. A recent petition on John's part to the pope to unite etc. the vicarages and rectory to the said monastery, for as long as John should preside over the monastery, if he were to be provided to it, stated that the monastery's fruits etc. are, as a result of several unfortunate events, so slender that the abbot for the time being cannot conveniently support himself from them in accordance with abbatial dignity and discharge the burdens incumbent on him); and John asserts that the annual value of the fruits etc. of the monastery does not exceed 16, and of the vicarages and rectory together, 20, marks sterling. The pope, therefore, hereby commands that the above three (or two or one of them), if, having summoned Maurus, (?)Thady, Cornelius and Honorius and others concerned, they find the monastery (which is not customarily disposed of consistorially) and the said vicarages and rectory to be vacant (howsoever etc.), shall (even if provision of the monastery be specially or generally reserved, and the vicarages and rectory be specially reserved etc.) make provision of John to the monastery and appoint him abbot, committing the care, rule and administration of the monastery to him in spiritualities and temporalities, and unite etc. the vicarages and rectory to the monastery, with all their rights and appurtenances, for as long as John presides over the monastery in the event of the pope providing him to it; inducting him etc. into corporal possession of the annexed vicarages and rectory and the rights and appurtenances aforesaid, having removed Maurus, Cornelius, (?)Thady and Honorius and any other unlawful detainers and causing due obedience and reverence to be given to John by the convent and customary services and rights by the vassals and other subjects of the monastery, and [causing] the fruits etc., rights and obventions of the vicarages and rectory to be delivered to him. [Curbing] gainsayers etc. Notwithstanding etc. The pope's will is, however, that the above vicarages and rectory shall not, on account of this union etc., be defrauded of due services and the cure of souls in them shall not be neglected; but that their customary burdens shall be supported; and that on John's death or his resignation etc. of the rule and administration of the monastery this union etc. shall be dissolved and be so deemed and the vicarages and rectory shall revert to their original condition automatically. Given at Palo, d. Porto.

Ex suscepte servitutis officio solicitudine pulsamur assidua …
.Je Benzon / JoA: / :JoA: L: Nardinus

1   *alias capellania monachorum nuncuptata* [!]
2   *licet … rectoriam* (?)*predictas* …; 'et vicarias' does not occur, and the final 's' of *predictas* may well be struck out. Nevertheless, the context – set by the opening narrative which listed five vicarages as well as the rectory – requires 'rectoriam et vicarias predictas'.
3   MS: *Julianus* (a slip for Thadeus?) in the first instance; thereafter his name is given (thrice altogether) as Thadeus (variously inflected). Thady seems the more likely name for an OBrien.

612   22 June 1516   *Reg. Lat.* 1344, fos 186ᵛ-187ᵛ

To William Busbi, rector of the parish church of B. Mary the Virgin, Hoo, d. Rochester (who, as he asserts, is a BA). Dispensation and indult etc. [as above, no. 2].

Vite ac morum honestas …
P Lambert(us) / M / M Lx de Campania

613   18 June 1516   *Reg. Lat.* 1344, fos 188ʳ-189ᵛ

Union etc. At a recent petition on the part of Richard Davi *alias* Davies, perpetual beneficed cleric, called the prebendary of Denys [also spelt *Denis*], in the parish church of Chulmelegh [also spelt *Chulmelemgh*¹], d. Exeter, the pope hereby unites etc. the parish church of Burklond [also spelt *Burkolond*], d. Winchester, and the perpetual vicarage of the parish church of Brodhambery, d. Exeter, (whose annual values do not exceed 5 and 11 pounds sterling [respectively]), which he holds together with the perpetual simple benefice, called the prebend of Denys, in the said church of Chulmelegh, by apostolic dispensation, with all rights and appurtenances, to the said benefice, for as long as Richard holds the latter,² to the effect that he may, on his own authority, in person or by proxy, continue in, or take anew, and retain corporal possession of the church of Burklond, the vicarage and the rights and appurtenances aforesaid, for as long as he holds the said benefice,³ and convert their fruits etc. to his own uses and those of the church of Burklond, the vicarage and the benefice aforesaid, without licence of the local diocesan or of anyone else. Notwithstanding etc. The pope's will is, however, that the said church of Burklond and the vicarage shall not, on account of this union etc., be defrauded of due services and the cure of souls in them shall not be neglected; but that their customary burdens shall be supported; and that on Richard's death or his resignation etc. of the benefice this union etc. shall be dissolved and be so deemed and the church of Burklond and the vicarage shall revert to their original condition and be deemed vacant automatically.

Ad futuram rei memoriam. Romanum decet pontificem votis illis gratum prestare assensum ...
.Je Benzon / M / M xxxv de Campania

1   written *Cuhu-* the first 'u' being deleted
2   MS: *quamdiu ipse Ricardus illud* [sc. perpetual simple benefice] *obtinuerit*; thus the second part of the narrative and the operative part of the letter. But the first part of the narrative has (wrongly): *quamdiu ipse Ricardus ecclesiam de Burklond et vicariam huiusmodi obtinuerit*
3   *see above*, note 2

614   19 June 1516   *Reg. Lat.* 1344, fos 261ʳ-262ᵛ

To the abbot of the monastery of B Mary, Wyndhm', d. Norwich, the prior of the church of Norwich, and the official of Norwich, mandate in favour of Thomas Hawnel, cleric or layman, d. Norwich. A recent petition to the pope on Thomas' part stated that when, at another time, a law suit had arisen between Thomas and John Compton', cleric or layman, and Agnes Fyllys *alias* Robynson' or Compton', woman, London, co-litigants in this regard, over the marriage contracted between Thomas and Agnes or over its dissolution (*divortio*), before Walter Stone, auditor of causes of the court of the archbishop of Canterbury, legate born of the apostolic see in those parts, Walter – proceeding wrongly in the case and (although it was clear to him from several witnesses who were beyond objection that Thomas had a good right) following the testimony of certain witnesses produced and examined on Agnes and John's part – promulgated an unjust or null, definitive (as he said) sentence, in favour of Agnes and John and against Thomas, from which, on Thomas' part, appeal was made to the apostolic see. At the supplication to the pope to commit to some upright men in those parts the causes: of the aforesaid appeal and of anything attempted and innovated after and against it; of the nullity of the process and sentence of Walter and of each and every other thing done in any way by him and any other judges and persons to Thomas' prejudice in connection with the above; and of the whole principal matter, the pope [hereby] commands that the above three (or two or one of them), having summoned Agnes and John and others concerned and having heard both sides, taking cognizance even of the principal matter, shall decree what is canonical, without appeal, causing by ecclesiastical censure, what they have decreed to be strictly observed; and moreover compel witnesses, etc.[1] Notwithstanding etc.; and that the above three are not of the class of persons to whom such cases have customarily been committed by the apostolic see, etc.

Humilibus et cetera.
.P. lanbertus / M / M xv de Campania

1   Unexpected: the *Testes* clause (which, unusually, is here fully extended and not abbreviated with 'et cetera')
     is not, as a rule, given in marriage cases.

615   22 June 1516   *Reg. Lat.* 1344, fos 311ʳ-312ʳ

To John Dolman' and William Haryngton', canons of the church of London, and
Richard Tollett[1], canon of the church of Exeter, mandate in favour of James Slake,
layman, d. Lincoln. A recent petition to the pope on James' part stated that when, at
another time, he sued Thomas Colynson *alias* Hilston', cleric or layman, said d. – who
had rashly contravened a certain oath [made to][2] James which he [i.e. Thomas] was
bound by law to observe – before Cuthbert Tunscall', auditor of causes cognizance of
which belongs to the archbishop of Canterbury for the time being by reason of the
office of legate born appointed by William, archbishop of Canterbury, legate born of
the apostolic see in those parts, praying *inter alia* over this that he be condemned, and
either coerced and compelled to observe the said oath or declared to have incurred the
guilt of perjury, Walter Stone, appointed auditor of such causes by archbishop William
when Cuthbert was absent, proceeding wrongly in the case, promulgated an unjust or
null definitive (as he said) sentence in Thomas' favour and against James, from which,
on James' part, appeal was made to the apostolic see. At the supplication to commit to
some upright men in those parts the causes: of the aforesaid appeal and of anything
attempted and innovated after and against it; of the nullity and nullities of Walter's
process and sentence and of each and every other thing done in any way by Walter and
any other judges and persons to James' prejudice in connection with the above; and of
the whole principal matter, the pope [hereby] commands that the above three (or two
or one of them), having summoned Thomas and others concerned and having heard
both sides, taking cognizance even of the principal matter, shall decree what is just,
without appeal, causing by ecclesiastical censure what they have decreed to be strictly
observed. Notwithstanding etc.

Humilibus et cetera.
P. lanb(er)tus / JoA: / :JoA: xij: Nardi(nus):

1   'tt' read sympathetically
2   MS: *iuramentum (?)ab (?)eodem Jacobo prestitum*; *recte*:'… eidem Jacobo …'?

616   22 April 1516   *Reg. Lat.* 1345, fos 21ʳ-22ʳ

To John Hekker, rector of the parish church of Asshe, d. Norwich. Dispensation and
indult etc. [as above, no. 2]. Given at Palo, d. Porto.

Vite ac morum honestas …
A. de. s. severino / JoA: / :JoA: Lx: Nardinus

617   13 April 1516   *Reg. Lat.* 1345, fos 22ʳ-23ʳ

To William Lyntoke, canon of the monastery of B. Mary Magdalene, Pentenen[1] [also spelt *Pentenee*], OSA, d. Norwich. Dispensation – at his supplication – to him, who, as he asserts, is expressly professed of the above order,[2] to receive and retain for life any benefice, with or without cure, usually held by secular clerics, etc. [as above, no. 43]. Given at Magliana, d. Porto.

Religionis zelus, vite ac morum honestas …
A. de. s. severino / JoA: / :JoA: xxx: Nardinus

1   or possibly *Penteney*
2   This information comes from a notwithstanding clause.

618   26 March 1516   *Reg. Lat.* 1345, fos 52ʳ-55ᵛ

To Felineus Omulrrian' and Dermot Omulrrian', canons of the church of Emly, and Cornelius Macnoniara, canon of the church of Killaloe, mandate in favour of Donat Macnomara, cleric, d. Killaloe. The pope has learned that the precentorship [of the church] of Killaloe and a canonry and prebend [of the church] of Moyn', [also spelt *Moyyn*], d. Limerick,[1] and the perpetual vicarages of the parish churches of Kylldsenaulyc' [also spelt *Kyllsenaulien*,[2] *Kylldeseuanlye'*], Kylloguede [also spelt *Kyllloguede*[3]], Kyllsogene [also spelt *Kyllsogeme*[4]] and of Kylcuayn[5] [also spelt *Kyllacayn*,[6] *Kyllarayn*, *Kyllcuayn*] (which, as is asserted, was at another time an integral part (*membrum*) of the treasurership [of the church] of Limerick), d. Killaloe and said d. Limerick, are vacant *certo modo* at present and have been vacant for so long that by the Lateran statutes their collation has lawfully devolved on the apostolic see, although Andrew Crees[7] has detained the canonry and prebend, Donald Obrien'[8] the precentorship and the vicarages of Kylloguede and Kyllsogene and John Macconomara the vicarages of Kylldsenaulyc' and Kylcuayn – bearing themselves as clerics – with no title,[9] temerariously and *de facto*, for a certain [time][10], as they still do. At a recent petition on the part of Donat (who asserts that he is of noble birth by both parents; and that the annual value of the canonry and prebend of the church of Moyn' and of the precentorship and vicarages aforesaid does not exceed 50 marks sterling) to the pope to erect and institute the vicarage of Kylldsenaulyc' into a simple prebend of a canonry in the said church of Killaloe, for as long as Donat should hold the canonry, if conferred on him by virtue of the presents; and to unite etc. the vicarages of Kylloguede, Kyllsogene and Kylcuayn and also the canonry and prebend of [the church of] Moyn' and the precentorship aforesaid to the proposed [prebend][11], the pope hereby commands that the above three (or two or one of them), if, having summoned Andrew, Donald and John and as regards the erection the bishop and chapter of Killaloe and others concerned, they find the [precentorship][12], which is a dignity, not however major *post pontificalem*, and the canonry and prebend of the church of Moyn' and the vicarages in question to be vacant (howsoever etc.; even if specially reserved etc.) shall erect and institute the vicarage of Kylldsenaulyc' into a simple prebend of the above canonry in the church of Killaloe which is to be conferred on Donat, for as long as he should hold this canonry, without prejudice to anyone; and collate and assign this canonry and the prebend thus erected and instituted to Donat, with plenitude of canon law; and also unite etc. the canonry of the church of Moyn', the precentorship and the vicarages of Kylloguede, Kyllsogene and Kylcuayn to the proposed prebend, for as long as Donat should hold the latter, inducting him etc. into corporal possession of the canonry to be conferred and prebend to be erected and thus then of the annexes and rights and appurtenances aforesaid, having removed Andrew, Donald, John and any other unlawful detainers from the same; and causing Donat (or his proctor) to be received as a canon of the church of Killaloe; and shall assign him a stall in the choir and a place in the chapter of the church of Killaloe, with plenitude of canon law; and [causing] the fruits etc., rights and obventions of the said canonry, proposed prebend and annexes to be delivered to him. [Curbing] gainsayers etc. Notwithstanding etc. The pope's will is, however, that the canonry and prebend of the church of Moyn' and the precentorship and vicarages aforesaid shall not, on account of this union etc., be defrauded of due services and the cure of souls in the vicarages and (if any) the precentorship shall not be neglected; but that their customary burdens shall be supported; and that on Donat's death or his resignation etc. of the canonry [of the church of Killaloe] to be conferred on him, the above erection and institution shall be extinguished and union etc. shall be dissolved and so deemed and the canonry and prebend [of the church of Moyn'], the precentorship and vicarages shall revert to their original condition automatically.

Apostolice sedis providencia circumspecta votis illis gratum prestat assensum...
J. Benzon / JoA: / :JoA: xxxx: Nardinus

1   *sic: Limiricen. dioc(esis)*
2   or perhaps *-liey*
3   *sic*
4   or *-gene* or even possibly *-gewe*
5   the '-cu-' uncertain; possibly '-en-', '-m-' etc.
6   the '-c-' uncertain; maybe a 'r'
7   reading *Andreas Crees*; but both names are uncertain.
8   uncertain (esp. the 'b')
9   'nullove iuris adminiculo' (or suchlike) does not occur.
10   'tempus' wanting
11   MS: (?)*preforende*; *recte*: 'prebende'?
12   *preceptoriam*; *recte*: 'precentoriam'

619   27 March 1516   *Reg. Lat.* 1345, fos 57ᵛ-60ʳ

To the abbot of the monastery of BB. Peter and Paul, Clogher,[1] and the official of Clogher, mandate in favour of Philip Macieneir, cleric, d. Clogher. The pope has learned that the perpetual vicarage of the parish church of Rannchinalas.[2] *alias* Plebis Clochran,[3] d. Clogher, is vacant *certo modo* at present and has been vacant for so long that by the Lateran statutes its collation has lawfully devolved on the apostolic see, although Nielanus[4] Oluan,[5] who bears himself as a priest, has detained the vicarage, with no title and no support of law, of his own temerity and *de facto*, for a certain time, and does so. At a recent petition on Philip's part to the pope to erect[6] a canonry in the church of Clogher and the said vicarage into a simple prebend of it, for his lifetime, the pope hereby commands that the above two (or one of them), if, having summoned Nicholas[7] and the bishop and chapter of Clogher as regards the erection[8] and others concerned, they find the vicarage (whose annual value does not exceed 5 marks sterling) to be vacant (howsoever etc.) shall erect a canonry in the said church of Clogher and the vicarage (even if specially reserved etc.) into a simple prebend of the said canonry, for Philip's lifetime, without prejudice to anyone; and, in that event, collate and assign the newly erected canonry and prebend, being then vacant, with plenitude of canon law and all rights and appurtenances to Philip, inducting him etc. having removed any other[9] unlawful detainer and causing Philip (or his proctor) to be received as a canon in the church of Clogher, and shall assign him a stall in the choir and a place in the chapter of the church of Clogher, with plenitude of the said law, and [causing] their fruits etc., rights and obventions to be delivered to him. [Curbing] gainsayers etc. Notwithstanding etc. The pope's will is, however, that on Philip's death or his resignation etc. of the canonry and prebend the said erection shall be extinguished and the vicarage shall revert to its original condition automatically.[10]

Apostolice sedis providentia circumspecta ...
Ge. de prato / JoA: / JoA: xx: tertio Id(us) aprilis Anno Quarto: [11 April 1516], *Nardinus*

1   MS: *Clochoren.*
2   possibly a letter (or letters) after the 's'; but illegible
3   *-ran* uncertain
4   MS: *Nielanus*; definitely not 'Nicolaus'. But the detainer's name is written *Nicolaus* (*Nicola-*) thrice below.
5   uncertain
6   'et institueretur' does not occur here or (differently inflected) below.
7   MS: *Nicolao* (and, close by, *Nicolai, Nicolaus*). *Cf.* above, note 4.
8   'institutionem' does not occur here or (differently inflected) below.
9   MS: *amoto exinde quolibet alio illicito detentore*; oddly, Nielanus/Nicholas is not named.
10   The usual formula safeguarding the parochial benefice's cure of souls etc., which commonly finds place in the Volumus clause, does not occur.

620   29 April 1516   *Reg. Lat.* 1345, fos 84ᵛ-85ᵛ

To William Browne, BDec, perpetual vicar of the parish church of St Fininus (*Sancti Finini*), Demore [also spelt *Demor'*], d. Meath. Dispensation and indult etc. [as above, no. 2].[1]

Litterarum scientia, vite ac morum honestas ...
.P. Lambertus / JoA: / JoA: Lx: Nardinus

1   The Notwithstanding clauses include the constitutions of Otto and Ottobuono, formerly legates of the apostolic see in the kingdom of England, thereby giving Browne the option of holding benefices in England.

621 [–]¹   *Reg. Lat.* 1345, fo 86ᵛ

Abortive entry: start only of conditional union, at the petition of John Alyn, canon of Lincoln, UID, of the parish church of Sowgh Wokyngton'², d. London, to Alyn's canonry and prebend of Lincoln (to which the vicarage of Cheslet, d. Canterbury, is temporarily united by apostolic authority).

Occupies lower two-thirds of page; stops at foot of page, at end of last line (the eighteenth) soon after start of operative part:

Nos igitur qui dudum inter alia voluimus quod petentes beneficia ecclesiastica aliis uniri [stops]

An unrelated letter, drawn under 27 March 1516, begins at the top of fo 87ʳ (the first of a new quintern). The previous letter (also unrelated), the end of which occupies the top third of fo 86ᵛ (the last page of the quintern), is drawn under 21 April 1516.

No administrative notes: no note of abbreviator's name; and no initial or subscription of registry master. The proem is the usual one for this class of letter: *Ad futuram rei memoriam. Romanum decet pontificem et cetera provideri.*

Cancelled (by striking through); but no explanatory note. So far as it goes, matches³ the union in favour of Alyn, drawn under 7 February 1516, enregistered by the same scribe at fos 117ᵛ-118ᵛ of another register, namely *Reg. Lat.* 1341 (no. 582 above). Presumably, the same document was behind both entries.

Curiously, the start of no.582 practically mimics the present entry: it occupies the lower two-thirds of a verso page (117ᵛ), runs to eighteen lines, and extends to *uniri* – the end of the last line on the page. As the top third of fo 117ᵛ is blank the arrangement was evidently deliberate. The circumstance argues that fo 117ᵛ was a re-write of the present fragment; and that fos 118ʳ⁻ᵛ (i.e. the rest of no. 582) is effectively the continuation of the present entry. As noted, the present entry was started on the last page of a quintern. The switch to a partially completed quintern may be explicable in terms of a new (i.e. blank) quintern not being to hand.

1   The entry does not reach the dating clause.
2   the 'k' over a 'g' in the first instance
3   Minor differences apart, that is. Where the present entry has *quibusque* no. 582 has *et quibus*; and where this has *eisdem canonicatui et prebende* no. 582 has *eidem canonicatui et prebende*. The differences are attributable to copyist error (if that is the word) by the *scriptor registri*.

622   **7 April 1516**   *Reg. Lat.* 1345, fos 97ᵛ-98ᵛ

To William Stable, rector of the parish church of Donnyngton',¹ d. York. Dispensation and indult etc. [as above, no. 2].

Vite ac morum honestas …
.P. Lambertus. / C / C. Lx. Barotius

1   first occurrence written on two lines: *Do'-* | *nyngton'*

623   23 April 1516   *Reg. Lat.* 1345, fos 125ʳ-127ᵛ

To the archdeacon of the church of Ossory and Peter Obecayn and James Oduyn, canons of the church of Kildare, mandate in favour of James Corryn, canon of [the church of][1] Leighlin. The pope has learned that the perpetual vicarages of the parish churches of Clnyuuaceys[2] and Hacha [also spelt *Acha*] and Killsynayn [also spelt *Kellsynayn*] and the church without cure of Balyycaron,[3] d. Leighlin, <which is of lay patronage and at another time>[4] was erected <into>[4] a simple prebend of the church of Leighlin, for the lifetime of Gerald Magduyll, who bears himself as a cleric, are vacant *certo modo* at present and have been vacant for so long that by the Lateran statutes their collation has devolved on the apostolic see, although Gerald has detained the church without cure and the said vicarage of Clnyuuaceys and Donald Omachassa, who bears himself as a priest of the said diocese, has detained the said vicarages of Hacha and Killsynayn, with no title and no support of law, of their own temerity and *de facto*, for a certain time, and do so.[5] Petition was made recently on the part of James (who asserts that some time ago – after he, notwithstanding a defect of birth as the son of an archpriest otherwise dean of the said church of Leighlin and a nun professed of the Augustinian or another order, had been marked with clerical character; and it had been mandated that canonries and prebends of the churches of Leighlin and Dublin, then vacant *certo modo*, be provided to him by apostolic authority – he was dispensed by apostolic authority to receive and retain the said canonries and prebends and also any number of other mutually incompatible benefices, with and without cure, if he obtained them otherwise canonically, and to be promoted to all, even sacred and priest's, orders; and that afterwards he had been duly promoted to all the orders in question and, by the said dispensation, holds a canonry and prebend of the church of Dublin, which was canonically conferred on him while vacant *certo modo*; and also that the annual value of the church without cure and vicarages aforesaid together does not exceed 12 marks sterling) to the pope to unite etc. the church without cure and the vicarages to the said canonry and prebend of the church of Leighlin, for as long as he holds the latter. The pope hereby commands that the above three (or two or one of them). if, having summoned Gerald and Donald and others concerned, they find the church without cure and the vicarages to be vacant (howsoever etc.) shall collate and assign them (even if reserved etc.) with all rights and appurtenances, to the said canonry and prebend of the church of Leighlin, for as long as he holds the latter; to the effect that James may, on his own authority, in person or by proxy, take and retain corporal possession of the church without cure and vicarages and rights and appurtenances aforesaid, for as long as he holds the said canonry and prebend of the church of Leighlin, and convert their fruits etc. to his own uses and those of the canonry and prebend of the church of Leighlin and the church without cure and vicarages aforesaid without licence of the local diocesan or of anyone else. Notwithstanding etc. The pope's will is, however, that the above church without cure and vicarages shall not, on account of this union etc., be defrauded of due services and the cure of souls in the vicarages shall not be neglected; but that their customary burdens and those of the church without cure shall be supported; and that on James's death or his resignation etc. of the canonry and prebend this union etc. shall be dissolved and be so deemed and the church without cure and the vicarages shall revert to their original condition automatically. Given at Palo, d. Porto.

Romanum decet pontificem votis illis gratum prestare assensum ...
G de Prato. | JoA: | JoA: xx: Nardinus

1   'ecclesie' does not occur
2   the minims variously readable
3   or perhaps *Balyycarog*
4   MS: ... *parrochialium ecclesiarum perpetue vicarie* [*nec non que alias in* deleted, initialled *C* at the start of
    the deletion; *Ba* at the end] <*ac que de iure patronatus laicorum existit et alias in* > *simplicem prebendam*
    ... The passage enclosed in angled brackets is inserted in the margin; *C* above the insertion; *cassatu(m) et*
    additu(m) de man(da)to .R. .p. D. Regentis Barotius after it. The sandwich all in the same (second) hand.
5   *detinebat*; *recte*: 'detineant' Small slips such as this occur throughout the entry.

624   22 April 1516   *Reg. Lat.* 1345, fos 128ʳ-132ʳ

<To the abbot of the monastery *de Legedei* [Abbeyleix], d. Leighlin, and James
Ocuryn, canon of the church of Leighlin, and Maurice Obecayn, canon of the church
of Kildare>[1], mandate in favour of Nicholas Marrostella[2] *alias* Nogola, priest, d.
[Kildare].[3] The pope has learned that the perpetual vicarage of the parish church of
Nerim [also spelt *Nerin*] *alias* Balyyrin[4] (which some time ago, as is asserted, was
erected into a simple prebend of the church of Kildare, for the lifetime of Gilbert
Omenay [also spelt *Omaynay*], priest, of the same diocese [Kildare]; and the rectory of
the parish church of Nerim and also the rectory, called *plebania*, of the parish church
of Gysel, of the said diocese [Kildare] (which some time ago (*olim*) were united by
apostolic authority in perpetuity to the monastery of Kylley, OSA, of the said diocese
[Kildare]); and the rectories, called chapels, of the parish churches of Cloymdahor
[also spelt *Coloyundahort*] and Disart [also spelt *Lisart*], d. Kildare (which are of lay
patronage) are vacant *certo modo* at present and have been vacant for so long that by
the Lateran statutes their collation has lawfully devolved on the apostolic see, although
Rory Ocuucalret[5] – bearing himself as a canon OSA – has detained the rectory of
Nerim, John Ymaynay has detained the rectories of Colymdahor and Disart, and
Gilbert Omenay has detained the vicarage of Nerim – bearing themselves as priests –
with no title or support of law, of their own temerity and *de facto*, for a certain time,
and do so. Recently, on Nicholas's part petition was made to the pope to collate a
canonry of the church of Kildare to him and erect the said vicarage into a simple
prebend of it, for his lifetime; and also to unite etc. the said rectories to the canonry and
prebend in question, for as long as he should hold the canonry and prebend; and it was
asserted on Nicholas's part that, at another time – after he had been duly marked with
clerical character notwithstanding a defect of birth as the son of a priest and a married
woman; and then, after he had been dispensed by pretext of certain falsely expedited
apostolic letters (of which Nicholas was completely ignorant) to be promoted to all,
even sacred and priest's, orders and to hold the said erected benefice,[6] even if it had
cure of souls – he was dispensed by apostolic authority by virtue of other duly
expedited apostolic letters[7] to be promoted to all the above orders and to hold a
benefice, even if it had cure of souls, and then had been duly promoted to all the orders
in question; and that the annual value of the above vicarage and rectories together did
not exceed 24 marks[8] sterling). At this petition, the pope hereby commands that the

above three,[9] if, having summoned John, Gilbert and Rory and as regards the erection the bishop and chapter of Kildare and others concerned, they find the vicarage and rectories to be vacant (howsoever etc.), shall erect and institute the vicarage into a simple prebend of the said church of Kildare, for Nicholas's lifetime, without prejudice to anyone, and collate and assign it, thus erected, and a canonry of the said church of Kildare to Nicholas; and unite etc. the said rectories (even if they and the said vicarage be specially reserved etc.) to the said canonry and prebend, for as long as Nicholas should hold the latter, if conferred on him as above, with plenitude of canon law and the annexes in question and also all rights and appurtenances, inducting Nicholas (or his proctor) into corporal possession of the canonry and prebend and annexed rectories and rights and appurtenances aforesaid, having removed Rory, John and Gilbert or any other unlawful detainers, and causing Nicholas (or his proctor) to be received as a canon of the church of Kildare, and shall assign him a stall in the choir and a place in the chapter of the church of Kildare, with plenitude of canon law, and [causing] the fruits etc., rights and obventions of the said canonry and prebend and annexed rectories to be delivered to him. [Curbing] gainsayers etc. Notwithstanding etc. Also the pope dispenses Nicholas to receive the said canonry and prebend, if [acquired] by virtue of the presents, and, with them, any benefice, with or without cure, of any order, even the Cluniac, even if a priory, *prepositura*, *prepositatus*, dignity, *personatus*, administration or office, even if the priory etc. should be customarily elective and have cure of souls, if he obtains it otherwise canonically, and retain the canonry and prebend *in titulum* and the regular benefice *in commendam*, for life; and to resign this regular benefice as often as he pleases and cede the commend, and in its place receive another, with or without cure, of any regular order, even the Cluniac (which, however, may not be a conventual dignity or claustral office), and retain it *in commendam* for life, as above; he may – due and customary burdens of the regular benefice having been supported – make disposition of the rest of its fruits etc. just as those holding it *in titulum* could and ought to do, alienation of immovable goods and precious movables being however forbidden, notwithstanding the above defect etc. The pope's will is, however, that the vicarage and rectories and regular benefice in question shall not, on this account, be defrauded of due services and the cure of souls in them shall not be neglected; but that customary burdens of the vicarage and rectories and the aforesaid burdens of the regular benefice shall be supported; and that on Nicholas's death or his resignation etc. of the canonry and prebend this erection shall be extinguished and union etc. be dissolved and be so deemed and the vicarage and rectories shall revert to their original condition automatically. Given at Palo, d. Porto.

Apostolice sedis providentia circumspecta ...
[–][10] / JoA: / JoA: xxx: Nardinus

1　　The entire address clause after *Leo et cetera* (that is, from *dilectis filiis abbati monasterii* to *ecclesiarum canonicis salutem* [et cetera]) visibly entered later (in enregistering scribe's hand) in space left blank for the purpose.
2　　the second 'r' blotched
3　　MS: *dicti* [!] *diocesis*, evidently referring to Kildare
4　　or *Balyynn*
5　　the *-t* doubtful

6   MS: *beneficium predictum errectum* [!]. Ordinarily, we would expect 'beneficium ecclesiasticum' here.
      Moreover, the vicarage of Nerim *alias* Balyyrin – the only 'said erected benefice' – sits uncomfortably in the
      context. However, as the relevant letters are stated to be false, the unexpected formula may follow their tenor
      and we hesitate to dismiss it as an error of the draftsman who framed the present letters or of the *scriptor
      registri* who copied them.
7   otherwise unknown, seemingly, to the *CPL*
8   *duc(atorum)* deleted and initialled *JoA.*
9   MS: *discretioni vestre per apostolica scripta mandamus quatenus si vocatis Johanne ...* 'vos vel duo aut unus
      vestrum', which we would expect after *mandamus*, does not occur.
10   abbreviator's name wanting

625   31 March 1516   *Reg. Lat.* 1345, fos 148ᵛ-152ᵛ

To William Offlauuma,[1] canon of Cashel, mandate in favour of Maurice Hyerla, cleric,
d. Cloyne. A petition[2] to the pope on Maurice's part stated that at another time –
following the renewal by Paul II of all papal sentences of excommunication,
suspension and interdict and other sentences, censures and pains against simoniacs (his
will being that every simoniac, manifest or occult, should incur them automatically)
and his reservation of their absolution and relaxation to himself and his successors
alone (except on the point of death) – Maurice reached a compact with the (?)then
bishop of Cloyne[3] that if the said bishop would collate and make provision of the
perpetual vicarage of the parish church of Assada [also spelt *Afada*, *Affado*, *Alfado*,
Afado],[4] then vacant *certo modo*, to him by ordinary authority, he, Maurice, would pay
the bishop a certain sum of money then expressed; [and], following this compact, the
bishop collated and made provision of the vicarage, vacant as above, to him by the said
authority, albeit *de facto*; and Maurice, by pretext of this collation and provision, took
possession of the vicarage and held[5] it for some time, as he still detains[5] it – receiving
the fruits etc. (of annual value not exceeding 4 marks sterling) arising from it – also *de
facto*, and – in accordance with the said compact – paid the said sum, genuinely and
with effect, to the bishop, incurring simony and the sentences, censures and pains
aforesaid. Since however, according to the foregoing, the said collation and provision
do not hold good; and, as the pope has learned, the vicarage of Assada is vacant still as
above, and the deanery of the church of Cloyne[6] and the perpetual vicarages of the
parish churches of the places of Balliborne [also spelt *Baliborne*] and Thechteseyn
[also spelt *Thethegen*, *Thetesyn*, *Theehtesyn*, *Thechtesyn*,[7] *Thetiegen*,[8] *Thetesym*]
(which is of lay patronage), said diocese,[9] are vacant *certo modo* at present and have
been vacant for so long that by the Lateran statutes their collation has lawfully
devolved on the apostolic see, although Thady Okyme has detained the deanery, and
Cornelius Ohyarhi[10] [also spelt *Ohyrla*, *Ohylac*] has detained the vicarage of
Balliborne and Cornelius Obreyn [also spelt *Obrean*] that of Thechteseyn – bearing
themselves as priests – with no title,[11] temerariously and *de facto*, for a certain time, as
they still do. At the supplication on the part of Maurice (who asserts that the annual
value of the deanery and annexes thereto and of the vicarages aforesaid[12] together does
not exceed 28 like marks) to the pope to erect and institute a canonry in the church of
Cloyne and the vicarage of Assada into a simple prebend of the same, for his lifetime;
and to unite etc. the vicarages of Balliborne and Thechteseyn to the proposed prebend
after it has been erected and instituted, for as long as Maurice should hold this prebend;

and to command that he be absolved from simony and the other sentences, censures and pains aforesaid, the pope hereby commands the above canon to absolve Maurice, if he so requests, from simony and also from the sentences of excommunication and other ecclesiastical sentences, censures and pains in the customary form of the church, having enjoined a salutary penance on him etc.; to dispense him on account of irregularity, if, as may be, he contracted it by taking part in divine offices while bound by the said sentences, censures and pains, not, however, in contempt of the keys; and to rehabilitate him on account of all disability and infamy contracted by him on this occasion; and if, in the event of this absolution, dispensation and rehabilitation, the above canon finds the vicarage of Assada and (having summoned Thady, Cornelius Ohyarhi and Cornelius Obreyn and as regards the erection the bishop and chapter of Cloyne and others concerned) the vicarages of Balliborne and Thechteseyn and the deanery (which is a dignity major *post pontificalem*), to be vacant (howsoever etc.), the pope commands the canon (even if the vicarage of Assada has been vacant for so long that by the Lateran statutes its collation has lawfully devolved on the apostolic see, and the deanery and vicarages are specially reserved, and the deanery (as a major dignity) is generally reserved, etc.) to erect and institute a canonry in the church of Cloyne and the vicarage of Assada into a simple prebend of it, without prejudice to anyone, for Maurice's lifetime; to collate and assign the newly erected canonry and prebend, being then vacant, [and] the deanery to Maurice; and to unite etc. the vicarages of Balliborne and Thechteseyn to the canonry and prebend, for as long as Maurice should hold the latter, inducting him etc. into corporal possession of the deanery, canonry and prebend, annexes and rights and appurtenances aforesaid, having removed Thady and Cornelius Ohylac and Cornelius Obreyn and any other unlawful detainers from the same, and causing Maurice (or his proctor) to be received as a canon of the church of Cloyne, and to assign him a stall in the choir and a place in the chapter of the said church of Cloyne, with plenitude of canon law, and [causing] him to be admitted to the deanery and its fruits etc., rights and obventions and those of the canonry and prebend and annexes aforesaid[13] to be delivered to him. Curbing gainsayers by the pope's authority etc. Notwithstanding etc. The pope's will is, however, that the said vicarages shall not, on this account, be defrauded of due services and the cure of souls in them shall not be neglected, but that their customary burdens shall be supported; and that on Maurice's death or his resignation etc. of the canonry and prebend this erection and institution shall be extinguished and union etc. shall be dissolved and so deemed and the vicarages shall revert to their original condition automatically; and that before the above canon begins to proceed to the execution of the presents in any way Maurice shall resign the vicarages into his hands genuinely and completely.

Sedes apostolica, pia mater, recurentibus[14] *ad eam cum humilitate ...*
Je Benzon / JoA: / JoA: xxxxv: Nardinus

1   the *-uuma* very uncertain
2   'nuper' does not occur.
3   *prefat(us) Mauritius qui cum episcopo Colnen.* [*sic*] *tunc pepigit et convenit ...* A near repetition, which occurs a little later in the narrative, has been cancelled: *prefatus Mauritius cum tunc episcopo* (?)*Colnen. pepigit et convenit* deleted and initialled *JoA* in two places.
4   diocese not stated; actually Cloyne
5   MS: ... *illam quamdiu tenuit prout aduc*[!] *detinet*

6   here (and elsewhere) spelt *Colonen.*; also spelt *Elonen.* (once), and (as usual) *Clonen.*
7   or *Thechyesyn*; the 'y' overwritten by 't' or vice versa
8   the 'h' and 'ti' uncertain
9   diocese of previous benefice not stated; actually Cloyne
10   final 'i' long; or *Ohyarly*
11   MS: ... *nullo titulo* | *sibi desuper suffragante*; 'iurisve adminiculo' (or suchlike) does not occur
12   MS: *decanatus et illi annexorum ac vicariarum predictarum* ... This is the sole mention of (existing) annexes
     to the deanery and their identity is nowhere revealed. (The 'annexes aforesaid' mentioned later [indicated by
     note 13] are, of course, the named vicarages which – under the terms of the present letter – are to be united
     to the canonry and prebend).
13   *see* note 12
14   *sic*: not '-rr-'

626   14 April 1516   *Reg. Lat.* 1345, fos 152ᵛ-155ᵛ

To Thady Orronain[1] and John *etiam* Orrnan[2] and William Offlavuan, canons of the
church of Lismore, mandate in favour of Thady[3] Mackrad, rector of the parish church
of Clume,[4] d. Lismore. Following the pope's reservation some time ago of all dignities
major *post pontificalem* in cathedral churches vacated then and in the future to his own
collation and disposition, the deanery of the church of Lismore, which is a dignity
major *post pontificalem*, and which, John Philippi Maegubu' *alias* de Geraldinis, its
late dean, held while he lived, became vacant by his death outside the Roman curia and
is vacant at present, being reserved as above. A recent petition to the pope on Thady's
part stated that if the above parish church (which Thady holds and to which the
perpetual vicarage of Culligen', said diocese, is canonically united, for as long as he
holds the parish church[5]), were to be united etc. to the said deanery, for as long as
Thady should hold the deanery[6] if it were to be conferred on him by virtue of the
presents, it would be of advantage to Thady (who asserts that William Butler – a former
(*alias*) canon, who bears himself as a cleric – has detained the deanery with no title, at
least no canonical title, and no support of law, temerariously and *de facto*, but not for
a year, as he still does at present; and that the annual value of the deanery and of the
prebend[7] and the deanery's other annexes, does not exceed 24 marks sterling in money
of those parts). At this supplication, the pope hereby commands that the above three
(or two or one of them) shall unite etc. the parish church, with the said annex[8] and all
other rights and appurtenances, to the deanery, for as long as Thady should hold the
latter;[9] to the effect that he may, on his own authority, in person or by proxy, continue
in, or take anew, and retain corporal possession of the parish church and the annexes
thereto and rights and appurtenances aforesaid, for as long as he should hold the
deanery, and convert their fruits etc. to his own uses and those of the parish church and
deanery, without licence of the local diocesan or of anyone else; and, having
summoned William and others concerned, collate and assign the deanery (vacant as
above or howsoever etc.; even if it has been vacant for so long that by the Lateran
statutes its collation has lawfully devolved on the apostolic see etc.) with the annexes
and all other rights and appurtenances, to Thady, inducting him etc. having removed
William and any other unlawful detainer and causing Thady (or his proctor) to be
admitted to the deanery and its fruits etc., rights and obventions to be delivered to him.
Curbing gainsayers etc. Notwithstanding etc. The pope's will is, however, that the said

parish church shall not, on account of this union etc., be defrauded of due services and the cure of souls in it shall not be neglected; but that its customary burdens shall be supported; and that on Thady's death or his resignation etc. of the deanery this union etc. shall be dissolved and be so deemed and the said parish church shall revert to its original condition and be deemed vacant automatically.

Apostolice sedis providentia circumspecta ...
.Je Benzon / JoA: / :JoA: xxvj: Nardinus

1   or -*am*
2   *sic*; the *etiam* indicates that John has the same surname as Thady.
3   The petitioner's name occurs (variously inflected) as: *Zade-*, (?)*Zacder-* (reworked; the *d* over (?)*h*), *Zacher-*, *Zacde-*, *Tade-*, *Thade-*
4   or *Clunie*
5   MS: *illam* (with evident reference to Clume)
6   MS again has *illam*; *recte* 'illum'; *cf.* note 9 below.
7   MS: *dicti decanatus et preb(ende) ac aliorum illi an(n)exorum.* This is the only mention of a prebend.
8   MS: *cum annexa huiusmodi*: i.e. the vicarage
9   MS: *eidem decanatui quamdiu dictus Zadeus illam*[!] *obtinuerit dumtaxat*; *cf.* note 6 above.

627   28 March 1516   *Reg. Lat.* 1345, fos 170ʳ-174ʳ

To the abbot of the monastery of Mothel (*de Motalia*), d. Lismore, the archdeacon of Ossory, and Felineus (*Felineo*) Omulrrean, canon of Emly, mandate in favour of William Yflavvnan[1] [also spelt *Offlavvnan, Offlavunan, Offlavvan, Offlavvnan, Off'lavvnan, Oflavvnan, Osslavvnan, Yflavunan, Yflauunan*], cleric, d. Lismore. A recent petition to the pope on William's part stated that, at another time, when there was no lawful impediment and no relevant dispensation had been obtained, he did not have himself promoted to the order of the priesthood while he was in peaceful possession, for a year and more, of the perpetual vicarages of the parish churches of Kylnulog [also spelt *Kilnulog, Kyllnuloch, Ryllunloge*], Kyllsyrche [also spelt *Kyllsyreche*] *alias* Colnian, Kyllbrachyc [also spelt *Kyllbrachhyc*], and Tollachinean [also spelt *Tollachincan, Tollachnuan*], d. Cashel, (which, when they were vacant *certo modo*, had been united together by (?)ordinary authority[2] for as long as William should hold them, and thereupon collated to him), and, without renewing his title, he detained the vicarages after the said year had elapsed, receiving and collecting the fruits etc from them, albeit *de facto*; that he then obtained an order by the said (?)apostolic authority[3] for the erection of a canonry of the church of Cashel and, as if they had been held canonically by him, for the erection of the three first-named vicarages into its prebend, for as long as William should hold the canonry, and for the collation to him of the newly erected canonry and prebend, being vacant, and he continued receiving the proceeds, again *de facto*; that thereafter David Oduyr, who bears himself as a cleric – falsely alleging that by law the aforesaid (*predictas*) vicarages belonged to him – by expression of falsehood[4] and [suppression][5] of the truth impetrated apostolic letters to the abbot of the monastery of B Mary, Rock of Cashel (*de Rupecasellis*), d. Cashel, his proper name not expressed, and certain other colleagues of his in that regard, and by pretext of them he caused William to be summoned to judgement in the said cause before the then abbot of the monastery; and that the abbot, or another to whom the abbot had committed his powers over this, proceeding wrongly in the case, promulgated an unjust or null definitive sentence in favour of David and against William, from which on William's part, appeal was made to the apostolic see. However, as the said petition added, it is asserted by some persons that the right in or to the aforesaid (*predictis*) vicarages does not belong even to David; and, as the pope has learned, the canonry and prebend of Hasmer, of the church of Lismore, which the late John de Geraldinis, canon of the church of Lismore, held while he lived, and the perpetual vicarages of the parish churches of Killgobonat [also spelt *Kyllgobonat*] and Kinogonat [also spelt *Kimogonat, Rinogonat, Rynogonat*], d. Lismore, are vacant at present – the canonry and prebend by John's death outside the Roman curia, the vicarages *certo modo* – and have been vacant for so long that by the Lateran statutes their collation has lawfully devolved on the apostolic see, although Donat Omurrycuus[6] and William Omulruome [also spelt *Omulrroan, Omulrronan, Vmulrronan*], who bear themselves as priests, have, without title, temerariously and *de facto*, detained the vicarages of Killgobonat and Kinogonat respectively unlawfully occupied (as they still do) for a year and more; and, as the said petition added, it would be to William Yflavvnan's advantage if a canonry was to be erected in the church of Cashel for as long as he should hold it, if conferred on him by virtue of the presents, and the vicarage of Kylnulog was to be instituted into its simple prebend, and the vicarages of Kyllsyrche, Tollachinean, Killgobonat, and Kinogonat[7] were to be united etc to the proposed prebend for the same time. At the supplication of William Yflavvnan (who asserts that the fruits etc unlawfully received by him do not exceed 10 marks sterling, that the fruits etc of the vicarages do not exceed an annual value of 19 marks sterling, and the fruits etc of the vacant canonry and prebend do not exceed an annual value of 5 marks sterling[8]) to order that a canonry be erected in the church of Cashel, that the vicarage of Kylnulog be instituted into its simple prebend, and that the vicarages of Kyllsyrche, Kyllbrachyc, and Tollachinean and also of Killgobonat and Kinogonat be united etc to the proposed prebend, as above; and to commit to some upright men in those parts the cause of the said appeal, the pope – wishing to grant a special grace to William Yflavvnan and rehabilitate him on account of all disability and infamy contracted by him by occasion of the foregoing – hereby commands that the above three (or two or one of them), having summoned, respectively, the archbishop and chapter of Cashel as regards the erection and David and William Omulruome and Donat as regards the prosecution of the cause and the collation mentioned below and others concerned, [shall hear][9] the causes[10] of the appeal and of the whole principal matter, and having heard both sides, decree what is just, without appeal, causing by ecclesiastical censure what they have decreed to be strictly observed; and moreover compel witnesses, etc. And if it is lawfully established before the above three that even David has no right in or to the first mentioned (*primo dictis*) vicarages, they are, on the pope's authority, without prejudice to anyone, to erect a canonry in the church of Cashel, and, for as long as William Yflavvnan holds the canonry, if conferred on him by virtue of the presents, institute the vicarage of Kylnulog [into][11] its simple prebend, and unite etc the remaining vicarages to the said prebend for the same period of time and no longer, and then collate and assign to William Yflavvnan the canonry and prebend thus erected and the canonry and prebend of the church of Lismore, howsoever vacant etc, with plenitude of canon law, their annexes, and all their rights and appurtenances, inducting, in person or by proxy, the said William Yflavvnan (or his proctor), into corporal possession of the canonries and prebends and annexes and rights and appurtenances aforesaid, etc, having removed David, Donat, and William Omulruome, and any other unlawful detainers from the same, and causing William Yflavvnan (or his proctor) to be received as a canon and equal (*fratrem*), in respect of the said prebends, in the churches of Cashel and Lismore, having assigned to him, with plenitude of canon law, a stall in the choir and a place in the chapter of each of the said churches, and causing the fruits etc of the said canonries and prebends and vicarages to be delivered to him; curbing gainsayers by the pope's authority, without appeal. Notwithstanding [the statutes and customs][12] of the church of Cashel (even ones concerning a fixed number of canons) and of the church of Lismore, etc. The pope's will is, however, that the said vicarages shall not be defrauded of due services and the cure of souls in them shall not be neglected on account of the said erection, institution, union, and annexation but that their customary burdens shall be supported; and that on William Yflavvnan's death or resignation etc of the said canonry of the church of Cashel the aforesaid erection and institution shall be extinguished and the union etc shall be dissolved and be so deemed and the said vicarages shall revert to their original condition automatically; and that before the above shall proceed in any way to the execution of the presents as regards the [(?)erection][13] and union of the vicarages held by William Yflavvnan, the said William is to relinquish possession of them, utterly and genuinely, into their hands or the hands of one of them.

Sedes apostolica pia mater recurrentibus ad eam cum humilitate filiis post excessum libenter se propiciam exhibet ...
Ie Benzon / JoA: / JoA: xxxxv: decimoctavo k(a)l(endas) maj Anno Quarto [14 April 1516]: *Nard(inus).*

1   ·or - *vvuan*
2   MS: *ordinaria auctoritate unitas*; but *see* next note
3   MS: *dicta apostolica sibi auctoritate conferri mandari obtinuit*; *recte*: 'dicta ordinaria sibi auctoritate ...'? So far, ordinary authority has been mentioned, but not apostolic (*see* previous note); and no such mandate is known to the *CPL*.
4   MS: *per* (?)*false expressionem*; *recte*: 'falsi'?
5   MS: *et veri surreptionem*; *recte*: 'suppressionem'?
6   the *-cuus* very doubtful; perhaps *-ceo*
7   Though mentioned below the vicarage of Kyllbrachyc is not mentioned here.
8   MS: *asserentis per eum indebite perceptos decem et vicariarum decem novem ac canonicatus et prebende vacantium huiusmodi fructus redditus et proventus quinque marcarum sterlingorum secundum communem extimationem valorem annuum non excedere*
9   MS wants 'audiatis' (or suchlike)
10   inflexion smudged and uncertain; reading *causas*
11   MS wants 'in'
12   omission in MS: *Non obstantibus ... ordinationibus ac dictarum Casalen. etiam de certo canonicorum numero et Lismoren. *** ecclesiis in canonicos sint recepti ...* Of the lost passage 'statutis et consuetudinibus' supplied from common form:
13   MS: *assecutionem*; *recte* 'erectionem'?

628   7 April 1516   *Reg. Lat.* 1345, fos 182[r]-187[r]

To William Offlaiban and Cormac Ohey, canons of the churches of Lismore and Emly, and the official of Cashel, mandate in favour of Felmeus Omolrean, cleric, d. Emly. The pope has learned that the monastery of the Holy Cross, Huottdealaun,[1] OCist, and the canonry and prebend of Disertlauiis,[2] church of Emly, and the perpetual vicarages of the parish churches of the places of Kylhoscoly [also spelt *Kyllhoscoly*], Kyllyenagaranu[3] [also spelt *Kyllronagaranu*] *alias* Aglisygonyn [also spelt *Aglisygruin*], Seraduualy [also spelt *Scrauialy*, *Seradvualy*, *Seraduunalo*, *Seradiuuale*[4]] *alias* Cloynarc, Kayrkyl [also spelt *Kayekyl*, *Kayrkyll'*], Lodyn, Killneelluyn [also spelt *Kylmellayn*, *Kyllmeluyn*, *Kyllmelayn*, *Kylmelayn*], Vilistoan [also spelt *Vilistan*, *Villesen*, *Villeson*, *Villeston*[5]], and lastly Kyllmury [*Kyllmvrey*,[6] *Killmury*], ds. Cashel, Killaloe, Emly and Limerick, are vacant *certo modo* at present and have been vacant for so long that by the Lateran statutes the collation of the canonry and prebend and of the vicarages has lawfully devolved on the apostolic see, although William Oduyr [also spelt *Odouyr*], who bears himself as abbot of the <monastery>[7] and – bearing themselves as priests and clerics – <William Olydy>[7] [also spelt *Olyde*, *Olydi*][8] has detained the canonry and prebend, and Cornelius Omulrean [also spelt *Omullrean*] has detained the vicarage of Kylhoscoly, Rory Omulrean [also spelt *Omullrean*] that of Killneelluyn, Philip Omulrean [also spelt *Omullrean*] that of Kyllyenagaranu, William Omulrean that of Seraduualy, Donald Omulrean that of Kayrkyl, Walter de Burgo those of Vilistoan and Kyllmury and Philip Scach [also spelt *Schac*, *Sehec*] that of Lodyn with no title,[9] temerariously and *de facto*, for a certain time, as they still do; and that the said Felmeus desires to enter the convent of the above monastery under the regular habit. Recently, supplication was made on the part of Felmeus (who asserts that he is of noble birth by both parents; and that the annual value of the vacant canonry and prebend [sc. Emly] and the vicarages together does not exceed 40, and that of the monastery – except for uncertain voluntary alms or oblations which are bestowed on the monastery or its church in honour of the Holy Cross – does not exceed 60, marks sterling) to the pope to erect and institute the vicarage of Kylhoscoly into a simple prebend of a canonry of the church of Cashel, for as long as Felmeus should hold the latter,[10] if conferred on him by virtue of the presents; and, at the same time, unite etc. the vicarages of Kyllyenagaranu, Seraduualy, Kayrkyl, Lodyn, Killneelayn, Vilistoan and Kyllmury, being vacant, and the above canonry and prebend [sc. Emly] to the proposed prebend [sc. Cashel]. Wishing to make provision of a capable and suitable governor to the monastery to rule and direct it as well as to assist Felmeus to support himself more conveniently, the pope hereby commands that the above three (or two or one of them), if, having summoned William Oduyr, William Olydy and Cornelius, Rory, Philip and William Omulrean and Donald [Omulrean], Walter [de Burgo] and Philip Scach and the archbishop and chapter of Cashel (as regards the erection) and others concerned, they find the monastery, the first canonry and prebend [sc. Emly] and the vicarages to be vacant (howsoever etc.), shall (even if disposition of the monastery pertains to the apostolic see, and the said vacant canonry and prebend [sc. Emly] and the vicarages be specially reserved etc.) erect and institute the vicarage of Kylhoscoly into a simple prebend of the said canonry in the church of Cashel which is to be conferred on Felmeus, for as long as he should hold this canonry, without prejudice to anyone; and shall, with plenitude of canon law, collate and assign the erected and instituted prebend of the said canonry of the church of Cashel to Felmeus; and shall commend the monastery to Felmeus to be held, ruled and governed by him for six months calculated from the day of his having peaceful quasi-possession of its rule and administration, even together with the other said canonry and prebend [sc. Cashel] which are to be conferred on him, and with all other benefices, with and without cure, secular and regular of the above and any other order, which Felmeus holds *in titulum* or *commendam* and shall hold in the future, and with annual pensions, assigned to him on any ecclesiastical proceeds, which he receives and shall receive in the future; Felmeus may in the interim – after due and customary burdens of the monastery and convent have been supported and after a fourth part (if the abbatial *mensa* is separate from the conventual) or after a third part (if there is one common *mensa* there) of the fruits etc. of the said monastery has been altogether deducted, annually, to be directed towards the restoration of the fabric, or the purchase or repair of ornaments, vestments or sacred furniture, or the sustenance and maintenance of the poor and of the members of the convent, according to the greater need[11] – make disposition of the rest of the monastery's fruits etc., just as abbots of the monastery could and ought to do, alienation of the monastery's immovable goods and precious movables being however forbidden; and the above three etc. shall next (or even before), if Felmeus wishes to enter the monastery under the regular habit and if he is suitable and there is no canonical obstacle, receive him as a monk of the monastery, bestow the regular habit on him in accordance with the custom of the monastery, receive and admit into their own hands (or the hands of one of them) the usual regular profession made by monks of the said monastery from Felmeus, if he spontaneously wishes to make it and cause him to be given charitable treatment therein; and then, after he has taken the habit and made his profession, make provision of Felmeus to the said monastery and appoint him abbot, and commit the care, rule and administration of the monastery to him in spiritualities and temporalities; and shall unite etc. the first canonry and prebend [sc. Emly] and also the vicarages of Killneelluyn, Seraduualy, Kayrkyl, Lodyn, Kyllyenagaranu, Vilistoan and Kyllmury to the proposed prebend [sc. Cashel], for as long as Felmeus should hold the latter, inducting Felmeus (or his proctor) into corporal possession of the canonry and proposed prebend and annexes and rights and appurtenances, having removed William Oduyr, William Olydy, Cornelius [Omulrean], Walter [de Burgo], Philip Omulrean, William Omulrean, Donald [Omulrean] and Philip Scach and any other unlawful detainers and causing Felmeus to be given obedience and reverence by the convent and customary services and other rights by the monastery's vassals and other subjects; and [causing] Felmeus (or his proctor) to be received as a canon in the church of Cashel; and shall assign him a stall in the choir and a place in the chapter of the church of Cashel, with plenitude of canon law; and [causing] the fruits etc., rights and obventions of these canonries and prebends and vicarages to be delivered to him. [Curbing] gainsayers etc. Notwithstanding etc. and [notwithstanding] the privileges, indults and apostolic letters granted to the Cistercian order, confirmed, approved and repeatedly renewed, in particular those in which it is said to be expressly stipulated that monasteries and benefices of the said order cannot be commended to anyone save cardinals of the Holy Roman church or those who have expressly professed the said order and [only then] with the consent of the abbot for the time being and convent of the monastery of Cîteaux, d. Chalon-sur-Saône; and that commends of them made otherwise, even by the apostolic see, are of no force or moment; the which privileges etc. (which shall otherwise remain in force) the pope, for this once only, hereby specially and expressly derogates, deeming their tenors to be sufficiently expressed by the presents, as if they were inserted verbatim, even if, for their sufficient derogation, special, specific, express and individual mention or any other expression was to be made of them and of their whole tenors, verbatim and not by general clauses importing the same, or even if any other uncommon form was to be observed. The pope's will is, however, that – during the commend in question – divine worship in the said monastery shall not be neglected and the usual number of monks and ministers shall not be diminished; and that the first canonry and prebend [sc. Emly] and the vicarages shall not, on account of the said erection, institution and union etc., be defrauded of due services and the cure of souls in the vicarages shall not be neglected; but that the customary burdens of the vicarages and the aforesaid burdens of the monastery and convent shall be supported; and that on the death of Felmeus or his resignation etc. of the canonry [sc. Cashel] to be conferred on him the said erection and institution shall be extinguished and union etc. shall be dissolved and be so deemed and the first canonry and prebend [sc. Emly] and the vicarages shall revert to their original condition; [and] that – within the said six months – Felmeus shall take the habit and make his profession, otherwise the said commend shall be deemed to cease automatically; and that, after he has taken the habit of a professed [monk] and worn it for a period of three days,[12] or after the year of his probation has elapsed, or even before if it appears that he has resolved to completely change his way of life, Felmeus is bound to resign and cede all the benefices which he will hold in the interim and in which and to which he has a right in any way, the which benefices the pope decrees vacant thenceforth; and he is bound to cede the right in question completely.

Apostolice sedis providentia circumspecta cupientibus vitam ducere regularem ...
Je Benzon / JoA: / JoA: Lxxv: Nardinus

1   Though there is a dot above and a little to the left of the first minim of the penultimate letter ('u').
2   Two, perhaps three, letters between the 'au' and the 'iis' are deleted by blacking out; the blacked out letters have no ascenders or descenders.
3   the four final minims (read as -*nu*) variously readable
4   uncertain
5   or *Villeson*
6   penultimate letter doubtful
7   MS: ... *qui pro abbate <monasterii et Vuillialmus de Olydy> se gerit dictos canonicatum et prebendam...* The insertion, which is made in the margin, is initialled *JoA*.
8   neither spelling preceded by 'de'; *cf.* above, note 7.
9   'iurisve adminiculo' (or suchlike), which we would expect here, does not occur.
10   reading *illu(m)* (in reference to the canonry)
11   Note that the section: (*Itaquod liceat ...*) *debitis et consuetis monasterii et conventus predictorum supportatis oneribus et si abbatialis mensa ... prout maior exegerit et suaserit necessitas annis singulis convertenda deducta* (*de residuis eiusdem monasterii fructibus ...*) (summarised here as '– after due and customary burdens ... according to the greater need –') is a variant form. The arrangements for the maintenance of the convent differ from those in nos 298, 303, 346 (itself a semi-variant), 347, and 366 above; and where the present entry has *convertenda deducta* the others have *impertita*.
12   *quodque postquam habitum susceperit ac per triduum illum gestaverit professor(is)*

629   27 March 1516   *Reg. Lat.* 1345, fos 223ᵛ-226ʳ

To the dean, the archdeacon and Arthur Maguin,[1] canon, of the church of Armagh,
mandate in favour of Matthew[2] Mactheon, priest, d. Armagh. The pope has learned that
the sacristy of the church of Armagh and the rectory of the parish church of
Carmaseyll[3] and Kylboyssyll, d. Armagh, are vacant *certo modo* at present and have
been vacant for so long that by the Lateran statutes their collation has lawfully
devolved on the apostolic see. At a recent petition to the pope on the part of Matthew
(who asserts that the annual value of the sacristy and rectory does not exceed 9 marks
sterling) to erect and institute a canonry in the church of Armagh and the rectory into
a simple prebend of it, and unite etc. the canonry and prebend, thus erected and
instituted, to the sacristy, for as long as Matthew should hold the sacristy, if conferred
on him by virtue of the presents, the pope hereby commands that the above three (or
two or one of them), having summoned the archbishop and chapter of Armagh and
others concerned, shall erect and institute a canonry in the church of Armagh and the
rectory into a simple prebend of the said canonry, for Matthew's lifetime, without
prejudice to anyone; and also unite etc. the canonry and prebend, thus erected and
instituted, to the sacristy, for as long as Matthew should hold the latter; and collate and
assign the sacristy (which is an office) – in whatever way the sacristy and rectory may
be vacant, even if still by the free resignation of Patrick Hunmuleheran[4], sometime
(*olim*) sacristan, or of Patrick Ydonyl[5], [sometime] rector, or of anyone else, etc. even
if the sacristy and rectory are specially reserved etc. with the united canonry and
prebend and all other rights and appurtenances, to Matthew, inducting him etc. into
corporal possession of the sacristy and rectory and canonry and prebend and rights and
appurtenances aforesaid, having removed any unlawful detainers from the same and
causing Matthew (or his proctor) to be received as a canon of the church of Armagh;
and shall assign him a stall in the choir and a place in the chapter of the church of
Armagh, with plenitude of [canon] law, and [causing] him to be admitted to the sacristy
and its fruits etc., rights and obventions and those [(?)of the church of Lyna[6]] and of
the other annexes at that time to be delivered to him. [Curbing] gainsayers etc.
Notwithstanding etc. The pope's will is, however, that the above rectory shall not, on
account of this erection and institution and union etc., be defrauded of due services and
the cure of souls in it shall not be neglected, but that customary burdens shall be
supported; and that on Matthew's death or his resignation etc. of the sacristy this
erection and institution shall be extinguished and union etc. shall be dissolved and so
deemed and the rectory shall revert to its original condition automatically.

Apostolice sedis providentia circumspecta votis illis gratum prestat assensum ...
.Je Benzon / JoA: / :JoA: xxx: Septimo Id(us) ap(ri)lis Anno quarto [7 April 1516],
:Nardinus

1   the *-uin* uncertain: minims variously readable
2   spelt *Mathe-* in most instances; but also occurs as: *Macte-, Mate-, Mohte-, Natehe-* (once in each case)
3   the 'rm' uncertain
4   the minims here read as *-unmu-* capable of various readings
5   MS: *Patricii etiam Ydonyl.* As no surname resembling 'Ydonyl' occurs previously, it is difficult to account
     for the 'etiam'.
6   *ecclesie de Lyna*: very unsafe

630   18 April 1516   *Reg. Lat.* 1345, fos 335ᵛ-336ᵛ

To Reginald Metcalf, perpetual vicar of the parish church of Bersted [also spelt *Besced*, *Bersied*[1]], d. Canterbury. Dispensation and indult etc. [as above, no. 2 to '... Notwithstanding etc. '].[2] And relaxation of the oath perhaps taken[3] by Reginald on acquisition of the above vicarage (or other benefices) to reside at it in accordance with the constitutions of Otto and Ottobuono formerly legates of the apostolic see in the kingdom of England. With the proviso that the vicarage and other, even incompatible, benefices shall not, on this account, be defrauded of due services and the cure of souls in the vicarage and (if any) the other, even incompatible, benefices shall not be neglected; but that customary burdens of those benefices in which he shall not reside shall be supported. Given at Magliana, d. Porto.

Vite ac morum honestas ...
.P. lanb(er)tus / JoA: / JoA: Lxx: Nardinus

1   the 'i' uncertain
2   Save that the order of clauses in the indult is not identical.
3   apparently *p(rese)ntium*; for 'prestitum'

631   12 June 1516   *Reg. Lat.* 1346, fos 47ᵛ-48ᵛ

To Michael Hunttbache, perpetual vicar of the parish church, called vicarage,[1] of B. Mary, Weschport *alias* Westport, Melduna *alias* Malmesbury,[2] d. Salisbury. Dispensation and indult etc. [as above, no. 2].

Vite ac morum honestas ...
Jo. danielo / JoA: / JoA: Lx: Nard(inus)

1   *... parrochialis ecclesie vicarie nuncupate ...* This unusual formulation is repeated in the narrative below.
2   *... de Weschport alias de Westport de Melduna alias Malmesbury Saresbirien' diocesis ...*

632   12 June 1516   *Reg. Lat.* 1346, fos 49ʳ-50ʳ

To John Northe, rector of the parish church of Boronghclere, d. Winchester. Dispensation and indult etc. [as above, no. 2].

Vite ac morum honestas ...
Jo. danielo / JoA: / JoA: Lx: Nardinus

633   12 June 1516   *Reg. Lat.* 1346, fos 50ᵛ-51ᵛ

To John Deane, perpetual vicar of the parish church of Longdon, d. Coventry and
Lichfield. Dispensation and indult etc. [as above, no. 2].

Vite ac morum honestas ...
Jo. danielo / JoA: / JoA: Lx: Nardinus

634   13 June 1516   *Reg. Lat.* 1346, fo 52ʳ⁻ᵛ

To George Grene, monk of the monastery of Hyde, OSB, d. Winchester. Dispensation
– at his supplication – to him, who, as he asserts, is expressly professed of the above
order,[1] to receive and retain for life any benefice, with or without cure, usually held by
secular clerics, etc. [as above, no. 43].

Religionis[2] zelus, vite ac morum honestas ...
jo. danielo / JoA: / JoA: xxx: Nardinus

1   This information comes from a notwithstanding clause.
2   *Vite ac morum honestas* deleted (but not initialled) before *Religionis*

635   12 June 1516   *Reg. Lat.* 1346, fo 53ʳ⁻ᵛ

To Thomas Dunwell', canon of the monastery, called a house or hospital, of St
Leonard, York, OSA. Dispensation – at his supplication – to him, who, as he asserts, is
expressly professed of the above order,[1] to receive and retain any benefice, with or
without cure, usually held by secular clerics, etc. [as above, no. 43].

Religionis zelus, vite ac morum honestas ...
Jo. danielo / JoA: / JoA: xxx: Nardinus

1   This information comes from a notwithstanding clause.

636   22 June 1516   *Reg. Lat.* 1346, fos 61ʳ-62ʳ

To John Moris, perpetual vicar of the parish church of Cary,[1] d. Bath and Wells.
Dispensation and indult etc. [as above, no. 2].

Vite ac morum honestas ...
Jo. danielo / JoA: / JoA: Lx Nardinus

1   first occurrence written: *Carij*

637   9 May 1516   *Reg. Lat.* 1346, fos 97ᵛ-98ʳ

To Thomas Maysmore, canon of the priory of Llanthony (*de Lantona*), OSA, d. Worcester. Dispensation and indult – at his supplication – to him, who, as he asserts, is expressly professed of the above order,[1] to receive and retain any benefice, with or without cure, usually held by secular clerics, etc. [as above, no. 43, to '… defined as above'[2]]; and – until such time as he is promoted[3] – to transfer to another place of the above order and serve the Almighty therein. Notwithstanding etc.

Religionis zelus, vite ac morum honestas …
A. de. s severino / JoA: / JoA: xxxx: Nardinus

1   This information comes from a notwithstanding clause.
2   Save that in the present instance 'simpliciter vel ex causa permutationis' ('simply or for exchange') does not occur.
3   *donec promotus fueris* – referring, presumably, either to orders required for benefice holding or to his actual preferment

638   20 May 1516   *Reg. Lat.* 1346, fos 133ʳ-134ʳ

Union etc. with indult for non-residence. At a recent petition on the part of William Taylard, UID, rector of the parish church of Abbott'[1] Ripton' [also spelt *Abbot Ripton*, *Abbott' Ripton*], d. Lincoln, the pope hereby unites etc. the parish church of Offord Dacy [also spelt *Offord Daci*], d. Lincoln (whose annual value does not exceed 6 pounds sterling), with all rights and appurtenances, to the above church of Abbott' Ripton' (to which the parish church of Stathern' [also spelt *Stathurn'*], d. Lincoln, is united by apostolic authority, for as long as William holds Abbott' Ripton'), which William holds together with the church of Offord Dacy by apostolic dispensation, likewise for as long as he holds Abbot' Ripton', to the effect that he may, on his own authority, in person or by proxy, take anew, or continue in, and retain corporal possession of Offord Dacy and the rights and appurtenances aforesaid, for as long as he holds Abbott' Ripton', and convert its fruits etc. to his own uses and those of the said churches of Abbott' Ripton' and Offord Dacy, without licence of the local diocesan or of anyone else. And the pope indulges William, for life, while attending a *studium generale* or residing in the Roman curia or any one of his benefices, not to be bound to reside in his other benefices, nor to be liable to be compelled to do so by anyone against his will. Notwithstanding etc. The pope's will is, however, that the church of Offord Dacy and other benefices in question shall not, on account of this union etc., be defrauded of due services and the cure of souls in that church and (if any) the other benefices shall not be neglected; but that customary burdens of the church of Offord Dacy and of other benefices in which he shall not reside shall be supported; and that on William's death or his resignation etc. of the church of Abbott' Ripton' this union etc. shall be dissolved and be so deemed and the church of Offord Dacy shall revert to its original condition automatically.

Ad futuram rei memoria(m). Romanum decet pontificem et cetera.
.P. Lambertus / . JoA: / :JoA: xxxxv: Nardinus

1   Here and below the mark at the end (actually a development of the cross to the '-tt-') is equivocal.

639   [–]¹   *Reg. Lat.* 1346, fo 134ʳ

Abortive entry: address clause only, viz.:
> *Leo et cetera dilecto filio Willelmo Harbotell' monacho monasterii Beate Marie de Coggeshall' Cistertien. diocesis*[!] *Londonien. diocesis salutem et cetera.* [ends]

Occupies two lines half way down the page, between the end of one entry (no. 638 above) and the start of another, namely a Spanish letter drawn under 22 April 1516. The present entry and the adjacent ones are all the work of the same scribe.

No administrative notes: no abbreviator's name; no magistral initial or magistral subscription.

Deleted; but no explanatory note.

Matches the start of the dispensation *ad unum* in favour of William Harbottle enregistered by the same scribe farther on in the same quintern (no. 643 below).² Though the same grant, or projected grant, is probably behind both entries, on the available data it is impossible to say whether they were both copied from the same document. Unclear why the present entry was abandoned. As the successful entry comes later in the quintern it was probably not because the letter had already been enregistered. In effect, it appears to be a case of deferred enregistration. Perhaps there were reasons for suddenly prioritising the Spanish letter.

1   Entry does not extend to dating clause.
2   Save that where the present fragment has *diocesis*[!] no. 643 has (correctly) *ordinis*. The spelling of
     Coggeshall also differs.

640   20 May 1516   *Reg. Lat.* 1346, fo 135ʳ⁻ᵛ

To Thomas Rowsewell', MA, perpetual vicar of the parish church of Bradeford, d. Bath and Wells. Dispensation and indult etc. [as above, no. 2].

Litterarum scientia, vite ac morum honestas ...
.P. Lambertus. / JoA: / JoA: Lx: Nardinus

641¹   20 May 1516   *Reg. Lat.* 1346, fos 135ᵛ-136ᵛ

To John Balle, cantor of the chantry of the Holy Trinity in the parish church of Bransterde,² d. Exeter. Dispensation – at his supplication – to receive and retain for life, together with the above chantry (which is incompatible with another incompatible benefice), one, and without them, any two other benefices etc. [as above, no. 2, to '… retain them together for life, as above']; and indult, for life, while attending a *studium generale* etc. [as above, no. 2].

Vite ac morum honestas …
.P. Lambertus / JoA: / JoA: Lx: Nardi(nus): –

1   *Cf. Reg. Suppl.* 1523, fo. 103^{r-v}.
2   The first occurrence of the name has an equivocal mark above the 'n'; both occurrences have the 's' long, but in the second occurrence it is written over another letter, almost certainly a 'd'. The supplication has *Branstede*.

642[1]   **20 May 1516**   *Reg. Lat.* 1346, fos 136^v-137^r

To Richard Whyte, canon of the monastery, called a house or priory, of Leysshe Parva, OSA, d. Lincoln.[2] Dispensation – at his supplication – to him (who, as he asserts, is expressly professed of the above order),[3] to receive and retain any benefice, with or without cure, usually held by secular clerics, etc. [as above, no. 43].

Relligionis[4] *zelus, vite ac morum honestas …*
P. Lambertus / JoA: / JoA: xxx: Nardinus

1   No 681 below is a similar grant.
2   *Sic*; *recte*: 'London'; no. 681 has Lincoln corrected to London.
3   This information comes from a notwithstanding clause.
4   *sic*

643   **20 May 1516**   *Reg. Lat.* 1346, fos 147^v-148^r

To William Harbotell', monk of the monastery of B. Mary, Coggessall', OCist, d. London. Dispensation and indult – at his supplication – to receive and retain any benefice, with or without cure, usually held by secular clerics, even if a parish church or its perpetual vicarage, or a chantry, free chapel, hospital or annual service, usually assigned to secular clerics in title of a perpetual ecclesiastical benefice, and of lay patronage and of whatsoever tax or annual value, if he obtains it otherwise canonically, to resign it, simply or for exchange, as often as he pleases, and in its place receive and retain another, similar or dissimilar, benefice, with or without cure, defined as above; and – even after he acquires the said benefice – to receive the usual monachal portion received by monks of the above monastery, OCist, of which he is a monk and is, as he asserts, expressly professed of the order, and to have, for life, a stall in the choir and a place and an active and a passive voice in the chapter of the said monastery and otherwise as before, without limitation, just as if he had not acquired the benefice. Notwithstanding etc.

Relligionis[1] *zelus, vite ac morum honestas ...*
.P. Lambertus. / . JoA: / JoA: Lx: Nardinus

1   *sic*

644[1]   **2 June 1516**   *Reg. Lat.* 1346, fos 163ᵛ-164ʳ

Union etc. At a recent petition on the part of John Bryme, canon of the church of
Honedona',[2] d. York, the pope hereby unites etc. the parish church of St Michael,
Milkeshma,[3] d. Salisbury (whose annual value does not exceed 20 pounds sterling),
with all rights and appurtenances, to the canonry and prebend of the above church of
Honedona,[4] which John holds together with the above parish church, for as long as he
holds the canonry and prebend, to the effect that he may, on his own authority, in
person or by proxy, continue in, or take anew, and retain corporal possession of the
parish church and the rights and appurtenances aforesaid, for as long as he holds the
canonry and prebend, and convert its fruits etc. to his own uses and those of the
canonry and prebend and of the parish church, without licence of the local diocesan or
of anyone else. Notwithstanding etc. The pope's will is, however, that the parish church
shall not, on account of this union etc., be defrauded of due services and the cure of
souls in it shall not be neglected; but that its customary burdens shall be supported; and
that on John's death or his resignation etc. of the canonry and prebend this union etc.
shall be dissolved and be so deemed and the parish church shall revert to its original
condition automatically.

Ad futuram rei memoriam. Romanum decet pontificem et cetera provideri.
.P. Lambertus. / JoA: / JoA: xxxv: Nardinus

1   Corresponding or related petitions are at *Reg. Suppl.* 1524, fo. 246ʳ⁻ᵛ and 1523, fo.274ʳ.
2   the 'a' superscript
3   the 'a' superscript
4   as in note 2 above

645[1]   **(?)1516 [or potentially 1517]**[2]   *Reg. Lat.* 1346, fos 168ᵛ-169ʳ

To Thomas Ashewood, rector of the parish church of Mason, d. Salisbury. Dispensation
[and indult][3] – at his supplication – to receive and retain for life, together with the
above parish church, one, and without them, any two other benefices, with cure or
otherwise mutually incompatible, even if parish churches or their perpetual vicarages,
or chantries, free chapels, hospitals or annual services, usually assigned to secular
clerics in title of a perpetual ecclesiastical benefice, or dignities, *personatus*,
administrations or offices in cathedral, even metropolitan ...[4] major *post pontificalem*
or principal in collegiate churches, or a combination etc. [as above, no. 2].

Vite ac morum honestas …
[–]⁵ / [–]⁶ / [–]⁷

1   The entry is struck through by a line (broad and smudgy) on each page. The text – which, as it stands, is
     wanting in various respects (*see below*, notes 2-7) – was probably copied into a register gathering from a
     draft, before the engrossment was expedited. The letter may have been successfully enregistered elsewhere
     (=no. 1034 below?).
2   dating clause incomplete, viz: *Dat. Rome apud Sanctum Petrum anno et cetera millesimo quingentesimo
     sextodecimo* [ends] – which leaves the date of the entry, potentially, any date from 25 March 1516 to 24
     March 1517 inclusive.
3   Common form for an indult of non-residence (as above, no. 2) occurs in the body of the letter; but though
     the pope dispenses, *dispensamus* is *not* followed by the standard words: 'tibique pariter indulgemus'.
     Likewise, 'indulti' is *not* listed in the *Nulli* clause.
4   The passage – 'vel collegiatis et dignitates ipse in cathedralibus etiam metropolitanis' (or suchlike) – is
     wanting.
5   no abbreviator's name
6   no magistral initial
7   no magistral subscription

646   9 June 1516   *Reg. Lat.* 1346, fos 184ᵛ-185ʳ

To William Berey, perpetual vicar of the parish church, called chapel, of the Blessed
(*dive*) Magdalene, Taunton [also spelt *Taunton*'], d. Bath and Wells. Dispensation and
indult etc. [as above, no. 2].¹

Vite ac morum honestas …
P. Lambertus / JoA: / JoA: Lx: Nardinus

1   Save that the list of types of benefices wants 'perpetue vicarie' where the scribe reached the end of a line;
     i.e. MS here has: … *parrochiales ecclesie vel earum | aut cantarie …*

647   9 June 1516   *Reg. Lat.* 1346, fos 185r-186r

To James Trevethen', MA, perpetual vicar of the parish church of St Gwennap (*Sancte
Weneppe*), d. Exeter. Dispensation and indult etc. [as above, no. 2].

Litterarum scientia, vite ac morum honestas …
.P. Lambertus / JoA: / JoA: Lx: Nar(dinus)

648   17 June 1516   *Reg. Lat.* 1346, fos 205ᵛ-206ᵛ

To John Bekwith', cleric, d. York. Dispensation and indult – at his supplication – to
him, who, as he asserts, is in his thirteenth year of age and expects to be presented [for]
the   parish   church   [of]¹   Southholeyngten'   [also   spelt   *Southholeymgten'*,

Sauthholeyngten',[2] *Sohout.,*[3] *Southh.*], d. York, by its patrons when it falls vacant,[4] to
receive – henceforth – the above parish church or another [benefice with cure or
incompatible], and – when he reaches his twentieth year – together with the said parish
church or benefice, one, or without them, any two [other] benefices, with cure or
otherwise mutually incompatible, etc. [as above, no. 2, to ' … he obtains them
otherwise canonically'], and to retain – henceforth until he reaches the lawful age – the
above parish church, or without it, [another benefice] *in commendam*; and then – when
he reaches his twentieth year – another with it, or without them, two other [benefices]
in titulum, for life; to resign them, at once or successively, simply or for exchange, as
often as he pleases, and cede the commend and in [their] place receive up to two [other,
similar or dissimilar],[5] incompatible benefices, and to retain – henceforth until he
reaches the lawful age – one benefice *in commendam*; and then – when he reaches his
said twentieth year – another with it, or without them, two others *in titulum*, for life, as
above; he may – due and customary burdens of the above parish church or other
benefice retained *in commendam* having been supported – make disposition of the rest
of its fruits etc. just as those holding it *in titulum* could and ought to do, alienation [of
immovable goods or precious movables][6] of the said parish church or other benefice
being however forbidden. And the pope indulges John, also for life, while residing in
the Roman curia or any one of his benefices or attending a *studium generale*, not to be
bound to reside in his other benefices nor to be liable to be compelled to do so by
anyone against his will. Notwithstanding the defect of age which he shall suffer in his
said twentieth year, etc. With the proviso that the above parish church and other
benefices shall not, on this account, be defrauded of due services and the cure of souls
in the said church and (if any) the other, even incompatible, benefices shall not be
neglected; but that customary burdens of the said church, or other [benefice], retained
in commendam, shall, during the said commend, be supported and so shall customary
burdens of those [benefices] in which he shall not reside.

Laudabilia tue puerilis etatis indicia …
.P. lambertus / JoA: / JoA: Lxxxx: Nardinus

1   'de' does not occur.
2   the penultimate letter ('e') and the final mark (bar) doubtful
3   The dot at the end indicates that the name is abbreviated.
4   MS appears to want 'ad' after *ac*: … *ac parrochialem ecclesiam … eius vacatione occasione p(er) illius
     patronos presentari speras …*
5   indicated in MS by *et cetera.*
6   as note 5

649   14 May 1516   *Reg. Lat.* 1346, fos 210ʳ-212ᵛ

To James, elect of Moray, exemption etc., as below. This day the pope, on the advice
of the cardinals, has provided James to the church of Moray, then vacant *certo modo*,
appointing him bishop, as is more fully contained in his letters drawn up in that regard.[1]
Hereby the pope, *motu proprio* – with the express consent for this of Andrew,
archbishop of St Andrews,[2] given through Gilbert Strathanchm, cleric, d. St Andrews,

his specially appointed proctor – utterly exempts and frees James and the aforesaid church of Moray, and any other cathedral or metropolitan [church] to which he happens to be translated, together with all churches, lands, and lordships annexed, united, and belonging to the same, and also all and any churches, monasteries, priories, and ecclesiastical benefices, with and without cure, secular and regular of any order, held in any way by James then and from time to time, and James's affairs (*res*) and any movable and immovable goods, present and future, and his officials, subjects, diocesans, parishioners, and familiars, whosoever, present and future, from all jurisdiction, superiority, dominion, power, visitation, and correction of Andrew, archbishop of St Andrews, primate of the whole kingdom of Scotland, and legate born, and of the archbishop of St Andrews, primate etc. for the time being, even jurisdiction etc. by reason of the primacy, of the legateship born, of the plenary power of a legate *de latere*, or of any other privileges granted from time to time to the said Andrew or the archbishop of St Andrews for the time being, and from the jurisdiction etc. of any other archbishops, bishops, and local ordinaries established (*consistentium*) in the said kingdom, and any of their vicars, officials, commissaries, and delegates for the time being; takes James and the aforesaid church of Moray, etc under the protection of the pope and the apostolic see, and makes them immediately subject and only subject to the pope, to the pope for the time being, and to the apostolic see; and decrees that they are exempt, free, taken under protection and made subject; to the effect that the aforesaid Andrew, archbishop of St Andrews, primate etc, and the other archbishops, etc and their vicars, etc, present and future, jointly or severally, cannot and ought not to exercise any jurisdiction, superiority, authority, dominion, power, visitation or correction, even by reason of the legateship born or faculty of a legate *de latere* or privileges aforesaid, against James and the church of Moray or any other cathedral or metropolitan church to which he happens to be translated, or against the aforesaid churches, monasteries, ecclesiastical benefices, affairs and goods, or against his officials, subjects, etc, seeing that they are absolutely exempt, and cannot and ought not to exercise any civil or criminal jurisdiction etc, against them even by reason of a delict, contract, domicile, or matter about which there is an action, wherever the delict is committed, contract entered into, domicile stands, or matter rests, or promulgate [sentences] of excommunication, suspension, or interdict and other ecclesiastical censures and pains against them; but the aforesaid subjects, diocesans, parishioners, and familiars who, themselves litigating (*de se querelantibus*), are bound to answer in law only before James or his officials, and, in the causes of any appeals lodged from time to time from James or his officials, they are bound to answer only before the apostolic see, and similarly James is answerable only before the apostolic see or its special delegates; strictly inhibiting archbishop Andrew and the archbishop of St Andrews for the time being, primate and legate born, and the other archbishops, bishops, etc aforesaid, present and future, lest they presume in any way to exercise any jurisdiction, dominion, superiority, visitation, or correction against James and the church of Moray or any other church to which he perhaps transfers or against any other churches, monasteries, priories, and benefices held by him in any way from time to time in the said kingdom, or against his affairs and goods, and also his officials, subjects, etc, even arising from any civil, criminal, or mixed cause, or presume hereafter to molest, obstruct, or disturb James etc in any way by any far-fetched pretext, method, or reason. Notwithstanding Innocent IV's constitution in respect to exempted persons which begins "Volentes"[3], and other apostolic constitutions, even the one published by the pope in the present Lateran council,[4] etc.

With executory[5] to the bishop of Cavaillon, the prior of the church of St Andrews, and the dean of the church of Dunblane.

E[xi]gentibus meritis tue devotionis quam ad nos et Romanam ecclesiam gerere ... The executory begins: *Hodie motu proprio ...*
f. Bregeon; phi. de Agnellis / C / C. CL. L. Barotius

1   *See below*, no.1027.
2   This is the third mention of archbishop Andrew; his other titles are not mentioned in this context.
3   *Sext*, V.7.1 (Friedberg 1082-3)
4   At its tenth session, on 4 May 1515, the V Lateran Council had approved the bull *Regimini universalis ecclesiae* aimed at curbing exemptions enjoyed by selected categories in the church (G.D. Mansi, *Sacrorum Conciliorum nova et amplissima collectio*, vol. XXXII, cols. 907-912; *Magnum Bullarium Romanum*, I [Luxemburg, 1742], pp. 551-553; Hergenroether, no. 15298; *cf.* C.J.von Hefele and J. Hergenroether, *Conciliengeschichte*, VIII [Freiburg im Breisgau, 1887], pp. 646-650).
5   The exemption of James is here stated to be 'for life' (*quoadvixerit*) – a statement which does not occur in the principal letter. Though it does not say so explicitly the exemption of the church of Moray etc. is presumably to last only so long as James holds it.

650   19 May 1516   *Reg. Lat.* 1346, fos 273ʳ-274ᵛ

Mandate to collate and assign to Theodericus Scholl, perpetual vicar at the altar of Sts Giles, Felix and Regula in the church of B. Mary the Virgin of the town of Eisenach (*Isinacen.*), d. Mainz, a vacant canonry and prebend in the said church.

The 'abbot of the monastery of St James *Scotorum* of the town of Erfurt (*Ersurden.*), d. Mainz' is one of the three mandataries. Entry otherwise of no interest to the Calendar.

Vite ac morum honestas ...
A de Alvarot(tis) / JoA: /:JoA: xxv: Vndecimo K(a)l(endas) Julij Ano Quarto: [21 June 1516], *Nardinus*

651   8 January 1517   *Reg. Lat.* 1347, fos 5ᵛ-7ʳ

To the abbot of the monastery of Beaulieu Regis (*de Bello Loco*), called Beuueley, d. Winchester, and the chancellor of the church of Salisbury, mandate in favour of Richard, bishop of Winchester and rector, called master, and the scholars of Pembroke (*Penbrorhie*) College in the university (*universitate studii*) of the town of Cambridge (*Cantabrigue*), d. Ely, co-litigants in this regard. A recent petition to the pope on the co-litigants' part stated that at another time – after the late Thomas, bishop of Winchester, had, in his testament or last will, bequeathed to the said college 40 pounds of English[1] money and a gold or gilded frontal (*tabulam*) for the <altar> of the chapel[2] and had ordered that they be given and handed over by the hands of certain executors appointed by bishop Thomas in the said testament or last will, and after the said executors had unduly delayed to give and hand [them] over, as they were bound, to the co- litigants – the co- litigants sued (not by apostolic delegation) John Withers, priest, executor of the said testament or last will, who was the only one of the executors then alive, before the archbishop of Canterbury, primate of the whole kingdom of England and legate born of the apostolic see in those parts, or before a certain auditor, then expressed, appointed by the said archbishop, of causes which arise from time to time in the court of the office of the legate born (*legationis nate*) of the archbishop, praying *inter alia* that John be condemned and coerced and compelled to give and hand over the pounds and the frontal, if it existed, [or its] true value; and that the said auditor, proceeding duly in the case, promulgated a definitive sentence in favour of the co-litigants and against John, with condemnation in costs, from which John – falsely asserting that it was unjust – appealed to the apostolic see. At the co-litigants' supplication to the pope to order the inhibition of any judges and persons, as appropriate, even under ecclesiastical censures and pains; to commit to some upright men in those parts the causes: of the aforesaid appeal and of anything perhaps attempted and innovated after and against it; of anything done to the prejudice of the co- litigants in connection with the above, and of the whole principal matter; and, in the event of it being lawfully established that the judgement is final, to order that the above sentence be duly put into execution and that it be confirmed,[3] the pope [hereby] commands that the above two (or one of them), having summoned John and others concerned, having inhibited any judges and persons, as appropriate, under the said pains and censures, in accordance with the law, and having heard both sides, taking cognizance even of the principal matter, shall decree what is just, and further, if it appears to them that the above sentence has become a final judgement, duly put it into execution, causing, by the pope's authority in the case of the said bishop and by ecclesiastical censure in the case of the others, what they have decreed to be strictly observed, [and moreover compel] witnesses, etc. Notwithstanding etc.

Humilibus et cetera.
.P. lanb(er)tus / M / M xviij de Campania

1   MS: *anglicale*; *recte*: ' anglicane'
2   MS: originally *pro capalla* [*sic*]; then *altari* inserted in margin but *capalla* not re-inflected: *pro < altari>* *capalla*; the insertion (in hand of enregistering scribe) initialled *M*
3   MS: *et in eventum quod ius de re iudicata huiusmodi legitime constiterit illam executioni debite demandari sententiamque ipsam confirmari mandare*; 'vobis' does not occur

652   1 July 1516   *Reg. Lat.* 1348, fos 12ʳ-14ʳ

To the abbot of the monastery of B. Mary, *de Arnicampo* [Kilcooly], d. Cashel, and Cornelius Olochnayn and Theobald Butheler, canons of the church of Cashel, mandate in favour of John Cantuel, priest of Cashel.[1] A recent petition to the pope on John's part

stated that at another time – [after]² the chancellorship of the church of Ossory, which
was then vacant *certo modo*, [had been (canonically) collated to John and provision
made of it to him and he had accepted it]³ by virtue of certain apostolic letters of
expectative grace (in which the said chancellorship was comprehended) granted to him
motu proprio by Julius II; and (after) Julius had learned that John suffered a defect of
birth (as the son of a cleric and an unmarried woman) and had been dispensed by
apostolic authority, notwithstanding this defect, to be promoted to all, even sacred,
orders and to hold a benefice, even if it should have cure of souls; and it was stated
that, by virtue of this dispensation, John had been duly promoted to the said orders and
that he was of the diocese of Ossory – by certain [other letters]⁴ Julius [dispensed]⁴
John [to hold]⁴ benefices which were comprehended under the aforesaid letters,⁵ but
not under the dispensation, [which had been (canonically) collated]⁴ to him, the said
defect notwithstanding, and by virtue of these letters⁶ he acquired possession of the
chancellorship and holds it at present, receiving fruits from the same. However, as the
same petition added, John fears that the acceptance and provision in question do not,
for certain reasons, hold good; and, as the pope has learned, the chancellorship is
understood to be still vacant. Wishing to give John (who asserts that he is the son of a
priest, a canon regular, OSA; and that he never was of the diocese of Ossory, but of
Cashel⁷) a special grace, the pope hereby commands that the above three, or two or one
of them, in person or by proxy, shall collate and assign the chancellorship (which is a
dignity, not however major *post pontificalem*; and whose annual value does not exceed
9 marks sterling) vacant howsoever etc.; even if vacant for so long that by the Lateran
statutes its collation has lawfully devolved on the apostolic see etc., with all rights and
appurtenances, to John, inducting him etc. having removed any unlawful detainer and
causing John (or his proctor) to be admitted to the chancellorship and its fruits etc.,
rights and obventions to be delivered to him. [Curbing] gainsayers etc.
Notwithstanding etc. Also the pope dispenses John to receive and retain a canonry and
prebend,⁸ if conferred on him by virtue of the presents, notwithstanding the above
defect etc.

Vite ac morum honestas …
*Phy de Agnellis / JoA: / JoA: xx: Decimo sept(im)o k(a)l(endas) Sept(embris) Anno
Quarto:* [16 August 1516], *Nardinus*

1   *diocesis* does not occur here; *cf.* below, note 7
2   MS: *per*; *recte*: 'postquam'
3   Conjectural restoration of text evidently wanting. The omission here was arguably triggered by 'acceperat'
    occurring twice in proximate positions.
4   Conjectural restoration of text evidently wanting. The omission is implied by *quasdam* (which expects 'alias
    litteras'); by *idem predecessor* (which expects verb) and by *cum dicto Johanne* (which expects the verb to
    be 'dispensavit' [or other tense/mood]).
5   i.e. the letters of expectative grace (which are unknown to the *CPL*)
6   i.e. Julius's 'other letters' (which are unknown to the *CPL*)
7   … *nunquam Osseren. sed Cassallen. dioc'* …
8   … *ut canonicatum et prebendam si sibi vigore presentium conferrantur recipere et retinere* … This is the first
    mention of a canonry and prebend (tied to the chancellorship?).

653   23 July 1516   *Reg. Lat.* 1348, fos 14ᵛ-16ᵛ

To the abbots of the monasteries of B. Mary, *de Arnicampo* [Kilcooly], d. Cashel, and
of B. Mary, *de Legedei* [Abbeyleix], d. Leighlin, and Patrick Cantuuel, canon of the
church of Ossory, mandate in favour of Dermot Mcostilla *alias* Nogul, monk of the
monastery of B. Mary, Rosglas, OCist, d. Kildare (who, as he asserts, notwithstanding
a defect of birth as the son of a cleric and an unmarried or married woman, has been
marked with clerical character otherwise duly, and in the said monastery has taken the
usual habit worn by its monks and made the usual regular profession made by the said
monks; and then had himself promoted to all, even sacred and priest's, orders). The
pope has learned that the perpetual vicarage of the parish church of Balleyscham, d.
Kildare, is vacant *certo modo* at present and has been vacant for so long that by the
Lateran statutes its collation has lawfully devolved on the apostolic see, although
David Sculyn,[1] who bears himself as a priest, has detained it with no title and no
support of law, of his own temerity and *de facto*, for a certain time, as he still does. He
hereby commands that the above three (or two or one of them), if, having summoned
David and others concerned, they find the vicarage (whose annual value does not
exceed 4 marks sterling), to be vacant (howsoever etc.) shall commend it (even if
specially reserved etc.), with all rights and appurtenances, to Dermot to be held, ruled
and governed by him for life; he may – due and customary burdens of the vicarage
having been supported – make disposition of the rest of its fruits etc. just as those
holding it *in titulum* could and ought to do, alienation of immovable goods and
precious movables being however forbidden; inducting Dermot etc. having removed
David and any other unlawful detainer; and causing Dermot (or his proctor) to be
admitted to the vicarage and its fruits etc., rights and obventions to be delivered to him.
Curbing [gainsayers] etc. Notwithstanding etc. Also the pope dispenses Dermot (who
suffers the above defect of birth) to receive and retain the above vicarage (if
commended to him by virtue of the presents) *in commendam* for life, notwithstanding
etc. With the proviso that the said vicarage shall not, on account of this commend, be
defrauded of due services and the cure of souls in it shall not be neglected; but that its
aforesaid burdens shall be supported.

Religionis zelus, vite ac morum honestas ...
Phy de Agnellis / JoA. / JoA: xx: Septimo k(a)l(endas) Sept(embris) Anno Quarto: [26
August 1516], *Nar(dinus)*

1   or *Scubyn* etc.

654   16 July 1516   *Reg. Lat.* 1348, fos 17ʳ-20ʳ

To the abbots of the monasteries of B. Mary, Rock of Cashel (*de Rupecasellis*), and of
B. Mary, *de Arvicampo* [Kilcooly], and of the Holy Cross, Motorlan, d. Cashel,
mandate in favour of John Yhoohenece, cleric, d. Cashel. The pope has learned that the
perpetual vicarages of the parish churches of St Nicholas, Balymtrany[1] *alias*

Scadanysdum, and B. Mary, Knoleac, and St James, Piperta', d. Cashel, are vacant *certo modo* at present and have been vacant for so long that by the Lateran statutes their collation has lawfully devolved on the apostolic see, although Thady Ohyfernan has detained St Nicholas's and James Brit has detained B. Mary's and St James's – bearing themselves as priests – with no title and no support of law, of their own temerity and *de facto*, for a certain time, as they still do. At a recent petition on the part of John (who asserts that the annual value of the vicarages together does not exceed 9 marks sterling) to the pope to erect and institute St Nicholas's into a simple prebend of the church of Cashel, for his lifetime;and to unite etc. the other vicarages to the erected prebend, the pope – not having certain knowledge of the foregoing – hereby commands that the above three (or two or one of them), if, having summoned Thady and James and, as regards the erection, the archbishop and chapter of Cashel and others concerned, they find the vicarages to be vacant (howsoever etc.), shall erect and institute a canonry in the said church of Cashel and St Nicholas's into a simple prebend of it, without prejudice to anyone, and unite etc.the other vicarages (even if specially reserved etc.) to the canonry and prebend thus erected, for John's lifetime; and in the event of this erection and institution and union etc. collate and assign the newly erected canonry and prebend, being then vacant, with plenitude of canon law and the annexes in question and all rights and appurtenances, to John, inducting him etc. having removed Thady and James and any other unlawful detainers from them, and causing John (or his proctor) to be received as a canon in the church of Cashel, with plenitude of canon law, and [causing] the fruits etc., rights and obventions of the said canonry and prebend and annexes to be delivered to him. [Curbing] gainsayers etc. Notwithstanding etc. It is the pope's will, however, that the said vicarages shall not, on this account, be defrauded of due services and the cure of souls in them shall not be neglected; but that their customary burdens shall be supported; and that on John's death or his resignation etc. of the canonry and prebend this erection and institution shall be extinguished and the union etc. shall be dissolved and be so deemed and the vicarages shall revert to their original condition automatically.

Apostolice sedis circumspecta benignitas ad ea libenter intendit ...
Phy Agnellis / JoA: / JoA: xxx: Decimo Septimo k(a)l(endas) Sept(embris) anno Quarto: [16 August 1516], *Nardinus*

1   or *Balynitrany*: the third minim is dotted

655   1 July 1516   *Reg. Lat.* 1348, fos 20^r-23^r

To the abbots of the monasteries of B. Mary *de Arvicampo* [Kilcooly], and Rock of Cashel (*de Rupecassellis*), d. Cashel, mandate in favour of Edmund Emeachyr, cleric, d. Cashel. The pope has learned that the rectory of the parish church of Kyllconyll, d. Cashel (which is of lay patronage) is vacant *certo modo* at present and has been vacant for so long that by the Lateran statutes its collation has lawfully devolved on the apostolic see, although Nicholas Odul la cinta, who bears himself as a priest, has detained it with no title and no support of law, of his own temerity and *de facto*, for a certain time, and does so. At a recent petition to the pope on Edmund's part to erect a canonry in the church of Cashel and the said rectory into a simple prebend of it, for his lifetime, the pope hereby commands that the above two (or one of them),[1] if, having summoned Nicholas and as regards the erection the archbishop and chapter of Cashel and others concerned, they find the rectory (which is with cure and whose annual value does not exceed 12 marks sterling) to be vacant (howsoever etc.), shall erect a canonry in the church of Cashel and the rectory (even if specially reserved to apostolic disposition etc.) into a simple prebend of it, for Edmund's lifetime, without prejudice to anyone;and in that event, collate and assign the newly erected canonry and prebend, being then vacant, with plenitude of canon law and all rights and appurtenances, to Edmund, inducting him etc. into corporal possession of the canonry and prebend and all rights and appurtenances, having removed Nicholas and any other unlawful detainer and causing Edmund (or his proctor) to be received as a canon in the church of Cashel; and shall assign him a stall in the choir and a place in the chapter of the church of Cashel, with plenitude of canon law; and [causing] the fruits etc., rights and obventions of the canonry and prebend to be delivered to him. [Curbing] gainsayers etc. Notwithstanding etc. The pope's will is, however, that the above rectory shall not, on account of this erection, be defrauded of due services and the cure of souls in it shall not be neglected, but that customary burdens shall be supported; and that on Edmund's death or his resignation etc. of the canonry and prebend this erection shall be extinguished and be so deemed and the rectory shall revert to its original condition automatically.

Apostolice sedis circumspecta providentia ...
Ge de Prato / JoA: / JoA: xxv: Sexto k(a)l(endas) Sept(embris) Anno Quarto: [27 August 1516], *Nardinus*

1   MS: *vos vel duo vel alter vestrum: vel duo* is redundant: there are only two mandataries.

656   28 August 1516   *Reg. Lat.* 1348, fos 86ᵛ-88ᵛ

To James Cantuel and Patrick Cantuel, canons of the church of Ossory, and Cornelius Olocuayn, canon of the church of Cashel, mandate in favour of John Ymuluuardayn *alias* Ybroth, abbot of the monastery of B. Mary, *de Arvicanpo alias* Kycule, OCist, d. Cashel. The pope has learned that the perpetual vicarage of the parish church of St Michael, Hermicoda, d. Ossory, and the perpetual vicarage of the parish church of B. Mary, Balignari [also spelt *Balyngari*], d. Cashel (which is a sacerdotal prebend of the church of Cashel), are vacant *certo modo* at present and have been vacant for so long that by the Lateran statutes their collation has lawfully devolved on the apostolic see, although William Machoda *alias* Ascaykyn' has detained the vicarage of St Michael and Thomas Fanyn has detained that of Balignari – bearing themselves as a priest and a cleric respectively – with no title and no support of law, of their own temerity and *de facto*, for a certain time, as they still do. At a recent petition on the part of John – who asserts that he suffers a defect of birth as the son of an unmarried man and an unmarried woman; that he presides over the said monastery and holds the perpetual vicarage of the parish church of St [Brendan?],[1] d. Cashel, with its annexes *in commendam* by apostolic dispensation; and that the annual value of the vacant vicarages does not exceed 18 and of the monastery and its annexes 20, marks sterling – to the pope to unite etc. the vacant vicarages to the said monastery, for as long as he presides over the latter, the pope hereby commands that the above three (or two or one of them), if, having summoned William and Thomas and others concerned, they find the vicarages to be vacant (howsoever etc.) shall unite etc. them (even if specially reserved etc.), with all rights and appurtenances, to the monastery, for as long as John presides over it, and shall remove William and Thomas and any other unlawful detainers from them; to the effect that John may, on his own authority, in person or by proxy, take and retain corporal possession of the vacant vicarages and the rights and appurtenances aforesaid, for as long as he presides over the said monastery,; and convert their fruits etc. to his own uses and those of the monastery, without licence of the local diocesan or of anyone else. Notwithstanding etc. It is the pope's will, however, that the said vacant vicarages shall not, on this account, be defrauded of due services and the cure of souls in them shall not be neglected; but that their customary burdens shall be supported; and that on John's death or his resignation of the monastery, this union etc. shall be dissolved and the "vacant" vicarages shall revert to their original condition and be deemed vacant automatically.[2]

Votis fidelium omnium ex quibus precipue eorum commoditatibus consulitur libenter anuimus …
.Phy. Agnell(is) / JoA: / JoA: xx: Duodecimo K(a)l(endas) octobris Anno Quarto: [20 September 1516], *Nardinus*

1   MS: *Sancti Bernardini* (i.e. S. Bernardino); *recte*: St Brendan (*cf. CPL* XVIII, no. 740)? No name for the place.
2   MS: *ipseque vicarie vacant(es) … vacare censeantur eo ipso:* meaning clear from context; but formulation not altogether happy

657   21 July 1516   *Reg. Lat.* 1348, fos 300ʳ-303ʳ

To the abbot of the monastery of B. Mary, de *Arvica'po*, [Kilcooly], d. Cashel, and the prior of the monastery, usually governed by a prior, of B. Mary, Carhyrduneso, d. Lismore, and Geoffrey Kychin,[1] canon of the church of Cashel, mandate in favour of James Butyler, canon of Lismore. The pope has learned that the deanery of the church of Lismore and the perpetual vicarage of the parish church of the vill of Collomell, d. Lismore, have been vacant *certo modo* and are vacant at present,[2] although Nicholas Machaurric, who bears himself as a cleric, has detained the vicarage with no title and no support of law, of his own temerity and *de facto*, for a certain time, as he still does. A recent petition on James's part to the pope to unite etc. the said vicarage to the canonry and prebend of Socsgynun of the said church of Lismore (which James holds), for as long as he holds the latter, stated that it would be of benefit to James (who asserts that at another time he was dispensed by apostolic authority notwithstanding a defect of birth as the son of an unmarried man and an unmarried woman to be marked with clerical character otherwise however duly, and then, the said defect notwithstanding, to be promoted to all, even sacred and priest's, orders, and also to receive and retain any number of mutually [(?)compatible][3] benefices, even if they should be canonries and prebends, dignities, *personatus*, administrations or offices in cathedral, even metropolitan, or collegiate churches, or parish churches or their perpetual vicarages, even if the dignities etc. should be customarily elective and have cure of souls, if he obtained them otherwise canonically – provided that the dignities in question were not major *post pontificalem* in cathedral, even metropolitan, churches, or principal in collegiate churches; and that, by virtue of this dispensation, he acquired the said canonry and prebend, which were then vacant *certo modo* and canonically collated to him; and that the annual value of the said vicarage and deanery together does not exceed 42 marks sterling). Wishing to give James a special grace and to honour him further in the said church of Lismore the pope hereby commands that the above three (or two or one of them), having summoned Nicholas and others concerned, shall collate and assign the deanery (which is a dignity major *post pontificalem*) to James, and unite etc. the vicarage (howsoever etc. the deanery and vicarage are vacant; even if they have been vacant for so long that by the Lateran statutes their collation has lawfully devolved on the apostolic see, and the deanery and vicarage be specially reserved and the dignity (as a major dignity) be generally reserved etc.) to the canonry and prebend, for as long as James should hold the latter), inducting James into corporal possession of the deanery and vicarage and rights and appurtenances aforesaid, having removed Nicholas and any other unlawful detainers and causing James (or his proctor) to be admitted to the deanery and its fruits etc., rights and obventions and those of the vicarage to be delivered to him. [Curbing] gainsayers etc. Notwithstanding etc. Also the pope dispenses James to receive and retain the said deanery, if conferred on him by virtue of the presents, notwithstanding the above defect etc. The pope's will is, however, that the vicarage shall not, on this account, be defrauded of due services and the cure of souls shall not be neglected; but that its customary burdens shall be supported; and that on James's death or his resignation etc. of the canonry and prebend this union etc. shall be dissolved and so deemed and the vicarage shall revert to its original condition and be deemed vacant automatically.

Vite ac morum honestas ...
Phy Agnellis / JoA: / JoA: xx: pridie Id(us) Aug(us)ti Anno Quarto: [12 August 1516], *Nardinus*

1   or *Kyctim*
2   'et tanto tempore ... quod eorum collatio iuxta Lateranen. statuta concilii est ad sedem apostolicam legitime
    devoluta' does not occur here (though it occurs below among the vacancy clauses).
3   MS: *si*[!] *invicem incompatientia* [!]

658   1 July 1516   *Reg. Lat.* 1348, fos 303ᵛ-307ᵛ

To the abbot of the monastery of B. Mary, *de Arvicampo*¹ [Kilcooly], d. Cashel, mandate in favour of James Maghvuyr, cleric, d. Leighlin. A recent petition to the pope on James's part stated that at another time – following the renewal by Paul II of all papal sentences of excommunication, suspension and interdict and other ecclesiastical sentences, censures and pains against simoniacs (his will being that every simoniac, manifest or occult, should incur them automatically) and his reservation of their absolution and relaxation to himself and his successors alone (except on the point of death); and after James himself, notwithstanding a defect of birth as the son of a then canon, afterwards bishop, of Leighlin, and an unmarried woman, had been marked with clerical character by the said bishop his father² – the said James, ambitiously aspiring to the precentorship of the church of Ossory, promised the then bishop of Ossory – if the bishop would confer the precentorship, then vacant *certo modo*, on him – and [promised] several clerics and laymen – if he acquired the precentorship by their efforts – several sums of money; and next the said bishop [of Ossory], at the instance also of the said clerics and laymen, by ordinary authority collated and made provision of the precentorship, thus vacant, to James (who did not have any dispensation in respect of his above defect of birth), albeit *de facto*; and James, by pretext of this collation and provision and by the power of the said clerics and laymen, took possession of the precentorship and held and holds it and receive(?)s fruits from it (of a value not exceeding 6 gold ducats of the camera), and, perhaps, paid the promised sum of money to the said bishop and clerics and laymen, incurring simony and also the sentences, censures and pains aforesaid and disability. Moreover since, according to the foregoing, the said collation and provision do not hold good; and, as the pope has learned, the precentorship is vacant still and also the archdeaconry of the church of Ferns and the perpetual vicarages of the parish churches of Jerpoint (*de Geriponte*) and Kylhago [also spelt *Kilhago*] and also the perpetual vicarage of the parish church, called *plebania*, of Maruen³ [also spelt *Marben'*], ds. Ossory and Ferns, are vacant *certo modo* at present and have been vacant for so long that by the Lateran statutes their collation has lawfully devolved on the apostolic see, although John Fremss⁴ has detained the archdeaconry, Thomas Ocorigayn the vicarage of Jerpoint and Maurice Ofortyryn⁵ the vicarages of Maruen and Kylhago – bearing themselves as priests – with no title and no support of law, of their own temerity and *de facto*, for a certain time, as they still do. At the said petition on the part of James (who asserts that the annual value of the precentorship does not exceed 9, and of the archdeaconry and vicarages together, 60, marks sterling) to the pope that James be absolved from simony and the other sentences, censures and pains aforesaid, and to unite etc. the archdeaconry and vicarages to the precentorship, for as long as James holds the latter, the pope hereby commands the above abbot to absolve James, if he so requests, from simony and the sentence of excommunication and other sentences, censures and pains incurred by him, for this once only, in the customary form of the church, having enjoined a salutary penance on him etc.; to dispense him for irregularity, if, perhaps, he contracted it by taking part in divine offices while bound by the said sentences, censures and pains, not, however, in contempt of the keys; and to rehabilitate him on account of all disability and infamy contracted by him by occasion of the foregoing; and, in the event of this absolution, dispensation and rehabilitation, collate and assign the precentorship (which is a dignity, not however major *post pontificalem*, in the said church of Ossory) to James; and also [having summoned] John, Thomas and Maurice and others concerned, unite etc. the archdeaconry (which is a dignity major *post pontificalem* in the said church of Ferns) and the vicarages (vacant howsoever etc.; even if specially reserved etc.) to the precentorship, for as long as James should hold the latter, with all rights and appurtenances, inducting James etc. into corporal possession of the precentorship and annexes and rights and appurtenances aforesaid, having removed John, Thomas, Maurice and any other unlawful detainers and causing James (or his proctor) to be admitted to the precentorship and its fruits etc., rights and obventions and those of the said annexes to be delivered to him. [Curbing] gainsayers etc. Notwithstanding etc. Also the pope dispenses James to use the said character and be promoted to all, even sacred and priest's, orders and to receive and retain the precentorship, if conferred on him by virtue of the presents, with the annexes in question, notwithstanding etc. The pope's will is, however, that the archdeaconry and vicarages shall not, on account of this union etc., be defrauded of due services and the cure of souls in the vicarages [and] (if any) the archdeaconry shall not be neglected, but that their customary burdens shall be supported; and that on James's death or his resignation etc. of the precentorship (after it has been conferred on him by virtue of the presents), this union etc. shall be dissolved and be so deemed and the archdeaconry and vicarages shall revert to their original condition and be deemed vacant automatically; and that before the above abbot shall proceed to the execution of the presents in any way, James shall resign the precentorship into his hands genuinely and completely.

Sedes apostolica pia mater recurentium ad eam post excessum …
Phy Agnellis / JoA: / JoA: xxxv: Nardinus

1   or *Arni-*
2   MS: *de tunc canonico postmodum episcopo Legilinen.* [!] *genitus et soluta ab eodem episcopo patre suo clericali caractere insignitus fuerat*
3   *Marven*?
4   changed from *Feemss*?
5   the second 'o' indistinct; perhaps an 'e'

659   20 September 1516   *Reg. Lat.* 1348, fos 413ᵛ-417ʳ

To Henry Branagayiy and Thady Okassy, canons of the church of Annaghdown, and Florence Okernaym, canon of the church of Clonfert, mandate in favour of Theobald de Burgo, cleric, d. Tuam. The pope has learned that the canonry and prebend of Kylmian [also spelt *Kyllmian, Kylmyan*], in the church of Tuam, and the canonry and prebend of Synwyr,[1] in the church of Clonfert, the rectories of the parish churches of Hanary, Arddrayn[2] and Kyllthomys [also spelt *Kyllchomys*] and the perpetual vicarages of the said parish church of Hanary and of the parish churches of Killcomyne[3] [also spelt *Kyllcomym*][4] and Kylmian, ds. Tuam, Clonfert, Annaghdown and Kilmacduagh, are vacant *certo modo* at present and have been vacant for so long that by the Lateran statutes their collation has lawfully devolved on the apostolic see, although Richard (*Restardus*) de Burgo and Walter de Burgo junior have for some time detained the canonries and prebends of the churches of Tuam and Clonfert, dividing their fruits between themselves, Hubert[5] Machmylot,[6] Thomas de Burgo senior and Thomas de Burgo junior have for some time detained the vicarage of Kylmian and the rectory and vicarage of Hanary, dividing their fruits between themselves, and Walter de Burgo senior and Thomas Macnauuyn, have for some time detained the rectories of Arddrayn and Kyllthomys and the vicarage of Killcomyne, (?)dividing their fruits between themselves – bearing themselves as clerics and priests of the dioceses of Tuam, Clonfert, Annaghdown and Kilmacduagh – with no title and no support of law, of their own temerity and *de facto*, for a certain time, as they still do. At a recent petition on the part of Theobald (who asserts that some time ago, notwithstanding a defect of birth as the son of a canon of a cathedral church and an unmarried woman, he had been dispensed first by ordinary authority to be marked with clerical character and to hold a benefice without cure,[7] and then by apostolic authority to be promoted to all, even sacred and priest's, orders, and to hold a benefice, even if [it should have cure of souls];[8] and that by virtue of the said first dispensation he had been duly marked with clerical character; and that the annual value of the said canonries and prebends, rectories and vicarages together does not exceed 120 marks sterling) to the pope to unite etc. the rectories and vicarages to the canonry and prebend of the church of Tuam, for as long as Theobald should hold the latter, if conferred on him as above, the pope hereby commands that the above three (or two or one of them), if, having summoned Richard, Walter junior, Walter senior, Hubert, Thomas de Burgo senior, Thomas de Burgo junior and Thomas Macnauuyn and others concerned, they find the canonries and prebends, rectories and vicarages to be vacant (howsoever etc.), shall unite etc. the rectories and vicarages to this canonry and prebend of the church of Tuam, for as long as Theobald should hold the latter; and collate and assign the canonries and prebends aforesaid (even if specially reserved etc.) to Theobald, with plenitude of canon law and the annexes in question and all rights and appurtenances, inducting him etc. into corporal possession of the canonries and prebends, rectories and vicarages and rights and appurtenances aforesaid, having removed Richard, Walter junior, Walter senior, Thomas de Burgo senior, Thomas de Burgo junior and Thomas Macnauuyn and any other unlawful detainers from them and causing Theobald (or his proctor) to be received as a canon of the said churches of Tuam and Clonfert, and shall assign him a stall in the choirs and places in the chapter[9] of those churches, with plenitude of canon law; and [causing] the fruits etc., rights and obventions of the canonries and prebends and of the annexed rectories and vicarages to be delivered to him. [Curbing] gainsayers etc. Notwithstanding etc. Also the pope dispenses Theobald, (who suffers the above defect of birth), to receive and retain the said canonries and prebends, if conferred on him by virtue of the presents, notwithstanding etc. The pope's will is, however, that the rectories and vicarages shall not, on account of this union etc., be defrauded of due services and the cure of souls in them shall not be neglected; but that their customary burdens shall be supported; and that on Theobald's death or his resignation etc. of the canonry and prebend of the church of Tuam, this union etc. shall be dissolved and be so deemed and the rectories and vicarages shall revert to their original condition and be deemed vacant automatically. Given at Monterosi, d. Nepi.

Vite ac morum honestas …
Phy Agnellis' / JoA: / JoA: xxxx: Sept(im)o K(a)l(endas) octobris Anno Quarto: [25
September 1516], *Nardinus*

1   uncertain
2   in second occurrence the 'r' uncertain and possibly deleted
3   uncertain
4   final letter reworked and uncertain
5   *Hubertus*; also spelt: *Unbert-, Umbert-*
6   the '-ot' uncertain
7   *See below*, note 8.
8   MS: *curam non*[!] *haberet animarum*; *recte*: 'curam haberet animarum'
9   MS: *stallo sibi in coris et locis in capitulo*; 'loco in capitulis'?

660   10 October 1516   *Reg. Lat.* 1349, fos 142ᵛ-143ʳ

To Andrew Brown[e][1] *alias* Walsham, monk of the monastery of St Benedict, Hulme
(*de Holmo*), OSB,[2] d. Norwich. Dispensation – at his supplication – to receive and
retain any benefice, with or without cure, usually held by secular clerics, etc. [as above,
no. 19, to '… and in its place receive and retain another, similar or dissimilar, benefice,
with or without cure, defined as above']; and – even before he has acquired the said
benefice – to wear the usual habit worn by monks of the above monastery, OSB,[3] of
which he is a monk and is, as he assserts, expressly professed of the order, under an
honest priestly garment or robe of any fitting and honest colour, without incurring
apostasy or other ecclesiastical censure; and not to be bound to wear the habit in
another way, nor to be liable to be compelled to do so against his will by the superiors
of the said order or by anyone else. Notwithstanding etc. Given at Corneto.

Religionis zelus, vite ac morum honestas …
P. lanbertus / JoA: / JoA: xxxx: Nardinus

1   final letter somewhat obscured by ink blot; confirmed by index reading
2   MS: *ordinis eiusdem sancti* +. Plainly *eiusdem* refers to *Benedicti*. The cross (which has points to form an
    asteriscus) could signify an omission (of 'Benedicti') – or it may be a reference mark (even though there is
    no corresponding mark or accompanying note in the margin).
3   as note 2 above

661   9 March 1517   *Reg. Lat.* 1349, fos 143ʳ-144ʳ

Indulgences as below. The pope has learned that James Hyde, esquire, and Elisabeth
Hyde, a married couple, and Nicholas Hyde their son, led by piety and after long
reflection on their own salvation and the end of their life, have chosen to be buried in
the church of St John, called the Savore hospital, d. London, to which they are
singularly devoted, and that they have caused to be built therein a notable monument
or tomb[1] for the interment of their bodies when they have died. The pope – wishing

that the said church be suitably honoured and that the priests and other faithful of Christ visiting it readily and devoutly pray to God for the prosperous estate of the said James, Elisabeth and Nicholas in this life and, after their deaths, for the salvation of their souls and the souls of the other faithful departed, because they see that they could thus be refreshed by the [(?)gift][2] of celestial grace – assured of the mercy of Almighty God and of the authority of His Apostles BB. Peter and Paul, relaxes [1] for all priests who, *inter missarum solemnia,* in the place where by custom they are wont to pray for the living and the dead, have devoutly prayed for James, Elisabeth and Nicholas: five years and as many quarantines of enjoined penance for each time they have done it; and [2] for all the faithful of both sexes who, being truly penitent and confessed, have devoutly visited the said church annually on the feasts of the Nativity, Resurrection and Ascension of our Lord, and also on the feasts of Pentecost and the Nativity of St John the Baptist, and, kneeling before the tomb or monument of James, Elisabeth and Nicholas, after it has been built,[3] have devoutly said and recited once the Lord's Prayer with the Angelic Salutation for their prosperous estate in this life and that of all their relatives and benefactors and, after their deaths, for the salvation of their souls and of the souls of the other faithful departed: five years and as many quarantines of enjoined penance for each time they have done it, available on each one of the above feasts. The present letters shall last for all time.

Universis Christifidelibus presentes litteras inspecturis [...] De salute gregis dominice[4]
meritis licet inparibus divina dispositione nobis commissi solicite cogitantes .. ...
/ Jo carotius; JoA: / :JoA: xx:- Nardinus

1   MS: *... et inibi notabile monumentum seu tumulum pro eorum corporibus cum ab hac luce decesserint
     sepeliendis construi fecerint*
2   MS: *celestis gratie devotione*; *recte*: 'dono'?
3   MS: *... et ante tumulum seu monumentum ipsorum Jacobi et Elizabeth ac Nicolai postquam constructum
     fuerit*
4   *sic*; 'dominici'?

662   31 July 1516   *Reg. Lat.* 1349, fos 333ᵛ-334ᵛ

To Thomas Bebry *alias* Princhett, monk, OSB,[1] d. (?)...[2] Dispensation – at his supplication – to him, who, as he asserts, is a monk, OSB,[3] to receive and retain any benefice, with or without cure, usually held by secular clerics, etc. [as above, no. 43, to '... receive and retain another, similar or dissimilar, benefice, with or without cure'], usually held by secular clerics.[4] Notwithstanding etc.

Religionis zelus, vite ac morum honestas ...
G. prato / JoA: / JoA: xxx: Nardinus

1   MS: *monacho ordinis Sancti Benedicti Woavicen. dioc(esis)* – i.e. the grantee is (most unusually) styled a
     monk of the Benedictine order and not a monk of a (named) Benedictine house.
2   MS: *Woavicen*: perhaps 'Norwich'; though no house is mentioned the cathedral priory (Benedictine) may lie
     behind the statement. The grantee's surname looks English; and reference to the legatine constitutions of

Otto and Ottobuono among the notwithstanding clauses implies an English (or Welsh) connection of some sort.

3   This information comes from a notwithstanding clause. MS: *ac ordinis Sancti Benedicti cuius monachus existis*; at this point it would have been usual to state that the grantee was a monk of a (named) house of the order (*cf.* above, note 1) with the further statement: 'et ut asseris ordinem ipsum expresse professus existis' (or suchlike).

4   Of course, this latter phrase reflects a variation from no. 43 merely in the formulation – not the tenor – of the Latin.

663   8 May 1517   *Reg. Lat.* 1350, fos 21ʳ-23ʳ

To Dermot Omerchayr, canon of the church of Killaloe, and William Macgilfadrig and John Ohylin, canons of the church of Ossory, mandate in favour of Nemeas Omhayier, cleric, d. Killaloe. The pope has learned that the canonry and prebend of Kyllurac of the church of Cashel and the perpetual vicarages of the parish churches of St Nicholas, Beruan, and of B. Mary, Buryn, and also of St Cronan [*Sancti Coronani/Cronani*], Roscec, ds. Cashel and Killaloe, are vacant *certo modo* at present and have been vacant for so long that by the Lateran statutes their collation has lawfully devolved on the apostolic see, although Thady Olahe has detained the canonry and prebend and John Olrearruyll [also spelt *Yceruall'*, *Oceruall'*, *Oueruall'*] the vicarage of St Cronan's – bearing themselves as clerics – and John Omechaue [also spelt *Omaher*] the vicarage of St Nicholas's – bearing himself as a priest – and Donald Omechayr the vicarage of B. Mary's – bearing himself as a canon regular OSA – with no title and no support of law,[1] of their own temerity and *de facto*, for a certain time, as they still[2] do. At a recent petition on the part of Nemeas (who asserts that, notwithstanding a defect of birth as the son – incestuously begot – of an unmarried man and unmarried woman, he has been marked with clerical character by ordinary authority; that he is in his fifteenth year of age; and that the annual value of the canonry and prebend and vicarages aforesaid together does not exceed 32[3] marks sterling) to the pope to unite etc. the above vicarages to the canonry and prebend, for as long as Nemeas should hold the latter, he hereby commands that the above three (or two or one of them, if, having summoned Thady, John Omechaue, John Olrearruyll and Donald aforesaid and others concerned, they find the canonry and prebend and the vicarages to be vacant (howsoever etc.), shall collate and assign the canonry and prebend to Nemeas and unite etc. the vicarages (even if specially reserved etc.) to the canonry and prebend, for as long as Nemeas should hold the latter, with plenitude of canon law and all rights and appurtenances, inducting Nemeas (or his proctor) into corporal possession of the canonry and prebend and annexes and rights and appurtenances aforesaid, having removed Thady, John Omechaue, John Olrearruyll and Donald and any other unlawful detainers and causing Nemeas (or his proctor) to be received as a canon of the church of Cashel, and shall assign him a stall in the choir and a place in the chapter of the church of Cashel, with plenitude of canon law, and [causing] the fruits etc., rights and obventions of the canonry and prebend and annexes in question to be delivered to him. Curbing gainsayers by the pope's authority. Notwithstanding etc. Also the pope dispenses Nemeas to receive and retain the said canonry and prebend, notwithstanding the above defect [of birth], etc. The pope's will is, however, that the said vicarages shall not, on account of this union etc., be defrauded of due services and the cure of souls in them shall not be neglected; but that their customary <burdens>[4] shall be supported; and that on Nemeas's death or his resignation etc. of the canonry and prebend this union etc. shall be dissolved and the vicarages shall revert to their original <condition>[5] and be deemed vacant automatically.

Vite ac morum honestas ...
Phy d(e) Angellis / JoA: / JoA: xxv: Nardi(nus):-

1   MS: *dilecti filii Beate Marie ecclesiarum vicarias huiusmodi nullo titulo iurisve*; there is a cross (signalling error) in the left margin against this line; but no action was taken.
2   *ad hunc*; *recte*: 'adhuc'
3   MS: *triginta [ducatorum* deleted and initialled *JoA.] duarum marcarum sterlingorum*
4   *consueta* occurs in line, but not 'onera'; *consueta onera* was inserted in the margin (in enregistering scribe's hand), but not initialled; *consueta* being then smeared out, likewise not initialled.
5   *statum* inserted in margin in enregistering scribe's hand, not initialled

664   8 May 1517   *Reg. Lat.* 1350, fos 23ᵛ-24ᵛ

To Dermot Omechayr, canon of the church of Killaloe, and William Macgilfadrig and John Ohylin, canons of the church of Ossory, mandate in favour of Dermot Omechayr, priest, d. Cashel. A recent petition to the pope on Dermot's part stated that at another time when the perpetual vicarage of the parish [church][1] of Heyne, d. Cashel, was vacant *certo modo*, the archbishop of Cashel collated and made provision of it, thus vacant, to Dermot by ordinary authority; and, by virtue of this collation and provision, he acquired possession of it. However, as the said petition added, Dermot fears that the said collation and provision do not, for certain reasons, hold good; and, as the pope has learned, the said vicarage is understood to be vacant still, as above. The pope hereby commands that the above three, or two or one of them, in person or by proxy, shall collate and assign the vicarage (whose annual value does not exceed 3 marks sterling) (vacant howsoever etc.; even if vacant for so long that by the Lateran statutes its collation has lawfully devolved on the apostolic see, etc.), with all rights and appurtenances, to Dermot, inducting him etc. having removed any unlawful detainer and causing Dermot (or his proctor) to be admitted to the vicarage and its fruits etc., rights and obventions to be delivered to him. Curbing gainsayers by the pope's authority etc. Notwithstanding etc.

Vite ac morum honestas ...
Phy. de Angellis / JoA: / JoA: x: Quinto k(a)l(endas) Junij Anno Quinto:- [28 May 1517], *Nardinus*

1   'ecclesie' does not occur

665   **17 September 1517**   *Reg. Lat.* 1350, fos 174ʳ-177ʳ

To the archdeacon of Moithwille'[1] of the church of Salisbury, and John Dowman and William Harington, canons of the church of London, mandate in favour of Richard Hamlett, <layman>[2], d. Lincoln, executor of the testament or last will of the late Thomas Bunett[3] [also spelt *Bunnett*[4]] of Iseldon, cleric or layman, d. London. A recent petition to the pope on Richard Hamlett's part stated that although, at another time, the said Thomas, being of sound mind, made the said testament or last will and in it appointed Richard Hamlett and the late Richard Du'kerley its executors, and although Richard Hamlett and Richard Du'kerley administered Thomas's goods and made disposition of them in accordance with his dispositions, Emma[5] Bunett, relict of the said Thomas – falsely asserting that the said testament or last will was not the true one and that she was appointed executrix in the true testament or last will – nevertheless sued Richard Hamlett and Richard Du'kerley over this, not by apostolic delegation, before Thomas Wodington', official of the court of Canterbury, who was, she said, a competent judge for this; that although, on the part of Richard Hamlett and Richard Du'kerley, several articles and material drawn up in articles (by which *inter alia* it was articulated and set forth that Thomas was of sound mind at the time the testament or last will in which Richard Hamlett and Richard Du'kerley had been appointed executors was made) and several witnesses to prove the said articles and material drawn up in articles had been exhibited and produced before the said official at a suitable time and place, nevertheless the official, proceeding wrongly in the case, did not, as he ought to have done, examine the said witnesses as to whether, at the time the testament or last will in which Richard Hamlett and Richard Du'kerley had been appointed executors was made, the said Thomas [(?) was of sound mind][6]; that after the publication of the said witnesses' depositions, Emma had set forth before the said official, by certain material drawn up in articles, that at the time the testament or last will in which Richard Hamlett and Richard Du'kerley had been appointed executors was made Thomas was mad (*furiosus*) and suffering from insanity; that Richard Hamlett and Richard Du'kerley had therefore prayed that the said witnesses be examined anew[7], over this, by the said official, exhibited material directly contrary to the material put forward on Emma's part, and prayed with due instance that they be admitted to prove the material; that the said official, proceeding wrongly in the case, refused, tacitly at least, to examine the said witnesses anew or cause a repeat and to admit the said material last exhibited before him on Richard Hamlett's part, and he decreed, albeit *de facto*, the publication of the said witnesses in the case on Emma's part,[8] wherefore on the part of Richard Hamlett, who felt *inter alia* unduly aggrieved thereby, appeal was made to the apostolic see, Richard Du'kerley being then dead; that the official unlawfully refused to admit the appeal, which he was unwilling to read, and by his interlocutory sentence pronounced that proceedings to further matters in the case were due, wherefore on the part of Richard Hamlett, who felt *inter alia* unduly aggrieved thereby, appeal was similarly made to the apostolic see and that the said official – regardless of the appeals of which he was not ignorant and while Richard Hamlett was still well within the time for prosecuting them – rashly proceeding to further matters, promulgated an unjust or null, definitive (as he said) sentence, by which *inter alia* he declared that at the time when the testament or last will in which Richard Hamlett and Richard Du'kerley were appointed executors was made Thomas was of unsound mind, that the testament or last will in which Emma was appointed was valid and true, and that under the provincial constitutions of those parts Richard Hamlett had incurred sentence of greater excommunication,[9] and he also condemned him in the costs run up in the case, from which, on Richard Hamlett's part, appeal was again made to the apostolic see. At the supplication to the pope to order that Richard Hamlett be absolved from the said sentence of excommunication and other sentences, censures, and pains promulgated against him on the above occasion and to commit to some upright men in those parts the causes: of each of the aforesaid appeals and of anything attempted and innovated after and against them and each one of them; of the nullity and nullities of the process and sentence of the said official and of each and every other thing done in any way by the official and any other judges and persons to Richard Hamlett's prejudice in connection with the above; and of the whole principal matter, the pope [hereby] commands that the above three (or two or one of them), having summoned Emma and others concerned, shall, on the pope's authority, for this once only, bestow on Richard Hamlett, if he so requests, the benefit of absolution *ad cautelam* from the said sentence of excommunication and other sentences, censures, and pains, if and as it is just, having, however, first received from him suitable security in respect of that for which he is perhaps deemed excommunicate and caught by the other sentences, censures, and pains, that if they find that the said sentence of excommunication, etc were justly inflicted on him he will obey their mandates and those of the church; as to the other things, having heard both sides, taking cognizance even of the principal matter, decree what is just, without appeal, [causing by ecclesiastical censure what they have decreed to be strictly] observed,[10] [and moreover compel] witnesses, etc. Notwithstanding etc.

Humilibus et cetera.
P. lanb(er)tus / JoA / JoA: xij: Nardinus

1   or *Morthwillt'* = North Wilts? Only 'archdeacons of Wiltshire' are known to John Le Neve, *Fasti Ecclesiae Anglicanae 1300-1541*, III: Salisbury Diocese, compiled by J.M. Horn (London, 1962), pp. 13-14; but an "Archidecanat' de North Wiltes' " is known to near contemporary record (*cf. Valor Ecclesiasticus temp. Henr. VIII*, vol. II [Record Commission, 1814], p. 147).
2   *laici* inserted in margin, initialled *JoA*.
3   the four minims variously readable
4   the six minims variously readable
5   read sympathetically; the name recurs repeatedly throughout the entry but occasionally appears to be written 'Emina' and certainly in one instance the fourth minim is dotted.
6   MS: *an idem Thomas tempore conditi testamenti seu ultime voluntatis huiusmodi in quo seu qua prefacti Ricardus Hamlett et Ricardus Du'kerley executores deputati fuerant *** ut debebat examinare non examinavit*; apparent omission tentatively supplied
7   very tentatively reading *denuo*
8   MS: *ac ad publicationem dictorum testium in huiusmodi causa pro parte prefacte Emme decrevit*; 'productorum' does not occur; neither does ' depositionum' (or suchlike).
9   perhaps under *Statutum bonae memoriae* of archbishop John Stratford (*Cf.* G. Lyndwood, *Provinciale*, Lib. III, Tit. 13, Cap. 5 [Oxford, 1679, pp. 171-179])
10   MS: *decernatis et cetera observari*. Supplied from common form.

666   12 August 1517   *Reg. Lat.* 1350, fos 375ʳ-376ᵛ

To the dean of the church of Dunblane, mandate in favour of Andrew Sym,[1] senior, priest, d. St Andrews. Following the pope's reservation some time ago of all benefices, with or without cure, vacated then or in the future at the apostolic see to his own collation and disposition, the perpetual vicarage of the parish church of Comri,[2] d. Dunblane, became vacant by the free resignation of James Belsis, recently perpetual vicar of this church which he was then holding, made through Adam Symsson, cleric, d. Dunkeld, his specially appointed proctor, spontaneously into the hands of the pope and admitted by him at the said see, and is vacant at present, being reserved as above. The pope hereby commands the above dean, if through diligent examination he finds Andrew to be suitable – concerning which the pope burdens the dean's conscience – to collate and assign the vicarage, whose annual value does not exceed 4 pounds sterling (vacant as above or howsoever etc.; even if it has been vacant for so long that by the Lateran statutes its collation has lawfully devolved on the apostolic see, etc.), with all rights and appurtenances, to Andrew, inducting him etc. having removed any detainer[3] and causing Andrew (or his proctor) to be admitted to the vicarage and its fruits etc., rights and obventions to be delivered to him. [Curbing] gainsayers etc. Notwithstanding etc.

Dignum arbitramur et congruum et cetera suffragantur.
[–]⁴ / *JoA:* / *JoA: xx: Septimo Id(us) Septenbris Anno Quinto:* [7 September 1517], *Nardi(nus)*

1   The 'm' has a long tail which might indicate abbreviation.
2   sympathetic; readable as *Coven*
3   'illicito' does not occur.
4   abbreviator's name wanting

667   8 July 1516   *Reg. Lat.* 1351, fos 318ʳ-321ᵛ

To the abbot of the monastery of B. Mary, Suir (*de Surio*) and the prior of the monastery, usually governed by a prior, of B. Mary, Cakyrdunese,[1] d. Lismore, and Geoffrey Kyetyn' (who is staying in the said diocese), canon of the church of Cashel, mandate in favour of James Tobyn, priest, d. [Lismore].[2] The pope has learned that the perpetual vicarages of the parish churches of Kylloluayn [also spelt *Kylloluyn*] and Karonan, d. Lismore, have been vacant *certo modo* and are vacant at present, although James Butyler has detained the vicarage of Kylloluayn and Walter *etiam* Mutiler[3] that of Karonan – bearing themselves as clerics – with no title and no support of law, of their own temerity and *de facto*, for a certain time, as they still do. At a recent petition on the part of James Tobyn (who asserts that the annual value of the vicarages does not exceed 9 marks sterling) to the pope to erect and institute a canonry in the church of Lismore and the vicarages into a simple prebend of it, for his lifetime, the pope hereby commands that the above three (or two or one of them), if, having summoned James Butyler and Walter and as regards the erection the bishop and chapter of Lismore and others concerned, they find the vicarages to be vacant (howsoever etc.), shall erect and institute a canonry in the church of Lismore and the above vicarages (even if they have been vacant for so long that by the Lateran statutes their collation has lawfully devolved on the apostolic see, etc.) into a simple prebend of it, for the lifetime of James Tobyn, without prejudice to anyone; and in that event collate and assign the newly erected canonry and prebend, then being vacant, to James Tobyn, with plenitude of canon law and all rights and appurtenances, inducting him etc. having removed James Butyler and Walter and any other unlawful detainers, and causing James Tobyn to be received as a canon of the church of Lismore, and shall assign him a stall in the choir and a place in the chapter of the church of Lismore, with plenitude of canon law, and [causing] the fruits etc., rights and obventions of the canonry and prebend to be delivered to him. Curbing gainsayers etc. Notwithstanding etc. The pope's will is, however, that the above vicarages shall not, on this account, be defrauded of due services and the cure of souls in them shall not be negected; but that their customary burdens shall be supported; and that on James Tobyn's death or his resignation etc. of the canonry and prebend, this erection and institution shall be extinguished and so deemed and the vicarages shall revert to their original condition automatically.

Ex iniuncto nobis desuper apostolice servitutis officio ad ea libenter intendimus …
Phi: de Angnellis / JoA: / JoA: xv: Quarto k(a)l(endas) Augusti Anno Quarto: [29 July 1516], *Nardinus*

1   the final letter uncertain; perhaps: 'r'
2   *dicte diocesis* – evidently referring to Lismore
3   *cf. Butyler*

668   1 July 1516   *Reg. Lat.* 1351, fos 321ᵛ-325ᵛ

To the abbot of the monastery of B. Mary, *de Arvicampo* [Kilcooly], d. Cashel, and Eugene Machani and Thady Octoni, canons of the church of Raphoe, mandate in favour of Philip Yketllalaen,[1] priest, d. Derry.[2] The pope has learned that the rectory and vicarage of the parish church of Lephadrac, d. Derry [also spelt *Dyren.*, *Diren.*], are vacant *certo modo* at present and have been vacant for so long that by the Lateran statutes their collation has lawfully devolved on the apostolic see, although Donat Okerwalaen [also spelt *Ykawulen*, *Oketwalaen*,[3] *Okeruualaen*], who bears himself as a priest, has detained the rectory, and Donat Okawul [also spelt *Ykawul*], who bears himself as a cleric, has detained the vicarage, with no title and no support of law, of their own temerity and *de facto*, for a certain time, as they still do. At a recent petition on the part of Philip (who asserts that some time ago, notwithstanding a defect of birth as the son of a cleric and an unmarried woman, he was dispensed first by ordinary authority to be marked with clerical character, and then by apostolic authority to be promoted to all, even sacred and priest's, orders, and to hold a benefice, even if it should have cure of souls; and that by virtue of the dispensation in question he was duly promoted to the said orders; and that the annual value of the rectory and vicarage does not exceed 5 marks sterling), to the pope to erect and institute a canonry in the church of Derry and the rectory and vicarage into a simple prebend of it, for his lifetime, the pope – not having certain knowledge of the foregoing – hereby commands that the above three (or two or one of them), if, having summoned Donat Okerwalaen and Donat Okawul and, as regards the erection, the bishop and chapter of Derry and others concerned, they find the rectory and vicarage to be vacant (howsoever etc.), shall erect and institute a canonry in the church of Derry and the rectory and vicarage (even if specially reserved etc.) into a simple prebend of it, for Philip's lifetime, without prejudice to anyone; and, in that event, collate and assign the newly erected canonry and prebend, being then vacant, to Philip, with plenitude of canon law and all rights and appurtenances, inducting him etc. having removed Donat Okerwalaen and Donat Okawul and any other unlawful detainers, and causing Philip (or his proctor) to be received as a canon of the church of Derry, and shall assign him a stall in the choir and a place in the chapter of the church of Derry, with plenitude of canon law, and [causing] the fruits etc., rights and obventions of the canonry and prebend to be delivered to him. Curbing gainsayers etc. Notwithstanding etc. Also the pope dispenses Philip to receive and retain the above canonry and prebend, if conferred on him by virtue of the presents, notwithstanding the above defect [of birth] etc. The pope's will is, however, that the rectory and vicarage shall not, on account of this erection and institution, be defrauded of due services and the cure of souls in them shall not be neglected, but that their customary burdens shall be supported; and that on Philip's death or his resignation etc. of the canonry and prebend this erection and institution shall be extinguished and be so deemed and the rectory and vicarage shall revert to their original condition automatically.

Apostolice sedis circumspecta benignitas ad ea libenter intendit …
Phi de Angnellis / JoA: / JoA: xx: Duodecimo k(a)l(endas) Augusti Anno Quarto: [21 July 1516]*, Nardi(nus): –*

1   or *Or-*
2   MS: *dicte diocesis* – evidently referring to Derry
3   the first part (*Oketw-*) obscure

669   16 November 1516   *Reg. Lat.* 1352, fo 33ʳ⁻ᵛ

To Richard Sansan,[1] LLD, cleric, d. Norwich. Dispensation and indult – at his supplication – to receive and retain together for life any three benefices, with cure or otherwise mutually incompatible, even if dignities, *personatus*, administrations or offices in cathedral, even metropolitan, or collegiate churches, even if the dignities in question should be major *post pontificalem* in cathedral, even metropolitan, churches or principal in collegiate churches, or chantries, free chapels, hospitals or annual services usually assigned to secular benefices in title of a perpetual ecclesiastical benefice, or two of them be parish churches or their perpetual vicarages, or a combination, and even if the dignities etc. should be customarily elective and have cure of souls, if he obtains them otherwise canonically, to resign them, at once or successively, simply or for exchange, as often as he pleases, and in their place [receive up to]² three [other, similar or dissimilar]², incompatible benefices – provided that of three such benefices not more than two be parish churches or their perpetual vicarages – and retain them together for life, as above; and, for life, while attending a *studium generale* or residing in the Roman curia or any one of his benefices, not to be bound to reside in his other benefices, nor to be liable to be compelled to do so by anyone against his will. Notwithstanding etc. With the proviso that the incompatible and other benefices in question shall not, on this account, be defrauded of due services and the cure of souls in them shall not be neglected; but that customary burdens of those benefices in which he shall not reside shall be supported. Given at Magliana, d. Porto.

Litterarum scientia, vite ac morum honestas …
.P. Lambertus / JoA: / JoA: C: Nardinus

1   possibly *-son*
2   MS: *loco dimissi et cetera ecclesiastica tria.* Supplied from common form.

670   16 November 1516   *Reg. Lat.* 1352, fos 42ʳ-43ʳ

Union etc. At a recent petition on the part of Thomas Wyse, LLB, canon of the church of St C[a]rantocus, d. Exeter, the pope hereby unites etc. the parish church of St Stephen, Exeter (whose annual value does not exceed 8 pounds sterling) and the perpetual vicarage of the parish church of St Gorran in Cornwall (*Sancti Gorran' in Cornub'*), d. Exeter (whose annual value does not exceed 13 pounds 6 shillings and 8 pence), with all their rights and appurtenances, to the canonry and prebend of ?Ancarum¹ of the above church of St C[a]rantocus (to which canonry and prebend the parish church of St Euninus, d. Exeter is united etc. by apostolic authority, for as long as Thomas holds the canonry and prebend) which Thomas holds together with the above church of St Stephen and the above vicarage by apostolic dispensation, likewise for as long as Thomas holds the said canonry and prebend, to the effect that he may, on his own authority, in person or by proxy, continue in, or take anew, and retain corporal possession of the church of St Stephen, of the vicarage and of the rights and appurtenances aforesaid, and convert their fruits etc. to his own uses and those of the canonry and prebend, of St Stephen's and of the vicarage, without licence of the local diocesan or of anyone else. And the pope indulges Thomas, for life, while residing in the Roman curia or any one of his benefices, or attending a *studium generale*, not to be bound to reside in his other benefices, nor to be liable to be compelled to do so by anyone against his will. Notwithstanding etc. The pope's will is, however, that St Stephen's and the vicarage and other benefices in which he shall not reside shall not be defrauded of due services and the cure of souls in St Stephen's and the vicarage and (if any) the other benefices shall not be neglected; but that customary burdens shall be supported; and that on Thomas's death or his resignation etc. of the canonry and prebend this union etc. shall be dissolved and be so deemed and St Stephen's and the vicarage shall revert to their original condition automatically. Given at Magliana, d. Porto.

Ad futuram rei memoriam. Romanum decet pontificem et cetera provideri.
.P. Lambertus. / JoA: / JoA. L: Nardinus

1   very doubtful reading

671   16 November 1516   *Reg. Lat.* 1352, fos 43ᵛ-44ᵛ

To Peter Carslegh, MTheol, canon of Exeter. Dispensation; with indult for non-residence and relaxation of oath to reside. Some time ago, Innocent VIII by his letters dispensed Peter to receive and retain together for life any two benefices, etc. [as above, no. 6, to '… retain them together for life'[1]], as is more fully contained in those letters.[2] The pope – at his supplication – hereby dispenses Peter, who, as he asserts, holds canonries and prebends[3] of the churches of Exeter and Wells and, by the said dispensation, the portion of Pytte in the parish church of Tiverton', usually ruled by two or more rectors[4], and also the perpetual vicarage of the parish church of Myhynet, d. Exeter, to receive and retain for life, together with the said portion [and] vicarage, or any two other incompatible benefices held by him at the time by virtue of the said dispensation, any third benefice etc. [as above, no. 6, to '… retain it for life, as above']; and indulges him, while attending a *studium generale* or residing in the Roman curia or any one of his benefices, not to be bound to reside in his other benefices, nor to be liable to be compelled to do so by anyone against his will. Notwithstanding etc. With relaxation of the oath to reside in them taken by Peter on acquisition of the portion and vicarage aforesaid (and of other benefices held by him at the time). With the proviso that the third incompatible and other benefices in question shall not, on this account, be defrauded of due services and the cure of souls in them shall not be neglected; but that customary burdens of benefices in which he shall not reside shall be supported. Given at Magliana, d. Porto.

Litterarum scientia, vite ac morum honestas …
P. Lambertus / JoA: / JoA: Lxxxx: Nardi(nus): –

1   Save that 'or a combination' ('aut talia mixtim') does not occur in the present entry.
2   summarised among the Addenda to *CPL* XV printed in *CPL* XVI at p. cxxvi (where he is described as MA, but not MTheol)
3   number not specified (though likely to be just one canonry and prebend at each of the two churches)
4   *sic: portionem de Pytte in Tiverton' per duos vel plures rectores regi solite necnon… parrochialium ecclesiarum*

672   16 November 1516   *Reg. Lat.* 1352, fo 45ʳ-ᵛ

To Robert Molton',[1] abbot of the monastery, called house, of Torney [also spelt *Tornei*], OSB, d. Ely. Dispensation and indult – at his supplication – to receive and retain *in commendam* for life, together with the above monastery, over which he is understood to preside, or with any other of the said order which he might be appointed to and preside over, or with any office of the said order which he might hold, any two, and without them, any three other benefices, with or without cure, even if chantries, free chapels, hospitals or annual services, usually assigned to secular clerics in title of a perpetual ecclesiastical benefice, [even if] two of them be parish churches or their perpetual vicarages, and [even if] the said [three][2] benefices be of lay patronage and of whatsoever tax or annual value, if he obtains them otherwise canonically, to resign them, at once or successively,[3] as often as he pleases, and cede the commend, and in their place receive up to three benefices, with or without cure, usually assigned to secular clerics in title of a [perpetual][4] ecclesiastical benefice – provided that of three such benefices not more than two be parish churches or their perpetual vicarages – and retain them *in commendam* for life, as above; he may – due and customary burdens of the said benefices having been supported – make disposition of the rest of their fruits etc. just as those holding them *in titulum* could and ought to do, alienation [of precious movables and immovable valuables][5] being however forbidden; and, while attending a *studium generale*, or [residing][6] in the Roman curia or any one of his benefices, not to be bound to reside in his other benefices, nor to be liable to be compelled to do so by anyone against his will. Notwithstanding etc. With the proviso that the benefices in question shall not, on this account, be defrauded of due services and the cure of souls in them (if any) shall not be neglected, but that customary burdens of the said benefices retained *in commendam* and in which he shall not reside shall be supported. Given at Magliana, d. Porto.

Personam tuam et cetera oportuna.
.P. Lambertus. | JoA: | JoA: Cx: Nardinus

1   Surnames of abbots to whom the letters are addressed are not usually given in the registers, except (as here)
    in the case of abbots of lesser houses.
2   MS: *illa*; here taken to refer to *tria alia ... beneficia*
3   'simpliciter vel ex causa permutationis' does not occur
4   'perpetui' "omitted" at point of transition between lines: ... *in titulum* | *beneficii* ...
5   MS: *alienatione tamen et cetera eorundem beneficiorum*. Supplied from common form.
6   'residendo' wanting

673   2 December 1516   *Reg. Lat.* 1352, fos 45ᵛ-47ʳ

Union etc. At a recent petition on the part of Edward Molyneux, rector of the parish church of Seston' [also spelt *Sexton'*, *Seston*], d. Coventry and Lichfield, the pope hereby unites etc. the perpetual vicarage of the parish church of Layland,[1] said diocese (whose annual value does not exceed 8 pounds sterling), with all its rights and appurtenances, to the above church of Seston', which Edward holds together with the above vicarage by apostolic dispensation, for as long as he holds the church of Seston', to the effect that he may, on his own authority, in person or by proxy, continue in, or take anew, and retain corporal possession of the vicarage and the rights and appurtenances aforesaid, for as long as he holds the church of Seston', and convert its fruits etc. to his own uses and those of the church of Seston' and the vicarage, without licence of the local diocesan or of anyone else. Notwithstanding etc. The pope's will is, however, that the vicarage shall not, on account of this union etc., be defrauded of due services and the cure of souls in it shall not be neglected; but that customary burdens shall be supported; and that on Edward's death or his resignation etc. of the church of Seston' this union etc. shall be dissolved and be so deemed and the vicarage shall revert to its original condition automatically.

Ad futuram rei memoriam. Romanum decet pontificem et cetera provideri.
.P. Lambertus. / JoA / :JoA: xxxv: Nardinus

1   or possibly *Layland'*: the mark is equivocal

674   2 December 1516   *Reg. Lat.* 1352, fo 47^{r-v}

To Robert Lynton, rector of the parish church of Hennay Magna, d. London. Dispensation etc. [as above, no. 161].

Vite ac morum honestas …
.P. Lambertus / JoA. / JoA: L. Nardi(nus):

675   9 September 1516   *Reg. Lat.* 1352, fo 48^{r-v}

To Nicholas Everard, <BDec>,[1] rector of the parish church of Copford, d. <London>.[2] Dispensation and indult etc. [as above, no. 2].

Litterarum scientia, vite ac morum honestas …
.P. Lambertus. / JoA. / JoA: Lx: Nardinus

1   *bachalario in decretis* inserted in left margin (first hand i.e. enregistering scribe's hand); not initialled; arguably not a correction ordered by the regent of the chancery
2   (?)*Laudaven.* in line deleted and initialled *JoA.* (second hand); with *Londonien.* inserted in left margin (first hand); and above it (second hand): *JoA.*; and beneath it (second hand): *cassat(um) et correct(um) ut supra Nar.* Presumably, 'supra' is a mistake for 'infra', since a corresponding correction occurs below in the body of the letter, viz.: (?)*Landaven.* in line deleted and initialled *JoA* (second hand); with *Londonien.* inserted in left margin (first hand); above it (second hand): *JoA.*; beneath it (second hand): *cassat(um) et correct(um) de man(da)to D(omi)ni Regentis Nar* (second hand)

676   28 October 1516   *Reg. Lat.* 1352, fos 51^{v}-52^{r}

To William Danyell', <perpetual>[1] vicar of the parish church of Banuton', d. Exeter. Indult for life – at his supplication – to him (who, as he asserts, holds the parish churches of Kynsdon' [also spelt *Kynsdon*] and Hampriston' [also spelt *Hampriston*] and the perpetual vicarage of the above parish church of Banuton', d. Bath and Wells, d. Salisbury and d. Exeter, by apostolic dispensation) while attending a *studium generale* or residing in the Roman curia or one of the said churches or any other benefice of his, not to be bound to reside in his other benefices, nor to be liable to be compelled to do so by anyone against his will. Notwithstanding etc. With the proviso that the churches of Kynsdon' and Hampriston' and the vicarage and other benefices in question shall not, on this account, be defrauded of due services and the cure of souls in the above churches and vicarage and (if any) in the other benefices shall not be neglected; but that the cure shall be exercised and things divine served by good and sufficient vicars maintained from the proceeds of the churches of Kynsdon' and Hampriston' and the vicarage and other benefices in question; and that customary burdens of the other benefices aforesaid shall be supported.

Vite ac morum honestas ...
.P. Lambertus. / JoA. / JoA: xx: Nardinus

1   *perpetuo* inserted above the line, initialled *JoA*

677   16 November 1516   *Reg. Lat.* 1352, fo 64[r-v]

To Thomas Dyconson', rector of the parish [church][1] of St Peter in the Fields (*in Campis*), Bedford (*Bedfordia*), d. Lincoln. Dispensation and indult etc. [as above, no. 2]. Given at Magliana, d. Porto.

Vite ac morum honestas ...
.P. Lambertus / JoA: / JoA: Lx: Nardinus

1   'ecclesie' wanting in address clause; but *ecclesiam* occurs in body of letter

678   16 November 1516   *Reg. Lat.* 1352, fo 65[r-v]

To John Orchard, canon of the monastery, called house or priory, of Erdebury [also spelt *Eedeburi*], OSA, d. Coventry and Lichfield. Dispensation – at his supplication – to him, who, as he asserts, is expressly professed of the above order,[1] to receive and retain any benefice, with or without cure, usually held by secular clerics, etc. [as above, no. 43]. Given at Magliana, d. Porto.

Relligionis[2] *zelus, vite ac morum honestas* ...
.P. Lambertus. / JoA: / JoA: xxx: Nardinus

1   This information comes from a notwithstanding clause.
2   *sic*

679   16 November 1516   *Reg. Lat.* 1352, fos 65ᵛ-66ʳ

To John Granger, rector of the parish church of Bramshill', d. Coventry and Lichfield. Dispensation and indult etc. [as above, no. 2]. Given at Magliana, d. Porto.

Vite ac morum honestas ...
.P. Lambertus / JoA: / JoA: Lx: Nardinus

680   17 October 1516   *Reg. Lat.* 1352, fos 67ᵛ-68ʳ

To Edward Estgate *alias* Coper, monk of the monastery, called house, of St Swithin, OSB, Winchester, d. Winchester.[1] Dispensation – at his supplication – to him, who, as he asserts, is expressly professed of the above order,[2] to receive and retain any benefice, with or without cure, usually held by secular clerics, etc. [as above, no. 43]. Given at Magliana, d. Porto.

Relligionis[3] *zelus, vite ac morum honestas ...*
.P. lambertus / JoA: / JoA: xxx: Nardinus

1   MS: *Wintonien. Wintonien. diocesis*
2   This information comes from a notwithstanding clause.
3   *sic*

681   20 May 1516   *Reg. Lat.* 1352, fo 68ʳ⁻ᵛ

To Richard Whyte, canon of the monastery, called a house or priory, of Laysse Parva, OSA, d. < London >.[1] Dispensation – at his supplication – to him (who, as asserts, is expressly professed of the above order),[2] to receive and retain any benefice, with or without cure, usually held by secular clerics, etc. [as above, no. 43].

Relligionis[3] *zelus, vite ac morum honestas ...*
.P. Lambertus / JoA: / JoA: xxx: Nardi(nus): –

1   (?) *Landavien.* in line deleted and initialled *JoA*; *Londonien.* inserted in margin (second – i.e. not the enregistering scribe's – hand); above it *JoA* (second hand); below it: *cassat(um) et correctu(m) de man(da)to D(omi)ni Regent(is) Nard(inus)* (second hand).
       The name of the diocese was corrected again (below, in a notwithstanding clause) by order of the regent of the chancery, viz.: (?)*Lincolinen.* (*sic*) in line deleted and initialled *Jo* (*sic*); *Londonien.* inserted in margin (second hand); above it: *JoA* (second hand); below it: *cassat(um) et correctum ut supra Nard(inus)* (second hand).
2   This information comes from a notwithstanding clause.
3   *sic*

682   10 October 1516   *Reg. Lat.* 1352, fo 72[r-v]

To Augustine Horsey, cleric, d. Salisbury. Dispensation – at his supplication – to him, who, as he asserts, is in his eighteenth year of age, to receive and retain any benefice, with cure or otherwise incompatible, etc. [as above, no. 56, to '… in its place receive and retain another, similar or dissimilar, incompatible benefice']. Notwithstanding the said defect of age etc. With the proviso that the benefice in question shall not, on this account, be defrauded of due services and the cure of souls in it (if any) shall not be neglected. Given at Corneto.

Vite ac morum honestas …
.P. Lambertus. / M / M xx de Campania

683   31 October 1516   *Reg. Lat.* 1352, fo 104[r-v]

To the bishop of Coventry and Lichfield and the abbot of the monastery of Vallis Crucis (*de Walle Crucis*), d. St Asaph, mandate in favour of John Wcham' and Lewis Apres, perpetual vicars in the church of Bangor, Maurice Glyn[1], rector of the parish church of Nan Saturni and Hugh Aphoell', rector[2] of the parish church of Nan Negehyd, city or d. Bangor, joint parties in this regard. A recent petition to the pope on the joint parties' part stated that although the vicars John and Lewis, who, by reason of the perpetual vicarages which they hold in the church of Bangor, which is also a parish church, have the cure of souls of its parishioners, and the rectors Maurice and Hugh[3] have never committed anything on account of which they ought (or had ought) to be defamed, Richard, the present prior of the house of St Dominic, OP, said city, has nevertheless hitherto presumed and is presuming, to the peril of his soul and to the considerable prejudice and grievance of the joint parties, to wickedly accuse (*diffamare*) them, before honest and important people, of several crimes and delicts, and to denigrate them, and to usurp the canonical portion due to the joint parties, by reason of the said churches and vicarages respectively, of the bequests and testamentary trusts (*fidecommissorum*) left from time to time by the faithful, and other parish dues (*parrochialia*) of the said churches and vicarages, and to seriously injure and molest them in connection with the above, on account of which the joint parties assert that they have had expenses and incurred serious damage. At the joint parties' supplication to the pope to commit to some upright men in those parts all the causes which they intend to move in connection with the above against Richard and any others, jointly or singly, disputing their interest, the pope [hereby] commands that the above two (or one of them), having summoned Richard and others concerned and having heard both sides, shall, in matters not involving the penalty of death or mutilation, decree what is just, without appeal, causing [by ecclesiastical censure] what they have decreed to be [strictly] observed.[4] Notwithstanding etc.

Humilibus et cetera.
.Jo. Copis. / JoA: / JoA: x: Nardinus

1 written *Glijn*
2 MS: *necnon Mauritii Glijn de Nan Saturni et Ugonis Aphoell' de Nan Negehyd parrochialium ecclesiarum Bangoren. civitatis seu diocesis rectorum*
3 MS: *Mauritius Saturnus et Ugo rectores prefati*; text errs: *Saturnus* is not a rector but part of a place name; *see above*, note 2.
4 MS: *quod decreveritis et cetera observari.* Supplied from common form. The 'Testes' clause does not occur.

684   28 October 1516   *Reg. Lat.* 1352, fo 107ʳ⁻ᵛ

To Roger Dudden', perpetual vicar of the parish [church]¹ of St Peter, Coussold, d. Chichester. Dispensation and indult etc. [as above, no. 2].

Vite ac morum honestas …
.P. Lambertus / JoA: / JoA: Lx: Nardi(nus)

1 'ecclesie' wanting in address clause; but does occur in body of letter

685   28 October 1516   *Reg. Lat.* 1352, fo 108ʳ⁻ᵛ

To Miles Hagge, rector of the parish church of Bentworth' *alias* Byntworth', d. Winchester. Dispensation and indult etc. [as above, no. 2].

Vite ac morum honestas …
.P. Lambertus / JoA. / JoA: Lx: Nardinus

686   28 October 1516   *Reg. Lat.* 1352, fos 115ᵛ-116ʳ

To James Gorton', rector of the parish church of Tatam', d. York. Dispensation and indult etc. [as above, no. 2].

Vite ac morum honestas …
.P. Lambertus / JoA: / JoA: Lx: Nardinus

687   28 October 1516   *Reg. Lat.* 1352, fos 116ʳ-117ʳ

To John Powys, rector of the parish church of Parva Wenlock', d. Hereford. Dispensation etc. [as above, no. 161].

Vite ac morum honestas …
P lanbert(us) / JoA: / JoA: L: Nardinus

688[1]   **26 June 1516**   *Reg. Lat.* 1352, fos 134ᵛ-135ʳ

To John Ebuston, canon of the monastery, called priory, of Canons Hasshby, OSA, d. Lincoln. Dispensation – at his supplication – to him, who, as he asserts, is expressly professed of the above order,[2] to receive and retain any benefice, with or without cure, usually held by secular clerics, etc. [as above, no. 43].

Relligionis[3] *zelus, vite ac morum honestas ...*
P. Lambertus. / JoA: / JoA: xxx: Nardinus

1   Copy in WRO, Reg. Campeggio, fo. 80ʳ. The condition of the engrossment from which the copy was made, specifically the seal-cords, evidently raised doubts about its authenticity and prompted the following footnote in the episcopal register: *Bulla plumbea erat dependens litteris originalibus cum filis rubei et crocei colorum sed videbantur ac si fuissent abscissa* [or possibly *-ssi*] *et iterum connodati supra plumbum suspiciose. Sed dictus d. Jo. Ibutson'* [spelt *Ebutson'* in the bishop's copy of Leo's letter] *dixit quod mures corroserunt.* Perhaps it was just mice: trifles apart, papal and episcopal register-copies agree.
2   This information comes from a notwithstanding clause.
3   *sic*

689   **26 June 1516**   *Reg. Lat.* 1352, fo 135ʳ⁻ᵛ

To William Tailor, canon of the monastery, called house or priory, of St Gregory, outside the walls of Canterbury, OSA, d. Canterbury. Dispensation – at his supplication – to him, who, as he asserts, is expressly professed of the above order,[1] to receive and retain any benefice, with or without cure, usually held by secular clerics, etc. [as above, no. 43].

Relligionis[2] *zelus, vite ac morum honestas ...*
.P. Lambertus / JoA: / JoA: xxx: Nardinus

1   This information comes from a notwithstanding clause.
2   *sic*

690   **26 June 1516**   *Reg. Lat.* 1352, fos 135ᵛ-136ᵛ

To William Hulle, MA, rector of the parish church of Elmeleylovet,[1] d. Worcester. Dispensation and indult etc. [as above, no. 2].

Litterarum scientia, vite ac morum honestas ...
.P. Lambertus. / M / M Lx de Campania

1   the 'v' equally readable as 'n' or 'u' (in both occurrences of the name)

691   31 July 1516   *Reg. Lat.* 1352, fos 140ᵛ-141ʳ

To Thomas Yeysse, MA, rector of the parish church of Hemston' <Perna>,¹ d. Exeter.
Dispensation and indult etc. [as above, no. 2].

Litterarum scientia, vite ac morum honestas ...
.P. Lambertus / JoA. / JoA: Lx: Nardinus

1   *Perna* is inserted by the scribe in the margin initialled *JoA*; the scribe appears to have noticed his omission
     almost immediately – since just a few lines below the full name is written correctly in the line.

692   31 July 1516   *Reg. Lat.* 1352, fos 141ᵛ-142ʳ

To William Ffleshmonger,¹ DDec, rector of the parish church of Stedhm' and Heyshet,²
d. Chichester. Dispensation and indult etc. [as above, no. 2].

Litterarum scientia, vite ac morum honestas ...
.P. Lambertus / JoA. / JoA: Lx: Nardi(nus)

1   There is also an 'o' written above the 'm'.
2   final letter doubtful: 't' or 'r'

693   31 July 1516   *Reg. Lat.* 1352, fo 142ʳ⁻ᵛ

To John Halle, perpetual vicar of the parish church of Remyll', d. Salisbury.
Dispensation and indult etc. [as above, no. 2].

Vite ac morum honestas ...
P Lambertus / JoA: / JoA: Lx: Nardinus

694   31 July 1516   *Reg. Lat.* 1352, fo 143ʳ⁻ᵛ

To John Bovnde, rector of the parish church of Barton' Sigrane,¹ d. Lincoln.
Dispensation and indult etc. [as above, no. 2].

Vite ac morum honestas ...
.P. Lambertus / JoA: / :JoA: Lx: Nardi(nus)

1   *Barton'* occurs twice in MS, each time (as it happens) at the end of a line. Directly after the first (but not the
     second) occurrence, *Sigrane* is written in the margin in the hand of the enregistering scribe, perhaps later.

695   31 July 1516   *Reg. Lat.* 1352, fos 143ᵛ-144ᵛ

To Walter Kerchener, perpetual vicar of the parish church of Orston', d. York.
Dispensation and indult etc. [as above, no. 2].

Vite ac morum honestas ...
.P. Lambertus. / JoA: / :JoA: Lx: Nardinus

696   25 July 1516   *Reg. Lat.* 1352, fos 144ᵛ-145ᵛ

To abbot John and the convent of the monastery of Whalley (*de Whalleya, de Walleya*),
OCist, d. Coventry and Lichfield. Indult – at the supplication of [abbot John and the
convent][1] – to John and his successors, abbots of the said monastery for the time being,
to use embroidered mitre adorned with gems, dalmatic, episcopal gloves adorned with
gems, sandals, grey almuce, ring, pastoral staff and other episcopal *insignia*; and also
– in the said monastery as well as in any other monasteries, priories and churches
subject to the said monastery and dependencies of it, albeit not by full authority, in
which abbot John and his successors shall have some superiority and in which they
shall from time to time celebrate in pontificals – to bestow, after the solemnities of
mass, vespers, matins and other divine offices, the solemn benediction over the people
then and there present – provided that no bishop or legate of the apostolic see is present
or (if present) provided that he has expressly consented; and, within the precincts of
the said monastery of Whalley or of the other monasteries, to promote to the four minor
orders, all under one or all together or separately, as expedient, each and every monk,
servant and novice of the said monastery of Whalley and, with the consent and licence
of the local ordinaries, any others, and confer the said orders on them; to bless images,
crosses, and each and every ornament and item of ecclesiastical furnishing, even things
sacerdotal, and bells, and also any vestments, vessels and tabernacles – even ones in
which the sacrament of the Eucharist is kept and relics are secured – dedicated to
divine service, of altars, churches and any other ecclesiastical places; to reconcile the
church of the monastery of Whalley and any other churches subject to that monastery
and dependencies of it, or over which abbot John and his successors shall have
superiority, and their cemeteries and other ecclesiastical places polluted by effusion of
blood or semen or in any other way, the water[2] having, however, been blessed
beforehand by any catholic bishop, as is the custom; and also to demolish the walls of
the said churches and priories or other regular places (subject as above) to achieve their
repair or restoration, and then to repair and restore them; and also to cause the altars of
the said churches, priories[3] and places to be moved from one place to another for their
more convenient use, and to cause the altars thus moved, to be repaired, as necessity
requires. Notwithstanding the constitution "Abbates" of Alexander [IV],[4] etc. With
indulgence to abbot John and his successors and the faithful who are present at the
benedictions which are to be bestowed by abbot John and his successors, as above, that
they may obtain an indulgence of forty days.
    The pope's will is, however, that this shall not be prejudicial to the constitution

which lays down that such reconciliations are only [to be performed][5] by bishops.[6]

Exposcit vestre devotionis sinceritas et cetera attollamus.
.P. Lambertus / JoA: / :JoA: Cxx: Nardi(nus): –

1   MS: *Hinc est quod nos* ['vos' here wanting ?] *et vestrum singulos … vestris in hac parte supplicationibus inclinati …*
2   MS: *a q(u)a*; *rectius*: 'aqua'
3   or possibly altars of the churches of priories and such places
4   MS: *III*; *recte*: 'IIII'; *cf. Sext*, V.7.3 (Friedberg, 1084).
5   'fieri' wanting
6   *Cf. Decretals*, III.40.9 (Friedberg, 635).

697 7 April 1516[1]   *Reg. Lat.* 1352, fos 155ʳ-156ʳ

To James Beale, perpetual chaplain, called cantor, at the altar of St Mary Magdalene in the parish church of <St Peter>,[2] Hereford. Dispensation – at his supplication – to receive and retain for life, together with the above chaplaincy (which is incompatible with another incompatible benefice), one, and without them, any two other benefices, etc. [as above, no. 2, to '… retain them together for life, as above']. And indult for life, while residing in the Roman curia or any one of his benefices or attending a *studium generale*, not to be bound to reside in his other benefices, nor to be liable to be compelled to do so by anyone against his will. Notwithstanding etc. With relaxation of the oath to reside at the chaplaincy taken by James on his acquisition of it. With the proviso that the chaplaincy and other (even incompatible) benefices shall not, on this account, be defrauded of due services and the cure of souls in them (if any) shall not be neglected; but that customary burdens of those benefices in which he shall not reside shall be supported.

Vite ac morum honestas …
.P. Lampertus / JoA: / JoA: Lx: Nardinus

1   Ordinarily the dating clause is written by the enregistering scribe in its entirety. Here the number of the pontifical year ([…*anno*] *quarto*) has evidently been entered later, in a different hand and ink. Not initialled.
2   *Sancti Petri* inserted in margin (in second – i.e. not enregistering scribe's – hand) initialled *JoA*

698   25 April 1516   *Reg. Lat.* 1352, fos 158ʳ-159ʳ

Union etc. At a recent petition on the part of John Brygges, UIB, rector of the parish church of Chylmerke [also spelt *Chylmerche*, *Chilmerke*], d. Salisbury, the pope hereby unites etc. the perpetual vicarage of the parish church of Tysbury, d. Salisbury (whose annual value does not exceed 6 pounds 13 shillings and 4 pence sterling), with all its rights and appurtenances, to the above church of Chylmerke, which John holds together with the vicarage of Tysbury by apostolic dispensation, for as long as he holds the church of Chylmerke, to the effect that he may, on his own authority, in person or by proxy, take anew, or continue in, and retain corporal possession of the vicarage and the rights and appurtenances aforesaid, for as long as he holds the church of Chylmerke, and convert its fruits etc. to his own uses and those of the church of Chylmerke and the vicarage of Tysbury, without licence of the local diocesan or of anyone else. Notwithstanding etc. The pope's will is, however, that the above vicarage shall not, on account of this union etc., be defrauded of due services and the cure of souls in it shall not be neglected; but that its customary burdens shall be supported; and that on John's death or his resignation etc. of the church of Chylmerke this union etc. shall be dissolved and be so deemed and the vicarage shall revert to its original condition automatically. Given at Palo, d. Porto.

Ad futuram rei memoriam. Romanum decet pontificem et cetera provideri.
P. Lambertus. / JoA: / JoA: xxxv: Nardinus

699   31 July 1516   *Reg. Lat.* 1352, fo 167ʳ⁻ᵛ

To Thomas Ambrose *alias* Williams, monk of the monastery, called house, of St Alban (*Sancti Albini*), OSB, d. Lincoln. Dispensation – at his supplication – to him, who, as he asserts, is expressly professed of the above order,[1] to receive and retain for life any benefice, with or without cure, usually held by secular clerics, etc. [as above, no. 43].

Relligionis² zelus, vite ac morum honestas ...
P. Lambertus / JoA: / JoA: xxx: Nardinus

1   This information comes from a notwithstanding clause.
2   *sic*

700   31 July 1516   *Reg. Lat.* 1352, fos 167ᵛ-168ᵛ

To John, abbot of the monastery of B. Mary, Swynneshede [also spelt *Suuynneshede*], OCist, d. Lincoln, dispensation. Wishing to enable John to keep up his position in accordance with abbatial dignity more fittingly, the pope – at his supplication – hereby dispenses him to receive and retain *in commendam* for life together with the above monastery, called house, over which he presides, or any other monastery over which he might preside in the future, one, and without them, any two other benefices, with or without cure, regular, of the aforesaid or any other order, even the Cluniac, or secular, even if the regular benefices should be priories, *prepositure, prepositatus*, dignities, *personatus*, administrations or offices and the secular be parish churches or their perpetual vicarages, or chantries, free chapels, hospitals or annual services, usually assigned to secular clerics in title of a perpetual ecclesiastical benefice, and [even if] the secular benefices as well as the regular benefices should be of abbot John's patronage by reason of his own person or of the said monastery, or of the patronage of any other persons, ecclesiastical or secular,[1] and of whatsoever tax or annual value, and [even if] the benefices pertain at the time in any way to his collation, provision, presentation or any other disposition, and even if the priories etc. should be customarily elective and have cure of souls, if he obtains them otherwise canonically; and to resign them, at once or successively, as often as he pleases, and cede the commend and in their place receive up to two other, similar or dissimilar, benefices, with or without cure, secular or regular of the aforesaid or any other order, even the Cluniac and – provided that the regular benefices be not conventual or claustral – retain them *in commendam* for life, as above; he may – due and customary burdens of the said benefices having been supported – make disposition of the rest of their fruits etc. just as those holding them *in titulum* at the time could and ought to do, alienation of immovable goods and precious movables being however forbidden. Notwithstanding etc. With the proviso that the above benefices shall not, on this account, be defrauded of due services and the cure of souls in them (if any) shall not be neglected, but that their aforesaid burdens shall be supported.

Personam tuam nobis et apostolice sedi devotam tuis exigentibus meritis paterna benivolentia prosequen(tes) ...
.P. Lambertus[2] / JoA: / :JoA: L: Nardi(nus):-

1   MS: *secularium. Cf.* above, nos. 555, 569 and below no. 719.
2   above it: (?)*P. Lambertus* heavily deleted (but not initialled)

701   9 September 1516   *Reg. Lat.* 1352, fo 170[r-v]

To Edmund Hord, DDec, cleric, d. Coventry and Lichfield. Dispensation and indult – at his supplication – to receive and retain for life, any two benefices, etc. [as above, no. 2, to '... Notwithstanding etc.']. With the proviso that the incompatible and other benefices shall not, on this account, be defrauded of due services and the cure of souls in them ([if] any) shall not be neglected; but that customary burdens of those benefices in which he shall not reside shall be supported.

Litterarum scientia, vite ac morum honestas ...
.P. Lambertus / JoA: / JoA: Lx: Nardinus

702   25 September 1516   *Reg. Lat.* 1352, fo 194[r-v]

To John Moreman', MA, perpetual vicar of the parish church of St John the Baptist, Midsom' Norton' *alias* Horton' Canonico [also spelt *Midson Norton' alias Horton Canonico*], d. Bath and Wells. Dispensation and indult etc. [as above, no. 2]. Given at Viterbo.[1]

Litterarum scientia, vite ac morum honestas …
.P. Lambertus / M / M Lx de Campania

1   *Ro* deleted – probably the start of 'Rome apud Sanctum Petrum' – occurs directly before *Viterbii*

703   25 September 1516   *Reg. Lat.* 1352, fo 195[r-v]

To Percival Pety, BDec, rector of the parish church of St John, Stanuton' [also spelt *Stameton*'], d. Lincoln. Dispensation and indult etc. [as above, no. 2]. Given at Viterbo.

Litterarum scientia, vite ac morum honestas …
.P. Lambertus. / M / M Lx de Campania

704   26 December 1516   *Reg. Lat.* 1352, fos 206[r]-207[r]

To Robert Stinchecome, BDec, rector of the parish church of All Saints, vill of Gloucester (*Gloucestrie*), d. Worcester. Dispensation and indult etc. [as above, no. 2].[1]

Litterarum scientia, vite ac morum honestas …
.P. Lambertus / JoA: / JoA: Lx: Nardinus

1   Save that the present entry wants 'vicarie' after *perpetue* in the list of types of benefices.

705   26 December 1516   *Reg. Lat.* 1352, fos 207[r]-208[r]

To Thomas Huls, rector of the parish church of Tacley, d. Lincoln. Dispensation and indult etc. [as above, no. 2].

Vite ac morum honestas …
.P. Lambertus / JoA: / JoA: Lx: Nardinus

706   26 December 1516   *Reg. Lat.* 1352, fos 208[r]-209[r]

To Christopher Channey, perpetual vicar of the parish [church][1] of Sabrichesworth' [also spelt *Sabrechesworth*'], d. London. Dispensation and indult etc. [as above, no. 2].

Vite ac morum honestas …
.P. Lambertus. / JoA: / JoA: Lx: Nardinus

1   'ecclesie' wanting in address clause; but does occur in body of letter.

707   26 December 1516   *Reg. Lat.* 1352, fos 209[r-v]

To Ralph Hopwood, rector of the parish church of Thonersham,[1] d. Ely. Dispensation and indult – at his supplication – to receive and retain for life, together with the above parish church, one, and without them, any two other benefices, etc. [as above, no. 2, to '… if he obtains them otherwise canonically'];[2] and, for life, while attending a *studium generale* etc. [as above, no. 2].

Vite ac morum honestas …
.P. Lambertus / JoA: / JoA: Lx. Nardi(nus)

1   the 'n' readable as a 'v'
2   Standard clauses permitting exchange of benefices (*cf.* no. 2: 'to resign them … and retain them together for life, as above') do not (through inadvertence?) occur in the present entry.

708   26 December 1516   *Reg. Lat.* 1352, fos 210[r-v]

To John Ffawne, MTheol, perpetual vicar of the parish church of the Holy Cross, vill of Southt', d. Winchester. Dispensation and indult etc. [as above, no. 2].

Litterarum scientia, vite ac morum honestas …
.P. Lambertus. / JoA: / JoA: Lx Nardi(nus):

709   31 July 1516   *Reg. Lat.* 1352, fo 211[r-v]

To John Palmer, monk of the monastery, called house, of St Mary Graces by the tower (*Beate Marie de Gratiis iuxta Turrim*), city of London, OCist, d. London. Dispensation and indult – at his supplication – to receive and retain any benefice, with or without cure, usually held by secular clerics, etc. [as above, no. 643,[1] to '…and to have, for life, a stall in the choir and a place and an active and a passive voice in the chapter'] and a room in the dormitory of the said monastery like the other monks, and otherwise as before, without limitation, just as if he had not acquired the benefice. Notwithstanding etc.

Relligionis[2] *zelus, vite ac morum honestas …*
.P. Lambertus / JoA: / JoA: Lx: Nardinus

1   Save that the present entry wants 'recipere' before *et retinere.*
2   *sic*

710   26 December 1516   *Reg. Lat.* 1352, fos 220ᵛ-221ᵛ

Union etc. At a recent petition on the part of James Daddisley, rector of the parish
church of St Peter, Hamnes, d. Chichester, the pope hereby unites etc. the parish church
of St Andrew *in Foro*, Lewis, d. Chichester – which is of lay patronage and for which
when it was vacant *certo modo* James was presented by its patron or patrons (who were
in peaceful quasi-possession of the right of presenting a suitable person for St
Andrew's at a time of vacancy within the lawful time) – assuming James were to be
instituted at this presentation in the rectorship of the church of St Andrew, whose
annual value does not exceed 4 pounds and 10 shillings sterling in English money, with
all its rights and appurtenances, to the above church of St Peter, which James holds, for
as long as he holds St Peter's, to the effect that he may, on his own authority, in person
or by proxy, take and retain corporal possession of St Andrew's and the rights and
appurtenances aforesaid, for as long as he holds St Peter's, and convert its fruits etc. to
his own uses and those of St Peter's and St Andrew's, without licence of the local
diocesan or of anyone else. Notwithstanding etc. The pope's will is, however, that St
Andrew's shall not, on account of this union etc., be defrauded of due services and the
cure of souls in it shall not be neglected; but that its customary burdens shall be
supported; and that on James's death or his resignation etc. of St Peter's this union etc.
shall be dissolved and be so deemed and St Andrew's shall revert to its original
condition automatically.

Ad futuram rei memoriam. Romanum decet pontificem et cetera provideri.
.P. Lambertus. / JoA: / :JoA: xxxv: Nardi(nus):

711   26 December 1516   *Reg. Lat.* 1352, fos 222ʳ-223ʳ

Union etc.; with indult for non-residence and relaxation of oath to reside. At a recent
petition on the part of William Burghill', rector of the parish church of St Michael the
Archangel, vill of Gloucester (*Gloucestrie*), d. Worcester, the pope hereby unites etc.
the perpetual vicarage of the parish church of Broketrope, d. Worcester (whose annual
value does not exceed 4 pounds sterling), with all rights and appurtenances, to the
above church of St Michael, which William holds together with the vicarage of
Broketrope by apostolic dispensation, for as long as he holds St Michael's, to the effect
that he may, on his own authority, in person or by proxy, continue in, or take anew, and
retain corporal possession of the vicarage and the rights and appurtenances aforesaid,
for as long as he holds St Michael's, and convert its fruits etc. to his own uses and those
of St Michael's and the vicarage of Broketrope, without licence of the local diocesan
or of anyone else. And the pope indulges William, for life, while residing in the Roman
curia or any one of his benefices, or attending a *studium generale*, not to be bound to
reside in his other benefices, nor to be liable to be compelled to do so by anyone
against his will. Notwithstanding etc. and [notwithstanding] the oath to reside in the
said vicarage perhaps taken by William on acquisition of it, which the pope relaxes in
this regard. His will is, however, that the vicarage and other benefices in which

William shall not reside shall not, on this account, be defrauded of due services and the cure of souls in the vicarage and (if any) the other benefices shall not be neglected; but that their customary burdens shall be supported; and that on William's death or his resignation etc. of the church of St Michael this union etc. shall be dissolved and be so deemed and the vicarage shall revert to its original condition automatically.

Ad futuram[1] *rei memoriam. Romanum decet pontificem et cetera.*
.P. Lambertus / JoA: / :JoA. L: Nardi(nus): –

1   *P* (the start of 'Perpetuam'?) is deleted before *Futuram*.

712   27 September 1516[1]   *Reg. Lat.* 1353, fo 83[r-v]

To Richard Caly, MA, perpetual vicar of the parish church of Rodyngton [also spelt *Rodyngton*'], d. York. Dispensation and indult etc. [as above, no. 2]. Given at Viterbo.

Litterarum scientia, vite ac morum honestas ...
.P. Lambertus. / JoA. / JoA: Lx: Nardi(nus)

1   Date more heavily inked than preceding text: added later?

713[1]   **15 September 1516**   *Reg. Lat.* 1353, fo 84[r-v]

To John Coliman,[2] perpetual vicar of the parish church of Estredforde [also spelt *Esterforde*], d. York. Dispensation and indult – at his supplication – to receive and retain for life together with the perpetual vicarage of the above parish church, one, and without them, any two other benefices, with cure or otherwise mutually incompatible, even if parish churches or their perpetual vicarages, or chantries,[3] etc. [as above, no.2, to '...retain them together for life, as above']; and, for life, while attending a *studium generale* or residing in the Roman curia or any one of his benefices, not to be bound to reside in his other benefices, nor to be liable to be compelled to do so by anyone against his will. Notwithstanding etc. and also [notwithstanding] the foundations of the said chantries and any last wishes of the deceased and other dispositions made by them to the contrary,[4] and anything else to the contrary. With relaxation in this regard of the oath taken by John on acquisition of the vicarage and other benefices. With the proviso that the vicarage and other, even incompatible, benefices shall not, on this account, be defrauded of due services and the cure of souls in the vicarage and (if any) in the other, even incompatible, benefices shall not be neglected; but that customary burdens of those benefices in which he shall not reside shall be supported.

Vite ac morum honestas ...
[...][5] / [...][6] / [...][7]

1   This and the next entry (*q.v.*) have much in common. Both are written in the hand of the same scribe, who probably enregistered them at the same time. They bear the same date; and they contain the same elements of legal matter, viz.: dispensation *ad duo* and indult for non-residence (very common); relaxation of oath (fairly common); and a most unusual clause relating to the dispositions of the deceased. All this, together with the fact that they share a York provenance (albeit one is the diocese, the other the church) make it likely that both bits of quite separate business at the curia were conducted by one and the same proctor acting for each man. Furthermore, like the next entry, this entry has not been cancelled; yet it bears none of the usual marks of official authentication (*see* notes 5, 6 and 7 below); and there is no explanatory note. Both entries could well have been enregistered from the same unofficial draft (in a more or less accurate manner); and the absence of all official marks of authentication suggests that both letters may never have been expedited (at least by the chancery).

2   or *Coltinan*

3   'chantries' occurs here merely as part of this standard list of eligible benefices.

4   MS: ... *necnon* <u>*cantariarum huiusmodi*</u> *fundationibus ac quibusvis defunctorum ultimis voluntatibus et aliis etiam per eosdem defunctos in contrarium factis dispositionibus ceterisque contrariis nequaquam obstantibus* ... As no chantries have been mentioned by name, there is nothing other than the 'chantries' in the description of eligible benefices (note 3 above) to which *cantariarum huiusmodi* might refer – and such reference hardly seems plausible. Indeed, it would even be rash to assume that the inclusion in this entry of the quoted passage was carefully thought out by an abbreviator. It appears to make no sense in this particular letter; and yet – since it is rare – cannot have been included routinely. Assuredly, some special factor must have applied. And – taking into account the demonstrable links between this entry and the next – the most likely factor was, arguably, confusion at the point of enregistration over the details of the two letters requested. In other words, if, as is by no means unheard of, two broadly similar letters were enregistered from a single source (especially an unofficial draft in a somewhat sketchy state) containing details relating to both letters, a clause could creep into the enregistration of one letter on the basis of details applicable only to the other letter. The next entry concerns a named chantry; the present one does not. The fact that the enregistration of neither of our two letters got official authentication supports our contention.

5   no abbreviator's name

6   no magistral initial

7   no magistral subscription

714¹   15 September 1516   *Reg. Lat.* 1353, fo 85^(r-v)

To John Bentley, cantor at the altar of St Laurence in the church of York. Dispensation and indult – at his supplication – to him, who, as he asserts, holds a chantry at the above altar, which is incompatible with another incompatible benefice, to receive and retain for life together with the above chantry, one, and without them, any two other benefices, with cure or otherwise mutually incompatible, even if parish churches or their perpetual vicarages, or chantries,² etc. [as above, no.2, to '... retain them together for life, as above']; and, for life, while attending a *studium generale* or residing in the Roman curia or any one of his benefices, not to be bound to reside in his other benefices, nor to be liable to be compelled to do so by anyone against his will. Notwithstanding etc. and also [notwithstanding] the foundations of the said chantries and any last wishes of the deceased and other dispositions made by them to the contrary,³ and anything else to the contrary. With relaxation in this regard of the oath taken by John on acquisition of the chantry and other benefices. With the proviso that the chantry and other, even incompatible, benefices shall not, on this account, be defrauded of due services and the cure of souls in the vicarage and (if any) in other, even incompatible, benefices shall not be neglected; but that customary burdens of those benefices in which he shall not reside shall be supported.

Vite ac morum honestas ...
[...]⁴ / [...]⁵ / [...]⁶

1   Like the previous entry (*q.v.*) this entry has not been cancelled; yet it bears none of the usual marks of official authentication (*see* notes 4, 5 and 6 below); and there is no explanatory note. Furthermore, it contains a most unusual clause relating to the dispositions of the deceased (*see* note 3 below; *cf.* also above, no.713, especially note 4) whose presence cannot be entirely accounted for in terms of the content of the letter as enregistered. The obvious explanation is, of course, that unusual issues of concern to the petitioner existed in the foundation of the one chantry he already held (and possibly also – since the Latin is definitely in the plural – of some other chantry, or chantries, he might get). But if so the rest of the entry does not enlighten us. The close association of this entry with the previous entry —where the same unusual clause occurs despite its apparent irrelevance to that entry – ought to make us wary of placing undue reliance on the evidential value of either entry. Both entries could well have been enregistered from the same unofficial draft (in a more or less accurate manner); and the absence of all official marks of authentication suggests that both letters may never have been expedited (at least by the chancery).
2   'chantries' occurs here merely as part of this standard list of eligible benefices.
3   *necnon cantariarum huiusmodi fundationibus ac quibusvis defunctorum ultimis voluntatibus et aliis etiam per eosdem defunctos in contrarium factis dispositionibus*: most unusual (even in a letter to the holder of a chantry)
4   no abbreviator's name
5   no magistral initial
6   no magistral subscription

715   27 September 1516   *Reg. Lat.* 1353, fos 86ʳ-87ʳ

Union etc. At a recent petition[1] on the part of William Danson,[2] MA, rector of the parish church of Ffordhm', d. London, the pope hereby unites etc. the <parish>[3] church of Aldham and the church <without cure>[4] of Ffakenhm'[5] Parva, ds. London and Norwich (the annual value of Aldham not exceeding 26 shillings and 8 pence and of Ffakenhm' Parva 3 pounds 6 shillings and 8 pence sterling), with all their rights and appurtenances, to <the above church>[6] of Ffordhm', which William holds together with Aldham by apostolic dispensation[7] and Ffakenhm' Parva <aforesaid>[8], for as long as he holds Ffordham', to the effect that he may,[9] in person or by proxy, continue in, or take anew, and retain corporal possession of the churches of Aldham and Ffakenhm' Parva and of the rights and appurtenances aforesaid, for as long as he holds Ffordhm', and convert their fruits etc. to his own uses and those of the said churches without licence of the local diocesan or of anyone else. Notwithstanding etc. The pope's will is, however, that the churches of Aldham and Ffakenhm' Parva shall not, on account of this union etc., be defrauded of due services and the cure of souls in <the said church of Aldham>[10] shall not be neglected; but that their customary burdens shall be supported; and that on William's death or his resignation etc. of the church of Ffordhm' this union etc. shall be dissolved and be so deemed and the churches of Aldham and Ffakenhm' shall revert to their original condition automatically. Given at Viterbo.

Ad <futuram>[11] rei memoriam. Romanum decet pontificem et cetera provideri.
.P. Lambertus. / M / M xxxv de Campania

1   Opening narrative much corrected, viz.: ... *quod si <parrochialis> de Aldham et <sine cura> de*

Ffake<n>hm' Parva Londonien. predicte et Norwicen. dioc(esium) [*parrochiales* deleted, initialled *JoA*] *ecclesie <prefate ecclesie> de Ffordhm' quam et* [*predictas* deleted, initialled *JoA*] *de Aldham <ex dispensatione apostolica> ac de Ffakenhm' Parva ecclesias <predictas> dictus Willelmus* [*ex dispensatione apostolica* deleted, initialled *JoA* in two places] *inter alia obtinet* ... (angled brackets enclose insertions, square brackets deletions).

2   the third letter equally readable as 'u' or 'n'. R. Newcourt, *Repertorium ecclesiasticum parochiale Londinense*, vol. 2 (London, 1710) has both 'Dawson' (p.6) and 'Danson' (p.270).

3   *parrochialis* inserted in margin (hand of Nardini?): *JoA* above it; *cassat(um) et correctu(m) de man(da)to D. Rege(n)tis Nardi(nus)* beneath (*see above*, note 1)

4   *sine cura* inserted in margin (Nardini's hand?): *JoA* above it; *cassat(um) et correctu(m) ut sup(ra) Nar* beneath (*see above*, note 1)

5   In the first occurrence (*see above*, note 1) the 'n' is inserted above the line by the enregistering scribe. Mostly thereafter written *Ffakenhm'* but twice (?)*Ffakenhnm'* (last two letters uncertain: a row of five minims).

6   *prefate ecclesie* inserted in the margin (Nardini's hand?); beneath it: *correctu(m) ut sup(ra) Nardi(nus)* (*see above*, note 1)

7   *ex dispensatione apostolica* inserted here in the margin (Nardini's hand?); after it: *JoA correctu(m) ut sup(ra) Nardi(nus):-* There is a corresponding deletion below. (*See above*, note 1)

8   *predictas* inserted in the margin (Nardini's hand?); beneath it: *correctu(m) ut sup(ra) Nardi(nus)* (*see above*, note 1)

9   'propria auctoritate' does not occur (though common form)

10   *dicta ecclesia de Aldham* inserted in the margin (Nardini's hand?); not initialled and no explanatory note; in the line: *eis* deleted (not initialled)

11   *perpetuam* deleted; *futuram* (as appropriate for a temporary union) inserted above the line, initialled *M*

716   27 September 1516   *Reg. Lat.* 1353, fo 87[r-v]

To Robert Coket,[1] perpetual vicar of the parish church of <Iford>,[2] d. Chichester. Dispensation and indult etc. [as above, no. 2].[3] Given at Viterbo.

Vite ac morum honestas ...
.P. Lambertus. / M / M Lx de Campania

1   or perhaps *Coker*

2   (?)*Iner* deleted in line, initialled *JoA*; with *Iford* inserted in margin: *JoA* above it; *cassat(um) et correctu(m) de man(da)to D(omi)ni Rege(n)tis nardinus* beneath. The insertion and explanatory note is all in the hand of Nardini (a *magister registri*) and not in the enregistering scribe's.
     There is a corresponding correction in the narrative: (?)*Iner* deleted in line, initialled *JoA*; with *Iford* inserted in margin; *JoA* above the insertion; *correctu(m) ut sup(ra) nardi(nus)* beneath.

3   The entry is remarkable for the extension by a registry master of passages of standard formulary which the enregistering scribe had abbreviated with *et cetera*. Where the scribe had written *et loco dimissi et cetera ecclesiastica* M de Campania has deleted the *et cetera* and inserted in the margin: *vel dimissorum aliud vel alia simile vel dissimile aut similia vel dissimilia beneficium seu beneficia ecclesiasticum vel*. And again, where the scribe had written *Octonis et cetera legatorum* M de Campania has deleted the *et cetera* and inserted in the margin: [*et*] *Octoboni olim in Regno Anglie apostolice sedis*. Though visibly in M de Campania's hand the insertions are authenticated by Nardini. The former has *JoA* above it and *Aditu(m) nardinus* after it; the latter has *JoA* above it and *nardi(nus)* after it.

717   7 April 1516   *Reg. Lat.* 1353, fos 95ʳ-96ʳ

To William Dodwell', MA, rector of the parish church of Gayton', d. Lincoln, dispensation. The pope has learned that it is expressly stipulated in the foundation or statutes and ordinances of the college of B. Mary the Virgin, Northyenell', d. Lincoln, founded by the late John Trally, knight, in his lifetime, that none of the members (*collegiatorum*) of the said college may, under pain of deprivation of the advantages (*commodorum*) of the college, hold any parish church or other ecclesiastical benefice requiring personal residence and that no chaplain who has been received as master or a member of the said college and been accepted (*probatus*) in it for a year may afterwards desert the college on his own authority unless he truly wishes to escape to a better or perfect life[1] and has obtained from all the remaining members of the college, with their spontaneous and unanimous consent, without coercion, by their letters strengthened with their common seal, licence and faculty to leave. The pope – wishing to promote William, who, as he asserts, holds the above parish church and whom the present master and members of the college desire to elect as a member and to receive and admit to a place in the college – hereby dispenses William – at his supplication – to receive and retain for life together with the above parish church, a place in the said college, or another [incompatible benefice with cure], and without them, any two other benefices, with cure or otherwise mutually incompatible, etc. [as above, no. 2, to ' … retain them together for life, as above']; and also to be elected as a member of the college by the master and college-members aforesaid and to be received and admitted to a place in it; and also, after he has been elected, received and admitted as above, to be able to use, possess and enjoy each and every one of the privileges, graces, exemptions, liberties, grants, indults, prerogatives, rights and emoluments which other members of the college use, possess and enjoy in any way now and in the future. And the pope indulges William, for life, while attending a *studium generale* or residing in the Roman curia or any one of his benefices, not to be bound to reside in his other benefices nor to be liable to be compelled to do so by anyone against his will. Notwithstanding etc. and also [notwithstanding] the said foundation and the above-mentioned statutes and ordinances[2] all of which the pope (deeming them and their whole tenors to be expressed by the presents as if they were inserted verbatim), for this once only, specially and expressly derogates, etc. With the proviso that the above parish church of Gayton' and the other, even incompatible, benefices shall not, on this account, be defrauded of due services and the cure of souls in the church and (if any) the other, even incompatible, benefices shall not be neglected; but that customary burdens of those benefices in which he shall not reside shall be supported.

Litterarum scientia, vite ac morum honestas …
.P. Lambertus. / M / M lxx de Campania

1   *nisi ad melioris seu perfectionis vite frugem vere et non ficte convolare voluerit*; it probably means become a religious.
2   MS: … *ac supradictis … necnon ecclesiarum … statutis et consuetudinibus* …; but the expression above is *statutis et ordinationibus*

718   27 September 1516   *Reg. Lat.* 1353, fo 99[r-v]

To William Web, professor, OCarm. Dispensation and indult – at his supplication – to him, who, as he asserts, is expressly professed in a house of B. Mary[1], OCarm, d. London, to receive and retain any benefice, with or without cure, usually held by secular clerics, even if a parish church or its perpetual vicarage, or a chantry, free chapel, hospital or annual service, usually assigned to secular clerics in title of a perpetual ecclesiastical benefice, and of lay patronage and of whatsoever tax or annual value, if he obtains it otherwise canonically, to resign it, simply or for exchange, as often as he pleases, and in its place receive and retain another, similar or dissimilar, secular benefice, with or without cure, as above; and, for life, to be able to remain in the said house – even after he shall have acquired the benefice – if he wishes, and also to have a stall in the choir and a place and an active and a passive voice in the chapter of the said house and otherwise as before, without limitation, just as if he had not acquired the benefice. Notwithstanding etc. Given at Viterbo.

Relligionis[2] *zelus, vite ac morum honestas …*
.P. Lambertus / JoA: / JoA: L: Nardi(nus):

1   This reads as a dedication: *in domo beate Marie ordinis eiusdem beate Marie de Monte Carmelo*
2   *sic*

719   14 July 1516   *Reg. Lat.* 1353, fos 106[v]-107[r]

To William Rolfhe, abbot of the monastery, called house, of B. Mary the Virgin, Keynsham, OSA, d. Bath and Wells. Dispensation – at his supplication – to receive and retain *in commendam* for life together with the above monastery, over which he is understood to preside, or with any other monastery which he might be appointed to and preside over, two, and without them, any three other benefices, [secular], with or without cure, or regular, of the above or any other order, even the Cluniac or Cistercian, even if the secular benefices should be chantries, free chapels, hospitals or annual services usually assigned to secular clerics in title of a perpetual ecclesiastical benefice, or two of them be parish churches or their perpetual vicarages, and the regular benefices should be priories, *prepositure, prepositatus,* dignities (even conventual), *personatus,* administrations or offices, and the regular as well as the secular benefices should be of abbot William's patronage by reason of his own person or of the above monastery or of the patronage of any persons, ecclesiastical[1] or secular,[2] and of whatsoever tax or annual value, and should pertain to his collation, provision, presentation or any other disposition in any way at the time, and even if the priories etc. should be customarily elective and have cure of souls, if he obtains them otherwise canonically, to resign them, at once or successively, as often as he pleases, and cede the commend, and in their place receive up to three [other benefices],[3] with or without cure, secular or regular of the above or any other order, even the Cluniac or Cistercian – provided that the regular benefices in question be not claustral offices and that of three such secular benefices not more than two be parish churches or their perpetual vicarages – and retain them *in commendam* for life as above; he may – due and customary burdens of the benefices having been supported – make disposition of the rest of their fruits etc. just as those holding them *in titulum* could and ought to do, alienation [of immovable goods and movable valuables][3] being however forbidden. Notwithstanding etc. With the proviso that the benefices in question shall not, on this account, be defrauded of due services and the cure of souls in them (if any) shall not be neglected; but that their aforesaid customary burdens shall be supported.

Personam tuam nobis et apostolice sedi devotam tuis exigentibus meritis paterna benivolentia prosequentes illa tibi et cetera oportuna.
.P. Lambertus. / JoA: / JoA: C: Nardinus

1   The word is abridged in MS and could be read *ecclesiarum*; but the context requires 'ecclesiasticarum'.
2   MS: *secularium. Cf.* above, nos. 555, 569 and 700.
3   MS: *loco dimissi et cetera ecclesiastica tria duntaxat.* Supplied from common form.

720   31 July 1516   *Reg. Lat.* 1353, fos 110[r]-111[r]

Union etc. At a recent petition on the part of Geoffrey Wren', MA, rector, called master or warden, of the hospital of B. Mary Magdalene, Sharbourne, d. Durham, the pope hereby unites etc. the perpetual vicarage of the parish church of New Windsor (*de Windesora Nova*), d. Salisbury, for which, at another time, when it was vacant *certo modo*, Geoffrey was presented by the then abbot and the convent of the monastery of the Holy Cross,[1] Waltham, London[2] – since the presentation of a suitable person for the said vicarage at a time of vacancy belongs to the abbot for the time being and the convent of the said monastery by ancient [and approved custom hitherto peacefully observed][3] – to the local ordinary, within the due time, assuming Geoffrey were to be canonically instituted at this presentation as perpetual vicar of the said church (whose annual value does not exceed 20 pounds sterling), with all its rights and appurtenances, to the said hospital which Geoffrey holds, for as long as he holds the latter, to the effect that he may, on his own authority, in person or by proxy, take and retain corporal possession of the vicarage and of the rights and appurtenances aforesaid, for as long as he holds the hospital, and convert its fruits etc. to his own uses and those of the vicarage and hospital without licence of the local diocesan or of anyone else. Notwithstanding etc. The pope's will is, however, that the vicarage shall not, on account of this union etc., be defrauded of due services and the cure of souls in it shall not be neglected, and that on Geoffrey's death or his resignation etc. of the hospital the union etc. shall be dissolved and be so deemed and the vicarage shall revert to its original condition automatically.

Ad futuram rei memoriam. Romanum decet pontificem et cetera provideri.
.J. Benzon. / JoA: / :JoA: xxxv: Nardinus

1   order not stated

2   'diocesis' does not occur
3   MS: *de antiqua et cetera pertineat.* Supplied from common form.

721   6 February 1517   *Reg. Lat.* 1353, fo 124[r-v]

To Leonard Constable, cleric, d. York. Dispensation – at his supplication – to him
(who, as he asserts, is in his eleventh year of age and, notwithstanding a defect of birth
as the son of a married man of noble birth and an unmarried woman, has been duly
marked with clerical character) to receive henceforth the parish church of Morston
[also spelt *Marston*], d. York, or without it, any other benefice, with cure or otherwise
incompatible, even if a parish church or its perpetual vicarage, or a chantry, free
chapel, hospital or annual service, usually assigned to secular clerics in title of a
perpetual ecclesiastical benefice, or a dignity, *personatus*, administration or office in a
cathedral, even metropolitan, or collegiate church, even if the dignity should be major
post pontificalem in a cathedral, even metropolitan, church or principal in a collegiate
church, even if the dignity etc. should be customarily elective and have cure of souls,
if he obtains it otherwise canonically, and retain it *in commendam* until he reaches the
lawful age, and thereafter *in titulum*, to resign it, simply or for exchange, as often as he
pleases, and in its place receive another, similar or dissimilar, incompatible benefice,
and retain it henceforth *in commendam* until the lawful age, and thereafter *in titulum*,
as above; during the commend, he may – due and customary burdens of the above
church or other incompatible benefice having been supported, make disposition of the
rest of its fruits etc. just as those holding it *in titulum* could and ought to do, alienation
[of immovable goods and precious movables][1] of the church of Morston or other
<incompatible>[2] benefice being however forbidden. Notwithstanding the above defect
[of birth], etc. With the proviso that the church of Morston and other incompatible
benefice shall not, on this account, be defrauded of due services and the cure of souls
in the church of Morston and (if any) the other incompatible benefice shall not be
neglected; but that the aforesaid burdens shall be supported.

Laudabilia tue puerilis etatis indicia ...
.P. Lambertus / JoA: / JoA L: Nardi(nus)

1   MS: *alienatione tamen et cetera.* Supplied from common form.
2   *incompatibilis* inserted in margin (enregistering scribe's hand) initialled *JoA*

722   10 December 1516   *Reg. Lat.* 1353, fo 128[r-v]

To Richard Botler, perpetual vicar of the parish church of Arsefelde, d. Worcester.
Dispensation and indult etc. [as above, no. 2].

Vite ac morum honestas ...
.P. Lambertus / JoA: / JoA: Lx: Nardinus

723   5 December 1516   *Reg. Lat.* 1353, fo 138ᵛ

To John Champernen' *alias* Chamborn, rector of the parish church of Shepton, d. Bath and Wells. Indult for life – at his supplication – to him, who, as he asserts, holds the above parish church and the perpetual vicarage of the parish church of Kyngysterey, d. Bath and Wells, not to be bound, while attending a *studium generale* etc. [as above, no. 433].

Vite ac morum honestas …
.P. lambertus / JoA: / JoA: XX: Nardinus

724   7 January 1517   *Reg. Lat.* 1353, fo 162ʳ⁻ᵛ

To Robert Hewghson', BDec, perpetual vicar of the parish church of Clyston' [also spelt *Clyston*], d. York. Dispensation and indult etc. [as above, no. 2].

Litterarum scientia, vite ac morum honestas …
.P. (?)Lambirtus¹ / JoA: / JoA: Lx: Nardinus

1   altered; but not indisputably to 'Lambertus' as might be expected

725   23 January 1517   *Reg. Lat.* 1353, fo 163ʳ⁻ᵛ

To John Colchestrie *alias* Newlond, monk of the monastery, called house, of St Edmund, Bury, OSB, d. Norwich. Dispensation and indult – at his supplication – to receive and retain any benefice, with or without cure, usually held by secular clerics, etc. [as above, no. 19, to '… if he obtains it otherwise canonically']; and to wear the usual habit worn by monks of the above monastery, OSB, of whose number he is <and> is, as he asserts, expressly professed of this order, under a robe or garment of any honest and decent colour; and also to preach the Word of God wherever he pleases, licensed by local ordinaries or others to whom licensing belongs at the time; and not to be bound to wear the habit in another way; and also, for life, not to be bound, while attending a *studium generale* or residing in the Roman curia or any one of his benefices, to reside in his other benefices, nor to be liable to be compelled to do so by anyone against his will. Notwithstanding etc. With the proviso that the benefices in which he shall not reside shall not, on this account, be defrauded of due services and the cure of souls in them (if any) shall not be neglected; but that their customary burdens shall be supported.

Relligionis¹ zelus, vite ac morum honestas …
.P. Lambertus. / JoA: / JoA: L: Nardinus

1   *sic*

726   7 January 1517   *Reg. Lat.* 1353, fos 163ᵛ-164ʳ

To John Cleanger, perpetual vicar of the parish church of Dean Prioris, d. Exeter.
Dispensation and indult etc. [as above, no. 2].

Vite ac morum honestas ...
P lambertus / JoA: / JoA: Lx: Nardinus

727   16 January 1517   *Reg. Lat.* 1353, fos 164ᵛ-165ʳ

To John Chylderley, perpetual vicar of the parish church of Gyldesburgh, d. Lincoln.
Dispensation and indult etc. [as above, no. 2].

Vite ac morum honestas ...
.P. Lambertus / JoA: / JoA: Lx: Nardinus

728   16 January 1517   *Reg. Lat.* 1353, fos 165ʳ-166ʳ

To Henry Dochson', perpetual vicar of the parish church of Stanton' Harencourt, d.
Lincoln. Dispensation and indult etc. [as above, no. 2].

Vite ac morum honestas ...
.P. lambertus / JoA: / JoA: Lx: Nardinus

729   5 February 1517   *Reg. Lat.* 1353, fos 227ʳ-229ᵛ

To the prior of the monastery, usually governed by a prior, of B. Mary, Hacros, d.
Killala, and John Odonnayayn and Dermot Odonnagayn, canons of the church of
Killala, mandate in favour of Roger Odubhda, cleric, d. Killala. The pope has learned
that the perpetual vicarages of the parish churches of Scrincamhanam[1] [also spelt
*Scrnicemhanam, Serincaraharr[a]m, Serrucamhanam, Serineamhanam,
Serimcamhanam*], Castro Conchubayr [also spelt *Castro Co(n)chubayr*] and Ardnaria[2]
[also spelt *Andaria, Ardvaria, Ardaria*], d. Killala, are vacant *certo modo* at present and
have been vacant for so long that by the Lateran statutes their collation has lawfully
devolved on the apostolic see, although Donald Otenchubhand has detained the
vicarage of Scrincamhanam, Donat Macdomnayll [also spelt *Macdonnayll,
Macdonayll*] that of Castro Conchubayr and Donat Ocuyn that of Ardnaria – bearing
themselves as clerics – with no title or support of law, of their own temerity and *de
facto*, for a certain time, and so do. At a recent petition on the part of Roger (who
asserts that some time ago he was dispensed by apostolic authority – notwithstanding

a defect of birth as the son of the incestuous union of an unmarried man and an unmarried woman, and also [notwithstanding] a certain homicide accidently committed by him and the irregularity contracted thereby – to be promoted to all, even sacred and priest's, orders and to receive and retain any number of mutually compatible benefices, with and without cure, if he obtains them otherwise canonically; and also asserts that the annual value of the vicarage of Scrincamhanam does not exceed 8, and of Castro Conchubayr also 8, and of Ardnaria, 1½, marks sterling) to the pope to unite etc. the vicarages of Castro Conchubayr and Ardnaria to the vicarage of Scrincamhanam, for as long as Roger should hold the latter, [if] conferred on him as above, the pope hereby commands that the above three (or two or one of them), if, having summoned Donald and Donat Macdomnayll and Donat Ocuyn and others concerned, they find the said vicarages to be vacant (howsoever etc.), shall collate and assign the vicarage of Scrincamhanam to Roger, and unite etc. the vicarages of Castro Conchubayr and Ardnaria (even if specially reserved etc.) to that of Scrincamhanam, for as long as Roger should hold the latter, if conferred on him as above, with all rights and appurtenances, inducting him etc. into corporal possession of Scrincamhanam, Castro Conchubayr and Ardnaria and the rights and appurtenances aforesaid, having removed Donald and Donat Macdomnayll and Donat Ocuyn and any other unlawful detainers, and causing Roger (or his proctor) to be admitted to the vicarage of Scrincamhanam and the fruits etc., rights and obventions of these vicarages to be delivered to him. [Curbing] gainsayers etc. Notwithstanding etc. The pope's will is, however, that the vicarages of Castro Conchubayr and Ardnaria shall not, on account of this union etc., be defrauded of due services and the cure of souls in them shall not be neglected, but that their customary burdens shall be supported; and that on Roger's death or his resignation etc. of the vicarage of Scrincamhanam this union etc. shall be dissolved and be so deemed and the vicarages of Castro Conchubayr and Ardnaria shall revert to their original condition automatically.

Vite ac morum honestas …
P lambert(us) / JoA: / JoA: xxv: Quarto: K(a)l(endas) martij Anno Quarto: [26 February 1517]*, Nardinus*

1   first occurrence, the reading of which is very uncertain
2   or *Arduaria*

730   26 February 1517   *Reg. Lat.* 1353, fos 258^r-260^v

To the abbot of the monastery of B. Mary, *de Kyrieleyson* [Abbeydorney], and the prior of the monastery, usually governed by a prior, of St Michael, *de Rupe* [Ballinskelligs], d. Ardfert, and the archdeacon of Agnolo[1] in the church of Ardfert, mandate in favour of Thomas Hosse, priest, d. Ardfert. The pope has learned that the perpetual vicarage of the parish church of Kylmaylicedayr and the perpetual vicarage and rectory of the parish church of Balenacurthe [also spelt *Balenacurte*] *alias Ville pontis*, d. Ardfert, (which are of lay patronage)[2] are vacant *certo modo* at present and have been vacant for so long that by the Lateran statutes their collation has lawfully devolved on the

apostolic see, although Philip de Geraldinis has detained the vicarage of
Kylmaylicedayr and Corgarius[3] Omurthytir has detained the vicarage and rectory of
Balenacurthe, with no title and no support of law, of their own temerity and *de facto*,
for a certain time, and do so. At a recent petition on the part of Thomas (who asserts
that the annual value of the vicarage of Kylmaylicedayr does not exceed 8, and of the
vicarage of Balenacurthe 4, and of the rectory of Balenacurthe also 4, marks sterling)
to the pope to unite etc. the vicarage of Kylmaylicedayr and the rectory of
Balenacurthe to the vicarage of Balenacurthe, for as long as Thomas holds the latter, if
conferred on him by virtue of the presents, the pope hereby commands that the above
three (or two or one of them), if, having summoned Philip and Corgarius and others
concerned, they find the vicarages and rectory to be vacant (howsoever etc.), shall
collate and assign the vicarage of Balenacurthe to Thomas, and unite etc. the vicarage
of Kylmaylicedayr and the rectory of Balenacurthe (even if specially reserved etc.) to
the vicarage of Balenacurthe, for as long as Thomas detains [*sic*] the latter, if conferred
on him as above, with all their rights and appurtenances, inducting him etc. into
corporal possession of the vicarages of Balenacurthe *alias Ville pontis* and
Kylmaylicedayr and also of the rectory and of the rights and appurtenances aforesaid,
having removed Philip and Corgarius and any other unlawful detainers and causing
Thomas (or his proctor) to be admitted to the vicarage of Balenacurthe and the fruits
etc., rights and obventions of the vicarages and rectory to be delivered to him.
[Curbing] gainsayers etc. Notwithstanding etc. The pope's will is that the vicarage of
Kylmaylicedayr and the rectory of Balenacurthe shall not, on account of this union etc.,
be defrauded of due services and the cure of souls in them shall not be neglected; but
that their customary burdens shall be supported; and that on Thomas's death or his
resignation etc. of the vicarage of Balenacurthe this union etc. shall be dissolved and
be so deemed and the vicarage of Kylmaylicedayr and the rectory [of Balenacurthe]
shall revert to their original condition automatically.

Vite ac morum honestas ...
P Lambert(us) / JoA: / JoA: xxv: Nardinus

1   *sic*; a corruption of 'Agado'
2   referring (as is clear from the syntax) just to the perpetual vicarage and rectory of Balenacurthe
3   thus in the first instance; thereafter once spelt *Gergari-* and twice *Corgari-* (changed from *G-*)

731   20 February 1517   *Reg. Lat.* 1353, fos 260ᵛ-263ᵛ

To the prior of the monastery, usually governed by a prior, of B. Mary, *de Insula
Munribayd* [Inishmurray], d. Elphin, and Thomas Obeanhaeheayn,[1] and Roger
Ocunchubayr, canons of the church of Elphin, mandate in favour of Magonius
Yconcubayr, cleric of Elphin.[2] The pope has learned that the perpetual vicarage of the
parish church of Rillea[3] Spacgbroyn and the rectory of the parish church of Mubhusg[4]
alias inter Duos Pontes[5], d. Elphin, are vacant *certo modo* at present and have been
vacant for so long that by the Lateran statutes their collation has lawfully devolved on

the apostolic see, although Andrew Okarrayd has detained the vicarage and Dermot Oconchubayr[6] the rectory – bearing themselves as clerics – with no title and no support of law, of their own temerity and *de facto*, for a certain time, as they still do. At a recent petition on the part of Magonius (who asserts that at another time he, notwithstanding a defect of birth as the son of an unmarried man and an unmarried woman, was duly marked with clerical character; and also that the annual value of the vicarage does not exceed 4, and of the rectory, 24, marks sterling) to the pope to erect and institute the vicarage into a simple prebend of the church of Elphin for his lifetime, and to unite etc. the rectory to the prebend thus erected, the pope hereby commands that the above three (or two or one of them), if, having summoned Andrew and Dermot and, as regards the erection, the bishop and chapter of Elphin and others concerned and those interested in the union, they find the vicarage and rectory to be vacant (howsoever etc.) shall erect and institute the vicarage into a simple prebend of the church of Elphin, without prejudice to anyone, and unite etc. the rectory to the prebend thus erected (even if they are specially reserved etc.), for as long as Magonius should hold the prebend, if conferred on him by virtue of the presents; and in the event of this erection, institution, union etc. collate and assign the newly erected prebend, being vacant, and also a canonry of the said church of Elphin to Magonius, with plenitude of canon law and the annex in question and with all rights and appurtenances; inducting Magonius etc. into corporal possession of the canonry and prebend, annex and rights and appurtenances aforesaid, having removed Andrew and Dermot and any other unlawful detainers and causing Magonius (or his proctor) to be received as a canon of the church of Elphin, and assign him a stall in the choir and a place in the chapter of the church of Elphin, with plenitude of canon law, and [causing] the fruits etc., rights and obventions of the canonry and prebend and the annex to be delivered to him. [Curbing] gainsayers etc. Notwithstanding etc. Also the pope dispenses Magonius to receive and retain the canonry and prebend, if conferred on him by virtue of the presents, notwithstanding etc. The pope's will is, however, that the vicarage and rectory shall not, on this account, be defrauded of due services and the cure of souls in them shall not be neglected; but that their customary services shall be supported; and that on Magonius's death or his resignation etc. of the canonry and prebend this erection and institution shall be extinguished and union etc. be dissolved and so deemed and the vicarage and rectory shall revert to their original condition automatically.

Apostolice sedis circumspecta benignitas ad ea libenter intendit …
Phy Agnell(is) / JoA: / JoA: xxv: Nardinus

1   or *Obenuhachcayn*
2   'diocesis' does not occur
3   or just possibly *Killea*; *cf.* the spelling 'Chillea' in the corresponding entry edited in *Annates, Elphin*, no. 110.
4   uncertain; *cf.* the spelling 'Murbhrisc' in the corresponding entry edited in *Annates, Elphin*, no. 110.
5   The appellation 'inter duos pontes' is known to a Lateran Register of Martin V (*CPL*, VII, p. 545) and also to the annates records; *see Annates, Elphin*, nos. 27, 32 and 44; *cf.* also no. 20.
6   directly before this spelling, (?)*0conba* has been deleted and initialled *JoA*

732   1 February 1517   *Reg. Lat.* 1353, fos 284ᵛ-286ʳ

Union etc. At a recent petition on the part of George Hermege,[1] BDec, rector of the parish church of Bonynguuorth' [also spelt *Benynguuorth', Benynguurth',*[2] *Benynguurth, Benynguuurgh,*[3] *Benynguurch*], d. Lincoln, the pope hereby unites etc. the parish church of Flixburgh [also spelt *Filixburgh, Flixbuurgh*], said d. Lincoln, (whose annual value does not exceed 9 pounds sterling), with all its rights and appurtenances, to the above church of Bonynguuorth', which George holds together with that of Flixburgh, by apostolic dispensation, for as long as he holds Bonynguuorth', to the effect that he may, on his own authority, in person or by proxy, continue in, or take anew, and retain corporal possession of Flixburgh and of the rights and appurtenances aforesaid, for as long as he holds Bonynguuorth', and convert its fruits etc. to his own uses and those of the said churches without licence of the local diocesan or of anyone else. Notwithstanding etc. The pope's will is, however, that the church of Flixburgh shall not, on account of this union etc., be defrauded of due services and the cure of souls in it [(if any)] shall not be neglected, but that its customary burdens shall be supported, and that on George's death or his resignation etc. of the church of Bonynguuorth' this union etc. shall be (?)utterly[4] dissolved and so deemed and the church of Flixburgh shall revert to its original condition and be deemed vacant automatically.

Ad futuram rei memoriam. Romanum decet pontificem votis illis gratum prestare assensum ...
.p. lanb(er)tus / M / M xxxv de Campania

1   the '-rm-' uncertain; possibly '–nn–'
2   the 'g' converted from 'h'?
3   the '-gh' very uncertain
4   (?)*penitus*

733   9 June 1516   *Reg. Lat.* 1353, fos 332ᵛ-333ᵛ

To Simon Rumsey, monk of the monastery, called <house>,[1] of Malmesbure, OSB, d. Salisbury. Dispensation and indult – at his supplication – to receive and retain any benefice, with or without cure, usually held by secular clerics, etc. [as above, no. 19, to ' ...and, to have, for life a stall in the choir and also an active and a passive voice in the chapter'] and a room in the dormitory of the said monastery like the other monks and otherwise as before, without limitation, just as if he had not acquired the benefice. Notwithstanding etc.

Religionis zelus, vite ac morum honestas ...
.P. lanbertus / JoA: / JoA: Lx: Nardinus

1   *domus* inserted in margin initialled by (and in the hand of?) *JoA*

734   3 November 1516   *Reg. Lat.* 1353, fos 334ʳ-335ʳ

To Thomas Ffrankeleyn', cleric, d. Lincoln. Dispensation – at his supplication – to him (who, as he asserts, is in his fifteenth year of age and is of noble birth) to receive the parish church of Botell', d. Durham, and without it, any [other] benefice, with cure or otherwise incompatible, even if a parish church or its perpetual vicarage, or a chantry, free chapel, hospital or annual service usually assigned to secular clerics in title of a perpetual ecclesiastical benefice, or a dignity, *personatus*, administration or office in a cathedral, even metropolitan, or collegiate church, even if the dignity should be major *post pontificalem* in a cathedral, even metropolitan, church or principal in a collegiate church, and even if the dignity etc. should be customarily elective and have cure of souls, if he obtains it otherwise canonically, and retain it *in commendam* up to the lawful age and thereafter *in titulum*; to resign it when he pleases and cede the commend and in its place receive another, similar or dissimilar, benefice, with cure or otherwise incompatible, and retain it *in commendam* up to the lawful age and thereafter *in titulum*, as above; he may – due and customary burdens of the church of Botell' or the other incompatible benefice, during the commend, having been supported – make disposition of the rest of its fruits etc. just as those holding it *in titulum* could and ought to do, alienation of immovable goods and precious movables of the church of Botell' or the other incompatible benefice being however forbidden. Notwithstanding etc. With the proviso that the church of Botell' or the other incompatible benefice, during the said commend, shall not, on this account, be defrauded of due services and the cure of souls in the church of Botell' or (if any) the other incompatible benefices shall not be neglected, but that, during the commend, the aforesaid burdens shall be supported.

Nobilitas generis, vite ac morum honestas ...
P lanb(er)tus / JoA: / :JoA: xxxx:- Nardinus

735   26 May 1516   *Reg. Lat.* 1353, fos 410ʳ-415ᵛ

Mandate to commend (up to his eighteenth year) and then (when he has taken the habit and made his profession) collate and assign to Cesar Franciottus – cleric of Rome, in his seventh year or thereabouts, illegitimate son of Andrew de Franciottis, and a continual commensal familiar of Sixtus, cardinal priest of the title of St Peter *ad Vincula*, vicechancellor of the holy Roman church – the preceptory of St John *de Templo*, Lucca, OHosp, whose annual value does not exceed 140 gold ducats of the camera, which had been commended to the said Sixtus on the resignation into the pope's hands of the said Andrew, its preceptor, and which, with the ending of the commend by the cession this day of Sixtus, is vacant at the apostolic see still in the way in which it was vacant before it was commended and is reserved to the pope's disposition. With dispensation to receive and retain the preceptory.

    The 'bishop of Worcester' is one of the three mandataries. Entry otherwise of no interest to the Calendar.

Apostolice sedis circumspecta benignitas cupientibus vitam ducere regularem ...
P. de Castello / JoA. /: JoA: Grat(is) p(ro) fam(iliari) Vicecancell(arii) Nardinus

736   9 September 1516   *Reg. Lat.* 1355, fos 119ᵛ-120ᵛ

Union etc. At a recent petition on the part of Hugh Sannders, MTheol, canon of
London, the pope hereby unites etc. the parish [church],[1] called the white chapel, of B.
Mary, Marselon (*capella alba nuncupata Beate Marie de Marselon*), d. London
(whose annual value does not exceed 19 pounds sterling), with all its rights and
appurtenances, to the canonry and prebend of Ealdstrete, church of London, which
Hugh holds together with the said parish church, for as long as he holds the canonry
and prebend, to the effect that he may,[2] in person or by proxy, continue in, or take anew,
and retain corporal possession of the parish church and of the rights and appurtenances
aforesaid, for as long as he holds the canonry and prebend, and convert its fruits etc. to
his own uses and those of the canonry and prebend and of the parish church, without
licence of the local diocesan or of anyone else. Also the pope indulges Hugh, for life,
not to be bound, while attending a *studium generale* or residing in the Roman curia or
any one of his benefices, to reside in his other benefices, nor to be liable to be
compelled by anyone to do so against his will. Notwithstanding etc. The pope's will is,
however, that the parish church and other benefices in question shall not, on this
account, be defrauded of due services and the cure of souls in the parish church and (if
any) the other benefices shall not be neglected, but that customary burdens of the
parish church and other benefices in which Hugh shall not reside shall be supported;
and that on Hugh's death or his resignation etc. of the canonry and prebend this union
etc. shall be dissolved and be so deemed and the parish church shall revert to its
original condition automatically.

Ad futuram rei memoriam. Romanum decet pontificem et cetera provideri.
.P. Lambertus / JoA: / JoA: xxxx: Nardinus

1   'ecclesia' does not occur here (but does below wherever appropriate)
2   'propria auctoritate' does not occur (though common form)

737   10 December 1516   *Reg. Lat.* 1355, fos 193ʳ-195ᵛ

To Peter Burnell, DDec, perpetual vicar of the parish church of Hendon, d. London.
Dispensation and indult as below, to Peter who, some time ago, as he asserts, was
dispensed by apostolic authority to receive and retain for life any two benefices, etc.
[as above, no. 6, to '...and in their place receive up to two other, similar or dissimilar,
incompatible benefices and retain them together for life]; and holds the perpetual
vicarage of the above parish church of Hendon, d. London, and the parish church of
Aylton, d. Lincoln, by virtue of the said dispensation, and also a canonry and one of

the two prebends of the church of St Martin le Grand, London, which were founded by the late Herbert[1] while he was a canon of St Martin's. The pope hereby dispenses further and indulges Peter – at his supplication – to receive and retain for life, together with the above vicarage and the above church of Aylton, or with any two other incompatible benefices held by him at the time by virtue of the said dispensation, any third benefice, with cure or otherwise incompatible, even if a [parish church or its perpetual vicarage],[2] or a chantry, etc. [as above, no. 6, to '... and in its place receive another, similar or dissimilar, third incompatible benefice and – provided that of three such benefices not more than two be parish churches or their perpetual vicarages[3] – retain it for life, as above']; and, for life, while residing in the Roman curia or any one of his benefices or attending a *studium generale*, not to be bound to reside in his other benefices nor to be liable to be compelled by anyone to do so against his will. Notwithstanding etc. and [notwithstanding] the foundation of the said prebends in which it is said to be expressly stipulated that those holding them from time to time are bound to reside personally in the said church of St Martin, and cannot absent themselves from St Martin's except with the consent or licence of the dean (or [his] deputy) of St Martin's for the time being; and that they are bound to take a corporal oath to observe the above; even if Peter has hitherto taken an oath in any way, in person or by proxy, to observe the said foundation (which oath the pope hereby relaxes), and [notwithstanding] anything else to the contrary. And the pope, specially and expressly, hereby derogates the said foundation (which shall otherwise remain in force) even if, for its sufficient derogation, special, specific and individual mention [or] any other expression ought to be made of it and its whole tenor, verbatim, and not by general clauses importing the same, or a carefully devised form [ought to be observed]. With the proviso that the third incompatible and other benefices in which he shall not reside shall not, on this account, be defrauded of due services and the cure of souls in them ([if] any) shall not be neglected; but that customary burdens of the canonry and prebend and the other benefices in which he shall not reside shall be supported.

Litterarum scientia, vite ac morum honestas ...
P lambertus / M / M C de Campania

1   *sic*; i.e. no second name supplied
2   wanting at this point in MS – but, as usual, alluded to below; *see* note 3
3   a standard proviso of dispensations *ad tertium*

738   15 November 1516   *Reg. Lat.* 1355, fos 208^r-209v

To Geoffrey Wren', MA, rector, called master or warden of the hospital of B. Mary Magdalene, Shierburn, d. Durham, validation as below. Some time ago, representation was made to the pope on Geoffrey's part that if the perpetual vicarage of the parish church of Windsor (*Windesora*[1]), d. Salisbury, (for which Geoffrey had been presented when it was vacant *certo modo* by the then abbot and the convent of the monastery of the Holy Cross, Walthm', OSB,[2] d. London – to whom the presentation of a suitable person for the said vicarage at a time of vacancy belonged by ancient and approved custom hitherto peacefully observed – [and] assuming Geoffrey had been instituted at this presentation as perpetual vicar of the said church), were to be united etc. to the above hospital (usually assigned in title of a perpetual ecclesiastical benefice) which he was holding even then, for as long as he should hold the latter, it would be of advantage to him. And, at that time, the pope – at Geoffrey's supplication – united etc. the vicarage, assuming Geoffrey had been instituted at this presentation as vicar, with all its rights and appurtenances, to the said hospital, for as long as he should hold the latter, as is more fully contained in the pope's letters drawn up in that regard.[3] However, as a recent petition to the pope on Geoffrey's part stated, at the time of the said letters the vicarage had not yet been vacated or Geoffrey had [not yet] been presented for it; he was, however, expecting to be presented by the said abbot and convent as soon as it should next fall vacant by the free resignation of its then perpetual vicar; but shortly afterwards Geoffrey was presented for the vicarage – then vacant by the death outside the Roman curia of its last perpetual vicar – by the said abbot and convent, and at this presentation Geoffrey was instituted as vicar of the said church by ordinary authority, and, by virtue of this presentation and institution he took possession of the vicarage; and, on this account, Geoffrey fears that the said letters could be surreptitious and be less useful to him, and that he could be molested over them in time to come. Lest, on this account, the effect of the said letters be frustrated, the pope – at Geoffrey's supplication – hereby wills and grants that the letters, with each and every one of the clauses contained therein, and the union etc. of the said vicarage to the said hospital and whatsoever ensued therefrom shall, from the date of the presents, be valid and have full force and be of support to Geoffrey, without limitation, just as if at the time of the said letters the vicarage had been vacant by the said death, as above, and Geoffrey had been presented for it by the said abbot and convent. Notwithstanding etc. Given at Magliana, d. Porto.

Litterarum scientia, vite ac morum honestas …
.p. Lambertus. / JoA: / JoA: xvj: Nardinus:

1   'de' does not occur; neither does 'Nova'; *cf.* above, no. 720
2   *sic*
3   above, no. 720

739   13 February 1517   *Reg. Lat.* 1355, fos 306ʳ-307ʳ

To the archdeacon of the church of Clogher, mandate in favour of Magonius Magniathune,[1] canon of the monastery of Sts Peter and Paul the Apostles, Clinose,[2] OSA, d. Clogher. The pope has learned that the above monastery has been vacant *certo modo* and is vacant at present, and he wishes – lest it be exposed to the inconvenience of a long vacancy – to make provision of a capable and suitable person to rule and direct it. And Magonius asserts that some time ago he was dispensed by apostolic authority, notwithstanding a defect of birth as the son of a priest of noble birth and an unmarried woman in an incestuous union, to be promoted to all, even sacred and priest's, orders and to hold a benefice even if it should have cure of souls; that afterwards he was duly marked with clerical character; that he is expressly professed of the said order; and also that he was elected abbot of the monastery by the convent of the same at a time when the monastery was vacant as above, albeit *de facto*. The pope – not having certain knowledge [of the foregoing] – hereby commands the above archdeacon to inform himself as to the merits and suitability of Magonius and if the archdeacon finds him to be capable and suitable for the rule and administration of the monastery – concerning which the pope burdens the archdeacon's conscience – make provision of Magonius to the monastery (whose annual value does not exceed 24 marks sterling), vacant howsoever etc., and appoint him abbot, committing the care, rule and administration of the monastery to him in spiritualities and temporalities and causing due obedience and reverence to be given him by the convent and customary services and rights by the vassals and other subjects of the monastery. [Curbing] gainsayers etc. Notwithstanding etc. Also the pope dispenses Magonius to be appointed to and preside over the said monastery as abbot and perform and exercise its care, rule and administration in spiritualities and temporalities, notwithstanding the above defect etc.

Solicite considerationis indagine ...
phi de agnellis / JoA: / JoA: xxxx: Nardinus

1   not readily readable as 'Magma–': the third minim is dotted.
2   three minims (none dotted); variously readable

740   5 March 1517   *Reg. Lat.* 1355, fos 335^r-336^v

To George Naper, rector of the parish church of Haryngby, d. Norwich. Dispensation and indult etc. [as above, no. 2]. Given at Magliana, d. Porto.[1]

[Vite ac morum honestas ...][2]
.p. lanbertus / JoA. / JoA: Lx: Nardinus

1   *Rome* (written directly after *Datum*) has been deleted, initialled *JoA*
2   MS: *Salutem et cetera. Hinc est ...* i.e. 'et cetera' here comprehends not only the rest of the greeting (as usual); but also the proem (which – in the case of a letter such as this addressed to a secular cleric without a degree – is appropriately: 'Vite ac morum honestas...')

741   7 March 1517   *Reg. Lat.* 1355, fos 336^v-338^r

To John Bulgen', MA, perpetual vicar of the parish church of Coggelhall' [also spelt *Coggeshall'*], d. London. Dispensation and indult etc. [as above, no. 2]. Given at Magliana, d. Porto.

[Litterarum scientia, vite ac morum honestas ...][1]
.p. lanbertus / JoA. / JoA: Lx: Nardi(nus)

1   MS: *Salutem et cetera. Hinc est ...* (*Cf.* the previous entry, note 2). The incipit of the proem – in the case of
     a letter such as this addressed to a secular cleric who holds a degree – is appropriately: 'Litterarum scientia,
     vite ac morum honestas ...'

742   6 March 1517   *Reg. Lat.* 1355, fos 338[r]-339[v]

To Christopher Barns, MA, rector of the parish church of St Martin, Blandon [also
spelt *Blandon*'], d. Lincoln. Dispensation and indult etc. [as above, no. 2]. Given at
Magliana, d. Porto.

[Litterarum scientia, vite ac morum honestas ...][1]
.p. lanbertus / JoA. / JoA: Lx: Nardinus

1   enregistered by the same scribe as the previous entry, *q.v.*

743   13 February 1517   *Reg. Lat.* 1355, fos 339[v]-341[v]

To Lewis Eall, rector of the parish church of Chepparton', d. London. Some time ago,
as he asserts, Lewis (after he – having kept silent about a defect of birth as the son of
a priest and an unmarried woman[1] – had had himself promoted to all, even sacred and,
perhaps, priest's, orders, otherwise duly) had been dispensed to minister in the orders
he had taken, notwithstanding the defect and other things aforesaid,[2] by a certain
someone who was then the appointed collector of the fruits and proceeds due to the
apostolic camera in those parts and who asserted that he had sufficient faculty for this
by letters of the apostolic see; and Lewis – without having obtained any dispensation
in this regard – had had the above parish church, then vacant *certo modo*, canonically
conferred on him, albeit *de facto*, and – taking possession of it, without however
receiving any fruits from it – had been dispensed by apostolic authority to retain the
said church, and he holds it by the dispensation in question. Dispensation and indult
etc. [as above, no. 2].

Dudum ...[3]
.p. lambert(us) / JoA / :JoA. Lxx: Nardinus

1   *solita*; *recte*: 'soluta'
2   *defectu et alis* [*sic*; 'aliis' ?] *prem[i]ssis*; referring to his birth and, necessarily, his silence
3   MS: *Salutem et cetera. Dudum ...* Enregistered by the same scribe as no. 740, *q.v.*

744   6 March 1517   *Reg. Lat.* 1355, fos 341ᵛ-342ᵛ

To John Wylbore, MA, perpetual vicar of the parish church of Lambrest, d. Rochester.
Dispensation and indult etc. [as above, no. 2]. Given at Magliana, d. Porto.

[*Litterarum scientia, vite ac morum* ...]¹
.p. lanbertus / JoA. / JoA. Lx: Nardi(nus)

1   enregistered by the same scribe as no. 741, *q.v.*

745   30 April 1516   *Reg. Lat.* 1355, fos 349ʳ-351ʳ

To John Yong, canon of the church of London, John Taylor, canon of the church of
Lichfield (*Richfelden.*), and the official of London, mandate in favour of William
Crissi¹, <cleric>², <d.>³ Lincoln. A petition⁴ to the pope on William's part stated that
<although>⁵ he had never had carnal knowledge of Elisabeth, his household servant,
but rather, as far as human frailty allows, he had abstained from illicit acts of the flesh,
nevertheless, firstly, John Incent, LLD, bearing himself as official or commissary
general of the abbot and convent of the monastery of St Alban, OSB or another order,
said d., and then <Thomas>⁶ Marshal, monk of the said monastery, who bears himself
as commissary of the archdeacon of the monastery [and] of its archidiaconal
jurisdiction, alleging that by ancient, approved, and lawfully prescribed custom, the
correction and punishment of delinquent clerics <and priests>⁷ who were subject to the
said archdeacon (among whom, he said, William was numbered) appertained to the
said archdeacon, *ex officio*, as they said, warned and ordered William, who was not
then accused (*diffamatum*) of adultery committed with the said Elisabeth, to appear
personally before them, within a certain too short term then expressed, to reply to
certain articles and claims (*petitionibus*) or inquiries, framed or to be framed,⁸
concerning the crime of the said adultery; that then, after John had desisted from the
said inquiry and process and Thomas had adopted John as his assistant in the said
matter, and after William had put forward certain lawful objections of mistrust
(*suspitionum*) and protest (*recusationum*) against the person of the said John the
assistant which he had also offered lawfully to prove, Thomas – having recklessly
rejected the said objections and proceeding to further matters in the cause of the
inquiry – by his definitive sentence (as he said) he *inter cetera* enjoined (*indixit*)
canonical purgation on William, by reason of the foregoing, within a certain term then
expressed, with the oath (*manu*) of twelve men living in a certain street (vico) of St
Peter of the town of St Alban (*de Sancto Albano*), said d.; that although, afterwards,
within the said term, William, together with twelve honest, <upright>⁹, and wholly
unobjectionable men, William's neighbours, appeared before Thomas, and was
prepared to purge himself in accordance with the said injunction (*inditionem*) (but only
as to the number of compurgators), and the said compurgators were prepared for it, and
although William alleged in excuse (*allegaverit*) that he was unable <to offer>¹⁰ twelve
men from St Peter's street in accordance with the injunction made to him <because the

men who>[11] were living in the street did not dare to come and appear before Thomas
the commissary to perform the purgation from a just fear, which could overcome a
steadfast person, of William's[12] enemies, viz. of George Sripwiht and of the said John,
adopted as above, the assistants; nevertheless Thomas – unlawfully refusing to admit
the compurgation of William then offered – assigned a certain too short term to
William to prove the said fear, and, while the term was pending, he rejected[13] and
unlawfully refused to admit certain witnesses whom William had produced before
Thomas to prove the fear and the twelve upright, honest, and wholly unobjectionable
men, William's neighbours, whom William had produced for the said compurgation,
and, proceeding to further matters, he promulgated his unjust and null sentence[14] by
which he declared *inter alia* that William had failed in the purgation and that he was
convicted of the said adultery; that William, feeling himself thereby unduly aggrieved,
appealed from the sentence repeatedly to the apostolic see; and that Thomas,
regardless[15] of the appeals of which he was not ignorant and while William was still
well within the time for prosecuting them, excommunicated William and threatened
that he was minded to declare him excommunicate, and, though lawfully asked to on
William's part, he unlawfully refused to hand over to William a copy of the
excommunication and other acts, or order a copy to be handed over, wherefore on
William's part appeal was again made to the apostolic see. [At the supplication to the
pope][16] to order that William be absolved *ad cautelam* from the sentence of
excommunication and other sentences censures and pains perhaps promulgated against
him by reason of the foregoing and to commit to some upright men in those parts the
causes: of each one of the said appeals and of anything attempted and innovated after
and against them and each one of them; of the nullity of the said process and sentence
and of each and every other thing done in any way to William's prejudice in connection
with the above; and of the whole principal matter, the pope [hereby] commands that
the above three (or two, or one of them), having summoned Thomas and others
concerned, shall, [on the pope's authority bestow] on William, [for this once only] if
he so requests, [the benefit of absolution] *ad cautelam* from the [sentence] of
excommunication and the other [sentences, censures, and pains], inasmuch as it is just,
having, however, first received from him suitable security in respect of that for which
he is perhaps deemed excommunicate and caught by the other sentences, censures, and
pains aforesaid, that if they find that the sentence of excommunication etc were justly
inflicted on him he will obey their mandates and those of the church; as to the other
things, having heard both sides, taking cognizance even of the principal matter, in
matters not involving the penalty of death or mutilation (*penam sanguinis*), decree
what is just without appeal causing [by ecclesiastical censure] what they have decreed
[to be strictly observed, [and moreover compel] witnesses, [etc]. Notwithstanding, etc.

Humilibus et cetera.
Jo Copis / M / M xiiij de Campania

1   or *Crssi*
2   *clerici* inserted at end of line; not initialled
3   *diocesis* inserted in margin, initialled *M*
4   'nuper' (usually rendered in the Calendar by 'recent') does not occur
5   squeezed in in line; not initialled

6   marginal insertion; not initialled
7   *et presbyterorum* inserted in margin; not initialled
8   reading *formatis seu formandis*; MS ill-written and also affected by ink-bleed. In places the readings are
     tentative.
9   *et probis* inserted at end of line; not initialled
10   *dare* (or possibly *fare* – the initial letter is blotched and ill-written) inserted in margin; initialled *M*
11   MS: ... *pro eo (?)quod* [deleted] *<quod homines qui> morabantur* ...; the insertion, which is in the margin,
     is not initialled.
12   MS: ... *ipsius Wull(e)rmi* | | [fo 350ʳ] *ipsius W(i)ll(e)rmi* ...; innocent repetition
13   reading *reiecit*
14   The sentence is not stated to be 'definitive'.
15   MS: *contentis* for 'contemptis'
16   The end of the narrative and the operative part of the letter is abbreviated (by *et cetera*) in several places.
     Supplied from common form.

746   14 December 1517   *Reg. Lat.* 1356, fos 28ʳ-30ʳ

To James Stewart, cleric, d. St Andrews, reservation etc. as below. This day the above
James Stewart, who was holding the monastery of Arbroth *alias* Aberbrodoch, OSB, d.
St Andrews, *in commendam* by apostolic concession at the time, spontaneously and
freely ceded the commend into the pope's hands, and the pope admitted this cession
and, on the advice of the cardinals, commended the monastery, then [vacant] *certo
modo* (which the pope willed vacant as expressed) to James, archbishop of Glasgow,
to be held, ruled and governed by him for life, as is more fully contained in the pope's
letters drawn up in that regard.[1] The pope – quashing and extinguishing, with the
express consent of Andrew, archbishop of St Andrews, the annual pension of 1000
pounds Scots formerly reserved, established and assigned by apostolic authority to
archbishop Andrew for life and payable in full to him (or to his specially mandated
proctor) on the monastery's fruits etc. by the above James Stewart and his successors
holding the monastery at the time, each year, on certain terms and under ecclesiastical
censures and pains then expressed; and decreeing that the said archbishop James and
his successors, the abbots or commendatory abbots of the said monastery for the time
being, are not bound to pay the said pension to archbishop Andrew and do not incur
the said censures or pains on account of the non-payment – lest James Stewart should
suffer excessive loss by this cession, *motu proprio* hereby reserves, establishes and
assigns a like annual pension of 1000 pounds Scots, not exceeding 240 pounds sterling,
on the monastery's fruits etc., payable to James Stewart (or to his specially mandated
proctor) by archbishop James (who has expressly assented to this) and by his said
successors, in full, each year, viz.: one half on the feast of the Nativity of B. John the
Baptist and the other on that of Jesus Christ; decreeing that archbishop James and his
successors are bound to make payment in full to James Stewart in accordance with the
above reservation, constitution and assignment; and willing and establishing that if
archbishop James (or any one of his successors) fails to make payment of the pension
reserved by the presents on the said feasts or at least within the thirty days immediately
following, the archbishop or other bishop shall, after the said days have elapsed, be put
under interdict *ab ingressu ecclesiae*[2] (or, should the individual concerned be inferior
to an archbishop or bishop, he shall incur sentence of excommunication) and he shall

be denied relaxation of the interdict (or absolution from the sentence of excommunication), except on the point of death, until he has made satisfaction in full or reached agreement in respect of it with James Stewart (or his proctor) and, if he remains obdurate under that interdict (or that sentence of excommunication) for a further six months, he shall thereupon be deprived in perpetuity of the rule and administration of the monastery which shall be deemed vacant automatically. Notwithstanding etc.

Executory to the bishops of Caserta, Dunkeld and Dunblane, or two or one of them, acting in person or by proxy.

Vite ac morum honestas ... The executory begins: *Hodie dilecto filio Jacobo Stewart...* *f. bregeon; phi de agnellis / . phi. / . phi. xxx. xx. de Senis*

1   Cf. no. 1227 below.
2   MS: *ingressus ecclesie ei interdictus existat*

747   17 September 1518   *Reg. Lat.* 1356, fos 92ᵛ-94ᵛ

To Robert Elphinstorm',[1] canon of Glasgow, mandate in favour of John Morisom, cleric, d. Glasgow. Following the pope's reservation of all benefices vacated then and in the future at the apostolic see to his own collation and disposition, the perpetual chaplaincy at the altar of Sts Peter and Paul in the church of Glasgow (founded[2] by the late Thomas Forsith, sometime canon of Ross) became vacant by the free resignation of its recent perpetual chaplain, another Thomas Forsith, who was holding the perpetual chaplaincy at the time, made through Adam Symson, cleric of Dunkeld, his specially appointed proctor, spontaneously into the hands of the pope who admitted this resignation at the said see; and the perpetual chaplaincy is vacant at present, being reserved as above. Wishing to honour John, the pope hereby commands the above canon Robert, if through diligent examination he finds John to be suitable – concerning which the pope burdens canon Robert's conscience – to collate and assign the chaplaincy (which is without cure and whose annual value does not exceed 4 pounds sterling), whether vacant as above or howsoever etc.; even if it has been vacant for so long that by the Lateran statutes its collation has lawfully devolved on the apostolic see etc., with all its rights and appurtenances, to John, inducting him etc. having removed any unlawful detainer and causing John (or his proctor) to be admitted to the chaplaincy and its fruits etc., rights and obventions to be delivered to him. [Curbing] gainsayers etc. Notwithstanding etc. and [notwithstanding] the chaplaincy's foundation in which it is said to be expressly stipulated that at a time of vacancy the chaplaincy must be collated to a cleric who is a close blood-relation (*propinquiori consanguineo*) of the founder and otherwise qualified *certo modo*, the which foundation the pope specially and expressly derogates for this once only; and [notwithstanding] that John is not qualified in accordance with the said foundation. Given at Stimigliano, d. Sabina.

Dignum arbitramur et cetera.

Jo. danyelo / JoA. / :JoA xxx: Decimo K(a)l(endas) nove(m)bris Anno Sexto [23 October 1518],*: nardinus*

1 initial letter read sympathetically; readable as 'C'
2 *funda*; *recte*: 'fundata'?

748 29 December 1517

Reg. Lat. 1356, fo 122^{r-v}

To Gregory Charlett,[1] MA, rector of the parish church of Herpeden', d. Lincoln. Dispensation and indult etc. [as above, no. 2].

Litterarum scientia, vite ac morum honestas ...
P Lanb(er)tus / JoA. / JoA. Lx: Nardinus

1 or *Chadett*

749 27 July 1517

Reg. Lat. 1356, fos 167^v-169^r

To Robert Catton, prior of the church of Norwich, OSB, dispensation as below. Some time ago, prior Robert was, as he asserts, dispensed by apostolic authority, to receive together with [the priory] of the above church (which he was holding at that time too), or with any other priory, monastery, dignity or office of the said order held by him at the time, two, and without them, any three other benefices, with or without cure, regular, of the aforesaid or any other order, even the Cluniac or Cistercian, or secular, even if the regular benefices should be priories, *prepositure, prepositatus,* dignities, *personatus,* administrations or offices, or the secular be chantries, free chapels, hospitals or annual services usually assigned to secular clerics in title of a perpetual ecclesiastical benefice, and two of them be parish churches or their perpetual vicarages, even if the priories etc. should be customarily elective and have cure of souls, if he obtained them otherwise canonically, and to retain whichever one of the said regular benefices he chose, even if it should be a priory or other conventual dignity, *in titulum,* and the other two regular benefices, or the secular benefices, *in commendam,* for life, to resign them, at once or successively, simply or for exchange, as often as he pleased, and cede the commend, and in their place receive up to three other, similar or dissimilar, regular or secular, benefices, with or without cure, and to retain whichever one of the regular benefices he chose *in titulum,* and the other regular benefices, or the secular benefices, *in commendam,* for life, as above. And by the said dispensation he holds the priory of the church of Norwich *in titulum* and the perpetual vicarages of the parish churches of Martham and Worstede,[1] d. Norwich, *in commendam.* At prior Robert's supplication, the pope hereby dispenses him to receive together with the above priory and vicarages, any fourth benefice, secular or regular of the above or any other order, even if the secular benefice should be a parish church or its perpetual vicarage, or a chantry, free chapel, hospital or annual service, usually

assigned to secular clerics in title of a perpetual ecclesiastical benefice, or a canonry
and prebend, dignity, *personatus*, administration or office in a cathedral, even
metropolitan, or collegiate, church, and even if the dignity should be *post pontificalem*
in a cathedral, even metropolitan, church, or principal in a collegiate church, or the
regular benefice should be a priory, *prepositura*[2] or other dignity, even conventual or
major *post pontificalem*, or a *personatus*, administration or office, even in the above
church of Norwich or other regular cathedral, even metropolitan, church, and even if
the priory, *prepositura*,[3] dignity etc. should be customarily elective and have cure of
souls, and two of the said four benefices should be dissimilar under one and the same
roof of one and the same church, if he obtains them otherwise canonically, and to retain
them *in commendam* for life, and to resign them, at once or successively,[4] as often as
he pleases, and cede the commend, and in their place receive other, similar or
dissimilar benefices, viz.: a fourth benefice, with or without cure, secular or regular of
the above or any other order, or two dissimilar benefices under one and the same roof
– provided that of the said four benefices not more than one be conventual or claustral
and not more than two be parish churches or their perpetual vicarages, and retain them
in commendam, for life, as above; he may – due and customary burdens of this fourth
benefice having been supported – make disposition of its fruits etc. just as those
holding it *in titulum* could and ought to do, alienation of immovable goods and
precious movables of the said fourth benefice being however forbidden.
Notwithstanding etc. With the proviso that the fourth benefice (secular or regular) and
the above benefices under the same roof shall not, on this account, be defrauded of due
services and the cure of souls in them (if any) shall not be neglected; but that customary
burdens of the fourth benefice (regular or secular) and of the same[5] benefices under the
same roof shall be supported.

Religionis zelus, vite ac morum honestas ...
O de Cesis / Je. / Je. xc. De laporta

1   sympathetic reading; readable as *Worsele*
2   'prepositatus' does not occur here; but not wanting: omitted deliberately (*see below*, note 3).
3   *prepositatum* here deleted and initialled *Je*
4   *simpliciter vel ex causa permutationis*, deleted and initialled *Je*
5   MS: *eorundem* (perhaps supporting the contention that the petitioner had particular benefices in mind)

750   27 September 1516   *Reg. Lat.* 1356, fos 218[r]-219[r]

To John Palsgrawe, warden of the wardenship of Coberlay, d. Worcester (who, as he
asserts, holds the above wardenship which is incompatible with another incompatible
benefice). Dispensation and indult etc. [as above, no. 2]. Given at Viterbo.

Vite ac morum honestas ...
p. lanb(er)tus / JoA. / JoA Lx: nardinus

RUBRICELLAE OF LOST LETTERS

Note. Aside from fragments in *Ind.* 355, the original *rubricellae* or brief summaries of Leo's chancery registers have not survived. We have the titles of the original *rubricellae*, or rather a list of the registers which were rubricated [i.e. the 'stocktaking list', above, p. lxiv, note 1, p. lxv, note 18], but, except for those covering the registers of consistorial provisions, not the *rubricellae* themselves. However, we do have an index to the registers which, though anonymous and undated, visibly forms part of a series of folio indices compiled in the mid-eighteenth century under the auspices of the pro-datary. The index occupies five large folio volumes (each approx. 22.5 x 34 cms.), namely *Ind.* 350 (foliated 1-413), *Ind.* 351 (ff. 1-336), *Ind.* 352 (ff. 1-358), *Ind.* 353 (ff. 1-320), and *Ind.* 354 (ff. 1-194). The volumes, which are in uniform parchment bindings, do not have title pages; but they make up a complete set. The spines are lettered (in gilt): LEO P·P· X· | ANNI PRIMI | TOMVS PRIMVS; LEO P.P. X. | ANNI II · ET III · | TOMVS II.; LEO P.P. X | ANNI IV ET V | TOMVS III.; LEO PP. X. | TOMVS IV. | ANNI. VI. VII.; and LEO PP. X. | TOM. V. | ANN. VIII. IX. respectively.

The C18 re-rubrication project and the character and limitations of the *rubricellae* have been discussed in a previous volume (*CPL* XVI, pp. xliv-liv). For the purposes of the project the medieval registers were dealt with in terms of an artificial scheme of *Libri* and *Anni*. The 227 Leo registers were divided into nine *Anni*, viz. *Annus* I of 50 *libri* (I - XXXXX) *Anni* II-VIII of 25 *libri* (I-XXV) each, and *Annus* IX of 2 *libri* (I & II). The relationship between the artificial *signatura* employed by the index and the actual titles and other *signaturae* is shown in the Conspectus (above, pp. xlvii-lxxiv). The letters in each register or *liber* were indexed under the relevant diocese in alphabetical order and each tome of the index was arranged as a single alphabet. Summaries of letters in the same register are thus dispersed throughout the index tome covering the *liber* in question.

Ind. 355 (ff. 1-230) contains miscellaneous *rubricellae* and other contemporary matter (notably quintern 'wrapper' or index leaves) relating to the registers of Leo X and Hadrian VI. The parchment binding (approx. 22x28.5 cms), which may indicate the date when the material was collected together, is probably not later than the earlier C18 and could be significantly older. The Leo chancery *rubricellae* (at fos 6r-43v) only cover the nine registers of provisions, that is nos 49 and 219-226 in Thierry's C17 numeration (above, pp. lv, lxiii), and stray consistorial items in other registers (e.g. the commend of Inchaffray to Alexander Stewart in what is now *Reg. Lat.* 1316 [nos. 303-305 above] noted at fo 11v of *Ind.* 355) . One example, not necessarily wholly representative, will serve to illustrate the overall character of the early *rubricellae* and their relationship with the C18 ones. Thus Calendar entry no. 103 above is rubricated (at *Ind.* 355, fo 8r) as:

> Glasgnen. Jacobus Archiepiscopus Glasgnen. super Monasterio Beate Marie Kilwyuyn   139 [old fol.]

The C18 index, which perhaps tends to be stronger on matter and weaker on names, has (at *Ind.* 354, fo 73v) under *XVII Anni VIII*:

> Glasgnen. Jacobus Archiepiscopus Glasgnen.   Subrogatio in Iuribus Collitigantis   139
> Monasterium   super Monasterio ordinis S. Benedicti

The present volume of the Calendar collects and transcribes all the *rubricellae* of lost letters of British and Irish interest in the C18 index and presents them in re-assembled register order. The method of editing is that established in earlier volumes (*cf. CPL* XVI, pp. xliv-liv). As can be seen, the *rubricellae* relate to letters in 92 of the 96[*] registers lost subsequent to the compilation of the index. The others – known to the index as *II Anni III*, *III Anni V*, *XV Anni VI*, and *XIV Anni VII* – either did not contain any letters of interest to the Calendar or they were passed over by the rubricators. Unhappily, any British and Irish letters in the one register certainly lost before the index was compiled (i.e. [16 AN. 6]) are, probably, beyond recovery. In dealing with the provisions, I have taken the usually fuller C18 index entries as the basis and only referred to the early *rubricellae* when they add particulars or differ significantly.

The *rubricellae* in the C18 index – our principal source – are undated and we turn naturally to the index reference as an indicator of date. As it happens there is a fair measure of coincidence between the year of the reference and the year of the register's original title and thus (presumptively) of the letters contained in it. However, the numbers of single-year *libri* produced by the registry did not match the artificial scheme and there was obviously no place in the scheme for the 35 or so multi-year *libri*. In consequence fact and fiction were often 'out of sync' and the *Annus* of the index can be highly misleading. For example, nos 787 and 788 below, which are referred by the index to *liber IX Anni I*, do indeed belong to the first year; but no. 1367, referred to *liber XXV Anni VII*, probably belongs to the very end of the 8th year. However, with the aid of the Conspectus (above, pp. xlvii-lxxiv) we can match the index reference with the *liber*'s original title (albeit conjectured) and thus, within limits, date the letters with reasonable confidence.

That the year of a *liber*'s original title is the year of the letters contained in it can, of course, be established from the extant registers and there is no reason to suppose that what is true for extant registers does not hold good for lost ones. Occasionally, where we have independent evidence of the date from other records, we can test the credentials of the exercise. For example, the Conspectus shows that the dispensation in favour of Edward Powell (no. 916 below) was probably enregistered in *liber* 'xiiii[us]

---

[*]   The figure assumes that nos. 186 and 210 in the C17 numeration equate with *XXV Anni VIII* and *I Anni IX* of the C18 index (*cf.* above, p. lxxiii, notes 243 and 270).

diversarum bullarum anno 2º Leonis pp. X^{mi}' (I expand the Conspectus's short title) and thus datable to the year 19 March 1514 - 18 March 1515; a copy in an episcopal register is dated 30 Nov 1514 (no. 916 *note*), well inside the expected limits. Moreover, as the example suggests, the ordinal number of the conjectured *liber* is an additional indicator of the date and, potentially, a means of narrowing the limits of the time-frame. The registry produced 25 registers of the 2nd year and the 14th *liber* is, by position, within a month or so of the time-slot argued by the crude arithmetic.

The pontifical year of the register's original title should be a generally reliable guide to the pontifical year of a lost letter; and the ordinal number of the title is a useful, but fallible, pointer to one part of the year rather than another. However, the papal bureaucracy did not run like clockwork and the exercise must be variously caveated. Several factors can undermine its validity. In the first place, letters were enregistered in the order in which they were expedited, not in the order in which they were granted and dated. Although, as a rule, the order of expedition roughly followed the order of grant a small proportion of letters were expedited well after the date they were granted. Delays of a few years' were not uncommon and in rare cases, expedition could be delayed for up to thirty years (*cf. CPL* XVI, pp. xxxv-xxxviii). Ordinarily, most of the latecomers were enregistered in *Mixtus* volumes; but a few rogue letters found their way into the mainstream series (ibid., p. xlix note 8). Secondly, the main sequence of registers for each year was sapped by the practice of forming some letters into multi-year registers and calculations based on the total number in the main series can be badly flawed. Thirdly, although the ordinal number no doubt reflected the order in which *libri* were completed, the registry was staffed by twelve scribes and two or more *libri* were in course of production simultaneously. In consequence, there is no close correlation between the order of the registers and the order in which letters were enregistered. Finally, the flow of letters fluctuated throughout the year, with obvious implication.

In the circumstances we must exercise extreme caution, particularly with regard to the ordinal number. There is obviously an overall probability that the number of the *liber* will point approximately to the month-dates of the letters contained in it. The lower the number, the earlier in the pontifical year; the higher the number, the later. But there is always a strong possibility that the lost letter in question could, for one reason or another, be effectively misplaced. In part, the ability of the *liber*'s title to mislead turns on the *liber*'s place in the year and the pontificate. Supplications were granted daily and over time the proportion of delayed letters in the pipeline naturally increased. In consequence, the possibility that a particular letter may be misplaced as to its month-date becomes stronger towards the end of the pontifical year in question; and, we may add, the possibility of misplacement as to the year is strengthened as the pontificate is protracted and the number of years multiplied. As always, the indicia must be sensitively evaluated.

Ind.		DIOCESE	PERSON	MATTER	LIBER	FOLIO
751	350,fo118r	*Exeter*	Rugerus Kennguet alias Nueit	Dispensatio ad incompatibilia	I Anni I	252
752	350,fo 118r	*York*	Joannes Prowgh alias Kinugisbure	*The like*	I Anni I	253
753	350,fo 110r	*Down*[1]	Guillermus de Bertis	Commissio vigore appellationis	I Anni I	254
754	350,fo180r	*Lincoln*	Rogerus Vytton	Dispensatio ad incompatibilia	I Anni I	338
755	350,fo180r	*London*	Thomas Waren	Littere Apostolice in forma Provisionis nostre super unione parochialis	I Anni I	348
756	350,fo 60v	*Chichester*	Willelmus Smyth	Dispensatio ad incompatibilia	I Anni I	364
757	350,fo 180r	*Lincoln*	Robertus Purdy	*The like*	I Anni I	365
758	350,fo 180r	*London*	Willelmus Huat	*The like*	I Anni I	367
759	350,fo 118r	*York*	Georgius Wastnes	*The like*	I Anni I	368
760	350,fo 118r	*Same*	Robertus Tutler	Dispensatio ad incompatibilia In forma Rationi congruit	I Anni I	369
761	350,fo 180r	*Lincoln*	Rogerus Geodueygbart alias Ifelten	Dispensatio ad incompatibilia	I Anni I	374
762	350,fo110r	*Dromore*	Gelasius Magnassa	Commissio vigore appellationis	IV Anni I	45
763	350,fo 62r	*Canterbury*	Joannes Champneg	*The like*	IV Anni I	156
764	350,fo 31v	*Bangor*	Joannes Santhey	*The like*	IV Anni I	226
765	350,fo 62r	*Cork*	Edimundus Ymurchi	*The like*	IV Anni I	294
766	350,fo 62r	*Same*	Joannes Oherrlathy	*The like*	IV Anni I	296
767	350,fo182r	*Lincoln*	Rogerius Novell cum aliis	*The like*	IV Anni I	299
768	350,fo 182r	*Same*	Robertus Gonde	*The like*	IV Anni I	319

Ind.		DIOCESE	PERSON	MATTER	LIBER	FOLIO
769	350,fo182r	*Same*	Joannes Sinyth	*The like*	IV Anni I	320
770	350,fo183r	*London*	Christophorus [Bainbridge] tituli Sancte Praxedis Presbyter Cardinalis	Indultum visitandi corrigendi et reformandi quoddam Monasterium	VI Anni I	116
771	350,fo 183v	*Same*	Riccardus Vowel monachus	Dispensatio ad incompatibilia In forma Rationi congruit	VI Anni I	141
772	350,fo 315v	*St Andrews*	Georgius [Brown] episcopus Dunkelden cum aliis	Locatio et concessio nonnullorum bonorum cuiusdam monasterii. si in evidentem	VI Anni I	202
773	350,fo 119r	*York*	Abbates Monasteriorum Ordinis Pre-monstraten. Regni Anglie et Regi Anglie subjectorum	Exemptio ab omni iurisdictione et superioritate abbatis generalis dicti ordinis	VI Anni I	207
774	350,fo 316r	*St Andrews*	Riccardus Thomsone	Pensio super quadam domo regulari ad effectum subeundi oneribus sui officii	VI Anni I	352
775	350,fo 301v	*Ross*	Joannes Caldor	Vicaria parrochialis per resignationem	VII Anni I	102
776	350,fo302r	[*Rochester*][2]	Milo Tomlynson	Littere in forma nove provisionis[3] super nova provisione vicarie parochialis	VII Anni I	163
777	350,fo 241v	*Norwich*	Willelmus Wangdem alias Willemson	Dispensatio ad incompatibile	VII Anni I	164
778	350,fo 65r	*Carlisle*	Joannes Hering	Ampliatio dispensationis ad incompatibilia	VII Anni I	165
779	350,fos 33r, 371r	*Bath & Wells*	Walterus[4] Piers	*The like*	VII Anni I	185
780	350,fo 371r	*Winchester*	[----][5]	Indulgentia pro visitantibus cappellam in ecclesia Vintonien. Ad futuram	VII Anni I	191

Ind.		DIOCESE	PERSON	MATTER	LIBER	FOLIO
781	350,fo 184v	*Lincoln*	Riccardus Fowler	Dispensatio ad incompatibilia	VII Anni I	203
782	350,fos 65r, 184v	*Coventry & Lichfield*	Gullielmus Crodocco	*The like*	VII Anni I	204
783	350,fos 33r, 371r	*Bath & Wells*	Thomas Wathel	*The like*	VII Anni I	246
784	350,fos 33r, 371r	*Same*	Willelmus Newton[6]	*The like*	VII Anni I	247
785	350,fo119r	*York*	Nicolaus Chelteman	*The like*	VII Anni I	261
786	350,fo 67v	*Cork*	Ranaldus Oncurchyly	Parochialis certo modo	IX Anni I	102
787	350,fo 67v	*Same*	Ranaldus Omuchyly	Canonicatus per devolutionem	IX Anni I	134
788[8]	350,fo 67v	*Cloyne; Cork*	Thomas Yeclay	Vicarie parochialium per dissolutionem	IX Anni I	136
789	350,fo 372v	*Worcester*	Stephanus Francisci	Commissio hospitalis per devolutionem unionis	IX Anni I	172
790	350,fo 144r	*Glasgow*	Jacobus Herot	Parochialis per resignationem	X Anni I	265
791	350,fo 302v	*Raphoe*	Magister Thomas Halsey	Decanatus per obitum In forma Rationi congruit	X Anni I	297
792	350,fo 70v	*Canterbury*	Joannes We'lbe	Dispensatio ad incompatibilia	XII Anni I	210
793	350,fo 319r	*Salisbury*	Willhelmus Nulve	*The like*	XII Anni I	211
794	350,fo 374v	*Rome*[9]	Christophorus [Bainbridge] tituli Sancte Praxedis Presbyter Cardinalis	Licentia testandi	XII Anni I	307
795	350,fo 189v	*Lincoln*	Christophorus [Bainbridge] tituli Sancte Praxedis Presbyter Cardinalis	Licentia seu facultas eligendi quatuor viros ex collegio scholarum studii Oxonie ut essent Magistri etiam (?)sectores[10] Theologie. Ad perpetuam	XII Anni I	308
796	350,fo 221r	*Moray*	Gilbertus Strarthanc'hm	Pensio super canonicatu ex causa litis In forma Rationi congruit	XIII Anni I	112

Ind.		DIOCESE	PERSON	MATTER	LIBER	FOLIO
797	350,fo 73r	*Canterbury*[11]	Guillelmus Boval	Pensio super preceptoria regulari In forma Rationi Congruit	XIII Anni I	162
798	350,fo 319v	*St Andrews*	Alexander Elphinston	Dispensatio ad incompatibilia non obstante defectu etatis	XIII Anni I	173
799	350,fo 319v	*Same*	Andreas Stewart	Dispensatio ad incompatibilia	XIII Anni I	173
800	350,fo 145r	*Glasgow*	Joannes Lokert	Pensio super domo regulari	XIII Anni I	177
801	350,fo 73v	*Cloyne*	Dernutius[12] Ohyauyan	Simplex certo modo	XIII Anni I	260
802	350,fo 319v	*St Andrews*	Willermus Vawan	Cancellariatus monasterii per obitum In forma Rationi congruit	XIII Anni I	281
803	350,fo 319v	*Same*	David Seton	Dispensatio ad incompatibilia	XIII Anni I	300
804	350,fo 192v	*London*	Joannes Asshewell	Commissio vigore appellationis	XVI Anni I	13
805	350,fo 377v	*Winchester*	Thomas [Skevington] episcopus Bangoren.	Indultum exercendi omnimoda[m] iurisdictionem in monasterio de Bello Loco Regis nuncupato Cistercien. Ordinis atque in aliis monasteriis eidem monasterio subiectis quandiu ipse Thomas Episcopus idem monasterium in Commendam retinuerit	XVI Anni I	29
806	350,fo112r	*Dunblane*	Walterus Derummona suo et aliorum nomine	Commissio vigore appellationis	XVI Anni I	137
807	350,fo 321r	*St Andrews*	Henricus Barre'	Parochialis per resignationem	XVI Anni I	139
808	350,fo 77v	*Coventry*[13]	Jacobus Machiriman	Mandatum de facienda unione vicarie parochialis alteri simili vicarie in eventum provisionis ipsius Jacobi de hac quandiu hanc ipse obtinuerit	XVI Anni I	292
809	350,fo 122r	*Elphin*	Joannes Margyllarmy	Vicaria parochialis certo modo	XIX Anni I	38
810	350,fo 41v	*Bath*	Thomas Spryngar et alii	Commissio vigore appellationis	XIX Anni I	151

Ind.		DIOCESE	PERSON	MATTER	LIBER	FOLIO
811	350,fo 122r	*York*	Margaritha Vanesour	Commissio vigore appellationis	XIX Anni I	235
812	350,fo 195v	*Lincoln*	Richardus Ward	Dispensatio ad incompatibilia	XXII Anni I	43
813	350,fo195v	*Same*	Georgius Homond	*The like*	XXII Anni I	44
814	350,fo 82v	*Chichester*	Willelmus Atkis	*The like*	XXII Anni I	46
815	350,fo122v	*Exeter*	Richardus Carlion	Unio parochialis per ipsum obtente canonicatui etiam per ipsum obtento quamdiu ipse illos obtinuerit. Ad futuram	XXII Anni I	47
816	350,fo 82v	*Canterbury*	Thomas Sayer canonicatus[14] Premonstraten. Ordinis	Dispensatio ad incompatibile per seculares obtineri solitum	XXII Anni I	48
817	350,fo195v	*Lincoln*	Thomas Dyllani	Dispensatio super defectu etatis ad incompatibile	XXII Anni I	58
818	350,fo195v	*Same*	William Wilton	Ampliatio dispensationis ad incompatibilia	XXII Anni I	76
819	350,fos 43r, 381v	*Bath & Wells*	Laurentius Feliphi	Dispensatio ad incompatibilia	XXII Anni I	99
820	350,fo195v	*Lincoln*	Prior et conventus prioratus de Kyrkeby super Wretek Ordinis Sancti Augustini	Indulgentia pro visitantibus ecclesiam dicti prioratus et porrigentibus manus adiutrices ad eiusdem ecclesie conservationem. Ad Perpetuam	XXII Anni I	111
821	350,fo 147r	*Glasgow*	Joannes Duncani	Pensio super precentoria cathedralis In forma Rationi congruit	XXII Anni I	115
822	350,fo 324r	*Salisbury*	Richardus Chapina	Dispensatio ad incompatibilia	XXII Anni I	171
823	350,fo 122v	*York*	Villelmus Howsden	*The like*	XXII Anni I	173
824	350,fo 122v	*Same*	Christophorus Salery	*The like*	XXII Anni I	176

Ind.		DIOCESE	PERSON	MATTER	LIBER	FOLIO
825	350,fo 324r	Salisbury	Willelmus Mylton abbas et conventus monasterii de Mylton Ordinis Sancti Benedicti	Indulgentia perpetua pro visitantibus ecclesiam dicti monasterii	XXII Anni I	177
826	350,fos 43r, 382r	Bath & Wells	Richardus Bromefeldi	Dispensatio ad incompatibilia	XXII Anni I	227
827	350,fo 196r	Lincoln	Galfridus Wren	Dispensatio ad incompatibilia In forma Rationi congruit	XXII Anni I	228
828	350,fo 382r	Winchester	Joannes Clerke	Dispensatio ad incompatibilia	XXII Anni I	231
829	350,fo 248v	Nullius expresse diecesis in Anglia	Gilbertus Gilberd	Unio parochialis per ipsum obtente alteri etiam per ipsum obtente quamdiu ipse hanc obtinuerit	XXII Anni I	232
830	350,fo 196r	London	Joannes Longlond	Unio parochialis per ipsum obtente alteri etiam per ipsum obtente quamdiu ipse hanc obtinuerit. Ad futuram	XXII Anni I	233
831	350,fo196r	Lincoln	Antonius Cariswall	Dispensatio ad incompatibilia	XXII Anni I	235
832	350,fo 122v	York	Richardus Shaa	[——][15]	XXII Anni I	236
833	350,fo 122v	Ely	Radulphus Wleitehede	Dispensatio ad incompatibilia	XXII Anni I	238
834	350,fo 196r	Lincoln	Joannes Egirton	The like	XXII Anni I	239
835	350,fo 122v	York	Georgius Palmes	The like	XXII Anni I	240
836	350,fo 196r	London	Willermus Harington	Indultum non residendi apud beneficia obtenta residendo in Romana Curia vel in loco alicuius eorum sive studii generalis	XXII Anni I	242
837	350,fo122v	York[16]	Robertus Granelle	Pensio super canonicatu	XXII Anni I	279
838	350,fo122v	Exeter	Joannes Chymos	Dispensatio ad incompatibilia	XXII Anni I	287
839	350,fo 248v	Nullius expresse diocesis[17]	Joannes Storke	The like	XXII Anni I	288

Ind.		DIOCESE	PERSON	MATTER	LIBER	FOLIO
840	350,fo 382r	*Worcester*	Joannes Webbe	Dispensatio ad incompatibile	XXII Anni I	288
841	350,fo 196r	*London*	Richardus Rawllyns	Unio parochialis per ipsum obtente canonicatui etiam per ipsum obtento quamdiu ipse hanc obtinuerit. Ad futuram	XXII Anni I	383
842	350,fo 324v	*Salisbury*	Joannes Bryme	Unio parochialis canonicatui per dictum Joannem obtento ad eius vitam tantum seu quamdiu hanc obtinuerit. Ad futuram	XXIII Anni I	127
843	350,fo 324v	*Same*	Willelmus Balle	Indultum deputandi presbyterum seu presbyteros idoneos in exercitio cure animarum ratione senectutis	XXIII Anni I	285
844	350,fo 308v	*Ross*	Joannes Hexburne	Parochialis per resignationem	XXXII Anni I	70
845	350,fo 93r	*Carlisle*	Christophorus Sser[18]	Dispensatio ad incompatibilia in forma Rationi congruit	XXXII Anni I	122
846	350,fo 232v	*St David's*	Joannes Alyer	Dispensatio ad incompatibilia	XXXVI Anni I	29
847	350,fo 95v	*Coventry*	N. Seth Wodecok[19]	Indultum percipiendi fructus beneficii in absentia	XXXVI Anni I	30
848	350,fo 204r	*London*	Robertus Bukuall	Unio parochialis alteri ad vitam dicti Roberti aut quamdiu primam obtinuerit. Ad futuram	XXXVI Anni I	31
849	350,fo 389v	*Winchester*	Willelmus Stynt	Dispensatio ad incompatibilia	XXXVI Anni I	40
850	350,fo 253r	*Nullius*[20]	Joannes Spryugwell	*The like*	XXXVI Anni I	58
851	350,fo 204r	*London*	Christophorus Leynacy	*The like*	XXXVI Anni I	108
852	350,fo 125r	*York*	Joannes Hastinge	*The like*	XXXVI Anni I	148
853	350,fos 98r, 205v	*Coventry & Lichfield* Perpetua[21]	Ivo Willelmi abbas monasterii Ordinis Sancti Benedicti	Indultum seu facultas utendi pontificalibus pro se et successoribus cum aliis gratiis. Ad perpetuam	XXXIX Anni I	174
854	350,fo 331r	*St Andrews*	Willelmus Myrtoneri	Pensio super vicaria	XXXIX Anni I	256

Ind.		DIOCESE	PERSON	MATTER	LIBER	FOLIO
855	350,fo 331v	Same	Joannes Treri	Erectio cappellanie cum certis statutis et ordinationibus. Ad perpetuam	XXXXI Anni I	145
856	350,fo 394r	Worcester	Hugo Veysy	Dispensatio ad incompatibilia	XXXXIV Anni I	103
857	350,fo 102r	Chichester	Joannes Kirkelon	Commissio vigore appellationis	XXXXIV Anni I	145
858	350,fo 126v	York[22]	(?)Dolorus Offlangen	Parochialis certo modo	XXXXIV Anni I	340
859	350,fo 27r	Killala	Ristarchus de Burgo	Prioratus regularis certo modo	XXXXV Anni I	56
860	350,fo 333v	St Andrews	Robertus Crechton	Dispensatio ad incompatibilia	XXXXV Anni I	166
861	350,fo 103r	Canterbury	Thomas Payn	The like	XXXXV Anni I	246
862	350,fo 209r	London	Stephanus Pertini	The like	XXXXV Anni I	276
863	350,fo 114v	Dunblane	Wilhelmus Drummond	Decanatus cathedralis per permutationem	XXXXVIII Anni I	134
864	350,fo 115r	Same	Gilbertus Strachanchia	Canonicatus per permutationem	XXXXVIII Anni I	136
865	350,fo 106v	Canterbury	Thomas Linarie	Dispensatio ad incompatibilia	XXXXVIII Anni I	301
866	350,fo 57v	Bath Perpetua	Habitatores et incole loci capelle Sancti Michaelis de Stokelave Bathonien. diocesis	Licentia perpetua quod presbyter ab ipsis conductus pro celebratione misse quotidiane ad altare in dicta capella ab eodem servitio et celebratione missarum huiusmodi a nullo superiore amoveri possit. Ad perpetuam	XXXXX Anni I	159
867	350,fo 256r	Norwich	Riccardus Hoobon	Indultum non residendi	XXXXX Anni I	245
868	350,fo 256r	Same	Robertus Smyth	Dispensatio ad incompatibilia	XXXXX Anni I	247
869	350,fo 211v	Lincoln	Joannes Waylot	The like	XXXXX Anni I	248
870	351,fo 177v	Moray	Galbinus Lesly	Si Neutri super canonicatu	II Anni II	140
871	351,fo 152v	Lincoln	Thomas [?Halsey] electus Seglinen.[23]	Unio parochialis ecclesiae Seglinen. ad vitam dicti Thome aut quamdiu dictam ecclesiam obtinuerit. Ad futuram	IV Anni II	301

Ind.		DIOCESE	PERSON	MATTER	LIBER	FOLIO
872	351,fo 96r	York	Wilhelmus Monton	Commissio vigore appellationis	VII Anni II	24
873	351,fo 153v	Lichfield	Thomas Longworthe	Dispensatio ad incompatibilia	VII Anni II	47
874	351,fo 265v	Salisbury	Joannes Rut	The like	X Anni II	199
875	351,fo 265v	Same	Thomas Ausell	The like	X Anni II	200
876	351,fo 96v	York	Mattheus Marcharelli	Commissio vigore appellationis	X Anni II	323
877	351,fo 155v	Lincoln	Ugo Hortis	Dispensatio ad incompatibilia	XIII Anni II	114
878	351,fo 155v	London	Jacobus Maler	Unio parochialis vicarie ad vitam dicti Jacobi aut quamdiu dictam vicariam obtinuerit. Ad futuram	XIII Anni II	149
879	351,fo 155v	Same	Willelmus Robson	Dispensatio ad incompatibilia	XIII Anni II	245
880	351,fo 96v	York	Oliverius Wodorff	The like	XIII Anni II	247
881	351,fo 156r	Lincoln	Thomas Smyth	The like	XIII Anni II	248
882	351,fo 307r	Wells	Edmundus Coscer	The like	XIII Anni II	248
883	351,fo 307r	Winchester	Joannes Corker	The like	XIII Anni II	249
884	351,fo 156r	Lincoln	Willelmus Clifson	Unio parochialis alteri ad vitam dicti Wilelmi aut quamdiu primam obtinuerit. Ad futuram	XIII Anni II	250
885	351,fo 156r	London	Robertus Philipson	Indultum non residendi in loco beneficii causa studii	XIII Anni II	280
886	351,fo 267r	Salisbury	Joannes Haakehet	Dispensatio ad incompatibilia	XVI Anni II	36
887	351,fo 202r	Norwich	Robertus Trower	The like	XVI Anni II	37
888	351,fo 156v	Lincoln	Riccardus Lincoll	The like	XVI Anni II	40
889	351,fo 156v	Same	Jacobus Balcombe	The like	XVI Anni II	45
890	351,fo 59r	Coventry	Joannes Chircheman	The like	XVI Anni II	46
891	351,fo 308v	Worcester	Thomas Wade	The like	XVI Anni II	47

Ind.		DIOCESE	PERSON	MATTER	LIBER	FOLIO
892[24]	351,fos 33v, 308v	*Bath & Wells*	Willelmus Mors	Unio vicarie ecclesie par(r)ochiali ad vitam dicti Willelmi aut quamdiu dictam parochialem obtinuerit. Ad futuram[25]	XVI Anni II	81
893	351,fo 156v	*Lincoln*	Laurentius Thonison	Unio vicarie ecclesie parochiali ad vitam dicti Laurentii aut quamdiu dictam parochialem obtinuerit. Ad futuram	XVI Anni II	93
894[26]	351,fo 308v	*Worcester*	Willelmus Dyngley	Dispensatio ad incompatibilia	XVI Anni II	94
895	351,fo 267v	*Salisbury*	Thomas Leegh	*The like*	XVI Anni II	124
896	351,fo 202r	*Norwich*	Willermus Cootre	*The like*	XVI Anni II	265
897	351,fo 254v	*Ross*	Joannes Sanchart	Pensio super cancellaria	XVIII Anni II	15
898	351,fo 60r	*Coventry*[27]	Petrus Altabegoti	Simplex per resignationem	XVIII Anni II	47
899	351,fo 90r	*Dunblane*	Gilbertus Strathanthini	Decanatus per obitum	XVIII Anni II	152
900	351,fo 254v	*Ross*	Joannes Miaclud	Reservatio fructuum canonicatus resignat[or]i	XVIII Anni II	179
901	351,fo 158r	*Lincoln*	Eduardus Miller	Dispensatio ad incompatibilia	XIX Anni II	1
902	351,fo 309v	*Worcester*	Philippus Weldon	*The like*	XIX Anni II	1
903[28]	351,fo 97v	*Exeter*	Franciscus de Marcheville	Indultum deputandi (?)alios pro visitatione locorum archidiaconatui subiectorum	XIX Anni II	11
904	351,fo 203r	*Norwich*	Willelmus Botey	Indulgentia pro ecclesia parochiali	XIX Anni II	35
905	351,fos 8r, 146r	*Armagh; Kilmore*	Bernardus Mhakayegke et Riccardus etiam Mhakayegke[29]	Concessio in emphiteusim aliquarum terrarum ad archiepiscopatum Armacan. spectantium	XIX Anni II	47
906	351,fo 97v	*Exeter*	Thomas Lloyde	Dispensatio ad incompatibilia	XIX Anni II	48
907	351,fo 158r	*London*	Jacobus Blieton	*The like*	XIX Anni II	49
908	351,fo 60v	*Coventry*	Bernardus Travers	*The like*	XIX Anni II	50

Ind.		DIOCESE	PERSON	MATTER	LIBER	FOLIO
909	351,fo 97v	York	Jacobus Cokville	The like	XIX Anni II	56
910	351,fo 158r	Lincoln	Eduardus Sheffeld	Unio vicarie canonicatui ad vitam dicti Eduardi aut quamdiu dictum canonicatum obtinuerit. Ad futuram	XIX Anni II	61
911	351,fo 203r	Norwich	Joannes Wynckylse	Dispensatio ad incompatibilia	XIX Anni II	63
912	351,fo 34v	Bath	Edmundus Coker	Indultum seu concessio permanendi in uno monasterio et quod non possit a superioribus amoveri	XIX Anni II	66
913	351,fo 97v	Exeter	Eduardus Higgyus	Indultum seu licentia absen(tan)di a loco beneficii	XIX Anni II	68
914	351,fo 158r	Lincoln	Brianus Higdon	Unio parochialis alteri ad vitam dicti Briani aut quamdiu primam obtinuerit	XIX Anni II	79
915	351,fo 60v	Coventry	Richardus Egerton	Unio parochialis alteri ad vitam dicti Richardi aut quamdiu primam obtinuerit	XIX Anni II	81
916[30]	351,fo 268v	Salisbury	Edwardus Powell	Dispensatio ad incompatibilia	XIX Anni II	82
917	351,fo 128v	Hereford	Willermus Marble	The like	XIX Anni II	84
918	351,fo 158r	Lichfield	Edmundus Stretoy	The like	XIX Anni II	85
919	351,fo 310r	Worcester	Thomas Fuse	The like	XIX Anni II	86
920	351,fo 158r	Lincoln	Nicolaus Greue	The like	XIX Anni II	87
921	351,fo 158r	Same	Joannes Greue	Unio parochialis alteri ad vitam dicti Joannis aut quamdiu primam obtinuerit. Ad futuram	XIX Anni II	93
922	351,fo 204v	Norwich	Willelmus Vyburgh alias Wydelsteldi	Indultum absentie	XXIII Anni II	46
923	351,fo 270r	St Andrews	Gilbertus Strathanchin	Rectoria parochialis per resignationem	XXIII Anni II	65
924	351,fo 270r	Same	David Seton	Reservatio fructuum parochialis	XXIII Anni II	67
925	351,fo 160r	Lincoln	Eduardus Hilton	Dispensatio ad incompatibilia	XXIII Anni II	88

Ind.		DIOCESE	PERSON	MATTER	LIBER	FOLIO
926	351,fo 311r	*Worcester*	Joannes Langeford	*The like*	XXIII Anni II	89
927	351,fo 160r	*London*	Willelmus Goodrich	*The like*	XXIII Anni II	90
928	351,fo 160r	*Lincoln* <u>Perpetua</u>	Universi confratres utriusque sexus confraternitatis gilde nuncupate sub invocatione Beate Marie apud ecclesiam Sancti Botulphi ville Bosson Lincolinen. diocesis	Extensio et ampliatio litterarum Innocentii PP VIII super nonnullis gratiis et privilegiis eidem confraternitati concessis ac statutum et ordinatio super eisdem. Ad perpetuam	XXIII Anni II	144
929	351,fo 63v	*Canterbury*	Joannes Carter	Dispensatio ad incompatibilia	XXIII Anni II	155
930	351,fo 98r	*York*	Edmundus Etioikton	Dispensatio ad incompatibilia cum indulto non residendo	XXIII Anni II	218
931	351,fos 63v, 160r	*Coventry & Lichfield; Lincoln*	Seth Wodecok[31]	Unio vicarie parochialis per ipsum obtente alteri vicarie (parochiali)[32] etiam per ipsum obtente quamdiu ipse hanc obtinuerit. Ad futuram	XXIII Anni II	219
932	351,fo 63v	*Chichester*	Willelmus Braben	Dispensatio ad incompatibilia	XXIII Anni II	232
933	351,fo 63v	*Coventry*	Laurentius Travers	*The like*	XXIII Anni II	233
934	351,fo 63v	*Chichester*	Georgius Shelley	*The like*	XXIII Anni II	234
935	351,fo 146v	*Kilmore* <u>Si in evidentem</u>	Bernardus Mhakayghe et Richardus etiam Mhakayghe	Licentia locandi in emphiteusim perpetuam ipsi Bernardo et Richardo nonnullas terras spectantes ad cappellam subiectam parochiali ab archidiacono de Renlys in ecclesia Miden' obtente ipsi archidiacono concessa. Si in evidentem	XXIII Anni II	236
936	351,fo 160v	*London*	Thomas Godwin	Dispensatio ad incompatibilia	XXIII Anni II	236
937	351,fo 36v	*Bath*	Waltherus Perrett	*The like*	XXIII Anni II	242
938	351,fo 64r	*Canterbury*	Willelmus Pen	*The like*	XXIII Anni II	243

Ind.		DIOCESE	PERSON	MATTER	LIBER	FOLIO
939	351,fos 160v, 270r	*London; Salisbury*	Robertus de Becausouu[33]	Unio parochialis Londonien. diocesis etiam per ipsum obtente simplici quamdiu ipse hoc obtinuerit. Ad futuram[34]	XXIII Anni II	276
940	351,fos 64r, 160v	*Coventry & Lichfield*	Richardus Egerton	Indultum non residendi	XXIII Anni II	302
941	351,fo 161v	*Lincoln*	Robertus Onael	Dispensatio ad incompatibilia	I Anni III	77
942	351,fos 37v, 313r	*Bath & Wells*	Riccardus[35] Germoni	*The like*	I Anni III	203
943	351,fo 256v	Rochester	Richardus Darrell	*The like*	I Anni III	220
944[36]	351,fo 165r	*London*	Joannes Goodryk	Dispensatio ad incompatibilia	VIII Anni III	89
945[37]	351,fo 165r	*Same*	Hugo Guibesson	*The like*	VIII Anni III	90
946[38]	351,fo 100r	*Exeter*	Willelmus Colles	*The like*	VIII Anni III	96
947[39]	351,fo 165r	*London*	Joannes Cooke	*The like*	VIII Anni III	124
948[40]	351,fos 40r, 315v	*Bath & Wells*	Willelmus Ratyliff	*The like*	VIII Anni III	125
949[41]	351,fo 165r	*London*	(?)Eudonus Aspelon	*The like*	VIII Anni III	126
950[42]	351,fo 273v	*Salisbury*	Willelmus Cynnes	*The like*	VIII Anni III	128
951[43]	351,fo 316r	*Worcester*	Willelmus Barcow	*The like*	VIII Anni III	129
952	351,fo 165r	*Lincoln*	Thomas Barcer	Unio parochialis alteri ad vitam dicti Thome aut quamdiu primam obtinuerit	VIII Anni III	130
953	351,fo 165r	*Same*	Willelmus Bastard	Unio parochialis canonicatui ad vitam dicti Willelmi aut quamdiu canonicatum obtinuerit	VIII Anni III	132
954	351,fo 165v	*London*	Willelmus Venori	Commissio vigore appellationis	VIII Anni III	351
955	351,fos 100r, 190r	*Elphin; Thérouanne*[44]	Wllialmus Oscyngin[45]	Mandatum de erigendis in simplicem prebendam ecclesie Elfinen. parochiali Morinen et quartis episcopalibus par(r)ochialium Elfinen. (respective)[46] diocesis ad vitam ipsius Wllialmi dictaque[47] simplici prebenda erecta eidem (Wlialmo)[48] conferenda	IX Anni III	118

Ind.		DIOCESE	PERSON	MATTER	LIBER	FOLIO
956	351,fo 165v	Lismore	Joannes Buther	Unio parochialium Lismoren. et Ossoren. canonicatui Lismoren. quamdiu ipse hunc obtinuerit	IX Anni III	321
957	351,fo 100v	York	Richardus Octirburn	Ampliatio dispensationis ad incompatibilia	X Anni III	12
958	351,fos 40v, 316v	Bath & Wells	Robertus (de)[49] Hardeconis	Dispensatio ad incompatibilia	X Anni III	20
959	351,fo 73v	Cloyne	Joannes de Gerladinis	Commissio vigore appellationis	X Anni III	78
960	351,fo 110r	Ferns	Oddo Abardan prior monasterii Sancti Joannis Evangeliste Ordinis Sancti Augustini	Unio rectorie parochialis et simplicis prioratui dicti monasterii quamdiu ipse hunc obtinuerit	X Anni III	122
961	351,fo 110r	Same	Vllialmus Miedull	Unio rectorie parochialis monasterio Premonstraten. Ordinis per ipsum obtento quamdiu ipse hoc obtinuerit	X Anni III	124
962	351,fos 73v, 166r	Coventry & Lichfield	Robertus Blythe[50]	Dispensatio ad incompatibilia	X Anni III	197
963	351,fo 130r	Hereford	Joannes Mawncell	The like	X Anni III	200
964	351,fos 41r, 317r	Bath & Wells	Thomas Lowell[51]	Unio vicarie parochialis per ipsum obtente (canonicatui)[52] quamdiu ipse hunc[53] obtinuerit	X Anni III	338
965	351,fo 317r	Worcester	Richardus Bredshay	Dispensatio super defectu etatis et ad incompatibile	X Anni III	339
966	351,fo 43r	Bath	Richardus Olben	Commissio vigore appellationis	XV Anni III	58
967	351,fo 259v	Raphoe	Joannes Ygaltur	Unio canonicatus parochiali ad vitam dicti Joannis aut quamdiu illam obtinuerit	XV Anni III	131
968	351,fo 77r	Cashel	Dominicus Oduyr	Thesauraria et canonicatus certo modo	XV Anni III	141
969	351,fo 111v	Ferns	Mauritius Offertheryn	Rectoria certo modo	XV Anni III	148

Ind.	DIOCESE	PERSON	MATTER	LIBER	FOLIO
970 351,fo 298r	*Tuam*	Seleuccy de Burgo	Archidiaconatus certo modo	XV Anni III	151
971 351,fo 111v	*Ferns*	Oddo Oderramy	Parochialis certo modo	XV Anni III	162
972 351,fo 77r	*Cashel*	Antonius Maymomy	Prepositura per cessionem	XV Anni III	167
973 351,fo 92v	(?)*Derry*[54]	Laurentius Mecorta	Parochialis certo modo	XV Anni III	186
974 351,fo 168v	*Lismore*	Thomas Omurissa	Vicaria certo modo	XV Anni III	202
975 351,fo 77v	*Coventry*	Richardus Carter	Dispensatio ad incompatibilia	XV Anni III	222
976[55] 351,fo 168v	*Lincoln*	Robertus Heggys	*The like*	XV Anni III	223
977 351,fo 101r	*Elphin*	Rodericus Mardermuda	Vicaria parochialis certo modo	XV Anni III	232
978 351,fo 77v	*Cashel*	Cornelius Olechnay	Parochiales certo modo	XV Anni III	237
979 351,fo 77v	*Same*	Cornelius Olachnayn	Vicarie certo modo cum unione canonicatui ad vitam dicti Cornelii aut quamdiu dictum canonicatum obtinuerit	XV Anni III	250
980 351,fo 259v	*Raphoe*	Bernardus Murarmie	Dispensatio super defectu natalium ad quecumque	XV Anni III	255
981 351,fo 168v	*Killaloe*	Eugenius Marmohaue	Vicaria certo modo	XV Anni III	259
982 351,fo 92v	*Kildare*[56]	Arturus Y Galanbayr	Vicaria parochialis certo modo	XV Anni III	265
983 351,fo 298r	*Tuam*	Felix de Burgo	Vicarie certo modo	XV Anni III	267
984 351,fo 168r	*Lismore*	Joannes Bonylur	Commissio vigore appellationis	XV Anni III	308
985 351,fo 45r	*Bangor*	Joannes Godfrey	*The like*	XX Anni III	47
986 351,fo 171v	*Leighlin*	Donatus Homorta	Vicarie ac rectoria parochialium per devolutionem	XX Anni III	48
987 351,fo 261r	*Raphoe*	Eugenius Marmemar'	Vicaria parrochialis per devolutionem et certo modo	XX Anni III	122

Ind.		DIOCESE	PERSON	MATTER	LIBER	FOLIO
988	351,fo 221r	*Ossory*	Jacobus Bultaz	Unio rectoriarum et vicariarum parochialium canonicatui quamdiu ipse illas et illum post unionem huiusmodi sibi conferendas et conferendum obtinuerit	XX Anni III	167
989	351,fo 211r	*Norwich*	Robertus Beckham	Dispensatio ad incompatibilia	XX Anni III	173
990	351,fo 211r	Nullius in Anglia	Willelmus Breme Anglicus Ordinis Fratrum B.M. de Monte Carmelo	*The like*	XX Anni III	207
991	351,fo 45v	(?)*Carlisle*[57]	Agnes Sothy alias Lancaster	Commissio vigore appellationis	XX Anni III	263
992	351,fo 194r	*Meath*	Cornelius Maghilagan	*The like*	XX Anni III	275
993	351,fos 82v, 172r	*Coventry & Lichfield*	Radulphus Holland	Unio parochialis canonicatui quamdiu ipse hunc obtinuerit	XX Anni III	290
994	351,fo 172r	*Lincoln*	Stephanus La Der	Dispensatio ad incompatibilia	XX Anni III	295
995	351,fo 320v	*Worcester*	Eliseus Benett	*The like*	XX Anni III	295
996	351,fo 320v	*Winchester*	Hugo Assheton	*The like*	XX Anni III	297
997	351,fo 173v	*Lismore*	Donaldus Oconarius	Erectio rectorie sine cura in canonicatum cathedrali[s] ad vitam dicti Donaldi in eventum provisionis Donaldi (?)met de huiusmodi canonicatu nec non unio vicarie parochialis dicto canonicatu[i] quamdiu ipse hunc obtinuerit	XXIII Anni III	83
998	351,fo 23r	*Ardfert*	Nicolaus de Geraldinis	Unio rectorie parochialis archidiaconatui quamdiu ipse hunc obtinuerit	XXIII Anni III	139
999	351,fo 23r	*Same*	Joannes Offyn	Mandatum de erigendo in dicta ecclesia canonicatu ex vicaria parochialis ad vitam dicti Joannis de huiusmodi canonicatu providendi	XXIII Anni III	142

Ind.		DIOCESE	PERSON	MATTER	LIBER	FOLIO
1000	351,fo 23r	Killala	Cormacus Odulna	Mandatum de erigendo canonicatu ecclesie Arteferten. ex vicaria parochialis ad vitam ipsius Cormanni de huiusmodi canonicatu providendi et de canonicatui (?)predicto unienda altera vicaria parochialis etiam ad vitam dicti Cormani	XXIII Anni III	149
1001	351,fo 102v	Elphin	Mattheus[58]	Vicaria parochialis per devolutionem	XXIII Anni III	153
1002	351,fo 173v	Lismore	Edmundus de Geraldinis	Perind(e vale)re super mandato erigendi canonicatum in cathdrali ex vicariis parochialium ad vitam dicti Edmundi de huiusmodi canonicatu providendi	XXIII Anni III	194
1003	351,fo 141v	Emly	Cornelius Macbrien	Dispensatio ad incompatibilia	XXIII Anni III	262
1004[59]	351,fo 85r	Coventry	Richardus Prestolomei	The like	XXIV Anni III	66
1005	351,fo 23v	Killala	Thomas Ohenices	Parochiales per devolutionem	XXIV Anni III	154
1006	351,fo 47r	Kildare	Thaddeus de Calderanis	Cappellania per cessionem	XXIV Anni III	175
1007	351,fo 174r	Lismore	Mauritius [FitzGerald] archiepiscopus Casalen.	Parochialis certo modo	XXIV Anni III	248
1008	352,fo 157v	Lincoln	Edwardus Phelipp	Dispensatio ad incompatibilia	II Anni IV	28
1009	352,fo 103r	York	Christophorus Latoner	The like	II Anni IV	29
1010	352,fo 103r	Same	Jacobus Twistefeld	The like	II Anni IV	30
1011	352,fos 27v, 323v	Bath & Wells	Joannes Oxlei	The like	II Anni IV	42
1012	352,fo 323v	Winchester	Walterus Yeman	The like	II Anni IV	45

Ind.		DIOCESE	PERSON	MATTER	LIBER	FOLIO
1013	352,fos 103r, 158r	*York;* *London*	Joannes Docwre[60]	Unio parochialis Eboracen. alteri Londovien. respective dioc. quamdiu ipse hanc obtinuerit	II Anni IV	338
1014	352,fo 158r	*London*	Raynaldus Brayo	Dispensatio super defectu etatis et ad incompatibile	II Anni IV	339
1015[61]	352,fos 52v, 158r	*Coventry & Lichfield*	Willelmus Honie	Ampliatio dispensationis ad incompatibilia	II Anni IV	344
1016	352,fo 161r	*London*[62]	Robertus Brighe	Indultum pres(en)tandi ad vicariam parochialis pro unica vice tantum	VIII Anni IV	51
1017	352,fo 57v	*Chichester*	Ricchardus Selwoode	Dispensatio ad incompatibilia	VIII Anni IV	114
1018	352,fo 161v	*London*[63]	Robertus Bright	Indultum presentandi ad parochialem pro unica vice tantum	VIII Anni IV	223
1019	352,fo 58r	*Canterbury*	Georgius Polery	Dispensatio ad incompatibilia	VIII Anni IV	303
1020	352,fo 104r	*York*	Christophorus Burgh	*The like*	VIII Anni IV	326
1021	352,fo 265r	*Rochester*	Thomas Hedde	Unio cantorie parochiali ad vitam tantum seu quamdiu hanc obtinuerit	VIII Anni IV	358
1022	352,fo 162r	*London*	Antonius Axlmer	Dispensatio ad incompatibilia	X Anni IV	74
1023	352, fo 279v	*St Andrews*	Nicolaus Crethon	*The like*	X Anni IV	234
1024	352,fo 327r	*Wells*	Joannes Fox	*The like*	X Anni IV	312
1025	352,fo 279v	*St Andrews*	Alexander Colinle	Reservatio fructuum canonicatus	X Anni IV	331
1026	352,fo 279v	*Same*	Willelmus Colinle	Canonicatus per resignationem	X Anni IV	333
1027	352,fo 189r	*Moray Ecclesia*	Jacobus [Hepburn] electus Moranien.	Ecclesia per translationem	XIV Anni IV	72
1028	352,fo 189r	*Same*	*Same*	*Same*[64]	XIV Anni IV	74
1029	352,fo 63r	*Whithorn*	Jacobus [Hepburn] electus Moranien.	Retentio parochialis	XIV Anni IV	75
1030	352,fo 189r	*Moray*	*Same*	Munus	XIV Anni IV	76
1031	352,fo 189r	*Same*	Jacobus Hepbury electus Moranien.	Absolutio	XIV Anni IV	77

Ind.		DIOCESE	PERSON	MATTER	LIBER	FOLIO
1032	352,fo 329r	*Worcester*	Joannes Abynton	Dispensatio ad incompatibilia	XIV Anni IV	170
1033	352,fo 8v	*St Asaph*	Joannes Gitton	*The like*	XIV Anni IV	238
1034[65]	352,fo 282r	*Salisbury*	Thomas Asshewood	*The like*	XIV Anni IV	362
1035[66]	352,fo 63v	*Canterbury*	Joannes Stodard	*The like*	XIV Anni IV	363
1036[67]	352,fo 105v	*Exeter*	Walterus Hillerdson	*The like*	XIV Anni IV	363
1037[68]	352,fo 282r	*Salisbury*	Joannes Noble	*The like*	XIV Anni IV	364
1038[69]	352,fos 63v, 165r	*Coventry & Lichfield*	Rodulphus[70] Oldon	*The like*	XIV Anni IV	366
1039	352,fo 165r	*Lincoln*	Joannes Charnerght	*The like*	XIV Anni IV	366
1040[71]	352,fo 165r	*Same*	Joannes Constable	Unio parochialis decanatui ad eius vitam seu quamdiu hunc obtinuerit	XIV Anni IV	369
1041[72]	352,fo 105v	*York*	Gamaliel Clifton	Unio parochialis canonicatui ad eius vitam tantum seu quamdiu hunc obtinuerit	XIV Anni IV	370
1042	352,fo 211r	*Nullius*	Robertus Cambrigge	Dispensatio ad incompatibilia	XIV Anni IV	378
1043	352,fo 165r	*Lincoln*	Richardus Roston	*The like*	XIV Anni IV	381
1044	352,fo 63v	*Chichester*	Thomas Combe	*The like*	XIV Anni IV	382
1045	352,fo 282r	*Salisbury*	Richardus Belton	*The like*	XIV Anni IV	382
1046	352,fo 282r	*Same*	Nicolaus Punffolde	*The like*	XV Anni IV	58
1047	352,fo 165r	*Lincoln*	Joannes Burgos	*The like*	XV Anni IV	59
1048	352,fo 165r	*Same*	Benedictus Dabis	*The like*	XV Anni IV	60
1049	352,fo 189r	*St David's*	Joannes Limtoloy	*The like*	XV Anni IV	62
1050	352,fo 211v	*Norwich*	Robertus Nolison	*The like*	XV Anni IV	117
1051	352,fos 33r, 329v	*Bath & Wells*	Thomas Treman[73]	*The like*	XV Anni IV	118

Ind.		DIOCESE	PERSON	MATTER	LIBER	FOLIO
1052	352,fos 33r, *Same* 329v		Simon Seward	*The like*	XV Anni IV	121
1053	352,fo 9r	*Ardfert*	Mauritius Ocantuor	Vicarie parochialium certo modo	XV Anni IV	137
1054	352,fo 165r	*Lincoln*	Simon Astley	Dispensatio ad incompatibilia	XV Anni IV	145
1055	352,fo 266v	*Ross*	Willelmus Tudes	Nova provisio canonicatus	XV Anni IV	167
1056	352,fo 64r	*Carlisle*	Jacobus Chaubot	Dispensatio ad incompatibilia	XV Anni IV	191
1057	352,fos 105v, *Ely*; 329v	*Winchester*	Thomas Ifnyrlton[74]	*The like*	XV Anni IV	193
1058	352,fo 64r	*Chichester*	Willelmus Lee	Unio parochialis sacristie ad eius vitam tantum seu quamdiu hanc obtinuerit	XV Anni IV	348
1059	352,fo 105v	*Exeter*	Thomas Gollcorne	Dispensatio ad incompatibilia	XV Anni IV	351
1060	352,fo 64v	*Canterbury*	Thomas Wellis	Unio parochialis alteri ad eius vitam tantum seu quamdiu hanc obtinuerit	XVI Anni IV	92
1061	352,fo 64v	*Same*	Richardus Master	Dispensatio ad incompatibilia	XVI Anni IV	94
1062	352,fos 33v, *Bath* 330r	*& Wells*	Abbas et conventus monasterii Glasten'[75] Ordinis S(ancti) Benedicti Bathonien. et Wellen.	Commissio vigore appellationis	XVI Anni IV	132
1063	352,fo 106r	*York*	Thomas Hale	Dispensatio ad incompatibilia	XVI Anni IV	205
1064	352,fo 225v	*Clogher*[76]	Adam Magenhin	Vicaria parochialis certo modo	XVI Anni IV	312
1065	352,fo 106r	*Exeter*	Robertus Body	Dispensatio ad incompatibilia	XVI Anni IV	313
1066[77]	352,fo 106r	*Elphin*	Donatus Ocellay	Prioratus regularis certo modo	XVI Anni IV	364
1067	352,fo 166r	*Lincoln*	[——][78]	Indulgentia pro elargientibus eleemosynas pro edificatione cuiusdam cappelle	XVII Anni IV	4
1068	352,fo 166r	*Same*	Joannes Brysbone	Dispensatio ad incompatibilia	XVII Anni IV	252
1069	352,fo 212r	*Norwich*	Richardus Shelton	*The like*	XVII Anni IV	274

Ind.	DIOCESE	PERSON	MATTER	LIBER	FOLIO
1070 352,fo 166r	*Lincoln*	Joannes Berobrowne	*The like*	XVII Anni IV	276
1071 352,fo 212r	*Norwich*	Rogerus Darlei	*The like*	XVII Anni IV	285
1072 352,fo 106r	*Exeter*	Laurentius Tranesle	*The like*	XVII Anni IV	287
1073 352,fo 106r	*Same*	Bernardus (?)Trauesse	*The like*	XVII Anni IV	288
1074 352,fo 106r	*Same*	Adam (?)Trauesse	*The like*	XVII Anni IV	289
1075 352,fos 34v, 330v	*Bath & Wells*	Rogerus Sandow	*The like*	XVII Anni IV	291
1076 352,fo 65v	*Clogher*	Donaldus Ohaurachtayd	Nova provisio parochialis	XVII Anni IV	333
1077 352,fo 212r	*Norwich*	Leonardus Cotton	Unio parochialis alteri ad eius vitam tantum seu quamdiu hanc obtinuerit	XVII Anni IV	350
1078 352,fo 66r	*Cashel*	Jacobus Cantuel	Unio precentorie canonicatui ad eius vitam tantum seu quamdiu hunc obtinuerit	XVIII Anni IV	1
1079 352,fo 66r	*Same*	Malachia Ymechair	Erectio quarumdam parochialium in simplicem prebendam pro eodem ad eius vitam tantum seu quamdiu hanc obtinuerit	XVIII Anni IV	6
1080 352,fo 66r	*Same*	Philippus Crai	Unio parochialis canonicatui ad eius vitam tantum seu quamdiu hunc obtinuerit	XVIII Anni IV	9
1081 352,fo 226r	*Ossory*	Robinotus Purrell	Erectio vicarie in simplicem prebendam ad eius vitam tantum seu quamdiu hanc obtinuerit	XVIII Anni IV	18
1082 352,fo 226r	*Same*	Anastasia Contuevvoll	Monasterium monialium certo modo	XVIII Anni IV	21
1083[79] 352,fo 10v	*Ardfert*	Nicolaus Oburan	Parochiales unite certo modo	XVIII Anni IV	32
1084 352,fo 66r	*Clogher*	Magonius Ohaurachtaye	Canonicatus certo modo	XVIII Anni IV	62
1085 352,fo 212v	*Norwich*	Willelmus Eglyn	Dispensatio ad incompatibilia	XVIII Anni IV	282

Ind.		DIOCESE	PERSON	MATTER	LIBER	FOLIO
1086	352,fo 167r	*Killaloe*	Philippus Ohaly	Perinde (vale)re super parochiali	XVIII Anni IV	363
1087	352,fo 283v	*St Andrews*	Jacobus Johinston	Commissio vigore appellationis	XIX Anni IV	106
1088	352,fo 12v	*Aberdeen*	Archibaldus Luydesay	Reservatio fructuum cantorie	XXII Anni IV	102
1089	352,fo 12v	*Same*	David Disthurwtbue	Cantoria per resignationem	XXII Anni IV	104
1090	352,fo 168v	*Lichfield*	Joannes Pemanr	Dispensatio ad incompatibilia	XXII Anni IV	126
1091	352,fo 284v	*St Andrews*	Georgeus Hepburne	*The like*	XXII Anni IV	142
1092	352,fo 284v	*Same*	Adam Hepburne	*The like*	XXII Anni IV	143
1093[80]	352,fo 106v	*Elphin*	Thomas Obeathathane	Prioratus ruralis[81] certo modo	XXII Anni IV	213
1094	352,fo 213r	*Norwich*	Joannes Mayr	Commissio vigore appellationis	XXII Anni IV	343
1095	352,fo 285r	*Salisbury*	Robertus Ridlei	Dispensatio ad incompatibilia	XXIII Anni IV	137
1096	352,fo 69v	*Carlisle*	Joannes Robruxone	*The like*	XXIII Anni IV	139
1097	352,fos 37r, 333r	*Bath & Wells*	Robertus Toker	*The like*	XXIII Anni IV	322
1098	352,fo 169r	*London*	Catharina Gronhuist	Commissio vigore appellationis	XXIII Anni IV	357
1099	352,fo 333v	*Winchester*	Willelmus Crosse	Dispensatio ad incompatibilia	XXIV Anni IV	78
1100	352,fo 169r	*London*	Henricus Croste	*The like*	XXIV Anni IV	91
1101	352,fo 70v	*Chichester*	Thomas Spire	*The like*	XXIV Anni IV	100
1102	352,fo 70v	*Same*	Hugo Bolfe	*The like*	XXIV Anni IV	101
1103	352,fo 194r	*Moray*	Galbinus Dumbard Junior	Decanatus per resignationem	XXV Anni IV	183
1104	352,fo 194r	*Same*	Galbinus Dumbard Senior	Reservatio fructuum decanatus	XXV Anni IV	185

Ind.		DIOCESE	PERSON	MATTER	LIBER	FOLIO
1105	352,fo 72r	*Coventry*	Willelmus Palden	Dispensatio ad incompatibilia	I Anni V	207
1106	352,fo 73r	*Whithorn*	Joannes Mekeraken	*The like*	II Anni V	137
1107	352,fo 170v	*Lincoln*	Joannes Cortese	*The like*	II Anni V	319
1108	352,fo 128r	*Glasgow*	Parochialis ecclesia Sancti Michaelis de Machlyn Glasgnen. dioc.	Indulgentia pro visitantibus eamdem parochialem ecclesiam. Ad perpetuam	IV Anni V	78
1109	352,fo 107v	*York*	Thomas Maymomid	Dispensatio ad incompatibilia	IV Anni V	172
1110	352,fo 107v	*Same*	Egidius Paman	*The like*	IV Anni V	223
1111	352,fos 17r, 100v	*Armagh; Kildare*	Jacobus Megunsonano[82]	Erectio parochialium in simplicem prebendam ad vitam ipsius[83]	VIII Anni V	20
1112	352,fo 17v	*Armagh*	Donatus Ohard	*The like*	VIII Anni V	160
1113	352,fo 17v	*Same*	Malachias Ohard	Erectio vicarie parochialis in simplicem prebendam ad vitam ipsius	VIII Anni V	163
1114	352,fos 17v, 100v	*Armagh; Kildare*	Bernardus Magunsenam[84]	Erectio vicarie in simplicem prebendam ad vitam ipsius[85]	VIII Anni V	166
1115	352,fo 128v	*Glasgow*	Joannes Turnrug	Pensio super parrochiali	VIII Anni V	181
1116	352,fo 313r	*Tuam*	Joannes Ohalluran'	Erectio vicariarum in simplicem prebendam ad vitam dicti Joannis	VIII Anni V	213
1117[86]	352,fo 313r	*Same*	Donaldus Oflart	Unio parochialium decanatui per dictum Donaldum ad eius vitam tantum	VIII Anni V	217
1118	352,fo 17v	*Killala*	Vinleelmus Dondonaill	Vicarie paro[chi]alium et prebenda certo modo	VIII Anni V	230
1119	352,fo 17v	*Same*	Willelmus Obruchayn	Erectio simplicium in simplicem prebendam ad eius vitam tantum	VIII Anni V	349

Ind.		DIOCESE	PERSON	MATTER	LIBER	FOLIO
1120	352,fo 18v	*Armagh*	Touiletus Y Dongale	Erectio vicarie in[87] parochialium in simplicem prebendam ad vitam ipsius	XI Anni V	49
1121[88]	352,fo 81r	*Cashel*	Donatus Yhora	Erectio parochialium in simplicem prebendam ad vitam ipsius	XI Anni V	53
1122	352,fo 81r	*Clogher*	Eugenius Magunsenan	Erectio parochialium in simplicem prebendam ad vitam ipsius	XI Anni V	65
1123[89]	352,fo 174r	*Killaloe*	Roricus Oglosayn	Decanatus et parochiales certo modo	XI Anni V	69
1124	352,fo 199r	*Meath*	Roricus Y Sachuyr	Unio prioratus monasterii alteri ad eius vitam tantum seu quamdiu hunc obtinuerit	XI Anni V	97
1125	352,fo 338r	*Worcester*	Richardus Solde	Dispensatio ad incompatibilia	XI Anni V	193
1126	352,fo 338r	*Same*	Nicolaus (?)Huband	*The like*	XI Anni V	259
1127	352,fo 81v	*Clogher*	Mauritius Macdonaill	Erectio vicarie in simplicem prebendam ad eius vitam tantum	XI Anni V	293
1128	352,fo 338r	*Winchester*	Joannes Hungete	Dispensatio ad incompatibilia	XII Anni V	213
1129	352,fo 174v	*Lincoln*	Nicolaus Euerardi	*The like*	XII Anni V	214
1130	352,fos 43v, 338r	*Bath & Wells*	Willermus Gilber	*The like*	XII Anni V	297
1131	352,fo 290v	*Salisbury*	Joannes Bromwiche	Unio parochialis alteri ad eius vitam tantum seu quamdiu hanc obtinuerit	XIV Anni V	37
1132	352,fos 44r, 339r	*Bath & Wells*	Robertus Garlont[90]	Dispensatio ad incompatibilia	XIV Anni V	98
1133	352,fo 217v	*Norwich*	Hugo Walker	Unio parochialis vicarie ad eius vitam tantum seu quamdiu hanc obtinuerit	XIV Anni V	100
1134	352,fo 109r	*Exeter*	Henricus Iferman	Unio parochialis alteri ad eius vitam tantum seu quamdiu hanc obtinuerit	XIV Anni V	101
1135	352,fo 175v	*London*	Laurentius Leycestre	Dispensatio ad incompatibilia	XIV Anni V	121

Ind.		DIOCESE	PERSON	MATTER	LIBER	FOLIO
1136	352,fo 175v	*Lincoln*	Joannes Well	*The like*	XIV Anni V	121
1137	352,fo 109r	*York*	Georgeus Wyndhm	*The like*	XIV Anni V	122
1138	352,fo 109r	*Ely*	Henricus Iforthe	*The like*	XIV Anni V	123
1139	352,fo 175v	Llandaff	Joannes Ap Jeban	*The like*	XIV Anni V	126
1140	352,fo 109r	*Exeter*	Joannes Esse alias Asthe	Unio parochialis alteri ad eius vitam tantum seu quamdiu hanc obtinuerit	XIV Anni V	128
1141	352,fo 175v	*Lincoln*	Thomas Maguins	*The like*	XIV Anni V	130
1142	352,fo 175v	*Same*	Joannes Groyne	Dispensatio ad incompatibilia	XIV Anni V	132
1143	352,fo 175v	*London*	Joannes Smithe	Unio vicarie canonicatui ad eius vitam tantum seu quamdiu hunc obtinuerit	XIV Anni V	134
1144	352,fos 83r, 175v	*Coventry & Lichfield*	Richardus Mynshull[91]	Dispensatio ad incompatibilia	XIV Anni V	136
1145	352,fo 339r	*Worcester*	Joannes Quare	*The like*	XIV Anni V	137
1146	352,fo 339r	*Winchester*	Willelmus Ryllych	*The like*	XIV Anni V	138
1147	352,fo 83r	*Canterbury*	Nicolaus Wotton	*The like*	XIV Anni V	139
1148	352,fo 101r	*Dublin*	Edwardus Dyllon	*The like*	XIV Anni V	144
1149	352,fo 109r	*Ely*	Willelmus Masse	*The like*	XIV Anni V	197
1150	352,fos 83v, 175v	*Coventry & Lichfield*	Edwardus Melyneux[92]	*The like*	XIV Anni V	237
1151	352,fo 176r	*Lincoln*	Edwardus Welshe	*The like*	XIV Anni V	263
1152	352,fo 176r	*London*	Willelmus Pace	Unio vicarie parochiali ad eius vitam tantum seu quamdiu hanc obtinuerit	XIV Anni V	312
1153	352,fo 217v	*Norwich*	Robertus Carter	Dispensatio ad incompatibilia	XIV Anni V	313
1154	352,fo 176r	*Lincoln*	Thomas Norley	*The like*	XIV Anni V	315
1155	352,fo 176r	*Same*	Joannes Lambe	*The like*	XIV Anni V	316

Ind.	DIOCESE	PERSON	MATTER	LIBER	FOLIO
1156	352,fo 176r *Lincoln*	Joannes Willynghen	*The like*	XIV Anni V	333
1157	352,fo 200v *St David's*	Ludovicus Guffith	Unio parochialis alteri ad eius vitam tantum seu quamdiu hanc obtinuerit	XV Anni V	3
1158	352,fo 109r *York*	Joannes Wodalh	Dispensatio ad incompatibilia	XV Anni V	4
1159	352,fo 176r (*?*)*London*[93]	Radulphus Tynlei	*The like*	XV Anni V	6
1160	352,fo 291r Salisbury	Thomas Hopar	*The like*	XV Anni V	8
1161	352,fo 176v (*?*)*London*[94]	Christophorus Seynteler	*The like*	XV Anni V	48
1162	352,fo 339v *Worcester*	Joannes More	*The like*	XV Anni V	59
1163	352,fos 44v, 339v	*Bath & Wells* Joannes Moxne[95]	Unio parochialis canonicatui ad eius vitam tantum seu quamdiu hunc obtinuerit	XV Anni V	61
1164	352,fo 109r *York*	Rombertus Wemberfley	Unio vicarie parochialis parochiali ad eius vitam tantum seu quamdiu hanc obtinuerit	XV Anni V	62
1165	352,fo 218r *Norwich*	Joannes Ryse	Dispensatio ad incompatibilia	XV Anni V	69
1166	352,fos 44v, 339v	*Bath & Wells* Willelmus Rawllins[96]	*The like*	XV Anni V	70
1167	352,fo 176v *Lincoln*	Rogerius Bulle	*The like*	XV Anni V	97
1168	352,fo 218r *Nullius*[97]	Joannes Clerk	Unio parochalis alteri ad eius vitam tantum seu quamdiu hanc obtinuerit	XV Anni V	140
1169	352,fos 44v, 340r	*Bath & Wells* Joannes Backer[98]	Dispensatio ad incompatibilia	XV Anni V	207
1170	352,fo 272r *Rochester*	Jacobus Hubys	Unio parochialis alteri ad eius vitam tantum seu quamdiu hanc obtinuerit	XV Anni V	212
1171	352,fo 109v *York*	Willelmus Faire	*The like*	XV Anni V	214
1172	352,fo 84r *Canterbury*	Joannes Viwove	Dispensatio ad incompatibilia	XV Anni V	259
1173	352,fo 291r *Salisbury*	Richardus Norcott	*The like*	XV Anni V	261

Ind.		DIOCESE	PERSON	MATTER	LIBER	FOLIO
1174	352,fos 84r, 177r	Coventry & Lichfield	Richardus Stakylei[99]	The like	XV Anni V	361
1175[100]	352,fo 20v	Ardfert	Mauritius Stack	Decanatus certo modo	XV Anni V	402
1176	352,fo 218r	Norwich	Willelmus Clerk	Unio parochialis alteri ad eius vitam tantum seu quamdiu hanc obtinuerit	XVI Anni V	28
1177	352,fo 177r	Lincoln	Thomas Peert	Unio parochialis alteri ad eius vitam tantum seu quamdiu hanc obtinuerit	XVI Anni V	30
1178	352,fos 291v, 340r	Salisbury; Winchester	Bernardus Olyden[101]	Unio parochialium canonicatui ad eius vitam tantum seu quamdiu hunc obtinuerit	XVI Anni V	47
1179	352,fos 45r, 340r	Bath & Wells	Joannes Waleys	Dispensatio ad incompatibilia	XVI Anni V	57
1180	352,fo 177r	Lincoln	Thomas Besten	The like	XVI Anni V	58
1181	352,fo 177r	London	Willelmus Capo	Unio parochialis alteri ad eius vitam tantum seu quamdiu hanc obtinuerit	XVI Anni V	59
1182	352,fo 218r	Norwich	Thomas Wotton	The like	XVI Anni V	62
1183	352,fo 177r	Lincoln	Robertus Nenton	Dispensatio ad incompatibilia	XVI Anni V	108
1184	352,fo 177r	Same	Eduardus Elson alias Baker	The like	XVI Anni V	118
1185	352,fo 84v	Canterbury	Willelmus Wygtham	The like	XVI Anni V	119
1186	352,fo 109v	York	Robertus Nobel	Dispensatio ad incompatibilia	XVI Anni V	134
1187	352,fo 109v	Ely	Richardus Baynton	The like	XVI Anni V	135
1188	352,fo 177r	Lincoln	Thomas Hawe	The like	XVI Anni V	137
1189	352,fo 84v	Canterbury	Thomas Dodyng	The like	XVI Anni V	138
1190	352,fo 109v	York	Joannes Wodhall	Unio parochialis alteri ad eius vitam tantum seu quamdiu hanc obtinuerit	XVI Anni V	139
1191	352,fo 177r	London	Henricus Hirman	The like	XVI Anni V	141
1192	352,fo 109v	York	Thomas Batterfeld	Dispensatio ad incompatibilia	XVI Anni V	278

Ind.	DIOCESE	PERSON	MATTER	LIBER	FOLIO
1193 352,fo 340v	*Worcester*	Willelmus Brewet	Unio cantorie parochiali ad eius vitam tantum seu quamdiu hanc obtinuerit	XVI Anni V	278
1194 352,fo 201r	*St David's*	Willelmus Here alias Morgan	Dispensatio ad incompatibilia	XVI Anni V	308
1195 352,fos 109v, 317r	*Elphin Tuam*	Nicolaus Ylanuagay	Erectio vicarie in simplicem prebendam ad vitam ipsius[102]	XVII Anni V	41
1196[103] 352,fo 272v	*Ross*	Oddo Yedersceoyll	Unio archidiaconatus vicarie et rectorie parochialis canonicatui ad eius vitam tantum seu quamdiu hunc obtinuerit	XVII Anni V	44
1197 352,fo 46v	*Bangor*	Mauritius Glyn	Unio parochialium canonicatui ad eius vitam tantum seu quamdiu hunc obtinuerit	XIX Anni V	48
1198 352,fo 110r	*York*	Lausflorus Claxton	Unio parochialis decanatui ad eius vitam tantum seu quamdiu hunc obtinuerit	XIX Anni V	57
1199 352,fo 341v	*Winchester*	Ricardus Awsell	Dispensatio ad incompatibilia	XIX Anni V	98
1200 352,fo 341v	*Worcester*	Thomas Tfumckyen	*The like*	XIX Anni V	99
1201 352,fo 178v	*London*	Henricus David	*The like*	XIX Anni V	130
1202 352,fo 110r	*Exeter*	Halnotheus Arstote	*The like*	XIX Anni V	131
1203 352,fo 178v	*London*	Christophorus Seynteler	*The like*	XIX Anni V	133
1204 352,fo 341v	*Worcester*	Joannes Sabage	*The like*	XIX Anni V	134
1205 352,fo 110r	*Exeter*	Oliverius Wiso	*The like*	XIX Anni V	135
1206 352,fo 341v	*Winchester*	Radulphus Barnache	*The like*	XIX Anni V	137
1207 352,fo 137v	*Hereford*	Rogerius Broyn	Unio parochialis canonicatui ad eius vitam tantum seu quamdiu hunc obtinuerit	XIX Anni V	138

Ind.		DIOCESE	PERSON	MATTER	LIBER	FOLIO
1208	352,fo 178v	*Lincoln*	Nicolaus Bothe	Commissio vigore appellationis	XIX Anni V	140
1209	352,fos 87v, 178v	*Coventry & Lichfield*	Edemundus Eyre	Dispensatio ad incompatibilia	XIX Anni V	165
1210	352,fo 341v	*Worcester*	Richardus Ruig	Dispensatio ad incompatibilia	XIX Anni V	174
1211	352,fos 87v, 178v	*Coventry & Lichfield*	Robertus Whitinton	*The like*	XIX Anni V	175
1212	352,fos 178v	*London*	Thomas Womberosley	*The like*	XIX Anni V	176
1213	352,fos 46v, 341v	*Bath & Wells*	Joannes Bonell	*The like*	XIX Anni V	177
1214	352,fos 46v, 341v	*Same*	Thomas Beuett	*The like*	XIX Anni V	184
1215	352,fo 110r	*Exeter*	Richardus Bowdun	*The like*	XIX Anni V	185
1216	352,fo 341v	*Winchester*	Willelmus Ripon alias Newhoso	*The like*	XIX Anni V	215
1217	352,fo 341v	*Same*	Ricardus Hutton	*The like*	XIX Anni V	231
1218	352,fo 341v	*Same*	Riccardus Moyrett alias Hamyton	*The like*	XIX Anni V	233
1219	352,fo 179r	*Lincoln*	Joannes Haloyes	*The like*	XIX Anni V	240
1220	352,fo 292v	*Salisbury*	Willelmus Wedehoke	*The like*	XIX Anni V	240
1221	352,fo 292v	*Same*	Thomas Holcuube	*The like*	XIX Anni V	256
1222	352,fo 110r	*York*	Willelmus Cunstable	*The like*	XIX Anni V	257
1223	352,fo 101v	*Durham*	Hugo Assheton	Unio parochialis canonicatui ad eius vitam tantum seu quamdiu hunc obtinuerit	XIX Anni V	258
1224	352,fo 179r	*Lincoln*	Thomas Meres	Dispensatio ad incompatibilia	XIX Anni V	260
1225	352,fo 110r	*York*	Willelmus Stayley	*The like*	XIX Anni V	263

Ind.		DIOCESE	PERSON	MATTER	LIBER	FOLIO
1226[104]	352,fos 22r, 273r	*Ardfert;* *Ross*	Donaldus Yhyngardayll	Unio vicariarum parochialium parochiali ad eius vitam tantum seu quamdiu hanc obtinuerit	XIX Anni V	382
1227[105]	352,fo 294r	*St Andrews*	Jacobus [Betoun] archiepiscopus Glasgnen.	Monasterium per cessionem	XXII Anni V	200
1228	352,fo 294r	*Same*	*Same*	Absolutio	XXII Anni V	204
1229	352,fo 294r	*Same*	*[Same]*	Commissio	XXII Anni V	204
1230	352,fo 110v	*Elphin*	Edmundus Oflanuagam	Vicaria certo modo	XXII Anni V	219
1231	352,fo 110v	*Same*	Malachias Oflanuagam	Prebenda certo modo	XXII Anni V	222
1232	352,fo 111r	*Exeter*	Robertus Chalvet	Dispensatio ad incompatibilia	XXIII Anni V	7
1233	352,fo 111r	*Ely*	Alexander Barelay	*The like*	XXIII Anni V	55
1234	352,fos 91v, 180v	*Coventry* *& Lichfield*	Willelmus Smyths[106] et Maria Herres	Dispensatio matrimonialis	XXIII Anni V	177
1235	352,fo 180v	*Lincoln*	Thomas Newton	Dispensatio ad incompatibilia	XXIII Anni V	178
1236[107]	352,fo 181r	*Llandaff*	Egidius Sonnet	Canonicatus per resignationem	XXIV Anni V	6
1237	352,fo 48v	*Bangor*	Joannes Aybell	Dispensatio ad incompatibilia	XXIV Anni V	74
1238	352,fo 343v	*Winchester*	Willelmus Bartholomei	*The like*	XXIV Anni V	76
1239[108]	352,fo 181r	*Llandaff*	Jacobus Chahone	Canonicatus per resignationem	XXIV Anni V	229
1240	352,fo 181r	*London*	Prior et conventus prioratus Sanctissime Trinitatis Londoven. Sancti Augustini seu alterius ordinis et Elisabeth Ghiffordi	Commissio vigore appellationis	XXIV Anni V	255
1241	352,fo 230v	*Ossory*	Dernutius Magilladrin	Erectio vicariarum in canonicatum et simplicem prebendam ad eius vitam tantum	XXIV Anni V	291

Ind.		DIOCESE	PERSON	MATTER	LIBER	FOLIO
1242	352,fo 230v	*Same*	Joannes Yduygyn	Erectio parochialium in simplicem prebendam ad eius vitam tantum	XXIV Anni V	293
1243	353,fo 121r	*Hereford*	Rogerius Bempti	Unio vicarie parochialis canonicatui ad vitam dicti Rogerii aut quamdiu dictum canonicatum obtinuerit. Ad futuram	I Anni VI	346
1244	353,fo 241r	*St Andrews*	Damianus Wenys	Commissio vigore appellationis	VI Anni VI	59
1245[109]	353,fo 140r	*London*	Elisabetha Bentori[110]	Indulgentia pro ecclesia Ordinis Fratrum Predicatorum et in altare Sancti Thome de Aquino	VI Anni VI	134
1246	353,fo 140r	*Lincoln*	Robertus Wrygkt	Dispensatio ad incompatibilia	VI Anni VI	161
1247	353,fo 140v	*London*	Thomas Neruuan	*The like*	VI Anni VI	165
1248	353,fo 140v	*Lincoln*	Stephanus Harondi	*The like*	VI Anni VI	169
1249	353,fo 140v	*Same*	Robertus Brulbera	*The like*	VI Anni VI	171
1250	353,fo 284r	*Worcester*	Edmundus Gledhyll	*The like*	VI Anni VI	172
1251	353,fo 140v	*London*	Jacobus Hall	*The like*	VI Anni VI	174
1252	353,fo 140v	*Lincoln*	Richardus Gardesall	*The like*	VI Anni VI	185
1253	353,fo 96r	*Same*	Robertus Westan	*The like*	VI Anni VI	186
1254	353,fo 230r	*Rochester*	Thomas Bable	*The like*	VI Anni VI	188
1255	353,fo 53r	*Canterbury*	Rolandus Philippus	Unio vicarie ecclesie parochiali ad vitam dicti Rolandi aut quamdiu dictam parochialem obtinuerit. Ad futuram	VI Anni VI	189
1256	353,fo 140v	*Lincoln*	Joannes Grittoni	Commissio vigore appellationis	VI Anni VI	201
1257	353,fo 184r	*Norwich*	Joannes Syngaykin	Dispensatio ad incompatibilia	VI Anni VI	287
1258	353,fo 140v	*Lincoln*	Joannes Beyman	*The like*	VI Anni VI	316

Ind.		DIOCESE	PERSON	MATTER	LIBER	FOLIO
1259	353,fo 140v	*Same*	Ricardus Porker	*The like*	VI Anni VI	318
1260	353,fo 53v	*Canterbury*	Edwardus Hyggonis	Unio parochialis alteri ad vitam dicti Edwardi aut quamdiu primam obtinuerit. Ad futuram	VI Anni VI	332
1261	353,fo 140v	*Lichfield*	Willelmus Atkinsei	Unio parochialis alteri ad vitam dicti Willelmi aut quamdiu primam obtinuerit. Ad futuram	VI Anni VI	333
1262	353,fo 284r	*Worcester*	Edmundus Gyfford	Unio vicarie parochiali ad vitam dicti Edmundi aut quamdiu dictam parochialem obtinuerit. Ad futuram	VI Anni VI	335
1263	353,fo 241v	*Salisbury*	Georgius Sydenhans[111]	Unio parochialis canonicatui ad vitam dicti Georgii aut quamdiu dictum canonicatum obtinuerit	VI Anni VI	336
1264	353,fo 284r	*Worcester*	Thomas Stockke	Dispensatio ad incompatibilia	VI Anni VI	355
1265	353,fo 164r	*St David's*	Joannes Vaghany	Indultum deputandi alios pro visitatione ecclesiarum et locorum sub iurisdictione archidiaconi existentium	VI Anni VI	370
1266	353,fo 147r	*Killaloe*	Cornelius Gennyr	Vicaria parochialis certo modo	XVII Anni VI	21
1267	353,fo 147r	*Same*	Theodricus Obrica	Canonicatus et vicarie certo modo	XVII Anni VI	24
1268	353,fo 232v	*Ross*	Philippus Hynaifrayn	Rectoria et vicaria certo modo	XVII Anni VI	25
1269	353,fo 147r	*Killaloe*[112]	Guillelmus et Michaelles Autrectz	Commissio vigore appellationis	XVII Anni VI	45
1270	353,fo 266r	*Tuam*	Ristardus de Burgo	Unio vicarie et semivicarie canonicatui per dictum Ristardum obtento ad eius vitam tantum	XVII Anni VI	46

Ind.		DIOCESE	PERSON	MATTER	LIBER	FOLIO
1271	353,fo 308r	Zamora	Rector et scholares collegii pauperum clericorum scholasticorum Sancti Thome archiepiscopi Cantuerien. in civitate Salamantin. instituti	Unio parochialis eidem collegio. Ad perpetuam	XVII Anni VI	80
1272	353,fo 232v	Ross	Willialmus Horga	Cancellaria et vicaria certo modo	XVII Anni VI (?)	113
1273	353,fo 10r	Ardfert	Donatus Occuncuyr	Erectio vicarie in simplicem prebendam ad eius vitam tantum	XVII Anni VI	156
1274	353,fo 170v	Moray	Willelmus Gaderar	Commissio vigore appellationis	XVII Anni VI	206
1275	353,fo 97v	Exeter	Robertus prior prioratus Sancti Germani Ordinis Sancti Augustini Exovien. diocesis	Dispensatio ad incompatibilia	XVII Anni VI	223
1276	353,fo 11r	Armagh	Thomas Oquelluye	Canonicatus certo modo	XVII Anni VI	266
1277	353,fo 232v	Ross	Donaldus Odonylbayn	Unio parochialium decanatui per dictum Donaldum obtento ad eius vitam tantum seu quamdiu hunc obtinuerit	XVII Anni VI	275
1278	353,fo 65v	Cashel	Philippus Purcell	Vicarie parochialium certo modo	XVII Anni VI	279
1279	353,fo 247v	St Andrews	Andreas [Forman] archiepiscopus Sancti Andree	Indultum regrediendi ad prioratum regularem	XXI Anni VI	126
1280	353,fo 68v	Chichester	Joannes [Young] episcopus Calipolen.	Unio canonicatus mense episcopali Calipolen. ad eius vitam tantum seu quandiu ipse Joannes episcopus prefate ecclesie prefueris. Ad futuram	XXI Anni VI	200
1281	353,fo 149v	Lincoln	Richardus Waweu alias Lache	Commissio vigore appellationis	XXIII Anni VI	50

Ind.		DIOCESE	PERSON	MATTER	LIBER	FOLIO
1282	350,fo 98v	*Exeter*	Joannes Pollard	Dispensatio ad incompatibilia	XXIII Anni VI	290
1283	353,fo 172v	*St David's*	Richardus Clemens	*The like*	XXIII Anni VI	291
1284	353,fos 35v, 292v	*Bath & Wells*	Willemus Vycary	*The like*	XXIII Anni VI	350
1285	353,fo 149v	*Lincoln*	Willelmus White	*The like*	XXIII Anni VI	350
1286	353,fo 98v	*York*	Villelmus Cowper	*The like*	XXIV Anni VI	27
1287	353,fo 149v	*Lincoln*	Richardus Walman	*The like*	XXIV Anni VI	47
1288	353,fo 149v	*Lichfield*	Georgius Traffard	Commissio vigore appellationis	XXIV Anni VI	62
1289	353,fo 292v	*Winchester*	Richardus Awussell	Dispensatio ad incompatibilia	XXIV Anni VI	70
1290	353,fo 293r	*Worcester*	Prior et conventus prioratus Beate Virginis Marie de Lanthomo iuxta Glowensettam Ordinis Sancti Augustini canonicorum regularium Wigorimen. diocesis	Commissio vigore appellationis	XXIV Anni VI	134
1291	353,fo 149v	*Lincoln*	Michael Browae	Dispensatio ad incompatibilia	XXIV Anni VI	213
1292	353,fo 98v	*Exeter*	Joannes Esse alias Affssh	*The like*	XXIV Anni VI	300
1293	353,fo 98v	*Same*	Willemus Bowrat	Unio parochialis canonicatui per dictum Willelmum obtento ad eius vitam tantum seu quamdiu hunc obtinuerit	XXIV Anni VI	302
1294	353,fo 149v	*Lincoln*	Willelmus Hunterodd	Unio parochialis alteri per dictum Willelmum obtente ad eius vitam tantum seu quamdiu hanc obtinuerit	XXIV Anni VI	303
1295	353,fo 293v	*Winchester*	Joannes Palines	Dispensatio ad incompatibilia	I Anni VII	65

Ind.		DIOCESE	PERSON	MATTER	LIBER	FOLIO
1296	353,fo 99r	*Exeter*	Joannes Greneway	Indulgentia pro elargientibus eleemosinas cuidam parochiali ecclesie	I Anni VII	122
1297	353,fo 249v	*Salisbury*	Thomas Whitewode	Dispensatio ad incompatibilia	I Anni VII	240
1298	353,fo 249v	*Same*	Joannes Grolleau	*The like*	I Anni VII	241
1299	353,fo 190r	*Norwich*	Robertus Webstar	*The like*	I Anni VII	296
1300	353,fo 99r	*Exeter*	Joannes Corke	*The like*	I Anni VII	297
1301	353,fo 150v	*Lichfield*	Thomas Radelyffez	Commissio vigore appellationis	I Anni VII	323
1302	353,fo 71v	*Canterbury*	Mermeducus Walby	Dispensatio ad incompatibilia	I Anni VII	332
1303	353,fo 150v	*Lincoln*	Willelmus Wade	*The like*	II Anni VII	34
1304	353,fo 150v	*Same*	Joannes Scott	*The like*	II Anni VII	35
1305	353,fo 99r	*York*	Jacobus Lewyus	*The like*	II Anni VII	36
1306	353,fo 190r	*Norwich*	Nicolaus Hauson	*The like*	II Anni VII	37
1307	353,fo 190r	*Same*	Robertus Treswell	The like	II Anni VII	38
1308	353,fo 190r	*Same*	Ricardus Roberd	Unio parochialis vicarie per dictum Ricardum obtente ad eius vitam tantum seu quamdiu hanc obtinuerit	II Anni VII	39
1309	353,fo 190r	*Same*	Thomas Reyny	Unio parochialis alteri per dictum Thomam obtente ad eius vitam tantum seu quamdiu hanc obtinuerit	II Anni VII	40
1310	353,fos 72r, 150v	*Coventry & Lichfield*	Joannes Halle	Dispensatio ad incompatibilia	II Anni VII	104
1311	353,fo 72r	*Chichester*	Thomas Schelley	*The like*	II Anni VII	207
1312	353,fo 99r	*York*	Henricus Lautor	*The like*	II Anni VII	208
1313	353,fo 190r	*Norwich*	Willelmus Loweak	*The like*	II Anni VII	260

Ind.		DIOCESE	PERSON	MATTER	LIBER	FOLIO
1314	353,fo 190r	*Same*	Willelmus de Ordemer	Unio parochialis alteri per dictum Willelmum obtente ad eius vitam tantum seu quamdiu hanc obtinuerit	II Anni VII	351
1315	353,fos 37v, 295r	*Bath & Wells*	Joannes de Well	Unio parochialis vicarie per dictum Joannem obtente ad eius vitam tantum seu quamdiu hanc[114] obtinuerit. Ad futuram	IV Anni VII	35[113]
1316	353,fo 190v	*Norwich*	Georgius Grey	Unio parochialis decanatui per dictum Georgium obtento ad eius vitam tantum seu quamdiu hunc obtinuerit. Ad futuram	IV Anni VII	37
1317	353,fo 234v	*Ross*	Robertus Fresail	Reservatio fructuum decanatus	IV Anni VII	102
1318	353,fo 73v	*Chichester*	Willelmus Bussoy	Unio parochialis alteri per dictum Willelmum obtente ad eius vitam tantum seu quamdiu hanc obtinuerit	IV Anni VII	164
1319	353,fo 151v	*Llandaff*	Willelmus More	Dispensatio ad incompatibilia	IV Anni VII	171
1320	353,fo 151v	*Lincoln*	Willelmus Curteys	*The like*	IV Anni VII	172
1321	353,fo 151v	*Same*	Joannes Legh	*The like*	IV Anni VII	173
1322	353,fo 73v	*Canterbury*	Rogerus Waleot	*The like*	IV Anni VII	200
1323	353,fo 151v	*London*	Radulphus Hamsterley	Indulgentia pro visitantibus quamdam ecclesiam	IV Anni VII	212
1324	353,fo 99v	*Exeter*	Joannes Wanen	Dispensatio ad incompatibilia	IV Anni VII	263
1325	353,fo 152v	*Lincoln*	Carolus Sinyth	*The like*	VII Anni VII	133
1326	353,fo 152v	*London*	Robertus Daudy	*The like*	VII Anni VII	231
1327	353,fos 80r, 155v	*Coventry & Lichfield*	Joannes Mogryche	Unio parochialium vicarie ad vitam tantum dicti Joannis seu quamdiu hanc obtinuerit. Ad futuram	XIII Anni VII	197
1328	353,fo 252v	*Salisbury*	Willelmus Hille	Dispensatio ad incompatibilia	XIII Anni VII	225
1329	353,fo 100v	*York*	Edwardus Basset	*The like*	XIII Anni VII	289

Ind.	DIOCESE	PERSON	MATTER	LIBER	FOLIO
1330 353,fo 117v	*Glasgow*	Archibaldus Stewart	Commissio vigore appellationis	XV Anni VII	36
1331 353,fo 101r	*Exeter*	Joannes Waby	Dispensatio ad incompatibilia	XV Anni VII	49
1332 353,fo 156r	*Lincoln*	Robertus Kirkton	*The like*	XV Anni VII	74
1333 353,fos 80v, 156r	*Coventry & Lichfield*	Edmundus Coll cum eius coniuge	Commissio vigore appellationis	XV Anni VII	75
1334 353,fo 156r	*Lincoln*	Edmundus Pergyter	Dispensatio ad incompatibilia	XV Anni VII	95
1335 353,fo 298v	*Worcester*	Alexander Pourlewent	Commissio vigore appellationis	XV Anni VII	121
1336 353,fo 101r	*York*	Richardus Ronudale	Dispensatio ad incompatibilia	XV Anni VII	137
1337 353,fo 101r	*Ely*	Willelmus Spicer	Commissio vigore appellationis	XV Anni VII	140
1338 353,fo 156r	*London*	Andreas Powes	Dispensatio ad incompatibilia	XV Anni VII	143
1339 353,fo 156r	*Lincoln*	Willelmus Bedforde	*The like*	XV Anni VII	144
1340 353,fo 156r	*Same*	Willelmus Lowude	*The like*	XV Anni VII	144
1341 353,fo 253v	*St Andrews*	Alexander Iuglis de Trebert cum aliis	Commissio vigore appellationis	XV Anni VII	272
1342 353,fo 178r	*Moray*	Thomas Brouen	*The like*	XV Anni VII	274
1343 353,fo 179v	*Meath*	Walterus Cusake	Dispensatio ad incompatibilia	XX Anni VII	8
1344 353,fo 300r	*Winchester*	Henricus Andrewe	*The like*	XX Anni VII	9
1345 353,fo 194r	*Norwich*	Willelmus Styllygton	Unio parochialis canonicatui per dictum Willelmum obtento ad eius vitam tantum seu quamdiu hunc obtinuerit. Ad futuram	XX Anni VII	11
1346 353,fo 157v	*Lincoln*	Willelmus Tomlynson	Dispensatio ad incompatibilia	XX Anni VII	73
1347 353,fos 43v, 300r	*Bath & Wells*	Rogerus Crugge	*The like*	XX Anni VII	74

Ind.		DIOCESE	PERSON	MATTER	LIBER	FOLIO
1348	353,fo 101v	*York*	Joannes Tomlynson	*The like*	XX Anni VII	74
1349	353,fo 157v	*London*	Willelmus Pase	Litere apostolice in forma Provisionis nostre Ad futuram	XX Anni VII	79
1350	353,fo 237r	*Rochester*	Rodulphus Mallynerer	Dispensatio ad incompatibilia	XX Anni VII	238
1351	353,fo 254v	*Salisbury*	Joannes Mason	Unio parochialis alteri per dictum Joannem obtente ad eius vitam tantum seu quamdiu hanc obtinuerit. Ad futuram	XX Anni VII	239
1352	353,fo 158r	*(?)London*[115]	Radulphus Bornache	Dispensatio ad incompatibilia	XX Anni VII	292
1353	353,fo 101v	*York*	Henricus Jakson	*The like*	XX Anni VII	320
1354	353,fo 158r	*Lincoln*	Joannes Constabile	Unio parochialis decanatui per dictum Joannem obtente [!] ad eius vitam tantum seu quamdiu hunc obtinuerit. Ad futuram	XX Anni VII	321
1355	353,fo 254v	*Salisbury*	Thomas Mawer	Dispensatio ad incompatibilia	XX Anni VII	340
1356	353,fo 85v	*Clogher*	Eugenius Machamahuna	Erectio vicarie parochialis in simplicem prebendam ad vitam tantum dicti Eugenii seu quamdiu hanc obtinuerit	XXIII Anni VII	9
1357	353,fo 195r	*Norwich*	Willelmus Jacson	Unio parochialis alteri per dictum Willelmum obtente ad eius vitam tantum seu quamdiu hanc obtinuerit. Ad futuram	XXIII Anni VII	139
1358	353,fo 195r	*Same*	Joannes Carne alias Buckenhem	Dispensatio ad incompatibilia	XXIII Anni VII	141
1359	353,fo 195v	*Norwich*	Henricus Bacon	*The like*	XXV Anni VII	32
1360	353,fo 124v	*Hereford*	Richardus Robertii	Unio parochialis canonicatui. Ad futuram.	XXV Anni VII	47
1361	353,fo 102v	*York*	Joannes Cley	Commissio vigore appellationis	XXV Anni VII	48
1362	353,fo 102v	*Exeter*	Joannes Davy	Dispensatio ad incompatibilia	XXV Anni VII	51
1363	353,fo 255v	*Salisbury*	Joannes Vebbe	*The like*	XXV Anni VII	52

Ind.		DIOCESE	PERSON	MATTER	LIBER	FOLIO
1364	353,fo 159v	*Lincoln*	Jacobus Milner	*The like*	XXV Anni VII	127
1365	353,fo 124v	*Hereford*	Eduardus Dalow	Commissio vigore appellationis	XXV Anni VII	169
1366	353,fos 88r, 159v	*Coventry & Lichfield*	Villelmus[116] Traffordi	Dispensatio ad incompatibilia	XXV Anni VII	207
1367[117]	353,fo 124v	*Hereford*	Ricardus Bonson	*The like*	XXV Anni VII	225
1368	353,fo 301v	*Worcester*	Hugo Lydezate	*The like*	XXV Anni VII	227
1369	353,fo 159v	*Lincoln*	Thomas Smyth	*The like*	XXV Anni VII	228
1370	353,fo 88r	*Chichester*	Robertus Marynge	*The like*	XXV Anni VII	229
1371	353,fo 159v	*(?)London*[118]	Joannes Lichefeld	*The like*	XXV Anni VII	291
1372	353,fos 45v, 301v	*Bath & Wells*	Joannes Staci	*The like*	XXV Anni VII	298
1373	353,fo 124v	*Hereford*	Eduardus Dalow	Commissio vigore appellationis	XXV Anni VII	311
1374	353,fo 159v	*Lincoln*	Richardus Mabott	Unio vicarie parochialis alteri per dictum Richardum obtente ad eius vitam tantum seu quamdiu hanc obtinuerit. Ad futuram	XXV Anni VII	338
1375	353,fo 159v	*London*	Richardus Parkar	Unio parochialis alteri per dictum Richardum obtente ad eius vitam tantum seu quamdiu hanc obtinuerit. Ad futuram	XXV Anni VII	339
1376	354,fo 93r	*Leighlin*	Mauritius Ymota	Parochialis certo modo	I Anni VIII	13
1377	354,fo 59r	*Exeter*	Robertus Vyllyany	Dispensatio ad incompatibilia	I Anni VIII	55
1378	354,fo 59r	*York*	Rolandus Lece	*The like*	I Anni VIII	57
1379	354,fo 93r	*Lincoln*	Robertus Pacher	*The like*	I Anni VIII	180
1380	354,fo 93r	*Same*	Thomas Lyliwe	*The like*	I Anni VIII	181
1381	354,fo 93r	*Same*	Thomas Lasynghy	*The like*	I Anni VIII	182
1382	354,fo 31r	*Canterbury*	Joannes Clerke	*The like*	I Anni VIII	200
1383	354,fo 93r	*London*	Joannes Golinez	*The like*	I Anni VIII	201

Ind.		DIOCESE	PERSON	MATTER	LIBER	FOLIO
1384	354,fo 93r	*Same*	Joannes Quarre	Unio parochialis prepositure ad vitam dicti Joannis aut quamdiu ipsam obtinuerit	I Anni VIII	250
1385	354,fo 117r	*Norwich*	Milones Ragon	Unio parochialis canonicatui ad vitam ipsius aut quamdiu dictum canonicatum obtinuerit	IV Anni VIII	127
1386[119]	354,fos 33v, 145v	*Cork; Ross*	Thaddeus[120] Yhederscoll	Vicarie certo modo	IV Anni VIII	130
1387	354,fo 154r	*Salisbury*	Thomas Wener	Unio parochialis alteri ad vitam ipsius aut quamdiu primam obtinuerit	IV Anni VIII	133
1388	354,fo 94v	*Lincoln*	Willelmus Deche	Dispensatio ad incompatibilia	IV Anni VIII	218
1389	354,fo 19v	*Bath*	Robertus Wilton	*The like*	IV Anni VIII	221
1390	354,fo 180v	*Winchester*	Willelmus Pichenam	Unio vicarie favore[121] ecclesie parochialis ad vitam ipsius aut quamdiu parochialem obtinuerit	IV Anni VIII	222
1391	354,fo 59v	*York*	Thomas Berisson	Dispensatio ad incompatibilia	IV Anni VIII	260
1392	354,fo 154v	*Salisbury*	Willelmus Wryhoc	*The like*	IV Anni VIII	320
1393	354,fo 94v	*Lincoln*	Riccardus Leblix alias Pigotti	*The like*	IV Anni VIII	322
1394	354,fo 89r	Carlisle	Willelmus Burbanke alias Smythson	*The like*	V Anni VIII	46
1395	354,fo 95r	*Killaloe*	Bernardus Macinhauna	Monasterium per devolutionem	V Anni VIII	118
1396	354,fo 59v	*Exeter*	Thomas Colyns	Ampliatio dispensationis ad incompatibilia	V Anni VIII	211
1397	354,fo 106v	*St David's*	Joannes Starty	Perind(e vale)re super dispensatione ad incompatibilia	V Anni VIII	320
1398	354,fo 155r	*Salisbury*	Decanus et canonici ecclesie Saresbirien. et alii	Commissio vigore appellationis	V Anni VIII	336
1399	354,fo 95v	*Lincoln*	Joannes Burges	Dispensatio ad incompatibilia	VII Anni VIII	65

Ind.		DIOCESE	PERSON	MATTER	LIBER	FOLIO
1400	354,fo 71v	*Glasgow*	Vinfiedus Colguhom et alii	Commissio vigore appellationis	VII Anni VIII	185
1401	354,fo 20v	*Brechin*	Jacobus Schrymgeour	Cantoria precentoria nuncupata per resignationem	VIII Anni VIII	13
1402	354,fo 20v	*Same*	Georgeus Fery	Reservatio fructuum dicte cantorie[122]	VIII Anni VIII	15
1403	354,fo 20v	*Same*	Alexander Paniter	Pensio super canonicatu	VIII Anni VIII	25
1404	354,fo 155v	*St Andrews*	Wilhelmus Balze	Reservatio fructuum parochialis	VIII Anni VIII	61
1405	354,fo 20v	*Brechin*	Alexander Setton	Canonicatus cathedralis per resignationem	VIII Anni VIII	83
1406	354,fo 53v	*Kildare*	Patritius Stic	Unio parochialium monasterio regulari ad eius vitam tantum seu.	VIII Anni VIII	179
1407	354,fo 37r	*Chichester*	Willermus Cradoli	Commissio vigore appellationis	IX Anni VIII	21
1408	354,fo 146v	*Rochester*	Oliverus Godfray	Dispensatio ad incompatibilia	IX Anni VIII	87
1409	354,fo 4v	*St Asaph*	Joannes Ayryse alias Kyston	*The like*	IX Anni VIII	189
1410	354,fo 118v	*Norwich*	Richardus Dracke	*The like*	IX Anni VIII	201
1411	354,fo 156r	*Salisbury*	Thomas Claghton	*The like*	IX Anni VIII	201
1412	354,fo 182r	*Winchester*	Joannes Wylford	*The like*	IX Anni VIII	208
1413	354,fos 53v, 96v	*Durham; Lincoln*	Willelmus Franchelun[123]	Unio parochialis Lincolinen. canonicatui Dunelinen. ad eius vitam tantum seu.	IX Anni VIII	250
1414	354,fo 60r	*York*	Robert Aliscundut	Indultum percipiendi fructuum in absentia	IX Anni VIII	250
1415	354,fo 156r	*Salisbury*	Joannes Fyster	Dispensatio ad incompatibilia	IX Anni VIII	278
1416	354,fo 118v	*Norwich*	Richardus Richoman	Commissio vigore appellationis	IX Anni VIII	282
1417	354,fo 182r	*Worcester*	Willelmus Man'	Dispensatio ad incompatibilia	IX Anni VIII	313

Ind.		DIOCESE	PERSON	MATTER	LIBER	FOLIO
1418	354,fo 118v	*Norwich*	Willelmus Walsyngham alias Bett	Dispensatio ad incompatibile	IX Anni VIII	346
1419	354,fo 108r	*St David's*	Thomas Lloide	Dispensatio ad incompatibilia	IX Anni VIII	347
1420	354,fo 21v	*Bath*	Thomas Panvischier	Unio vicarie parochiali ad eius vitam tantum seu.	X Anni VIII	123
1421	354,fo 182r	*Winchester*	Bernardus Holden	Unio parochialis canonicatui ad eius vitam tantum seu.	X Anni VIII	185
1422	354,fo 38r	*Chichester*	Joannes Raspas	Dispensatio ad incompatibilia	X Anni VIII	192
1423	354,fo 96v	*(?)London*[124]	Joannes Boher	*The like*	X Anni VIII	195
1424	354,fo 96v	*(?)Llandaff*[125]	Joannes Appievan	Commissio vigore appellationis	X Anni VIII	230
1425	354,fo 182v	*Winchester*	Willelmus [Hogieson?] episcopus Barier[126]	Dispensatio ad incompatibilia	X Anni VIII	234
1426	354,fo 96v	*Lincoln*	Joannes Fitzarbert	*The like*	X Anni VIII	247
1427	354,fo 96v	*London*	Thomas Warde	*The like*	X Anni VIII	247
1428	354,fo 72r	*Glasgow*	Joannes Reid	Vicaria parochialis per resignationem	X Anni VIII	275
1429	354,fo 72r	*Same*	Robertus Staw	Reservatio fructuum dicte vicarie[127]	X Anni VIII	277
1430	354,fo 97r	*Lincoln*	Abbas et conventus monasterii Ordinis Sancti Benedicti	Commissio vigore appellationis	X Anni VIII	295
1431	354,fo 156r	*Salisbury*	Jannottus Baoret	Dispensatio ad incompatibilia	X Anni VIII	316
1432	354,fo 97r	*London*	Joannes Wisset	*The like*	X Anni VIII	317
1433	354,fo 21v	*Bath*	Robertus Webe	*The like*	X Anni VIII	318
1434	354,fo 97r	*Lincoln*	Georgeus Appulyerde	*The like*	X Anni VIII	319
1435	354,fo 38v	*Coventry*	Joannes Wallier	*The like*	X Anni VIII	354

Ind.		DIOCESE	PERSON	MATTER	LIBER	FOLIO
1436	354,fo 21v	*Bath*	Joannes Newburgh	Commissio vigore appellationis	X Anni VIII	357
1437	354,fos 6v, 40v	*Armagh; Clogher*	Patritius Ochad[128]	Mandatum super facienda unione vicariarum parochialium Clocoren. et Armachan. respective diocesis alteri vicarie parrochialis Armachan. diocesis ad eius vitam tantum seu et cetera[129]	XIV Anni VIII	18
1438	354,fo 89v	*Kilmore*	Thomas Macbrian	Absolutio ab excessu casuali privationis oculo cuiusdam mulieris ac dispensatio super irregularitate ac (?)provisio vicarie parochialis per devolutionem	XIV Anni VIII	81
1439	354,fo 6v	*Achonry*	Thaddeus Macdayr	Vicaria parrochialis per devolutionem	XIV Anni VIII	83
1440	354,fo 98v	*London*	Willelmus Dawsoon	Commissio vigore appellationis	XIV Anni VIII	228
1441	354,fo 98v	*Lincoln*	Joannes Lambe	Ampliatio dispensationis ad incompatibilia	XIV Anni VIII	235
1442	354,fo 110r	*St David's*	Joannes (?)Aphrru	Dispensatio ad incompatibilia	XIV Anni VIII	264
1443	354,fo 147v	*Rochester*	Richardus Gharpe	*The like*	XIV Anni VIII	300
1444[130]	354,fo 24v	*Brechin* Ecclesia	Joannes [Hepburn] electus Brechinen.	Ecclesia per obitum	XX Anni VIII	82
1445	354,fo 24v	*Same*	*Same*	Munus	XX Anni VIII	86
1446	354,fo 24v	*Same*	*[Same]*	Absolutio	XX Anni VIII	86
1447	354,fo 149r	*Ross*	Joannes [Hepburn] electus Brechinen.	Retentio	XX Anni VIII	86
1448	354,fo 24v	*Brechin*	*Same*	Dispensatio super defectu etatis	XX Anni VIII	88
1449[131]	354,fo 101v	*Lydda* Ecclesia	Joannes Brainfort electus Liden.	Ecclesia certo modo	XX Anni VIII	103
1450	354,fo 101v	*Same*	*Same*	Dispensatio de non residendo	XX Anni VIII	106
1451	354,fo 101v	*Same*	*[Same]*	Absolutio	XX Anni VIII	106

Ind.		DIOCESE	PERSON	MATTER	LIBER	FOLIO
1452	354,fo 101v	Same	[Same]	Munus	XX Anni VIII	106
1453	354,fo 101v	Lincoln	Same	Retentio	XX Anni VIII	107
1454[132]	354,fo 10v	Aberdeen Ecclesia	Alexander Gordoni electus Aberdonen.	Ecclesia per cessionem	XX Anni VIII	182
1455	354,fo 10v	Same	Same	Absolutio	XX Anni VIII	187
1456	354,fo 10v	Same	[Same]	Munus	XX Anni VIII	187
1457[133]	354,fo 101v	Llandaff[134] Ecclesia	Georgeus [de Athequa] Electus Laudunen.	Ecclesia per obitum	XX Anni VIII	220
1458	354,fo 101v	Same	Same	Absolutio	XX Anni VIII	222
1459	354,fo 101v	Same	[Same]	Munus	XX Anni VIII	222
1460[135]	354,fo 78v	Hereford Ecclesia	Carolus Bothi electus Hereforden.	Ecclesia per obitum	XX Anni VIII	235
1461	354,fo 78v	Same	Same	Absolutio	XX Anni VIII	238
1462	354,fo 78v	Same	[Same]	Dispensatio	XX Anni VIII	238
1463	354,fo 78v	Same	[Same]	Munus	XX Anni VIII	238
1464[136]	354,fo 120v	Negroponte Ecclesia	Riccardus [Wilson] electus Nigroponten.	Ecclesia in partibus	XX Anni VIII	239
1465	354,fo 120v	Same	Same	Absolutio	XX Anni VIII	240
1466	354, fo 120v	Same	[Same]	Munus	XX Anni VIII	240
1467	354,fo 120v	Same	[Same]	Dispensatio de non residendo	XX Anni VIII	240
1468[137]	354,fo 11r	St Asaph Ecclesia	Henricus Standysh electus Assanen.	Ecclesia per obitum	XXI Anni VIII	27
1469	354,fo 11r	Same	Same	Absolutio	XXI Anni VIII	28
1470	354,fo 11r	Same	[Same]	Munus	XXI Anni VIII	28

Ind.	DIOCESE	PERSON	MATTER	LIBER	FOLIO
1471[138] 354,fo 11r	*Ardagh* *Ecclesia* electus Ardehaden.	Rogerius [Ó Maoileóin]	Ecclesia per obitum	XXI Anni VIII	30
1472 354,fo 11r	*Same*	*Same*	Absolutio	XXI Anni VIII	31
1473 354,fo 11r	*Same*	*[Same]*	Munus	XXI Anni VIII	31
1474[139] 354,fo 101v	*Lismore* *Ecclesia*	Nicolaus [Comin] episcopus Lismoren.	Ecclesia per cessionem	XXI Anni VIII	51
1475 354,fo 101v	*Same*	*Same*	Absolutio	XXI Anni VIII	52
1476 354,fo 101v	*Same*	*[Same]*	Munus	XXI Anni VIII	52
1477[140] 354,fo 67r	*Ferns* *Ecclesia*	Joannes Purcell electus Fernen.	Ecclesia per cessionem	XXI Anni VIII	55
1478 354,fo 67r	*Same*	*Same*	Absolutio	XXI Anni VIII	56
1479 354,fo 67r	*Same*	*[Same]*	Munus	XXI Anni VIII	56
1480[141] 354,fo 44r	Connor *Ecclesia*	Robertus [Blyth] electus Conueren.	Ecclesia per obitum	XXI Anni VIII	89
1481 354,fo 44r	*Same*	*Same*	Absolutio	XXI Anni VIII	91
1482 354,fo 44r	*Same*	*[Same]*	Munus	XXI Anni VIII	91
1483[142] 354,fo 149r	*Ross* *Ecclesia*	Joannes Omurkuly electus Rossen.	Ecclesia per cessionem	XXI Anni VIII	111
1484 354,fo 149r	*Same*	*Same*	Absolutio	XXI Anni VIII	110
1485 354,fo 149r	*Same*	*[Same]*	Munus	XXI Anni VIII	110
1486[143] 354,fo 44v	*Clogher* *Ecclesia*	Patritius Oculuyz electus Clocoren.	Ecclesia per obitum	XXI Anni VIII	146
1487 354,fo 44v	*Same*	*Same*	Absolutio	XXI Anni VIII	147
1488 354,fo 44v	*Same*	*[Same]*	Munus	XXI Anni VIII	147

Ind.		DIOCESE	PERSON	MATTER	LIBER	FOLIO
1489	354,fo 160r	Sunen. Ecclesia	Riccardus [Burgh] Electus Sunen.	Ecclesia certo modo	XXI Anni VIII	155
1490	354,fo 160r	Same	Same	Absolutio	XXI Anni VIII	155
1491	354,fo 160r	Same	Same	Indultum non accedendi	XXI Anni VIII	156
1492	354,fo 112r	Maiocen. Ecclesia	Willelmus [Gilbert] Electus Maiotan.	Ecclesia certo modo	XXI Anni VIII	176
1493	354,fo 112r	Same	Same	Absolutio	XXI Anni VIII	176
1494	354,fo 112r	Same	Same	Munus	XXI Anni VIII	177
1495	354,fo 160r	Syenen. Ecclesia	Joannes Pinnock Electus Syenen.	Ecclesia certo modo	XXI Anni VIII	264
1496	354,fo 160r	Same	Same	Absolutio	XXI Anni VIII	264
1497	354,fo 160r	Same	Same	Munus	XXI Anni VIII	265
1498[147]	354,fo 159v	St Andrews Monasterium	Alexander [Myln?] abbas monasterii Ordinis Sancti Augustini	Monasterium per cessionem	XXI Anni VIII	324
1499	354,fo 159v	Same	Same	Absolutio	XXI Anni VIII	325
1500	354,fo 159v	Same	[Same]	Munus	XXI Anni VIII	325
1501[148]	354,fo 61v	Exeter Ecclesia	Joannes [Veysey] electus Exomen.	Ecclesia per obitum	XXII Anni VIII	22
1502	354,fo 61v	Same	Same	Absolutio	XXII Anni VIII	26
1503	354,fo 61v	Same	[Same]	Munus	XXII Anni VIII	26
1504[149]	354,fo 161r	St Andrews	Edwardus Schewil abbas monasterii de Newbottil Ordinis Cistercien.	Monasterium per cessionem	XXII Anni VIII	174

Ind.	DIOCESE	PERSON	MATTER	LIBER	FOLIO
1505 354,fo 161r	*Same*	*Same*	Absolutio	XXII Anni VIII	175
1506 354,fo 161r	*Same*	*[Same]*	Munus	XXII Anni VIII	175
1507[150] 354,fo 45v	*Caithness Ecclesia*	Andreas Stelbart electus Cathenen.	Ecclesia per obitum	XXII Anni VIII	193
1508 354,fo 45v	*Same*	*Same*	Absolutio	XXII Anni VIII	194
1509 354,fo 45v	*Same*	*[Same]*	Munus	XXII Anni VIII	194
1510[151] 354,fo 46v	*Canterbury; Chichester*	Georgeus [Cromer] electus Armachan.	Retentio	XXII Anni VIII	216
1511 354,fos 14r, 54v,162r	*Aberdeen; Dunblane; St Andrews*	Patritius Panter	Reservatio ecclesiarum et rectorie sive omnium fructuum quam plurium ecclesiarum[152]	XXV Anni VIII	18
1512 354,fos 62r, 103v	*York; Lincoln*	Robertus Carter	Unio parochialis hospitali ad eius vitam tantum seu.	XXV Anni VIII	50
1513 354,fo162r	*Salisbury*	Joannes Clyffi	Unio parochialis cappelle ad eius vitam tantum seu.	XXV Anni VIII	50
1514 354,fo103v	*London*	Joannes Chume	Dispensatio ad incompatibilia	XXV Anni VIII	52
1515 354,fo103v	*Same*	Wolwinus Prynco	*The like*	XXV Anni VIII	52
1516 354,fo162r	*St Andrews*	Joannes Irwyn	Parochialis per resignationem	XXV Anni VIII	82
1517 354,fo14r	*Aberdeen*	Robertus Monorgound	Canonicatus per resignationem	XXV Anni VIII	83
1518 354,fo 162r	*St Andrews*	Joannes Forbeser	Pensio super parochiali	XXV Anni VIII	84
1519 354,fo 74v	*Glasgow*	Robertus Crechton	Pensio super canonicatu	XXV Anni VIII	88
1520 354,fo 162v	*St Andrews*	Willelmus Dundai et eius uxor	Commissio vigore appellationis	XXV Anni VIII	140
1521 354,fo 122r	*Norwich*	Riccardus Hocker alias Craffeld	Dispensatio ad incompatibilia	XXV Anni VIII	248
1522 354,fo 122r	*Same*	Robertus Warles	*The like*	XXV Anni VIII	249
1523 354,fo 189r	*Worcester*	Joannes Hanchyth	*The like*	XXV Anni VIII	249

Ind.		DIOCESE	PERSON	MATTER	LIBER	FOLIO
1524	354,fo 62r	*York*	Riccardus Sakhon	*The like*	XXV Anni VIII	250
1525	354,fo 162v	*Salisbury*	Willelmus Marthefeld	*The like*	XXV Anni VIII	250
1526	354,fo 104r	(*?*)*Llandaff*[153]	Willelmus Nowell	Unio parochialis alteri ad eius vitam tantum seu et cetera	XXV Anni VIII	253
1527	354,fo 62r	*Exeter*	Willelmus Tayrchayr	Ampliatio dispensationis ad incompatibilia	XXV Anni VIII	254
1528	354,fo 49r	*Carlisle*	Joannes Dacre	Ampliacio dispensationis super defectu etatis ad incompatibilia	XXV Anni VIII	257
1529	354,fo 114r	*Meath*	Eduardus Dyllon	Ampliatio dispensationis ad incompatibilia	XXV Anni VIII	257
1530	354,fo 27v	*Bath*	Thomas Benet	Dispensatio ad incompatibilia	I Anni IX	72

1   MS: *Dunen.*: the usual index form for Down; but the grantee is an unconvincing Irishman. Perhaps the diocese is mistaken or the surname corrupt. An aggrieved 'foreigner' (Italian?) cannot, of course, be ruled out.

2   MS: *Rossen.*; *recte* 'Roffen.'

3   *sic*; in error for 'provisionis nostre' (i.e. an exemplification)?

4   thus fo 33r (Bath); fo 371r (Wells) has *Walterius*

5   MS: has no entry under this head.

6   thus fo 33r (Bath); fo 371r (Wells) has *Nowton*

7   *Cf. Annates, Cork*, no. 102 (5 June 1513).

8   *Cf. Annates, Cloyne*, no. 103 (7 July 1513).

9   MS: *Urbis*

10   apparently; *recte* 'doctores' or possibly 'lectores' ?

11   MS: *Cantuarien.*; but the matter casts doubt on its correctness.

12   *sic*; 'Dermitius' ?

13   MS: *Conventien.* (a common index variant of 'Conventren.'); but the matter raises a question about its correctness: English unions of benefices during tenure are normally drawn in *forma gratiosa* (almost invariably in the form *Ad futuram rei memoriam*), not in *forma commissoria*.

14   *sic*; *recte*: 'canonicus'

15   MS: has no entry under this head.

16   *sic*: MS: *Eboracen.*; but the matter is unexpected and casts doubt on the correctness of the diocese.

17   potentially of British and Irish interest; perhaps a friar

18   *sic*; a corruption of 'Ff~' (itself a corruption of 'F~')?

19   written *N. Sethwodecok*; the 'N.' of uncertain value: not part of the forename

20   potentially of British and Irish interest; perhaps a friar

21   occurs on fo 98r (Coventry) only

22   *sic*: *Eboracen.*; in error,presumably,for an Irish diocese. At *Reg Suppl.* 1506, fo 66r there is a petition, captioned *per devolutionem*, of Dorlotus Offlangan, canon of the Augustinian monastery of B. Mary, (?)Devenish (*Dayno*), d. (?)Clogher (*Clocacen.*). The petition, which may be related to the letter summarised in the index, is dated Florence, 23 Dec. 1515. *Clocacen.* (or close spelling) could easily

be misread as *Eboracen.*

23   *sic*; *recte*: 'Leglinen.' (Leighlin)?

24   *Cf.* petition of William Mors for union of perpetual vicarage of parish church of St Andrew, Pydmyster,d. Bath & Wells,to parish church of St Benet Gracechirche in the city of London,d. London. The petition is dated Nepi 1 October 1514 (*Reg. Suppl.* 1468,fo 79r-v). *And see CPL* XVII, part II, pp. cxxiv-cxxv.

25   occurs on fo 308v (Wells) only

26   *Cf.* petition, for a dispensation, of William Dyngley,scholar,d. Worcester. The petition is dated Nepi 1 October 1514 (*Reg. Suppl.* 1468,fo 79v).

27   *sic*: MS: *Conventren.*; but the surname and particularly the matter cast doubt on the correctness of the diocese.

28   Entered under the usual index form for Exeter (*Exouien.*). It is always possible that the grantee's name is mistaken.

29   thus fo 8r (Armagh) in both instances; fo 146r (Kilmore) has *Mhakayeghe* in both instances and *Richardus*

30   *Cf.* dispensation *ad tertium*, dated 30 Nov. 1514, in favour of Edward Powell, MTheol, who holds, under a dispensation *ad duo* of Julius II (= *CPL* XVIII, no. 336), the provostship of the church of St Edmund, Salisbury (*Novi Saresbirien.*), d. Salisbury, and the parish church of Bleadon (*Bledon'*), d. Bath and Wells (WRO, Reg. Audley, fo 164r-v).

31   thus fo 63v (Coventry); fo 160r (Lincoln) has *Vodcock*

32   occurs on fo 63v (Coventry) only

33   thus fo 160v (London); fo 270r (Salisbury) has *Becausauu*

34   thus fo 160v (London); fo 270r (Salisbury) has: ... *diocesis per ipsum obtente simplici etiam per ipsum obtento quamdiu* ...

35   thus fo 37v (Bath); fo 313r (Wells) has *Richardus*

36   *Cf.* petition, for a dispensation *ad duo*, of John (?)Goodregh,rector of the parish church of Hadley,d. London. The petition is dated Florence 30 January 1516 (*Reg. Suppl.* 1512, fo 48r).

37   *Cf.* petition,for a dispensation *ad duo* ,of Hugh Guibason, cleric, d. London. The petition is dated Florence 30 January 1516 (*Reg. Suppl.* 1512, fo 47v).

38   *Cf.* petition, for a dispensation *ad duo*, of
     William Colles, BDec, perpetual vicar of
     the parish church of Begebelugh, d.
     Exeter. The petition is dated Florence 30
     January 1516 (*Reg. Suppl.* 1512,fos 47v-
     48r).

39   *Cf.* petition, for dispensation *ad duo*, of
     John Cooke, cantarist of the chantry of St
     John the Baptist, Braintree (*in Magna
     Reynes alias Branetre*), d. London. The
     petition is dated 14 March 1516. (*Reg.
     Suppl.* 1514, fo 168r).

40   *Cf.* petition, for dispensation *ad duo*, of
     William Redcliffe (*Ratclyff*), cantarist of
     the chantry of Sancti [? Dub] raci in the
     parish church of Porlock (*Parlok*), d. Bath
     and Wells. The petition is dated 14 March
     1516. (*Reg. Suppl.* 1514, fo. 167v).

41   *Cf.* petition, for dispensation *ad duo*, of
     (?)Eudo ?Asplen (*Aspelon'*), BDec, rector
     of the parish church of Holy Trinity,
     Leyton (*Leydon'*), d. London. The petition
     is dated 14 March 1516 (*Reg. Suppl.* 1514,
     fo 168r).

42   *Cf.* petition, for dispensation *ad duo*, of
     William Cynnes ((?)*Cymies*), vicar of the
     parish church of Hagbourne
     ((?)*Hagbrerne*), d. Salisbury. The petition
     is dated 14 March 1516 (*Reg. Suppl.* 1514,
     fo 167r-v).

43   *Cf.* petition, for dispensation *ad duo*, of
     William Barowe ((?)*Barrevw*), LLB, rector
     of the parish church of Shipton Moyne
     (*Synthon'* (?)*Mogyn*), d. Worcester. The
     petition is dated 14 March 1516 (*Reg.
     Suppl.* 1514, fo 168r).

44   *sic*: *Morinen.*; in error,perhaps,for an Irish
     diocese (perhaps 'Ma(g)ionen.')

45   thus fo 100r (Elphin); fo 190r
     (Thérouanne) has *Ostyngui*

46   occurs on fo 100r (Elphin) only

47   thus fo 100r (Elphin); fo 190r (Morinen.)
     has *atque*

48   occurs on fo 100r (Elphin) only

49   occurs on fo 40v (Bath) only

50   thus fo 73v (Coventry); fo 166r (Lichfield)
     has *Bytle*

51   thus fo 41r (Bath); fo 317r (Wells) has
     Lovell

52   occurs on fo 317r (Wells) only

53   thus fo 41r (Bath); fo 317r (Wells) has
     (with difference of meaning) *hanc*

54   MS: *Diren.*

55   *Cf.* text of dispensation and indult, in
     favour of Robert Heggys, monk of the
     Cistercian (*Cicestren.* [!]) monastery of
     BMV, Bruern (*de Bruera*), d. Lincoln,
     enabling him to hold a secular benefice
     and wear his habit under the garment or
     robe of a secular cleric or priest. The
     dating clause of the letter, which is drawn
     in the name of Leo, is incomplete: *Dat.
     Rome apud Sanctum Petrum anno
     incarnacionis domini* [!] *millesimo
     quingentesimo quintodecimo* [ends]
     (HWRO, Reg. XXVI: Reg. Silvestro de'
     Gigli, fos 126v-127r / pp. 242-3 [mod.
     pencil]).

56   MS: *Daren.*; *recte*: 'Deren.'?

57   MS: *Barliolen.*; *recte*: 'Carleolen.'?

58   no surname

59   *Cf.* petition, for dispensation *ad duo*,of
     Richard P(re)stoland , rector of the parish
     church of (?)Thunstymley,d. Coventry &
     Lichfield. The petition is dated Florence 1
     February 1516 (*Reg. Suppl.* 1512, fo 30r-
     v).

60   thus fo 103r (York); fo 158r (London) has
     Docowre

61   *Cf.* petition, for dispensation *ad tertium*, of
     William Hone, dean of the church of
     Tamworth (*Tamworth'*), d. Coventry and
     Lichfield. The petition is dated Palo, d.
     Porto, 25 April 1516 (*Reg. Suppl.* 1521,
     fos 111v-112r).

62   MS: *Landonien.*; *cf.* no. 1019 below.

63   MS: *Londouien.*; *cf.* no. 1017 above.

64   MS: *Idem* with reference,seemingly, to
     Ecclesia per translationem; what letter is
     meant is unclear.

65   *Cf.* petition, for dispensation *ad duo*, of
     Thomas Asshewood, rector of the parish
     church of Mason', d. Salisbury. The
     petition is dated 29 May 1516 (*Reg. Suppl.*
     1523,fo 273v).

66   *Cf.* petition, for dispensation *ad duo*, of
     John Stodard,perpetual vicar of the parish
     church of Dynnford, d. Canterbury. The
     petition is dated 29 May 1516 (*Reg. Suppl.*
     1523, fo 273r).

67   *Cf.* petition, for dispensation *ad duo*, of
     Walter Hillesdon', rector of the parish
     church of Weyne Giffard, d. Exeter. The
     petition is dated 29 May 1516 (*Reg. Suppl.*
     1523,fo 273r).

68 *Cf.* petition, for dispensation *ad duo*, of John Noble', LLB, perpetual vicar of the parish church of Thachin, d. Salisbury. The petition is dated 29 May 1516 (*Reg. Suppl.* 1523, fo 273r-v).

69 *Cf.* petition, for dispensation in respect of age,of Ralph (Radulphus) Oldoy,cleric, d. Coventry & Lichfield. The petition is dated 29 May 1516 (*Reg. Suppl.* 1523, for 273v).

70 thus fo 63v (Coventry); fo 165r (Lichfield) has *Radulphus*

71 *Cf.* petition of John Constable,DDec,for union of parish church of Connyngesby, d. Lincoln, to the deanery of the church of Lincoln. The petition is dated 8 June 1516 (*Reg. Suppl.* 1524, fo 230v).

72 *Cf.* petition of Gamaliel Clyston', DDec, for union of parish church of Wylforth', d. York, to canonry and prebend of Wystaw in the church of York. The petition is dated 8 June 1516 (*Reg. Suppl.* 1524, fo 230r-v).

73 thus fo 33r (Bath); fo 329v (Wells) has *Freman*

74 thus fo 105v (Ely); fo 329v (Winchester) has *Chyfurlton*

75 thus fo 33v (Bath); fo 330r (Wells) has (?)*Glosten'*

76 MS: *Olocoren.*; *recte*: 'Clochoren.'

77 *Cf. Annates, Elphin*, no. 111 (28 Feb. 1517).

78 MS: has no entry under this head.

79 *Cf. Annates, Ardfert*, no. 143 (19 Sept. 1516).

80 *Cf. Annates, Elphin*, no. 112 (5 Feb. 1517).

81 apparently; 'regularis'?

82 thus fo 17r (Armagh); fo 100v (Kildare) has *Megunsonan*

83 thus fo 17r (Armagh); fo 100v (Kildare) has: ... *prebendam ad eius vitam tantum*

84 thus fo 17v (Armagh); fo 100v (Kildare) has *Magunsanam*

85 thus fo 17v (Armagh); fo 100v (Kildare) has: ... *prebendam ad eius vitam tantum*

86 *Cf. Annates, Tuam Province*, no. 343 (19 March 1517).

87 apparently; *recte* 'et'?

88 *Cf. Annates, Cashel*, no. 69 (6 May 1517).

89 *Cf. Annates, Killaloe*, no. 254 (29 May 1517).

90 thus fo 44r (Bath); fo 339r (Wells) has *Gallant*

91 thus fo 83r (Coventry); fo 175v (Lichfield) has *Mynshul*

92 thus fo 83r (Coventry); fo 175v (Lichfield) has *Melineux*

93 MS: *Laudouien.*

94 MS: *Lodouien.*

95 thus fo 45v (Bath); fo 339v (Wells) has *Maxne*

96 thus fo 45v (Bath); fo 339v (Wells) has *Rawlins*

97 odd, given the matter

98 thus fo 45v (Bath); fo 340r (Wells) has *Baker*

99 thus fo 84r (Coventry); fo 177r (Lichfield) has *Stakyley*

100 *Cf. Annates, Ardfert*, no. 147 (18 Nov. 1517).

101 thus fo 291v (Salisbury); fo 340r (Winchester) has *Holiden*

102 thus fo 109v (Elphin); fo 317r (Tuam) has: ... *ad eius vitam*

103 *Cf. Annates, Ross*, no. 43 (19 Feb. 1518).

104 *Cf. Annates, Ross*, no. 42 (13 Feb. 1518).

105 *Cf.* Betoun's provision as commendator to the Benedictine monastery of Arbroath, 14 Dec. 1517 (Brady, I, p. 165; *cf.* no. 746 above).

106 thus fo 91v (Coventry); fo 180v (Lichfield) has *Smiths*

107 MS: *Laudanen.* (a variant form of 'Landaven.'); but the other particulars argue that the diocese may be incorrect.

108 as previous note

109 *Cf.* indulgence (specified), dated 26 June 1518, for the altar of St Thomas Aquinas and B. S[c]ita the Virgin (*B. Site Virginis*) in the church of the Dominican house, London, where Elisabeth Denton (*Dentori*), of the illustrious family of Jerningham (*Jarnynghin Majori*) of Somerleyton (*de Homerleto Unhatt*), d. Norwich (*Nortonen.*) and, by appointment of Henry VII, governess (*directrix* and *curatrix*), when they were of tender age, of Henry VIII and of his sister [sc. Margaret *or* Mary], has elected to have her tomb (*BOP*, pp. 368-9, item LXXXVIII., printed from copy *ex Archivo Apostolico Lib. CLVI fol. 104* [*sic*]).

110 the 'B' badly written and doubtful

111 written *Syden hans*

112 MS: *Laonen.*: the usual index form for Killaloe; but the grantee does not look Irish; perhaps written in error for 'Leonen.' (St-Pol-de-Léon).

113 thus fo 37v (Bath); fo 295r (Wells) has *37*

114 thus fo 37v (Bath); fo 295r (Wells) has (incorrectly) *hunc*

115 MS: *Laudouien.*

116 thus fo 88r (Coventry); fo 159v (Lichfield) has *Willelmus*

117 *Cf.* dispensation *ad incompatibilia*, dated 18 March 1521, in favour of Richard Benson, portioner of the parish church of Burford, d. Hereford (BL, Stowe Charter 588; Bell, no. 283).

118 MS: *Laudunen.*

119 *Cf. Annates, Ross*, no. 45 (6 March 1520).

120 thus fo 33v (Cork); fo 145v (Ross) has *Thade*

121 apparently; *recte* 'rectorie'?

122 with reference,presumably,to previous entry

123 thus fo 53v (Durham); fo 96v (Lincoln) has *Franckelun'*

124 MS: *Londoven.*

125 MS: *Laudunen.*

126 apparently; *recte*: 'Darien.'?

127 The reference is to no. 1428.

128 thus fo 6v (Armagh); fo 40v (Clogher) has *Patricius Ohacdh*

129 thus fo 6v (Armagh); fo 40v (Clogher) simply has: *Unio vicariarum parochialium alteri ad eius vitam tantum seu et cetera*

130 *Cf.* Dowden, p. 189 (29 Oct. 1516).

131 *Cf.* Eubel, III², p. 225 (26 Feb. 1517); *Ind.* 355, fo 40v has: *Braynfort*

132 *Cf.* Eubel, III²,p.91 (6 June 1516).

133 *Cf.* provision, dated 11 Feb. 1517, of George de Athequa (*Acrca*), OP, beloved (*grato*) of Henry, king of England and confessor of Catherine, queen of England, to the church of Llandaff, vacant by the death of Miles [Salley], its late bishop (BOP , p. 402, printed from copy *Ex Archivo Apostolico Lib. CCXXII fol. 220*).

134 MS: *Laudunen.*; *recte*: 'Landaven.'

135 *Cf.* Eubel, III², p. 209 (21 July 1516).

136 *Cf.* Eubel, III², p. 259 (21 July 1516).

137 28 May 1518: Brady, I, pp. 85-6; Eubel,III², p. 120. *Ind.* 355, fo 22r has: *6⁰ Henricus Standish Electus*

138 *Cf.* Brady, I, p. 289 (2 Dec. 1517) and Eubel, III², p. 116 (14 Dec. 1517); both citing (different) consistorial records. The latter is probably to be preferred. *Ind.* 355, fo 22r has: *5⁰ Rogerus Electus*

139 13 Apr. 1519: Brady, I, p. 67; Eubel, III², p. 226. *Ind.* 355, fo 22v has: *Lismoren. et Waterforden. 7⁰ Nicolaus episcopus*

140 13 Apr. 1519: Brady, I, p. 374; Eubel, III², p. 195

141 16 Apr. 1520: Brady, I, p. 262; Eubel, III², p. 189. *Ind.* 355, fo. 23r has: *Dunen. et Conneren. 8[⁰] Robertus electus*

142 4 Nov. 1517: Brady ,II, pp. 108-9; Eubel III², p. 287. Though not indexed there was a Retentio (*cf. Annates, Ross*, no. 41). *Ind.* 355, fo 23r has: *5⁰ Joannes Omurhuly electus*

143 Eubel III², p. 170 (11 Feb. 1517); Brady, II, pp. 258-259 (correcting vol. I, p. 251), 362. *Ind.* 355, fo 23v has: *4⁰ Patricius Oculny electus*

144 Citing different consistorial records, Eubel III², p. 307 (under Syronen.) gives 9 Sept. 1519 as the date of provision; Brady, I, pp. 111-112 (under Surien.) gives 14 Sept. 1519; the former date perhaps to be preferred.

145 Brady, I, p. 111 and Eubel, III², p. 233 (both under Maioren.) give 13 May 1519 as the date of provision.

146 Brady, I, pp. 110-111 (under Syennen.) and Eubel, III², p. 299 (under Sidonien.) both give 10 Nov. 1518 as the date of provision; *Ind.* 355, fo. 25r has: *Syenen. 4⁰ Johannes Pinnok electus*

147 *Cf.* provision of 8 Aug. 1519 to Cambuskenneth: Brady ,I, p. 169; *cf. National Library of Scotland. Catalogue of Manuscripts Acquired since 1925*, vol. II (Edinburgh, HMSO, 1966), p. 352, Ch. 2137 (=conclusion to vassals); *Ind.* 355, fo. 26r has: *7⁰ Alexander Abbas Sancte Marie Virginis de Cambus[...?]*.

148 31 Aug. 1519: Brady, I, p. 42; Eubel III², p. 193

149 16 Apr. 1520 (Brady, I, p. 202). *Ind.* 355, fo 19v has: *Edoardus Schervil Abbas de Harvotil*

150 2 or 14 Dec. 1517: Brady, I, p. 149; Eubel, III², p. 159; Dowden, p. 248. Probably 14 Dec. *Ind.* 355, fo. 20r has: *5⁰ Andreas Steuuart electus*

151 2 Oct. 1521: Brady, I, p. 216; Eubel, III², p. 118

152 thus fo 14r (Aberdeen); fo 54v (Dunblane) has: *Reservatio fructuum quam plurium beneficiorum*; so does fo 162r (St Andrews) with the addition of *et iurium* after *fructuum*

153 MS: *Laudanen.*

INDEX OF PERSONS AND PLACES

Note. The present index covers the Calendar Text, the *Rubricellae* of Lost Letters, and selectively the preliminary matter. Unless preceded by 'p.', references are to serial numbers of entries. Irish surnames are under their Mac and O prefixes. As in the Indexes to CPL XVII Parts I and II names of places are collected under counties as well as under dioceses; and the names of persons are collected under dioceses. The sub-entries of the relevant main entries are, typically : "cathedral church"; "bishop"; "diocese". Under "diocese, persons of" the reader will find listed both persons who are locally designated by diocese alone as well as persons beneficed in that diocese, either currently or prospectively (e.g. by virtue of a mandate of provision), or otherwise connected with it. To avoid repetition, persons encountered elsewhere in the main entry (e.g. as canons under "cathedral church") are generally excluded from the listing under diocese. Archdeacons are entered below "bishop", not under "cathedral church". Diacritics are often omitted.

A

Abardan *see* OBardon

[Abbey, *in* Stirling, co. Stirling] *see* Cambuskenneth

Abbeydorney [*in* ODorney, co. Kerry], [Cistercian] monastery of B. Mary, *de Kyrieleyson*, abbot of, papal mandatary, 730

[Abbeygormacan, co. Galway], place in *see* Finnure

Abbeyleix [co. Laois], Cistercian monastery of B. / St Mary, *de Legedei*, 141

......,......,....., prospective union to, of the vicarages of Dysartenos, Kilcolmanbane, Straboe *alias* ?Shaen, and ?Timogue *alias* Ballintubbert, 141

......,......,....., abbot of, papal mandatary, 145, 151, 624, 653

......,......,....., detainer of *see* OMore, Donat

......,......,....., monk of *see* OLalor, Donat

Abbeyshrule [co. Longford], [Cistercian] abbey *de Flumine Dei*, abbot of, papal mandatary, 307

[Abbotskerswell, Devon], place in *see* Kerswell

Abbots Ripton (Abbott' Ripton') *see* Ripton, Abbots

Aberbrodoch, alias of Arbroth, *q.v.*

Aberbrothock, alias of Arbroath, *q.v.*

Aberdeen [co. Aberdeen], layman (named) of, 137

......, **[cathedral] church** of [*at* Old Aberdeen, co. Aberdeen], treasurer of, papal judge delegate, 522

......,......, chantership [=precentorship] of, collation of, 1089

......,......,....., reservation of fruits of, 1088

......,......, chanters [=precentors] of *see* Dischington, David; *cf.* Lindsay, Archibald

......,......, canonry and prebend of Banchory-Devenick in, resignation, vacancy, and provision of, 65, 66

......,......, fruits of, reservation of, 66

......,......, canonry and prebend of Kinkell in, 137, 590

......,......, canonry and prebend of Turriff in, collation of, 247

......,......,....., fruits of, reservation of pension on, 247, 522

......,......,......,....., pension reserved on, alleged non-payment of, 522

......,......, canonry of, collation of, 1517

---

1   The register note of the abbreviator's signature is variously punctuated, capitalised, and abbreviated.

[Ahamplish, co. Sligo], place in *see* Inishmurray

Ahassagrachaman *see* Tisrara

Airlie (Arlit)[co. Forfar], James, Malcolm, and Thomas Ogilvie of, *q.v.*

de Alagon, Lucas, *abbreviator de parco minori*, letter expedited by:

.*L. Dalago*, 298

Albany, duke of *see* [Stewart], John

Albert, SRE cardinal priest and chancellor, 494

Alby [Norf], parish church of, rector of, 394

Alchurche *see* Alvechurch

Alcock (Alcok), Thomas, archdeacon of the church of Worcester, 134

......,......,....., proceedings by as papal judge delegate, 134

Alderley (Alderlay)[Ches], parish church of, rector of, 528

Aldham [Essex], parish church of, holder of, 715

......,....., union of, to the parish church of Great Fordham, 715

Alekary *see* ?Athlacca

Alen (Alyn), John, holder of canonry and prebend of Lincoln (with vicarage of Chislet), prospective holder of parish church of South Ockendon, 582, 621

......,....., canon of Lincoln, papal judge delegate, 572

......,......,....., living in the city of London, 572

Alessandria [Italy], bishop of, papal mandatary, 259

Alexander III, written in error, 696 *note*

Alexander [IV], constitution "Abbates" of, 696

Alexander VI, letters of, 55, 230, 238, 470, 473

Aliscundut, Robert, of York diocese, indulged to receive fruits while absent [from benefice], 1414

Allare *see* Aller

[All Cannings] *see* [Cannings, All]

Aller (Allare)[*now represented by* Aller's Copse *in* Crediton, Devon], a prebend in the church of Crediton, *q.v.*

Almondsbury (Almondesbury)[Glos], parish church of B. Mary the Virgin, vicarage of, prospective holder of, 189

......,......,....., vacancy of, 189

......,......,....., presentation of person for, by the abbot and convent of the [Augustinian] monastery of St Augustine near Bristol, 189

......,......,....., union (conditional) of, to the parish church of Newington, 189

Alnym *see* Athlone

Aloisius, *scriptor apostolicus*, signature of, as *computator see* frontispiece

?Alphington (Absinten')[Devon], parish church of, rector of, 201

Alps, a divide in financial administration of camera, 133

Alscott *see* Alvescot

Alsey *see* Halsey

Altabegoti, Peter, to have simple benefice, Coventry [and Lichfield] diocese, 898

Altarnon (Alternon)[Corn], parish church of, vicarage of, holder of, 456

de Alvarottis, Alvarottus, *abbreviator de parco maiori*, letters expedited by:[1]

A de Alvaroctis, 138

A de Alvarottis, 146, 375-378, 650

A de Alverottis, 298, 303, 305

A de Averottis, 304

---

1   The register note of the abbreviator's signature is variously punctuated, capitalised, and abbreviated.

Banke (*contd*)

......,....,...., deprivation of, 434

......,...., capital enemy of *see* [Stanley, Thomas]

Banuton' *see* ?Bampton

Banwell (Bauwel) [Som], parish church of, annexed or appropriated to the Augustinian monastery of Bruton, 154

......, jurisdiction in, of abbot of Bruton, 154

Baoret, Jannottus, of Salisbury diocese, dispensed for plurality, 1431

Barcelona [Spain], diocese of, person of *see* Salvago, Panthaleon

......,...., places in *see* 'Caual' ; 'Marmellario'

Barcer *see* ?Barker

Barcher *see* Barker

Barckwey *see* Barkway

Barclay *cf.* Barelay

Barcow, *see* Barowe

Barelay, Alexander, of Ely diocese, dispensed for plurality, 1233

......, *cf.* Barclay

Baret *see* Barrett

Barfreystone (Berfreyston) [*or* Barfreston, Kent], parish church of, rector of, 325

Barier *see* Daria

Barkeley *see* Berkeley

Barker and ?Barker (Barcer, Barcher), Thomas, prior of the Augustinian monastery of Newburgh, 167

......,....,...., holder of the parish church of Epworth, 167

......,...., union for, of one of his parish churches to another, Lincoln diocese, 952

Barkway (Barckwey) [Herts], parish church of, vicar of, 547

Barlinch (Barlyche) [*in* Brompton Regis, Som], Augustinian monastery of St Nicholas, prior of *see* Byrde, Thomas

Barmondesey *see* Bermondsey

Barnack (Barnache), Ralph, of Winchester diocese, dispensed for plurality, 1206

Barnane-Ely (Beruan) [co. Tipperary], parish church of St Nicholas, vicarage of, 663

......,....,...., prospective union of, with other benefices, to canonry and prebend of Killea in Cashel, 663

Barnes (Barns), Christopher, rector of St Martin's, Bladon, 742

......, Geoffrey, canon of the Augustinian monastery of St Peter, Ipswich, 439

Barnwell (Bernewell') [*modern* St Andrew the Less *in* Abbey Ward, Cambridge, Cambs], Augustinian] priory of, prior of, papal judge delegate, 134

Barotius, Cristoforus, *magister registri*, entries signed by:[1]

    C Barotius, 92-96, 140, 161, 162, 177, 178, 199, 214, 218, 222-225, 242, 250, 254, 280, 283, 284, 286, 287, 379-385, 421, 434, 497, 519, 622, 649

......,....,...., alterations to register ordered by regent of chancery signed (*C* and *Ba*; *C Barotius*) by, 273 *note*, 424 *note*, 623 *note*

......,....,...., other alterations to register initialled (*C*, *C* and *Ba*) by, 199 *note*, 284 *note*, 286 *note*, 424 *note*

Barowe (Barcow), William, of Worcester diocese, dispensed for plurality, 951

......,...., rector of Shipton Moyne, petition of, 951 *note*

Barre, Barre' *see* Barry

Barrett (Baret, Bauod), James, canon of Limerick, papal mandatary, 229

......, Richard, ostensible cleric, detainer of deanery of Killala, 571

---

1   When it is punctuated the punctuation of the signature varies.

Barrett (*contd*)

......, Richard [another?], bishop of Killala, grievances of, 219

.........,...., provision of to Killala, 219

......, alias of OMalley, Robert, *q.v.*

Barry (Barre, Barre'), Henry, cleric of Brechin diocese, 233

.......,........,...., provision to, of the parish church of Collace, 233; *cf.* 807

.......,........,...., assent of, to reservation to previous holder of pension on fruits of church of Collace, 233

.........,...., late rector of Collace, 240

.........,...., collation to, of parish church, St Andrews diocese, 807

......, John, senior, vicar of Dundee, resignation of, 232, 234

.......,.......,........,...., collector of the camera [in Scotland], 232

.......,........,...., proctor of *see* Fagnoy, John

.......,........,...., priest of Brechin diocese, 234

.......,........,........,...., reservation for, of pension on fruits of vicarage of Dundee, 234

......John, [senior?], holder of parish church of Collace, resignation of, 233

.......,........,...., priest of Brechin diocese, 233

.......,........,........,...., reservation for, of pension on fruits of parish church of Collace, 233

......, John, junior, cleric of Brechin diocese, 232, 234

.......,........,........,...., to have vicarage of Dundee, 232

.......,........,........,...., provision to, of vicarage of Dundee, 234

.......,........,........,...., assent of, to reservation to previous holder of pension on fruits of vicarage of Dundee, 234

Barsted' *see* Bersted

Bartholomew (Bartholomei), William, of Winchester diocese, dispensed for plurality, 1238

Barton (Berton') [Cambs], parish church of, vicar of, 465

Barton (Barton') *or* [Barton], Andrew, of Coventry and Lichfield diocese, 190

.......,........,...., blood relative and prospective spouse of *see* Stanley, Agnes

......, John, prior of the Augustinian monastery of Burscough, litigant, 134

.......,........,...., deprived, 134

......, William, abbot of the Augustinian monastery of B. Mary, Oseney, 133, 293, 360, 567; *and see* 11, 130

.......,........,........,...., lifetime of, validity of letters conservatory for Oseney limited to, 360

.......,........,........,...., holder *in commendam* of vicarage of St Mary Magdalen, Oxford, 133

......, William [*another*], bishop of Salona, 57

.......,........,...., holder of canonry of Salisbury and prebend of Beminster Prima, parish church of Monxton *alias* Anna de Becco, and vicarage of Britford, 57

Barton Seagrave (Barton' Sigrane) [Northants], parish church of, rector of, 694

Barwell [Leics], parish church of, rector of, 410

Bascharche *see* Baschurche, Thomas

de Baschenis, Antonius [*magister registri supplicationum*], alterations to register ordered by referendary made by, 519 *note*

Baschurch (Baschcurche) [Salop], parish church of, vicarage of, incumbent of, 433

Baschurche (Bascharche), Thomas, rector of Newington and prospective holder of the vicarage of Almondsbury, 189

Bashani *see* Bosham

Basset, Edward, of York diocese, dispensed for plurality, 1329

Bastard, William, union for, of his parish church to his canonry, Lincoln diocese, 953

Beckensaw (*contd*)

......, Robert, union for, of his parish church in London diocese to his simple benefice in Salisbury diocese, 939

Beckham, Robert, of Norwich diocese, dispensed for plurality, 989

Beckington (Bekyngton') [Som], parish church of St George, rector of, 2

Beckwith (Bekwith'), John, cleric of York diocese, 648

......,......,....., expects to be presented for the parish church of South Otterington, 648

Bedford [Beds], parish church of St John the Baptist, vacancy of, 519

.........,...., patrons of, presentation by, 519

.........,...., prospective holder of, 519

.........,...., prospective union of, to canonry and prebend of Iveston of the church of Lanchester, 519

......, parish church of St Peter in the Fields, rector of, 677

Bedford [Beds], archdeaconry of in the church of Lincoln, 207

.........,...., holder of *see* Cosyn, William

[Bedford, co. of], places in *see* Bedford; Cranfield; Houghton Conquest; Northill; Oakley; Tingrith

Bedford (Bedforde), William, of Lincoln diocese, dispensed for plurality, 1339

Bedmynye *see* Bodmin

Bedow (Bedoo), Richard, vicar of Lewknor, 435

[Beeding, Upper], place in *see* Sele

Beeleigh (Bildgh, Bylley) [*in* Maldon, Essex], Premonstratensian monastery of B Mary and St Nicholas, abbot of, papal judge delegate, 572

.........,...., abbot and convent of, presentation by, of canon for the church of ?Dengie, 425

Beeleigh (*contd*)

.........,....., benefices in the patronage of *see* ?Dengie; Ulting

.........,....., canons of *see* Copsheffe, John; Purfoot, Henry

Begebelugh *see* ?Bickleigh

Bekan (Cillurquur *alias* Racurnay) [co. Mayo], parish church of, vicarage of, 246

Bekehem *see* Becham

Bekwith' *see* Beckwith

Bekyngton' *see* Beckington

Belay, Robert, rector of the Augustinian hospital of St Bartholomew, West Smithfield, London, 542

......, *cf.* Beyley

Bellingham (Bellynghm'), John, cantor of the chantry of St Catherine in the church of B. Mary the Virgin, Gillingham, 46

de Bello Loco (Regis) see Beaulieu Regis

Bellynghm' *see* Bellingham

Bellzo *alias* Kelso *see* Kelso

Belshaw (Belschaw), Thomas, rector of Nailstone, appellant in case of disputed provision, 215

Belsis, James, vicar of Comrie, resignation of, 666

.........,....., proctor of *see* Simson, Adam

Belton, Richard, of Salisbury diocese, dispensed for plurality, 1045

Beminster Prima (Bemester Prima) [*in* Netherbury, Dors], a prebend in Salisbury cathedral, *q.v.*

Bempti, Roger, union for, of his vicarage to his canonry, Hereford diocese, 1243

Benedict XIII, register of, p. lxv note 17

Benedict XIV, register of, pp. l, li, lii, lxv note 17

de Benedictione Dei see Kilbeggan

Berna(r)di, .H., presumptively an *abbreviator de parco minori* or *de prima visione*, letter expedited by:

.H. Berna(r)di, 298

Bernewell' *see* Barnwell

Berobrowne, John, of Lincoln diocese, dispensed for plurality, 1070

Berriman (Buryman'), Alice, the late, woman, parishioner of Stow, 279

.....,.....,.....,.....,....., will of, executors of *see* Bewe, John; Hill, Richard

Berry (Byry), Ralph, the late, vicar of St James's, Shaftesbury, 269

.....,.....,.....,.....,....., will of, executor of, 269

......, *cf.* Berey

Bersted *see* Bearstead

Bersted (Barsted') [*or* South B~, Sussex], parish church of, vicar of, 47

de Bertinis (Bertini), James, the late, rector of the parish church of St Michael, Villaga, 259

......, Leonard, scriptor and papal familiar, 140

.....,.....,....., proctor of Alexander Inglis, 140

de Bertis, William, of Down diocese, commission by virtue of an appeal, 753

Berton' *see* Barton

Beruan *see* Barnane-Ely

Berwick (Berewyk) [*modern* B~ St John, Wilts], parish church of St John the Baptist, united to parish church of Fugglestone, 486

Berwick (Berwyke) [*modern variously* B~ St Leonard *or* B~ - in - Tisbury, Wilts], parish church of St Leonard, rector of, 532

[Berwick, co. of], place in *see* Dryburgh

Berwyke *see* Berwick

Besançon [*dép.* Doubs, France], diocese of, persons of *see* Esteueno, Ludovicus; Perrot de Lavantio, Claudius

Besançon (*contd*)

.....,....., place in *see* Mont-sous-Vaudrey

Besten, Thomas, of Lincoln diocese, dispensed for plurality, 1180

......, *cf.* Boston

Beswick *cf.* Bexwyk

Betesson *see* Betson

Betoun (Beton), David, archbishop of St Andrews, investiture with pallium, 385 *note*

......, James, archbishop of Glasgow, 103-105, 746

.....,.....,....., absolution of preliminary to surrogation and commend, 104

.....,.....,....., surrogation of, to another's right to Benedictine monastery of Kilwinning, 103, 105

.....,.....,....., commend to, of Kilwinning, 103, 105; *and see* p. 526

.....,.....,....., to take oath of fealty, 103, 105

.....,.....,....., grant *in commendam* to, of Benedictine monastery of Arbroath or Aberbrothock, 746, 1227 *note*

.....,.....,....., assent of, to reservation to previous commendatory abbot of pension on fruits of monastery, 746

.....,.....,....., provision to, of monastery, St Andrews diocese, 1227

.....,.....,....., absolution of preliminary to provision, 1228

.....,.....,....., commission [*probably* for reception of his oath of fealty], 1229

......, Walter, canon of Glasgow and prebendary of Govan, 497

.....,.....,....., assent of, to reservation of pension on tithes and fruits etc. of his canonry and prebend, 497

.....,.....,....., proctor of *see* Simson, Adam

Betson (Betesson), John, rector of Ringsfield, 251

Bett, alias of Walsingham, William, *q.v.*

de Blanchis, Blanchus, cleric of Lucca, 149

......,....,...., appointment of, as vicar in rule and administration of the parish church of St Mary, Villa Basilica, 149

......,....,...., reservation for, of pension on fruits of same, 149

Blandford Forum (Blanford Fori) [Dors], parish church of, vicar of, 288

......,...., parish of, places in see 'Ffonage'; 'Hurles Plaic'; 'Noosend'

......,...., annexed to Augustinian monastery of Twynham, 288

Blandon see Bladon

Blanford Fori see Blandford Forum

Blankafort see Blancafort

Bleadon [Som], parish church of, holder of, 916 note

Blenluce see Glenluce

Blieton, James, of London diocese, dispensed for plurality, 907

Blockley (Blocley) [Glos (formerly Worcs)], parish church of, vicarage of, united to the parish church of Bishop's Hampton, 429

Blofield (Blowfold) [Norf], parish church of, rector of, 440

Blondus, Paulus, secretarius apostolicus, letter expedited by:

.P. Blund(us), 460

Blowfold see Blofield

Blund(us) see Blondus

[Blyth] or Blythe (Blyeth'), Geoffrey, bishop of Coventry and Lichfield, litigation before and proceedings by, 134

......,....,...., deprivation by, 134

......, James, cleric of York diocese, 459

......, Robert, of Coventry and Lichfield diocese, dispensed for plurality, 962

......,...., absolution of preliminary to provision, 1481

[Blyth] or Blythe (contd)

......,...., provision of to Connor, 1480

......,...., [bishop-] elect of Connor, 1480

......,....,...., faculty for consecration, 1482

Bnyght' see Knight

Boccarde see Bouquehault

Bochyng see Bocking, Richard

Bocking (Bockyng) [Essex], parish church of, rector of, 162

......,...., union to, of the parish church of Southchurch, 162

Bocking (Bochyng), Richard, monk of the [Cluniac] monastery, called house or priory, of B. Mary the Virgin, Thetford, 564

Bockyng see Bocking

Boconnoc (Bokonck) [Corn], parish church of, rector of, 213

Bodmin (Bedmynye, Bodmyn') [Corn], parish church of St Petroc, vicar of, 12

......, Augustinian priory, called house, of B. Mary and St Petroc, 595

......,....,....,...., prior of see Vivian, Thomas

Body, Robert, of Exeter diocese, dispensed for plurality, 1065

Boher, John, of (?)London diocese, dispensed for plurality, 1423

Bokonck see Boconnoc

Bolas (Bollas) [modern B~ Magna, Salop], parish church of, rector of, 562

Bolfe, Hugh, of Chichester diocese, dispensed for plurality, 1102

Bolla see ?Rolla

Bollas see Bolas

Bologna [Italy], studium generale of, student at see Colman, Thomas

......, Benedictine monastery of St Stephen, convent of, conclusion to, 73, 177

......,...., commend of, 73, 177, 178

Brechin (*contd*)

......, **bishop** of, to receive oath of fealty, 303, 305, 366; *cf.* 298; *and see* 368 *note*

............,...., papal mandatary, 241, 305

......, [bishop-] elect of *see* [Hepburn], James

......, official of, papal mandatary, 232

......, church of, provision to, 1444

......, city or diocese of, person of *see* Painter *alias* Lam, William

......, **diocese** of, persons of *see* Barry, Henry, John, junior and senior/priest; Nudre, Thomas; Painter, Alexander ; Painter *alias* Lam, William

............,...., places in *see* Dundee; Dunnichen; Montrose

......, 234

[Brecon, co. of], place in *see* Cantriff

Bredshay, Richard, of Worcester diocese, dispensed for minority and to hold an incompatible benefice, 965

......, *cf.* Bradshaw

Bredy, Long (Longbredy) [Dors], parish church of, rector of, 474

Bregeon, Franciscus, *abbreviator de parco maiori*, letters expedited by:[1]

    F Bregeon, 89-91, 97-102, 155, 177, 178, 214, 588, 590, 649, 746

    F Bregion, 135-137

    F Bregon (*Bregon'*), 322, 369-371

    F Brigon', 103-105

......,....,....,...., *and see* Benzon, F

Breme *see* Bream

?Bremhill (Remyll') [Wilts], parish church of, vicar of, 693

Brenton *see* Bruton

Bressanone [*modern* B~ - Brixen, prov. Bolzano, Italy], [cathedral church of], person mis-described as canon of, 239

Brewet, William, union for, of his chantry to his parish church, Worcester diocese, 1193

Bridford *see* Britford

Bridford (Brydfford) [Devon], parish church of, rector of, 560

Bridges *cf.* Brygges

Bridlington (Beydlynton') [Yorks], Augustinian monastery, called house, of B. Mary the Virgin, canon of *see* Whitehead, Gilbert

......,....,....,...., canons of, canonical portion received by, 188

Bright (Brighe, Bryght', Brygth'), Robert, rector of St Peter's, Northampton and prospective vicar of St John's, [Margate], in the Isle of Thanet, 538

......,...., cleric, commissary of the official of London, proceedings by, 243

......,...., indulged to present person for vicarage of parish church, London diocese, for one turn only, 1016

......,...., indulged to present person for parish church, London diocese, for one turn only, 1018

Brikehede *see* Birkhead

Brington [Hunts], parish church of, rector of, 499

Bristol (*Bristollie*) [Glos and Som], vill of, 602

......, parish church of St Michael the Archangel (on the Hill), holder of, 428, 565

......,...., union of, to the parish church of Suckley, 428

......,...., union of, to the vicarage of ?Elberton, 565

......, Augustinian (Victorine) monastery, called house, of St Augustine at or near, abbot of, papal judge delegate, 602

......,....,....,....,...., *see* Eliot, Robert

1   The register note of the abbreviator's signature is variously punctuated and capitalised.

Bristol (*contd*)

.....,...., abbot and convent of, presentation by, of person for vicarage of Almondsbury, 189

Bristowe, John, monk of the Cluniac monastery of Lewes, 301

Brit *see* Britt

Britford (Bridford) [Wilts], parish church of, vicarage of, holder of, 57

Britt (Brit), James, ostensible priest, detainer of vicarages of B. Mary's, Cooleagh and St James's, Peppardstown, 654

Brixen *see* Bressanone

Broad Chalke *see* Chalke, Broad

Broadhembury (Brodhambery) [Devon], parish church of, vicarage of, holder of, 613

.....,....,...., union of, to the prebend of Denes in the parish church of Chu(l)mleigh, 613

[Brocklesby, Lincs], place in *see* Newsham *alias* Newhouse

Brode Chalke, Brode Thalke *see* Chalke, Broad

Brodhambery *see* Broadhembury

Broghton' *see* Broughton [Hunts]

Broketrope *see* Brookthorpe

Broklondon *see* Brookland

Bromfield (Bromefeldi), Richard, of Bath and Wells diocese, dispensed for plurality, 826

Bromiard, Bromiard' *see* Bromyard

[Brompton Regis, Som], place in *see* Barlinch

Bromwich (Bromwiche), John, union for, of one of his parish churches to another, Salisbury diocese, 1131

Bromyard (Bromiard, Bromiard') [Heref], [putative collegiate or prebendal] church of, canonry and prebend / portion of, union to, of the parish church of B. Mary the Virgin, Patching, 206, 437

Bromyard (*contd*)

.....,...., canon / portionary of *see* Myllyng, Thomas

Brondesbury (Brordsburry) [*or* Broomesbury *in* Willesden, Midd], a prebend in London cathedral, *q.v.*

......, mis-described as a prebend of Llandaff, 583

Brongh'ton' *see* Broughton [Northants]

Brookland (Broklondon) [Kent], parish church of, vicar of, 204

Brookthorpe (Broketrope) [Glos], parish church of, vicarage of, holder of, 711

.....,....,...., union of, to the parish church of St Michael the Archangel, Gloucester, 711

[Broomesbury] *see* Brondesbury

Brordsburry *see* Brondesbury

Brouen *see* Brown

Broughton (Broghton') [Hunts], parish church of, rector of, 442

Broughton (Brongh'ton') [*in* Rothwell deanery, Northants], parish church of, rector of, 300

Broughton (Broughton') [one of the eight parishes of this name in Lincoln diocese; *probably* B~, Lincs, *or perhaps* B~ Poggs, Oxon; *possibly* B~, Oxon, *or perhaps* B~ Astley, Leics], parish church of, holder of, 545

.....,...., union of, to the parish church of Chenies, 545

Brough under Stainmore (Burghe) [Westm], vill of, inhabitants etc of, 1

.....,....,...., increase in number of, 1

.....,...., new building in, 1

.....,...., parish church of, vicar of, 1

.....,....,...., united to the Queen's college, Oxford, 1

.....,...., oratory in honour of the Most Glorious Virgin Mary and hospital built in by John Brunskill, 1

Bryght', Brygth' *see* Bright

Bryme, John, canon of the church of Howden and holder of the parish church of St Michael, Melksham, 644

.........,...., union for, of his parish church to his canonry, Salisbury diocese, 842

Bryne *cf.* Bryme

Bryngwyn (Bryngoyn) [co. Radnor], parish church of, united to canonry and prebend of Clyro in the church of Abergwilly, 579

Brysbone, John, of Lincoln diocese, dispensed for plurality, 1068

[Buckingham, co. of], places in *see* Burnham; Chenies; Drayton Parslow; Ivinghoe; Lavendon; [Newton Longville]; Woughton on the Green

Buckingham (Buckynham), William, vicar of the parish church of the Holy Sepulchre, Cambridge, 453

Buckland (Burklond) [Surrey], parish church of, holder of, 613

.........,...., union of, to the prebend of Denes in the parish church of Chu(l)mleigh, 613

[Bucknall, Lincs] *see* ' Bukenehull' '

?Bucknall (Bukuall), Robert, union for, of one of his parish churches to another, London diocese, 848

[Bucknell, Oxon] *see* ' Bukenehull' '

Buckworth (Bukvorte) [Hunts], parish church of All Saints, rector of, 332

Buckynham *see* Buckingham

Bucotbrogkton' *see* Brant Broughton

[de Bucy], Michael, the late, archbishop of Bourges, 171

Budleigh (Budley) [*modern* East B~, Devon], parish church of, vicarage of, holder of, 22

.........,...., union of, to the parish church of St Dominic, 22

'Bukenehull'', diocese of Lincoln [*unidentified*; *either* Bucknall, Lincs *or* Bucknell, Oxon], parish church of, united to parish church of Nettleton, 570

[?Bukler], William, ostensible abbot of the Premonstratensian monastery of St Radegund, 242

.........,....,...., confirmed or otherwise appointed by the abbot of 'Newerque', 242

Bukuall *see* ?Bucknall

Bukvorte *see* Buckworth

Bulgyn (Bulgen'), John, vicar of Coggeshall, 741

Bulle (Bull'), John, vicar choral in the collegiate church of Southwell, 37; *and see* p. lxxv

......, Richard, vicar of Brookland, 204

.........,...., cantor of the chantry, called chapel, of B. Mary the Virgin, Wolverhampton 'Pyxwell', 209

......, Roger, of Lincoln diocese, dispensed for plurality, 1167

Bullis *see* Boyle

Bultaz, James, to have rectories and vicarages of parish churches and canonry collated to him and have the rectories and vicarages united to the canonry, Ossory diocese, 988

......, *cf.* Butler

Bunbury (Bunbrery) [Ches], [secular collegiate] church of St Boniface, keepership or wardenship in, 448

.........,....,...., holder of, 448

Bunch (Bwuch), William, monk / abbot of the Benedictine monastery of B. Mary, Kilwinning, 103-105

.........,....,....,...., provision of, to Kilwinning, 103

.........,....,....,...., litigant over the monastery, 103, 105

.........,....,....,....,...., cession of, 103, 104

Bunett, Emma, relict of the late Thomas Bunett, executrix of his will, litigant, 665

......, Thomas, the late, of Islington, cleric or layman of London diocese, 665

Butler (*contd*)

......, John, to have parish churches of Lismore and Ossory dioceses united to canonry of Lismore, 956

......, Peter, captain, to be inhibited, 317

......, Theobald, canon of Cashel, papal mandatary, 652

......, Walter, ostensible cleric, detainer of vicarage of Rathronan, 667

......, William, sometime canon [of Lismore?], ostensible cleric, and detainer of deanery of Lismore, 626

......, *cf.* Bonylur; Bultaz

Butley (Buttley) [Suff], Augustinian monastery of B. Mary, canon of *see* Duttley, Thomas

Butterfield *cf.* Batterfeld

Buttley *see* Butley

Butyler, Butyller *see* Butler

[Buyuk-Cekmece] *see* Natura

Bwuch *see* Bunch

Bygrave (Bigrave) [Herts], parish church of, rector of, 186

Byland [*at* Byland Abbey *in* Coxwold, York], [Cistercian] monastery of, abbot of, papal judge delegate, 434

Bylley *see* Beeleigh

Byngesten' Baptist *see* ?Kingston Bagpuize

Byntworth', alias of Bentworth, *q.v.*

Byrde, Thomas, prior of the Augustinian monastery of St Nicholas, Barlinch, 479

Byry *see* Berry

C

[de Caccialupis] de Sancto Severino, Antonius, *abbreviator de parco maiori*, letters expedited by:[1]

A de Sancto Severino, 44- 49, 110-113, 130, 149, 167, 284, 493, 616, 617, 637

Cade, Thomas, rector of All Saints', Buckworth, 332

[Caerleon] *see* Llantarnam

Caher (Cakyrdunese, Carhyrduneso) [*or* Cahir, co. Tipperary], [Augustinian] monastery of B. Mary, prior of, papal mandatary, 657, 667

Caherelly (Kayrillei, Kayrkyl) [co. Limerick], parish church of, vicarage of, 237, 628

......,.....,....., to be united, with other benefices, to canonry and prebend of Inch St Lawrence in Emly, 237

......,.....,....., to be united, with other benefices, to projected prebend of Killoscully in Cashel, 628

[Cahir, co. Tipperary] *see* Caher

Caithness, [cathedral] church of [*at* Dornoch, co. Sutherland], provision to, 1507

......, [bishop-] elect of *see* Stewart, Andrew

Cakyrdunese *see* Caher

Calais [*dép.* Pas-de-Calais, France], parish church of St Peter near, rector of, 458

Calder (Caldor), John, collation to, of vicarage, Ross diocese, 775

de Calderanis, Thady, to have chaplaincy, Kildare diocese, 1006

Caldor *see* Calder

Caley (Caly), Richard, vicar of Ruddington, 712

Calipolen. see Gallipoli

---

1   The register note of the abbreviator's signature is variously punctuated, capitalised and abbreviated.

Canterbury (*contd*)

..........,...., other persons of peculiars *see* Myllyng, Thomas; Pyere, Thomas; Woodington, Thomas

..........,...., places in *see* Barfreystone; Bearstead; Benenden; Boxley; Brookland; Charing; Chislet; Eynsford [*in d. Rochester*]; Eythorne; Harbledown; Harrow [*in d. London*]; Hernhill; Malling, South [*in d. Chichester*] ; [Margate]; Newington [*in d. Winchester*]; St Radegund; Sandhurst; Smarden; Snave; Stanmer [*in d. Chichester*]; Stone; Thanet, Isle of; ?Tonbridge; Westwell; ?Wimbledon [*in d. Winchester*]; *and see* Faversham; Folkestone

..........,......,...., other peculiars described by diocese in which situate *see* Bersted; Bocking; ?Patching; Southchurch

......, provincial constitutions of, 169, *cf.* 533, 665

Cantriff (Cantres') [co. Brecon], parish church of, rector of, 359

Cantwell (Canchowll, Cantuel, Cantuuel, Cantwell', Contuevvoll), Anastasia, to have nunnery, Ossory diocese, 1082

......, James, canon of Ossory, papal mandatary, 656

..........,....,...., papal judge delegate, 352

..........,...., to have precentorship united to canonry, Cashel diocese, 1078

......, John, canon of Ossory, papal mandatary, 60

..........,...., priest of Cashel, 652

..........,....,...., not of Ossory diocese, 652

..........,......,...., to have chancellorship of Ossory anew (?)and canonry and prebend, 652

......, Patrick, canon of Ossory, papal mandatary, 653, 656

Capachac *see* Cappagh

Capo *see* Capol

Capodimonte [prov. Viterbo, Italy], letter dated at, 335

Capol (Capo), William, vicar of Barkway, 547

..........,...., union for, of one of his parish churches to another, London diocese, 1181

Cappagh (Capachac) [co. Tyrone], parish church, called rectory, of, 150

..........,......,..........,...., to be erected into a prebend of Derry, 150

[Cardigan, co. of], places in *see* Llanarth; Llangoedmore

Careggi [*presumably* Villa Medicea di C~, *in* com. of Florence, Italy], letters dated at, 523, 532, 538, 545

Carhyrduneso *see* Caher

Carin'dine *see* ?Carmarthen

Cariswall *see* ?Carswell

'Carlile', diocese of Glasgow [*unidentified*; *in* civil vicariate of Dumfries], [lordship of][*centred on* Carlyle family castle *in* parish of Torthorwald, *q.v.*], temporal lord of *see* [?Carlyle], William

..........,......,...., damsel of *see* Douglas, Margaret

Carlion, Carlion' *see* Carlyan

Carlisle [Cumb], bishop of, oratory and hospital built with licence of, 1

..........,...., consent of, to agreement concerning oblations, contemplated, 1

..........,...., *see* [Leybourne], Roger

......, official of, approval and confirmation of agreement committed to, 1

..........,...., proceedings by, 1

......, **diocese** of, persons of *see* Brunskill, John; Burbank alias Smithson, William; Chaubot, James; [de Clifford], Henry; Collinson, Christopher; Crackenthorpe, George; Dacre, John; Hering, John; Musgrave, Edward; [Redman], Richard; Rigge, Thomas; Robruxone, John; Sothy alias Lancaster, Agnes; Spenser, Miles; Sser, Christopher; Stephynson, Edward; ?W(h)arton, Thomas

..........,...., places in *see* Brough under Stainmore; Musgrave; Newbiggin; Shap

---

1   The register note of the abbreviator's signature is variously punctuated and abbreviated.

de Cesi(i)s, P [*in all probability registry mistranscriptions of* 'O de Cesis', *q.v.*; *just possibly* letters expedited by Paulus Emilius de Cesis *either as* substitute of O de Cesis *or as* regent of the chancery], name noted in register in position reserved for abbreviator:

P. *de Cesiis*, 324

P *de Cesis*, 157

Cetra, Cetram *see* Chitterne

Chahone, James, to have canonry, Llandaff diocese, 1239

Chalke, Broad (Brode Chalke) [Wilts], parish church of, rector of, 64

......,....,...., vicar of, 35

[Chalkis] *see* Negroponte

Chalmer (Thawmer), Thomas, cleric of Aberdeen diocese, 344

......,....,...., to have succentorship of Moray, 344

Chalon-sur-Saône [*dép.* Saône et Loire, France], diocese of, place in *see* Cîteaux

Chalvet, Robert, of Exeter diocese, dispensed for plurality, 1232

Champernon *alias* Chambourn (Champernen' *alias* Chamborn), John, rector of Shepton Beauchamp and incumbent of the vicarage of Kingsbury, 723

?Champney (Champneg), John, of Canterbury diocese, commission by virtue of an appeal, 763

Chaneforo, Chanesoto *see* Canford

Channey, Christopher, vicar of Sawbridgeworth, 706

Chapel Martel (Martyll) [*in* Particles, co. Limerick], chapel, called particle of land, of, 333

......,....,....,...., to be erected, with other benefices, into a prebend of Limerick, 333

Chapina, Richard, of Salisbury diocese, dispensed for plurality, 822

Chapman, Robert, rector of St John the Baptist's, Trimingham, 450

[Chard], Thomas, bishop of Selimbria, commendator of the Cluniac priory of Kerswell and of the parish church of Little Torrington, 281

Charelbery *see* Charlbury

Charing (Charryng) [Kent], parish church of, vicar of, 553

Charlbury (Charelbery) [Oxon], parish church of, vicarage of, holder of, 55

Charles, bishop of Tournai *see* [de Hautbois], Charles

Charlett, Gregory, rector of Harpsden, 748

Charlton Mackrell (Charteton Macrelle) [Som], parish church of St Mary, rector of, 21

Charnerght, John, of Lincoln diocese, dispensed for plurality, 1039

Charryng *see* Charing

Charteton Macrelle *see* Charlton Mackrell

Chaubot, James, of Carlisle diocese, dispensed for plurality, 1056

Chelerey *see* Childrey

Chellisworth' *see* Chelsworth

Chelmsford (Chelmesford) [Essex], parish church of B. Mary the Virgin, rector of, 473

......,....,.... parish church of St Michael, Smarden, united to, 473

Chelsworth (Chellisworth') [Suff], parish church of, rector of, 451

Chelteman, Nicholas, of York diocese, dispensed for plurality, 785

Cheminart, Johannes, *scriptor apostolicus*, signature of as *rescribendarius see* frontispiece

Chenies (Isenhamsted Cheyny, Isenhm'sted Theyne) [Bucks], parish church of, rector of, 51, 545

Chenies (*contd*)

.....,...., union to, of the parish church of Broughton and, conditionally, of the parish church of Tingrith, 545

Cheppard, Richard, vicar of Charing, 553

......, *cf.* Sheppard

Chepparton' *see* ?Shepperton

Chepstow (Strugulior [*now represented by* Striguil castle *in* Chepstow] *alias* Chepstowe) [Monm], parish church of, vicarage of, holder of, 517

.....,....,...., union of, to the parish church of Newport, 517

Chesilchurst *see* Chislehurst

Cheslet *see* Chislet

[Chester, co. of], places in *see* Alderley; Bunbury; ?Thurstaston

Chewton (Chewton') [*modern* Chewton Mendip, Som], parish church of, rector of, bound to provide priest-chaplain for the chapel of Farrington, 223

.....,...., vicar of, refusing to provide chaplain, 223

.....,...., boundary of, chapel of Farrington in, 223

......, place in *see* Farrington

Chichele, Henry, archbishop of Canterbury, investiture with pallium, 385 *note*

Chichester [Sussex], [**cathedral church** of], canonry of, *cf.* 1280

.....,...., canon of, *cf.* Yonge, John

.....,...., **diocese** of, persons of *see* Atkis, William; Bolfe, Hugh; Braben, William; Bristowe, John; Bussoy, William; Cockett, Robert; Coke *alias* Reeve, Richard; Combe, Thomas; Cosyng, John; Cradoli, William; Crowmer, George; Daddisley, James; Dudden', Roger; Fleshmonger, William; Fowler, Simon; Fransbysh, John; Gcynyssh, John; Henauge, William; Inskippe, John; Kirkelon, John; Lee, William; Marynge

Chichester (*contd*)

Robert; Miles, Thomas; Patching, John; Respise, John; Robinson, William; Selwood, Richard; Sewell, Thomas;Shelley, George and Thomas; Skenner, Henry; Smith, William; Spire, Thomas; Stephynson, Edward

.....,...., persons of Canterbury peculiars in *see* Myllyng, Thomas; Pyere, Thomas; Rothelay, John; Wykes, Robert

.....,...., places in *see* Angmering, East; Arlington; Bersted [*Canterbury peculiar*]; Bosham; Boxgrove; Cowfold; Durford; Eastbourne; Felpham; Guldeford; Hamsey; Heyshott; Iford; Lewes; Patching [*Canterbury peculiar*]; Rudgwick; Rye; Sele; Sidlesham; Stedham; Steyning

.....,...., other Canterbury peculiars in *see* Malling, South; Stanmer

Chiericati, Francesco, canon of 'Castonen.', living in the city or diocese of London, 316

.....,....,...., papal judge delegate, 316

.....,...., cleric of Vicenza, 345

.....,....,...., to have chaplaincy at altar of St Mary in parish church of St Mary, Cologna Veneta, 345

......, John, bishop of Cattaro, the late, 345

.....,....,...., commendator of chaplaincy at altar of St Mary in parish church of St Mary, Cologna Veneta, 345

Child Okeford, Child Okford *see* Okeford, Childe

Childrey (Chelerey) [Berks], parish church of the Assumption of B. Mary the Virgin, bell- tower of, bell (named) in, 580

.....,...., [monument of Elisabeth and William Fettiplace in], 580

.....,...., visitors to, indulgences obtainable by, 580

Chilmark (Chylmerke) [Wilts], parish church of, rector of, 698

[Ciocchi del Monte Sansovino] (*contd*)

.....,.....,....., proceedings by, 103

Cirencester (*Cirencestren.*, *Cirencestria*, *Cirencestrie alias* Ccessetur) [Glos], Augustinian monastery (of St Mary) of, abbot and convent of, privileges etc of, to be enjoyed by abbot and convent of the Augustinian monastery of Bruton, 154

.....,.....,.....,....., to be enjoyed by prior and convent of Augustinian monastery of Bradenstoke, 494

.....,....., former dependency of *see* Bradenstoke

.....,....., (?) secular from its foundations, 494

......, church of, jurisdiction of, prior and brethren of Augustinian church of Bradenstoke freed from, 494

.....,....., canon of *see* Burford *alias* Lambard, William

Cîteaux [*dép.* Côte d'Or, France], monastery of, abbot and convent of, consent of a requirement for commends of monasteries of the order, 628

Civita Castellana [prov. Viterbo, Italy], letter dated at, 292

Civitavecchia [prov. Rome, Italy], letters dated at, 18, 501

Claghton *see* Claughton

Clamdacbocdoc *see* Clondavaddog

Clankelly (Clanchellovyd) *see* Clones and Clankelly

Clare [a quarter *in* Tiverton, Devon], a portion of the parish church of Tiverton, 6

.....,....., collation of, 6

......, portioner of, 6

[Clare, co. of], places in *see* ?Crumlin; ?Faha; Feakle; ?Gleninagh; Kilfenora; ?Killana; ?Killeely; ?Killofin; Killokennedy; Killuran; ?Kilnasoolagh; Kilquane; ?Kilseily; Kilshanny; Kiltenanlea; Kiltoraght; Ogonnelloe; Rath; [St Munchin's]; Tomgraney; Tulla

Clashmore (Hasmer) [co. Waterford], a prebend of Lismore, *q.v.*

Claughton [Lancs], rectory of, 184 *note*

Claughton (Claghton), Thomas, of Salisbury diocese, dispensed for plurality, 1411

Claxton, Lausflorus, union for, of his parish church to his deanery, York diocese, 1198

Clay (Cley), John, of York diocese, commission by virtue of an appeal, 1361

Cleanger, John, vicar of Dean Prior, 726

Clement V, constitution [*Quamvis sacris*] of, 425 note, 521

Clement VII, register of, p. lxv notes 12 and 17

Clement XII, register of, pp. l, lxv note 17

Clement (Clemens), Richard, of St David's diocese, dispensed for plurality, 1283

Clendesyll *see* Killeshin

Clerk (Clerke), John, rector of Portishead, 161, 327, 328

.....,....., of Canterbury diocese, dispensed for plurality, 1382

.....,....., of Winchester diocese, dispensed for plurality, 828

.....,....., *nullius diocesis*, union for, of one of his parish churches to another, 1168

......, Thomas, prior of the Augustinian priory of B. Mary the Virgin and All Saints, Westacre, 419

......, William, chaplain in the parish church of Towcester, 9

.....,....., union for, of one of his parish churches to another, Norwich diocese, 1176

......, alias of Marston, William, *q.v.*

Clero *see* Clyro

Cley next the Sea, parish church of, holder of, 540

Cley *see* Clay

Cliddesden (Cludysden') [Hants], parish church of, rector of, 414

.........,...., union to, of the parish church of Chilton Candover and, conditionally, of the chantry of St Catherine in the parish church of St Peter, Marlborough, 414

Cliff cf. Clyffe

[de Clifford], Henry, temporal lord of Clifford and Westmorland, 1

Clifson, William, union for, of one of his parish churches to another, Lincoln diocese, 884

......, cf. Clifton

?Clifton, North (Clyston') [Notts], parish church of, vicar of, 724

Clifton (Cliston, Clyston'), Gamaliel, canon of York, papal judge delegate, 535

.........,...., union for, of his parish church to his canonry, York diocese, 1041

.........,...., petition of, for union of parish church of Wilford to canonry and prebend of Wistow in York cathedral, 1041 note

......, cf. Clifson

Clinose see Clones

Clist see Clyst

Cliston see Clifton

'Clnyuuaceys', diocese of Leighlin [unidentified], parish church of, vicarage of, 623

.........,....,........,...., to be united, with other benefices, to canonry and prebend of Leighlin, 623

Clogher (Plebis Clochran) [co. Tyrone], [Augustinian] monastery of B. Mary, abbot of, papal mandatary, 578

......, [cathedral] church of, dean of, papal mandatary, 338

.........,...., chapter of, to be summoned over erection of canonry and prebend, 310, 619

.........,...., canonry of, to be collated, 1084

Clogher (contd)

.........,...., (canonries and) prebends to be erected in, 310, 619; cf. 1122, 1127, 1356

.........,...., projected prebends in see Galloon and Dartree, Clones and Clankelly, and Drummully; ?Rackwallace alias Clogher

.........,...., canons of see Maccrenyr, Magonius; MacMahon, Patrick; OCullen, John

........,........,...., prospective see Macieneir, Philip; OHanratty, Magonius; and cf. MacDonnell, Maurice; MacMahon, Eugene; Magunshenan, Eugene

......, bishop of, episcopal fourth of Drummully customarily given in farm for annual payment at pleasure of, 310

.........,...., consent of a pre-condition of the erection of episcopal fourth of Drummully into a prebend, 310

.........,...., to be summoned over erection of canonry and prebend, 310, 619

......, [bishop-] elect of see OCullen, Patrick

......, official of, papal mandatary, 619

......, (church of), provision to, 1486

.........,...., archdeacon of, papal mandatary, 256, 739

......, diocese of, persons of see MacArdle, Philip; MacGrath, Thoroletus; MacMahon, Magonius and Patrick; Magenhin, Adam; Meyayn, John; OCallan, Donat; Ochonant, John; Offlangen, ?Dolorus/Dolotus, Ohaed, Patrick; OHanratty, Donald ; Oluan, Nielanus; Osyche, Terence

.........,...., places in see Clankelly; Clones; Dartree; (?)Devenish; Drummully; Galloon; 'Macgareroche'; [Magher-across]; [Magheross]; ?Rackwallace; St Patrick's Purgatory; Tedavnet ; Tehallan

......, alias of ?Rackwallace, q.v.

.........,.......,, monastery of BB. Peter and Paul, [Clones] erroneously stated to be at, 619

Clomarean alias Stradnali see ?Cloon Island alias Stradbally

Clonyhurc (Cloymdahor) [co. Offaly], parish church of, rectory, called chapel, of, 624

......,....,....,....,...., to be united, with other benefices, to newly erected canonry of Kildare and prebend of Nurney, 624

?Cloon Island (Clomarean, Cloynarc) [in the Shannon at Castleconnell, in Stradbally, co. Limerick] alias Stradbally (Seraduualy, Stradnali) [and vice versa, co. Limerick], parish church of, vicarage of, 263, 628

......,....,...., to be united, with other benefices, to canonry and prebend of Tomgraney in Killaloe, 263

......,....,...., to be united, with other benefices, to projected prebend of Killoscully in Cashel, 628

Cloontuskert (Cluntoskeyt nasyna) [co. Roscommon], [Augustinian] monastery of, prior of, papal mandatary, 228

Cloymdahor see Clonyhurc

Cloynarc, alias of Seraduualy, q.v.

Cloyne [co. Cork], **[cathedral] church** of, deanery of, 625

......,....,...., detainer of see OKeeffe, Thady

.........,...., dean of, prospective see Hyerla, Maurice

.........,...., chapter of, to be summoned over erection of canonry and prebend, 625

.........,...., projected canonry and prebend of Aghada in, proposed union to, of the vicarages of Ballintemple and Titeskin, 625

.........,...., canons of see ?MacAuliffe, Donat; MacCarthy, Cormac; Okyellyry, Thomas; Olyche', John; Valetio, Peter; and see Hyerla, Maurice (prospective)

......, **bishop** of, simoniacal compact with, 625

.........,...., to be summoned over erection of canonry and prebend, 625

.........,...., papal mandatary, 333

Cloyne (contd)

......, **diocese** of, persons of see de Geraldinis, James Redimundi and John; de Lacy, Hugh alias Ulick; Magner, David; OBrien, Cornelius; Ohyarhi, Cornelius; Ohyauyan, Dernutius; OSheehan, William; Yeclay, Thomas

.........,...., places in see Aghada; Ballintemple; Castlemagner; 'Moiranoach' ; Ros(s)keen; Shandrum; Titeskin

......, written in error for Clonmacnois, 369-371

Cludysden' see Cliddesden

Clueneynec see Clonenagh

Cluenos and Clanchellovyd see Clones and Clankelly

Cluhan see OCluvane

Clume see ?Clonea

Cluntoskeyt nasyna see Cloontuskert

[Cluny, co. Aberdeen], place in see Kinnernie

Clyffe (Clyffi), John, rector of Whaddon, 255

.........,...., union for, of his parish church to his chapel, Salisbury diocese, 1513

......, cf. Cliff

Clyro (Rayte and Clero) [co. Radnor], a prebend of the church of Abergwilly, q.v.

Clyst (Clist) [modern Clyst (or Clist) St George, Devon], parish church of St George, rector of, 45

Clyston' see ?Clifton, North

Clyston' see Clifton, Gamaliel

Coale cf. Coole

Coberley (Coberlay) [Glos], wardenship of, warden of, 750

Cobham [Kent], [secular] college or chantry of, master of see Crowmer, George

---

1   When it is punctuated the punctuation of the signature varies.

Compton (*contd*)

......,......,....., co-litigant and implied wife of *see* Fyllys *alias* Robinson or Compton, Agnes

......, alias of Fyllys *alias* Robinson or Compton, Agnes, *q.v.*

Comrie (Comri) [co. Perth], parish church of, recent vicar of, 666

......,....., vicarage of, resignation, vacancy, and prospective collation of, 666

......,....., prospective vicar of, 666

Condon *cf.* Condour

Condour, James, scholar of diocese of Ross [*probably* Ireland, *possibly* Scotland], 286

......, *cf.* Condon

Cong (*de Conga*) [cos. Galway and Mayo], Augustinian monastery of St Mary, 610

......,....., detainer and ostensible abbot of *see* MacDonnell, Eneas

......,....., to be united to canonry of Tuam and newly erected prebend of Kilmainebeg, 610

Congiren' *see* Tomgraney

Coningsby (Connyngesby) [Lincs], parish church of, proposed union to the deanery of Lincoln, 1040 *note*

Conmor *see* Cumnor

Connor [co. Antrim], **[cathedral] church** of, canon of *see* Ochilla, Odo

......, bishop of, 350 *note*

......, [bishop-] elect of *see* [Blyth], Robert

......, church of, provision to, 1480

......, [church of], archdeacon of, papal mandatary, 603

......, diocese of, persons of *see* Macgelarinan, Magonius and Patrick; Machrecani, Odo; Maquelurmna, Dermot, John, and Magonius; Obyge, Andrew; ?ODurnin, William; OMurray, Donat and Philip

Connor (*contd*)

......,....., places in *see* ?Ballymena; 'Balmalmad'; Doagh; Kells; Kilbride; Moblusk; Rashee; Templepatrick; Woodburn

......, place in *see* Kells

Connyngesby *see* Coningsby

Constable (Constabile, Cunstable), John, union for, of his parish church to his deanery, Lincoln diocese, 1040

......,....., petition of, for union of parish church of Coningsby to deanery of Lincoln, 1040 *note*

......,......,....., of [another?] parish church held by him to his deanery, Lincoln diocese, 1354

......, Leonard, cleric of York diocese, 721

......,......,....., dispensed to receive the parish church of Long Marston, 721

......, William, of York diocese, dispensed for plurality, 1222

Constal *see* Tunstal

Constantinople (*Constantinopolitan.*) [Turkey], archbishop of, subjection to, of church of Natura, 126

......,......,....., of church of Panados, 120

?Controne (Courrono) [*perhaps* San Gimignano di C~ *or* Pieve di C~, *both in* com. of Bagni di Lucca, prov. Lucca, Italy], parish church of St Geminianus, resignation of, 461

......,....., commend of, 461

Contuevvoll *see* Cantwell

Conveth (Convecht) [*modern* Laurencekirk, co. Kincardine], parish church of, fruits of, reserved, 102

......,....., re-entry and entry to, grant of, 102

Cook (Cooke), John, of London diocese, dispensed for plurality, 947

......,....., cantor of the chantry of St John the Baptist, Braintree, petition of, 947 *note*

......, *cf.* Coke *alias* Reeve

---

1   The register note of the abbreviator's signature is variously punctuated and capitalised.

?Crumlin (Cromlyn) [*in* Killonaghan, co. Clare], parish church of, vicarage of, 611

......,....,...., to be united, with other benefices, to the Augustinian monastery of B. Mary, Kilshanny, 611

Cudgtinglon', Cudgtington' *see* Kidlington

Cuirni *see* ?OCurran

Cukam *alias* Tempul padrig *see* Templepatrick

Culase, Cullace *see* Collace

?Cullan (Caluanen'), Alexander, canon of Aberdeen, papal judge sub-delegate, 137

......,....,....,...., proceedings by, 137

Cullicolman *see* ?Kilcolman

Culligen' *see* Colligan

Culmacuenam *see* Kilmacrenan

Cumberegge, John, rector of Colsterworth, 39

[Cumberland, co. of], place in *see* Carlisle

Cumnor (Conmor) [Berks], parish church of St Michael the [Arch]angel, vicarage of, holder of, 206

Cundall', Henry, vicar of Barton, 465

Cunstable *see* Constable

Cunstall' *see* Tunstal

Cuper, alias of Colchester, Robert, *q.v.*

Curreyn, Curryn *see* ?OCurran

Curtas (Curteys), William, of Lincoln diocese, dispensed for plurality, 1320

Cusack (Cusake), Walter, of Meath diocese, dispensed for plurality, 1343

Cuselegh' *see* Carsley

Cusin *see* Cosyn

Cutcombe (Cuttrombe) [Som], parish church of, vicar of, 185

......,...., vicarage of, union to, of the vicarage of Winsford, 185

Cutler, Alexander, vicar of St Botolph's, Saxilby, 452

Cuttrombe *see* Cutcombe

Cyllcairill *see* Termonamongan

Cynnes, William, of Salisbury diocese, dispensed for plurality, 950

.........,...., vicar of Hagbourne, petition of, 950 *note*

D

Dabis *see* Davy

Dacre, John, of Carlisle diocese, further dispensed in respect of minority for plurality, 1528

Daddisley, James, rector of St Peter's, Hamsey and prospective rector of St Andrew's *in Foro*, Lewes, 710

Dalago, .L. see de Alagon

Dalby, Thomas, archdeacon of Richmond in the church of York, 268; *cf.* 270

......,....,...., holder of provostship of the church of St John, Beverley, 268, 270

......,....,....,...., holder of parish church of Brant Broughton, 268, 270

......,....,....,....,...., perhaps deprived, appellant, 268; *cf.* 270

Dalow, Edward, of Hereford diocese, commission by virtue of an appeal, 1365, 1373

[Dalton in Furness, Lancs], place in *see* Furness

Dalton (Dalton'), John, ostensible cleric or monk of the Cistercian monastery of Furness, 434

......,....,...., appointed abbot of Furness, 434

Damyon (Damyan'), John, OFM, 444

?Dandy (Daudy), Robert, of London diocese, dispensed for plurality, 1326

Dane *see* ?Dean, West

Danielo, Johannes, *abbreviator de parco maiori*, letters expedited by:[1]

Jo Danielo, 241, 247, 631- 636

Jo Danyelo, 587, 747

---

1 The register note of the abbreviator's signature is variously punctuated and capitalised.

Danson, William, rector of All Saints, Great Fordham, 446, 715

......,....,....,...., holder of the parish church of Aldham and the church of Fakenham Parva, 715

......, cf. Dauson; Dawson

Dansoy see ?Dengie

Danyell (Danyell'), William, vicar of ?Bampton and incumbent of Kingsdon and Hampreston, 676

[Daonium] see Daria

La Darbi see Derby

Darby, Edward, archdeacon of Stow in the church of Lincoln and incumbent of Charlbury, 55

Darean see Derrane

[Dareja] see Daria

Darforth see Durford

Daria (Barier recte Darien.) [in partibus infidelium] unidentified [possibly Darien. recte Danen., i.e. Daonium in Thrace, modern Eski-Eregli, on the northern coast of the Sea of Marmara, European Turkey; Dareja in Syria has also been suggested], bishop of see [Hogeson], William

......, provision to, p. lxxiv note 294

Darley (Darlei), Roger, of Norwich diocese, dispensed for plurality, 1071

Darragh (Dermachno) [co. Limerick], parish church of, vicarage of, 333

......,....,...., to be erected, with other benefices, into a prebend of Limerick, 333

Darrell, Richard, of Rochester diocese, dispensed for plurality, 943

Dartree (Darteny) see Galloon [and] Dartree

Darwent, George, vicar of ?Dilhorne, appellant in case of allegedly false accusation, 498

Daudy see ?Dandy

Dauson cf. Danson; Dawson

Dauyd Duy, Griffin see Griffin [ap] David Duy

Daventry (Daventre) [Northants], Benedictine priory of St Augustine, priory of, 88, 205

......,...., prior of see [Ilston], Thomas

Davi alias Davies see Davys

David, Henry, of London diocese, dispensed for plurality, 1201

David, bishop of Lismore see [Hamilton], David

David [ab Owain], the late, bishop of St Asaph, 89, 91

Davies, alias of Davi, q.v.

Davy (Dabis), Benedict, of Lincoln diocese, dispensed for plurality, 1048

......, John, of Exeter diocese, dispensed for plurality, 1362

Davys (Davi alias Davies), Richard, prebendary of Denes in the parish church of Chu(l)mleigh and holder of the parish church of Buckland and the vicarage of Broadhembury, 613

Dawson (Dawsoon), William, layman of Lincoln diocese, litigant, 218

......,....,...., adjudged wife of see Choney, Cicely, 218

......,...., of London diocese, commission by virtue of an appeal, 1440

......, cf. Danson; Dauson

Dayly alias Doyly, Thomas, vicar of All Saints', Marcham, 294

?Dean, West (Dane) [Wilts], land of lying nearest and most convenient to the land [i.e. holdings?] of Bradenstoke monastery, gifted to the monastery, 494

Deane, John, vicar of Longdon, 633

Dean Prior (Dean Prioris) [Devon], parish church of, vicar of, 726

Debrena, John, ostensible priest, detainer of vicarage of ?Agha, 348

Deche, William, of Lincoln diocese, dispensed for plurality, 1388

Delge, Delig see Kildellig

Demore see Diamor

[Denbigh, co. of], place in see Vallis Crucis

Denes (Denys) [probably in Chu(l)mleigh, Devon], a prebend in the parish church of Chu(l)mleigh, q.v.

?Dengie (Dansoy) [modern St Lawrence Newland, Essex], church of St Laurence, rectory with cure of, holder of, 425

......,....,...., in the patronage of the abbot and convent of Beeleigh, 425

..........,...., presentation of canon of Beeleigh for, 425

Denham, John, rector of North Kilworth and prospective holder of the parish church of Tinwell, 290

Dennington (Donynglon') [Suff], parish church of St Mary, incumbent of, 418

Denton (Bentori), Elisabeth, indulgence impetrated by, for a Dominican church, London diocese,and the altar of St Thomas Aquinas therein, 1245

..........,...., of the illustrious family of Jerningham of Somerleyton, 1245 note

..........,...., governess of Henry VIII and of his sister, 1245 note

..........,...., to be buried by the altar of St Thomas Aquinas and B. S[c]ita the Virgin in church of Dominican house, London, 1245 note

......, James, rector of St Olave the Martyr's in Southwark, 128

Denys see Denes

Derby [Derb], archdeacon of in the church of Lichfield, papal judge delegate, 462

[Derby, co. of], places in see Aston on Trent; Derby; ?Marston; Repton; Rolleston

Derby (La Darbi) [Derb], present earl of see [Stanley, Thomas]

Dermachno see Darragh

Derrane (Darean, Doran) [in Kilbride, co. Roscommon], Augustinian monastery of B. Mary, prior of, papal mandatary, 245, 330

Derry [co. Londonderry], [Augustinian] monastery of Celemegre, abbot of, benefice or office (not named) pertaining to collation of, 347

......,....,...., see ?OFriel, Conatius

..........,...., prospective commendator of see OMulfall, Nillanus

..........,...., goods of, alleged dilapidation of, 347

..........,...., wrongly described as Cistercian, 347

......, [cathedral] church of [at Derry or Londonderry, co. Londonderry], dean of see MacCloskey, [forename wanting]

..........,...., chapter of, to be summoned over erection of canonry and prebend, 668

..........,...., canonries and prebends to be erected in, 150, 668

..........,...., projected prebends in see Cappagh; Leckpatrick

..........,...., canons of, see Macantaggart, John; OBoyle, Bernard; OCarolan, Nillanus; OMorrissey, Cormac and William

......,....,...., prospective see Macnarthan', Terence; OCarolan, Philip

......, bishop of, to be summoned over erection of canonry and prebend, 668

......, archdeacon of see MacCloskey, [forename wanting]

......, diocese of, persons of see MacGrath, Thoroletus; Magnacman, Emundus; Mecorta, Laurence; OCarolan, Donat and Philip; OGormley, Magonius; OKane, Cornelius; Okawul, Donat; and cf. OGallagher, Arthur

..........,...., places in see Agivey; Cappagh; Derry; Dungiven; Termonamongan; Urney

......, Kildare written in error for, 111 note, 112 note; and see also 982 note

Disertlauiis *see* Inch St Lawrence

Disseacthenis *see* Dysartenos

Disthurwtbue *see* Dischington

Ditcheat (Dychet) [Som], parish church of, parish of, married couple (named) of, 316

Doagh (Duochayn *alias* Dumdean) [*in* Grange of Doagh, co. Antrim], parish church of St Archanata, vicarage of, vicar of, 606

.....,....,...., prospective union to, of rectory of Kilbride, 606

Dochson', Henry, vicar of Stanton Harcourt, 728

Docwra (Docwre), John, union for, of his parish church in York diocese to his parish church in London diocese, 1013

Dodd (Dodde), Robert, of Coventry and Lichfield diocese, 289, 295

.....,....,...., spiritual relative and prospective spouse of *see* Cotton, Cicely

Dodding (Dodyng), Thomas, of Canterbury diocese, dispensed for plurality, 1189

Dodwell (Dodwell'), William, rector of Gayton and prospective member of the college of B. Mary the Virgin, Northill, 717

Dodyng *see* Dodding

Dolman, Dolman' *see* Dowman

Domacdrchyny *see* ?Modreeny

Doma'omer *see* Donaghmore

Dominic, [cardinal] bishop of Porto *see* [de Grimanis], Dominic

Donaghmore (Doma'omer, Donachinor) [co. Laois], parish church of St Patrick, rectory of, 265, 601

.....,....,...., to be erected into a prebend of Ossory with rectory of Kildellig and vicarage of B. Mary's, Rathdowney united thereto, 601

Donaldi [*deleted*], Maurice, 338 *note*

Dondonaill, William, to have vicarages of parish churches and a prebend, Killala diocese, 1118

[Donegal, co. of], places in *see* Clondavaddog; Inishkeel; Inver; Kilmacrenan; Raphoe; ?Ray; Raymoghy; St Patrick's Purgatory; Termon; Tullaghobegly; Urney

Donnyngton' *see* Dunnington

Donynglon' *see* Dennington

[Donyrish *in* Particles, co. Limerick] *see* Down Innish

Donyson *see* Thomson

Doran *see* Derrane

Dorchester (Dorchestre) [Dors], parish church of the Holy Trinity, rector of, 33

.....,...., collation of, 33

[Dornoch, co. Sutherland], [cathedral] church of Caithness at, *q.v.*

Dorset, archdeaconry of in the church of Salisbury, 343, 361

.....,...., visitation of by deputy, 343, 361

......, archdeacon of, 343, 361

[Dorset, co. of], places in *see* Beminster Prima; Bindon; Blandford Forum; Bradpole; Bredy, Long; Canford; Corfe Castle; Dorchester; Fifehead Neville; Gillingham; Hampreston; ?Manston; Milton; Milton Abbas; Okeford, Childe; Pimperne; Shaftesbury; Stratton; 'Wualde Fletayn' [*in* Canford]

Douglas (Dowglas), Gavin, provost of the church of B. Giles, Edinburgh, 375, 376, 378

.....,....,....,...., absolution of preliminary to provision, 376

.....,....,....,...., provision of to Dunkeld, 375, 377, 378

.....,...., [bishop-] elect of Dunkeld, 375, 377, 378

.....,....,...., faculty for consecration, 377

Douglas (*contd*)

......,.....,....., to take oath of fealty, 377

..........,....., holder of canonry of Dunbar and prebend of Hauch, 378

......,.....,....., dispensed to retain provostship and canonry and prebend, 378

......, Margaret, damsel (of 'Carlile'), 135, 320

......,.....,....., litigant over tithe-fruits of parish church of Torthorwald, 320

[Doulting, Som], place in *see* Stoke Lane

Dow *see* Dull

Dowglas *see* Douglas

Dowman (Dolman, Dolman'), John, canon of London, papal judge delegate, 535, 615, 665

Down, diocese of [*seated* at Downpatrick, *in* Down, co. Down], person of *see* de Bertis, William

..........,....., place in *see* Moville

[Down, co. of], places in *see* Down; Moville

Downehm' *see* Downham

Down Gadmond (Dulgadmac) [*or* Dungadmon *in* Particles, co. Limerick], chapel, called particle of land, of, 333

......,.....,.....,....., to be erected, with other benefices, into a prebend of Limerick, 333

Downham (Downehm') [Essex], parish church of St Margaret, holder of, 299

..........,....., union of, to the parish church of B. Mary the Virgin, Whatfield, 299

Down Innish (Dwnyrys) [*or* Donyrish *in* Particles, co. Limerick], chapel, called particle of land, of, 333

......,.....,.....,....., to be erected, with other benefices, into a prebend of Limerick, 333

[Downpatrick] *see* Down

Doynton [Glos], parish church of the Holy Trinity, rector of, 18

Dracke *see* Drake

Draiton Paslow *see* Drayton Parslow

Drake (Dracke), Richard, of Norwich diocese, dispensed for plurality, 1410

Drax (Drakys *alias* Drax) [Yorks], Augustinian monastery of St Nicholas, canons of *see* Norcliffe, Robert; Wilkinson, John

Draycott Le Moors (Dreycot' Delemoers) [Staffs], parish church of, rector of, 467

Drayton Parslow (Draiton Paslow) [Bucks], parish church of, holder of, 573

Dreycot' Delemoers *see* Draycott Le Moors

Driburgch, Driburght, Driburgrh *see* Dryburgh

Drommyche' *see* Drummully

Dromore [co. Down], diocese of, persons of *see* Magennis, Gelasius

Dron [co. Perth], parish church of, sometime vicar of, 239

..........,....., vicarage of, litigation over, 239

......,.....,....., fruits of, sequestration of, 239

?Drumlane (*de Torsolato*) [co. Cavan], [Augustinian] monastery of St Mary, prior of, papal mandatary, 310

Drummond, William, collation to, of deanery of Dunblane, 863

......, *cf.* Derummona

Drummully (Drommyche', Drumonilche) [cos Fermanagh and Monaghan], parish of, episcopal fourth of, 310

......,.....,....., customarily given in farm at the bishop of Clogher's pleasure for an annual payment, 310

......,.....,....., with the bishop of Clogher's consent to be erected, with other benefices, into a prebend of Clogher, 310

......, parish church of St Cormac, vicarage of, collation of, 338

Duochayn *alias* Dumdean *see* Doagh

inter Duos Pontes, alias of Mubhusg, *q.v.*

Durford (Darforth) [*in* Rogate, Sussex], Premonstratensian monastery, called house, of B. Mary and St John the Baptist, canon of *see* Skenner, Henry

Durham [Durh], Benedictine monastery of St Cuthbert, prior and convent of, presentation by, of person for vicarage of Heighington, 199

......, **bishop** of, papal letters directed to, 287

..........,..., papal mandatary, 207; *cf.* 287

..........,..., papal judge delegate, 268

..........,..., special licence of, a requisite for bishop *in partibus* to exercise the pontifical office in city and diocese, 124

..........,..., [peculiar jurisdiction of, church in] *cf.* Osmotherley

..........,..., *see* [Booth], Laurence

......, church of, archdeaconry of, 519

..........,..., archdeacon of *see* Franklin, William

......, **city and diocese** of, bishop *in partibus* indulged to exercise pontifical office in *see* Slater, Richard

..........,......, diocese of, persons of *see* Ashton, Hugh; Franklin, Thomas; Patenson, Thomas; Richardson, William; Wren, Geoffrey; *and see* Newman, John

..........,..., places in *see* Auckland; Bothal; Heighington; Kepier; Lanchester; Sherburn; Stranton; *and see* Osmotherley

......, *and see* Kepier

[Durham, co. of], places in *see* Auckland; Durham; Heighington; Iveston; Kepier; Lanchester; Sherburn; Stranton

Dusque *alias* St Saviour *see* Graiguenamanagh

Duthil (Duchel) [cos. Inverness and Moray], a prebend of Moray cathedral, *q.v.*

Duttley, Thomas, canon of the Augustinian monastery of B. Mary, Butley, 574

Duy, Griffin David *see* Griffin [ap] David Duy

Dwnyrys *see* Down Innish

Dwsq(ue) *alias* St Saviour *see* Graiguenamanagh

Dychet *see* Ditcheat

Dyconson' *see* Dickenson

Dyker (Dykar), Robert, canon of Wells, papal judge delegate, 222

..........,..., chancellor of Wells, 277

..........,.....,...., oath taken by, on admission to chancellorship, 277

..........,.....,...., indulged not to lecture, 277

Dyllani, Dyllon *see* Dillon

Dyngley *see* Dingley

Dynnford *see* Eynsford

Dysartenos (Disseacthenis) [co. Laois], parish church of, vicarage of, 141

..........,.....,...., to be united, with other benefices, to the Cistercian monastery of St Mary, *de Legedei*, Abbeyleix, 141

Dysertynyn *see* ?Disert Fincheall

E

Ealdstreet (Ealdstrete) [*in* Shoreditch, Midd], a prebend of London cathedral, *q.v.*

Eall, Lewis, rector of ?Shepperton, 743

East Angmering *see* Angmering, East

Eastbourne (Estburne) [Sussex], parish church of, rector or vicar of, 426

..........,..., confraternity in dedicated to the Name of Jesus and St [S]citha the Virgin, 426

..........,.....,...., chaplain (named) of, 426

..........,.....,...., guardians and keepers of, 426

..........,..., indulgence obtainable by those visiting and contributing to the confraternity and its chaplain, 426

Fedamore (Frademur) [co. Limerick], in the lordship of John, son of Thomas the earl of Desmond, 236

......,parish church of, disrepair of, 236

........,...., vicarage of, poverty of, 236

.........,......,...., grant of patronage of, conditional on increased endowment and repair of church, 236

Federesso *see* Fetteresso

Fedun *see* Fiddown

Felany, Felavyn *see* ?OPhelan

Feliphi *see* Philips

Fell (Fell'), William, rector of Theydon Mount, 14

Felpham (Ffelgam) [Sussex], parish church of B. Mary the Virgin, vicar of, 515

Feltwell (Ffoltwe'll) [Norf], parish church of St Nicholas, united to chantry of St Leonard, [Sheffield], 540

Feriby (Fferyby), Richard, rector of Stratford, 487

......, *cf.* Ferriby

[Fermanagh, co. of], places in *see* Clankelly; Clones; (?) Devenish; Drummully; Galloon; [Magheracross]

Ferne *cf.* Fery

Ferns [co. Wexford], **[cathedral] church** of, precentorship of, 599

......,....,...., detainer of *see* Ewart, John

......,......,...., to be united to vicarage of Reisk for OMorrissey, William, 599

........,...., chapter of, to be summoned over erection of canonry and prebend, 355

........,...., benefice, called prebend, in parish church of Toome customarily conferred on one of the numerary canons, 355

......,....,......,....,...., detained by William Lacy and Thomas Quenurthwn, 355

........,...., canonry and prebend to be erected in, 355

Ferns (*contd*)

.........,...., projected prebend in *see* 'Issertkainain', 'Karmilla' *alias* 'Karnodia', Preban, and Toome

.........,...., canon(s), of *see* Lacy, Donald; Sutton, William

......,......,...., prospective *see* Ygyhyn, Patrick

......, **bishop** of, to be summoned over erection of canonry and prebend, 355

........,...., *see* Neville, [Laurence]

......, [bishop-] elect of *see* Purcell, John

......, church of, provision to, 1477

........,...., archdeaconry of, 658

......,......,...., to be united, with other benefices, to the precentorship of Ossory, 658

......,......,...., detainer of *see* Fremss, John

......, **diocese** of, persons of *see* Lawless, John; MacMurphy, Maurice; Miedull, William; Neville, Richard; OBardon, Odo; Oderramy, Odo; OFortin, Maurice; Ogemnan, Nicholas; Ostosgat, Maurice; *and see* Kawall, Richard

........,...., places in *see* Clonmore; Enniscorthy; 'Issertkainain'; 'Karmilla' *alias* 'Karnodia'; 'Maruen'; Preban; Ross, Old; Toome

Ferriby *cf.* Feriby

Ferta and Cilcumata *alias* Maentemayn *see* Fuerty and Kilcomnata

Fery, George, reservation to, of fruits of chantership, called precentorship, of Brechin, 1402

........,...., chanter, called precentor, of Brechin, resignation of, *cf.* 1401 and 1402

........,. *cf.* Ferne

Fetteresso (Federesso) [co. Kincardine], parish church of, fruits of, specified sum reserved on, 102

........,...., a prebend in the church of St Mary of the Rock, St Andrews, 102

........,...., re-entry and entry to, grant of, 102

Green *cf.* Grene

Greenway (Greneway), John, indulgence impretrated by, for those giving alms to a certain parish church, Exeter diocese, 1296

Gregory X, constitution [*Exigit*] of, 343

Greig, Thomas, canon of Dunkeld, papal judge delegate, 530

Grene (Greue), George, monk of the Benedictine monastery of Hyde, 634

......, John, union for, of one of his parish churches to another, Lincoln diocese, 921

......, Nicholas, of Lincoln diocese, dispensed for plurality, 920

......, Thomas, vicar of 'Nevntonluyll', diocese of Lincoln, 559

......, *cf.* Green

Greneway *see* Greenway

Gresham, Thomas, rector of Southrepps and holder of Wiveton, 357

Greue *see* Grene

Grey, [Lord] George, union for, of his parish church to his deanery, Norwich diocese, 1316

......, Thomas, rector of St Augustine's, Snave, 187

Gridson', Edward, ostensible precentor of Crediton, accusations against, 462

......,......,....., litigant, 462

[Griffi], Peter, bishop of Forlì, 220

......,......,....., scriptor of the archive of the Roman curia, 220

......,......,....., though not proficient in English dispensed to receive benefices in England, 220

Griffin [ap] David (Dauyd) Duy [*cf.* Dewi], rector of St Giles the Abbot, Wendlebury and holder of the vicarage of the parish church of St ?Miliceus, Llanarth, 25

Griffith *and* ?Griffith (Griffith', Guffith), John, treasurer of St David's cathedral and incumbent of Burton Ferry, 539

......,Lewis, union for, of one of his parish churches to another, St David's diocese, 1157

......,*cf.* Gruffudd

Griffith Ap Giryn', Hugh Ap *see* Hugh Ap Griffith Ap Giryn'

[de Grimanis], Dominic, [cardinal] bishop of Porto, fruits of Cistercian monastery of Glenluce reserved to, 366

Grittoni, John, of Lincoln diocese, commission by virtue of an appeal, 1256

Grolleau, John, of Salisbury diocese, dispensed for plurality, 1298

Gronhuist, Catherine, of London diocese, commission by virtue of an appeal, 1098

Groyne, John, of Lincoln diocese, dispensed for plurality, 1142

Gruffudd *cf.* Griffith

Gudbuerum *see* Woodburn

de Gueraldinis see de Geraldinis

Guffith *see* ?Griffith

Guibesson (Guibason), Hugh, of London diocese, dispensed for plurality, 945 and *note*

Guidottis (de Guinzano), Paulus Nicolai, cleric of Lucca, 146

......,......,....., continual commensal familiar of cardinal Sixtus [de Franciottis de Rovere], 146

......,......,......,....., to have the priorship of the church of St Donatus outside the walls of Lucca, 146

.........,...., detainer of and litigant over the parish church, called priory, of St Stephen, Tassignano, 147

......,......,...., cession of, 147

[Ham, West, Essex], place in *see* Stratford

Hamikan', John, canon of Lismore, papal mandatary, 581

[Hamilton], David, bishop of Lismore, 366-368

......,....,...., absolution of preliminary to commend, 367

......,....,...., commend to, of Cistercian monastery of Glenluce, 366, 368

......,....,...., to take oath of fealty, 366, 368

Hamlet (Hamlett), Richard, layman of Lincoln diocese, 665

......,....,...., executor of the will of the late Thomas Bunett of Islington, appellant, 665

Hammond (Homond), George, of Lincoln diocese, dispensed for plurality, 813

Hamnes *see* Hamsey

Hampreston (Hampriston') [Dors], parish church of, incumbent of, 676

[Hampshire], places in *see* Beaulieu Regis; Bentworth; Burghclere; Candover, Chilton; Cliddesden; Havant; Hyde; Meonstoke; Monxton *alias* Anna de Becco; Quarley; Southampton; Twynham; Winchester; Worthy, Headbourne; Wymering

Hampton, Bishop's [*or* Hampton Lucy, Warw], parish church of, holder of, 429

......,...., vicarage of Blockley united to, 429

Hampton (Hampton', Hamyton), alias of Moyne, Richard, *q.v.*

Hampton Episcopi *see* Hampton, Bishop's

[Hampton Lucy] *see* Hampton, Bishop's

Hamsey (Hamnes) [Sussex], parish church of St Peter, rector of, 710

......,...., union (conditional) to, of the parish church of St Andrew *in Foro*, Lewes, 710

Hamsterley, Ralph, indulgence impetrated by, for those visiting a certain church, London diocese, 1323

Hamyton *see* Hampton

Hanary *see* Athenry

Hanch *see* Hauch

Hanchyth, John, of Worcester diocese, dispensed for plurality, 1523

Haney *see* Hanney

Haniball' *see* Hannyball

Hanney (Haney) [*modern* West H~, Berks], parish church of, vicarage of, holder of, 3

......,....,...., union of, to the parish church of Lockinge, 3

Hannyball (Haniball', Han(n)ybale), Thomas, rector of Alvechurch and holder of the parish church of East Ilsley, 501

......,...., vicar general in spirituals of the bishop of Worcester or official of Worcester, 134

......,....,...., commissary of bishop of Lincoln, 134

......,....,....,...., allegedly absented himself from place of trial, 134

......,...., canon of York, papal judge delegate, 218

Hanson (Hauson), Nicholas, of Norwich diocese, dispensed for plurality, 1306

Harbledown (Harbaldoune) [Kent], parish church of St Michael the Archangel, rector of, 50

Harbottle (Harbotell'), William, monk of the Cistercian monastery of B. Mary, Coggeshall, 639, 643

(de) Hardeconis, Robert, of Bath and Wells diocese, dispensed for plurality, 958

Harden, John, rector of Headbourne Worthy and holder of the parish church of Upton Lovell, 4

Harenhyll *see* Hernhill

Haresfield (Arsefelde) [Glos], parish church of, vicar of, 722

Haringron, Harington *see* Haryn(g)don

[Harington, John and Elisabeth his wife], chantry of *see under* Porlock

Harondi, Stephen, of Lincoln diocese, dispensed for plurality, 1248

Harou *see* Harrow

Harpsden (Herpeden') [Oxon], parish church of, rector of, 748

Harris (Harrys, Herres), Mary, of Coventry and Lichfield diocese, to be dispensed for marriage, 1234

......,......, (future) spouse of *see* Smith, William

......,Richard, rector of Holy Trinity, Doynton, 18

Harrow (Harou) [*modern* Harrow on the Hill, Midd], parish church of, rector of, 184

Harrys *see* Harris

Hart *cf.* Hortis

Hartpury (Hertbury) [Glos], parish church of, vicar of, 488

Harvey (Harwy), Robert, ostensible Augustinian canon, 134

......,......,......, provision to, of Augustinian priory of Burscough, 134

Haryman (Harymany), Joan, ostensible nun or prioress of the Benedictine nunnery of Usk, 602

......,......,......, supporters of *see* Hopkyn ap Pukyn'; Philip ap Llewellyn; Thomas ap John

Haryngby *see* Herringby

Haryn(g)don (Haringron, Harington, Haryngton'), William, canon of London, papal judge delegate, 535, 615, 665

......,......, indult for non residence in usual form, 836

Hasmer *see* Clashmore

Hasting (Hastinge), John, of York diocese, dispensed for plurality, 852

Hathington *see* Haddington

Hau, Thomas, cleric of St Andrews diocese, 241

......,......,......, secretary of John [Stewart], duke of Albany, 241

......,......,......,......, to have deanery of Brechin cathedral, 241

Hauch (Hanch) [*i.e.* Prestonhaugh, *modern* Prestonkirk *or* East Linton, co. Haddington], a prebend in church of Dunbar, *q.v.*

Hauson *see* Hanson

[de Hautbois], Charles, recently bishop of Tournai, cession of, 78, 81

Havant (Halbant) [Hants], parish church of, rector of, 291

Hawe, Thomas, of Lincoln diocese, dispensed for plurality, 1188

Hawnel, Thomas, cleric or layman of Norwich diocese, 614

......,......,......, appellant in marriage case, 614

......,......,......, alleged wife of *see* Fyllys *alias* Robinson or Compton, Agnes

Hay (Hai, Haye), Alexander, canon of Aberdeen and prebendary of Turriff, 522

......,......,......, pursued over non-payment of pension, appellant, 522

......,......, canon of Moray, papal judge sub-delegate, 137

......,......,......,......, proceedings by, 137

Headbourne Worthy *see* Worthy, Headbourne

Heal (Hele), John, layman, parishioner of the chapel of Farrington in Chewton, appellant, 223

......, William, layman, parishioner of the chapel of Farrington in Chewton, appellant, 223

Hecton', Gilbert, vicar of Leigh, 407

......, *cf.* Ecton

Hedde, Thomas, union for, of his chantry to his parish church, Rochester diocese, 1021

Henshaw, Nicholas, rector of St George's, Clyst, 45

.........,...., canon of the [secular collegiate] church of Ottery, holder of the vicarages of Holbeton and Thorverton, 417

Henton (Henton'), John, the younger, layman, parishioner of the chapel of Farrington in Chewton, appellant, 223

......,Robert, layman, parishioner of the chapel of Farrington in Chewton, appellant, 223

Heoke, Henry, cleric or layman of Exeter diocese, appellant, 222

Hepburn (Hepbuene, Hepburne, Hepbury, Hexburne), Adam, cleric of St Andrews diocese, 283

......,.....,...., to have vicarage of Haddington, 283; cf. 285

.........,...., of St Andrews diocese, dispensed for plurality, 1092

......, Alexander, cleric of St Andrews diocese, 284

......,.....,...., to have vicarage of Gamrie, 284

......, George, vicar of Haddington, resignation of, 283

......,.....,...., proctor of see Strachan, Gilbert

......, George [another], cleric of St Andrews diocese, 412

......, George, of St Andrews diocese, dispensed for plurality, 1091

......, James, [bishop-] elect of Moray, 649, 1027-1029; and see p. lxxi note 164

......,.....,...., faculty for consecration, 1030

......,.....,...., dispensed to retain parish church, Whithorn diocese, 1029

.........,...., provision of, to Moray, 649, 1027, 1028

......,.....,...., absolution of preliminary to provision, 1031

.........,...., exemption of, from the jurisdiction of the archbishop of St Andrews, 649

Hepburn (contd)

......, John, collation to of parish church, Ross diocese, 844

.........,...., provision of to Brechin, 1444

......,.....,...., absolution of preliminary to provision, 1446

.........,...., dispensed for minority, 1448

......,.....,...., [bishop-] elect of Brechin, 1444, 1447

......,.....,.....,...., faculty for consecration, 1445

......,.....,.....,...., dispensed to retain benefice(s), Ross diocese, 1447

Heraclea (Irachien.) [Thrace, modern Marmaraereglisi on the northern shore of the Sea of Marmara, European Turkey], archbishop of, subjection to, of the church of Gallipoli, 94

Herbert, late canon of St Martin le Grand, London, and founder of two prebends therein, 737

Here alias Morgan, William, of St David's diocese, dispensed for plurality, 1194

Hereford [Heref], parish church of St Peter, altar of St Mary Magdalene in, chaplaincy at, 697

......,.....,...., chaplain, called cantor, at see Beale, James

......, [cathedral] church of, prebends of see Ewithington; Withington [Parva]

......,.....,...., canonry and prebend of Ewithington, union to, of St Nicholas's, Southam, 427

.........,...., canons of see Martyn, Henry; Pole, Ranulph

......, bishop of see [Mayeu], Richard

......, [bishop-] elect of see Booth, Charles

......, church of, provision to, 1460

......, diocese of, persons in see Bempti, Roger; Benson, Richard; Broyn, Roger; Dalow, Edward; Marble, William; Maunsell, John; Myllyng, Thomas; Parkhurst, Richard; Powys, John; Roberts, Richard; Slade, Thomas

Ireland (*contd*)

......, all, primate of *see* [De Palatio], Octavian

......, collector of the camera in *see* Theodorici, John

Ireland (Yrlande, Yslande), William, canon of Dunkeld, papal judge delegate, 137, 530

Irwin (Irwyn), John, collation to, of parish church, St Andrews diocese, 1516

Isabel *see* Otto and Isabel

Iscerdagrych *see* Desertcreat

Iseldon *see* Islington

Isenhamsted Cheyny, Isenhm'sted Theyne *see* Chenies

[Isertlaurence, co. Limerick] *see* Inch St Lawrence

[Ishartmon, co. Wexford] *see* 'Issertkainain'

[Isles, The] *see* Sodor

[Isleworth, Midd], place in *see* Syon

Islington (Iseldon) [Midd], person of *see* Bunett, Thomas

'Issertkainain', diocese of Ferns [*unidentified*; *perhaps* Ishartmon, co. Wexford], parish church of, rectory of, 355

......,......,......,......, to be erected, with other benefices, into a prebend of Ferns, 355

Iuglis de Trebert *see* Inglis of Tarvit

de Iustinis Civitatis Castelli, Paulus Amadei, *abbreviator de parco maiori*, letters expedited by:[1]

　　P de Castello, 17, 18, 74-77, 114-117, 255, 279, 338, 372- 374, 379-385, 437, 438, 462, 523-526, 531, 532, 565, 735

[Ivernoon, co. Roscommon] *see* Rindown

Iveston (Ystune) [*in* Lanchester, Durh], a prebend of the [secular collegiate] church of Lanchester, *q.v.*

Ivinghoe (Yvingho) [Bucks], parish church of, vicarage of, holder of, 36

......,......,......, union of, to the parish church of Limington, 36

Ixworth (Yxworth) [Suff], [Augustinian] priory of, prior of, papal judge delegate, 224

J

Jackson (Jacson, Jakson), Henry, of York diocese, dispensed for plurality, 1353

......, William, union for, of one of his parish churches to another, Norwich diocese, 1357

James (Jamys), John, layman, parishioner of the chapel of Farrington in Chewton, appellant, 223

James [V], king of Scots, 97, 101, 103, 241, 303, 366 *note*, 590; *cf.* 298

......,......, a minor, 241

......,......, conclusion to, 97, 103, 303, 366, 375, 588 [B]; *cf.* 298

......,......, counsellor of *see* Ogilvie, James

......,......, secretary of *see* Painter, Patrick

......,......, tutor of *see* [Stewart], John, duke of Albany

James, archbishop of Glasgow *see* [Betoun], James

James, bishop of Ely *see* [Stanley], James

James, [bishop-] elect of Moray *see* [Hepburn], James

Jamys *see* James

Jativa (Xatina) [prov. Valencia, Spain], [collegiate] church of B Mary, canonry and prebend of, 235

1　The register note of the abbreviator's signature is variously punctuated, normally capitalised, and very occasionally abbreviated.

Jativa (*contd*)

....., ..., ..., former holder of, 235

....., ..., ..., collation of, 235

Jeban, John Ap *see* John Ap Jevan

Jeffrey, Walter, rector of All Saints's, Radwell, 129

......,*cf.* Geffrey

Jenkinson (Jenkynson'), William, rector of Alby, 394

Jennings (Jenyn, Jeuyn'), Richard, prior of the Augustinian priory of B. Mary the Virgin, Maiden Bradley, 416, 449

Jenyns *cf.* Jennings

Jerningham of Somerleyton, illustrious family of, 1245 *note*

......,....., member of *see* Denton, Elisabeth

Jerpoint (*de Geriponte*) [*modern* Jerpointchurch, co. Kilkenny], parish church of, vicarage of, 658

......,.....,....., to be united, with other benefices, to the precentorship of Ossory, 658

Jerusalem [Palestine], Holy Sepulchre in, military order of, knight of *see* Pillet, John

......, knight of the military order of the Holy Sepulchre returning from, 587

......, Hospital of St John of *see* Hospitallers *in* Index of Subjects

......, *and see* Holy Land, the

Jervaulx [*in* East Witton, Yorks], Cistercian monastery, called house, of B. Mary, abbot of *see* Thornton, Robert

Jeuyn' *see* Jennings

Jevan, John Ap *see* John Ap Jevan

Johacd *see* Ohaed

Johannis *see* Johns

Johinston *see* Johnston

John Ap Jevan (Jeban), of Llandaff diocese, dispensed for plurality, 1139

John Ap Jevan (*contd*)

......, of (?)Llandaff diocese, commission by virtue of an appeal, 1424

John ap Rice (Ayryse) alias Kyston, of St Asaph diocese, dispensed for plurality, 1409

John, Thomas ap *see* Thomas ap John

John, abbot of Rewley *see* [?Rytoner], John

John, abbot of Swineshead *see* [Addingham], John

John, [archbishop-] elect / archbishop of Armagh *see* Kite, John

John, bishop of Cattaro *see* [Chiericati], John

John, [bishop-] elect of Gallipoli *see* Yonge, John

John, bishop of Sibenik *see* [Staphyleus], John

John, duke of Albany *see* [Stewart], John

John [no surname], 585 *note*

Johns (Johannis, Joh'ns), Philip, rector of Cantriff, 359

......, Roger, layman, parishioner of the chapel of Farrington in Chewton, appellant, 223

Johnston (Johinston), James, of St Andrews diocese, commission by virtue of an appeal, 1087

Joyce *cf.* Joye

Joye, Christopher, cleric of London diocese, 69

......,......,....., a nephew of cardinal [Bainbridge], 69

Julius II, grant by, effectuation of, 35, 55, 64, 128, 129, 149, 155, 168, 179, 203, 214, 225, 247

......, letters of, 6, 15, 127, 153, 154, 167 *note*, 181, 194, 207, 219, 239, 282, 287, 291, 293, 324, 365, 427, 429, 448, 494, 506, 521, 539, 567, 570, 579, 652, 916 *note*; *and cf.* 40 *note*

......, register of, exemplification from, 579

......, reservation by, 171

K

Kakilworthi, Robert, canon of the Augustinian priory of Sts Peter and Paul, Taunton, 337

Kamanach see Kavanagh

Kareketaeyll' see Carrickittle

'Karmilla' alias 'Karnodia', diocese of Ferns [unidentified; perhaps Carn(e), co. Wexford], parish church of, vicarage of, 355

......,....,....,...., presentation of person for allegedly pertains to abbess and convent of Augustinian monastery of Graney, 355

......,....,....,...., to be erected, with other benefices, into a prebend of Ferns, 355

Karonan see Rathronan

[Kastoria] see Castoria

Kathblamac see Rath

Katholona see Rathdowney

Kavanagh (Kamanach), Maurus, canon and prebendary of Leighlin, 349

......,....,...., to have archdeaconry of Leighlin with rectory of Killeshin united thereto, 349

Kawall, Richard, of Ferns diocese, 230 note

......, cf. Neville

Kayrillei, Kayrkyl see Caherelly

Keating (Kychin, Kyetyn'), Geoffrey, canon of Cashel, 657, 667

......,....,...., papal mandatary, 657

......,....,...., staying in diocese of Lismore, 667

[Keith Hall and Kinkell] see Kinkell

Kelalban see Killabban

Kellet (Keller), Edward, ostensible commissary or deputy of the official of the court or consistory of York, process of, 271

Kells (de Deserto [Fonte Conneri]) [in Connor, co. Antrim], monastery of B. Mary, abbot of, papal mandatary, 603

Kells (Renlys) [co. Meath], archdeacon of in the church of Meath, q.v.

Kelly [Devon], parish church of B. Mary the Virgin, rector of, 54

Kelso (Bellzo alias Kelso) [co. Roxburgh], Benedictine monastery of, grant of access to, 172

......,....,...., prospective commendator of see [Forman], Andrew

Kemey, Thomas, rector of Newport and holder of the vicarage of Chepstow, 517

Kendal (Kyrkbi in Kendal) [Westm], parish church of, vicarage of, incumbent of, 184

Kennguet alias Nueit, Roger, of Exeter diocese, dispensed for plurality, 751

[Kent, co. of], places in see Barfreystone; Bearstead; Benenden; Boxley; Brookland; Canterbury; Charing; Chislehurst; Chislet; Cobham; Eynsford; Eythorne; Faversham; Folkestone; Harbledown; Hernhill; Hoo; Lamberhurst; Leybourne; [Margate]; Ridley; Rochester; St Radegund; Sandhurst; Smarden; Snave; Stone; Thanet, Isle of; ?Tonbridge; Westwell

Kepier (Kepyer) [in parish of St Giles, Durham, Durh], hospital of St Giles of, holder of, 519

Kerchener, Walter, vicar of Orston, 695

......, cf. Kitchener

[Kerry, co. of], places in see Abbeydorney; Aghadoe; Ballinskelligs; Ballynacourty; Kilmalkedar

Kerswell (Carswell') [in Abbotskerswell, Devon], Cluniac priory, called cell, of, 281

......,...., union to, of the parish church of Little Torrington, 281

......,...., commendator of see [Chard], Thomas

---

1 The register note of the abbreviator's signature is variously punctuated, capitalised, and abbreviated. For present purposes, *La'bertus* is expanded as *Lambertus*, *Lambert'* as *Lambertus*.

Lambertus (*contd*)

P *Lambertus*, 3-5, 8, 9, 11, 12, 15, 22, 30, 33-36, 39- 41, 43, 50-52, 55-58, 61-68, 70, 127, 128, 133, 139-145, 148, 150, 152, 154, 156, 158-162, 164, 166, 168, 170, 179-190, 192-195, 199, 202, 205-209, 211, 216, 217, 219, 220, 222-227, 231-234, 238, 239, 251-254, 258, 261, 266, 267, 272-276, 278, 280-282, 289-294, 296, 297, 299- 302, 307, 311-315, 323, 325, 327-329, 337, 344, 348, 355, 357-360,, 362-365, 391-408, 412-424, 427-429, 431-433, 435, 436, 439-442, 444-449, 454-456, 458, 459, 464- 474, 476, 478- 490, 494-497, 499-506, 509-518, 520, 522, 527, 528, 530, 533, 534, 537, 539, 540, 542-564, 566-570, 573, 574, 579, 581, 584-586, 612, 620, 622, 638, 640-644, 646-648, 669-682, 684-686, 688-696, 698-712, 715-719, 721-723, 725- 730, 736-738, 743

P *Lambirtus*, 724

P *Lampertus*, 697

P *Lamtus*, 213,

P *Lanbertus*, 23, 320, 321, 575, 614, 615, 630, 651, 660, 665, 687, 732-734, 740-742, 744, 748, 750

..........,.........,....., name of, deleted, 565 *note*, 700 *note*

..........,.........,.........,....., in apostolic secretaries' position, 323

Lambrest *see* Lamberhurst

Lame *alias* Panter *see* Painter *alias* Lam

[Lanark, co. of], places in *see* Carnwath; Glasgow; Govan

Lancaster [Lancs], town of, Dominican house of, chapter-house of, Cistercian abbot ordered to appear before visitor in, 434

..........,....., governor of *see* Derby, earl of

[Lancaster, co. of], places in *see* Burscough; Claughton; Furness; Lancaster; Leigh; Leyland; Manchester; Radcliffe; Rufford; Sefton; Tatham; Upholland; Whalley

Lancaster, alias of Sothy, Agnes, *q.v.*

Lanchester (Langehestre) [Durh], [secular collegiate] church of, canonry and prebend of Iveston of, 519

..........,.........,....., prospective union to, of the parish church of St John the Baptist, Bedford, and of one of the two portions of the parish church of All Saints, Houghton Conquest, 519

..........,....., canon of *see* Franklin, William

......, place in *see* Iveston

Lane, John, layman, parishioner of the chapel of Farrington in Chewton, appellant, 223

......, Thomas, vicar of Chewton, litigant over chapel of Farrington, 223

Langeford *see* Langford

de *Langeforet, Stephani see* Langford, Stephen of

Langeforo *see* Langford

Langehestre *see* Lanchester

Langford (Langeforo) [*either* Little L~ *or* Steeple L~ *or* Hanging L~ (*in* Steeple L~), Wilts], vill of, land in, gifted to the Augustinian monastery of Bradenstoke, 494

Langford (*de Langeforet*), Stephen of, property of, gifted to Augustinian monastery of Bradenstoke, 494

Langford (Langeford), John, of Worcester diocese, dispensed for plurality, 926

Langham [Essex], parish church of, rector of, 406

Langley (Langlei) [Norf],Premonstratensian monastery of, convent of, election of abbot by, 425

..........,....., abbot of *see* Purfoot, Henry

Langton (Langton'), John, the late, abbot of the Cistercian monastery of B Mary Graces by the tower of London, 165

..........,.........,.........,....., salvation of soul of, prayer etc. for, 292

Lovel (Loell, Lovell', Lowell), Thomas, canon of Wells, appellant, 287

........,...., union for, of his vicarage to [his] canonry, Bath and Wells diocese, 964

........,...., ostensible vicar general in spirituals of the bishop of Bath and Wells, 316

........,....,...., *ex officio* proceedings by, 316

Lowcht *see* Louth

Loweak, William, of Norwich diocese, dispensed for plurality, 1313

Lowell *see* Lovel

Loweth *see* Lowth

Lownd *see* Lound

Lowth (Loweth, Lowth'), Ambrose, cleric or layman of Colchester, appellant, 572

......, William, canon, formerly holder of the priorship, of the Augustinian monastery of Walsingham, 329

......,....,....,....,...., pension and house reserved for, 329

Lowude *see* Lound

de Loyz *see* de Lacy

Lucca [Italy], secular collegiate church of St Donatus outside the walls of, priorship of, 146

......,....,...., collation of, 146

........,...., commendatory prior of *see* [de' Gigli], Silvester

......,Hospitaller preceptory of St John *de Templo*, commend of, 735

........,...., preceptor of *see* de Franciottis, Andrew

........,...., commendator of *see* de Franciottis, Cesar; *and see* [de Franciottis de Rovere], Sixtus

......, clerics of *see* de Blanchis, Blanchus; de Ciampantibus, Hercules; Guidottis de Guinzano, Paulus Nicolai

......, diocese of, persons of *see* de Nellinis, Galeatius and Geminianus Damiani

Lucca (*contd*)

........,...., places in *see* ?Controne; Tassignano; Villa Basilica

[Luce, Old] *see* Glenluce

Lucius III, letter of, 494

[Ludd] *see* Lydda

Ludden (Lodyn, Lugden') [co. Limerick], parish church of, vicarage of, 237, 628

......,....,...., to be united, with other benefices, to canonry and prebend of Inch St Lawrence in Emly, 237

......,....,...., to be united, with other benefices, to projected prebend of Killoscully in Cashel, 628

Lufford *see* Rufford

Lugden' *see* Ludden

Lussell', Henry, vicar of Wistow, 402

Luydesay *see* Lindsay

Lydda [*ancient* Lod, *modern* Lidd, Lod *or* Ludd, *in* Palestine, *now in* Israel], church of [*in partibus infidelium*], provision to, 1449

......,[bishop-] elect of *see* Brainfort, John

Lydezate, Hugh, of Worcester diocese, dispensed for plurality, 1368

Lydiate *cf.* Lydezate

Lye, Edward, rector of Bolas, 562

Lyell (Lyell'), Thomas, OCarm, 274

Lyle (Lile), Jonet, noblewoman, damsel, relict of the late James Ogilvie of Airlie and executor of his will, appellant, 136

Lyliwe, Thomas, of Lincoln diocese, dispensed for plurality, 1380

Lymyngton' *see* Limington

'Lyna' [*unidentified*; *possibly identifiable with* 'Lena', d. Armagh, *known to* Reg. Swayne], church of, annexed to sacristy of Armagh, 629

[Lyneham, Wilts], place in *see* Bradenstoke

Moblusk (*contd*)

.....,.....,....., to be united, with other benefices, to rectory, of ?Ballymena, 603

Mocody *see* Macody

?Modreeny (Domacdrchyny) [co. Tipperary], parish church of, rectory of, 319

.....,.....,....., to be united, with another benefice, to newly erected canonry and prebend of ?Modreeny in Killaloe, 319

.....,....., vicarage of, 319

.....,.....,....., to be erected into prebend of Killaloe, 319

Mogriche *and* ?Mogriche (Mogerii, Mogryche), John, canon of the church of B. Mary, Stafford, holder of the prebend of Swetnam in the same, holder of the parish church of Wigginton, 554

.....,....., general commissary of Silvester [de' Gigli], bishop of Worcester, process of, 279

.....,....., union for, of his parish churches to his vicarage, Coventry and Lichfield diocese, 1327

......, *cf.* Mogridge

Mogridge *cf.* Mogriche

Mogryche *see* Mogriche

'Moiranoach', diocese of Cloyne [*unidentified; but in vicinity of* Castlemagner and Ros(s)keen, co. Cork], parish church of, vicarage of, 143

.....,.....,....., united with vicarage of Castlemagner, 143

.....,.....,....., prospective union to, of vicarage of Ros(s)keen, 143

Moithwille' *see* ?Wiltshire, North

Molton' *see* Moulton

Molusk *see* Moblusk

Molyndkearr *see* Mullingar

Molyneux (Melyneux), Edward, rector of Sefton, 399, 673

Molyneux (*contd*)

.....,.....,....., holder of the vicarage of Leyland, 673

.....,....., of Coventry and Lichfield diocese, dispensed for plurality, 1150

[Monaghan, co. Monaghan], place in *see* ?Rackwallace

[Monaghan, co. of], places in *see* Clones; Dartree; Drummully; [Magheross]; [Monaghan]; ?Rackwallace; Tedavnet; Tehallan

Monaincha (*de Insul(l)a Viventium*) [*in* Corbally, co. Tipperary], Augustinian monastery of the Holy Cross, priory of, prospective union to, of vicarages of St James', Borris(o)leigh, Leigh, B.Mary's, Ballymurreen, and St Nicholas's, Boythstown, 257

.....,....., prior of, papal mandatary, 151, 262, 265

.....,.....,....., *see* OMeagher, Donald

Monasteranenagh (*de Magio*) [co. Limerick], [Cistercian] monastery of B. Mary, abbot of, papal mandatary, 141

Monasterevin (Rosglas) [co. Kildare], Cistercian monastery of B. Mary, monks of, habit and profession of, 653

.....,....., monk of *see* MacCostelloe *alias* Nangle, Dermot

Mone, John and his wife Joan, of Ditcheat parish, appellants, 316

Monkyston' *alias* Anebek *see* Monxton *alias* Anna de Becco

[Monmouth, co. of], places in *see* Chepstow; Llantarnam; Usk

Monorgund (Monorgond, Monorgound), Robert, detainer of parish church of Collace, 240

.....,....., collation to, of canonry of Aberdeen, 1517

Montefiascone [prov. Viterbo, Italy], letters dated at, 340, 341, 409, 410, 510-517

......, diocese of, place in *see* Capodimonte

---

1   signature normally punctuated; the colon, though not invariable, is characteristic.

Narthaston *see* Aston, North

Nash (Nasche), William, layman, parishioner of the chapel of Farrington in Chewton, appellant, 223

Natura (*Naturen.*) [*ancient* Athyra, Thrace; *modern* Buyuk-Cekmece, *on* northern shore of Sea of Marmora to west of Istanbul, European Turkey], church of, *in partibus infidelium*, 124, 125

.........,...., subject to archbishop of Constantinople, 126

.........,...., fruits and proceeds of, nil receipts from, 125

.........,...., provision to, 122-126, 202

......, [bishop-] elect of *see* Slater, Richard

......, city and diocese of, 122, 124

Nawbrugh' *see* Newburgh

Nayleson *alias* Nayleston' *see* Nailstone

[Nazareth] *see* Maioren.

Neblond *see* Newlond

Neel (Neell'), Richard, vicar of Westwell, 514

Negala *see* Nangle

Negeyll' *see* Nagle

Negroponte (Nigroponten.) [*or* Euboia, *an island in the* Aegean, *adjacent to the mainland*, Greece], church of [*seated at* Khalkis *or* Chalkis], provision to, 1464

.........,...., *in partibus* [*infidelium*], 1464

......, [bishop-] elect of *see* [Wilson], Richard

de Nellinis, Galeatius, rector of the parish church of St Geminianus, ?Controne, 461

......,....,....,...., resignation of, 461

.........,...., proctor of *see* [de' Gigli], Silvester

......, Geminianus Damiani, scholar of Lucca diocese, 461

......,....,...., prospective commend to, of parish church of St Geminianus, ?Controne, 461

Nembery *see* Newbury

Nenagh (Lenaenach) [co. Tipperary], [*Fratres Cruciferi*] monastery of St John, prior of, papal mandatary, 257

Nenton *see* Newton

Nepi [*in* prov. of Viterbo, Italy], letters dated at, 127, 294

......, petitions dated at, 892 *note*, 894 *note*

......, diocese of, place in *see* Monterosi

Nerim *alias* Balyyrin *see* Nurney

Neruuan, Thomas, of London diocese, dispensed for plurality, 1247

[Netherbury, Dors], place in *see* Beminster Prima

Nettleton (Nettillon) [Lincs], parish church of, holder of, 570

.........,...., parish church of 'Bukenehull' ' united to, 570

Neville (Newyll'), [Laurence, bishop of Ferns, 1479-1503], son of *cf.* Neville, Richard

......, Richard, cleric of Ferns diocese, 230

......,....,...., father of *cf.* Neville, [Laurence]

......, *cf.* Kawall

'Nevntonluyll', diocese of Lincoln [*unidentified*; a corresponding petition has *Nevnton' Will'* (*Reg. Suppl.* 1506, fo. 176ʳ); *possibly* Newton Longville, Bucks *or* Newton, Lincs], parish church of, vicar of, 559

Newbattle (Newbottil) [co. Midlothian], Cistercian monastery of, provision to, 1504

.........,...., abbot of *see* Schewill, Edward

Newbiggin (Newbiggynge) [St Edmund, 6 m NW Appleby, Westm], parish church of, rector of, 160

Newbottil *see* Newbattle

Newburgh (Nawbrugh', *de Novo Burgo*) [*in* Coxwold, Yorks], Augustinian monastery of, called house, 432

Norwich [Norf], city of, inhabitant (named) of, 541

......, Benedictine **[cathedral priory] (church)** of, prior of, papal judge delegate, 475, 614

..........,...., *see* Catton, Robert

..........,...., monk of *cf.* Bebry *alias* Princhett, Thomas

......, **bishop** of, to receive oath of fealty, 382, 384, 385[A], 385[B]

..........,...., to assign pallium, 385[A], 385[B]

..........,...., papal (commissary and) mandatary, 24, 384, 494

..........,...., papal judge delegate, 134, 425, 462

......,....,....., sub-delegate of *see* Wilton, William

..........,...., reservation by, of pension on fruits of monastery and house in its precinct for canon who had resigned priorship, 329

..........,...., special faculty from, for his vicar general to reserve pension on fruits of monastery and house in its precinct for canon who had resigned priorship, 329

......, bishop (or his vicar general) of, admission by, of resignation of priorship made into hands of, 329

......, official of, litigation before and proceedings by, 541

..........,...., papal judge delegate, 614

......, church of, archdeacon of Suffolk of, *q.v.*

......, **diocese** of, persons of *see* Bacon, Henry; Balkey, Thomas; Barnes, Geoffrey; Baxter, Rowland; Beckham, Robert; Betson, John; Bocking, Richard; Bolte, Denise; Botey, William; Brown[e] *alias* Walsham, Andrew; Butler, John; Carne alias Buckenhem, John; Carre, Nicholas; Carter, Robert; Chapman, Robert; Clerk, Thomas and William; Colchester *alias* Cuper, Robert; Colchester *alias* Newlond, John; Colet, John; Cotton, Leonard; Cootre, William; ?Creswell, Robert; Danson, William; Darley, Roger; Drake, Richard; Duttley,

Norwich (*contd*)

Thomas; Eden, Richard; Eglin, William; Freeman *alias* Fuller, Robert; Glover, Henry; Gresham, Thomas; Grey, George; Hanson, Nicholas; Hawnel, Thomas; Hekker, John; Hocker alias Craffeld, Richard; Hone, Robert; Hoobon, Richard; Jackson, William; Jenkinson, William; Knight, Geoffrey; London, John; Loweak, William; Lowth, William; Lyntoke, William; Mawer, Gregory; Mayer, John; More, Henry; Naper, George; Nolison, Robert; de Ordemer, William; Purfoot, Henry; Ragon, Miles; Rainey, Thomas; Rice, John; Richoman, Richard; Roberts, Richard; Rodding, Thomas; Sampson, Richard; Sebby, Cuthbert; Shelton, Richard; Shorton, Robert; Smith, John and Robert; Stillington, William; Syngaykin, John; Trower, Robert; Vyburgh alias Wydelsteldi, William; Walker, Hugh; Walsingham alias Bett, William; Walters, Elisabeth; Wangdem alias Williamson, William; Warles, Robert; Webster, Robert; White, John; Winchelsea, John; Wotton, Thomas; Wyott, John; *and see* Denton, Elisabeth; Walters, John

..........,...., places in *see* Bury; Butley; Campsea Ashe; Chelsworth; Dennington; Fakenham Parva; Gosbeck; Icklingham; Ipswich; Ixworth; Melford, Long; Ringsfield; Somerleyton; Stratford; Thrandeston; Tuddenham; Ufford; Waldingfield, Great; Whatfield; ?Wickham Market; *and* places *listed above under* [Norfolk, co. of]

..........,...., place in wrongly stated to be in diocese of York, 540

[Nottingham, co. of], places in *see* ?Bunny; ?Clifton, North; Orston; Retford, East; Ruddington; Southwell; Welbeck; Wilford

Novell, Roger, of Lincoln diocese, commission by virtue of an appeal, 767

de Novo Burgo see Newburgh

Nowell, William, union for, of one of his parish churches to another (?) Llandaff diocese, 1526

Nudre (Midre), Thomas, cleric of Brechin diocese, 247

......,....,...., proctor of Thomas Dickson, 247

.........,...., archdeacon of the church of Moray, 175, 176

......,....,...., notary of the pope, 175, 176

.....,.....,.....,...., envoy of Andrew [Forman], 175, 176

......,.....,.....,.....,...., to deliver pallium, 175, 176

Nueit, alias of Kennguet, Roger, *q.v.*

Nullius diocesis, persons expressly stated to be (in *rubricellae*) see Bream, William, OCarm; Cambridge, Robert; Clerk, John; Gilbert, Gilbert; ?Springwell, John; Stork, John

......, *and see* Birkhead, Edmund, OFM; Damyon, John, OFM; Graunt, William, OESA; Lyell, Thomas, OCarm; Mowtter, John, OFM; de Nuy, Edmund, OP; OKelly, Maurice, OFM; Rodoke, Nicholas, OFM

Nulve, William, of Salisbury diocese, dispensed for plurality, 793

Nuneaton (Noneton') [Warw], parish church of, vicarage of, holder of, 579

Nurney (Nerim *alias* Balyyrin) [*in* West Offaly barony, co. Kildare], parish church of, rectory of, 624

......,.....,...., united to Augustinian monastery of Killeigh, 624

......,.....,...., to be united, with other benefices, to newly erected canonry of Kildare and prebend of Nurney, 624

.........,...., vicarage of, 624

......,.....,...., allegedly erected into prebend of Kildare, 624

......,.....,...., to be erected into a prebend of Kildare, 624

de Nuy, Edmund, OP, 183

O

Oakley (Ocley) [Beds], parish church of, vicar of, 13

OBanaghan (Obeanhaeheayn, Obeathathane), Thomas, canon of Elphin, papal mandatary, 731

.........,...., to have regular priory, Elphin diocese, 1093

OBardon (Abardan), Odo, prior of the Augustinian monastery of St John the Evangelist, [Enniscorthy], 960

......,.....,...., to have rectory of parish church and simple benefice, Ferns diocese, united to priorship of monastery, 960

Obeanhaeheayn, Obeathathane *see* (?) OBanaghan

Obecayn, Obechan, Obechayn *see* OBehan

Obegnuim, Donald, ostensible cleric or priest, detainer of vicarage of Rathjordan, 237

OBehan (Obecayn, Obechan, Obechayn, Ybecan'), Donald, vicar of Kilclonfert, 148

......,.....,...., to have the rectory united to his vicarage, 148

......, Maurice, canon of ?Kildare, papal mandatary, 145, 624

......, Peter, canon of Kildare, papal mandatary, 151, 623

OBeirne (Obern, Obernd), Malachy, canon of Elphin, papal mandatary, 248

......, Odo, canon of Elphin, papal mandatary, 331

?OBoran (Oburan), Nicholas, to have united parish churches, 1083

OBoyle (Obugill), Bernard, canon of Derry, papal mandatary, 258

Obreyn *see* OBrien

Obrica, Theodoric, to have canonry and vicarages, Killaloe diocese, 1267

[OCorkery] *see* OMulcorkery

OCormachan (Ocormacam), John, ostensible dean of Killaloe, detainer of the rectory of Killuran, Feakle, Ogonnelloe, ?Faha, [and] ?Killana, 607

......, *cf.* Ochonimochan'

?OCornan (Okernain), alias of OKelly, *q.v.*

OCorrigan (Ocorigayn), Thomas, ostensible priest, detainer of vicarage of Jerpoint, 658

OCrun, Donat, ostensible priest, detainer of vicarages of Killasser and *?cell sestnain*, 575

Octavian, archbishop of Armagh *see* [De Palatio], Octavian

Octirburn, Richard, of York diocese, further dispensed for plurality, 957

Octoni, Thady, canon of Raphoe, papal mandatary, 668

Oculean *see* OCullen

OCullane (Oculeayn), David, canon of Tuam, papal mandatary, 358

......, *cf.* Ohilliman

OCullen (Oculean, Oculuyz), John, canon of Clogher, papal mandatary, 577

......, Patrick, provision of to Clogher, 1486

......,...., absolution of preliminary to provision, 1487

......,...., [bishop-] elect of Clogher, 1486

......,....,...., faculty for consecration, 1488

OCullinane *cf.* Ohilliman

Oculuyz *see* OCullen

Ocuncenayn, Ocunoenayn *see* OConcannon

Ocunchubayr *see* OConnor

?OCurran [*or* ?OCurrin] (Corryn, Cuirni, Curreyn, Curryn, Ocurryn, Ocuryn), James, canon of Leighlin, papal mandatary, 606, 608, 624

......,...., canon of Dublin, papal mandatary, 597, 598

?OCurran (*contd*)

......,...., canon and prebendary of Leighlin, 623

......,....,...., son of archpriest otherwise dean of Leighlin, 623

......,....,....,...., canon and prebendary of Dublin, 623

......,....,....,....,...., to have sinecure of 'Balyycaron' and vicarages of Agha, 'Clnyuuaceys', and 'Killsynayn' united to his canonry and prebend of Leighlin, 623

......, *cf.* Ocuzryhyn

Ocuucalret, Rory, ostensible Augustinian canon, detainer of rectory of Nurney, 624

Ocuyn *see* OQuinn

Ocuzryhyn, Thady, ostensible priest, detainer of rectory of 'Carygwaspayn', 476

......, Thady [*another*], ostensible priest, detainer of parish church, called vicarage, of Ballon, 476

......*cf.* ?OCurran

ODaly (Odalig), Eugene, cleric of Cork diocese, 341

......,....,...., to have canonry and prebend of Killanully of Cork cathedral with rectory of Kilmiddy and vicarage of Liscleary united thereto, 341

ODeegan *cf.* ODuigan

ODelahunty (Odul la cinta), Nicholas, ostensible priest, detainer of rectory of Kilconnell, 655

Odenenir *see* OConnor

Oderramy, Odo, to have parish church, Ferns diocese, 971

Odidchn, Thady, ostensible cleric, detainer of vicarage of Rathreagh, 571

......, *cf.* ODowda

Odnygyn *see* ODuigan

ODoherty *cf.* Oduchard

Odonaill, Odonaill', Odonayll *see* ODonnell

OFlavahan *cf.* OFlahavan

OFlynn (Offlayn), Rory, ostensible cleric, detainer of canonry and prebend of Killanully of Cork cathedral, 341

......, *and see under* OFlahiff

OFortin (Offertheryn, Ofortyryn), Maurice, ostensible priest, detainer of vicarages of 'Kylhago' and 'Maruen', 658

.........,..., to have rectory, Ferns diocese, 969

Ofribel, Thady, ostensible priest, detainer of rectory of Kilmacrenan, 354

......, *cf.* OFriel

?OFriel (Oseegil), Conatius, abbot of the [Augustinian] monastery of *Celemegre*, Derry, 347

......,....,....,..., accusations against, 347

......,....,....,..., to be deprived, 347

......, *cf.* Ofribel

OGallagher (Ogallcuyr, YGalanbayr), Arthur, to have vicarage, (?) Derry diocese, 982

......, Laurence, ostensible priest, detainer of deanery of Raphoe, 256

......, alias of MacGilligan, Laurence, *q.v.*

......, *cf.* Ygaltur

Ogbourne (Ocborne) [*modern* O~ St Andrew, Wilts], parish church of, vicarage of, incumbent of, 424

Ogemnan, Nicholas, ostensible priest, detainer of vicarage of 'Karmilla' *alias* 'Karnodia', 355

Ogilvie (Ogilvi, Ogilvy), James, the late, of Airlie, knight, 136

......,....,....,..., will of, executors of, 136

......,....,....,....,..., litigation over, 136

......,....,....,..., relict of *see* Lyle, Jonet

......, James, canon of Aberdeen, 588 [A & C], 589, 590

......,....,...., prebendary of Kinkell, 590

Ogilvie (*contd*)

......,....,...., counsellor of James [V], 590

......,....,...., Master of Requests of the kingdom of Scotland, 590

......,....,...., absolution of preliminary to commend, 589

......,....,...., commend to, of Premonstratensian monaastery of Dryburgh, 588 [A], 590

......,....,...., to take oath of fealty, 590; *cf.* 588 [C]

......, Malcolm, [of Airlie], nobleman, litigant over will of the late James Ogilvie of Airlie, 136

......, Thomas, [of Airlie], nobleman, knight, litigant over will of the late James Ogilvie of Airlie, 136

OGleeson *cf.* Oglosayn

Oglosayn, Rory, to have deanery and parish churches, Killaloe diocese, 1123

Ogonnelloe (Hyconyly) *see* Killuran, Feakle, Ogonnelloe, ?Faha, [and] ?Killana

OGormley (Ygarme Leigaydh), Magonius, vicar of Urney, 258

......,....,...., to have rectory of Termonamongan united to his vicarage, 258

OGrady (Ograda, Ogradi, Ogrida), John, ostensible priest, detainer of vicarage of Tomgraney, 608

......, Thomas, ostensible cleric, detainer of canonry and prebend of Tomgraney in Killaloe, 263

.........,...., canon of Killaloe and prebendary of Tomgraney, 608

......,....,...., to have treasurership of Killaloe and vicarage of Tomgraney united to his canonry and prebend, 608

Ohaed (Johacd, Ochad, Ohard), Conacius / Conocius, canon of Armagh, papal mandatary, 576

.........,...., rector of Aghaloo, 577

Ohilliman, David, canon of Tuam, papal mandatary, 610

......, cf. OCullane; OCullinane

OHingerdell (Yhyngardayll), Donald, to have vicarages united to parish church, Ardfert and Ross dioceses, 1226

OHogan (Hogan, Ohogayn), John, ostensible canon, OSA, detainer of vicarage of Liscleary, 341

........,...., canon of Killaloe, papal mandatary, 607

......, Malachy, canon of Killaloe, papal mandatary, 317-319

OHolian cf. Ohuluyn

OHoolahan (Ohullachan), Cornelius, priest of Ross diocese, 309

......,....,...., to have vicarage of Kilcrohane, 309

?OHora (Yhora), Donat, to have parish churches erected into prebend, Cashel diocese, 1121

?OHorgan (Horga), William, to have chancellorship and vicarage, Ross diocese, 1272

Ohullachan see OHoolahan

Ohuluyn, William, canon of Tuam, papal mandatary, 358

......, cf. OHolian

Ohyarhi, Cornelius, ostensible priest, detainer of vicarage of Ballintemple, 625

......, cf. Hyerla; OHylan

Ohyauyan, Dernutius, to have simple benefice, Cloyne diocese, 801

Ohydscoll' see ODriscoll

Ohyfernan see OHeffernan

OHylan cf. Hyerla; Ohyarhi

Ohylin, John, canon of Ossory, papal mandatary, 663, 664

Ohynaga', Odo, priest of Achonry diocese, 575

Ohynaga' (contd)

......,....,...., to have specially united vicarages of Killasser and ?cell sestnain, 575

......, cf. OHenaghan

Okahan, Okahan' see OKane

Okaillyd' see OKelly

OKane (Okahan, Okahan'), Cornelius, cleric of Derry (diocese), 110-112

......,....,...., absolution of preliminary to provision, 111

......,....,...., dispensed for illegitimacy, 112

......,....,...., provision of, to Raphoe, 110, 113

......,....,...., [bishop-] elect of Raphoe, 110, 113

......,....,...., faculty for consecration, 113

......,....,...., to take oath of fealty, 113

......,....,...., petition on behalf of, by Henry [VIII], 110

Okarrayd see OCarry

Okassy see OCasey

Okawul, Donat, ostensible cleric, detainer of vicarage of Leckpatrick, 668

......, cf. OCarolan

Okcallachan see OCallaghan

Okearwayll see OCarroll

OKeeffe (Okyme), Thady, ostensible priest, detainer of deanery of Cloyne, 625

Okeford, Childe (Child Okeford, Child Okford) [Dors], (North [a moiety?]), parish church of, rector of, 566

......,....,....,...., union to, of the parish church of Fifehead Neville and, conditionally, of the parish church of Childe Okeford, (South [a moiety?]), 566

......,...., (South), parish church of, prospective rector of, 566

......,....,....,...., vacancy of, 566

......,....,....,...., patron of, presentation by, 566

Olochlynd *see* OLoughlin

Olochnayn, Olocuayn *see* OLoughnane

OLongan (de Ylongayn), John, priest of Limerick diocese, 333

......,....,...., to have canonry of Limerick and vicarages of Cloncrew, Corcomohide, Ardpatrick, and Darragh, the rectory of Kilflyn, and the chapels of Down Innish, Down Gadmond, Chapel Martel, and Ineycahal erected into a prebend, 333

OLoonan *cf.* Oluan

OLoughlin (Olochlynd), Honorius, ostensible cleric of diocese of Kilfenora or Killaloe, detainer of rectory of 'Aglinmena *alias* Nova', 611

OLoughnane (Olach..an, Olachnaym, Olachnayn, Olachuayn, Olacuayn, Olechnay, Olochanyn, Olochnayn, Olocuayn), Cornelius, canon of Cashel, papal mandatary, 355, 477, 600, 601, 652, 656

......,...., ostensible cleric, detainer of vicarages of St James', Borris(o)leigh, Leigh, B.Mary's, Ballymurreen, and St Nicholas's, Boythstown, 257

......,...., to have parish churches, Cashel diocese, 978

......,...., to have vicarage united to canonry, Cashel diocese, 979

......, *cf.* Olocamahayn

Olrearruyl *see* OCarroll

Oluan, Nielanus, ostensible priest, detainer of vicarage of ?Rackwallace *alias* Clogher, 619

......, *cf.* OLoonan

Olyche', John, canon of Cloyne, papal mandatary, 336

Olyden *see* Holden

Olydy *see* OLiddy

Omablpadrig *see* OMulpatrick

OMackesy (Omachassa, Omakassa), Donald, vicar of 'Killsynayn', 348

......,....,...., to have canonry of Leighlin, his vicarage of 'Killsynayn' erected into a prebend, and the vicarages of ?Lorum and ?Agha united to the newly erected canonry and prebend, 348

......,...., ostensible priest of Leighlin diocese, 623

......,....,...., detainer of vicarages of Agha and 'Killsynayn', 623

Omadyn, Maurice, canon of Emly, papal mandatary, 609

OMahony (Omathunna), Richard, detainer of vicarage of Kilcrohane, 309

Omakassa *see* OMackesy

Omale *alias* Baret *see* OMalley *alias* Barrett

?OMallane (Ymallayn), John, Augustinian canon and ex-Franciscan, 611

......,....,...., to have Augustinian monastery of B. Mary, Kilshanny with vicarages of Kiltoraght, ?Gleninagh, 'Aglaysni in Ballayn', ?Crumlin, and Rath, and rectory of 'Aglinmena *alias* Nova' united thereto, 611

OMalley *alias* Barrett (Omale *alias* Baret), Robert, cleric of Tuam diocese, 358

......,....,...., to have vicarage of ?Kilgeever, 358

Omalryayn *see* OMulryan

Omanay, Magonius, canon of Annaghdown, papal mandatary, 605

......,...., canon of Tuam, papal mandatary, 610

......, Thomas, cleric of Tuam, 604

......,....,...., to have simple benefice, called semi-vicarage or semi-office or semi-stipend, in Tuam cathedral, 604

......, *cf.* OMannin; OMeany

OMannin *cf.* Omanay; Ymaynay

Omurysci *see* OMorrissey

On.cadam, John, canon of Ossory, papal mandatary, 246

Onael, Robert, of Lincoln diocese, dispensed for plurality, 941

Oncurchyly *see* OMurilly

Oneda, Edmund, ostensible priest, detainer of vicarage of ?Lorum, 348

Ongar, High (Onger Alta) [Essex], parish church of, rector of, 199

......,....,...., union (conditional) to, of the vicarage of Heighington, 199

Onibury (Oniburi) [Salop], parish church of, rector of, 484

Oola (Vlay) [co. Limerick], parish church of, vicarage of, 250

......,....,...., to be united to deanery of Emly, 250

OPhelan and ?OPhelan (Felany, Felavyn, Offellan, Offellayn, Offilayn), Cormac, ostensible cleric or priest, detainer of vicarage of Darragh, 333

......, Maurice, canon of Limerick, papal mandatary, 237

......,...., priest of Limerick diocese, 229

......,....,...., collation (of doubtful validity) to, of vicarages of Kilmallock and Tankardstown, 229

......,....,...., to have canonry of Emly and vicarages of ?Athlacca, Kilmallock, 'Stagno', and Tankardstown erected into a prebend, 229

......,...., ostensible priest, detainer of vicarages of Kilmallock and Tankardstown, 335

......, William, ostensible cleric or priest, detainer of vicarage of B. Mary's, Rathdowney, 601

OQuan *cf.* Oquari

Oquari, Matthew, canon of Elphin, papal mandatary, 575

Oquelluye, Thomas, to have canonry of Armagh, 1276

OQuinn (Ochoyn, Ocuyn), Bernard, cleric of Emly diocese, 609

......,....,...., proctor of Rory OMarkahan, *q.v.*

......, Donat, detainer of vicarage of Ardnaree, 729

Oran (Vrauinathe) [co. Roscommon], prebend, called canonical, in Elphin, 248

Orchard, John, canon of the Augustinian monastery of Arbury, 678

de Ordemer, William, union for, of one of his parish churches to another, Norwich diocese, 1314

Oreanayn *see* ORonan

Orenge, Edward, cleric of London diocese, 56

Orihuela [prov. Alicante, Spain], diocese of, persons of *see* Rolla, Ieronimus and Peter

......,...., place in *cf.* ?Villajoyosa

[Ormskirk, Lancs], place in *see* Burscough

ORonan (Oreanayn, Orrnan, Orronain, Orronan), James, late vicar of Cloncrew, 333

......,....,...., death of, at the apostolic see, 333

......, John, canon of Lismore, papal mandatary, 626

......, Thady, canon of Lismore, papal mandatary, 335, 336, 340-342, 626,

Orston (Orston') [Notts], parish church of, vicar of, 695

OScallan *cf.* Sculyn

OScingin (Oscyngin), William, to have parish church in diocese of Thérouanne [!] and episcopal fourths of the parish churches of Elphin erected into a prebend of Elphin, 955

......, *cf.* Ostyn[g]in'

Oseegil *see* ?OFriel

Oxford (*contd*)

......,......,...., master and members of, non-appearance of following summons, 1

......, *studium* at, college of scholars of, cardinal [Bainbridge] licensed to choose four men from to be MTheol or (?) DTheol, 795

......, places at *see* Oseney; Rewley

[Oxford, co. of], places in *see* Alvescot; Ardley; Aston, North; Bladon; (?) Broughton; Bruern; 'Bukenehull''; Charlbury; Ewelme; Harpsden; Henley-on-Thames; Kidlington; Lewknor; Norton, Hook; Oseney; Oxford; Rewley; Rotherfield; ? Standlake; Stanton Harcourt; Stanton St John; Tackley; Wendlebury; Wigginton; Wootton

Oxley (Oxlei), John, of Bath and Wells diocese, dispensed for plurality, 1011

Oylledres *see* Kildress

P

Pacchyng, Pacchyng' *see* Patching

Pace *or* Pacey (Pase), (master) Richard, papal notary, 177, 178, 343, 361

......,......,...., cleric of York, 177, 178

......,......,......,...., absolution of preliminary to commend, 178

......,......,......,...., commend to, of the Benedictine monastery of St Stephen, Bologna, 177

......,......,......,...., archdeacon of Dorset in the church of Salisbury, 343, 361

......, William, union for, of his vicarage to his parish church, London diocese, 1152

......,....., of London diocese, exemplification [of enregistered letter], 1349

Pacher, Robert, of Lincoln diocese, dispensed for plurality, 1379

......, *cf.* Paget

Pachyng *see* Patching, John

Paget *cf.* Pacher

Painestown (Poyneston) [cos Carlow and Kildare], prebend, called rectory, in Leighlin cathedral, 60

......,......,......,...., to be united, with other benefices, to canonry and prebend in Leighlin, 60

Painter (Paniter, Panter), Alexander, [reservation to], of pension over canonry of Brechin, 1403

......, Patrick, cleric of Brechin diocese, 97-99, 101

......,......,...., secretary of James [V], 97, 101

......,......,...., absolution of preliminary to provision, 99

......,......,...., provision of, to Augustinian monastery of Cambuskenneth, 97, 100, 102

......,......,...., to be received as canon of Cambuskenneth, habited, and professed, 101

......,......,...., dispensed to be abbot for a year without taking habit or making profession, 98, 102

......,....., abbot of Cambuskenneth, 97, 100, 102

......,......,...., faculty for ordination and blessing, 100

......,......,...., to take oath of fealty, 100

......,....., commend to, of Hospitaller preceptory of Torphichen, 102

......,....., litigant over Torphichen, 102

......,....., reservation to, of fruits of archdeaconry of Moray, 102

......,......,...., of fruits of canonry and prebend of Kinnell of church of St Salvator, St Andrews, 102

......,......,...., of fruits of parish church of Conveth, 102

......,......,...., of specified sum on fruits of parish church of Fetteresso, a prebend in church of St Mary of the Rock, St Andrews, 102

Painter (*contd*)

.........,...., grant to, of entry and re-entry to benefices whose fruits reserved, 102

.........,...., dispensed, even after taking habit, making profession, and acquiring Cambuskenneth, to retain preceptory (if he wins it) *in commendam* for life and receive the reserved fruits, and (in event of re-entry and entry) to retain archdeaconry, canonry and prebend, and parish churches for a year, 102

.........,...., reservation to, of fruits of numerous benefices, Aberdeen, Dunblane, and St Andrews dioceses, 1511

.........,...., late dean of Brechin cathedral, 241

Painter (Paniter, Panter) *alias* Lam (Lame) *and* vice versa, William, cleric of Brechin diocese, 247

......,....,...., sometime holder of the canonry and prebend of Duthil of Moray cathedral, 247

......,....,...., resigned his canonry and prebend to facilitate acquisition by Thomas Dickson of canonry and prebend of Turriff of Aberdeen cathedral, 247

......,....,...., reservation for, of pension on fruits of canonry and prebend of Turriff, 247, 522

.........,...., ostensible cleric of city or diocese of Brechin, 522

......,....,...., litigant over non-payment of pension, 522

[De Palatio], Octavian, archbishop of Armagh, 438

......,....,...., primate of all Ireland, 438

......,....,....,...., proceedings by, 438

.........,...., the late, archbishop of Armagh, 114, 115

Palden, William, of Coventry [and Lichfield] diocese, dispensed for plurality, 1105

Palgrave (Palsgrawe), John, warden of Coberley, 750

Palines, John, of Winchester diocese, dispensed for plurality, 1295

Palmer, John, monk of the Cistercian monastery of St Mary Graces by the Tower, London, 709

Palmes, George, of York diocese, dispensed for plurality, 835

Palo [*in* com. of Cerveteri, prov. Rome, Italy], letters dated at, 7, 308, 332, 611, 616, 623, 624, 698

......, petition dated at, 1015 *note*

Palsgrawe *see* Palgrave

Paman, Giles, of York diocese, dispensed for plurality, 1110

Panados (*Panaden.*) [*or* Banados, *anciently* Panium, *in* Thrace, *on* northern coast of Sea of Marmara, European Turkey], church of, *in partibus infidelium*, 16, 121, 579

.........,...., subject to archbishop of Constantinople, 120

.........,...., provision to, 118-121; *and see* p. lxxiv note 297

......, bishop (-elect) of *see* Graunt, William; *and see* [Sutton], William

......, bishop of *see* [Wele], Thomas

......, city and diocese, 118, 121

......, episcopal *mensa* of, nil receipts from, 16

Paniter *see* Painter

Paniter *alias* Lam *see* Painter *alias* Lam

Pannfford (Pannffordt), John, cleric or layman of Exeter diocese, appellant, 222

......, Thomas, cleric or layman of Exeter diocese, appellant, 222

Pannycuyk *see* Pennycuick

Panter *see* Painter

Panter, alias of Lame, *q.v.*

Panvischier, Thomas, union for, of his vicarage to his parish church, Bath [and Wells] diocese, 1420

Porlock [Som], parish church of [St Dubricus], [Harington] chantry of Sancti [?Dub]raci in, cantor of, 948 *note*

de la Porta, Hieronimus, *magister registri*, entries signed by:

Je. De laporta, 749

Je- De laporta—, 596

....,....,...., alterations to register initialled (*Je*) by, 749 *note*

Portishead (Porteshed, Porteshed', Porteshet) [Som], parish church of, rector of, 161, 327, 328

Porto [suburbicarian see *near* Fiumicino, *in* com. of Rome, Italy], [cardinal] bishop of *see* [de Grimanis], Dominic

......, diocese of, places in *see* Cerveteri; Magliana; Palo

........,...., wanting in register entry, 334 *note*

Potter (Pottere), Thomas, priest, ostensible vicar of St James's, Shaftesbury, 269

....,....,....,....,...., litigant over vicarage buildings, 269

[Poulton, Kent], place in *see* St Radegund

Pourlewent, Alexander, of Worcester diocese, commission by virtue of an appeal, 1335

Powell, Edward, of Salisbury diocese, dispensed for plurality, 916; *and see* p. 526

........,...., holder of provostship of [secular collegiate] church of St Edmund, Salisbury, and of the parish church of Bleadon, petition of, 916 *note*

Powes, Andrew, of London diocese, dispensed for plurality, 1338

Powne, John, rector of Chu(l)mleigh, 472

Powys, John, rector of Little Wenlock, 687

Poxwell (Poxwel), William, rector of Childe Okeford, (North), holder of the parish church of Fifehead Neville, and prospective rector of Childe Okeford, (South), 566

Poyneston *see* Painestown

Poynings (Ponyng), Edward, nobleman, captain of Henry [VIII], lord of Folkestone, 242

........,....,....,....,...., patron of the Premonstratensian monastery of St Radegund, grievances of, 242

Poyntz, Humphrey, cleric of Worcester diocese, 397

de Prato, Genesius, *abbreviator de parco maiori*, letters expedited by:[1]

G de Prato, 5, 65, 129, 259, 283, 306, 332, 354, 430, 497, 603, 607-609, 623; *and cf.* 317

Ge de Prato, 233, 234, 244, 347, 350, 463, 619, 655

G Prato, 140, 662

........,....,...., name of, deleted, 284 *note*

......, Raynaldus [of Modena], continual commensal familiar of cardinal Christopher [Bainbridge], 259

........,....,...., collation to, of the parish church of St Michael, Villaga, 259

Preban (Preben) [co. Wicklow], parish church of, rectory of, 355

......,....,...., to be erected, with other benefices, into a prebend of Ferns, 355

Prehest, Richard, prior of the Cistercian monastery of B Mary Graces by the tower of London, 165

........,....,...., election of, as abbot, 165

......,....,....,....,...., approval and confirmation of, 165

........,...., abbot of B Mary the Virgin of Graces by the tower of London, 292

......,....,...., devotion of, to monastery's church, 292

---

1   The register note of the abbreviator's signature is variously punctuated, capitalised and abbreviated.

Prémontré [*dép.* Aisne, France], monastery of, abbot of, conclusion to, 588 [B]

.....,...., present (father) abbot of *see* [Bachimont, Jacques de]

.....,....,...., jurisdiction and superiority of, exemption from, of abbots of Premonstratensian monasteries of the kingdom of England and subject to the king of England, *cf.* 773

Prestland *cf.* Prestoland

Prestoland (Prestolomei), Richard, of Coventry [and Lichfield] diocese, dispensed for plurality, 1004

.....,...., rector of ' (?) Thurstaston, 1004 *note*

Preston, Henry, vicar of Gamrie, resignation of, 284

.....,....,...., proctor of *see* Strachan, Gilbert

[Prestonhaugh, *modern* Prestonkirk co. Haddington] *see* Hauch

?Prince (Prynco), Wolwinus, of London diocese, dispensed for plurality, 1515

Princhett, alias of Bebry, Thomas, *q.v.*

[Prior, co. Kerry], place in *see* Ballinskelligs

?Prizren (*Purien.*) [*probably* a corruption of 'Pizrien.' *traditionally identified as* Prizren *also called* Perzerin *and* Prizrendl, *in* rep. Macedonia, *nr* border with Albania, Yugoslavia], church of, *in partibus infidelium*, 87, 88, 205

.....,...., subject to the archbishop of ?Prjeslav, 85

.....,...., fruits and proceeds of, nil receipts from, 88, 205

.....,...., provision to, 84-88, 205

......, [bishop-] elect of *see* [Ilston], Thomas

?Prjeslav (*Procamen.*) [*probably* a corruption of ' Prosc(h)almen.' *traditionally identified as* Prjeslav (Prost (h) laven.) *also called* Eski-Stambul, *in* prov. Shumla, Bulgaria], archbishop of, subjection to, of church of ?Prizren, 85

Prowgh alias ?Kingsbury (Kinugisbure), John, of York diocese, dispensed for plurality, 752

Prynco *see* ?Prince

Puccius, Pucius see de Putiis

Pukyn', Hopkyn ap *see* Hopkyn ap Pukyn'

Punffolde *see* Pinfold

Punscal *see* Tunstal

Purcell (Purrell), John, provision of, to Ferns, 1477

.....,...., absolution of preliminary to provision, 1478

.....,...., [bishop-] elect of Ferns, 1477

.....,....,...., faculty for consecration, 1479

......, Philip, to have vicarages, Cashel diocese, 1278

......, Robinotus, to have vicarage erected into prebend, Ossory diocese, 1081

Purdy, Robert, of Lincoln diocese, dispensed for plurality, 757

Purfoot (Purforte), Henry, canon of the Premonstratensian monastery of B Mary and St Nicholas, Beeleigh, 425

.....,....,....,...., holder of the vicarage of Ulting and the rectory with cure of St Laurence, ?Dengie, 425

.....,...., abbot of the Premonstratensian monastery of Langley, 425

.....,....,...., litigant over rectory of ?Dengie, 425

Purien. see ?Prizren

Purrell *see* Purcell

de Putiis, Laurentius Antonii, *abbreviator de parco maiori*, letters expedited by:[1]

L *Puccius*, 31, 32, 71, 72, 92-96, 171-176, 221

L *Pucius*, 118-121, 191, 200, 201

L *Putius*, 122-126

Pydmyster *see* Pitminster

---

1   The register note of the abbreviator's signature is variously punctuated and capitalised.

de Sancto Severino, A see [de Caccialupis] de Sancto Severino, Antonius

Sandall (Sandwall') [one of several prebends which had shared the name of Whitgreave (*in* Stafford St Mary, Staffs)], a prebend of the church of B. Mary, Stafford, *q.v.*

Sandford (Sondeforth'), Roger, rector of St Clement [Danes]'s, London and incumbent of Morchard Bishop, 470

Sandhurst (Sandhirst) [Kent], parish church of, vacancy and provision of, 478

......,...., provisee of, 478

......,...., union of, to canonry and prebend of Pipa Parva of Lichfield cathedral, 478

Sandon (Sandow), Roger, of Bath and Wells diocese, dispensed for plurality, 1075

Sandronin *see* Shandrum

Sandwall' *see* Sandall

Sanlake *see* ? Standlake

Sannders *see* Saunders

Sanquhar *cf.* Sanchart

Sansan *see* Sampson

Santhey, John, of Bangor diocese, commission by virtue of an appeal, 764

Santiago de Compostela (Compostella) [prov. Corunna, Spain], [cathedral church of St James the Apostle], tomb of St James at, vow to visit, 155, 292

Saresbrigie, de Saresburia, Gualteri see Salisbury, Walter of

......, *Guillelmi see* Salisbury, William [fitz Patrick], earl of

[of Sassello], Francis, [OFM], bishop of Castoria, 316 *note*

Saunders (Sannders), Hugh, holder of canonry and prebend of Ealdstreet of London cathedral and of the parish church of B. Mary Matfellon, Whitechapel, 736

Savage (Sanage), Edward, of York diocese, 52

Savage (*contd*)

......,....,...., late wife (not named) of, 52

......,....,...., mistress of and current spouse's blood relative *see* Slylay, Elisabeth

......,....,...., current spouse of *see* Knight, Alice

......, *cf.* Sabage

Sawbridgeworth (Sabrichesworth') [Herts], parish church of, vicar of, 706

Saxilby (Saxhilby) [Lincs], parish church of St Botolph, vicar of, 452

Sayer, Thomas, canon OPrem, of Canterbury diocese, dispensed to hold a secular benefice, 816

Scach *see* Stack

Scaddanstown (Balymtrany *alias* Scadanysdum) [*or* St Johnstown, co. Tipperary], parish church of St Nicholas, vicarage of, 654

......,....,...., to be erected into a prebend of Cashel, 654

Scale *see* Sele

Scawceby (Scanceby), Thomas, vicar of Broad Chalke, 35, 64

......,....,...., holder of the chantry of St Thomas in York cathedral, 35

Schaw *see* Shaw

Schaw (Staw), Robert, reservation to of fruits of vicarage, Glasgow diocese, 1429

......,...., vicar of parish church in Glasgow diocese, resignation of, *cf.* 1428 *and* 1429

Schelley *see* Shelley

Scherborn *see* Sherburn [Yorks]

Scherman *see* Sherman

Schewill (Schewil), Edward, provision of, to Cistercian monastery of Newbattle, 1504

......,...., absolution of preliminary to provision, 1505

......,...., abbot of Newbattle, 1504

......,....,...., faculty to be blessed, 1506

Scholl, Theodericus, vicar at altar of Sts Giles, Felix, and Regula in the church of B Mary the Virgin, Eisenach, 650

.......,...., to have canonry and prebend in same, 650

Schrymgeour *see* Scrymgeour

Sclater *see* Slater

Scotland, kingdom of, governor of *see* [Stewart], John, duke of Albany

.......,...., Master of Requests of *see* Ogilvie, James

.......,...., money current in, 233, 234

......, collector of the camera in *cf.* Barry, John, senior

Scots, king of , *see* James [V]

.......,...., provostship of church of B. Giles, Edinburgh, in patronage of, 378

Scott (Scotte), John, of Lincoln diocese, dispensed for plurality, 1304

Scrabo *alias* Syan *see* Straboe *alias* ?Shaen

Scrincamhanam *see* Skreen

Scrymgeour (Schrymgeour), James, collation to, of chantership, called precentorship, of Brechin, 1401

Sculyn, David, ostensible priest, detainer of vicarage of ?Ballyshannon, 653

......, *cf.* OScallan

Seal (Shele) [Leics], parish church of St Peter, rector of, 401

.......,...., union to, of the parish church of St Andrew, Bosherston, 401

Sebby, Cuthbert, layman of Tuddenham parish, appellant in tithes case, 224

Sefton (Seston') [*or* Sephton, Lancs], parish church of, rector of, 399, 673

.......,...., union to, of the vicarage of Leyland, 673

Seglinen. *see* Leighlin

Sele (Scale) [*at* Sele Priory *in* Upper Beeding (*formerly* Sele), co. Sussex], Carmelite house, called priory, professor of *see* Coke *alias* Reeve, Richard

Selimbria (*Solubrien.*) [*or* Selymbria *or* Selembria, *modern* Silivri, *on* northern coast of Sea of Marmara, European Turkey], present bishop of, resident in city or diocese of London, papal judge delegate, 462

......, bishop of *see* [Chard], Thomas

Selwood (Selwoode), Richard, of Chichester diocese, dispensed for plurality, 1017

Selwood (Selwoode) *alias* Tanner, John, monk of the Benedictine monastery of B. Mary the Virgin, Glastonbury, 273

de Senis, Philippus, *magister registri*, letters signed by:[1]

Phi de Senis, 31, 32, 50, 149, 216, 221, 251, 252, 329

Phi d(e) Senis, 51

phi de Senis, 215, 498, 603, 609, 746

......,....,...., alterations to register ordered by regent of chancery signed (*phi. d(e) Senis*) by, 262 *note*

Sephton *see* Sefton

Seraduualy *alias* Cloynarc *see* Stradbally *alias* ?Cloon Island

Seskinan (Socsgynun) [co. Waterford], a prebend of Lismore, *q.v.*

Seston' *see* Sefton

Seton (Setton), Alexander, collation to, of canonry of Brechin, 1405

......, David, of St Andrews diocese, dispensed for plurality, 803

.......,...., reservation to, of fruits of parish church, St Andrews diocese, 924

Seward, Simon, of Bath and Wells diocese, dispensed for plurality, 1052

---

1   The punctuation of the signature varies.

Sewell (Sewell'), Thomas, holder of canonry and prebend of Hoxton of London cathedral and of the parish church of Leybourne and the vicarage of Rye, 26

Seynteler, Christopher, of (?)London diocese, dispensed for plurality, 1161, 1203

Shaa, Richard, of York diocese, 832

?Shaen, alias of Straboe, *q.v.*

Shaftesbury [Dorset], vill of, 269

......, parish church of St James, successive vicars of, 269

.........,...., buildings assigned for use of vicar, alleged ruinous state of, 269

......, parish church of St Romuald, rector of, 433

......, layman of *see* Gill, Walter

Shandrum (Sandronin) [co. Cork], parish church of, vicarage of, 335

.........,....,...., to be united, with other benefices, to canonry and prebend of Lismore, 335

Shap (Shappe) [Westm], Premonstratensian monastery of, abbots or commendators of, to appoint chaplain and Latin master at oratory and hospital built by John Brunskill at Brough under Stainmore, 1

.........,...., commendator of *see* [Redman], Richard

Sharbourne *see* Sherburn [Durh]

?Sharpe (Gharpe), of Rochester diocese, dispensed for plurality, 1443

Shaw (Schaw), Thomas, master of the hospital of the Holy Trinity, Fossgate, York, 464

Sheff, John, cleric or layman of Canterbury diocese, appellant in marriage case, 536

.........,....,...., adjudged wife of *see* Taylor, Margaret

Sheffeld *see* Sheffield, Edward

[Sheffield, Yorks], chantry [free chapel or hospital] of St Leonard [on "Spittal Hill"], holder of, 540

.........,...., parish church of St Nicholas, Feltwell, united to, 540

Sheffield (Sheffeld), Edward, union for, of his vicarage to his canonry, Lincoln diocese, 910

Shele *see* Seal

Shelley (Schelley), George, of Chichester diocese, dispensed for plurality, 934

......, Thomas, of Chichester diocese, dispensed for plurality, 1311

Shelton, Richard, of Norwich diocese, dispensed for plurality, 1069

Sheppard *cf.* Cheppard

?Shepperton (Chepparton') [Midd], parish church of, rector of, 743

Shepton Beauchamp (Shepton) [Som], parish church of, rector of, 723

Sherburn (Sharbourne, Shierburn) [in Pittington, Durh], hospital of B. Mary Magdalene, union (conditional) to, of the vicarage of New Windsor, 720, 738

.........,...., rector, called master or warden, of *see* Wren, Geoffrey

Sherburn (Scherborn) [either S~ - in -Elmet, WR *or* S~ *in* Buckrose deanery, ER, Yorks], parish church of, vicar of, 131

Sherman (Scherman), Roger, vicar of Pelynt, 29

Shierburn *see* Sherburn [*in* Pittington, Durh]

Shipton Moyne [Glos], parish church of, rector of, 951 *note*

[Shoreditch, Midd], place in *see* Ealdstreet; Hoxton

Shorton (Shorton'), Robert, rector of Kettering, vicar of Hoo [St Werburgh], and prospective holder of Long Melford, 537

Skipwith (*contd*)

......, Richard, holder of canonry and prebend of St Michael of the church of B. Mary the Virgin, Warwick and of the parish church of St Alban in Wood Street, London, 321

Skirling (Skerling), Robert, the late, 530

......,......,...., relict of *see* Wardlaw, Christine

Skreen (Scrincamhanam) [co. Sligo], parish church of, vicarage of, 729

......,......,...., prospective union to, of the vicarages of Ardnaree and Castleconor, 729

Skypwith *see* Skipwith

Slade, Thomas, rector of Onibury, 484

Slake, James, layman of Lincoln diocese, 615

......,......,...., appellant in case concerning oath, 615

Slapton (Slapton') [Devon], [secular] college of, church called chapel of, rector of, 158

......,......,...., foundation of, stipulations in concerning rector's duty to reside, assist at mass etc., and preside over priests and clerics living in college, 158

Slater (Sclater), Richard, canon of the Augustinian monastery of Guisborough, 122, 123

......,......,...., absolution of preliminary to provision, 123

......,......,...., provision of, to Natura, 122, 124-126, 202

......,......, [bishop-] elect of Natura, 122, 124-126, 202

......,......,...., faculty for consecration, 126

......,......,...., to take oath of fealty, 126

......,......,...., holder of vicarage of Stranton, 125

......,......,......,...., dispensed to retain vicarage, 125, 202

Slater (*contd*)

......,......,...., indulged to exercise the pontifical office in city and diocese of Durham, 124

Sleatty (Sleti) [co. Laois], parish church of, rectory of, united to treasurership of Leighlin, 61

Sligo (Mubhusg *alias inter Duos Pontes*) [co. Sligo], parish church of, rectory of, 731

......,......,...., to be united to newly erected prebend of Killaspugbrone in Elphin , 731

[Sligo, co. of], places in *see* Achonry; Ardnaree; Aughris; Castleconor; Inishmurray; Killaspugbrone ; Skreen; Sligo

Slimbridge (Slimbrige) [Glos], parish church of St John the Evangelist, rector of, 511

Sloo, William, monk of the [Cluniac] monastery of St Saviour, Bermondsey, 196, 480

Slow *cf.* Sloo

Slylay, Elisabeth, of York diocese, 52

......,......,...., mistress of Edward Savage and mother of his children, 52

......,......,...., first husband (not named) of, 52

......,......,...., current husband (not named) of, 52

......,......,......, blood relative of *see* Knight, Alice

Smarden (Smerden') [Kent], parish church of St Michael, united to parish church of B. Mary the Virgin, Chelmsford, 473

Smith (Simyth', Sinyth, Smithe, Smyth, Smyth', Smyths, Sthmydt) *and* [Smith], Charles, of Lincoln diocese, dispensed for plurality, 1325

......, Elisabeth, of St Stephen's parish, London, 535

......,...., appellant in marriage case, 535

......,...., husband of *see* Hypping, Robert

......, John, rector of Chelsworth, 451

Sothy alias Lancaster, Agnes, of (?)Carlisle diocese, commission by virtue of an appeal, 991

Southam (Sontham') [Warw], parish church of St Nicholas, holder of, 427

.........,...., union of, to canonry of Hereford and prebend of Ewithington, 427

Southampton (Southt', Sudhamten') [Hants], vill of, 164, 708

.........,...., parish church of the Holy Cross, vicar of, 708

.........,.........,...., vicarage of, holder of, 164

.........,.........,.........,...., union of, to the parish church of Corfe Castle, 164

South Bersted see Bersted

Southchurch (Sowthchirche) [Essex], parish church of, incumbent of, 162

.........,...., union of, to the parish church of Bocking, 162

Southcott (Sonthcott), Walter, rector of Bridford, 560

Southe Reppes see Southrepps

Southholeyngten' see Otterington, South

[South Leith] see [Leith, South]

South Malling, Southmallyng see Malling, South

South Moreton see Moreton, South

South Ockendon see Ockendon, South

South Otterington see Otterington, South

South'pole, South Pool see Pool, South

Southrepps (Southe Reppes) [Norf], parish church of, rector of, 357

.........,...., union to, of parish church of Wiveton, 357

Southt' see Southampton

Southwark (Gnthwark, So'thwerk, Southwrk) [Surrey], parish church of St Olave the Martyr in, rector of, 128

......, Bermondsey in, 196, 480

Southwell (Suthwell') [Notts], collegiate church of, vicarage choral in, 37; *and see* p. lxxv

.........,...., vicar choral in *see* Bulle, John

Southwrk *see* Southwark

Sowgh Wokyngton, Sowgh Wokyngton' *see* Ockendon, South

Sowthchirche *see* Southchurch

Sowthe Mallyng *see* Malling, South

Spalding (Spaldyng) [Lincs], [Benedictine] monastery of, prior of, papal judge delegate, 218

Spens, David, canon of Moray, papal judge delegate, 137

......, Hugh, sub-conservator of privileges of St Andrews university, 530

.........,.........,...., litigation before and proceedings of, 530

Spenser (Spensar), Miles, cleric of Carlisle diocese, 156

.........,.........,...., a nephew of cardinal [Bainbridge], 156

Spicer, William, of Ely diocese, commission by virtue of an appeal, 1337

Spinelli *cf.* Spynnell'

Spire, Thomas, of Chichester diocese, dispensed for plurality, 1101

Sponne, [William], chantry of *see under* Towcester

Spott (Spot) [co. Haddington], parish church of, rector of, 530

Spreule (Sprente), John, commissary of archbishop of Glasgow, 320

.........,.........,...., proceedinngs by, 320

Springar (Spryngar), Thomas, guardian or churchwarden of the chapel of Farrington in Chewton, appellant, 223

.........,...., of Bath [and Wells] diocese, commission by virtue of an appeal, 810

?Springwell (Spryugwell), John, *nullius diocesis*, dispensed for plurality, 850

Stanmer (*contd*)

.........,...., statutory visits to, by penitentiary of South Malling, 30

Stanton Harcourt (Stanton' Harencourt) [Oxon], parish church of, vicar of, 728

Stanton St John (Stanuton') [Oxon], parish church of St John, rector of, 703

Stanyng *see* Steyning

[Staphyleus], John, bishop of Sibenik, *locumtenens* auditor of causes of the apostolic palace, commission of case to, 239

Starston (Sterston') [Norf], parish church of, rector of, 481

Starty, John, of St David's diocese, validation for, of dispensation for plurality, 1397

Stathern (Stathern') [Leics], parish church of, united to parish church of Abbots Ripton, 638

Stauerton' *see* Staverton

Stauley *see* Stanley

Staverton (Stauerton') [Devon], parish church of, vicar of, 456

.........,...., vicarage of, union to, of the vicarage of Altarnon and, conditionally, of the vicarage of Ipplepen, 456

Staw *see* Schaw

Stayley, William, of York diocese, dispensed for plurality, 1225

Stedham and Heyshott (Stedhm' and Heyshet) [Sussex], [united parishes of], parish church of, rector of, 692

Steeple Ashton *see* Ashton, Steeple

Stelbart *see* Stewart

Stephenson *cf.* Stephynson

Stephynson, Edward, holder of the canonry and prebend of Apuldram of the [secular collegiate] church of Bosham and holder of the parish church of Musgrave, 469

......, *cf.* Stephenson

Stepulashton *see* Ashton, Steeple

Sterlingen. , Sterlingnen. see Stirling

Sterston' *see* Starston

Steuart, Steuuar' , Steuuart *see* Stewart

Stevont, James, canon of Aberdeen and prebendary of Kinkell, appellant, 137

.........,...., sometime numbered among scholars and rectors of the *studium* of St Andrews, 137

Stewart (Stelbart , Steuart, Steuuar', Steuuart, Steward, Stuart) *and* [Stewart], Alexander, detainer of deanery of Brechin cathedral, 241

.........,...., cleric of St Andrews diocese, 303, 304; *cf.* 298

.........,....,...., absolution of preliminary to commend, 304; *cf.* 298

.........,....,...., commend to, of Augustinian monastery of Inchaffray, 303, 305; *cf.* 298; *and see* p. 525

.........,....,...., to take oath of fealty, 303, 305; *cf.* 298

......, Andrew, cleric of St Andrews diocese, 497

.........,....,...., alleged provision to, of canonry of Glasgow and prebend of Govan, 497

.........,....,....,...., cession of, 497

.........,....,...., reservation to, of pension on tithes and fruits etc. of ceded canonry and prebend, 497

.........,...., of St Andrews diocese, dispensed for plurality, 799

.........,...., provision of to Caithness, 1507

.........,...., absolution of preliminary to provision, 1508

.........,...., [bishop-] elect of Caithness, 1507

.........,....,...., faculty for consecration, 1509

......, Archibald, canon of Glasgow, papal judge delegate, 320

.........,...., of Glasgow diocese, commission by virtue of an appeal, 1330

Stone (contd)

.........,....., ostensible deputy of Cuthbert Tunstal, 583

.........,.......,..., proceedings by, 583

Stork (Storke), John, nullius diocesis, dispensed for plurality, 839

Stortford (Strotford) [modern Bishop's S~ , Herts], parish church of, vicar of, 549

Stow (Stowe) [modern Stow-on-the-Wold, Glos], [parish church] of St Edward the King, parishioner (named) of, 279

Stow (Stowe) [Lincs], archdeaconry of in the church of Lincoln, 55

......, archdeacon of see Darby, Edward

Straboe (Scrabo) [co. Laois] alias ?Shaen (Syan) [in Straboe, co. Laois], parish church of, vicarage of, 141

.........,.......,..., to be united, with other benefices, to the Cistercian monastery of St Mary, de Legedei, Abbeyleix, 141

Strachan [or Strathauchin] (Strachanchia, Stracthanthyn, Strarthanc'hm, Strathanchin, Strathanchm, Strathanchm', Strathanthini, Strathanthm), Gilbert, cleric of St Andrews diocese, 649

.........,.......,..., proctor of Andrew [Forman], archbishop of St Andrews, 649

..........,...., canon of Brechin, 239, 283, 284

.........,.......,..., proctor of George Hepburn, 283

.........,.......,..., proctor of Henry Preston, 284

.........,.......,..., proctor of James Wilson, 239

..........,...., wrongly described as canon of Brixen, 239

.........,....., reservation to, by reason of litigation, of pension over canonry, Moray diocese, effectuation of, 796

..........,...., collation to, of canonry of Dunblane, 864

.........,.......,..., of deanery of Dunblane, 899

.........,.......,..., of rectory of parish church, St Andrews diocese, 923

Stradbally (Stradnali) [co. Limerick], alias of ?Cloon Island, q.v.

......, place in see ?Cloon Island

Stradbally alias ?Cloon Island see ?Cloon Island alias Stradbally

Stradford see Stratford [Suff]

Stradling, William, chancellor of St David's cathedral and incumbent of ?St Athan's, 181

Stradnali see Stradbally

Strafford see Stafford

Stranton (Strancton', Stremton') [Durh], parish church of, vicarage of, 125, 202

.........,.......,..., holder of, 125, 202

Strarthanc'hm see Strachan

Strata Marcella [II] [in Welshpool, co. Montgomery], Cistercian monastery of B. Mary the Virgin at, monk of see Godson, Benjamin

Stratford [at Stratford Langthorn(e) in West Ham, Essex], Cistercian monastery of B Mary, abbot of, papal judge delegate, 572

.........,....., ostensible abbot of see [Hicheman], William

Stratford (Stradford) [either S~ St Andrew in Orford deanery or S~ St Mary in Samford deanery, Suff], parish church of, rector of, 487

Stratford Tony (Stratford' Tony) [Wilts], parish church of, rector of, 393

Strathanchin, Strathanchm, Strathanchm', Strathanthm, Strathanthini see Strachan

Stratton [Corn], parish church of, vicarage of, holder of, 551

.........,.......,..., union of, to canonry and prebend of the church of Glasney, 551

Stratton [Dors], a prebend in Salisbury cathedral, q.v.

Stremton' see Stranton

Stretoy, Edmund, of [Coventry and] Lichfield diocese, dispensed for plurality, 918

Strotford *see* Stortford

Strugulior *alias* Chepstowe *see* Chepstow

Stuart *see* Stewart

Styfkey, Styfkey St Johns *see* Stiffkey

Styllygton *see* Stillington

Stynchecombe (Stinchecome), Robert, rector of All Saints's, Gloucester, 704

Stynt, William, rector of Havant and holder of the parish church of Meonstoke, 291

.....,....., of Winchester diocese, dispensed for plurality, 849

Suckley (Suckeley) [Worcs], parish church of, rector of, 428

.....,....., union to, of the parish church of St Michael the Archangel on the Hill, Bristol, 428

Sudhamten' *see* Southampton

Suffolk, archdeacon of, in the church of Norwich, 288

.....,.....,....., papal judge delegate, 288

[Suffolk, co. of], places in *see* Bury; Butley; Campsea Ashe; Chelsworth; Dennington; Fakenham Parva; Gosbeck; Icklingham; Ipswich; Ixworth; Melford, Long; Ringsfield; Somerleyton; Stratford; Thetford; Thrandeston; Tuddenham; Ufford; Waldingfield, Great; Whatfield; ?Wickham Market

Suir (*de Surio*) *see* Inishlounaght

Sulham[Berks], parish church of, rector of, 421

Sunen. *or* Surien. [*unidentified; traditionally identified, tentatively, as* Syros *or* Syra, *anciently* Syria, *on* Syros, *an island in the Aegean, Greece*], church of, [*in partibus inifidelium*], provision to, 1489

......, [bishop-] elect of *see* [Burgh], Richard

de Surio see Suir

[Surrey, co. of], places in *see* Bermondsey; Buckland; Merton; Newington; Southwark; ?Wimbledon

[Sussex, co. of], places in *see* Apuldram; Chichester; Malling, South; Stanmer; *and* places *listed above under* Chichester, diocese of

[Sutherland, co. of], place in *see* [Dornoch]

Suthwell' *see* Southwell

Suth Wokyngton *see* Ockendon, South

Sutri [prov. Viterbo, Italy], diocese of, place in *see* Ronciglione

Sutton *and* [Sutton], William, canon of Ferns, papal mandatary, 477

.....,....., provision of, to Panados, p. lxxiv note 297

Swale, Christopher, vicar of Messing, 221

Swetnam (Swenam *alias* Wichenhm') [one of several prebends which had shared the name of Whitgreave (*in* Stafford St Mary, Staffs)], a prebend of the church of B. Mary, Stafford, *q.v.*

Swhynesched' *see* Swineshead

Swillington, Robert, of York diocese, 193

.....,.....,.....,....., spiritual relative and prospective spouse of *see* Bewick, Margaret

Swineshead (Swhynesched' , Swynneshede) [Lincs], Cistercian monastery of B. Mary, abbot of , papal judge delegate, 218

.....,.....,....., *see* [Addingham], John

[?Swymmer], Robert, prior of the Augustinian priory of St Germans, dispensed for plurality, 1275

Swynneshede *see* Swineshead

Syan, alias of Scrabo, *q.v.*

Sydelesham *see* Sidlesham

Sydenham (Sydenhans), George, union for, of his parish church to his canonry, Salisbury diocese, 1263

Syenen. [*unidentified; on the basis of other records* Pinnock's provision *has been referred to* Sidon, *modern* Saida, Lebanon], church of [*in partibus infidelium*], provision to, 1495

Taylor (Tailer, Tailloure, Tailor, Tayllour), John, canon of Lichfield, papal judge delegate, 745

......, Margaret, woman of Canterbury diocese, litigant in marriage case, 536

......,....,....., adjudged husband of *see* Sheff, John

......, Robert, canon of the Augustinian monastery of Tiptree, 527

......, William, rector of Quarrington, 44

......,....., canon of the Augustinian monastery of St Gregory outside the walls of Canterbury, 689

Tayrchayr, William, of Exeter diocese, further dispensed for plurality, 1527

Tedavnet (Tethdannada) [co. Monaghan], parish church of, 578

......,....., prospective union of, to the parish church of Tehallan, 578

Tehallan (Tethalen) [co. Monaghan], parish church of, rector of, 578

......,....., prospective union to, of the parish church of Tedavnet, 578

[Templeboy, co. Sligo], place in *see* Aughris

Templebredon (Tempul Hybrydeayin) [cos. Limerick and Tipperary], parish church of, vicarage of, 609

......,....,....., to be united to chancellorship of Emly, 609

......, place in *see* ?Killeenagallive

[Templecarn, co. Donegal], place in *see* St Patrick's Purgatory

[Templecrone, co. Donegal], place in *see* Termon

[Templemurry, co. Mayo], place in *see* Rathfran

Templepatrick (Cukam *alias* Tempul padrig) [co. Antrim], parish church of, rectory of, 350

......,....., vicarage of, annexed to rectory, 350

......, place in *see* Moblusk

Tempul Hybrydeayin *see* Templebredon

Tempul padrig, alias of Cukam, *q.v.*

Termon (Termancrona) [*in* Templecrone, co. Donegal], parish church of, rectory of, 256

......,....,....., to be united, with other benefices, to the deanery of Raphoe, 256

Termonamongan (Cyllcairill) [co. Tyrone], parish church of, rectory of, 258

......,....,....., to be united to vicarage of Urney, 258

Terzi, Bartolomeo, *custos registri bullarum*, p. lxvi note 22

[Tessaragh] *see* Tisrara

Tethalen *see* Tehallan

Tethdannada *see* Tedavnet

Teversham (Thonersham) [Cambs], parish church of, rector of, 707

Tfumckyen, Thomas, of Worcester diocese, dispensed for plurality, 1200

Thachin *see* Thatcham

Thames (Tauusiazo), place on *see* Henley

Thanet, Isle of [Kent], parish church of St John in [*at* Margate], vicarage of, prospective vicar of, 538

......,....,....., vacancy of, 538

......,....,....., presentation for, by the abbot and convent of the [Benedictine] monastery of St Augustine outside the walls of Canterbury, 538

......,....,....., union (conditional) of, to the parish church of St Peter, Northampton, 538

Thatcham (Thachin) [Berks], parish church of, vicar of, 1037 *note*

Thawmer *see* Chalmer

Thaydon' at Mount *see* Theydon Mount

Theachbuy *see* Taghboy

Thechteseyn *see* Titeskin

Thedford *see* Thetford

Theoclugyn *see* Tuoghcluggin

de' Tornabuoni (*contd*)

......,....,...., notary and continual commensal familiar of pope, 346

......,....,....,...., commend to, of Basilian monastery of 'St ?Nicander', 346

Torney *see* Thorney

Torphichen (Torsihen) [co. Linlithgow], Hospitaller preceptory of, commend of, 102

......,...., litigation over, 102

......,...., commendator of *see* Painter, Patrick

Torrays *see* Turriff

Torrington, Little (Parva Torynton') [Devon], parish church of, commendator of, 281

......,....,...., union of, to the Cluniac priory of Kerswell, 281

Torsihen *see* Torphichen

de Torsolato see ?Drumlane

Torthorwald (Torthowald) [co. Dumfries], parish church of, tithe-fruits of, 320

......,....,...., farmer of *see* [?Carlyle], William

......,....,...., litigation over, 320

......, *and see* 'Carlile'

Toscanella [*modern* Tuscania, prov. Viterbo, Italy], letters dated at, 520, 567

Totild, William, rector of Kings Ripton, 32

Touch *cf.* Toncht

Tournai [prov. Hainaut, Belgium], [cathedral] church of, chapter of, conclusion to, 78

......, bishop of *see* [de Hautbois], Charles

......, [bishop-] elect *see* Guillart, Louis

......, church of, appointment of administrator of then provision of bishop to, 78-83

......,...., administrator of *see* Guillart, Louis

......,...., subject to archbishop of Reims, 83

......,...., vassals of, conclusion to, 78

Tournai (*contd*)

......, city and diocese of, clergy of, conclusion to, 78

......,...., people of, conclusion to, 78

Towcester (Tawcestre, Tawcetur) [Northants], parish church of, chaplaincy in, foundation of, 9

......,...., chaplaincy called "Spones' Chauntrey" in, foundation of, 163

......,...., chaplains in *see* Clerk, William; Mabot, Richard

Townley, Nicholas, vicar of Stortford, 549

Tradley *see* Cradley

Trafford (Traffard, Traffordi), William, of Coventry and Lichfield diocese, dispensed for plurality, 1366

......, George, of [Coventry and] Lichfield diocese, commission by virtue of an appeal, 1288

[Trail] *see* St Mary's Isle

Trally *see* Traylly

Tranesle, Laurence, of Exeter diocese, dispensed for plurality, 1072

......, *cf.* Travers

Travers (Travesse, (?)Trauesse) , Adam, vicar of ?Winkleigh, 436

......,...., of Exeter diocese, dispensed for plurality, 1074

......, Bernard, of Coventry [and Lichfield] diocese, dispensed for plurality, 908

......,...., of Exeter diocese, dispensed for plurality, 1073

......, Laurence, of Coventry [and Lichfield] diocese, dispensed for plurality, 933

......, *cf.* Tranesle

Traylly *or* Trailli (Trally), John, knight, the late, founder of the college of B. Mary the Virgin, Northill, 717

Trebert *see* Tarvit

Valt *alias* Killmali *see* ?Killeenagallive

Vanesour *see* Vavasour

Vanzon see Venzon

Vastina *see* Kilbride Veston

Vaughan (Vaghany) *and* [Vaughan], Edward, sometime holder of canonry of London and prebend of Brondesbury, 583

........,....., bishop of St David's, appellant, 583

......, John, archdeacon of St David's, indulged to visit his archdeaconry by proxy, 1265

Vavasour (Vanesour), Margaret, of York diocese, commission by virtue of an appeal, 811

Vaven', Vawan *see* Wawane

Vebbe *see* Webbe

Venice [Italy], merchants of, knight captured by Moors bound himself to in respect of ransom, 587

Venori, William, of London diocese, commission by virtue of an appeal, 954

Venzon, Johannes Hieronimus, *abbreviator de parco maiori*, letters expedited by:[1]

I or *J Benzon*, 1, 6, 7, 16, 24, 84-88, 106-109, 163, 169, 334, 386-388, 409, 410, 457, 508, 521, 577, 578, 618, 720

Je Benzon, 286, 591-595, 611, 613, 625-627, 629

Je Bonzon, 628

Vanzon, 203

Je Venzon, 228, 235

........,.....,.....,....., *and see* 10, 538

Vernon (Wernon'), Arthur, rector of St Peter's, Seal and holder of St Andrew's, Bosherston, 401

Veroli (*Verulis*) [prov. Frosinone, Italy], letters dated at, 494

Veysey (Veysy) , Hugh, of Worcester diocese, dispensed for plurality, 856

......, John, dean of Exeter, 134

........,.....,....., commissary of bishop of Lincoln, 134

........,....., provision of to Exeter, 1501; *and see* p. lxxiv note 292

........,....., absolution of preliminary to provision, 1502

........,....., [bishop-] elect of Exeter, 1501

........,.....,....., faculty for consecration, 1503

Vicary (Vycary), William, of Bath and Wells diocese, dispensed for plurality, 1284

Vicenza [Italy], bishop of, vicar general of, papal mandatary, 259

......, diocese of, persons of *see* Bertini, James; Chiericati, Francesco and John; de Podio Catini, Silvester; de Prato, Raynaldus; *and see* [Bainbridge], Christopher

........,....., places in *see* Cologna Veneta; Villaga

Vienne [*dép.* Isère], general council of, constitution of concerning dietae, *cf.* 425 *note*, 521

Vilechota *see* Wilcot

Vilistoan *see* Willestown

Villa Basilica [prov. Lucca, Italy], parish church, called *plebs*, of St Mary, litigation over, 149

......,.....,.....,....., rule and administration of, appointment of vicar in, 149

......,.....,.....,....., fruits of, reservation of pension on, 149

de Villafontis, alias of Tymolk, *q.v.*

Villaga (Viraga) [*near* Barbarano Vicentino, prov. Vicenza, Italy], parish church of St Michael, 259

---

1 The register note of the abbreviator's signature is variously punctuated and capitalised.

[Wawne or Waghen, Yorks], place in *see* Meaux

Waylett *cf.* Waylot,

Waylot, John, of Lincoln diocese, dispensed for plurality, 869

Wayte (Waytt), John, rector of St Nicholas's, Newbury, 20

Wcham', John, vicar in Bangor cathedral, 683

.....,.....,....., litigant in case concerning defamation and parish dues, 683

Weare Giffard (Weyne Giffard) [Devon], parish church of, rector of, 1036 *note*

Webbe (Vebbe, Web, Webe), John, of Salisbury diocese, dispensed for plurality, 1363

.....,....., of Worcester diocese, dispensed for plurality, 840

......, Robert, of Bath [and Wells] diocese, dispensed for plurality, 1433

......, William, sacrist of Lichfield cathedral, 49

.....,....., professor of a Carmelite house of B. Mary [*presumably* White Friars, London *or* Maldon, Essex], diocese of London, 718

Webster (Webstar), Robert, of Norwich diocese, dispensed for plurality, 1299

Wedehoke, William, of Salisbury diocese, dispensed for plurality, 1220

Weir (Weyr), John, vicar in the church of Carnwath, 140

.....,....., collation to, of vicarage, called *pensionaria*, in church of Carnwath, 140

.....,....., pension reserved for, on fruits of benefice, called prebend, of Carnwath in Glasgow cathedral, 140

.....,.....,.....,.....,....., nullification of, consent to, 140

We'lbe, John, of Canterbury diocese, dispensed for plurality, 792

Welbeck (Welbeke) [extra parochial place, *near* Worksop, Notts], Premonstratensian monastery of, abbot of, 471

.....,....., possible dependency of *see* Lavendon

......, *and see* 'Newerque'

Weldon, Philip, of Worcester diocese, dispensed for plurality, 902

[Wele], Thomas, bishop of Panados, 579

.....,.....,....., holder of canonry and prebend of Clyro (with parish church of Bryngwyn united thereto) in church of Abergwilly and of vicarage of Nuneaton, 579

.....,.....,....., exemplification for, 579

Welkynson *see* Wilkinson

Well (de Well), John, of Lincoln diocese, dispensed for plurality, 1136

.....,....., union for, of his parish church to his vicarage, diocese of Bath and Wells, 1315

Wellesley (Wellysley), Walter, papal judge delegate, 491

.....,.....,....., proceedings by, 491

Wellie *see* Wells

Wellis *see* Wells, Thomas

Wells (Wellie) [Som], parish church of St Cuthbert, vicar of, 448

......, **[cathedral] church** of, deanery of, 207

.....,....., dean of, residence customarily kept by, 287

.....,.....,....., accustomed, when bishop absent, to attend chapter and hear causes in place of bishop, 287

.....,.....,....., *see* Cosyn, William

.....,....., sub-dean of *see* West, Reginald

.....,....., chancellorship of, oath on admission to, 277

.....,....., chancellor of, obligation of to lecture in theology or the decretals, 277

.....,.....,....., *see* Dyker, Robert

Winchelsea (Wynckylse), John, of Norwich diocese, dispensed for plurality, 911

Winchester [Hants], Benedictine monastery [i.e. cathedral priory], called house, of St Swithin, 680

....., ..., ..., ..., monk of *see* Eastgate *alias* Cooper, Edward

....., [cathedral priory] church of, dean [!] of, papal judge delegate, 536

....., ..., chapel in, indulgence for those visiting, 780

....., bishop of, (?)papal judge delegate, person summoned before, 277

....., ..., papal judge delegate, 243, 268, 270, 271, 287

....., ..., to assign pallium, 17[A], 17[B], 385[A], 385[B]

....., ..., to receive oath of fealty, 17[A], 17[B], 382, 384, 385[A], 385[B]

....., ..., papal commissary and mandatary, 384

....., ..., *see* [Fox], Richard; [Langton], Thomas

....., church of, archdeacon of, papal judge delegate, 536

....., **diocese** of, persons of *see* Andrew, Henry; ?Ansell, Richard; Ashton, Henry and Hugh; Barnack, Ralph; Bartholomew, William; [Barton], William; Clerk, John; Corker, John; Crosse, William; Davys, Richard; Denton, James; Fawne, John; Garnet, Miles; Grene, George; Hagge, Miles; Harden, John; [Hogeson], William; Holden, Bernard; Hungete, John; Hutton, Richard; Ifnyrlton, Thomas; Moyne *alias* Hampton, Richard; North, John; Palines, John; Pichenam, William; Ripon alias ?Newhouse, William; Ryllych, William; [Skevington], Thomas; Sloo, William; Stynt, William; Tuker, Henry; Wilcockes, John; Wylford, John; Yeman, Walter

....., ..., persons of Canterbury peculiars in *see* Baschurche, Thomas; Wykes, Robert

Winchester (*contd*)

....., ..., places in *see* Beaulieu Regis; Bentworth; Bermondsey; Buckland; Burghclere; Candover, Chilton; Cliddesden; Havant; Hyde; Meonstoke; Merton; Monxton *alias* Anna de Becco; Quarley; Southampton; Southwark; Twynham; Worthy, Headbourne; Wymering

....., ..., Canterbury peculiars in *see* Newington; ?Wimbledon

....., *and see* Hyde

Windham (Wyndhm), George, of York diocese, dispensed for plurality, 1137

Windsor, New [Berks], parish church of, vicarage of, (prospective) vicar of, 720, 738

....., ..., ..., ..., vacancy of, 720, 738

....., ..., ..., ..., presentation for, by the abbot and convent of the [Augustinian] monastery of the Holy Cross, Waltham, 720, 738

....., ..., ..., ..., union (conditional) of, to the hospital of B. Mary Magdalene, Sherburn, 720, 738

....., [secular collegiate] church, called chapel royal [*in* Windsor Castle *at* New Windsor], dean of , papal judge delegate, 287

....., ..., ..., ..., *see* West, Nicholas

?Winkleigh (Wynkelley) [Devon], parish church of, vicar of, 436

Winsford (Wynnysford) [Som], parish church of, vicarage of, holder of, 185

....., ..., ..., union of, to the vicarage of Cutcombe, 185

Winterbourne (Wyntbora') [Glos], chantry of, cantor of, 210

Wisbech (Wisbych') [Cambs], parish church of, vicar of, 540

Wise (Wiso), Oliver, of Exeter diocese, dispensed for plurality, 1205

Wolsey (*contd*)

.....,....,...., translation of to York, 379, 382, 384, 385[A]

..........,...., archbishop-elect of York, 382, 384, 385[A], 385[B]

.....,........,...., to take oath of fealty, 382, 384, 385[A], 385[B]

.....,.........,...., pallium requested by, 385[A], 385[B]

.....,.........,...., to be assigned pallium, 385[A], 385[B]; *and see* frontispiece

.....,.........,...., envoy of *see* Gentile, Andrea

..........,...., and bishopric of Tournai, 78 *note*

..........,...., *and see* 316 *note*

Wolverhampton (Wolnerhampton') [Staffs] 'Pyxwell' [*unidentified; just possibly* Pelsall, a dependent chapel in Wolverhampton], chantry, called chapel, of B. Mary the Virgin, cantor of, 209

Wombersley (Womberosley), Thomas, of London diocese, dispensed for plurality, 1212

......, *cf.* Wemberfley

Woodburn (Gudbuerum) [*in* Carrickfergus, co. Antrim], [Premonstratensian] monastery of, abbot of, papal mandatary, 606

Woodcock *cf.* Wodecoke

Woode, Richard, vicar of Brackley, 48

Woodhall (Wodhall), John, union for, of one of his parish churches to another, York diocese, 1190

......, *cf.* Wodalh

Woodington (Woddingten', Wodington', Wodyngton', Wudyngton'), Thomas, holder of canonry and prebend of London, rector of Bocking, and incumbent of the parish church of Southchurch, 162

..........,...., official or president of (the court of) Canterbury, 169, 222, 224, 462, 665

Woodington (*contd*)

.....,........,...., proceedings by, 169, 222, 224, 665

..........,...., dean of B Mary le Bow, London, 224

.....,........,........,...., litigation before, 224

..........,...., official of the primatial court of Canterbury, 279

.....,........,...., declaration by, 462

?Woodroff (Wodorff), Oliver, of York diocese, dispensed for plurality, 880

[Wool, Dors], place in *see* Bindon

Woolfe, Ralph, cantor at the altar of St Catherine in St Paul's cathedral, London, 192

Wootton (Wotton) [Oxon], parish church of, rector of, 526

Worcester [Worcs], parish church of St Helen, rector of, 314

......, bishop of (or his vicar general), presentation to, of person for institution to vicarage, 189

......, bishop of, vicar general in spirituals of *see* Hannyball, Thomas

..........,...., papal mandatary (foreign business), 147, 149, 463, 735

..........,...., *see* [de' Gigli], Silvester

......, official of *see* Hannyball, Thomas

......, church of, archdeacon of, papal judge delegate, 134

.....,........,...., *see* Alcock, Thomas

......, **diocese** of, persons of *see* Abynton, John; Barowe, William; Baschurche, Thomas; Bennet, Eliseus; Berriman, Alice; Bewe, John; Blamire, John; Botler, Richard; Bredshay, Richard; Brewet, William; Brown, William; Burford *alias* Lambard, William; Burghill, William; Dingley, William; Eliot, Robert; Francis, Stephen; Fuse, Thomas; Gifford, Edmund; Gledhill, Edmund; Hall, Thomas; Hanchyth, John; Hannyball,

INDEX OF SUBJECTS

Note. The present index covers the Calendar Text and the *Rubricellae* of Lost Letters. References are to serial number of entries. Cross references to proper names of persons and places are to the INDEX OF PERSONS AND PLACES.

A

Abbots, blessing of, faculties for, 100, 141, 1500, 1506

......,.....,....., granted by Julius II; clarified (in certain respects) by Leo X, 154

......, dispensed to retain the following benefices together with monastery:- archdeaconry, canonry and prebend and two parish churches (for one year), 102

......, election of, by convent, 425, 739

......,.....,....., confirmed by superior abbot, and by pope, 165

......,.....,....., confirmed by visitor, disputed by noble lay patron, 242

......, grants to, to receive blessing from any catholic bishop, 100, 141; *cf.* 1500, 1506

......, indult etc. to: use pontificals, give benediction, confer minor orders, bless images etc., reconcile polluted churches etc., demolish church fabric in course of restoration etc., move and repair altars, 696

......, granted indulgence along with those present at abbatial benediction, 696

......., mandate to, to dispense married couple to remarry, 52

......, of named house, change of status (from prior) to, granted by Julius II; clarified and extended by Leo X, 154

......, *see also* Provisions *and under individual religious orders*

Abbreviatores see under Rome, court of, chancery

Absence (from benefices), indults for, (*rubricellae* of), 913, 922

......, *and cf.* Residence

......, *and see under* Fruits

Absolution, as preliminary to promotion etc. to archbishopric, bishopric or headship of religious house, 72, 77, 79, 86, 90, 96, 99, 104, 107, 111, 115, 119, 123, 174, 178, 304, 367, 370, 374, 376, 380, 383, 387, 589, 594; (*rubricellae* of) 1031, 1228, 1446, 1451, 1455, 1458, 1461, 1465, 1469, 1472, 1475, 1478, 1481, 1484, 1487, 1490, 1493, 1496, 1499, 1502, 1505, 1508; *and cf.* 298

......, by appointed confessors, from all sins (even reserved, except those specified in *Coena Domini*), 155, 292

......, by chosen confessor, from all sins (except reserved), of confraternity-members, 168

......, conditional, from sentence of excommunication, 135, 136, 169, 222, 268, 269, 271, 287, 288, 316, 320, 389, 434, 475, 492, 522, 535, 536, 541, 572, 602, 665, 745

......, faculty for, granted to prior of Augustinian house in respect of parishioners of the monastery (and of places united or subject to it etc.), from all sins (except reserved), 494

......,....., granted to abbot of Augustinian house in respect of parishioners of the monastery and of a specified parish church annexed thereto, 154

......, from apostasy, 455

......, from excess, (*rubricellae* of), 1438

......, from incest, 52, 533

......, from homicide and mutilation etc., 141

......, from sentence of greater excommunication, 665

......, from simony, 625, 658

......, *see also under* Excommunication

Appeals, to apostolic see, (*rubricellae* of),
753, 762-769, 804, 806, 810, 811, 857,
872, 876, 954, 959, 966, 984, 985, 991,
992, 1062, 1087, 1094, 1098, 1208, 1240,
1244, 1256, 1269, 1274, 1281, 1288,
1290, 1301, 1330, 1333, 1335, 1337,
1341, 1361, 1365, 1373, 1398, 1400,
1407, 1416, 1424, 1430, 1436, 1440,
1520

..........,...., from *de facto* collation of priory, 134

..........,...., from definitive sentence, 134, 136,
137, 169, 215, 216, 218, 222-224, 239,
243, 269, 288, 320, 352, 389, 438, 475,
498, 530, 535, 536, 572, 583, 614, 615,
627, 651, 665

..........,...., from grievances, 279, 287, 316, 425,
434, 491, 492, 521, 522, 541, 665

..........,...., from revocation of definitive
sentence, 352

..........,...., from sentence and from collation
etc. of parish church, 326

..........,...., from sentence(s), 135, 320, 745

..........,...., in testamentary case, 137

..........,...., in tithes case, 320

..........,...., intervention of local bishop in
dispute involving, 352

..........,...., not prosecuted within proper time,
136, 320, 475, 491, 492, 530

..........,...., over perpetual vicarage(s), 352, 627

..........,...., extra-judicial, 268, 271

..........,...., over rector's suit against laymen for
cutting down trees etc., 169

..........,...., over rights of jurisdiction or over
money etc., 135

......, from investigation by local bishop, to
apostolic see, then to local metropolitan
court, then again to apostolic see; then the
other party appealed to apostolic see, 462

......, to archbishop of Canterbury / papal
legate, over priory, 134

......, to legate of apostolic see in "those
parts" (England), 541

Appeals (*contd*)

......, to local metropolitan court, 498

Appropriation *see* Unions

Archbishops *see under* Bishops and
Archbishops *and under individual sees*

Archdeacons, indults to, to visit by deputy
and receive procurations in ready money,
343, 361; (*rubricellae* of), 903, 1265

......, marriage case between persons in
jurisdiction of, 218

......, of monastery of St Albans, jurisdiction
of, 745

......, other reference to, 935

Archives and Rolls *see under* Rolls

Arson, 317

Arts, *for graduates in see under* Degrees

Auditor of causes of the apostolic palace *see
under* Rome, apostolic palace

Auditor of court of audience of archbishop
of Canterbury *see* Tunstal, Cuthbert

Augustinian Hermits, Order of:-

professor of, provided to bishopric *in
partibus infidelium*, 118

Augustinian Order:-

privileges etc. of houses of the Lateran
congregation to be enjoyed by named
houses and their personnel in England,
154, 494

privileges etc. granted to English houses
by Julius II, approval and extension of,
494

...., clarification and extension of, 154

statutes etc. of hospital, 24

abbots of, dispensed to be appointed to
and preside over monastery for a year
without taking habit or making
profession, 98; *and cf.* 97

...., dispensed to hold a regular or secular
benefice *in commendam* with house, 293

Benefices (*contd*)

....,....,...., to hold for life, resign and exchange, two incompatible, 2, 6, 9, 12-15, 18, 20, 21, 27-29, 31-33, 35, 37-39, 41, 42, 44-51, 53-55, 58, 62, 64, 129, 131, 132, 153, 156, 159-161, 163, 179, 181, 186, 187, 191, 192, 194, 198, 200, 201, 203, 204, 209, 210, 212-214, 221, 231, 238, 251, 252, 254, 255, 261, 266, 275, 291, 296, 300, 302, 314, 315, 324, 325, 328, 332, 356, 362, 365, 392-394, 399, 400, 402-407, 410, 418, 420, 421, 435, 436, 442, 446, 448, 450-454, 457, 458, 464-467, 470, 472-474, 481-484, 487-489, 493, 496, 499, 500, 502-506, 511-516, 518, 524-526, 528, 532, 539, 546-549, 553, 556-562, 568, 570, 586, 612, 616, 620, 622, 630-633, 636, 640, 641, 645-648, 671, 674, 675, 677, 679, 684-687, 690-695, 697, 701-706, 708, 712-714, 716, 722, 724, 726-728, 737, 740-744, 748, 750; *and see* 184, 207, 424, 425, 433

....,....,...., to hold for life, two incompatible (without clauses providing for resignation and exchange), 61, 707

....,....,...., to hold for life, resign and exchange two incompatible benefices and any number of compatible, 230, 609

....,....,...., to hold for life, resign and exchange, three incompatible, 128, 272, 440, 669 *and see* 676

....,....,...., to hold for life, three benefices, with or without cure, even canonries and prebends, 229

....,....,...., to hold for life, three (specified) benefices, later disputed, 268

....,....,...., to hold for life, resign and exchange a third incompatible, 6, 15, 35, 55, 181, 194, 203, 291, 324, 418, 470, 473, 506, 539, 737; *and see* 238

....,....,...., to hold for life, resign and exchange a third incompatible (but if the third is a parish church (etc.) hold it for one year only), 156, 328, 570

Benefices (*contd*)

....,....,...., to hold for life, resign and exchange three incompatible (but if the third is a parish church hold it for one year only), 157

....,....,...., to hold for life, resign and exchange, four (i.e. two in addition to two already held) incompatible, 365

....,....,...., to hold for life, resign and exchange, four incompatible (but if the third is a parish church hold it for six months only; and hold the fourth for two years only); extended to: hold the third (if a parish church) for an additional six months, and hold the fourth for life, 429

....,....,...., to hold for life, resign and exchange, any fourth incompatible, 570

....,....,...., to hold for life five benefices (including three incompatibles), subject to restrictions, 238

....,....,...., to hold canonry and prebend and one benefice with cure for life, and resign and exchange them for up to two benefices with cure, 351

....,....,...., to hold with canonry and prebend two benefices with cure for life, and resign and exchange the two benefices, 265

....,....,...., to hold canonry and prebend and two benefices with cure and any number of compatibles for life; and resign and exchange the two benefices etc., 534

....,....,...., to hold certain canonries and prebends and any number of incompatible, 623

....,....,...., to hold any number of compatible, 657, 729

....,....,...., to hold any compatible (without clauses providing for resignation and exchange), 310

....,....,...., to retain parish church acquired without appropriate dispensation, 743

....,....,...., to retain incompatible benefice with another, 33

Bridgettine Order, house of, in England *see* Syon (described as Augustinian)

Brief, papal, 127

Buildings, construction of, great hall by confraternity, 24

.........,...., new houses etc., in vill with popular oratory, 1

......,...., oratory and hospital, by layman under bishop's licence, 1

......,...., oratory or church within parishes subject to monastery, to be permitted only under licence of prior and local diocesan, 494

.........,...., indulgence for those contributing to, (*rubricellae* of), 1067

......, demolition of ecclesiastical fabric for restoration purposes, abbot granted indult for, 696

......, maintenance of, alleged neglect of, 137, 583

.........,...., apportionment of monastery's fruits for, 303, 347, 366, 628

.........,...., indulgence for those contributing to, 292, 460; (*rubricellae*) of, 820; *and cf.* 155

.........,...., vicar's house (and its offices etc.), litigation over, 269

......, restoration of parish churches, to be undertaken by temporal lord in return for perpetual right of patronage and presentation, 236

Bull *in Coena Domini*, 155, 292

Burial, of those dying in hospital and of confraternity-members, 168

......, 494, 661

C

Camera, apostolic, *see under* Rome, court of

Canon law *see* Decretals

Canonical hours, penitentiary indulged not to be compelled to attend at, for seven years while residing in Roman curia etc., 30

......, recitation of in churches etc. subject to monastery, prior empowered to reform, 494

......, abbot empowered to reform in conformity with ancient custom of monastery, 154

Canonries *see under* Cathedral churches

Captains, in Ireland, [of their respective nations], 317

Cardinals *see under* Rome, titular churches in *and also see under* Porto

Carmelite Order:-

professors of, dispensed to hold a secular benefice, 390

...., dispensed and indulged to hold a secular benefice and nevertheless remain in his house and have stall in choir and place and voice in chapter, 718

...., dispensed to hold a secular benefice with conventual portion and have voice in order and usual privileges, 274

[....], dispensed to hold incompatible benefices, 990

house of, in England *see* Sele

Castle *see* Carmarthen

Cathedral churches, canonries and prebends of, papal decree invalidating provisions to persons who have not completed their fourteenth year, 69, 286

......, in England, chancellor of, indulged not to be compelled to give annual lecture as required by statute, 277

.........,...., dean of, duties and functions of, 287

1 Place-names which may derive from a dedication are also included.

Dedications of churches (*contd*)

St Just *see* St Just

St Laurence *see* 'Caual'; ?Dengie; York

St Leonard *see* Berwick; Colchester; [Sheffield]; York

St Malachy *see* Addergoole

St Margaret *see* Cley next the Sea; Downham

St Martial *see* Newsham or Newhouse

St Martin *see* Bladon; Thompson; ?Wimbledon; Withcall

St Martin le Grand *see under* London

B. Mary *see* Abbeydorney; Abbeyleix; Abington; Aughris; Ballingarry; Ballymurreen; Beaulieu; Boston; Bourney; Bradenstoke; Bruton; Butley; Caher; Coggeshall; Connor; Cooleagh; Coverham; Derrane; ?Devenish; Furness; Inishlounaght (Suir); Inishmurray; Jativa; Jervaulx; Kilbeggan; Kilcooly; Kilshanny; Kilwinning; London; Manchester; Monasteranenagh; Monasterevin; Mont-sous-Vaudrey; Mucklestone; Mullingar; Oseney; Rathdowney; Rathkeale; Reading; Rock of Cashel (Hore Abbey); Rome; Ross, Old; Rufford; Stafford; Steyning; Stratford; Suir; Swineshead; Tuddenham; Walsingham; Westport; Whitechapel; Wymondham; York; *and see* 718

B. Mary Graces *see* London

B. Mary, St Benedict and All Holy Virgins *see* Ramsey

B. Mary and St John the Baptist *see* Durford

B. Mary and St Nicholas *see* Beeleigh

B. Mary and St Petroc *see* Bodmin

B. Mary le Bow *see* London

BVM *see* Almondsbury; Arbury; Aston, North; Bridlington; Bruern; Chelmsford; Colchester; Eisenach; Felpham; Gillingham; Glastonbury; Hoo; Kelly; Keynsham; Lanthony II by Gloucester; London [city of] (Woolnoth); Louth; Maiden Bradley; Northill; Oseney; Patching; Rewley; Rome; Rouncivall; Rye; Strata Marcella; Thetford; Thrandeston; Usk; Warwick; Wells; Wendling; Whatfield; Wolford; Wolverhampton 'Pyxwell'; *and cf.* Brough under Stainmore

BVM and All Saints *see* Westacre

BVM and BB. John and James the Apostles *see* Reading

BVM and St John the Baptist *see* Lavendon

BVM and St John the Evangelist *see* 'Stagno'

...., *and see under* Holy Trinity and BVM

St Mary *see* Abbeyleix; Charlton Mackrell; Cirencester; Cologna Veneta; Cong; Coverham; Dennington; ?Drumlane; Ottery; St Andrews; St Mary's Isle; Villa Basilica

S Maria della Pace *see* Rome

S Maria in Porto *see* Ravenna

St Mary the Virgin *see under* St Saviour and Sts Mary the Virgin and Bridget

St Mary Graces *see* London

B. (Mary) Magdalene *see* Pentney; Sherburn [Durh]; Taunton

St Mary Magdalen *see* Oxford

St Mary Magdalene *see* Hereford

St Michael *see* Ballinskelligs; Erke; Hernhill; 'Marmellario'; Mauchline; Mayo; Melksham; Smarden; Stoke Lane; Villaga; Warwick

St Michael the Archangel *see* Bristol; Cascob; Cunmor; Gloucester; Harbledown; Oxford

St Mildred *see* Canterbury

St ?Miliceus *see* Llanarth

Dedications of churches (*contd*)

St Nicholas *see* Barlinch; Barnane-ely; Boythstown; Burscough; Colchester; Drax; Feltwell; Milton Abbas; Newbury; St Johnstown or Scaddanstown; Southam; York

...., *and see under* B. Mary and St Nicholas

S Nicandro *see* 'St ?Nicander'

St Olave the Martyr *see* Southwark

St Paternus *see* Madron

St Patrick *see* Donaghmore; St Patrick's Purgatory

BB. Peter and Paul (the Apostles) *see* Clogher; Eythorne; Kilmallock; Ridley

St Paul *see* London; Piacenza

...., *see under* Sts Peter and Paul

St Peter *see* Bedford; Calais; Cowfold; Derry; Hamsey; Hereford; Ipswich; Marlborough; Northampton; Peterborough; St Albans; Seal; Trim

St Peter *ad Vincula see under* Rome, titular churches in

Sts Peter and Paul *see* Armagh; Athlone; Clones; Glasgow; Kilmallock; Taunton

St Petroc *see* Bodmin

...., *cf. also under* B. Mary and St Petroc

S Prassede *see under* Rome, titular churches in

St Radegund *see* St Radegund

St Regula *see under* Sts Giles, Felix and Regula

St Romuald *see* Shaftesbury

St Salvator *see* St Andrews

St Sampson the Bishop *see* Milton

St Saviour *see* Bermondsey; Graiguenamanagh

Dedications of churches (*contd*)

St Saviour and Sts Mary the Virgin and Bridget *see* Syon

B. S[c]ita / [S]citha the Virgin *see under* Name of Jesus and St [S]citha the Virgin *and under* St Thomas Aquinas and B. S[c]ita the Virgin

S Sisto *see under* Rome, titular churches in

St Stephen *see* Bologna; Exeter; London [city of]; Tassignano; Westminster

St Swithin *see* Winchester

St Thomas *see* York

St Thomas Aquinas and B. S[c]ita the Virgin *see under* London [city of]

St Thomas the archbishop of Canterbury *see* Argenteuil; Salamanca

St Thomas the Martyr *see* Dublin; Upholland

St Thomas the Martyr of Acon *see* London [city of]

St Tiernach *see* Clones and Clankelly

St Vincent *see* Caythorpe

S Vincenzo and S Anastasio *see under* Rome

S Vitale *see under* Rome, titular churches in

......, corrected by order of the regent of the chancery, 471

Defamation, potential, of two women related by consanguinity to each other and sexually linked to the same man, 52

Defects, of age *see* Age

......, of birth *see* Illegitimacy

......, non-disclosure of, 265, 601, 743

Defence, of self and country, plea of, 141

Degrees[1]:-

Arts, bachelor of *see* Busby, William; Colcot *alias* Colocot, Thomas; Grene,

---

1   Though not so treated by the chancery the BA is, for convenience, included here among the degrees.

I

N

Q

Quarters, episcopal *see* Fourths

Queen, of England *see* Catherine [of Aragon]

R

Ransom *cf.* 587

Reconciliation, of polluted churches etc. and cemeteries, indults etc. granted for:-

to abbot, 154, 696

to prior, 494

Re-entry, indults for, 66, 67, 322, 584; 1279

......, granted, 102

Regress *see* Re-entry

Rehabilitation *see* Disability

Relaxaton *see under* Oaths

Relic, head of St Anne, veneration of, 292

Religious house, questioned status of, letters of successive popes relating to, 154

Religious Orders etc. *see* Augustinian Hermits; Augustinian Order; Benedictine Order; Carmelite Order; Cistercian Order; Cluniac Order; Dominican Order; Franciscan Order; Hospitallers; Order of the Knights of the Holy Sepulchre; Order of St Basil; Order of St Lazarus; Premonstratensian Order; Victorine Order; *and cf. Fratres conscripti*

......, dispensation for widower with offspring to enter Augustinian Order etc., 447

......, members of, indulged to remain in particular monastery, 912

.........,...., indulged to transfer to another place of same order until promoted, 637

.........,...., translated from one to another, 611

......, persons joining named house without consent of abbot and convent and refusing to leave, to incur excommunication automatically, 154

Religious Orders (*contd*)

......, persons joining named house without consent of prior and convent and refusing to leave, to incur excommunication automatically, 494

......, reception of new members in named house, to be subject to consent of abbot and convent, 154

.........,...., to be subject to consent of prior and convent, 494

......, runaway members of (from named houses), to incur excommunication automatically, 154, 494

.........,...., those assisting them, to incur excommunication automatically, 154, 494

Remission of sins, appointed confessors granted faculty for, 155

......, by chosen confessor of confraternity-members, 168

......, 292

Removal by superior, of priest celebrating mass in chapel, licence preventing, (*rubricellae* of), 866

......, of [religious] from monastery, indult preventing, (*rubricellae* of), 912

Requests, Master of, of kingdom of Scotland *see* Ogilvie, James

Reservation, of collations etc. to pope:-

general, all qualifying benefices below specified value falling vacant in specified months [alternate 'apostolic months'] during specified term, 240

.........,...., extended to all benefices of any value, 240

.........,.........,...., renewal of, 240

...., of archbishoprics, vacated at the apostolic see, 78, 232, 259, 283-285, 338, 344, 382, 411, 585, 609, 666, 747

...., of benefices vacated at the apostolic see, 65, 68, 110, 285

...., of major dignities, 241, 626